NCE

y of

Politics and
International Relations

Garrett Wallace Brown is a Professor of Political Theory and Global
Health Policy in the School of Politics and International Studies at
the University of Leeds.

Iain McLean is an Official Fellow in Politics at Nuffield College,
Oxford, and Professor of Politics at the University of Oxford.

Alistair McMillan is a Senior Lecturer in Politics at the University
of Sheffield.

 SEE WEB LINKS

For recommended web links for this title, visit
www.oxfordreference.com/page/pol when you see this sign.

VISIT ONLINE

OXFORD QUICK REFERENCE

The most authoritative and up-to-date reference books for both students and the general reader.

Accounting
Animal Behaviour
Archaeology
Architecture and Landscape Architecture
Art and Artists
Art Terms
Arthurian Literature and Legend
Astronomy
Battles
Bible
Biology
Biomedicine
British History
British Place-Names
Business and Management
Card Games
Chemical Engineering
Chemistry
Christian Art and Architecture
Christian Church
Classical Literature
Computing
Construction, Surveying, and Civil Engineering
Cosmology
Countries of the World
Critical Theory
Dance
Dentistry
Ecology
Economics
Education
English Etymology
English Grammar
English Idioms
English Literature
English Surnames
Environment and Conservation
Everyday Grammar
Film Studies
Finance and Banking
Foreign Words and Phrases
Forensic Science
Geography
Geology and Earth Sciences
Hinduism
Human Geography
Humorous Quotations

Irish History
Islam
Journalism
Kings and Queens of Britain
Law
Law Enforcement
Linguistics
Literary Terms
London Place-Names
Marketing
Mathematics
Mechanical Engineering
Media and Communication
Medical
Modern Poetry
Modern Slang
Music
Musical Terms
Nursing
Opera Characters
Philosophy
Physics
Plant Sciences
Plays
Pocket Fowler's Modern English Usage
Political Quotations
Politics
Popes
Proverbs
Psychology
Quotations
Quotations by Subject
Reference and Allusion
Rhyming
Rhyming Slang
Saints
Science
Scottish History
Shakespeare
Slang
Social Work and Social Care
Sociology
Statistics
Synonyms and Antonyms
Weather
Weights, Measures, and Units
Word Origins
Zoology

Many of these titles are also available online at
www.Oxfordreference.com

The Concise Oxford Dictionary of

Politics and International Relations

FOURTH EDITION

Edited by
GARRETT WALLACE BROWN,
IAIN McLEAN,
and ALISTAIR McMILLAN

OXFORD
UNIVERSITY PRESS

OXFORD
UNIVERSITY PRESS

Great Clarendon Street, Oxford, OX2 6DP,
United Kingdom

Oxford University Press is a department of the University of Oxford.
It furthers the University's objective of excellence in research, scholarship,
and education by publishing worldwide. Oxford is a registered trade mark of
Oxford University Press in the UK and in certain other countries

First published as *The Concise Oxford Dictionary of Politics* 1996
Second edition 2003
Third edition 2009

Fourth edition published as *The Concise Oxford Dictionary of Politics and International
Relations* 2018

Impression: 5

Published in the United States of America by Oxford University Press
198 Madison Avenue, New York, NY 10016, United States of America

British Library Cataloguing in Publication Data
Data available

Library of Congress Control Number: 2017944688

ISBN 978-0-19-967084-0
ebook ISBN 978-0-19-254584-8

Printed in Great Britain by
Clays Ltd, Elcograf S.p.A.

Contents

List of Contributors

Executive Editor: Garrett Wallace Brown
Professor of Political Theory and Global Health Policy, University of Leeds

Executive Editor: Alistair McMillan
Senior Lecturer in Politics, University of Sheffield

Consulting Editor: Iain McLean
Official Fellow, Nuffield College, Oxford; Professor of Politics, University of Oxford

KA	Katharine Adeney	*Professor in Politics, University of Nottingham*
LA	Lincoln Allison	*Emeritus Reader in Politics, University of Warwick, and Professor in the Politics of Sport, Brighton University*
AA	Alan Apperley	*Senior Lecturer in Media, Communication and Cultural Studies, University of Wolverhampton*
PA	Paul Arthur	*Professor of Politics, University of Ulster*
IB	Ian Bache	*Professor of Politics, University of Sheffield*
AB	Andrew Baker	*Professor of Political Economy, University of Sheffield*
CB	Cyril Barrett	*Formerly Tutor in Philosophy, Campion Hall, Oxford*
RB	Ross Bellaby	*Lecturer in Security Studies, University of Sheffield*
AMB	Alexandra Bohm	*Senior Lecturer in Law, University of Lincoln*
FB	Francesca Borgonovi	*Research Fellow, Centre for Analysis of Social Exclusion, London School of Economics*
JBr	Jonathan Bradbury	*Professor in Politics, University of Wales, Swansea*
WB	William Brown	*Senior Lecturer in Government and Politics, Open University*
RBu	Russell Buchan	*Senior Lecturer in International Law, University of Sheffield*
VB	Vittorio Bufacchi	*Senior Lecturer in Philosophy, University College Cork*
JBu	Jim Bulpitt	*Formerly Professor of Politics, University of Warwick*
BBz	Barbara Buraczynska	*Fellow in International Relations and Quantitative Methods, University of York*
TB	Tania Burchardt	*Associate Professor in Political Science and Director of CASE, London School of Economics*
PBl	Peter Burnell	*Emeritus Professor of Politics, University of Warwick*
PBm	Peter Burnham	*Professor of Politics and International Studies, University of Birmingham*
BB	Barry Buzan	*Emeritus Professor of International Relations, London School of Economics*
PBy	Peter Byrd	*University Senior Tutor, University of Warwick*
LC	Luis Cabrera	*Associate Professor in Political Science and International Studies, Griffiths Business School*

IC	Ian Campbell	*Formerly Senior Lecturer in Politics, University of Warwick*
SDC	Sean D. Carey	*Lecturer in Politics and Quantitative Methods, University of Mannheim*
DC	David Carlton	*Emeritus Professor in International Studies, University of Warwick*
MC	Mick Carpenter	*Professor in Social Policy, Department of Sociology, University of Warwick*
SC	Steven Casper	*Assistant Professor in Management & Commercialization of Biomedical Science, Keck Graduate Institute, Claremont, USA*
RTC	Richard Coggins	*College Lecturer in Politics, New College, University of Oxford*
VC	Vivien Collingwood	*Freelance writer, translator, and editor*
RJC	Richard Crampton	*Professor of East European History, University of Oxford*
AD	Alix Dietzel	*Lecturer in Environmental Politics, University of Bristol*
KD	Keith Dowding	*Professor of Political Science, Australian National University*
KDr	Kyril Drezov	*Lecturer in Politics, Keele University*
SF	Stephen Fisher	*Associate Professor in Political Sociology, University of Oxford*
MF	Mathew Frank	*Associate Professor in International History, University of Leeds*
IF	Ian Fraser	*Senior Lecturer in Political Theory, Loughborough University*
AG	Adrian Gallagher	*Senior Lecture in International Relations, University of Leeds*
RG	Richard Gillespie	*Professor of Politics, University of Liverpool*
LGM	Laura Gomez-Mera	*Department of International Studies, University of Miami*
FG	Francisco E. González	*Associate Professor, Johns Hopkins University*
WG	Wyn Grant	*Professor of Politics, University of Warwick*
JG	Jack Gray	*Formerly Research Fellow, Institute of Development Studies, University of Sussex*
JH	John Halliday	*Formerly Senior Lecturer in Politics, University of Warwick*
GH	Graham Harrison	*Professor of African Politics, University of Sheffield*
AH	Angela Hobbs	*Professor in the Public Understanding of Philosophy, University of Sheffield*
JMH	John Hobson	*Professor of Political Economy and International Relations, University of Sheffield*
AHr	Alexandra Homolar	*Associate Professor in International Security, University of Warwick*
JHa	Justa Hopma	*Research Fellow in International Relations, University of Sheffield*

DH	David Howarth	*Honorary Professor in Politics, University of Edinburgh and Professor of Politics, University of Luxembourg*
MH	Mathew Humphrey	*Professor in Political Philosophy, University of Nottingham*
AHu	Andrew Hurrell	*Montague Burton Professor of International Relations, University of Oxford*
PI	Paul Ingram	*Executive Director, British American Security Information Council*
CJ	Charles Jones	*Emeritus Reader in International Relations, University of Cambridge*
JJ	Jonathan Joseph	*Professor of International Relations, University of Sheffield*
YFK	Yuen Foong Khong	*Fellow of Nuffield College, University of Oxford*
ZLH	Zig Layton-Henry	*Professor of Politics, University of Warwick*
GLB	Genevieve LeBaron	*Senior Lecturer in Political Economy, University of Sheffield*
GL	Geraldine Lievesley	*Senior Lecturer in Politics, Manchester Metropolitan University*
JM	John McEldowney	*Professor of Law, University of Warwick*
AMQ	Alison McQueen	*Assistant Professor in Political Science, Stanford University*
WM	William Maley	*Director, Asia-Pacific College of Diplomacy, Australian National University*
PM	Paul Martin	*Fellow and Tutor in Politics, Wadham College, University of Oxford*
DM	David Mervin	*Emeritus Reader in Politics, University of Warwick*
TM	Tariq Modood	*Director of the Centre for the Study of Ethnicity and Citizenship, University of Bristol*
AM	Andrew Mumford	*Associate Professor in Politics and International Relations, University of Nottingham*
IO	Ivan Oliver	*Formerly Fellow, Department of Sociology, University of Warwick*
IP	Istvan Pogany	*Professor of Law, University of Warwick*
SR	Shirin Rai	*Professor of Politics and International Studies, University of Warwick*
AR	Andrew Reeve	*Professor of Politics, University of Warwick*
MRM	Melanie Richter-Montpetit	*Lecturer in International Relations, University of Sheffield*
BR	Berthold Rittberger	*Professor of Political Science and Contemporary History, University of Mannheim*
BAR	Barbara Allen Roberson	*Professor in International Relations, University of Warwick*
SRt	Simon Rushton	*Lecturer in Global Health Policy and International Relations, University of Sheffield*
CSa	Clara Sandelind	*Research Fellow in the Politics of Migration, University of Sheffield*

PS	Petra Schleiter	*Fellow and Tutor in Politics, St Hilda's College, University of Oxford*
LSb	Laura Sjoberg	*Associate Professor in International Relations, University of Florida*
MS	Matt Sleat	*Reader in Politics, University of Sheffield*
CS	Carl Slevin	*Formerly Lecturer in Politics, University of Warwick*
LSz	Lisa Stampnitzky	*Lecturer in International Security, University of Sheffield*
LS	Liam Stanley	*Lecturer in Political Economy, University of Sheffield*
DS	David Stasavage	*Associate Professor of Politics, New York University*
AT	Andrew Taylor	*Professor of Politics, University of Sheffield*
KT	Keith Taylor	*Formerly Head of Politics and International Relations, University of Westminster*
ST	Stan Taylor	*Academic Staff Development Officer, University of Durham*
STh	Suruchi Thapar-Bjorkert	*Senior Lecturer in Sociology, Uppsala University*
CT	Claire Thomas	*Lecturer in Politics, University of Sheffield*
KCU	Kristian Coates Ulrichsen	*Fellow for the Middle East, Rice University's Baker Institute for Public Policy*
GU	Geoffrey R. D. Underhill	*Professor of International Governance, Universiteit van Amsterdam*
FV	Federico Varese	*Professor of Criminology, University of Oxford*
SWe	Stuart White	*Professor in Politics, Jesus College, University of Oxford*
SWh	Stephen Whitefield	*Professor of Politics, University of Oxford*
RW	Rick Wilford	*Professor of Politics, Queen's University Belfast*
DW	Daniel Wincott	*Professor of European and Comparative Politics, University of Birmingham*
MW	Matt Wood	*Lecturer in Politics, University of Sheffield*
SW	Stewart Wood	*Fellow in Politics, Magdalen College, University of Oxford*
FZ	Fariborz Zelli	*Senior Lecturer in Political Science, University of Lund*

Preface to the Fourth Edition

As with previous versions of this dictionary, the fourth edition contains many changes and additional new entries. These have been made to reflect new political concepts (e.g. wellbeing), new political movements (e.g. ISIS), new institutional arrangements (e.g. SDGs), new norms (e.g. R2P), a need to honour important scholars who have passed away (e.g. Kenneth Waltz), and new events that have dramatically changed the political lexicon (e.g. Brexit, financial crisis, Syrian Civil War, etc.). These are just a few of the hundreds of new and updated entries contained within this edition. It is our hope that this dictionary will continue to be a valued and important source of information for students, scholars, politicians, journalists, and laypeople alike.

Again, as with former editions, the fourth edition has remained faithful to the editorial process adopted in the Preface to the Original Edition (1996). Thus, we have continued the policy of not adding entries for living political figures or scholars as well as continued the practice of placing an asterisk (*) in front of words or terms that are themselves entries, as a means of cross-referencing.

That said, unlike past versions, the fourth edition has introduced a significant and important change. This is because this edition represents the first iterative move from *The Concise Oxford Dictionary of Politics* to *The Concise Oxford Dictionary of Politics and International Relations*. As a result, the most significant change found within its pages is the systematic inclusion of the field of international relations.

One consideration for this expanded coverage of international relations was the need to find space. In order to be able to back-fill the catalogue of international relations scholarship into the dictionary we had to add a considerable number of entries (of nearly 20,000 words). To make room, the decision was made to remove the country list of primary office holders from the print edition of the dictionary (although these lists are still included online). We felt, rightly or wrongly, that this material was now easily located on the Internet and that very few people would continue to make reference to it. Most importantly, by removing this section we were also able to find significant room for the new entries without also having to be brutal in culling existing entries.

Moreover, including comprehensive coverage of such a prominent discipline as international relations also required a refined and reformulated entry selection process. This is because the constraints on word space also required us to be rather discriminating in our choices without also short-changing the richness of the discipline. In order to try to obtain the right balance, we developed an entry selection process that consulted and triangulated three sets of resources. First, we began our process by reviewing three leading and widely used IR textbooks in order to help populate a long-list of common IR terms, approaches, ideas, and thinkers. The logic for doing so was uncomplicated. If all three textbooks referred to the same material consistently, then that material must be crucial to the understanding of international relations, and thus a candidate for inclusion. Second, five popular and long-established IR course guides were reviewed (one from the USA, one from the UK, one from Japan, one from Australia, and one from South Africa). This was done to help locate and reconfirm important themes, approaches, concepts, and thinkers that would be of the most relevance to students of international relations across different regions. Third, as with past editions of the dictionary, we commissioned a large number of experts in their respective areas as contributors and prompted them to tell us what we missed. Overall we found this process extremely fruitful and rewarding, and we are very grateful to all of our contributors, since they enriched the dictionary significantly. Finally, as editors, we relied on our combined eighty years of experience and knowledge in the fields of politics and international relations. From these efforts, and given the difficult choices that had to be made, we are confident that this fourth edition is comprehensive and complementary to the study and practice of both politics and international relations. Of course, any remaining deficiencies are ours alone.

Lastly, we are extremely grateful to those who have sent in their comments and suggestions to the dictionary over the years. We are also grateful to the external reviews that were enlisted for this edition. And we are grateful to the entire staff at Oxford University Press. They have shown incredible patience and support during what has turned out to be a longer process than expected. As we have discovered, like our editorial predecessors, the editorship of the dictionary is both an honour and a curse.

Preface to the Third Edition

Politics may appear to be ephemeral, moving with the shifting sands of current affairs, but the preparation of this new edition of *The Concise Oxford Dictionary of Politics* shows the deep foundations on which the study of politics is built. We sought to reflect the influence of contemporary events on the concepts and institutions which underpin the understanding of politics, as well as developments in the study and interpretation of politics.

The contributions to this dictionary are written by a team of academics, specialists in the areas which they cover. The team of contributors has expanded, as new concepts have emerged and the events and focus across the study of politics change. We are extremely grateful to the contributors to previous editions who have updated and revised their entries, and to the new members of the team who have enabled us to expand and refresh the coverage. We also would like to thank readers and colleagues who have sent us comments or suggestions, which are reflected in new entries or changes to the existing ones.

The changing discipline of politics is reflected in new entries covering concepts such as cosmopolitanism, the clash of civilizations, deliberative democracy, and the politics of fear. The influence of contemporary events and our concern to broaden the geographical range of our coverage sees new entries on the Bolivarian revolution and pink tide, oligarchs, and aid. Incidents and events which have broad political resonance are reflected in new entries on Darfur and Rwanda. Many new and revised entries cross-reference (indicated by an asterisk, *) the entry on the attacks of 11 September 2001. Coverage of the response to these attacks includes new entries on the Director of National Intelligence, Guantanamo Bay, and rendition. Institutional changes in the world of politics see new entries on the African Union, the International Atomic Energy Agency, the International Criminal Court, and the Organization for Security and Cooperation in Europe.

Our criteria for the inclusion of political theorists and politicians remain the same as in previous editions and are outlined in the Preface to the Original Edition (1996). Whilst conceptual contributions can be made whilst living, we only provide individual entries for those who have died. Those unfortunate to have met this qualification in time for this revised edition include John Rawls (1921-2002), Jacques Derrida (1930-2004), Murray Bookchin (1921-2006), Iris Marion Young (1949-2006), and Richard Rorty (1931-2007).

This edition introduces web links, provided via the *Dictionary of Politics* companion website: www.oxfordreference.com/page/pol. We believe that this resource extends our coverage through information made publicly available on the Internet, whilst maintaining the authority and selectivity of this academic reference work. We are grateful to the staff at Oxford University Press for their support and suggestions for new innovations in our coverage, and their patience and application in preparing this edition of the dictionary for publication.

Preface to the Second Edition

The Editors were half-delighted and half-apprehensive when Oxford University Press approached us about preparing a second edition of this Dictionary: delighted that it has been useful enough to need a new edition; apprehensive of the volume of work it would take to update it.

It is a tribute to the calibre of our contributors that the entries have in fact worn very well, so that the work necessary to update the Dictionary was less than we feared it would be. We read every entry in the Dictionary to decide whether it should be updated, expanded, or compressed. In most cases our contributors were happy to oblige by updating their entries. There are about 200 new entries, some commissioned from the original team, some from a distinguished panel of new contributors.

Sadly, one original contributor was unable to contribute this time around. Jim Bulpitt died in April 1999. Jim was a refreshingly grumpy colleague. A political conservative but an academic radical, he pioneered the study of statecraft. His work on the statecraft of Margaret Thatcher is now hailed as a classic.

As some reviewers seem to have missed the point of our selection criteria, we ask them (and our new readers) to read the second and third paragraphs of the original Preface with care. We thought we had explained ourselves clearly and we have stuck with our selection criteria. Unfortunately, some scholars and politicians who did not qualify for an entry in the first edition now do. Examples are Mancur Olson (1932–98) and Robert Nozick (1939–2002).

We are very grateful to our team, old and new, for their unfailing good humour; to the staff at Oxford University Press who have dealt with the Dictionary; to Nuffield College Oxford for its facilities; and to all users of the Dictionary who have made helpful suggestions about what should be in it.

Preface to the Original Edition (1996)

This is a new dictionary, written by a team of political scientists and political theorists centred around the Department of Politics and International Studies at the University of Warwick, one of the leading departments in this field in the United Kingdom. We hope that it will be useful to many sorts of reader, but the reader we have had most in mind is the university (or equivalent) student who is fairly new to the study of politics.

'Politics' is one of the many words ('geography' and 'history' are two more) that describe both an activity and the study of that activity. This is a dictionary of politics in the second sense, not the first. In other words, it is not a dictionary of events, nor a dictionary of politicians, nor a dictionary of countries and regions where politics go on (i.e. everywhere). There are many such dictionaries, and there is no point in adding to their number. This dictionary aims to cover the concepts, people, and institutions most commonly referred to in academic and scholarly writing about politics. 'Concepts' and 'institutions' are more or less self-explanatory. People must meet two criteria to earn an entry. First, they must have made a distinct contribution to political theory, the design and structure of political institutions, or political science; secondly, they must have died before April 1994. The second criterion was introduced because we do not wish to get into endless and sterile controversy about who are the greatest living political scientists and political theorists. Living writers whose work seems certain to endure are discussed under the relevant concepts or institutions.

In considering whether to include entries on politicians, therefore, we have applied a 'politician plus' test. A politician gains an entry for having helped to design some important institution or promote some theory or ideology. In the latter case, the 'ism' test has been applied: politicians who have a doctrine or practice named after them are much more likely to be included than those who have not, usually under the name of the doctrine or practice. This rule could not be inflexible. Unlike the *Oxford English Dictionary*, this dictionary has no entry on Majorism, because we do not know what it is. However, there are entries on Thomas Jefferson and Abraham Lincoln—Jefferson qualifies twice over, as a political theorist and as a designer of institutions. The fact that there is an entry on Jean Monnet and none on Winston Churchill does not therefore imply that we think Monnet was a greater politician than Churchill (nor that we do not). However, we have included an Appendix giving the names (and parties, where appropriate) of the principal political leaders of all the main English-speaking countries and of the most influential countries in the world. In most cases these lists begin in 1945, but in cases where older names often appear in writing about politics the lists go back further in time.

In our coverage of place and time, we have been guided by politics as it is generally taught in English-speaking universities. Thus our coverage begins with classical Greece and extends to the present day. We have tried to be comprehensive in listing the main political institutions of the democratic world, with most detail on the United Kingdom and the United States. Limitations of space have meant that we have had to be more sparing towards the rest of the world, although we have tried to be as generous as possible to China and the Middle East. We will certainly be attacked for ethnocentrism. Our defence is that we are trying to serve the needs of students of the subject as it is, not as we would like it to be.

In his preface to the companion *Concise Oxford Dictionary of Sociology*, Gordon Marshall wrote that 'Sociology itself has a clear theoretical core but an irretrievably opaque perimeter'. This is just as true of politics, and, as with sociology, it may be regarded as 'one of the subject's principal merits, since it facilitates study of genuinely interdisciplinary problems'. The interdisciplinary nature of politics is what attracts and excites us as researchers. But it causes us problems as dictionary writers and editors. For fringe subjects, we have applied the test, 'Would one expect the reader who comes across this term and wishes to know more about it to turn to a dictionary of politics?' This means that unlike some of our rivals we have no excursions to discuss such fascinating subjects as *Scots law* or *fiscal drag*.

We shall probably be criticized for some of these decisions. Our only defence is that we have done what we have done, and we have not done what we have not done. We hope we have at least been consistent and produced something that our readers find useful.

All contributions, except those written by the Editors, are signed. An asterisk (*) placed before a word in a definition indicates that additional relevant information will be found under this heading. Some entries simply refer the reader to another entry, indicating either that they are synonyms or that they are most conveniently explained, together with related terms, in one of the dictionary's longer articles.

abortion *See* PRO-CHOICE; PRO-LIFE; RIGHT TO LIFE.

absolutism Originally (1733) a theological concept referring to God's total power to decide about salvation. Extended to politics indicating a *regime in which the ruler might legitimately decide anything. Usually applied to monarchical regimes of the early modern period, chiefly that of Louis XIV of France, although the term was not used politically until towards the end of the eighteenth century when many such regimes were about to disappear. Unlike tyrannies, absolutist regimes are usually seen to have been legitimate, as indicated by Louis XVI of France in November 1788, just before the *French Revolution, when he said to his cousin, the duc d'Orléans (father of the future king Louis Philippe, 1830–48), that any decision he made was legal because he willed it. Some contemporary historians deny that absolutism ever referred to an unlimited power or authority, but was always restricted by traditions and practices which effectively limited its scope. CS

accountability The requirement for representatives to answer to the represented on the disposal of their powers and duties, act upon criticisms or requirements made of them, and accept (some) responsibility for failure, incompetence, or deceit. Members of a legislature may be brought to account for their voting record by party officials such as *whips, their local parties, or their constituents. Government ministers are accountable additionally for government decisions to a legislature and the voting public. In Britain it is intended that ministers observe the concepts of both individual *ministerial responsibility and *collective responsibility. Parliamentary debate, select committee investigations, and the media

are the key forums in which their accountability is maintained. The accountability of bureaucrats varies according to their level of politicization. For example, in the USA officials of an administration are political appointees who may be required to take personal responsibility for their actions. In Britain, however, while they may be asked to answer questions before a *select committee, departmental civil servants are nominally neutral and are made accountable for their actions only in cases of maladministration. Otherwise it is assumed that their actions are taken on behalf of ministers, and, hence, accountability for their actions is maintained through the concept of individual *ministerial responsibility.

Arguments may be advanced that politicians and officials can be made too accountable, thus hampering them in carrying out their duties and powers. However, in Britain concern is more frequently expressed about the problems of maintaining accountability. Ministers in practice often do not observe the concept of ministerial responsibility, and the extent to which they are compelled to account for their actions is often dependent upon the political context. At the same time, the creation of executive agencies since the late 1980s has revised the hierarchic organization of the civil service which underpinned the concept of ministerial responsibility. This reform was designed to separate accountability for departmental policy-making functions, which remained with ministers, and accountability for executive agency policy execution functions, which was placed with agency chief executives. A review in 2002 concluded that the agency model, involving direct accountability of chief executives to parliamentary scrutiny, had generally worked well. However, in two cases—the child support agency and the prison service agency—there were long-running problems, and the issue of where accountability for policy and management failings respectively began and ended became a major issue of public debate. In these cases the chief executive resigned or was dismissed rather than the minister, leading to accusations that ministers were able to avoid accountability. More generally, complaint is made that there is a lack of accountability for key parts of government activity, such as the *intelligence services.　JBr

activist One who takes an active part, usually as a volunteer, in a political party or interest group. Because activism is costly, activists are unusual people. Either they enjoy political activity for its own sake, or they have off-median views (*see* MEDIAN VOTER) which give them an incentive to pull the party or interest group towards the position they favour, rather than the position it would take to maximize its vote or influence. Hence some have argued for a 'law of curvilinear disparity' which holds that activists hold more extreme views than either the mass electorate or the party leadership. There is some empirical support for this 'law' but it has rarely been tested carefully.

Adams, John (1735–1826) American revolutionary politician and political theorist. Trained as a lawyer in Massachusetts, he helped formulate the argument that the US colonies had never legitimately been subject to the jurisdiction of the British parliament. After independence he was the intellectual leader of the conservative wing of the revolution, arguing in his *Defence of the Constitutions . . . of the USA* (1787) that the Senate ought to be chosen from among the rich and the intelligent. Until 1796 he nevertheless retained a friendship with the much more radical *Jefferson, perhaps because of their common exposure to the French *Enlightenment when they had been diplomats in the 1780s. The friendship was broken by Adams's partisan Presidency (1797–1801), although Adams was less extreme in his partisanship of urban, commercial policies than the fiery *Hamilton. It was resumed in 1812 and led to a warm and wise exchange of letters which ended with the death of both men on the same day—4 July 1826, the fiftieth anniversary of the signing of the Declaration of Independence.

additional member system (AMS) Any system of *proportional representation in which a set of representatives is chosen to supplement those chosen by some other route in such a way that the house, overall, is proportionately representative of the votes cast. The additional members are sometimes also called 'top-up' members. The best-known AMS is used for the German parliament, where voters have two votes. With the first, they elect a single constituency MP by the *plurality ('first-past-the-post') rule. With the second, they shape the overall party composition of the house. Additional members (additional, that is, to those elected in the single-member districts) are elected in such numbers as required to ensure that the house reflects the vote shares gained by the parties in the second votes. The electoral systems in Belgium, Denmark, and Sweden also have an AMS component.

The combination of locally accountable members and a roughly proportional outcome has made AMS systems popular in new democracies across Eastern Europe, as well as in countries considering electoral reform. New Zealand voted to switch from a first-past-the-post system to AMS in 1993, and in the same year Japan switched to AMS from the single non-transferable vote. The devolved assemblies/parliaments of Scotland, Wales, and London use AMS systems.

Adenauer, Konrad (1876–1967) West Germany's first Chancellor (1949–63). Adenauer was deposed as Mayor of Cologne (Köln) by the Nazis in 1933, and imprisoned twice before 1945. After the war, he led the newly constituted centre-right Christian Democratic Union. His tenure as Chancellor was notable for Germany's accession to NATO, the co-founding of the EEC in 1957, and the construction of the 'social market economy' combining free market capitalism with state responsibility for citizens' welfare.　SW

adjournment (debate) The procedure by which the sitting of a legislature is brought to a close. In the UK House of Commons each day's sitting ends with a motion 'That this House do now adjourn', when, in a debate lasting half an hour, members can raise any matter of concern; one of the few opportunities for private members to initiate debate. The House may adjourn if Members are disorderly, or if there is not a *quorum of members present. During a debate an adjournment motion may be proposed as a means of blocking the passage of a measure. Unless the measure is backed by the government, adjournment normally means that it fails.

administration Administration refers to the organization and management of public and governmental administrative systems. Organization refers to the structure of public government, while management refers to its function. The organization aspects of administration can be defined as the structure of authoritative and habitual personal interrelations in an administrative system. Organization in this respect is not coterminous with institution, which refers to a more long-term embedded set of rules and norms. Management aspects of administration are defined as action intended to achieve rational cooperation within an administrative system. This is the set of practices that create and sustain the organization (*see* BUREAUCRACY), which in turn structures those processes of management in the administrative system as a whole.

This definition is a combination of two separate ways of viewing the administration of government and public-sector bodies: synchronic and diachronic. Viewing administration as organization involves taking a 'snapshot' of how the relationship between actors within the administrative system 'looks' at a particular moment in time. By contrast, viewing administration as management involves a 'dynamic' focus on the practices undertaken. Taken together, these approaches make up the sub-discipline of *public administration.

Recently, administration has become more complex, particularly as government and public services have been outsourced to private-sector firms or quasi-governmental bodies. Administrative systems are now often composed of multiple organizations, rather than individual public bodies. *Public–private partnerships, for instance, involve administrative interaction between public-sector and private-sector organizations. Moreover, management has come to include action intended to achieve rational cooperation across or between multiple organizations. For example, 'transnational administration' involves *European Union

bodies tasked with coordinating policy across multiple member states. These developments highlight the 'systemic' aspect of administration, its composition of potentially private and public bodies aimed at governing a particular policy issue. It also highlights that administration is not a given, but must constantly be created and sustained collaboratively. Administration should therefore be defined as the emergence of management and organization in governing administrative systems.   MW

administrative law The law relating to the control of government power, including the detailed rules which govern the exercise of administrative decision taking. Despite A. V. Dicey's reluctance in his *Law of the Constitution* (1885) to accept the idea of specific and specialized legal rules governing administrative decisions, English law has developed administrative law especially since *c.*1960. Lord Diplock in 1982 regarded the development of English administrative law 'as having been the greatest achievement of the English Courts in my judicial lifetime'. Primarily the courts have developed general principles to ensure that all public authorities must act within the powers granted to them by Act of Parliament. Such principles include reasonableness in making decisions and principles of natural justice to ensure fair procedure. Discretion must not be abused and decisions must be made according to law and not outside the powers of the Act, which might make them *ultra vires.* Under section 31 of the Supreme Court Act 1981, and Rules of the Supreme Court, Order 53, an applicant may seek *judicial review. This procedure permits an application for such remedies as a judicial order or damages as is appropriate to the facts of the case. The various remedies available under English law are mandamus, prohibition, or *certiorari* and the private law group of remedies such as declaration, injunction, or damages. Leave to apply for judicial review must first be obtained in the Crown Office before a judge and usually on affidavit or written evidence. Once leave is granted there may be a hearing of the case where all the parties may be represented. The matter which is the subject of complaint must be a 'public law' question and the courts have defined the exact meaning of this term on a case-by-case basis since the House of Lords decision in *O'Reilly* v. *Mackman* [1983] AC 237. Applications for judicial review have steadily increased since 1981. The subjects for review extend from immigration disputes, housing, local government, and planning matters.

The English system of administrative law has developed on a case-by-case basis in marked contrast to administrative law in both the United States and in France, which owes its development to the nature of the written constitution in both jurisdictions. JM

Adorno, Theodor W. (1903–69) German philosopher, leading figure of the *Frankfurt School and exponent of Marxist Critical Theory. He also published widely on music and aesthetics. His main philosophical works were *Dialectic of Enlightenment* (1947 with Max Horkheimer); *Minima Moralia* (1951); and *Negative Dialectics* (1966). In *Dialectic of Enlightenment* Adorno glossed Walter Benjamin and Friedrich Pollock. Benjamin was disenchanted with the Marxist faith in historical progress while Pollock argued that intervention in the economy had dissipated socialism as an alternative to authoritarian or democratic forms of state capitalism. Such arguments led Adorno to see capital's domination as permeating the whole of society. Control and manipulation of the masses took place through a standardized 'culture industry' which negated individuality and freedom. Such an ideological stranglehold led Adorno to conclude that working-class resistance was all but extinguished. *Minima Moralia* marked his rejection of Hegelian Marxism with his assertion that 'the whole is the false' in contradistinction to *Hegel's claim that 'the true is the whole'. This was reasserted in *Negative Dialectics* where he argued that the dialectic did not reach a unity between universal and particular as Hegel had thought. Rather, it led to a non-identity where universality is in the ascendant over particularity. This argument, coupled with his observation that philosophy lives on only because the moment to realize it was missed, encapsulates the pessimism of Adorno's thought within the Marxist tradition. In empirical work, Adorno was also associated with the development of the concept of the *Authoritarian Personality. *See also* REIFICATION. IF

adversary politics Term coined by S. E. *Finer in his edited book *Adversary Politics and Electoral Reform* (1975) for the British parliamentary system, which he characterized as 'a stand-up fight between two adversaries for the favour of the lookers-on'. He argued that the Labour and Conservative parties had become locked into sterile confrontation of extremisms, which might be broken by electoral reform, to which he was a recent convert. Supporters of the adversary politics hypothesis point to the debasement of parliamentary debate and Question Time; opponents variously argue that the adversaries were not adversarial on everything (for instance, in their common opposition to electoral reform) and that adversary politics was a temporary pathology.

affirmative action Policy designed to correct past practices of discrimination against racial minorities, women, the disabled, and other historically disadvantaged groups. The advocates of affirmative action programmes argue that it is not sufficient to pass legislation aimed at eliminating discrimination in education, employment, and other areas of human activity. Such legislation where it was successful could help eliminate discrimination in the long run, but more drastic measures were required if progress, at an acceptable pace, was to occur in the short term.

In the United States in 1970, for instance, more blacks than ever were going into higher education, yet it remained the case that while blacks made up nearly 12 per cent of the population only 2.2 per cent of doctors and 2.8 per cent of medical students were black. Statistics such as these appeared to justify admissions procedures used in the 1970s by the medical school of the University of California at Davis. Under these arrangements 16 out of 100 places were reserved for minority students, mainly blacks, Chicanos, and Asian-Americans. Allen Bakke, a white applicant who achieved far better test scores than minority students who were admitted, was denied admission. Bakke challenged the legitimacy of this decision in the courts and eventually the matter was addressed by the United States Supreme Court.

In a confusing judgment the Court said that the use of quotas violated the *Fourteenth Amendment to the Constitution and directed that Bakke should be admitted. At the same time the justices said that it was constitutionally acceptable for race to be taken into account in making admissions decisions—affirmative action, in other words, was constitutional.

Affirmative action nevertheless continues to be intensely controversial in the United States. Opponents of such policies insist that they undermine one of the most cherished values of American political culture, the commitment to equality of opportunity. Affirmative action is also condemned for standing in the way of meritocracy—a society where success in life is based on merit rather than birth, class, race, or some other spurious criterion. Critics argue further that affirmative action is ultimately destructive of the goal of eliminating discrimination—that it creates discrimination itself, a reverse discrimination where white males such as Bakke, for example, are denied opportunities for no other reason than their race and sex. *See also* MAJORITY-MINORITY DISTRICTING.   DM

Afghanistan War (1979–1989) Following a military coup in April 1978, the communist People's Democratic Party of Afghanistan took power. The party was riven by sectarian disputes and, in December 1979, the Soviet Union intervened in support of Babrak Karmal who was installed as president. Military conflict ensued between the Afghan army and opposition Mujahedin forces, who were themselves factionalized. The Soviet Union became involved, committing thousands of troops to action. This failed, however, to secure stability for the new communist regime and security beyond the area around the capital, Kabul, was never established.

Soviet military involvement in Afghanistan was a key factor leading to the end of *détente and to more hostile relations between Moscow and the United States in the first half of the 1980s. The large number of Soviet casualties also had a profoundly radicalizing impact on politics in the Soviet Union itself after the election of Mikhail Gorbachev as General Secretary of the Communist Party of the Soviet Union in March 1985 and the introduction of perestroika. In line with Gorbachev's policy of 'new political thinking', the Soviet Union announced a timetable for withdrawal from Afghanistan which was

completed in 1989. The Afghan communist regime fell in 1992.   swh

Afghanistan War (2001) On 7 October 2001 the United States of America commenced air strikes against targets in Afghanistan associated with the ruling Taliban movement, and Osama bin Laden's *al-Qaeda terrorist network which the Taliban had nurtured. Prompted by al-Qaeda's attacks on the World Trade Center in New York and the Pentagon Building in Washington DC on *11 September 2001, these strikes resulted in the dispersal of the Taliban movement, the routing of al-Qaeda forces, and the occupation of the Afghan capital Kabul by anti-Taliban 'United Front' forces on 13 November 2001.

The outbreak of this conflict was actually the culmination of years of turbulence in Afghanistan, involving the progressive breakdown of the Afghan state in the period following the Soviet invasion of Afghanistan in December 1979, and the promotion by neighbouring countries, especially Pakistan, of surrogate forces after the collapse of communist rule in April 1992. The last such force was the Taliban movement, a mixture of Muslim students, former communists, and opportunistic members of the Pushtun ethnic group, which took shape in late 1994 and with backing from bin Laden and Pakistan managed to seize Kabul in September 1996. This did not put an end to conflict: the forces of the 'Islamic State of Afghanistan', despite their displacement from Kabul, retained control of the north-east of Afghanistan, and continued to occupy Afghanistan's seat in the United Nations General Assembly. The armed forces of the Islamic State, led by former Defence Minister Ahmad Shah Massoud, formed the core of the 'United Front'. However, the USA did not make any effort to cultivate these forces, despite al-Qaeda attacks in August 1998 on US Embassies in Kenya and Tanzania, preferring instead to seek to use the Taliban's patron Pakistan as an intermediary to secure the handover of Bin Laden for trial.

On 9 September 2001 Massoud was assassinated by two al-Qaeda operatives posing as journalists. His death, however, did not lead to the fragmentation of his forces, which to Pakistan's consternation became principal partners in the US campaign to obliterate al-Qaeda and the Taliban. The overthrow of the Taliban was accomplished with relative ease, for Pakistan, under intense US pressure, was obliged to abandon its backing for the movement, at which point the Taliban's lack of legitimacy left it with little in the way of concrete support, either normative or prudential. Air attacks using B-52 bombers, AC-130 gunships, Tomahawk cruise missiles, and 2,000-pound Joint Direct Attack Munitions shattered Taliban morale. Cities across the north of Afghanistan fell to the United Front in a cascade from 9 to 13 November, and on 7 December, the Taliban abandoned their last stronghold, Kandahar, and their leader, Mullah Muhammad Omar, went into hiding. While mopping-up operations, directed mainly at pockets of Arab and Pakistani extremists, continued into 2002, on 22 December 2001, a new 'Afghan Interim Administration', chaired by Hamed Karzai, was sworn into office in Kabul with the support of the United Nations and the international community.

Under President George W. Bush operations in the aftermath of the Afghanistan War remained largely ineffective in restabilizing the country and the general mission continued to operate on an ad hoc basis, with *NATO support eventually evaporating into a largely token presence. The election of President Barack Obama in 2008 initiated the start of a significant drawdown of US forces in Afghanistan, with operations being rebranded as a stabilizing effort; with a reduced military presence, a focus on retraining the Afghan army, and the use of pinpointed military operations. The result is that Afghanistan continues to be fractured and largely unstable with recent signs of Taliban resurgence. WM

African National Congress See ANC.

African Union Originally the Organization of African Unity (OAU), restyled the African Union in July 2002. The OAU was established in 1963 at Addis Ababa, with a continent-wide membership (although Morocco withdrew in 1984, applying to rejoin in July 2016), a rotating system for choosing the chairman, and decision-making based on consensus. It aimed to promote unity and cohesion among the newly independent African states, to advance their economic development, and

to accelerate the liberation of those still under colonial or white rule. It recognized the sovereignty of existing African states within their colonial frontiers, subscribed to a policy of non-intervention in domestic affairs, and refused to countenance attempts at secession. The OAU showed little capacity to intervene effectively in any of the crises affecting Africa.

The creation of the African Union sought to expand the remit of the OAU, and craft an expanded institutional structure, along similar lines to the *European Union. An Assembly of the African Heads of State and Government holds annual meetings, a Pan-African Parliament was created in 2004, and provision was made for the establishment of a financial infrastructure including an African Central Bank. The African Union has greater powers to intervene in the politics of member states, and provided a peacekeeping force in the *Darfur region of Sudan from 2005. The peacekeeping role in Darfur was extended as part of a United Nations mission, but criticized as ineffective and under-resourced. The African Union responded tentatively to the crisis in Zimbabwe over the leadership of Robert Mugabe in 2008 and responded more effectively to the Ebola epidemic in 2014 by mobilizing resources to infected areas. The aspiration of the African Union is ambitious, and the institutional and political resources required to fulfil its promise are not presently available.

(⊕) SEE WEB LINKS
• African Union website.

age The different attitudes and behaviours displayed by people of different ages add an important dynamic aspect to politics. This can be seen through the effects of general demographic changes, and studied at the level of individual and generational change over time.

Age, along with migration and immigration, affects the demographic composition of a country, relating to the structure and development of the population. This in turn can be seen to affect the relative importance of particular policies and attitudes. In the West, low birth rates and increased life expectancy have led to a larger proportion of elderly people within society. Issues such as pension provision and the personal health services provided in old age have moved up the political agenda, amidst concern that the shift in ratio of working to non-working population could have serious implications for public service provision. In Europe, this demographic change has been marked by the emergence of Pensioners' parties to campaign for the political rights of the elderly; and in the United States the emergence of activist groups such as the Gray Panthers. Other countries with rapidly growing populations, such as India, where 40 per cent of the population is under 18, face different social priorities, with more focus on, for instance, education and youth employment.

Age differences have been shown to be associated with very different political attitudes and behaviour. The British Election Survey has shown that the elderly are more likely to have right-wing views; whilst the young are less likely to be members of political parties or to turn out to vote. Two different age effects can be discerned, when studying political change; a cohort (or generational) effect and a life-cycle effect. People brought up in a particular period, known as an age cohort, can be seen to have certain shared experiences and values which are reflected in their political choices. In *Political Change in Britain* (1969) Butler and Stokes argue that the elderly were less likely to vote Labour partly because their formative years of political activity occurred before the party was a major force in British politics. Life-cycle effects reflect the changing material interests of individuals as they pass through different stages of life—with the elderly more interested in issues related to pension provision, those with young children more interested in educational provision, the young more interested in licensing laws, etc. Older people tend to have higher incomes, and are more likely to favour parties offering low taxation, such as the Conservatives in Britain. Distinguishing between life-cycle and cohort effects needs careful study of change over time, through tools such as *panel survey studies.

The rights of particular age groups have been championed by a variety of organizations, and opposition to ageism has become an integral part of campaigns for human rights. In 1989 the United Nations adopted a *Convention on the Rights of the Child*, which sought to enhance the protection and treatment of children throughout the world. Ageism, evident when the elderly face discrimination or stereotyped attitudes, has received increasing attention since the 1960s. Since age is a constantly changing attribute of individuals, as we all grow older, it requires a different conceptual treatment from attributes such as sex or race; although there is also a gender aspect to ageism, since women tend to live longer than men.

Concern has been raised that the young are becoming increasingly disillusioned with party politics; and are turning to single-issue campaigns and protest movements. Here again, it is important to distinguish between cohort effects and life-cycle issues. The changes in technology and the media mean that the young generation have different opportunities and approaches to political issues, whilst events such as the fall of the Soviet Union have radically changed the context of political discourse. Hence, the younger generations have to work out new modes of political discourse to reflect their perceptions of the modern world. In terms of life-cycle issues, parliamentary politics is a middle-aged game, and is likely to stay that way. Youth protest has been a highlight of campaigns against the *Vietnam War, the French *Fifth Republic, and the *poll tax in Britain. However, as they grow older, young militant campaigners have tended to be assimilated into (or even shape) the established political culture. AM

agency In social science, agency refers to the ability to act. Indeed agents may be said to have this particular power or capability. There is significant dispute, however, about the extent of agency and about what counts as an agent. In particular, the question of agency is often bound up with that of structure. The *structure/agency question deals with the weight given to each of these. Those favouring structure emphasize the context or conditions that shape the way that agents act. Others emphasize their mutual interdependence. In looking at what is distinctive about agency, it is possible to point to such qualities as intentionality, reflexivity, and adaptability. It is worth considering this in relation to recent arguments by approaches such as actor network theory and new materialism. They suggest that all kinds of objects can have agency and that humans and non-human entities form complex assemblages. A response to this argument is to maintain that only sentient beings have agency and that the new approaches confuse agency with causal powers. A distinction might also be made between actors—perhaps states or organizations— and agents, both individual and collective. It might be wondered, for example, whether states have agency or act by virtue of the agents within them. JJ

agenda setting The art or science of controlling an agenda so as to maximize the probability of getting a favourable outcome. As many *social choice procedures have the property that a given set of preferences can lead to different outcomes if votes are taken in a different order, there is often scope for manipulative agenda setting. The phrase is also used more broadly for efforts to change the political agenda by adding or subtracting issues.

aggregation This term refers to the conversion of political demands into alternative courses of action, usually by political parties. It formed part of the *structural functionalist approach to the study of politics. WG

agrarian parties Parties representing farmers have been a significant feature of many Western political systems, but are now declining in importance. As urbanization and industrialization reduce the share of the rural population in the electorate, agrarian parties have found it more difficult to sustain an electoral base, and a number have either faded away, or have converted themselves into parties with a more general electoral appeal. The interests of farmers may be more effectively represented by national farmers' organizations with close links with the national agricultural ministry, the pattern that has been followed in Britain and Germany. Agrarian parties have been particularly important in Nordic countries (Denmark, Finland, Norway, and Sweden), and have appeared in some of the new democracies of Eastern and Central Europe, such as Hungary and Poland. They have been particularly influential in Poland, joining coalition governments. To some extent the electoral weakness of agrarian parties in

urbanized societies is offset by their organizational strength, based on their links with a network of rural and farming organizations; high memberships and high membership ratios; an ability to mobilize their members; and stable leadership and internal party unity. Particularly in political systems based on *proportional representation with a strong tradition of coalition government, agrarian parties that have converted themselves into centre parties with a broader appeal have been frequent participants in government. The *Keskustapuolue* (KESK) in Finland has one of the most impressive records of postwar office for a party with a rural base, although the Swiss Volkspartei (formerly the BGB, the Burghers, Artisans and Peasants Party) has been represented in the Federal Council since 1929. In general, the electoral base for an agrarian party is too narrow to make it an effective presence in most Western political systems. WG

aid International aid generally encompasses any transfer of resources between states which is not undertaken on a commercial basis. Normatively, most would exclude military assistance from their definitions of foreign aid, which highlights how the politics of aid is largely conducted through discourses of humanitarianism and economic development. Indeed, aid is closely associated with the notion of development, and this association is in itself structured through a distinction between 'developed' and 'developing' countries. The vast majority of aid moves from the former to the latter.

Official aid may be handled on a bilateral basis, through intergovernmental transfers from developed states to developing states; or through transfers from multilateral institutions (e.g. the United Nations Development Programme or aspects of the World Bank's lending) to developing states. Another important multilateral aid institution which has a unique structure is the *Global Fund. The European Union has its own aid strategies, focused on the African, Caribbean, and Pacific post-colonies. Other sources of aid include non-governmental organizations, funded through private donations and 'home' governments.

Since the mid-1950s, aid has emerged as a key aspect of global politics, and the politics of international aid has become a prominent issue, rising up the agenda of G7/8, OECD, and other intergovernmental meetings. There is concern about the efficacy of aid; after \$2.3 trillion of aid has been disbursed over the last fifty years, it is questionable whether aid makes much of a difference to development. Aid can also be seen to influence the relationship between donors and recipients. Questions have been raised about the motivations of aid givers, especially in respect to donor states, whose geopolitical and economic interests may affect how aid is allocated. In terms of aid strategy, forms of aid differ widely and donor institutions always attach projects, plans, and preferences to aid, commonly known as *conditionality and tied aid. Aid can be seen to lead to dependence, establishing a hierarchy of giver and receiver and allowing for intervention in developing states by developed states. *See also* MARSHALL AID.   GH

alderman An alderman was an indirectly elected member of county and county borough councils in England and Wales prior to the 1972 Local Government Act. The aldermen, who were elected by councillors generally from among their own number, composed a third of the council, and served for six years, one half seeking re-election every three years. Abolition resulted from the conflict with the principle of direct election in local government, as well as the unscrupulous use of their majority by dominant party groups in aldermanic elections.

The term is also used to denote elected local council representatives in US cities, especially in the Northeast.   JBR

alienation The root meaning of 'alienation' denoted a relationship to property. One could, for example, alienate one's property by transferring it to another person, or to an institution. During the seventeenth century, the focus of the term shifted from material to immaterial possessions such as rights, and sovereignty over oneself. It came to be accepted by thinkers such as *Grotius and *Locke that alienating certain rights or powers was a necessary prerequisite for legitimate political society. Alienation in this sense became the basis of social contract theory.

A more recent sense connoted a loss of reason or personality, so that one was alienated or estranged from one's true or rational

self through mental disorder ('alienist' is an obsolete word for a psychiatrist). In the eighteenth century, thinkers such as *Paine argued, for example, that certain rights were not just accidental to human character, but essential. Hence such rights were 'inalienable', and to lose such rights either by giving them away or by having them removed against one's will, was to lose an essential part of one's humanity.

Although *Rousseau did not specifically use the term, the first systematic account of alienation by a political theorist is to be found in his *Discourse on the Origin of Inequality* (1755). Here, alienation is uncompromisingly a condition of developed society, where systems of law—moral/religious, political and economic—rob one of the responsibility of setting the parameters of one's own liberty. Under such conditions one will remain alienated from one's potential, moral self, unless and until one can reconstruct society to enable one to participate in the setting of such boundaries. *The Social Contract* (1762) proposes one form which such a society might take.

The most important accounts of alienation from the point of view of political theory are those of *Hegel and *Marx. Hegel believed the purpose of history to be the progressive overcoming of the gap between the particular consciousness and the universal consciousness until a final unity of the two is achieved (absolute self-consciousness). This gap between the particular and the universal constitutes, for Hegel, a central and necessary element of alienation. History is therefore the story of humanity's progress towards freedom from alienation. For Hegel, alienation is through and through a historical concept.

Marx accepts this latter point, but (under the influence of *Feuerbach) rejects Hegel's emphasis on consciousness for two main reasons. First, it implies that alienation originates within the individual, whereas for Marx alienation originates in the material conditions of existence—the 'ensemble of social relations'—within which the individual is enmeshed. Second, Hegel's view makes the individual responsible for his or her own release from alienation, since all that is required is an effort of will. For Marx, overcoming alienation requires a change in the material conditions of productive social existence, and such a change cannot be wrought by individuals. Alienation, for Marx, must therefore be overcome by the activity of a historically specific class.

Marx believes humanity to be capable of producing freely and creatively, overcoming the tyranny of immediate, basic needs that characterizes the rest of the animal kingdom. Under conditions which enable free, creative production, one's personality can be expressed in the objects one produces. This investing of oneself in one's products is a form of alienation, but it is a positive form. It must exist wherever and whenever human beings freely create things, including communist society. But where the conditions for free, creative production do not exist alienation will become distorted into negative forms.

Under capitalism, for instance, factory work (through the division of labour) turns labour from a social activity into an individuated process, alienating workers from each other. Factory work dehumanizes workers by giving them repetitive tasks which require no free, creative input. Thus workers are alienated from their human potential. The products one produces fail any longer to express one's personality. For Marx, then, the superseding of capitalism is a necessary prerequisite for ridding alienation of its distorted elements.

Since Marx, writers across a number of disciplines have developed accounts of alienation, notably in existentialist philosophy (*Sartre), social psychology (Erich Fromm), and various hybrids of Marxism (*Marcuse's psychoanalytic version, for example). As a result of its dissemination across a range of disciplines, the term has been loosely applied to describe the sometimes debilitating effects of life in modern, large-scale societies. AA

Allende Gossens, Salvador (1908–73) Chilean politician. Born on 26 July 1908, Allende became a student leader at Valparaíso University, where he studied medicine. While working for the public health service in 1933, he helped create the Socialist Party of Chile. He was elected to the Chamber of Deputies in 1937 and served as health minister in the Popular Front government elected in 1938. He was general secretary of his party from 1943 to 1970.

Allende's political career was mainly in the Senate, which he presided over in the 1960s. He also became the left's presidential candidate, eventually triumphing at the head of the Popular Unity alliance in 1970. The new coalition was handicapped by internal divisions, its lack of a majority in Congress, and strong US opposition. Electoral support for Popular Unity reached 44 per cent in 1973 but its economic policies were inflationary and provoked active middle-class opposition. Eventually Allende took his own life on 11 September 1973, during a US-backed coup led by General Augusto Pinochet.

Internationally, Allende is associated with the conviction that socialism can be introduced by parliamentary means. Left-wing opinion was deeply divided over the significance of Allende's defeat. Some simply made US imperialism a scapegoat; others decided that Allende's policies had been too ambitious; others concluded that socialism could not be introduced by reformist methods—the state would subvert the socialist government by means of military intervention. RG

alliances An informal or formal relationship between groups, parties, peoples, states, or organizations for common purpose and mutual strategic and political benefit. In the study of politics, alliances often denote a political or economic relationship between political parties seeking to form a *coalition government or to counterbalance the authority of an existing party in power. In the study of *international relations, alliances mainly refer to military agreements between states or between military factions. Those in military alliances generally refer to themselves as 'allies', such as the 'allied forces' in World War II. *NATO is a current alliance with considerable political significance within the *international system.

al-Qaeda A terrorist organization ('The Base') led by Osama Bin Laden, responsible for major attacks on US targets. Born into a wealthy family on 10 March 1957 in Riyadh, Saudi Arabia, Bin Laden studied at the King Abdul Aziz University in Jedda and was influenced by a Palestinian radical, Dr Abdullah Azzam. Following the Soviet invasion of Afghanistan, he backed the Mujahedin resistance to the Soviet occupation, especially the radical Hezb-e Islami of Gulbuddin

Hekmatyar. From 1984 he ran a guesthouse for Arab volunteers in Peshawar in Pakistan entitled the Beit al-Ansar ('House of Supporters'). In 1986 he set up a base in the Jaji area of Paktia in eastern Afghanistan, known as Maasadat Al-Ansar, and in 1989 he formed the al-Qaeda organization. But shortly thereafter, in the wake of the Soviet withdrawal from Afghanistan and the assassination of Abdullah Azzam, he returned to Saudi Arabia, which he was then not allowed to leave. During the 1991 *Gulf War, he developed a profound hatred of the USA; the Western deployment in Saudi Arabia seems to have struck him as the very violation he was called upon to resist. He finally left Saudi Arabia in April 1991, fired with the conviction that the experience of the Soviets in Afghanistan had proved the vulnerability even of superpowers when confronted with true believers. After leaving Saudi Arabia, he revisited Afghanistan and Pakistan, before making his way to Sudan, where he settled in late 1991. In April 1994 he was deprived of Saudi citizenship; in May 1996 he left Sudan for Afghanistan, where he was a significant financier of the Taliban takeover of Kabul in September of that year.

On 7 August 1998 al-Qaeda operatives struck simultaneously at the US Embassies in Kenya and Tanzania; vehicles packed with explosives destroyed both buildings and killed hundreds of people. The US responded with Tomahawk cruise missile attacks against camps in eastern Afghanistan at which al-Qaeda was believed to be engaged in terrorist training. Bin Laden survived the attacks, and also a US campaign, embodied in both unilateral sanctions and multilateral sanctions imposed by UN Security Council resolutions 1267 and 1333, directed at forcing the Taliban leadership to surrender him for trial. Bin Laden's most dramatic attacks came in September 2001. On 9 September suicide bombers posing as journalists killed the military leader of the anti-Taliban forces in Afghanistan, Ahmad Shah Massoud. Two days later, on *September 11th 2001, planes hijacked by al-Qaeda operatives were deliberately flown into the Pentagon building in Washington DC and the twin towers of the World Trade Center in New York, killing over 2,000 people. The direct consequence of this was 'Operation Enduring Freedom', a military campaign led by the US to destroy the Taliban regime and the al-Qaeda organization. In the former aim it was successful; Kabul fell to anti-Taliban forces on 13 November 2001. However, Bin Laden's whereabouts remained unclear, as did the extent to which the activities of al-Qaeda had been fundamentally undermined, as opposed to temporarily disrupted. Since 2001, al-Qaeda or networks associated with it have been variously blamed for bombings in Bali, Madrid, and London, as well as in a number of other cities, and for the assassination in December 2007 of former Pakistan Prime Minister Benazir Bhutto. However, the precise nature of al-Qaeda's involvement, if any, in these attacks remains a matter of speculation. Bin Laden was eventually tracked down to a secure compound in the Pakistani town of Abbottabad, where he was killed in a US military raid in 2011. The saliency of al-Qaeda has recently waned, particularly with the rise of *ISIS and its unifying call for an Islamic caliphate. The rise of ISIS has attracted many followers who might have otherwise been attracted to al-Qaeda. Furthermore, the tactics of ISIS have been largely criticized by al-Qaeda, who view ISIS as illegitimate, hence an alliance between the two is not forthcoming. *See also* AFGHANISTAN WAR (2001).   WM

alternative vote (AV) A procedure for selecting a candidate who can command a majority. Voters rank the candidates. First preferences are counted, and any candidate with more than half of them is declared elected. If no candidate is elected, the candidate with fewest first preferences is eliminated and their votes redistributed; this is repeated as often as required until a candidate wins more than half of the valid votes cast. (The process of vote transfers is similar to the *single transferable vote used in multi-member constituencies.)

AV is used in the lower house of the Australian parliament. Its near relations, double-ballot and exhaustive ballot, are used respectively in French national elections and in British trade-union and Labour Party internal elections. As they are majoritarian, not proportional systems, they do not achieve proportionality in multimember assemblies. They also may fail to select the *Condorcet winner, and are thus far from ideal majoritarian schemes.

Althusius, Johannes (1557–1638) *See* FEDERALISM.

Althusser, Louis (1918–90) French Marxist philosopher who rose to intellectual prominence in the 1960s. Associated with the school of 'structural Marxism', which emphasizes 'scientific' rather than humanist elements of Marx's thought, and develops a multilayered structuralist account of historical determinism.

While claiming with Marx that society is determined by productive forces within the economy 'in the last instance', Althusser conceived of economic determination itself in terms of a complex of interrelated structures exercising various economic, political, and ideological forces within the social body. Within each of these levels of social reality, specific processes of 'contradiction' between the relevant productive forces and production relations effect transformation. But the coexistence and inseparability of these processes within the social whole means that there can be no single dominant dialectical force propelling social development—rather, social formation is 'overdetermined' by an intricate dynamic resulting from the interaction of heterogeneous 'practices'. Furthermore, as a result of the relative autonomy of individual structures and the possibility of their uneven development, a plurality of institutional and social forms is compatible with the notion of economic determinism.

Althusser was an important figure in the extension of Marxist arguments to related fields of philosophy and the social sciences. In particular, he pioneered an epistemological theory according to which knowledge is conceived as a practice of conceptual production rather than the discovery of an external order. Althusser's selective reading of Marx and his attempt to marry Marxist materialism with causal pluralism have been controversial yet highly influential contributions to neo-Marxist debate. In 1980 Althusser murdered his wife. He was found unfit to plead and was confined to a psychiatric hospital for three years. sw

altruism Benefiting other persons or interest-bearers. The common contrast with selfishness reveals some variations in the understanding of altruism, which may refer to a disposition, to an intention, or to behaviour. Hence an altruistic person might intend to benefit others, but fail to do so when executing that intention. Altruism is sometimes understood as giving more consideration to others than oneself, and sometimes as giving equal consideration to oneself and others. Since there are commonly more 'others' than the decision-maker, the distinction usually lacks practical importance, but it may be significant in two-person cases. In discussions informed by *game theory, a contrast is drawn between reciprocal altruism and universal altruism. Reciprocal altruists display that behaviour towards those from whom they have received it, or from whom they expect to receive it. Universal altruism, often seen as the central ethical prescription of Christianity, is unconditional. In sociobiological applications, it can be shown that the survival chances of individuals and groups depend not only on the incidence of selfishness and altruism, but also on the type of altruism in question. AR

Ambedkar, Bhimrao Ramji (1891–1956) Indian politician, who helped frame the Constitution, and has become a symbol of the struggle against oppression and discrimination in modern politics. A member of an Untouchable caste, Ambedkar was raised in poverty and faced caste discrimination throughout his life. Through the sponsorship of the Maharaja of Baroda, he attended Columbia University, and then moved to London, where he studied at the London School of Economics and trained for the Bar. On his return to India, Ambedkar became a spokesman for the Untouchables, campaigning for social, economic, and political rights. His opposition to the Indian National *Congress, which he saw as being dominated by caste Hindus, brought him into conflict with *Gandhi. Upon Independence Ambedkar was inducted into the Congress-led administration, and given a powerful role as Chair of the Drafting Committee of the Constitution. Here he used his legal expertise to mould a document which combined the existing political arrangements with aspects of the American *Bill of Rights and guaranteed protection for the most disadvantaged groups in society. Ambedkar's political philosophy combined a rational individualism with a social critique which sought to undermine the constraints which held back personal development, particularly caste discrimination and economic disparities. His disillusionment with Hinduism led him on a search for an alternative religion more compatible with his political outlook, and in 1956 Ambedkar converted, followed by some three million followers, to Buddhism. His assertive championing of the socially and economically disadvantaged, and reputation as the Untouchable who framed the Constitution, has given him an iconic status amongst the poor of modern India. AM

amendment The official change or formal alteration to an existing piece of legislation, law, constitution, or legal code. In contrast to the creation of a new legislative document, an amendment is added on to existing legislation or legal code so as to redirect, better define, or expand the provisions of existing law. In the United States, the word 'amendment' usually refers to constitutional amendments, which are formally attached to the US Constitution. The most famous amendments in US law are the *Bill of Rights, which refers to the first ten amendments of the US Constitution and which outlines the key rights individuals hold against the power of the state.

amenity Term denoting, in a very broad way, the public benefits accruing from the condition of a place, such as aesthetic beauty, clean air and water, or good street lighting. The function of the concept of amenity is therefore to embrace those factors in a decision about environmental development which are excluded from, and sometimes in contradiction to, considerations of commercial productivity.

In UK politics, the 'amenity clause'—a requirement that public bodies pay due regard to the interests of amenity—was first mentioned in legislation concerned with hydroelectric power in Scotland in 1943. It became a general duty of all public bodies with respect to the countryside in 1968, though the requirement necessarily weakened during the acts of privatization during the 1980s, being replaced by a number of regulative and 'watchdog' bodies.

The 'amenity movement' refers to private organizations defending the interests of amenity, especially pressure groups concerned with particular towns or areas. The

number of these grew rapidly in the 1970s and declined only slowly, if at all, in subsequent decades. *See also* PUBLIC GOOD.   LA

America Often used to refer solely to the United States of America, the term has far richer connotations. The most positive of these centre upon liberation, purity, novelty, and separation. A minority of early Spanish writers viewed orderly pre-Columbian polities as signs of the uniformity and wholeness of natural creation. However, displacement of indigenous peoples, and the creation of independent republics across most of the continent following wars of liberation between 1775 and 1830, made America synonymous with the ideal of republican government within open frontiers. For tens of millions of Europeans, chafing at urban industrialism and autocratic rule, free migration and expanding American agriculture permitted some realization of this ideal, most of all in Canada, the United States, and the southern states of Latin America. But the ideal of liberation was always denied by widespread slavery and coerced labour affecting many millions of Africans and native Americans, while that of purity, wilderness, or naturalness also came under stress in the twentieth century as urbanization and unprecedentedly energy-intensive and consumerist patterns of industrialization took hold and frontiers closed. American claims to novelty and separation from a corrupt Old World wore thin. Already, in 1893, Oscar Wilde could jibe that 'the youth of America is their oldest tradition'.

Once the United States had emerged as the dominant economic, military, and political power in the world, the notion of America became associated with the aggressive promotion of the interests of the United States through its economic and foreign policy. These policies were justified as measures to promote freedom, peace, and democracy, but could also be seen as a modern form of *imperialism. From the *Vietnam War, Chile, and Iran in the 1970s through to Afghanistan and Iraq in the early years of the new century, the United States was open to charges of ill-considered interference with bloody consequences. The advocacy of capitalism and free trade could also be seen as self-serving, directed towards opening up markets for American corporations and ensuring cheap supplies of raw materials. Anti-Americanism became a focus for groups including anti-globalization protestors and those opposed to US policy in the Persian Gulf and its support for Israel (*see also* WEST).   CJ

American Enlightenment   *See* ENLIGHTENMENT, AMERICAN.

American Revolution The process whereby colonists in North America broke free from the British Empire to found the United States.

Despite the political upheavals of the previous century, Britain itself in the middle of the eighteenth century remained a rigidly hierarchical society, still rooted in its feudal past. By contrast, on the other side of the Atlantic, Puritanism and the experience of frontier life had generated anti-authority, individualistic attitudes, while the absence of an aristocracy and the ease with which land could be acquired made possible a degree of social mobility unheard of in Europe. The original charters establishing the colonies had provided for self-government, and, subsequently, successive British administrations allowed the colonists great freedom to conduct their own affairs. By the mid-eighteenth century a large proportion of adult white males in the colonies possessed the suffrage while also enjoying the privileges of a free press and some freedom of religious worship. The colonies, in other words, had grown apart from the mother country, their inhabitants had begun to think of themselves as Americans, and, not surprisingly, they proved unreceptive to attempts to bring them to heel.

British politicians, for their part, with the ending of the Seven Years War (1756–63) turned their attention to the problems of administering an empire. In order to meet the large debt incurred by war with France and the continuing costs of protecting the western frontier and defending the colonists from the American Indians the British government sought new sources of revenue. Believing, not unreasonably, that those same colonists should contribute to the funds necessary for their defence Parliament passed the Revenue Act, otherwise known as the 'Sugar Act', in 1764, and the Stamp Act in 1765. The latter required the affixing of a stamp, which had to be purchased, to a wide range of legal documents, newspapers, pamphlets, playing cards, and other items.

It was the fact that this and other legislation was introduced solely for the purpose of raising revenue that made it so offensive to Americans. As they saw it, this was to infringe one of the most hallowed principles of good government, the right of free people not to be taxed without their consent. Accordingly, the representatives of nine colonies at the Stamp Act Congress of 1765 agreed a number of resolutions, including one asserting, 'That it is inseparably essential to the freedom of a people, and the undoubted rights of Englishmen, that no taxes should be imposed on them, but with their own consent, given personally, or by their representatives'. On the same occasion the Congress rejected categorically the claim of the British government that no basic rights had been violated because colonists enjoyed '*virtual representation' in the House of Commons.

The Stamp Act proved unenforceable and, a year after its passage, was repealed, but Parliament remained unwilling to forgo its claim to paramountcy and continued to pass legislation based on that assumption. The Quebec Act 1774 was the most threatening, empowering as it did the French Canadians and any Indian allies to settle in the Ohio and Mississippi valleys, thus potentially cutting off the expansion of the colonies to the west. Growing resentment in the colonies led to the convening of the First Continental Congress in 1774. This gathering claimed for the people of the colonies the right to enjoy without infringement 'life, liberty and property'; rejected again the relevance of virtual representation in their case; and repeatedly asserted their entitlement to all the rights and immunities of freeborn Englishmen. The first shots in the Revolutionary War were fired at Lexington in April 1775 and the *Declaration of Independence formally breaking the link between the colonies and Britain was signed on 4 July 1776.

The American Revolution was essentially a political revolution. Even though the revolutionaries in this case were motivated in part by a concern for property rights this was not a conflict primarily about economics, but about the values of democratic government. This was also, in several senses, a conservative revolution. Many of those prominent in the movement towards independence were most reluctant to break the link with Britain and only accepted the need to do so as a last resort. They also insisted that in resisting the British government they were merely asserting their rights as Englishmen—that it was the government in London that had first disrupted the *status quo* by enforcing illegitimate measures in the colonies. Furthermore, unlike subsequent revolutions in France and Russia the American version involved no fundamental reordering of existing economic or social structures. DM

amicus curiae Literally, a friend of the court, who may give evidence in court cases, acting either as a disinterested adviser or in order to represent the views of people or bodies that, although not directly involved in the particular case, may be affected by its outcome. The term is used mostly in US law.

Amnesty International International non-governmental organization, formed in 1961, which campaigns against violations of human rights. Originally established to highlight cases of unjust imprisonment, it has led campaigns against the use of torture, the death penalty, and state violence; and sought to promote the protection of individual and group rights. Widely respected, and awarded the Nobel peace prize in 1977, its monitoring of human rights issues through *Amnesty International Reports* has provided information widely used by policy makers and political scientists.

(⊕) SEE WEB LINKS

• Official site, with history, reports, and campaign information.

AMS *See* ADDITIONAL MEMBER SYSTEM.

Amsterdam Treaty (1997) *See* EUROPEAN UNION.

anarchism The view that society can and should be organized without a coercive state. This specialized usage of the word differs markedly from common usage, which takes anarchism as a synonym for moral and political disorder. This pejorative usage is as old as the Greek origins of the word. It was reinforced by an offshoot from mainstream anarchism that for a time carried out spectacular political assassinations, such as those of Tsar Alexander II of Russia (1881), President Carnot of France (1894), and President McKinley of the USA (1901). There is no single positive anarchist doctrine, and apart from their rejection of the state, anarchist thinkers differ fundamentally, supporting a range of proposals from the most extreme *individualism to complete *collectivism.

While supporters of the state see it as necessary to solve problems of security and order (and in many cases, to provide other services), anarchists reverse the argument, and see such problems as a direct consequence of its existence whatever form it may take. The earliest developed theory of anarchism, although not by that name, was *An Enquiry Concerning Political Justice* (1793), by William *Godwin. He said that governments keep their power only by misleading and corrupting their subjects. As individual human reason and judgement grow, and as they lead necessarily to justice and right, governments will become less and less capable of doing this. They will eventually vanish.

*Stirner, although he rejected the word 'anarchism', which he applied to liberalism, was the most extreme individualist, denying any idea of obligation or truth. When the individual recognizes himself as the only value, he will reject every moral and institutional structure, and will be able to live with others in a 'union of egoists' based solely on self-interest. Other individualist anarchists have been far less extreme. Benjamin Tucker (1854–1939), for example, suggested that each individual should enjoy the maximum liberty compatible with that of others, and that society would best be organized as a free market without any authoritative institutions. Since 1945, this line of thought has been continued and sometimes modified in *libertarianism.

Pierre-Joseph *Proudhon (1809–65), recognized by *Marx as the founder of scientific socialism (until 1846 when Proudhon rejected Marx as too authoritarian), became the leading revolutionary thinker in Europe as a result of his book *What is Property?* (1840). His answer to the question was, 'Property is theft'. Proudhon saw society (and indeed the universe) as contradictory, something which could not be changed, but which could be regulated by balancing its necessary pluralisms to avoid disastrous extremes. Proudhon rejected the ideas of God and the state, along with the institutions deriving from them, as the two connected sources of human enslavement. He was one of the first to assert that groups and society exist as such, and are not simply aggregations of individuals. In his theory of exploitation, the surplus taken by capitalists is the result of cooperation between workers rather than (as in Marx) what each produces individually beyond the level of subsistence. In place of the state, Proudhon proposed economic and territorial federalism, with each productive unit managed by its workers and each area by its inhabitants. This system would be continually renewed. Relations between every different level of organization, from the smallest group to the whole of humanity, would be negotiated by delegates. By this means, Proudhon was able to propose that artisans and peasants remain in modern society alongside industrial production. This still reflects the French economy better than Marx's model.

Mikhail *Bakunin was a follower of Proudhon. He saw the wage labourer, necessarily a slave, as typical, and therefore proposed collective ownership. Both the governed and the governors in a society based on the state were corrupted by it, losing their status as human beings. Bakunin opposed Marx, who wished to transform rather than abolish the state, in the First International, which as a result disappeared in 1876.

Peter *Kropotkin (1842–1921) attempted to provide a scientific foundation based on *Darwin for his form of anarchism. In *Mutual Aid* (1897), he argued that evolutionary success was a function of the extent to which members of particular species had adopted the practice of helping each other in ways which did not necessarily benefit the individual. His application of this to humanity, however, finished with the medieval city, which he saw as the most perfect form of society so far achieved. A few examples of cooperation had survived, but it would become dominant only with the revolution which would result from the combination of mass revolutionary feelings with the ideas of anarchist intellectuals.

Almost by definition, there are as many forms of anarchism as there are supporters of it. The main criteria in terms of which they differ concern the legitimacy of different means ranging from the violence of the assassins to the pacifism of *Tolstoy (1828–1910), as well as the social forms already examined. In the reaction against the so-called *totalitarian states of Hitler and Stalin, anarchism played little part in contrast to *liberalism, although the two have been combined in *libertarianism. cs

anarcho-syndicalism A variety of *anarchism, relatively prominent in early twentieth-century France, whose proponents believed that the state should be replaced by trade unions (French *syndicats*). Anarcho-syndicalism had some influence in Spain during the Civil War and a little, but not so much as the government thought, in Britain between 1910 and 1914.

anarchy Lack of centralized authority as opposed to within polities, where social relations are hierarchically ordered by the state or other social institutions. In the discipline of *international relations, anarchy refers to the fact that there is no world government. It is often regarded as the starting point for theorizing international relations as it underpins the distinction between *national* and *international* relations. Whereas at the domestic level, states have a government that oversees societal relations, at the international level there is no such government. Accordingly, states find themselves operating in an anarchical realm. This is widely accepted, but there are two prominent debates regarding anarchy at the international level. The first refers to the implications that stem from anarchy. This was famously captured in Alexander Wendt's statement 'anarchy is what states make of it'. In so doing, he challenged the dominant neo-realist viewpoint argued by *Kenneth Waltz, which claims that the structural nature of anarchy causes states to behave in a certain way. This illustrates that whilst each international relations approach accepts anarchy, they remain divided over its effects. Second, regarding hierarchy, traditional explanations of anarchy claimed that the lack of a world government dictates that there is no hierarchy at the international level. However, this has been challenged by revisionists who claim that hierarchy can still exist within anarchy. AG

ANC (African National Congress) The African National Congress was the first African liberation movement, formed in 1912 in response to the creation of the South African Union which entrenched white minority rule. The ANC, with its middle-class, professional leadership and commitment to liberal principles, multiracialism, and non-violence, had little impact at home or abroad until it expanded its base and broadened its appeal in the 1940s. The Youth League was formed in 1943, with Nelson Mandela and Oliver Tambo, in support of a radical Programme of Action, later adopted by the ANC as the basis of the Defiance Campaign of the 1950s. This pronounced shift leftwards coincided with a National Party government in 1948 committed to *apartheid. The next decade saw ANC support for mass action with the formation of a Congress Alliance, including the Indian Congress, the Coloured People's Congress, and the white Congress of Democrats, influenced by the recently banned Communist Party. In 1955 the ANC adopted the Freedom Charter which reaffirmed its commitment to an inclusive form of nationalism, proclaiming 'that South Africa belongs to all who live in it'. This provoked the departure of a militant Africanist minority in 1959 to form the Pan-Africanist Congress. Both movements were banned in 1960 following the Sharpeville shootings, after which the ANC organized a clandestine military wing, *Umkhonto We Sizwe* (MK), committed to armed struggle. This phase ended in 1963-4, with the arrest, trial, and imprisonment of most of the leadership, while the ANC was forced into exile.

The ANC remained largely in abeyance for the next decade until after the Soweto student uprising of 1976, when a generation of young activists left South Africa to join ANC training camps abroad. With the regime in Pretoria under increasing pressure at home and abroad, the ANC became once again the principal focus of opposition. The movement benefited from the widespread unrest in 1984-6 that accompanied the introduction of a new constitution on racial lines, with no provision for representation of the African majority. The change of leadership in South

Africa in 1989, under F. W. de Klerk, saw the release of Nelson Mandela the following year, the unbanning of the African political organizations, and the beginning of talks on the enfranchisement of the African majority in a new political dispensation. The ANC agreed to suspension of the armed struggle and entered into talks with the government and other parties. September 1992 saw the conclusion of a Record of Understanding, between the government and the ANC, which led to the ANC election victory of April 1994 and the installation of Nelson Mandela as President of South Africa. Thabo Mbeki succeeded Mandela as leader of the ANC in 1997, and became president in 1999. In 2007, after a divisive contest, Jacob Zuma defeated Mbeki to become the President of the ANC.

In recent years the ANC has suffered from a number of corruption scandals, including allegations against President Jacob Zuma for fraud and the misappropriation of public funds. The growing unpopularity of the ANC is compounded by the lack of general economic advancement for black South Africans as well as continued power struggles within the ANC itself, which has resulted in a left-wing splinter group called the Economic Freedom Fighters (EFF). Consequently there has been rising mistrust of the ANC more generally and a growing perception that the ANC will not deliver on its original post-apartheid promises. This growing scepticism about the ANC has also helped the rise of other opposition parties in South Africa, such as the Democratic Alliance, who have won key seats and Provinces in recent South African elections. IC

(⊕) SEE WEB LINKS

• Official site, with historical documents and speeches and writings of Presidents, including Nelson Mandela.

Anglo-Irish Agreement (1985) *See* NORTHERN IRELAND.

Anglo-Saxon capitalism A system of capitalism characterized by extensive market coordination by economic actors and relatively neutral patterns of governmental market regulation aimed at maintaining property right institutions without privileging particular social actors. Though closely tied to liberal political theory, the term 'Anglo-Saxon capitalism' was recently popularized by Michel Albert in his book *Capitalism Vs. Capitalism* (1993) and is central to recent research on 'varieties of capitalism'. Anglo-Saxon capitalism is associated with the United Kingdom and the United States, but also characterizes Canada, Australia, New Zealand, and Ireland. Non-market or associational patterns of economic coordination are weak within Anglo-Saxon capitalism. Markets or relatively short-term pacts between firms are used to coordinate most patterns of economic activity. Unions, employers groups, or other social actors have few statutory bargaining rights within the economy or the governance of firms. Anglo-Saxon capitalism is associated with generally deregulated labour markets, primarily firm-level patterns of wage bargaining, a system of corporate governance dominated by the financial owners of the firm, and a system of finance depending primarily on capital market-based financing rather than long-term bank debt.

Political research on Anglo-Saxon capitalism draws on liberal political theory and neoclassical economic thought. Within economic policy debates, advocates of the Anglo-Saxon model note the strong economic performance of the UK and especially the US during the 1990s to bolster claims that the 'liberal market' model of capitalism is superior to the Rhenish version. Extremely flexible labour markets and financial markets within Anglo-Saxon economies are seen as creating competitive advantages in newly developing or 'radically innovative' industries such as biotechnology or computer software.

Marxist scholars developed the earliest and perhaps most systematic critiques of Anglo-Saxon capitalism, noting a high degree of inequality and a property rights system favouring the owners of capital over other 'stakeholders' within the firm. Critics have pointed to patterns of 'social democracy' associated with Rhenish capitalism and suggested that the introduction of a 'stakeholder' system of corporate governance within Anglo-Saxon economies could have similar effects. Others have pointed to the historically short-term nature of capital investments within Anglo-Saxon economies, associated with the long-term decline of industrial manufacturing and, according to

critics, a shift from higher-paying (and unionized) jobs to lower-paying (and typically un-unionized) jobs in the service sector. SC

animal rights The claim that animals have rights reflects a belief that (at least some) animals are worthy of the protection and security afforded by a set of politically enforced rights. This belief may be grounded in utilitarianism, on the grounds that (*a*) animals can feel pleasure and suffer pain, (*b*) the world is a better place if animals do not suffer unnecessarily, and (*c*) such unnecessary suffering is best avoided through the invocation of rights. It may also be grounded in a deontological argument that all 'subjects of a life' have a basic moral right to be treated with respect. Amongst animal rights theorists the first approach is exemplified in the work of Peter Singer and the second in that of Tom Regan.

The claim for equal rights is not a claim for equal treatment. Whilst both animals and humans can be said to have an interest in not being tortured, cows are not generally thought to have an interest in a right to vote. Thus the claim is for rights appropriate to the capacities of a species.

Problems with animal rights are raised by those who believe that rights must be accompanied by duties—how can animals be rights bearers when they can never be under moral obligation? Environmentalists who believe that a serious moral belief in animal rights would see humans interfering in natural processes of predation and disease have also raised objections. *See also* ANTHROPOCENTRISM and ECOCENTRISM. MH

anomie *See* DURKHEIM.

Antarctic Treaty International agreement which seeks to protect Antarctica from military exploitation and promote international cooperation in scientific investigation. Negotiated in 1959, it was ratified by twelve countries, including the United States and USSR, in June 1961. By 2008 46 countries had signed the treaty. The Protocol on Environmental Protection to the Antarctic Treaty, which was signed in Madrid in 1991, restricts the commercial exploitation of mineral resources in Antarctica, reaffirming the designation of the area as 'a natural reserve, devoted to peace and science'. The environmental protocol runs to 2048. The Antarctic Treaty did not resolve territorial disputes in Antarctica, but sought to prevent new territorial claims. This has not stopped claims for rights to resource exploitation in the Antarctic waters, including an extended claim by the UK, put to the United Nations Commission on the Limits of the Continental Shelf in 2007.

((⊕)) SEE WEB LINKS

• Details of the Antarctic Treaty from the British Antarctic Survey.

anthropocentrism A term from environmental political philosophy denoting a human-centred ethical system, usually contrasted with *ecocentrism. The question of the distribution of value across human and non-human nature has been one of the central preoccupations of environmental ethics over the last thirty years. The anthropocentric belief is that human beings are the sole bearers of intrinsic value or possess greater intrinsic value than non-human nature. It is therefore acceptable to employ the resources of the natural world for only human ends—a view that has come in for sustained criticism from ecocentric philosophers, who argue that it amounts to little more than a species bias, or 'human racism'.

Recent ecological defences of anthropocentrism claim that an anthropocentric ethics is adequate to the task of grounding care for the natural environment. A sufficiently complex or enlightened understanding of human well-being will acknowledge the value of the non-human world to humans in more than merely economic-instrumental terms. If the existence of a non-anthropogenic environment is taken as essential to human well-being, then demands for environmental protection can be anthropocentric in origin but no more contingent than ecocentrism claims to be; the advantage of anthropocentrism being that it allows these demands to be made within a familiar moral framework.   MH

anthropology Anthropology literally means the science or study of mankind, and the word was used in this broad sense in English for several centuries. In the eighteenth century, and even for most of the nineteenth century, it was conceived as a primarily physiological study, though there were always those who insisted that anthropology should study body, soul, and the relations between them. With the development of zoology, sociology, and economics, anthropology lost a great deal of its territory, although physical anthropology was partly absorbed in the new genetics after the discovery of the structure of DNA in 1953. What remained was primarily 'cultural' anthropology and an emphasis on the variety of human societies. In practice, this has meant an emphasis on 'primitive' societies which can be studied in a more comprehensive way than is usually possible with more 'advanced' societies. This has often cast the anthropologist in the role of defender as well as interpreter of the values of such societies.   LA

Anti-Ballistic Missile Treaty *See* DISARMAMENT.

anticlericalism The belief that the influence of the, or any, church in politics ought to be diminished. Strongest in some Roman Catholic countries, in reaction to the claims (real or supposed) of the Catholic Church. In Europe, it has been traditionally strong in France, representing social divisions that go back before 1789: areas that supported the *French Revolution tend to remain anticlerical.

anti-globalization An umbrella term invoking a common element of opposition to globalization amongst a diverse range of protest movements. Anti-globalization brings together campaigns about labour conditions (including child labour and slave labour), environmental destruction, biohazards, animal rights, social justice, third-world development and debt, and politically oppressive regimes. As well as these specific protests anti-globalization has also attracted groups more generally opposed to liberal capitalism, such as anarchists. Opposition to globalization focuses on two areas. First there is the perceived growth in the power of *multinational corporations. These firms are deemed to wield significant political and economic power without being subject to the constraints of democratic accountability. Secondly, international bodies such as the *World Bank, *International Monetary Fund, and *World Trade Organization are held by anti-globalization protestors to sponsor and facilitate this corporate power, and their meetings have thus also been the targets of protest. Not all protestors against global capitalism accept the 'anti-globalization' label, claiming instead to be seeking an alternative form of globalization—the term 'alterglobalization' has been developed to denote this view.

Major anti-globalization demonstrations have occurred at a number of meetings of international financial and trade organizations, including the World Trade Organization ministerial meeting in Seattle in November 1999, the meeting of the World Economic Forum in Davos in January 2000, those of the World Bank and International Monetary Fund in Washington in April 2000 and again in Prague in September of that year, the Summit of Americas in Quebec in April 2001, and the G8 summit in Genoa in July 2001. There have been more recent demonstrations at the G8 summit in Heiligendamm, Germany, in June 2007, and the Asia-Pacific Economic Cooperation Leaders' Summit in Sydney in September 2007. The period since 2001 has also seen the development of the *World Social Forum and its regional offshoots.

More recent anti-globalization demonstrations were witnessed in response to the 2008 *Financial Crisis and the high-risk global financial systems that made the crisis possible. The most prominent of these protests was called the 'Occupy movement', which saw prolonged sit-in demonstrations at all major financial centres across the globe as well as sit-in protests in a number of other locations worldwide. The focus of these protests was not necessarily a full repudiation of globalization per se, but that globalization seemingly favours the 'elite 1 per cent' at the expense of 'the 99 per cent' of ordinary people. MH

anti-Semitism Literally, persecution of or discrimination against the Jews. The first use of the term, which came into being in the 1870s, is variously attributed to the German Wilhelm Marr and the Frenchman Ernest Renan. In one respect it was a misnomer from the beginning since, in the jargon of the racial theory of the period, 'Semites' were a broad group of non-European ethnic groups including Arabs, whereas anti-Semitism was taken to mean, and has continued to

mean, an anti-Jewish racism. Anti-Semitism differs from the anti-Jewish ideas and theories which pre-dated the rise of racial theory in the 1850s in that it identifies Jewish characteristics as congenital rather than as specifically religious or broadly cultural (and, therefore, capable of rejection by individual Jews). The persecution of Jews is as old as the 'Diaspora' which spread Jewish population throughout Europe and the Mediterranean after the Romans expelled the Jews from Palestine in AD 79; Jews were expelled from several countries in the later Middle Ages. Anti-Semitism differs from most other forms of racism which emphasize merely the inferiority of certain races (especially those of African origin). Doctrines of racial inferiority usually recognize the possibility of racial harmony provided that the inferior race is kept in its proper, inferior, social place. But anti-Semitism emphasizes the innate hostility of Jews to the interests of non-Jews rather than their inferiority as such. LA

anti-system party A political party that wishes to change or destroy the political system in which it is operating. Used extensively in the 1950s and 1960s to describe fascist, communist, and *Poujadist parties, the term is less in favour now, as it is widely thought to be a product of the *Cold War. In particular, most communist parties since 1945 have not been anti-system in any strong sense.

ANZUS Treaty signed in 1951 by Australia, New Zealand, and the United States, pledging mutual protection, with the aim of discouraging communist expansion and increasing US influence in the Pacific region.

ANZUS was superseded by the broader-based *SEATO, but was used by the United States to put pressure on Australia and New Zealand to become more involved in the *Vietnam War. The failure of the military campaign in Vietnam, and the growth of opposition to nuclear weapons in New Zealand, have meant that, though still technically operative, ANZUS has little practical relevance.

(((⊕))) SEE WEB LINKS

• Text of the ANZUS treaty.

apartheid Afrikaans word meaning, literally, 'separateness'. In South Africa, an official government policy between 1948 and 1989 of racial segregation. The term originated as a political slogan coined by Dr D. F. Malan, leader of the South African National Party, in 1944, and derived from the Afrikaans word denoting 'apartness' or separation. It featured prominently in the party's successful election campaign in 1948, cementing a coalition of disparate Afrikaner groups and classes, and would serve for the next four decades as the rationale for the regime's racial programme. Segregation had long been practised by white governments in South Africa. White workers were traditionally privileged in an economy otherwise heavily dependent on black labour. The African population, three-quarters of the total, was disenfranchised and subject to coercion backed by law. And 70 per cent of the land had been reserved for white occupation. After 1948, under the new apartheid measures, racial differentiation and separation, already comprehensive, became rigid and systematized, with no further prospect of assimilation or integration.

The key legislation enacted 1948–50 dealt with Population Registration, the Prohibition of Mixed Marriages, demarcation of Group Areas and restructuring of Bantu Education, as well as the Suppression of Communism. The main architect of apartheid was H. F. Verwoerd (1901–66), the leading intellectual and ideologue of the National Party. Determined to resist the movement towards self-determination and independence elsewhere in Africa, Verwoerd insisted that in South Africa self-determination for the white and other racial minorities was incompatible with majority African rule. Instead the government proposed to implement a programme of separate development, promising eventual independence for the various ethnic groups that were held to comprise the African population. Having been assigned a national homeland, or Bantustan, Africans settled and working in South Africa would lose their residence and other rights and became liable to deportation in the event of political unrest or large-scale unemployment. Under the guise of 'trusteeship', government policy was to confine the African majority to reserves that could not support them, thus ensuring the continuation of a cheap, compliant labour force.

Within South Africa opposition to apartheid was forcibly suppressed, with the main African political movements banned after 1960 and their leaders imprisoned or exiled. Through the 1970s, however, there was mounting criticism, not only from white liberals, but also from a younger generation of Africans who had grown up under apartheid and were attracted by Black Consciousness ideology. Resistance to the regime continued after the Soweto uprising of 1976, reinforced by the collapse of white rule elsewhere in southern Africa, and by growing international pressure for sanctions. Among 'enlightened' whites it was already clear that apartheid was unworkable (and increasingly unprofitable) in a closely integrated, urban society, with a growing industrial base looking for a wider domestic market and heavily dependent on a skilled, educated African labour force. The gradual scrapping of petty apartheid discrimination, and the recognition accorded black trade unions in 1979 were evidence of revisionist thinking among Verwoerd's political successors. Meanwhile, without infrastructure or resources, deprived of investment, and denied international recognition, the four 'independent' and six self-governing homelands offered no prospect of development and served only to underline the contradictions inherent in official policy. After 1978 the term apartheid was itself rejected by the new Prime Minister, P. W. Botha.

It was 1984, however, before constitutional changes were made, providing for an executive-style President and a tricameral legislature. Structured along racial lines and with no provision for the African majority, the 'reform' provoked sustained unrest throughout South Africa during 1984–6, with the state declaring a state of emergency and exceptional levels of violence on both sides. The international community responded with further sanctions, while foreign banks withheld investment, precipitating a financial crisis in an economy already experiencing prolonged recession and record unemployment. With the end of the Cold War in southern Africa, and independence for Namibia, there was growing pressure for democratization in South Africa itself. Meanwhile apartheid no longer commanded the loyalty of the white electorate as a whole, or even of its entrenched Afrikaner component. Like the English-speaking community the Afrikaners now had much to lose from domestic conflict generating widespread insecurity. The far right had quit the National Party as early as 1982 to form the Conservative Party and, by 1989, there was majority support for new leadership, under F. W. de Klerk, and a new political dispensation.

De Klerk freed Mandela and the other political detainees, unbanned the nationalist parties and the Communists and, by 1992, had repealed all the principal apartheid legislation. The Dutch Reformed Church, which had claimed scriptural backing for apartheid, split with the white branch, which was prepared to acknowledge that apartheid was a serious error, if not a heresy. Even the *Broederbond*, the original inspiration for apartheid, whose select membership has been credited with a disproportionate influence on government, considered the admission of non-whites. *See also* ANC.   IC

apparat A Russian word literally meaning 'apparatus', used to denote the machinery of state administration. Its primary use in English is pejorative, denoting a faceless, privileged, and all-powerful communist bureaucracy; its members are referred to as apparatchiki. In the narrowest sense in official Soviet discourse, the word did not have a negative connotation. Rather, it may best be understood as designating that part of the state—the permanent commissions of the Council of Ministers and the state committees such as State Committee for Planning (Gosplan) or the State Committee for Material and Technical Supply (Gossnab)—primarily concerned with issuing regulations and instructions to other bodies—the industrial ministries—which were operationally responsible for carrying them out. Members of the latter bodies were frequently called *khozyaystvenniki* (economic executives).   swh

apparentement In France, a legally recognized alliance between parties. Before the 1951 legislative elections the governing centre parties introduced changes in the electoral system which aimed to neutralize pressure from the two political extremes, *Gaullists and Communists, both opposed to the regime and expected to benefit from a proportional system that favoured the strongest parties in the distribution of seats.

By changing the law to provide (among other things) for *alliance* or *apparentement* the centre parties were able to pool their votes, maximize their share of seats, and achieve a workable majority in the legislature. When he came to power at the outset of the *Fifth Republic, General de Gaulle was able to discriminate even more effectively against the political extremes by replacing proportional representation with a double-ballot system.   IC

appeasement A policy of acceding to hostile demands in order to gain peace. The term is today normally used in a pejorative sense by most politicians and communicators. Its alleged practitioners are usually held to be willing, in an ignoble or cowardly fashion, to sacrifice other people's territories or rights in an attempt to buy off an aggressor or wrong-doer. Moreover 'appeasement' is supposed never to succeed for long: the aggressor always returns demanding further concessions. And the implication is usually that refusal to 'appease' would, by contrast, have a happy ending as in any morality play.

'Appeasement' has often been seen in these terms ever since the outbreak of the European war over Poland in 1939. But the word had no such connotations when it first became fashionable during the 1920s and early 1930s. As late as 1936 British Foreign Secretary Anthony Eden, later widely thought of as an 'anti-appeaser', stated in the House of Commons that 'it is the appeasement of Europe as a whole that we have continually before us'. A consensus had developed in most countries, and in Great Britain in particular, that the Peace Settlement of 1919, based on questionable assumptions about war guilt, had been too severe to the First World War's defeated powers. Hence it was thought that the way to avoid a second such war was for the victors to try to meet the reasonably justified grievances of the losers. This meant working by negotiation to end reparations, to address German grievances with respect to permitted levels of armaments, to evacuate those parts of Germany that were occupied by the victors, and to meet claims for frontier adjustments in cases involving a denial of the principle of self-determination. At first, France, supported by some of her East European allies, was hesitant about accepting this approach. But gradually Great Britain, supported by most other countries, broke down French resistance.

The rise to power of Adolf Hitler in Germany in 1933 did not at first make much difference to this pursuit of 'appeasement' by the victors of 1918. It was widely hoped that he would become more moderate as he gained experience in office and as Germany's reasonable grievances were met. Thus Great Britain and France did nothing to prevent Hitler's proclamation that 'illegal' German rearmament was taking place, his remilitarization of the Rhineland and the *Anschluss* (annexation) with Austria. Nor would public opinion in Great Britain or France, still less in the United States, have favoured war over these issues. A war against Mussolini's Italy for attacking Abyssinia would have been more popular, but the British and French governments were too afraid of the growing strength of Germany and Japan to take any serious risk of joining in a conflict that did not directly affect their interests.

The public mood in Great Britain and France changed only in 1938–9—largely as a result of Hitler's treatment of Czechoslovakia. Hitler seemed at first to have a reasonable case when he drew attention to the discontent of the German-speaking minority of Czechoslovak citizens living in the Sudetenland area that was contiguous to Germany. And British Prime Minister Neville Chamberlain was generally applauded when he masterminded the transfer of this territory to Germany at the Munich Conference held in September 1938. But Winston Churchill led a vociferous minority who claimed that Hitler had behaved in such a threatening manner that he had effectively humiliated Great Britain and France and that he was really aiming at European mastery if not world conquest.

In March 1939 Churchill appeared to have been vindicated when Germany invaded the remainder of Czechoslovakia without serious justification. It seems probable that Chamberlain's initial inclination was nevertheless to continue with the policy of 'appeasement' as long as Hitler continued to move east. For he recognized that Great Britain had never seen Eastern Europe as an area of vital interest and he was aware that in any case the military balance of forces was not such as to make it easy to check Hitler in

that region. And he had no desire to ally with the Soviet Union whose communist system he detested even more than fascism. But the majority in the British Cabinet, responding to public opinion, decided to abandon 'appeasement'. Accordingly, a 'security guarantee' was given to Poland and this was honoured with an Anglo-French declaration of war in September 1939 when Germany invaded. The policy of 'appeasement' was thus discredited and has remained so among ordinary people ever since.

Some historians have attempted to launch 'revisionist' accounts that support Chamberlain's broad approach. They point out that Great Britain and France were unable to defeat Germany in 1939–40—with the result that Poland was to be subjugated for half a century. As A. J. P. Taylor, an early 'revisionist', wrote: 'Less than one hundred thousand Czechs died during the war. Six and a half million Poles were killed. Which was better— to be a betrayed Czech or a saved Pole?'   DC

appellate jurisdiction The authority of a court of appeal to review decisions made by a lower court.

apportionment Allocation of seats to regional units, or to parties under systems of proportional representation.

Territorial apportionment is usually a process of adjusting the seats allocated to each unit to reflect changes in population. Under the US Constitution, seats in the House of Representatives are divided among the states once every ten years (after each census), with no seat crossing a state line. The UK Boundary Commissions redistribute parliamentary seats every twelve to fifteen years, and normally no parliamentary seat crosses county boundaries.

Within territorial units, the apportionment process then involves the (re-)drawing of constituency boundaries (in the US known as redistricting, in India delimitation), usually with the aim of equalizing the population (or electorate) per seat, in accordance with the principle of 'one person, one vote, one value'. This is usually done with regard to stated constraints of administrative convenience, contiguity, geographical, and communication factors; and unstated influences of party-political advantage. Such a process is open to political manipulation, or *gerrymandering.

Alternatively, apportionment may refer to the allocation of seats according to the number of votes a party has received, particularly in the case of list *proportional representation. In the *Northern Ireland Assembly ministerial portfolios are apportioned according to the number of votes each party attained, according to the d'Hondt formula. Applications of apportionment have a common mathematical structure (and hence face common *impossibility theorems) but this has not generally been realized by reformers who periodically reinvent systems of apportionment that are already in use under another name somewhere else. *See* D'HONDT; SAINTE-LAGÜE; JEFFERSON; WEBSTER.

appropriation The allocation of money by public officials for specific purposes. Control by the legislature over the raising of revenue and the expenditure of public funds has been seen historically as an essential requirement of democratic government. In practice in the United Kingdom, control over the purse strings lies with the government. Theoretically, back-bench members of the House of Commons may reduce or delete proposed appropriations, but they are unable to initiate expenditures without the agreement of the executive. No such restrictions exist in the United States Congress, where legislative control over appropriations is complete (apart from rare Presidential vetoes) and, as such, a bulwark of the considerable power of the legislature. DM

approval voting An electoral system in which voters may cast up to as many votes as there are candidates, but may not cast more than one vote for one candidate (which would be *cumulative voting). The effect is that each voter may partition the list of candidates into two classes: 'those I approve of' and 'those I do not approve of'. Approval voting has influential academic support in the United States and is used in some society and local elections there. It produces better results than other unranked voting systems (such as *first-past-the-post) but uses less information than some systems which ask voters to rank-order the candidates (such as *single transferable vote).

Aquinas, St Thomas (*c.*1225–74) Catholic theologian and political philosopher, regarded as one of the great figures of medieval thought. The tradition he founded became known as 'Thomism'. The basis of his political theory is contained in his commentary on Aristotle's *Politics*, in *De regimine principum* (On the Rule of Sovereigns), written while at the papal court in Italy (1259–68) and completed by others, and in the *Summa Theologiae*, II, First Part, Questions 90–7.

Following *Aristotle, he held that the state is a natural, not a conventional (such as a society, company, or club), institution; and it is a perfect society (*communitas perfecta*). It is natural, not conventional because human beings are social animals. They need to form a society for their survival, prosperity, and cultural development. Gregarious animals do this by instinct; humans do it by using reason. It is perfect in that (in principle) it can satisfy all the ends of human life, and is not dependent on any higher society, unlike the family (also a natural society), which is dependent on a larger community for survival and material and cultural development.

All power, according to Aquinas, comes from God since it involves the power of life and death which, in Church doctrine, is the prerogative of God—here Aquinas deviates from Aristotle. But he returns on stream when he argues that (1) sovereignty (be it monarchy, parliamentary government, or popular government) is natural, and that (2) it comes (albeit from God) through the people governed. It is natural in that without a governing body capable of making binding decisions anarchy would result and people could destroy each other. It comes through the people, because, whatever the form of government, it must reflect the wishes of the governed. The sovereign or government, in the view of Aquinas, is the representative of the governed (popularly called 'the people'): 'If the people (*multitudo*) do not have the power to institute laws freely or to rescind laws imposed by a superior power, a custom prevailing among such people, however, obtains the force of law, insofar it is by it [the custom] that those who impose them on the people are allowed to do so' (*ST*, II, First Part, Question 97, Article 3).

The State is, therefore, not in any way dependent on the Church. Each has a separate end and a separate role. But Aquinas believed in a supernatural end for humankind. In the pursuit of this end the Church is a perfect society, since in this respect, it does not depend on any other body. Moreover, unlike the State, it is an autonomous perfect society. In the Thomist view the Church as such is in no way subordinate to the State, whereas the State must take the interests of the Church into account, since its end is loftier and it is the ultimate end of the citizen. Aquinas likens the relationship of Church to State to that of the soul to the body. Each has its own particular role to play but ultimately the soul's is higher.

This unity of purpose comes about in the citizen who has one end but separate spiritual and material needs. The citizen's relationship to the State is also holistic. He is subordinate to the State as the part is to the whole, the members to the body. But this does not give the State unlimited power over its subjects. For one thing, it is never permissible to obey a law which is contrary to divine law. For another, civil laws and decrees that are contrary to natural (i.e. moral) law are invalid. In this Aquinas was voicing the views of most medieval political theorists, as in his support for the legitimacy of tyrannicide. As political power, after God, rested with the governed, the government holds power in trust. If the ruler or rulers abuse that trust by tyrannical behaviour, it can be withdrawn, even if this means deposing the tyrant. CB

Arab–Israeli conflict *See* INTIFADA; PLO; ZIONISM.

Arab League Organization, officially The League of Arab States, which seeks to promote political, cultural, and economic cooperation between member states. It was formed in 1945, with Egypt, Iraq, Jordan (then Transjordan), Lebanon, Saudi Arabia, and Syria the original members. In 2008 it had 22 full members, including representatives of Palestine from the *PLO. The Arab League coordinated an economic boycott of Israel, which ran from 1948 to 1993, but has struggled to present a coherent political programme on broader issues, and economic cooperation has been limited.

Such failure has partly resulted from the organization's design: decisions are binding only for members who voted on them. In addition, internal factors such as state form (e.g. monarchic or republican rule) have informed Arab states' diverging policies. External relations also divide Arab states; for example, the existence of ties with either the US or the USSR during the *Cold War. More recently, the nature of relations with various external actors determined Arab actors' action and inaction during the events of the *Arab Spring. In 2011, the Arab League denounced Muammar Gadaffi's human rights abuses and called for the imposition of a no-fly zone over *Libya in an unprecedented request for UN *Security Council intervention. JHA

((🌐)) SEE WEB LINKS
• Site of the Arab League (League of Arab States), including a list of member states and historical documents (in Arabic).

Arab Spring In the spring of 2011 popular protests brought an end to Tunisian dictator Zine El Abidene Ben Ali's twenty-three-year rule. The events in Tunisia inspired protests against authoritarian rule in Egypt, *Libya, *Syria, Yemen, Sudan, Iraq, Jordan, Bahrain, and Oman. The protests emerged suddenly and were largely unanticipated by the majority of academic commentators. Whilst protests quickly spread from one country to the next, general *regime change across the Middle East has not come as quickly as it appeared in Tunisia. Between 2010 and the present, thousands of peaceful protesters in various Arab countries have been tortured, imprisoned, or sentenced to death. The overall civilian death toll of the 'Arab Spring' continues to mount, partly as the result of air strikes and continued civil war in Libya, Syria, and Yemen. As a result of the ongoing conflicts, the optimism that characterized international reaction to the uprisings of 2010–2012, which in many cases characterized the 'Arab Spring' as a democratic movement, has gradually given way to pessimism.

The Arab countries that have experienced similar revolutions and counter-revolutions share a number of commonalities, but it is important to recognize that their own unique domestic politics and international relations have shaped their recent histories. The protesters who took to the street in 2010–12 were bound by their rejection of authoritarian rule and a desire for constitutional and representative government. Nevertheless, manifold differences exist between Arab states. Understanding these differences is vital to explain the divergent outcomes of the revolutionary trajectories of the 'Arab Spring'.

Facile analyses of the 'Arab Spring' have disproportionately focused on the influence of social media and the significance of bread riots. Arab countries' 'youth bulge' is another factor that is frequently emphasized. Whilst these factors are important, considered in isolation they do not explain why the revolutions occurred when they did, and why—in spite of these commonalities—there were vastly divergent outcomes in different states. Three broader themes are particularly important in developing a deeper understanding of the state of turmoil in which the Arab region has found itself since 2011: economic failure, state repression, and geopolitical context.

First, poor long-term economic growth across the region contributed to popular dissatisfaction. Overall economic growth in the Arab world was negative for the last three decades of the twentieth century, and rates of unemployment, underemployment, and poverty remained amongst the highest in the world in 2010. Market liberalization, privatization, deregulation, and fiscal discipline aggravated the economic ailments of many Arab countries, and social inequalities increased amidst the corruption and clientelist practices of ruling elites. The Tunisian revolution began because an informal street vendor, Mohamed Bouazizi, set himself on fire when he could no longer pay police bribes. Whilst Bouazizi's act was the result of his desperate economic situation, it is important to note that the proverbial 'final straw' was the lack of respect the authorities showed Bouazizi. The episode resonated with millions across the region, and, taken as analogy, the incident highlights the Arab Spring's economic and political dimensions. Arabs going onto the street wanted to secure democratic freedoms and improve government accountability, but they also wanted recognition of their rights as citizens and protection from repression at the hands of the state and its agents.

It is also important to highlight the international dimension of these dynamics.

Whilst the orientalist portrayal of the Arab region and peoples as 'ungovernable' and deserving of despotic rule lives on, external actors share responsibility for ill-targeted economic policies and hard-line state repression. The negative impact of *IMF policies on Arab employment rates has been well-documented, and the promotion of export economies by external actors such as the *European Union has actively shaped Arab economic policies.

In addition to shaping the region's economy, external actors had supported the late dictatorships for decades and often continued to do so when revolutions began. As a result of concerns for stability, their prioritization of anti-terrorism policies, and consideration for their bilateral relations with Israel, Western actors were often hesitant to express their support for the protesters. Within the region, Arab actors such as Saudi Arabia, Qatar, and Iran influenced the outcome of uprisings by supporting existing regimes and/or proxy organizations. Saudi Arabia, for example, actively supported existing dictatorial regimes, except in the cases of Libya, Yemen, and Syria. Likewise, Iran has intervened in various conflicts that emerged as a result of the 'Arab Spring', increasing its support for Hamas and other Shia militia organizations.

Finally, it is important to note that the state of analysis of the events collectively referred to as the 'Arab Spring' remains fragmented and largely superficial. This is partly because of the limited time which has elapsed since the onset of the events, but also because insufficient attention is being paid to the long history of the contributing factors to the Arab Spring and the diverse experiences of Arab countries in this context. JHa

Arendt, Hannah (1906–75) Political theorist, who was born in Königsberg (then in Germany, now Kaliningrad in Russia) and studied *existentialism under *Heidegger and Karl Jaspers. During the Nazi era she emigrated first to France and then to the United States, and published her best-known work in English. Her first major work was *The Origins Of Totalitarianism* (1951), which attempted to understand the horror of both Nazism, in terms of the concentration camps, and Stalinism, with reference to the ruthlessness of the purges. Arendt saw *totalitarianism occurring through two particular factors: the destruction of the legal and territorial nation-state by imperialism and the tendency for individuals to identify themselves with races as opposed to citizens or members of a class. Through the concept of 'superfluousness' she shows how these factors could lead to a political system where human beings become quickly and simply expendable. This led to her conception of 'the banality of [the] evil' represented by the Nazi war criminal Adolf Eichmann: what he lacked was ordinary understanding of how the world looked from inside other people's minds. In *The Human Condition* (1958) she attempts to analyse particular concepts, such as labour, work, and action, in terms of how they were linguistically understood in previous cultures. The motive for this was to try to give an insight into the very experiences which people felt in earlier ages and thereby reveal possibilities in our own human condition which have become lost in modern language. In *On Revolution* (1963) she attempted to reinstate human action, rather than simply historical processes, as the essence of a revolution. Such a focus on the capacity for individuals to act led her to support popular councils for self-government and to stress the importance of public freedom. Thus the paradigm revolution was not the *French or *Russian, but the *American. She saw her emphasis on human action and human capacity as the distinguishing factor between her own and preceding political theory. Some have seen the collapse of East European communism as an Arendtian moment of free human action; others see her as a precursor of *post-modernism. IF

aristocracy Rule by the best. The basis upon which the best are to be identified or chosen may be variously specified; for example, fitness to govern may be assessed in technical, meritocratic terms, or in historical, or dynastic ways. Since, by definition, the best are a select group, the distinction between aristocracy and *oligarchy may become blurred, and oligarchy has often been presented as a corrupt form of aristocracy. AR

Aristotle (*c.*384–322 BC) Greek philosopher. He was born into a wealthy family in northern Greece, where his father was physician to the King of Macedon. In 367 he came to Athens and associated himself with *Plato's Academy, where he studied and taught until Plato's death in 347. After several years travelling and researching in the eastern Aegean, he was invited by Philip of Macedon to be tutor to the young Alexander the Great. In 335 he returned to Athens and established his own school of philosophy, the Lyceaum, where he worked until strong anti-Macedonian feeling prompted him to retire to Euboea; he died the following year.

His first independent researches were principally in biology, and the methods and concepts of the natural scientist permeated his thought throughout his life. His range of interests and learning was vast: apart from several fine biological works, he wrote treatises on physics, metaphysics, logic, psychology, aesthetics, ethics, and politics. He divided the sciences into three main branches: the theoretical, the productive, and the practical. Ethics and politics are practical sciences, aimed not just at knowledge but also at action, at changing the way people conduct their lives. In a move away from Plato, Aristotle believed that these practical sciences should be based on empirical data and taxonomy, and together with a team of students he researched the political structure and history of 158 constitutions, though only the *Constitution of Athens* has survived. Some of the results of these researches, however, can be found in his most famous political work, the *Politics*, which, in its mixture of analysis, prescription, and description, gives accounts of a number of constitutions, including Sparta, Crete, and Carthage. Aristotle also describes and analyses the political theories (or his versions of them) of other philosophers, notably Plato.

The biological framework of his thought also shapes his analysis of the nature, origin, and purpose of the state. Whereas some of the *sophists had claimed an antithesis between nature and culture, Aristotle seeks to demonstrate that 'man is a political animal', by which he means the kind of animal that naturally lives in a *polis* or city-state. First, he examines the way the city-state comes to be. There are, he believes, two basic forms of human association: the association of male with female for the purposes of procreation; and the association of master and 'natural slave' for the purposes of mutual preservation. From these associations the household is formed. Households group together to form villages and villages group together to form the *polis*, which Aristotle perceives as a self-sufficient community bonded together by shared practices and values. Living in a *polis*, therefore, is for humans the natural result of the two fundamental natural forms of association. There is no antithesis between nature and culture, and no artificial '*social contract'.

The second argument rests on an analysis of human nature and human flourishing which is referred to in the *Politics* but expounded in most detail in the *Nicomachean Ethics*. To flourish, we need to exercise the intellectual and moral capacities which we possess as members of the human species: such capacities, and in particular our capacity to act justly, cannot be exercised outside the context of the state. It is precisely because the state provides everything necessary for the good and flourishing life that it is said to be self-sufficient; and it is in the provision of this good life that its main purpose lies. Here again, therefore, the state accords with human nature. Indeed, Aristotle claims that the state itself is a natural entity: not only does it have its origins in the natural associations of male and female, and of master and slave, but it is the natural end of all the earlier associations, and 'nature is itself an end'; it follows therefore 'that the state belongs to the class of objects which exist by nature' (*Politics* I. 2). This can lead Aristotle to talk of the state as a kind of suprabeing of which individuals are merely the parts, of no independent worth. Such tendencies in his thought have led to charges of totalitarianism: at one point the citizen is actually said to belong to the state (*Politics* VIII. 1).

But who are to count as citizens? Aristotle distinguishes three basic elements in government, the deliberative, the executive, and the judicial, and he defines citizenship as active participation in at least the deliberative and judicial functions. Such active participation requires directive reasoning powers and a certain amount of leisure and education; he further holds that these requirements will mean that only freeborn, non-artisan males can be citizens. Some

humans, Aristotle believes, have only sufficient reasoning powers to obey the directions of others; they cannot deliberate for themselves. Such humans are 'natural slaves' and are not capable of taking part in political decision-making: indeed they will be much happier if someone else directs their lives for them. This is why the master–slave relation is basic and natural. Women will also be happier if they are directed by someone else, for though they possess the ability to reason for themselves, this faculty is not authoritative in them, being at the mercy of their emotions. Artisans and manual labourers are to be excluded on the grounds that their occupation deprives them of the leisure required both for active political participation and for the intellectual development such participation demands. As resident aliens are also to be denied citizenship, the result will be that only a comparatively small number of those living in a state are to count as its citizens. Indeed, Aristotle sometimes writes as if these non-citizens are not even to count as members of the state, but simply as its *sine qua non* (cf. *Politics* III. 3 and VII. 8)—a view which, at least in the case of women and slaves, would appear to be at odds with the argument in Book I for the development of the state from the household.

In Books III and IV of the *Politics* Aristotle undertakes a taxonomy and analysis of the different kinds of constitution. One way of roughly distinguishing constitutions is by asking two fundamental questions: who rules and on whose behalf? Rule may be exercised by one, few, or many, and it may be exercised well, on behalf of the population as a whole, or badly, on behalf of the rulers themselves. The three correct constitutions are monarchy, aristocracy, and 'polity', and the three corresponding deviations tyranny, oligarchy, and democracy. In practice, however, the few will be rich and the majority poor; thus economic status will be at least as important a defining feature as number. In helping to shape the goals and values of those in power, economic conditions are also partly responsible for giving each constitution its own distinguishing mark: the goal of oligarchy, for instance, is more wealth; that of democracy, freedom. Later Aristotle qualifies this broad taxonomy. He stresses that there are several varieties of each of the six basic types and that all these varieties can be combined in a number of ways: indeed it is really more accurate to speak of a constitution as possessing, for instance, certain democratic features.

Aristotle's views on the relative merits of these constitutions are complex. He is clear that all constitutions which aim at the common good are preferable to those which look solely to sectional interests, and he is also clear that the common good must be firmly based on a notion of distributive justice, according to which the greater share of goods and honours is distributed to the citizens who contribute most to the state. The question of which form of constitution is best, however, depends on circumstances. Should a supremely wise and good person arise, who contributes supremely to the state, then according to the transactional principles of distributive justice such a man should be given supreme power, and be permitted to rule above the law; the same argument would apply to a supremely virtuous group. In the probable absence of such an ideal monarchy or aristocracy, however, the best constitution for the majority of states is 'polity', a mixture of democracy and oligarchy in which power is in the hands of those of moderate wealth. This middle class, Aristotle believes, will be the most likely to act in accordance with reason, and the least likely to suffer from faction and the extremes that both wealth and poverty encourage; he explicitly, if problematically, links it to the 'mean' which in the *Nicomachean Ethics* is said to constitute virtue. The decisions of the middle class are also most likely to win general acceptance. All these factors will make for stability.

Political stability is for Aristotle one of the greatest goods, and in Books V and VI of the *Politics* he devotes considerable space to examining the features which promote and undermine it. He considers it worthwhile to include measures for preserving even the 'deviant' constitutions, though in the case of tyranny he may regard an understanding of the tyrant's tactics as the best insurance against his emergence. The chief reason for constitutional instability and revolution is said to be discontent arising from perceived inequality. Everyone agrees that there should be justice, and that this is proportional equality, but there is no agreement on what the criterion for this should be: democrats will claim it is freedom and oligarchs that it is wealth.

The way to ensure stability, therefore, is to prevent such discontent by giving as many people as possible at least some share of honours, offices, and profit. Laws should be passed to guard against extremes of wealth and poverty, and to increase the numbers of the middle class; indeed, the support of this class in general will be critical for those in power. It is also vital to seek to incorporate opponents of the constitution into its structure. The most effective safeguard of all, however, is education: through education, the state can habituate its young to the ways of the constitution; without such habituation, the laws are powerless.

This pragmatic approach to political theory is also evident in the unfinished sketch of his ideal state in Books VII and VIII of the *Politics*: even an ideal, Aristotle stresses, should remain always within the bounds of possibility. Given that the purpose of the state is to provide the good life, and this—as he argues—is the life of virtue, the ideal state will be that which best facilitates the exercise of virtue in its citizens. For this, certain physical conditions are required, and advice is given on territory, food supply, defence, and size of the population (Aristotle would consider almost all modern 'states' far too large to count as states at all). Easily the most important factor, however, is again education, the principal aim of which is to create good citizens. Since the good life and good citizenship are for Aristotle matters of objective fact, education for citizenship must be based on objective principles and must be the same for all; this will also ensure homogeneity, and thus stability. The only way of guaranteeing that education is the same for all is if it is organized by the state. To what extent females are to be included in this 'all' is a vexed question: as they are excluded from citizenship, one would not expect them to require the same training as males; yet Aristotle makes it clear that they are to receive at least some education.

For all his emphasis on moderation and practicability, Aristotle is strongly authoritarian. His ideal state decides when an individual may produce children and have non-reproductive sex; it decides what works of art may be seen or heard, and even what musical instruments a child may learn. Like Plato, Aristotle not only believes that the good life is objective, but also that knowledge of this good is possible and entitles its possessor to prescribe it for others. The possibility of a right to decline such prescriptions is never raised.

The *Politics* has influenced philosophers as diverse as *Aquinas and *Hegel, and is essential background to *Machiavelli, *Bodin, and *Hooker. More recently, many of its notions have informed *communitarian thinkers such as Alasdair MacIntyre and Michael Sandel. AH

arms control *See* DISARMAMENT.

arms races During the First World War, the Quaker physicist L. F. *Richardson (1881–1953), noted that Anglo-German arms races had had the property that the number of extra ships built by Britain in period two partly reflected the number built by Germany in period one, and the number built by Germany in period three partly reflected the number built by Britain in period two. Richardson modelled this as a difference equation system which might have a stable or (as in 1914) an unstable outcome. After many decades of neglect, Richardson arms races are again studied both in *international relations and in evolutionary biology. *See also* SECURITY DILEMMA.

Arrow's theorem *See* IMPOSSIBILITY THEOREM.

articulation This term was used in the structural functional approach to politics, referring to the formation of political demands, for example by *interest groups, which could then be aggregated into policy alternatives. WG

ASEAN In 1967 Indonesia, Malaysia, Singapore, Thailand, and the Philippines formed the Association of Southeast Asian Nations (ASEAN) as a non-provocative display of solidarity against communist expansion in Vietnam and insurgency within their own borders. Following the Bali summit of 1976, the organization embarked on a programme of economic cooperation, which foundered in the mid-1980s only to be revived around a 1991 Thai proposal for a regional *free trade area. ASEAN has been joined by Brunei, Vietnam, Laos, Myanmar (Burma), and Cambodia; and has pressed forward with the establishment of the ASEAN Free Trade Area. The policy of 'constructive engagement' with the oppressive government of Myanmar exposed the political timidity of ASEAN, particularly in the light of the suppression of anti-government protests in 2007 and the insular response to cyclone Nargis in 2008. CJ

(((○))) **SEE WEB LINKS**

• ASEAN official site.

Asiatic mode of production Referred to in *Marxist texts as a specific mode of production prevalent in pre-capitalist Asia. It was used to explain the difference between the Asiatic and Occidental social relations, in particular the nature and role of the state in the two systems. Two chief characteristics were highlighted by *Marx and *Engels in 1853. First, there was the absence of private property, which led, according to Marx and Engels, to stagnant social and economic relations. In particular they criticized the self-sufficient nature of the village life in Asiatic societies that was supported by this absence of private property, and did not allow for the transformation of social and economic relations in the countryside. In this context Marx wrote of the 'regenerative role of imperialism' which would pierce this shell of self-sufficiency and introduce capitalist relations into these stagnant economies. Second, there was the geographical and climatic feature of Asiatic societies that made them dependent on irrigation and which in turn required centralized planning and administration, thus increasing the role of the central state in these societies, which in turn led to an '*oriental despotism'. This ethnocentric view assumes that the way forward for Asiatic societies is to tread the well-beaten path of capitalist development that Europe had walked down. The Asiatic mode of production (AMP) became the focus of debate in the 1960s and 1970s among Third World development theorists, who were concerned in particular to understand the role of the state in the post-colonial context. They looked to AMP to understand the traditions of state intervention in Asiatic social and economic relations which might allow the *post-colonial states to continue to be involved in developing the economic infrastructure of Asiatic societies. SR

Association of Southeast Asian Nations *See* ASEAN.

asylum *See* POLITICAL ASYLUM; REFUGEE CRISIS.

asymmetrical warfare A term used to describe the use of untraditional tactics of warfare—usually by a smaller force—in order to exploit inflexibilities and weaknesses of a larger and more regimented standing army. The term is often used synonymously with *guerrilla warfare, *insurgency, and *counter-insurgency. Modern forms of asymmetrical warfare are visible by insurgents in the *Afghanistan War and *Iraq War, particularly against US efforts to stabilize those territories post-conflict.

Athenian democracy From about 500 BC to 321 BC the city-state of Athens was a direct democracy. Any citizen could (and all public-spirited citizens were expected to) attend the sovereign Assembly. The agenda for the Assembly and the daily government of the city were controlled by the Council; judicial and auditing functions were conducted by large juries. Membership of both Council and juries was by lot; any citizen had a better-than-evens chance of being president of Athens for one day, and chief justice for another.

Pericles, who flourished *c.*430 BC, was the first ideologue of democracy, which he justified on the grounds that it promoted tolerance and public-spiritedness. He also introduced attendance payments, at about the same level as a workman's daily income, for jurors (later extended to council and assembly members). As *Aristotle noted, this slanted attendance towards the poor, who otherwise would have had no opportunity to take part. Like our other principal sources, *Plato and *Thucydides, Aristotle was no friend of democracy; they pictured it as expropriating the propertied and vulnerable to ignorant demagogues. However, a relic of the democratic enthusiasm for participation survived in the language we inherited from the Greeks; in classical Greek, *idiotes* means 'private citizen' and the pejorative meaning which gives English 'idiot' derives from democratic ideals.

Serious discussion of Athenian democracy as a possible model did not revive till our own time when it began to be explored as a possibly viable alternative to representative democracy in an age when computer technology has removed the barriers to large-scale participation in decision-making. *See also* DELIBERATIVE DEMOCRACY.

Augustine, St (354–430) Theologian and political philosopher. Augustine's political theory is incidental to his theology and philosophy of history. The principal source is *De Civitate Dei* (The City of God), written in response to those who attributed the fall of Rome (AD 410) to the abolition of pagan worship. This occasioned a sweeping account of the historical roles of Church and State, and a philosophico-theological discussion of the relationship between them.

Augustine postulates two symbolic cities, Jerusalem (the City of God) and Babylon. These are primarily moral and spiritual symbols: the celestial or spiritual, and the terrestrial or worldly. The one is governed by the love of God, the other by the love of self. But these cities cannot be equated with Church or State. An officer of State may belong to the celestial city, and a Church official to the terrestrial, depending on whether love of God or self-love motivates them.

Augustine defines a state as 'a multitude of rational creatures associated in common agreement as to the things which it loves' (*De Civitate Dei* 19. 24). The things which it loves, however, can be good or bad. Of itself it is neither just nor moral; it is worldly. This is a consequence of original sin. Yet, it is for this very reason it is necessary to have a State. For the State to be just and moral it must follow the Christian principles of love of God and of each other for his sake. It is the duty of the Church to imbue the State with these principles. This gives the Church superiority over the State, though no right to interfere in secular matters. It may, however, invoke the power of the State, e.g. to suppress heresy. Thus were sown the seeds of the medieval Church–State controversy. CB

austerity The reduction or tightening of state spending. Following the 2008 global *financial crisis, the term 'austerity' took on a renewed meaning as Western liberal democracies dealt with increasing budget deficits, swelling state debt, and, in some cases, *sovereign debt crises. Reducing the gap between state revenues and expenditures through cuts to public spending therefore became a central strategy for many European states in the post-2008 period. During this period, the term 'austerity' developed an extended meaning as a way of denoting and characterizing the slowdown of economic activity, reduced living conditions, and general pessimistic public feeling that characterized the post-crisis period.

Although popularized in public discourse following the global financial crisis, austerity has numerous uses in politics and international relations. For example, the term 'permanent austerity' is used by political scientists to denote the sustained period of welfare retrenchment in the 1980s and beyond, following the post-war expansion of social protection policies. Fiscal austerity is also noted as a key prescription of the *Washington Consensus policy paradigm that underpinned the *World Bank and *IMF's approach to development in the 1980s and 1990s. Regardless of these different contexts, austerity measures typically centre on reducing or privatizing public services, reducing access to or the generosity of social protection, and cutting public-sector workers and pay.   LS

Australian ballot A ballot prepared by public officials listing all the candidates for office. So called by late nineteenth-century American reformers, who wished to substitute such ballots, as used in Australia, for the earlier American practice whereby parties prepared their own lists of their candidates and handed them to their supporters. As 'Australian' ballots are now virtually universal, the term is obsolete.

autarchy, autarky These two derivatives of similar but different Greek roots (*archein*, to rule; *arkeein*, to suffice) are frequently confused. 'Autarchy' means self-government, usually nowadays without pejorative overtones. 'Autarky' is invariably used pejoratively to mean self-government in a manner condemned by the speaker. A regime is autarkic if it tries to be self-sufficient by cutting off trade and intercourse with the rest of the world.

authoritarian personality Title of 1940s study by Berkeley researchers into the psychological origins of *anti-Semitism. The term was used to refer to an 'ethnocentric' personality pattern characterized by traits such as obedience, dogmatism, prejudice, contempt for weakness, low tolerance for ambiguity, hostility to members of 'outgroups', and superstition.   SW

authoritarianism A style of government in which the rulers demand unquestioning obedience from the ruled. Traditionally, 'authoritarians' have argued for a high degree of determination by governments of belief and behaviour and a correspondingly smaller significance for individual choice. But it is possible to be authoritarian in some spheres while being more liberal in others. Frederick the Great is alleged to have said, 'I have an agreement with my people: they can say what they like and I can do what I like'.

Authoritarianism has become simply a 'boo' word, referring to overweening and intolerant government irrespective of the justification, or lack of it, of such practices. Thus it often means exactly the same as despotism, an older word. A number of American political scientists in the Cold War period distinguished between 'authoritarian' and 'totalitarian' governments. The former (mainly military regimes) had two advantages over the latter: they did not last as long and, though they could repress their political opponents as brutally as any known regimes, they left a larger sphere for private life. (Totalitarian regimes were, in this context, invariably communist.) Thus, where conditions were not yet ripe for democracy, there were relative advantages to authoritarianism.   LA

authority The right or the capacity, or both, to have proposals or prescriptions or instructions accepted without recourse to persuasion, bargaining, or force. Systems of rules, including legal systems, typically entitle particular office-bearers to make decisions or issue instructions: such office-bearers have authority conferred on them by the rules and the practices which constitute the relevant activity. Umpires and referees, for example, have authority under the rules and practices constitutive of most sporting contests. Law enforcement officers are authorized to issue instructions, but they also receive the right to behave in ways which would not be acceptable in the absence of authorization: for example, to search persons or premises. To have authority in these ways is to be the bearer of an office and to be able to point to the relation between that office and a set of rules. In itself, this says nothing about the capacity in fact of such an office-holder to have proposals and so forth accepted without introducing persuasion, bargaining, or force. A referee, for example, may possess authority under the rules of the game, but in fact be challenged or ignored by the players. A distinction is therefore drawn between *de jure* authority—in which a right to behave in particular ways may be appealed to—and *de facto* authority—in which there is practical success. A different distinction is drawn between a person who is in authority as an office-bearer and a person who is an authority on a subject. The latter typically has special knowledge or special access to information not available to those who accept the person's status as an authority. Sometimes the two forms are found together: for example, the Speaker of the Commons *possesses* authority (to regulate the business of the House, under its rules of procedure), and is also *an* authority (on its rules of procedure). Attempts have been made to find common features between these two usages. These focus primarily on the 'internal' relationship between the authority-holder and the authority-subject, the process of recognition of the status involved, and on the willingness of the authority-subject to adopt the judgement of the authority-holder (instead of his or her own, or in the absence of the ability to formulate one). AR

autogestion *See* INDUSTRIAL DEMOCRACY.

autonomous republic Soviet federalism designated a hierarchy of subunits from the centre: republics, given the ethnic name of the titular majority and with the official right to secede; autonomous republics, mainly in the Russian Federation, with an ethnic identity but without the right to secede; and autonomous regions, with some geographical or historical identity but without an ethnic basis. The independence movement in the Chechen Republic challenged Russian

federal control, leading to violent military conflict between 1994 and 2000.

autonomy Self-government. The term may be applied both to the individual person and to a group or an institution. An autonomous person is, fundamentally, one able to act according to his or her own direction—the prerequisite for rational human action, according to *Kant. An autonomous institution is one able to regulate its own affairs. The relation between the self-government of a group and individual autonomy is complicated by the need to distinguish between the collective self-government of a group and the self-direction of an individual member of that group, as *Rousseau's writings illustrate. Ideas about individual autonomy are closely linked to conceptions of *freedom. For example, to act according to my own direction may (on some views of freedom) require access to resources I presently lack, in which case to provide me with them would enhance both my liberty and my autonomy. Further, this problem is connected to notions of the constitution of the self. For example, it may be held that I am not truly 'self'-governing if my action is driven by powerful phobias 'I' cannot regulate, any more than if my actions are determined by external circumstances beyond my control. AR

AV *See* ALTERNATIVE VOTE.

Averroës, Ibn Rushd (Abu-l-Walid Muhammad ibn Ahmad ibn Muhammad) (1126–98) Better known in Europe as Averroës, he was the last and most famous of the Andalusian philosophers and the last of the great Arab rationalists, taking rationalism further than anyone else. Born in Cordoba, he came from a prominent family of jurists. He studied theology, jurisprudence, mathematics, medicine, and philosophy. He served as a chief Qadi and was a jurist of the Maliki school of jurisprudence. His lasting fame is due to his philosophical writings and his 38 commentaries on the works of *Aristotle. Within the Arab world he is known both for his fatwas and for his defence of Aristotelian philosophy in the face of Al-Ghazali's condemnation of philosophy.

Ibn Rushd's translations of Aristotle into Arabic with accompanying commentaries were themselves first translated into Latin in Toledo, then a centre for such translation. They facilitated the interaction between the ideas of Aristotle and Church doctrine in the intellectual renaissance associated with thirteenth-century scholastic philosophy (*see also* MEDIEVAL POLITICAL THEORY).

In contrast, the Church in the East had been permeated by the influence of the Greek philosophers. When Islam burst upon the scene from the seventh century onward and Arabic became the language of the region, the intellectual heritage of Indian, Persian, and Graeco-Alexandrian learning was taken up with astonishing enthusiasm. The translation of Greek, Syriac, Pahlavi, and Sanskrit texts into Arabic which took place during the mid-eighth to early tenth centuries led to the emergence of Islamic philosophy between the ninth century to the thirteenth century. The Peripatetic school, which combined Neoplatonic and Aristotelian teachings, became known to the scholastic movement through Al-Kindi (801–66), Al-Farabi (870–950), and Ibn Sina (Avicenna) (980–1037). Nonetheless, it is Ibn Rushd, with his concentration on the works of Aristotle, whose influence was greater in Europe. His translations contained only limited interjections of his theological frame of reference. He attempted faithfully to reproduce the ideas of Aristotle where they were clearly stated, and elaborated on those that were ambiguous. At this time, the little that was known of Aristotle's ideas was being shaped to conform to Christian theology. The objectivity of Ibn Rushd's translations and the cogency of his commentaries allowed European scholars to examine the ideas of Aristotle in greater depth.

The political views of Ibn Rushd are contained in his commentaries on *Plato's Republic* and Aristotle's *Nicomachean Ethics* (he was not familiar with Aristotle's *Politics*). From the *Republic*, he concluded that, in practice, political rule would require the ability of the ruler to communicate the virtues to the differing strata comprising the community: this required the ruler to be thoroughly grounded in the understanding of the virtues. He believed that the *Nicomachean Ethics* would serve as a foundation for the practice of politics.

In the course of his defence of philosophers from Al-Ghazali's accusation of heresy, it becomes apparent that Ibn Rushd regarded Aristotle as an intellectually flawless man whose philosophical findings were absolute and infallible truth.   BAR

Avicenna *See* AVERROËS.

Ayatollah *Ayat Allah,* 'a miraculous sign, a mark, an exemplar of God'. This is a designation which came into use in the late nineteenth and twentieth centuries among the Imamis, or Twelvers, the majority tradition in Shi'i Islam. Ayatollahs are found in Iran, Iraq, and Lebanon. 'Ayatollah' denotes a religious scholar of outstanding quality and reputation. He is a *mujtahid*, a specialist in law who is capable of formulating through independent reasoning interpretations (*ijtihad*) in legal and theological matters based on the Jafari school of jurisprudence. *Mujtahids* are *ulama* (recognized religious scholars). Among the Imamis, by the end of the seventeenth and into the eighteenth centuries, *mujtahids* came to perform a more enhanced role within the Shi'i *ulama*.

During the fourteenth century, a practice had emerged that all Shi'i throughout their lifetime should follow the religious guidance of a *mujtahid* and, should the *mujtahid* die, choose a successor. The individual Shi'i decides which *mujtahid* he or she will follow. A *mujtahid* of the Imamis came to be regarded as representing the will of the Hidden Imam (the twelfth Imam), as His deputy until His return. By the early nineteenth century, a further development in the differentiation of the Shi'i *ulama* led to the recognition of the *marja i taqlid* (source of imitation), that is, the most pre-eminent of the *mujtahids*. As the number of *marja i taqlid* grew, the designation 'Ayatollah' began to be used in the twentieth century to refer to the outstanding *marja*. Thus, a hierarchy came to exist among the Shi'i *ulama* unlike the Sunni *ulama*. Those that become pre-eminent among the *mujtahids* evidenced by the number of followers that they can attract emerge as Ayatollahs. Among the Ayatollahs a few will become known as Grand Ayatollahs (*Ayat Allah al-uzma*). It is from these that the one that is able to attract an exceptional following will emerge as the *marja*—the apex of the Shi'i hierarchy. This particular evolution of an informal hierarchy arrived at via consensus within the Shi'i *ulama* had the effect, amongst other things, of facilitating the accommodation of the religion to the changing times.

Ayatollahs also act as administrators: as collectors of religious taxes, managing pious gifts and property, dispensers of grants and alms, responsible for schools, orphanages, publishing houses, libraries and other social services institutions. Ayatollahs can at times attract considerable following abroad as evidenced by the popularity of the now deceased Ayatollah al-Khu'i, well known for his erudition in Shi'i jurisprudence and pious works in many countries. BAR

Ba'athism Refers to the political philosophy of the Arab Socialist Ba'ath Party (hizb al-ba'ath al-arabi al-ishtiraki). This party is the result of the 1952 merger of two parties—the Arab Ba'ath Party founded in 1947 and the Arab Socialist Party. The Arab Ba'ath or Renaissance Party was founded by three French-educated Syrian intellectuals: Michel Aflaq, a Greek Orthodox Christian; Salah al-Din Bitar, a Sunni Muslim, both of whom had a particular vision of Arab socialism and nationalism; and Zaki al-Arsuzi, an Alawi, who first used the term al-ba'ath al arabi for his followers but never joined the official party.

Michel Aflaq, the party's philosopher, took the idea of the Arab nation elaborated 'scientifically' by the Syrian Sati al Husri, a notion which became popular in Pan-Arab nationalism taken up by many groups, and grafted onto the idea of the Arab nation the doctrine of Arab socialism (unrelated to Marxism) to form the guiding principles of Ba'athism. The slogan of the Arab revolution was Unity, Freedom (from colonialism), and Socialism. In Aflaq's view, there was no Syrian or Egyptian or other nation in the Middle East. There was only the Arab nation from which a single Arab state would eventually emerge. The unity of the Arab Nation would lead to the regeneration of the Arab character and society. Arab socialism did not focus on the needs of a dispossessed class but on the people as a whole. It was, in effect, a spiritual marriage of nationalism and socialism. Ba'athi doctrine indicated little confidence in gradual reform achieved through elections and pluralistic politics. For Aflaq, Islam was a part of Arabism and not incompatible with nationalism.

The Party's pan-Arab ideology affected its organization. It began in Syria but soon spread to other Arab countries and local party organizations were set up in Jordan, Lebanon, Palestine, Saudi Arabia, Iraq, and Tunisia. As it spread, the parties were viewed as regional extensions of the umbrella organization, each of the states became a 'region' of the future all-embracing single Arab state.

From 1953 onward, the Ba'ath gradually became a mass party in Syria. In 1957–8, it was in a position to support and press for the unity of Syria with a somewhat reluctant Egypt to form the United Arab Republic. The idea of unity with Egypt had considerable appeal in Syrian politics as an antidote to domestic instability and regional threats. However, at the time that a merger between Egypt and Syria was proposed, the Ba'ath party, fearing that their position was being undermined by leftist forces in the country, sought political unification in order to preserve and enhance their position. As a condition of the merger, Jamal Abd al-Nasir (President of Egypt) required that all political parties and their activities, including the Ba'ath party, be suspended. After three years, the expectations engendered by the original enthusiasm for union dissipated in the inability of the merger to address the domestic political and economic concerns of crucial Syrian interest groups. Subsequent attempts at merger in 1963 also failed. Even when Ba'athist governments committed ideologically to Arab unity were involved (Syria and Iraq), attempts at political unity foundered on political realities—internal and factional divisions, ideological competition on a regional level, and a regional security environment that tempered attempts at cooperation. In these circumstances, though the vision of Arab unity remained embedded in Ba'ath ideology, the reality of regional as well as domestic politics required that Ba'athist states pursue national interests. As a consequence, the idea of a national state emerged in tension with the legitimacy of a state founded on the greater interests of the Arab nation.

Both Syria and Iraq since the 1960s have had Ba'athist governments. In both cases, the Ba'ath Party became an instrument of the government concerned and no longer a telling influence on their policies. In the aftermath of the United States-led invasion of Iraq and the removal of Saddam Hussein's government, the Ba'ath Party was banned, and a process of de-Ba'athification introduced in 2003. This sought to remove the influence of pro-Saddam officials, but was seen to destabilize the whole administration, and attempts were made to reverse the measure in 2008 with little success. The Syrian Ba'ath Party remains at the centre of the ongoing *Syrian Civil War between Syrian President Bashar al-Assad and rebel groups aimed to overthrow his government. One trigger of the civil war was when governmental troops violently responded to the burning down of the Ba'ath Party headquarters in 2011 during the *Arab Spring protests. Instability remains in both Iraq and Syria. BAR

Babeuf, François-Noel, known as 'Gracchus' (1760–97) French socialist. Before the *French Revolution, he proposed moderate reform of land tenure based on collective leases. After it, he proposed a centralized distribution system for all produce to ensure complete equality, and collectivization of the industrial sector. He was executed after failure of a *coup d'état based on that of the *sans-culottes in 1793. CS

Babri Masjid *See* HINDU NATIONALISM.

back-bencher Legislator who is a member neither of the government nor of the opposition leadership. Traditionally, especially in Britain, party leaders sit on the front benches of the legislature and their followers sit behind them.

backlash Hostile reaction to reform, especially white backlash against *civil rights, and anti-feminist backlash. *See also* REACTIONARY.

Bagehot, Walter (1826–77) English journalist; editor of *The Economist* 1861–77. Best known for *The English Constitution* (1867), in which he distinguished between the 'dignified' and the 'efficient' parts of the constitution. The monarchy and other dignified parts of the constitution existed to give popular legitimacy to the inconspicuous cabinet—the

'buckle' which fastened the legislature to the executive. Bagehot wished to distinguish the 'living reality' of the constitution, in contrast to its 'paper description'—an aim which has made him an enduring source for political scientists ever since.

b

Baker* v. *Carr *See* CIVIL RIGHTS.

Bakke (US Supreme Court case) *See* CIVIL RIGHTS; AFFIRMATIVE ACTION.

Bakunin, Mikhail (1814–76) Russian *anarchist and revolutionary activist. Representing the *libertarian wing of the First International (1864–76), he attacked *Marx as an authoritarian. Where Marx advocated a centralist revolution based upon the dictatorship of the proletariat, Bakunin wanted a federal arrangement with workers' control and the abolition of the state at the earliest possible moment. Bakunin's revolutionary philosophy was an apocalyptic one with the emphasis upon the destruction of the old order as a prelude to the creation of the new, his most important text being *The State and Anarchism* (1873). He influenced the development of the Russian, Italian, Swiss, and Spanish anarchist movements. He created a number of semi- and totally fantastic revolutionary networks, the most viable being the International Alliance of Social Democracy (founded in 1868) which called for 'the definitive abolition of classes and the political, economic and social equalization of the two sexes'.

His reputation was damaged by his relationship with Sergei Nechayev, whose nihilist creed was expressed in *The Revolutionary Catechism* (1870) and who was later implicated in murder and blackmail (the story was used by Dostoevsky in *The Possessed*). Marx used this as a pretext to effect Bakunin's expulsion from the International and the removal of its Secretariat from Europe to New York where it soon collapsed. GL

balance of power Probably the oldest concept in the study of *International Relations going back at least to the work of *Thucydides. It is closely associated with both diplomatic parlance and *realism. Its logic derives from the self-help imperative of the international system's anarchic structure, in which states are obliged to give priority to survival and security. In pursuing this logic, states will usually join together to oppose any expansionist centre of power that threatens to dominate the system and thus threaten their sovereignty. Balance of power behaviour is central to conceptions of the national interest and to alliance policy. If successful, it preserves individual states and the anarchic structure of the system as a whole. Its opposite is *bandwagoning, in which states seek security by joining with the dominant power. Realists conceive balance of power as an automatic tendency in state behaviour. In an international society perspective, balance of power is a conscious policy shared amongst a group of states, and serving as the principle by which they regulate their relations. Neither 'balance' nor 'power' are measurable, and their interpretation is much debated.

Balkanization The division of a state into smaller territorial units. The term tends to imply a policy of 'divide and rule', whereby the strength of a united country is diluted by the creation of internal division. The term came to prominence in the aftermath of the First World War, but has contemporary resonance in the light of recent *Balkan politics.

Balkan politics The Balkans, or southeastern Europe, may be defined as the states of Albania, Bulgaria, Romania, and those which constituted the former Yugoslavia. They all share experiences of communism and of post-communist transition. For this reason Greece and European Turkey, though geographically part of the Balkans, are excluded from this account.

Since the collapse of European communism in 1989–91 the Balkans have been more at the forefront of European and world affairs than at any time since the First World War. For this reason the evolution of Balkan politics has been determined as much by external as by internal factors. The area has seen: the first preventive deployment of UN forces, along the Macedonian borders in 1992; the first use of UN peacekeepers in mainland Europe; the first military action by NATO in 1994 (against Bosnian Serbs) and the first offensive NATO war in 1999 (against Yugoslavia), the latter being also the first exclusive air war; and also the highest casualties, the most extensive ethnic cleansing, and the greatest number of displaced persons in

Europe since the immediate aftermath of the Second World War. In 2001 it witnessed the first return of an exiled king as prime minister in Europe (in Bulgaria).

The centre of international attention was the collapse of the Yugoslav federation in 1991–2, from which four new states—Slovenia, Croatia, Bosnia and Hercegovina, and Macedonia—emerged. In April 1992 a new Yugoslav federation, consisting of Serbia and Montenegro, was formed, to be peacefully dissolved in 2006. Of the four new states proclaimed in 1991–2, only Macedonia emerged without conflict with Serbia and the local Serbs. The secession of Slovenia in the summer of 1991 was relatively easy despite the initial intervention of the Yugoslav National Army, but Croatia's departure was much more bitterly disputed, not least because it, unlike Slovenia, contained large numbers of Serbs who did not wish to be included in a Croatian national state. Most bloody of all, however, was the fighting in Bosnia which lasted for over three years. It was not a war in the traditional sense of one side battling against another because the three main elements, Bosnian Muslim, Croat, and Serb, shifted their alliances and all at one point or another fought the others. The United Nations forces originally deployed in Croatia extended their mission to Bosnia, initially to guarantee the flow of humanitarian supplies through Sarajevo airport. Later, as the fighting intensified, the UN passed to NATO the task of preventing further escalation of the conflict; this meant, primarily, acting against Bosnian Serbs. In the summer of 1995 NATO bombing raids on Bosnian Serb communications systems, provoked by the shelling of a market place in Sarajevo, combined with the defeat of Serbian Krajina forces in Croatia at last hastened the move towards a settlement. A peace was agreed at Dayton, Ohio, in December 1995.

The Dayton peace process pacified Bosnia, but catalysed conflagration in Kosovo, a part of Serbia inhabited primarily by Albanians. Dayton was seen as rewarding violent secession and ethnic cleansing, thus undermining Kosovo Albanians' non-violent struggle for independence post-1989. Moreover, Kosovo was ignored in Dayton, and after it Western governments officially recognized the new federal Yugoslavia and its territorial integrity, leaving Kosovo within Serbia. From 1997 the Kosovo Liberation Army (KLA), increasingly backed by local Albanians, was in conflict with Serbian forces. At first KLA was considered a prima facie terrorist group by Western governments, but eventually dislike of Milosevic and his methods brought KLA under Western protection. Bombing of Yugoslavia began in March 1999 and continued until June. Thereafter Kosovo passed effectively into UN and NATO control with elections to its assembly finally taking place in 2001. The minority situation in Kosovo after 1999 remained dismal, with Serbs and Roma as the victims this time.

Interestingly, none of the states bordering the former Yugoslavia, many of which had historic claims on parts of it, intervened. This was in no small measure because the external actors, primarily the EU, the USA, and the international financial institutions, upon which the Balkan states depended for economic regeneration, have insisted that no borders may be changed by force. Political reconstruction, though at times difficult, was much easier than economic regeneration. It was a relatively simple process to dismantle the apparatus of communist party control and to enact constitutional guarantees of individual liberties, press freedom, and political pluralism, and to dissolve the links between the former ruling party and social organizations such as the trade unions. By the end of 1995 all the states of south-eastern Europe had, at least in theory, multi-party systems with assemblies elected by universal suffrage. In all states, except Bosnia and Hercegovina, general elections have brought about a change of government, though in Serbia in October 2000 it required considerable popular pressure on the streets to persuade the incumbent Slobodan Milosevic to relinquish power in Yugoslavia. There was also political violence in Romania in 1990 and 1991 when miners from the Jiu valley were brought to Bucharest to intimidate student protestors and the government. Changes of government also came about as a result of street pressure in Bulgaria in 1990 and 1997, and in Albania in 1997, though a third attempt by the Jiu miners to march on the Romanian capital was prevented in 1999.

Ethnic differences which did much to destabilize and then ruin the old Yugoslav federation were always a factor in Balkan politics. In general, ethnic tensions have been contained. In Romania the main party of the Hungarian minority has been included in every government since 1996 and promises of more education in Hungarian have been given, if not always fulfilled. In Bulgaria the Turkish minority party had strong influence on the formation of cabinets in 1992–4 and has been continuously in government since 2001, winning a number of concessions for the Turkish and Islamic communities. After some tension in the early 1990s Albania too has promised that it will improve conditions for its largest minority, the Greeks. Slovenia has few non-Slovenes amongst its population, and since the end of the Tudjman era in late 1999 the Croatian government has been much less strident in its nationalist rhetoric and policies. Macedonia has faced the most severe problems, with unrest amongst the local Albanians (a quarter of the population) leading to intervention by the EU and NATO in 2001, followed by constitutional changes that improved the position of the Albanians. A persistent and more difficult problem centres upon the Roma who are found in all Balkan states (*see* MULTICULTURALISM). Most Balkan governments have made efforts to improve the lot of the Roma but the latter still find many reasons for complaint.

Corruption and crime are also endemic. Both were much encouraged by the imposition of sanctions on Yugoslavia, the profits to be made from sanctions-busting being so great that few could resist the temptation. A related phenomenon was the burgeoning of pyramid selling schemes. In states where personal financing was little developed, state welfare benefits were minimal, and inflation raged, the chance to make a great deal of money in a short space of time proved irresistible. In Albania the collapse of pyramid schemes early in 1997 unleashed such fury that national government broke down and a semblance of order could be restored only with the help of an international force led by Italy.

The new political systems created in the Balkans after the fall of communism varied. In Romania, Croatia, and, initially, in Albania, the executive was more powerful than the legislative arm; in the other states the balance of power tended to favour the latter, though in most states there were still disputed areas between the president and the premier; control of the intelligence services was an issue particularly prone to dispute. In Bosnia and Hercegovina a modern state in the generally accepted meaning of the term could scarcely be said to exist. There remained in essence two entities, the Bosnian-Croat federation and the Republika Srpska, but real authority rested with the international High Representative, a post created after Dayton. One of the most surprising features of the 1990s in the Balkans was that the military played so little part in domestic politics. Proportional representation, one variant or another of which was adopted in all states except Albania and Slovenia, meant that coalition governments were the norm.

The political parties which emerged in the Balkans were of four main types: the former ruling communist parties; anti-communist electoral alliances; resurrected parties; and new parties. The former communist parties changed their names and liberalized their structures. The strongest amongst them were those of Serbia, Montenegro, Romania, Bulgaria, and Albania, all of which remained united and most of which continued the close association with nationalism established before 1989. Cohesion and continuity amongst the anti-communist electoral alliances were rare, though not unknown. Generally, these were loose associations which fell apart once their one unifying demand, the removal of the communists from office, had been achieved. The third group of parties, those resurrected from the past, has played very little part in the evolution of the area since 1989. Most had little in the way of infrastructure or funds and their leadership, though venerated, was old and had been too long in exile to be in touch with contemporary affairs. In general, newly formed parties were much more important than resurrected ones. But they too faced considerable difficulties. Communist rule had meant the elimination of former distinctions of class, status, and wealth upon which old party divisions were frequently based, and there had not been time for market forces to create or recreate the social bases for bourgeois parties. Some new parties were founded on issues such as the environment and most countries soon had their green party or its equivalent. Parties representing ethnic

majorities and minorities appeared in all states. KDr

⊕ SEE WEB LINKS
• The text of the Dayton peace agreement.

ballot Secret voting; a vote conducted by this method. Voting by dropping a pebble (*psephos*—hence *psephology) into an urn was an invention of ancient Greek democrats, resurrected in the eighteenth century. Though J. S. *Mill argued that voting in public encouraged more responsible behaviour, most regimes decided that intimidation and corruption necessitated secret voting, introduced in the United Kingdom in 1872.

banana republic A dictatorship run in the interests of foreign commercial exploitation. The term originates as a description of Latin American countries (such as Honduras, Costa Rica, and Guatemala) in the early twentieth century. Foreign fruit-trading companies (such as the United Fruit Company) used corruption and bribery to control the government, in order to protect agricultural interests and provide an infrastructure which suited their commercial requirements.

bandwagoning The idea that strategically weaker states may join with stronger states, adversarial powers, or superior *alliances for the purpose of offsetting a *balance of power and thus obtaining an overall strategic advantage, even if, by doing so, the stronger state or dominant members receive widely disproportionate gains.

Banzhaf index A power index devised by John F. Banzhaf III, a lawyer. In a seminal article entitled 'Weighted Voting Doesn't Work' (1965), he noted that the power of a bloc of votes to affect the outcome depends on whether the bloc's withdrawal from a coalition would turn it from a winner into a loser. The Banzhaf index, which examines all possible combinations of blocs, measures a bloc's influence on policy. The *Shapley-Shubik index, which operates on permutations of blocs, measures a bloc's capacity to win spoils.

bargaining theory The branch of *game theory dealing with non-*zero-sum games, in which both (all) parties have a common interest in bargaining for a solution which improves the outcome for at least some and worsens it for none. Bargaining models are much more sophisticated in economics than in politics, but have obvious applications in both.

Barnett formula A formula for the allocation of tax revenues from the UK government to be spent by the devolved governments of Scotland, Wales, and Northern Ireland. The formula pre-dates political devolution; for its first twenty years it was used to assign block grant to the executive departments that ran the devolved administrations of the three territories. It takes its name from Joel Barnett (1923–2014), Chief Secretary to the Treasury 1974–9. In 1978, when the formula was devised, Scotland was receiving far more spending per head than the poorer regions of England and Wales, not because it was poorer than them but because it posed the credible threat to the UK of a Scottish nationalist secession. Barnett and his officials had two aims. The first was to prevent rounding up, which had occurred when Scottish officials negotiated with the Treasury one service at a time, and always made a special claim for that service. By substituting a block, which it was up to the territories to assign, for grants for one service at a time, Barnett succeeded. The second aim (not acknowledged at first) was to whittle away the Scottish advantage by having spending per head converge in the four territories of the UK. This aim was always flawed, because Scotland, Wales, and Northern Ireland do need more spending per head than England to obtain an equivalent level of service. The formula ought to have ceased to operate when spending per head had been brought into line with needs per head. Because of extensive *rent-seeking in the territories, there was in fact no convergence in Scotland until 1999. There was convergence in Wales, which was inappropriate because spending was probably below needs. This led to a revolt in which the London-approved leader of the Welsh executive was toppled in 2000. Barnett is clearly unstable but no agreed substitute has been found.

Barry, Brian (1936–2009) British moral and political philosopher, best known for interdisciplinary research combining both *political theory and *social choice theory in order to advance *liberal and *cosmopolitan theories of *social justice and social *equality.

base/superstructure By 'base' is meant the economic foundations of a society, and by 'superstructure' is meant the social, political, and legal relations which are said to be built upon the base.

This topographical metaphor, attributed to Karl *Marx, has given rise to much confusion within social and political science, assuming particular importance in discussions of the *state in capitalism. The distinction between the 'economic base/basis/ substructure' of society and its corresponding 'ideological/political superstructure' was initially formulated in part one of *The German Ideology* written by Marx and Engels in 1845–6. It is most clearly stated by Marx in a famous passage in the 1859 *Preface to a Contribution to a Critique of Political Economy* (part one), where he writes: 'In the social production of their existence, men inevitably enter into definite relations, which are independent of their will, namely relations of production appropriate to a given stage in the development of their material forces of production. The totality of these relations of production constitutes the economic structure of society, the real foundation, on which arises a legal and political superstructure and to which correspond definite forms of social consciousness. The mode of production of material life conditions the general process of social, political and intellectual life . . . changes in the economic foundation lead sooner or later to the transformation of the whole immense superstructure.'

Within the Marxist tradition there are two broad ways of interpreting this metaphor. The first, and the dominant, interpretation is to see the base/superstructure metaphor as a characterization of the essence of the *materialist conception of history. This view takes literally the notion that changes in production relations give rise to new forms of politics, law, and ideology. In this 'hard structural determinist' reading, exemplified by Soviet Marxism–Leninism, the economic base determines the political superstructure, thus rendering a serious analysis of politics redundant. Although Engels later tried to soften this view by introducing the notion of 'determinant in the last instance', this has done little to dissuade structuralist

Marxists (and technological determinists) that the economy should be awarded primacy when studying social formations. The state in this model is seen as epiphenomenal, its existence reducible to the economic base; changes in state policy are understood as merely reflecting changing economic relations. The notion of *relative autonomy has been developed by a number of contemporary Marxists who subscribe to the base/superstructure metaphor but who wish to correct this 'reductionist' and 'monistic' overemphasis on the economic side of the historical process.

The second way of interpreting the base/superstructure metaphor is to see it as a provisional level of abstraction useful for limited analytical purposes only. This view, found in the 'softer' more 'humanistic' currents of Marxism (including *Gramsci, the *Frankfurt School, and most versions of Western Marxism) realizes that the metaphor is all but useless as theory and denies that Marx would have accepted its hard structuralist reading. Humanistic Marxists therefore replace this monocausal economism with the dialectical notion that social relations of production only exist in the form of economic, legal, and political relations. It is not simply that each of these relations exercise reciprocal and causative influence, but that antagonistic class relations are always manifest in social, political, and cultural forms. In this way 'economics' rests as firmly on 'politics' and 'law' as vice versa. According to this view, determinists understand 'economics' in a technicist apolitical sense and do not give sufficient attention to Marx's stress on the social relations of production. For most Western Marxists the base/superstructure metaphor is more an affirmation of Marx's materialism (in opposition to philosophical idealism) than a guide to historical research. The distinctiveness of Marx's method is not his alleged emphasis on the 'economic base' but his insistence on understanding capitalist society in terms of class relations and class struggle.   PBM

Bay of Pigs Planned by the United States *CIA, the Bay of Pigs invasion was a failed attempt to topple the Cuban government of Fidel Castro. Planning was instigated under President Eisenhower, and was well advanced when John F. Kennedy became President in January 1961. The aim was for Cuban exiles, covertly supported by the United States, to invade Cuba, spark a popular uprising, and unseat Castro. In April 1961 a force of some 1500 Cuban exiles, trained in Guatemala by the CIA, landed at the 'Bay of Pigs', but within three days the Cuban military had defeated the invasion.

The CIA believed it could support the action without US involvement becoming public, and this led to confused planning and operations. Air attacks on Cuban airbases exposed US involvement, and the denials from the United States Ambassador to the United Nations, Adlai Stevenson, were quickly shown to be false. The event was a deeply embarrassing policy failure for the Kennedy government, and made it even more hostile to Castro. In November 1961 the Kennedy government established Operation Mongoose, which sought to sabotage and destabilize the Cuban government and economy, and included plans to assassinate Castro. The reaction to the Bay of Pigs events influenced the development of the *Cuban Missile Crisis, and the mistakes in the planning of the operation were used by Irving Janis as an illustration of *groupthink.

Beccaria, Cesare (1735–94) Italian philosopher whose *Dei delitti e delle pene* (On Crime and Punishment) (1764) made the first reasoned case for the abolition of the death penalty. Influential on thinkers of the French *Enlightenment, especially *Voltaire and *Condorcet.

Beck, Ulrich (1944–2015) German political sociologist, best known for his work on 'reflective modernization' in an age of 'second modernity'. In essence, Beck argued that the modern age (second modernity) is characterized by revolutionary processes of *globalization which create new uncertainties and new reflections about collective 'risk'. These new reflections cause societies to reorganize their responses to globalized risk in new ways, which sociologically favours greater global interconnection—forming new cosmopolitan perceptions of a global 'risk society'. According to Beck, global issues, such as *climate change, are creating new perceptions of global risk society and thus undermining the saliency of the *state system towards a form of *cosmopolitanism.

beggar-thy-neighbour politics A term coined by Adam *Smith to refer to economic policies that seek to resolve domestic problems at the intended or unintended expense of surrounding countries or trading partners. Often used in *game theory to highlight adverse knock-on effects of policies. Contemporary examples often occur between trading partners when one partner rapidly devalues its currency to boost its exports at the expense of its trading partner.

behaviour(al)ism 1. Behaviourism is a school of psychology that takes the objective observation of behaviour, as measured by responses to stimuli, as the only proper subject for study (in humans or other animals) and the only basis for its theory, without any reference to conscious experience. It is driven by the belief that the mind is unexaminable, except in anatomical specimens. It led some psychologists, notably B. F. Skinner in his briefly notorious *Beyond Freedom and Dignity* (1971), to reject the whole of political philosophy and ethics in favour of producing desired social effects by conditioning. A similar gritty positivism underlies economists' insistence that their proper study is revealed preference: what people do as revealed by their choices, rather than what they say they do.

2. Behaviouralism is a movement in political science which insists on analysing (only) the observable behaviour of political actors. It has much intellectual background in common with psychological behaviourism. Behaviouralism in political science emerged in the 1940s and was dominant in the United States until the early 1970s. It was driven by similar but less extreme impatience with studying what people said or (said they) thought. Armed with the newly developed tools of *survey research, it turned away from the study of constitutions and from saying how states ought to be ruled to the study of the behaviour of political actors and to statements about how states actually were ruled. Behaviourists were mostly drawn to subjects about which quantitative data could be obtained, and thus the study of mass political behaviour was promoted at the expense of studying elites. Behaviourism and *rational choice were initially hostile to each other, but have become reconciled.

Belfast Agreement (also known as **Good Friday Agreement)** The Agreement, arrived at on 10 April 1998, created the opportunity to restore a devolved, power-sharing government to *Northern Ireland for the first time since 1973.

Endorsed by referendums in both Northern Ireland and the Irish Republic on 23 May 1998, the Agreement established a unicameral 108-member Assembly elected on 25 June 1998 and a voluntary power-sharing Executive Committee. These are integral democratic institutions of Strand One of the Agreement, which also provided for the establishment of a consultative Civic Forum, comprising representatives of the voluntary, business, and trade union sectors.

Strand Two of the Agreement established a North–South Ministerial Council. It consists of Ministers from the Executive Committee and their Irish counterparts, that meet in both sectoral and plenary formats to develop consultation, cooperation, and action across the island of Ireland on matters of mutual interest within the competence of the Administrations on each side of the border. Such cooperation is effected through six implementation bodies and six cross-border bodies, also created under the terms of the Agreement.

Strand Three of the Agreement established a British–Irish Council, encompassing the British and Irish Governments, the devolved institutions in Northern Ireland, Scotland, and Wales, together with representatives of the Channel islands and the Isle of Man and, prospectively, of English regional assemblies if they are established. Strand Three also paved the way for a new British–Irish Agreement between the two Governments and established a standing British–Irish Intergovernmental Conference designed to promote bilateral cooperation on all matters of mutual interest within the competence of both Governments. The institutions of all three strands interlock: none can stand alone.

Elsewhere, the Agreement created the Northern Ireland Human Rights Commission and confirmed the merger of Northern Ireland's four existing anti-discrimination agencies into one Equality Commission. The Agreement witnessed the affirmation by its signatories of a new culture of human rights, equality of opportunity, and of mutual respect for the identity and ethos of both communities. They also acknowledged the needs of victims of the violence and pledged to support those organizations committed to develop reconciliation, mutual respect and understanding between and within communities in Northern Ireland and between it and the Republic of Ireland. The Agreement obliged its signatories to use their influence to achieve the decommissioning of all paramilitary weapons within two years of the confirmatory referendums, and to work in good faith with the Independent International Commission on Decommissioning to that end. The British Government also undertook to normalize security arrangements in Northern Ireland, contingent upon perceived threat levels, and to put in place an accelerated prisoner release programme applicable to those organizations maintaining a complete and unequivocal ceasefire. The Agreement also set in train reviews of both the policing and criminal justice systems in Northern Ireland. RW

(⊕) SEE WEB LINKS

• An outline and text of the Belfast Agreement, from the UK Northern Ireland Office.

beltway 'Inside the beltway' is used to refer to the often inward-looking and self-absorbed political community of Washington. Events in the country directly affecting ordinary Americans are referred to as 'outside the beltway'. The name is taken from the ring road which encircles Washington, DC. WG

Benelux Belgium, the Netherlands, and Luxembourg. Since the foundation of the EEC (now the *European Union) the three countries have frequently acted as a bloc.

Bentham, Jeremy (1748–1832) Economist, political and legal philosopher, and social reformer. Born in Houndsditch in London, the son of a prosperous attorney and entrepreneur, sent to Westminster school at the age of 7 and then to Queen's College Oxford at the age of 12, Jeremy Bentham graduated at the age of 16. To further his legal education, he attended the Court of Kings Bench in the student's seat secured by his ambitious father. The law, however, was not his sole concern, despite a lifelong commitment to legal reform, and to penal reform

in particular. And, although admitted to the Bar, he did not actually practise law. Instead, he became an eclectic, studying the experimental sciences of chemistry and physics as well as the classics, ranging widely from Cicero to Homer. He also read widely in European philosophy, particularly *Hume, *Montesquieu, Joseph Priestley, Hartley, and *Beccaria, adopting as a consequence a familiar and orthodox empiricism. In 1768, during the course of this reading, he came across the expression 'the greatest good of the greatest number' in Priestley's *Essay on Government*. This discovery led to a kind of inner ecstasy. From this point, Bentham became the leading and tireless English advocate of *utilitarianism. It was part of Bentham's utilitarianism that each person was to count as one and no more than one, a form of radical egalitarianism which made him unpopular with many contemporaries, a radicalism both confirmed and developed by his association with James *Mill which began in 1808. And, although Bentham did not write or campaign publicly for universal suffrage until 1817, after this point he was firmly committed to representative democracy, open government, and annual parliaments, even though he never wavered in his critique of French revolutionary radicalism and its classic doctrines of imprescriptible natural rights and of a revocable *social contract. In the hands of the French, these doctrines were not only politically dangerous, but also philosophically nonsensical. As a liberal constitutional thinker, Bentham can also be plausibly interpreted as a precursor of those who defend the modern welfare state. In his view, the ends of legislation quite properly included subsistence, security, abundance, and equality, and, at different times and in different places, Bentham can also be found advocating sickness benefit, free education, and minimum wages. Perhaps the final word, however, should be left to John Stuart *Mill, a radical who was specifically educated to fully develop the legacy of Bentham. In his view, Bentham was the great questioner of established and customary procedures. With his restless and questioning mind, he had been primarily responsible for breaking 'the yoke of authority' and for making it necessary for each person to have reasons for his opinions and not merely impulses derived from tradition, habit, or authority. In fact, before Bentham and his utilitarianism, no one had really dared to question the habits of the British constitution and the idiosyncrasies of the English legal system. Bentham's own massive enthusiasm was the instigation of much beneficial practical reform. Without him, and despite his obsessive concerns with the model prison the Panopticon, the cause of liberal-reformism would have been so much weaker and would certainly have rested upon far less substantial intellectual concerns. JH

Bentley, A. F. (1870–1957) American political scientist; founder of *pluralism. Bentley argued that every interest would form its interest group and that the interplay of these interest groups was definitive of democracy: 'when the groups are adequately stated, everything is stated. When I say everything, I mean everything', he wrote in *The Process of Government* (1908). Bentley's approach was refreshingly empirical and pragmatic for its time, but it is no longer accepted that to every potential group there corresponds an actual group. Some 'groups' never come into existence, for various reasons; therefore Bentley's normative justification of interest-group lobbying cannot be sustained.

Berlin, Isaiah (1909–97) Historian of ideas and political philosopher, holding the Chichele Professorship in Social and Political Thought at All Souls College Oxford University, from 1957 to 1967; also the first President of Wolfson College Oxford from 1966 to 1975. Berlin's major works include *Karl Marx: His Life and Environment* (1939), *The Age of Enlightenment: The Eighteenth Century Philosophers* (1956), *Four Essays on Liberty* (1969), *Russian Thinkers* (1978), *Concepts and Categories* (1978), *Against the Current: Essays in the History of Ideas* (1979), *The Crooked Timber of Humanity: Chapters in the History of Ideas* (1990), *The Magus of the North: J. G. Hamann and the Origins of Modern Irrationalism* (1993), and *The Sense of Reality: Studies in Ideas and their History* (1996). Berlin is probably best known for his influential essay 'Two Concepts of Liberty' (1958). Berlin argues that there are two traditions of thinking about liberty in political thought. One tradition, associated with the rise of liberalism, is committed to the idea of negative liberty, the liberty of people to do as they wish without interference by others. The second tradition is committed to positive liberty, a form of self-mastery which consists in conforming one's actions to the demands of reason or to a normatively preferable higher self. Some thinkers in this tradition have identified the demands of reason or the higher self with the commands of the state, with what Berlin sees as alarming authoritarian implications. Related to the critique of positive liberty is Berlin's thesis of value pluralism, developed in this essay and in many of his works. Whereas theorists of positive liberty tend to think that there is a rationally discernible harmony of values, Berlin holds that there are a plurality of objective goods which are not fully combinable and which are also incommensurable. Individuals and societies must make nonrational 'radical choices' between these goods. For Berlin, negative liberty, and liberal institutions which uphold this type of liberty, are of great value because they enable individuals the opportunity to shape their lives through radical choice. Critics argue that the thesis of value pluralism is a weak and uncertain foundation for liberalism. If the thesis is true, then the goods that a liberal society secures will presumably be uncombinable with, and so enjoyed at the expense of, other goods that are secured in non-liberal societies. Since the various goods in question are also presumably incommensurable, we will have no basis on which rationally to prefer a liberal society to a non-liberal society. Much of Berlin's work in the history of ideas focused on retrieving, and making vivid, counter-Enlightenment perspectives which challenge contemporary liberal assumptions. Relatedly, his work explores nationalist philosophies, and can be seen in part as a sustained reflection on the relationship between nationalist and liberal values. *See also* FREEDOM. SWE

Berlin Wall The Berlin Wall was erected in September 1961 to prevent the outflow of skilled manpower from the German Democratic Republic and other Soviet bloc countries into the Western-controlled sectors of the city and thence into the West as a whole. It came to symbolize the *Cold War and the rigid division of Europe into two armed camps. Its removal in November 1989 had precisely the opposite implications, culminating in *German unification and the end of the Cold War. DC

Bernstein, Eduard (1850–1932) Leading member of the German Social Democratic Party before 1914. Initiated the debate on *revisionism. His *The Premises of Socialism and the Tasks of Social Democracy* (1899—sometimes known as *Evolutionary Socialism*) argued that socialism was already being realized and there was no need for revolution. GL

Beveridge (Report) William Henry Beveridge (1879–1963) was author of the 'Beveridge Report' (*Report on Social Insurance and Allied Services*, 1942), which proposed a comprehensive 'cradle to the grave' scheme of social insurance covering all citizens irrespective of income, and which shaped much subsequent British legislation. Beveridge also wrote two influential reports on unemployment (1909 and 1944) and directed labour exchanges while a civil servant at the Board of Trade. *See also* WELFARE STATE. SW

Bharatiya Janata Party *See* HINDU NATIONALISM.

bicameralism The view that a legislative chamber should be properly composed of two houses. In the majority of states, the second or upper house has a more restricted role, for example limited to checking or delaying legislation introduced in the lower house, but an important exception is the United States where both the *Senate and the *House of Representatives play an important role in the legislative process. In such a system where the two houses have broadly equivalent power, it is necessary to provide a mechanism to resolve differences between them, such as *joint committees. In *federal systems, the upper house often represents the units of the federation, which may be given an equal number of seats regardless of their size, as in the United States. In Germany, the consent of the upper house, the Bundesrat, which is not directly elected, is necessary in those areas which directly affect the competence of the federal units or Länder. Purely appointed bodies such as the Canadian Senate, whose members are appointed by the federal prime

minister, may lack *legitimacy, although it has provided ministers from provinces where the governing party is weak. Second chambers differ considerably in their methods of appointment or election, legitimacy, powers, and effective political role, making it difficult to advance a coherent philosophy of bicameralism. In the UK, this incoherence has been evident in the repeated attempts to reform the *House of Lords, with conflicting claims about the nature of the relationship with the *House of Commons and the need for representativeness, independence, and accountability. WG

Big Brother In George *Orwell's *1984*, the embodiment of state power is 'Big Brother', a middle-aged man pictured almost everywhere and said to be always watching the people. Big Brother was, thus, a powerful, literary image of totalitarianism. For Orwell, he combined elements of Hitler and Stalin, but perhaps also Lord Reith (the first chairman of the BBC), God, and Winston Churchill. The image of Big Brother has entered political language and propaganda and is used to connote the all-embracing power of the state. LA

bilateralism Affecting two parties; often used in relation to negotiations or agreement between two countries. International relations are often conducted between two countries, seeking mutually beneficial solutions to disputes, and improved collaboration and cooperation. Bilateralism can be contrasted with *unilateralism, and many international organizations are designed to encourage *multilateral negotiations. Bilateral agreements can be easier to negotiate, involving only two parties, but outcomes can be seen to serve a narrow set of interests. Bilateral negotiations have a similar interpretation in domestic politics. The prime ministerial style of Tony Blair, involving an emphasis on bilateral meetings between himself and ministers, was seen to reduce the influence of the *Cabinet and undermine collective decision-making.

bill Proposed legislation which has not yet been enacted. In the United Kingdom Parliament there are two types of bill: public and private. *Public bills presented by ministers in the House of Commons, which take up the

most parliamentary time, follow a set procedure, which is also followed for other public bills and private bills but with some
variations. A bill initially is merely a short
title, usually with an explanatory memoran-
dum signed on the back by the minister in
charge. It is read for the first time in the
House of Commons. Upon passing, a complete draft of parts or chapters, classes, and
schedules is drawn up and submitted for a
second reading in the House. Here members
debate the general principle and purposes of
the bill. If the vote to confirm the second
reading is won the bill is then committed
to a public bill committee to debate the
detail. Complex bills may be referred to a
select committee first, which then passes its
recommendations to the public bill committee. For some bills, notably finance bills, the
detail is debated by a committee of the whole
house and/or a public bill committee. A bill
is then reported to the House complete with
suggested amendments from the committee
stage. During the report stage these and any
further amendments are debated in the
House. Ultimately, the bill complete with
agreed amendments is then given its third
reading, and upon passing is submitted to
the House of Lords. Generally, the Lords
agree suggested amendments to the bill
after which it is returned to the Commons.
Members may then debate only the amendments suggested by the Lords and pass on
their views. This continues until agreement
is reached. The bill in its final form is then
taken to the monarch by the clerks of the
House of Lords for royal assent. When this
is received the bill becomes an act and a date
of commencement for the act coming into
force may be set. A bill may be defeated on a
vote at any of the three readings in the House
of Commons and by the House of Lords.
A bill may also be lost by being talked out
in the Commons and in committee. Governments anxious to prevent this resort to the
*guillotine procedure, by which a time limit
for each stage of a bill's passage is set. Ultimately, the Commons has supremacy under
the 1911 and 1949 Parliament Acts and can
override a Lords' veto by passing a bill twice
in successive sessions.

The process for passing bills in the UK
House of Commons is well established but
a notable revision since the 1990s has been
the practice in some cases of publishing a bill

in draft form and having pre-legislative scrutiny by select committees. This has generally
been welcomed as a way of influencing
Government intentions before the formal
presentation of a bill for first reading. More
generally, devolution has had the most
impact on the legislative process. Since
its creation in 1999 the unicameral Scottish
Parliament has assumed responsibility for
the preparation of all bills in non-reserved
areas for Scotland and has its own procedures for scrutiny, amendment, and completion. Nevertheless, through the passing of
Sewel motions (named after Lord Sewel,
who suggested this amendment included in
the 1998 Scotland Act), bills being passed in
the UK Parliament in non-reserved areas
may also be given legislative effect in Scotland. Between 1999 and 2007 this was a fairly
common practice. Under the 1998 Government of Wales Act, the National Assembly for
Wales, with the sponsorship of the Wales
Office, was able to propose Government
Wales-only bills for passage through Parliament. Under the 2006 Government of Wales
Act, a new procedure was established by
which the Assembly proposed legislative
competence orders, which were deliberated
and granted through an orders in council
procedure at Westminster. Once the legislative competence was granted the Assembly
was able to introduce its own 'measures' as a
way of directly and more extensively making
primary law with effect only in Wales. The
Northern Ireland Assembly, established in
1998, also has powers to prepare bills in a
number of prescribed domestic policy areas,
although until 2007 the Assembly had largely
been suspended. Whether bills lie within the
legislative competence of these devolved
bodies can be referred by a UK government
minister to the judicial committee of the
privy council. For their bills to become acts
they also have to receive royal assent. Theoretically, the UK Parliament remains sovereign in the making of law, although it is
expected that in practice this is unlikely to
be invoked to block bills of devolved bodies.

The principal basis upon which bill procedures are criticized is the extent to which
they are influenced by partisanship. Party
interest has been seen to undermine the
quality of parliamentary debate in both the
time provided for deliberation, and in particular the approach taken to detailed work

at committee stage. More recently, devolution in Scotland has raised the issue of whether it is right for Scottish MPs to vote in the House of Commons on bills relating only to England on issues which in Scotland are the responsibility of the Scottish Parliament, when English MPs are denied any reciprocal say on the same issues in Scotland because of devolution. The Blair Governments were able to pass controversial education and health bills for England only because of the support of Scottish Labour MPs. Nevertheless, addressing this issue is fraught with difficulty primarily because of the complexity of most bills in how they directly or indirectly affect different parts of the UK.

Similar procedures to those of the UK Parliament are in force in the US Congress, whose procedural rules were derived from eighteenth-century British parliamentary usage, except that the *separation of powers ensures that there is no such thing as a government bill. However, Congress, like other genuinely *bicameral legislatures, requires a conference procedure to reconcile versions of bills produced by the two houses. JBT

(⊕) SEE WEB LINKS

• UK Parliament site, with details of current legislation and previous statutes.

bill of attainder A law that indicates the guilt of an individual without trial. In effect, this transfers the functions of ascertaining guilt and sentencing from the judiciary to the legislature. Under Article One, sections nine and ten of the US Constitution, 'No Bill of Attainder shall be passed by either Congress or State legislature'. Acts of Attainder were employed by the British Parliament between the fifteenth and early eighteenth century, but have not been used since.

bill of rights A statement of the privileges, immunities, and authorities to act that may be legally and morally claimed by the citizens of a state within the bounds of reason, truth, and the accepted standards of behaviour.

Written constitutions normally include clauses designed to protect fundamental human rights against encroachment by the state. In France this was the purpose of the Declaration of the Rights of Man of 1789 and the Preamble to the Constitution of 1946, both of which were incorporated in the Constitution of the Fifth Republic of 1958. The first ten amendments to the United States Constitution provide one of the best-known examples of a bill of rights. The *First Amendment, for instance, enshrines the freedom of religion, the right of free speech and of the press, and the right of the people to assemble and to petition the government for the redress of grievances. The Second Amendment concedes the right 'to keep and bear Arms' while the *Fifth protects individuals against self-incrimination and requires that no one 'be deprived of life, liberty or property without due process of law'. Originally, these provisions were added to the Constitution to ensure that the rights of the people were not violated by the federal government, but in the twentieth century the US Supreme Court has drawn on the *Fourteenth Amendment, adopted after the Civil War, to apply the bill of rights to the governments of the states. Statutory law cannot alter the provisions of a bill of rights such as those found in the United States, Germany, and France; like the rest of the constitution they are part of the 'higher law' not subject to change except by the extraordinary processes of constitutional amendment.

The idea of fundamental, inviolable, human rights is rooted deep in the history of Western civilization. Magna Carta (1215) was, in part, a statement of human rights, including most famously in clause 39 the right to due process: 'No free man shall be taken or imprisoned or dispossessed, or outlawed, or banished, or in any way destroyed, nor will we go upon him, nor send upon him, except by the legal judgment of his peers or by the law of the land.' But Magna Carta was an accord between King John and his barons rather than constitutional or even statutory law. On the other hand, the Bill of Rights, enacted by Parliament in 1689, was a statute concerned primarily with curtailing royal prerogative and asserting the rights of the legislature while also including some provisions designed to protect individual rights. Subjects were accorded the right to petition the monarch; provided they were Protestants they were allowed to retain arms for their defence and they were granted immunity from excessive bail or fines. However, this was not a bill of rights comparable to those that later emerged in other countries in that it could be overturned by an Act of Parliament. A better precedent was provided by the Charter or Fundamental Laws of West New Jersey (1677). This secured the right to due process and trial by jury and protected religious freedom while specifically excluding the possibility of such rights and privileges being denied by legislative authority.

It is frequently argued that a bill of rights is needed in the United Kingdom to defend the rights of the individual against overbearing public authorities. Opponents of this view argue that human rights are adequately protected by common and statutory law. Others claim that the introduction of a bill of rights would lead to a politicization of the judiciary and express concern that the entrenchment of such rights in a written constitution would compromise the sovereignty of Parliament, supposedly one of the cornerstones of democracy in the United Kingdom. DM

binomial distribution The probability distribution for the frequency of a particular event given that the event has the same probability of occurring in each of several independent trials. For example, the number of heads observed in several coin tosses follows a binomial distribution. SF

bioethics The study of ethical controversies and moral tensions associated with advancements in biological and medical sciences as well as in the determination of appropriate social policy in response to those advancements. Bioethical arguments have become widely used in policy debates about the moral appropriateness of animal testing, the ethical limits to genetic modification, the use of human medical trials, and the broader social effects associated with the prevalence of pharmaceuticals. For example, there have been significant ethical and policy debates surrounding the appropriateness of genetic engineering for animal and human cloning, as well as debates regarding the regulation of genetically modified food production. In many ways bioethics attempts to negotiate between opposing ethical goods (e.g. animal welfare versus life-saving drug testing) in cases where clear moral or empirical answers are not always available. As a result, it is often the case that bioethical

arguments change as new evidence comes to light or as public opinion transforms in light of other emerging ethical norms.

bipartisanship Agreement or collaboration between two parties. In the US and UK, where the national legislatures have tended to be dominated by two parties, bipartisanship can be seen to represent a political consensus, most often relating to foreign policy. The *separation of powers often requires an element of bipartisanship, and, as entrenched within the US constitution, this can be seen within the US *Congress and in relations between the Congress and the President. It has a similar effect to the system of *cohabitation in the French system of government. Bipartisanship is prevalent in foreign policy, often appealing to a unified conception of national interest, but can be seen to stifle criticism and may be used by dominant parties to keep potentially divisive issues off the political agenda.

bipolarity An *international system characterized by two relatively equal military *superpowers (or power blocs). The term 'bipolarity' is often associated with the international system during the *Cold War, where the system was dominated by the *NATO Alliance (backed by the United States) and the *Warsaw Pact (underwritten by the Soviet Union). According to *neorealism, the existence of these two relatively equal superpowers created a natural equilibrium and *balance of power that caused the system to remain fairly stable and peaceful. However, critics of neorealism have suggested that this bipolarity also led to a dangerous nuclear *arms race between the superpowers as well as the pursuit of hegemonic ambition via *proxy wars and the strategic use of *soft power.

Black Caucus An informal organization of African-American legislators found in the United States *Congress, and in some state legislatures. The Congressional Black Caucus, established in 1971, exists to influence the making of public policy and to advance the interests of black Americans. DM

(⊕) SEE WEB LINKS

• Homepage of the Congressional Black Caucus.

Black, Duncan (1908–91) Scottish economist; one of the modern pioneers of analytically rigorous political science. From his time as a student of physics and economics in Glasgow (1929–33), he dreamt of formulating a 'Pure Science of Politics' in which any political system could be represented by a set of definitions and axioms. His most important contribution, the *median voter theorem, came to him in 1942. It states that if all members of a voting body (committee, legislature, or electorate) recognize one main dimension in politics (left–right, for example, so that all leftists like the rightmost option least, all rightists like the leftmost option least, and everybody else dislikes an option more the further it is from their favourite position), then the median voter's favourite position will win in any reasonable voting procedure. Hence the median voter may stand for the whole voting body. The median voter theorem does not necessarily hold in more than one dimension, as Black was the first to see, because then there is always the possibility of majority-rule *cycling. But where one dimension dominates the others, as in Congressional committees or (probably) UK voting behaviour in general elections, it is a powerful predictor of convergence on the median voter's position. In the long run, politicians who diverge far from this are unlikely to be successful, even if protected by an electoral system for some time.

Black Panthers The Black Panther Party, formed in California in 1966 by Huey Newton and Bobby Seale, comprised a relatively small body of vociferous black militants, who dabbled in Marxism–Leninism, made some use of revolutionary rhetoric, and became involved in shoot-outs with police in California and New York. Despite a great deal of wild talk, however, the published programme of the Black Panthers was moderate, non-Marxist and non-revolutionary. By 1975 the party had become small and insignificant and fully committed to working within the existing system.   DM

black power A movement calling for fuller rights and more resources for black people, especially in the United States.

Initially, a vague and provocative slogan used by some radical black leaders in the United States during the 1960s, the most notable being Stokely *Carmichael. For a while the ambiguity of the phrase appeared to be tactically deliberate, but Carmichael, in collaboration with Charles Hamilton, eventually provided an exposition of its meaning in *Black Power* (1967). This made it clear that those who advocated black power were part of the black nationalist tradition exemplified by Marcus Garvey and later, *Malcolm X. They similarly emphasized the need for African-Americans to glorify in their blackness; they called on them to exhibit pride in their history and culture, and exhorted them to develop a sense of community embracing all members of their race. The evils of white racism were denounced, parallels were drawn between the conditions of blacks in the United States and the circumstances of oppressed colonial people elsewhere, and the integrationist tactics of moderate black leaders like Martin Luther King, were condemned as ineffective and futile.

There was no point in African-Americans allying themselves with the left wing of the Democratic party, trade unions, or any other groups, because it was self-defeating for weak groups to enter alliances with the strong. 'Coalitions of conscience', in other words, were unacceptable, but the exponents of black power, unlike black separatists, were not opposed to coalitions in principle, or indeed, to pluralism as such. However, 'before a group can enter the open society it must first close ranks. By this we mean that group solidarity is necessary before a group can operate effectively from a bargaining position of strength in a pluralistic society' (*Black Power*, p. 58).

Contrary to popular impressions at the time therefore, black power was not about overturning the existing system, but about preparing African-Americans for participation within it. This meant instilling them with a new sense of militancy and solidarity. They were urged, furthermore, to build their own organizational structures, and to develop their economic and political resources so that they would then be able to participate in the American pluralist system not as subordinates, as had been the case hitherto, but as full and equal partners.   DM

black sections In the 1980s there was a campaign to create special sections of the Labour Party for members from ethnic minorities. The campaign for black sections was stimulated by the frustration of aspiring black politicians who were unable to gain selection for winnable parliamentary seats. In the general election of 1983 only one black Labour candidate was selected, and this was for a safe Conservative seat. At the 1984 Labour Party Conference the campaign secured the support of 25 constituency parties and one trade union. The Labour leadership opposed their solutions as divisive and marginalizing for black members; the resolutions were heavily defeated at this and subsequent conferences. The election of four black Labour MPs in 1987 and of growing numbers of black councillors took some of the heat out of the campaign. In 1990 the Labour Party agreed to set up a Black Socialist Society in an effort to accommodate some of the aspirations of black Party members. ZLH

Blanqui, Louis-Auguste (1805–81) French insurrectionary communist who failed completely in all his attempted *coups d'état*, and spent more than thirty years in prison. In his theory of revolutionary organization, based on the cell structure, he was a precursor of *Lenin and of many communist and terrorist movements after the *Russian Revolution (1917). CS

block grant A central grant in general aid of local government services, distributed on one or more of the criteria of local needs, resource equalization, or relief of local taxation. Often called general grants, block grants are predominant as the form of central grant subvention to local government in the United Kingdom and Europe, in contrast to the United States where specific service-targeted grants are still more common. Confusingly, some US government grants made to local authorities for discretionary usage within a broad policy area, such as education, are also called block grants. JBr

block vote (weighted vote) Any procedure whereby members of some federation vote in blocks proportionate to their size: for example the Electoral College for the US Presidency, where each state has as many votes as it has members of Congress; and the EU Council of Ministers. Criticism of block voting rules concentrates on the cases

where a block-vote rule is combined with a unit rule: that is, where the block first decides how to cast its votes, and all of them are then cast in favour of the largest opinion within the block. This is the case in the British Labour Party Conference and usually in the Electoral College. In this case, larger blocks usually have disproportionate power. A square-root rule (each block to have votes in proportion to the square root of its size) has sometimes been proposed to overcome this, but would not work where blocks had the option of dividing themselves into smaller blocks in order to gain votes.

Block vote is also used to describe electoral systems for multi-member constituencies, where the voter has the same number of votes as there are seats to fill, but can only cast one vote for each candidate. In a five-member constituency, the five candidates with the largest number of votes are elected. The system is similar to the *first-past-the-post system, and tends to disproportionately favour larger parties.

Bodin, Jean (1529–96) French philosopher and legal theorist, most famous for the doctrine of sovereignty in his *Six livres de la république* of 1576. Bodin presented a complete system of knowledge divided between religious history (why God had created the universe and what he had established for human guidance), natural history (the physical laws of the universe), and human history (the structure and development of government). The problem faced by Bodin was that although the political order should reflect the divine order, France, during the Wars of Religion (1559–89), embodied disorder and civil war. He proposed that any properly constituted political society (*république* in the ancient sense of *res publica*) must have a sovereign which can make and break the law for the good of the society. Bodin is often seen as a predecessor of *Hobbes in his view of sovereignty, but his system was based on Christianity, and did not approach what later became the doctrine of *absolutism. Bodin's sovereign has the right to do anything but only in order to realize the divine plan. This was not an empty limitation (as it may have been for Hobbes) but involved the practical defence and maintenance of the established rights and liberties of individuals and groups, something Bodin saw as superior to heredity as the basis for sovereignty. CS

Bolingbroke, Viscount (1678–1751) Tory member of parliament from 1701 to 1708 and again from 1710 to 1712 before being raised to the House of Lords. He held office as Secretary for War and as Secretary of State for the North. He flirted with *Jacobitism, and spent two periods in exile after the accession of George I in 1714. Later, however, he became reconciled to the new, near-republican form of the English constitution and was chiefly concerned to move people away from what he regarded as an outdated party division between Whigs and Tories, and to build a broad coalition against the Whig Prime Minister Sir Robert Walpole. *A Dissertation upon Parties* (1735) expresses these sentiments and establishes Boling-broke's place in the evolution of Tory thought. LA

Bolivarian revolution Term used by President Hugo Chávez to describe the political process he promoted in Venezuela from his first election in 1998 until his death in office in 2013. The allusion is to the war of continental liberation from the Spanish led by Simón Bolívar in the early nineteenth century. To its critics, the Bolivarian revolution masked Chávez's personal ambitions and an increasingly authoritarian style of government. Those who offer critical support point to the fact that he did not embark upon a transformation of domestic modes and patterns of ownership and the Venezuelan elite remains entrenched. To his supporters—in Venezuela and across Latin America—the revolution represents a commitment to popular empowerment and the transformation of conventional politics. GL

(⊕) SEE WEB LINKS

• Alianza Bolivariana para los Pueblos de Nuestra América (ALBA; Bolivarian Alliance of the Peoples of Our America) website (in Spanish).

Bolshevism Political theory and practice of the Bolshevik Party which, under Lenin, came to power during the *Russian Revolution of October 1917. The Bolshevik (meaning 'majority') radical communist faction within the Russian Social Democratic Labour party emerged during the 1903 Party Congress following the split with the more moderate *Mensheviks (meaning 'minority'). After a period of intermittent collaboration and schism with the latter, the Bolshevik Party was formally constituted in 1912.

The 1905 Revolution took the Bolsheviks by surprise and there was little formal activity. The ensuing repression forced the party into clandestinity, and contact with the exiles, led by Lenin, was difficult. After the outbreak of the First World War, whilst Lenin proclaimed 'revolutionary defeatism', the Bolshevik organization inside Russia was practically moribund. The February Revolution of 1917 found the Bolsheviks unprepared. The majority of the Central Committee and the editorial board of *Pravda* (headed by Stalin) gave conditional support to the Provisional Government and entered unity discussions with the Mensheviks. Party membership soared, exiles returned, but there were problems of loss of direction. On his return to Russia, Lenin's *April Theses* (no support for the Provisional Government; the Revolution was passing from the democratic to the socialist stage; under a Bolshevik majority the *Soviets must assume state power) were poorly received. He found the Party divided between a group which advocated an immediate uprising and a Central Committee which desired a peaceful accretion of power. Lenin appealed to the rank-and-file, arguing that 'the masses are a hundred times to the left of us'. However, he resisted calls for insurrection in both June and July, declaring that 'one wrong move on our part can wreck everything'. The Party remained divided right up to the October insurrection; Zinoviev and Kamenev opposed it, and Lenin was forced to threaten resignation unless the uprising took place.

The immediate post-revolutionary situation—the period of war communism—saw the beginning of the transformation of the Communist Party into a bureaucratically organized, top–down apparatus, the eclipse of the soviets and the trade unions, and the suppression of opposition (although socialist and anarchist critics experienced alternate persecution and semi-legality). The Party also continued to be racked by internal divisions. Many objected to the Brest Litovsk treaty in March 1918, which ceded vast tracts of Russia to Germany, and the Left Communists criticized the use of bourgeois 'experts' in government and army. The Workers' Opposition (1920-1) declared that the leadership had violated 'the spirit of the Revolution' and championed workers' control in industry. Meanwhile right-wing dissidents called for a prolonged period of state capitalism as Russia was not ready for socialism.

The end of the civil war marked the transition from a temporary dictatorship to a peacetime institutionalization of repression. The tenth Party Congress (1921) was a decisive event. The introduction of the New Economic Policy (*NEP) coincided with the ban on factions and the bloody suppression of the Kronstadt rebels. Before his death in 1924, Lenin criticized the existence of 'a workers' state with bureaucratic distortions' and appealed unsuccessfully to Trotsky to work with him to oust Stalin whose role as head of the central Party apparatus gave him enormous power.

*Bukharin and Stalin championed *socialism in one country (retreat from the world stage, the enrichment of the peasantry, and the permanent retention of the NEP). Trotsky and the Left Opposition (1923-4) argued that this would destroy the socialist character of the Revolution and create a new ruling class. They advocated rapid industrialization to be financed by what Preobrazhensky termed 'primitive socialist accumulation' (the unequal exchange of resources between industry and agriculture to the benefit of the former). When Stalin and Bukharin launched the First Five Year Plan in 1928 they adopted much of the left's programme although the latter would not have defended forced collectivization and the horrors this unleashed.

The Left Opposition offered the most trenchant critique of *Stalinism in its description of the widening gap between party hierarchy and masses and the growing bureaucratization of soviet state and society. The social profile of the Party had changed qualitatively: the civil war decimated a generation of militants and the 'Lenin Levy' of 1924 swamped it with 240,000 career-minded new members. The Left Opposition represented the last serious challenge to Stalin. By 1929 he had removed the Bolshevik Old Guard from power and sent them to exile, prison, show trial, or execution.

Bolshevism may be characterized by strong organization, a commitment to world revolution, and a political practice guided by what Lenin called *democratic centralism. Whether Bolshevism inevitably transmuted into Stalinism or whether historical circumstances caused the deformation is still in dispute. GL

Bonapartism Following the practices of Napoléon Bonaparte, First Consul and subsequently Emperor of France between 1799 and 1815, and/or his nephew Louis Bonaparte (Napoléon III), Emperor of France between 1851 and 1870. The term was given its specific meanings by *Marx (see especially his *Eighteenth Brumaire of Louis Bonaparte*, 1852). For Marx, Bonapartism was an opportunistic and populist alliance between part of the bourgeoisie and the *lumpenproletariat* ('proletariat in rags'), which relied on *plebiscites, in which Bonaparte set the questions, to secure legitimacy for the regime. For Marxists, Bonapartism represents the autonomy that the state may achieve when class forces in society are precisely balanced. Historically, Bonapartism stood for strong leadership and conservative nationalism without advocating a return to the *ancien régime*. swh

Bookchin, Murray (1921–2006) One of the leading *anarchist social philosophers of the late twentieth century and a pioneering figure in the emerging green movement. In *Post-Scarcity Anarchism* (1971), Bookchin argues that capitalism has developed productive technology to a point which makes possible a transition to a society of general affluence and free time based on decentralized, self-governing communities, a social vision akin to that of anarcho-communists such as *Kropotkin. At the same time, Bookchin argues, capitalism threatens environmental catastrophe, making it essential to effect a transition to an environmentally sustainable post-capitalist society of this kind. Bookchin further developed his philosophy of what he came to call 'social ecology' in *The Ecology of Freedom* (1982) and in polemics with other radical thinkers. Against 'deep green' thinkers, Bookchin asserted the distinctive value of humanity and the importance of rationalism and scientific development (*Re-enchanting Humanity*, 1984).

He criticized currents of anarchist thought which he saw as privileging politically disengaged individualism above the claims of collective struggle and comprehensive social change (*Social Anarchism or Lifestyle Anarchism: An Unbridgeable Chasm*, 1995). He undertook an impressive survey of participatory democratic currents in the French, Russian, and other revolutions (*The Third Revolution*, four volumes, 1996–2005). His political theory is perhaps ultimately best understood as a form of radical civic republicanism which encourages local communities to take direct democratic control over the management of their social and economic needs ('libertarian municipalism' or 'communalism').   swe

Borda, J. C. de (1733–99) French engineer, naval officer, and voting theorist. In 1770 Borda first proposed what is now generally known as the Borda count. Under the Borda count, each voter ranks the candidates or options from best to worst. These numbers are added up, and the candidate who on average scores highest is declared the winner. The Borda count is often used in selecting candidates for jobs, but rarely for other voting tasks. It has a number of attractive properties, including simplicity; but it sometimes fails to choose the *Condorcet winner.

Boundary Commission (in full **Parliamentary Boundary Commission)** One of four bodies, one for each component part of the United Kingdom, which determines parliamentary boundaries every twelve to fifteen years. A separate commission determines local government boundaries. The commissions are non-partisan, in contrast to the position in the United States where drawing district boundaries is either partisan (controlled by the local governing party) or bipartisan (controlled by a body containing representatives of both parties). *See also* APPORTIONMENT.

(((∰))) SEE WEB LINKS
• Electoral Commission page linking to Parliamentary Boundary Commissions.

Bourdieu, Pierre (1930–2002) *See* SOCIAL CAPITAL.

bourgeoisie Term originally referring simply to those who lived in urban areas.

However, during the seventeenth and eighteenth centuries it became increasingly identified with a particular stratum of town-dwellers, the merchants who traded for profit and who employed others to work for them, and with what were seen as this group's distinctive values, including thrift, hard work, moral uprightness, the sanctity of the family, and respect for private property and the law. Both the profit orientation of the bourgeoisie and their values were viewed with distaste by sections of the land-owning classes and the former became objects of satire, so the term acquired pejorative connotations of money-grubbing, exploiting others, and dull conformity. As such it was seized upon by *Marx to describe the dominant class of capitalist society which existed by exploiting the wage labour of the proletariat and which was ultimately doomed to extinction. Subsequently, 'bourgeois' became a term of abuse on the left for attacking its enemies, as in 'bourgeois values', 'bourgeois democracy', or 'bourgeois social science'. Although capitalism has come back into fashion, the word itself has remained a term of abuse. Sociologists use the term 'petty bourgeoisie' in social class schema to denote self-employed businessmen who employ just a small number of people, such as small shop keepers.   ST

boycott An orchestrated way of showing disapproval, such as by not attending a meeting or avoiding a country's or company's products, so as to punish or apply pressure for change of policy or behaviour. The term originated with Captain Boycott, an Irish landlord who was subjected to this treatment in 1880.   PBI

Brandt Report (1st Report 1980, 2nd Report 1983) Name given to findings and recommendations of an international study group led by former West German Chancellor Willy Brandt. The Reports drew attention to inequalities between *North and *South, and recommended a restructuring of the world monetary regime, redistribution of income through larger global commitments to 'development funds', and negotiations to reform the international economic system.   SW

Bretton Woods A New Hampshire resort where in 1944 a forty-four-country agreement was signed to establish a post-war international monetary and payments system. Hence 'Bretton Woods system' refers to the institutions and their workings thus established. This process had begun as Anglo-American wartime collaboration.

Mindful of the economic disasters of the 1930s and the failure of the inter-war international monetary system known as the Gold Standard, the delegates recognized that a successful replacement had to be compatible with the domestic policy priorities and objectives of participating countries. A stable monetary and payments system was seen as the necessary underpinning of a liberal international trade regime (*see* WORLD TRADE ORGANIZATION). The outcome of the negotiations would have important distributional consequences for national economies and would provide the framework for the international financial system and capital flows. As the *Cold War emerged in 1946-7, the agreement in practice became limited to countries of the Western alliance and the developing world. The Bretton Woods institutions entrenched the interests of the most developed market economies among this group.

The delegates devised a payments system and exchange rate mechanism based on fixed but adjustable exchange rates pegged to the American dollar, dollar–gold convertibility at a fixed price ($35.00/ounce), international cooperation in the control of short-term capital flows, and two crucial public international institutions, the International Monetary Fund (*IMF) and the International Bank for Reconstruction and Development (IBRD or *World Bank). Members of these organizations with payments difficulties and related exchange-rate problems would be able to borrow from the IMF in the short term and the IBRD would provide long-term financing for economic reconstruction and development. The authors of the agreement intended that public *multilateral cooperative institutions would underpin the exchange rate and payments system, as opposed to private market processes or unilateral nationalist policies of the most powerful states, as during the inter-war disaster.

In the event, the resources provided for the two institutions were grossly inadequate for the task in the immediate post-war years, and the attempt to establish what came to be

known as the Bretton Woods system collapsed in 1947. The inadequate level of resources largely reflected the concerns of the US Congress: as the only country in the immediate post-war period with a sustainable payments surplus, a still isolationist Congress was unwilling unilaterally to finance recovery in Europe and the Far East. From 1947 the plan was put on hold until currencies other than the US dollar could sustain convertibility, for most from 1959 onwards. Meanwhile, through the *Marshall Plan and other programmes of aid to allies in the early Cold War, unilateral United States aid effectively replaced the IMF and World Bank as providers of international liquidity and the American dollar became the principal reserve currency in the system. The World Bank's activities became limited to the problems of the Less Developed Countries in the global economy, a role which continues to this day.

The Bretton Woods 'system' which emerged post-convertibility differed in important respects from the original plan. The US dollar functioned as a 'key currency' in the system, with dollar outflows eclipsing the meagre resources of the IMF in financing international trade and payments. The US Treasury and Federal Reserve were thus primarily responsible and dominant in the system through their discretionary manipulation of the dollar, thus side-stepping the prescribed role of the IMF. As the dollar became overvalued through a failure on the part of the United States to adjust to intensified trade competition and to keep inflation in check, confidence in the exchange rate parities declined. In addition, growing off-shore capital markets began to exert pressure on the exchange rate mechanism and international payments equilibrium. The commitment of the US government to convert dollars to gold at a fixed rate was challenged by speculators, and the United States unilaterally abrogated the system in August 1971. There were attempts at reform of the system, but differences among the big market economies prevented re-establishment with new parities and rules. The era known as Bretton Woods officially came to an end with the 'Jamaica' amendments to the IMF Articles of Agreement in 1976 instituting a 'non-system' of floating exchange rates. GU

Brexit Yet another clever abbreviated term by the British. Literally shorthand for 'British exit', 'Brexit' refers to the build-up and continuing debates associated with the 23 June 2016 referendum for Britain to 'leave' the *European Union. Triggered by then Prime Minister David Cameron in order to appease pressures from *backbenchers in his *Conservative Party, the Brexit referendum quickly became a toxic and misleading debate between *eurosceptics ('leave') and pro-Europeans ('remain'), which transcended all party and political affiliations. For eurosceptics, the argument to leave the EU was about democratic accountability, the protection of *sovereignty, *self-determination, and reducing immigration into Britain as permitted under EU rules for the free movement of EU nationals. For 'remainers', the argument was about the economic and trade benefits associated the European common market, issues of maintaining ongoing stability and peace via European membership, as well as the social opportunity costs involved with leaving the EU.

The result of Brexit was a slim referendum majority to 'leave' the EU (52 to 48 per cent), with Wales and England holding small majorities to leave. This was in contrast to Scotland, Northern Ireland, and the greater London area, which voted to 'remain' in the EU with significant margins. Although the referendum result signalled for the government to 'leave', the UK did not immediately trigger Article 50 of the EU Charter, which would automatically start a two-year period of exit negotiations between the UK and the EU.

The result of delay has been something of a constitutional crisis within the UK (as well as in the EU), with debates about whether to trigger Article 50 quickly with immediate effect ('hard Brexit') or to delay triggering Article 50 further so as to allow opportunities to prepare and plan for a gentle exit from the EU ('soft Brexit'). In addition, constitutional questions about the role of parliament in negotiating Brexit as well as whether Scotland will hold a new referendum to leave the UK (yet remain in the EU) have emerged. That said, the distinctions between soft and hard Brexit are seemingly redundant and irrelevant, since the EU Charter is clear about withdrawal timelines, and EU bodies

have been unwilling to start negotiations prior to the triggering of Article 50. Although market destabilizing did not occur as predicted by the 'remain' campaigners, the British pound did fall sharply and there are ongoing investment fears, particularly for foreign investors uncertain about continued access to the EU common market via the UK.

In Europe, the Brexit referendum has stirred renewed questions about ongoing EU integration efforts, the future saliency of the EU itself, and its continued lack of perceived legitimacy as an 'elite project'. Furthermore, the successful 'leave' vote in the UK has emboldened eurosceptics in other EU member states, particularly in France, Denmark, and Holland. This adds uncertainty about the future of the EU and whether other members will also hold referendums to leave the union. Therefore, perhaps the key words associated with Brexit and its ongoing implications are 'unpredictability' and 'uncertainty', and thus the saga continues in unabbreviated form.

BRIC/BRICS An acronym for the emerging economies of Brazil, Russia, India, China, and now South Africa. The acronym was first used in 2001 by the asset management firm Goldman Sachs to reference the four (Brazil, Russia, India and China—BRIC) fastest-emerging economies and their ascendency as new global economic forces. On 24 December 2010 South Africa became the fifth member, representing the group's current status as BRICS. Since 2009 the BRICS have held annual summits to discuss and agree on issues of cooperative development, joint investment, and strategic foreign policy alignment.

There remains considerable debate about the long-term importance and impact of the BRICS. Although the BRICS did launch the New Development Bank, which many argued would be a strategic alternative to the development policies of the *World Bank and the West, it did not receive the financial pledges made by BRICS members themselves, with China having to underwrite most of its reserves. In addition, slow economic growth from BRICS countries has significantly weakened its coherency as a group of ascending powers, thus seemingly undermining claims that it provides an alternative to Western-led *global governance.

brinkmanship Usually associated with the *Cold War practice of the superpowers wherein either might precipitate a crisis involving a potential nuclear holocaust ('going to the brink') in the hope that the adversary would make concessions on the issue in question (e.g. the 1961 crisis over Berlin or the 1962 *Cuban Missile Crisis). By analogy the term may include any high-stakes political 'gamesmanship', particularly in international politics. GU

British National Party *See* NATIONAL FRONT (UK).

Brown v. Board of Education of Topeka *See* CIVIL RIGHTS.

Bryce, James (1838–1922) British politician, diplomat, jurist, and historian. He became a professor of law at Oxford before becoming a Member of Parliament in 1880. He held office in several Liberal governments. From 1907 to 1913 he was British Ambassador to the United States. His most important academic work *The American Commonwealth*, first published in 1888, was a detailed and highly sympathetic study of the politics of the United States in the late nineteenth century. DM

buck-passing In political terms, buck-passing is the unwillingness or failure to accept responsibility for the consequences of a policy decision and blame another person or institution instead. States can also be guilty of passing the buck when they defer responsibility to deal with a local or regional conflict. The etymology of the phrase purportedly stems from poker when a player can defer their chance to deal the cards to the next player. The policy of *appeasement that occurred during the early 1930s when the UK, France, and the USSR all tried to avoid war with the Nazi regime can be seen as an international example of buck-passing whereby security arrangements for annexed countries were overlooked in favour of avoiding direct confrontation with Hitler. US President Harry S. Truman (1945–53) famously kept on his desk in the Oval Office a sign that read 'The Buck Stops Here' as a reminder of what he felt was the ultimate responsibility of the office. AM

budgeting The process of determining the financial resources necessary to meet the cost of given policy aims. The origins of modern budgeting may be traced to the reorganization of French finances, on the restoration of the monarchy in 1815. An ad hoc system of tax raising was replaced by a systematic process of presenting to parliament an evaluation of government financial needs and means of raising the necessary resources. Following this it was established that the budgeting process should occur annually, that it should embrace all government finance needs, that on being passed by parliament it should give legal effect to appropriate tax-raising powers, and that at the end of a financial year the accounts of an implemented budget should be open to official audit. The political economy underpinning the content of budgeting in the nineteenth century was free trade. Hence, indirect taxation, notably import tariffs, were replaced gradually by levies for direct taxation in order to pay for public expenditure. The annual ritual of British budget day, created by Gladstone in the 1850s, developed precisely because of the need to legitimize new forms of direct taxation with an account of the state of the nation and an explanation of the benefits that would flow from free trade. The principle of balancing outgoings against revenues in each year also commonly underpinned budgeting. Hence, in this period governments of whatever party were locked into fiscal rectitude and had little room to play party politics.

Public budgets grew as a proportion of gross domestic product in North America and Europe in the late nineteenth and early twentieth centuries as welfare expenditure was increased. In addition, the First World War necessitated greater public expenditure to meet immediate needs, but also initiated state expenditure which became permanent as citizens in the victorious countries sought a 'peace dividend'. Budgeting merely expanded in scope as a process to meet these new demands, drawing most heavily on increases in direct taxation, notably taxes that were progressively related to income. The influence of public expectations and *Keynesian economics expanded from the 1940s, bringing about the demise of the orthodoxy of balanced annual budgeting for flexible budgeting over a given period, thus allowing governments greater freedom to indulge in party politics. Budget surpluses could be built up in the first years of a government to allow fiscal give-aways in the budget preceding an election. Hence, manipulation of the budget for economic ends, which was intended by Keynes, turned into manipulation for political ends via the logic of party competition.

The contemporary problems of budgeting arise from two broad dilemmas of political economy which have emerged since the 1960s. First, continued incremental budget growth to provide for the needs of different sections of electorates has resulted in the emergence of health, social security, and education spending to dominate state budgets or at least stand comparison with longer-held commitments to defence. Whilst this spending has increased it has nevertheless occurred simultaneously with a squeeze on the fiscal capacity to afford increased public spending in large parts of the West. Budgetary control is particularly hazardous because of uncontrollable commitments such as inflation-linked pensions, and because of the electoral implications of budget reduction for the party of government responsible. Secondly, in responding to the conflict between expectations of public expenditure and the pressures of fiscal stress, continued expectations of governmental responsibility for macroeconomic management coexist uneasily with new political economies such as monetarism and old orthodoxies such as balanced budgets.

Since the 1970s, in its attempts to respond to these problems of needing to hold public spending and debt down while also continuing to respond to both policy and political expectations of government, UK budgeting has become increasingly systematic. Each year the process starts with departmental estimates of spending needs being submitted to and then summarized in the Public Expenditure Survey Committee (PESC). Bilateral relations between the Treasury and spending departments then lead to proposals being considered in cabinet committees for approval, with a 'Star Chamber' cabinet committee being used to resolve disputes. The budget is then consolidated in a finance bill presented to the House of Commons each November, in which since 1993

both expenditure and taxation and other income measures have been announced. Public spending has tended to be set at around 40 per cent of annual gross domestic product. Governments have sought to hold down levels of direct taxation, with a greater proportion of revenue raised through domestic indirect taxation.

The Blair Governments have been innovative in guaranteeing three-year departmental expenditure limits, thereby giving departments clearer expectations of what they can spend over a longer period but at the same time imposing aggregate limits. Equally, there has been a move to resource accounting budgeting, to count expenditure when commitments are made rather than when it is implemented; to comprehensive spending reviews, to replace incremental departmental budget growth with fundamental reallocations of departmental funding to address government priorities; and to the pooling of departmental budgets to address the so-called 'wicked issues' of government, such as juvenile delinquency, which cut across departmental boundaries. These reforms indicate the tendency towards continual technical innovation in order to gain greater value for money in government budgeting, a tendency that can be seen to a greater or lesser extent across states. JBr

Bukharin, Nikolay Ivanovich (1888–1938) A Soviet Communist politician and writer, Bukharin is best remembered for his association with the New Economic Policy (*NEP) and for his execution after a show trial at which he was falsely charged with counter-revolutionary activity. He was also referred to by Lenin as the 'darling of the party', although Lenin thought he had never fully 'understood the dialectic'. Bukharin was rehabilitated in 1988 with the return to vogue of many of his ideas during *perestroika.

Despite his 'liberal' reputation, Bukharin was one of the 'Left Communists' who opposed the peace treaty with Germany and Austria-Hungary as a deal with imperialism. He favoured a rapid transition to total state control of the economy during the Civil War 1918–20. Moreover, in this period, he produced a rather doctrinaire textbook, *The ABC of Communism*. However, Bukharin became the leading proponent of NEP, advocating the radicalization of the policy at various critical junctures. Famously, he enjoined the Russian peasantry to 'enrich' themselves. With the NEP's demise, Bukharin's political career effectively ended. He was removed from the Politburo in 1929, although he was re-elected to the Central Committee in 1934 when he became editor of *Izvestiya*. In 1937 he was arrested and, after threats had been made against his wife and son, confessed to the charges.   swh

Bull, Hedley (1932–85) International relations theorist. Hedley Bull is widely acknowledged as one of the most prominent members of the *English School or *international society approach in *international relations. Born in Sydney, Australia, Bull left Australia in 1953 for the University of Oxford where he was taught, and influenced by, H.L.A. Hart. Bull went on to be appointed in the London School of Economics as an assistant lecturer in 1955. He was appointed Reader following the publication of his first monograph *The Control of the Arms Race* in 1961, and took up a Professorship at the Australian National University in 1967. A decade on, Bull published *The Anarchical Society: A Study of Order in World Politics*, which is widely regarded as one of the most influential monographs in international ielations.

The Anarchical Society advances the idea that a 'society of states' exists at the international level. Two years prior to Kenneth *Waltz's *Theory of International Politics*, Bull claimed that even though states operate within an anarchical realm they establish rules, values, principles, norms, and institutions which facilitate international order. Notably, these are conditions of social order and thus this order has a moral value in its own right. In so doing, Bull exposes the tension between order and justice at the international level, which continues to be a central feature of studies in international relations and global governance. In addition, international society should not be viewed as fixed. It has been created, and is an ongoing process that is shaped by the decisions made by states (Bull's focus was very much on the *great powers). Bull put forward the *pluralist and *solidarist visions of international society. These reflect different interpretations of reality as well as normative commitments to alternative world orders.

Pluralists prioritize the dignity found in diversity. States should be allowed to forge their own culture, values, belief systems, and practices without the interference of other states. In doing so, they uphold the norms of state sovereignty and non-intervention. In contrast, solidarists believe that state sovereignty is not a right but a responsibility, and that governments that fail to fulfil this responsibility—for example, by committing *crimes against humanity—forfeit the right to be treated as a legitimate *sovereign authority. At this point, the international community has a responsibility to protect the populations being targeted, even if this involves military intervention.

Methodologically, Bull applied 'the classical approach' which reflected 'theorizing that derives from philosophy, history, and law, and that is characterized above all by explicit reliance upon the exercise of judgement and by the assumptions that if we confine ourselves to strict standards of verification and proof there is very little of significance that can be said about international relations'. The statement provides an insight into both what Bull stands for and stands against. Regarding the former, Bull's commitment to interdisciplinary research is evident, and forty years on has become a current trend in both the social and natural sciences. Regarding the latter, it reflects Bull's anti-positivist stance, which dominated the discipline at the time. This methodological position continues to be a central distinguishing feature of the English School four decades later.   AG

bureaucracy Government by permanent office-holders. The term was coined in eighteenth-century France, and first appeared in English in 1818, in both cases with pejorative overtones built in from the beginning. The pejorative overtones are still current in everyday usage and in semi-jocular references to such maxims of bureaucracy as Parkinson's Law ('Work expands to fill the time available for it').

The first writer to view bureaucracy more favourably was Max *Weber. Weber argued that working to the rules in a hierarchical office in which appointment and promotion went by merit was more rational than making appointments on other bases such as *patronage. Weber also stressed the tension between bureaucrats and elected officials. The latter may wish to give favours to their supporters in return for votes. Bureaucrats may be expected to obstruct this.

Most subsequent sociological writing on bureaucracy has been an extended footnote to Weber. An important extension, due especially to Michel Crozier (*The Bureaucratic Phenomenon*, English edition, 1964) stresses the difference in motives between the bureaucrat at the top of the organization and the bureaucrat at the bottom. The latter wants a quiet life which may best be ensured by slavish adherence to the rules, whatever they are. The former may have more elevated aims for the bureaucracy which are frustrated by inability to force the routine employee to have the same aims as the bureau. Generally, means become ends in themselves. This difficulty is shared with firms. Indeed, the Weberian analysis of bureaucracy is intended to apply just as much to the firm as to the government office. Therefore it gives no support to the 'New Right' proposition that governments are less efficient than markets.

Many of the economists who have investigated bureaucracy, however, have made precisely that claim. W. A. Niskanen, in *Bureaucracy and Representative Government* (1971), argues that the bureaucrat seeks to maximize his or her budget and therefore systematically to overproduce bureau goods and services. The politician to whom the bureau reports would like to control its costs, but faces what economists call an 'agency problem'. The only reliable information on the costs of the bureau comes from the bureau itself, unless the politicians erect a second bureau to check on the costs of the first. This is done to a limited extent (for instance by the *Office of Management and Budget in the United States and the audit office, which has gone by various names and which serves the *Public Accounts Committee, in the UK Parliament). But who is to check on the costs of the second agency, or check that the audit agency is not conniving with the agency it is auditing? Once again, however, note that these problems are shared by public and private bureaucracy. Auditing has not prevented a number of notable scandals in recent company history. Therefore, although the Niskanen model is elegant and has spawned many studies of

bureaucracy, it provides less ammunition for the *privatization programme of governments in the 1980s than its partisans claim.

Burke, Edmund (1729–97) *Whig politician who sat in parliament, apart from a brief interlude, from 1766 until his death. He espoused the cause of his native Ireland in many ways, by opposing absentee landlordism, by pressing the case of Ireland's commercial rights, and by advocating steps towards Catholic emancipation. He was also sympathetic to the cause of the American colonies, being London agent of the state of New York and writing on the injustice of the taxation of the colonies and in favour of reconciliation with them. As a supporter of Lord Rockingham, he opposed the revival of the influence of the King, George III, in Parliament. He was also concerned with maladministration by the East India Company and was involved in the impeachment of Warren Hastings.

It is a great irony that a Whig politician and one who might (anachronistically) be said to be associated with a variety of progressive causes should come to be regarded as one of the supreme articulators of conservative thought and sentiment, producing what some have seen as the definitive statement of such thought. The reason for Burke's status in this respect lies in his reaction to the events of 1789 in France, contained in his *Reflections on the Revolution in France* (1790). Burke was most of all opposed to the assumption by the revolutionaries that they could redesign a system of government on abstract and universal principles. His book was directly stimulated by the support of one of his old adversaries, Richard *Price, for the principles of revolution.

In opposing the Declaration of the Rights of Man, Burke drew upon arguments about social practice and political constitutions which he had developed in relation to other issues. Custom and practice define society; they have developed over a long period and can be changed only slowly. Law comes out of custom and must be in tune with it. Reform of all sorts is possible, but it must preserve and extend the harmony between established social practice and policy. Revolution, in the sense of a new system of government and social relations, based on principles not well founded in the society in question, can only end in chaos or tyranny. Real rights are prescriptive: that is, they are established by the laws of a society and based on its customs. 'Natural' rights, based on abstract principles about the human condition, are nonsensical and dangerous.

Burke sounds his most reactionary in bemoaning the fate of France in general and Marie Antoinette in particular: 'The age of chivalry is gone. That of sophisters, economists and calculators has succeeded: and the glory of Europe is extinguished for ever.' Tom *Paine commented, 'He pities the plumage, but sees not the dying bird,' and Mary *Wollstonecraft beseeched him to acknowledge that if he were a Frenchman he would be a revolutionary. After all, he was not a supporter of absolutist, unparliamentary, and inefficient government in Britain and its colonies, so it was perverse to be sentimental about the *ancien régime*.

These reactionary sentiments were probably real, but certainly untypical. Burke believed in a commercial society. He thought government rested ultimately on popular sovereignty and should seek to maximize the general well-being. However, these beliefs are doubly obscured in his writings. First, he was much more politician than philosopher, concerned more to develop his arguments in a passionate rhetorical style and to a practical purpose than to examine their premisses. Second, he believed in the obfuscation of principles, because he thought that principles like popular sovereignty and utility might prove dangerous and counterproductive if made too explicit; he was a kind of 'blinded utilitarian' who thought that custom and our sense of moderation were better guides to utility than the (abstract) principle of utility itself.

One important application of these principles was Burke's theory of the role and duties of a parliamentary representative, most famously expressed in a speech at Bristol when he was elected there in November 1774. He intended, he said, to put 'great weight' on the wishes of his constituents and accord their opinions 'high respect'. Even so, he did not intend to be instructed by them, but by his reason and conscience, for 'Your representative owes you, not his industry only, but his judgement'. Only to a limited degree was it a representative's job to protect the interests of his constituents; the

more important role was to play a part in 'a deliberative assembly of *one* nation with *one* interest, that of the whole' (Burke's italics). This 'Burkean' doctrine of representation has had resonance wherever there have been elected parliaments, and has had supporters and opponents inside parties of the 'left' as well as those of the 'right'.

It may be ironic that Burke is seen as definitively conservative, but the perception is also accurate and revealing. Burke's stance against the French Revolution and the 'abstract' ideas arising out of the Enlightenment is prototypically conservative; the importance he attributed to local and national traditions, his capacity to support reform, and his belief in putting custom and moderation before absolute principle have all contributed to the style and outlook of conservatism. In the last two or three years of his life (he died in 1797) Burke's attitude to the French Revolution hardened to a loathing more crudely based on religious condemnation, but his writings from this period are little read today whereas the more subtle arguments he deployed in 1790 are still widely read and generally considered to be an important influence on conservative thought.   LA

Bush Doctrine Catchphrase to characterize the foreign policy of US President George W. Bush. While it changed several times throughout the 43rd President's two terms in office, the Bush Doctrine has four pillars centred on US military superiority: (1) *unilateralism; (2) a 'with us or with the terrorists' logic; (3) pre-emption; and (4) *regime change.

The Bush administration turned towards a *realist 'America First' approach to international engagement soon after taking office in January 2001. This found first expression in the US withdrawal from the Kyoto Protocol six months into the new presidency. Following the terrorist attacks on American soil on September 11th, 2001, the Bush administration combined unilateralist leanings with military interventionism directed at countries presumed to harbour terrorists. In October 2001 the US launched war against the Taliban government in *Afghanistan, and in March 2003 invaded *Iraq as part of the War on Terror.

The pillars of the Bush Doctrine were codified in three prominent texts: (1) Bush's 2002 State of the Union Address, which included the terminology of the 'axis of evil' to characterize Iran, Iran, and North Korea; (2) the 2002 National Security Strategy (updated in 2006); (3) the President's 2003 State of the Union Address.   AHr

Butskellism Term popularized in Great Britain during the 1950s, coined in *The Economist* by merging the names of two successive Chancellors of the Exchequer, Labour's Hugh Gaitskell (1950–1) and the Conservative R. A. Butler (1951–5). Both favoured a 'mixed economy', a strong welfare state, and Keynesian demand management designed to ensure full employment.   DC

butterfly-ballot A confusing design of ballot paper in which the column for indicating preferences is located between two staggered lists of options, rather than left or right of a single list. This phrase was made commonplace in reporting of the disputed US Presidential election of 2000, having been used in parts of the pivotal State of Florida.   PM

cabinet 1. A regular meeting of ministers, chaired by a head of government, with authority to make decisions on behalf of the government as a whole. Such a cabinet is common in parliamentary forms of government, including that in the United Kingdom, where it has been imitated in the devolved parliaments and assemblies for Scotland, Wales, and Northern Ireland.

Cabinet systems of government share two common principles. First, they observe the principle of *collective responsibility. Cabinet ministers share in the process of making cabinet decisions and are duly bound to defend those decisions in public irrespective of private opinion. Secondly, they observe the principle of parliamentary *accountability. However, whilst the principles of cabinet government are universal, the structure, membership, and operations of cabinet in practice are open to considerable variation.

Cabinets vary in size between roughly ten and forty members. Size is principally a function of absolute levels of public expenditure and the amount of governmental business this engenders. However, it is also determined by decisions taken on the proportion of government ministers to be included in the cabinet. In Canada virtually all ministers are included as a result of the need for territorial as well as departmental representation in the cabinet, meaning that there are between thirty and forty cabinet ministers at any one time. By contrast, the United Kingdom, which has generally over a hundred government ministers, has only a fifth of them in the cabinet.

Cabinets also vary according to their use of committees. Cabinet government in Luxembourg, Iceland, and Sweden under the Social Democrats is notable for making no use of committees. In the first two cases the extent of government business is sufficiently limited to allow it to be dispatched by the meetings of full cabinet. In other cabinet systems delegation of cabinet business to committees is commonplace. It is usual that there are standing committees on foreign affairs, defence, economic policy, and budgetary policy. Beyond this there is considerable variation in both standing and ad hoc committees.

Membership of full cabinet and of cabinet committees is formally determined by the prime minister. In practice many prime ministers face many constraints. Much is made of the case of Labour governments in Australia and New Zealand, where cabinet membership has been determined by parliamentary party election, the power of the prime minister being limited to the apportionment of specific cabinet portfolios. However, it is also commonplace in countries which are federal, or have strong regional government, for prime ministers to have to ensure appropriate territorial representation, and in coalition governments for each of the coalition partners to have bargained representation in cabinet and cabinet committees. Small parties which are nevertheless crucial to the forming of any government can dictate continuous control of particular cabinet portfolios, as was the case with the Free Democrats in Germany. Even where single party majority control is long-standing, the apportionment of cabinet positions may have to be sensitive to intra-party factionalism, as was the case with the Liberal Democrat governments in Japan.

Differences in the operation of cabinet government reflect differences in structure and membership, and the role of the prime minister that they incorporate. In multi-party coalition governments a prime minister's ability to control the cabinet agenda, use cabinet debates as a means to arbitrate between ministers in dispute, and coordinate the overall policy of the government is very weak. Even in more consensual cabinets derived from more than one party, or based on diverse territorial representation, decision-making can be slow and chaotic. This has led to the charge that cabinet government is managerially inefficient.

In the United Kingdom the Cabinet is generally drawn from parliamentary members of the single majority party. As a result cabinet government is based upon relative cohesion in purpose. In addition, the leading role of the Prime Minister as *primus inter pares* ('first among equals') is not questioned. Ever since the modern cabinet system evolved during the First World War, when formal cabinet meetings were convened with written agendas and staffed by a cabinet secretariat, the Prime Minister has had clear powers of agenda control. The Prime Minister has also had power to appoint cabinet committees and determine their terms of reference, allowing their recommendations to become effectively the policy of the government. This has led to the charge that in Britain cabinet government has fallen prey, not to chaos and inefficiency, but to an overriding power of the Prime Minister. Over time there is considerable evidence of prime ministers bypassing cabinet and potential cabinet opposition on economic and defence-related issues by resort to carefully selected cabinet committees. This was true, for example, of Attlee's approach to framing policy on an independent nuclear deterrent 1945–51. A more general thesis of prime ministerial government gained credence with the publication of the Crossman diaries detailing the practice of the Wilson governments 1964–70, and with the apparent contempt for collective decision-making shown by Mrs Thatcher during her premiership 1979–90. Equally, the decision to go to war in Iraq in 2003 was widely perceived as evidence of a prime minister's ability to make key decisions, which could be pushed through both Cabinet and Parliament with the command of party support, irrespective of opposition. More broadly, the advent of a Labour government in 1997 arguably ushered in a period of dual prime ministerial government. Tony Blair and his Chancellor, Gordon Brown, decided most key policies either singly or together while cabinet meetings were reduced to a perfunctory weekly meeting lasting less than an hour.

The practice of cabinet government in the UK, however, remains contingent on prime ministerial style, elite political culture, and political position. Attlee delegated considerable power in domestic policy areas to his ministers working on cabinet committees. Churchill and Macmillan prided themselves on a patrician style that allowed full debate in cabinet of all key issues. Callaghan used the full processes of cabinet decision-making to deal with the financial crisis in 1976. Even Mrs Thatcher relented on a number of policy ideas against cabinet opposition and eventually fell because she did not do so more. The Major Government 1990–97 actively sought to re-establish the notion of consensual cabinet government as a way of rebinding a Conservative Party tearing itself apart over European policy. As part of this, the secrecy surrounding cabinet government was eroded. In May 1992 *Questions of Procedure for Ministers*, which is the nearest thing Britain has to a constitution for cabinet government, was published. This disclosed the names, membership, and purposes of sixteen standing cabinet committees and ten cabinet subcommittees. The secretary to the cabinet made it clear that while only Treasury ministers had the right to challenge committee decisions in full cabinet, any alliance of five or more ministers could effectively do likewise and have a chance of success. This suggests that prime ministerial government has not only political but also constitutional limits. Equally, the Brown premiership from 2007 sought to establish a more consensual tone after the controversies of the Blair years.

In recent years study of the cabinet in comparative political science has been refreshed by new theories that have focused on the power of prime ministers, notably those of presidentialisation and prime ministerial predominance. These have sought to take into account both the increasing importance of executive responses to media scrutiny and the increasing complexity of governmental responsibilities in accounts of how power is wielded at the top. At the same time the turn towards governance has sought to reconceptualise the focus of the study of political elite decision-making to that of the core executive. In this approach, much greater significance can be allocated to non-governmental actors and the role, for example, of policy networks, which demands a re-evaluation of the roles that formal institutions such as cabinet, and indeed individual actors such as the prime minister, play in the conduct of politics. Cabinet and the context in which it is studied remain, therefore, of enduring interest.

2. A regular meeting of ministers which is consultative to a head of government, not sharing responsibility for final decisions. Such a cabinet is exemplified in the American presidential system.

3. (In this meaning often spelt in italics and pronounced as in French, to indicate its origins and the distinction from senses 1 and 2.) A group of political advisers which is consultative to an individual minister. Ministerial *cabinets* exist in a number of European executives. JBr

cadre The word cadre originally referred to 'the permanent skeleton of a military unit, the commissioned and non-commissioned officers, etc., around whom the rank and file may be quickly grouped' (Chambers Dictionary). Thence it was applied in Russia to 'a cell of trained Communist leaders, or to a member of such a cell'.

The political use of this military term indicated the intention of the Leninist leadership of the Russian Revolution to create a disciplined, hierarchically organized, and swiftly responsive system of control of the revolutionary movement. The cadre system was also the embodiment of the 'vanguard party' which Lenin believed was made necessary by the inability of the working class to achieve class consciousness spontaneously. Cells were established in all neighbourhoods, work places, and social organizations, and their cadres owed their entire loyalty not to the members of the organization within which they worked, but to the Party cadres at the level above. The control from above of appointments and postings of the cadre force was the basis of Stalin's rise to power. JG

cadre party *See* PARTY ORGANIZATION.

Calhoun, John C. (1782–1850) Calhoun has three claims to fame. One stems from his prominence as an American politician between 1811 and 1850. During that period he was, successively, an important member of the House of Representatives (1811–17), Secretary of War (1817–25), Vice-President of the United States (1825–32), senator for South Carolina (1832–44), Secretary of State (1844–5) and, yet again, senator for South Carolina (1845–50). In his lifetime his reputation as a politician was mixed. He was variously described as a patriot, a nationalist, an apologist for the slave-owning South, 'first amongst second rate men', an opportunist, and the destroyer of the Union. What is clear is that for the last twenty years of his life he was one of the leaders of the Old South in its attempts to defend its interests in the Union.

As a political theorist his claim to fame rests largely on three works, *The South Carolina Exposition and Protest* (1828), *A Disquisition on Government*, and *A Discourse on the Constitution and Government of the United States* (both published after his death in 1850). The *Exposition* presents the case for state nullification of federal laws, the *Discourse* is a states' right tract incorporating ideas for a plural executive, and the *Disquisition* presses the case for a ruling concurrent majority, that is, one rooted not in numbers but in interests, each of which possesses a 'mutual negative'. These ideas were all attempts to avoid the South's secession. The problem was that although presented in a scholarly fashion they all suffered from the same crucial weakness—their success depended on acceptance by Northern politicians. For a theorist obsessed with power this was, to say the least, a significant weakness.

Calhoun's final claim to fame rests on the analytical problems he bequeathed to politicians and theorists who followed him. One of these is the role of *pressure groups. The other, and more important problem, is how, short of secession, the interests of territorial minorities can be defended in wider Unions. Calhoun never resolved these problems, but neither has anyone else. In short, Calhoun remains important because of the problems which defeated him. JBU

Calvin, Jean (1509–64) Swiss theologian and religious leader. Born at Noyon, he studied arts in Paris, and law at Orléans. In 1536 he fled persecution in France. In Basle he published *Christianae Religionis Institutio*, an exposition of Reformation doctrine in which predestination figured prominently. He settled in Geneva in 1537. In 1541 he founded a theocracy where all matters of state and of social and individual life were governed by the Reformed Church.

Calvin's assertion of the supremacy of Church over State far exceeded any papal claims and is akin to that of Israeli and Islamic fundamentalists today. But the theocratic State was democratic, not hierarchical. The Church was to be governed by elders (presbyters—hence, Presbyterianism) all of equal status. Moreover, the Church was to play a supervisory role only. Church and State were independent of each other with their own specific roles. Clergy could not be State officials, nor State officials members of the clergy. According to the *Ecclesiastical Ordinances* of 1541 the Church, in a consistory, comprising pastors and elders, supervised the citizens and maintained discipline.

Calvin's political theory was Scholastic. He regarded both Church and State as natural groups; man having a tendency to group. He insisted magistrates should uphold natural law as well as divine positive law. He also held that the purpose of the State is the administration of justice, not only retributive and natural justice (equity), but also distributive justice (fair shares). Whether he allowed subversion for just reasons is unclear. CB

Campaign for Nuclear Disarmament
See CND.

Camus, Albert (1913–60) Novelist and philosopher, whose work addressed the alienation inherent in modern life, and explored the basis of morality and politics. Born in Algeria to a French father (killed in the First World War) and Spanish mother, Camus attended the University of Algeria, and played regular club football, noting that sport provided 'my only lessons in ethics'. Camus worked as a journalist, and in 1940 moved to Paris, fighting with the resistance during the Second World War. In *Le Mythe de Sisyphe* (The Myth of Sisyphus: 1942) Camus dealt with 'the absurd'—the impossibility of the human search for logic and order amidst a chaotic and uncertain world. Escape from the deadening routine of everyday life would lead only to a sense of displacement. This work, and novels such as *L'Etranger* (The Outsider: 1942) brought Camus close to the *existentialism of Jean-

Paul *Sartre. Camus, however, saw the roots of German fascism in the moral and intellectual nihilism of the 1930s, and sought to provide some sort of basis for a political system which would promote justice and liberty. In *L'Homme révolté* (The Rebel: 1951) he advocated rebellion in order to build a new social system that, instead of trying to replace one misplaced orthodoxy with another, promoted moderation and social justice. Camus combined his belief in the subjectivity of truth and the futility of rational approaches to politics, with a humanitarianism that led to his rejection of violence and extremism. These two elements of his work were never completely reconciled.

candidate selection In democratic political systems the selection of candidates is critically important as political parties and the party preferences of voters have come to dominate electoral politics. Party selection of candidates thus effectively determines the public's choice of who will represent them. In electoral areas which are dominated by a single party, that party's choice of candidate also then effectively determines who is elected.

In Britain and Europe the political parties are responsible for selecting their candidates. This is done on either a local, regional, or national basis. Britain's *first-past-the-post electoral system has in the past facilitated localized constituency party selection. Here, the 'selectorate' may be limited to branch delegates or a local party electoral college, but most parties have now embraced the principle of one member one vote (OMOV). The national party role may involve simply routine endorsement of local party decisions. However, in recent years central party involvement has increased primarily so as to vet potential candidates' ability to withstand media scrutiny and support party views. Central party intervention has been the greatest in the Labour Party to ensure better female representation. This resulted in the practice of imposed all-women shortlists, made legal by legislation allowing positive discrimination in 2002.

In countries where list elections are held either on their own or as part of mixed member electoral systems, candidate selection focuses not simply on the selection of candidates but on their ranking on party lists.

Historically, list selection has been associated with greater central party influence over selection and ranking. Although this has been diluted by recent trends towards party democratization, in list selection too there is evidence of central party intervention to ensure better female representation. In Britain, Plaid Cymru innovated in 'zipping' list candidate selection for the National Assembly for Wales by placing a woman at the top of each of their regional lists, followed by a man, another woman, and so on.

In some political systems parties have involved the electorate directly in candidate selection. In part of the United States a system of *primary elections was introduced in the late nineteenth and early twentieth centuries to overcome the corruption which had developed through selection by party *convention or *caucus. The primary election transfers responsibility for selecting the candidate from the party to the electorate: either the electorate at large or those members of the electorate who have registered with the public authorities as supporters of the party. Moreover, the primary election is part of the official business of government; it ceases to be part of an internal party process and the party has to accept the outcome of the primary election. Primaries are held to establish candidates both for the Congress (both Houses) and, on a loosely organized state-by-state basis, for presidential elections.   PBy/JBr

canvassing The activity of soliciting votes and locating supporters. Traditionally done by tramping the streets from house to house, culminating in what (in British English only) is known as 'knocking up' (viz. persuading those who have previously promised to support one's party to come out and vote for it). Now largely done by telephone.

CAP (Common Agricultural Policy) The Common Agricultural Policy of the *European Union (EU). The objectives, set out in the Treaty of *Rome, included increased productivity, provision of a fair standard of living for the agricultural community, the stabilization of markets, security of food supplies, and provision of food to consumers at reasonable prices. In effect, it involves a massive transfer of resources from non-farmers to farmers, has protected EU farmers from international competition, and has artificially inflated food prices. The CAP is expected to consume over a third of the budget of the EU between 2007 and 2013: in the 1970s the proportion was around two-thirds. Some pressure for reform has come through EU participation in *World Trade Organization negotiations and with the expansion of the EU into eastern Europe, although vested interests have been effective in ameliorating their losses.

(((•))) SEE WEB LINKS

• European Union information on agriculture.

capitalism A term denoting a distinct form of social organization, based on generalized commodity production, in which there is private ownership and/or control of the means of production. The word 'capitalism' is a relative latecomer in social science, with the *OED* citing its first use in 1854 ('capitalist' in 1792). Originally popularized by Marxist writers (Marx preferred to speak of the capitalist mode of production or bourgeois society), it is a term which has increasingly gained credence across the political spectrum, although this has inevitably produced inconsistency in its employment. At least three present-day usages are discernible.

1 The meaning derived from the work of Werner *Sombart and Max *Weber. Sombart describes capitalism in terms of a synthesis of the spirit of enterprise with the 'bourgeois spirit' of calculation and rationality. This *geist* or spirit is deemed to be an aspect of human nature and is seen to have finally taken a suitable form for itself in the shape of the economic organization of modern society. On this basis, Weber (in *The Protestant Ethic and the Spirit of Capitalism*) charts how the 'spirit of capitalism' transformed other modes of economic activity designated as 'traditionalist'. A traditionalistic worker does not consider maximization of the daily wage as a primary objective, but opts instead to work to secure an accustomed style of life. The capitalist enterprise, by contrast, is based on a rational reorganization of production and is directed solely towards maximizing productive efficiency. Although Weber stops short of suggesting that the Protestant ethic produced capitalism, he believes that the

origins of the capitalist spirit can be traced particularly to the ethics associated with *Calvinism. Capitalism is therefore less the result of the introduction of new technology than the consequence of a new spirit of entrepreneurial enterprise. Weber (in *General Economic History*) develops an account of the rise of modern capitalism in post-feudal Europe, emphasizing characteristics broadly similar to those discussed by Marx. The spirit of rational calculation fosters a capitalist economic system in which wage-labourers are legally 'free' to sell their labour power; restrictions on economic exchange in the market-place are removed; technology is constructed and organized on the basis of rational principles; and there is a clear separation of home and workplace. Furthermore, capitalism enables the consolidation of the legal form of business corporation, the expansion of public credit, organized exchanges for trading in all commodities, and the organization of enterprises for the production of commodities rather than simply for trade. Above all, capitalism is characterized by the increased rationalization of social life, and the further advance of *bureaucracy is seen as inevitable in the modern world. Capitalism, for Weber, is clearly the most advanced economic system ever created. However, its technical rationality threatens to constrict and extinguish the most distinctive values of Western civilization. Humanity is therefore trapped in an 'iron cage' of its own making.

2 The sense which identifies capitalism with the organization of production for markets. This is a usage derived from the German Historical School, with its primary distinction between the 'natural economy' of the medieval world and the 'monetary economy' of the modern age. This definition of capitalism as a commercial system is commonly buttressed by an emphasis on a certain type of motive, the profit motive. Although this definition has affinities with the Sombart/Weber view, its emphasis on the market economy lends it a substantially different focus.

3 Karl Marx sought the essence of capitalism neither in rational calculation nor in production for markets with the desire for gain (a system termed by Marx, 'simple commodity production'). For Marx capitalism is a historically specific mode of production, in which capital (in its many forms) is the principal means of production. A mode of production is not defined by technology but refers to the way in which the conditions of production are owned and controlled and to the social relations between individuals which result from their connection with the process of production. Each mode of production is distinguished by how the dominant class, controlling the conditions of production, ensures the extraction of the surplus from the dominated class. As Marx clarifies in a famous passage, the really distinctive feature of each society is not how the bulk of labour is done, but how the extraction of the surplus from the immediate producer is secured: 'It is in each case the direct relationship of the owners of the conditions of production to the immediate producers . . . in which we find the innermost secret, the hidden basis of the entire social edifice, and hence also the political form of the relationship of sovereignty and dependence, in short the specific form of state in each case' (*Capital*, vol. iii, ch. 47). Capitalism is thus perceived as a transient form of class society in which the production of capital predominates, and dominates all other forms of production (generalized commodity production). Capital is not a thing, not simply money or machinery, but money or machinery inserted within a specific set of social relations whose aim is the expansion of value (the accumulation of capital). Capitalism is therefore built on a social relation of struggle between the bourgeoisie and the working class. Its historical prerequisite was the concentration of ownership in the hands of the ruling class and the consequential and 'bloody' emergence of a propertyless class for whom the sale of labour-power is their only source of livelihood. The distinction between the sale of labour and the sale of labour-power (the capacity to labour) is crucial, Marx argues, for understanding how all profit derives from the unpaid and therefore exploited labour of the worker. Capitalism therefore combines formal and legal equality in exchange with subordination and exploitation in production. The existence of

trade, rational calculation, production for the market, the use of money, and the presence of financiers is not enough to constitute a capitalist society. For Marx, capitalism is based on a specific form of private property which enables capital to yoke labour to create surplus value in production. Like Weber, Marx portrayed capitalist society as the most developed historical organization of production. Unlike Weber, Marx envisaged that class struggle would intensify and produce an ever-expanding union of workers who, as a self-conscious, independent movement of the majority, would rise up and abolish capitalism.

All periodizations of capitalism are problematical. Whilst Marx claims that in Western Europe bourgeois society began to evolve in the sixteenth century and was making giant strides towards maturity in the eighteenth century, Karl Polanyi concludes that capitalism did not emerge until the Poor Law Reform Act of 1834. Capital existed in many forms—commercial capital and money-dealing capital—long before industrialization. For this reason the period between the sixteenth and eighteenth centuries is often referred to as the merchant capital phase of capitalism. Industrial capitalism, which Marx dates from the last third of the eighteenth century, finally establishes the domination of the capitalist mode of production.

For most analysts, mid- to late-nineteenth-century Britain is seen as the apotheosis of the laissez-faire phase of capitalism. This phase took off in Britain in the 1840s with the Repeal of the Corn Laws, and the Navigation Acts, and the passing of the Banking Act. In line with the teachings of classical political economy (Adam *Smith and David Ricardo), the state adopted a liberal form which encouraged competition and fostered the development of a 'self-regulating' market society. Liberal and conservative thinkers have been keen to identify this particular phase of capitalism with the essence of capitalism itself. This has encouraged some theorists to dispense with the term completely when describing societies in the post-1945 period. Hence during the post-war long boom (1950–70), an explosion of terms—industrial society; post-industrial society; welfare statism; post-capitalist society—

threatened to displace the centrality of the concept of capitalism. The waves of economic and political crises experienced since this period, however, led many commentators to reinstate the term, particularly under the influence of the *New Right (*Hayek and Friedman). In contrast to liberals, writers in the Marxist tradition understand twentieth-century developments in terms of the movement from the laissez-faire phase of capitalism to the monopoly stage of capitalism. On the basis of *Lenin's famous pamphlet, *Imperialism: The Highest Stage of Capitalism*, the monopoly stage is said to exist when: the export of capital alongside the export of commodities becomes of prime importance; banking and industrial capital merge to form finance capital; production and distribution are centralized in huge trusts and cartels; international monopoly combines of capitalists divide up the world into spheres of interest; and national states seek to defend capitalist interests thus perpetuating the likelihood of war (*see also* IMPERIALISM).

Since the extension of the franchise in nineteenth-century Britain there has been a hotly contested debate on the relationship between democracy and capitalism. The experience of the twentieth century, however, shows that there are a variety of political forms—liberal democratic, social democratic, fascist, statist, republican, monarchical—which can accompany capitalist economies. This constitutes the basis for the study of the *state in capitalism.

Although the world market has always formed the backdrop to the development of capitalism, a number of recent changes, associated with both the 'globalization of capital', and the demise of the Soviet Union, have strengthened the claim that capitalism should now be viewed as a world system. *See also* ANGLO-SAXON CAPITALISM; RHENISH CAPITALISM. PBM

carbon trading A market-based approach to combating climate change that centres around finical incentives for lowering global carbon dioxide (CO_2) emission levels. Part of a wider approach referred to as 'emissions trading', which can include the trading of any greenhouse gas or gases (such as methane, chlorofluorocarbons, and nitrous oxide). Carbon trading is currently the most common type of emissions trading.

The majority of carbon trading regimes operate as a 'cap and trade' system. Under this kind of regime, an upper limit of emissions is set and emissions are then traded within this cap. A country, city, or corporation that has high emissions can pay for the right to emit more than their allocated share by buying permits from actors with low emissions. This offers a financial incentive for reducing emissions, since selling off emission permits is profitable. Carbon markets are said to allow emission cuts at the lowest possible cost, because they do not require adoption of green technology from all actors. Carbon trading is a central element of the Kyoto Protocol, in the form of the Clean Development Mechanism, and a key policy of the *European Union, whose Emissions Trading System is the largest in the world. *See also* CLIMATE CHANGE.   AD

Carlyle, Thomas (1795–1881) Scottish literary and political writer. Born in Ecclefechan close to the English border, son of a master stonemason in a Calvinist household, Carlyle was schooled at Annan Academy and Edinburgh University. He took up tutorships in mathematics, taught himself German and French, and soon developed into a leading Victorian critic of mechanistic materialism. In part, this was from the general philosophic standpoint of German Romanticism, but it also stemmed from an intense personal admiration of Goethe, Schiller, and *Coleridge. At times, this contempt for materialism issued as an irritable disdain for science and scientific procedures. It also produced an antipathy to *Benthamism and to the whole 'mechanico-corpuscular' philosophy of utilitarianism. Carlyle also advocated a historical perspective in literary criticism, though his famous history of the French Revolution (1837) had the prime didactic purpose of warning the British to take up social reform. Indeed, his own study of Chartism, 1839, was an attempt to interpret for the Tories that new and unfamiliar class of industrial workers whose only property was their labour power. As he became more successful and wealthier Carlyle inclined more and more to the politics of deference, with captains of industry becoming the new lords of the manor and with a new and profound spiritualism being encouraged by devices analogous to the *clerisy.   JH

Carmichael, Stokely (Kwame Ture) (1941–98) *Civil rights campaigner, advocate of *black power, and leader of the *Black Panthers. Carmichael was born in Trinidad, and moved to New York in 1951. He was active in the civil rights campaign, repeatedly gaoled for his role highlighting racism in the Southern United States, and in 1966 became leader of the Student Nonviolent Coordinating Committee. As leader, Carmichael advocated a programme of black assertion, which would recognize the distinctiveness of the black community, rather than merely demand racial integration into society. He popularized the slogan 'Black is Beautiful', and promoted a distinctive Black–African heritage. His views were expounded in *Black Power* (1967), written with Charles Hamilton. He questioned the rationale of non-violence, and was bitterly hostile to the Vietnam War. His radical stance was seen as unnecessarily hostile to whites, and Carmichael became distanced from groups such as the National Association for the Advancement of Colored People and the leadership of Martin Luther *King. He became 'prime minister' of the Black Panthers in 1968, but left the United States in 1969 to live in Guinea, West Africa, promoting *Pan-Africanism, working as an adviser to the prime minister, Sekou Toure, and writing *Stokely Speaks: Black Power Back to Pan-Africanism* (1971). He adopted the name Kwame Ture (from African Nationalist leaders Kwame *Nkrumah and Sekou Toure).

carpet-bagger *See* CIVIL RIGHTS.

Carr, E. H. Edward Hallett Carr (1892–1982) was a British diplomat, journalist, historian, and international relations theorist. He spent the first twenty years of his career (1916–1936) at the British Foreign Office. In 1936 he left the Foreign Office to accept the Woodrow Wilson Chair in the Department of International Politics at the University of Wales, Aberystwyth. During his eleven years in this position he wrote a number of books on international politics. However, his lasting contribution to the field of international relations was *The Twenty Years' Crisis* (1939), which argued for the importance of 'peaceful change' and accepting the realities of power. According to Carr, the *study* of international politics was initially dominated by idealist or utopian scholars who were prescriptive, fact-insensitive, and optimistic that human reason can bring an end to war. This early *utopianism was superseded by a realist (*see* REALISM, CLASSICAL) approach that was analytical, fact-sensitive, and resigned to ineradicable conflict. Utopianism and realism are also recurrent tendencies in the practice of international politics. While Carr would ultimately be labelled a 'realist' (particularly by his *Cold War American readers), his position is more nuanced. He argues that utopianism and realism must serve as dialectical checks on one another. Realists expose the ways in which the moralistic rhetoric of utopians serves as a cover for power interests, while utopians reveal the moral poverty of pure realism.   AMQ

Carroll, Lewis *See* DODGSON, C. L.

casino capitalism The high-risk and potentially high-impact character of financial *globalization. Popularized by *international relations scholar Susan *Strange, the casino metaphor was intended to illustrate how global financial markets increasingly resemble a game that is rapidly detaching from genuine social purpose, despite the potentially disastrous implications of resulting financial crises.   LS

caste A group of people bound together through Hindu religious sanctions and rituals. Broadly speaking, the origins of the caste system, first articulated in the *Law Book of Manu* between 200 BC and AD 200, were functional. The four major caste groups (varnas) were characterized according to the social functions they performed. Brahmins were the educators, kshatriyas the producers and warriors, vaishyas the merchants, and shudras the labourers. Tasks perceived as involving pollution were undertaken by the *avarna*, or Untouchables. Castes are further divided into subcastes (jatis) which are more important in their impact on the daily lives of people. Those belonging to a *jati* form a *biradari* which is the specific sociocultural unit within which caste roles are performed.

Under the Indian Constitution (1950) caste discrimination and the practice of Untouchability were made a criminal offence. However, those such as *Nehru who thought that caste was an outdated social institution which would wither away have been disappointed. Instead it has remained an important factor in the Indian political system, primarily because of the politics of *reservation.   SR

Castroism Theory and practice associated with Fidel Castro (b. 1926), leader of the Cuban Revolution since 1959. Its first public statement was Castro's *History Will Absolve Me* (1953) which stressed nationalism, democracy, and social justice, but not socialism (the debate continues as to whether Castro was always a Marxist or 'became' one in 1961 in order to secure Soviet support against the United States; *see* CUBAN MISSILE CRISIS).

The *Second Declaration of Havana* (1962) called upon all progressive forces to participate in an anti-feudal and anti-imperialist revolution. Revolutions depended upon the conjunction of objective and subjective conditions in each country. The latter (propaganda, organization, and leadership) matured in response to the former, which included exploitation, the development of a mass revolutionary consciousness, a general crisis of imperialism, and the emergence of national liberation forces. There was no need to create an idealized vanguard party, and neither was the proletariat the only revolutionary class—peasants, students, radical Christians, could all join the movement.

Castroism exercised a strong influence over the *New Left. In power, the institutionalization of the Revolution under the Cuban Communist Party produced an uneasy blend of bureaucracy, selective repression, artistic conformity, social welfare, mass mobilization, support for other revolutions (Angola), promotion of Latin American unity (for example, in the debt crisis), and, above all, charismatic leadership.   GL

catastrophe theory Catastrophe theory provides a systematic classification of sudden changes from one stable condition to another, applicable to phenomena as disparate as the freezing of a liquid, the collapse of an empire, the buckling of metal, or a prison riot. Developed by 1965, the theory began to be tentatively applied to the social sciences by Christopher Zeeman (1925–2016) and others in the following decade, and became an object of popular controversy after 1975. Its appeal to non-mathematicians was twofold. First, it forms part of the mathematics of surfaces, topology, which—rather more than most fields of mathematics—yields ideas of great generality which non-mathematicians are able to grasp through spatial intuition. Secondly, catastrophe theory offered an explanation of just those kinds of discontinuous change and radical divergence from nearly identical initial conditions that had seemed most resistant to scientific explanation in the Newtonian tradition and were thought peculiarly characteristic of social and political phenomena. Like *chaos theory a decade later, catastrophe theory has intrigued students of politics without achieving an assured place in the discipline, having had more success as a heuristic device than in detailed applications. Its impact has accordingly been less than that of *game theory. CJ

catch-all party *See* PARTY ORGANIZATION.

categorical variable *See* DISCRETE VARIABLE.

catholic parties Parties which seek to advance the programme or policies of the Roman Catholic Church. Given that the Catholic Church often has its strongest following among the poor and devout, the programme of Catholic parties is typically conservative on matters covered by Catholic social teaching, but in favour of redistribution, and generally mildly leftist on economic matters.

caucus An exclusive meeting of the members of a party, or faction for organizational and/or strategic purposes. In the United States there are nominating caucuses and congressional caucuses. In some states caucuses of local party members are held as the first step in a multistage process to determine the membership of the state party's delegation to the National Convention where presidential candidates are selected. The best-known caucuses of this type take place in Iowa. These caucuses select delegates to county conventions in accordance with the presidential preferences of those who attend. *Primary elections provide an alternative means whereby rank- and-file party members may participate in the process of selecting presidential candidates.

The word caucus is also used in the United States in reference to party organizational structures in Congress. The parties in each house periodically hold private meetings to elect officers, to make nominations, and where substantive policy issues may also be considered. Among Democrats such gatherings are known as caucus meetings whereas Republicans in modern times come together in a 'conference'. The significance of the congressional caucus or conference has varied over time. They have also usually been more important in the House than in the Senate and Democrats have tended to take them more seriously than Republicans.

In the early years of the republic congressional caucuses took upon themselves the responsibility for selecting candidates for President and Vice-President. Congressional party leaders have periodically sought to use caucus mechanisms to instil party discipline in the legislature. This occurred during Thomas *Jefferson's and Woodrow Wilson's presidencies. In the latter period, the Democratic caucus in the House debated legislative proposals and ruled that when two-thirds of those present agreed to support a bill this would, with certain qualifications, be binding on party members in the House. In the early twentieth century, the Republican leadership in the House also made use of the caucus in efforts to maintain party discipline and later, in 1925, expelled rebels who supported Robert LaFollette, the Progressive candidate for the Presidency in 1924, as did the House Democratic caucus against two Democrats who supported Barry Goldwater, the Republican presidential candidate in 1964.

In the 1970s the Democratic caucus in the House abolished the *seniority rule in favour of making Committee chairmanship nominations subject to caucus approval. In 1974 three chairmen were deposed. The caucus was further strengthened by making the appointment of *Rules Committee members and Appropriations Committee Chairmen subject to its approval. A further rule change conferred on the principal committee of the Democratic caucus, the Steering and Policy Committee, the right to nominate standing committee members, subject to caucus approval.

The word is also used for informal organizations of members who share common interests and come together in attempting to influence the agenda. These bodies often have cross-party membership. One of the best-known examples is the Congressional Black Caucus, an organization of African-American legislators. There is also a Hispanic Caucus, and many others. DM

caudillismo The system of rule by a caudillo (from Latin *capitellum*, meaning head). A caudillo is a political boss or overlord, the leader or chief of a politically distinctive territory. Caudillismo surfaced as a consequence of the wars of independence in Latin America after 1810. The power vacuum left by the fall of the Spanish empire in the Americas was filled in by the rise of caudillos—usually regional military officers—who became the guarantors of basic social peace and political stability in the regions they controlled militarily. Their ruling style was a combination of two of Max *Weber's types of political domination: traditional and charismatic. Examples include Juan Vicente Gómez (1857–1935) in Venezuela, Plutarco Elías Calles (1877–1945) in Mexico, and Juan *Perón in Argentina. On the left notable caudillos include Fidel *Castro and Hugo Chávez (1954–2013). Ultimate authority rests with the caudillo thanks to his alliance with both the military and important sectors of society organized from below. FG

Central Bank The Central Bank is a financial institution charged with several different functions, the most important of which is managing a country's monetary policy. In addition, central banks typically manage a government's debt, they participate in the formulation of exchange rate policy, together with the government, and in many countries they are the principal regulator for the financial sector. Modern central banks were first developed during the late seventeenth century, most notably with the foundation of the Bank of England in 1694. While many major central banks before 1945 were privately owned, today central banks operate as agencies of government. Recently, there has been much debate over the extent to which central banks should be independent from political control when they set monetary policy. During the post-war period governments in many OECD countries retained the authority to intervene with or override central bank decisions. This was a provision seen as a necessary corrective to the perceived failure of policies pursued by several central banks during the 1930s. Since the 1980s, with the increasing popularity of rational expectations models of monetary policy and the perceived post-war success of independent central banks like Germany's Bundesbank, it has become increasingly popular to emphasize the benefits of making central banks independent from day-to-day political interference. This intellectual shift has helped lead to reforms of central bank statutes in numerous countries, while also influencing the development of the European Central Bank, which has a very high degree of legal independence. Political scientists have begun to examine a number of issues related to this debate, asking whether *de jure* independence will only result in *de facto* independence in certain types of political systems, whether independence can only result in both low inflation and low unemployment if it is accompanied by centralized wage-bargaining institutions, and more generally how partisan political considerations influence central bank policy. DS

central committee The centre of power in a Communist Party run on the Leninist principle of *democratic centralism. Each level of the party controls the personnel of the level below, and each level is bound to obey the rulings of the level above. Thus a majority in the central committee is enough to commit the whole party at every level.

Central Intelligence Agency *See* CIA.

central–local relations In Western pluralist countries all central governments, except those in micro-polities, confront a twofold governing dilemma: (1) how do they organize public policy delivery and control in 'the country', that is outside the central departmental structures in the capital city; and (2) to what extent do they allow local citizens, or local elites, to manage the delivery of public services in their own areas. In short, central governments confront problems of territorial administration and territorial politics. This is, or ought to be, the subject-matter of central–local relations. It is a dilemma which engages both *federal and non-federal systems. In the present context, consideration will be given only to the latter, commonly called unitary systems.

In terms of territorial administrative patterns central governments have a number of options. The local delivery of public services can be entrusted to local offices of the central departments, or to ad hoc agencies composed of local people chosen by the central government, or to elected local authorities, or to some combination of these options. A further set of options concerns the centre's supervision of these various policy delivery agencies. Supervision (or control) can be divided between the relevant central departments in the capital city, or entrusted, comprehensively, to centrally appointed career officials in various areas of the country, or to specific central departments (and ministers) responsible for particular parts of the national territory.

The actual process of central–local relations is often highly influenced by political factors. Some central governments may try to exert detailed supervision over local governments, especially elected local authorities. A principal weapon of control in these circumstances is finance: the extent to which local governments have their own sources of revenue and the degree to which they rely on central grants-in-aid. An alternative strategy is to shift local public services into the private sector and allow the discipline of market forces to act as the control mechanism. This can be done either on ideological grounds or simply because detailed central control of local governments is a complex, time-consuming, difficult task. JBU

centre party Obviously, a centre party is one which lies between parties of the *left and of the *right; but as these two terms are so elusive, so is 'centre party'. The easiest examples to define are those in countries where politics is mostly dominated by the single dimension of economic policy, such as the Liberal Democrats in Britain and the Free Democrats in Germany. In the French *Fourth Republic there were strong and clearly defined centre parties. In the *Fifth Republic, however, the two-round electoral system has tended to produce two coalitions. On the left, the Socialists may be regarded as more centrist than the Communists (though the label is seldom used); but which are the more centrist of the Gaullists and the non-

Gaullist right? A further complication comes from Scandinavia, where right-wing parties renamed themselves 'centre' in order to increase their appeal.

Even in Britain and Germany, the 'centre' label can be misleading. The British Liberal Democrats are indeed centrist on economic matters (the leadership more to the left, those who vote for them more to the right) but socially liberal on a liberal–authoritarian scale. The Free Democrats are the most economically liberal (and therefore, on one definition, the rightmost) of the three main German parties.

centre–periphery politics This particular approach to political analysis comes in three forms. First, the commonly called modern *world system analysis is a theory of the international political economy rooted in a perspective which argues that since the rise of capitalism and the nation state in the sixteenth century global market forces, not domestic ones, have determined national economic development or underdevelopment. The structural form of this process, which has persisted over time, is one in which core manufacturing states dominate, exploit, and make dependent, peripheral (and sometimes semi-peripheral) states which operate primarily as raw material producers for the core. In short, peripheral countries exist, and have always existed, to service the economies of core countries. World politics must be understood in terms of this unequal division of labour. Hence capitalism, rather than contributing to the development of the global periphery, ensures the 'development of underdevelopment'. The theory does allow for dominant centres within the core. Examples would be Britain in the nineteenth century and the United States in the twentieth century.

Second, the theory of *internal colonialism is in many ways an offshoot of the first. Here the stress is on the unequal division of labour, exploitation, and dependency within singleton core or peripheral countries. Internal colonialism is concerned with patterns of domestic territorial inequality and with the various ways (not just economic) a core, or centre region, controls and exploits a peripheral region or regions.

Thirdly, the centre–periphery framework has been employed by some analysts as an approach to *central–local relations, alternative to the intergovernmentalist bias of the traditional literature. Here the emphasis is on the variety of mechanisms by which the political centre seeks to control, or manage, or avoid dealing with, the rest of the national territory (the periphery or peripheries). This certainly opens up the study of central–local relations and inserts a much-needed concern with the centre. On the other hand, it suffers from a degree of uncertainty about the precise principal actor focus in the periphery. JBU

chad A fragment of paper separated from a ballot by the action of a hole-punch in certain kinds of voting machine; also used to classify incompletely punched ballots (hanging, pregnant, or dimpled chad). The word was made commonplace in reporting of the disputed US Presidential election of 2000, being crucial in the counting of the vote in the pivotal State of Florida. PM

Chancellor of the Duchy of Lancaster UK Cabinet post, which, because of the negligible departmental duties, is usually given to someone in order to deal with an ad hoc measure, or one not covered by another government department.

chancellor of the exchequer The finance minister of the UK. The title goes back to the reign of Henry III of England in the thirteenth century.

chaos theory Mathematical theory which analyses the arbitrarily unpredictable consequences of an arbitrarily small shift from *equilibrium in a complex system. Frequently referred to by variants of the claim that 'a flutter of a butterfly's wing may cause a thunderstorm'. Used in politics and international relations more to debunk claims to scientific precision than to advance formal models of chaos.

charisma Originally a term from Christian theology, meaning 'a favour specially given by God's grace', the word was appropriated by *Weber to mean 'a certain quality of an individual personality by virtue of which he is set apart from ordinary men and treated as endowed with supernatural . . . or . . . exceptional powers or qualities'. The term was used to refer to the spellbinding powers which apparently enabled Hitler to have such a hold over the German people. Weber gave interesting examples of how charisma comes to be 'routinized' as by its nature it cannot be passed on. Critics of Weber query whether the term can be defined in a sufficiently precise way to be of use.

charity The word 'charity' derives from the Latin for affection, and in general connotes (Christian) love and benevolence.

There is no statutory definition of a charitable organization, but case law in England and Wales has identified four principal charitable purposes, namely trust for: (1) the relief of poverty; (2) the advancement of education; (3) the advancement of religion; (4) other purposes beneficial to the community, not falling under the previous heads. In Scottish law charity identifies trusts for the relief of poverty. The wider account is used by the Inland Revenue, which accords certain fiscal privileges to the charitable form of voluntary organization. There are many thousands of charities registered with the Charity Commissioners for England and Wales, who exercise the quasi-judicial function of giving advice, investigating, and checking abuse.

In UK law political objects are not charitable, and so political parties and institutions which exist in order to influence government policy on particular issues (i.e. *pressure groups) cannot normally be regarded as charitable. However, a charity may conduct reasonable advocacy of causes which directly further its objects and are ancillary to the achievement of those objects. PBl

chemical and biological warfare *See* WEAPONS OF MASS DESTRUCTION.

Chicago School An approach to economics developed at the University of Chicago, which was the intellectual forebear to *neoliberalism. Associated with economists such as Friedrich *Hayek, Frank Knight, Milton Friedman, and Gary Becker, the approach emphasized the virtues of free markets and political decentralization. In the context of the rise of *Keynesian and *Marxist paradigms, and alongside the creation of the Mont Pèlerin Society, the approach was explicitly formed as a transnational intellectual movement to promote liberal ideas inside and outside of academia.

Although the School's neoliberal doctrine emerged over time, four key features can be identified. First, in contrast to classical *liberalism in which it is assumed that liberty and a flourishing market would emerge naturally due to human nature, neoliberals acknowledged that the state was actively required to establish the success of the market. Second, Chicago neoliberalism adopted a neoclassical model of the economy, in which human actors are imagined as utility-maximizing agents. Third, Friedman's famous argument for a supposed separation between positive (scientific) and normative economics was part of a wider embrace of scientific discourse and techniques. Fourth, the Chicago School was at the forefront of extending neoclassical models to politics and to life itself, paving the way for *public choice theory. LS

Chicken Game which takes its name from 'dare' games said to be played by Californian teenagers: two people are driving head-on at one another on a narrow road; the first to swerve is chicken. When two people are playing, Chicken is best represented by the following diagram:

	You swerve	You keep going
I swerve	b, b	c, a
I keep going	a, c	d, d

where $a > b > c > d$ and in each box the letter before the comma is what I get and the letter after the comma is what you get. The paradoxical feature of Chicken is that each player has an incentive to try to lock the other into cooperating (here, swerving) by announcing in advance that he or she will defect (here, keep going). If this works, the defector will get a (the best result) and the cooperator c (the third-best). But if both players do it and neither swerves, both get d, their worst outcome: something which was widely feared in the *Cuban Missile Crisis of 1962. Furthermore, the *supergame faced by each Chicken player in deciding whether to precommit him- or herself to defection is itself a Chicken game. Chicken is thus very different from *Prisoners' Dilemma despite a close superficial resemblance. Real-life contributors' dilemmas usually resemble one or the other. Everybody is tempted to *free ride, that is let others contribute and benefit from their contributions without paying oneself. If universal free-riding leads to the worst outcome for everybody, the game is a form of Chicken. If it leads to a suboptimal, but not the worst, outcome for everybody, it is probably a form of Prisoners' Dilemma.

chief secretary to the Treasury UK post created in 1961 to relieve some of the increasing workload on the *chancellor of the exchequer. The chief secretary monitors each department's spending plans, and helps set departmental budgets for the annual spending round.

Chiltern Hundreds A procedural device by which a British Member of Parliament resigns. An MP is not allowed to occupy a position of profit under the crown, and by accepting one, such as the stewardship of the Chiltern Hundreds, the MP is deemed to have resigned.

Chinese democracy movement See TIANANMEN SQUARE.

Chinese political thought Chinese classical thought was directed primarily to politics in the wider sense, yet China produced relatively little systematic political philosophy. The Chinese cities of the Warring States period (481–221 BC) were not, like Athens, the home of maritime traders with wide experience of other cultures, but centres of Chinese acculturation of the surrounding areas. China did not experience Christendom's struggle between Church and State, nor the enforced religious pluralism which succeeded the European wars of religion. Feudalism, which in Europe provided the basis for constitutionalism, disappeared from China with the war chariot; indeed it was the collapse of feudalism which created the problems with which China's ancient thinkers were preoccupied. Finally, the emphasis on finding new means of maintaining social harmony led Chinese philosophers to think less in terms of abstract principles and more in terms of the processes of socialization. As a result, China produced a political culture rather than a political philosophy.

The agenda of Chinese philosophy was set by *Confucius, and after two centuries of debate Confucianism became dominant in the version created by Mencius (d. 289 BC). However, in the disorder which followed the fall of the Han dynasty (202 BC–AD 220), during which Buddhism, imported into China in the first century AD, became a serious rival, Confucianism suffered a decline. In attempting to attract support away from Buddhism, the *Ru* (the Confucian scholars) turned their attention to cosmology and metaphysics, and their concern with public values and public service declined. However, after many centuries the commitment began to be revived, paradoxically by giving it a new metaphysical basis in continued rivalry with Buddhism. Zhu Xi (1130–1200), using metaphysical arguments, reasserted the claim of Confucianism as a means to control erring emperors.

Every phenomenon, argued Zhu Xi, is an imperfect expression of its own eternal principle. Good government also expresses such principles. The emperors, however, were quick to make themselves the supreme interpreters of principle. Zhu Xi's philosophy, thus captured by the throne, remained the official orthodoxy until modern times.

Wang Yangming (1472–1529), in opposition to this orthodox view, asserted that moral principles were created by the response of an active conscience to individual experience. He developed the Zen idea that if, through meditation (which to Wang meant essentially introspection) a man can clear his mind of prejudice, fear, and self-interest, he will be able to act with the speed and strength of the tiger. Wang also argued that knowledge was incomplete until applied in action. There is a clear implication that consciousness thus attained will itself motivate to moral action.

In the late seventeenth century three scholars who had retired from affairs after participating in the popular but unsuccessful guerrilla defence of central China against the Manchu conquest of 1644, sought to explain why the Ming dynasty had collapsed. Gu Yanwu (1613–82) argued that China was at her weakest when the central government was strongest, and at her strongest when her local communities were strong. Huang Zongxi (1610–95) reasserted the belief that the true guardians of morality were the Confucian gentry, and advocated that the emperors should have to choose their councillors from the independent Confucian academies. Wang

Fuzhi (1619–92) demystified the ancient idea of the Mandate of Heaven by which successful revolt against a failing dynasty was justified after the event, and the new dynasty said to have received the Mandate. He argued that the struggle for the throne was usually a struggle among rogues, but that the rogue who won was obliged to rise to the responsibilities of empire. He thus secularized China's moral legitimation of government. All three in different ways were asserting the primacy of civil society.

The political culture was, in the same way, full of alternative possibilities. First, although the theory of government was autocratic and totalitarian, in practice Chinese communities largely governed themselves, and the emperor's official representative made the best bargain he could with them; he was more of a British District Officer than a French prefect. Second, while official Chinese society was elaborately hierarchical, informal egalitarian associations flourished. Third, while the normal way to deal with potential conflict was to suppress it, there was a strong belief in the virtues of moderation and a widespread belief that the best solution to many problems was a bargain which gave something to both sides. Fourth, in spite of the attempted atomization of Chinese society and the refusal to acknowledge the legitimacy of special interests, voluntary associations flourished in China on a scale more characteristic of a modern democracy than of an ancient monarchy. Political thought in China was closely related, both as cause and effect, to such habits and assumptions. Thus the political culture offered some, at least, of the means of creating a pluralist system.

On the other hand, political thought and culture offered certain stubborn obstacles to institutional control of the emperors. Patron–client relationships prevented impartial administration. The stress on harmony led to fear of conflict—even of the legitimized controlled conflict which is the content of democracy. There was resistance to the idea of precise law, reflecting Confucian hostility to Legalism as well as the problems of the acculturation of local communities with differing customs.

From China's defeat in the First Anglo-Chinese War (1837–43) onwards, China faced an increasing threat which required an increasingly drastic response. In 1912 the

Manchu ruling house was forced to abdicate. The result, however, was not the hoped-for democratic republic but the beginning of brutal civil wars among the provincial military commanders, while the new parliament, massively bribed, supported whatever puppet of the ruling warlord faction held power in the capital. In 1919 the willingness of one of this succession of governments to make concessions to Japan at Versailles led to student riots in Beijing (the May Fourth Movement), an event which crystallized the opinions of the new generation. This was the watershed, at which Confucianism was repudiated by almost all of educated China, dethroned to make way for 'science and democracy'.

The writers of the European Enlightenment and their nineteenth-century successors were now being read in China by people who faced the task of founding a new state, indeed of creating a nation, where hitherto there had only been a culture. This culture, however, was too deeply based and rich in alternatives to be swept aside. Western ideas were assimilated in terms of Chinese heresies ignored until then. Western individualism was interpreted in terms of Wang Yangming, and Western ideas of the relation of civil society to the state in terms of the seventeenth-century patriot thinkers. Typical of the new synthetic thought was the philosophy of Yang Changji. After a classical education, he studied in Germany and in Scotland. He accepted, as most of his generation did, the idea that the liberation of the individual was the source of the wealth and strength of modern societies. He then attempted to determine how individuals could be expected to behave in socially responsible ways. This chimed with Confucian (and Buddhist) stress on self-cultivation. Yang also accepted T. H. *Green's idea that consciousness of the gap between ideal possibility and ugly reality itself motivates the 'conscious man' to moral action, and he related this to Paulsen's theory of the will; this chimed with Wang Yangming's Zen-derived idea of the uninhibited power of a man to act when his consciousness is cleared of the distractions of self-interest and habit. He accepted, largely out of his commitment to the ideas of the seventeenth century patriots (especially of Huang Zongxi), the Western assumption that civil society

creates the norms and the task of the state is to safeguard them. In sum, 'conscious men' would be compelled to throw themselves into the reform of society. They would create new norms and a new society, and the new society would create a new nation and a new state. Yang's theories were the basis of *Mao Zedong's interpretation of Marxism.

Such ideas were addressed to the conscious few. They were not, however, given an elitist interpretation. The revolution would not be from the top. On this, virtually all Chinese radicals agreed. The most eloquent advocate of the duty of the intellectual elite to 'go down to the countryside' and induce a new consciousness among the whole mass of the Chinese people was Li Dazhao, later a founder of the Communist Party of China. Many intellectuals accepted his urging, and spent years in the villages. Their example was one of the origins of Mao Zedong's theory of the 'mass line'. Such liberal forms of synthesis between Chinese and Western ideas were known to the whole May Fourth generation, including Mao Zedong. Yang Changji was his philosophy teacher. It seemed clear to this generation of Chinese that democracy and nationalism were two sides of a single coin, and that each was instrumental in achieving the other. All knew Gu Yanwu's assertion that 'when the Empire falls, everyone is responsible'. Only a democratic system could create a sense of common responsibility.

Socialist ideas began to be widely discussed in China only after the *Russian Revolution of 1917. They were readily received. The Chinese still entertained the distaste for capitalism general in pre-modern societies where trade is perceived as the exploitation of scarcities, and credit means usury at the expense of the distressed. And in a culture which attached supreme value to social harmony, capitalism was bound to be regarded as divisive and therefore deplorable. No party in China advocated uncontrolled free enterprise. All advocated redistribution of the land, at least a degree of cooperativization of agriculture, the development of local and village resources, and state control of the commanding heights of industry.

Socialism, however, was seen in the now accepted terms of revolution from below. Li Dazhao, with twenty of Lenin's titles available to him, showed interest only in *State and Revolution*, in which Lenin committed himself (theoretically) to a communalist view of socialism. It could be said that Chinese theories of democracy and of socialism paid too little attention to questions of law and institutions, for two reasons, one historical and one contemporary. The first was the traditional distaste for fixed law; the Chinese principle was 'a government of men, not of laws'. The second was the cynical constitution-mongering of the warlords and the venality of their puppet parliaments. Democracy was seen, for example by Li Dazhao, as 'a sort of spirit', not a set of laws and institutions guaranteeing specific rights. Mao Zedong inherited this scepticism towards institutionalized democracy.   JG

Chinese Revolution The seizure of power in China by the Communist Party under *Mao, which controlled the whole of the Chinese mainland by 1949. *See also* CHINESE POLITICAL THOUGHT; GREAT LEAP FORWARD; CULTURAL REVOLUTION.

Christian democracy Christian democracy has been a successful post-war political movement in Western Europe and, to a lesser extent, Latin America. Its sociological and ideological origins, however, lie in the mobilization of Catholics in response to the emergence of liberal capitalism in the nineteenth century. The explicit challenge to the position of the Church launched by the French Revolution forced Catholics to accept democratic political forms and defend Catholic interests through the promotion of Catholic secondary associations (particularly Catholic unions and schools). Traditional institutions central to Christian practice—in particular, the family and a harmonious social order—were considered to be facing a dual attack: first, from the corrosive effects of industrialization and laissez-faire liberalism, and secondly, from increasing state regulation of social life. From the 1850s onwards, Vatican-sponsored 'Catholic Action Groups' campaigned to limit the power of the emerging Italian state, and sizeable political Catholic groups emerged in the German-speaking areas of Europe.

Pope Leo XIII's *Rerum Novarum* (1891) liberated Catholicism from moral opposition to democracy, and stimulated further political mobilization. Electoral success came first to the Italian 'Popular Party' under the leadership of Luigi Sturzo in 1919, while the German 'Centre' Party was a coalition mainstay of the Weimar Republic. By this time, political Catholicism had developed an ambiguous stance towards the exertion of state power: while hostility to socialism and communist forms of ownership remained a dominant theme, the initial opposition to capitalism had by 1914 moderated into recommendations for social improvement through strong welfare legislation. This ambivalence towards the role of government is reflected in the work of the foremost theorist of Christian Democracy, Jacques Maritain, whose contempt for strong states is coupled with specific provisions for state intervention given the failure of industrial capitalism to serve 'the common good'.

Fascism repressed and discredited most of these political groups—most offered weak resistance to right-wing extremism, some (e.g. the Austrian Christian-Social Party) gave it support. At war's end in 1945, however, the strains of mild conservatism and scepticism towards active government held formidable appeal. Promoted heavily by the victorious Allies as a bulwark against communism, newly constituted Christian Democratic parties in Italy, Germany, France, Austria, Belgium, and the Netherlands won office, either as single-party administrations or as important elements of ruling coalitions. The popularity of these post-war parties rests more on their inoffensive centrism than on any distinctive ideological platform. Consequently, and somewhat ironically given the ideological ancestry of Christian Democracy, electoral support derives from a largely middle-class and interdenominational suspicion of threats to the liberal capitalist order (particularly from 'the left'). In the 1960s and 1970s, Christian Democracy suffered a relative demise as the threat of communism receded, and socialist opponents moderated their platforms. In Latin America, however, Christian Democratic parties, championing democratic stability through restraint of traditionally overactive states, achieved brief electoral success during this period (notably in Chile and Venezuela, and in the 1980s in Ecuador, Guatemala, and El Salvador). In Mexico, the Partido Acción Nacional (PAN) emerged as a powerful electoral force after the presidential election of 2000, won by Vicente Fox. During the 1980s, Christian Democracy enjoyed a resurgence as part of the general rightward swing of European electorates (with the partial exception of the spectacular collapse of the DC in Italy in 1993). SW

Christian fundamentalism A reaction by Protestants in Britain and the United States from the 1800s onwards to modernist readings of the Bible which challenged the literal truth of the supernatural and miraculous episodes of biblical history, and the status of Scripture as a direct and unchallengeable revelation of the word of God. In particular, fundamentalists resisted the teaching of Darwinian evolutionary science in American public schools (culminating in the famous Scopes 'Monkey trial' in Tennessee in 1925, in which a teacher was convicted under a state law which forbade the teaching of *Darwinism).

The more overtly political incarnation of Christian fundamentalism stems from the alliance of religious and political conservatism in the American South. From the 1970s onwards, groups such as the 'Moral Majority' became powerful populist lobbies in state and national politics on issues ranging from family and welfare policy to defence and foreign affairs, particularly during the Presidency of Ronald Reagan. More recently, Christian fundamentalism has underwritten what is known as the *Tea Party, which has been successful in mobilizing grassroots efforts to change the *Republican Party platform towards the right as well as to help elect the reality TV star and real-estate billionaire Donald J. Trump to the US Presidency in 2016. SW

Christian socialism This doctrine—which grows out of the adherents' Christianity, so that the term is more specific than merely indicating those socialists who also happen to be Christian—attempts to relate the teachings of Christ (as for instance given in the Sermon on the Mount) with the political practice of socialism. In Britain Christian socialism was a mainly nineteenth-century movement, associated both with the High Church revival and its attempts to spread Christianity into the working classes and also with the growth of Nonconformism, especially Methodism, which placed importance on its social ministry. Many Labour politicians

in Britain argued that their party owed more to Methodism than to Marx. Christian socialist thinking favoured alternatives to capitalism in such ideas as co-operatives, and stressed the importance of industrial reconciliation and justice between workers and owners, the moral responsibilities of the better-off towards the poor, and the importance of public education. The Christian socialist strand of the Labour Party was boosted under Tony Blair's leadership.

Post-war *Christian Democratic parties in Europe are not a variant of Christian socialism but represent a version of conservatism which accommodates (mainly Catholic) social doctrine. The Christian Social Union in Bavaria is Christian Democrat, not Christian Socialist. PBY

Church and State The relationship between Church and State can be described as the institutional form of the relation between religion and politics. As a problem, 'Church and State' has been a particularly Western and Christian concern. This is not only because Western secularization has required a limit to the powers of religious authorities, but it has its origins in a much earlier period, in the development of separate Church and State institutions in Christendom which were natural rivals (with rival claims of authority and law enforcement) to a degree incomprehensible in the realms of other prominent religions. Thus the rivalry between Emperor and Pope was a key feature of the politics of Europe in the Middle Ages and in the twelfth, thirteenth, and fourteenth centuries the rivalry between Guelphs (or Guelfs) and Ghibellines was the greatest contest in Italian politics. It had started as a feud between South German tribes but became a partisan quarrel between the papal faction (Guelfs) and the imperial Ghibellines.

Western society thus has a long history of rivalry between Church and State (*see e.g.* AUGUSTINE; AQUINAS; BODIN; and CALVIN) which has helped foster secular and anticlerical movements. Many modern states and parties welcome the separation of Church and State, but a suspicion has often attached to Catholic politicians in predominantly Protestant countries, such as John F. Kennedy, that they are, whatever they may say, religiously committed to extending the influence of their Church over the State.

In the early twenty-first century issues of Church and State were in many Western countries more contested than they had been for some time. This was partly because 'fundamentalists', usually either Christian or Muslim, challenged schools and other state institutions to permit more expression of religious belief. In France, for example, this endemic issue centred on the wearing of headscarves in school whereas in the United States there were controversies about the display of religious texts on public property and expressions of belief by children in schools. In many cases these demands for religious expression were matched by more militant expressions of secularism and atheism. Generally, these controversies were more intense in secular republics than in those parts of the United Kingdom and Scandinavia which still had established churches. In the United Kingdom there was a general debate about 'faith' schools, raising the general question of the extent to which the public purse should fund religious schools and the more divisive question of which 'faiths' should be acknowledged in this way. LA

CIA (Central Intelligence Agency) The US government agency charged with collecting and analysing intelligence. The agency was established in 1947 to advise the *National Security Council. The Intelligence Directorate assesses economic and military information on foreign countries, and the Operations Directorate coordinates covert operations. Involvement in the *Bay of Pigs fiasco, the *Watergate break-in, and the Iran–Contra affair have led to the role of the CIA being questioned, and a growth in Congressional oversight. The failure of the agency to anticipate the attacks on the US on *September 11th 2001 brought criticism, and led to the creation of the Office of the *Director of National Intelligence in 2005. *See also* INTELLIGENCE SERVICES.

(((⊕))) SEE WEB LINKS
• CIA website.

Cicero, Marcus Tullius (106–43 BC) Roman jurist and political theorist. His *De finibus* (On the purposes of human life) might be said to have laid foundations for a political philosophy. *De officiis* (On duty), a moral treatise, bears on political behaviour. *De legibus* (On laws) is positivist: it deals with natural and sacred laws, law courts, and the rulings of magistrates. *De re publica* (*The Republic*) does deal with political philosophy in a *utopian way. There is satirical criticism of forms of government; a model state (the Roman state idealized); the ideal politician (the best among the good). The basis of government is justice and harmony among the people (*res populi*). In a crisis there should be a sole ruler, who would rule constitutionally, not for remuneration or fame, but for immortality.

To find Cicero's real political philosophy we must turn to his life and speeches. He was born into a wealthy but not noble family. He was the greatest Roman orator, part barrister and part politician. He was guided by the notion of constitutionality, the rule of the senate, and the consensus of all good people, not the rule of the *optimates* (aristocrats), much less of a self-appointed triumvirate, such as established itself in 62 BC. He agreed to a single leader in time of crisis, but not at other times or permanently. In 31 BC, after the battle of Actium, Octavian became sole ruler of the Roman empire. So ended Cicero's dream of senatorial constitutional rule. CB

citizenship The status of being a citizen, usually determined by law. In the republican tradition, qualifications for citizenship are associated with particular rights and duties of citizens, and a commitment to equality between citizens is compatible with considerable exclusivity in the qualifying conditions. For example, classical republics excluded slaves, women, and certain classes of workmen from citizenship. In general, qualifications for citizenship reflect a conception of the purposes of the political community and a view about which persons are able to contribute to, or enjoy the benefits of, the common good, or the freedom of the city. Although the concept of citizenship may refer to a status conferred by law, it may also be deployed to argue that persons have entitlements as a consequence of their position within a community or polity. This approach suggests that since individuals, as a matter of fact, participate in a common life, they have rights and duties as a consequence. Hence, it has been argued, we have moral obligations to one another because of that shared existence, whether what is shared be characterized as economic activity, culture, or political obligation. There may, then, be an uncertain connection between the ideas of membership of a community and citizenship of a polity. Both membership and citizenship may be construed as conferred statuses or as empirically determined positions; membership of a community may be asserted as a qualification for citizenship; the common good may be seen as what gives value to both community and political organization. And both membership and citizenship may be valued partly because they are not universally available. AR

civic culture A political culture characterized by (1) most citizens' acceptance of the authority of the state, but also (2) a general belief in participation in civic duties. The term was systematically deployed in Gabriel Almond and Sidney Verba's influential 1963 book, *The Civic Culture*, and revived in their *The Civic Culture Revisited* (1980). Prompted by a concern about a perceived problem of political stability in Western democracies, the civic culture model suggested that a polity in which citizens were informed about political issues, and involved in the political process, could not of itself sustain a stable democratic government. The civic culture is seen as an allegiant political culture in which political participation is mixed with passivity, trust, and deference to authority. Traditionality and commitment to parochial values are seen as balancing involvement and rationality. *The Civic Culture* provided a five-nation study of citizen values and attitudes viewed as supportive of a democratic political system. In the mainstream of behavioural analysis when it was first published, the book has been somewhat eclipsed by the emphasis on policy analysis, although its influence can be seen in more recent work on *social capital. Its concerns about the survival of democracy in Western societies now seem somewhat misplaced. The spread of higher levels of education through the population has encouraged new forms of participation in politics, such as *social movements and campaigning *interest groups. WG

civic humanism A body of ideas about politics which stresses the merits of a sturdy and independent way of life (often in an image of rural yeomen). Virtue consists in public-spiritedness, and a participatory orientation. Professional or standing armies, and a separate political class, are much disfavoured. There is an opposition to luxury, and to commercial self-interest and corruption. AR

civil disobedience A political act involving disobeying governmental authority on grounds of moral objection, with the aim of promoting a just society. The term was first used by H. D. *Thoreau in his essay *On the Duty of Civil Disobedience*, 1849.

Civil disobedience occurs when someone intentionally and publicly violates certain laws. The law being violated may be the target of one's protest, for example dodging conscription to the army. Alternatively the civil disobedient may have no objection to the law being violated, but may do so as a symbolic act to draw attention to other laws that are deemed unjust, as in the case of sit-ins in public places during the Vietnam War. The civil disobedient differs from a mere criminal primarily in terms of motive, since the ordinary criminal acts out of self-interest, while the civil disobedient violates penal statutes in order to make society more just. Furthermore the civil disobedient objects to the injustice of a particular law or policy, while maintaining fidelity to the system as a whole, therefore unlike the revolutionary the civil disobedient has no desire to overthrow the system entirely.

There are at least three issues that divide scholars on civil disobedience. Should the civil disobedient accept the punishment for breaking the *law, or is resistance to the agents of law and order justified? Accepting one's punishment is seen by some as necessary in order to emphasize that civil disobedience is a public act done for the public good, not an excuse to run riot. Those who reject this argument point to the fact that tactical considerations must be taken into account, therefore resisting arrest may be justified if doing so furthers the goal of defeating the unjust law.

Is *violence ever justified during acts of civil disobedience? Following *Gandhi, it may be argued that non-violence is intrinsic to civil disobedience, although many feel that some form of violence, within limits, is acceptable. The *suffragettes for example used violence against property, smashing windows and slashing paintings in art galleries, although they never directed their violence against other people.

Finally, there is the question whether civil disobedience is a right bestowed on all citizens of a just society, or alternatively, as famously argued by Thoreau, whether upholding justice means that we have a duty to engage in acts of civil disobedience.   SR/VB

civil liberties Those freedoms which are, or should be, guaranteed to persons to protect an area of non-interference from others, particularly power holders and legal authorities. Civil liberties are especially invoked to limit the justifiable coercive power of the state: for example, freedom from arbitrary arrest or detention, and *habeas corpus; *freedom of speech; freedom of lawful assembly; freedom of association and of movement; and the right not to incriminate oneself. Some civil liberties are seen as implications of respect for the rule of law; for example, the right to a fair trial. The importance of civil liberties has been reflected in attempts to provide constitutional guarantees for them. After the *September 11th 2001 attacks on the United States, a heightened perception of a terrorist threat has led to what some see as moves to curtail civil liberties, for instance through the detention of suspects without trial.   AR

civil rights The political, social, and economic rights that each citizen has by virtue of simply being a citizen, and which are usually upheld by law. The meaning of the phrase is shaded by its commonest reference: to the civil rights of ethnic minorities in the United States. In this and similar usages, there is at least as much stress on the rights of a (minority) group as on the rights of the individual.

Nevertheless the phrase is older and more general. Any state which gives constitutional or legal guarantees to its citizens confers civil rights. However, constitutions sometimes state rights without giving the citizen any means of enforcing them against the state. In the *French Revolution for instance, the Declaration of the Rights of Man and the Citizen (1789) was modelled on contemporary American attempts to guarantee certain individual freedoms, which appear in the US Constitution (1787) and its first ten amendments, collectively known as the *Bill of Rights (1791). The French Declaration remains in force in that it was incorporated into the preamble to the constitutions of the *Fourth and *Fifth Republics. However, French practice, unlike American, gives the citizen no legal channel to claim the rights guaranteed in 1789.

Both the French and the American declarations guarantee the citizen freedom of speech, assembly, and religion, and also offer procedural guarantees of fair trials and fair taxation. But the American Bill of Rights is part of the Federal Constitution; therefore from 1787 to 1868 it protected citizens only from the federal authorities, not from states or other levels of government. Indeed the Tenth Amendment, part of the Bill of Rights, specifies that 'the powers not delegated to the United States by the Constitution, nor prohibited by it to the States, are reserved to the States respectively, or to the people'. Not until the end of the Civil War were any civil rights against the states guaranteed. Then, the Thirteenth Amendment (1865) outlawed slavery; the *Fourteenth (1868) extended the rights guarantees in the original constitution and Bill of Rights to the states; and the Fifteenth (1870) forbade the United States or any state to restrict voting rights on the grounds of 'race, color, or previous condition of servitude'. It is the programme of these three amendments that has come to summarize 'civil rights' in the United States.

Despite the unambiguous language of the three 'Reconstruction Amendments', civil rights were not protected for almost a century longer. In the immediate aftermath of the Civil War, those who had supported the 'rebellion' in the Southern states were disenfranchised, and the state governments were run by 'carpet-baggers': politicians from the North who packed their belongings in capacious carpet-bags and went to run the Southern states, supported by black votes. Their enemies alleged that they put as much into their carpet-bags to take north with them again. A bargain was struck in 1876 whereby the Republicans were allowed to claim victory in the disputed presidential election of that year on condition that Northern troops were withdrawn from the South. That marked the end for the carpet-baggers, but also for Southern blacks. A succession of discriminatory laws and practices in Southern state laws were upheld by the courts, in spite of their apparently blatant inconsistency with the Reconstruction Amendments. In the key case of *Plessy* v. *Ferguson* (1896), the Supreme Court upheld a Louisiana segregation law on the grounds that segregation does not mark 'the colored race with a badge of inferiority' unless 'the colored race chooses to put that construction on it'. The judgment in *Plessy* v. *Ferguson* was not reversed until the ruling in *Brown* v. *Board of Education of Topeka* (1954) that separate facilities were inherently unequal. *Brown* and *Baker* v. *Carr* (1962, enforcing equal-sized electoral districts) were the most important of a series of Supreme Court judgments that restored civil rights in law to what a non-lawyer would believe the Reconstruction Amendments meant. These cases also helped to solidify the doctrine of the incorporation of the Bill of Rights into the Fourteenth Amendment, thereby extending its guarantees to the state and local levels.

But the Supreme Court commands no armies. Civil rights could not become effective until both the executive and the legislature had also put their weight behind them. The executive did so by sending federal forces to the South to enforce desegregation; the legislature did so by passing, especially, the Civil Rights Act 1964 and the Voting Rights Act 1965. Voting rights have become self-enforcing: now that black citizens have the vote, politicians have to balance their votes against those of white supremacists. Voting rights are now safe, but not all civil rights are. Some parts of the Deep South remain segregated.

A difficult problem in civil rights is whether all minorities can, or should, receive equal protection. In 1978 a would-be student, Alan Bakke, complained that his Fourteenth Amendment rights had been violated because he had been refused a place whereas minority ethnic group students with poorer qualifications had gained places in the quota which had been set aside for them. In *Regents of the University of California* v. *Bakke* (1978) a divided Supreme Court held that Bakke had been unlawfully excluded but that *affirmative action to redress past racial discrimination was not unlawful. Affirmative action continues, notably in higher education, but much more cautiously than before *Bakke*.

In the United Kingdom, the currency of the term 'civil rights' is largely due to the Northern Ireland Civil Rights Association, which copied American methods in its protests against religious discrimination in the 1960s. Unlike their American counterparts, the Northern Ireland protesters had no constitutionally guaranteed rights, because nobody in the United Kingdom then did. However, UK legislation now bans discrimination on the grounds of race, sex, sexual orientation, or religion. Thus citizens may enforce some rights against the state, an example being the embarrassment of the UK armed services in the 1990s at having to pay substantial sums in compensation to servicewomen who had been unlawfully dismissed on becoming pregnant. The *European Convention on Human Rights has now been incorporated into UK law.

civil service Term generally referring to administrators paid for implementing the policies of national governments. The term derives from British civilian (as opposed to military) officials working in India in the nineteenth century. The UK civil service is the body of officials, paid for out of the public purse, who work in the departments of state and those associated bodies and agencies which are headed by a secretary of state in the cabinet. It developed out of the ad hoc system of service to the pre-nineteenth century executive and a number of historic departments, notably the Treasury, the Home and Foreign Offices, and the Board of Trade. The growth of governmental responsibilities from the late nineteenth century involved the creation of more departments: the majority, such as Education, Employment, and Environment, functionally defined; but some territorially defined, these being the Scotland, Northern Ireland, and Wales Offices.

The origins of the civil service as a modern bureaucracy lie in the implementation of the Northcote–Trevelyan reforms in the second half of the nineteenth century. These ensured, first, that entrance to the civil service was by competitive examination, both for the administrative (highest) and executive (intermediate) classes. Promotion was also on merit. Secondly, the civil service became a life career and hence a profession for the educated to enter into. Thirdly, the tasks of civil servants were divided into the intellectual and routine. This meant that departments developed as hierarchic: those drawn from the administrative class filled senior policy advice positions; those from the executive class filled positions defined by their superiors; and those on clerical grades—the least intellectual—carried out routine work. Fourthly, the civil service as a permanent institution of government developed an ethos of political neutrality, willing and able to advise and serve an elected government of any party programme. This clearly closely mirrors *Weber's ideal type of bureaucracy.

Unification of the civil service, with centralized schemes of recruitment, standardized terms of pay and conditions, scope for mobility and promotion between departments, and a corporate ethos, was achieved between 1919 and 1939. Responsibility lay chiefly with Sir Warren Fisher, who was both permanent secretary to the Treasury and head of the civil service, and established unity through the exertion of Treasury control. Apart from some modernization during the Second World War, the British civil service remained largely intact up until the 1970s.

Under the Conservatives after 1979, however, the British civil service changed markedly. Governmental growth was checked, and the privatization or marketization of some responsibilities led to contraction in some areas of government. Such quantitative change was matched by qualitative change. First, entrance to the civil service was widened to take in the employment of those who have been successful in the private sector. Secondly, this move to diversify recruitment weakened the idea of the civil service as a life career. It became more acceptable to move freely between work in the civil service and the private sector, and to enter the civil service at a later stage after attaining some 'life experience'. Thirdly, civil servants were evaluated less by their pure intellectual power and more by their perceived management skills. At the same time, the departmental basis of the civil service was partly broken up. Departments of state were retained as core policy advice bodies, but those departmental functions

which were considered to involve the mere implementation of ministerial policy were hived off into executive agencies, associated with their former department, but now with their own budget, mission statement, and cost centre manager. From 1991 civil service functions were explicitly market tested so see whether better value for money might be achieved by contracting out civil service responsibilities to private providers. This process led to a number of executive agencies, such as Her Majesty's Stationery Office, being sold to the private sector. Fourthly, the political neutrality of the civil service came increasingly under attack. The Thatcher governments were accused of promoting civil servants on the basis of 'Is he one of us?' Controversies over the rights and duties of civil servants who disagreed with their minister or who thought the minister might be misleading Parliament led to the issue of new guidelines on the duties and responsibilities of civil servants in relation to ministers in 1985. These changes taken together weakened the unity of the civil service—a fact that pleased some and horrified others. The introduction of citizens' charters heralded a further development towards output-oriented management in which fragmentation was accompanied by a move to limit bureaucratic autonomy through customer performance review.

The Labour Government after 1997 endorsed the changed approach to recruitment, career development, and the skills mix required of civil servants, as well as the organizational move to a new core-agency civil service. Nevertheless, it sought to assert different emphases in civil service development towards policy outputs, defined in terms of best quality standards as well as value for money. The Government defined the next stage as combining bureaucratic flexibility with joined-up government to deal with problems which cut across departmental and agency boundaries. The development of e-government was identified as a key tool for these aims. At the same time a focus was put on developing target-setting and evaluation in civil service performance. Civil servants were encouraged into a culture of risk as a further extension of the innovation to be gained from use of private sector methods. The market testing regime was also replaced with a better quality services initiative, which in the context of a general public–private partnership policy sought to focus on identifying the best provider of a service in terms of value and quality, without a necessary predilection towards privatization. The Government's focus on policy outputs also led to the commissioning of the Gershon Review which in 2004 recommended the phasing out of 84,000 civil service jobs to allow the redirection of funds to front-line services. All of these developments necessitated more central political control. Two major developments which facilitated this were Labour's extensive use of special advisers to assist ministers in directing policy according to governmental priorities, and the creation of task forces to focus on specific problems and raise fresh approaches. These developments were again not without considerable controversy.

The changes wrought on the 'classic' British civil service appeared to have their origins in a number of factors. First, key changes were consistent with recommendations for greater efficiency and effectiveness in the Fulton Report (1968), which responded to demands for the modernization of government to arrest British relative decline by copying successful practice from other countries. Secondly, the changes were consistent with a more contemporary ideological preference for market or quasi-market forms of supply associated with the new right. In the case of Labour after 1997, this was related to third-way ideas of modernized social democracy that accepted market solutions to public policy problems. Thirdly, the move from hierarchic departments to functionally segregated agencies appeared to give a public sector mirror the move from '*fordist' mass production methods to post-fordist 'small is beautiful' flexible production units in the private sector. Finally, fragmentation and politicization were entirely consistent with the result of elected governments believing that the civil service had a political agenda of its own that had undermined previous governments and must not be allowed its head again.

Australia, Canada, and France are examples of other countries with a more or less unified and hierarchical civil service. The United States displays a distinctly different pattern, because each incoming administration normally replaces the existing heads of each department and agency with its own nominees (*see* SPOILS SYSTEM). The Weberian model therefore applies to lower-level civil servants but not to upper-level ones. JBr

civil society The set of intermediate associations which are neither the state nor the (extended) family; civil society therefore includes voluntary associations and firms and other corporate bodies. The term has been used with different meanings by various writers since the eighteenth century, but this main current usage is derived from *Hegel. One definitional characteristic in current usage is the distinction between political parties and civil society. Whereas political parties seek direct political power, via election and public office, civil society organizations seek to change the political agenda through forms of political activity but do not directly seek political office.

The need to (re)build civil society after the collapse of communism in eastern Europe has been a common theme of reformers and commentators there since 1991. The communist regime had disapproved of the institutions of civil society. Therefore, apart from hardy examples such as the Catholic Church in Poland, there was not a lot of it about. Current scholarship on civil society is focused on how these organizations can influence policymaking and hold institutions to account. A key feature of civil society, therefore, is its ability to transform political decision-making and represent alternative voices.

civil war Military conflict centred on territory within a state, involving combatants from that state, over the political right to control that territory. Civil wars usually involve government forces, and the territorial aspect of the conflict means that civilian involvement and civilian deaths are usually high. In practice, it is sometimes difficult to differentiate between a civil war and terrorist activity, *coup d'état*, *ethnic cleansing, or international war. Academic attempts to quantify the incidence of civil war, for instance through the *Correlates of War studies, have emphasized the requirement that state violence should be sustained and reciprocated, with significant numbers of casualties (typically more than 1,000 deaths, with significant casualties on each side of the conflict). Nicholas Sambanis has identified the onset of 119 civil wars between 1945 and 1999.

Historical examples show the variety of causes and the range of situations in which civil wars can occur. The English Civil War (1642–6) can crudely be characterized as the battle between forces loyal to parliament and forces loyal to the monarch. It did, however, encompass many other issues, notably religious toleration and the relationship between Church and State, and other countries, notably Scotland, Wales, and Ireland. The American Civil War (1861–5), fought between the southern Confederate states and the federal Union forces, centred on the rights of states within the Union, the legitimacy of secession from the Union, and the issue of slavery. The *Russian Revolution (1917) was accompanied by civil war, with the conflict lasting until 1923. The fall of the Russian Tsar, and the international instability following the end of the first World War, also led to civil war in Finland in 1917. The Spanish Civil War (1936–9) pitted left-wing Republican forces against the right-wing Nationalist army. The schisms exposed by civil wars tend to be deep, and are often entrenched in the partisan and institutional politics of a state for years after the conflict has ended.

Attempts to explain and analyse the outbreak of civil war have overlapped with the study of *revolution and *war. Studies have looked at the incentives which may trigger civil conflict, the structural factors common to conflict situations, and the factors which lead to civil wars being sustained. Influences on the incidence of civil wars have included the roles of elites and the relationship between the government and military forces; economic factors, such as the distribution of wealth and income and the control of natural resources; religious, cultural, and ethnic divisions in society; and international intervention. The prevalence of civil wars in contemporary politics shows that greater understanding of their causes does not easily translate into measures to prevent them occurring.

clash of civilizations A concept first used by Samuel *Huntington (1927–2008) in a 1993 *Foreign Affairs* article. He argued that, in the context of the end of the Cold War, conflict in international relations increasingly would be due to clashes between civilizations rather than to ideology or economic interests. Huntington conceived of civilizations as the highest level of cultural grouping, identified by features such as language, history, or religion. He identified eight such civilizations—Western, Confucian, Japanese, Islamic, Hindu, Slavic-Orthodox, Latin American, and African—and predicted that conflict was most likely on the borders between civilizations.

The concept of a clash of civilizations has been used widely since 1993, but it has also been widely criticized. Critics question whether a civilization or culture can be self-contained in an age of *multiculturalism, and claim the thesis creates a polarized view of the other. Concern that the idea could become a self-fulfilling prophecy has led to the concept of a 'dialogue of civilizations' in response.

Since the attacks of *September 11th 2001 on the US, the clash of civilizations concept has received increased attention. It has been a convenient framework to use to interpret these events and the 'war on terror' that followed. Despite attempts by politicians to distance themselves from a West versus Islam narrative, the events are often reported and interpreted in this way.   CT

class The *Oxford English Dictionary* definition is 'a division or order of society according to status; a rank or grade of society'. But this confuses as much as it clarifies. It is not what *Marx or *Weber mean by class; and Weber specifically distinguishes class from status. As, however, the *OED* meaning is the everyday one, there is great confusion as writers about class slither around between one (implied) definition and another.

For Marx, class is defined by one's relationship to the means of production. One either controls a factor of production or one does not. In the first case, one belongs to the landlord or capitalist class. In the second, when one has nothing to offer but one's labour power, one belongs to the *proletariat. Marx and Engels believed that 'Society as a whole is more and more splitting up into two great... classes directly facing each other: *Bourgeoisie and Proletariat' and that 'the executive of the modern State is but a committee for managing the common affairs of the bourgeoisie' (*Communist Manifesto*, 1848). The bourgeoisie and the proletariat have starkly contradictory class interests. Politics and economics are a *zero-sum game.

However, Marx refined and (some would say) muddied his two-class model. First, he stressed that a 'class in itself' is not necessarily a 'class for itself'. Only when the proletariat became conscious of its common interest and common opposition to the bourgeoisie could it expect to become a revolutionary class. People may suffer from *false consciousness and fail to realize where their true class interests lie. But Marx by no means always sticks with the schematic two-class model. In the *Communist Manifesto* itself, for instance, he and Engels note how the working class may 'compel...legislative recognition of particular interests of the workers, by taking advantage of the divisions of the bourgeoisie itself. Thus the ten-hour bill in England was carried.' (The Ten Hours Act 1847, restricting maximum working hours, was carried with predominantly Tory support against most of the Whigs.) In his journalism and political commentary, Marx recognized complex ebbs and flows of class alignment, as when he claimed that 'the aristocracy of finance, the industrial bourgeoisie, the middle class, the petty bourgeois, the army, the lumpenproletariat...intellectual lights, the clergy and the rural population' united against an urban proletarian revolt in Paris in 1848, or that '[Louis] *Bonaparte represents a class, and the most numerous class of French society at that, the small-holding peasants' (*The Eighteenth Brumaire of Louis Bonaparte*, 1852).

It fell to *Weber to make explicit the distinction between a class and a status-group. As he put it: 'status position...is not determined by class position alone: possession of money or the position of entrepreneur are not in themselves status qualifications, although they can become such; propertylessness is not in itself status disqualification, although it can become such.' There is the plot summary of every Victorian melodrama and modern sitcom. The Duke of Omnium and his self-employed window-cleaner are in the same class (owners of a factor of production) but not in the same status-group. The Duke's window-cleaner and his daughter who cleans the windows in the factory where she works are in the same status-group but different classes.

Unfortunately, English uses 'class' to cover both concepts, whereas Marx's and Weber's native German distinguishes them. Usually, discussions about class and politics are really discussions of status-group and politics. For instance, studies of class and vote in the UK have traditionally divided the electorate by the classification scheme used by the Market Research Society. For many years, this has run along the following lines:

A	Higher managerial, administrative or professional
B	Intermediate managerial, administrative or professional
C1	Supervisory, clerical; junior managerial, administrative or professional
C2	Skilled manual worker
D	Semi-skilled and unskilled manual worker
E	State pensioner, casual worker

Such a scale is perfectly appropriate for market research but not for politics. Advertisers need to know which medium is read by ABs and which by DEs because they need to know the consumption patterns of the audience reached by the medium. It is pointless to advertise AB goods in a DE medium, and vice versa. But this has nothing much to do with class. The consumption habits of self-employed window-cleaners and of employed window-cleaners are very similar; their voting behaviour is not. Likewise for salaried managers and capitalist business owners. A better class scheme for voting studies is the one now used in the British Election Study. This separates owners from managers, and *petite bourgeoisie (small proprietors) from the rest of the 'working class'. Modern Marxists debate extensively whether such people as managers (who control people and capital although they do not own them) and small tradespeople (who own capital but too little of it to have much control over their own environment, let alone other people's) should be described as occupying 'contradictory class locations' (*see e.g.* POULANTZAS). Arguably, though, it does not matter into which box people are put so long as their class characteristics are understood. *See also* MIDDLE CLASS; WORKING CLASS; CLASS CONSCIOUSNESS.

class action suit Lawsuit in which the case of an individual is taken as representative of the cases of a larger group, hence obviating the need for separate individual trials. Chiefly American.

class consciousness Awareness of social divisions in society and of belonging to a particular social rank. *Hegel made a distinction between the existence of a *class and the subjective awareness of class. *Marx argued, however, that a class whose members were not aware of their common relationship to the means of production was not effectively a class. For example, of peasants under feudalism Marx asserted that 'the identity of their interests begets no community, no national bond, and no political organization among them, they do not form a class'. To Marx, the clearest example of a class characterized by consciousness of class is the modern *proletariat, who have identical interests and are aware of this, who are concentrated in cities and who create their own political organizations. Marx knew, however, that the working class did not always behave with the sense of solidarity which this analysis implies, and some of his successors became convinced that the working class was incapable, without assistance from outside its own ranks, of developing a consciousness of common interests, expressed in political organization. *Lenin asserted this, while Rosa *Luxemburg denied it. Hence Lenin argued for the necessity of a 'vanguard party', with important consequences for the development of socialism in Russia and beyond. The basis of Marx's expectation that the working class would develop the sense of 'common destiny' was his belief that the interests of the working class are identical, they are in constant communication because concentrated in factories and cities, they are subject to the erosion of the differentials among themselves, they are subject to increasing immiseration, and they form an increasingly large majority of the population.

In the event, the working class now seem further away from class consciousness than they were when Marx wrote. Their interests are less and less obviously identical; they are increasingly differentiated in function and incomes as technology advances, the spread of prosperity has led more and more workers to cease to identify themselves with the deprived, and blue-collar employees in private employment are now a shrinking minority in all advanced countries. Much the same has occurred in Communist systems—witness the expression of despair of *Mao Zedong, faced with the chaos which had overwhelmed his Great Proletarian Cultural Revolution: 'Who would have believed that the working class could be so divided?' *See also* FALSE CONSCIOUSNESS. JG

classical economics The economics derived from a number of leading theorists of the late eighteenth and early nineteenth centuries, especially Adam *Smith, David Ricardo, and Thomas *Malthus. Though the classical economists disagreed about many things, they all agreed that governments were less likely to produce wealth than were markets. They therefore favoured free trade and laissez-faire. Classical economics began to be revived in the late nineteenth century, when its claims were mathematically formalized and made more precise. *See also* NEOCLASSICAL ECONOMICS.

Clausewitz, Carl von (1780–1831) Prussian soldier and author of *On War* (1832), which deals with military strategy, the nature of war, and the relationship between war and politics. Famous for his quote that 'war is politics by other means'.

cleavage Term borrowed from its geological meaning to denote the splitting of a political system along ethnic or ideological lines. The term is used rather loosely, sometimes to indicate the division between dimensions (as in 'cleavage structure'), sometimes just as a synonym for disagreement within a dimension.

clerisy An idea or proposal for a publicly endowed national class or order, in whom the culture and learning of a nation is embodied, a class or order composed not merely of theologians and divines but of non-sectarian thinkers capable of advancing learning in all branches of knowledge. This idea or proposal was first advanced in *Coleridge's *On the Constitution of the Church and State* (1830), a work which also contained the suggestion that a few members of the clerisy should reside at university with the rest being distributed throughout the country. Also, incidentally, an idea quite strongly favoured in the Broad Church movement and one taken up enthusiastically by liberals such as John Stuart *Mill who were permanently preoccupied with enhancing the role of intellectuals in politics. JH

clientelism An early definition of clientelism emphasized the exchange of votes for favours, over a long period of time, among actors with asymmetric power, the clients having little power. Politicians would reward a portion of their supporters with public resources in return for electoral support. Scholars have found this definition increasingly wanting: first, clients can offer politicians financial contributions and other nonmonetary resources, not just votes. Second, clients could be rather 'powerful'. Third, the sale of one's vote in exchange for a benefit to which the client is not otherwise entitled qualifies as *corruption.

It is more fruitful to understand clientelism as a type of *principal–agent relationship. Clientelism involves three actors, a principal, an agent, and a 'client'. Typically, a client (say, a politician's supporter and financier) transfers resources over which he has control to the agent (the politician). The agent will then transfer resources he obtains from the principal (the electorate) back to his client. The criterion of allocation is particularistic, rather than universalistic: clients are rewarded with public contracts, appointments and the like not because of merit or qualifications but prior support. Given the nature of this exchange, the relationship between agent and client tends to be long-term.

Contrary to corruption, the clientelistic exchange is done in the open and contravenes neither a legal provision nor a custom: the US president openly appoints trusted friends and supporters to ambassadorships around the world. To the extent that such an allocation breaches a legal provision and is done secretly, clientelism turns into corruption, the exchange occurring in an illegal market. If the exchange goes counter to public sentiments, it still qualifies as clientelism although the public frowns upon it. FV

climate change Referring, as a political problem, to the build-up of additional CO_2 and other greenhouse gases (GHGs) due to human activity, which increases the amount of reflected solar radiation that remains trapped at atmospheric levels.

This anthropogenic phenomenon (otherwise known as 'global warming') adds to the natural greenhouse effect and variability of the global climate. Since 1970, cumulative anthropogenic CO_2 emissions have at least tripled, with the largest increase rates occurring in recent years. Total anthropogenic GHG emissions from 2000 to 2010 were the highest in human history, growing on average by 2.2 per cent annually and reaching 49 (± 4.5) gigatonnes CO_2 equivalent per year in 2010. Without additional efforts to reduce emissions, global mean surface temperatures are expected to increase by 2100 between 2.5 and 7.8°C.

Apart from the uncertainty over the exact extent of both global warming and its consequences (such as sea level rise, species loss and shifts, or precipitation changes), climate change exhibits extreme material complexity. It unfolds into a series of sub-issues such as mitigation, adaptation to climate change, and emissions from land use, while at the same time touching upon numerous other policy fields such as biodiversity, trade, transportation, energy, health, migration, and the north–south divide. This has led some observers to speak of a 'super wicked' political problem with manifold problem perceptions, interrelated causes, knowledge gaps about possible solutions, and limited opportunities to test them. As a result, the public and policymakers largely end up in carbon 'lock-ins', taking decisions that disregard overwhelming evidence of risks and impacts and reflect very short time horizons.

The material complexity is reflected in a highly complex *climate governance system with a UN negotiations process at its core. These produced legally binding treaties with the 1997 Kyoto Protocol and the 2015 Paris Agreement, but Kyoto targets were missed, and policy pledges submitted in the run-up to Paris would result in a global warming of at least 2.7°C. Many commitments rely on so-called negative emissions through speculative technologies such as bio-energy with carbon capture and storage. Apart from the envisaged ratcheting up of pledges over time, an effective political response therefore requires scaling up technology research and developing a cross-institutional strategy. MH/FZ

(⊕) SEE WEB LINKS
• United Nations Framework Convention on Climate Change site.

climate governance All forms of collective steering, by public and private actors, to prevent or adapt to dangerous anthropogenic interference with the climate system. The pervasiveness of climate change is mirrored in a fragmented governance system, which can be roughly divided into international or intergovernmental, national, and transnational domains.

The first milestone in international climate governance was the 1992 United Nations Framework Convention on Climate Change (UNFCCC). Crucial momentum had been provided by the first report of the Intergovernmental Panel on Climate Change (IPCC), initiated by governments to assess the state of scientific knowledge. The 1997 Kyoto Protocol to the Convention elaborated differentiated responsibilities between the *Global North and the *Global South, obligating thirty-eight developed countries to reduce their greenhouse gas emissions by 5.2 per cent under 1990 levels during 2008–12. To achieve this goal, the Protocol introduced market-based 'flexible mechanisms', like trading in emissions permits. After failing to forge a new climate treaty for the post-2012 period in Copenhagen in 2009, UNFCCC parties adopted the Paris Agreement in 2015, aiming to limit temperature increase above pre-industrial levels to well below 2°C. While the Agreement includes all countries in its mitigation effort, it allows each party to set its own 'nationally determined contributions'. These are to be ratcheted up over time with the help of international transparency and review mechanisms.

Aside from mitigation, UN climate negotiations seek to reduce vulnerability and build resilience to assist developing counties in adapting to *climate change, but so far remain fairly general on this issue. Developed countries further promised up to US $100 billion annually by 2020 for the Green Climate Fund and additional progression after 2025. The last years saw the introduction of a mechanism to Reduce Emissions from Deforestation and Forest Degradation (REDD+) and several technology-related bodies under the UNFCCC. New themes are frequently added to official or informal discussions in the wider UN context, such as short-lived climate pollutants or climate geo-engineering.

Major intergovernmental institutions from related policy fields also have a stake in climate governance, among others: the Convention on Biological Diversity and the Montreal Protocol; the *World Bank; the *World Trade Organization; international civil aviation and shipping institutions; the *UN Security Council, Human Rights Council, and High Commissioner for Refugees. Since the mid-2000s, several minilateral initiatives, mostly mitigation- and technology-oriented clubs of fewer than twenty-five member countries, add to this intergovernmental landscape.

National climate-change laws and policies worldwide have doubled every five years since 1997, with 804 in place by the end of 2014. Adoptions are occurring faster in developing countries, with the share of world population covered by national climate policy doubling between 2007 and 2012.

Finally, transnational climate change initiatives emerged rapidly after 2000. About 7,000 cities are estimated to take climate action, many collaborating in forums like the C40 Cities Climate Leadership Group. Some private-led transnational initiatives provide standards for voluntary markets or specialize in the transparency of corporate greenhouse gas emissions, such as the CDP. Business-led approaches include investor networks and a series of emission reduction commitments, while civil society engagement spans a range of activities from petitions to climate marches. Hybrid initiatives such as public–private climate governance partnerships can serve different purposes, from dialogue to implementation.

The inherent complexity of international, national, and transnational climate governance provides ample opportunities for involving a wide range of actors and governance experiments. However, it is increasingly difficult to ascertain coherence and legitimacy across so many approaches, and, most crucially, to assess whether they can reach their principal objectives. Future success will depend on a cross-institutional strategy that continuously enhances and implements commitments by both states and non-state actors. FZ

closed/open rules Closed rules set time limits on debate and restrict the passage of amendments; open rules permit amendment from the floor of the house. In the US Congress the passage of legislation through the House of Representatives is controlled by these rules, which are set by the House Rules Committee.

closed shop Workplace where only workers who are the members of a particular trade union can be employed. Closed shops were outlawed in Britain in 1988, and in the United States by the Taft–Hartley Act of 1947.

closure/cloture Any procedure for limiting or curtailing debate in a legislature, forcing the matter to a vote even when there are members still wanting to speak. One form in the United Kingdom is the '*guillotine' resolution which restricts discussion on the remaining clauses of a government bill. Used to save parliamentary time by preventing *filibusters.

CND (Campaign for Nuclear Disarmament) UK *unilateralist pressure group set up in 1958, at a time of public concern over the British Government's drive to maintain an independent nuclear capability, the doctrine of 'massive retaliation', and poor relations between the United States and the Soviet Union.

Although much of the support for CND came from the unaligned middle classes, politically its support came from the Labour left and the trade union movement. At the 1960 Labour Party Conference a motion calling for a unilateralist defence policy was passed, despite the fervent opposition of the leader, Hugh Gaitskell, who condemned CND as 'pacifists, unilateralists, and fellow travellers', and swore to 'fight and fight and fight again to save the party we love'. The unilateralist vote was reversed in 1961. The divisions in the Labour Party were matched by schisms in CND, between the Committee of 100, which called for civil disobedience, and members who favoured constitutional campaigning. Internal disunity led to falling support, and by 1963 the organization was virtually moribund.

The resurgence of CND came with the escalation in nuclear tension between the superpowers at the end of the 1970s.

The campaign in the 1980s centred on opposition to the Conservative government's agreement with the United States to replace the existing Polaris nuclear missiles with the Trident system, and to site American cruise missiles in Britain. This led to an upsurge in membership of CND, and demonstrations at the sites chosen as cruise missile bases. Again the growth of the unilateralist movement influenced the Labour Party, and again it led to splits in the party. Disagreement about the incorporation of a commitment to unilateral disarmament in the Labour Party programme in 1980 was one of the main reasons for the breakaway of the Social Democratic Party in 1981.

The association of CND with left-wing politics reduced the Labour Party's appeal, and contributed to its electoral failure throughout the 1980s. As relations between the United States and the Soviet Union improved, following the accession of President Gorbachev, concern about the risk from nuclear weapons diminished. A short-term consequence was a boost for the sister organization END (European Nuclear Disarmament), but by the end of the 1980s CND had, again, lost mass support.

(((●))) SEE WEB LINKS
• CND website.

coalition Any combination of separate players (such as political parties) to win a voting game. The commonest form of coalition arises where legislation requires a majority to pass, but no one party controls as many as half of the seats in the assembly.

It is traditional in countries where single-party governments are common (such as the UK) for politicians to be suspicious of coalitions. They point out that ahead of an election in which no party wins half of the seats, the voters cannot know what coalition will result from their votes in aggregate and hence may be deprived of information they need in order to decide how to vote. The issue is entangled with the choice of an *electoral system, because the *plurality system tends to boost the proportion of seats held by the leading two parties, and hence the likelihood that one of them will form a government unaided; whereas *proportional representation may increase the number of parties represented, and will decrease the likelihood that one party will win more than half of the seats. One consequence is that in a plurality system, large parties are themselves coalitions of widely differing points of view, so that the problems of coalition games are removed from the floor of the legislature only to surface in the party office.

Coalition theory is the study of which of the available coalitions tends to form. One prediction, derived from the theory of *zero-sum games, is that, of the possible coalitions, the one which forms a majority with the smallest number of seats 'to spare' is the likeliest to form. The reasoning is that the prize—government and the spoils that flow from it—is of fixed size, which it is best to distribute among as few people as possible. The rival prediction is that those coalitions which are ideologically closest are the most likely to form. This seems better supported by the evidence, although it faces a problem in measuring 'ideological closeness'. Measures of the power of a party in coalition bargaining include the *Shapley-Shubik and *Banzhaf indices.

coat-tail effect The ability of the candidate heading a party ticket to help carry into office lesser candidates from the same party who appear on the same ballot. A negative coat-tail effect can occur when an unpopular candidate heading the party ticket is a disadvantage for other candidates of the same party.

co-decision *See* EUROPEAN PARLIAMENT.

cohabitation French term for cooperation between parties without forming a coalition. This situation arises whenever the presidency and the legislature are controlled by different parties, for instance in 1986, when a President of the left, François Mitterrand, was confronted by a government of the right under Jacques Chirac. This represented a major test for the hybrid *Fifth Republic whose constitution allocates powers and responsibilities in a vague and sometimes contradictory manner between President, prime minister, and government. Cohabitation is essentially a conflictual relationship, but one involving a temporary collaboration where responsibilities overlap. The government legislates for domestic matters with the President confined to advice and arbitration.

Foreign and European policy are shared although as head of state the President retains his traditional privileged status. Defence, nuclear strategy, and the deterrent, however, remained the exclusive preserve of the President.   IC

cohort effect *See* AGE.

Cold War The name normally given to the period of intense conflict between the United States and the Soviet Union in the period after the Second World War.

In 1945 the United States and the Soviet Union emerged as the two leading powers in Europe, with the Soviet Union effectively occupying the countries of Eastern Europe and the United States as the liberator (or in the case of Britain creditor and underwriter) of the countries of Western Europe. In Germany these two 'superpowers', along with France and Britain, established zones of occupation and a framework for four-power control. In the conferences at Yalta (February) and Potsdam (July/August) 1945 the two superpowers and Britain attempted to define the framework for a post-war settlement in Europe. However, by the time of the Potsdam conference serious differences had emerged, in particular over the future development of Germany and Eastern Europe. Both conferences also discussed the Far East, in particular the entry of the Soviet Union into the war against Japan.

By 1947 a general 'East-West' division of states was emerging. The Soviets were intent, according to the West, on undermining democracy and establishing puppet communist regimes in Eastern Europe, and in Germany on crippling her wealth and creating an exclusive influence in their zone of occupation. The Soviets defended their actions in Eastern Europe in terms of establishing broadly based anti-Fascist governments which were friendly towards the Soviet Union. Other conflicts elsewhere emerged and the two states began to denounce each other in increasingly violent ideological terms—the Soviet Union portraying the United States as bent on destroying communism while the United States portrayed the Soviet Union as intent on undermining liberal democracy in Western Europe and the United States itself.

The Cold War from 1947 onwards is marked by the Berlin Blockade Crisis of 1948–9, the victory of Mao's Red Army over the American-backed Nationalist Government in China in 1949, the *Korean War in 1950, the Soviet military occupation of Hungary in 1956, Soviet pressure on Berlin from 1958 culminating in the Berlin Wall crisis of 1961, and the *Cuban Missile Crisis of 1962. During this period the Americans consolidated their new role as leader of the West: they offered assistance to the economies of the Western European states through the *Marshall Plan of 1947; formally allied themselves to an emerging alliance of Western European states in the North Atlantic Treaty of 1949; took the lead in establishing the Federal Republic of Germany from the three Western zones of occupation in 1949 and in the early 1950s worked for the rearmament of this new state and its full membership of *NATO in 1955. The Soviet Union proclaimed its zone of occupation in Germany as the German Democratic Republic in 1949 and established a formal alliance with its Eastern European 'partners' in 1955 (the *Warsaw Pact Treaty Organization).

In Asia the Americans concluded an alliance and then a peace treaty with Japan in 1951 and 1952 and brought other states, including Australia, New Zealand, Thailand, and the Philippines, within a series of alliances, while the Soviet Union concluded an alliance with China in 1950. The war in Korea ended in 1953 but the Americans gradually became entangled in a more complex war in Vietnam in which it supported the Republic of (South) Vietnam against the Democratic Republic of (North) Vietnam which was backed by the Soviet Union and China.

Throughout this period the two sides also pursued policies of nuclear rearmament and developed long-range weapons with which they could strike the homeland of the other. After the Cuban Missile Crisis relations improved. Agreements were concluded to 'normalize' the situation in Europe, particularly the Quadripartite Agreement on Berlin in 1971, agreements which led to the two German states entering the United Nations in 1973 and the Helsinki Accords agreed by the Conference on Security and Cooperation in Europe (*see* ORGANIZATION FOR SECURITY AND COOPERATION IN EUROPE) in 1975 which appeared to mark a tacit peace treaty to conclude both the Second World War and the Cold War. Agreements limiting the nuclear arms race were also concluded. Conflict between the superpowers continued even through this period of détente, particularly in new areas of rivalry such as Southern Africa, the Horn of Africa (i.e. north-eastern Africa), and the Middle East. However, improved relations between the United States and China, the work of President Nixon, Secretary of State Kissinger, and Premier Chou En-Lai, together with the détente between the United States and the Soviet Union and the worsening of relations between the Soviet Union and China, gave a new shape to relations between the two (or perhaps three) superpowers in the 1970s.

By the mid-1970s the Cold War in its original form can be said to have died away. The *arms race between East and West had all the characteristics of a classic 'action-reaction' model of international conflict in which each side reacts to an earlier step by the other side. The explanation of the origins of the conflict is more complex, though three broad categories of explanation can be identified. First, some analysts have emphasized that the Cold War occurred primarily as a result of the destruction of German power, the resulting 'power vacuum' in Central Europe and the new bipolar balance of power between the superpowers. From this perspective, the Cold War was a traditional great power conflict in which ideological rivalry was essentially secondary and the structural constraints of bipolarity crucial in throwing the two sides apart. A second explanation, sometimes called the orthodox or liberal interpretation, stresses the American desire for a return to a much more limited international role after the Second World War. However, after having begun to disarm and disengage from Europe, the Americans were obliged by Soviet expansionism in Eastern Europe to take up in 1947 a much more active, and unsought for, role in Europe in order to contain Soviet power. A third explanation stresses the long-term objective of the American capitalist power to undermine communism and to expand American power throughout Europe, the Middle East, and the Far East. Some writers in this category thus trace the Cold War back to American opposition to the 1917 Russian Revolution. Of course, many accounts weave together two or even all three of these broad categories.

In the 1980s there was a short-lived but intensive reawakening of the Cold War, sometimes called the New Cold War. Détente petered out in the late 1970s, arms control faltered, and in December 1979 the Soviet Union occupied *Afghanistan. From 1980 onwards the Soviet Union exerted intense pressure over the government of Poland. In the United States and in Britain the governments of Reagan and Thatcher denounced the Soviet Union in ideological terms unheard since the worst days of the Cold War. On the Western side there was rearmament in Europe, under the so-called double-track policy of NATO, changes in the American doctrine of deterrence which appeared to emphasize the political utility of limited nuclear war, and the American pursuit of defences against Soviet missiles (the Strategic Defense Initiative). As in the post-1945 period it is difficult to disentangle action and reaction between the two sides.

In any case, by 1987 the two superpowers had moved decisively back towards agreement and by 1989 Soviet power itself had crumbled. The US and Russian agreements to work together against terrorism after *September 11th 2001 mark the most dramatic change in their relations since the start of the Cold War.   PBY

Cole, G. D. H. (1889–1959) Prolific writer of politics, philosophy, economics, social history, and fiction, collaborating, for some purposes, with his wife, Margaret. He is chiefly remembered for those early writings which developed the idea of *guild socialism, a variant of syndicalism in which workers control their own lives through a democratic workplace and in which the state has a much smaller role than in many other socialist proposals. Cole's early work is of abundant interest because of its development of ideas of pluralism and of industrial democracy.   LA

Coleridge, Samuel Taylor (1772–1834) Born in Devon, educated intermittently at Jesus College Cambridge, which he left in 1794 without a degree. Coleridge was 'myriad-minded', to borrow his own phrase about Shakespeare, making significant contributions not just to poetry, but also to theology, philosophy, psychology, political theory, and criticism. His initial political sympathies were to radical dissent and anarcho-communism. And there was a strong, if not permanent, attachment to the 'pantisocratic' schemes of Robert Southey: small communities dedicated to the equal government of all. Events in revolutionary France and the extremes of Jacobinism gave Coleridge a more favourable view of both government and property, as well as a strong antipathy to natural rights doctrines, which he thought were harmful abstractions from national culture. His main philosophic enemy, however, was Godless materialism, a crude and dangerous habit of mind, which he associated with radicals such as Paine and Godwin, and utilitarians such as *Bentham. And one of Coleridge's most enduring beliefs was that only the grand tradition of Christian Platonism was an adequate antidote to both materialism and rationalism. The 'Lay Sermons' in particular explore this very theme. The last published statement of his political philosophy, *On the Constitution of the Church and State*, 1830, avoided the prevailing platitudes of Anglicanism, while advancing the notion of a *clerisy and arguing strongly for a positive end for government to develop all of man's powers.   JH

collateral damage Collateral damage is a phrase that has been used by Western militaries, especially the American armed forces, to describe the unintended loss of civilian life during military operations. The term became popularized during the *NATO bombing missions to push Serbian forces out of Kosovo in 1999. Critics of the phrase argue that it euphemistically dehumanizes the victims of war and perceive 'collateral damage' as a *war crime.   AM

collective action problem Any situation in which the uncoordinated actions of each player may not result in the best outcome he or she can achieve. Two famous examples are *Chicken and *Prisoners' Dilemma, another class of collective action problem is the Assurance Game. In a typical Assurance game, you and I have agreed to meet in London tomorrow, but we have forgotten to specify where and when. So each of us must try to think what the other is likely to be thinking (which of course includes my thinking what you are thinking that I am thinking, and so on). If each of us thinks that the other thinks (that the other thinks . . .) that the likeliest venue is, say, in front of the National Gallery at noon, then the collective action problem is optimally solved; otherwise not.

Assurance games are trivial once the parties can communicate; other collective action problems including both Chicken and Prisoners' Dilemma may be harder to solve. These often involve free-riding dilemmas which are important in politics (should I voluntarily pay taxes, clean up the environment, vote . . . ?). It would be best if everybody did, but each individual is usually better off to try to free-ride and let others provide the good. However, if all or most people free-ride, the good is not provided. *See also* PUBLIC GOOD.

collective goods A term used in politics and economics to denote goods that are of benefit to all members of the public and thus cannot be withheld or reduced for some members of the public without affecting all members. Examples of collective goods are a clean environment or a national defence provision, since once the good has been produced, all members of the public benefit, while reducing the good would create a level of cost or diminished benefit for all members. *See also* PUBLIC GOOD.

collective leadership Historically, this was asserted within the Soviet party hierarchy immediately after the General Secretary's death or ouster; thus, after Lenin's death in 1924, after Stalin's death in 1953, and after the removal of Khrushchev in 1964. The pre-eminence of the new General Secretary, however, was soon reasserted.   swh

collective responsibility A convention applied in the operations of the UK cabinet that decisions on important issues of policy should not be taken by individual ministers in advance of cabinet meetings, and that decisions, once taken in cabinet, should be actively supported by all members of the government. The importance of the convention in the United Kingdom is reflected in the fact that failure to observe it in both speeches and parliamentary voting normally obliges ministers to resign. Rigorous observation of

the convention is believed to be necessary to maintain stable government, and has been followed by the shadow cabinet, wishing to offer a stable alternative government for the next election. Critics suggest that its observation stifles political debate and provides a cloak of legitimacy for policies pursued by a prime minister which may in reality be opposed by the majority of his or her government. The resignations of Michael Heseltine in 1986 over the Westland affair and Robin Cook and Claire Short in 2003 over the decision to go to war in Iraq are celebrated but rare examples of cabinet ministers resigning because of disagreement with government policy and a refusal to be bound by collective responsibility. However, the relaxation of the convention is routine in the case of private members' bills, and has occurred exceptionally in cases of a government being completely split on a major policy, which may bring about its demise. For example, the cabinet of 1974–5 allowed members of the government to follow their conscience in the referendum on membership of the EEC.   JBr

collective security A system for maintaining world peace and security by the concerted action and agreement of all nations. The central idea of collective security is to institutionalize a permanent arrangement of the balance of power in which the entire international community agrees to oppose military aggression by any member. The logic of the scheme is that no state can stand up to all of the other members of the system together, and that aggression will therefore be permanently deterred (an assumption made difficult when there are nuclear powers in the system). The necessary conditions for collective security are very demanding. First, all states must accept the *status quo* sufficiently to renounce the use of force for any purpose other than defence of their own territory. Second, all states must agree on a clear definition of aggression so that paralysis can be avoided if cases arise. Third, all states, and especially the large powers, must be willing to commit their own armed forces and/or funds (or to create, pay for, and find means of controlling, an international armed force) to prevent aggression even if it is remote from, or opposed to, their immediate interests.

Fourth, all states must prevent actively any breaches of sanctions that might assist the declared outlaw. Attempts by the *League of Nations to implement collective security failed because of inability to meet these conditions. The United Nations Security Council is a mechanism for collective security, and its operation in 1991 against Iraq's invasion of Kuwait might be seen as an instance of successful implementation of the idea.   BB

collectivism Originally used in reference to *Bakunin's *anarchism, collectivism in political terms affirmed the moral status of the collective, a freely formed and self-governing association, in contrast to the primacy of the individual or of the state. However, since the late nineteenth century collectivism has come to refer to a set of related propositions on goals and procedures of decision-making appropriate to modern industrial society. First, collectivism is often used to refer to any doctrine which argues for the priority of some version of 'the public good' over individual interests. In particular, collectivism is associated with the goal of equality among citizens. Secondly, the pursuit of these goals is seen to require the extension of public responsibility and state intervention in the form of regulations, subsidies, or public ownership. Thirdly, the substitution of market allocation by administrative decision-making has generated an association between collectivism, bureaucracy, and the centralization of power. A more precise understanding of the concept is as a theory of representation in industrial society (see S. Beer, *Modern British Politics*, 1965). In this sense, collectivism involves the incorporation of organized producer groups into policy construction and government administration, often referred to as 'functional representation' (*see also* CORPORATISM).

Collectivism has therefore emerged as a somewhat ill-defined term to designate various features of modern political life. In recent years, the institutions and principles of collectivism have come under considerable rhetorical attack from neoliberal critics throughout the West, although the prominence of the state and of organized interest groups have proven extremely resilient.   SW

collectivization The process of abolishing private ownership of land in favour of state or (supposedly) communal ownership. Following the difficulties in procurement of agricultural products in the Soviet Union in 1927-8, Stalin led the party towards full collectivization of the peasantry in 1929. Large collective farms (*kolkhozy*) were established based on expropriated land on which peasants were then effectively employed, although officially the peasantry comprised a distinct class from other state employees. In line with the campaigning spirit of the times, collectivization proceeded as rapidly as possible, and all goods and livestock were initially appropriated. Many of the best (and sometimes wealthiest) farmers were designated *kulaks and exiled or killed, as part of the drive to 'liquidate the kulaks as a class'. Some relaxation of life for the peasantry occurred subsequently, but those who survived were unable, until the 1960s, to move to other jobs without official permission. The policy did immense damage to agricultural production, by destroying the peasants' skills and their attachment to the land. Moreover, with further relaxation of state control, farm output stagnated as peasants worked the private plots they had been allowed. Ironically, and partly as a result of the abandonment of farming by the most able, efforts to abolish collective farms have faced considerable opposition in the post-Soviet period from those who fear the operation of the market.   swh

Collingwood, Robin George (1889–1943) British philosopher and archaeologist (specializing on Roman Britain), Wayneflete Professor of Metaphysical Philosophy, Magdalen College, Oxford University, 1935–41. Collingwood's work as a philosopher was wide-ranging, covering metaphysics, aesthetics, the philosophy of mind and of history. His *The Idea of History*, published posthumously in 1945, received particular attention by later philosophers of history. Collingwood also produced an important work of political philosophy, *The New Leviathan* (1942). In this work, he seeks to provide a theoretical defence of liberalism in the face of contemporary opposition from fascism and Nazism. Collingwood articulates a liberalism which owes much to T. H. *Green and his followers, and to his Italian contemporary, Guido de Ruggiero (author of *The History of European Liberalism*, 1927, translated by Collingwood for Oxford University Press). Freedom, properly understood, consists in self-direction in accordance with a moral will: a will based on a recognition of the claims of other people to self-direction. It is the task of the liberal state to create the conditions under which this distinctively free personality can emerge and express itself. Collingwood places a particular emphasis on the educative governance necessary for the creation of free persons, and on the need to extend liberal principles to interstate relations. swe

colonialism The policy and practice of a strong power extending its control territorially over a weaker nation or people. Originally the Latin *colonia* simply meant a country estate. But already in classical Latin it acquired the meaning of such an estate deliberately settled among foreigners. This sort of colonization was commonplace in the classical Mediterranean and in medieval Europe. Medieval and early modern English governments colonized both Wales and Ireland in this classical sense, intending the English farmers to defend English rule against the hostile Welsh or Irish. The pattern of settlement in, for instance, the west of Ulster reflects this to the present day, with Protestant 'colonial settlers' planted amongst the native Catholics. In his influential book *Internal Colonialism*, Michael Hechter (1975) has examined the *internal colonialism of the British Isles, claiming that peripheral regions were internal colonies of England.

But 'colonial' must be in distancing quotation marks because, where such colonization occurred a long time ago, the descendants of the settlers feel themselves as much part of the territory as those whose ancestors they displaced (in South Africa, for instance). Colonialism is more often thought of as an attribute of the late nineteenth-century imperialists who conquered large tracts of the globe to find themselves ruling, in Rudyard Kipling's phrase, 'new-caught, sullen peoples, | Half-devil and half-child' (*The White Man's Burden*). It is usually used pejoratively to denote an unwarranted sense of racial superiority and the set of attitudes, beliefs, and practices that sprang from this sense. It has been often argued that racism and xenophobia are colonialism brought home. *See also* POST-COLONIALISM.

comitology An idiomatic term used to describe the procedures by which decisions to implement *European Union legislation are made. These procedures involve numerous committees, made up of representatives from member states and chaired by the *European Commission (EC), whereby the member states can exercise some control over implementing powers delegated to the EC. According to the procedure which is applied, member states can exercise different degrees of influence over how the EC intends to implement legislation. BR

committee Literally, a small group of people to whom a larger group has delegated the power to act or formulate recommendations. In ordinary usage, however, a committee is not always a subgroup of a larger one ('the Committee of 100' was a free-standing group in *CND in the 1960s, for instance), and a committee may be regarded as any small group of voters.

committee of the whole (house) Legislative committees are normally restricted in their membership, whereas all members are entitled to participate when a legislature meets as a committee of the whole. This device is extensively used in the United States House of Representatives (although not in the Senate) as a means of expediting legislative business. An appointee of the Speaker chairs the proceedings, formal rules are suspended, and a quorum of only 100 is required instead of the 218 otherwise needed. At Westminster committees of the whole have been used for the discussion of matters of especial importance where it is thought that any member should, in principle, be allowed to participate. Thus for centuries prior to procedural changes in the 1960s all bills authorizing taxation or expenditure were first considered by the House of Commons sitting as a committee of the whole. In 1993 the committee stage of the Maastricht bill was dealt with under this procedure. DM

⊕ **SEE WEB LINKS**

• UK Parliament guide to procedure.

Committee on Standards in Public Life The UK Committee on Standards in Public Life was set up in October 1994 and issued its first report in 1995, under the chairmanship of Lord Nolan. It was established in order to investigate concerns about the conduct of members of parliament, after allegations that MPs had taken cash for putting down *parliamentary questions. The Committee Report set out seven principles of public life: selflessness, integrity, objectivity, accountability, openness, honesty, and leadership. The 'Nolan reforms' established a new post of Parliamentary Commissioner for Standards (see OMBUDSMAN) whose job was to maintain the Register of Members' Interests and investigate the conduct of MPs; to set up a House of Commons Committee on Standards and Privileges; and to set down a Code of Conduct for MPs. In 1998 the Committee issued a report on the funding of political parties, which rejected calls for state funding.

((( ))) SEE WEB LINKS
• Site of the Committee on Standards in Public Life.

committee stage In the UK Parliament, each bill which reaches this stage is examined clause by clause and amended by a committee, usually a standing committee of about twenty MPs who form a microcosm of the party composition of the house. For extremely important bills the entire House may act as the committee (see also COMMITTEE OF THE WHOLE; BILL). In the United States, congressional committees have more independence.

commodity-fetishism An idea added into the second edition of *Marx's *Capital*. In general, the analysis of the commodity is held to reveal the microscopic anatomy of bourgeois society, and also to show that capitalist wealth is always bound to appear as commodities. However, according to Marx, the mystical or fetishistic characters of these commodities does not lie in their use-value but in the fact that they are labour products, such that definite social relations between men assume the fantastic and alienated form of a relationship between things. Here fetishism is taken to be involved whenever human relationships come to be seen as properties of inanimate objects. Following *Feuerbach, his mentor until 1845, Marx sees the true analogy in religion. In religion

in general and idolatry in particular, what are no more than productions of the human brain appear as independent beings with a life of their own. Just as gods are inseparable from their human creators, so fetishism is inseparable from the production of commodities. This concept is now often taken to show the permanence of Marx's early concern with human *alienation and with the estrangement of labour.   JH

Common Agricultural Policy See CAP.

Common Foreign and Security Policy (CFSP) Policy areas covered by the second of the three pillars of the European Union (EU), established by the *Maastricht Treaty of 1992. (The Lisbon Treaty sought to collapse the three-pillar structure but this will not, in itself, have a major impact on decision-making on CFSP matters.) The EU member states which called for the creation of a CFSP aimed to reinforce existing intergovernmental cooperation on foreign policy carried out in the context of European Political Cooperation, in place since the early 1970s. In particular, the German government sought to introduce a stronger supranational element to CFSP policy-making but met strong French and British resistance, although there was general agreement that reforms were necessary. CFSP introduced two new decision-making instruments to the EU: common positions to establish cooperation on a day-to-day basis and joint actions to allow Member States to act together on the basis of Council decisions as to the specific scope, objectives, duration, and means of such actions, and procedures for carrying them out. Council decisions were based on unanimity but specific joint actions (in areas agreed upon) could be based on *Qualified Majority Voting (QMV).

The CFSP has enjoyed only qualified success. More frequently, EU member states have failed to reach agreement on coordinated policy stances and joint actions. The use of QMV to implement joint actions has been avoided due to the sensitive and frequently controversial nature of interventions and the preference for unanimity. There were also problems establishing and operating the CFSP unit in the Council secretariat, the body of national foreign policy officials responsible for improving coordination. The

Amsterdam Treaty of 1997 included an attempt to resolve these difficulties with the creation of the Policy Planning and Early Warning Unit, the lack of which was seen as one of the main weaknesses of CFSP. The reluctance of member states to share sensitive information has limited the effectiveness of this unit and the EU member states continue to rely upon NATO security information.

The Amsterdam Treaty also created the position of EU High Representative on Foreign and Security Policy attached to the Council secretariat. The aim was to give the CFSP a higher profile and to contribute to the formulation and implementation of policy. Javier Solana, the former head of NATO, was appointed as the first High Representative in 1998. In post for two terms, he had only marginal success in asserting his leadership role in relation to successive Council presidents. The creation of EU foreign minister is one of the institutional innovations of the non-ratified Constitutional Treaty of 2004, with the less controversial label of High Representative restored in the Lisbon Treaty of 2007. The new High Representative will serve for two and a half years and will sit astride both the Council and the Commission, replacing the EU External Affairs Commissioner. The reform is designed to increase the coherence of EU foreign policy making and the visibility of the EU as an international actor.

Humanitarian missions, peacekeeping operations, policing, and evacuation of expatriates (labelled the *Petersberg Tasks) were incorporated into the EU by the Amsterdam Treaty and supplemented by the more aggressive peacemaking operations. The Lisbon Treaty of 2007 proposed a range of additional military operations in which the EU can engage. The establishment of a European *Rapid Reaction Force (ERRF) was agreed in 1999, with participating member states contributing specialized troops and equipment in order to give the EU the capability of carrying out the Petersberg Tasks. Eight years later the ERRF was not yet operational. The Nice Treaty (2001) brought the *Western European Union (WEU) into the CFSP and created a Common European Security and Defence Policy (CESDP). This is a misnomer as joint defence—although established as a goal of the EU—was the one element of the WEU which the British refused to allow to be

incorporated. Reflecting ongoing French and German efforts to reinforce the CESDP, the Lisbon Treaty includes a Collective Defence provision which allows those member states wishing to reach agreements in this area to do so and to use EU institutions, without obligating the participation of other member states. The solidarity clause in the Lisbon Treaty requires member states to provide mutual assistance in the event that one suffers a terrorist attack and allows them to provide military assistance. DH

(((⊕))) SEE WEB LINKS

• European Union guide to the CFSP.

common good The good which is common to—that is, shared by—a number of persons; or, the good of a collectivity which cannot be disaggregated. The first standpoint takes the view that the good of a collectivity can be no more than the good of particular persons. The second supposes that the good or well-being of an entity like an association may be divorced, to some degree, from that of specific individuals presently constituting it. The whole notion of a common good was attacked by *Schumpeter, who claimed that democratic theory had aimed to promote it, but that it was impossible to discover its content. However, peace and community may be quoted as examples of such goods, for each is obtainable by anybody only if attainable by (almost) everybody. AR

common law (*lex communis*) In modern usage, frequently used to denote unwritten law which is generally derived from cases decided by courts, and not from the express authority contained in a statute. As a general term the common law may express the general customs of English law (and those in legal systems derived from England, such as that in the United States), originating from its medieval inheritance, which refers to early laws, unwritten in form but administered by the common law courts.

The common law may also refer to the earlier development of English law administered by the common law courts before the Judicature Acts 1873-5. Then, the distinction between Common Law courts and the Court of Chancery which administered *equity was an important one. After the Judicature Acts and especially since the Judicature Act 1925 which set up the *Supreme Court, the courts have developed common law principles alongside doctrines in equity. In English law the Supreme Court is distinct from countries with written constitutions that provide for a Supreme Court to have ultimate legal authority. The Supreme Court does not have such a jurisdiction in the United Kingdom as its decisions may be overturned by Act of Parliament.

The common law includes both civil and criminal law. The former refers to the law of contract and tort. The latter refers to the law of crime.

As the common law is developed by the judges, so it is not found in a written form comparable to statutory law. Instead the principles of the common law have developed gradually on the strength of decided cases. The inherent flexibility of the common law has been a strength of the English legal system and permitted continuity with change. Milsom has written 'the common law is the by-product of an administrative triumph, the way in which the government of England came to be centralized and specialized during the centuries after the conquest' (*Historical Foundations of the Common Law*, 1981). The future of the common law is constrained by the predisposition to statutory enactments as part of the development of European law. The vast detail and complexity of the law is more often found in European directives and laws as a requirement of modern government. For that reason, the term common law may best be understood to refer to techniques of interpretation and analysis employed by judges to understand and interpret statutes. Judges will continue to shape and guide the future development of English law, drawing on the flexibility of principles inherent in the common law tradition.   JM

common market When the integration of a group of national economies is taken beyond the stage of a *customs union by the adoption of common economic policies and the facilitation of free movement of capital and labour, a common market results. The most accomplished example is the *European Union.   CJ

Commonwealth (British) The Commonwealth evolved from the meetings between Britain and the self-governing dominions of Australia, Canada, South Africa, and New Zealand during and after the First World War. The *Statute of Westminster, 1931, confirmed the dominions' status as quasi-sovereign states, bound together voluntarily by the British Crown. During the Second World War the dominions assumed the powers of sovereign states (they, rather than Britain, declared war on Germany, and the dominion of Ireland decided to remain neutral). In 1947 India, Pakistan, and Ceylon became dominions and members of the Commonwealth, Burma chose not to join on gaining independence in 1948, and in 1949 Ireland left the Commonwealth.

The Commonwealth is dominated numerically by poor states in Africa, Asia, the Caribbean, and the Pacific who joined on obtaining independence. Dependencies such as the Falklands are not members. Namibia, which was formerly ruled by South Africa, chose to become a member in 1990. Six states have left: Ireland, South Africa in 1961 (though it rejoined in 1994), Fiji in 1987 (re-admitted 1997, expelled 2006, re-admitted 2014), The Gambia in 2013, and the Maldives in 2016. Pakistan left in 1972 but rejoined in 1989, and has been suspended and re-admitted twice since then. Cameroon, Mozambique and Rwanda have joined, although they had limited or no colonial links with Britain.

In 1965 a small secretariat was established. Heads of government meet biennially to discuss a broad agenda, and other ministers also meet regularly. In the 1980s the Commonwealth's agenda was dominated by *apartheid, and, on the issue of sanctions against South Africa, Britain was frequently in an awkward minority of one. However, the Commonwealth operates by consensus and persuasion, rather than by binding vote. About 70 per cent of Britain's state-to-state development aid continues to go to Commonwealth states. The organization also serves as a useful consultative mechanism for its members, but its significance in foreign and economic policies of its members, including Britain, is gently subsiding.   PBY

(🌐) SEE WEB LINKS

- Site of the Commonwealth Secretariat, including a history and membership of the organization.

Commonwealth of Independent States (CIS) The CIS was formed by the leaders of Russia, Ukraine, and Belarus (formerly Byelorussia) in Minsk on 8 December 1991. With the exception of Georgia and the Baltic states, other former Soviet republics joined in Alma-Ata on 21 December. Georgia became a member in 1993 but withdrew in 2009; Ukraine withdrew in May 2018. The creation of the CIS precipitated the final demise of the Soviet Union. Whilst moves have been made to develop the CIS as the basis of a free trade area or defence pact, progress has been largely determined by *bilateral relations between Russia and the separate states. swh

(⊕) SEE WEB LINKS

• Commonwealth of Independent States site, with details of history and membership.

communalism Associated (1) with support for the autonomous rule of localized political units, such as the Paris Commune of 1871; and (2) in South Asia with the antagonistic polarization of politics between religious and ethnic groups, particularly conflict between Hindus and Muslims.

commune In its older and neutral senses, the lowest unit of local government in a number of countries, especially France. Two ideologically charged meanings have emerged for historical reasons:

1 The (politicians who controlled the) Paris Commune of 1870–1 included radical socialists who tried to run the government on revolutionary principles until their military defeat. Their use of the title echoed its use by the similarly revolutionary Commune which controlled Paris (and could often coerce the National Convention) between 1792 and 1794. The Commune of 1870–1 was idealized by *Marx.

2 Any group of people living together and sharing possessions; but used usually with the implication that the people in question hold radical or revolutionary views.

communism In its usually acknowledged form, a process of class conflict and revolutionary struggle, resulting in victory for the proletariat and the establishment of a classless, socialist society in which private ownership has been abolished and the means of

production and subsistence belong to the community.

The notion of communism has a long history. Writers such as *Babeuf and *Owen are sometimes regarded as communists (*see also* PRIMITIVE COMMUNISM), but 'communist' first appeared in English in 1841 and 'communism' in 1843. It is now mainly understood to mean either the end of history predicted by Marxist thinkers, or the reality of life in conditions of Communist Party rule. Though one can still hear advocates insist that communism is possible despite the experience of Eastern Europe, the utopian element has been largely discredited by the political practice.

The Marxist argument for communism has both normative and positive components. The main characteristic of human life is *alienation. Communism ought to be desirable because it entails the full realization of human freedom. Marx here follows Hegel in conceiving freedom not merely as the absence of constraints but as action having moral content. Not only does communism allow people to do what they want but it puts humans in such conditions and in such relations with one another that they would not wish or have need for wrong-doing or evil. Whereas for Hegel, the unfolding of this ethical life (*sittlichkeit*) in history is mainly cognitively motivated—hence the importance of philosophers—for Marx, communism emerged from material, especially productive, development. Thus, he jibes that philosophers had hitherto only sought to interpret the world, when the point was to change it.

Marx himself says little about the non-alienated world of communism. It is clear that it entails superabundance in which there is no limit to the projects that humans may choose; one could be a painter in the morning, a fisherman in the afternoon, a writer in the evening, and a lover at night. In the slogan that was adopted by the communist movement, communism was a world in which 'each gave according to his abilities, and received according to his needs'. Since morality had been abolished along with want, the main criteria governing the choice of life projects were aesthetic or scientific; communist society was not expected to be consumerist.

As a normative enterprise, therefore, communism appealed to many circles, uniting not only the poor person struggling under want, but also the high-minded intellectual who saw transcendental virtue in his work. Marx's achievement and lasting significance, however, was to add to this utopia a positive scientific theory of how society was moving in a law-governed way towards communism and, with some tension, a political theory that explained why human agency—revolutionary activity—was required to bring it about. These latter aspects, particularly as developed by Lenin, provided the underpinning for both the dogmatic and mobilizing features of twentieth-century Communist Parties.

In *Capital* and other 'scientific' works, Marx claims to have uncovered the laws of capitalist development. All societies must solve the problem of reproducing human life, but at each historical stage, the level of development of the productive forces shapes the pattern of human organization. The combination of productive forces and human relations comprises a 'mode of production', and each mode has its own distinctive laws arising from the manner in which production is accomplished and the relationship among its social elements—historically these have mainly been classes. Capitalism is characterized by commodity production or production of goods with exchange value. Profit results from the ability of those controlling the means of production to treat labour as a commodity like any other, which they can employ to produce goods with value greater than that paid in wages. There is constant competition among capitalists to extract the greatest amount of surplus value. A number of laws are deduced from these premises: constant overproduction and underconsumption which leads to periodic economic crises in which the productive potential of capital and labour is wasted; ever greater mechanization and a diminution in the share of labour in the production process; a long-run tendency for the rate of profit to decline; the relative impoverishment of the working class in comparison to the amount of surplus value it produces; and the rise of an absolutely impoverished lumpenproletariat.

At this point, the normative and positive elements meet. The massive productive potential of capitalism, undreamt of in human history, to free people from want to pursue their own projects, increasingly comes into conflict with the reality of increased alienation. At the same time, the character of production tends to increase social interaction and homogeneity among those exploited, and on a global scale. Capitalism, therefore, creates its own 'gravediggers' in a working class who have 'no country' and 'nothing to lose but their chains'. The overthrow of capitalism is possible because the process of production has already been socialized. However, with the expropriation of capitalists, the international, homogenous working class has neither reason nor interest to introduce another exploitative social order. Thus the productive potential of advanced machinery may be harnessed with non-exploitative social relations—in a word, communism.

Marx and Engels certainly believed that by offering a scientific explanation of the possibility, indeed necessity, of communism they were distinguishing themselves from lesser 'utopian' socialists. However, although periodic economic crises have taken place with enormous waste of human and other capital, there has not occurred either a tendency for the rate of profit to decline or for an inexorable fall in the share of labour as opposed to machinery across all sectors of industry. Indeed, capitalism has proved extraordinarily revolutionary and able to revitalize itself, even by Marx's own very high estimates of its capacity. Moreover the impoverishment of the working class did not take place, at least in the advanced capitalist world where Marx predicted revolution would take place, and evidence suggests that the size of the underclass is a function of political and institutional factors rather than an inevitable consequence of capitalism itself.

Perhaps the biggest problems in Marx's own theory were identified by Lenin. First, he argued, workers did not go beyond their narrow economic demands for higher pay and conditions to make explicitly political demands for the overthrow of capitalism. Only intellectuals could properly understand the emancipatory potential of communism, which was beyond workers' experience, however much production may have been socialized. A steadfast, resolute, and organized party of intellectuals, acting as the workers' vanguard, and armed with the knowledge given by Marxist theory, was therefore required if the transition to the freedom of communism was to be achieved. Secondly, not only did workers orient their demands on economic improvements, but capitalism, at least in some circumstances, was quite capable of granting concessions. Thus, the impoverishment and, more importantly for Lenin, the homogeneity of workers was not a spontaneous result of capitalist production. Imperialism allowed capitalists particular opportunities to reward workers in the metropolis with money derived from the super-exploited in the colonies. Moreover, the alliance of a 'labour aristocracy' with sections of *imperialist capital resulted in working-class nationalism which, in Lenin's view, led to the break-up of the international socialist movement at the outbreak of the First World War. The road to communism, therefore, would take a different path in which the 'weak links in the imperialist chain' would be the first to break with capitalism, with Russia the first to fall in 1917 after defeat in the war.

The effort to build communism in Russia, however, raised significant further theoretical and practical problems. The theory had presumed that revolution would occur where the socialization of production, potential for abundance, and a large working class were already in place. Russia was the poorest country in Europe with an enormous, illiterate peasantry and little industry. In these circumstances, it was not only necessary for the party to educate workers beyond narrow economism, but to create the working class itself. For this reason, the socialist *Mensheviks had opposed the communist *Bolsheviks in their demand for socialist revolution before capitalism had been established. In seizing power, the Bolsheviks found themselves without a programme beyond their pragmatic and politically successful slogans, 'peace, bread, and land', which had tapped the massive public desire for an end to the war and privation, and the peasants' demand for land redistribution. As Lenin himself was fond of saying, there was no blueprint for socialism on the road to communism. Indeed, there could not have been since, to use Marx's metaphor, communism should have matured within the womb of capitalist society, ready to emerge, if not fully formed, then requiring only a short period of transition before being up and running.

Like the early Christians, the Bolsheviks acted almost immediately, as if the millennium was upon them. In the years of War Communism 1918–20, in the middle of a civil war, all property was nationalized and money for a period abolished. When mutiny and peasant unrest resulted, Lenin declared a short breathing space in 1921 (the *NEP) before 'the heavens' of communism could once again be assaulted. However, in the last three years of his life, Lenin also showed a growing awareness of the difficulties of building communism in Russia, which necessitated a prolonged transition period in which both antagonistic social classes and commodity relations would be maintained under the watchful and guiding eyes of the Party.

Political and institutional factors conspired to foreshorten this transitional phase. While the Communist Party and industrial institutions such as the Supreme Council for the National Economy had been operationally responsible for running the country under War Communism, NEP was controlled largely by experts frequently of bourgeois origin and of Menshevik or right-wing political persuasion. When NEP ran into difficulties, it was difficult for the Party and other bodies to resist the claim that the abolition of market relations and the liquidation of 'exploiting' classes such as the *kulaks or the small traders (NEPmen) was a better strategy. Since political power continued to rest with the Party, which was hardly content to kick its heels while capitalist relations were given time to develop, NEP was unlikely to survive. These political and institutional obstacles to NEP were magnified by personal competition in the leadership which saw Stalin using his control over personnel to shift policy to the left in 1929.

The Stalinist version of socialism, with some important modifications, ruled the Soviet Union for the next fifty-six years. It began in a spirit of enormous optimism about the possibilities of building communism via a massive industrialization and collectivization programme. The rapid development of industry, and above all the victory of the Soviet Union in the Second World War, maintained this optimism even into the *Khrushchev period, 1953–64, when the Party adopted a programme in which it promised the establishment of communism within thirty years.

However, more evidence emerged which in the end dented faith in the possibility and desirability of communism irrevocably. First, Khrushchev himself revealed the enormity of repression that had taken place. Second, industrial development had been organized by state institutions which began to act as a dead, conservative hand on further progress. As growth declined, so *rent-seeking and corruption by state officials increased, which dented the legitimacy of the system. Third, the allies which the Soviet Union had won by war in Eastern Europe, and as a result of the collapse of imperialism in Africa and Asia, became a financial and military burden. Finally, while Soviet development slowed, that of the capitalist West accelerated, and introduced new technological developments that the Soviet economy could not match. No communist revolutions had occurred in the capitalist centres of the West. By the 1980s, therefore, faith in the capacity of the Soviet Union to make the transition to communism had evaporated. swh

Communist Party Despite its title, the 'Manifesto of the Communist Party' argued that the 'communists do not form a separate party opposed to the other working class parties'. Rather, Marx and Engels claimed, the role of communists was to point out that working-class aims could only be achieved by the overthrow of 'all existing social conditions'.

Until the collapse of the Second Socialist International in 1914, Marxists worked within social democratic parties. The Russian Social Democratic and Labour Party, however, had split into the radical Bolshevik (majority) and the more moderate Menshevik (minority) factions in 1903. Lenin had developed a theory of a 'party of a new type' in *What is to be Done?* written in 1902. Only a highly centralized and disciplined party of professional revolutionaries, which would act as 'the vanguard of the proletariat', was capable of overthrowing autocracy. After the victory of the Bolsheviks in the October 1917 Russian Revolution, Lenin's 'democratic centralist' party became the model for Communist Parties around the world.

Communist Parties outside the Soviet Union met with varying success. In the inter-war period, the German party was the strongest in Europe, but was crushed by

Nazism. In Asia, notably China in 1949, and Vietnam as a whole after United States withdrawal, the communists were able to win power on their own. In India Communist Parties have been electorally successful in the States of Kerala and West Bengal. In Eastern Europe, with the exception of Yugoslavia, communists relied on Soviet support to win and maintain power after 1945. In Western Europe, particularly in Italy and France, mass Communist Parties wielded considerable influence, as they did in some Latin American countries, notably Chile, but never held power.

With the collapse of communism in the Soviet Union and Eastern Europe, Communist Parties appeared to suffer irretrievable damage. However, in a number of European states such as Poland, Lithuania, Italy, and Russia itself, successor parties have achieved significant electoral success. swh

communitarianism Advocacy of a social order in which individuals are bound together by common values that foster close communal bonds. A label used loosely to describe the ideas of a number of writers particularly critical of modern liberal political thought, because of the importance they attach to '*community'. Hence an antagonism has been presented between communitarianism and liberalism, which may, however, be overdrawn. Frequently identified communitarians are Alasdair MacIntyre, Michael Sandel, Michael Walzer, and Charles Taylor. The fundamental division is said to be about the nature of the self. Communitarianism insists upon the interaction of the social context and individuals' self-conceptions, while liberalism allegedly works with an atomized individual artificially if not incoherently divorced from his or her social surroundings. The intellectual origins of communitarianism are various, but *Hegel and the English Idealists, notably T. H. *Green, provide important perspectives, because of Hegel's concept of *sittlichkeit, or the shared values of the community, and the English Idealists' emphasis on the obligations of citizenship. The socialist tradition, notably through its concern with fraternity, and the anarchist tradition, with its focus on the possibility of community in the absence of state coercion, are also important. Ferdinand Tonnies's work on

Community and Society drew attention to the value of community, and the threat posed to it by *industrial society. Fundamental questions about the desirable relationships between 'the community', 'the nation', and 'the state' remain intellectually contentious and hotly contested in practical politics. AR

community A group of people who are socially related by virtue of identity with a particular location. The nature of the social relationship and location are, however, ideologically contested. Traditional conservative thought emphasizes the idea that community is based upon commonality of origin—the blood, kinship, and historic ties—of a people living in a particular location. Village localities as much as national groups are considered to cohere on such a basis. As in such terms as the 'Jewish community', commonality of origin may also have been derived in another location or by reference to a homeland. Socialist thought identifies conservative versions of community as hegemonic devices to bind both the haves and have-nots together in capitalist society, preventing them from seeing their real clash of economic interests and thus averting social conflict. Reformist socialists seeking to attain this goal may construct community on the basis of enjoining wealthier locations with poorer ones to effect redistribution of wealth and create the desired social relations at the local level.

Conservatives and socialists may stress different bases for the existence of community, but both identify the social relations inherent in community as something greater than the concerns and interests of each individual living in it added together, and as providing the basis for the longevity of a community. Liberals are reluctant to conceptualize community on the same elevated basis because of their commitment to individual freedom. Instead they see community as based on the freely chosen associations of individuals with common interests and needs. Such associations may be strongly locationally based. For example, 'financial community' suggests both a group of people who have common work-related interests and needs and a particular work location such as the City of London or Wall Street. Similarly, 'travel to work area' suggests the

locational setting of motorists, commuters, and shoppers who have shared needs, and would be deemed to be a suitable basis for a community. However, given that they are based upon freely chosen association and the individual imperatives which drive employment and economic and social change, such communities may change both in nature and in location. For example, deregulation and information technology have changed the organization of financial markets, and suburbanization and the development of transport infrastructure have changed travel to work areas. In the practical domain, however, all too often 'community' is given no explicit meaning and used instead for the general sympathy it attracts as a legitimizing concept for any political programme. This is illustrated well by the rhetorical focus on a politics of the community by Tony Blair, the reformist 'New Labour' leader of the Labour Party in the UK, as opposed to previous emphases on the state by the Labour Party and on the individual by the Conservatives under the Thatcher and Major Governments. JBR

community politics Term invented by candidates of the Liberal Party in Britain in the 1970s to denote the tactic of fighting elections on issues of importance to small, local communities. As a process, community politics both draws on the identity of a local community and its shared interests, particularly those which it has in preserving and enhancing the local environment, and helps build the community by making people more aware of those interests and by raising their estimation of the relative importance of local issues. The process and the tactic are, therefore, relevant to a much wider context than Britain. Opponents of community politics have often been contemptuous of the pettiness of the issues it brings to the fore, an attitude to which one Liberal candidate, Bill Pitt, replied by saying, 'You cannot reach for the stars when you always have to look at your feet to make sure you are not treading in dog dirt'. LA

community power The question of who makes decisions within a community was a debate prominent in American political science in the 1950s and 1960s, and reflected in discussions in other countries including

Britain. In 1953, Floyd Hunter's *Community Power Structure* suggested that power in the community he studied (not named in the book, but Atlanta, Georgia) was dominated by business elites to the exclusion of ordinary people, and the total exclusion of black people. In 1961, Robert Dahl's riposte, *Who Governs?*, suggested that in New Haven, Connecticut, no one group did: that power was dispersed among interest communities. Of course, both writers could have been right about their particular place and time. In themselves, the books permitted no generalization except that those who look for elites will probably find them, whereas *pluralist writers will expect to find, and probably will find, that there is no controlling elite. The community power debate therefore became rather sterile. In response to Dahl, it was claimed that powerful groups could keep issues off the agenda, a process labelled 'mobilization of bias'. The best such study is Matthew Crenson's *The Unpolitics of Air Pollution* (1971), which was published when air pollution in the United States had just become extremely political.

comparative government The systematic study of the government of more than one country. One of the main subdivisions of the study of politics. Until recently, however, it was usually very unsystematic. Much of what passed for comparative government was simply the study of the government of a small number of large countries. A typical course or textbook would cover two or three parliamentary democracies and one or two communist regimes. While it is certainly useful for any student of politics to know something about the institutions of three or more countries, that is not comparative politics until it involves some comparisons.

What comparisons are useful? The oldest form of comparative government is the study of constitutions. The first known such work is *Aristotle's compilation of the constitutions and practice of 158 Greek city-states, of which only the *Constitution of Athens* survives. Undoubtedly, however, comparisons between different city-states underpin some of the generalizations in Aristotle's *Politics*, just as comparisons between different living organisms underpin his biological writing.

Biology has made great strides since Aristotle; the comparative study of constitutions has not. This is partly because it is difficult to get the right level of generality. Some studies compare all the countries in the world. Some useful statistical generalizations can be made about them. But there is no scholarly agreement on such basic questions as the relationship between the economic development of a country and its level of democracy. Another approach is to look at all cases of a common phenomenon—such as revolutions, totalitarian states, or transitions to democracy. In some cases these are dogged by difficulties of definition. For instance, what is to count as a revolution?

The commonest form of comparative government remains the detailed study of some policy area in two or more countries. Sensitive researchers are always aware of the problem of 'too few cases, too many variables'. Consider a popular research programme in the 1980s and 1990s: the impact of *corporatism on gross national product. It is clearly not straightforward. Some corporatist and some anticorporatist countries have had fast economic growth; some corporatist and some anticorporatist countries have had slow economic growth. There can be many reasons why a country becomes corporatist, and many reasons why an economy grows fast (or not). No researcher, or even collaborative team, can hope to know enough about more than perhaps five countries to talk about each of their institutions in a well-informed way. So they can never be sure whether the factors they identify as the causes of growth really are the true causes. In recent years, this literature has improved, with several large multiple-regression-based studies of all countries, all democracies, or all *OECD countries.

These difficulties have always surrounded comparative government. Nevertheless, researchers are far more sensitive to the difficulties of generalization than they once were, and accordingly more tentative in their conclusions.

competitive party system Political system in which more than one political party has a reasonable expectation of winning an election, or of being in a winning coalition. *First-past-the-post electoral systems are associated with party systems which superficially do not appear to be competitive. For instance, presidential elections in the United

States have shown long periods of one-party dominance: Democratic from 1828 to 1856, Republican from 1896 to 1928, and Democratic from 1932 to 1968, for example. Likewise, the Conservatives were dominant in the British party system from 1922 to 1997, and the Liberals and Whigs were equally dominant between 1846 and 1874. However, even in these systems ruling parties know that the exaggerated majorities which keep them in may one day throw them out; if they forget, they need only note the reduction of the Canadian Progressive Conservatives from 170 seats to 2 in the 1993 election there.

On this view, every party system in a democracy is competitive. Others would insist that there is a useful distinction between systems such as those mentioned above and systems in which shifting coalitions guarantee that the composition of the government is constantly changing. Finally, it is worth noting that some *centre parties such as the German Free Democrats and, until 1992, the Italian Republicans were in almost every government, even though the party system could be labelled as competitive.

completeness *See* ECONOMIC MAN.

Comprehensive   Nuclear-Test-Ban Treaty (CTBT) The treaty commits states to a ban on the testing of nuclear weapons, and establishes the Comprehensive Nuclear-Test-Ban Treaty Organization to ensure that the provisions of the treaty are implemented. Negotiated in the early 1990s, by February 2008 it had been signed by 178 nations, and ratified by 144. The United States signed the treaty, but the Senate rejected the treaty in 1999 and the administration of George W. Bush was opposed to the treaty. Other states known to have nuclear weapon programmes, such as India, Israel, North Korea, and Pakistan, have not signed. *See also* NUCLEAR NON-PROLIFERATION TREATY.

SEE WEB LINKS

• Site of the Preparatory Commission for the Comprehensive Nuclear-Test-Ban Treaty Organization.

compulsory voting Law in force in Australia and Belgium, and in some other regimes in the past, which stipulates that it is compulsory to vote and lays down penalties for failing to vote. The main effects in Australia are thought to be: (1) slightly greater support for parties of the left than there would otherwise be, because in a typical election their supporters are less strongly motivated to vote; (2) the 'donkey vote', in which resentful or uninterested voters simply vote for the first few names on the list presented to them. Until elaborate procedures for randomizing names on the ballot paper and rotating their order were devised, this gave a significant advantage to parties which could find candidates with names early in the alphabet.

Comte,   Isidore-Auguste-Marie-François-Xavier (1798–1857) French sociologist (he invented the word 'sociology' in 1838 although he always had doubts about the combination of Latin and Greek roots) and political philosopher. Auguste Comte based his system of ideas on *positivism, originally a theory of knowledge which he had a large part in developing, but which also became the title usually applied to his substantive theories. He was greatly influenced by his time at the École Polytechnique (one of the *Grandes Écoles), and by *Saint-Simon by whom he was employed as secretary from 1817 to 1824.

In the *Cours de philosophie positive* (published in six volumes between 1830 and 1842), Comte was concerned with philosophy, which he saw as a necessary basis for the rest of science. Later, in the *Système de politique positive* (four volumes, 1851–4), he was concerned with political restructuring. However, the basis of nearly all his later work in both parts had appeared in four essays written in the 1820s. Comte was not only a system builder, but he also remained committed to the same basic system from his first formulation of it at the age of 24.

In the first part, he advocated positivism as epistemology, rejecting the possibility of knowledge other than of correlative laws showing the connections between phenomena, generated by the application of reason to empirical observations. In the past, human knowledge had passed through two earlier stages, the theological (itself progressing from fetishism through polytheism to monotheism) and the metaphysical. This pattern of development constitutes Comte's philosophy of history (*historicism). In the theological stage, humanity had invented imaginary beings to explain why things were as they were, and this stage had lasted more than 3,000 years. The metaphysical stage had been much shorter, from the fourteenth century to the eighteenth, and consisted in effect of a critique of the theological stage. It still posed questions in the form of 'Why?', but substituted abstractions such as nature for supernatural beings. This did not constitute a viable alternative to the theological explanation, and the metaphysical stage was essentially transitional. The positive stage was in process of replacing the earlier ones in Comte's day, and had substituted the question 'How?' This law of the three stages was extremely influential, and was accepted in its general form, for example, by John Stuart *Mill, who rejected most of the rest of Comte's ideas.

Comte divided sociology into social statics and social dynamics. The latter consists of the philosophy of history, the former of Comte's analysis of human nature. He classified these as the sciences of progress and order respectively. Every change in the social order brought about by human beings depended for Comte upon the intellectual system in operation. Because the *French Revolution had been based on the metaphysical stage, it had not been able to produce a viable replacement for the *ancien régime* which it had destroyed.

The primacy of theory over action produced in Comte's social thought a division between spiritual and temporal powers, with the latter subordinated to the former. The temporal power was to be exercised by industrialists and bankers who would achieve the maximum economic development through their expertise. Comte dismissed any element of democracy because it would allow ignorance to dominate knowledge. Even in industrial society, however, some moral foundation beyond mere efficiency and well-being would be necessary, and this would be provided by the spiritual power. It was to be exercised by leading intellectuals who would provide it through the religion of humanity.

Despite the ridicule which his religion of humanity generally attracted (although it was to have considerable success in, for example, Brazil), Comte has been remarkably influential. He was important to

*Spencer, Renan, Taine, *Durkheim, and Lévy-Bruhl as well as John Stuart Mill. Echoes of his thought can be found in logical positivism, analytical philosophy, and particularly in one of the most widespread approaches in twentieth-century American political science, *behaviouralism. CS

Concorde fallacy Name given by evolutionary biologists to a form of suboptimal behaviour found among wasps and policymakers. Certain species of wasp are observed to defend their nests with an amount of energy proportionate to the amount they have spent on building the nest. It would be more efficient for them to defend them with an amount of energy proportionate to the cost of an alternative and the strength of the aggressor. Likewise, wasteful public expenditure on the supersonic aircraft Concorde was defended on the grounds that a great deal had already been spent. But this argument is fallacious. What has been spent has been spent, regardless of what happens now. Spilt milk cannot be unspilt. Spending on Concorde should have been judged by the expected value of the extra spending being contemplated, and on that alone.

The Concorde fallacy is extremely widespread in human reasoning, with the result that policymakers who commit it are rarely punished for doing so.

concurrent majorities Majorities in each of several bodies, such as houses in a legislature. Used specifically by John C. *Calhoun for the claim that a policy (on slavery, for instance) should not be implemented unless a majority in both areas affected agreed with it. This would of course have resulted in no policy on slavery being adopted at all. Many constitutions require concurrent majorities for certain sorts of weighty decisions.

conditionality Idea that external credit or funding should be advanced to a government only where a programme of economic or political reforms was to be implemented. The concept is associated with funding provided by the *IMF, particularly since the 1970s, when conditionality was seen as a way of enhancing government credit without generating inflationary or foreign exchange pressures. Financial support would be forthcoming only with agreements on macro-economic policy and reform of trading policy, with the hope that such measures would enhance a government's economic credibility and credit-worthiness. Since the 1980s, as the IMF and *World Bank have extended lending and funding programmes in the Third World and the post-communist states, the focus of conditionality has been on the establishment of open economies and other aspects of *structural adjustment. From 2000, conditionality has been a major component of 'performance-based financing' models for *aid delivery, where fund disbursement is 'conditioned' on the fulfilment of certain corresponding performance targets by the recipient country/institution. Since conditionality is based on the existence of external constraints to ensure virtuous government behaviour in the long term, there are always likely to be tensions between short-term domestic incentives and the expectations of international funding bodies. Yet, proponents of conditionality suggest that conditionality curbs corruption by recipients and increases accountability. In foreign policy, conditionality is also often viewed as a useful mechanism to generate norm compliance or as a way to exert *soft power. However, conditionality has been criticized for imposing the model of Western political liberalism on countries where it may not be appropriate or supported by the people; exposing poor countries to competition and exploitation from companies in wealthier countries; and focusing on economic growth rather than promotion of social reform and equality. Thus, critics highlight the negative externalities and forms of unequal power associated with conditionalities and the harm they can produce. For example, even by World Bank accounts, the structural adjustments associated with IMF and World Bank assistance in the 1990s caused significant harm to many recipients and resulted in substantial human harm. *See also* DEVELOPMENT.

Condorcet, M. J. A. N. de Caritat, marquis de (1743–94) French scientist, revolutionary, and political theorist. Born into the aristocracy, and originally intended to be a priest or a soldier, Condorcet escaped both by becoming a mathematician and soon being taken under the wings of powerful patrons associated with the Academy of Sciences in Paris and with the *Encyclopédie*. His professional career was made in the Academy, whose permanent secretary he became. In the 1760s he established himself as a leading mathematician with his work on integral calculus. Condorcet was associated with *Voltaire and other figures of the French *Enlightenment in their campaigns against the legal system, which had led to the persecution and judicial murder of religious dissidents. This led him towards his grand project of applying probability theory to social science in the shape of his *jury theorem.

In Condorcet's view, social science should be studied with the same tools as engineering or biology. Probability was the key to all the sciences. For example, a naval engineer cannot design an unsinkable ship, but can design one that would sink only in the most improbably violent storm—say, one that occurred only once in every 400 years. Analogously, a designer of jury systems cannot design one that will never convict an innocent suspect. But if a jury system is set up in which the reliability of each juror—the probability that the juror will make the correct observation on whether the accused is guilty or not—is known, the probability that an innocent person will be convicted can be held down to an acceptable level by requiring a majority of a certain number of jurors to convict. Condorcet was the first to apply the advances in probability theory made by Thomas Bayes (*see* RICHARD PRICE) and the Bernoulli family to social science.

Condorcet's probability theory had an uneasy relationship with his theory of voting. His chief work is the *Essai sur l'application de l'analyse à la probabilité des décisions rendues à la pluralité des voix* (Essay on the application of mathematics to the probability of majority decisions, 1785). This is so difficult that even the meaning of the title is hard for the non-specialist to understand. The first clear exposition of it was by *Black in 1958, and the *Essai* was not fully understood until the 1980s. In it, Condorcet tries to select the voting procedure that is most likely to select the 'correct' result. This is open to the objection that, generally, there is no such thing. In a jury trial, the accused either did or did not commit the crime as charged. There is a correct answer to this question, which the jury tries to find. But there is no correct answer to the question 'Which party should govern Britain for the next five years?'; there are merely interests and opinions. However, Condorcet's method led him to a discovery which, although it all but made his own approach unworkable, came to create the entirely new subject of *social choice, nearly 200 years after Condorcet's death. This was the discovery of majority-rule *cycles. When there are at least three voters and at least three options, it is always possible that option A beats B by a majority, B beats C, and C beats A, all at the same time. Condorcet proposed ways of identifying what he regarded as the 'true' majority winner whether or not there was a cycle among the winning options (*see* CONDORCET WINNER).

Condorcet is also well known for his *Esquisse d'un tableau historique des progrès de l'esprit humain* (Sketch of a history of the progress of the human mind, 1795). The philosopher of the Enlightenment, in hiding from the murderous politicians of the revolutionary Terror who were soon to claim his life, paints a serene picture of the progress of humanity from superstition, religion, and barbarism to mathematics, probability, and enlightenment. Widely regarded as the most tragi-comic product of the French Enlightenment, the *Esquisse* is gaining renewed attention as its connection with Condorcet's scientific work is understood. It was the unacknowledged precursor of *Comte's similar work. Condorcet was also one of the first feminist political writers.

Condorcet was first involved in practical politics as a trusted aide of *Turgot during the latter's brief ministry. He returned to politics as the *French Revolution progressed. The height of his power was as a leading member of the Legislative Assembly and the National Convention in 1792-3. He drafted a report on public instruction that was immediately overtaken by wars and riots, but came to inspire the centralized and uniform French school system as it has remained to this day. And he wrote a constitution for France embodying his ideal voting procedures. This was debated in early 1793, and Condorcet's voting procedures were actually implemented in neighbouring Geneva (with chaotic results). But in June 1793 the *Girondin members of the Convention were expelled at the demand of rioting

members of the *Commune of Paris. Condorcet was not a Girondin, but he joined them in defeat by complaining that the victorious *Jacobins had scrapped his constitution in favour of one written by *Robespierre which failed to understand the theory of voting. This sealed Condorcet's fate. He was expelled from the Convention, hid in the house of a brave Parisian landlady, escaped from there in order to avoid her being guillotined for harbouring an outlaw, was arrested when he turned up, starving, in a village inn which happened to be run by an informer for the Committee of Public Safety, and was found dead in prison the next day.

Condorcet's ideas were more influential than his contemporaries recognized. Through his friendship with *Jefferson, he tried to influence the American constitution-making process. In this, as in other areas, his true stature is only now emerging.

Condorcet (Grouchy), Sophie, marquise de (1764-1822) French feminist writer. Alleged by their enemies to be the malign influence behind her husband *Condorcet's support for republicanism and feminism during the *French Revolution. Her best-known work over her own name is a French translation of *Smith's *Theory of Moral Sentiments*. She played a large part in the feminist writings published either jointly or over her husband's name. These argued that the biological differences between men and women did not constitute any reason for treating them differently in education, the job market, or civil rights.

Condorcet winner The option, or candidate, in a multicandidate election, which wins a simple majority against each of the others when every pair of candidates is compared. Voting rules inspired by *Condorcet seek to find the Condorcet winner if one exists. If there is a *cycle among the leading candidates, then there is no Condorcet winner, and some tie-breaking procedure is needed. Various candidates for such a procedure have been suggested, but there is (and probably can be) no agreement on which is the best.

confederation A term applied to a union of states which is less binding in its character than a federation. In principle, the states in a confederation would not lose their separate identity through confederation, and would retain the right of secession. In practice, this right might be difficult to exercise, and the constituent units of a long-standing confederation might appear to be little different from those of any other federal state. Thus, although the cantons in the Swiss confederation are designated as 'sovereign', and enjoy considerable decision-making autonomy, the powers of the federal government have grown over time, and secession would not seem to be a practical possibility. The replacement of the term 'confederated states' by 'federal state' in descriptions of the American constitution following the Civil War reflects both the negative connotations of the term 'confederacy' following its appropriation in the war by the secessionist states of the South, and the growing power of the federal government.   WG

conference committee *See* JOINT COMMITTEE.

Conference on Security and Co-operation in Europe (CSCE) *See* ORGANIZATION FOR SECURITY AND COOPERATION IN EUROPE (OSCE).

confidence motion Short for 'a motion of no confidence', a confidence motion refers to a vote or formal statement made against a senior party or government leader so as to indicate that they are no longer deemed fit to hold their post. Votes of 'no confidence' can often be a response to corruption, a lack of leadership ability, unpopularity with voters, an inability to unite a party, a public scandal, or political infighting. Depending on the constitution of a state, a successful motion of no confidence will either lead to mandatory resignation or result in a formal, but not mandatory, request to step down. Either way, both are far more civilized than a *coup d'état.

conflict resolution The methods and process of negotiation, arbitration, and institution building which promote the peaceful ending of social conflict and war.

Confucius (551–479 BC) Confucius was the founder of the philosophy which came to dominate Chinese life from AD 124 to 1906, and spread to Japan, Korea, and Vietnam.

Little is known of Confucius himself. The provenance of most of the texts associated with him is uncertain. They are written in the literary language, *wenyan*, a sort of elegant grammarless telegraphese full of ambiguities, so that the texts themselves have become dwarfed by accumulated exegesis; but these very uncertainties stimulated interpretations which were often in themselves valuable philosophical innovations.

At first sight, his work seems to be concerned mainly with moral self-cultivation. However, the premisses of this process of self-improvement are of some importance for political philosophy. They are: that knowledge is not knowledge until applied in action; that knowledge unrelated to values is vain; that self-fulfilment is possible only through participation in the public sphere; and that only the enlightened scholar can explain and predict the rise and fall of states, and the scholars are thus the repository of accumulated political wisdom and of social norms. In this theory of the rise and fall of power, only government by consent can create and sustain a strong state. The aim of the enlightened man should be to serve as a minister. In doing so, he represents not just himself, but the collective wisdom of the scholars who are in a sense the leaders of civil society. In this role the scholar-counsellor should be completely loyal, but loyalty does not mean subservience; faced with a ruler who decides to commit evil or folly, loyalty dictates that he should be opposed. If necessary, the enlightened man should retire, or in extreme cases accept martyrdom. Implicit in Confucius' philosophy is the assumption that human nature is perfectible; it is perfected through 'reciprocity'; justice will be responded to with justice, generosity with generosity. And this is the basis of political consent. Socialization begins in the home. A well-regulated family in which the child experiences affection, rational discipline, and mutual responsibility is the source of altruism. Regulation is through a hierarchy by generation, age and sex, headed by the paterfamilias. The greatest virtue is filial piety, which covers all the family relationships involved. This is still, in spite of revolution, a deep-rooted view in China: in an opinion poll in the 1980s, in which respondents were asked to rank certain social vices, a large majority named lack of filial piety as the worst misdemeanour. Society is the family writ large, and is based on similar hierarchical relations, but Confucius stressed that the senior in the relationship had responsibilities to the junior as great as the junior had to the senior. Only through the acceptance of the mutual ties of hierarchy do rights and obligations come into existence. These rights and obligations create the loyalties which held society together.

Confucius' philosophy was essentially secular. He occasionally deferred to Heaven as if personified, but this idea was never pursued, and he instructed his followers that, while as a social duty they should participate in religious ceremonies, they should 'keep the spirits at a distance'. No religious belief was required of his students. His acceptance of religious ceremonial illustrates his belief that ritual was a vital influence in sustaining society. Much of the Analects is concerned with the importance of the ritualization of behaviour, which imparts a sort of sanctity to social ties.

Several centuries of debate began from his teaching. The debate produced three main schools of thought. On the one hand, the Legalists asserted that human nature was incorrigibly selfish and therefore society could be sustained only by strict laws ruthlessly enforced. On the other hand, the Daoists insisted that human beings were naturally sociable, and that the intervention of authority could only deprave them. Confucians offered, at least by implication, a middle position: human nature was not perfect, but perfectible, and government was necessary because socialization could not be totally effective.

Confucius' theory was essentially anti-despotic, and although he proposed no specific institutional controls of despotism, the first emperor of reunited China, Chin Shu Huang Di (255 BC) took Confucianism seriously enough to attempt to destroy the Confucian texts and put the scholars to death, but his ruthless tyranny was destroyed within a generation by widespread rebellion, an event which thereafter was flourished by the Confucians as proof that consent was the necessary basis of government.

Mencius, in striking epigrams and vivid illustrations, launched Confucianism afresh. On the question of human nature, he asserted that human beings were instinctively good: 'when a child falls down a well, we do not ask ourselves whose child it is before we pull it out'. On government by consent he said, on the occasion of the assassination of the tyrant Zhou Wang: 'I did not hear that a king was murdered, only that a knave called Zhou was killed.'

The first ruler of the Han dynasty (202 BC–AD 220) made Confucianism the doctrine of the state, but this victory was somewhat hollow: the emperors, from claiming to be the supreme patrons of the sages, soon claimed to be the supreme sages. In the Sui dynasty (AD 581–618) the system of public examination was established as a means to recruit able officials. When the reigning emperor saw the first examinees assemble, he said: 'The heroes of the Empire have fallen within range of my bow.' Yet the moral authority of the Confucian officials was never wholly fraudulent. *See* CHINESE POLITICAL THOUGHT. JG

Congress (India) The Indian National Congress, which, as the foremost political party in India, led the national movement and took over power from the British in 1947, was formed in 1885. Initially a middle-class organization representing the interests of a growing number of educated Indians who wanted to play an increasing part in the governance of their country, it later became a mass organization under the leadership of *Gandhi and *Nehru. Always a centre party, Congress, influenced by Nehru, remained an ideological amalgam of nationalism, *Fabian socialism, and a commitment to modernization of the country's economy. Self-reliance was another theme pursued by Nehru that led India to follow *non-alignment as its foreign policy, and to pursue an economic policy based on import-substitution. The importance of the Congress to India's national movement, a strong leadership with a specific and well-articulated political agenda, and the ability to respond to opposition movements led to Indian politics being characterized as a one-party dominant system. Under the leadership of Nehru's daughter, Indira Gandhi, the Congress Party faced internal division and greater challenges from opposition parties, and responded with populist slogans and a centralized organization. Failure to deliver its promises led to growing popular discontent, to which the Congress government responded by imposing a state of Emergency, lasting from 1975 to 1977, when the fundamental rights of Indian citizens were suspended. The Congress lost the subsequent election after further breakaways, and in the face of an opposition united against the excesses of one-party rule.

Indira Gandhi returned to power at the head of a Congress government in 1980, but the party lacked the ideological and organizational coherence which had characterized its early years of rule under Nehru. The central government's manipulation of politics in the Punjab gave rise to a separatist movement, and the escalating violence led to the assassination of Indira Gandhi in 1984. Increasingly associated with government corruption, organizationally weak, with no clear political platform and a leadership that failed to resist the lure of the Gandhi dynasty (first calling on Rajiv and later on Sonia, his wife), the party has had to adjust to declining electoral fortunes and increased competition from both regional and identity based parties. The party returned to power in 2004 and increased its representation in the 2009 elections. Their administration, however, was plagued by corruption scandals and the party became increasingly unpopular as the economy slowed and inflation increased. In 2014, a resurgent and partisan Bharatiya Janata Party (BJP), under the leadership of Narendra Modi, swept to power with an overall majority in parliament, while Congress slumped to 44 seats, their worst ever parliamentary result.   SR

⊕ SEE WEB LINKS

• Congress Party site, with historical coverage, party constitution, and recent election manifestos.

Congress of People's Deputies (Russia) Directly elected lower tier of the Russian legislature during the transitional period of 1990–93 during which Russia evolved from a USSR Union Republic to independent statehood. The Congress of People's Deputies was elected as the assembly of the RSFSR in competitive elections in March 1990. It was extremely large, numbering 1,068 deputies and it was no standing parliament—Congress met only once or twice annually for several weeks or even just days. Nonetheless, the Russian constitution gave Congress

extensive powers. It could alter the constitution, or adopt a new one (Constitution Art. 104.1), determine the guidelines of foreign and domestic policy (Art. 104.2), and influence government composition (Art. 104.10). Congress delegated the power to adopt all normal legislation to a subset of 252 of its deputies who formed the Supreme Soviet, a smaller, bicameral standing parliament elected by Congress itself. With the exception of the Supreme Soviet members Congress deputies were part-time legislators. Parties played very little role in Congress. Once elected, deputies formed only weakly disciplined and volatile factions, most of which lacked links to parties outside parliament. To organize congressional business, deputies used a Soviet inheritance, the speaker and the presidium, an administrative organ chaired by the speaker.

The decisions taken by Russia's Congress of People's Deputies played a central role in shaping Russian politics during the decline and collapse of the USSR, and the first year of independent Russian statehood. Key Congress decisions included the declaration of sovereignty and the creation of the republic's executive presidency. Congressional opposition to the economic policies of Russia's first president, Boris Yeltsin, eventually precipitated a constitutional conflict that culminated in the shelling of Congress by the president, and the collapse of Russia's First Republic in October 1993. It was replaced by the *Federal Assembly.   PS

Congress (USA) The bicameral, national legislature of the United States. According to Article I, Section 1 of the Constitution, 'All legislative powers herein granted shall be vested in a Congress of the United States, which shall consist of a Senate and House of Representatives'. The Senate has a hundred members, two from each state, elected for six-year terms in two-year cycles of staggered elections under *first-past-the-post arrangements. First-past-the-post also applies in the election of 435 members of the House of Representatives. Representatives are elected to simultaneous two-year terms with the number of seats per state determined by the size of the population, although every state is entitled to at least one member. A redistribution of House seats occurs after each decennial census (*see* APPORTIONMENT), and, within the states, the determination of congressional boundaries is the responsibility of the state legislatures.

The House and the Senate are co-equal in status, but nevertheless different institutions. All bills must pass both houses and, since the passage of the Seventeenth Amendment in 1913, the members of both have been popularly elected (previously, senators were chosen by the state legislatures). The two-year term tends to tie members of the House of Representatives more closely to their constituents, whereas senators enjoy not only more independence, but also greater visibility. The larger membership of the House requires more formal organization than in the Senate, where a club-like atmosphere traditionally prevails. In financial matters, the House lays claim to superiority on the strength of Article I, Section 7 of the Constitution, which states that 'All Bills for raising Revenue shall originate in the House of Representatives'. Meanwhile, the Senate draws on its constitutional prerogatives in treaty-making to support assumptions of primacy in foreign affairs. Its role in confirming presidential appointments (especially to the judiciary) is likewise a source of its power.

The United States Congress is often characterized as the most powerful legislature in the world. It has, undoubtedly, lost ground to the executive branch in the twentieth century, but, as many recent Presidents would confirm, it is far from being reduced to the position of impotence that has befallen many of its counterparts elsewhere. There are three related phenomena that help to account for this: the Constitution, American political parties, and congressional committees.

In drawing up the Constitution the Founding Fathers were bent on ensuring that too much power did not fall into too few hands. Accordingly they devised a complex system of checks and balances which to this day provides for 'separated institutions sharing powers'. Modern Presidents are expected to lead in both foreign and domestic policy-making, but Congress, from which members of the executive branch are excluded, constitutes an awesome obstacle to the fulfilment of those responsibilities. The appointment of executive officials is subject to the 'Advice and Consent of the Senate'; every bill, every demand for revenue, and every request for expenditure must be approved by a body marked by a centrifugal distribution of power and notorious for its unwillingness to act as a mere 'rubber stamp'.

In parliamentary systems, it is possible for strong parties, with significant leaders and disciplinary means, to bring order to the legislature and thereby facilitate executive dominance. No such parties exist in the United States Congress. There are parties and party leaders, but the ability of the latter to control members is limited. Party loyalty in Congress is a most fragile commodity. The seniority system, which for a long time substituted for party as an organizing device, was seriously weakened by reforms of procedure after *Watergate.

The weakness of party helps to explain the potency of congressional committees, the great powerhouses of the national legislature in the United States. More than a century ago Woodrow Wilson noted that 'Congress in session is Congress on public exhibition, whilst Congress in its committee rooms is Congress at work'. This is no less true today. Debates on the floor of either chamber are rarely meaningful; the fate of legislative proposals is decided in specialist committees; it is here where the great issues are thrashed out, where the executive is called to account and where policy is made. In other systems committees are chaired by party loyalists and voting takes place along party lines, but congressional committees are institutions of a quite different order.   DM

⊕ SEE WEB LINKS
- US Senate website.
- US House of Representatives website.

Conseil Constitutionnel A body set up under the constitution of the French *Fifth Republic to ensure the regularity of elections and referenda and, in certain cases, to rule on the constitutionality of laws. There is no appeal from its decisions as the intention was to confine the legislature, formerly the repository of national sovereignty, within a new more limited role. Accordingly, the *Conseil* can rule on the constitutionality of parliamentary laws but executive actions are reserved for the *Conseil d'État*. Appointed for nine years and in equal proportions by the President of the Republic and the two parliamentary presidents, the *Conseil*

Constitutionnel acted at first to uphold executive supremacy. After 1974 President Giscard d'Estaing provided for more generous access by deputies and senators to the *Conseil*. This right was increasingly exercised through the 1980s by the parliamentary opposition, while successive administrations, Socialist and Conservative, have complained of 'government by judges'. In 1985 *Conseil Constitutionnel* ruled that the constitution was superior to parliamentary legislation. The government now finds itself subject to judicial constraints from an unexpected quarter, while parliament and opposition, much circumscribed by the constitution, have been quick to exploit their new privileges. IC

(⊕) SEE WEB LINKS
• Conseil Constitutionnel website (in French).

Conseil d'État The *Conseil d'État* is the highest administrative court in France with final jurisdiction over cases involving misuse of administrative power. Executive action is subject to its review, as is the conduct of the bureaucracy, and it may make recommendations on administrative reform. It must also be consulted in advance concerning certain types of legislation initiated by government for submission to parliament, while the government may seek advisory opinions. Individual citizens have access to the *Conseil d'État*, ensuring a degree of personal accountability for administrative acts and providing a check on the use or abuse of discretionary powers. Acts may be annulled where the administration has exceeded its powers or has not complied with formal procedures. Under the *Fifth Republic the Conseil d'État* has consciously acted to extend its judicial control to keep pace with the expansion of executive power: a reversal of its role under previous republics where it was more concerned to strengthen a weak executive. The *Conseil d'État* is among the leading *grands corps*, with its members serving the state at all levels and in the highest offices. IC

(⊕) SEE WEB LINKS
• *Conseil d'État* website (in French).

consensus Max *Weber defined consensus as existing when expectations about the behaviour of others are realistic because the others will usually accept these expectations

as valid for themselves, even without an explicit agreement. For *Marxists, consensus is a highly ideological concept used to perpetuate class rule by attempting to disguise the extent of conflict within society. The idea of consensus became associated with the debate about 'the end of ideology', and the supposed replacement of conflict about basic values and goals by harmony about the ends to be attained. In analyses of postwar politics in Britain and other Western countries, consensus came to be used to refer to cross-party agreement about procedures and constitutional conventions, but also about broad policy objectives such as the maintenance of a national health service and a welfare state, and the use of neo-Keynesian techniques of demand management to ensure full employment. D. Kavanagh and P. Morris define consensus in the sense that it was used in post-war British politics as 'a set of parameters which bounded the set of policy options regarded by senior politicians and civil servants as administratively practicable, economically affordable and politically acceptable'. Conflict between the parties was then confined to a few symbolic but highly charged issues such as *nationalization. Such broad agreement about objectives tended to make much policy-making a technical argument about incremental adjustments to existing policies, enhancing the opportunities open to *interest groups to exert influence within a generally agreed set of goals. Post-war consensus politics in Western polities reached its most highly developed form in the long-lasting post-war coalition of the two main parties in Austria (1945–66), and the shorter but politically significant 'Grand Coalition' in West Germany (1966–9). The grand coalition in Germany stimulated the emergence of an extraparliamentary opposition on the left and right made up of citizens who felt excluded from the dominant centrist consensus. In Britain, increasing economic difficulties in the 1970s called into question consensus politics based on funding increased public expenditure out of growth. Under Margaret Thatcher's leadership, the Conservative Party moved away from consensus politics to a conviction politics based on strongly held beliefs seen as distinct from those of the Labour Party which itself moved to the left. The 1990s saw a partial return to more consensual politics. Even during the Thatcher period, consensus about political procedures was largely maintained, and some measure of agreement about decision-making procedures is necessary if a polity is to survive as a working entity. WG

consent Acquiescence or agreement. More elaborately, the attachment of an agent's will to a proposal, action, or outcome, such that the agent accepts (some share of the) responsibility for the consequences and/or legitimizes an action or state of affairs which, in the absence of consent, would lack legitimacy or legality. For example, the difference between rape and ordinary sexual relations depends upon consent. Legal systems do not always allow consent to remove the illegality of an act, in the sense that the consent of the 'victim' will not always be treated as a defence. This may be because the law exhibits *paternalism, or because it is intending to enforce a moral code which sees particular acts as wrong irrespective of their consensual nature. The presence of consent has been an important test of political legitimacy in many theories, it being argued that the state or government would have no right to direct a person's behaviour unless that person's consent to be governed had been given. Consent conceptually embraces a wide range of attitudes, from grudging acquiescence to enthusiastic agreement. Arguments about the legitimizing force of consent need to accommodate this fact. When consent is given explicitly and expressly, its legitimizing force is at least plausible. Difficulties arise, however, when the presence or absence of consent has to be inferred from a person's actions (or inactions), because that explicitness is absent. Is anything short of active dissent to be construed as tacit consent? *Locke recognized this problem, although the answer he provided to it has not been regarded as satisfactory. He distinguished between express consent and tacit consent. A person gave tacit consent by behaving (or failing to behave) in particular ways. Since the giving of consent has been taken to have these important consequences for responsibility and legitimacy, attention has naturally focused on the circumstances in which consent is given: for example, are those circumstances free from coercion or improper

influence? Does the agent have a genuine choice? Is the consent given by a person with adequate knowledge of what his or her decision involves? This last question has produced the notion of informed consent: that is, consent given by a person who has the information required to give meaning to the attachment of his or her will to the proposal, action, or outcome. Clearly, a person with incomplete or inadequate knowledge might consent enthusiastically to a proposal that would be rejected if that person had a fuller understanding of what was involved. Because of the connection between consent and the conferral of legitimacy, both the state of mind and the maturity of the agent have to be considered. For example, contracts entered into under undue stress might be considered voidable; children are debarred from consenting to many proposals because they are considered to lack the necessary decision-making competence. Many attempts have been made to refine our understanding of consent, leading to further distinctions between actual and hypothetical consent, between prospective and retrospective consent, and between strong and weak consent. AR

consequentialism In ethics, consequentialist doctrines are those which judge actions by their effects (or, sometimes, their intended effects) rather than by their conformance to rules, rights, or obligations. Consequentialist ethics are normally contrasted with deontological moral arguments (from the Greek *deontos*, meaning duty), which have been the overwhelmingly predominant form of moral judgements for most of human history. The most important tradition of consequentialist ethics is *utilitarianism. LA

conservation Political action or belief which seeks to keep something in being. Etymologically, there is no significant difference between conserving something and preserving it in any of the languages which contain these two verbs. In Victorian England those who favoured what would now be called conservation tended to refer to the 'preservation' of the things they regarded as important (footpaths, ancient buildings, or species, for example) and what is now the Council for the Protection of Rural England was founded in 1926 with the word 'preservation' in its title instead of 'protection'.

However, an important nuance has come to distinguish conservation from preservation: conservation accepts that you cannot literally keep things as they are, but only manage change to preserve what is valuable. Thus conserving a forest does not just mean preventing anyone from chopping down the trees, it means planting new trees and even new types of tree if that is what is needed in order to maintain a healthy forest.   LA

conservatism In general terms, a political philosophy which aspires to the preservation of what is thought to be the best in established society, and opposes radical change. However, it is much easier to locate the historical context in which conservatism evolved than it is to specify what it is that conservatives believe. Modern European conservatism evolved in the period between 1750 and 1850 as a response to the rapid series of changes and prospects for change which convulsed European societies; these included the ideas of the *Enlightenment, the *French Revolution, industrialization (especially in England), and the demands for an extended or universal, generally male, suffrage. The name 'Conservative' for the English political party which had previously been called the Tory Party became established during the debate about electoral reform which led to the Reform Act of 1832.

The nature of conservative reactions to change has varied considerably. Sometimes it has been outright opposition, based on an existing model of society that is considered right for all time. It can take a 'reactionary' form, harking back to, and attempting to reconstruct, forms of society which existed in an earlier period. Other forms of conservatism acknowledge no perpetually preferable form of society but are principally concerned with the nature of change, insisting that it can only be gradual in pace and evolutionary in style. Perhaps the most unifying feature of conservatism has been an opposition to certain kinds of justification for change, particularly those which are idealistic, justified by 'abstract' ideas, and not a development of existing practices.

It is clear that, ideologically, conservatism can take many different forms. Liberal individualists, as well as clerical monarchists, nostalgic reactionaries, and unprincipled realists, have all been called 'conservatives', regarded themselves as conservative, and demonstrated the typically conservative responses to projects for change. Particular conservative writers have founded their conservatism on individualism as often as on collectivism, on atheism as much as on religious belief, and on the idealistic philosophy of *Hegel as well as on profound scepticism or vulgar materialism. Furthermore conservatism has been primarily a political reaction, and only secondarily a body of ideas: those who are defending their interests against projects for change often have little interest in philosophical ideas or treat them on the basis of 'any port in a storm'.

A further complication is that many people might be properly described as conservatives who would not describe themselves as such. A principal reason for this is that the image of conservatism in much of continental Europe became tainted, during the first half of the twentieth century, first by association with a defunct clerical-monarchist outlook and later by alliance with fascist and National Socialist movements. Thus, although the word 'conservatism' exists in French, German, and Italian, the number of prominent intellectuals and politicians who have described themselves as 'conservative' since 1945 is extremely small. When a 'Conservative' group existed in the European Parliament between 1989 and 1992, it had only English and Danish members. In some respects, other political movements, especially *Christian Democracy, have become forms of conservatism 'that durst not speak its name', but even Christian Democracy is quite distinct from conservatism in its origins and principles.

*Burke's *Reflections on the Revolution in France* has been taken as definitive and formative of modern conservatism, with its opposition to radical reform based on abstract principles and its pleas for the virtues, often hidden, of established, evolved institutions. But Burke himself was not a conservative. Not only did his literary and political careers precede the existence of conservatism, but he was a Whig with reformist and protoliberal views on the principal issues of the day, including India,

Ireland, America, and Parliament. Until the 1920s he was claimed and cited as often by Liberals as by Conservatives. There is every reason to suppose he would have opposed 'Conservatism' when it emerged in 1832.

Much theoretical commentary on conservatism has contributed to the inherent confusion of the subject by starting with false assumptions. Often, the commentators are not merely hostile, but contemptuous, in the tradition of J. S. *Mill's comment that the Conservative Party was, 'by the law of their existence the stupidest party'. The assumption has been that conservative ideas are essentially flawed as well as being chosen for their political utility rather than their theoretical coherence. Alternatively, a spurious theoretical unity is attributed to conservatism, so that all conservatives are thought to believe in psychological pessimism, or the *organic nature of society, or the importance of national traditions. Nor have many of the taxonomies of conservatism— for example, between 'high' and 'low', 'wet' and 'dry', 'true' and 'neo', 'old' and 'new', Tory and Conservative—afforded much insight, the distinctions having been made in too many different and contradictory ways without any one version establishing itself. A further source of unclarity is the common resort to a confused notion of a political 'spectrum' or 'continuum' which suggests that to be deeply conservative is to be on the 'extreme right', along with (mysteriously) divine right monarchists, libertarian anarchists, and National Socialists.

*Mannheim, faced with the considerable differences between Continental and English traditions of conservatism, concluded that the drive behind conservatism was a 'universal psychic inclination' towards traditionalism, the doctrinal form that expressed this inclination differing between contexts. But he does detect a common negative strand to all conservatism, a critical response to 'natural law thinking'. Conservative ideas are, thus, more genuine and profound than many critics suggest, but such unity as they have is purely negative, definable only by its opposition and rejection of abstract, universal, and ideal principles and the projects which follow from them.

This analysis of conservatism, as having only a negative doctrinal unity that allows for a vast range of positive doctrines, would seem to be the least misleading picture of what conservatism is as a general political phenomenon. It generates an intellectual method that can be described as a sceptical reductionism, which demands, of grand proposals and principles, 'Is it really a good idea, given local conditions?' This kind of questioning is common to Edmund Burke, Benjamin Disraeli, Lord Salisbury, Michael *Oakeshott, and Margaret Thatcher; it may well be all that they have in common as conservatives.

Thus conservative reformism is quite central to the conservative tradition, rather than aberrant or peripheral. The idea of radical conservatism is less easy to accept. In so far as radicalism is interpreted according to its original meaning, which suggests that radicals propose a systematic replacement of institutions and practices, from the roots up, then radical conservatism is a contradiction in terms. It is more acceptable at a less literal level as meaning a belief, in a particular context, that drastic, immediate change is required to preserve the underlying virtues of the system. For example, the belief that a severe combination of reductions in public expenditure, the privatization of services, and high unemployment was necessary to preserve the underlying vitality of the capitalist system, might fall into this category. However, an extreme belief in 'free' markets and a minimal state of a kind which has never existed, or existed only in the distant past, could not properly be called conservatism at all.

In the nineteenth century conservatism was preoccupied with what might reasonably be called the liberal agenda of extended rights. To different degrees in different contexts it won or lost these struggles or simply took over what had been its opponents' policies in earlier periods. Nineteenth-century conservatism appears more successful when judged as a procedural doctrine preoccupied with the nature of change, than as a substantive doctrine concerned with the value of particular social forms. In the twentieth century conservatism has been so preoccupied with the struggle against forms of socialism that many people have made the mistake of identifying conservatism purely with anti-socialism. If this perception were correct then the demise of socialism would also be the demise of conservatism. But in fact there is never any shortage of the kind of belief to which conservatism is inherently opposed. We can be assured that forms of feminism, ecologism, radical democratic theory, and human rights doctrines will, *inter alia*, continue to provide the kind of political projects which serve as both opposition and stimulus to conservatism. LA

Conservative Party The British Conservative Party is often said to have origins which are 'lost in the mists of history'. Samuel Beer traces a lineage back to the supporters of the Tudor court in the sixteenth century. Less tendentiously, there is an unbroken descent from the parliamentary *Tories of the late seventeenth century whose original defining belief was Stuart legitimism, but whose *raison d'être* under the Hanoverian monarchy of the eighteenth century became opposition to the ideas and entrenched power of the *Whig oligarchy. Only in the nineteenth century did Tories become (also) Conservatives, the name being used in the debate about electoral change which culminated in the Reform Act of 1832. 'Conservative' was accepted as a self-description by one of the most prominent Tories, Sir Robert Peel, in the statement known as the Tamworth Manifesto in 1834. The reform debate also brought into being the first real extraparliamentary Conservative institution, the Carlton Club, which was founded in 1831.

The second Reform Act of 1867, which doubled the electorate, proved the stimulus for the creation of a national, extraparliamentary Conservative Party. The parliamentary Conservative Party responded by creating a National Union of Conservative Associations, a 'handmaid' of the Party as one of its founders (H. C. Raikes, MP) was to describe it. The principal purpose of the National Union was to bring a local party association into being in every constituency. In 1870 Conservative Central Office was founded as a body of professional party workers to coordinate the essentially volunteer army of supporters in the constituencies. Thus a modern party was brought into being with great rapidity as an extension of an ancient parliamentary faction and in response to the challenge of a mass electorate. Further reform was stimulated by the heavy electoral defeat by the Liberals in 1905–6 and a Chairman of the Party Organization was appointed in 1911.

The Conservative Party is one of the oldest political parties in the world and also one of the most successful, having held office, usually as sole governing party, for more than half of the period of its existence. The secret of its success largely consists of the loyalty with which constituency associations, who provide much of its resources and whose ultimate autonomy is very great, have been prepared to support both their elected member and their party leader, sometimes studiously ignoring the differences between the two. This support has been possible because the party is, in many respects, the least politicized of political parties, capable of subordinating argument and factionalism to an overwhelming desire to keep opposing parties out of office. Thus, although the party has always contained factions, including, in the late twentieth century, 'wets' (in favour of selective state intervention in the economy) and 'dries' (supporters of Margaret Thatcher's project to 'roll back the state') as well as pro- and anti-Europeans, it has not experienced a serious split since the Corn Law controversies of the 1840s. Even so, during its time out of office in 1997–2010 Conservatives could be forgiven for feeling some nostalgia for a clear socialist opponent which had proved capable of uniting them in hostility whereas such issues as global warming, European integration, and human rights continued to divide them.

However, the Conservatives returned to government in 2010 as the major party in a coalition with the Liberal Democrats (which restricted some of their more radical policy objectives) and after 2015 as a Conservative administration, following a successful general election campaign under the leadership of David Cameron. Nevertheless, the longevity of Cameron's leadership was cut short by his willingness to appease *back-benchers and hold a UK referendum as to whether the UK should 'remain' in or 'leave' the *European Union. The result of the referendum, known as *Brexit, was a slim majority to leave the European Union, which forced the resignation of Cameron as Prime Minister. He was quickly replaced with Theresa May as Prime Minister. LA

(⊕) SEE WEB LINKS

• Conservative Party website.

consociational democracy Term developed by the Dutch political scientist Arend Lijphart to explain the mechanisms of political stability in societies with deep social cleavages. Through government by an elite cartel, a democracy with a fragmented political culture was stabilized, e.g. Austria, Belgium, the Netherlands. The settlement in *Northern Ireland could be regarded as essentially consociational. *See also* PILLARIZATION. WG

constituency Area whose electorate returns a representative to a national parliament, or other elected legislature or assembly. There are 646 serving the United Kingdom House of Commons, their number and dimensions continually subject to reform under the House of Commons (Redistribution of Seats) Act. The functional equivalent is a 'district' in (for instance) the United States, and a 'riding' in Canada. 'Constituency' may be taken to mean more broadly the support which a politician appeals to or seeks. The amount of constituency representation, the roles performed, and the reasons for providing constituency representation have become a major focus for research. *See also* APPORTIONMENT. JBr

constitution The set of fundamental rules governing the politics of a nation or subnational body. The word was first used in this sense after the 'Glorious Revolution' of 1688 in Britain, when the deposed king, James II, was accused of having violated the 'fundamental constitution of the kingdom'. But though the word in this sense is a British invention, it is much harder to determine what the British constitution actually is than that of almost anywhere else.

A typical constitution is written, short, general, and entrenched. The oldest and (except from 1861 to 1865) most successful constitution in the world, that of the United States, illustrates all these points. It was written at a Constitutional Convention in 1787 and ratified by all the existing states except Rhode Island. The US Constitution and all its subsequent amendments run to only around 8,000 words. It contains no rules about what must be done, except procedural rules governing the election of Presidents and Congress and the nomination of Supreme Court justices and other senior officials. It contains many rules about what Congress,

the executive, and (since the Civil War) the states may not do. And it contains the rules for its own amendment: proposals must emanate from either two-thirds of each house of Congress, or a convention called at the request of two-thirds of the state legislatures, and to succeed they must be ratified by three-quarters of the states.

Most other written constitutions are longer than that of the United States, and they often contain particular rules (a popular example being clauses like 'The national anthem is the *Marseillaise*' from the constitution of the French Fifth Republic, Title 1, Article 2). But they all entrench themselves by making themselves more difficult to amend than ordinary laws. Many go beyond the procedural rights guaranteed in the US Constitution to guarantee substantive rights as well: for instance, 'Every individual has the duty to work and the right to employment' (France); 'Citizens of the USSR have the right to rest and leisure' (USSR constitution of 1977). They are typically less forthcoming about how the citizen who feels deprived of these rights may seek redress.

Given the tradition of *parliamentary sovereignty, how can it be said that a British constitution exists? As it is a fundamental idea of parliamentary sovereignty that Parliament can do anything except bind its successor, it follows that anything which purports to be a constitutional guarantee enshrined in a British Act of Parliament could simply be amended by a later parliament. Thus for instance the five-year maximum term of a parliament is set by the Parliament Act 1911, but if a parliament which was near the end of its term decided that it would rather not face a general election, there would be no legal impediment to its simply repealing the 1911 Act, so long as both houses agreed. When commentators state that the British constitution is unwritten, they are expressing the nature of entrenchment in Britain in a very misleading way by saying that there is an unwritten understanding that no parliament would actually do that. But unwritten understandings are not always understood until somebody writes them down (and not necessarily then). Those who argue that Britain ought to have a written constitution claim that some of the supposed unwritten understandings have ceased to be understood, pointing in particular to the decline of *collective responsibility and claiming that the British executive treats the legislature increasingly arrogantly and unaccountably. Those opposed to a written constitution argue that decisions on constitutional matters ought not to be transferred from elected politicians to unelected lawyers.

constitutional law (UK) The set of rules that define the distribution of governmental power; the study of those rules. The term is not to be found defined in a statute book and it has not been the subject of exact judicial definition in any case decided by the courts. No special pre-eminence is given to constitutional law largely due to the absence of a written *constitution for the United Kingdom. John Austin, whose opinion on sovereignty in English law has been influential, identified constitutional law as extremely simple 'for it merely determines the person who shall bear the sovereignty'. In modern usage this view is too narrow. The law relating to Parliament, the executive, including cabinet government, and the judiciary are relevant to constitutional law today.

In the absence of a written constitution in the United Kingdom, constitutional law is not primarily the concern of the courts. Parliament and its privileges, and the scope and extent of *prerogative powers, all fit for convenience into the general description of constitutional law. As F. W. Maitland observed, constitutional law has 'no special sanctity'. Thus demarcation lines between what is and what is not constitutional law are extremely difficult. Definition appears to be a matter of convenience. Constitutional law is sufficiently broad and flexible to refer to the structure and the broad rules, whether or not enforceable by the courts, that describe how power is exercised by government.

Rigid classification of English law is inappropriate to its understanding compared to other European countries where law is codified. A. V. Dicey claimed that three guiding principles were apparent. First, the legislative sovereignty of Parliament, second, the 'universal rule or supremacy throughout the constitution of ordinary law', and thirdly, the dependence in the last resort on unwritten conventions as part of the law of the constitution. This last may be regarded as a 'more doubtful and speculative

ground' to advance a definition. The inclusion of conventions refers to the unwritten but no less important 'morality of the constitution'. For example, the doctrine of ministerial responsibility for the decisions of a government department provides that ministers may be held accountable to Parliament. However, today ministerial resignation appears more a matter of political expediency rather than constitutional propriety.

Constitutional law might have been codified if *Bentham's Constitutional Code had been adopted in the nineteenth century. More recently, codification has come closer with the constitutional changes introduced by the Labour governments of 1997 and 2001, the most important of these being the incorporation of the European Convention on Human Rights into UK law. JM

constructivism A philosophical term used in both epistemological debates and theoretical mathematics. In regard to epistemology, constructivism is a theory which asserts that human knowledge and understanding are constructed through social institutions and practices. The implication is that knowledge of the material world becomes reality not through the discovery of objective truths or facts, but through intersubjective socialization and constructed understanding. In this regard, any theoretical reliance on claims of objective reality or knowledge is questioned by many constructivists. They maintain that political claims to universal objective truth cannot be grounded through independent knowledge, but through individual interpretation and social intersubjectivity. In this regard, humans not only interpret, construct, and invent their knowledge of the material world, but also allow this constructed perception to influence their political actions and social thinking at both the normative and political level. *See also* EPISTEMOLOGY.

containment First articulated by President Truman in 1947, containment involved maintaining the US military presence around the world, as well as supporting 'friendly' regimes economically and militarily. It was the foreign policy of the United States during the Cold War, aimed at preventing Soviet expansion. *See also* TRUMAN DOCTRINE.

context The circumstances surrounding an event, usually the writing or publication of a book. Amongst such circumstances, contemporary political and intellectual debates are often seen as especially important. Knowledge of the context of intellectual production may help to explain what an author was trying to achieve, and the meaning of what was produced, but this is a disputed matter in the study of the history of ideas. 'Contextualism' is associated in the United Kingdom with political philosophers in Cambridge (*see* HERMENEUTICS), while the rival approach of confining oneself to the analysis of the arguments of the text is associated with political philosophers in Oxford. Intelligent discussion of political theory requires both.   AR

continuous revolution A phrase especially associated with *Mao Zedong. In 1958 Mao, in an intra-Party document, criticized Stalin and the Soviet party for having allowed the Soviet Union to drift into a state in which the institutions hastily created to bring the resources of society under communist control had been accepted as having permanent and universal validity. This was the consequence of a centralized command structure which suppressed political activity, and it was given ideological expression in Stalin's assertion that there were no contradictions in socialist society. Mao argued that the nationalization of industry and commerce and the collectivization of agriculture represented only the first step to socialism; the assumption of ownership and control achieved no more than the opportunity to transform the relations of production; hence his apparently perverse accusation that those of his fellow leaders who were content to operate the state sector by management methods inherited from capitalism were 'following the capitalist road'. The same applied to the Soviet-inspired use of state tractor stations to control the management of agriculture.

At the theoretical level, Mao insisted that dialectical materialism applied as much to socialist society as to the capitalist phase. Contradictions continued to exist, and were indeed the driving force—the only driving force—of progress towards a truly and effectively socialist system. He expressed this idea in his speech 'How to Handle Contradictions Among the People'. The rectification movement of 1957, in which Mao widened the Hundred Flowers policy of permitting debate in scientific and academic affairs to include political criticism; the *Great Leap, which sought to encourage full popular participation in the development process; and the *Cultural Revolution, which was intended to open a dialogue on the basic issues of socialism, are all illustrations of his belief that revolution must be continuous, that if it is not going forward it is going backwards. The idea of continuous revolution implied that the function of the Communist Party was not to staff an authoritarian bureaucracy, but to enable and guarantee a process of development which gave a Marxist form to popular aspirations and to supervise a continuous process of change. Mao's continuous revolution should be distinguished from *Trotsky's 'permanent revolution', which was concerned with the situation before, not after, the achievement of socialist power, advocating that social democrats should not, following the bourgeois revolution, relax in the drive to achieve the social revolution.   JG

continuous variable In *quantitative research there are two broad types of variable: *discrete and continuous. A continuous variable is one for which a subject or observation takes a value from an interval of real numbers. For example, if age can be measured precisely enough it takes any value from 0 upwards.   SF

contract An agreement made between two or more persons to secure a result which each intends should benefit him or her. Although every participant anticipates a gain, it does not follow that each will benefit to an equal amount; indeed, one or more may lose in the event. Legal systems and their students are concerned with questions like: Which contracts should be legally enforceable? Should contracts be enforced by requiring that they be carried out, or by assessing compensation due to the aggrieved party if they are not? What is the proper way to analyse a contract—as a pair of promises, as an offer coupled with an acceptance, as a promise given for a reasonable consideration? Contracts are also of importance in exemplifying the relation between rights and duties, which seems particularly symmetrical in the case of consensual contract. Each party acquires duties and rights as a result of the contract, and one person's right has a clear relation with other persons' duties. An important political application has been the *social contract, under which the state, the political community, or legitimate authority is seen as the consequence of a contract drawn up to secure that result. The idea of a social contract has been criticized for historical inadequacy, and for misconceiving the relation between individuals and society or the state. Nevertheless, the contractarian tradition still flourishes in political theory. For example, John *Rawls, in *A Theory of Justice*, has asked what individuals in specified conditions would hypothetically agree to, what sort of contract they would accept, if they were trying to agree on critical standards of justice—although whether this approach is illuminating is disputed. AR

contradiction Term adapted from its ordinary meaning by *Hegel and *Marx to refer to dialectical conflicts in history and society. According to Marxist theory, contradiction is a tenet of dialectical reasoning rather than a logical error. Contradiction is held to be present in all phenomena and to be the principal reason for their motion and development. In *Dialectics of Nature*, *Engels presents examples from both natural science and mathematics intended to defend this proposition. However, the doctrine of contradiction as the main source of development is most easily understood with respect to society. Marx and Engels argued in the *Manifesto of the Communist Party* that, 'the history of society is the history of class struggle'. Social classes, particularly bourgeois and proletarians under capitalism, found themselves with contradictory interests, and their interaction produced not only historical but social transformation. Marx and Engels predicted the victory of proletarians and the eventual abolition of class relations. Given the ubiquity of contradictions, Soviet ideologists were faced with initial difficulty in characterizing social relations under socialism. They resolved the problem by developing the notion of antagonistic and non-antagonistic contradictions; thus, unlike bourgeois and proletarians under capitalism, workers and peasants in the Soviet Union did not have antagonistically contradictory interests, merely non-antagonistically contradictory ones. swh

Convention 1. A meeting of persons with a common concern or purpose, for example the intention to create a constitution. *See also* PARTY CONVENTION.

2. A shared practice, or a practice widely followed, usually in the absence of any written prescription and sometimes without the backing of (formal) sanctions. Conventions governing property and government were especially important in the writings of *Hume, for whom they provided an alternative explanation of political institutions to the (for him) discredited theory of a *social contract. Conventions have also been important to *anarchist writers as examples of social cooperation in the absence of centralized coercion. The unwritten 'constitution' of the United Kingdom is often described as conventional, meaning that it is thought appropriate to do what has been done before. Here it is not so much that a practice is widely followed (as there may be few examples of a particular situation having arisen) as that there is a general inclination to follow alleged precedents. Because of the possibilities of uncoerced social cooperation apparently offered by conventions, the dynamics of their emergence have attracted sociological and philosophical attention. *See also* NATURE. AR

cooperative movement The idea of replacing economic competition by the mutual cooperation of producers and/or consumers was central to the nineteenth-century socialist tradition, particularly Robert *Owen and his followers. In principle all economic activities related to the processes of production, distribution, and exchange might be included in a scheme for a 'Co-operative Commonwealth', implying the total abolition of capitalist industrial ownership and management, and the establishment of a network of voluntary associations owned and run by groups of workers or (in the case of consumer cooperatives) by consumers. It is one of the key principles of economic cooperation that net earnings are redistributed directly (usually on an annual basis) to the 'members' of the association or undertaking, and do not serve as profit for a separate group of owners or investors. In practice, cooperatives of many kinds have emerged and flourished across the world: in farming, industry, and the service sector, and in the form of consumer societies and housing associations. Cooperatives have been more common and in many respects more successful in capitalist societies (including the United States) than under systems of socialist economic planning. Yet for many democratic socialists and anarchists the cooperative principle, linked to the ideal of *workers' control, remains an important starting point for building a vision of an alternative society to both capitalism and state socialism.   KT

Copenhagen School The Copenhagen School represents one of the most sustained and influential attempts by *constructivists and *critical security studies to analyse how language can shape and impact real-world security issues through its central concept of *securitization. The key Copenhagen School scholars include Barry Buzan, whose influential work broadened security to include five sectors: the political, military, societal, economic, and environmental; Ole Weaver, who developed the concept of securitization; and Jaap de Wilde. The framework they developed offers a means of analysing the process by which something becomes a security issue and in turn how politics therefore tries to solve it. The Copenhagen School envisions a spectrum on which issues can exist—ranging from the non-political, through the political, where issues are dealt with as part of the ordinary policy process—up into the security realm, where issues represent an existential threat requiring emergency measures and justifying responses outside the normal bounds of the political procedure. What is important for the Copenhagen School is looking at the process; namely, how something is raised up to the security sphere, who has power to do it, and what makes them special, and under what conditions it can be achieved. This is the main focus of the Copenhagen School as it uses language theory to characterize securitization as a 'speech act'. That is, when the word 'security' is communicated—through spoken or written text—it is not merely a description or statement of reality, but a means by which reality is constructed. It is an action that seeks to label an issue as being

something special and in doing so moves it out of the political sphere and places it in the extraordinary security realm.

The Copenhagen School outlines the conditions required to make this process of securitization a success, which do not necessarily have to be real but are presented as being so. First an issue must be presented as an existential threat—a threat to the existence of something valued. This is aided if it can be tied into an issue that is already seen as being a security concern. Second, those making the speech act must be recognized as having the authority to do so, whether because of the position they hold or because they are recognized as being especially knowledgeable on the issue. The Copenhagen School therefore focuses on analysing the declarations made by political elites and examining how they control and utilize an issue. Finally, the securitization must be accepted by an audience—media, other political elites, or broad population support—whose recognition makes an issue a security concern.

There is also recognition that not all pressing issues should be securitized. By raising it up into the security sphere, it can create heightened pressure to deal with the problem urgently. This gives power holders enormous opportunity to exploit the threat for political gain as ordinary legal and democratic avenues are silenced in order to deal with the problem as quickly as possible. Also, once in the security sphere there is a tendency to tackle issues through traditional militarized means, which can be unsuitable. Therefore there is also a need for 'de-securitization'—the process by which a topic is transferred from the security agenda and placed in the political arena where normal democratic procedures can be utilized to address them.   RB

corporation A group of people legally authorized to act as if it were a single person. Once such a group with a common purpose is incorporated, whether by royal charter (the Hudson's Bay Company (1670), or the British Broadcasting Corporation (1926), or under successive facilitatory Companies Acts of the kind passed in Anglo-Saxon legal systems since the middle of the nineteenth century, it has legal personality. This means that it can sue and be sued in the courts as though it were an individual. Under British law an office held by an individual may also be corporate in character, to allow distinction in law between, for example, the Crown and the reigning monarch. There are in addition some bodies, notably trade unions and *quangos, which have from time to time enjoyed effective corporate status under different legal instruments. Together these form the chief institutions of mediation between individual and state under *corporatism. In Britain the term is now much less frequently used than in the past to refer to local government authorities—perhaps in recognition of their diminished autonomy—and has therefore become virtually synonymous with the incorporated business firm or company. Originally devised in early modern Europe chiefly to permit provision of utilities or services of a clearly public character (banking, insurance, the defence of a trade route, or consular and diplomatic services), incorporation is now almost universally linked to the principle of limited liability of shareholders and is resorted to for the whole range of enterprises undertaken for profit, whether or not they have strong public implications. CJ

corporatism The central core of corporatism is the notion of a system of interest intermediation linking producer interests and the state, in which explicitly recognized interest organizations are incorporated into the policy-making process, both in terms of the negotiation of policy and of securing compliance from their members with the agreed policy. However, one of the characteristics of the debate in the social sciences from the mid-1970s onwards about corporatism was the failure of the participants to agree about the meaning of the term. There was agreement that the area being studied was that of relations between organized interests and the state. There was some agreement that the discussion was particularly concerned with interests that arose from the division of labour in society, and particularly attempts to reconcile conflicts between capital and labour. However, while some analysts insisted that corporatist arrangements had to be tripartite, involving the state, organized employers, and organized labour, others insisted that they could be bipartite between the state and one of the other 'social partners', or between the 'social partners'

themselves. There was a measure of agreement that whereas conventional *pressure groups made representations about the content of public policy, corporatism involved a mixture of representation and control. In return for being involved in the formulation of public policy, corporatist interest groups were expected to assist in its implementation. This was sometimes captured through the idea of 'intermediation' which some analysts saw as central to the idea of corporatism (A. Cawson), although others doubted whether intermediation was unique to corporatism and therefore could be regarded as its distinguishing feature.

Although the modern debate started in the mid-1970s, the idea of corporatism has a long history. Guilds or corporations were important institutions in medieval life, but attracted little attention from political theorists. Conscious reflection about the potential prescriptive value of corporatist arrangements really started in the last quarter of the nineteenth century. In the papal encyclical *Rerum Novarum* (1891), Leo XIII tackled the problems of the poverty of the working classes, the development of trade unions, and the prevalent 'spirit of revolutionary change'. It was argued that class conflict was not inevitable, but that capital and labour were mutually dependent. Noting the general growth of associative action, Leo XIII argued that problems such as working conditions and health and safety could be dealt with by specially established organizations or boards, with the state sanctioning and protecting such arrangements. The object of proceeding in this way was 'in order to supersede undue interference on the part of the State'. This concern with limiting direct state intervention, and finding alternative forms of state-sanctioned associative action, has remained a central theme of the corporatist debate. The association between corporatism and Catholic social theory has also remained a strong one.

After the First World War, the idea of corporatism was taken up by the radical right, in particular by Mussolini, who placed it at the centre of the fascist regime in Italy. As a consequence, corporatism suffered from guilt by association. It came to be regarded as a synonym for fascism and disappeared from most political discussion, although it survived in Spain and especially Portugal.

There was, nevertheless, an alternative liberal version of corporatism which was clearly distinct from the surviving remnants of authoritarian corporatism. Samuel Beer made use of the term in his *Modern British Politics* (1965), forecasting that 'The further development of corporatism is surely to be expected'. Andrew Shonfield's *Modern Capitalism*, published in the same year and one of the most influential mid-century works on political economy, discussed the concept in terms of a corporatist management of economic planning in which the main interest groups were brought together to conclude bargains about their future behaviour.

The index entry for 'corporatism' in Shonfield's book reads 'see also Fascism', and it was the objective of the new generation of neocorporatist writers, led by Philippe Schmitter, to strip corporatism of its fascist associations, and to reinvent the concept as a means of analysing observable changes in a number of Western democracies. In 1974, Schmitter published *Still the Century of Corporatism?*, the title referring to Mihail Manoilesco's 1934 prediction that, just as the nineteenth century was that of liberalism, the twentieth century would be that of corporatism. Schmitter wished to escape from what he saw as an unhelpful dominance of pluralist analysis in American political science.

Schmitter triggered off an academic 'growth industry' on corporatism. In part, this was because it helped the understanding of long-term political phenomena such as the social pacts in Sweden and Switzerland, or the Parity Commission in Austria. Corporatism's appeal was wider, however, than explaining the politics of some of the more prosperous smaller European democracies where it was always difficult to decide whether corporatism promoted prosperity, or prosperity made corporatism possible because everyone came away from the bargaining table with something. Modern neocorporatism can best be understood as part of the breakdown of neo-Keynesianism. In the post-war period, Western governments had attempted to maintain full employment through techniques of aggregate demand management. This had, however, led to inflationary pressures, which became much worse after the first oil shock in 1973. Hence, governments increasingly turned to incomes policies as a means of restraining inflation while maintaining a demand management policy. This inevitably led them into agreements with the large producer groups, even in countries like Britain which had a predisposition for liberal solutions to economic problems. In particular, the unions were often offered concessions on social issues (employment law, taxation, social benefits) in return for agreeing to assist in the restraint of wage increases. The organized employers were also brought into the bargaining picture, in part because their assistance might be required in relation to price restraint, but also to act as a counterweight to the unions. The link between incomes policy and corporatism is illustrated in a study by Helander of the development of incomes policy in Finland which required the creation of new institutions and alterations in the functions of some existing ones. The Finnish political system changed into a two-tier one with parliamentary and corporatist subsystems.

Although the debate on corporatism produced a considerable volume of research output, it is often regarded as flawed for a number of reasons. First, there was the failure to agree on what was actually being discussed. Second, although corporatism claimed to be distinct from pluralism, it shared many of pluralism's assumptions, and could be presented by its opponents as little more than a subtype of pluralism. Third, the debate really developed just as the phenomena it was examining became less central to the political process. More liberal solutions to problems of economic policy became favoured in a number of European countries in the 1980s as social democratic parties lost power. Moreover the focus of debate moved away from the politics of production to the politics of collective consumption, as issues such as environmental problems moved higher up the political agenda. They are less amenable to corporatist solutions, and the relevance of a modernist concept like corporatism to more *post-modernist forms of politics is open to question. Fourth, the debate was characterized by a failure to separate analysis and prescription. Many, although not all, of the writers on corporatism were either openly (C. Crouch) or covertly sympathetic to its use as a means of providing a 'middle way' that would satisfy the legitimate aspirations of organized labour whilst maintaining a capitalist mode of production. Corporatism was often defended in terms of its effectiveness in securing desired economic goals (high growth, low inflation, low unemployment), but there was a recognition that it could have undesirable political consequences. It lacked *legitimacy as a mode of governance, emphasizing functional rather than territorial representation. It tended to bypass legislatures by creating new unelected bodies, such as economic councils of various kinds, and while it included some interests, it excluded others (smaller businesses, consumers). Fifth, as the debate developed in the 1980s, it focused increasingly on examples of sectoral or meso corporatism rather than at the macro level. Although many examples of corporatism were uncovered in particular policy areas (such as training policy and many areas of agricultural policy), the explanatory value of corporatism as a model of the polity as a whole was thereby diminished. Sixth, corporatism depended on autonomous domestic politics and was therefore undermined by the onset of *globalization.

Schmitter's article made a clear distinction between societal corporatism to be found in countries such as Sweden, Switzerland, and the Netherlands, and state corporatism to be found in countries such as Spain, Portugal, and Mexico, as well as Fascist Italy and Pétinist France. Much of the subsequent debate focused on societal (or 'liberal') corporatism, although Coleman showed that the concept of state corporatism could be applied in a liberal democracy through his analysis of Quebec.

The concept of corporatism has been applied to the European Community, which certainly has been influenced by the Catholic tradition of 'social partnership', exemplified by the 'val Duchesse' discussions between the Community, employers, and labour initiated in 1985. The protocol on social policy in the *Maastricht treaty includes provisions both for consultation with management and labour, and arrangements for the joint implementation of directives by management and labour. This is an unambiguously corporatist arrangement, but if the Community had generally followed a corporatist path, the Economic and Social Committee would have been a central institution, instead of being marginalized.

The corporatist debate stimulated comparative empirical research on pressure groups as, for example, in the Organization of Business interests project coordinated by Schmitter and Wolfgang Streeck. Whether it provided theoretical 'value added' beyond the insights provided by *pluralism remains contentious. WG

Correlates of War Research project, established in 1963 by J. David Singer, which sought to examine the incidence and extent of armed conflict in the post-Napoleonic period (1816 to the present). The data collected have provided the basis for numerous quantitative studies of a range of issues, including *arms races, military strategy, and international conflict.

(⊕) SEE WEB LINKS

• Correlates of War website, including a variety of data sets.

corruption Corruption obtains when an official transfers a benefit to an individual who may or may not be entitled to the benefit, in exchange for an illegal payment (the bribe). By taking the bribe, the official breaks a legally binding promise he gave to his 'principal' (usually the state administration or a private company) to allocate the benefit to those entitled to it. Corruption is neither a property of a social system or an institution, nor a trait of an individual's character, but rather an illegal exchange. Nowadays scholars have abandoned the classic view of corruption as the degradation of an individual's ethical sense, or lack of moral integrity. If corruption is a type of exchange it can, at least in principle, be the subject of empirical, cross-country examination. For data, scholars turn mainly to three sources, the German-based NGO Transparency International; the *World Bank, and, to a lesser extent, Freedom House. These agencies all produce large cross-national surveys and ranking of countries, although the data come with a variety of biases. Naturally, illegality makes it hard to measure corruption.

Still, a set of empirical regularities has emerged. A positive relation appears to exist between the extent of bribery and: the level of 'red tape'; tiers of government; Spanish colonial domination; the amount of time spent by managers with public officials; the cost of capital and investment; and the degree of regulatory discretion on the part of officials. Other studies show a negative relation between corruption and economic growth; Protestant religious traditions; former British colonial status; openness to trade; current democratic government; and long exposure to democracy.

Empirical regularities are no substitute for explanatory mechanisms. Is corruption a function of red tape or is red tape a function of corruption? If corruption were a function of red tape, bribes could be an efficient way to get round red tape. Contrary to this view, many argue that in the long term corruption breeds inefficiency. Also, with multiple officials and many potential bribers, corruption can generate further corruption, leading a country to fall into a 'trap' where bribery is pervasive. In extreme cases, where everybody takes bribes, the concept loses analytical clout.

In accordance with its own empirical findings, the World Bank promotes policies fostering economic deregulation and liberalization, civil liberties, and the rule of law. Yet, no single recipe exists to eradicate corruption and more work is needed to isolate mechanisms that fetter this social bad.   FV

cosmopolitanism The philosophical idea that human beings have equal moral and political obligations to each other based solely on their humanity, without reference to state citizenship, national identity, religious affiliation, ethnicity, or place of birth. The term originates from the Greek philosopher Diogenes of Sinope who responded to questions about his citizenship and political allegiance by claiming that he was a *Kosmopolite* ('citizen of the world'). Cosmopolitans argue that all human beings share a capacity for reason and are therefore, by nature, members of a universal community. From this, cosmopolitanism makes the normative claim that political boundaries and national identities are morally arbitrary and that all human beings should be held as the primary units of moral worth, as if they were equal citizens of a universal political community. Contemporary cosmopolitan arguments tend to make both moral and institutional claims, suggesting not only that human beings have equal and universal moral worth, but also that political institutions at

the global level should reflect, to various degrees, these cosmopolitan moral values. Consequently, many recent cosmopolitan debates have focused on promoting a condition of global justice and providing a challenge to the traditional Westphalian notion of state sovereignty. Ancient cosmopolitan thinkers include such philosophers as Zeno of Citium, Chrysippus, *Marcus Cicero, Marcus Aurelius, and Seneca. Modern cosmopolitan thinkers include Immanuel *Kant, Charles Beitz, *Brian Barry, Thomas Pogge, Jürgen Habermas, Simon Caney, and David Held.

cost-benefit analysis A technique of constructing a balance sheet of the consequences of a project or activity. By definition, it is a method of assessment which uses monetary units. When used by a private company it is essentially a way of calculating what profit or loss can be expected, but it goes beyond simple versions of such a calculation by insisting on a 'full balance sheet'. On the cost side, for example, this would include the 'opportunity cost' of the resources involved, including the income which might be derived from investing available money in assets which carry the minimum risk. Benefits might include good publicity for the company, so that a nominal loss on a project might be shown by cost-benefit analysis to be a real gain.

In the sphere of public investment, cost-benefit analysis takes on extra dimensions of complexity, since it is required to assess the full range of costs and benefits not just to the municipal or nationalized company involved, nor even to the government, but to the whole population. In such a calculation all social costs and benefits must be assessed, including those which are 'external' to the transactions involved, which would not be considered by a private company. A calculation as broad as that is tantamount to duplicating the felicific calculus of Benthamite *utilitarianism in terms of money, a point which has been generally accepted by enthusiasts and critics alike.

Supporters of cost-benefit analysis argue that it is part of the very idea of rational decision-making. How else are we to find out whether it is better to spend our investment in health or saving lives or alleviating pain? What else can tell us whether the advantages of a new motorway or airport outweigh its disadvantages? Critics regard it as a pseudo-science, a distortion of the values it seeks to assess and an attempt to reduce the serious and evaluative problems of political decision-making to bogus technicalities. LA

Council of Ministers of the European Union The Council should not be confused with the ministerial cabinets of some countries such as France, which use the same title, nor with the European Council (regular European Union summit meeting). The Council refers to a collection of fifteen theme-specific sectoral councils—ranging in coverage from agriculture to financial and economic matters and involving different groups of ministers and civil servants—as well as to the sector-specific councils themselves. These sectoral councils meet with different frequency, with the foreign ministers tending to meet most often in the General Affairs Council. The Council is responsible for approving *European Union (EU) legislation and is composed of the ministers of the member states under a presidency which rotates among members semi-annually. This arrangement implies that European integration requires member states' agreement to proceed. In this sense it is paradoxically both a basic constraint on the Commission and European Parliament's pro-integration ambitions, and the main driving force behind what has been achieved. The idea that integration is 'imposed from Brussels' has therefore little grounding in reality. Important as the Council is in terms of decision-making, however, it does not fully control the agenda: it can only adopt legislation on a proposal of the Commission, and approval of an increasing breadth of legislative matters takes place in 'co-decision' with the Parliament. The Council passes legislation with a *qualified majority voting (QMV) system with different member states holding different numbers of votes, corresponding very roughly to population size. Roughly 70 per cent of the votes are needed to pass legislation, with the implicit rule that at least 50 per cent of countries should approve and, since the Nice Treaty (2001), that the approving member states should include at least 62 per cent of the total population of the EU. The Commission

is responsible for implementation in cooperation with member states.

The issue of voting has, not surprisingly, been controversial in the operation of the Council. The various EU treaties assigned unanimity to certain Council decisions, and QMV to others. In 1966 the Luxembourg Compromise established unanimity as the accepted practice. The *Single European Act and subsequent Treaties of Maastricht, Amsterdam, and Nice have redefined and reinforced the role of QMV, particularly with respect to Single Market issues, thus enhancing the supranational qualities of the EU. QMV now applies to approximately 70 per cent of laws adopted at the EU level. The extension of QMV was considered necessary in the context of enlargement to prevent the increased number and diversity of member states from paralysing EU law-making. The Lisbon Treaty simplifies and redefines QMV as 55 per cent of the member states with 65 per cent of the population. DH

( ) SEE WEB LINKS

• Official site, including constitutional and policy documents.

counter-insurgency Military strategy, aimed at undermining anti-government forces within a territory. In particular, it is associated with attempts to undermine popular support for insurgents through the use of propaganda. During the *Vietnam War, the United States developed a 'hearts and minds' campaign, which sought to reach out to the Vietnamese public, and the strategy was used again in the aftermath of the *Iraq War.

coup d'état The sudden, forcible, and illegal removal of a government, usually by the military or some part thereof, often precipitated by more immediate grievances bearing directly on the military. The coup may be the prelude to some form of military rule, with a greater or lesser degree of civilian collaboration, perhaps requiring the collaboration of the civil service and members of the professional and middle classes, or involving the co-optation of sympathetic politicians and parties and of occupational groups, such as peasant and union leaders. While the focus of the coup is on the remedy of specific or immediate grievances, the outcome is unlikely to involve wide-ranging changes in the social order. More often a coup is seen as an effective means of pre-empting revolutionary change from below by imposing some measure of 'reform' from above. However, repeated military intervention has seldom contributed to a resolution of long-term social and economic problems.

Although not unknown in developed industrial societies, coups have been exceptional wherever governments, popular or not, are accorded a large degree of legitimacy and where there are widely accepted procedures for effecting a regular and orderly change of administration. In Europe the most recent cases of military intervention have been precipitated either by failures of decolonization (France 1958, Portugal 1974), or by rapid economic change and political polarization (Greece 1967), or have been linked to the crisis of communism in Eastern Europe (Poland 1981). The strengthening of the European Union, with democracy as a condition of membership, has also been seen as a stabilizing factor. Moreover here the military has available to it constitutional means for advancing its corporate and professional interests. In developing and underdeveloped countries, however, military intervention was commonplace until the 1980s; in much of Africa it remains so. The nature and frequency of coups has varied both by country and by context. Latin America has the longest experience of military involvement and intervention, dating almost from the inception of the republics, and even affecting relatively advanced states like Brazil, Chile, and Argentina. With independence in Africa coups quickly became the accepted means of changing governments in the absence of free and regular elections, and in circumstances where governments are highly personalized, have little authority, and command almost no legitimacy.

There are several distinct but related schools of thought about coups and their causes. Some seek to explain them largely as a response to social upheaval, economic collapse, and political and institutional failure. On that view intervention is a military response to acute social and political unrest in societies where the level of political culture is low or minimal. The military acts, almost by default, to fill a power vacuum at the centre. Others have looked instead for specifically 'military' explanations for intervention, focusing on the organizational strengths of the armed forces (e.g. discipline, centralized command structure, cohesion), compared with civilian institutions in underdeveloped countries. Intervention, according to this view, is likely to be the result of acute frustration with civilian incompetence and corruption. Others again have focused on the internal politics of the armed forces, insisting that coups are more or less random phenomena, arising from and inspired by a mix of personal ambitions, corporate interests, constituency rivalries, and often intense manifestations of ethnic and sectional loyalty. The appearance in Latin America of authoritarian military regimes, from the 1960s through to the 1980s, has been attributed to the failure of one particular model of economic development, based on import substitution, and the need to attract substantial foreign investment to promote export-based recovery and sustained industrial growth. The military was determined to stay in power to restructure society and create a climate more appropriate to such investment.

It is doubtful whether such a complex and variable phenomenon can be explained in terms of one or a small number of variables. Meanwhile military regimes have been increasingly concerned with the problems of withdrawal: how to extricate themselves from government without at the same time creating the conditions for renewed intervention. Since the 1980s there have been additional pressures arising from the debt crisis, and growing demands from creditor states for good governance. International monetary bodies have also begun to insist on multiparty democracy as a condition for further aid. Consequently, there has been a sharp decline in military intervention in the developing world, measured in terms of the incidence of coups. IC

covenant An undertaking about a future action or other performance understood to be binding on the person giving it. A covenant shares certain features with a promise, but the two have been distinguished in various ways. Covenants were legally enforceable when bare promises were not. Thomas *Hobbes denied that a mere promise created a (moral) obligation, but argued that a covenant (in certain circumstances) did. For Hobbes, a covenant involved the promise of future performance given in return for a benefit either received or expected, whereas a promise was a simple statement about the will of the promissor. In Hobbes's writings, and more generally, an especially important covenant involved a promise of obedience or allegiance sufficient to ground a political *obligation: his version of the *social contract which creates the state was a covenant of every man with every other man to relinquish rights of self-government in favour of the sovereign. This was more than a mere promise, because each man received the benefit of the undertakings given by others. AR

credible threat A threat that one's opponent has good grounds for believing will be carried out. Especially during the nuclear arms race, many threats were seen as incredible. A threat to launch a nuclear-armed weapon on a nuclear-armed enemy seemed incredible because it would lead to nuclear retaliation. Domestically, Scotland and Northern Ireland pose credible threats to the UK polity (it is credible that they could secede), whereas Wales and the English regions do not. Accordingly, Scotland and Northern Ireland receive far the most public spending per head of any UK regions.

Crimea Crisis The Crimea Crisis peaked in February–March 2014 when Russia annexed the Crimea region of south Ukraine and occupied the eastern Donbas region of the country. The crisis stemmed from the decision by Ukrainian President Viktor Yanukovych to renege on a deal to bring Ukraine closer to the European Union and instead tighten links with Moscow. This sparked the so-called 'Euromaidan' protests in Kiev that led to violent clashes with security forces in which eight-two people were killed in and around Maidan Square. President Yanukovych fled to Russia. Soon afterwards, the Russian military started to undertake covert military operations with so-called 'little green men' (Russian soldiers in uniforms that had all insignia removed) in the majority Russian-speaking Crimea, where the Russians already had a major naval base at Sevastopol on the Black Sea. On 27 February the Russian military had taken the Crimean parliament building in Simiferopol. On 6 March Crimean policymakers authorized a vote for independence from Ukraine. The referendum was held on 16 March and saw 97 per cent of people vote for Crimea to become part of Russia. Despite heaping opprobrium on the government of Vladimir Putin for its actions, the West did not launch any counteracting military operations to return Crimea to Ukrainian control. AM

crimes against humanity The origins of the term are often traced back to the Hague Convention of 1907, which set out 'laws of humanity' based on existing state practice. Contemporary understandings often invoke the legal definition set out in the 1998 Rome Statute. Acts such as murder, extermination, enslavement, torture, and rape, amongst others, constitute crimes against humanity 'when committed as part of a widespread or systematic attack directed against any civilian population, with knowledge of the attack'. AG

critical elections A pair (or longer series) of elections in which political alignments change fundamentally. The term was coined by *V. O. Key in 1955 to denote the US Presidential Elections of 1928 and 1932, in which various social groups (especially urban 'ethnics' and blacks) switched from Republican to Democratic support, and stayed switched. As the term implies a shift which is not reversed, it is impossible for a single election to be critical, but the term is often used loosely and incorrectly to mean 'any election in which there is a big swing'.

critical realism A branch of scientific realism associated with the British philosopher Roy Bhaskar. Early work contributed to philosophy of science by asking the *ontological question of what the world must be like for science to be possible. Extending this to social science, Bhaskar develops a critical naturalist view that the social world, like the natural world, is relatively enduring and open to investigation. Critical realism is comprised of ontological realism—the belief in a world 'out there', epistemological relativism (*see* EPISTEMOLOGY) based on distinguishing between this reality and the knowledge we have of it, and judgemental rationalism which, contra *post-modernism, says that there are still rational grounds for judging knowledge claims. Other critical realists, such as Margaret Archer and Colin Hay, have contributed to arguments about the *structure/agency question. Critical realism argues that agents always operate in a pre-existing structural context that they reproduce and occasionally transform. Moreover, this structural context is socially stratified with unintended consequences. Social structure is an underlying and unobservable, but nevertheless real, social feature. Later critical realism adds dialectical and transcendental arguments, though these have been disputed. Initially intended as a philosophical *meta-theory, it can be disputed whether critical realism has overextended itself into making substantial claims about society and human beings. JJ

critical security studies An approach to the study of security within *international relations that falls outside of, or in opposition to, traditional approaches to security. In particular, critical scholars often reject *classical realism and its foundational and methodological presuppositions. Critical scholars tend to advance a *post-structural approach and methodology to the study of security, thus operating outside the mainstream. That said, critical approaches have been on the rise for some time, which raises questions about what is 'mainstream'. There are a number of varying approaches and political commitments within critical security studies writ large, which are often called 'schools', such as the Welsh School (with a commitment to *emancipation and against processes of *securitization), the *Copenhagen School (with a focus on social dimensions), and the Paris School (a focus on cultural dimensions and reiterations of control). Although each school is somewhat unique, most critical approaches share a common methodology and commitment to critically examine existing epistemological, ontological, and sociological foundations.

critical theory Critical theory has been defined as 'theory which can provide the analytical and ethical foundation needed to uncover the structure of underlying social practices and to reveal the possible distortion of social life embodied in them' (Shawn Rosenberg). As a body of theory, it is complex and multidisciplinary, seeking to explain the whole phenomenon of consciousness and to undermine the ways in which existing consciousness perpetuates existing societies. It is particularly associated with the '*Frankfurt School', founded in 1923. The most influential theorists of the first generation were *Adorno and Max Horkheimer (1895–1973), though *Marcuse, who stayed in the United States when the Frankfurt School returned from exile in 1950, found a larger audience. More recent developments have been dominated by Jürgen Habermas (b. 1929).

In a sense, critical theory starts with *Marx, but quickly abandons the philosophical materialism, the theory of historical development, and the crucial role of the proletariat, which are key features of most Marxism. What is retained is the sort of explanations of *false consciousness and of *alienation which are to be found in Marx's earlier writings. It then draws on a variety of insights into the formation and structure of consciousness (more specifically, 'modern' consciousness), including Jean Piaget's accounts of how children learn language and thought, Ludwig Wittgenstein's philosophy of language, and *Heidegger's hermeneutics. But, in each case, it goes beyond these forms of inquiry into a broader, Marx-like account of the political and economic processes upon which the workings of consciousness are said to depend.

Critical theory is thus able to develop a sharp, subtle, and derogatory account of modern consciousness which undermines much we believe by showing us the influences which have moulded our beliefs. These influences are contrasted with rationality and with the conditions for rational argument that would allow what Habermas calls the 'ideal speech act'. Critical theory has therefore had a considerable influence, often indirect, on such 'counter-culture' movements as feminism and the green movement because it allows them to point to the structure and irrational origins of our 'patriarchal' or 'industrial' thought.

The most criticized weakness of critical theory is its failure to engage in what many writers would regard as genuine ethical or political argument: only very rarely do critical theorists offer reasoned alternatives to capitalism, democracy, or 'positivist' science, which are among their most frequent targets. Nor do they clarify what would count as acceptable criteria for the resolution of such arguments. LA

cronyism *See* CLIENTELISM.

Crosland, C. A. R. (1918–77) British Labour politician and socialist theorist. C. A. R. (Tony) Crosland's *The Future of Socialism* (1956) was a revisionist critique of socialism which had an important impact on the British Labour Party, and on Continental socialist parties.

Crosland defined the goals of modern socialism as the pursuit of political liberalism and political/social equality. Egalitarianism distinguished socialism from other political creeds. It required high levels of government expenditure on services and the redistribution of income and wealth which, he argued, was politically feasible when the economy was expanding. Keynesian demand management of a mixed economy, with some direct government ownership but within a system of predominantly private ownership, was the means to ensure economic growth. Crosland argued that additional nationalization and state ownership of industry was an unnecessary objective of socialism in Britain, which should instead apply state control and regulation of industry. Educational egalitarianism through the replacement of grammar and secondary modern schools by neighbourhood comprehensive schools, together with the expansion of opportunities in higher education, was another important aspect of Crosland's socialism.

Crosland entered the cabinet of the Labour government in 1965, and was a prominent figure, until his untimely death in 1977 while serving as foreign secretary. His arguments undoubtedly contributed to the comprehensive school movement and to the scepticism of many socialists with further nationalization, although in contrast with many other socialists who shared generally similar views, Crosland was not an enthusiastic exponent of membership of the European Community. PBY

cross-bench Seats in the House of Lords between the government and opposition benches, where peers not aligned to any political party sit.

cross-sectional analysis The study of a population at a single point in time. This normally refers to the analysis of large-scale sample surveys, such as the British Election Study. Cross-sectional analysis is useful for studying the association and correlation between variables at the individual, rather than aggregate level, and thus avoiding the ecological fallacy (*see* ECOLOGICAL ASSOCIATION). However, *longitudinal studies, including *time-series and *panel studies are usually more appropriate for studying change. SF

CSCE *See* ORGANIZATION FOR SECURITY AND COOPERATION IN EUROPE.

Cuban Missile Crisis The Cuban Missile Crisis of October 1962 is generally regarded as the most dangerous moment of the Cold War, one in which the world moved perceptibly close to nuclear conflict between the superpowers.

In the period after Fidel Castro's successful revolution in Cuba, 1959, the Americans considered various plans to restore an anti-Communist government. In April 1961 these plans culminated in the unsuccessful *Bay of Pigs invasion which the American government authorized and supported. This was followed by a build-up of Soviet forces in Cuba. Throughout 1962 the issue of Cuba caused difficult relations between the superpowers, already tense as a result of the Berlin Wall crisis of the previous year. The Americans publicly signalled that they would not tolerate the Soviets placing 'offensive' nuclear missiles in Cuba, which lay only about one hundred miles from the coast of Florida. Nikita Khrushchev, the Soviet leader, appeared to understand and to comply with this demand. President Kennedy stated on 13 September that if Cuba were to become an offensive military base then he would take whatever steps were necessary to protect American security. During September the first missiles and the equipment to build the launchers arrived in Cuba.

On 14 October photographs from U2 aircraft revealed that medium-range missiles were being installed and on 16 October the Executive Committee of the National Security Council (ExCom) held the first of its meetings to resolve what the American government regarded as a direct threat to its security. President Kennedy announced on television the detection of the missiles, demanded their removal, and the ExCom went into semi-permanent session to consider the next American steps. A variety of strategies was considered, including doing nothing (which was quickly dismissed), various forms of diplomatic action (which ran the risk of leading to negotiation and hence counter-concessions by the Americans) over the missiles' removal, invasion, an air strike against the missiles, and a blockade. Kennedy initially favoured military action of some sort and the possibility of invasion and air strike was held in reserve throughout the crisis. However, a blockade to prevent further missiles reaching Cuba emerged as the preferred solution. A blockade, accompanied by demands for the removal of the existing missiles, offered various advantages. It demonstrated American resolve and willingness to use military force, it capitalized on America's local naval superiority, it gave time for Khrushchev to back down, and it threw back onto him the difficult next step of escalating further the crisis if he were not to comply. The ultimatum, in short, offered the 'last clear chance' to avoid an uncontrollable confrontation which might probably end in nuclear war.

At first Khrushchev appeared reluctant to comply. He made a good deal both of the American threat to Cuba's integrity and the deployment of American medium-range missiles in Turkey. Kennedy was reluctant to make any deal which traded the Turkish for the Cuban missiles, though he personally had ordered the removal of the missiles from Turkey several months earlier on the grounds that they were unnecessary to American security and provocative to the Soviet Union. The imposition of the American blockade went ahead and the risks of incidents between the two naval forces became apparent.

In the days after 16 October the tension increased and the two states appeared to be moving to war as the Soviets showed no willingness to back down. On 26 October the Americans received in secret what they interpreted as a personal letter from Khrushchev which offered the possibility of a solution. The letter, in effect, offered to remove the missiles in return for the Americans removing the blockade and agreeing not to invade Cuba. The following day Khrushchev sent a public letter which was both more belligerent in tone and which demanded the removal of the missiles from Turkey in return for removal of the missiles from Cuba. The Americans were adamant that such a deal was unacceptable, moreover the tone of the letter suggested to them that Khrushchev might have lost control within the Presidium to more hawkish elements. The same day Soviet surface-to-air missiles in Cuba shot down an American plane. American military action appeared imminent. At that point Robert Kennedy, brother of the President, suggested that the Americans agree to Khrushchev's first (secret) letter, publicize the 'agreement', and in that way attempt to lure Khrushchev into acceptance—making clear at the same time that the burden of failure and responsibility for war would fall onto Khrushchev if he failed to accept.

The following day the crisis ended on these terms. The Americans had secured a great diplomatic victory, though by running enormous risks, and Kennedy's prestige stood at its new peak. The Soviets got much less out of the crisis, though they were able to share public credit for the resolution of the crisis. However, they had got the American promise not to invade Cuba and, some time later, they saw the Americans remove their medium-range missiles not merely from Turkey but from Europe as a whole. The Soviet withdrawal appears to have fatally undermined Khrushchev's prestige within the Presidium and to have led to his overthrow two years later. The Americans consolidated their leadership within NATO which had been threatened by their inability to prevent the Soviet gains in Berlin in 1961.

The successful resolution of the crisis led to an immediate improvement in superpower relations. The 'hot line' was installed to give direct communications between the leaderships in Washington and Moscow, and in 1963 the two powers, with Britain playing an important minor role, went on to conclude the Partial Test Ban Treaty which outlawed nuclear testing in the atmosphere. Above all, the mutual realization of how close the world had come to war led the two superpowers to give renewed attention to their doctrines of nuclear deterrence. In the West the missile crisis was taken as a paradigm case of a new science or art of 'crisis management', and the decision-making processes within ExCom were analysed in order to learn the 'rules' or conventions of the new science. In particular the importance of manipulating risk, or brinkmanship, emerged as a key element in coercive diplomacy—using the risk of war to push the opponent into backing down—together with the equal importance of allowing the opponent a last clear chance to avoid uncontrollable escalation. Kennedy himself laid great emphasis on finding terms to offer to Khrushchev that would not be so humiliating that in fact he would decline to take them.   PBY

Cuban Revolution *See* CASTROISM.

cube law, better known as **cube rule** A relationship discovered by David Butler in 1949, when he observed that the effect of the *first-past-the-post electoral system in Britain was to produce a ratio of seats between the (two) parties which was the cube of their ratio of votes. For instance, a party which won a British general election by 55 to 45 per cent of the vote would win seats in the ratio 64.6 per cent to 35.6 per cent (55^3 to 45^3). Subsequent research has shown that the cube ratio was a product of the geographical distribution of the voters for each party, and that the exaggerative effect of the operation of the system in Britain has tended to decline.

Note that the cube rule and its generalization apply only to the ratio of votes between the two leading parties. Third parties such as the British Liberal Democrats suffer much more severely from underrepresentation if their vote is evenly dispersed, while concentrated third parties such as the Ulster unionists may obtain as high or higher a ratio of seats as of votes.

cultural imperialism The process whereby one country/region imposes its own culture on other countries/regions to reshape the receiver's culture. For *Marxists this was often associated with the 'coca-colonization' or the *McDonaldization of the world. Gradually, this notion dovetailed with the critique of *globalization. Thus for Marxism, globalization is associated with the *neo-liberalization* of non-Western societies in which the international financial institutions—the *World Bank, the *IMF, and the *World Trade Organization—culturally convert such

societies according to *neoliberal norms and processes such that their own forms of productions are sacrificed on the altar of neoliberal capitalism. In this vision, cultural imperialism is 'superstructural' in that it is 'epiphenomenal'; i.e., that it is driven and informed by fundamental capitalist–economic requirements, such that the analysis of capitalism occupies front and centre. However, beginning with Edward *Said's theory of *orientalism, which launched *post-colonialism, the imposition of cultural imperialism is viewed not as an epiphenomenon of capitalism but is foundational to Western identity and culture. Thus the belief in the inherent inferiority of the non-Western world leads to the Western imperialist desire (originally dubbed 'the white man's burden') to culturally convert the economic, political, and cultural foundation of such societies to that of Western civilization through a 'civilizing' mission.   JMH

cultural relativism The view that cultural belief systems such as ethics, morality, and social meaning differ from culture to culture and are equally valid relative to each culture. Cultural relativists often argue that no culture can/should be judged as better than another, since the value of that culture is relative to its members' belief systems. Often accredited to Franz Boas and most prevalent within political anthropology, cultural relativism seeks to understand how belief systems are constructed and practised while problematizing arguments that claim universal morality or deep senses of common humanity. In international relations, cultural relativism is often used as a means to critique Western *hard power and *soft power, *globalization, and *post-colonialism, and to argue against *cosmopolitanism. Although relativism offers a number of explanatory benefits, it suffers from a number of contradictions and limitations. First, cultural relativism often treats cultures as static entities and thus falsely 'freezes' their historic and future potentialities for cross-cultural intersubjectivity and mutual identification. Secondly, the relativist claim against universalism is inconsistent with its own normative claim that relativism demands universal equal consideration and respect. Lastly, critics suggest that relativism cannot respond to the collective action problems associated with globalization and therefore is a dying notion of 'authenticity' rooted in a human experience now long gone.

Cultural Revolution In September 1965 an article appeared in a Shanghai newspaper criticizing a historical play written in 1961, on the subject of the Ming official Hai Rui, renowned for his principled opposition to the Emperor. The play was a political parable, which had been carefully prepared and endlessly discussed to sharpen its political point. It was one of a number of works of literature from the period after the collapse of the *Great Leap Forward in which historical figures were used as political parallels. It was an attack on *Mao Zedong; its main point was the implicit identification of Hai Rui with Marshal Peng Dehuai, whom Mao had dismissed from his posts for his tenacious opposition to the Great Leap Forward. The critical article was published in Shanghai because Mao no longer had sufficient influence in the capital to secure its publication there.

Facing resistance to his condemnation of the offending play, Mao appealed to the young of China to launch their own criticism of privilege and the policies which bred privilege. The attack was not intended to be against persons; it was the system that had to be criticized on the grounds that in spite of the socialization of the means of production, relations between leaders and led were essentially still 'capitalist' and reforms modelled on those which had already begun in Eastern Europe would only make the system worse. Mao's amanuensis, Chen Boda, in planning a new revolutionary play, described its central character: a man of perfect integrity and infinite conscientiousness, yet a tyrant; but he is not personally a tyrant; it is the system which leaves him no choice.

Liu Shaoqi attempted to keep the movement within bounds by dispatching work teams to the universities and colleges. The students resisted. Mao sided with them, and published among their wall posters a poster of his own, 'Bombard the Headquarters', indicating that it was the Party leaders who should be the main target of attack, not a few intellectuals. This led to the escalation of the protest into a serious political movement. The seeds of bitter conflict had by then already been sown, when the 'Red Guards' (the student organizations) split into two factions: the so-called 'moderates' who were led largely by the favoured children of the Party leaders, and were moderate only in their attempts to protect their parents but were violently immoderate in their attacks on writers and artists; and the 'radicals' who were often led by the children of bourgeois families whose members had been persecuted and discriminated against, as well as by the children of workers and peasants. Meanwhile, the struggle widened as China's several million deprived casual workers and members of other disadvantaged classes joined the radical students. The new Cultural Revolution leadership, formed of Mao's closest associates, called on the People's Liberation Army to hold the ring and prevent the use of force. As a result, many army units joined in the struggle. Bloodshed and vicious persecution of opponents ensued, and there was an almost complete breakdown of government. The power of the radicals reached its peak when they proclaimed a 'Paris Commune' government of Shanghai to replace the Chinese Communist Party hierarchy. The idea spread to other cities. Mao Zedong stepped in and condemned the Paris Commune, insisting that the Communist Party could 'not yet' be superseded. He created a new governing institution, the 'revolutionary committee', which brought together representatives of the radicals, cadres who had not been condemned for abuse of power and privilege, and local army units. Through these the Communist Party was to be rebuilt on the basis of popular election of its cadres. This, however, ensured that with the help of sympathetic units of the armed forces the Party could reassert unchanged authority. Open and popular election of cadres almost never occurred. The rest of the story of the Cultural Revolution is one of a protracted rearguard action by the left, which continued until Mao's death, and the subsequent arrest of his supporters brought the movement to an end.

The Cultural Revolution has often been represented in the West as a struggle between pragmatism and radical ideology; but to reach this conclusion one must identify pragmatism with a marginally modified form of Stalinism, and ideology with Mao's determination to short-circuit Party bureaucracy by decentralizing decision-making to the local communities, and one must ignore the many millions of words concerning policy questions which the radicals poured out during the movement, and which expressed the belief that autocracy flourished on the existence of the centralized command economy. It is also interpreted as a struggle between unrepentant Stalinism (represented by Mao and the radicals) and reformed Communism; but this ignores the fact that the policies demanded by the radicals were based explicitly on Mao's rejection of Stalinism, now for the first time openly published by the Red Guards.

As the Cultural Revolution was more and more frustrated the ideas of those who had participated in the revolt evolved, through the Li Yi Zhe poster of 1974 to Chen Erjin's *Crossroads Socialism* and the *Fifth Modernization* of Wei Jingsheng of 1978, to the erection of the Goddess of Democracy in *Tiananmen Square. JG

cumulative vote A voting procedure in which voters have more than one vote in a multicandidate election and may choose to give one vote to each of several candidates or to give more than one to some. Used in some school boards in nineteenth-century England. If everybody votes sincerely, it may be used to judge the intensity of voters' feelings about the candidates. But, as pointed out by C. L. *Dodgson (Lewis Carroll), it is very vulnerable to manipulation. If any voter is tempted to 'plump' for (give all his or her votes to) a favourite candidate to maximize that candidate's chances, then every rational voter must, and cumulative vote degenerates to single non-transferable vote.

curvilinear disparity, law of *See* ACTIVIST.

Cusa, Nicholas of (Kryfts, Krebs) (1401–64) German theologian, philosopher, and voting theorist. Nicholas was born in Kues (Cusa) on the Moselle. He took a doctorate in canon law at Padua, and was ordained in 1426. In 1432 he was sent to the Council of Basle. This led him to favour the conciliar movement in the Church of his day. Reconciliation, unity, harmony, and concord were the principal concepts of his life and writings. The Council of Constance (1414–18) had brought the Great Schism to an end by deposing two rival popes and forcing a third to resign. This led Nicholas to think that the way to Christian unity lay in democratic rather than authoritarian rule. But he later came to believe that unity stood a better chance under one leader, the pope (apart from any scriptural claims to his supremacy). However, his papalism was not extreme. He never claimed the supremacy of the papal over secular power, not even the moderate Thomist 'indirect power'.

Nicholas's ultimate notion of concordance and harmony (*coincidentia oppositorum*) is to be found especially in *De Docta Ignorantia* (On Learned Ignorance). Opposites coincide in God in whom there are degrees of attributes and no distinctions between them. How this is so is beyond our comprehension, yet since God is infinite it must be so.

Nicholas also wrote three treatises on mathematics. His mathematical bent led him to propose what is known nowadays as the *Borda count (but which should perhaps be renamed the Cusanus count): that is, the rank-order method of voting. There is no evidence that any of his contemporaries understood the depth of his argument. CB/IM

Cusanus Latinized version of the name of Nicholas of *Cusa.

customs union A customs union, unlike a *free trade area, requires its members to adopt a common external tariff of customs duties. The objective, seldom in fact achieved, is to enable goods (but not labour or capital) to move freely throughout the union. CJ

cyber-attack Outside of the context of *cyber-terrorism and *cyber-crime, state-sponsored cyber-attacks and cyber-attacks committed by individuals pose a serious threat to the international community because they are designed to degrade, deny, or destroy information resident in computers, or to compromise computers themselves. This is done with the explicit intent to cause disruption, destruction, and even human loss. Cyber-attacks are being increasingly considered war-like attacks on states and are regulated primarily by the international legal framework relating to the use of force or, if committed during times of armed conflict, international humanitarian law. RBU

cyber-crime Cyber-crime often refers to traditional crimes that have migrated to cyberspace, such as money laundering and sexual exploitation, but can also include cyber-specific crimes such as illegal access to electronic information, trade secrets, or the creation and spread of harmful computer viruses. Cyber-crime is a foremost threat to individuals and industry, with losses from cyber-crime predicted to reach $2.1 trillion by 2019. Because of its magnitude and pervasiveness, cyber-crime can also question the function of the state if the latter persistently fails to control such criminal activity or suffers breakdowns in *cyber-security. The Council of Europe's Convention on Cybercrime (2001/2004) establishes a common criminal policy among state parties by adopting appropriate legislation and by fostering international cooperation. More specifically, states should criminalize illegal access, illegal interception, data interference, and system interference, and should cooperate in their investigation and prosecution.   RBU

cyber-security Cyberspace has become part of daily life and now permeates all aspects of modern society. Notwithstanding the enormous benefits afforded by cyberspace, this new domain has also emerged as a source of a number of security threats and vulnerabilities. The threat landscape in cyberspace is multifaceted and dynamic, and the most prominent cyber threats range from *cyber-terrorism and *cyber-crime to *cyber-attacks. The threat landscape is further complicated by the fact that cyber threats emanate not just from states but increasingly from non-state actors. In fact, because of the accessibility of the Internet, the anonymity it affords and its ease and speed of use, cyberspace provides a thriving environment for non-state actors to operate, and has greatly amplified the potential for non-state actors to engage in malicious and damaging cross-border conduct. This poses problems from the perspective of ensuring accountability and responsibility, because under international law it is states rather than non-state actors that are generally the objects of the international order. Generally speaking, under the law of state responsibility, states can be responsible for malicious cyber operations of non-state actors where that conduct is under the effective control of the state or, in the aftermath, the state adopts that conduct as its own. Otherwise, specific regimes of international law can impose upon states certain legal duties in relation to non-state actors operating within their jurisdiction.   RBU

cyber-terrorism Cyber-terrorism refers to the use of cyberspace by organizations with the intentional aim to promote terrorist propaganda, recruitment, incitement, revenue generation, training, and acts of disruption. The *United Nations Security Council has determined that such online terrorist activities threaten international peace and security, and has urged member states to prohibit incitement to commit terrorism, take active measures to prevent incitement, and deny safe haven to persons guilty of incitement. Importantly, it is incontrovertible that *cyber-security policies in cyberspace must comply with prevailing international human rights law standards relating to, for example, the freedom of speech and association and the right to privacy. Terrorists can also use cyberspace as an additional domain to carry out *cyber-attacks. These may be confined to cyberspace by targeting computers and networks that sustain military, governmental, or other public infrastructure, but cyberspace may also be utilized to perpetrate acts of terror that produce physical, real-world damage. Through a patchwork of international agreements designed for the suppression of terrorism generally, and more recently cyber-terrorism in particular, states are subject to various international legal obligations that require they deter and suppress the use of cyber infrastructure that is located on their territory for terrorist purposes. The United Nations Security Council has also adopted various resolutions requiring member states to address terrorist activities within their borders, including the criminalization of terrorist-related activities. In extreme instances, terrorists can also incur individual criminal responsibility under international criminal law where their conduct amounts to *war crimes, aggression, *crimes against humanity, or *genocide.   RBU

cycle Any situation in which a voting procedure, choosing among multiple options, would choose A over B, B over C..., i over j, and j over A. The best-known example is the cycle in simple majority rule, discovered by *Condorcet in 1785, but any majority rule short of unanimity may generate a cycle. Even if A beats B only if at least all the voters except one prefer A to B, there may still be a cycle. When a cycle exists, the will of the people is undetermined. Whatever is chosen, a majority of the people would rather have had something else.

Da'esh *See* ISLAMIC STATE OF IRAQ AND SYRIA.

Dante Alighieri (1265–1321) Italian poet and philosopher, born in Florence. Very little is known for certain about his life. From 1295 he took an active part in local politics, which led to his exile. Having wandered for a time, spending part of it in Verona, he finally settled in Ravenna, where he died.

On the death of Beatrice Portinari with whom he was secretly in love, he turned to philosophy (*c.*1290) of the Thomist variety. He differs from Thomas *Aquinas in not conceding even indirect power to the papacy. Secular and ecclesiastical authorities are separate and independent; neither has a right to interfere in the other's affairs. Dante regarded peace as paramount in any civilized social system and this he believed could only be achieved by a 'universal monarchy' along the lines of the Roman Empire, which he regarded as ordained by divine providence. This theory is developed in *De Monarchia*, written probably around the time of the visit of the Emperor Henry VII to Italy (1310–13). His theory has its origin in St *Augustine's *City of God*. According to Dante a universal monarch could create a *humana civilitas* which would unify all peoples of all faiths, which the papacy could not do. This in itself could ensure peace. But added to that is the fact that 'The monarch has nought that he can desire, for his jurisdiction is bounded by the ocean alone, which is not the case with other princes, since their principalities are bounded by others'. He would also be an ideal court of appeal since he has nothing to gain, 'whence it follows that the monarch may be the purest subject of justice among mortals'. *De Monarchia* was publicly burnt in Bologna and remained on the index of prohibited books until the nineteenth century. Was this simply because of its content or was

it possibly because in another book Dante put Pope Boniface VIII in hell? CB

Darfur Darfur is the westernmost state in Sudan. Despite its long and complex history, it has gained international attention only since 2003 when an insurgency emerged in the region, triggering a humanitarian emergency that has involved African states, the African Union, major Western states, the United Nations, and various non-governmental organizations.

Darfur's etymology derives from the Arabic 'land of the Fur'. This refers to the establishing of an Islamic sultanate in that area during the sixteenth century. Up until the advent of European colonialism, the Darfur sultanate consolidated a complex system of trade, political authority, and social interaction. In contrast to its marginal status today within the modern Sudanese state, Darfur was a central and relatively 'modern' social system in north Africa's Islamicizing and fluid Afro–Arab region.

The annexation of Sudan in 1821 created an imperial administrative centre in Khartoum, which from 1875 served as the base for the colonization of Sudan by the British and Egyptians. The period from 1875 to 1916 was unstable and contingent for Darfur and indeed the rest of Sudan—subject as it was to Egyptian rule which was established through the authority of Britain. The British–Egyptian 'condominium' was subjected to various forms of resistance, mainly from Mahdist attempts to create a purified Islamic state in Sudan. During this period Darfur's political system was modified and disrupted but it was only in 1916 that Darfur was fully annexed to the colonized Sudanese state.

From 1916 to independence in 1956, the British colonial administration, with its focus on Khartoum and the Blue Nile river basin, established Darfur's modern marginality.

Darfur's population was disempowered and located at the border of a state consolidated through European colonization.

If British colonialism achieved the subordinate incorporation of Darfur into Sudan, the bulk of the post-colonial period affirmed Darfur's subordination fairly consistently through regime changes between military, civilian, secular, and Islamic. A powerful aspect of the ruling ideology of the elites within Khartoum has been a perception that peoples to the west and south are inferior. This political schism has expressed itself largely through a protracted war between north and south, until 2004. Throughout this period, Darfur remained fluid, unstable, and marginal: part of a complex frontier of migration, insurgency, and militarism which involved Chadian and Libyan as well as Sudanese politics.

In 2001 Darfur's structures of authority broke down, and two years later an insurgency against the state emerged when the Sudanese Liberation Army and later the Justice and Equality Movement attacked government buildings, personnel, and property. The Sudanese government response caused the humanitarian crisis which has made Darfur synonymous with displaced and desperate people and the predations of *counter-insurgent militias. Suffering from the same historic weakness of all Sudanese governments in Darfur, the government mobilized diffuse mobile armed groups into what is known collectively as the *janjaweed*. These militias have raided and attacked civilian populations throughout Darfur, resulting in the displacement of millions and the deaths of hundreds of thousands from raids, starvation, and disease. The Sudanese government has supported the *janjaweed* raids with air strikes. The severity of the humanitarian crisis and the direct involvement of the government have led to various calls within Africa and more widely for intervention, a humanitarian response, peacekeeping, and a ceasefire. The United States government has called the humanitarian disaster in Darfur *genocide, and although this categorization is contested very few would deny the severity of the crisis or the purposeful *ethnic cleansing that has taken place.

A slow response by the United Nations (UN) and others has been succeeded since 2006 by more concerted efforts. In Abuja during that year, a peace agreement was signed by the Sudanese government and some representatives of the insurgency. This facilitated the arrival of an African Union–UN peacekeeping mission which replaced an incumbent African Union force. In the interregnum between the UN resolution enabling the UN military force and its arrival, the Sudanese government stepped up its war against the insurgency and the people of Darfur.

Darfur's plight has been projected through campaign groups, human rights organizations, politicians, and celebrities. In 2008, the *International Criminal Court prosecutor for Darfur, Luis Moreno-Ocampo, requested an arrest warrant for the Sudanese President Omar Bashir on charges of genocide, crimes against humanity, and war crimes. Although international liberal opinion is resolved that the Sudanese government is responsible for a major humanitarian crisis, views on how to intervene effectively and/or create peace are not easy to come by. Although some refugees have now returned from camps in neighbouring Chad, there remains an uneasy ceasefire, with new tensions flaring in the south between Sudanese forces and forces loyal to the newly formed South Sudan.   GH

Darwinism The body of scientific ideas deriving from Charles Darwin (1809–82); in particular, his theory of the evolution of all animal and plant species through natural selection. Darwinism may usefully be considered both as a general doctrine about man and nature and also as a specific theory of biological evolution. As the former, it is firmly in the camp of materialism and physicalism suggesting, as it does, a single universal law governing all animate phenomena. Just as late Victorians tended to believe in one fundamental law of association for all mental activity, so Darwinism suggested one natural law of development for all forms of life. Not surprisingly perhaps, Darwin himself took immense pleasure in the idea that man and other animals were 'netted together'. Indeed, many Darwinists held that there was no longer an objective basis for elevating one species above another. Needless to say, Darwinism is also fatal for all arguments from design and special creation. As a specific biological theory, Darwinism shifted the biologist's concern from a concentration on specific types, each with its own fixed form and essence, to a concentration on populations whose boundaries were neither fixed nor predetermined. As a result of unremitting selection pressure, some organisms would be rejected, either by death or by sterility, favouring those organisms better adapted to their niche or environment. In this way, populations evolved by natural selection of favourable, heritable variants. Herbert *Spencer's phrase 'survival of the fittest' is often accepted as a synonym for natural selection; 'survival of the fitter' would in fact be more appropriate. *See also* SOCIAL DARWINISM. JH

Dayton peace agreement (1995) *See* BALKAN POLITICS.

dealignment The concept that voters in Western liberal democracies, who were formerly aligned into well-defined social groups on the basis of commonalities such as class, religion, and ethnicity, and exhibited high partisan identification as a result, have over time become more loosely attached to such allegiances and have more aleatory and fleeting preferences in electoral competition. The concept is opposed to that of *realignment, in which voters lose attachments to prior allegiances but instead gain new ones, and a distinction is usual between social dealignments and partisan dealignments.

The concept of dealignment became widespread during the 1980s, and three major causes can be identified. First, some writers observed an apparent general weakening of social and political group identities in Western societies, evidenced by, for example, falling labour union membership, political party membership, and religious observance, and this was associated with the rise of cross-group identities and consciousness found by sociological works such as John Goldthorpe's 'Affluent Worker' studies in the UK. Simple ideas of voter alignment seemed ill-suited to rising social complexity, and were sometimes linked to materialist conceptions of politics equally ill-suited to represent the rise of new issues identified in Ronald Inglehart's post-materialism thesis. Secondly, in the US, the temporal pattern of realignments at *critical elections appeared to have been broken, with no clear new alignment arising from the partial disintegration of the New Deal

coalition. Thirdly, rational choice models of behaviour, which had become increasingly popular, implied a consumerist model of voting in which choice rather than identity was crucial.

However, the extent of dealignment has been strongly contested: levels of party identification have ceased to fall in the US, and the extent and meaning of *class dealignment in UK voting is the subject of a lengthy and vigorous dispute. *See also* CRITICAL ELECTIONS. PM

de Beauvoir, Simone (1908–86) Philosopher, associated with the *existentialist movement, who wrote on a wide range of issues, including radical politics, feminism, and ageism. Born in Paris, de Beauvoir met Jean-Paul *Sartre in 1929, whilst studying philosophy at the Sorbonne, and the two shared a tumultuous relationship. In her writings she combined a political concern with autobiographical insight and an existentialist striving against the limitations imposed by society. *The Second Sex* (1949) sought to assert a positive feminine identity, as opposed to one defined by and in the interests of the dominant male. She traced the marginalization of women through a history of masculine-dominated cultural and social development, and outlined the contemporary position of women within society. She criticized marriage and motherhood as constraints on the freedom of women, and saw socialist economic restructuring as a key to enhancing the status of women. De Beauvoir became actively involved in the *women's movement in the early 1970s, campaigning on a variety of feminist issues, particularly the legalization of abortion and the provision of contraception. In *The Coming of Age* (1970) she presented an analysis of the treatment of the elderly across various cultures and throughout history. Again, de Beauvoir showed how patterns of discrimination were built into social norms and practices.

debt crisis A tendency for highly indebted poor states to reach a point where they are unable to meet repayment schedules. Debt might be incurred as a result of multilateral lending by the *World Bank or *IMF, or lending by commercial banks. The management of a country's debt 'package' is commonly the outcome of a series of agreements between a debtor state and the World Bank/IMF. High levels of debt per se are not necessarily a sign of 'crisis', however. Crisis occurs when the agreed repayment schedules (interest and capital) can no longer be adhered to, creating situations in which debtor states stop, or threaten to stop, payments. The political responses by all interested parties constitute the contours of any particular crisis and this produces considerable variation in how crises are dealt with and—in a sense—resolved. Nevertheless, the debt crisis has its origins in a number of general tendencies and patterns of global politics since the early 1980s.

The causes of the debt crisis included aggressive lending by multilateral and commercial banks from 1974 onwards which allowed high levels of debt to accumulate; the prosecution of poorly conceived or executed development strategies by many indebted states which reduced the ability to repay interest; interest rate hikes in the United States in the early 1980s which made the holding of international debt more expensive; and falling global prices for the main export commodities of the world's poorest states, undermining the ability to earn hard currency to repay debts. The impacts of the debt crisis were sharpened social hardship and political instability and protest as debt repayments were continued in the context of widespread poverty; the introduction of a range of write-off and rescheduling agreements; and an increasingly prominent role for the World Bank and IMF in the economic management of indebted countries.   GH

debt relief Debt relief refers to the total or partial cancellation of debt. It can be granted to individuals, companies, or nations. Notable instances of international debt relief include the 1953 agreement writing off Germany's First World War reparations and debt relief granted to developing countries towards the end of the twentieth century. The latter involved a 1989 *IMF scheme to reduce the debt burdens of some Latin American countries, and in 1996 the IMF and *World Bank's Highly Indebted Poor Countries (HIPC) initiative. HIPC granted debt relief for poor countries (mainly in Africa) which met certain criteria including

an established track record of economic policy reform and the development of plans to use the funds made available for poverty reduction (codified as Poverty Reduction Strategy Papers, or PRSPs). The HIPC scheme was expanded in 1999 and joined in 2005 by the Multilateral Debt Relief Initiative (MDRI), which granted 100 per cent debt relief on debts owed to the IMF, the World Bank, and the African Development Bank. In the 2010s debt relief also became a prominent concern in Eurozone negotiations over the provision of loans to Greece, a move supported by the IMF but opposed by the European Central Bank (see SOVEREIGN DEBT CRISIS). Debt relief is sometimes criticized on the grounds of 'moral hazard', the potential misuse of funds by elites, and because the conditions attached to debt relief by institutions such as the IMF are economically and socially damaging.   WB

decision theory The theory of how rational individuals (should) behave under risk and uncertainty. One branch deals with the individual against an uncertain environment ('Nature'); the other, *game theory, with the interactions of rational individuals who jointly produce an outcome that no one can control. Decision theory uses a set of axioms about how rational individuals behave which has been widely challenged on both empirical and theoretical grounds, but there is no agreed substitute for them.

Declaration of Independence The statement agreed by the Continental Congress on 4 July 1776 proclaiming the freedom and independence of thirteen British colonies in North America and announcing the creation of the United States of America. The Declaration can be divided into four parts. It begins with a preamble revealing that the statement's primary purpose is to provide a justification for dissolving the ties binding the colonies to Britain. The second part claims that people are duty bound to throw off governments that fail to meet the requirements of that theory. Part three is a catalogue of grievances against George III prior to a concluding section asserting that the former colonies were now 'FREE and INDEPENDENT STATES; that they are Absolved from all Allegiance to the British Crown, and that all political connection between them and the

State of Great Britain, is and ought to be, totally dissolved'.

For Americans, the Declaration of Independence, authored primarily by Thomas *Jefferson, is second only to the US Constitution as a hallowed document symbolizing the founding of the nation. However, Congress actually announced the independence of the colonies on 2 July, two days before the Declaration of Independence was agreed. Furthermore, many of the grievances listed in the Declaration are of dubious validity, but even if they are accepted they do not support the sweeping allegations of absolute despotism and tyranny 'with circumstances of cruelty and perfidy, scarcely paralleled in the most barbarous ages'. George III and his ministers were insensitive, short-sighted, and incompetent, but hardly tyrants.

It was in any case inappropriate for the Declaration to direct its fire so exclusively at the person of the King, at one point even going so far as to accuse him of inciting 'the merciless Indian savages' against his colonial subjects. In fact, Parliament and government ministers were the principal parties to the dispute with the colonies even though they receive no direct mention in the Declaration.

The most enduring and universally significant part of the Declaration of Independence is to be found in its second paragraph: 'We hold these truths to be self-evident: that all men are created equal; that they are endowed, by their Creator, with certain unalienable rights; that among these are life, liberty and the pursuit of happiness. That to secure these rights, governments are instituted among men, deriving their just powers from the consent of the governed; that when any form of government becomes destructive of these ends, it is the right of the people to alter or abolish it, and to institute a new government.... The history of the present King of Great Britain is a history of repeated injuries and usurpations, all having in direct object the establishment of an absolute tyranny over these states.' This famous passage encapsulates several of the canons of liberal democracy including the principle of equality, natural rights, government by consent, and limited government. The influence of John *Locke on Jefferson and his colleagues has been widely noted and it is evident that the Declaration states briefly many of the themes developed at greater length in Locke's *Second Treatise of Government*. DM

 SEE WEB LINKS

• Text of the Declaration of Independence.

decolonization The process of decolonization refers to a form of regime shift, a changed relationship between the colonizing power and colony, usually in the context of the end of European empires in the developing world after the pressures of the Second World War. It reflects a changed power relationship between colonial powers and colonial nationalist movements which arose to assert national self-determination and challenge traditional imperial hegemony. The era of European decolonization is generally held to run from the creation of an independent India, Pakistan, Ceylon (now Sri Lanka), Burma (renamed Myanmar in 1989), and Indonesia in the late 1940s up to the creation of Zimbabwe from Rhodesia in 1980, or even the democratization of apartheid South Africa in 1994 and the return to communist China of Hong Kong and Macau in 1997 and 1999 respectively. The African *annus mirabilis* of 1960 when fifteen mainly French colonies on the continent gained independence may perhaps be taken as the high point of the phenomenon.

The process can be broken into stages. At the most immediate level, decolonization refers to the grant of formal constitutional independence by the departing colonial power. Independence is conferred and the new state takes its place in the international system, including membership of international bodies such as the United Nations. Political sovereignty is conferred upon the new state by its acceptance into the Westphalian state system and the international community.

More broadly, it refers to the change in government of the new state from bureaucratic-authoritarian government by the colonizing power, whether authoritarian, paternalistic, or by a colonial settler racial minority, to a locally legitimized government. The process may require agreement between the departing colonial power and its designated successor regime. Agreement may arise from military defeat by nationalist forces, a recognition of the unfeasible or overly costly continuation of colonial rule in the face of colonial nationalism, or an implicit arrangement between the metropole and incoming political rulers to confer independence without fundamentally altering the power relationship. Initial moves to replace colonial bureaucrats with representative and then responsible government institutions can be accelerated by the radicalization of colonial nationalism, outflanking the colonizing power's controlled pace of change as it seeks post-independence collaborative government.

At the broadest level, decolonization can be taken to mean the establishment of a fully independent state freed from economic and cultural dependence on the former colonial power (*see* IMPERIALISM). This dependence is usually thought of in terms of development aid, or the continued use of colonial rather than local languages. In this sense it also requires the freedom to seek alliances with other potential great powers, alliances not necessarily meeting with the approval of the former metropole. It is a matter for debate whether this broader process has occurred in each individual state, given the prolonged indebtedness of many developing countries both to former colonial powers and to multilateral institutions such as the *IMF (International Monetary Fund) and the *World Bank.

Definition of the term is complicated by the varying definitions of colonial rule. If it is taken to be merely the formal grant of independence, the ending of many clearly imperialist power relations (for example, Britain and France's role in controlling the finances of the Suez Canal) are omitted. If it is defined to encompass the restitution of full economic, diplomatic, and cultural sovereignty, it may be so broad as to imply no act of complete decolonization has been achieved in the twentieth century. In addition, the term does not generally imply that the departing colonial power bequeaths a democratized state; many military regimes and one-party states have arisen in the immediate aftermath of twentieth-century decolonization. As an alternative, the term *disimperialism* has been proposed to cover the changed diplomatic and constitutional relationship, while leaving open the question of economic independence.   RTC

deep ecology *See* ECOLOGY.

defensive realism A form of *neorealism associated with Kenneth *Waltz as well as some *classical realists who argue that the anarchical structure of the *international system encourages states to pursue moderate, defensive, and measured policies so as to maintain state security and promote international order. *See also* OFFENSIVE REALISM.

deflation The dictionary definition is 'an economic situation characterized by a rise in the value of money and a fall in prices, wages, and credit, usually accompanied by a rise in unemployment' (*OED*). However, in politics it is generally used much more loosely to mean a government-imposed squeeze on credit and/or rise in interest rates leading to increased unemployment.

de Gaulle, Charles *See* GAULLISM.

delegate A person on whom an individual or group confers the capacity to act on his or their behalf. The central idea of delegation is that the person who delegates passes authority or responsibility to the person who is delegated to carry out a task or assume a role: hence a delegate may also be a representative (*see also* REPRESENTATION). The relationship between the principal (who delegates) and the agent may be variously understood. For example, a delegate may be sent to a meeting only in order to report back to his or her principals, or may be sent with authority to bind his or her principals to a decision. Delegation thus involves the notions of authorization, accountability, and responsibility, but any specific act of delegation will contain particular applications of these ideas.   AR

delegated legislation Delegated (or secondary) legislation is law made by ministers under powers given to them by parliamentary acts (primary legislation) in order to implement and administer the requirements of the acts. It has equal effect in law although ministers can be challenged in the courts on the grounds that specific pieces of delegated legislation are not properly based on powers given by acts. In the United Kingdom, delegated legislation, typically, is made through the force of *statutory instruments in the form of ministerial regulations, orders in council, and codes of practice. The amount and scope of delegated legislation has grown as a result of the increasing pressure on parliamentary time. Advocates suggest that it represents an efficient way of relieving Parliament, that much of its subject-matter is uncontroversial, and that Parliament voluntarily gave up power in such irksome business. Critics object to the growing legislative autonomy of the executive from Parliament, and point out that deeply controversial matters, such as immigration rules, have been treated as delegated legislation. Increasing political concern was reflected in the House of Lords' successful defeat in February 2000 of an affirmative instrument by which government sought to deny candidates a free mailshot in the 2000 London Mayor election. Devolution to Northern Ireland (1998) and Scotland (1999) means that the assembly and parliament respectively make their own arrangements for primary and delegated legislation. The creation of the National Assembly for Wales in 1999 established an elected institution that was unique in being solely responsible for the creation, scrutiny, and implementation of delegated legislation from primary legislation still drawn up by the UK Parliament, although the 2006 Government of Wales provided mechanisms for the gradual development of its own primary law as well. JBR

(⊕) SEE WEB LINKS

• UK Parliament page on delegated legislation.

deliberative democracy A critical response to traditional models of democracy. Although deliberative democracy encompasses a broad spectrum of ideas, the motivational aim of deliberative theory is to legitimize political decisions by creating procedures that allow democratic decisions to be a result of mutual understanding, publicly expressed reason, and broadened political inclusion. This position is contrasted with democratic models that have traditionally relied on ideas of competing elites, vote aggregation, and private interest maximization. Whereas traditional models focus on aggregative outcomes (by elites or individuals), deliberative theory focuses on broadening the deliberative input from all participants, on creating a sense of public reason, and on creating procedures that can be seen as acceptable by all stakeholders involved. By doing so, deliberative

democrats seek to transform current systems of governance, which are often associated with social exclusion, power asymmetries, and mutual distrust. Deliberative theorists maintain that political decisions are best created (and thus can be seen as more legitimate) through a process of public reason formation, which will decrease the *democratic deficits that are currently experienced in most democracies.

delimitation *See* APPORTIONMENT.

demagogue Like democracy, the idea of a demagogue has its roots in the ambiguous Greek word *demos* meaning 'the people', but in the sense of either 'the population' or 'the mob'. Thus a demagogue was, even in classical times, the leader of the mob, but also the leader of a popular state in which sovereignty was vested in the whole adult male citizenry. In this defunct, neutral, sense all modern Western leaders are, to some degree, demagogues. But the modern significance of the idea of a demagogue lies in its pejorative sense, as the leader of a mob, with the implication that those who rouse the rabble always do so for ignoble purposes.   LA

demarchy Term introduced by J. Burnheim, 1985, to denote democracy implemented by selection of people and courses of action by lot rather than by election. Burnheim's criticisms of representative democracy are telling, but most critics have found his scheme of demarchy impracticable.

democracy Greek, 'rule by the people'. Since the people are rarely unanimous, democracy as a descriptive term is synonymous with *majority rule. In ancient Greece, and when the word was revived in the eighteenth century, most writers were opposed to what they called democracy. In modern times, the connotations of the word are so overwhelmingly favourable that regimes with no claim to it at all appropriated it (the German Democratic Republic, Democratic Kampuchea). Even when not used emptily as propaganda, 'democracy' and 'democratic' are frequently applied in ways which have no direct connection with majority rule: for instance, *The Democratic Intellect* (G. E. Davie) is a well-known discussion of the (supposed) egalitarianism of the Scottish educational system in the nineteenth century. Such uses of 'democracy' to mean 'what I approve of' are not considered further here. Issues relating to majority rule include:

1 *Who are to count as 'the people' and what is a 'majority' of them?* Ancient Athens called itself a democracy (from *c.*500 BC to *c.*330 BC) because all citizens could take part in political decisions. But women, slaves, and resident aliens (including people from other Greek cities) had no rights to participate. Citizens were thus less than a quarter of the adult population. Modern writers have nevertheless accepted the self-description of classical Athens as 'democratic' (*see also* ATHENIAN DEMOCRACY). Likewise, well under half the adult population of the United Kingdom had the vote before the first women were enfranchised in 1918; but 1918 is not usually given as the year in which Britain became a democracy. What minimum proportion of adults must be enfranchised before a regime may be called democratic? This simple question seems to lack simple answers.'Majority' appears to be more clear-cut than 'people'; it means 'more than half'. In votes between two options or candidates this poses no difficulty; in votes among three or more it does. The difficulty was studied by various isolated people (Pliny the Younger, *c.*AD 105; Ramon Lull in the thirteenth century; Nicolas *Cusanus in the fifteenth) but first systematically tackled by *Borda and *Condorcet in the late eighteenth century. The plurality rule ('Select the candidate with the largest single number of votes, even if that number is less than half of the votes cast') may select somebody whom the majority regard as the worst candidate. Nevertheless, countries using this rule for national elections (including Britain, the United States, and India) are normally described as 'democratic'. Borda proposed to select the candidate with the highest average ranking; Condorcet proposed to select the candidate who wins in pairwise comparisons with each of the others. Although these are the two best interpretations of 'majority rule' when there are more than two candidates, they do not always select the same candidate; and the *Condorcet winner—that is, the candidate who wins every pairwise comparison—sometimes does not exist. In this case, whichever candidate is chosen, there is always a majority who prefer some

other, and the meaning of 'majority rule' is unclear. Voting in legislatures is usually by the binary resolution-and-amendment procedure, which always ensures that the winning option has beaten its last rival by a majority (but does not solve the problems mentioned in the previous paragraph).

2 *Why (if at all) should majorities rule minorities?* The first argument for democracy in ancient Greece is that attributed by *Thucydides to Pericles, one of the democratic leaders of Athens, in 430 BC. Pericles argued that democracy is linked with toleration, but made no special claims for majority rule. *Plato and *Aristotle both deplored democracy, Plato on the grounds that it handed control of the government from experts in governing to populist *demagogues and Aristotle on the grounds that government by the people was in practice government by the poor, who could be expected to expropriate the rich. However, Aristotle did first mention as a justification of majority rule that 'the majority ought to be sovereign, rather than the best, where the best are few . . . .[A] feast to which all contribute is better than one given at one man's expense.' In medieval elections, the usual phrase was that the 'larger and (or "or") wiser part' ought to prevail. But every losing minority could claim that it was the wiser part. Only in the seventeenth century did a defence of democracy based on an assumption of equal rights for all citizens begin to re-emerge, perhaps as a by-product of the Protestant Reformation. *Hobbes and *Locke both assume the political equality of citizens, but neither draws explicitly democratic conclusions. A stronger claim of equality was asserted by Colonel Rainborough of Cromwell's army in 1647, with his claim that the 'poorest hee that is in England hath a life to live, as the greatest hee'.Significant widening of the franchise in Western regimes began in the late eighteenth century. In the French Revolution, the franchise was at first restricted to fairly substantial property-holders, but it was widened to something approaching manhood franchise in the constitution of 1791 and the proposed constitution of 1793. Many of the American colonies had broad suffrage before 1776, and the Constitution of 1787 lays the groundwork for democracy in federal elections by giving

each state representation in the House and in presidential elections in proportion to its population (except for Indians and slaves). Except between 1865 and the 1890s, however, Southern blacks remained disenfranchised until 1965. The first British act to widen the franchise was in 1832; universal suffrage was achieved in 1928. The leading commentators of the period from 1780 to 1920 all accepted the basic premiss that the 'poorest hee' (and for *Condorcet and J. S. *Mill the poorest she) had as good a right to a vote as the richest, although many of them were concerned about the '*tyranny of the majority' (see 4 below) and Mill proposed weighting votes in favour of the richer and the better-educated. *See also* MADISON; TOCQUEVILLE.

Another strand of democratic thought argues from equal competence rather than equal rights. This revives Aristotle's feast. Democrats who see politics as a matter of judgement rather than opinion (including *Rousseau and Condorcet) argue that, other things being equal, the more people who are involved in arriving at a decision the more likely the decision is to be correct. Condorcet formalized this in his *jury theorem, which states that, providing a large enough majority is required, a large number of only moderately competent people can be relied on to take the right decision.

3 *Direct v. representative democracy.* Athenian democracy was direct. All citizens were expected to participate, and the attendance at the sovereign Assembly may have been as high as 6,000. When decision-taking bodies had to be smaller, their members were selected by lot rather than by election. Every citizen of Athens had a reasonably high probability of being chief executive for a day. When democracy was reinvented in the eighteenth century, every system was indirect: voters elected representatives who took decisions for which they were answerable only at the next election. Rousseau argued that this was no democracy ('The people of England think they are free. They are gravely mistaken. They are free only during the election of Members of Parliament'), but was a lone voice. Interest in direct democracy revived in the 1890s when the *referendum became more popular, and to a greater extent in the 1960s, when many

people especially on the *New Left revived Rousseau's criticism of representation. Modern communications and computers have removed many of the technical obstacles to direct democracy, but it is not popular either among politicians (whose jobs it imperils) or among political philosophers (the majority of whom accept *Schumpeter's argument that direct democracy is incompatible with responsible government).

4 *Is democracy merely majority rule or are other features necessarily part of the definition?* Most of the classical theorists of democracy were liberals; and they all saw a tension between democracy and liberty. If the majority voted to invade the minority's rights, this could be tyrannical. Therefore Madison proposed the divisions of powers, both among branches of government and between levels of government, that are a feature of the US Constitution; and Mill proposed to weight the votes of the more educated. Although Madison's scheme protects only some groups from majority tyranny (until 1954 it did nothing for black people in Southern states), the Madisonian principle has been accepted by Schumpeter and many other modern theorists of democracy. Schumpeter's opponents argue that he 'posed a false dilemma' because the persecution of minorities 'cannot be squared with democratic procedure'. This suggestion leaves undetermined the many cases in the world where majorities vote to persecute minorities: not only are places like Kosovo not democracies, but they would not be democracies whichever faction controlled them. It is probably better to restrict 'democracy' narrowly to majority rule, and treat toleration, entrenchment of rights, and so on as preconditions for democracy but not as constitutive of democracy itself.

democratic centralism The official organizing and decision-making principle of *Communist Parties. Formally, the centralist aspect was asserted via the subordination of all lower bodies to the decisions taken by higher ones. Democracy consisted in the fact that the highest body of the Party was its congress to which delegates were elected by local organizations. In theory at least, therefore, although Party members were bound to carry out a policy once it had been adopted, there was room for democratic input in the pre-congress discussion and elections. In practice, criticism of Party leaders under any circumstances was considered disloyal and grounds for expulsion. Moreover, particularly where Communist Parties were in power, dependence of those below on higher Party officials for promotions and benefits effectively eroded democratic decision-making. Occasionally, Party leaders such as Stalin, Khrushchev, and Gorbachev, would seek to revive the 'democratic' aspect of the principle in campaigns against rivals in the leadership or those undermining the centre in the apparatus. However, the stability of the system and the interests of those at the grass roots were so adversely affected by such campaigns that they tended to be either of short duration or to spin out of control.   swh

democratic deficit The term denotes a perceived deficiency in the way a particular political arrangement works in practice against a benchmark as to how it is supposed to work in theory. Although this definition does not preclude any democratic systems of political domination from potentially suffering from a democratic deficit, the term features most prominently in the context of *European Union (EU) institutions and policy-making. The use of the term mirrors a general, yet multifaceted dissatisfaction with the way democracy works at the EU level. The use of the term usually implies a connotation with a *procedural* perspective of democratic legitimacy. Decisions are thereby viewed as legitimate if they fulfil certain procedural requirements, such as direct or indirect citizen participation through elections as well as scrutiny and accountability of policy-makers. Not only is there broad agreement on these principles across democratic states, within the EU there is also broad agreement that the delegation and pooling of sovereignty reduces the possibility of national parliaments and citizens to hold national policy-makers accountable. Yet, there is disagreement conerning solutions to the democratic deficit. For example, some see the empowerment of the powers of the directly elected *European Parliament the best solution to solve the democratic deficit. Others argue that national policymakers can only be accountable to national

parliaments and thus reject the proposal to empower the European Parliament. This diversity in opinion recurs most prominently to differences in national constitutional histories (e.g. the Federal State analogy in Germany and national *parliamentary sovereignty doctrine in the UK).   BR

Democratic Party (USA) The Democratic Party arose from the Democratic–Republican coalition which supported *Jefferson's presidential campaign of 1800. The Democratic-Republicans were strong in rural, southern, and western areas, opposed to the Federalists, led by John *Adams, whose strength was in the industrial and trading north and east. The party was refounded as the Democrats by Andrew Jackson, President from 1829 to 1837, the first frontiersman to be elected President. In the years leading up to the Civil War, therefore, the Democratic Party was a coalition of rural and frontier interests against urban and industrial interests. As most of the United States was rural and it had an enormous frontier, the Democratic coalition won most federal elections. Some have seen the raising of the slavery issue in national politics in the 1850s, associated with the foundation of the *Republican Party, as a deliberate attempt by the persistent losers to break up this Democratic coalition and thereby gain power. If so, it was successful, but at the cost of a civil war. The Civil War united rich and poor in the South behind the Democrats, and therefore when Southern whites were fully enfranchised after 1876 (*see also* CIVIL RIGHTS) the South became a Democratic one-party state in federal and many state and local elections.

The Democrats suffered a setback in the 1896 presidential election when a western faction under W. J. Bryan, which campaigned for an inflationary coinage of silver in order to relieve debtors, captured them. This campaign, of which *The Wizard of Oz* is an allegory (Dorothy's slippers should be silver, as in the book, not ruby, as in the film), recreated the Democratic Party of Jefferson and Jackson, but by now America was less rural and the party was correspondingly less successful. The next big change in Democratic fortunes came between 1928 and 1936, when the urban poor were consolidated and Northern blacks were brought into the fold for the first time, by the welfare policies of F. D. Roosevelt's *New Deal. This began a period of Democratic hegemony in federal politics which lasted until 1968. The New Deal coalition was extremely broad. In particular, it embraced most black Americans and most white racist Americans. Although they could agree on welfare policy, they obviously disagreed on race policy. Neither the executive nor the legislature could therefore enact *civil rights until 1964, in the wake of the assassination of President Kennedy.

Since then, scholars are unanimous that the 'New Deal alignment' has died, but are unclear as to what has taken its place. The Democratic Party controlled the House of Representatives until 1994 and recaptured it in 2006; it usually but not always controls the Senate, but between 1969 and 2017 it controlled the Presidency for only 20 years (1977–81, 1993–2001, 2009–17). It lost control of the House of Representatives in 2010 and of the Senate in 2014. In 2008, Barack Obama won the US Presidency for the Democrats and won a second term in 2012. Obama is the first black president in US history. His key accomplishments were his civil rights protections for homosexuals and his comprehensive, yet controversial, health-care legislation 'Obamacare'.

American parties are much weaker than parties in most European regimes. In most states, anybody who wishes may announce that he or she is a Democrat or Republican, vote in that party's *primary election, and run for office, acquiring the party label if successful in a primary (or, in some states, in a caucus). The parties do have some control over their members in Congress, especially in the allocation of committee places. Even here, however, seniority of membership of Congress remains important (though less important than it once was). Conservative Southern Democrats held safe seats and therefore easily gained seniority. However, this effect has faded as the South has become solidly Republican.

(⊕) SEE WEB LINKS

• Democratic Party site, including history and organizational information.

democratic peace The idea that democratic or republican states are more peaceful in their external relations and never (or almost never) fight each other. Modern democratic peace theory (DPT) builds on a long-standing tradition in liberal writing on *International Relations and is often associated with the German philosopher Immanuel *Kant (1724–1804)—hence references to 'Kantian peace'. However, it only formed one (and not the most central) part of Kant's political thought and had already become a liberal commonplace by the end of the eighteenth century. Other precursors of modern democratic peace theory include Karl Deutsch's writing in the 1950s on security communities—groups of states (such as North America, Scandinavia, and Western Europe) in which there is real assurance that the members of that community will not fight each other physically but will settle their disputes in some other way. Overlooked or neglected by many studies of war causation, the idea of the democratic peace theory was revived in the mid-1980s by the US political scientist Michael Doyle. It became a major theme of both academic writing in international relations and of political and public debate on the nature of the post-Cold War international order (as in the Clinton administration's policy of democratic enlargement or in the justifications for EU and NATO expansion).

The democratic peace hypothesis rests on two claims: (*a*) that democracies almost never fight each other and very rarely consider the use of force in their mutual relations; and (*b*) that other types of relations are much more conflictual including democracies' interactions with non-democracies. The claim is almost always made in probabilistic terms. Few claim that it is a determinstic law. It is not a general theory since it is agnostic or at least much less certain about relationship between democracies and non-democracies. But it provides some grounds for liberal optimism, even if only within the democratic zone and thus stands in striking contrast to realist and neorealist accounts of world politics. *Neorealists argue that even peacefully motivated democratic states in an anarchic self-help system will be forced to become involved in *arms races, crises, and conflicts with each other. This is not because of any drive for power and aggrandizement, but because of the security dilemma and the extent to which uncertainty and lack of information make it rational for states to behave in ways that foster conflict.

Democratic peace theorists argue that two sets of causal factors are important in explaining the democratic peace. In the first place, the structural constraints of democratic institutions and of democratic politics make it difficult or even impossible for war-prone leaders to drag their states into wars. They also stress the joint effect of these democratic constraints, together with the greater openness and transparency of liberal democracies. If both sides are governed by cautious, cost-sensitive politicians that only use force defensively, then conflict is far less likely to occur. Second, democratic peace theorists highlight the importance of normative mechanisms. Liberal and democratic norms involve shared understandings of appropriate behaviour, stabilized expectations of the future, and are embedded in both institutions and political culture. Rule-governed change is a basic principle; the use of coercive force outside the structure of rules is proscribed; and trust and reciprocity, and rule of law are at the heart of democratic politics. On this view, then, the democratic peace is produced by the way in which democracies externalize their domestic political norms of tolerance and compromise into their foreign relations, thus making war with others like them unlikely.

The main debates surrounding the democratic peace and the main issues raised by critics and sceptics include: (*a*) the reliability of the statistical evidence for the democratic peace, especially in the pre-1945 period; (*b*) the existence of alternative causal logics, especially in explaining regional clusters of peaceful states as in Western Europe or the Americas; (*c*) the difficulties of defining key terms in the theory, especially war and democracy; and (*d*) the problems raised by democratization processes and the evidence that, whilst fully consolidated democracies may be peaceful, democratizing states, especially in unstable regions, may be more conflict-prone than authoritarian regimes. *See* SEPARATE PEACE. AHU

democratic socialism In general, a label for any person or group who advocates the pursuit of socialism by democratic means. Used especially by parliamentary socialists who put parliamentarism ahead of socialism, and therefore oppose revolutionary action against democratically elected governments.

Less ambiguous than *social democracy, which has had, historically, the opposite meanings of (1) factions of Marxism, and (2) groupings on the right of socialist parties.

democratization The process of becoming a *democracy. The word was first used by *Bryce in 1888. Bryce identified the process as beginning with the *French Revolution. If democracy is equated with the *franchise, the first wave of democratization was a slow one, spreading from France and some states in the United States in the 1790s to most of the industrialized world by 1918. After both the First and Second World Wars, there were wavelets of democratization. Woodrow *Wilson's championing of self-determination encouraged the first one, and the second was encouraged by independence movements in Western colonies, particularly in Africa and in Asia. However, the rise of communism and fascism rolled back the first; and internal strife in former colonies rolled back the second. A so-called Third Wave of democratization started in the early 1970s. By the year 2000 there were, according to Freedom House, one hundred and twenty democracies in the world, the highest number yet recorded. Moreover, the proportion of countries in the world that are democratic vis-à-vis non-democratic ones is higher than ever before (63 per cent). The Third Wave started in Southern Europe with the demise of military dictatorships in Portugal (1974), Spain (1976), and Greece (1976), and then extended to Latin America, Central and Eastern Europe, the Far East, South-East Asia, and sub-Saharan Africa in the 1980s and 1990s.

Scholars followed a *substantive* approach to analyse democratization in the 1960s. The core assumptions underlying this approach are that democratization in any given country is a gradual, long-term historical process, and that democratization is a broad phenomenon, which is not only political, but also economic and social. This type of analysis emphasized the 'prerequisites of democracy'. The basic hypothesis was that the richer and more prosperous a country gets, the greater the chances that it will sustain democracy. The substantive approach's most important weakness was probably the fact that its core assumptions encouraged engagement with the analysis of long-run historical processes at the expense of assessing the short-run. This was clearly seen soon after the Third Wave of democratization started. The substantive approach was unable to account for the possibility of short-term political democratization, particularly in countries outside the core of Western industrialized democracies. Moreover, once democratization spread from Southern Europe in the 1970s to Latin America in the 1980s, and to Central and Eastern Europe and the Far East in the 1990s, this approach did not possess the tool kit to analyse short-term political conjunctures.

The so-called procedural approach shifted the attention from democracy (an outcome) to democratization (a dynamic process). D. A. Rustow concluded that the factors that keep a democracy stable are not necessarily the ones that brought it into existence. Explanations of democracy must distinguish between function and genesis. This crucial distinction allowed analysts to overcome the emphasis on the long-run and on democracy as an outcome, and to focus instead on the short-run and on the dynamic process of democratization. As the Third Wave of democratization showed, democratic regimes could be, and indeed were, born and developed in a couple of years throughout the world. The possibility of democratization processes in the short-run also allowed Rustow to establish concepts that became central to the study of the Third Wave such as *transitions* and *consolidation* (he called it 'habituation'). These concepts established a time horizon that permitted one to distinguish stages of democratization in the short-term.

The procedural approach's emphasis on the short-term was also complemented by the idea that democratization can be better studied by following a minimalist conception of democracy. This is the idea of *polyarchy, which concentrates on political institutions and procedures (free and fair political participation and contestation, and wide protection of civil rights), and excludes economic and social processes and indicators (the so-called relative autonomy of the political). By focusing on the short-term and on the criteria of polyarchy scholars have thus been able to analyse the first truly global democratization wave between the early 1970s and the dawning of the twenty-first century. FG

deontology *See* CONSEQUENTIALISM.

dependency A view of the relationship between developed and underdeveloped countries. Dependency theory built upon *Lenin's theory of *imperialism, and focused upon the economic penetration of the *Third World, particularly Latin America, by the large capitalist states. Emerging in the 1960s, dependency crystallized around a critique of the structural developmentalism associated with Raúl *Prebisch and the United Nations Economic Commission for Latin America (ECLA) which was founded in 1948 in Santiago, Chile.

ECLA characterized the world as divided into centre (the developed, industrialized North) and periphery (the underdeveloped agricultural South); the relationship between them was determined by the structure of the world economy. Latin American economic activity was based upon primary export production. This had been dealt a devastating blow during the Great Depression when the bottom fell out of the market. In place of classical trade theory's notion of a mutually advantageous relationship between centre and periphery, Prebisch argued that a model of unequal exchange operated, with Latin American economies facing a long-term secular decline in their terms of trade. This resulted in a chronic balance of payments crisis, with the periphery having to export more and more in order to maintain the same levels of manufactured imports. ECLA's solution was forced industrialization through protectionism and import substitution, and an interventionist role for the state in economic management and infrastructural development. The hope was that such programmes would reduce Latin America's vulnerability to sharp swings in international commodity prices.

Various governments attempted to apply the ECLA model but its performance was unimpressive and Prebisch admitted that it was flawed. Industrialization actually made Latin American economies more, not less, vulnerable to the vicissitudes of the world market. It distorted growth both between the industrial and agricultural sectors, and within industry, where the emphasis upon consumer durables facilitated greater involvement by transnational companies. Governments failed to introduce the structural reforms (such as changes in land ownership patterns and income redistribution) which would have facilitated the expansion of the domestic market and social modernization. In the 1970s ECLA's developmentalism was abandoned as military regimes followed *monetarist policies which opened up rather than protected domestic economics.

Dependency theory built upon ECLA's intellectual traditions. Andre Gunder Frank, in *Capitalism and Underdevelopment in Latin America* (1967), concentrated upon the external mechanisms of control exerted by the centre (or metropole) upon the periphery (or satellite). The centre maintained the periphery in a state of underdevelopment for purposes of superexploitation. Underdevelopment was not an original or inherent condition, rather it was the determined outcome of the historical relationship between dominant and subordinate states. As underdevelopment was a product of capitalist development, it would only end when the capitalist system itself collapsed. For Frank, socialist revolution was the only solution. Frank should perhaps be more accurately regarded as a *world systems theorist rather than a dependency writer. Perhaps a more seminal text was *Dependency and Development in Latin America* by Fernando Henrique Cardoso and Enzo Faletto (1969). This concentrated upon the domestic experience of dependency, involving an analysis of different types of export economy (the key issue being whether the export sector was foreign or nationally owned) and the impact these had upon class relations and the forms of the state they gave rise to. Unlike Frank, Cardoso and Faletto did not offer a deterministic view of dependency theory; they believed that social actors were faced with real choices and the variations in the structure of the dominant class explained different political outcomes. This led them to contend that independent development was not impossible and that revolution was not inevitable.

Critics of the dependency thesis have complained of careless terminology, simplistic class analysis, lack of conceptual rigour, and excessive polemic. Dependency should be regarded more as a tool of interpretation, a critical methodology rather than a fully developed theory. It has not provided answers to Latin American problems but has provoked debate. GL

SEE WEB LINKS
• Site of the the Economic Commission for Latin America (ECLA), including details of membership and institutional history.

Derrida, Jacques (1930–2004) French philosopher, often associated with *poststructuralism and the continental tradition. However, Derrida is also often labelled as being a postmodernist and a literary critic. These signifiers would trouble Derrida. This is because Derrida often argued against the use of broad generalizations in political and theoretical discourse, preferring to 'deconstruct' words, terminology, and assumed knowledge. This was often done to expose internal inconsistencies hidden within concepts, to highlight these tensions and to explore alternative meanings. In this regard, Derrida was largely interested in the relationship between language and philosophy, the indeterminacy often involved with philosophical knowledge and how we assume to 'know' the world around us. The impact of Derrida's works on politics remains contested. Many political theorists and analytical philosophers dismiss his works as prone to grandiloquence and ambiguity, and see them as more suitable to literary critique than political theory. Nevertheless, the works of Derrida continue to influence many post-structuralist scholars who have adapted his critical methodology in order to respond to many issues of contemporary relevance.

desegregation See CIVIL RIGHTS.

despotism Autocratic rule by one person. Thus in its original Greek sense a 'despot' was the lord or ruler of an unfree state. The Byzantine emperor was routinely referred to as a despot, the title was transferred to Christian rulers in provinces of the Turkish Empire, and remains in modern Greek as an old-fashioned word for a bishop, *Thespotis*.

*Aristotle began an important Western tradition of thought by distinguishing Persian 'despotism' from Greek tyranny. Tyranny was usurped, unstable power, wielded coercively, while despotism was persistent and stable, depending on the acquiescence of the people, often the only authority they knew and therefore essentially legal. It was thus an oriental phenomenon because free, Greek peoples would not tolerate it for long. The category of oriental despotism is almost universal in Western political thought. Most notably, *Montesquieu developed the category in his *L'Esprit des lois*, published in 1748. Even the most absolute of Western monarchies was not a despotism, he argued, because the monarch was bound by law whose legitimacy was justified by the same reasoning as was his authority. He did, though, note a tendency for the French monarchy to degenerate towards despotism, as did several of his contemporaries, and after the revolution of 1789 it became customary to refer to the *ancien régime* as a despotism.

Western theorists have used despotism as a limiting case, a *reductio ad absurdum* of the concentration of power. To Burke it was 'the simplest form of government', the domination of the will of a single man. To Bentham it was an evil form, the inverse of the evil of anarchy. Their shared assumptions about the actual working of the Ottoman, Chinese, Persian, and Moghul Empires can be said to be oversimplified where not actually wrong, and the use of the term has degenerated into a mere political boo-word, not really distinguishable from 'tyranny', 'dictatorship', or 'absolutism'.   LA

détente Literally 'loosening'. Détente was used to refer to periods of reduced tension in relations between the United States and the Soviet Union during the Cold War. It was closely associated with the process (and progress) of arms control, and the main period of détente ran from the Partial Test Ban Treaty in 1963 to the late 1970s. The term has fallen out of use with the end of the Cold War, but it has generic standing and can be used to describe any easing of tension in relations between states that are otherwise expected to be hostile.   BB

deterrence A policy of attempting to control the behaviour of other actors by the use of threats. The deterrer tries to convince the deterree that the costs of undertaking the actions that the deterrer wishes to prevent will be substantially higher than any gain that the deterree might anticipate making from the action. Deterrence is a general

principle for human behaviour, but with the deployment of nuclear weapons by states after the Second World War, it became the central theoretical idea in the sub-discipline of Strategic Studies. Nuclear weapons made it much easier to threaten very large punishments than it had ever been with conventional weapons. Nuclear weapons initially forced the adoption of deterrence as a policy for military security because there was no effective way for states to prevent some nuclear weapons from getting through if an attack was launched. The threat of a retaliatory counterstrike thus became the centrepiece of superpower military policy during the *Cold War. The desire to escape from deterrence led to pursuit of defences against ballistic missiles, but the technical difficulties of this option have not yet been overcome.

Deterrence is associated with nuclear retaliation, and is sometimes used in contrast to defence. The key distinction is between strategies of denial (seeking to block an attack directly by confronting the forces making it), and strategies of retaliation (inflicting punishment, usually elsewhere than on the attacking forces). Where there is geographical contiguity, as there was between the *NATO alliance and the *Warsaw Pact, then denial easily became part of deterrence policy. The strategy of NATO was to confront Soviet forces with a ladder of escalation, starting with conventional defence and moving up rungs to a full-scale nuclear strike.

Although simple in conception, deterrence can be extremely complicated in practice. If two nuclear powers confront each other, each fears that a first strike by the other could disable its retaliatory forces. Under these conditions, each side must pursue a secure second strike force: one that is large enough to survive a first strike and still inflict unacceptable damage in retaliation. Fear of becoming vulnerable to a first strike (and/or a desire to attain first-strike capability) gives technology a central role in deterrence, and tends to fuel a high-intensity qualitative arms race. Deterrence theory was shot through with many debates about problems of rationality, dangers of accidental war, and dangers of uncontrollable escalation from peripheral conflicts. Because it developed largely in the context of the Cold

War, deterrence theory is largely cast in terms of a two-party relationship, with much less thought having been given to the operation of deterrence logic in a multipolar system. For the United States and its allies the issue of extended deterrence became the core focus of NATO policy. Extended deterrence required the United States to give a nuclear guarantee to its allies, and the problem was how to make this threat credible once the Soviet Union acquired the ability to make nuclear strikes against North America. Maintaining credibility was seen as the central problem for American deterrence policy throughout the Cold War.

Deterrence theorists can be divided into two groups. On one side are those who think that nuclear weapons make deterrence easy. They tend to support policies of minimum deterrence, the logic being that deterrence is made effective by the appalling consequences of even small nuclear strikes. On the other side are those who think deterrence is difficult. They focus on the complexities of the escalation ladder, and the need to deter highly aggressive, risk-taking, opponents under all foreseeable contingencies. They tend to favour large and diverse nuclear force structures capable of dealing with all worst-case scenarios. Extended deterrence favoured the 'difficult' logic, and with the ending of the Cold War, there has been a general move towards minimum deterrence amongst the big nuclear powers. Nuclear deterrence has implications for nuclear proliferation. To the extent that the large powers rest their own security on nuclear threats, it makes it difficult for them to persuade other states that they should renounce their right to possess nuclear weapons. BB

de Tocqueville *See* TOCQUEVILLE.

development Development is a normative concept referring to a multidimensional process. Some people argue that development must be relative to time, place, and circumstance, and dismiss any universal formula.

Increased economic efficiency, expansion of national economic capacity, and technological advance are generally accepted as necessary conditions if development is to be sustainable, as are economic and industrial diversification and adaptability in the face of shocks. Additional ingredients, attached by writers from various social sciences, include changes in social structure, attitudes, and motivation or specify the purposes of economic improvement. Increases in gross national product (GNP) and average real incomes are means, not ends. In some accounts, the increase of general social welfare embraces even spiritual and cultural attainments, personal dignity and group esteem, development being defined as the fulfilment of the necessary conditions for the realization of the potential of human personality. At its simplest, development is the increasing satisfaction of basic needs such as for food. Controversy surrounds the extent of such needs. Is education one of them? Development is customarily translated into improvements in certain social indicators and indicators of the (physical) quality of life, such as life expectancy. Ideas of development engender debate over the theoretical and empirical relationships between the rate and pattern of economic growth, the distribution of the benefits and *equity.

Other conditions that have been included in development are increasing national self-determination, predicated on the notion that development is something a country does to itself and means reducing external *dependency. More fashionable now are notions of environmentally sustainable development, or development that meets the needs of the present without compromising the ability of future generations to meet their own needs, and feminist theories of development that emphasize gender and women's issues specifically. Democratization, accountable government, and a respect for human rights have also recently become more prominent, as features of political development contained by the generic sense of development.

Development, then, values increased freedom. After all, the most basic need of all may be the freedom to define your own needs, taking part in decisions that affect your own life. Economic development cannot be divorced from the other aspects of development. Its principal contribution is to enhance the range of human choice for all members of society without discrimination. Modern observers of developing countries argue that whatever else development is it must be participatory—a 'bottom up' exercise, where ordinary people understand, initiate, and control the process. The United Nations Development Programme offers a particularly influential account of human development that aims to promote not only material well-being but also freedom and dignity. The UNDP provides annual surveys of human development in countries all around the world, although the actual indicators it uses to measure human development focus more narrowly on life expectancy, literacy, education, and standard of living. *See also* POLITICAL DEVELOPMENT. PBl

devolution The grant of power by an upper level of government to a lower one. In contrast to *federalism, where each tier has protected areas of power, a devolved government remains constitutionally subordinate to the government which gave it its power and which could in principle revoke it.

There have been several experiments with devolution to subnational governments in the United Kingdom. The three Home Rule Bills (1886, 1893, and 1912) were all attempts to set up a devolved government in Ireland while retaining sovereignty at Westminster. They all failed, for a number of reasons. Most relevant of them today is what is now known as the 'West Lothian Question' (because it was constantly being put in the 1970s by Tam Dalyell, then MP (Lab) for West Lothian; like Mr Gladstone's Irish Question, it never received a satisfactory answer). In a generalized form, the West Lothian Question asks what are to be the numbers, powers, and duties of upper-tier (Westminster) MPs for a devolved territory. If their numbers are left untouched (as in the Scotland and Wales Acts 1978), the devolved territory is privileged vis-à-vis the rest of the country. If they are abolished (1886) the devolved territory suffers taxation without representation. If they are allowed to vote at Westminster on non-devolved matters but not on devolved ones (considered in 1893) the majority of votes on devolved matters might be for a different party to the majority of votes on non-devolved matters. The most coherent solution to the West Lothian Question is probably to reduce the numbers of such Westminster MPs and to ring-fence devolved matters in the devolved territory. This was adopted for Northern Ireland in the Government of Ireland Act 1920 but broke down in

1972 because Westminster could no longer refrain from intervening in the devolved affairs of Northern Ireland.

The difficulty of solving the West Lothian Question drove various parties (the Liberals in 1912 and the Labour Party in 1991–2) to propose schemes for 'Home Rule All Round', in which the whole country is given lower-tier assemblies. In the United Kingdom this produces further problems: either the whole of England is given one assembly (the 1912 proposal), in which case it becomes overwhelmingly stronger than the Scottish, Welsh, and Northern Irish assemblies and there is rather little left for Westminster to do; or each region of England is given an assembly (the 1991 proposal), a solution which has nothing in its favour except logic. A proposed elected assembly for the North-East of England was overwhelmingly defeated in a 2004 referendum.

Devolution to Scotland, Wales, and Northern Ireland was implemented in 1998 and 1999. In each case, it was legitimized by a referendum approving it—by a very narrow margin in Wales, but by comfortable margins in Scotland and Northern Ireland. A simultaneous referendum in the Republic of Ireland agreed overwhelmingly to abandon the Republic's territorial claim over Northern Ireland. This legitimation makes UK devolution much more stable than the failed attempts of 1886, 1893, 1912, and 1978. However, the problem of representation (the West Lothian Question) and the problem of finance (summarized as the '*Barnett Formula'; more accurately, the incorrect objectives of the formula coupled with its failure to achieve them) leave tensions in the devolution settlement.

d'Holbach *See* HOLBACH, PAUL HENRI DIETRICH D'.

d'Hondt, Victor (1841–1901) Belgian lawyer and enthusiast for *proportional representation. His formula for assigning seats to parties in multiseat districts was, unknown to him, the same as that proposed a century earlier by *Jefferson to assign seats to states in the US Congress after each decennial census (*see* APPORTIONMENT). The d'Hondt (Jefferson) system is biased in favour of large parties. Unsurprisingly, it is the most popular of the apportionment rules used nowadays by parties to assign each other seats in assemblies with proportional representation.

dialectical materialism A theory of nature formalized from the work of *Engels in particular by Soviet ideologists, dialectical materialism supposes that all phenomena consist of matter in motion. Motion itself is the result of the contradictions inherent among the elements in all objects. Moreover, arguing that they are putting *Hegel on a materialist basis, dialectical materialists assert that nature itself has a history governed by determinate laws such as quantity into quality, interpenetration of opposites, and the negation of the negation. The motion of matter has been subject to transformation and development, particularly the transformation of quantitative changes into qualitative differences. Mankind is considered to be the highest stage of material development. As with nature itself, so human development is subject to dialectal processes of development. The motion of any given stage of society is to be understood in terms of the character of the contradictions of its constituent social elements. At certain stages, and of necessity, quantitative changes occur in a given order which result in such heightened social contradictions that a new, qualitatively higher, stage of social development results. For Soviet dialectical materialists, the highest stage of social development was communism.   swh

dictatorship In modern usage, absolute rule unrestricted by law, constitutions, or other political or social factors within the state. The original dictators, however, were magistrates in ancient Italian cities (including Rome) who were allocated absolute power during a period of emergency. Their power was neither arbitrary nor unaccountable, being subject to law and requiring retrospective justification. There were no such dictators after the beginning of the second century BC, however, and later dictators such as Sulla and the Roman emperors conformed more to our image of the dictator as an autocrat and near-despot.

In the twentieth century the existence of a dictator has been a necessary and (to some) definitive component of totalitarian regimes: thus Stalin's Russia, Hitler's Germany, and Mussolini's Italy were generally referred to

as dictatorships. In the Soviet case the very word and idea of dictatorship were legitimized by Marx's idea of the historical necessity of a 'dictatorship of the proletariat' which would follow the revolution and eradicate the bourgeoisie.   LA

dictatorship of the proletariat For Marx, the transition period between capitalist and communist society 'in which the state can be nothing but the revolutionary dictatorship of the proletariat' (*Critique of the Gotha Programme*, 1875). The proletariat would assume state power aiming to eliminate the old relations of production. It would replace these relations with a class dictatorship which would both place the productive forces under proletarian control and pave the way for the abolition of class distinctions culminating in a classless society. *The Communist Manifesto* (1848) stated that the result would be 'an association in which the free development of each is the condition for the free development of all'.

Marx used the expression very infrequently and when he did employ it, he appeared to understand the word 'dictatorship' as meaning a concentration of power or forces rather than as a repressive situation. A different model of transition is offered in *The Civil War in France* (1871) based upon the experience of the Paris Commune. It stressed the immediate dismantling of the state apparatus, the decentralization of power and popular democratic control over and management of civil society. The 'commune' and 'dictatorship' models coexist uneasily in Marx's work.

Lenin discussed both models in *The State and Revolution* (1917). It can be argued that the establishment of war communism in the immediate post-revolutionary era was an attempt to implement the dictatorship.   GL

Diderot, Denis (1713–84) French philosopher and co-editor (with Jean d'Alembert) of the original seventeen-volume *Encyclopédie* (1751–65): one of the most remarkable works of the French *Enlightenment and a testament to the new intellectual enthusiasm of that age for secular rationalism and socially progressive ideas. The *Encyclopédie* issued a direct challenge to royal *absolutism and the religious supremacy of the Catholic Church throughout Europe.

Diderot's political ideas were rooted in his philosophical *materialism and atheism, and an awareness of the link between political institutions and a society's underlying culture and socio-economic characteristics: a view he shared with *Montesquieu and *Rousseau. Diderot desired to enhance conditions of human freedom, a goal which in his view required an open society and toleration of each individual's chosen route to happiness through the exercise of individual rights. Property rights served as the only rational basis of citizenship. A political ruler must act as a guardian of such rights in the national interest.

Towards the end of his life, influenced by the *American Revolution, Diderot advocated the principle of popular sovereignty, and defended the people's right of revolution against tyrannical authority. Although he died in 1784, his radical ideas were a key intellectual component in the early stages of the *French Revolution. KT

difference principle The principle that inequalities are acceptable only if they attach to positions open to all (*equal opportunity) and are of benefit to the worst-off members of society. This principle was put forward by John *Rawls (1921-2002), and first elaborated in his *A Theory of Justice*, to capture the requirements of social justice. It would, he asserts, be embraced by rational, prudential individuals asked to provide a standard of justice for their society, in ignorance of (among other things) their place in it. Although Rawls varied the precise formulation of the principles of justice in his later work, the key notion remains that stated above. AR

Diggers *See* WINSTANLEY, GERRARD.

dignified/efficient Walter *Bagehot, in *The English Constitution*, published in 1867, asserted that a constitution needed two parts, 'one to excite and preserve the reverence of the population' and the other to 'employ that homage in the work of government'. The first he called 'dignified' and the second 'efficient'. The monarch was the prime example of dignity in this sense and the cabinet of efficiency. Thus Queen Victoria, while lacking executive power, had an important constitutional role. The distinction

has survived and has been often cited in the twentieth century in the development of systematic theories of politics (in which the parts of a system are seen as functional in respect of the whole) and in prescriptive debates about the merits of an executive presidency vis-à-vis those of monarchy and other forms of 'symbolic' head of state. LA

diminishing marginal utility *See* ECONOMIC MAN.

diplomacy Diplomacy originated in the system of conducting relations between the states of classical Greece. It revived in medieval Europe and grew in importance in the relations between the city states of Renaissance Italy and the emerging states of post-Reformation Europe.

The Congress of Vienna, 1815, regularized a system of permanent diplomacy between states. The great powers exchanged embassies and ambassadors, while relations involving smaller powers were conducted through legations and ministers. A recognized diplomatic profession developed, characterized by the aristocracy of its members and the secrecy of its methods. After the First World War more open or 'democratic' diplomacy flourished for a short while. At the end of the Second World War the distinction between embassies and legations was abandoned, and ambassadors proliferated, especially when new states were formed from the European colonies.

Some writers have identified distinct styles of diplomacy—the European style with its emphasis on diplomacy as a mere instrument, and American, revolutionary, and Third World styles which, in differing ways, give more emphasis to the morality of recognizing and dealing with other states. However, in practice, diplomacy reflects strongly the European tradition: diplomats represent to their home government and to their host government the views and interests of the other and, in negotiation, attempt to reconcile the two. The diplomat is thus always liable to be misunderstood; popularity at home spells unpopularity with the host or, the more frequent case, vice versa.

Improved communications are often cited as having rendered diplomats obsolete. However, capital cities host large diplomatic communities. PBY

direct action A form of political protest aimed at placing pressure upon rulers for changes to policy, which employs methods that bypass 'official' channels such as parliaments or bureaucracy. It is the very 'directness' of direct action which is often of primary concern to the protestors, i.e. that the action is aimed at preventing, or at least significantly increasing the costs of, whatever policy it is that the protestors object to. In recent years this kind of activity has been particularly marked in the environmental policy area, with direct action groups operating in the areas of anti-roads protests (e.g. 'Reclaim the Streets'), the defence of what are seen as pristine areas of wilderness (Earth Liberation Front), climate change ('Rising Tide'), and animal rights (Animal Liberation Front).

As well as seeking to make a direct difference to the costs involved in pursuing certain policies (which will often involve covert forms of activity), direct action can have a more symbolic dimension as well, as it moves towards forms generally recognized as 'civil disobedience'. This may be exemplified by peace groups who cut a link in a fence and wait to be arrested for criminal damage, or anti-GM crop protestors who pull up one plant and also await arrest. This behaviour highlights a second aspect of direct action—as a method of attracting public attention to a particular policy area about which protestors are concerned, which involves being seen to take a clear moral stand on the relevant issue.

Where direct action protest takes place within a democratic context, critics often see it as inherently undemocratic and anti-deliberative. Small groups of self-elected activists take it upon themselves to decide what is right, and then seek to impose costs on others in order to get them to change their policy preferences. MH

direct democracy Democracy without representation, where those entitled to decide do so in sovereign assemblies, and where committees and executives are selected by lot rather than elected. Direct democracy was practised in ancient Athens, and was advocated by *Rousseau. Rousseauvian ideals revived under the influence of the *New Left in the 1960s and some argue that modern information technology now makes direct democracy possible even in populous places.

directed democracy A form of democracy whereby citizens remain engaged in democratic procedures continuously, and particularly between elections. Unlike *representational government structures (or indirect democracy), where individuals are most active in decision-making during an election through voting, directed democracy is where citizens maintain an active and continuous role in decision-making processes through a series of formal democratic mechanisms, such as automatic legislative review, *referendum, *recall, and policy ratification. This can be complementary to, but distinct from *deliberative democracy, which incorporates more informal structures of consultation, grass-root forums, and civil action.

directional theory of voting A set of models of voting behaviour in which a voter's strength of preference for a candidate depends on whether the voter and the candidate take the same side on a policy issue/dimension. These contrast with the theory of *spatial competition (or proximity model) in which voters prefer the candidate closest to them in the policy space irrespective of whether they lie on different sides of a neutral (or status-quo) point. In its simplest form, voters prefer candidates on the same side to those on the opposite side of a single dimension. If the single dimension is the left–right dimension, right-wing voters would prefer all the right-wing candidates to the left-wing candidates, even if they are closer to a left-wing candidate. This model can be extended to allow for different dimensions of varying importance or *salience. Rabinowitz and Macdonald (1989, *American Political Science Review*) elaborate further by incorporating 'intensity'. Both voters and candidates can vary in the extent to which they take a particular stance. This is modelled as distance from the neutral point. The utility function (strength of preference for a candidate) is the product of the voter and candidate intensities, accounting for direction. This implies that right-wing voters prefer the most right-wing candidate, no matter how right-wing they are themselves. The model therefore predicts that candidates have an incentive to be the most extreme candidate on their side of any particular dimension. Since this is an unattractive feature of the model, mechanisms have been proposed to constrain movement, such as a 'region of acceptability' outside of which candidates are penalized. SF

directive (EU) A legal act of the *European Union that dictates that a particular action must be performed or complied with but does not instruct means for how the directive must be implemented. Directives are distinctive from regulations (fully binding and detailed for all member states), recommendations (non-binding), decisions (fully binding on members it is directed to) and opinions (non-binding). The key aspect of a directive is that it leaves room for flexibility by member states, especially in terms of implementation, while still dictating compliance. There are a number of legislative mechanisms within the EU to create directives, yet most are created via the *European Commission and the *European Parliament.

Director of National Intelligence After criticism of the *CIA over its failure to prevent the *September 11th 2001 attacks on the United States, the Office of the Director of National Intelligence was created in 2005. The Director of National Intelligence was charged with the oversight of the US intelligence community, and providing advice to the President, the *National Security Council, and the Department of *Homeland Security.

(⊕) SEE WEB LINKS

• Office of the Director of National Intelligence website.

dirigisme Term derived from French word *diriger* (to direct) referring to the control of economic activity by the state. Intervention may take the form of legal requirements, financial incentives and penalties, nationalization, or comprehensive economic planning, though with an underlying commitment to private ownership. Used predominantly in connection with the practices of French governments of both Imperial and Republican varieties. SW

dirty public goods Dirty public goods are not necessarily public goods, in the technical sense that an act of consumption does not diminish their supply, but rather public projects assumed to be of net benefit to the population as a whole, but not to those living

near them. Power stations and airports are among the most common examples: they leave what some political geographers call their 'externality footprint' on their neighbours. Naturally the neighbours of such projects are likely to show a *NIMBY reaction. There has been considerable debate about the best decision-making procedures for taking into account the interests of both gainers and losers in such issues. In this debate it is generally argued that existing procedures are fundamentally flawed. LA

disarmament Reduction in fighting capacity. The word disarmament, as commonly used, invariably lacks precise meaning unless subject to careful qualification. For example, it can be multilateral, bilateral, or unilateral. And the extent of what could be involved varies greatly. General and complete disarmament is often piously held among negotiators to be the final objective. But in practice, states have usually concentrated on the less utopian goal of seeking agreement on partial measures intended to cover particular categories of weapons, or applying to designated geographical areas (as in the case of nuclear-weapon-free zones). And in this kind of strictly limited context the goal has sometimes been abolition, sometimes limited reduction, sometimes a freeze, sometimes even a mutually agreed increase. Now a freeze or a mutually agreed increase is not strictly speaking disarmament at all. And such measures may not even be intended to be a first step towards any kind of reduction or abolition. For the aim may simply be to promote stability in force structures. Hence a new term to cover such cases has become fashionable since the 1960s, namely, arms control.

The first practical efforts to limit armaments by general international agreement were made at conferences held at The Hague in 1899 and 1907 but no positive results were achieved. Much more serious were the efforts made under the auspices of the League of Nations after the First World War. Negotiations involving most countries and ostensibly covering all categories of weapons reached a climax in 1932 when the World Disarmament Conference opened in Geneva. By 1935 the Conference was, however, seen to have failed due to rising tensions among the great powers—not least between Germany and France following the rise of Hitler. But perhaps failure was in any case inevitable given the complexity of striking a fair balance among the force structures of a great variety of states with differing security concerns.

More successful were negotiations in the same period for naval arms limitation. In 1922 at the Washington Conference the United States, Great Britain, Japan, France, and Italy agreed on the size of their battleship fleets and in 1930 at the London Conference the first three extended the deal to cover all fighting vessels. Verification was easy and the issues uncomplicated. Nevertheless the Japanese in 1935 decided to abandon support for these treaties and hence a new naval arms race began.

Following the Second World War disarmament and arms control negotiations came to be dominated by the *Cold War alliances. There was much insincere posturing on both sides until the Soviets achieved nuclear parity with the Americans in the late 1960s. Thereafter negotiations, particularly concerning nuclear weapons, became more serious and notable agreements have been signed ranging from the *SALT Treaties of the 1970s to the *START Treaties. But experts disagree about the importance of the limitations thus achieved. There certainly have been financial savings, especially since the end of the Cold War (*see* PEACE DIVIDEND). And the spiralling and potentially destabilizing nuclear arms race between Moscow and Washington appears to have ended. On the other hand, the Russians have recently been troubled by two developments. First, in October 1999 the US Senate voted down ratification of the *Comprehensive Nuclear-Test-Ban Treaty. Secondly, in December 2001 the new Republican Administration of George W. Bush announced its unilateral withdrawal from the Anti-Ballistic Missile Treaty of 1972 in order to pursue a National Missile Defense programme (*Strategic Defense Initiative) designed to reduce vulnerability to missile attacks from so-called 'rogue states'—and maybe also China (although this was not proclaimed). And the fact is that both Russia and the United States still have a massive capacity to inflict assured destruction on any part of the planet, including each other's heartlands. These fears were relieved to some degree

with the signing of New START between the US and Russia in 2010. This treaty made significant pledges to reduce existing stockpiles of nuclear weapons as well as limited the design of new offensive nuclear weapons. That said, the future for New START is now unclear, since in 2017 US President Donald J. Trump signalled to the Russians that the treaty was disadvantageous to the US, and thus it may not survive until its stated end date of 2021 (*see also* START).

Even if in the long run the US–Russian strategic relationship can continue to be managed in a much more satisfactory way than during the Cold War, this may not unfortunately have much impact on the issue that is now causing greatest concern to advocates of disarmament and arms control: the proliferation of nuclear-weapon capability to more and more states. Thus both India and Pakistan openly carried out nuclear weapon tests in 1998 and did so for reasons of perceived national security interest that were probably beyond being influenced by any example, however noble, that Washington and Moscow had chosen to set. And the same will apply in the case of various other states if they come to feel vulnerable in their own regions to irresistible attacks with conventional forces.

Finally, efforts continue to be made to control the spread of chemical weapons under the Chemical Weapons Convention of 1993 and to keep in place the Biological Weapons Convention of 1972. But confidence in such measures of arms control, especially when unaccompanied by extensive means of *verification, has not been strengthened by the revelation that the Soviet Union in its last years successfully concealed consistent and systematic cheating on its obligations under the Biological Weapons Convention. Events in Tokyo during the mid-1990s, in the United States in the last months of 2001, and the use of chemical weapons in the *Syrian Civil War in 2014 underline the fear that the threat of the use of biological and chemical weapons may now come more from sub-state actors than from sovereign states. DC

discourse analysis A general term used to refer to the study and analysis of language (written and oral) to determine broader political meaning and its social implications. In the study of politics, discourse analysis is a methodological tool often used to examine political speeches, policy documents, institutional framework documents, and legal cases. Often associated with *post-positivism or *political sociology, discourse analysis argues that all language is a form of social interaction, which is socially constructed, contextualized, and embedded. As a result, the systematic analysis of political language/discourse can reveal key insights about the particular social understanding of a political issue, its social construction, embedding, its discursive practice, and its broader meaning (explicit or hidden).

discrete variable In *quantitative research there are two broad types of variable: discrete and *continuous. Discrete, or categorical, variables are those for which subjects or observations can be categorized. For example, vote choice is a discrete variable since there is a limited set of parties or candidates to vote for. SF

discrimination Originally the act of noting differences, discrimination now denotes differentiation between people on grounds such as gender, colour, sexuality, disability, or class. Discrimination in a political system can be explicit or covert. South Africa under apartheid would be a case of institutionalized exclusion of black people from public political life recognized by the state. Similar explicit exclusions are practised against women in many Middle Eastern countries. However, discrimination on grounds of ethnicity and gender can also be seen to operate at a more informal level. Levels of education, employment, and political representation, and percentages of those convicted of crimes, living in poverty, and so on, have been employed as measures by organizations monitoring discrimination in various societies to indicate how informal exclusions operate. In the UK, the Equality and Human Rights Commission was created in 2007, with the aspiration to 'eliminate discrimination, reduce inequality, protect human rights and to build good relations, ensuring that everyone has a fair chance to participate in society'. SR

disjointed incrementalism Disjointed incrementalism occurs when the making of policy is divided into stages, in such a way that by separately considering $p_1, p_2, \ldots, p_n$ we arrive at a conclusion less justifiable than if we had considered the whole, P. A paradigm example at the level of public decision-making occurs in road planning: A motorway is constructed from A to B. It creates such a large traffic flow entering B that there is a very powerful argument for extending it to C and so on to E. However, had we to consider a road from A to E per se, we might have seen more properly the disadvantages of such a scheme and either left well alone or built a railway. Disjointed incrementalism has acquired the nickname 'salami politics' for no better reason than that salami is a sausage almost invariably eaten in slices. LA

dissolution The act of bringing about the end of a parliament, followed by the issuing of writs for the election of a new one. In many countries parliaments have fixed terms leading to predictable dissolution. Other constitutions allow governments the right to determine the length of a parliament and the timing of a dissolution. The United Kingdom, by contrast, has few rules concerning dissolution, a situation which continues to fuel active debate. Under the 1911 Parliament Act it is laid down that no parliament should last longer than five years. Formally, dissolution is by royal proclamation. In practice, few parliaments run the full term. Prime ministers frequently request a dissolution at a time when an election could be held to keep or increase the governing party's majority. The monarch complies, although the proper response to such a request in the context of a *hung parliament is unclear. Alternatively, a prime minister may be forced to request a dissolution as a result of the government losing a vote of confidence in the House of Commons. Critics suggest that the power to dissolve is unfair to non-incumbents, and that fixed-term parliaments would be fairer. Alternatively, it is contested that fixed-term parliaments could saddle the country with weak minority or coalition governments as well as governments which have lost the confidence of the House of Commons and hence the capacity to take decisions on controversial issues. The flexibility in current practice allows for dissolutions which meet the need for effective governing majorities and changes in government. The Scottish Parliament, National Assembly for Wales, and Northern Ireland Assembly all have fixed terms, although there are provisions for dissolution and fresh elections in circumstances in which a government cannot be formed. JBT

distributive justice The principle or set of principles explaining what justice requires when some good (or bad) is distributed amongst persons. The general requirement of distributive justice is *suum cuique*, to each his or her due; but this does not yet explain how we should determine what is due to a person. Common bases for this calculation are needs, rights or entitlement, and desert. Hence what is due to a person would depend, respectively, on level of neediness, on rights or similar claims already possessed, or on desert. All three notions need further elaboration, and desert is especially open to interpretation. Disputes about distributive justice arise in three principal ways. The first dispute concerns the spheres in which we are willing to apply notions of distributive justice. Are the requirements of distributive justice to be applied to just any (dis)benefit persons may enjoy, or should its sphere be restricted—for example, is distributive justice relevant to developing friendship? A second source of difficulty arises if a measure of need, desert, or entitlement is required. For example, even those who might agree that distributive justice should respond to neediness or merit can disagree about how to assess it. Lastly, what is the proper response to the number of possible interpretations of *suum cuique*? For example, should we recognize only one distributive principle to be used across all spheres? Or should we take account of a plurality of principles, perhaps by using different principles within different spheres? What is to be done when the principles require conflicting distributions? *See also* GLOBAL JUSTICE. AR

divine right of kings The doctrine that the right to rule comes from God, and that kings are answerable to him alone. This theory has its origins in the medieval controversy between the Church and secular rulers as to the origin of political power. All were agreed that it came ultimately from God who alone held the right over life and death. What was at issue was the route. The papacy held that it came through God's representative, the Church and its ministers. Anti-papalists, such as *Dante, maintained that power in secular matters came directly from God to the monarch, whether he be elected or hereditary. The argument was revived in the sixteenth and seventeenth centuries with the rise of absolute monarchs in France and England. In its extreme form, as stated in *Basilikon Doron* by King James I, it says that: (1) political power comes directly from God to a hereditary monarch; (2) that monarch has absolute power which cannot be in any way restrained; and (3) anyone who opposes the monarch in any way is guilty of treason and liable to death, and, possibly, damnation. *Filmer gave divine right a *patriarchal base by attempting to ground it on the authority God gave to Adam, as the father of the human race.

The doctrine was opposed by the Jesuits—Bellarmine and *Suarez in particular. It was brutally set aside in England by Cromwell and in France by the Republic in 1792–3. In England it was revived by Charles II but died with the Glorious Revolution of 1688 (*see also* LOCKE). CB

division of labour The systematic (but not necessarily planned or imposed) division of functions, tasks, or activities. *Plato's Republic is built upon a functional division of labour: the Philosophers determine the law, the Auxiliaries act as a military force and executive branch, and the Producers undertake the economic activity necessary to provide everyone with sustenance and themselves with comfort. This particular division of labour, Plato argues, reflects the requirements of nature (since individuals have different natural capacities) while producing a harmonious whole. Other important forms of the division of labour are sexual, geographical, and social. Men and women have undertaken different activities, although contemporary understandings of what is conventional or the result of domination reject earlier views of what is natural in such arrangements. Geographical division of labour may emerge where different localities have different climatic and soil conditions; one form which has been thought important is the division of labour between town and country. Social division of labour refers to the separation of activities between individuals within society, and is often linked to the existence of *classes. The division of labour has been regarded as an important explanation of increased productivity in *industrial society, although it has also been identified with alienation, demoralization, and the imposition of labour discipline. These negative features of the division of labour have been particularly emphasized in relation to the removal of direct producers from the product market, and the intensification of the division of labour involved when one person repetitively performs the same detailed operation. Whether a 'harmonious whole' coexists with extensive division of labour, or how one might be achieved, remain fundamental issues. AR

Dodgson, Charles L. (1832–98) English mathematician and logician, who also wrote the children's classics *Alice's Adventures in Wonderland* and *Through the Looking Glass* under the pseudonym of Lewis Carroll. In the early 1870s Dodgson stumbled on the problem of *cycling independently of *Borda and *Condorcet (copies of whose works in the libraries Dodgson used remain uncut to this day). He proposed several voting procedures, including one for breaking a cycle should no Condorcet winner exist. In the 1880s he turned his attention to *proportional representation. Because of the eccentricity of his personality, all this work was totally ignored until recently.

domestic analogy An analogy between individuals in a state of nature and polities in the anarchical international system, often drawn by writers on international relations. This has permitted social contract theories to be applied to relations between states and the development of international society. The chief deficiency of this line of reasoning, first pointed out by *Rousseau, is that there is neither a natural limit to the growth of the state nor an organically constrained lifespan. It is therefore possible for states reacting to the *security dilemma to dedicate themselves to competition through trade and war to an extent and in a manner far exceeding the physical specialization of individual warriors. CJ

dominant party Term referring to a political party which dominates the government of a country over several decades, governing either on its own or as the leading partner in coalition governments. The classic examples were the Christian Democrats in Italy, the *Liberal Democrats in Japan, and the *Congress in India. One of the characteristics of a dominant party is that opposition politics often occurs within the dominant party, rather than through the formal opposition. Dominant parties have tended to become highly factionalized, with the selection of party leaders becoming a competition between the leading factions. WG

dominion A synonym for power in early modern English, the term later came to denote any realm over which a sovereign exercised authority. From the later nineteenth century it was adopted to refer to self-governing states within the British Empire, such as Canada (1867), New Zealand (1907), and South Africa (1910), as a way of distinguishing them from less autonomous dependencies, such as Crown colonies. CJ

domino theory Analogy, first propounded by US President Eisenhower in 1954, which suggests that events in one country could trigger similar events in neighbouring countries: 'You have a row of dominoes set up, you knock over the first one, and what will happen to the last one is the certainty that it will go over very quickly. So you could have a beginning of a disintegration that would have the most profound influences.' The theory was used to justify military intervention in *Vietnam, with the claim that if it were allowed to become a communist government many others might follow. A bombastic doctrine of communist contagion, the domino theory ignored country-specific factors and was used to undermine the development of democratic socialist governments. Despite the disaster of the Vietnam War, the domino theory was resurrected by Ronald Reagan, who used it to justify military intervention in Nicaragua in the 1980s.

donor fatigue A reluctance to commit to voluntary donations of resources or *altruistic behaviour in the light of repeated demands. Donor fatigue can be seen to be exacerbated by increased competition amongst specialist charities and NGOs (*non-governmental organizations), often dependent on voluntary donations, each of whom wish to present their issues as the most urgent and beneficial. Since every issue is presented as a crisis, it can be hard to distinguish where real need lies, and both overall levels and the distribution of resources become sub-optimal.

double ballot *See* SECOND BALLOT.

Downing Street Joint Declaration (1993) *See* NORTHERN IRELAND.

Droop, H. R. (*c.*1831–84) English lawyer and advocate of proportional representation. Modified earlier suggestions as to the correct quota which should entitle a party to one seat in a multiseat district. Where v votes have been cast in an n-member district, the Droop quota is $v/(n+1)$, usually rounded up to the next integer. Used in *single transferable vote.

due process The administration of justice in accordance with established rules and principles. This cardinal principle of limited government of great antiquity is embedded in clause 39 of Magna Carta (1215). 'No free man shall be taken or imprisoned, or dispossessed, or outlawed, or banished, or in any way destroyed, … except by the legal judgment of his peers or by the law of the land.' Subsequently this right was extended to all subjects and 'law of the land' became synonymous with 'due process of law'. It is this terminology that appears in key amendments to the United States Constitution. The *Fifth Amendment (1791), one of those that comprise the so-called *Bill of Rights, was designed to ensure that the federal government did not deprive citizens of their 'life, liberty, or property, without due process of law'. Identical wording is to be found in the *Fourteenth Amendment (1868) which provides Americans with similar protection against the governments of the states. This clause has played a dramatic part in the *judicial activism of the *Supreme Court since the 1950s, notably in *civil rights cases.   DM

Durkheim, Émile (1858–1917) French sociologist. Durkheim dominated the French educational system at all levels between 1906 and 1917 when he held the chair of education (renamed the chair of sociology in 1913)

at the Sorbonne. In *The Rules of Sociological Method* (1895), he attempted to establish sociology as a science with its own particular method, explaining a distinct reality separate from individuals, and restraining their behaviour. His most famous methodological proposition was that social facts must be considered as things. Throughout his career, Durkheim applied this view to the problem of social integration which he examined in all his principal works. In *The Division of Social Labour* (1893), he proposed a general theory to explain the evolution of societies from primitive, held together by mechanical solidarity (based on similarity between different individuals), to modern, held together by organic solidarity (based upon complementary differences between individuals). Unlike economists, whom he accused of tautology, Durkheim based this evolution towards greater division of labour on the social fact of increasing density of populations, which led to reduction in the level of mechanical solidarity, and therefore to consciousness of the change. Following their method, economists posited a deliberate choice of increased division of labour as the cause although it was also the effect. In *Suicide* (1897), less under the influence of *Comte than previously, he tried to find sociological explanations for what is apparently the most isolated action possible. He divided suicide into three (or perhaps even four) main types, one of which is the most important for his analysis. This is based on his concept of anomie, the breakdown of the individual's connection with society. He rejected what he saw as simplistic positivist explanations, as for example the thesis that suicide can be explained by differences in climate at different seasons. Social facts can only be explained by other social facts, not determined from outside. He saw anomie as a result of the rapidity of industrialization which was breaking down the existing moral order. In *The Elementary Forms of Religious Life* (1912), Durkheim again chose a particular problem to discover its general implications. He examined primitive Australian religion, and proposed that the general form of religion, repeated in all other examples, was as a system of collective beliefs separating sacred from profane. Whatever the particular forms asserted by different religions, the sacred was always society in general, the external force that imposed much of their behaviour on individuals. Durkheim attempted to turn morality into a science, and he always believed that sociology should be used to improve society rather than simply to explain it. The most important way in which this could be done was through education, a view he shared with the founders of the Third Republic. In a political sense, he was a liberal, but not an individualist. He examined socialism in 1893, and decided that while it was certainly a proper reaction to the evils of industrial society, its proposed solution would not improve human life. He was one of the chief proponents of the doctrine of solidarism which, as one of his followers asserted in 1907, became 'a sort of official philosophy for the Third Republic'. This formed the ideological basis of the Radical Party which was founded in 1905 and became the most important in the Republic.   cs

Duverger's law In *Political Parties* (English edition 1954), the French political scientist Maurice Duverger (1917–2014) proposed a law and a hypothesis about the relationship between the number of parties in a country and its electoral system. The law was that 'the simple majority, single ballot system favours the two-party system'; the hypothesis was that 'both the simple-majority system with second ballot and proportional representation favour multi-partism'. The division of these two statements into one law and one hypothesis is due to *Riker, who claims that the first is a generalization which can be backed by formal reasoning, whereas the second is an easily falsifiable contingent generalization about the cases actually studied by Duverger. The law is driven by the idea that in the long run rational politicians and voters will realize that it is hopeless to have more than two parties competing at national level. Although three parties may remain in contention for a few years, a party which begins to slide will rapidly disappear as everybody comes to realize that it will win no seats at all if its support is evenly dispersed. By contrast, the number of parties in a proportional electoral system may be determined more by social forces than by the system's opportunities to split without penalty: Austria and Germany are well-

known examples of countries with PR but only three or four parties.

The reasoning behind Duverger's law seems good, so why has three-party competition been so hardy in Britain? The struggle between the Liberals and the Labour Party to be the opposition to the Conservatives ran from 1918 to 1929, when it was won by Labour, and reopened in 1981. Because the Liberals (now Liberal Democrats) have some local fortresses, they have never been entirely wiped out, so that votes for them are not always obviously wasted. The need to modify Duverger's law to allow for differing patterns of two-party competition in different regions was pointed out by Douglas Rae (*The Political Consequences of Electoral Laws*, 1967). A similar pattern of competition between two locally strong parties, which might be different parties in different parts of the country, persists in Canada. One view voiced by G. Tullock is that 'Duverger's Law is true, but it may take 200 years to work itself out'.

dyad Pair (of countries, usually). The term is most used in international relations research (such as the *Correlates of War), especially peace studies, where all dyads are examined to investigate the causes of war—a line of research begun by L. F. *Richardson. It turns out that there are few wars between Switzerland and Nepal.

dyarchy System of dual rule, whereby government functions are shared between two bodies. Dyarchy was introduced in India between 1919 and 1935, with governmental functions divided between Provincial legislatures and the Governor's Executive Council. It proved unpopular, with disputes regarding overlapping functions and a lack of accountability. In *Northern Ireland a different form of dyarchy has been in operation since 1998. The devolved government established after the *Belfast Agreement has a system whereby the Assembly elects two leaders, one from each of the two main communities. These two leaders have identical powers (although called First Minister and Deputy First Minister) and serve jointly; if one ceases to hold office so must the other. In such a way it is hoped that both unionists and nationalists can be seen to have a share in the leadership of the devolved government.

Early Day Motion In the House of Commons, a motion put down by a back-bench MP nominally for discussion 'at an early day' but with no time fixed for it. As the parliamentary timetable is controlled by the leadership of the parties, Early Day Motions are almost never actually debated. They may be regarded as pure expressive gestures, as cheap talk in which an MP can strike attitudes at no cost, or as a serious basis for classifying MPs' ideologies.

SEE WEB LINKS
• Early Day Motion website and database from the UK Parliament.

East The word evokes some combination of (1) the sacred East to which Christians and Muslims both pray; (2) the Orient (which is simply the Latin for 'east') as traditional antithesis to the modern secular West; (3) the Orthodox or Eastern Church with its historic mission to preserve the orderly values of the Eastern Roman Empire, as much against a decadent West as against Islam; (4) the settled and tamed East coast of North America; and (5) the Eastern bloc of communist states, centred upon the USSR, which the United States and its allies opposed during the *Cold War. CJ

ecocentrism A term in ecological political philosophy used to denote a nature-centred, as opposed to human-centred, system of values. The justification for ecocentrism normally consists in an ontological belief and subsequent ethical claim. The ontological belief denies any existential divisions between human and non-human nature sufficient to ground a claim that humans are either (*a*) the sole bearers of intrinsic value or (*b*) possess greater intrinsic value than non-human nature. Thus the subsequent ethical claim is for an equality of intrinsic value across human and non-human nature, or 'biospherical egalitarianism'.

Ecocentrism is taken by its proponents to constitute a radical challenge to long-standing and deeply rooted *anthropocentric attitudes in Western culture, science, and politics. Anthropocentrism is alleged to leave the case for the protection of non-human nature subject to the demands of human utility, and thus never more than contingent on the demands of human welfare. An ecocentric ethic, by contrast, is believed to be necessary in order to develop a non-contingent basis for protecting the natural world. Critics of ecocentrism have argued that it opens the doors to an anti-humanist morality that risks sacrificing human well-being for the sake of an ill-defined 'greater good'. MH

ecological association In the sense used by political statisticians, ecological association is the association between two characteristics both measured at the aggregate level rather than the individual level, and has nothing to do with ecology. For instance, it may be shown that regions with high mining employment also display a high vote for the left-wing party. The ecological fallacy is to infer from this that miners vote for the left-wing party. From the given facts, nothing is known about the individuals in the region and there may (although in this case there is unlikely to) be some quite different reason for the association than the obvious one.

ecology From the Greek roots meaning 'house study'. The German writer Ernst Haeckel defined ecology as 'the science of relations between organisms and their environment', a general definition which has remained acceptable. He first published the word *Oekologie* in his *Generalle Morphologie* in 1866.

The concept of ecology has always had three separate dimensions. (1) Overtly, it refers to an intellectual pursuit, the study of the system of interactions involving living things. (2) But it is also used to refer to the system itself: the reality of causal relationships between species. (3) Finally, 'ecology' has always been used by some people, though not generally by professional ecologists, to mean a substantive morality and a political programme inspired by the perception of the existence of an ecological system. Typically, the morality criticizes current human practice for its destruction of ecological systems and seeks to (re)create harmony between man and nature. Whether these objectives are possible (or even coherent) and what their relations are with the perceptions of scientific ecology form the central questions of political ecology.

The political (as opposed to the scientific) use of the term only became established after the period of intense environmental awareness in the Western world in the late 1960s and early 1970s. This period also diverted the attention of moral philosophers, in particular, the Norwegian philosopher Arne Naess, to the implications of the idea of ecology. Naess distinguished 'Deep Ecology' which was not 'anthropocentric' and which recognized principles of 'biospherical egalitarianism', 'diversity and symbiosis', and decentralization, from 'Shallow Ecology', the merely anthropocentric environmentalism which sought to conserve the earth's resources (whether beauty or fossil fuels) for man's use. The suggestion was that man must shift to the outlook of 'Deep Ecology' even to attain the more modest aims of shallow ecology. On Naess's own account the distinction and the key principles of 'Deep Ecology' were far from clear, but this essay, among others, struck an important chord in the concerns of the time and stimulated the growth of 'green philosophy', which has existed and developed at popular, polemical, and academic levels since.

There is a fundmental problem for ecological political theory, in that scientific studies of ecology do not offer a model of ecological stability nor an idea of a harmonious role for *Homo sapiens* within the ecological system. Rather, they develop the *Darwinian model of an unstable, evolving system in which man, though not only man, crucially modifies the conditions of life for most other species, affecting their chances of survival, some for the worse, but perhaps even more for the better. Man cannot live in harmony with nature, if that means that his ecological role must be inert; nor can he fail to, in the sense that it is part of the role of all species within an ecological system to modify that system as an environment for other species.

Individual and collective choices cannot be ecologically right or ecologically wrong *per se*. However, there are powerful arguments for the looser suggestions that we should consider not only the detailed ecological consequences of our decisions, but also the nature of ecology, in considering the 'environmental' aspects of policy.   LA

Economic and Monetary Union (EMU)

The creation of a single European currency, the euro, managed by an independent European Central Bank (ECB), and the coordination of economic policies of participating member states which are expected to respect rules on convergence. The exchange rate parities of eleven participating national currencies were irrevocably fixed on 1 January 1999 and—following the admission of Greece—the euro replaced national currencies in the twelve 'Euro-zone' member states during the first months of 2002. There are presently fifteen member states, with Slovenia joining the Euro-zone in 2007 and Cyprus and Malta in 2008.

The EMU project of the *Maastricht Treaty involved the irrevocable fixing of exchange rates of national currencies from 1997—by unanimous vote if a majority of countries met the convergence criteria and were able to begin—or by 1999, automatically for those countries meeting the criteria. The project consisted of three stages: the first, which had already started in 1990, involved the liberalization of capital flows within the European Community and improved coordination of national economic policies (reinforced mutual surveillance) with the aim of sustainably low inflation rates. The second stage began in 1994 and involved the move to national central bank (NCB) independence, the reinforcement of economic policy convergence, and the creation of the European Monetary Institute (EMI) which with the European Commission would make the technical preparations for EMU and the introduction of the single currency. The third stage, beginning either in 1997 or 1999, would involve the irrevocable fixing of exchange rates, the transfer of monetary policy-making power from NCBs to the ECB, and the eventual introduction of the hard single currency and the withdrawal of national currencies.

European Union (EU) member states failing to meet the convergence criteria in 1999 would be admitted into Stage Three only when they succeeded in doing so. New EU member states were expected to join EMU—part of the *acquis communautaire*—but would initially only participate in Stage Two, proceeding to Stage Three individually once the criteria were met. These criteria are public spending deficits below 3 per cent of GDP; public debts below 60 per cent; inflation of within 1.5 per cent of the average of the three countries with the lowest rates; nominal interest rates on long-term government bonds within 2 per cent of the average of the three countries with the lowest rates (an indicator of the perceived durability of convergence); and exchange rate stability—no devaluation or severe tension within the Exchange Rate Mechanism (ERM; ERMII post-1999)—over at least a two-year period. Some margin of manoeuvre was allowed: on excessive deficits as long as they were declining 'substantially and continuously' or were considered to be 'exceptional and temporary'; and on excessive debt on the condition that this was 'sufficiently diminishing' and approaching the 60 per cent figure at 'a satisfactory pace'. The intention was to admit high debt countries such as Belgium and Italy into Stage Three. The German government—responding to domestic political pressure rooted in the concern that EMU would fail to maintain the monetary stability achieved over many years by the Bundesbank—insisted that the 3 per cent deficit be strictly respected as a condition of participation in Stage Three and beyond. The Germans also insisted upon the adoption of the Stability and Growth Pact, agreed in December 1996, which from 1999 enabled the Council to impose fines on member states which failed to respect the deficit criterion except in the case of a significant decline in the size of a member state's economy.

The negotiations on EMU began prior to German reunification, and the project was set out by national central bank governors in the Delors Committee's report of April 1989. Nonetheless, some observers have claimed that the geo-political dynamics of the early 1990s increased support for the project in countries like France, worried by the new dominance of a united Germany, and helped to convince the German Chancellor, Helmut Kohl, of the need for EMU to bind Germany to the EU and reassure Germany's neighbours. The British and Danish governments were resolutely hostile to the project and insisted upon their right to opt out of the third stage as the precondition for their accepting the Maastricht Treaty. Sweden, which joined the EU in 1995, also decided not to participate in the Euro-zone.

The creation of EMU has been justified in functionalist terms as the crowning of the *Single European Market. Some economists explain the logic of monetary union in terms of the 'triangle of incompatibility', arguing that the pursuit of exchange rate stability in the context of free capital mobility resulted in the end of monetary policy autonomy for all countries participating in the ERM except the country with the hardest (anchor) currency: Germany. In such circumstances, moving to a single currency enabled member states to avoid the exchange rate instability created by periodic bouts of currency speculation and to 'pool' control over monetary policy at the European level rather than follow German (Bundesbank) policy. However, many economists, principally Anglo-American, have criticized EMU on the grounds that the single currency area (the Euro-zone) is not an optimal currency zone, as it lacks the capacity to cope with asymmetrical economic shocks due to inadequate EU budget transfers, poor labour mobility between member states, and the constraints imposed on national economic policy-making. Since 1999, growing divergence in member state inflation and thus real interest rates have contributed to economic difficulties in many member states, stifling economic growth in some and reinforcing the possibility of boom–bust in others.

In operation, EMU and the ECB have been the object of much criticism. The euro lost over 20 per cent of its value in relation to the American dollar between 1 January 1999 and early 2002. The decline was explained in various ways: the confusion created by the virtual nature of the European currency and the 'communication' problem of the Euro-zone with the ECB and national govern-ments often sending conflicting messages to financial markets; and the lack of confidence in the Euro-zone's economies and the inad-equacy of national structural reforms. By the middle of the 2000s, the strength of the euro in relation to the dollar and other major international currencies was of great concern to most Euro-zone member states. Several member state governments have been crit-ical of what they see as the ECB's hawkish pursuit of low inflation. The independence of the ECB and its pursuit of low inflation as its primary goal have been ongoing matters of concern.

The Maastricht Treaty and the Stability and Growth Pact require all EU member state governments to submit medium-term stabilization plans to demonstrate their inten-tion of ensuring sustainably low budget def-icits (and ideally surpluses during periods of economic growth). Despite considerable pressure from the ECB, the European Com-mission, and other member states to respect the deficit criterion, Germany and France both exceeded the 3 per cent figure for several years from 2002. Together they called for and achieved (in November 2003) the suspension of the Pact's excessive deficit rules. They then engineered Pact reform (agreed in March 2005) which allowed for more margin of manoeuvre to governments in the determin-ation of excessive deficits and the application of the Pact's excessive deficit rules. *See also* FINANCIAL CRISIS (2008), SOVEREIGN DEBT CRISIS. DH

(⊕) SEE WEB LINKS

• Site of the European Central Bank (ECB), which administers Economic and Monetary Union.

Economic Commission for Latin America (ECLA) *See* DEPENDENCY.

economic man (rational economic man)
An imaginary person fought over by rival social scientists. The fights are full of sound and fury but usually signify nothing because of confusions between two meanings of 'eco-nomic man'. In the narrow meaning he is rational and selfish; in the broad meaning, rational but not necessarily selfish. Broad

economic man always observes the axioms of behaviour assumed in mainstream eco-nomic theory. At the deepest level, these are rules about transitivity, consistency, and completeness of preferences. 'Transitivity' means that if I prefer A to B and B to C, then I should prefer A to C. 'Consistency' means that if I choose A over B now, then I will continue to choose A over B every time I am confronted with the identical choice in identical circumstances. 'Completeness' means that for any goods (services, oppor-tunities) A and B, I can always make one of three choices: to prefer A, to prefer B, or to be indifferent between them. At a less abstract level, economic man is assumed to prefer more of any given good to less of it, but with diminishing marginal utility (so that each extra unit of the good is worth less to him than the one before). More generally, in his preferences for bundles comprising some quantity of one good and some of another, the more he already has of one good the more of it he would require in order to offset the loss of a unit of the other. This is called diminishing marginal substitutability.

All of these axioms are controversial. Psychologists have shown that individuals do not observe transitivity or consistency of choice when the 'frame' of the choice is altered. (For instance, people may accept a certain gamble when it is presented to them as a choice between gaining and standing still, but reject the identical gamble when it is presented to them as a choice between standing still and losing.) Completeness is unrealistically demanding. Diminishing mar-ginal utility is not always observed. However, much criticism of rational economic man is for his supposed selfishness, which the axioms of standard economic theory do not imply. Broad economic man maximizes his utility, but if giving money to famine relief makes him happier than anything else, he gives money to famine relief. Narrow eco-nomic man maximizes his personal wealth. Commonly, economics is attacked for assum-ing that most people are (or, worse, ought to be) narrow economic men; economists defend themselves by claiming that economic man is really broad economic man. However, neither side is consistent in its usage.

economics and politics *See* POLITICS AND ECONOMICS.

effective number of parties Political analysts regularly use terms like 'two-party system' and 'multi-party system' when the number of effective parties in a legislature is hard to measure. In the UK parliament of 2001, for instance, 10 parties were represented in the House of Commons, but seven of them returned only 28 MPs between them. A widely accepted algorithm due to M. Laakso and R. Taagepera calculates the effective number of parties in such circumstances. The formula is

$$N = 1/\Sigma p_i^2$$

where N denotes the effective number of parties and p_i denotes the ith party's fraction of the seats. The same process can be used for vote share for each party. This formula is the reciprocal of a well-known concentration index (the Herfindahl–Hirschman index) used in economics to study the degree to which ownership of firms in an industry is concentrated. Laakso and Taagepera correctly saw that the effective number of parties is simply an instance of the inverse measurement problem to that one. The index makes rough but fairly reliable international comparisons possible.

egalitarianism Political practice aimed at increasing *equality; the philosophical explanation and defence of the value of equality. The goods, benefits, or burdens of which an equal distribution is thought valuable may be variously specified. Considerable debate has surrounded what is required on egalitarian principles sensitive to the arguments of modern *liberalism. The focus is on the identification of inequalities which are arbitrary from a moral point of view—perhaps those which result from natural talent but not those which result from differential effort, for example. In general, the equality in question is an equality of outcome. Equalities of income, wealth, utility, and life-chances have been canvassed, as well as equal consideration (*see also* FRATERNITY) and equality of rights. Many egalitarians have been suspicious of the equality of formal rights, pointing to the substantive inequalities they may disguise or exacerbate. Critics have maintained that egalitarianism necessarily diminishes *freedom in unacceptable ways. *See also* EQUAL OPPORTUNITY; EQUAL PROTECTION. AR

Election/Electoral Commission A non-partisan body which determines election procedures and district boundaries and oversees the conduct of elections. Countries with long-established electoral commissions include India, Colombia, and Australia, the last being internationally regarded as one of the most successful. An Electoral Commission began work in the UK in 2001 and promptly began to worry whether the record fall of turnout in the 2001 General Election was its fault. (It was not.)

SEE WEB LINKS
• The site of the UK Electoral Commission.

Electoral College A mechanism for the indirect election of public officials. For the purpose of electing the President and Vice President of the United States a 538-member Electoral College is created with each state having as many electors as it has representatives and senators in the national legislature, plus three for the District of Columbia. To be elected, a candidate must obtain an absolute majority in the Electoral College, currently 270. If no candidate gains an absolute majority the US House of Representatives makes the choice, with the delegation from each state having one vote.

Most of these arrangements were devised in the Constitutional Convention of 1787 as a compromise between those who proposed a direct popular election of the President and those who preferred to make him subject to election by the legislature. As originally conceived, members of the Electoral College were expected to be prominent state worthies impervious to transient public moods. However, such notions were quickly overtaken by the emergence of parties and the popular election of electors in place of their appointment by state legislatures. The 'winner takes all' rule, or convention, that all of a state's Electoral College votes go to the candidate which wins the highest popular vote, is not in the US Constitution; two states (Maine and Nebraska) assign their electoral votes in proportion to the state vote for each candidate. Occasionally, states elect unpledged electors, or electors break their pledge and vote for a candidate other than the one they said they would. Because of the constitutional origins of the college, electors cannot be punished for this.

Reformers regularly query the merits of the Electoral College system for 'misfired' elections (where a loser gains more popular votes than the winner) and for the contingency arrangements that come into play when no candidate wins a majority in the Electoral College. The elections of 1824, 1876, 1888, and 2000 misfired, and misfires came perilously close in 1844, 1880, 1884, 1960, and 1968. Of these, 1876 and 2000 sparked legitimacy crises. That of 1876 was resolved by a 'corrupt bargain' whereby the Republicans kept the Presidency and the Democrats were allowed back into power in the South, where they resumed their oppression of African-Americans. That of 2000 was suddenly ended by the terrorist attacks of September 2001, which conferred legitimacy on President George Bush that his election by one vote in the Supreme Court had failed to do. If all states followed Maine and Nebraska and allocated electoral college votes in proportion to the popular vote in the state, misfires like 2000 would be less likely and misdemeanours in counting (such as those in Florida in 2000) less momentous.

When an election is thrown into the House the bargaining required to form a majority could also create a crisis of legitimacy. This occurred in 1800 and 1824 and might have happened in 1960, 1968, 1980, 1992, and 2000. There could also be a dangerous period of uncertainty in that the House would not make its decision until early January, a mere two weeks before the inauguration. DM

⊕ SEE WEB LINKS

• Operation and history of the Electoral College from the United States National Archives.

electoral geography Term covering the geography of elections, electoral systems, and *apportionment. Electoral geography first developed as a distinct subdiscipline in France, where *Siegfried established an association between different physical features of the terrain of western France and different voting patterns. Siegfried's *ecological association techniques were copied by a few others, notably V. O. *Key for the Southern United States, and Henry Pelling and other scholars working on Victorian and Edwardian Britain. These methods were eclipsed by survey-based methods in the 1960s because of concern about ecological fallacy, but have revived with more sophisticated techniques.

The geography of electoral systems is widely but patchily studied. *Plurality electoral systems reward small concentrated parties and punish small dispersed parties; they reward large dispersed parties and punish large concentrated parties. 'Small' and 'large' are defined in relation to the threshold of support at which a party tips from one to the other; in a three-party system this threshold is around one-third of the vote, in a four-party system around a quarter, and so on. Similar effects will be noted in any other electoral system short of the most fully proportional achievable.

The geography of apportionment deals with both the allocation of seats among multiseat units (such as states, multiseat districts, or counties), and the allocation of seats within them. The former raises the problem of allocating an integer number of seats when the exact proportion is a fractional number. The latter deals with *gerrymandering and with the computations needed to achieve optimal non-partisan districting.

electoral system Any set of rules whereby the votes of citizens determine the selection of executives and/or legislators. Electoral systems may be categorized in several ways. The most useful is probably a three-way division into *plurality, majoritarian, and *proportional systems. For national elections, plurality systems are found only in Great Britain and some former British colonies (including the United States and India) (*see* FIRST-PAST-THE-POST). Majoritarian systems are found in France and Australia for legislative elections, and in about half of the countries with directly elected chief executives (*see* SECOND BALLOT). There are many proportional systems in the democratic world; they differ widely and there is no agreed criterion whereby one may be judged better than another.

Each family of systems has a number of distinctive features. Plurality systems tend to concentrate the vote on the two leading parties (*see* DUVERGER'S LAW) except where there are concentrated regional parties. Majoritarian systems are appropriate for presidential elections, since there is only one president who ought to have majority support at least against the last rival left in the field; therefore systems such as *alternative vote are justifiable, though imperfect. However, using a majoritarian system to elect a legislature can lead to severe distortions. The number of parties elected under a proportional system is a function partly of the size of districts it employs (the more seats there are in each district, the more parties will tend to be represented), and partly of the underlying *cleavages in the society.

electoral volatility 1. The degree of change in voting behaviour between elections. There is a distinction between net volatility and total volatility. Net volatility relates to the change in the shares of the vote for each party. It is usually measured by the index of dissimilarity, or Pedersen index, which is the sum of the absolute changes in vote shares divided by 2. This gives a lower bound on the proportion of voters who changed their votes, assuming a stable voting population. Total or overall volatility is the total proportion who changed between the two elections. This can be measured with respect to those who voted at both elections, those who were eligible at both elections, or those who were eligible at either election. Since the 1960s in Britain overall volatility has been relatively stable despite large changes in net volatility.

2. The idea that voters have become more willing to switch between parties. This is related to the *dealignment thesis that voters are no longer consistent strong party identifiers with correspondingly stable voting behaviour, but free to choose who to vote for depending on the issues of the day. SF

elitism 1. The belief: that government ought in principle, always and everywhere, to be confined to elites. Rarely a worked-out doctrine in its own right, more often a piece of unexamined value judgement, or a view which follows from some more general argument in political philosophy, as for example in *Plato's *Republic*.

2. The belief: that government is in practice confined to elites; that, following a maxim of *Hume, 'ought implies can' (in other words, that there is no point in saying that government ought to be controlled by the people if in practice it cannot); and that we might just as well accept what we are bound to have anyhow. These views are especially associated with Mosca and with *Pareto in the early twentieth century, and with *Schumpeter in mid-century. All three writers shade into elitism in sense 1 because they go on to produce normative justifications of rule by elites in a democracy. However, their earlier arguments do not in themselves imply that if democratic control of the government were somehow achievable it would be undesirable.

3. The belief that government is in practice confined to elites; that this has often been justified by arguments from Plato or Schumpeter; but that this is undesirable because elite rule is in practice rule on behalf of the vested interests of (usually economic) elites. *See also* COMMUNITY POWER.

Elshtain, Jean Bethke (1941–2014) Jean Bethke Elshtain was a philosopher, political theorist, and ethicist who focused on the intersection between the ethical and the political. Elshtain's best-known work is *Women and War* (1985), in which she examines women's traditional roles in wars and the ways that those differ from (privileged) masculine roles. From highlighting gender subordination to arguing for traditional family structures, Elshtain's work was complicated, multidirectional, and path-breaking. What her diverse work shares across its many themes is emphasis on the connections between democratic thinking, ethical analysis, and religious commitment. Her work on the nature of democracy, on *just war theorizing, and on god in the state examines (in a variety of different ways) the politics and ethics of the state and its use of violence. Later in her life, Elshtain was one of a few scholars to explicitly *support* the US interventions in the *Afghanistan and *Iraq Wars, most notably in *Just War Against Terror* (2003), which used just war theorizing to argue *for* the 'war on terror' and to critique other academics' less bellicose positions. Whether cautioning against war or advocating for it, Elshtain's Christian realism provided a distinct voice in political analysis for four decades. LSB

emancipation The act or process of being set free from political, economic, cultural, and social restrictions and structures. In the study of politics and *international relations, emancipation usually is used in reference to informal or formal structures of *power with critical reflections on how to release or minimize the dominance of power on individuals and peoples. Key examples of emancipatory politics can be found in *post-colonial and anticolonial theory, in aspects of *Marxist thinking, and within *post-structuralism. However, a form of liberation politics is also a cornerstone of *liberal and enlightenment thinking, which in many ways seeks to emancipate individuals from arbitrary coercion and authoritative power. Whereas liberals and some Marxists are more assured that legitimate forms of power can coincide with freedom and emancipation, most post-structuralists believe that illegitimate power will always retrench itself and will always remain manifest in some form.

emergency powers An act of legislation or leadership decree that grants extraordinary powers to the government. Emergency powers are generally a response to a 'state of emergency' in which extraordinary events, such as war or natural disaster, compel the government to invoke stronger measures of control and coordination (e.g. the 1939 UK Parliamentary Defence Act prior to World War II). Emergency powers tend to be time-bound (at least in democracies) and are meant as a measure of last resort, since they typically suspend normal legislative and judicial procedures of democratic *accountability and *due process. That said, emergency powers are also often used as a justificatory veil for *authoritarianism and state violence. As a result, in the study of politics, the legitimacy of emergency power is usually qualified by the emergency in which those extra powers provide appropriate response. Nevertheless, even in cases of clear natural disaster, determining the legitimate use of emergency powers remains contested. *See also* SECURITIZATION.

emigration *See* MIGRATION.

EMILY's List United States *PAC which campaigns to increase the number of Democrat *pro-choice women legislators. EMILY is an acronym for 'Early Money Is Like Yeast'. There is a UK sister organization, which

seeks to increase the number of Labour women legislators.

SEE WEB LINKS
• US EMILY's List site.

eminent domain The right of the state, on behalf of the public, to take private property without the owner's consent. The term remains in wide current use in American property law and planning because American arrangements are framed by a republican constitution informed by the writings of *Locke, *Grotius, *Pufendorf, and others who suggest that the state can and must take public property on occasions, but has an absolute duty to compensate the owner justly; both the owner's and the state's rights are said to be derived from natural law. The requirement for 'due process and just compensation' are established by the *Fifth Amendment. LA

emission trading *See* CARBON TRADING.

empire Deriving from the Latin term (*imperator*) for a supreme military and, later, political leader, empire came to mean a territorial realm over which exclusive authority was exercised by a single sovereign. Thus the preamble of the English Act of Appeals (1533) justified denial of the right of subjects of the Crown to appeal to courts outside the realm or territory of England on the ground (however dubious) 'that this realm of England is an empire, and so hath been accepted in the world, governed by one supreme head and king'.

The term was also to be applied to the much more loosely controlled and heterogeneous domains of princes such as the Habsburgs. The power of the emperor Charles V (1500–58) was manifestly compromised and limited in many places, perhaps most of all within the so-called Holy Roman Empire from which he derived the title, by the continuing privileges of Church, lesser princes, cities, guilds, electors, and estates. Likewise, Queen Victoria adopted the style of Queen Empress in 1877 at precisely the moment when the addition of India and new African dependencies to her dominions led them to resemble the ramshackle constitutional amalgams of her Austrian and Russian cousins more than the older English ideal of a contiguous territory with a homogeneous population. Thereafter, 'empire' lost much of its original constitutional force and was generally taken to denote any extensive group of states, whether formed by colonization or conquest, subject to the authority of a metropolitan state, even when—as in the cases of France or the USSR—that dominant state became a republic. In this later sense, well established by the early years of the twentieth century, empire became closely associated with *imperialism. CJ

empirical analysis Research based on the objective observation of phenomena. Empirical analysis is concerned with describing and explaining reality following certain common principles for collecting and evaluating information. The general approach of empirical analysis is that only information acquired through experience and the senses is acceptable. Empirical analysis applied to the study of politics usually applies the scientific method to the study of human behaviour. Empirical analysis can be either *qualitative or *quantitative in nature. SDC

EMS (European Monetary System) The system in the *European Union intended to stabilize exchange rates between the currencies of participating member states, using the Exchange Rate Mechanism (ERM) and the balance-of-payments support process. It paved the way for *Economic and Monetary Union.

European monetary cooperation was not specifically mentioned in the *Treaty of Rome, but it was recognized that if the internal market were to avoid competitive distortions linked to exchange rate volatility, monetary cooperation would become an issue. Moreover, the operation of *CAP (Common Agricultural Policy) price support mechanisms was thought to require exchange rate stability. This led to the Barre Report of 1969, the Werner Report blueprint for monetary union of 1970, and the European 'snake' exchange rate system of 1971 as the first stage of the process to be completed by 1980. The snake died prematurely in the collapse of the *Bretton Woods gold–dollar system.

The Commission sponsored renewed efforts in 1977, unexpectedly supported by Germany and France and leading to the EMS agreement of March 1979, with Britain remaining outside. The EMS consisted first of the Exchange Rate Mechanism (ERM) fixing currency parities to +/−2.25 per cent in relation to the European Currency Unit, the value of which was determined by a weighted basket of currencies. Weaker currencies such as the lira were allowed to float or maintain wider parities of +/−6 per cent. Parity adjustment was frequent in the early 1980s, but by 1985 stability returned and agreement emerged on the need for further monetary integration as the Single Market Programme became a reality. The Delors Report on Economic and Monetary Union (1989) eventually became enshrined in the *Maastricht Treaty, for which the EMS was seen as an essential building block. Despite the clear success of the EMS, with even the UK participating by 1991, economic recession in the early 1990s and the turmoil of German reunification conspired to destabilize the ERM. Britain and Italy were forced to withdraw in September 1992 with Spain and Portugal devaluing, and by July 1993 ERM parities were allowed to fluctuate up to 15 per cent, essentially a float. The EMS crisis temporarily upset the move towards monetary union, but the development of common financial institutions and a more stable economic environment in the late 1990s saw most EU countries adopt the euro as a common currency. The ERM II came into existence in 1999, with participating currencies to remain within a margin of fluctuation of the euro. DH

EMU *See* ECONOMIC AND MONETARY UNION.

end of history A philosophical and political concept suggesting that the evolutionary and historical stages of political and economic organization could, or will, give way to a single system, or to a new unifying system, of political and economic order. This stage of organization will in essence represent the 'end of history', since all human and social evolution will be organized from within this new *post-modern condition. The concept is most notably present in the works of Thomas Moore, G. W. F. *Hegel, Karl *Marx, and, more recently, the works of international relations scholar Francis Fukuyama. In *The End of History and the Last Man*, Fukuyama argued that the end of the

*Cold War and the triumph of *liberalism and *democracy over *communism signalled an end of history. Needless to say, these views remain controversial.

endogeneity/endogenous Something is endogenous to a system if it is determined within the system, and exogenous if it is determined outside. It is relatively straightforward to determine whether a variable is endogenous or exogenous to a theoretical model. However, there is always an empirical question as to whether the model is adequate and thus whether variables that are theoretically exogenous are in fact endogenous to the system being modelled.

Sometimes there is only a tacit reference to the system. For instance, to say that 'technological development is endogenous' is to assume the reader understands that this means technological development depends on the state of the economy, i.e. the system is the economy.

In statistical regression models the exogeneity of the 'independent' variables, or regressors, is assumed. But this may be false and problematic if a regressor is correlated with the error term. The 'problem of endogeneity' arises when the factors that are supposed to affect a particular outcome, depend themselves on that outcome. For example, the effect of campaign spending on the chances of electoral success cannot easily be estimated since the level of campaign spending depends itself on the perceived chances. SF

Engels, Friedrich (1820–95) Born in Barmen near Düsseldorf, the eldest in a family of eight, Engels was the son of a wealthy mill owner who was as much dedicated to the pietist church and good works as he was to profit. At school he proved himself to be a gifted student of languages. He also quickly developed an enduring admiration for ancient Greek civilization. Later Engels was to combine his compulsory military service in the Prussian artillery with attendance at Berlin University. In Berlin he was influenced by the materialism and humanism of the *Young Hegelian critique of religion and, when in Cologne, he was strongly attracted by the communism of Moses Hess. He is remembered now, of course, as the lifelong friend, collaborator, and financial supporter of Karl *Marx, a collaboration which began in real earnest in 1845 with the joint writing of *The German Ideology*, the first full statement of *historical materialism. Orthodox Marxists are still rather inclined to assume that Marx and Engels were intellectual twins with a kind of composite personality. Nothing could be further from the truth. While there were large and unquestioned areas of agreement between Marx and Engels, most of all in political economy, the history of industry, and in the demands and tactics of the proletarian party, there were also crucial areas of disagreement, particularly, perhaps, in natural science and in the philosophy of nature. Engels was a *Darwinian of sorts and he kept abreast of modern developments in evolutionary biology. He also saw that modern materialism was inextricably bound up with the concept of evolution by natural selection and his *Introduction to the Dialectics of Nature*, first published in 1925, shows him to be very well informed about the history of the evolutionary idea. Marx, on the other hand, was a critic of Darwin, characterizing his method as crude and his results as inconclusive. He much preferred the environmentalism of the Frenchman Pierre Trémaux, a stance which led Marx to argue that the Confederate states would win the American Civil War because they were built on better soil. More important, perhaps, was that Engels was solely responsible for formulating the doctrine of *dialectical materialism and for attempting to rest Marxism on a dialectical philosophy of nature. In *Anti-Dühring* of 1876, Engels applied universal dialectical laws to geology, mathematics, history, philosophy, to thought itself, and even to grains of barley, the three main dialectical laws being negation of the negation, the interpenetration of opposites, and the transformation of quantity into quality. There is no evidence that Marx approved of this. Indeed, many scholars now insist that Engels was writing in a mode and with conclusions about dialectics that Marx could never have accepted.

Engels' influence on Marxism was greatly increased by the fact that he was editor of Marx's posthumous works. JH

English School The phrase 'the English School' was first coined in 1981 by a critic,

Roy Jones, who questioned the value of this approach to the study of *international relations. Despite Jones' 'call for closure', the English School or *international society approach has become increasingly prominent in the twenty-first century. The resurgence of the English School is indebted to Barry Buzan, whose famous call to 'reconvene the English School' in 1999 led to a significant rise in English School studies.

The origins of the English School remain somewhat contested. A common starting point is to acknowledge the influence of the Department of International Relations at the London School of Economics. At one point or another, it acted as home to C. W. Manning, Martin Wight, Hedley *Bull, and R. J. Vincent, who are often regarded as the founding fathers of the School. In contrast, some trace the English School approach back to the British Committee, which held its first formal meeting in January 1959. This was a Committee of scholars interested in international theory. From this perspective, Herbert Butterfield, Martin Wight, and Adam Watson act as the founding fathers of the English School. This reflects an alternative historical account, because Butterfield was not part of the London School of Economics, and Manning, who was part of the London School of Economics, was not a member of the British Committee. In addition, the notion of 'Englishness' is also misleading, as Manning was South African and Hedley Bull was Australian. In a strange twist, it was Roy Jones (a Welshman) who first referred to 'the English School', and the label has stuck.

Nowadays, the English School reflects a broad intellectual movement carried forward by the works of contemporary scholars such as Andrew Linklater, Adrian Gallagher, Barry Buzan, Chris Reus-Smit, Cornelia Navari, Edward Keene, Richard Little, Robert Jackson, Jason Ralph, John Williams, Hidemi Sugunami, William Bain, and Matthew S. Weinert, to name just a few. This movement remains distinct for a number of reasons. First, at the heart of the English School lies the idea that states form a society at the international level, hence the international society approach. Whereas some English School scholars, such as Edward Keene, treat international society as an 'ideal type' in a Weberian sense, others

invoke Hedley Bull's formulation that states have in fact forged an 'Anarchical Society'. Second, English School scholars focus on the institutions, rules, values, principles, and norms that make up international society. Third, English School scholarship tends to uphold a tripartite frame to theorize the relationship between 'international system' (associated with *realism and Thomas *Hobbes), 'international society' (associated with the English School and Hugo *Grotius), and 'international community' (associated with *cosmopolitanism and Immanuel *Kant). The English School view is that international relations is an ongoing conversation between different approaches, none of which have a monopoly on knowledge claims. Fourth, the English School upholds a commitment to methodological pluralism. This does not refer to a plurality of *ontologies and *epistemologies, but instead reflects an interdisciplinary approach that incorporates history, political theory, and law to theorize societal relations at the international level. Fifth, English School scholars have tended to focus on normative issues such as *human rights, *humanitarian intervention, and good international citizenship. Although these are now commonly studied by scholars from many different approaches, the English School is widely accepted to have been at the forefront of bringing such issues into the discipline of international relations. AG

Enlightenment, American A tradition in political thought imported to revolutionary America particularly by *Franklin, *Jefferson, *Madison, and *Paine. Jefferson drew on both the *French and the *Scottish Enlightenment; Paine especially on French Enlightenment and revolutionary thought. However, they did more than simply import Enlightenment ideas and views to America; they modified and applied them. In the *Declaration of Independence, drafted by Jefferson, in the Constitution, and in the *Bill of Rights, which was due among others to Jefferson (who had promulgated the Virginia Declaration of Religious Freedom on which the *First Amendment was modelled) and *Madison, American Enlightenment thought went beyond its teachers to produce documents that survive to this day. Jefferson also had a role in reimporting the

Enlightenment to France. The French Declaration of the Rights of Man and the Citizen of 1789, still incorporated in the modern French constitution (*see also* CONSTITUTION), is in part an American statement of rights and in part a *Rousseauvian statement of citizenship.

In the early nineteenth-century United States there was a reaction against the secular tone of Enlightenment thought. Jefferson had been a religious agnostic, but with a high opinion of Jesus as an ethical teacher, and Paine an antichristian deist. In the religious reaction that followed, Paine died in poverty and obscurity and Jefferson in his last years retreated to 'the consolations of a sound philosophy, equally indifferent to hope and fear'.

Enlightenment, French Name given to the French version of the most important movement of ideas during the eighteenth century. Other versions appeared mainly in Germany, Scotland, and the United States, and there were individual thinkers who were accepted as members from all over Europe. Although there were some differences between them, the Enlightenment was a self-consciously international, and more particularly European, movement. Europe was often seen as a single country divided into various provinces, but with a common way of thinking, a common set of values, and a common language, French, which had the same role as Latin in the Middle Ages. Belief in progress was universal among the thinkers of the Enlightenment, but it was not something that would appear by itself: they knew that they had to work for it. The word 'civilization', with its modern signification and values, was probably first used by Mirabeau (father of the French revolutionary figure) in 1757. Attempts to provide exact dates for the beginning or the end are little more than an imposed neatness. The origins of all Enlightenment thought can be found in the works of seventeenth-century thinkers such as *Hobbes, Descartes, *Locke, and Newton, who were far more original than their later followers, and provided them with basic assumptions and methods in epistemology, psychology, natural science, and the study of society.

After the Glorious Revolution of 1688, which provided a new model for political change, the thought of its liberal supporters

became the starting point for discussion in Europe in the early part of the eighteenth century. In the middle of the century came an explosion of ideas with *Montesquieu's *Esprit des lois* (1748), the first volumes of the *Encyclopédie* (1751), *Voltaire's *Le Siècle de Louis XIV* (1751), the start of Buffon's *Histoire naturelle* (1749) and, even if they belonged to a different style of thought, *Rousseau's two *Discourses* (1750 and 1754).

Thinkers of the French Enlightenment were by no means agreed in many areas but they all rejected authority as the basis for knowledge. Instead they accepted the rationalism developed in the previous century, whether in its deductive or empirical form. This did not automatically imply a rejection of religion, and various positions were held including atheism, deism, various forms of Protestantism, and even Catholicism. In practice, however, it meant rejecting the Church as the source of knowledge and therefore of the rules by which anyone should live. These could only be reached by the individual exercising his reason. The best example of this attitude was the *Encyclopédie*, edited by *Diderot and d'Alembert, which claimed to present all existing knowledge in an easily assimilable and usable form. This approach was applied to every subject, and included not only human nature, religion, and politics but also natural sciences, law, and the arts, as well as strictly practical subjects. Philosophy in a strict sense, especially ontology, suffered a decline.

Given this common starting point, the French Enlightenment was politically divided between those such as Voltaire who favoured strengthening the absolute monarchy as the most efficient way to achieve reform, and those such as Montesquieu who favoured restricting the monarchy to re-establish liberty. Various other positions existed, such as those of *Helvétius and *Holbach. Neither side proposed extreme change although their thought has often been seen as a factor leading to the *French Revolution. This was certainly not intended or foreseen, and the adherence of various absolute monarchs and other rulers in Europe, such as Frederick II of Prussia, Joseph II of Austria, and Catherine II of Russia, demonstrates the point. Rousseau is sometimes seen as a member of the French Enlightenment—he was for a time accepted by some of

e

its other members and contributed to the *Encyclopédie*—but his romanticism and (sometimes) irrationalism make this doubtful. cs

Enlightenment, Scottish The period from about 1730 to about 1800 was one of the brightest in the history of the Scottish universities (and one of the dimmest in the history of the English ones). Why this was so has never been established; it may perhaps be attributed to an influx of wealth and self-confidence following the Treaty of Union in 1707, coupled with lack of clerical control over the universities. The main figures of the Scottish Enlightenment were Francis Hutcheson (1694–1746), Adam Ferguson (1723–1816), David *Hume, Adam *Smith, and Dugald Stewart (1753–1828). It is difficult to generalize about the thought of a loosely connected group of people, but the Scottish Enlightenment tried to construct first principles of politics and society free from the religious underpinnings that had previously been thought essential even by liberals such as *Locke. Hume and Smith developed classical economics.

The Scottish Enlightenment had reciprocal links with France and America. Hume spent several years in France, where he wrote his *Treatise of Human Nature*. Smith and *Turgot admired each other's work. *Jefferson owed much to a Scottish teacher at William and Mary College, and much of mainstream liberal thought may have reached America through such routes. Although the Declaration of Independence sounds very Lockean, it reflects Locke inherited through the Scottish Enlightenment (and thus secularized) rather than directly.

entitlement A claim or *right defended by reference to what has already occurred, or an established procedure, particularly previous authorization under such a procedure. For example, a police officer may be entitled to enter premises by a search warrant. Robert *Nozick, in *Anarchy, State, and Utopia* (1974), propounded a historical entitlement theory of justice which depends on the pedigree of titles to *property. According to this theory, individuals have *natural rights and these ground the legitimate original acquisition (creating titles to property). These entitlements defeat the claims of others,

including a state, to those holdings, reducing the scope for redistribution to compensation for rights-violations. AR

entrenchment Literally, 'digging in'. The property of a framework document, such as a *constitution, that it makes itself difficult to amend.

entryism Term given to the tactic pursued by extremist parties of gaining power through covertly entering more moderate, electorally successful, parties. Within those parties they maintain a distinct organization while publicly denying the existence of a 'party within the party'. Entryism is a more acute problem for parties in two party/majoritarian systems than in multiparty/proportional systems. In majoritarian systems such as Britain there is no real political life to the left of Labour or to the right of Conservative, hence there is an incentive for extremist parties to enter Labour or Conservative. In proportional systems the 'barriers to' entry into the political system are lower.

Communist (Stalinist) and Trotskyist parties pursued entryism within the British Labour Party for many years after the Labour Party formally established itself as an anti-Communist party in the early 1920s. In the 1940s and early 1950s, during the *Cold War, Communists attempted to gain entry. From the 1960s onwards the main threat came from various Trotskyite groupings of which the most damaging to the party was the *Militant Tendency.

Entryism can also occur where extreme right-wing parties, normally fascist or racist, similarly attempt to gain entry into conservative/Christian Democratic parties. In Britain there has been periodic penetration of the Conservative Party by fascists or racists. In Germany neo-Nazis have sometimes sought to enter the Christian Democratic Union. PBY

environmentalism A belief in and concern for the importance and influence of environment within a society.

'Environment' is derived simply from the French verb *environner*, to surround. Our environment, literally, is no more and no less than our surroundings. The concept of the environment, though, arose in the mid-nineteenth century. It was given force by a range of new ideas that human beings are, to an important degree, formed by their surroundings. These included Darwin's discovery that the survival of species depends on their suitability to their surroundings and the German geographers' theories of the importance of the environment (*Umwelt*) in determining economic and cultural differences between peoples.

In the second half of the twentieth century environmentalism has come to refer to a combination of beliefs in the value and fragility of the environment, and a tendency to be conservationist with respect to it, leaving the expression 'environmental determinism' to cover the old meaning of the word. Unfortunately, what was intrinsically a very broad concept has been further stretched to the point of meaninglessness. Just as 'environmental studies' can embrace geography, biology, chemistry, law, history, politics, and many other disciplines, the concerns of environmentalism can range from architecture to the stratosphere, from the water supply to the diversity of species on the planet. Environmentalists can base arguments on virtually any known discipline or philosophical assumption, including those which are *anthropocentric (concerned only with benefits to human beings) and those which are studiously opposed to anthropocentrism, and insist that non-human entities have value in themselves. Fortunately, some constructive limitation has been suggested by the eco-philosophers, principally Arne Naess, who, since the 1970s, have expressed suspicion of 'mere environmentalism' which criticizes existing practices and policies affecting our surroundings only in terms of criteria derived from their effects on human interests. This suggests that environmentalism occupies a middle ground between those (rare) minds who see no disadvantages to current practices because of their effects on our surroundings and those eco-philosophers who seek to orient our entire approach away from anthropocentrism. *See also* ECOLOGY; ENVIRONMENTAL JUSTICE.   LA

environmental justice A normative approach or political/social aim adopted by academics, politicians, activists, and individuals alike. Originating in the United States, environmental justice initially concerned the relationship between race and poverty. The

approach has since rapidly expanded in scope and reach. *Social justice broadly concerns questions of 'who deserves what and why', and is often broken down into two main concerns: fair distribution of benefits and burdens (*distributive justice) and fair decision-making procedures (procedural justice). Environmental justice focuses on these concerns to analyse and understand environmental problems from an ethical perspective.

Environmental justice raises questions about how environmental concerns, including deforestation, *climate change, biodiversity loss, and pollution, will impact individuals, communities, animals, and the natural environment. The main emphasis is on how environmental impacts have been caused, whether those affected have a say in their management, and who is responsible for addressing the problem. Most fundamentally, environmental justice is concerned with making normative observations about how the environment, and people affected by the environment, should be treated.

Environmental justice has many subfields, including climate justice. Climate justice addresses questions such as who should be paying for climate change costs, which actors must lower their emissions, and what is owed to future generations.   AD

EPA (Environmental Protection Agency) This US federal agency gained great prominence in the *environmentalist 1970s, and has survived attempts by the Reagan administration to marginalize it. It is sometimes accused of being captured by those it regulates.

(⊕) SEE WEB LINKS
• EPA site, including a history and achievements.

epistemic communities An epistemic community is defined by Peter Haas as a 'network of professionals with recognized expertise and competence in a particular domain and an authoritative claim to policy-relevant knowledge within that domain or issue-area'. Aspects of international policy-making are complex, and political actors may rely on experts. If international experts share intellectual beliefs and have common assumptions, then this can be seen to shape international cooperation. The epistemic communities approach attempts to recognize the role of knowledge networks in shaping outcomes in areas such as environmental policy and economics. It shares some of the concerns and limitations of the *policy networks approach.

epistemic realism *See* EPISTEMOLOGY.

epistemology Espistemology is the theory or philosophy of knowledge. In contrast to *ontology, or theory of being, epistemology is not concerned with what is in the world, but rather with how—indeed whether—we can know it. Epistemology is concerned both with the extent of our knowledge and our degree of certainty about it. This also relates to questions of truthfulness. A significant philosophical dispute over the source of our knowledge is that between rationalism and empiricism. The latter holds that our knowledge derives from sense impressions rather than being innate. However, this is open to scepticism insofar as we cannot be sure whether our sense impressions correspond to things 'in themselves'. Another important distinction is between *a priori* knowledge that is prior to experience, and *a posteriori* knowledge that is subsequent to experience. Rationalists hold that knowledge derives from reason, empiricists that the source of our knowledge is experience, Kantians from their combination, and realists from the nature of the world itself. Important epistemological questions concern the status of our knowledge, the extent of our knowledge, its truthfulness, and its justification. JJ

equality A factual and/or normative assertion of the equal capacity or equal standing of persons, generating claims about *distributive justice. The quasi-empirical equality of individuals may refer to apparently physical characteristics—as in *Hobbes's view of man's equal natural insecurity—or to mental characteristics like rationality or the capacity for morality. Claims about the capacity for rationality or morality may be made as transcendental arguments. The normative claim involves four main 'applications' which are not wholly separable:

1 *Equal consideration within a scheme of (moral) decision-making.* In this sense, the claim to equal treatment is the claim to be taken equally into account, as in the *utilitarian concern that each count for one in the aggregation procedure. This is a fundamental but weak conception of equality: the purpose of the decision may be to differentiate, and it may aim at unequal distribution. (For example, a good may be distributed by competitive examination—equality 1 would require only that everyone be allowed to enter.)

2 *Even-handed treatment.* Here the claim to equal treatment is the claim that like cases be treated alike. This only contingently leads to equal outcomes (*see also* EQUITY).

3 *Equality in distribution.* The claim that equal treatment requires that each person receive an equal amount of a good. Such claims seem most plausible when there is a lack of information about the circumstances of the persons involved.

4 *Equality in outcome.* The claim that equal treatment requires that persons should end up in the same conditions, taking account of their situation before distribution and adjusting the amount to be distributed to each accordingly. This may be compared with *equal opportunity, which requires that persons should be equally placed with respect to opportunities to compete for a good. *See also* EGALITARIANISM. AR

Equality and Human Rights Commission *See* DISCRIMINATION.

equal opportunity Equal access to the procedure under which some office or benefit not available to all is allocated, with stipulations about the fairness of the procedure in view of its purposes. For example, nineteenth-century reforms of the civil service in the United Kingdom introduced the allocation of positions by competitive examination, to replace patronage or family connection as determinants of success. In this conception, equal opportunity is necessarily associated with rationing. 'Equal opportunity' is, however, sometimes misused to support an increase in the supply of some good, for example in the claim that equal opportunity requires that higher education be made available to all who want it. This is better characterized as a demand for *equality in distribution.

'Equal opportunity' is an elastic notion because of the problems of deciding at what point in a process it is appropriate to measure it. For example, a competitive examination may provide equal opportunity for candidates to be tested, but that does not mean they have had an equal opportunity to acquire the knowledge and skills required for success, and hence may not be a true guide to talent. The 'equal access' mentioned may then be applied to the circumstances in which individuals receive their education, it being argued that equal opportunity in the test requires equal opportunity to acquire the skills to be tested. This may lead to a demand for equal conditions in the period before the rationing, or a demand that, because those conditions have not in fact been equal, the procedure take account of the previous relative lack of resources or opportunities of some competitors by discriminating in their favour. *See also* AFFIRMATIVE ACTION; POSITIVE DISCRIMINATION.   AR

equal protection The *Fourteenth Amendment guarantees to Americans 'the equal protection of the laws'. State and federal law-makers are prohibited from arbitrarily discriminating against particular groups such as blacks, women, and the disabled. This is not to say that discrimination is never constitutionally permissible. Legislation that taxes people according to their ability to pay is regarded as reasonable. But state laws requiring or permitting segregation in public schools according to race were, in 1954, deemed to contravene the constitutional principle of 'equal protection' (*Brown* v. *The Board of Education at Topeka, Kansas* (1954)).   DM

equilibrium Balance; more particularly, any state of affairs which no actor has an individual incentive to disturb. The study of political equilibria derives from two traditions: the tradition of *balance of power in international relations; and the tradition of *game theory.

In a balance of power, aggression is deterred because it would overall do more harm than good to the aggressor. Analogously, a game is in equilibrium if no actor would benefit from shifting his strategy to another of those available to him or her. Some equilibria are defective: a notorious case is simple *prisoners' dilemma, in which each player would be better off if

both moved from the equilibrium in which both defect, but neither has an incentive to do so.

equity 1. Even-handed treatment. Equity requires that relevantly similar cases be treated in similar ways. For example, two persons doing the same job in the same way with similar results for the same employer would expect the same pay. Again, it would be inequitable if two individuals committed the same crime in similar circumstances, but received quite different sentences. Equity is therefore closely connected to *equality, and to the rule of *law. Controversy arises from the delineation of relevant similarity: the notions of equity and precedent both raise this problem.

2. An older meaning of equity referred to the need to modify the consequences of a strict application of the law to avoid unfair or unconscionable outcomes. From the sixteenth to the nineteenth century, some English courts were specifically designated as 'equity' courts in contrast to those dealing with *statute and *common law; since 1873 all English courts are supposed to follow the legal rules of equity.   AR

Erskine May The term refers to the guide to parliamentary practice, *Treatise upon the Law, Privileges, Proceedings, and Usage of Parliament* (1844), written by Thomas Erskine May (1815–86). The book, and its subsequent updated editions, provides rules of conduct for Members of Parliament and is referred to in those countries which have a legislature based on the Westminster Parliament.

essentially contested concepts 'Concepts...the proper use of which inevitably involves endless disputes about their proper use on the part of their users' (W. B. Gallie). Such concepts lie on a putative spectrum between the 'essentially straightforward' and the 'radically confused'. They are to be found in all the philosophic disciplines: Gallie's own principal three examples were 'art', 'democracy', and 'a Christian life'. In each of these cases the concept carries a positively appraisive character and there is agreement on an 'original exemplar', but there is a problem interpreting that exemplar's achievement in contemporary conditions and a requirement that argument sustains or develops the original exemplar's achievement.

The historical significance of Gallie's argument lies in his rejection of positivism and his insistence on the value of continued debate about meaning in such fields as aesthetics, theology, and political theory. For those reasons it has constituted an important candidate in arguments about the nature of political language and was increasingly taken up by opponents of positivism in the years after its publication. One of the commonest criticisms of Gallie's theory is that it requires us to hold a contradictory pair of beliefs before we can argue theoretically: we must continue to assume that disputes can be resolved whilst knowing that they cannot. LA

established Church A religious organization is established if the State recognizes it as having a unique or superior claim to the allegiance of the population in religious matters. However, there is no precise line to be drawn between established churches and those which have some other form of special status. For example, England has an established Church, the Anglican Church, which is Protestant and Episcopalian. The Queen, as head of State, is also head of the Church; she is also a member of the Church of Scotland, which is considerably different from the Church of England theologically and she, like her predecessors, worships in the appropriate Church depending on which side of the border she is at the time. Neither Wales nor Northern Ireland now has an established Church. The Republic of Ireland has no established Church, but its constitution acknowledges a 'special place' for the Roman Catholic Church in the hearts and minds of its citizens. There can be no doubt that this 'special place' has proved far more potent than has established status in England, where the specifically Anglican influence on policy has been very little.

Most Western constitutions have followed the American model and firmly eschewed all possibility of an established Church. However, forms of the Lutheran Church are still established in Denmark, Norway, and until 2000 Sweden, even though religious observance in Scandinavia is much lower than in most of Europe. *See also* RELIGION AND POLITICS. LA

estates general, states general Alternative translations of the French *États Généraux*, the body whose summons by Louis XVI in 1789 (for the first time since 1614) is usually held to mark the outbreak of the *French Revolution. Each 'estate' of the realm, namely, the nobility, the clergy, and the commons, was represented separately. However, the Estates voted to unite and turned themselves into the National Assembly.

ethnic cleansing A contested term used extensively from May 1992 onwards by the international media, Western politicians, and diplomats to describe a systematic policy of mass killings, deportation, rape, internment, and intimidation engaged in by rival ethnic groups of the former Yugoslav republic of Bosnia-Hercegovina with the goal of rendering ethnically mixed areas homogeneous and thereby establishing a *de facto* claim on ethnic grounds to sovereignty over disputed territory. Principally, though not exclusively, applied to the actions of Bosnian-Serb paramilitaries backed by elements of the Yugoslav People's Army. Subsequently used to refer to other instances of minority persecution worldwide, such as the mass killings in *Rwanda. The term is also increasingly employed anachronistically by historians, e.g. to refer to the expulsion of Greeks from Asia Minor in the 1920s or Germans from Eastern Europe in the 1940s.

The concept of 'cleansing' or 'purifying' undesirable elements from a community on the grounds of their ethnicity or otherwise is neither exclusively Balkan nor of recent vintage. Notable in this regard are the eugenics movement and the racial tenets of *National Socialism, e.g. areas of Nazi-occupied Europe were declared *judenrein* ('pure of Jews') once the Jewish population had been deported or exterminated. Similarly, the Russian term for the Stalinist purges of the 1930s is *chistki* ('the cleansings'). However, the exact origins of the term 'ethnic cleansing' are unclear. It is most probably a literal translation of the Serbo-Croatian *etnicko cišcenje*, references to which were already being made in Kosovo in the early 1980s. Its contemporary usage possibly derives from military jargon during the Croatian war of 1991 and was subsequently popularized by Western journalists.

From the outset, the term was considered by those critical of Western policy in Bosnia-Hercegovina to be a euphemism for *genocide cynically used by the international community to evade its obligation under the 1948 UN Convention to 'prevent and punish' recognized cases of genocide (which many at the time regarded the Bosnian Muslims victims of, as a UN tribunal has acknowledged). Its use was also condemned on the grounds that appropriating the language of the perpetrator inadvertently legitimized and sanitized the practice. Nevertheless, partly because of its ubiquity and descriptive power, the term subsequently assumed a moral force all of its own and came to imply both an obligation to act and a pretext for international intervention, as in the case of NATO's campaign against Serbia over Kosovo in 1999.

There have been recent attempts to draw a clearer theoretical distinction between genocide and 'ethnic cleansing' and thereby give the latter some terminological credibility. It has been argued that despite its emotive and graphic connotations 'ethnic cleansing' is a useful term to conceptualize the more extreme forms that modern state-building has taken over the last century and that it not only captures the motivation and mindset of the perpetrator but also communicates the process itself more graphically than bloodless terms such as population transfer or forced migration. When seen primarily in terms of its intent—i.e. the removal of an ethnic group from a given territory—'ethnic cleansing' can be conceived as a spectrum on which at one end lies genocide and at the other, milder administrative measures such as forms of legal discrimination. That is, genocide represents the most extreme form of 'ethnic cleansing', but not all forms of 'ethnic cleansing' are necessarily genocide. Seen as a process—i.e. the methods used to pursue that goal—'ethnic cleansing' is itself part of a continuum, situated towards but not at the extremity, next to but differentiated from genocide by lacking the crucial element of intent to kill in part or whole an ethnic group. However, both approaches are problematic. Does 'ethnic cleansing' have to involve overt violence? If not, then all manner of petty infringements of minority rights might be labelled 'ethnic cleansing', and categorizing these alongside genocide runs the serious risk of relativization. As a process, the

distinction between 'ethnic cleansing' and genocide is still unclear, especially when the former is genocidal in its consequences if perhaps not in its intent.

Although the UN and the US State Department both have working definitions of the term, it has no legal definition. All of the defendants at the Hague-based International Tribunal for War Crimes in the former Yugoslavia have been charged under existing UN statutes, including crimes against humanity and genocide. In none of the indictments is the term 'ethnic cleansing' used.

That said, at the United Nations World Summit in 2005 the *General Assembly unanimously endorsed the *responsibility to protect (R2P) principle, which states that every state has a responsibility to protect their population (not just citizens) from *genocide, *war crimes, *crimes against humanity, and *ethnic cleansing. Although the R2P has been invoked in over forty-five *Security Council resolutions, such as Resolutions 1970 and 1973 on Libya in 2011, it has not been consistently used or properly defined, and there have been signs recently that backing for the R2P has now waned.   MF/AG

ethnicity The only working general definition of ethnicity is that it involves the common consciousness of shared origins and traditions.

The Greek *ethnos* is variously translated 'tribe' or 'nation' and its meaning can be taken as being some way between the two. Ethnicity is the quality of belonging to an ethnic group. But the question of what is an ethnic group, as opposed to any other kind of group, is one which permits no simple answer. Ethnic groups are not races, since ethnicity can be more precisely defined than race or even logically independent: Serbs and Croats are also Slavs, and a Jew might be black or white. Nor does membership of an ethnic group relate a person necessarily to a particular territory in the way that nationality does. Nevertheless, 'ethnic conflict' can be the same thing as conflict between nations or races as it can also be conflict between religious groups. Ethnic conflict in Northern Ireland ('Catholic' and 'Protestant'), Lebanon (where Christian Arabs have been in conflict with Muslim Arabs), and in the Balkans (where Orthodox

Serbs differ from Catholic Croats and from Muslims principally in terms of religion) are all conflicts primarily identified by religious affiliation. Language, for the Basques, Welsh, or Georgians, for example, is a more important badge of ethnicity than race, nationality, or religion.

It does not matter, ultimately, whether shared origins and traditions in our opening definition can be said to exist as a matter of objective fact or whether they are 'invented' or 'selected'. Thus the kind of consciousness of ethnicity which gives rise to ethnic conflict can depend entirely on the context in which people form their consciousness and, particularly, on the other ethnic groups which they recognize as existing in that context. In England or the United States ethnicity is conceived primarily in terms of 'white', 'Caucasian', or 'white Anglo-Saxon Protestant' groups in contrast with others, notwithstanding that the most extreme ethnic conflicts in continental Europe take place between 'Caucasians'. In Australia it is common to refer to 'Anglo-Celts' because an important decision is perceived to exist between Australians who identify their origins in the British Isles and the 'New Australians' from other parts of the world. But in some cities of the British Isles, like Belfast and Glasgow, the most important ethnic conflict is precisely that between 'Anglos' and 'Celts'. Ethnicity remains one of the most elusive and mysterious aspects of social structures, but also one of the most fundamental and important. LA

ethnocentrism A view of society and politics shaped by one's own cultural expectations. An ethnocentric approach tends to view positively the beliefs of one's own community, culture, or nation, and view 'outsiders' negatively. Ethnocentrism has been used to explain ethnic conflict and nationalism, and also as part of a broader critique of claims to objectivity in the social sciences. The charge of Eurocentrism, whereby history and development have been analysed in ways which are narrowly focused on Western conceptions of progress, whilst minimizing the contribution from, and exploitation of, non-Western societies, has been levelled at a range of authors, including *Marx and *Weber. *See also* ORIENTALISM.

euro *See* ECONOMIC AND MONETARY UNION.

Eurocentrism *See* ETHNOCENTRISM.

Eurocommunism A body of thought developed within the Italian, Spanish, and French Communist Parties from 1975, characterized by three central theses. The first was that the Soviet Union was not the only model for socialist change. Each party operated in distinctive national conditions and must develop programmes to suit these. The second thesis proposed a convergence of all progressive forces (workers, peasants, intellectuals, students, women, clergy, the middle classes) to work for 'the democratic and socialist renewal of society', to isolate reactionary groups, and to confront capitalism's 'incapacity to meet the general demands of society's development' (Leghorn Statement of the PCI and PCE, July 1975). The third thesis was the need for Communist Parties to re-create themselves, democratizing organizational structures and engendering internal debate. Communist Parties must acknowledge the impact of changing patterns of economic activity upon class structures (the retraction of the traditional working class and the emergence of newly mobilized groups).

Eurocommunism brought the Italian Communist Party close to power before the collapse of the Soviet Union made both party and movement obsolete. GL

Europe Europe remains powerful yet ill-defined. Some of its members—Russia and Turkey—extend beyond its accepted geographical limits. Such unity as it possessed by the early twentieth century rested equivocally upon a shared though divisive Christianity and a rationalist philosophical and scientific tradition (both owing much to the Arab world), a common history of sustained internecine warfare, a fiction of racial homogeneity, and a claim to original responsibility for industrialization and modernity. This tense unity was first effectively projected beyond its own boundaries in the sixteenth century, reaching its greatest extent in the early twentieth century before dissolving in the great European civil wars of 1914–45. Its greatest continuing vulnerabilities are to nostalgia and racism. *See also* EUROPEAN UNION. CJ

European Central Bank *See* CENTRAL BANK; ECONOMIC AND MONETARY UNION.

European Commission The Commission of the *European Union most resembles the executive or civil service branch of government in the sense that it generates and executes policies, but does not legislate. It is useful to focus on the evolving relationship between the Commission and the *Council of Ministers in order to understand the role of the former. It is said that 'the Commission proposes, the Council disposes'. While the Council (representing the member states' governments) passes European Union legislation into law, it can only do so on a proposal of the Commission. Historically this simple pattern has not obtained: the work of the Commission and Council is often so interconnected as to be indistinguishable, and the source of the large majority of European Union legislative proposals is the member states via the Council. Successive Treaty amendments have furthermore steadily integrated the 'co-decision' role of the *European Parliament in European Union law-making.

In the first place, the twenty-eight-member Commission is appointed by member governments for a renewable term of five years. Complicated political jockeying takes place as member states attempt to place national candidates in key positions. Prior to the ratification of the Nice Treaty (2001), two commissioners came from each of the five largest member states. One commissioner now comes from each member state, while some of the most important portfolios have, to date, been held by commissioners heralding from the largest member states. The Nice Treaty also sets a maximum of twenty-seven Commission members with a rotation system to be established when the number of member states exceeds this number. This number was thought to be too large and the Lisbon Treaty sought to cap the total number of commissioners at eighteen with the rule that, for five years in any fifteen-year cycle, each country (regardless of size) would be without a commissioner. The Commission President is selected by unanimity in the European Council. The President can to an extent shape his 'team' and influence the appointment of key personnel among the twenty-three 'Directorates-General' (somewhat akin to ministerial departments) including agriculture, industry, competition, and external relations.

Most commissioners today are former leading politicians from their member state of origin and they may choose to re-enter national political life following their term at the Commission. Once appointed, commissioners are obliged to serve the interests of the Union as a whole, not their governments of provenance. This rule has held relatively well.

The Commission has demonstrated capacity for autonomous leadership in European policy-making. The Commission will propose legislation that is requested by the Council or several member states. That said, initiatives dear to a particular Commission may be submitted with relatively little overt support in the Council, whereupon the Commission attempts to mobilize lobbying and a coalition of forces behind it. The Commission presents white and green papers on various aspects of European Union policy-making with the aim of monitoring progress in an area and promoting new policy direction. The Commission oversees the implementation of legislation, but as Brussels staff is very limited it is usually national ministries or regional or local government which apply the legislation, monitored by the Commission and its agencies and if necessary prodded by the *European Court of Justice.

The power of the Commission to succeed with its proposals depends on a number of factors such as prevailing public opinion on the subject of European Union integration, economic circumstances, the dynamism of the commissioners (and particularly the President), the predispositions and the level of consensus or agreement among member state governments, and the authority assigned to the Commission by the various treaties. In this regard the prerogatives of the Commission have tended to grow over time, but the road has not been smooth nor the passage inevitable. Up to about 1964 the Commission was surprisingly successful at sponsoring new policies and indeed accelerating the integration process. The Commission's activism was challenged and significantly curtailed by the French government. However, the Commission continued to play a limited initiating role in particular policy areas and, under Roy Jenkins's presidency, helped France and Germany agree to create the *EMS (European Monetary System) in 1979. The Commission's activism and leadership was particularly important in shaping European integration during the two Commission terms led by Jacques Delors (1985–96). The Commission promoted the *Single European Act, to address European economic difficulties and unblock the decision-making machinery; proposed hundreds of pieces of legislation to free up the Internal Market; and led discussions on *Economic and Monetary Union. The Single European Act and the treaties of Maastricht (1992), Amsterdam (1997), Nice (2001) and Lisbon (2007) all extended the powers of the Commission, although this was balanced with the European Parliament's enhanced powers of scrutiny and ability to initiate legislation. Over time, then, the Commission along with the Parliament has been strengthened in relation to the member state governments, with more policies moving to the European Union and the Union taking on more supranational characteristics. However, the move to greater Commission influence has also been curtailed by institutional and policy-making developments. For example, the creation of a multi-annual Council presidency of the European Union (through the Lisbon Treaty) is bound to diminish the public profile of the Commission president.

Several member states continue to resist enhanced powers for the Commission. Moreover, the democratic legitimacy of the Commission as a policy-making body is constantly challenged on the grounds that it is unelected and appears remote to the citizens of the European Union. However, member states are unlikely to be willing to accept institutional reform that strengthens the democratic credentials of the Commission. DH

((⊕)) SEE WEB LINKS
• European Commission site.

European Community *See* EUROPEAN UNION.

European Convention for the Protection of Human Rights and Fundamental Freedoms The Convention, which was inspired in part by the 1948 Universal Declaration of Human Rights and was drafted under the auspices of the Council of Europe, entered into force in 1953. As of 15 April 2002, there are forty-two parties. The Convention is largely confined to civil and political rights,

including the right to life (Art. 2), freedom from torture (Art. 3), the right to respect for one's private and family life (Art. 8), freedom of thought, conscience, and religion (Art. 9), freedom of expression (Art. 10), and freedom of peaceful assembly (Art. 11). The European Social Charter, which entered into force in 1965, is concerned with the protection of various social and economic rights by member states of the Council of Europe.

Perhaps the most radical and innovatory features of the European Convention for the Protection of Human Rights and Fundamental Freedoms are the remedies conferred on victims of alleged human rights violations and the machinery of enforcement. Following the entry into force of Protocol No. 11, on 1 November 1998, a victim of an alleged violation of the Convention or of its Protocols, by one of the contracting states, may submit an application directly to the European Court of Human Rights, located in Strasbourg, France (Art. 34). Prior to the entry into force of Protocol No. 11, victims of alleged human rights violations could petition the European Commission on Human Rights (now abolished) provided that the defendant state had accepted the right of individual petition. However, the Commission lacked the power to adopt binding decisions and victims were unable to refer a dispute to the Court, although a limited exception to this was introduced as late as 1994 by Protocol No. 9.

In accordance with Protocol No. 11, submissions to the European Court of Human Rights, provided they are held to be admissible, are examined by a Chamber of the Court consisting of seven judges. In some circumstances, the examination may be conducted by a Grand Chamber consisting of seventeen judges (Art. 30). The parties to a case may opt for a friendly settlement and may be assisted in securing such a settlement by the Court (Art. 38(1)(b)). Failing this, the Court will proceed to a judgment. In 'exceptional cases', following the judgment of a Chamber, any party to the case may refer it to a Grand Chamber (Art. 43). The powers of the European Court of Human Rights are comparable to those of national courts. Thus, contracting states 'undertake to abide by the final judgement of the Court in any case to which they are parties' (Art. 46(1)). If the Court finds that there has been a violation of the Convention it may, in some circumstances, award 'just satisfaction' to the injured party, covering legal expenses, loss of earnings, etc. (Art. 41).

The judgements of the Court have had a significant impact on the protection of civil liberties in Europe. Since the early 1990s, many ex-Communist states of Central and Eastern Europe have become members of the Council of Europe and parties to the Convention. As a consequence, the European Court of Human Rights has come to play an increasingly critical role in securing appropriate levels of human rights protection in the former Communist states.

The United Kingdom, which is the only state in Europe that lacks a written constitution, enacted the Human Rights Act in 1998 to incorporate the Convention into its domestic law. Under the Act, Parliament remains free to pass legislation contrary to the Convention and the Act itself may be amended or repealed in the ordinary way. IP

(⊕) SEE WEB LINKS
• European Court of Human Rights site, which includes the text of the Convention.

European Council The European Council initially emerged as a series of summits, starting in 1969 in The Hague, between the heads of government and heads of state of the European Community. In 1974 these political leaders agreed to meet three times each year. They took the title of the European Council. It was not until the *Single European Act (1986) that the European Council came to have a treaty basis. It coordinates the various elements or 'pillars' of the European Union established by the *Maastricht Treaty on European Union (1992). However, the European Council remains outside the jurisdiction of the *European Court of Justice, and therefore arguably outside the European Union, narrowly defined. The original model of the Community envisaged a technocratic integration of the states of Europe, bypassing the high politics of the member states. As a result, the heads of government and heads of state had no role in the European Community. The European Council developed in response to the crisis in the legislative system of the European Community which began in the mid-1960s. The Council provided the impetus for the development of new consumer, environmental, and social policies, as well as initiating attempts at monetary union and foreign policy cooperation. Paradoxically the European Council played a key role in 'relaunching' the Community in the 1970s, while shifting the locus of initiative from the supranational Commission to the leaders of the member states. DW

(⊕) SEE WEB LINKS
• European Council site.

European Court of Human Rights *See* EUROPEAN CONVENTION FOR THE PROTECTION OF HUMAN RIGHTS AND FUNDAMENTAL FREEDOMS.

European Court of Justice The European Court of Justice (ECJ), which is based in Luxembourg, is an institution of the European Union (EU) and should not be confused with the European Court of Human Rights. The ECJ played a crucial part in the process of integration in Europe, particularly by interpreting the treaty basis of the Community, formally a species of international law, as internal law common to the member states. A series of judgments (starting with *Van Gend en Loos* 26/62 [1963] ECR 1 and *Costa* v. *ENEL* 6/64 [1964] ECR 585) interpreted the Treaty of Rome as a constitution for Europe, based on the doctrines of the 'direct effect' and 'supremacy' of Community law. Initially 'direct effect' meant that without further domestic legislation some articles of the Treaty of Rome became national law. It allowed individuals to rely on Community law as such before national courts. The doctrine of 'direct effect' raised the possibility of a conflict between Community and national law. The ECJ resolved this problem by developing the principle of the 'supremacy' of Community law. Another feature of the Community which marks it out from other international organizations is its capacity to pass secondary legislation (that is, rules with the force of law which are not passed directly by one or more legislatures, but are authorized by them). The ECJ has strengthened this capacity by applying doctrine of direct effect to some secondary legislation (*Van Duyn* v. *Home Office* 41/74 [1974] ECR 1337). Although they took place over the same period of time as a political crisis that increased the control of the member states in the Community's legislative process, these legal developments provoked little or no political criticism. The criticism that did emerge was mainly legal. However, even the courts of the most recalcitrant member states (Germany, Italy, and France) had more or less acknowledged the constitutional role of the ECJ by the middle of the 1980s. DW

(⊕) SEE WEB LINKS
• European Court of Justice site, including texts governing procedure and case law.

European Monetary System *See* EMS.

European Parliament *Democratic legitimacy in the *European Union (formerly European Community) is indirectly provided through national ministers meeting on the *Council of Ministers (Council), but the European Parliament over the years has played a growing role in this regard. As the discontent of citizens with the European Union has become apparent through, among other measurements, national referendums, the role of parliament and democratic accountability have become central to debates about European Union reform and further integration. Some members respond by resisting further cession of powers to the European Union level, while others push to develop 'state-like' democratic mechanisms within the European Union itself.

The European Union treaties originally created an 'Assembly', consisting of delegates from the member states' national parliaments, which declared itself a 'parliament' from 1962. The European Parliament had consultation powers on all European Community legislation and could also debate other areas of policy-making. Though the analogy with national legislatures is not yet fully sustainable, the role of the European Parliament has increased in important ways. The Treaty of Luxembourg (1970) established the European Parliament's influence over the European Union budgetary process, with the power to accept or reject the budget and amend a limited range of expenditure. Since 1979, the democratic legitimacy of the European Parliament through its link with voters has been enhanced through direct elections. The European Parliament gained greater power to amend European Community/European Union legislation in the *Single European Act (1986) and subsequent treaties. The *Maastricht Treaty gave the European Parliament the power to reject legislation in a limited range of areas, which was extended by the Amsterdam and Nice treaties. The Lisbon Treaty (2007) sought to extend this power to most areas where the European Union can make laws.

The European Parliament has limited powers of selection and dismissal over the College of Commissioners and must grant its assent to all treaties agreed between the EU and non-EU countries as well as European Union treaties. The European Parliament is thus slowly evolving as a legislature in the traditional meaning of the word, paralleling the evolution of the European Union as a quasi-federal political system. However, the European Parliament continues to lack several powers possessed by legislatures in liberal democracies, notably the power of the majority to select a government and the power to propose legislation. DH

(⊕) SEE WEB LINKS
• Official site, including information about policy-making and Members of the European Parliament.

European Security and Defence Policy *See* COMMON FOREIGN AND SECURITY POLICY.

European Union In November 1993 the official title of the European Community (EC) was changed to European Union (EU) as a result of ratification of the *Maastricht Treaty by the member states. The European Union consists of three pillars. The European Community pillar is considered supranational in that laws can be made on policy matters covered. The two other pillars are purely intergovernmental in that agreements reached on policy areas covered by them do not have a legal status. The second pillar is the *Common Foreign and Security Policy and the third is Justice and Home Affairs (relabelled Police and Judicial Cooperation following the ratification of the Amsterdam Treaty). The Lisbon Treaty (2007) sought to bring an end to this three-pillar structure. The European Community was properly known as the European Communi*ties*, in the plural. It began as three legally distinct but related organizations: the European Coal and Steel Community, the European Atomic Energy Community (Euratom), and the European Economic Community (EEC, sometimes referred to as the 'Common Market'). The institutions of these three communities were merged by the Merger Treaty of 1965, and the European Coal and Steel Community ceased formally to exist when the terms of the Treaty of Paris expired in 2002 and its activities and resources were absorbed by the EEC/EC pillar of the European Union.

The European Union is the most thoroughgoing example of regional economic and political integration. As an international organization it goes beyond traditional intergovernmentalism in policy-making and has substantial elements of supranationality, with policy processes often referred to as *multi-level governance. The various Union/Community treaties contain fairly open-ended if imprecise commitments to 'ever closer union' among the (currently) twenty-eight member states.

At the end of the Second World War, European economic and political cooperation was seen as an important element of postwar reconstruction, and was therefore supported by the United States. As a wholesale abrogation of national sovereignty seemed a distant reality, efforts focused on the *functionalist approach to integration as expressed in Jean *Monnet's Schumann Plan. Monnet's guiding idea was that war between France and Germany must never again disrupt the politics and prosperity of the continent. Italy and the three *Benelux states joined the ensuing negotiations.

The result was the European Coal and Steel Community (Treaty of Paris, signed 18 April 1951, implemented July 1952) among the so-called Original Six, which sought to integrate the coal and steel sectors in such a way that the parties could no longer maintain an independent capacity to make armaments and thus war on each other. The cooperation created by the European Coal and Steel Community and the importance of increased trade to economic growth in the 1950s provided impetus for further and broader integration, despite the failure of the Original Six to set up a European Defence Community in 1954. Plans for integration

across all economic sectors culminated in the *Treaty of Rome establishing the European Economic Community and Euratom, signed on 25 March 1957 by the Original Six with effect from 1 January 1958. The treaty established a common assembly and Court for all three, and a legally distinct Commission (see EUROPEAN COMMISSION) and *Council of Ministers for the two new communities. The United Kingdom had declined involvement, opting to establish a rival less institutionalized organization, the European Free Trade Area (EFTA).

The European Economic Community quickly became the focal point of efforts on European integration. Where the member states could agree, a concrete timetable for policy integration was specified. This led to the fairly rapid establishment of a customs union, a common external tariff, and a nascent common trade policy. Agreement on the removal of barriers to the free movement of labour and capital (required in principle by the Treaty of Rome) and services (an implied goal in the Treaty) proved more difficult to reach. Where agreement was difficult, the Treaty was vague about further steps towards integration. In this way the Treaty has ensured that the integration process has never progressed unless it was in line with member states' national interests.

The Treaty also put forward a long series of policy questions for negotiation among the members. It was hoped that the tangible economic benefits of common policies would provide ongoing impetus for the integration process. It was the responsibility of the Commission to develop legislative proposals aimed at common EC policies, integrating or replacing the policies of individual member states. Agriculture had been of great concern to the French government, being specifically mentioned in the Treaty as a priority, and in 1962 Regulation 25 was adopted establishing a Common Agricultural Policy (*CAP). To the present day, annual EC/EU expenditure on the Common Agricultural Policy exceeds that given to any other policy area. The European Union also developed its role in external relations through its assistance agreements with former French colonies, the Yaoundé Accords of 1963, succeeded in 1975 by the first Lomé Convention, and bilateral trade agreements with non-EU countries.

During the 1960s, the European Court established the supremacy of European Community laws over national laws and their direct effect in the member states, creating in effect a quasi-federal legal system.

The European Union has also undergone a considerable expansion of membership from six to twenty-eight, with the accession of the United Kingdom, Ireland, and Denmark in 1973; Greece in 1981; Spain and Portugal in 1986; Sweden, Austria, and Finland in 1995; Cyprus, the Czech Republic, Estonia, Hungary, Latvia, Lithuania, Malta, Poland, Slovakia, and Slovenia in 2004; Romania and Bulgaria in 2007; and Croatia in 2013.

As membership has widened, the policy jurisdiction of the European Union has 'deepened' dramatically. The monumental Single Market Programme followed the *Single European Act and has led to the rapid trans-border integration of national markets. Regional and social policy dimensions have been developed (if hesitantly). Foreign and military policy cooperation were enabled through the institutional framework of the Common Foreign and Security Policy pillar. Cooperation on immigration, asylum, and criminal matters was encouraged through the Justice and Home Affairs pillar. The most radical step so far is *Economic and Monetary Union which began on 1 January 1999. Economic and Monetary Union has involved the adoption of the euro as the single EU currency with a single monetary policy run by the European Central Bank and a degree of macroeconomic policy coordination by participating member state governments (sixteen in 2009). The introduction of the euro has also accelerated the process of market integration, building on the Single Market Programme. This process of policy deepening has been aided by institutional reforms contained in amendments to the treaties as with the Single European Act of 1986 and the Treaty of Maastricht. The more recent treaties of Amsterdam (1997), Nice (2001), and Lisbon (2007) extended this process of institutional reform, ostensibly to cope with EU enlargement. The increased use of opt-out provisions for individual member states (as with the UK and Denmark for Economic and Monetary Union, the UK for Justice and Home Affairs, and Denmark for Common Foreign and Security Policy) has allowed member states not wanting to proceed with integration in a particular area not to prevent others from proceeding.

By keeping the end goal indeterminate, 'Euroenthusiasts' and ardent supporters of national autonomy alike have usually been able to strike compromises which are understood to be in the common interest of all. This propels the process of integration, despite frequent turmoil and disagreement, and has seen the European Union emerge as an increasingly 'state-like' entity in the international system. As such the European Union is poised to alter traditional conceptions of *sovereignty and international organizations. However, the European Union finds itself post-euro at a crucial juncture. It has taken on many state-like attributes in a context of institutional underdevelopment. This fuels dilemmas for European Union authorities and member states alike. Deepening European integration has serious implications for traditional notions of national policy-making and *sovereignty, while the European Union clearly lacks a strong sense of collective identity at the level of *civil society, often portrayed as *democratic deficit. Economic adjustment processes resulting from integration are often difficult and the costs are unequally distributed across members and regions. These inequalities and tensions were recently witnessed in response to the 2008 *financial crisis and the bailout conditions associated with the Greek *sovereign debt crisis. These challenges come in the context of continuing challenges to state capacity in the form of new security dilemmas and global economic integration, which European Union-level policy is at least partially meant to address.

In addition, the post-financial crisis era has seen a number of renewed *populist and *nationalist anti-European or *eurosceptic movements, which have seemingly threatened the coherency of the European project as a whole. The most significant event took place in June 2016, when the United Kingdom held a referendum vote to 'leave' the European Union (labelled *Brexit). This vote has created considerable uncertainty about ongoing European integration and saliency, as well as given fuel to similar anti-European movements in France, Denmark, and Holland. DH

(🌐) SEE WEB LINKS
- European Union website, including treaties, details of policy, and information on institutional structure.

eurosceptic/euroscepticism   Literally meaning a person, a political party, or group of people who are sceptical of the *European Union and European integration. The range of euroscepticism can be a stronger anti-European position as well as more moderate positions against key aspects of the European project, such as the *Economic Monetary Union, its bureaucratic engrossment, its lack of democratic legitimacy, or the *European Convention for the Protection of Human Rights and Fundamental Freedoms. Euroscepticism can also act as a political platform for the establishment of a party (such as the United Kingdom Independence Party—UKIP). Nevertheless, in the mainstream, the term 'eurosceptic' has come to signify strong opposition to the European Union, particularly with claims that it 'erodes' the *self-determination and cultural uniqueness of nationality while also undermining state *sovereignty.   More recently, European rules governing the free movement of people have also attracted eurosceptic anti-immigration scrutiny with claims that free movement diminishes national unity and identity. Although euroscepticism has existed since the founding of the European Union, it has recently gained momentum politically, moving towards anti-Europeanism, as dramatically represented by the UK *Brexit referendum to leave the EU, as well as similar campaigns in other EU member states such as France and Holland.

euthanasia See RIGHT TO LIFE.

evolution One of a number of words including, *inter alia*, 'growth', 'development', and 'change', which imply a natural alteration of system or structure through time. 'Evolution', however, has been given the quite specific meaning of a gradual diversification of species over time through the action of natural selection. Yet even *Darwin, the joint author of the theory of natural selection with Alfred Russel Wallace, was very reluctant to use the word evolution. For most of his life he preferred, instead, to talk of transmutation, hence the famous

transmutation notebooks in which the theory of evolution by natural selection was first advanced. And, prior to the popularization of Darwinism, it was common to stick closely to classical usages deriving from the Latin verb *evolvere*, literally to unfold or disclose, the substantive form, *evolutio*, referring to the unfolding and reading of a scroll. The word evolution was not regularly and systematically used in a recognizably modern context until the debate between evolutionists and epigenists in the early eighteenth century. And, as has been suggested about *social Darwinism, despite the immense prestige attaching to modern evolutionary theory and to the idea of species variance, the biology of natural selection entailed nothing uniform either for sociological method or for specific political doctrine. There is not a single political doctrine appropriate to natural selection and the idea of evolution itself inspired many different creeds and many different methodologies, who used the inspiration of evolution not just in contrasting but also in competing ways.   JH

evolutionary game theory The branch of *game theory that studies the interaction of non-rational beings such as animals, or humans whose behaviour evolves under the influence of the environment in which they find themselves. At first sight, evolutionary game theory seems to contradict the basic premiss of game theory, namely that it formalizes the interdependence of rational actors. But actors may reach *Nash equilibrium by evolution as well as by reasoning. If they are human, they may notice that some strategies work and others do not, without understanding why the strategies that work do so. Or they may read successful business books at airports. If they are animals, then natural selection may select for successful strategies. Animals that 'play' (actually, that are hard-wired to act in accordance with) successful strategies survive to have more offspring than those that 'play' others. Therefore the gene for the successful strategy spreads in the population. A version of Nash equilibrium for evolutionary games is an evolutionarily stable strategy (ESS), a term invented by J. Maynard Smith in 1973 and popularized by Richard Dawkins, Robert Axelrod, and others. Ironically, an ESS may itself be unstable, because what is evolutionarily stable in a given population depends on the make-up of the rest of the population. If most of the rest of the population are aggressive 'hawks', it pays to be a 'dove'; if most of the rest of the population are pacifistic 'doves' (doves in the literary conception, not the biological one—doves are actually aggressive birds), it pays to be a hawk.

exchange theory Branch of sociology which sees most social interaction as exchange from which both, or all, parties benefit. The idea is derived from anthropology, and is parallel to the idea of *Pareto improvement in economics; sociologists in this tradition have therefore for practical purposes become indistinguishable from *rational choice analysts from other disciplines.

exchange value A quantitative relationship which expresses the worth of one commodity in terms of another commodity. For instance, if one pair of shoes can be exchanged for two chairs then the exchange value of a pair of shoes is two chairs and the exchange value of two chairs is a pair of shoes. When these exchange ratios are expressed in a money form (2 chairs = £40) then exchange value is the price of a particular commodity. From *Aristotle, who was the first to develop the concept, to the Classical Economists such as *Smith and Ricardo, the main problem lay in trying to discover the determinants of a commodity's exchange value. Utility, scarcity, and production costs of labour and capital were some of the solutions suggested. These debates culminated with the contribution of *Marx who argued that exchange value was not an expression of the labour time embodied in an article, as Ricardo had asserted, but rather the 'form' taken by 'value' in exchange. 'Value' itself is the socially necessary labour time of society expended on a commodity: that is, a portion of the labour time of society as a whole, which cannot be discovered until the commodity has been put on the market for exchange. This implied that the exchange of one commodity for another was a social relationship between people which 'appeared' as a quantitative relationship between things, that is, commodities. Outside of Marxism, however, theorists ignore the social basis of exchange and see exchange value simply as an expression of price which is determined by the dictates of supply and demand. IF

executive The branch of government concerned with the execution of policy. Three types of executive may be distinguished. Authoritarian executives vary in form according to the circumstances in which they were created and developed, but are distinctive by virtue of their powers being constrained only by the limits of the will of their members and the limits of the force at their disposal to impose that will on subject peoples. The presidential executive of the United States, which has developed in spite of the United States Constitution, is composed of ministers and senior officials appointed by and headed by the President. The President has ultimate say on the policies advocated by the executive branch. However, following the separation of powers principle, presidential authority is constrained by a separately elected congress and by an independent judiciary whose duty it is to see that executive action is not contrary to the articles of the Constitution. The parliamentary executive, typified by the United Kingdom, is based upon the principle of *cabinet government. In this ministers are appointed and headed by a prime minister but all executive decisions are collectively made and members of cabinet are collectively answerable to the legislature from which they are drawn and whose continued support they need to stay in office.

In practice the focus of executive decision-making both within presidential and parliamentary systems is more diverse than this would suggest. Presidential government is marked by the decentralization of decision-making within the executive branch, and by a reliance on congressional support. Analysts have observed the importance of iron triangles of executive agencies, congressional committees, and key interest groups, agreement between which is crucial to the effective formulation and implementation of policy. Such networks are highly fragmented between different policy areas, making policy co-ordination difficult if not impossible. Presidential power is greatest in the initial period of a new incumbent's tenure when public opinion may be mobilized on the back of election victory euphoria to the attainment of key election pledges. At other times presidential initiative is concentrated on the framing of the annual budget and the prosecution of foreign policy, success in which against potential opposition in Congress is again dependent upon mobilization of public opinion and successful relations with congressional leaders. Significant impediments to presidential success have been the tendency for a President to be faced with a Congress dominated by the rival party and for both parties to exhibit poor cohesion in policy aims, meaning that even a Democrat President working with a Democrat-controlled Congress will find it difficult to achieve success. Of course, policy initiatives originating in Congress may also be, and frequently have been, blocked by the President. The incoherence of executive authority in practice continues to provide grounds for believing that, particularly in domestic policy, effective government has been sacrificed to the preservation of the separation of powers principle underpinning the Constitution.

Parliamentary systems of government are also marked by a considerable range of executive decision-making foci, even in the United Kingdom. Many decisions are indeed taken by the cabinet, or cabinet committees in the name of the cabinet. However, with the growth of government, considerable executive authority has also been exercised by individual ministers at departmental level, or senior officials acting in their name; ministers whose remit covers more than one department of government; two ministers, generally one from a spending department and one from the Treasury, who bilaterally agree upon policy; more than two ministers from different departments who have a common concern which need not be put up to the Cabinet; and party business managers, who may wield significant influence over the Prime Minister. Where policy is decided at departmental level by ministers or officials it is also common to find selected interest groups being invited into the decision-making process either formally or informally. The role of political advisers has increased since the 1960s. The rapid turnover in ministerial appointments, which means that few ministers occupy the same position for more than two years, contrasts with the permanence of the civil servants. Hence, it may be suggested that if executive government is not highly fragmented, then it may be highly departmentalist. Those analysts who in turn view the senior civil service as highly cohesive in its strategic aims may go further and say that in practice real executive authority lies with unelected officials.

Solutions to the problems of executive government in liberal democracies rest uneasily upon a reliance on institutional modernization from above and greater opportunities for citizen participation from below. Whilst executives work in an age of big government they will continue to face the inevitable tensions between a small group of elected individuals attempting to control executive authority in a manner accountable to citizens and the limited capacity of those individuals to carry out executive government efficiently. The focus in recent academic research on broader conceptions of the core executive, rather than simply formal institutions such as cabinet, is providing more detailed understanding of how executives work in practice, and thus may yet facilitate more sophisticated prescriptions for reform. JBr

executive agreement Executive agreements enable the US President to make international arrangements without senatorial participation, as is constitutionally required for treaties. Presidents may thus circumvent the Constitution by calling treaties executive agreements.

Executive Office of the President Made up of the top agencies of the United States government, including the Office of Management and Budget, National Security Council, and White House Office, with the purpose of coordinating the activities of the executive, the emphasis being on programme and policy development. Some analysts see this as a rival *cabinet to the official one.

(⊕) SEE WEB LINKS

• Executive Office of the President website.

executive privilege The right of the executive to withhold information from the legislature or courts.

In the United States executive privilege has been used by the President, and executive officials given the right by the President, to refuse to appear before congressional committees. Executive privilege has no constitutional basis, but has been claimed as an inherent power based on the separation of powers, and in order to protect the national interest. The right was curtailed by the Supreme Court in 1974, in the case of *US* v. *Nixon*, which held that executive privilege was not absolute. The case followed President Nixon's claim that executive privilege meant he could withhold tapes concerning the *Watergate scandal from Congress.

existentialism Concept borrowed by twentieth-century European philosophers from the theologian Søren Kierkegaard (1813–55) but shorn of any religious meaning. First attested in English in 1941, apparently as a translation of German *Existentialismus*, itself derived from Kierkegaard's Danish neologism *Existents-Forhold*. *Nietzsche and *Heidegger are also formative influences on many (mostly literary figures rather than philosophers) who describe themselves as existentialists. Existentialism is very hard to define but may be summarized as the belief that people are all that there is. It is expressed in reaction to the grand designs in human history seen by *Hegel and his followers. In particular, it denies the existence of *natural law, an unchanging human nature, or indeed any objective rules. Each individual is cursed with freedom and must make his or her own way in the world, although many people resort to devices to hide this from themselves. Life is without ultimate meaning, but we are forced to make choices all the time. The spirit of existentialism is well summarized in a poem (1922) by A. E. Housman (1859–1936) on being an unacknowledged homosexual in a homophobic society:

> The laws of God, the laws of man,
> He may keep that will and can
> And how am I to face the odds
> Of man's bedevilment and God's?
> I, a stranger and afraid
> In a world I never made

See also SARTRE, JEAN-PAUL.

exit To leave, or 'to vote with one's feet'. According to A. O. Hirschman's economic analysis of the relationship between group members and group leaders, members of organizations may express their dissatisfaction with leaders by leaving the organization. While the option of leaving remains viable, members may use the threat of exit as a way of exerting pressure on leaders. The possibility, terms, and control of the 'exit option' are consequently viewed as important dimensions of intra-group politics. *See also* VOICE. SW

exit poll Opinion poll conducted at the exit from the polling station, when people have already voted. The advantages of an exit poll over a conventional opinion poll of voting intentions are:

1 People seem less likely to mislead about what they have already done than in their statements of what they intend to do.

2 Relatedly, an exit poll interviews only people who have voted and therefore avoids the errors inevitably associated with guessing how many of those who say they will vote, or abstain, will actually do what they say.

3 It is easier to interview the correct proportions of people of different socio-economic groups in an exit poll than in a conventional quota sample (*see* SURVEY RESEARCH).

In recent general elections in Britain and elsewhere, exit polls have produced predictions closer to the actual result than any preceding poll. It would be very disappointing if they did not. Exit polls will certainly continue to be used by media predictors of election results, who can bring powerful processing and computing resources to bear on the data in order to get a prediction of the national result before the votes have been counted. However, the limitations they share with all other quota samples make academic analysts cautious about using them, and their essential brevity limits the study of the underlying reasons for vote choice.

exogeneity/exogenous *See* ENDOGENEITY/ENDOGENOUS.

exploitation 1. Taking advantage of a resource, for example good weather.

2. Taking unfair advantage of persons, their characteristics, or their situations. The difficulties are in specifying the nature of the unfairness of the advantage, and the ways in which the opportunity to take advantage arises in the first place, and/or is seized on a particular occasion. For these reasons, the analysis of exploitation is linked inextricably to understandings of *power and *(in)justice. What is distinctive about exploitation as a particular form of injustice has been controversial; so, too, have been the ways in which (if any) exploitation is a form of power, rather than a possible consequence of it. A particular problem is the identification of exploitative transactions within consensual exchanges, which for some theorists disguise the presence of a power relation, but for others guarantee its absence. *See also* MARX. It may well be that the underlying complaint is that persons who are exploited are treated merely as things, linking the second sense to the first, but there is no agreement on how this is to be elaborated.   AR

externalities Costs and benefits which accrue to people who are not party to the economic decisions which bring them into being. They can arise out of decisions to produce or decisions to consume. A typical example of production with high external costs would be a glue factory: three groups (workers, owners, and purchasers) might all consider themselves to be better off as a result of the transactions involved in producing glue, but their decisions take no account of the smell on neighbours. An external cost of consumption might be incurred by my neighbour as a result of my playing the radio loudly.

Externalities show that markets are not necessarily maximizers of collective well-being. Of course, there are many arguments which support this suggestion, but the argument about external costs is the most demonstrable and unavoidable for orthodox economists. One alternative solution is a 'full privatization' model in which everything that incurs a cost on anyone is paid for: thus I would have to rent my right to play my radio from my neighbours. Most economists reject this in favour of state modification of prices through taxation.

Many of the most important externalities are public, either in the sense of accruing to an indefinite number of people or of affecting public goods—things like clean air which can be consumed without being reduced.

A recommendation to deal with these costs, formally accepted by a number of governments and international organizations since the 1970s, is the 'polluter pays principle' which requires producers to meet the full social cost of their production by the imposition of taxes and levies.   LA

extradition Legal process by which criminals or criminal suspects are transferred between one country and another. There is no international convention regarding extradition, which is mainly regulated through bilateral agreements between countries. Extradition is usually based on a shared recognition of serious crimes and the severity of the punishment involved. The European Arrest Warrant was introduced in 2004 to make extradition between members of the European Union easier, based on a shared recognition of the *European Convention for the Protection of Human Rights and Fundamental Freedoms. The extradition process is cumbersome, and states have circumvented it by abduction of suspects discovered overseas (for example, the case of Mordechai Vanunu) or through *extraordinary rendition.

extraordinary rendition Transfer of criminal or terrorist suspects from country to country without judicial authority. The term is associated with actions undertaken by the United States *CIA from the 1980s, when suspects were brought into US judicial authority without going through an *extradition process. Concern about the threat of international terrorism led the Clinton administration to allow the CIA to capture and transport suspects, but with the deliberate avoidance of a transfer into the US judicial system; and under the Bush administration extraordinary rendition became a key part of the response to the attacks of *September 11th 2001. In some cases this led to imprisonment at *Guantanamo Bay, and suspects were transferred (according to a Council of Europe Report) to CIA facilities in Poland and Romania, and to detention in other countries. Although the US administration claimed such measures were used rarely, and only for dealing with 'High Value Detainees', there have been accusations that the extra-judicial nature of these detentions enabled torture and maltreatment, and violated international law.

extreme-right parties Contemporary extreme-right, or radical-right, parties in Western Europe are variously characterized as *populist, *nationalist, *fascist, anti-system, anti-party, anti-Eu and/or anti-immigrant. While none of these are essential, anti-immigrant policy is common to the vast majority. Major examples include the Freedom Party (Austria), *National Front (France), Vlaams Belang (previously Vlaams Blok) (Belgium), Republikaner (Germany), the Danish and Norwegian Progress parties, Alleanza Nazionale (previously MSI) and Lega Nord (Italy), and in the UK the British National Party and *National Front. Many of these parties saw a marked increase in their vote share in the 1980s and 1990s so that among others, the French, Italian, Austrian, and Flemish extreme-right have all frequently achieved more than 10 per cent of the vote although some have received setbacks since 2000. While survey research shows that anti-immigrant sentiment is the main factor influencing individual citizen decisions to vote for the extreme-right, it is not the case that the varying fortunes of extreme-right parties can be accounted for by differences between countries in the hostility to immigrants. Instead it appears that the success of extreme-right parties are affected by the electoral system, the reactions of other parties and their own history prior to the immigration issue becoming prominent. SF

Fabianism The Fabian Society, which was established in London in 1884, took its name from Fabius Cunctator, the Roman General who applied carefully conceived tactics of preparation, attrition, and judicious timing of attack in defeating Hannibal. Fabianism refers especially to a particular position within British socialism, originally espoused by Sidney and Beatrice *Webb and George Bernard Shaw, three of the most prominent early Fabians. The early Fabians concentrated on the research of social issues, the results of which were forwarded in arguments for reform to intellectuals and leaders within both the Independent Labour Party and the Liberal Party. After the First World War the Fabian Society affiliated to the Labour Party, becoming a less high-profile group after the 1930s, but providing a basis for a more diverse set of socialist intellectuals to conduct debate on any issue of interest to the Labour Party.

The Webbs and Shaw believed in a Ricardian theory of rent, which determined that one part of rent should be apportioned to society, or, in practice, the state acting on behalf of society. This was the justification for progressive taxation to fund state expenditure directed at correcting social inequalities. State policies at both national and local levels were to aim at creating a 'national minimum' of social welfare which would liberate all individuals to fulfil their talents and act as good citizens. Thus, political democracy enshrined in the right to vote could be extended to a social democracy in which the values and injustices of unfettered capitalism could be eroded. At the same time, the Fabians advocated that the state should be staffed by trained experts in public administration, capable of rational consideration of public policy, dedicated to public service for the general good, and, thus, successful in delivering social democracy. The emphasis on the role of trained intelligence in good government derived from contempt for 'amateur' administrators, who by default had facilitated unfettered capitalism.

The Fabian approach to political action by way of calm intellectual reflection and considered rational planning, and advocacy that social democracy be engineered by a meritocratic state elite, have appealed to successive generations of senior parliamentary Labour Party figures and to socialists overseas, such as *Nehru. Fabianism has been criticized from the left for its rejection of notions of class struggle and its focus instead on creating social solidarity from above which underplays the problems of the working class. It is charged with being based on inherently elitist assumptions, born of its adherents' generally relatively comfortable upbringings and university education. Equally, it has been criticized from the right for ignoring the role of markets, in which benevolent administrators have a smaller role than in planned societies. With the advent of the modernization of the Labour Party from the mid-1980s, however, the Fabian Society has remained a forum for the debate of a diverse set of issues following the assumption of a smaller and territorially decentralized post-Thatcherite state in the UK. A 1992 Fabian Society pamphlet by Ed Balls is widely accredited with influencing the decision to make the Bank of England independent in 1997, and the report of the Fabian Society tax commission, chaired by Raymond Plant, in 2000 is considered to have influenced the decision to increase national insurance contributions in 2001 to fund new spending on the National Health Service. JBr

⊕ SEE WEB LINKS
• Site of the UK Fabian Society.

faction Generally, any political grouping the writer disapproves of. Thus, *Madison, in the two most famous numbers of *Federalist*, nos. 10 and 51, wished to design a set of institutions for the USA that would combat faction, and stipulated that 'Ambition must be made to counteract ambition' (no. 51). The extended republic of the United States would minimize the ill effects of faction because 'A rage for paper money, for an abolition of debts, for an equal division of property, or for any other improper or wicked project, will be less apt to pervade the whole body of the Union than a particular member of it' (no. 10). More specifically, an organized group within a political party, especially in a country where they have semi-permanent existence, such as Japan or Italy.

factor analysis A statistical model that attempts to explain the correlation between a number of observed *continuous variables in terms of a smaller number of latent, or unobserved, factors. The measured variables are assumed to depend on the underlying factors, but they also include random error. Factor analysis is particularly useful when direct measurement is impossible, as for social attitudes such as national sentiment, or psychological concepts such as intelligence. It is also used to detect summary dimensions in the pattern of correlation in a set of variables. For example, Arend Lijphart (*Patterns of Democracy*, 1999) found two dimensions (called executives-parties and federal-unitary) to be sufficient to explain the variation in ten measured characteristics of political institutions in democracies. Factor analysis is similar in its aims to principal component analysis. SF

factors of production The inputs involved in the production of goods and services. Sir William Petty (1623–87) first defined land and labour as factors of production. The factors of capital and entrepreneurship were added by the French *physiocrats. 'Land' includes resources within the land such as mineral deposits like coal and iron ore. Labour is the human effort, whether manual or mental, that contributes to production. Capital is usually denoted as machinery or tools which are used in combination with labour for the purpose of making goods. There can be fixed or circulating capital. The former relates to goods such as buildings or machinery while the latter refers

to the stock of goods a firm has ready for use in the future. Capital is the only factor of production which itself is created in the production process. Entrepreneurship refers to the managerial, innovative, and risk-taking qualities which an individual displays when combining the other factors of production in order to generate output. The returns or payments to each of these factors are rent for land, wage for labour, interest for capital, and profit for entrepreneurship. IF

fair trade Fair trade refers to trade that meets social, economic, and environmental standards relating to wages and conditions for those involved in the production or distribution of goods. Fair-trade schemes are promoted with the aim of improving the economic and social benefit of trade to producers in developing countries. Fair-trade schemes work by giving a product a fair trade certification, ensuring a minimum price is paid to producers and/or granting additional sums to be invested in producer community development projects such as schools, healthcare, or environmental protection. Fair-trade schemes can involve certification to small-scale farmers, seeking to ensure that they receive higher revenues for produce such as coffee and cotton. They can also be granted to larger farming enterprises for products such as bananas or tea, where the schemes seek to ensure that the employer meets certain criteria in relation to wages and conditions. Controversies around fair trade include whether fair-trade criteria are properly audited and enforced by fair-trade organizations; uncertainty as to how much benefit farmers actually get from fair-trade schemes; and whether the criteria used reflect the interests and values of northern consumers rather than those of the developing countries and farming communities involved. Others argue that fair trade is a distraction from the need to develop a more just international trading scheme. WB

Falklands war Military conflict fought between Argentina and the United Kingdom over a small group of islands in the South Atlantic, in 1982. Behind the conflict lay a long dispute over sovereignty of the islands (known by the Argentinians as Islas Malvinas); the political and economic troubles of the Argentinian military dictatorship of

General Leopoldo Galtieri; and a perception that the British would not, or could not, defend the islands. Argentinian forces occupied the islands on 2 April 1982. Attempts to find a diplomatic solution failed, and the British Prime Minister, Margaret Thatcher, ordered the preparation of a naval task force to retake control of the islands. The main landings by British troops began on 21 May, and the Argentinian forces surrendered on 14 June.

The loss of the Falklands campaign hastened the downfall of the Argentinian junta. In the UK, Margaret Thatcher's popularity soared, and she entrenched her reputation as a strong leader willing to take resolute action. She won a resounding victory at the 1983 general election. The resignation of the Foreign Secretary, Peter Carrington, who accepted the blame for the failures of his department in intelligence and preparation in the run-up to the invasion, has been seen as a rare example of the convention of *ministerial responsibility in practice.

false consciousness In its crudest form, false consciousness implies a misperception of reality, or of one's relationship to the world of which one is part. On this reading, *Plato's myth of the cave (*Republic*, bk. 7) might be said to be an account of false consciousness, as might *Rousseau's infamous claim (in *The Social Contract*) that those who oppose the general will might be 'forced to be free'.

Although he did not use it himself, the term is usually associated with *Marx, and subsequently with Marxism, especially of the *Frankfurt School variety. In Marx, the focus tends to be on the relationship of consciousness to reality as it is mediated through the prevailing mode of production (i.e. capitalism). It follows from this that false consciousness can be overcome only by addressing its economic source. But how is it possible to have knowledge of a consciousness which is false?

The danger with the concept of false consciousness lies in the possibility it affords to those willing and able to take it, to impose a 'correct' perception on the falsely conscious. This danger can be avoided only if it is the case that 'truth' and 'falsity' are self-evident. This in part explains Marxism's need to present itself as scientific, although the extent to which scientific analyses are themselves free from ideological dressing has itself been questioned, notably by Thomas Kuhn. *See also* FALSIFIABILITY.   AA

falsifiability The test that a theory is scientific, according to the influential views of Karl *Popper. Especially in *Conjectures and Refutations* (1963), Popper argued that science can never prove things to be true, but it can prove them to be false. It can never prove things to be true by what has been known since *Hume as the 'problem of induction'. 'All swans are white' is either part of the definition of the word 'swan', or a generalization about swans based on observations of all known examples. When settlers first saw black swans in Western Australia, they could have denied that what they saw were swans. As *Hobbes said, 'True and false are attributes of speech, not of things'. However, as a purely linguistic convention, it has been agreed that black swans are swans. Therefore 'All swans are white' is an example of a falsifiable, and false, scientific generalization. Thus a Popperian scientist must try to formulate a generalization which the scientist believes to be true but formulates in a way that is open to falsification.

The Popperian method is dominant but not unchallenged in empirical politics. All empirical work that uses statistical methods is explicitly or implicitly falsificationist in its approach. Other schools of thought argue that some aspects of political life may be unobservable, and the hypothesis that they exist unfalsifiable, but that they remain important topics of study. (*See* COMMUNITY POWER).

The Popperian programme has also been challenged on the grounds that scientists do not actually follow it, although they are trained to present their results as if they had. The most influential such critique has been Thomas Kuhn's *The Structure of Scientific Revolutions* (1962). Kuhn's critique does not undermine the falsificationist programme by as much as its literary adulators argue. Although historians of science cannot ignore it, it has had no impact on the way in which results continue to be presented and argued over.

Fanon, Frantz (1925–61) Theorist of revolution whose ideology is most clearly enunciated in his last book, *The Wretched of the*

Earth. Born in Martinique, he studied medicine in France, specializing in psychiatry. He joined the National Liberation Front (FLN) in Algeria in 1956, later serving as diplomatic representative in several African states. To Fanon colonialism was a system of racial oppression all the more insidious because its impact was mental as well as physical, distorting attitudes and behaviour alike. Genuine liberation could not therefore be achieved by peaceful negotiation, as was attempted elsewhere in black Africa in the 1960s, but only as a result of protracted violence involving direct, collective action by the masses as in Algeria. Even then Fanon had reservations about nationalist movements, on account of their privileged, urban, middle-class leadership, susceptible to colonial penetration. The only reliable revolutionary force was the peasantry, with nothing to lose and retaining the capacity for spontaneous protest and explosions of violence. Fanon died of leukaemia before Algeria finally acquired its independence in 1962.   IC

fascism A right-wing nationalist ideology or movement with a totalitarian and hierarchical structure that is fundamentally opposed to democracy and liberalism. In ancient Rome, the authority of the state was symbolized by the *fasces*, a bundle of rods bound together (signifying popular unity) with a protruding axe-head (denoting leadership). As such, it was appropriated by Mussolini to label the movement he led to power in Italy in 1922, but was subsequently generalized to cover a whole range of movements in Europe during the inter-war period. These include the *National Socialists in Germany, as well as others such as Action Française, the Arrow Cross in Hungary, or the Falangists in Spain. In the post-war period, the term has been used, often prefixed by 'neo', to describe what are viewed as successors to these movements, as well as *Peronism and, most recently, some movements in ex-Communist countries, such as Pamyat in Russia (*see* EXTREME-RIGHT PARTIES). Given such diversity, does the term have any meaning?

Genuinely fascist ideologies are: *monist*, that is to say, based upon the notion that there are fundamental and basic truths about humanity and the environment which do not admit to question; *simplistic*,

in the sense of ascribing complex phenomena to single causes and advancing single remedies; *fundamentalist*, that is, involving a division of the world into 'good' and 'bad' with nothing in between; and *conspiratorial*, that is, predicated on the existence of a secret world-wide conspiracy by a hostile group seeking to manipulate the masses to achieve and/or maintain a dominant position.

In content, these ideologies are distinguished by five main components: (1) extreme *nationalism, the belief that there is a clearly defined nation which has its own distinctive characteristics, culture, and interests, and which is superior to others; (2) an assertion of national decline—that at some point in the mythical past the nation was great, with harmonious social and political relationships, and dominant over others, and that subsequently it has disintegrated, become internally fractious and divided, and subordinate to lesser nations; (3) this process of national decline is often linked to a diminution of the racial purity of the nation—in some movements the nation is regarded as co-extensive with the race (the nation race), while in others, hierarchies of races are defined generically with nations located within them (the race nation), but in virtually all cases, the view is taken that the introduction of impurities has weakened the nation and been responsible for its plight; (4) the blame for national decline and/or racial miscegenation is laid at the door of a conspiracy on the part of other nations/races seen as competing in a desperate struggle for dominance; (5) in that struggle, both capitalism and its political form, liberal democracy, are seen as mere divisive devices designed to fragment the nation and subordinate it further in the world order.

With regard to prescriptive content, the first priority is the reconstitution of the nation as an entity by restoring its purity. The second is to restore national dominance by reorganizing the polity, the economy, and society. Means to this end include variously: (1) the institution of an authoritarian and antiliberal state dominated by a single party; (2) total control by the latter over political aggregation, communication, and socialization; (3) direction by the state of labour and consumption to create a productionist and self-sufficient economy; and (4) a charismatic leader embodying the 'real' interests of the nation and energizing the masses. With these priorities fulfilled, the nation would then be in a position to recapture its dominance, if necessary by military means.

Such priorities were explicit in the interwar fascist movements, which indulged in racial/ethnic 'cleansing', established totalitarian political systems, productionist economies, and dictatorships, and of course went to war in pursuit of international dominance. But such parties can no longer openly espouse these extremes, and national/racial purity now takes the form of opposition to continuing immigration and demands for repatriation; totalitarianism and dictatorship have been replaced by lesser demands for a significant strengthening in the authority of the state, allegedly within a democratic framework; productionism has become interventionism; and military glory has been largely eschewed. ST

Fatah *See* PLO.

fatwa A legal opinion on an issue of Islamic ritual or conduct or on issues of jurisprudence. The person who issues a fatwa is one who is versed in Islamic Law, a jurist (*mufti*).

favorite son American term for a presidential nominee whose support comes mainly from one state delegation. Usually nominated either as a token gesture of honour, or as a tactical move to keep a delegation's options open for a time, for instance to see whether a bandwagon effect is building behind any other candidates. With the prevalence of *primary elections, which have reduced the importance of the nominating convention (*see* PARTY CONVENTION), the number of favorite sons has declined.

The term has been borrowed outside the United States, with the vaguer meaning of 'local hero'.

FBI (Federal Bureau of Investigation) Division of the US Department of Justice, responsible for investigation of violations of federal law. The FBI was organized in 1934, under the direction of J. Edgar Hoover, and intended mainly as a fact-finding agency with responsibility for internal security. However, under the authoritarian control of Hoover the FBI systematically engaged in illegal activities, particularly aimed at undermining left-wing,

and civil rights, activists. Since the 1970s Congress has attempted to increase the accountability of the FBI, notably after the *Watergate affair. The Bureau was heavily criticized for failing to prevent the *September 11th 2001 attacks on the United States, despite having information which could have led to the bombers. The FBI and *CIA were both forced to reorganize their anti-terrorism operations, alongside a new Department of *Homeland Security and under a new *Director of National Intelligence. New powers to investigate terrorist subjects were conferred under the USA Patriot Act (2001), reauthorized in 2006 despite concerns that the legislation infringed civil liberties.

((⊕)) SEE WEB LINKS
• FBI website.

fear *See* POLITICS OF FEAR.

Federal Assembly (Russia) The Federal Assembly became Russia's parliament with the adoption of a new constitution and elections in December 1993. It was constituted in the shadow of the dissolution and shelling of its predecessor, the Russian *Congress of People's Deputies, by president Yeltsin in October 1993. The Federal Assembly is a bicameral parliament, composed of State Duma (the lower house) and Federation Council (the upper house). The first Duma served for a transitional term of two years. Since December 1995, Duma deputies have been elected to four-year terms.

The State Duma has 450 seats. Up to 2007 members of the lower house were elected through a mixed electoral system: 225 deputies were chosen by proportional representation from national party lists, subject to a 5 per cent threshold, and the remaining 225 deputies were elected through plurality elections in single member districts. President Vladimir Putin reformed the electoral system and the December 2007 Duma elections were held under a closed-list proportional representation system. Now all 450 deputies are elected from party lists in a single national electoral district. Parties must receive at least 7 per cent of the vote in order to gain seats, and seats are distributed in proportion to the vote-share won by parties. Votes for parties that do not cross the 7 per cent threshold are redistributed to benefit those parties which achieve Duma representation.

The Duma is Russia's principal legislative institution. Although the legislative process requires the Duma to cooperate with up to three other actors—the Federation Council, the president, and, in specified areas of economic legislation, the government too—no bill can become law without the Duma's endorsement. Moreover, the Duma has the power to approve or reject the president's choice of prime minister and can vote no confidence in the government.

Politically, the Duma's composition has changed markedly since 1993. The lower house was politically fragmented and worked without a governing majority throughout the 1990s. It was also largely hostile to President Boris Yeltsin, particularly after the December 1995 elections. Following his election in 2000, President Putin undertook a series of reforms to build a pro-presidential parliamentary majority. Changes to the Duma's electoral rules, the law on parties, and also electoral manipulation, especially in the 2003 and 2007 parliamentary elections, led to the increasing dominance of the pro-presidential United Russia party in the lower house. In the elections of 2007 United Russia won over 64 per cent of the vote, a result which, together with the redistribution of votes won by parties that did not cross the 7 per cent threshold, put it in control of 70 per cent of the Duma seats.

The upper house, the Federation Council, is composed of two representatives from each of the subjects of the Russian Federation, irrespective of federal status or population size. The Russian Constitution of 1993 does not specify how the upper house is to be composed and, after a transitional period in which Council members were elected, the Council was from 1995 composed *ex officio* of the heads of each federation subject's executive and legislative branch. As a consequence, the Federation Council became a part-time chamber, which gave regional officials a powerful voice in national politics. President Putin (elected in 2000) reformed the upper house. Senators can no longer be regional officials serving in an *ex officio* capacity but are now delegates, one elected by the regional legislature, the other nominated by the regional governor subject to confimation by the legislature. This reform reduced the direct voice of regional leaders in national politics. In addition, President Putin combined the reform of the upper house with federal reforms, which transformed governors, who used to be popularly elected, into presidential appointees. These changes have enhanced the president's ability to control the political composition of the upper house through his gubernatorial appointees.

The Federation Council may consider all legislation, but is not required to do so. The constitution requires the Council only to examine legislation in areas that are critical to federal relations in Russia including the budget, federal taxes and levies, financial matters, foreign currency, credit and customs regulation and money emission, the ratification and denunciation of international treaties, the status and protection of the Russian Federation's borders, and issues of war and peace. The Council has the power to reject bills that have been passed by the State Duma. A veto by the upper house can be overridden, but the override threshold is high, requiring a majority of no less than two-thirds of all Duma deputies. PS

Federal Bureau of Investigation *See* BFI.

federalism The term federalism (Latin: *foedus*, compact, covenant, agreement) is most commonly employed to denote an *organizational principle* of a political system, emphasizing both vertical power-sharing across different levels of governance (centre-region) and, at the same time, the integration of different territorial and socio-economic units, cultural and ethnic groups in one single polity. Federal political systems are hence often viewed as combining 'unity with diversity' (as in the motto of the United States, *e pluribus unum*). Yet, federal political systems come in different forms: one central dimension along which different types of federal polities can be compared is the autonomy and diversity of the corresponding units. Where the units of a federal polity are highly autonomous and possess exclusive competences over taxation and public policy-making, one can speak of a *confederal polity (or centrifugal federalism). However, a polity where the integration of different units, the sharing of competencies, and the equalization of living conditions among the different units is emphasized can be considered a decentralized unitary state (or centripetal federalism).

In the early seventeenth century, Johannes Althusius (1557-1638) conceived of a polity as a federally constructed edifice of multiple layers of 'consociations' such as family and kinship, guilds and estates, cities and provinces—in direct contrast to Jean *Bodin's conception and defence of the unitary monarchical state as guarantor for order and stability. Taken as a whole, the different consociations form a system of 'societal federalism' in which representation is functional (e.g. professional guilds) as well as territorial (cities and provinces). However, it was only with *Montesquieu that not only the idea of a 'separation of powers' but equally that of *federalism* as a core principle for the organization of polities entered the political debates, against the background of absolutist monarchical rule. One of the most lucid examples where enlightened political thought met the practical art of constitution-building was the *The Federalist Papers*, whose impact on political thought and practice echoed during the French Revolution and the nineteenth century reorganization of European states following Napoleon's fall.

The actual creation of federal polities has been either 'from below', through the consent of the constituent units such as, for example, in the United States and Switzerland, or 'from above', through imposition from the 'centre' and/or outside forces, such as in Germany after the Second World War, post-Franco Spain, or Belgium. The creation of a federal political system in the United States, following decolonization and the creation of independent states, was motivated by the desire of a majority of the constituent states to enhance the security and economic benefits of limiting the sovereignty of individual states by creating an 'extended republic' with a strong central authority. Security-induced and economic motives as well as the appreciation of cantonal autonomy and cultural diversity were behind the creation of the Swiss federal polity in 1848. The creation of a federal polity 'from above' in post-war Germany followed 'outside' pressure from the Allies to prevent the high degree of centralization experienced

under National Socialism ever being repeated. The 'Länder', however, were not generally based upon any ethnic groups, some were artificial whilst others had existed previously; in Spain, where cultural differences were suppressed under the Franco Regime, the federalization of Spain after 1978 was thus driven by the objective to abandon a centralized authoritarian state and to institutionally recognize the social and cultural regional differences; in Belgium, the growing rift between Flanders and the French-speaking Wallonian population rendered the maintenance of a centralized, unitary form of government impossible and, increasingly, the Belgian decision-making process became deadlocked by divisions along linguistic, rather than ideological lines. A gradual process of federalization with major constitutional revisions occurred throughout the 1970s and 1980s.

Federalism suggests that everybody can be satisfied (or nobody permanently disadvantaged) by nicely combining national and regional/territorial interests within a complex web of checks and balances between a general, or national, or federal government, on the one hand, and a multiplicity of regional governments, on the other. This concept purports to describe a method of arranging territorial government, and accommodating differing territorial interests that, at one and the same time, avoids both the perceived overcentralization of unitary systems and the extreme decentralization of confederations.

Its principal ambiguities are three. First, in operational terms federal systems operate in a variety of different political contexts and are associated with a variety of significantly different political outcomes. No one distinctively federal pattern of relations between the national and regional levels of government emerges. It is not at all clear that regional interests and governments are always better promoted and protected in most systems called federal than they are in many systems labelled unitary. Secondly, federal theory is similarly confused. The literature on the subject has produced three broad models: dual, cooperative, and organic federalism. If these are static, 'timeless' models—that is, at any particular point in time examples of all three will be present—then the problem is that the differences between them are too great to suggest that they apply to the same thing. If, however, it is argued they are developmental in character—such that dual federalism existed in the nineteenth century, cooperative federalism in the mid-twentieth century, and organic federalism in the late twentieth century—there seems to be very little difference between federal and unitary systems. 'Federalism' is a classic example of concept overstretch.

Thirdly, supporters of the federal 'idea' and the notion that federalism is a distinct principle of governing, are most plausible when they confine their analysis to formal constitutional or institutional matters. What they have never been able to do is to incorporate other political phenomena, political cultures, party systems, the influence of bureaucrats, and external pressures, into these notions of the distinctiveness of federalism and its commitment to decentralization. These academic ambiguities would not matter so much if federalism was not on so many occasions a symbol of serious division and conflict. This is curious, and dangerous, because federal enthusiasts in the political world often offer this symbol as a way of avoiding territorial conflict. In practice, people have been willing to fight and die to support or oppose the principle. This is because federalism usually becomes a 'live' political issue in two highly dangerous circumstances: (1) when a region wishes to secede from an existing federation; or (2) when an attempt is made to replace a loose confederation, or alliance, with a more centralized federation.   BR/JBU

Federalist Papers, The A series of newspaper articles appearing over the pseudonym Publius in New York city newspapers between 2 October 1787 and 16 August 1788. Most of these 85 articles were written by either Alexander *Hamilton or James *Madison, with a handful by John Jay. The purpose of these writings was to make the case for the ratification of the United States Constitution that had been formulated during the summer of 1787. *The Federalist Papers* remains a volume of great significance constantly cited by lawyers, scholars, and commentators seeking to comprehend the meaning of the various clauses of the Constitution. The papers address some of the key problems that arise from attempting

to establish liberal democratic government in a vast and diverse society. Topics covered include the nature of representative government, the separation of powers, federalism, pluralism, and judicial review. Among the more important papers can be included numbers 10, 51, 70, and 78.   DM

(⊕) SEE WEB LINKS

• *The Federalist Papers*, reproduced at the Library of Congress site.

Federalists (US political party) *See* DEMOCRATIC PARTY; REPUBLICAN PARTY.

feminism There are many feminisms, in politics, in the study of politics, and even within the many categories of feminism discussed here. If there is a universal understanding of feminism, it might be found in the idea that women *are not* and *should be* held equal to men in social, political, and economic life from the household to the international arena. There are many feminisms *ontologically* (that is, they differ in what they believe) as well as *functionally* (that is, they differ in what they *do*). Functionally, two main ways to look at feminism are as a political movement or series of movements or as a body of scholarly inquiry.

As a movement, feminism was once frequently and is still commonly described as a series of 'waves'—terminology coined in 1968 by Martha Lear in the *New York Times Magazine*. Traces of feminist thought (defined as advocacy for the equality of women) can be found in Enlightenment writings from Jean Jacques Rousseau, John Locke, and Mary Wollstonecraft, but the movement's 'first wave' is frequently mapped from the late nineteenth century to the mid-twentieth century, when *movements* advocated for the rights and equal treatment of women under the law. Many of these movements focused on women's suffrage or the right to vote. The 'second wave' was distinguished (or distinguished itself) by broadening the mission of the movement from legal (often political) equality to a wide variety of issues that affect women's daily lives: family structures, sexuality, workplace rights, domestic violence, sexual violence, and other places that women were (or are) held unequal to men under the law. Rebecca Walker identified the 'third wave' as breaking from the 'second wave' as it looked to break up feminism's often homogenized idea of the 'woman' and her needs, paying attention to women of colour, queer women, and others whose gendered experiences did not conform with white, heterosexual expectations. Kimberle Williams Crenshaw began to use the term 'intersectionality', referring to the intersection of experiences (particularly systems of oppression and domination) to which overlapping identity categories expose their holders.

Others have used different categories to distinguish different commitments within feminism, especially as a scholarly enterprise. Rather than the progressivist notion of 'waves', some have labelled feminism by substantive stakes, using categories such as standpoint feminism (which holds that feminist social science should be pursued from women's standpoints), empiricist feminism (which maintains commitments to traditional social-science epistemology and methods while pursuing research on women's emancipation), radical feminism (which seeks a rearrangement of social and political order to eliminate male dominance), and postmodern feminism (which views gender subordination as a complicated discursive construct).

These are among the categories that distinguish varieties of feminism by their *ontological commitments. Across political science, as across politics, different branches of feminism situated differently identify in different ways. For example, in *international relations (IR), where explicitly feminist work is pursued with more frequency than in comparative politics or American politics, feminists have used the theoretical categories that IR scholars use (e.g., *realism, *liberalism, *constructivism, *critical theory, *post-structuralism, decolonial theory) as shorthands to talk about the ways in which their feminist commitments fit into the *epistemological commitments of different branches of theorizing in the field.

There remains substantial debate about how much different types of feminism have in common, and the extent to which they can be considered a common enterprise, both in the academy and in the political realm. From the political realm, one of the most well-known examples of conflict *among* varieties

of feminism is what has been called the 'sex wars'. These were (are) a debate between those feminists who can be called anti-pornography feminists and those who can be called sex-positive feminists. Anti-pornography feminists argued that the economic exploitation and physical abuse that came along with the porn industry, as well as its exploitative depictions of women, meant that doing away with pornography entirely was (is) essential to sex equality. Sex-positive feminists, on the other hand, argued that it is necessary to understand and promote sex as an avenue of pleasure for women, and to take away the taboo on female sexuality. While both sides of this debate shared the *goal* of gender equality, each thought that the other side's path to promoting it was actually gender-oppressive.

Similar debates can be found in the exploration of women and gender in political science. In political science there are scholars who self-identify as feminists who are interested in gathering as much data as they can about the legal situation of women around the world, and analyzing that data to understand both the sources and implications of women's equality or inequality. Others call this sort of feminism 'liberal'; that is, both tied to the binary that there are two sexes (male and female) and focusing on their equality before the law. Those who would see the label 'liberal feminism' as pejorative contend that this perceives people to have essential characteristics based on sex, ignore the degree to which sex (as well as gender) is socially constructed, and do not reach the full spectrum of complex ways in which gender subordination affects people's lives. Intersectional, *queer theory, trans, decolonial, and/or socialist feminisms focus not only on deconstructing the male/female binary but also on looking at the complex webs of gender subordination in social and political life. The latter group of scholars often characterize the former's work as counterproductive to the goal of analyzing and ending gender subordination, whereas the former group often characterizes the latter's as politically ineffective and communicatively obfuscating.

Across this wide variety of feminism, some key questions for politics have been risen to salience in political science research, though to varying degrees in varying subfields.

Scholars such as Cynthia Enloe (originally) ask where the women are in (academic and media) stories of politics, which include only, or focus, on male actors. Scholars such as Judith Butler try to encourage unease with the simple understanding that people occupy sexed bodies that are not constructed, mapped, or rendered meaningful by social engagement; that is, they argue that not only gender but also sex is performative. Scholars such as Laura J. Shepherd look for where gender can be found, not only in comparisons of people in politics but also in accounts of states, state leaders, international organizations, policy initiatives, and policy results. Scholars such as Cynthia Weber ask what assumptions about sex and sexuality are necessary to create and maintain particular political organizations and orders, and how those assumptions can be revealed and questioned. Scholars such as Mona Lena Krook ask how women's under-representation in political life can be corrected, and what the consequences of various policy choices pursuing correction are. Scholars such as Jacqui True confront macropolitical narratives about how the relationship between (decreases in) violence and (increases in) gender equality are related, arguing that real, tangible, and serious gender subordination remains prevalent across the world. Scholars such as L. H. M. Ling map the ways in which subordination on the basis of gender intersects with and co-constitutes subordination based on race and nationality, both in politics and in political science. These are just a few of many lines of inquiry that a wide variety of feminist scholars, and their wide variety of scholarship, have contributed to both politics and the study of politics. LSb/SR

feudalism Feudalism was a system of society in which vassals acknowledged and fought for a lord in return for his protection for their persons and land tenure. The lord in turn paid allegiance to a king in return for his granting of their status, though this was very often a disputed relationship. Feudalism was thus a comprehensive social system which defined authority and property rights. It is most closely associated with France between the ninth and thirteenth centuries AD, but most parts of Europe experienced something

like a feudal system at some stage of their history and there were similar social systems as far away as Japan. England was subjected to a strong version of the feudal system after the Norman invasion of 1066, but it was always opposed by and compromised with non-feudal English institutions. Whereas the remaining rights and duties of *feodalité* were specifically abolished by the French National Assembly in 1789, there was never such a moment of formal change in England and there could not have been.

In the developmental theories of history offered by *Marx and others, feudalism is portrayed as a stage of history made necessary by the breakdown of the economic and military–political systems of antiquity, but itself necessarily spawning its successor, commercial capitalism. In informal contexts 'feudal' and 'feudalism' (like 'medieval') are often used to mean 'outdated' or 'old-fashioned, but not in a good way'. LA

Feuerbach, Ludwig Andreas (1804–72) Born in Bavaria, the son of a distinguished jurist and administrator, Ludwig Feuerbach studied theology at Heidelberg and philosophy under *Hegel in Berlin. His first postdoctoral published work, *Thoughts on Death and Immortality*, published in 1830, caught the attention of the police and censors and Feuerbach was barred from all future university posts. He married and moved to Bruckberg, where he lived in quiet isolation and material comfort for many years. He was most productive in the 1840s, publishing *The Essence of Christianity* in 1841, as well as, somewhat later, the *Preliminary Theses for the Reform of Philosophy* and the *Foundations of the Philosophy of the Future*. These works quickly established Feuerbach as the mentor of the left-Hegelian movement. He gave that movement a common conception of philosophy as nothing but the process of human self-understanding. He also provided a clear notion of human nature in terms of *species-being. Finally, he made possible a radical materialist critique of all religion and religious belief, in particular, perhaps, Judaism. Marx's criticism of Feuerbach's philosophy in his 1845 *Theses on Feuerbach* constituted the first statement of *historical materialism. JH

Fifteenth Amendment *See* CIVIL RIGHTS.

Fifth Amendment One of the ten 'Bill of Rights' amendments (1791) to the United States Constitution, this guarantees citizens that '*due process' will be observed by governing authorities in the event of their arrest or trial. Of particular importance is the right to avoid self-incrimination (known as 'taking the Fifth'). sw

(((●))) SEE WEB LINKS

• The full text of the Bill of Rights and the Fifth Amendment.

Fifth Republic, French The Fifth Republic was formed in response to a military rebellion in Algeria, in May 1958, which was directed more against the policies of the government in Paris than against the regime. Facing a protracted nationalist insurrection across the Mediterranean, the army wanted guarantees that Algeria would remain French, while opinion in France favoured a negotiated peace. The Fourth Republic could no longer command respect or authority and a crisis was avoided only by the appointment of General de Gaulle as Premier, on the understanding he would present a new constitution to the electorate for approval. The constitution of the Fifth Republic provided for a strong President whose powers, however, were shared with a Prime Minister answerable to a majority in the National Assembly. In accordance with de Gaulle's long-held views, Parliament was confined within a strictly legislative role with its jealously guarded sovereignty heavily circumscribed, while the government retained the initiative throughout the legislative process. The constitution was nevertheless ambivalent about the role of the President in the new system, and vague about his relationship with the Prime Minister and the government. The President appointed (and could presumably remove) the Prime Minister, and de Gaulle soon indicated that foreign affairs, defence, and Algeria were his own 'reserved domain'. Moreover, the end of the Algerian war in 1962 saw a clear shift towards presidential rule, with the President no longer chosen by electoral college but elected directly by popular vote.

In many respects the system was actually less presidential under de Gaulle (1958–69) than under his successors, if only because of the General's reluctance to involve himself in routine administration and domestic policy-making, which he entrusted to his Prime Ministers, who, in turn, commanded the support of the parliamentary majority. Later Presidents have intervened much more extensively. Presidential power was most in evidence from 1981 to 1986, when François Mitterrand, former leader of the Socialist Party, enjoyed unquestioning support from his lieutenants in the government, as well as commanding a disciplined Socialist majority in the National Assembly. Nevertheless, while the scope for presidential intervention has increased considerably and the office has become ever more personalized, there are obvious limits to executive discretion in a country with entrenched liberal traditions and powerful autonomous institutions. Even before 1986 and *cohabitation, Mitterrand had come increasingly to delegate responsibilities to the Prime Minister and the government and that trend has since continued. The wide-ranging emergency powers conferred on the President by Article 16 of the constitution were used only once, by de Gaulle. The provision for popular consultation by referendum was invaluable while the Algerian war lasted but has since proved a two-edged weapon. De Gaulle was forced to resign after the defeat of the 1969 referendum on regional powers, while the 1992 referendum on the Maastricht treaty produced a narrow majority in favour but at the cost of revealing the extent of the country's divisions on the issue.

Unlike its predecessors, the Fifth Republic has provided governmental stability and continuity of policy, notwithstanding the student and labour unrest in May 1968, the strains of cohabitation, and the economic problems of the 1970s. While the popularity of political leaders and governments has fluctuated widely, France's present institutions have enjoyed a legitimacy unprecedented since the Revolution. The domestic consensus on foreign policy, forged by de Gaulle, survives to the present, with remarkably few modifications. There is little sign of the *immobilisme* associated with the two previous regimes as governments have moved to tackle some of the country's most intractable problems. The Fifth Republic has seen the consolidation and completion of the Common Market, the modernization of French agriculture, industrial reform and economic liberalization, administrative decentralization, and significant changes in the educational system.

The Fifth Republic has also seen the smooth transfer of power from right to left and vice versa, along with a growing convergence of views about economic policy. This followed an abrupt change in Socialist thinking after 1982, with broad acceptance of free-market principles in place of the earlier emphasis on state control. The collapse of Communist support in the country also contributed to the climate of consensus and stability despite the increasing salience of new issues such as immigration, race, and environment. The traditional dividing line between left and right, so long a feature of the French electoral landscape, has weakened, and there is no obvious new line of demarcation.

The sudden eclipse of the Communists, the traditional party of protest, and the rapid rise of issue movements as dissimilar as the National Front and the Greens, has added to the sense of disorientation shared by party supporters and voters alike across the political spectrum. However, the Fifth Republic's malaise bears no comparison with the periodic crises of the Third and Fourth Republics. IC

( ) SEE WEB LINKS

- The text of the constitution of the French Fifth Republic on the site of the National Assembly.

filibuster Attempt to obstruct parliamentary proceedings by prolonging debate. Common in the US Senate, where the right of free discussion is protected. A minority of senators may attempt to delay and obstruct a measure by speaking on irrelevant subjects, and introducing dilatory motions. Legislatures have attempted to prevent filibusters by introducing procedures to curtail debates, such as *closure, *closed rules, and *guillotine motions.

Filmer, Sir Robert (1588–1653) English political thinker who defended the patriarchal thesis against doctrines based on consent. His main work, *Patriarcha*, was circulated in manuscript among his acquaintances during his lifetime, but only published in 1680 as a defence of Tory support for

Charles II in the Exclusion Crisis. Filmer is most famous for the fact that *Locke attacked his ideas directly in the First Treatise of Government, and provided an alternative position in the Second Treatise, both published in 1689, immediately after the Glorious Revolution. Filmer argued that all legitimate government is ultimately based on God's gift to Adam of absolute sovereignty and private property over the whole world, and their transmission by primogeniture. Fatherhood and political rule are in principle the same, but the relationship is of analogy, not of homology. In effect, however, because knowledge of the true heirs had been lost after the division of the world between the sons of Noah, Filmer was obliged to admit that any government that continued in power had to be accepted as legitimate whatever its origin. The patriarchal theory was bypassed in favour of a general assertion of divine authorization. Although he took the same view of the nature of sovereignty as *Hobbes and *Bodin, he rejected completely Hobbes's derivation of it from the supposed original freedom of individuals by means of the *social contract. Filmer's strongest argument was that in recognizing the continuation of legitimate rule over later generations without further consent, and in allowing private property established by fathers to be passed on to their sons, such theorists had in effect admitted his patriarchal theory. CS

Financial Crisis (2008) Financial crises involve a sudden pronounced drop in the market value or price of a financial asset or instrument. Falling asset prices are likely to result in an unwillingness to hold or buy a particular type of financial asset amongst market participants and investors. Many contemporary financial institutions' risk management models are price-sensitive, so that falling prices create an imperative to sell those assets. In a situation of falling market prices, a downward self-perpetuating spiral can quickly take hold, producing an investment downturn and further 'fire sales' of particular types of asset. Sudden price reversals and downward spirals of this sort effectively result in wealth vanishing.

The cause of such reversals and evaporations of wealth is most frequently the emergence of new information, or a reappraisal of existing information by a critical mass of market participants, that suggests assessments and estimates of future earnings and potential revenues have been overstated. Once such a reappraisal is under way, confidence in the viability and future returns on particular assets can evaporate quickly. Repeated instances of reversals in investor confidence have resulted in an argument that modern financial systems are characterized by an inherent *procyclicality* and instability. Procyclicality involves confidence accruing from rising asset prices, leading to an expansion in credit and endogenous money creation. New funds are in turn invested in rising assets, leading to a further expansion in available credit in an upswing phase of a cycle. Once confidence is shaken due to reappraisals of future prospects, the process goes into reverse, leading to plummeting asset prices and reduced credit as part of a self-sustaining downswing cycle of price movements.

Financial crises are political events because they unavoidably become distributional phenomena due to the sudden loss of wealth they entail. Where the losses are so great that large financial institutions are imperilled, sovereign governments may intervene to provide support for institutions because they are fearful of the systemic consequences of institutions collapsing. This is what governments in the United States and the United Kingdom did in 2008. Where sudden price reversals lead to a contraction in available credit, financial crises can feed into a more general macroeconomic slowdown and recession. In 2008 this very process resulted in an expansion in government annual fiscal deficits and resulted in a turn to austerity policies of public expenditure retrenchment across a number of advanced states. The financial crash of 2008 is widely regarded as a large one. The loss of market value was greater than in the crash of 1929. While government stimulus packages prevented a rerun of the Great Depression, central banks estimate world output was 6.5 per cent lower in 2009 and 11 per cent of global wealth was lost.

Some financial crises involve government finances coming under pressure due to capital flight and currency depreciation, creating short-term financing pressures for governments and banking systems, as international investors withdraw their investments from a particular national territory. This is essentially what happened in the case of the contagious South-East Asian crises of 1997–98, forcing these countries to seek emergency loans from the *International Monetary Fund (IMF) to restore financial confidence. These loans came with significant conditions attached to them, such as retrenchment in public spending, and requirements for governments to give foreign investors more freedom to trade in assets in their territories.

Consequently, public policy interventions to manage crises affect how the losses arising from the evaporation of wealth are shared out and the burdens and costs associated with that are distributed, creating perceptions of winners and losers. Realignments of interest calculation and new coalitions can result from the sudden losses of wealth and the distribution of those losses through public policy interventions. Financial crises can therefore spark intense forms of distributional struggle. Such struggles are in part a function of an existing distribution of power in society and the institutional access to decision-making which certain groups possess. Financial crises and their management consequently can very quickly become political moments and events, involving a competition for power and a process of coalition building as rival political parties, sectoral interests, and domestic and international agencies compete to define the nature of the crises, the appropriate public policy response, and how any financial losses should be shared out.

In their famous account of 800 years of financial crises, Carmel Reinhart and Kenneth Rogoff identified seven types of financial crisis, including inflationary crises, currency crashes, currency debasement, asset price bubbles bursting, banking crises, external debt crises, and domestic debt crises. In reality, crises are often fluid and flow into one another, so that in 2008 a problem of falling asset prices in securitized debt markets turned into a focus on the sustainability of widening government deficits by 2010. In this sense, modern financial markets and institutions operating in them are highly interconnected. This means that financial crises can be highly contagious, because they can cross market segments and national borders, with many financial institutions having global investment strategies and owning assets in many parts of the world. Financial crises consequently often require international cooperation and negotiations between governments and market actors to contain contagion.

Financial crises are of political importance for two further reasons. First, they have to be interpreted by technical policy elites, business groups, the media, NGOs, political parties, and the public at large, as each of these groups formulate and publicly forward diagnoses of complex events. Interactions between these groups through political and public processes of interpretation and debate concerning the nature of the crises and the necessary course of action mean that crises are often characterized by society-wide persuasive struggles between elites and mass publics. Different groups compete to define the nature of the crisis and create a dominant public understanding. In this sense, financial crises can be conceived of as something politically constructed and created by different political and institutional actors offering public explanations and interpretations, which draw on both cognitive understandings of the causes of crisis and calculations of self-interest.

Second, financial crises such as the Wall Street crash of 1929 (which led to the Great Depression) and the stagflationary crisis of the 1970s have been transformational moments, which change the trajectory of politics. The 1929 crisis eventually sewed the seeds for a more social democratic distributional and interventionist order, throughout the 1930s and after the World War II, leading to the *Bretton Woods system, of activist domestic economic management, the rise of *Keynesian policy regimes, *welfare states, public services, and national capital control that restricted international capital mobility. The 1970s produced a trajectory change towards financial liberalization, reduced trade union power, labour market, and welfare reform, and privatization, in a swing towards a more liberal set of economic ideas and policies often referred to as *neoliberalism. Financial crises have in the past, therefore, produced great transformations in the established political, institutional, and economic order. Such processes were themselves the result of processes of interpretation, contestation, and the political construction of crisis. ABr

Finer, S. E. (1915–93) Influential member of the first generation of British political scientists, educated at Oxford. After a first post at Balliol College, he became Professor of Government at the University of Keele, and then Professor of Government at the University of Manchester, finally returning to All Souls College Oxford at the end of his career. Like many political scientists of his generation, Finer developed eclectic interests, writing on political thought, public administration, local government, civil–military relations, and comparative government. One of his best known books remains *Anonymous Empire* (1958), which was a widely read pioneering account of pressure group activity in Britain. *See also* ADVERSARY POLITICS. WG

firm, theory of the A rationale for the existence of firms. Economists were slow to recognize that the existence of firms required explanation. The theory first developed by Ronald Coase in 1937 to account for these blisters of hierarchy on the skin of the market rested on the concept of transaction costs. Any market transaction between autonomous individuals required time and negotiation and therefore had a cost. Wherever and to whatever extent the firm, a fundamentally political entity, was able to coordinate production and exchange at less cost than the market, competition would allow it to prevail. As the public good of information became increasingly important in complex modern economies the advantage of firm over market increased in many sectors, leading to growth in the average size of firms. Information, once created, may very easily disperse across a large population without any diminution of its utility to each additional consumer. Because it is so easy to come by, unless protected, no individual has an incentive to declare and part with its true value. But if all refuse to pay, the incentive to create information disappears. The firm overcomes this problem by using authority to help ensure a return to those who acquire title to information, whether it be the location of a good, a technique for refining it, or an innovative and effective administrative system for bringing it to market. CJ

First Amendment One of the most important amendments to the United States

Constitution encapsulating several rights deemed essential to liberal democracy: freedom of religion, of speech, and of the press, and the right of the people to assemble and to petition the government. This amendment is one of those added to the Constitution as a *Bill of Rights immediately after it was first drawn in order to assuage the concerns of those who feared the emergence of an overbearing central government. The Supreme Court, drawing on the *due process wording of the Fourteenth Amendment, has argued that First Amendment freedoms are also protected from impairment by the states.   DM

(🌐) SEE WEB LINKS

• The full text of the Bill of Rights and the First Amendment.

First International *See* INTERNATIONAL SOCIALISM.

first-past-the-post A name for the *electoral system in which the person winning the most votes in a district or *constituency is elected. It is used in Britain, Canada, India, the USA, and other countries associated with British colonialism. It is also known as the (single ballot, single member) simple plurality electoral system. Sometimes it is referred to as a majoritarian or as the simple majority system, which is misleading since a candidate only has to win a plurality (i.e. the most votes), not a majority. Indeed, it is often the case that constituencies are won without a majority. It is also true that parties can win a majority of the seats in the legislature under this system without even a plurality of votes. In the British general election of 1951 the Conservatives won a majority of seats whilst winning fewer votes than the Labour party, and in February 1974 the Labour Party won a plurality of seats without a plurality of votes. Since then all British governments have won parliamentary majorities without a majority of the votes. Whilst these outcomes are seen as unfair by some, the system has been defended by others who believe that majority governments are preferable to minority or coalition governments for reasons of efficacy and accountability.

The system is thought to penalize small parties both in the aggregation of votes into seats and by providing incentives to vote *tactically. Thus *Duverger described a tendency towards a two-party system among countries using the first-past-the-post system.   SF

first strike Getting one's retaliation in first. In warfare the first (or pre-emptive) strike strategy aims to maximize damage to one's enemy; combining the element of surprise, the full deployment of offensive capability, and undermining an opponent's ability to respond. Particularly threatening when nuclear weapons are involved, strategists sought to minimize the attraction of a first strike in warfare by building up *second-strike capacity and formulating the theory of *mutually assured destruction. *See* DETERRENCE.

first world A term used to refer to a block of industrialized and developed countries allied with the United States after World War II. First world is distinguished from 'second world' and *third world, which refer to former soviet countries and developing or neutrally aligned countries respectively. In modern use, first world continues to refer to developed countries who share 'Western' values of democracy and capitalism, such as Australia, Britain, France, Germany, Japan, other European countries, and the USA. It is also synonymous with the term *Global North. Yet, with the fall of the soviet system, first world is now contrasted exclusively with developing countries or 'third world' countries, which are also often referred to as being part of the *Global South.

fiscal crisis Actual or supposed inability of the state to raise enough tax revenue to pay for its programme. Theories of fiscal crisis were widespread in the 1970s, both among Marxists such as James O'Connor (*The Fiscal Crisis of the State*, 1973), and non-Marxists such as Samuel Brittan (*The Economic Consequences of Democracy*, 1977). These writers argued that no government could extract more in tax revenue without imperilling liberal democracy, nor could it cut services. Theories of fiscal crisis appeared to be discredited in the 1980s. In the United Kingdom, the Thatcher administrations lowered the top marginal rates of income tax. Because the burden of tax was shifted to indirect taxes, especially value added tax, enough people seem to have believed the false claim that the burden of tax had been reduced for democracy to survive. In the United States, there were significant tax reforms in 1981 and 1986, which again broadened the tax base and cut marginal rates of income tax. New Zealand introduced a tax reform of similar scope. So long as taxes are collected in imperceptible ways—such as through National Insurance contributions— it seems that fiscal crisis can be put off.

But it may recur. The ageing of the population in advanced capitalist states means that health and social security expenditure per head must rise sharply to maintain the same level of service, to be paid for by levies on the economically active, who form a declining proportion of the population. Generally, politicians are unwilling to admit to this harsh truth, so it is predictable that talk of fiscal crisis will recur when the illusions cease to work. *See also* FINANCIAL CRISIS (2008).

fiscal policy A government's taxation and public expenditure policy. Tax enables the government to raise revenue in order to provide *public goods which would not otherwise be provided by the market, such as a police force, national defence, and so on. The tax system may also have an effect on the distribution of income, and the allocation of resources in the market. A government's fiscal policy will have a broader effect on economic activity, unemployment, and inflation. Under *Keynesian policies fiscal measures should be used to smooth out the cyclical, *stop-go, nature of economic development, by stimulating the economy during slumps, and deflating the economy during booms.

fixed-term parliament One whose term is exactly fixed by law or constitutional mandate. Thus for example the United States House of Representatives has a term of exactly two years, and each Senator one of six years, with a third retiring by rotation every two years. The UK House of Commons by contrast has variable terms: the law fixes the maximum but not the minimum length of a parliament, so that incumbent politicians are free to dissolve parliament at what seems to them the most propitious time. Whilst the House of Commons has retained the powers of *dissolution, the devolved assemblies and parliaments established in Scotland, Wales, and Northern Ireland, have fixed terms.

Fletcher, Andrew (1653–1716) Scottish politician and commentator, known as 'Fletcher of Saltoun', who gained a reputation as 'the patriot' for his opposition to Union with England. Influenced by *Machiavelli and *Harrington, Fletcher was primarily concerned with limiting the power of the monarchy; proposing an independent parliament, frequent elections, and the incorporation of citizens in a militia (as opposed to a standing army). A proponent of *confederation—whereby European states could exist under a regime of mutual cooperation between decentralized, self-governing units—his ideas have resonance with those who believe that Scotland could act independently within the European Union. Fletcher's views were propounded in a number of pamphlets and speeches in the Scottish parliament, and he can be seen as a precursor of the Scottish *Enlightenment. His principled stand against court patronage and bribery was not shared by a majority of his fellow members of the Scottish parliament, who voted for Union with England in 1707.

flexible response Military doctrine developed under the Kennedy administration in the United States, providing a conventional warfare strategy for *NATO alongside that of *massive retaliation and *mutual assured destruction.

floating voter A voter who does not vote consistently for one or other of the political parties but 'floats' between them. When, in the 1930s, research began on voting behaviour, it was found that large blocks of voters remained wedded to particular parties for election after election on the basis of their social group memberships, and that relatively few switched their vote. But these few 'floating voters', it was thought, corresponded to an ideal type of democratic voter in so far as they were informed and open-minded in making their choices. Such voters were widely considered by politicians and political analysts to hold the balance between the 'blocks' of committed partisans, and their support was seen as the key to political power. Subsequent research suggested that habitual 'floaters' were, in fact, less involved and informed about issues than others, and more inclined to vote on whimsical grounds. The extent to which there are distinct groups of floaters and loyalists, as opposed to various degrees of loyalty, is also debatable (*see* ELECTORAL VOLATILITY). ST

floor leader *See* MAJORITY/MINORITY LEADER.

focus group In market research, a group of people brought together for an in-depth discussion of their feeling about some consumer good such as a beer or a range of sauces. Used by political parties' market researchers since the 1980s to measure people's feelings, in a broad sense, for and against the 'brands' that parties embody. Focus groups, unlike quota or probability samples of the population, are not designed to be statistically representative, and are an example of *qualitative research.

forces of production A term, in German *Produktivkräfte*, that is part of the technical jargon of the theory of *historical materialism, as first formulated by *Marx and *Engels in *The German Ideology* of 1845–6, which can be translated both as productive forces and as productive powers. Unfortunately, Marx and Engels nowhere provide a list of these forces or powers and ambiguity still persists about the significance and correct usage of the term. In general, forces of production refers to means of production and labour power. And the term itself should be restricted to what materially facilitates the process of production. This does not resolve the more difficult and interesting question of whether historical materialism entails technological determinism. Nor does it fully explain why a contradiction between the forces of production and the *relations of production is the dynamic of the historical process. JH

fordism A term popularized in political science by the Sardinian Marxist Antonio *Gramsci in the early 1930s. Gramsci focused on the extent to which new American production techniques (in particular, moving assembly-lines and product standardization) and their attendant social relations, pioneered by Henry Ford, signalled the beginning of a new epoch in capitalist development. These techniques of 'scientific management' are sometimes called 'Taylorism' after a

leading early twentieth-century American exponent of them. In the early 1980s, under the influence of Marxist regulation theory, the term 'fordism' was used to describe a 'regime of accumulation' (said to exist in varying degrees in Western Europe between 1945 and 1973) in which mass production was linked to mass consumption, trade unions participated in tripartite negotiation with capital and the state (*see* CORPORATISM), a social and political consensus fostered increases in real wages and the consolidation of a welfare state, governments committed to full employment followed Keynesian demand management policies, and the *Bretton Woods agreements regulated international economic relations. The widespread introduction of flexible specialization, small-batch production, niche consumption, just-in-time management strategies, and the popularity of monetarist ideologies among governments, is said to signal the introduction in the 1980s of 'post-fordism'. PBM

foreign aid *See* AID.

formative elections In the *democratization process the first elections can be seen to have an important effect on the structure of political development, through the type of *party system which emerges or the institutions which are shaped under early administrations. If formative elections are held at a local or regional level it may take longer for national parties to emerge, and sub-national power structures may be entrenched. In post-colonial societies the electoral dominance of the parties which led the nationalist struggle have shaped the political discourse for many years (*see e.g.* CONGRESS (INDIA), ANC).

Foucault, Michel (1926–84) French philosopher. Born in Poitiers, Foucault studied at the École Normale Supérieure and the Sorbonne. In 1970 Foucault was appointed to the chair of Professor of the History of Systems of Thought at the Collège de France. Foucault's work ranges widely across many disciplines and deals with many topics, both contemporary and historical.

Foucault did not believe that there could be a single, unified history. This immediately differentiates Foucault from historicists such as *Hegel and *Marx, although Foucault's relationship with Marx is complex and subtle. Foucault, for whom history is characterized by discontinuity, rupture, and arbitrariness, eschewed reductionist explanatory devices such as 'class struggle' and 'reason'. He does not deny that we can give explanations of certain events, and indeed offers his own explanations of fundamental shifts in what he calls 'discursive formations' (what others might call 'epochs'). But the kind of explanation he gives avoids as far as possible the totalizing explanatory frameworks of other historical thinkers. He denies that historians can make universal claims based on a reading of history.

What Foucault's historical researches establish, he argues, is the existence of discourses, or discursive formations. These are not structures in the sense employed by structuralist writers such as Lévi-Strauss or *Althusser. In denying rigidly deterministic structures, Foucault creates a space in which political actors can act. This leads us to Foucault's concept of *power.

According to Foucault, power is not merely something that individuals, groups, or classes exercise, though of course it can be this. Foucault argues that discursive formations are networks of power within which we are all enmeshed. As he claimed on several occasions, power is everywhere and everything, and is therefore 'dangerous'. However, power, he argues, can be positive as well as negative, productive as well as repressive. What is more, he insists that every instance of power brings with it an instance of resistance to power. Foucault's concept of power has been criticized for its vagueness and its generality. However, his own historical writings provide illustrations of his understanding of power and its relationship to discursive formations.

Foucault's most important works include *Madness and Civilization* (1961), *Discipline and Punish* (1975), and his *History of Sexuality*, of which there are three published volumes (*An Introduction* (1976), *The Use of Pleasure* (1984), and *The Care of the Self* (1984). AA

Fourier, Charles (1772–1837) French social theorist who belongs to the traditions of nineteenth-century *utopianism and *socialism, and who was a savage critic of bourgeois 'civilization' and its values. Fourier's vision of a harmonious future was essentially communitarian, like that of his contemporary Robert *Owen. He advocated social experiments on the scale of between 1,500 and 1,800 people who would live in a 'Phalanx' organized to make labour both productive and attractive to workers (for example, through frequent changes of occupation and routine), and whose basic physical, mental, and even emotional needs would be met through processes of mutual support and democratic self-government. Women would achieve true equality with men, and a sexual revolution would liberate both men and women from the oppressiveness of the traditional family structure. A Fourierist movement enjoyed some success in both France and the United States in the 1830s and 1840s, and even *Marx and *Engels, while dismissing Fourier as a utopian (i.e. non-scientific) socialist, expressed admiration for his originality, and made use of many of his ideas, in particular his theory of attractive labour. KT

Fourteenth Amendment Adopted after the Civil War in 1869, this amendment to the US Constitution was intended to incorporate the 'privileges and immunities' enumerated in the Bill of Rights at the level of the states, and compel state authorities to ensure 'equal protection of the laws' for all their citizens. Although the purpose of the Amendment was to guarantee newly freed slaves recognition of their citizenship by state governments, it has been used subsequently to justify the modern Supreme Court's '*judicial activism' in a variety of policy areas (most notably in its 1954 *Brown* ruling outlawing segregation in state educational facilities). See also DUE PROCESS. SW

(⊕) SEE WEB LINKS
• The text of the Fourteenth Amendment.

Fourth International *See* INTERNATIONAL SOCIALISM.

Fourth Republic, French The constitution of the Fourth Republic was approved in 1946, with the National Assembly accorded more power than it could usefully exercise, while the President was assigned a largely ceremonial role which nevertheless allowed him some discretion in the many cabinet crises that followed. The parties were better structured and more clearly differentiated than previously, but two large anti-system forces, Communists and Gaullists, supported by nearly half of the electorate, did nothing to promote consensus or stability. With twenty-five governments in twelve years, effective power shifted by default to the highly effective administration. The Fourth Republic was never popular but managed some notable achievements, namely, the rapid post-war recovery and subsequent 'economic miracle', coupled with the introduction of indicative planning, innovations in industrial relations, and the extension of welfare provision. In foreign policy France was integrated into NATO, played a leading role in the creation of the European Community, prepared the way for decolonization in black Africa, and finally (and reluctantly), conceded independence in Indo-China. However, the Algerian problem finally exposed the fragility of the system. With opinion in France moving towards a negotiated settlement, in May 1958, the army in Algeria rebelled—not to overthrow the republic but to keep Algeria French. For the sequel, *see* FIFTH REPUBLIC. IC

franchise The right to vote. Universal franchise is a modern phenomenon. In Britain, male franchise was extended in 1832, 1867, and 1884, and became universal in 1918; female franchise was granted in part in 1918 and fully in 1928 (*see also* SUFFRAGE). Earlier, almost no democracy permitted all adult women to vote; *Athenian democracy disenfranchised women, slaves, and non-natives of Athens.

Franco(ism) Francisco Franco Bahamonde (1892–1975) was born at El Ferrol in northwest Spain, into a middle-class seafaring family, and entered the Toledo Military Academy in 1907, having been a mediocre pupil at school. At 33 Franco became the youngest general in Europe since Bonaparte. The left branded him 'the hangman of Asturias' for the brutal manner of his repression of insurrectionary Asturian miners in 1934.

Although Franco was too cautious a man to initiate the right-wing rebellion against the Spanish Republic in 1936, he quickly became the leader of the rebels and in September

1936 was proclaimed '*generalissimo*' of the Nationalist armies and head of state (although he did not govern Spain until the republic fell in 1939).

'Francoism' was not a distinctive ideology: Franco stood for traditional Catholic and military values and was an implacable enemy of liberal, left-wing, and separatist forces. Francoism as a term is mainly used to refer to Franco's regime. Although this had some features of *fascism, and its creation relied upon military support from Hitler (*see* NATIONAL SOCIALISM) and Mussolini, the regime was authoritarian rather than totalitarian.

Sociologist Juan Linz pointed to the existence of 'limited pluralism' within the regime. Franco avoided elite opposition by skilfully playing off different power groups against one another and by tolerating widespread corruption. RG

Frankfurt School The headquarters of *critical theory, founded at Frankfurt University in 1923, in exile in the United States from 1935 to 1953, and revitalized in Frankfurt under Jürgen Habermas, who taught there during the 1960s and from 1982.

A number of broad themes can be identified. One is that Marxism and psychoanalysis combine in critical analysis (*see also* ADORNO; AUTHORITARIAN PERSONALITY). In Habermas's work psychoanalysis, which seeks freedom from control by repressed forces, is a model for emancipation. His focus on language has produced an interest in 'systematically distorted communication' to be countered by 'ideal speech situations' through which all can participate in dialogue. All this is central to the idea of an emancipatory role for critical theory. This leads to a theory of 'communicative action' directed at the cooperative realization of understanding between participants. 'Legitimation crisis' is an important concept for the analysis of late capitalism. Here Habermas suggests that rulers may be unable to generate the consent and commitment of the ruled. IO

Franklin, Benjamin (1706–90) US politician and scientist. Franklin trained as a printer, and gained great popularity by the homespun philosophy of *Poor Richard's Almanack* (1732–67). Homespun philosophy matched a homespun personal style, which Franklin wielded to great effect in London and Paris, where he was sent as the first ambassador of the independent United States. As with *Gandhi, however, the calculated homespun style concealed a sophisticated intelligence, which Franklin put to work not only in science (through his invention of the lightning conductor) but also in politics, notably as the oldest and most revered member of the Constitutional Convention of 1787.

fraternity Brotherhood among a disparate body of people united in their interests, aims, beliefs, and so on. Although 'fraternity' was a political goal at a time when politics was dominated by men, no contemporary contrast with 'sisterhood' is intended by most of those who today embrace fraternity. The goal, rather, is to instantiate in the wider community the sorts of feelings for each other, and the sorts of behaviour towards each other, that brothers and sisters are taken to have or display. This has commonly been thought to be impossible without greater *equality, and one defence of that value is that it facilitates fraternity. Characterizing the sentiment and behaviour need not romanticize the family. What appears to be intended is a conscious or unconscious setting aside of calculations of self-interest for a greater willingness to recognize that others, too, have their projects and concerns. To this extent 'fraternity' suggests greater *altruism. But it also suggests some shared purposes, to be jointly pursued, so its antithesis would be self-absorption. In particular, perhaps, it suggests a common concern with the circumstances in which each person can develop most fully or most satisfyingly. Finally, it suggests a sense of belonging to a unit with which one can readily, if not naturally, identify: the community is a sort of extended family, rather than an 'anonymous' society outside it. AR

freedom Absence of interference or impediment. Unfortunately, and as a reflection of the importance which has been attached to ideas of freedom, almost every aspect of its characterization is controversial. Gerald MacCallum has suggested that all statements about freedom can be cast in the same form—*A* is free from *B* to *p* (*p*

stands for any verb of action)—and that disputes about freedom are disputes about the three terms involved, referring to the agent, the obstacle, and the action or state to be achieved, respectively. This may help to diagnose disagreement, and it does provide a formal framework in which various conceptions may be cast, but it does not itself provide a substantive account. There may be one concept of freedom (in this formal sense), but many conceptions of it (that is, many substantive ways of filling out the formula). Isaiah *Berlin proposed in a famous lecture that two accounts of liberty be distinguished: negative liberty, focusing on the absence of interference by others, and positive liberty, focusing on an agent's capacity to *p*. Berlin particularly emphasized the connection between the positive conception and a willingness to accept an intrapersonal notion of freedom, because he was suspicious of the idea of the self upon which such intrapersonal notions rested—they seemed to rely upon a higher self and a lower self, or a similar bifurcation. Three problems will illustrate how substantively different conceptions of freedom may be put forward. First, attempts have been made to distinguish freedom from ability. In most social contexts the concern is with interference or impediments which are the responsibility of other persons, suggesting to some a distinction between a person's ability to do something and his or her freedom to do it. Hence I am free to fly like a bird (no one is interfering or will impede me) but I am unable to do so; I am able to do many actions which I am legally unfree to do. If I break my wrist accidentally, I am unable to write; if you handcuff me I am unfree to do so. But in these last two examples the distinction between ability and freedom looks less straightforward than in the first two, because in both cases the immediately relevant impediment is physical. The most obvious description of the handcuff case is that I am unfree to write because disabled by you, suggesting ability is a condition of freedom. If ability is a condition of freedom, however, I am unable and therefore unfree to fly like a bird. Clearly, both the agent and others can affect physical capacity, and this in various ways: handcuffs are a temporary impediment, but some disabling conditions are not reversible; both the agent and others can affect an individual's abilities in an accidental way and in an intentional way. (Suppose I deliberately broke my wrist: is the relationship between my ability to write and my freedom now the same as if you had handcuffed me?) In Hillel Steiner's conception of freedom, a person is unfree if and only if his action is prevented by another person. Hence a person is unfree to *p* only if he is unable to *p* because of someone else—a conception which makes freedom depend on ability but only in interpersonal cases.

The second major difficulty arises specifically from the comparison of interpersonal and intrapersonal cases. Some, like Steiner, see freedom solely in interpersonal terms. Others, however, have wanted to extend the range of freedom-reducing impediments or obstacles with which a person may be faced to include those which arise from 'internal' characteristics or dispositions. Suppose I am unlucky enough to suffer from agoraphobia. No one else is responsible for my condition—it has not been imposed on me by others, even if they might be able to help me overcome it. If we say that my freedom would be enhanced by the removal of this phobia, we accept that freedom can be intrapersonal. Alternatively, if we restrict freedom to interpersonal cases, we may say that I am free to walk in open spaces but apparently psychologically unable to bring myself to do so.

A third problem is the relation between freedom and resources. To be able to achieve some objectives, or even to do particular actions, persons require access to the components of action—most fundamentally space and, often, funds. To describe someone who lacks the resources to *p* as free to *p* is to suggest that if he or she is now provided with the resources there has been no increase in freedom, only resources; and many writers accept that characterization of the situation. Others have suggested the need to distinguish formal freedom from substantive freedom. In the present case, there would be no change in the person's formal freedom, but an increase in his or her substantive freedom. (A similar point is made about *rights.) The freedom persons care about is substantive.

This suggestion raises another issue: whether it is plausible to characterize freedom independently of the reasons we might have for valuing it. Some hold that there are two quite separate questions: What is freedom? Why, if at all, is freedom valuable? Others regard the attempt at separation as implausible. For example, many discussions of freedom make reference to the value of individual choice or autonomy. Is the point of having freedom to enhance choice or autonomy, or is what freedom is the having of choice or autonomy? One approach is to distinguish between freedom in some general sense and particular freedoms (although it is not clear how 'freedoms' are to be aggregated). A class of apparently valueless freedoms—for example, to do the many things I am free to do but do not choose to do, or the things I am free to do but lack the resources to do—may be consistent with an explanation of the value of freedom. My wants may change, I may acquire the resources, and the value of freedom in general (it enables choice, it respects autonomy) is compatible with contingently valueless freedoms.

The various responses to the controversial aspects of 'freedom' mentioned here (and others) have generated many conceptions of freedom. Attempts to adjudicate between them have raised the charge that ideological preference masquerades as philosophical discrimination. AR

Freedom House index Measure of political rights and civil liberties. Collected since the 1970s by Freedom House, an American research institute, the index evaluates countries according to a wide range of criteria relating to democratic performance and the functioning of government. The index provides a broad indicator of change over time, and has been used to assess changes in democracy and human rights and their relationship with institutional structure and economic development.

(⌾) SEE WEB LINKS
• Freedom House assessments of the status of political rights and civil liberties across countries.

freedom of association The freedom of individuals to associate as an end in itself or with a view to pursuing common projects, e.g. through churches, trade unions, political parties, and sporting clubs. Freedom of association is widely seen by liberal political philosophers as a core personal liberty, warranting strict protection by the state, though the exact contours of the freedom, and how it is appropriately balanced against other values, are a matter of considerable and continuing dispute. John Stuart *Mill, in *On Liberty*, argues that citizens should have 'freedom to unite for any purpose not involving harm to others', a formulation which leaves open the question of what counts as sufficient harm to others to justify state interference. John *Rawls, in *Political Liberalism* (1993), argues that freedom of association is a 'basic liberty' because, and to the extent that, it is an extension of liberty of conscience. One major point of controversy concerns the extent to which freedom of association should be understood to include the right to refuse membership of a given association to others who may wish to join it. May and should the state strike down membership rules which exclude on the basis of ascriptive characteristics such as race and gender? A considerable body of case law has recently emerged in the United States on this issue. There, the Supreme Court has determined that the United States Constitution asserts two fundamental rights of free association: a right of intimate association and a right to associate for expressive (essentially, religious or political) purposes. Where associations fail to meet the Court's demanding criteria of intimacy, the Court has ruled that government may require associations to satisfy equal opportunity norms in their membership policies unless departure from these norms will clearly undermine the association's specific expressive purposes (see especially *Roberts, Acting Commissioner, Minnesota Department of Human Rights, et al.* v. *United States Jaycees*, 468 U.S. 609 (1984). Critics argue that it is unreasonable to expect associations to show that all membership policies are rationally derived from their expressive purposes. Such an expectation, critics claim, will inhibit the evolution of associations over time and thus make for a poorer associational life overall. Another major point of controversy concerns the extent to which individuals should have the right to refuse membership of associations that others would like them to join, e.g. a trade union at a given place of work. Enforced membership in such cases may violate liberty of conscience, though complete voluntarism may also result in situations where some individuals unfairly free-ride on the associational activism of others.   swe

freedom of information The free access of the public to information contained in government records. In many liberal democracies freedom of information is considered the hallmark of open government. Introduction of freedom of information acts in the United States and in continental Europe led to three major reforms in the United Kingdom. Under the 1986 Local Government (Access to Information) Act local government records are available within a short period. Under the 1998 Data Protection Act (reforming previous legislation) individuals have a right of access to their personal information held on all public authority files. Under the 2000 Freedom of Information Act the public has a broader statutory right of access to information from government and public authorities. In 2002 the Scottish Parliament passed its own Freedom of Information Act pertaining just to information from government and public authorities on devolved issues in Scotland.

Applications under freedom of information legislation have led to notable disclosures of records relating, for example, to government decision-making in the run-up to Black Wednesday in September 1992 when the UK suspended its membership of the European exchange rate mechanism; as well as on government policy on pensions in 1997–8 which changed pension entitlement rights. Despite such examples, however, the principle of administrative secrecy that was established in the UK during the period of absolute monarchy remains influential. Governments have generally established control over access to information by resort to the sovereignty of Parliament and parliamentary privilege. The spirit of the 2000 Act is no exception. It has several areas of blanket exemptions, including defence, national security, international relations, commercial security, and government policy-making. Government also may be expected in practice to take a restrictive approach to disclosure. Schemes setting out the information that public authorities would publish as a matter of course were delayed until 2002.

The Act created an Information Commissioner, who could adjudicate on decisions to withhold public information, but had no power to compel disclosure.

Disclosure of information is further constrained by the 1989 *Official Secrets Act, and other statutes. Civil servants are not allowed to keep diaries, and under civil service rules are bound to keep their work confidential. Information is otherwise disclosed under the public records acts, under which only a selection of the records of central government are available and then only after thirty years. That there have been developments in freedom of information reflects its importance to liberal democracy. Differences in national practice, however, reflect competing conceptions of liberal democracy, and disagreement over what freedom of information is supposed to achieve.   JBr

freedom of religion The right to practise the religion of one's choice, or to be a non-believer. The persecution of men and women for their religious beliefs has a long history and is, even yet, far from universally eradicated. In the United Kingdom, the worst forms of religious discrimination have long since disappeared, although the lack of any separation between Church and State remains offensive to many citizens who do not share the Anglican faith.

In the United States the principle is regarded far more seriously for several reasons. Many of the early settlers who founded the nation were fugitives from religious persecution in Europe and in modern times an extraordinary number of religions are represented in the country. The *First Amendment specifically prohibits the founding of an established church, or any other limitation on the freedom of religion.

The continued significance of these issues in the United States can be seen in the Supreme Court's school prayer rulings since 1962. In *Engel* v. *Vitale* (1962) the Court declared unconstitutional the preparation by a New York state agency of a prayer to be read aloud by children in public schools. Although the prayer was clearly non-denominational, the Supreme Court insisted that officially sponsored religious services were tantamount to the establishment of religion and were therefore unconstitutional. A year later the Court struck down a Pennsylvania state law calling for bible reading and a reading of the Lord's Prayer in that state's public schools. More recently, in 1992, the Court declared unconstitutional the offering of non-sectarian prayers at public school graduation ceremonies. These and other similar decisions have evoked bitter controversy and led to calls for constitutional amendment. Nevertheless these judgments are testimony to the continued importance of the principle of religious freedom in the United States.   DM

freedom of speech Liberty to express opinions and ideas without hindrance, and especially without fear of punishment. Despite the constitutional guarantee of free speech in the United States, legal systems have not treated freedom of speech as absolute. Among the more obvious restrictions on the freedom to say just what one likes where one likes are laws regulating incitement, sedition, defamation, slander and libel, blasphemy, the expression of racial hatred, and conspiracy. The liberal tradition has generally defended freedom of the sort of speech which does not violate others' rights or lead to predictable and avoidable harm, but it has been fierce in that defence because a free interchange of ideas is seen as an essential ingredient of democracy and resistance to tyranny, and as an important agent of improvement. The distinction between an action falling under the description of speech and one which does not is not clear cut, because many non-verbal actions can be seen as making a statement—for example, burning a flag or destroying a symbol. Again, valued freedom of speech embraces publication—writing, broadcasting, distributing recordings—as well as oral delivery of ideas.   AR

free rider One who benefits from a collective activity without participating in it. In Mancur *Olson's classic formulation (*The Logic of Collective Action*, 1965), the incentive to free-ride exists for every rational, self-interested member of any organization where collective action is required to secure a common good. The fact that a goal is common means that 'no one in the group is excluded from the benefit or satisfaction brought about by its achievement'. Each member therefore faces an incentive not to incur his or her share of the costs. Furthermore, if the organization is sufficiently large, the individual knows that his or her costless enjoyment will not affect the motivations of other members to alter their behaviour, because the withdrawal of his or her involvement 'will not noticeably increase the burden for any other one dues payer'. Provision of the good *is* threatened, however, if each and every member reasons in this way. Organizations thus face strong incentives to devise rules (regulating membership and admissible activity) to prevent free riding, both on instrumental grounds and on grounds of fairness. Taxation of citizens by states for the provision of *public goods, and trade union monopolies ('closed shops') are two well-known illustrations of such institutional devices. sw

free trade The absence of barriers to international trade. Up to the nineteenth century, under the system of *mercantilism, Europeans faced two main kinds of barriers to trade: first, duties, quotas, and prohibitions restricting the movement of goods from one customs area to another; second, controls on participation in particular trades imposed by corporations like the British or Dutch East India Companies.

In 1813 the British East India Company was deprived of its monopoly over trade between Britain and India. Following a prolonged public campaign, the repeal of the Corn Laws in 1846 opened the British market to cheap foreign grain. The exemplary force of these events was all the greater because they appeared to be applications of the cogent and appealing liberal economic theories of Adam *Smith and David Ricardo. Moreover, rapid growth in international trade, coinciding with increasing wealth and an extended period of general peace in Europe, at first appeared to confirm these theories.

Ricardo had argued in his theory of comparative advantage that free trade between nations would bring gains to both parties to an exchange, even when one was the more efficient producer of every good they traded. This was because trade encouraged even an unproductive national economy to devote resources to those branches of production in which they would be least inefficiently employed. But Ricardo never promised that

the gains from trade would be evenly distributed, and a nationalist critique of free trade pioneered by Alexander *Hamilton in the United States and Friedrich List in Germany gathered strength towards the end of the century. It even gained ground among traditionally liberal British businessmen, now buffeted by the trade cycle and threatened by new centres of manufacturing industry in continental Europe and North America.

The campaign for tariff reform in Britain was only one facet of a general drift away from free trade. By the 1930s not just the practice but even the ideology had been largely abandoned because it was held to provide disproportionate gains to established industrial economies and to provide insufficient opportunity for the realization of their potential comparative advantage by newly developing economies. In its place came bilateral systems of exchange within currency areas, the British system of *imperial preference within the sterling area being only one example.

Because bilateralism coincided with a sharp fall in the volume of international trade and was held by powerful members of the Roosevelt administration to have contributed indirectly to the outbreak of the Second World War, the allied powers reinstated a limited form of free trade within a dollar-exchange monetary system in the later 1940s. Under the GATT (General Agreement on Tariffs and Trade) of 1947 (*see* WORLD TRADE ORGANIZATION), successive rounds of multilateral trade negotiations (MTNs) outlawed quantitative restrictions on trade, such as quotas, and achieved greatly reduced tariffs on the principal classes of manufactured goods traded between leading industrialized economies. But although this contributed to a sharp increase in levels of trade and prosperity during the 1950s and 1960s, it became more and more evident that many non-tariff barriers—including complex administrative procedures, ingeniously drafted health and safety regulations, and nationalistic public procurement policies—still impeded free exchange of goods and services. Moreover the GATT had permitted a number of exceptions to its general principles from the outset. Trade in temperate-zone agricultural goods was not covered, nor in textiles and clothing, and both became subject to extremely restrictive regimes devised by the United States, Japan, and the European Community to protect their own producers. The GATT also allowed discrimination in favour of each other by groups of countries pledged to the formation of a *free trade area or *customs union, such as the *European Union.

Add to this the extent to which goods such as automotive components, oil, or aluminium are traded internationally within large multinational corporations at administered rather than market prices, together with the renewed prevalence of smuggling (especially of precious metals and illegal drugs), and it becomes hard to discern clearly any causal relation between global prosperity and the imperfect contemporary implementation of liberal free trade theory. Be this as it may, the most impressive rates of economic growth achieved in recent years have without exception been achieved by export-oriented countries, like Japan, Taiwan, South Korea, and China, that have relied very heavily on market access provided by this system of managed liberalism; and this has confirmed free trade once again as the effectively unchallenged ideal type of international commerce.   CJ

free trade area A group of countries, such as the North American Free Trade Area (Canada, Mexico, and the United States), pledged to remove barriers to mutual trade, though not to movements of labour or capital. Each member continues to determine its own commercial relations with non-members, so that a free trade area is distinguished from a *customs union by the need to prevent the most liberal of its members from providing an open door for imports. This is done by agreeing rules of origin, which set the terms on which goods manufactured outside the area may move from one state to another within it. *See also* SINGLE EUROPEAN ACT.   CJ

free vote A division in Parliament on which no formal party line applies, when MPs are free to vote as they see fit. Generally confined to moral issues, such as abortion and capital punishment.

freezing hypothesis A concept introduced by S. M. Lipset and Stein Rokkan in 1967 to denote the fact that *cleavages within Western European parties have remained largely 'frozen' since before 1920 and the introduction of women's *suffrage. Understanding this phenomenon has become a key component in the study of comparative politics, generating interesting insights on how party structures and constraints determine the way cleavages can form and how political movements are amalgamated into existing party structures.

French Enlightenment *See* ENLIGHTENMENT, FRENCH.

French Revolution (1789) The first modern revolution because it changed the structure of society, rather than simply replacing the existing ruler or even the political regime, and created new ideologies to explain its course when nothing suitable could be adopted from the past. It produced the modern doctrine of *nationalism, and spread it directly throughout Western Europe, something that has had enormous indirect consequences up to the present. The European wars of 1792–1815, sparked off by the French Revolution, spread both revolutionary ideas and nationalism (although the only newly free state created by the French Revolution was Haiti). The French Revolution also provided the empirical origin of modern theories of revolution, including that of *Marx, as well as an important model for subsequent revolutions. Part of the reason for this was that France was pre-industrial, just as many of the countries that underwent subsequent revolutions were to be. Interpretations of the French Revolution have varied enormously, depending upon the political position and historical views of the writer.

The relationship between the French *Enlightenment and the Revolution is extremely complex. *Burke blamed the Enlightenment, in which he included *Rousseau, for the Revolution. But while the Enlightenment spread a sceptical rationalism, it did not propose the extremism or the political solutions adopted during the Revolution.

Before 1789, France combined an absolute monarchy with feudalism. As *Tocqueville first suggested, the aristocracy was exempted from taxation in return for not interfering with the king's policy. The latter was, however, fundamentally limited by the former even under Louis XIV (reigned 1643–1714), the most absolute of French kings. Because the wealthy paid no taxes, there was a permanent *fiscal crisis, and the effects were only avoided by taxing the rest heavily, and by selling offices and letters of nobility. Because of its fiscal privilege, the aristocracy felt no need for a parliamentary system such as developed in England.

The Revolution proper started in 1789 and ended ten years later. A series of political and social crises led up to it, including widespread popular discontent because of poverty made worse by poor harvests. The royal treasury's normal state of near bankruptcy had become desperate because of help given to the American revolt against Britain. Attempts in 1787 and 1788 by ministers of Louis XVI (reigned 1774–92) to address the financial problem by reducing the privileges of the aristocracy (and the clergy) produced revolt on their part. They induced him to call, for May 1789, the first meeting since 1614 of the Estates General, an assembly of representatives of feudal society. This body consisted of the First Estate, the clergy, the Second, the aristocracy, and the Third, the rest. The aristocracy expected to dominate the Estates General and although the king had decided in December 1788 that the Third Estate would have the same number of representatives as the other two together, they were still intended to sit and vote separately. If the First and Second agreed, they would always have defeated the Third.

None of the estates was united. Each was divided between rich and poor members, and among different interest groups. When the Estates General met, the Third Estate withdrew and declared itself the National Assembly, inviting the others to join it. After some of the first two estates, especially the clergy, joined the Third, the king ordered them to combine into a single chamber, which then declared itself competent to give a new constitution to France.

On 14 July 1789, the fortress in Paris known as the Bastille, then used as a prison, was seized and demolished as a symbol of despotism. In fact, although this event has been celebrated almost ever since as a national holiday, it contained only seven prisoners, and it is even possible that the demolition had already been ordered by the existing regime.

On 4 August, remaining privileges, and effectively *feudalism, were abolished, although various remnants continued in dispute. The Revolution continued, becoming more and more extreme as different groups succeeded for a time in gaining control. The wealth of the clergy was transferred to the nation and priests were required to accept civil status, which led to papal condemnation.

Eventually, in 1791, the king attempted to escape from France, but was arrested. In 1792, the monarchy was abolished, France was proclaimed a Republic, and the king was put on trial. A new calendar was adopted, starting with Year I, with ten new months, named after prevailing weather conditions, in place of the old. In 1793, the king was executed, and Robespierre, leader of the *Jacobins, succeeded in becoming effective leader of the Committee of Public Safety, from which position he and his followers brought about the Terror in which thousands were summarily executed for supposed crimes against the Revolution. After a year, Robespierre fell, and was himself executed. Various schemes to reorganize government were tried, none of which worked for long, and eventually Napoleon Bonaparte succeeded with a *coup d'état* in 1799 which eventually led to his election as emperor in 1804.

Although started by the privileged, control of the Revolution rapidly passed to the middle classes and then, for a time, to the *sans-culottes* in Paris who were poor and extreme. Robespierre and the Jacobins obtained power with their support against their rivals, the *Girondins, mainly because they were willing to accept the *sans-culottes'* demand for strict control of food prices, especially bread. Their failure to carry out the policy in full explains why the *sans-culottes* did not intervene on Robespierre's behalf when he was under attack. The price of bread was crucial because even in normal times, it took half the expenditure of the majority of the population, and in difficult times, much more.

After Robespierre fell, control passed back to the middle classes. Napoleon's success represented a desire for internal order and victory abroad, although it was presented as the only way to keep the Revolution's achievements.

The view of the Revolution, following *Marx, as the replacement of a feudal economic system, based on agriculture and a rigid social hierarchy, by capitalism, based on industry with hierarchy established in the market, is far too crude. One aspect of the abolition of privilege was the reinforcement of the peasantry, both that which continued from before 1789 and the new members who joined it as a result of the disposal of land previously owned by the Church and some of the aristocracy. This class continues to exist and to wield considerable political influence. cs

front-bencher *See* BACK-BENCHERS.

Front National *See* NATIONAL FRONT (FRANCE).

front organization A body not officially sponsored by a Communist party but actually controlled by it. The term was coined during the hysteria which led to *McCarthyism in the United States. Front organizations have certainly existed, although there have never been as many of them as Senator McCarthy and his equivalents in other countries believed.

functionalism The doctrine that societies or social systems have 'needs' and that we can explain institutions and practices in terms of the 'functions' they perform for the survival of the whole. Functionalist explanation is prevalent in all traditions in social science and there is no single school of modern functionalism. However, it is characteristic for functionalist accounts to draw analogies between the biological organism and the social system, to view societies as made up of component parts whose interrelation contributes to the maintenance of the whole, and to focus on the problem of order specifying forces that bring cohesion, integration, and equilibrium to society.

The origins of modern functionalism can be traced to *Comte. Comte maintained that all of the institutions, beliefs, and morals of a society are interrelated as a whole, and so the method of explaining the existence of any one item is to discover the law which governs the coexistence of all phenomena. Through the work of *Durkheim this approach was developed and appropriated by the social anthropologist Bronislaw Malinowski (1884–1942) who was the first to coin the term after he had carried out ethnographic fieldwork among Australian aborigines and later Trobriand Islanders. Malinowski sought to explain the existence of institutions and practices in terms of the needs or functional requisites which had to be met to maintain society (religious rituals are functional for social adaptation). The anthropologist A. R. Radcliffe-Brown (1881–1955) further developed this approach under the title *structural functionalism.

Normative functionalists, strongly influenced by the American sociologist Talcott Parsons (1902–79), hold that there is a central value system in every society and stress the importance of *political socialization which teaches appropriate normative expectations and regulates the potential conflict which is inherent in situations of scarce resources. This view has been particularly influential in American political science, enabling theorists to posit a number of system functions (socialization, political recruitment, political communication) through which political systems are maintained and adapt to change. General functionalism (with its distinction between 'latent' and 'manifest' functions) and General Systems Theory (with its cybernetic analysis of positive and negative feedback loops) are more recent attempts to develop the insights of functionalism whilst rejecting both the 'oversocialized concept of man' characteristic of normative functionalism and the teleology implicit in early functionalist explanation.

A number of objections have been raised to functionalist explanation in social science. Most decisively it has been argued that all functionalist accounts rely on teleological explanation. To explain an event teleologically is to account for its occurrence on the grounds that it contributes to a goal or end-state and that this goal is sought or maintained by the system in which the event takes place. Explaining an event by showing that it has beneficial consequences for another is to treat an effect as a cause. To argue that the state exists to meet certain functions necessary for the maintenance of capitalism, is to use a consequence to explain a cause. This both defies orthodox logic and is clearly ahistorical. In addition, functionalist accounts have been criticized for lacking adequate accounts of human action (*see* STRUCTURATION), for failing to account for social change, and for introducing a conservative bias into methodology since every element in the 'status quo' becomes functional simply because it is present. Whilst functionalist accounts contain useful injunctions for political scientists—to look for relationships between institutions and social practices—functionalist methodology has come under increasing attack as its basic assumption that 'societies have needs' cannot be demonstrated.   PBM

functional representation Functional representation may be contrasted to the more usual form of territorial representation where a legislator is elected to represent a defined territorial unit and all the citizens who live within it. Samuel Beer defined the term as referring to 'any theory that finds the community divided into various strata, regards each of these strata as having a certain corporate unity, and holds that they ought to be represented in government'. In the twentieth century these were generally regarded as groupings emerging from the division of labour in society such as employers, labour, and farmers. Demands were made from time to time by leading politicians for an 'industrial parliament' in Britain. Such ideas took root in continental Europe, influenced by the corporate emphasis of Catholic social thought. Austria developed a series of chambers of commerce, labour, etc. with compulsory membership and a system of elections. Five of the six founding member states of the European Community had developed consultative bodies representing socio-economic interests, leading to the establishment at European level of an Economic and Social Committee with three groups of members: employers, workers, and other interests. The limited impact that this body has had on policy-making reflects a broader decline of interest in functional representation. It is associated with the idea of *corporatism which is far less popular than it once was. Twenty-first century societies are characterized by the disintegration of traditional social strata based on the division of labour and their replacement by a more fragmented social structure with multiple sources of identity which is less amenable to functional forms of representation.   WG

fundamentalism, Christian *See* CHRISTIAN FUNDAMENTALISM.

fundamentalism, Islamic *See* ISLAMIC FUNDAMENTALISM.

G20 The Group of Twenty (G20) represents a club of states that meets annually to discuss important economic, financial, and political issues. It is made up of the *G7 industrialized democratic countries, the five 'emerging' *BRICS countries, six other economically emerging countries, and the *European Union, which together as the G20 represent the twenty largest global economies, generating approximately 85 per cent of global GDP. Originating as a forum for central bankers in 1999, ongoing economic stability issues, as well as the 2008 *Financial Crisis, prompted the establishment of an annual G20 'Leaders Summit' (the first two years saw biannual summits in order to respond to the financial crisis). Although the G20 began as a forum to discuss global economic stability, its agenda has expanded to include the discussion of other topics, such as global security, global health, *development, gender, *climate change, *migration, the *Syrian Civil War, and the *refugee crisis.

There remains considerable debate about the usefulness and importance of the G20. Although once heralded as being a more representative and legitimate replacement for the G7/8, its policy effectiveness in comparison to the G7/8 is minor. Whereas the G7 has an established history of delivering a number of significant global initiatives, the G20 remains fairly stagnate and ineffective in its ability to generate dynamic global policy initiatives and general consensus. That said, the G20 does offer a unique forum to tackle global collective action problems. Given that the G20 represents two-thirds of the world's population and most of its economic viability, it has built-in potential to be a meaningful global policy forum, which could provide greater accountability and legitimacy than the G7 can offer.

G7 The Group of Seven (G7), formerly the G8, is a club of industrialized democratic states that meets annually to discuss important economic, financial, and political issues. The first summit, held in Rambouillet in 1975, was attended by the G5 (France, Germany, Japan, the US, and the UK) and Italy. Canada and the European Community joined in 1976 and 1977 respectively. Membership then remained constant until the end of the Cold War. From 1991 onwards, Russian Presidents attended select G7 meetings. Russian participation at the 1998 Birmingham Summit marked the birth of the G8, and Russia's status as a full member was confirmed when the nation hosted the G8 summit in St Petersburg in July 2006. However, Russia was kicked out of the G8 in response to its annexation of Crimea in 2014, and its membership is foreseeably suspended (*see* CRIMEA CRISIS).

G7 'summit diplomacy' has a number of functions. It provides a forum for world leaders to collaborate on collective problems, to manage the world economy, and to address issues arising from interdependence and globalization. It presents informal opportunities for leaders to forge good personal relations. G7 summits are also used to set international priorities, to identify and define issues, to set up new regimes and reinvigorate existing ones, and to provide guidance to international organizations. The G7 works closely with other organizations, in particular the International Monetary Fund (*IMF) and the Organization for Economic Co-operation and Development (OECD).

Unlike the United Nations or the Bretton Woods institutions, the G7 has no charter, formal rules, or permanent secretariat. The G7's unusual format dates back to 1975: the Rambouillet meeting was intended to be a 'one-time get-together' to discuss economic and monetary issues in the wake of the OPEC oil crisis and the collapse of the Bretton Woods monetary system. This one-off meeting became an annual summit. Although senior national officials—or 'sherpas'—prepare the summit agenda in advance, G7 leaders can deviate from it. The G7 reaches 'understandings' rather than resolutions, and relies on consensus formation rather than formal voting. Compliance rates vary according to country and issue-area. Whereas at the outset it was little more than an informal club, the G7 may now be described as a *system* consisting of complex, multi-levelled bodies. Since the 1980s, G7/G8 working groups and task forces have addressed specific problems, such as nuclear safety, *financial crisis, international security, *climate change, and organized crime. Certain issues have been shifted to the ministerial level: the 'Quadrilateral' of trade ministers from the US, Japan, Canada, and the EC has met annually since 1982, and foreign affairs ministers since 1984. Ad hoc meetings are occasionally convened in response to particular events, such as the Gulf War and the 1992 Rio Conference.

The G7's agenda has evolved over the years, reflecting changes in leadership and broader political and economic developments. Traditionally, G7/G8 summits have discussed macroeconomic issues such as international economic and financial management, trade, and relations with developing countries. Key achievements include the 1985 Plaza Agreement, which corrected G7 currency misalignments and coordinated interest rates, and the 1987 Louvre Accord, which stabilized the American dollar after it fell too rapidly. Following the accession of a new generation of politically conservative, pro-market leaders in the early 1980s, the G7 began to explicitly address political issues, with summit discussion of world events such as the Israeli invasion of Lebanon (1982), the deployment of US missiles in Europe (1983), and the situation in the Middle East, Cambodia, and South Africa (1988). Summits have also increasingly tackled 'microeconomic' issues such as employment and information technology.

In the 1990s, two issue-areas dominated the G7/G8 discussions: issues arising from the end of the *Cold War and the transnational challenges posed by economic globalization. After the collapse of communist regimes in Eastern Europe and the Soviet Union, the G7 explored means of assisting the transition to market democracy in post-communist states. At the 1989 Summit, the G7 established the Group of Twenty-Four (G24)—composed of the OECD and former Warsaw Pact states—in order to aid the process of transition. The G7 also set up the European Bank for Reconstruction and Development (EBRD) to finance transition. Second, G7 summits increasingly sought to find solutions to transnational problems, addressing issues such as the developing world debt crisis, the environment, global energy issues, trade, UN reform, financial crisis, global poverty, nuclear safety, *nonproliferation, world health, the 'digital divide', and conflict prevention.

At the beginning of the twenty-first century, the G7/8's traditional focus on macroeconomic issues and trade continued, combined with an expanding focus on the environment (e.g. the 2007 Heiligendamm Summit), meeting global development goals (e.g. the 2005 Gleneagles Summit), and cross-border security-related issues such as transnational crime and terrorism. G7/8 summits have also been used to air tensions between Russia and the West over military and security issues, in particular the US's planned missile defence system and the *Iraq War in 2003.

The G7 is not immune to criticism, and three major problem areas can be identified. First, non-governmental organizations (NGOs) and *anti-globalization protestors have highlighted the discrepancy between the G7's power and its perceived lack of accountability and transparency, most notably during the 2001 Genoa Summit riots and the 2005 'Make Poverty History' campaign. Summits are now characterized by 'ring of steel' security, and there are frequent clashes between protestors and police. Second, the summit's informal structure, while creating space for dialogue, limits the G7's ability to make binding commitments on issues of global importance. The absence of specific binding targets on reducing greenhouse gas emissions following the 2007 Summit, for example, reflects this ongoing dilemma.

Lastly, the G7 continues to face criticism concerning its representativeness and relevance in the global economy, in light of its exclusive nature. While G7 members still account for almost two-thirds of global economic output (measured by GNP), the non-inclusion of rising economic powers such as

China and India has been widely criticized. This issue was addressed at the 1999 Cologne Summit, when eleven states—including Brazil, Australia, Argentina, and South Africa—joined the G8 to form the *Group of Twenty (G20). The G20 aims to promote dialogue between systemically important economies, but has no decision-making powers. Further progress was made at the 2005 Gleneagles summit, when the 'G8+5' was created. The G8+5 is a separate set of meetings attended by the G7 Finance and Energy Ministers, in addition to those of China, Mexico, Brazil, India, and South Africa. The intention to fully institutionalize this dialogue was announced at the 2007 Heiligendamm Summit. VC

(⊕) SEE WEB LINKS

• G8 Information Centre at the University of Toronto.

G77 Established in 1964, the Group of 77 (G77) represents a loose coalition of (was seventy-seven, now 134) developing countries within the *United Nations who mutually promote their economic interests so as to advance development in the *Global South and to increase their collective negotiating capacity within the United Nations.

Gallup, George (1901–84) Founder of the US, now multinational, opinion polling company which bears his name. One of the first people to realize that reliable prediction of public attitudes can be made from a small sample, so long as the sample is carefully chosen.

game theory Branch of mathematics that has been applied to politics since *c.*1960. A game is any situation in which the outcomes ('pay-offs') are the product of the interaction of more than one rational player. The term therefore includes not only games in the ordinary sense, such as chess and football, but an enormously wide range of human interactions. (And it has been applied to animal interactions: *see* EVOLUTIONARY GAME THEORY.) Any human interaction from 'Should I drive on the left or the right side of the road?' to 'How should I behave in international negotiations?' may be treated as a game.

There are many ways of classifying games. The two most useful are between games with perfect information and those without; and between *zero-sum and non-zero-sum games. Chess is a game of perfect information. It is fully defined by the rules on what constitutes a legal move and what constitutes winning. In theory a computer could look at all the possible combinations of moves and responses to moves and specify a unique best strategy for both Black and White. When this happens, chess will cease to be an interesting game, but it is a long way off. Bridge is a game of imperfect information, in which players must not only calculate what it is rational for the other side to do, but also calculate the probabilities on which player holds each card they cannot see. Most human encounters are not games of perfect information. A zero-sum game is one in which the aggregate pay-off—the sum of the pay-offs for all the players put together—is the same in all outcomes (for instance if a player in a two-person game is paid £100 for winning, £50 for a tie, and nothing for a defeat). A non-zero-sum game is any other. If the pay-offs were £100 for winning, £60 for a draw, and nothing for a defeat, for instance, the players would have an incentive to agree to draw and to split the extra takings between them. This makes the game non-zero-sum, or one of partial cooperation. The games most often studied in politics, especially *chicken and *prisoners' dilemma, are non-zero-sum.

Though first formalized in the 1940s, game theory has a long prehistory. Elements of game-theoretic reasoning can be seen in the writings of many thinkers, including *Plato, *Hobbes, *Rousseau, and *Dodgson.

Gandhi, Mohandas Karamchand (1869–1948) Arguably the most influential figure of modern Indian politics, Gandhi became the symbol of Indian nationalism and was given the status of the Father of the Nation after India achieved independence in 1947. Gandhi's most significant contribution to Indian politics was perhaps his belief in the strength of ordinary people. Gandhi was able to mobilize the Indian people primarily because the demands his politics made upon the individual were not extraordinary. His insistence on *non-violence (*ahimsa*) which underpinned his campaigns of *civil disobedience (*satya-graha*) allowed people to participate in national politics in many different ways—none of which necessarily required a break with people's daily lives. Gandhi was able to create a national mood, which cut across castes, classes, religions, and regional loyalties by rejecting the boundaries that these created as irrelevant to the moral Truth that he made central to his discourse. This at times led him to limit the more radical aspects of nationalist aspirations of some within the *Congress and outside it. Another distinguishing feature of Gandhi's philosophy, one that was less influential, was his opposition to Western modernization as a model for India's development. He looked much more to India's villages and self-sufficient rural communities for inspiration in the economic sphere. Gandhi died on 30 January 1948, shot by a *Hindu nationalist militant. SR

garden city movement One of the crusades which arose out of the horrified reaction to the growth of cities in Victorian Britain. Its aims were encapsulated in Ebenezer Howard's book *Tomorrow: A Peaceful Path to Real Reform*, published in 1898. Howard assumed an environmental determinism which blamed poor surroundings for the moral and social failings of urban life. He proposed self-contained cities of about 30,000 people provided with extensive parks and surrounded by 'home farms' and in which every house would have its own garden. George Bernard Shaw described Howard as 'the heroic simpleton' because, though his theories of the urban condition were more simplistic than those of his rivals and his environmental determinism verged on the naive, his faith in his beliefs and his energy in implementing them were second to none.

In fact, only two true garden cities were ever built in England, Letchworth and Welwyn. After the first Town Planning Act was passed in 1909, the influence of the garden city idea was considerable, but compromised and diffused, in England as in the rest of the world. Its greatest influence was on the large number of garden suburbs built between 1918 and 1939. Many of the original ideas of the movement re-emerged in the planning of New Towns between the New Towns Act of 1946 and the abandonment of a New Towns policy in 1977. LA

GATS (General Agreement on Trade in Services) The Uruguay Round of GATT negotiations included a legally distinct series of negotiations to bring the services sector of the global economy under GATT disciplines and dispute settlement procedures, despite substantial initial resistance from less-developed countries. The successful accord or GATS (which entered into force on 1 January 1995) is now under the umbrella of the *World Trade Organization (WTO), which succeeds GATT as the core of the *multilateral trade regime. DH

(⊕) SEE WEB LINKS

• Text and related information from the World Trade Organization.

GATT (General Agreement on Tariffs and Trade) *See* WORLD TRADE ORGANIZATION.

Gaullism French political movement, originally associated with Charles de Gaulle (1890–1970) and the wartime Resistance. It subsequently provided a base for his opposition to the *Fourth Republic, with his insistence that only a strong executive presidency could defend French sovereignty and national independence, guarantee consensus and social cohesion, and promote rapid modernization. There have been numerous Gaullist parties, mirroring de Gaulle's long political career, from his opposition to the Fourth Republic to the defeat of the 1969 referendum, his subsequent retirement, and his death in 1970. A strongly pragmatic and flexible movement, with little in the way of ideology, Gaullism has undergone further change under the General's successors. The post-war Rally of the French People (RPF), with its militant nationalist and anti-regime views, contrasted with the accommodating conservatism of Georges Pompidou's Union for the Defence of the Republic (UDR), although there were some similarities with Jacques Chirac's stridently populist Rally for the Republic (RPR). IC

GCC *See* GULF CO-OPERATION COUNCIL.

GDP (gross domestic product) The aggregate output of the *factors of production in a country, regardless of who owns the factors. *See also* GNP.

Gellner, Ernest (1925–95) British–Czech philosopher, best known for his study of language, modernization, and nationalism. His major contribution to the study of politics is the sociological idea that nationalism and national identities are strongly linked to, and promoted by, processes of modernization, industrialization, and the unification of language via formal state curricula.

Gemeinschaft/Gesellschaft   Terms introduced into social science by the German sociologist Ferdinand Tönnies in 1887. Most commonly translated as 'community' and 'association', the concepts refer not only to idealized types of society but also more broadly to forms of social organization and social relationships. The movement from *Gemeinschaft* to *Gesellschaft* indicates the idealized transition from small, rural, tightly knit communities in which kinship ties and traditional values predominate, to an associational impersonal industrial society based on the rational pursuit of self-interest and contract characterized by heterogeneity and diverse belief-systems.

The spread of industrialization in the nineteenth century made such binary divisions appealing and similar distinctions are found in the work of Maine (from status to contract), *Bagehot (from custom to law), and most famously *Durkheim (from mechanical to organic solidarity). Although such distinctions are often represented in terms of evolutionary societal development, the concepts can also be applied to characterize relations within a society. In this way family relations can be thought of as pertaining to *Gemeinschaft* whilst commercial and legal dealings assume more the character of *Gesellschaft*. Within international relations, theorists interested in developing the notion of *international society have recently drawn on Tönnies' distinction to help explain the origin of the society of states.   PBM

gender and politics A series of contributions by feminists in the field of politics and political theory has focused on the ways in which women's issues, concerns, and participation are excluded from the public political arena because of the division between the private and public spheres, on the one hand, and the language and politics of universal political rights, on the other. Feminists

have challenged these constructs and have pointed out that the public and the universal have both historically been masculine in nature. From Mary *Wollstonecraft's concern with women's rights in the public sphere, shared in France by *Condorcet and his wife Sophie de Grouchy, to the slogan of second-wave *feminism—'the personal is political'—feminists have sought greater access to institutional politics, and to reconstitute the political world. While the concern of liberal feminism has been improving access for women to institutions of public power, through improved educational facilities, *equal opportunities legislation, and anti-discrimination politics, and therefore challenging political *patriarchy from within, other feminists, especially Marxists and radical groups, have challenged the very linking of the political to public. They believe that the reason why women have been systematically excluded from the political arena is the false distinction that has been made and sustained by patriarchy between the public and the private worlds. Feminists have also challenged the institutionalized, delegational form of politics in this context, emphasizing the importance of participation per se. Black feminists have contributed to the debate on politics by insisting upon the importance of race in Western societies, which does not allow them to participate in political life both as women and as black persons. Feminist groups have historically struggled with the question of making alliances with other groups. While some have wanted women's groups to be exclusive to women, others have sought alliances with men on specific issues affecting both sexes.   SR

gender mainstreaming If *women's inclusion* looks to add women to positions of opportunity and leadership in politics, *gender mainstreaming* is meant to be a more comprehensive idea where gender is taken into account in staffing, policy, and implementation in a wide variety of contexts. The terminology was first proposed as policy in the international arena in the 1985 Third World Conference on Women in Nairobi, Kenya, and formally featured in the policy conclusions of the 1995 Fourth World Conference on Women in Beijing. Adopted by institutions as wide-ranging as the *United Nations Security Council and the World

Health Organization, gender mainstreaming has become a mainstay of national and international bodies looking to address gender equality. Still, there remains significant confusion about how to implement gender mainstreaming either substantively or procedurally, the pros and cons of universally applying one standard of mainstreaming, and the ineffectiveness of some efforts at implementation. Over the last fifteen years, gender mainstreaming legislation in domestic and international arenas has focused on *how* to integrate gender across a wide variety of policy platforms, and how to apply that integration in not only policy-making but policy implementation. Many policy entrepreneurs are looking to combine grassroots-level experience and substantive expertise.   Lsb

General Agreement on Tariffs and Trade *See* WORLD TRADE ORGANIZATION.

General Agreement on Trade in Services *See* GATS.

General Assembly (UN) The main deliberative and policy-making body of the *United Nations. The General Assembly, also known as UNGA, is the only body within the six main branches of the UN where all members are represented equally. Presided over by a Secretary General, the main functions of the UNGA are to review the UN budget, to appoint non-permanent members to the *United Nations Security Council (UNSC), to review the activities of other UN bodies, and to debate and recommend UN resolutions. The UNGA can vote and debate any matter within the remit of the UN, including peace and security, except for issues currently under consideration by the UNSC. Critics of the UNGA suggest that it is far too fractured and weak (particularly in comparison to the UNSC) to enact fundamental and meaningful policy. However, supporters suggest that the UNGA is a key mechanism to enact more legitimate UN action and is thus a progressive mechanism for international policy—though admittedly, it is in serious need of reform alongside the UNSC.

General Election 2010 The 2010 UK General Election was held on 6 May 2010 (except in the Thirsk and Malton constituency where it was postponed to 27 May, due to the death of a candidate). The Conservative Party emerged as the largest party, with 307 seats (a net gain of 97) and 36.1 per cent of the vote, the Labour Party won 258 seats (a net loss of 91) with 29.0 per cent of the vote, the Liberal Democrat Party 57 seats (a net loss of 5) with 23.0 per cent of the vote, and other parties won 28 seats. Turnout was 65.1 per cent, an increase of 3.7 per cent from 2005.

The election was fought against the backdrop of an economic recession, and with the reputation of Members of Parliament suffering from a scandal over their expenses. The Labour Party campaign, led by the Prime Minister Gordon Brown, stressed the importance of sound economic management, but Brown's uneasy rapport with the public was highlighted when he was recorded in an unguarded moment describing a voter as a 'bigoted woman'. The Conservative Party campaign, led by David Cameron, emphasized the need for a change of government, although the theme of the 'big society' failed to resonate. Coverage of the campaign was dominated by the three televised debates between Gordon Brown, David Cameron, and Nick Clegg, leader of the Liberal Democrats.

With no party gaining an overall majority of the 650 House of Commons seats, the election resulted in a hung Parliament. Without formal constitutional rules in the case of such an outcome, Gordon Brown remained Prime Minister whilst talks were initiated between the Conservatives and the Liberal Democrats. There were also discussions about a possible Labour Liberal Democrat government requiring support from other parties. On 11 May 2010 Gordon Brown resigned, and David Cameron became Prime Minister at the head of a Conservative and Liberal Democrat coalition government. Nick Clegg became Deputy-Prime Minister, and an agreement was published setting out the programme for the coalition government.

General Strike The instrument by which *syndicalists believed capitalism would be brought to its knees. The General Strike in Britain in May 1926 was not led by syndicalists, nor was it successful.

General Systems Theory *See* FUNCTIONALISM.

general will Central political concept in the work of Jean-Jacques *Rousseau, for whom the general will is the result when citizens make political decisions considering the good of society as a whole rather than the particular interests of individuals and groups. Originally part of a theological debate concerning whether or not God had a general will that all men be saved or a particular will that some be not saved. Rousseau was influenced by the Jesuit philosopher, Malebranche (1638–1715), who rejected the idea of original sin central to *Calvinism.

According to Rousseau, the general will can only be achieved in a city-state analogous to those in the ancient world, or to his birthplace, Geneva. These had political systems based on direct democracy in which all citizens, a small minority of the population, had political rights, but no one else did. Citizens therefore enjoyed liberty in the ancient sense of participation in law-making, but not in the modern sense of having a sphere of life free from collective interference. The exercise of political rights formed part of a general ethos based on patriotism, and was a reflection of a set of values instilled into every member of the citizen class from birth. cs

genocide This word was created by Polish jurist Raphael Lemkin in 1944 and derives from the Greek word for people or tribe (*genos*) and the Latin suffix for murder (*cide*). Lemkin sought to criminalize acts that destroyed groups through physical and non-physical measures. Genocide was codified into international law via the 1948 United Nations Convention on the Prevention and Punishment of the Crime of Genocide. It defines genocide as the intent to destroy a national, ethnical, racial, or religious group, in whole or in part, through a range of acts, such as killing, mental harm, prevention of births, and the forcible transfer of children. It remains one of the most controversial and contested terms in *international relations as scholars reassess four key elements: (1) the complexity of establishing intent; (2) which groups should be included; (3) the range of acts contained within in the remit of 'destroy'; and (4) the scale of the crime regarding debates over whether a group has to be destroyed 'in whole' or 'in part'. *United Nations agencies have recognized genocide in *Rwanda, in the former Yugoslavia, and in the *Darfur region in Sudan. AG

geopolitics An approach to politics originating in late nineteenth-century Germany that stressed the constraints imposed on foreign policy by location and environment, geopolitics contributed to the emphasis on continuity in modern political realism. Mediated to policy-makers by Karl Haushofer, Halford Mackinder, and the United States authors N. Spykman and S. B. Cohen, the idea that control of the Eurasian land mass or heartland was a prerequisite for global dominance fed the successive preoccupation of the United States and its allies with Communist expansion into the so-called rimlands of South-East Asia, Eastern and Southern Europe, and the Middle East during the *Cold War. CJ

George, Henry (1839–97) American economist and social reformer best known for his *Progress and Poverty* (1879). George examined the reasons for the persistence of poverty in capitalist industrial societies (despite their steadily increasing levels of production) and also considered the causes of slumps and continuing economic depressions. In George's opinion, the key factor was the fluctuation of land values, which led to intense speculation in the interests of a small number of privileged landowners. His proposed remedy was a 'single tax' system which would levy a tax on land values, and would thus in effect create a kind of common property in land (without altering legal ownership), while at the same time other taxes on earned incomes would be abolished, thus providing strong incentives for free enterprise and productive labour. George's proposal revived the 'impot unique' idea associated with the *physiocrats. Single tax legislation, albeit on a limited (usually local) scale, has since been implemented in many countries of the world, including the United States, Canada, Australia, and New Zealand. In Britain George's ideas influenced the economic thinking of the *Fabian socialists, and the Liberal Government's 1909–10 budget included a proposal to value all land in England with a view to taxing it for the benefit of society as a whole. KT

German unification The German Federal Republic and the German Democratic Republic achieved full political unification in October 1990, thus ending a division between the two separate German states which had been a central problem of the *Cold War. Constitutionally unification was achieved by the territories of the former communist GDR becoming part of the Federal Republic, whose legal jurisdiction was now extended to encompass the six new eastern *Länder*, including Berlin.

The process of unification was precipitated by the collapse of the GDR's communist regime in 1989, which occurred against a background of intense struggle for social and political change throughout Eastern Europe. Widespread popular protest in the GDR, as well as a massive exodus of citizens to the West, made it clear that there was an irreversible demand for democratization and liberalization. KT

gerrymandering Drawing of district boundaries so as to favour one's own chances in future elections. In 1812 Governor Elbridge Gerry of Massachusetts drew boundaries for electoral districts in the state so as to maximize the chance of his party's winning seats. The cartoonist Elkanah Tisdale superimposed the head and tail of a salamander on a map showing some of Gerry's long, thin, and tortuous districts, and coined the word. Strategies for gerrymandering have been characterized as 'stacking', 'packing', 'racial gerrymandering', and 'cracking', each of which seeks to minimize the influence of those likely to vote for opponents. 'Stacking' occurs when boundaries are drawn so opponents are grouped in constituencies where they are a minority; 'packing' when opponents are concentrated in a small number of constituencies; racial gerrymandering when boundaries are drawn along racial lines or to limit racial influence; and 'cracking' when opponents are divided between a large number of constituencies. Concern that such methods were used to minimize the influence of black voters has led to the adoption of *majority-minority districting. Sometimes misspelt as 'jerrymandering'. *See also* APPORTIONMENT.

Gesellschaft *See* GEMEINSCHAFT/ GESELLSCHAFT.

Gibbard–Satterthwaite theorem All 'reasonable' methods of preference aggregation

can be manipulated by the misrepresentation of preferences. This was proved independently by both Gibbard (*Econometrica*, 1973) and Satterthwaite (*Journal of Economic Theory*, 1975). The theorem implies that under any determinate electoral system there may be incentives for voters to misrepresent their preferences and so engage in *tactical voting. SF

gift relationship, the Title of study (1970) by R. M. Titmuss of blood supply in Britain and the United States. Titmuss took his title from anthropological studies of reciprocal gift-giving, especially Marcel Mauss's *The Gift* (English translation 1954), and his data from a survey of UK donors. The study shows that more and purer blood was available in Britain than in the United States, although nobody was paid, nor received any other favour, for donating. Titmuss used his results to claim that humans are more altruistic than he believed *economic man to be, and that the success of altruistic systems of blood donation may be related to the highly developed networks of gift and counter-gift studied by anthropologists in Africa and Polynesia.

Girondins A group of deputies in the Assembly and Legislative Convention, many of them from the Gironde area around Bordeaux, established during the French Revolution. Centred around the figure of J.-P. Brissot, the 'faction of the Gironde' represented the resistance of the provinces to Parisian dominance, and opposition to the emerging dictatorship and terror under Robespierre. In June 1793 the Girondins were themselves expelled from the Convention and later killed. SW

glasnost Russian: literally 'the fact of being public; openness to public scrutiny'; the term may have been picked up from the writer Alexander Solzhenitsyn. The policy of Mikhail Gorbachev, General Secretary of the Communist Party of the Soviet Union 1985–91, of permitting more public discussion of current affairs than had been permitted earlier. It has been argued that the political liberalization symbolized by glasnost and *perestroika, unaccompanied until 1991 by significant economic liberalization, was unstable, and contributed to the fall of Gorbachev and of the Soviet Union.

Global Fund The Global Fund to Fight Aids, Malaria and Tuberculosis is a multi-sectoral global institution developed to respond to the world's three most devastating infectious diseases. Established in 2002, through a series of initiatives by the *G7/8 and *United Nations, the Global Fund was created to be an independent organization to collect funds from a broad range of governmental and private sources and to act as a unified global response to help those most affected by the three diseases. Although there is considerable debate within global health governance as to the success of the Global Fund (in terms of fostering genuine participation and eliminating power asymmetries between G7 and non-G7 countries, as well as its effectiveness in helping disease reduction), what continues to make the organization unique is its multisectoral decision-making procedures and its commitment to *public–private partnerships. It remains one of the few global institutions where all decisions are derived from the formal participation of donor governments, receiving governments, private foundations, NGOs, and the private sector, as well as a representative for those suffering from the diseases.

(⊕) SEE WEB LINKS

• Global Fund website.

global governance All coexisting forms of collective steering of social affairs, by public and private actors, that directly or in their repercussions transcend national frontiers.

Steering echoes the Latin and Greek roots of the term 'governance', which comprises, following Renate Mayntz, all forms of collective regulation, including self-regulation of civil society, the co-regulation of public and private actors, and authoritative regulation through public actors. These may imply formal or informal processes, institutionalized or ad hoc mechanisms; address specific problems or cut across policy fields; and serve different functions such as agenda-setting and policy formulation, decision-making, implementation, or evaluation. 'Global' here refers to the highest level of political activity, but acknowledges that local,

national, and regional processes may have implications for world politics. While 'global governance' is a highly contested concept among scholars and practitioners, there is consensus that it implies 'governing without government' (James Rosenau and Ernst-Otto Czempiel) in the absence of a global authority with the monopoly of force.

Notwithstanding its academic origins in the discipline of international relations, global governance deviates from neo-realist and liberal institutionalist understandings, as it neither suggests a mere focus on the international level, nor an a priori description of world politics as state-centrist and hierarchical. Yet, the more one accounts for multi-level, constructivist, or critical perspectives on international relations, the stronger the two concepts overlap. Likewise, 'transnationalism' originally concentrated on effects of societal interactions on domestic politics, but meanwhile, like global governance, recognizes the emergence of new spheres of authority and political interlinkages across borders.

Global governance has served as a heuristic tool in academic and political debates since the late 1990s—meant to capture key transformations in the international system in times of socioeconomic globalization. One of these trends is the ascent of new types of agency. Aside from classical roles as agenda-setters and information-brokers, *civil society and *non-governmental organizations (NGOs) came to monitor international commitments of states, serve as mediators and evaluators, and help put international norms into practice; e.g. implementing development assistance programmes administered by the *World Bank or bilateral donor agencies. Likewise, many corporations took over more visible roles as financial supporters, but also as political partners of (inter-)governmental actors, such as in the Global Compact, a voluntary corporate sustainability initiative under the UN. Transnational networks of scientists assumed a growing role in providing policy-relevant knowledge on uncertainty-laden problems. A prominent example is the Intergovernmental Panel on Climate Change (IPCC), an authoritative scientific body set up by governments that has accompanied UN climate negotiations from their inception (*see* CLIMATE GOVERNANCE). Public non-state actors also exert growing international influence, such as international bureaucracies and coalitions of cities. Ultimately, illicit networks such as transnational crime syndicates add to the new agency of global governance. The mix of functions these different actors perform varies considerably across policy fields, depending on governance gaps, the nature of the subject matter, or power and interest coalitions. It is further contingent on the openness of intergovernmental organizations towards non-state actors, which, for instance, differs significantly between the inclusive UN climate negotiations and the relatively closed world trade rounds.

A closely related transformation process in international politics is institutional proliferation and variation. Since the end of the *Cold War, intergovernmental institutions, and particularly the UN, initiated a series of mega-conferences, such as the so-called Earth Summit in Rio 1992, and comprehensive sets of principles, such as the *Millennium Development Goals and the *Sustainable Development Goals. In parallel, new global judicial actors were established, such as the *International Criminal Court or the Dispute Settlement Body of the *World Trade Organization. On the other hand, non- and sub-state actors gave rise to novel forms of cooperation, from looser networks to transnational standards and highly institutionalized initiatives that may exert considerable influence, for example, on consumer behaviour. A growing series of market-based mechanisms and hybrid initiatives such as *public–private partnerships complement this greatly diverse institutional architecture.

Another trend is the further globalization and diversification of subject matters. Whereas during the Cold War global political processes and institutions largely targeted security, trade and, to a lesser degree, development and human rights, other issue areas gained a stronger profile, most prominently environmental protection. Traditional domains meanwhile were redefined and broadened, visible, *inter alia*, in new paradigms such as Global War on Terrorism, *responsibility to protect, *human security, and good governance.

These agency-related, institutional, and thematic transformations went hand in hand with an increasing complexity. The governance systems of individual policy domains, and global governance as a whole, are marked by an unprecedented expansion and fragmentation of regulatory apparatuses and processes that differ in their constituencies, geographical scopes, and thematic foci. The resulting polycentric governance structures, as Elinor Ostrom called them, offer ample opportunities for a wide range of actors and political experiments, but they also pose new challenges to coherence, legitimacy, effectiveness, and evaluation.

In response to these developments, two typical perspectives on global governance have evolved. An analytical take offers methods to map, explain, or understand transformations in world politics. This position, reflected in the above definition, has materialized in respective social science study programmes at universities. While a theory of global governance in its own right has not been developed, the analytical strand draws eclectically on international relations, international political economy, discourse analysis, and other approaches for theoretical guidance.

In a second perspective, scholars and practitioners alike see the concept as a political programme. Global governance is here defined as the solution-oriented, decentralized steering of globalization and coping with its negative consequences in the absence of a global government. This normative understanding originated from influential political reports such as *Our Common Neighborhood* by the UN Commission on Global Governance (1995). A long-term project of global integration will be advanced, for instance, through more democratic structures and stronger inclusiveness towards civil society, especially in key UN organs and international financing institutions. More ambitious proposals called for a global constitution or social contract, and, ultimately, for a world government—or, on a slightly more realistic note, for potent problem-specific agencies such as a World Environment Organization.

In both its analytical and normative readings, global governance has drawn criticism from very different sides. For one, seeing global political issues as a matter of the right regulation was perceived as ideologically biased. For critical international political economy scholars such as Ulrich Brandt, the concept mirrors a market-oriented hegemonic discourse that looks for efficient solutions and avoids broaching the discontents of late capitalism. Similarly, others criticized a *Global North bias and disregard for regional contexts and global equity imbalances. *Neoconservatives, on the other hand, rejected global governance as an attempt to limit the influence of the US and other powerful countries.

Moreover, scholars attacked the unfounded optimism and, in light of developments such as the 2008 *financial crisis, observed a gridlock of global governance. Jan Aart Scholte argued that regulatory proliferation and complexity led to a fuzzy and weak system that lacks effectiveness and democratic credentials. New forms of agency and institutions may not close, and even widen, gaps in legitimacy and accountability, since they posit the interests of NGOs or businesses along with those of popularly elected governments. Others again doubt whether a shift in global policy-making in favour of non-governmental actors, and at the expense of the power of states, has taken place at all. FZ

globalization A central part of the rhetoric of contemporary world politics and the subject of increasing volumes of academic analysis. It resists any single or simple definition. Although often associated with claims that the present world system is undergoing transformation, it is an old idea. There is a long tradition of writers emphasizing the external economic constraints that act upon nation states and the transforming impact of global economic processes, with Marx being amongst the most powerful and prescient. Such themes were revived in the late 1960s and early 1970s when writers on interdependence and modernization argued that the rapid expansion of international trade and investment, the increased awareness of ecological interdependence, the declining utility of military power, and the increasing power of non-state actors (*multinational corporations but also religious organizations and terrorist groups) constituted a systemic shift that would increasingly undermine the traditional role and primacy of nation states. The 1970s literature on interdependence faded under pressure from two sources. First, the reappearance of superpower confrontation and the second Cold War appeared to justify those who took a more Hobbesian view of international life, dominated by military confrontation rather than economic exchange. Second, within academia, statists and realists responded vigorously, arguing, for example, that multinational corporations were closely tied to states and to patterns of interstate politics; that the state was still the most important institution of international order; that military power had not declined in its utility; and, most important of all, that the international political system with its dominant logic of power balancing remained the most important element of any theory of international politics.

However, with the end of the Cold War, academic interest shifted back to the role of external or global economic factors, this time under the broad banner of 'globalization'. It is far from easy to gather together the wide variety of meanings attached to the term globalization. At one level it appears simple. Globalization is about the universal process or set of processes which generate a multiplicity of linkages and interconnections which transcend the states and societies which make up the modern world system. It involves a dramatic increase in the density and depth of economic, ecological, and societal interdependence, with 'density' referring to the increased number, range, and scope of cross-border transactions; and 'depth' to the degree to which that interdependence affects, and is affected by, the ways in which societies are organized domestically.

In reality, much of the muddle and inconclusiveness of the debates on globalization stem from the ambiguities of the concept. Globalization is sometimes presented as a causal theory: certain sorts of global processes are held to cause certain kinds of outcomes; sometimes it is a collection of concepts, mapping (but not explaining) how the changing global system is to be understood; and sometimes it is understood as a particular kind of discourse or ideology (often associated with neo-liberalism). There are also important distinctions between economistic readings of globalization (that stress increased interstate transactions and flows of capital, labour, goods and services) and social and political readings (that stress the emergence of new forms of governance and authority, new arenas of political action ('deterritorialization' or the 'reconfiguration of social space'), or new understandings of identity or community). Within economistic readings, there are distinctions between a traditional focus on interstate economic transactions and broader shifts in transnational production-structures and the emergence of new kinds of deterritorialized markets. Distinctions are also drawn between globalization, internationalization, westernization, and modernization. And there is the important distinction between the claim that globalization should be seen as the continuation of a deep-rooted set of historical processes and the view that contemporary globalization represents a critical breakpoint or fundamental discontinuity in world politics.

Perhaps the most important single idea concerns the growing disjuncture between the notion of a sovereign state directing its own future, the dynamics of the contemporary global economy, and the increasing complexity of world society. More specifically, there are three broad categories of claim that globalization is having a deep, perhaps revolutionary, impact. In the first place, it is widely argued that certain sets of economic policy tools have ceased to be viable and that states face ever increasing pressures to adopt increasingly similar pro-market policies. Because of the increasing power of financial markets, governments are forced into pursuing macroeconomic policies that meet with the approval of these markets. Increasing trade also places governments under pressure to adopt pro-market policies, avoiding policies which would imply the need to harm business by taxation, or to raise interest rates as a consequence of increased borrowing. They also find themselves forced to cut back the role of the public economy in order to attract inward investment from increasingly footloose multinational companies quick to punish governments who stray from the path of economic righteousness by exercising their exit option. Consequently, the range of policy options open to governments is claimed to be dramatically reduced.

A second cluster of arguments relates to the degree to which globalization has created the conditions for an ever more intense and activist global or transnational civil society. The physical infrastructure of increased economic interdependence (new systems of communication and transportation) and the extent to which new technologies (satellites, computer networks, etc.) have increased the costs and difficulty for governments of controlling flows of information, has facilitated the diffusion of values, knowledge, and ideas, and enhanced the ability of like-minded groups to organize across national boundaries. Transnational civil society, then, refers to those self-organized intermediary groups that are relatively independent of both public authorities and private economic actors; that are capable of taking collective action in pursuit of their interests or values; and that act across state borders. Globalization writers have laid great emphasis on the roles played by *non-governmental organizations, social movements, and multinational corporations, but such activity also includes transnational drug and criminal groups and transnational terrorism. The analytical focus of much of this work has been on transnational networks—for example, knowledge-based networks of economists, lawyers, or scientists; or transnational advocacy networks which act as channels for flows of money and material resources but, more critically, of information and ideas.

A third cluster of arguments suggests that it is institutional enmeshment rather than economic transactions or the 'reconfiguration of social space' that has most constrained the state. On this view, states are increasingly rule-takers over a vast array of rules, laws, and norms that are promulgated internationally but which affect almost every aspect of how they organize their societies domestically. Proponents of this view highlight the tremendous growth in the number of international organizations; they point to the vast increase in both the number of international treaties and agreements and the scope and intrusiveness of such agreements; and they suggest that important changes are occurring in the character of the international legal system (the increased pluralism of the process by which new norms and rules emerge; the appearance of more and more 'islands of supranational governance' (such as the EU or the WTO); the blurring of municipal, international, and transnational law; and the increased importance of informal, yet norm-governed, governance mechanisms, often built around complex transnational and transgovernmental networks).

The critics attack along a number of fronts. First, they highlight the lack of clear and consistent definitions of globalization and the deep ambiguities as to what 'globalization theory' is supposed to involve or explain. Second, they point to the mounting empirical grounds for scepticism, for example: that levels of globalization are not higher or more intense than in earlier periods (especially the period before WW1); that there is no clear evidence of state retreat, of welfare states being cut back because of globalization pressures, of transnational capital standing in automatic opposition to social welfare, or of globalization being the most important factor in explaining levels of inequality in OECD countries. Whilst many of the changes and challenges of globalization are very real, the critics argue that they do not point in a single direction and certainly do not provide secure grounds for accepting the claim that some sort of deep change or transformation is under way. Third, the critics argue that globalization has been driven not by some unstoppable logic of technological innovation, but by specific sets of state policies, backed by specific political coalitions. This suggests that states themselves are not passive players and that the impact of globalization will often depend on national-level political and institutional factors. Equally, even where liberalizing effects can be attributed to globalization, it is not always the case that this implies state retreat—as in the process by which privatization and deregulation have involved re-regulation. Nor does globalization inevitably push governments towards declining state activism. It can, on the contrary, lead to increased pressure on government to provide protection against the economic and social dislocations that arise from increased liberalization and external vulnerability. Finally, the critics remain deeply unconvinced by the arguments for systemic transformation, highlighting the degree to which international institutions are created by states for particular purposes and the evident capacity of powerful states to resist or even abandon such institutions; the continued importance of military power controlled by states and of political

boundaries and of national allegiances even in regions of dense economic and societal interdependence; and the very deep resistance of the United States as the global hegemon to contemplate giving up its own sovereignty and the capacity of the United States to both shape and resist the course of globalization. AHU

global justice A common term in political and *international relations theory referring to debates about the scope and appropriateness of applying theories of *distributive justice and *social justice to the global level. In a nutshell, global justice is concerned with reducing existing global inequalities and with deriving the normative principles necessary to create a more fair and just distribution of benefits and burdens globally. Largely inspired by the work of John *Rawls (though he himself disliked the idea), many scholars of global justice have argued that the basic social structures which animated Rawls' relational theory of justice at the domestic level are now present globally under conditions of *globalization, thus demanding that the scope of *justice now applies at the global level. In this case, the argument is made that globalization has created relational conditions and basic structures between states and people where issues of justice become salient. In addition, many scholars associated with *cosmopolitanism and global activism have supplemented relational accounts of global justice, also suggesting that aspects of common humanity, *human rights, human dignity, and *natural law morally demand principles of global justice as well as institutional reforms to mitigate political, social, and economic inequalities. Debates within global justice tend to revolve around issues for the need for cultural and national identities as a basis relational solidarity, the demandingness of moral obligations for justice, and the types of 'goods' required to satisfy those demands of global justice. Needless to say, the debate continues, yet the debate has recently become more pertinent as collective action problems associated with global cohabitability, planetary sustainability, and human interdependence become more acute.

Global North The east–west conflict of the *Cold War, with its emphasis on military aspects of security, appeared to give way, during the détente of the 1970s, to disagreements over the material preconditions of security and welfare in which the Soviet Union was regarded as belonging, along with the United States, Japan, and other relatively wealthy and industrialized states like Australia, to a metaphorical North or 'global north', while the remaining states identified themselves, oppositionally, as the South or 'global south'. Negotiations during the 1970s over issues as diverse as trade, investment, intellectual property, and rights to sea-bed resources became known collectively as the North–South dialogue. In the 1990s this radical simplification of this opposition seemed less apposite because of the rise to wealth of former southern economies such as Taiwan, the acute economic problems experienced by some successor states of the 'northern' Soviet empire, and the redundancy of the east–west divide against which the *non-aligned South had originally defined itself.

However, the *Financial Crisis in 2008 has again brought notions of a divide between the wealth of the 'global north' and the needs of developing 'global south' into sharp contrast. In particular, there are criticisms that *globalization favours the global north (hence the remaining of the north/south divide as one of a global north and south). In addition, there have been considerable criticisms by developing countries around the failure of the *Millennium Development Goals (MDGs) and the dependency cycles that international aid places on the global south. This debate is enhanced by the rise of new alternative development programmes offered by the *BRICS, which have opened renewed calls for 'south–south' cooperation and which set themselves very much as an alternative to northern 'business as usual'. CJ

Global South Less cumbersome and specific than '*non-aligned', yet carrying the same aspiration of post-colonial states to dissociate themselves from the east–west division between the United States and the USSR, 'the South' was adopted from the 1960s as a shorthand for all poor countries, especially when acting together. *See also* GLOBAL NORTH, THIRD WORLD. CJ

global value chain The array of activities through which workers and companies bring a product or service from conception to sale. Multinational corporations steer these activities, through commercial contracts with arms-length supplier firms. Reorganizing global production into 'chains' will fragment the workforce behind a single product across dozens of national boundaries, worksites, and employers. GLB

global warming *See* CLIMATE CHANGE.

Glorious Revolution *See* HOUSE OF COMMONS.

GNP (gross national product) *GDP plus net factor income from abroad.

Godwin, William (1756–1836) British radical philosopher and exponent of a distinctly utopian social theory of *anarchism which saw all forms of government as evil, corrupt, and injurious to human happiness. Godwin wrote not only treatises on social and political questions, but also novels (such as *Caleb Williams*, 1794) embracing his philosophical world-view. *An Enquiry Concerning Political Justice* (1793) sets out Godwin's belief in the perfectibility of man through the development of reason, and in the necessary relationship between reason and justice as mediated by the principle of utility (*see also* UTILITARIANISM). KT

golden rule UK public expenditure rule introduced in 1997 which states that over the economic cycle, the Government will borrow only to invest and not to fund current spending.

Goldman, Emma (1869–1940) *Anarchist and *feminist, born in Lithuania, who campaigned throughout America and Europe for political and sexual freedom from the conventions of capitalist society. An effective propagandist, Goldman was vilified in the United States as 'Red Emma', and was deported from there in 1917 after terms in gaol for incitement to riot, suspected involvement in the assassination of President McKinley, distributing birth control information, and activities against conscription. After returning to Russia in 1919 Goldman became disillusioned with the oppression and persecution following the *Russian Revolution, leaving the country in 1921, but continued to support anarchist causes through her writing and campaigning, dying in Canada whilst on a tour in support of Spanish anarchists in the aftermath of the Spanish Civil War.

Good Friday Agreement (1998) *See* BELFAST AGREEMENT.

GOP *See* REPUBLICAN PARTY.

governability A literature emerged in the 1970s which suggested that a number of advanced industrial countries, notably Britain, were becoming ungovernable, or at least harder to govern. The concept was not well defined, but centred on the idea that, as the range of problems that the government was expected to deal with had increased, its capacity to solve them had been reduced. The government had become more ineffective because its ability to secure compliance with its policies had diminished. This was partly because of the intractability of the problems facing government, and excessive citizen expectations, but also reflected resistance to government authority from a variety of groups, notably trade unions. Critics of the concept argued that most European polities were not designed to be governable in the sense of having a central, unchallenged authority, but rather represented a form of compromise between competing groups in society. The term fell out of favour in the 1980s as governments of the right demonstrated a willingness both to reduce the functions of the state and to reassert their authority. WG

governance The process of collective decision-making and policy implementation, used distinctly from *government to reflect broader concern with norms and processes relating to the delivery of public goods. Its political usage developed in the UK in the 1990s, reflecting the *Thatcherite programme to restrict the role of the state, *privatization, and the contracting out of public services. The study of governance was seen to encompass the regulatory framework, delegated authority, and non-governmental provision of services—covering areas which the traditional focus on Westminster politics ignored. The perspective of governance has been used to reflect on non-governmental networks which influence the delivery of public goods, both positively and negatively.

This approach engages with aspects of civil society, community action, social capital, charity, and corruption. The *World Bank has developed measures of six dimensions of governance: voice and accountability, political stability and absence of violence/terrorism, government effectiveness, regulatory quality, rule of law, and control of corruption. 'Good governance' has become a mantra for politicians, bureaucrats, and employees of NGOs.

government The institutions, rules, and *administration of *state authority. *See also* EXECUTIVE.

governmentality Michel *Foucault's work on governmentality developed through a serious of lectures and represents a development of his work away from some of the positions outlined in his earlier work on disciplines and discourse. It refers to governing in a rather broad sense, but is distinctive in seeing the population as the target of governance. This concern, which develops in the modern period, highlights the exercise of power over population rather than territory, taking a less overtly coercive mode of operating.

Foucault traces the emergence of governmentality alongside established forms of *sovereignty and discipline, but these new forms of government are distinctive in taking population as their main target, political economy as their means of knowledge, and apparatuses of security as their main technical instrument. It is generally accepted that governmentality works in a less direct way, often from a distance, in order to influence the actions of others and encourage self-government. It has thus been described as the 'conduct of conduct'.

Inevitably, governmentality becomes associated with a *liberal form of rule that operates by encouraging the free conduct and *autonomy of the governed. This more narrow understanding of governmentality is disputed. Nevertheless, much of Foucault's own argument highlights this aspect of governmentality. Liberal governmentality works through a continual assessment of government's need to impose limitations on itself, respecting individual autonomy and the *natural laws of the market and private life. Governing, in its wider understanding, leaves things to other social institutions such as *civil society and to the private sphere.

The notion of governance as devolved away from a central point and as operating through different networks and the self-regulation of individuals themselves is strongly congruent with *neoliberal thinking, and Foucault himself dedicated a significant amount of his work to the study of this phenomenon. Neoliberalism as a form of governmentality is concerned to govern through the market. It is a reflexive form of governance, critical of established liberal approaches through its awareness of the need to more actively promote market mechanisms in all spheres of social life. Taken as a form of governance, neoliberalism, rather than being the retreat or 'hollowing out' of the state, is better understood as the governmentalization of the state according to the mechanisms of the market. It is a rationality intent on devolving power away from centralized state regulation in favour of working through a network of private and quasi-private bodies based on belief in the superiority of market forces.

There is dispute about how far this account relies on the interpretation of Foucault by the school of Anglo-Foucauldians such as Nikolas Rose, who advances the idea of 'governance from a distance' operating in 'advanced liberal' countries. This is particularly important when considering whether govermentality can help us understand international relations. There is first the issue of whether governmentality exists mainly in the 'advanced liberal' countries of the West, or whether it operates in different ways in other parts of the world. Then there is the question of *global governance as understood as global governmentality. Can we understand interventions by international organizations—*statebuilding, *democracy promotion, poverty reduction, *gender mainstreaming, *resilience building—as governmentality? These would seem to be targeted at populations, and they operate 'from a distance' through partnerships and local ownership. However, if the technologies and techniques of governance are those developed under 'advanced liberalism', to what extent can these really be applied to different parts of the world? Is the aim really to governmentalize the populations of these countries, or is this concern

with their security and *wellbeing merely a pretext to discipline poorer countries and their governments? JJ

Gracchus *See* BABEUF, FRANÇOIS-NOEL.

Gramsci, Antonio (1891–1937) Italian Marxist and journalist. Active in the Italian Socialist party from 1913. Co-founder (1919) and editor of the influential newspaper *L'ordine nuovo*; took an active role in the Turin factory council movement (which he saw as 'models of the proletarian state') during the *Biennio Rosso* ('the two red years') of 1919–20. In 1921 he became a member of the Central Committee of the new Italian Communist Party (PCI) and in 1922 went to Moscow as Italian representative on the Executive of the Communist International. Returned to Italy in 1924 and was elected to parliament. Became Secretary General of the PCI. Arrested by the fascist regime in 1926, sentenced (Mussolini reportedly saying 'We must keep this brain from functioning for twenty years'), and despite chronic ill health remained in prison until his death in 1937. His most important work is *The Prison Notebooks* (1928–37).

Gramsci wanted to understand why the revolution had failed to spread after 1917, how *capitalism had survived and why the *proletariat had not acquired *class consciousness and hence what strategies should be adopted by revolutionary parties operating in liberal democratic states. This led him to analyse the relationship between the economic base and the political superstructure, and to introduce the concept of *hegemony. In liberal democracies, class hegemony was based upon consent far more than on force. The *state had ultimate resort to its coercive machinery in periods of exceptional crisis, but generally maintained and justified its control through the intellectual and moral leadership it exercised in *civil society. The ideological superstructure—politics, education, culture, religion—shaped the framework of perception, understanding, and knowledge. The result of this socialization process was that the governed actively consented to their oppression. Class domination was preserved behind the veneer of social harmony—bourgeois relations were internalized and consequently the possibility of revolutionary activity receded.

What then should a revolutionary party do? Gramsci identified two complementary strategies: a war of manoeuvre, and a war of position. The former—which he relegated to a subsidiary role as inappropriate in the period of reaction following the October Revolution—represented a rapid frontal assault on the state. The latter involved what he called 'protracted trench warfare', that is multiple struggles based upon a variety of organizational forms and with differing political objectives (parliamentary, union, cultural, alliances with other progressive forces) but directed by the Communist Party. This did not imply gradualism; Gramsci never doubted that the question of state power would finally have to be addressed by revolutionary force.

The revolutionary party alone had a total conception of the world and the commitment needed to instil in the masses what he described as 'critical self-consciousness', which would lead them to overthrow the existing order and develop a new hegemonic socialist culture. Gramsci did not believe in the pure spontaneity of the working class—it needed the direction of the Communist Party, which had the ability to render explicit what was implicit. At the same time, he demanded far greater mass involvement in the formulation of Party policy. In *The Modern Prince*, Gramsci drew an analogy between the way *Machiavelli employed 'the Prince' as a mythic force capable of stimulating mass mobilization and creating community and the Party which represented 'the collective will' and acted as the catalyst of revolution. 'Traditional' intellectuals were closely linked to the dominant class and performed socializing tasks for it, but 'organic' intellectuals had the ability to cut themselves off, universalize their experience, and join the class of the future, the proletariat and its revolutionary party.

Gramsci's discussion of hegemony was grounded in his contention that 'man is essentially political'. He was critical of what he regarded as the dogmatism which had characterized much of Marxism since the death of Marx. He was influenced by Benedetto Croce's emphasis upon the importance of a subjective and cultural understanding of historical change which led him to reject the crude positivism of revisionist Marxist theory.

He distinguished between organic (long-term, objective trends) and conjunctural (subjective, immediate factors) forces in society. When the two came together they produced a 'historic bloc'—the coincidence of a pre-revolutionary situation and a class conscious movement. The individual/class/party must choose a fusion of theory and praxis, of intellectual rigour and revolutionary commitment ('pessimism of the intellect and optimism of the will').

Gramsci's belief that people could be conscious, deliberate actors in the processes of history had a tremendous impact upon the *New Left, *Guevara, and *Castroism, whilst his theories of hegemony and revolutionary strategy greatly influenced *Eurocommunism and the evolution of the PCI. GL

Grandes Écoles Collective name for the leading specialized higher-education institutions outside the university system in France. Their graduates provide most ministers, in governments of all persuasions, they educate the highest echelons of the public service, and provide three-quarters of managers in the 200 largest private companies, as well as filling a huge percentage of responsible posts elsewhere. The most prestigious is the École Polytechnique, followed by the École Normale d'Administration and the École Normale Supérieure. Despite differences in the subjects studied and in style, there is a certain intellectual community which gives a degree of continuity to governments of the left and the right, and to the other ruling groups. The *Grandes Écoles* demonstrate the hierarchical nature of education in France and its immense importance in political and economic life. CS

grandfather clause 1. Legal provision granting vote to persons whose ancestors had voted prior to 1867, used by Southern states in the US to disenfranchise blacks. Grandfather clauses were declared unconstitutional in 1915.

2. The phrase is now used non-pejoratively to denote existing rights protected by an Act which removes the entitlement to the right from any future claimants.

Great Leap Forward In 1958–61, the attempt, initiated by Mao Zedong, to resolve China's economic problems by rural industrialization.

China launched her First Five Year Plan in 1953. It was accompanied by the phased collectivization of agriculture and the nationalization, with compensation, of industry and commerce. The plan was based on the Soviet model: using concealed taxation of peasant incomes in the form of controlled low farm-gate prices, giving massive priority to heavy industry, concentration of industry in the cities, and comprehensive command planning of the economy. The plan, in its own terms, proved highly successful, but the ambivalence of many of China's leaders towards centralized planning on the Soviet model is obvious in the fact that the plan was not fully applied or fully published until 1955, was subjected to severe criticism by 1957, and was virtually superseded by the Great Leap of 1958, never to be fully restored. China's devotion to the centralized command economy (already under attack elsewhere in the communist world) was thus very brief.

*Mao Zedong had already begun to adumbrate an alternative from December 1955 (Preface to *The High Tide of Socialism in the Chinese Countryside*), fully expressed by 1958 in several subsequent intra-Party documents. It represented a reaction to Stalin's zero-sum-game economics, his exploitation of agriculture, and his stress on heavy industry and neglect of investment in agriculture and light industry. It was also a reaction against authoritarian bureaucracy, the unpopularity of which had been dramatically expressed during the Hundred Flowers and to which Mao was by temperament (and guerrilla experience) extremely hostile. The alternative sought also to deal with specific Chinese problems: (i) factor proportions characterized by a vast and rapidly increasing population, inadequate arable land, and lack of capital; (ii) the fact that an attempt to increase agricultural procurement quotas in the good harvest years of 1954 and 1955 had proved strongly counter-productive, showing the limits of peasant tolerance of state accumulation at their expense; (iii) the threat of military dependence on Khrushchev's Soviet Union, which could be avoided only by preparations for a decentralized guerrilla-style resistance dependent on local development of the means to maintain supplies of 'millet and rifles'. Mao's alternative owed much to his wartime experience in organizing scattered guerrilla bases and developing their economies in cooperative forms. It also quite clearly owed

much to Western development theory of the 1950s, with the stress on using surplus rural labour, via programmes of integrated rural development, to create local industry and improve local infrastructure.

In 1957 the Chinese government, following Soviet precedents, began to decentralize control of the state sector to provincial governments and, under their aegis, to individual enterprises. Under Mao's influence, this reform was overtaken by a contrasting form of decentralization directly to the village communities. A vast campaign began to encourage the rural communities to transform their own lives by self-initiated development. Subsequently, in mid-1958, the communes were created as an appropriate planning framework for this effort. The movement roused great enthusiasm at first; but its very achievements encouraged a change from enthusiasm to hubris: local leaders competed to outdo the promises of their neighbours. Wild local claims were accepted and turned into national targets. Ideas such as village iron and steel-making (perfectly viable where resources and traditional skills existed) were made virtually compulsory and universal. Persuasion gave way to coercion, in spite of the solemn public promises which had been elicited from all concerned before the movement was launched, that it would be a democratic movement, an application of the mass line. So many new tasks were undertaken that the rural labour force, normally 30 per cent surplus, was stretched to breaking point. Extremists announced that full communism had arrived; field kitchens, a practical necessity in view of the vast redeployment of labour, became to-each-according-to-his-needs institutions. Even the peasants' courtyards with their pigs and fruit trees were made communal property. China's local party cadres in fact did the only thing they knew how to do—they carried the Stalinist command economy right into the grassroots. The commune, quite against the original concept, was made a single vast farm. Prosperous villages were forced to invest for the benefit of poor villages swept into the same commune, and were bitterly resentful.

Mao condemned the requisition of peasant property and he justified peasant resistance. He demanded the restoration of the original concept of the Great Leap as a process in which voluntary participation in a successful effort of local economic development would create a new rural consciousness of the potentiality of communal planning. But he would not cancel the movement, and he could not in fact control it. Meanwhile bad weather struck and devastated an already weakened and demoralized rural economy. By 1961 mass starvation, not policy, had brought the Great Leap to an end. Those who lived through it now look back with a mixture of horror at its consequences and some pride in its vast and permanent achievements in the form of dams, roads, railways, and forests. At the time, however, the political consequence was to weaken Mao's authority, discredit his alternative to the command economy, destroy the commune and brigade enterprises which were the fulcrum of his effort—'our great and glorious hope for the future', as Mao had called them—and initiate a period of retreat from collectivism in the countryside.   JG

great power(s) A term used to denote a powerful state in relation to other 'small states', which can exert disproportionate influence and *hard power militarily and economically, as well as *soft power and *normative power. In many ways, the phrase 'great power' has become synonymous with *superpower, since a great power is a state either in a league of its own (*unipolarity) or among a small number of states who hold a position of *relative power between them (*bipolarity and *multipolarity). The concept of a 'great power' was established immediately following the Napoleonic Wars through the 1814 Treaty of Chaumont, which designated major European states as responsible for upholding a *balance of power in Europe. The term 'great powers' was also used frequently in World War I and World War II, and is currently used to refer to the 'permanent five' members of the *United Nations Security Council.

Greek political thought Political questions are raised by many of the pre-Classical Greek poets and thinkers, from Homer's thoughts on kingship (probably mid- to late eighth century BC), to the Athenian lawgiver and poet Solon *c.*600 BC. Nevertheless it is not until the mid-fifth century BC that *sophists such as Protagoras and Antiphon introduced

systematic political theory, supported by rational argument; their central concern was the relation between '*nature' and 'convention' and the question of whether obedience to the state's laws and conventions was to the individual's advantage. A keen interest in these and other political questions can also be found around this time in the works of the Athenian tragedians, and the historians Herodotus and *Thucydides. Methods of political analysis were greatly developed by *Socrates, and Greek political thinking in general reaches its culmination in the fourth century BC with the radical idealism of *Plato and the more conservative and pragmatic work of *Aristotle.

A number of historical reasons help explain why this relatively brief flourishing of systematic and practical political thought in Greece occurred when it did. By the mid-fifth century BC the independent city-state or *polis* (from which our word 'politics' derives) was well established as the basic unit of political organization in Greece, and the many different forms that the *polis* took—from the oligarchical and military regime of Sparta to the radical participatory democracy of Athens—prompted comparisons and the question of which form was best. Increasing travel and the nascent disciplines of history and anthropology provided further data for comparison, and the continuing practice of colonization around the Mediterranean gave real urgency to the question of how the *polis* should be structured, and provided a field for political experiment and theorizing. Nor is it a matter of chance that such theorizing tended to originate in Athens: her participatory democracy (albeit limited to adult free-born males) both encouraged political debate and offered the practical experience to inform such debate. Furthermore, though democracy was generally in the ascendant at Athens, oligarchical factions remained powerful and the tensions between the two parties required each to produce political theories in its support. Young men of either party who desired political influence required training in rhetoric and argument, and the sophists arose partly to supply such needs.

Thus when Philip of Macedon and his son Alexander the Great destroyed the autonomy of the *polis* in the last forty years of the fourth century BC, serious practical contributions to Greek political thought largely ceased. After this, philosophy tended to concentrate on the individual in isolation (as for instance in the philosophy of Epicurus), rather than on relations between the individual and the state. The intriguing Stoic notion of the 'cosmopolis' (perhaps influenced by Alexander's own ambitions to create a world-state) was not intended as a practical manifesto for reform. It is rather a utopian vision in which all separate states and political and economic institutions have crumbled, and individuals are united by the ties of friendship and common humanity alone.

Historical circumstances also account for many of the issues prevalent in Greek political theory: the range of data available gives rise to a tendency to rank constitutions and a corresponding tendency to create fictional ideal states (as opposed to the Stoic world community) to serve as the blueprints for such rankings: Plato's *Republic* and *Laws* and the last two books of Aristotle's *Politics* are notable examples. The very different criteria for citizenship employed by the different states also prompted the question of what citizenship really meant and who was eligible for it. As a result of the constant tensions between oligarchic and democratic factions the issue of stability was crucial for Plato and Aristotle; in contrast, the accent in Athenian democracy on individual participation raised the sense of the individual's importance, and highlighted the question of relations between individual and state.

Most significant of all in determining the themes of Greek political theory was the nature of the *polis* itself. Indeed, Aristotle's claim that 'man is a political animal', meaning that man is the kind of animal which naturally lives in a *polis*, suggests that political theory can only operate within such a context; he may also be implying that political theory is thus distinctively Greek. The most salient feature of the *polis* is that it was perceived as an association of people bonded together by a shared way of life and a shared morality. The whole was more important than any of its parts, and it remained a whole owing to the cohesive influence of its educational system, the purpose of which was to educate the young to be good citizens, sharing the state's moral code.

Such an active role for the state gave plenty of material to those sophists, such as Antiphon, who believed that the state acted

as a shackle on the true nature and freedom of the individual. To thinkers such as Plato and Aristotle, who accepted the *polis* as the natural and best context for man (though neither was entirely happy with any of the models currently on offer, and particularly not that of democratic Athens), it meant that political theory had a strongly ethical flavour and that the role of education was paramount, whereas such modern watchwords as representation and the protection of rights were barely considered. Their stress on training the individual to function correctly in the whole leads directly to the authoritarian tendencies of their very different visions of what that whole should be like.   AH

Greenham Common Site of US airbase in Berkshire which became the focus of the feminist peace movement in the 1980s. The Greenham Common Women's Peace Camp was formed in 1981, protesting about the presence of American cruise missiles in Britain.

greenhouse effect *See* CLIMATE CHANGE.

green parties Green parties grew out of the concern for the *ecological stability of the planet and the quality of life in industrial societies which sharpened perceptibly in the 1970s. The German greens, Die Grünen, were the most successful and influential; their movement grew out of a wide range of 'grass roots' and 'outsider' organizations which developed 'lists' of approved candidates at local elections and constituted themselves as a party in 1980. It was a remarkably successful party for a time. In 1983 it crossed the 5 per cent threshold in Bundestag elections and took 27 seats; at its peak in 1987 it had 8.2 per cent of the vote and 46 seats. Its best known figure was Petra Kelly (1947–92).

Many countries, including most in Western Europe, developed green parties during this period. Several existing parties renamed themselves as greens, including the Ecology Party in Britain and the Values Party in New Zealand. This partly was out of respectful imitation of Die Grünen, but also because the image of greenness, with its connotations of freshness and nature, was thought to have proved so powerful. It also carried the advantage, as a colour, of a certain ideological freshness; although the colour of Islam and of some nationalist movements, it was not tainted with images of the 'left' and the 'right' in politics, unlike blue, red, black, white, and others.

The nuclear accident at Chernobyl in 1986 proved a fillip to the green cause in many countries and green parties met with considerable electoral success in the late 1980s. In the elections to the European Parliament in 1989 most green parties achieved record performances, including a remarkable 14.9 per cent of the vote in Britain. Green parties entered national governments in Europe for the first time in the 1990s, in broad left coalition governments: in France in 1997 and in Germany in 1998. However, in the twenty-first century green parties have tended to decline even where it might be thought that they have won the argument. This is partly because they have demonstrated the natural fissiparity of radical movements and parties, but it is also because some of their analyses were adopted by larger parties with more resources. To use a nineteenth-century expression, their clothes were stolen by the established parties.   LA

Greenpeace Greenpeace was set up in 1971 by a small group of North American activists, who sailed their small boat into the US atomic test zone near Alaska. It is most famous for targeted and highly public direct action by small groups of individuals, but also engages in research and lobbying activities. Issues it campaigns on include climate change, nuclear weapons testing, toxic waste dumping, biodiversity, and whaling. Greenpeace is often in conflict with governments, most notably when the first *Rainbow Warrior* was bombed and sunk in New Zealand by French secret service agents.   PI

(⊕) SEE WEB LINKS

• Greenpeace site, including a history of the organization.

Green Revolution In the early 1960s developments in agricultural production, sponsored by international funding agencies, led to what came to be called the Green Revolution. These developments emphasized hybrid seeds, mechanization, and pest control as answers to the agricultural backwardness of the Third World. High-yielding varieties were promoted, as were the use of pesticides, and economies

of scale of production, which could be successful only through mechanization of agriculture. This initiative did result in much better production figures across a range of countries. However, the Green Revolution has been criticized by *environmentalists and others for resulting in environmental disasters in the countries where it was most effective. Mechanization of agriculture, where successful, led to changing work and social patterns, an exacerbation of class divisions in society, and the displacement of minority groups like tribal peoples and politically marginalized groups such as women from agricultural production. Further, new types of crops were not resistant to local diseases and required high levels of pesticides which polluted the local waterways, impoverished the land, and also increased the dependency of many Third World countries on the West with imports of pesticides. Moreover, the commercialization of agriculture led to the exporting of food out of the local areas, increasing the dependence of producers on market forces that did not always benefit the majority of producers.   SR

Green, Thomas Hill (1836–1882) Fellow of Balliol College Oxford, 1860–82, and Whyte's Professor of Moral Philosophy, Oxford University, 1878–82. Influenced by Kantian and post-Kantian German philosophy, as well as Aristotle's conception of the *polis* as a partnership for pursuit of the common good, Green's political philosophy exerted a strong influence on the development of liberalism in Britain in the late nineteenth and early twentieth century. His essay 'Liberal Legislation and Freedom of Contract', written as an address to Leicester Liberal association in 1881, argues that freedom should be understood as the power to develop our best selves in common with others: 'the ideal of true freedom is the maximum power for all members of human society alike to make the best of themselves'. The commercial freedoms defended by classical liberals have value, Green argues, only insofar as they promote freedom in this 'higher' sense, and should be restricted by the state if they impair such freedom. His work is thus sometimes seen as providing theoretical foundations for the construction of the British welfare state. But in some important respects, such as the treatment of property rights, his prescriptions do not move much beyond the classical liberal position. His major works, in which his political philosophy is developed in greater depth, were published posthumously. These include *Prolegomena to Ethics* (1883) and *Lectures on the Principles of Political Obligation* (1895). swe

Grotius, Hugo (Huig de Groot) (1583–1645) Grotius was born in Delft, South Holland. At the age of 16 he acquired a doctorate of laws and at 24 was advocate-general for Holland and Zeeland and for the rest of his life pursued a career as a diplomat. As a pioneer in international law, his writings have important political implications. His first book, *On the Law of Booty* (1604) concerned the claim of a Portuguese ship seized by the Dutch East India Company, but the principle of his solution—that the ocean is free to all nations—had wider implications. These were examined in his great work, *On the Law of War and Peace* (1625). This work is in the Aristotelian tradition. Grotius bases international law (*ius gentium*) on natural law, which, for him, embraces civil and even divine law. Civil, because, for him, each society naturally chooses its own form of government, but all nations are subject to the same basic or natural law (*ius naturale*). Divine, because natural law is founded in divine wisdom: they cannot be in conflict (*see also* SUAREZ). All this, in Grotius's view, is a product of ratiocination. He believed that the conflict between Protestants and Catholics could be solved by rational discussion.

Grotius also dabbled in theology and poetry. He regarded Christ's death not as expiation for sin, but as retributive or exemplary justice, demonstrating God's hatred of moral (as distinct from physical) evil. This theme, expressed in his poem *Adamus Exsul*, is said to have influenced Milton in writing *Paradise Lost*. CB

group representation Idea that a legislature should contain representatives who share the social characteristics of a particular group in society; for instance that women should be represented by female legislators. Although closely allied to the microcosm theory of *representation, proponents of group representation have tended to justify their claims in terms of discrimination against particular groups, who as a consequence find

themselves excluded from policy deliberation and determination. In order to enhance group representation a number of mechanisms have been introduced across the world, including *majority-minority districting for blacks in the US and *separate electorates. In the UK in the 1990s the Labour Party used a quota system to improve the chances of getting women elected to parliament. The idea that people can only be represented by those who share their social backgrounds has been a source of contention, and it has been argued that group representation prioritizes certain aspects of individual identity above (possibly) more politically germane aspects (*see* MINORITY POLITICS; POSITIVE DISCRIMINATION).

groupthink Situation where committees, cabinets, or other groups make suboptimal decisions, occurring when considerations of cohesiveness override a fully rational examination of the situation. The concept was developed by the social-psychologist Irving Janis in *Victims of Groupthink* (1972). Janis used examples of foreign policy failure in the United States to illustrate the idea, including the *Bay of Pigs invasion and escalation of the Vietnam War.

Guantanamo Bay Detention centre where the United States has held 'enemy combatants' and people suspected of terrorist activity. Guantanamo Bay has become a symbol of US disdain for the humane treatment of prisoners and its disrespect for international law.

Situated in Cuba, where the United States retains a naval base, the detention centre began to receive 'enemy combatants' from the *Afghanistan War in January 2002. The location and the designation 'enemy combatants' were designed to avoid the jurisdiction of US courts and international obligations, notably under the Geneva Convention. Terrorist suspects were also transported to Guantanamo Bay through the process of *extraordinary rendition. Over 700 people were detained in the centre, with citizens from a range of countries including Afghanistan, Pakistan, Saudi Arabia, and Yemen. The United States has faced criticism for the treatment of the prisoners, including accusations that inmates were tortured.

President George W. Bush argued that Guantanamo Bay was a key part of the response to the *September 11th 2001 attacks on the US, and those held at the centre included suspected bomb makers; terrorist trainers, recruiters, and facilitators; and potential suicide bombers. He commented that 'the only thing I know for certain is that these are bad people'. The Bush administration defended the use of 'enhanced interrogation techniques' and argued that fair judicial hearings could be provided by military commissions.

Although President Barack Obama signed an executive order to close Guantanamo Bay immediately after his 2008 presidential win, the order was refused budgetary support by the *Republicans in Congress, and there was public disapproval of Obama's plan to relocate prisoners to a facility in the US. As a result, despite increased legal processing and extradition of prisoners out of Guantanamo Bay, it remains in operation today, and there are new signals to suggest its reaccelerated use under new orders from President Donald J. Trump.

guerrilla warfare Armed struggles waged by irregular units, usually in the countryside and enjoying popular support, which demand socio-political transformation and challenge the power of the state. The strategy has been identified with Third World revolutions, particularly the Chinese, Vietnamese, and Cuban. GL

Guevara, Ernesto 'Che' (1929–67) Argentine Marxist and revolutionary. Having participated in the Cuban Revolution of 1959 and served as a government minister, he left Cuba in 1965 in order to support other Third World revolutions. He launched an abortive insurrection in Bolivia in 1967 but was caught and executed.

His *Guerrilla Warfare* (1960) was a practical guide. It proposed four theses: (1) Popular forces could win a war against a regular army providing the people realized that legal processes were no longer viable. (2) It was not necessary to wait for all objective conditions to exist before launching the guerrilla war; the revolutionary *foco* (Spanish for point of activity) could create them. The *foco* theory was misinterpreted by Regis Debray in *Revolution in the Revolution?* (1967), which stressed the military to the neglect of the political. Debray's misinterpretation had disastrous results in a number of countries (for

example, Peru in 1965). (3) The countryside would be the place for armed struggle, the city for clandestine activity. (4) The revolution must be international. His last message from Bolivia called for the creation of '2, 3 . . . many Vietnams'.

Guevara criticized orthodox communist policy in Latin America and argued against any slavish copying of the Soviet model. Revolutionary theory must be based upon practical experience of struggle in each country. Guevara advocated the development of a socialist political culture based upon moral rather than material incentives, and resulting in the creation of a 'New Man'. GL

guild socialism A short-lived but influential British socialist movement which flourished in the first quarter of the twentieth century, and which achieved its fullest exposition in the writings of G. D. H. *Cole. Inspired by the model of the medieval guilds, it offered a vision of decentralized socialism rooted in structures of *workers' control and *industrial democracy. KT

guillotine Term adopted in the United Kingdom and the United States in the late nineteenth century to describe the enforced closure of parliamentary debate, by analogy with the revolutionary guillotine of France. Formally an 'allocation of time motion' in the United Kingdom, a guillotine regulates the amount of time the House of Commons devotes to debate on a particular bill, either on the floor of the house or in committee. A guillotine was first used to manage debates in the House of Commons in 1881, when Irish MPs tried to *filibuster the Coercion Bill.

Gulag Russian acronym for 'Chief Administration of Corrective Labour Camps'. The ostensible purpose of these camps, dispersed throughout the less inhabited areas of the Soviet Union, was to imprison and reform citizens guilty of various 'crimes against the people'. Inmates were used as forced labour in the drive for rapid industrialization and infrastructural development. The atrocious conditions of the camps were publicized by the first-hand accounts of Solzhenitsyn, and it is estimated that the Gulags accounted for between 9.5 and 15 million deaths.   swh

Gulf Cooperation Council (GCC) A body formed in 1981 by six countries on the western side of the Persian Gulf (the United Arab Emirates, Bahrain, Saudi Arabia, Oman, Qatar, and Kuwait) for their collective security after the overthrow of the Shah of Iran followed by the emergence of the Islamic Republic of Iran, the Soviet invasion of Afghanistan, and the launching of the Iraq–Iran War. The vulnerability of the oil facilities of the Gulf states to air and sea attack was exposed by the war. In the face of these external threats, cooperation was forged amongst the six for purposes of coordinating defence through regional collective security.

The main goals of the GCC are: economic integration together with coordinated planning; a cohesive foreign policy towards the non-Arab world, and a framework for the discussion of Arab affairs; coordination of regional collective security; and educational cooperation and sociocultural understanding among member states. There has been success on each of these four fronts but the most successful area has been in the field of economic cooperation. A common market was established in 2008.

A Gulf Rapid Deployment Force with units from each member state, was set up in 1984. But with the Iraqi invasion of Kuwait in 1990, it was clear that this Rapid Deployment Force could not delay any large-scale assault until help could be organized for an effective defence. BAR

( ) SEE WEB LINKS

• Gulf Cooperation Council site, including charter, details of membership and organization, and history.

Gulf War (1991) A major war in the Middle East between Iraq and a range of Western and Arab powers led by the United States. On 2 August 1990 Iraq invaded its Arab neighbour Kuwait, following an escalating campaign of allegations and threats from the Iraqi regime of Saddam Hussein directed against the Emir of Kuwait. The invasion met with widespread international condemnation and a deployment of forces to Saudi Arabia by the United States and other Western powers ('Operation Desert Shield'), which culminated in massive air strikes from 17 January 1991 ('Operation Desert Storm') and a final ground attack from 24 February 1991 that culminated in an Iraqi

retreat and the liberation of Kuwait city and its surrounds.

The complex roots of the conflict lay in the personality of Iraq's leader, the damage which Iraq had experienced as a result of its lengthy war with Iran (1980–8), and Iraq's perception that Gulf states such as Kuwait were insufficiently grateful to it for what it perceived as its role in opposing Iran. A crisis in Iraq–Kuwait relations flared suddenly in July 1990 when the Iraqi Government accused Kuwait of 'stealing' Iraqi oil; the Iraqi invasion followed barely two weeks later. With the US Administration of President George Bush taking a leading role, the United Nations Security Council through Resolution 660 condemned the Iraqi invasion and demanded the immediate and unconditional withdrawal of all Iraqi forces. On 8 August Iraq announced the 'comprehensive and eternal merger' of Kuwait with Iraq. Iraq also responded to proposals for a military response to its invasion by seizing Western hostages, who were held from 16 August to 6 December 1990. The US responded by building a coalition of Arab and Western powers committed to achieving the withdrawal of Iraqi troops from Kuwait, through the application of force if necessary.

On 29 November 1990, as US deployments of military forces in Saudi Arabia under US General H. Norman Schwarzkopf gathered pace, the Security Council adopted Resolution 678, which authorized member states to use 'all necessary means' to give effect to UN Security Council resolutions, unless Iraq had fully complied with them on or before 15 January 1991. Iraq's failure to do so triggered US air strikes. These caused extensive damage to Iraqi military assets and infrastructure. Iraq, hoping to catalyse a break-up of the coalition arrayed against it, launched SCUD missile attacks on Israel from 18 January, but under US pressure, Israel did not respond. Iraq also embarked on a campaign of pillage and destruction in Kuwait; more than 500 Kuwaiti oil wells were set ablaze on the night of 21–2 February. Allied ground forces then smashed through Iraqi front lines, prompting a chaotic Iraqi flight from Kuwait on 27 February 1991, and capitulation in a letter from Iraqi Foreign Minister Tariq Aziz dated 28 February in which he stated that 'Iraq agrees to comply fully with Security Council resolution 660 (1990) and all the other Security Council resolutions'. This brought the war to an end. WM

habeas corpus Literally, 'that you have the body'. A writ directed to the person who has someone in detention or custody and commands the detained person to be produced before a court. It dates back to Edward I's reign and was not then intended to get people out of prison but to ensure that they were in lawful custody in prison. The writ has been subject to a large number of statutory interventions and cases decided by the courts. Its constitutional significance is that it is a remedy available against Crown servants or servants acting in the name of the Crown. It was imported into other states that shared the English legal tradition, notably the United States.

Habeas corpus is used to test the validity of detention by the police, detention in cases of deportation, and in cases where there is an alleged breach of immigration regulations. In determining the outcome of the application, the legality of the detention is usually examined by the judge. The Habeas Corpus Acts 1679 and 1816 strengthened the role of the courts, and allowed the courts to determine for themselves the existence of facts, rather than rely on the assertions made by the executive.

Within the United Kingdom, habeas corpus is restricted to the jurisdiction of the English courts. In *re Keenan* [1972] 1 QB 533, it was held that there was no jurisdiction in the English courts to issue habeas corpus to persons detained in Northern Ireland. There is doubt as to the jurisdiction of the English courts to issue habeas corpus to British subjects throughout the world where the country is 'a colony, or foreign dominion of the Crown' (Habeas Corpus Act 1862). Habeas corpus has a greater reputation than perhaps the historical evidence may support, for affording the citizen protection against abuse of power by the state. JM

Hagenbach-Bischoff, E. Nineteenth-century Swiss mathematician who proposed the formula, still used in Switzerland, for calculating the quota required to elect one representative under the *d'Hondt system of *proportional representation.

Hamilton, Alexander (1757–1804) American politician and political theorist. Hamilton was active in the American War of Independence and politics from a precociously young age. In 1787 he, James *Madison, and John Jay cooperated on writing *The Federalist Papers*. Hamilton was responsible, among others, for the number which recommended the *Electoral College for the indirect election of the President as a device to prevent the election being directly in the hands of the untrustworthy people, and for the numbers dealing with the Supreme Court, which Hamilton described as the 'least dangerous' branch of the government. In the 1790s Hamilton parted company with Madison and *Jefferson. The latter remained agrarians, suspicious of centralized government and warmer towards democracy (at least among free men) than Hamilton, who favoured strong central government pursuing pro-industrial policies. Hamilton was Secretary to the Treasury under Washington (1789–95) but tried to act rather as prime minister. He was killed in a duel with Aaron Burr, Jefferson's Vice-President.

Hamilton was the first proponent of what is now called the 'largest remainder' system of *proportional representation; he proposed it as a means to assign a whole number of seats to each state in the apportionment of representatives to states required by the Constitution after each census. He was overruled by a group of Virginians, including Jefferson, who proposed the *d'Hondt system, which awarded Virginia more seats than did the largest remainder system.

Hansard The Official Report of Debates in the UK Parliament. There are separate volumes for the House of Commons and House of Lords. Hansard contains a verbatim report of all speeches, questions and answers, and statements. Daily debates are published on the Hansard website by 8 a.m. the following morning. Hansard takes its name from Luke Hansard who succeeded William Cobbett shortly after he began the reporting of the House of Commons in 1807. JBR

(⊕) SEE WEB LINKS
• Hansard site, including history of the Department of the Official Report (Hansard).

hard power A term often used in the study of *international relations to denote both the threat and use of military measures and/or economic sanctions to exert coercive influence on states or other collective bodies within the *international system. This form of 'hard' coercion is often contrasted with *soft power, which prioritizes diplomacy, market incentives, and cultural elements to 'persuade' socializing compliance.

Hare, Thomas (1806–91) Self-taught British lawyer and enthusiast for *proportional representation. Hare's scheme was vigorously promoted by J. S. *Mill as the way to ensure that all, not just the majority, were represented in a legislature. The details were wildly impracticable, and its descendant, *single transferable vote, though often called the 'Hare scheme', in reality owes more to C. G. Andrae (1812–93) and H. R. *Droop than to Hare.

Harrington, Sir James (1611–77) Political theorist, active in the Interregnum (the interval between the execution of Charles I and the Restoration of Charles II). Harrington was convinced of the need to create a republican settlement, reflecting the distribution of property and thus establishing political stability in England. He set out his argument at length in *Oceana* (1656), drawing on classical sources and his knowledge of contemporary republican forms, and incorporating aspects of *Machiavelli's thought. He advocated a complicated mixed constitution in which each 'class' of citizens was allocated a role appropriate to its capacity and property. He adopted the idea of a citizen army and made elaborate stipulations about its formation

and training. The complexity of his proposals, and the level of detail he provided, invited both mockery and incomprehension, and he tried to present his central ideas in simpler form in response. AR

hawk and dove Terms used to signify individuals and political groups who favour and promote the use of *hard power and military might as a foreign policy tool (hawk) versus individuals and political groups who favour and promote the use of *soft power and other peaceful diplomatic means to exert influence and power (dove).

Hayek, F. A. von (1899–1992) Austrian political economist who spent much of his life in Britain. In *The Road to Serfdom* (1944) he portrayed state intervention and collectivism, even in their moderate forms, as inevitably leading to an erosion of liberty. In both Britain and the United States, the book became a text for supporters of laissez-faire and opponents of *Keynesian economics and the welfare state for more than three decades in which their views were largely unrepresented in government. Hayek was far from a simplistic supporter of laissez-faire and in *The Constitution of Liberty* (1961) he was concerned to explore the necessary framework of government and the rule of law in which freedom and commerce could prosper. Hayek denied being either a conservative or a libertarian and described himself as a *Whig. LA

head of government Person responsible for carrying on the business of government and for leading the team of ministers who control the central institutions of the government and the state. In democratic presidential systems such as Russia and the United States, the *head of state also serves as head of government. In parliamentary systems the head of government is normally the leader of the largest party in the legislature. In a presidential system the head of government draws legitimacy from popular election, in a parliamentary system from the strength of support in the legislature. In France the head of state, a president elected for a seven-year term, does not serve as head of government, but may chair meetings of the cabinet and exercises direct responsibility for matters of defence and foreign policy.

In addition, the president may also appoint and dismiss the prime minister. In non-democratic systems the head of government, who may also be head of state, may have been appointed as a result of military intervention, or some other device for managing power. PBY

head of state The head of state embodies the political community and continuity of the state, and carries out ceremonial functions associated with representing the state both at home and in foreign policy, for instance in committing the state to treaty obligations.

If the head of state does not also act as *head of government, the head of state attempts to appear above party politics and to represent the interests of the nation as a whole. Such a head of state may be a hereditary monarch, which is the situation in about thirty states, or a president elected indirectly by the legislature from amongst 'elder statesmen'. In Europe heads of state may be able to exercise some discretionary powers if the political process is temporarily deadlocked. In Italy, presidents have tried to represent the interests of the nation at large against the corruption of both government and Mafia, and in Spain King Juan Carlos played an important role in the transition from dictatorship to democracy and in cementing support for the democratic regime.

The British monarch plays two additional roles as head of state which have evolved from the nineteenth-century role of the Crown as King and Emperor (Queen and Empress). First, the monarch is head of the *Commonwealth, and recognized as such by the majority of members of the Commonwealth, which are either republics or have retained their own monarchy. Secondly, the monarch remains head of state of a few Commonwealth states, such as Canada, Australia, and New Zealand. In these states, from which most of the time of course she is absent, a Governor-General who carries out ceremonial functions on her behalf represents her. In 1999 Australians unexpectedly voted in a referendum not to substitute an indirectly elected head of state. PBY

hearts and minds *See* COUNTER-INSURGENCY.

Hegel, Georg Wilhelm Friedrich (1770–1831) German philosopher, born in Stuttgart in 1770; died of cholera in Berlin in 1831. He attended the Tübinger Stift where he studied philosophy and theology. After being employed as a house tutor Hegel eventually secured a position at the University of Jena in 1801 where he lectured on logic and metaphysics for four years until he was appointed as a professor. In 1816 he became Professor of Philosophy at the University of Heidelberg and lectured on political philosophy, history of philosophy, logic and metaphysics, anthropology and psychology, and aesthetics. Two years later Hegel took a professorship at the University of Berlin, where he remained until his death.

During his lifetime Hegel published four important philosophical works: *Phenomenology of Spirit* (1807); *Science of Logic* (1812-16); *Encyclopaedia of the Philosophical Sciences* (1817, 1827, 1830); and *Philosophy of Right* (1821). His lectures on the history of philosophy, and philosophies of history, aesthetics, and religion were all published after his death.

Hegel intended the *Phenomenology of Spirit* to serve as an introduction to his whole philosophical system, which was later to be explicated in the *Encyclopaedia*. His task in the *Phenomenology* is to present scientifically the contradictory development of consciousness from its most abstract state to the level of 'absolute knowledge'. For Hegel the aim of philosophy is to apprehend 'what truly is' but to do this we need first to reflect on the very way consciousness itself understands reality. Hegel does this by showing how consciousness develops dialectically through education to preserve and transcend previous modes of thought. As each form of consciousness becomes aware that it has not achieved 'absolute knowledge' it is forced to move on to a higher level of cognition. For Hegel this is why 'the history of the world is none other than the progress of the consciousness of freedom'.

The *Science of Logic* sees Hegel similarly concerned with the discovery of truth but also with the problem of a starting point for philosophical analysis. Initially, however, Hegel is concerned to show that the weakness of traditional logic is that it separates form from content. For instance, formal logic would regard the following as 'true': all men are stupid, Galileo was a man, therefore Galileo was stupid. In form this is correct, each statement can be deduced from one another, but in content it can only be decided by experience whether the main premiss and the conclusion are 'true'. In contrast, Hegel argues that 'real' logic can only come about if thought is allowed to develop itself free from the imposition of formal rules of traditional logic. Consequently, he wants to begin without any such presuppositions. He does this through abstracting thought to an indeterminate state as 'pure being' where it is 'nothing'. Yet this 'nothing' is itself 'something'—that is, it is nothing. Both 'being' and 'nothing' therefore become reducible to one another. Yet the movement which takes place between the two is a movement of 'becoming'. 'Being' becomes 'nothing' and 'nothing' becomes 'being'. From a state of indeterminacy we have moved to the determinacy of 'becoming' without assuming or presupposing anything. The rest of the *Logic* is an attempt by Hegel to develop further categories from the level of bare determinacy.

It is from this analysis that we begin to discern the outlines of Hegel's dialectical method. Hegel attempts to explain this as lucidly as is possible in the *Lesser Logic* which comprises part one of the *Encyclopaedia*. The rest of the *Encyclopaedia* covers the philosophy of nature and the philosophy of mind. Hegel argues that his logic consists of three moments: the Understanding, the Dialectic, and the Speculative. Thought which remains simply at the level of the Understanding holds determinations in a fixed manner and sees them as being distinct from one another. The Dialectic is the recognition of the movement between these 'fixed' determinations in terms of their opposites, such as 'being' and 'nothing', for example. The Speculative stage is where real truth is found. It is the stage of 'positive reason' which is the knowledge that the opposites themselves should be apprehended as contradictions within a unity. Speculative philosophy is concerned with grasping the truth which emerges out of the contradictory movement of the Dialectic itself.

In the *Philosophy of Right* this dialectical movement becomes expressed in the development of the concept of the will as it makes its progression along the path to freedom. The will moves through the moment of

'Abstract Right', where it manifests itself into material existence as it posits itself in property. It then passes through 'Morality', which allows it to realize the importance of moral norms, before it enters the realm of 'Ethical Life'. It is here that the will passes through the moments of the family, *civil society, and the state. It is through these mediating moments that a particular will comes into contact with other wills. Such interaction leads to the creation of institutions that attempt to bring the particular and universal will into a contradictory unity, for only then can people be truly free. The task for philosophy, according to Hegel, is to discern what is rational in this progression of the will. It is to try and penetrate the 'forms, appearances and shapes' which rationality takes in its external existence. Hence Hegel's claim, that 'What is rational is actual; and what is actual is rational', should be understood as a non-identity. The 'rational is actual' in that it exists in society but only in a particular 'form'. Speculative philosophy's task is to grasp the 'content' of that 'form' and thereby discover what is truly rational. If Hegel's legacy means anything it is the importance of carrying out this endeavour in order for human freedom to be fully realized. *See also* SITTLICHKEIT.   IF

hegemony When one social class exerts power over others, beyond that accounted for by coercion or law, it may be described as hegemonic, drawing on the Greek word *hegemon*, meaning chieftain. Thus the bourgeoisie was regarded as hegemonic within capitalist society by *Gramsci, who believed their power depended on the permeation by bourgeois values of all organs of society. Hegemony has also been attributed to other social institutions. Indeed, the phrase first entered the vocabulary of the left following the Russian Revolution of 1905 when Plekhanov used it to describe the relation of the Bolshevik party to the proletariat. Among contemporary North American international relations theorists, the term has been used rather differently. The influence of Britain beyond the boundaries of its formal Empire in the nineteenth century and the analogous power of the United States since 1945 were regarded as hegemonic by Charles Kindleberger and Robert Gilpin, the key to power residing latterly in the functioning of the hegemonic state—supposedly essential to a liberal international economic order and the security system, as provider of a range of *public goods including relatively open markets, a stable international trading currency, and a nuclear deterrent force. Such arguments have been used: to explain the depth and duration of the depression of the 1930s (said to have stemmed from lack of an effective hegemon); to warn of the possible consequences of current United States economic decline; and to argue that beneficiaries of this regime should contribute more to its costs, which are held to accrue disproportionately to the dominant provider, making hegemony a system with a built-in tendency to self-destruction.   CJ

Heidegger, Martin (1889–1976) German philosopher whose social and political ideas have been controversial because of his support for Hitler and *National Socialism in the early 1930s. Heidegger's *existentialist and anti-rationalist approach to exploring the nature of human existence ('Being') led him to question the *Enlightenment project of building an ever more progressive world rooted in science, industry, and technology. Heidegger rejected all notions of universal, objective rationality made manifest in mankind's increasing mastery and control of nature, and in enthusiasm for technocratic planning and social organization, as being incapable of harnessing the essentially human qualities of authentic, creative, and imaginative existence in a purposeful *polis* or political community.

Like *Nietzsche, Heidegger sought to elevate the aesthetic and mythological power of philosophy and poetry to a leading role in the shaping of human affairs. The emphasis of both these thinkers on the need for inspired political leadership in the cause of romantic and noble ideals—expressed through the imaginative use of mythological symbols and language—suggests linkages with the right-wing, nationalist, and irrationalist tendencies of European fascism after the First World War. Heidegger's excursion into political affairs was, to say the least, ambiguous and open to a variety of interpretations.   KT

Helvétius, Claude Adrien (1715–71) Utilitarian thinker of French *Enlightenment.

Not original or profound—although a significant influence on *Bentham. Reflected commonly held ideas in an extreme form. An egalitarian who believed that differences between men are the result of education. The sole human motivation is self-interest, so each family should be given a piece of land to ensure that all, working for themselves alone, contribute to the aggregate good.   CS

heresthetic(s) Term coined by W. H. *Riker in 1986 to denote the art and science of political manipulation. Intrigued that the root of *heresy* is from the Greek word meaning 'to find out', Riker coined 'heresthetics', and later dropped the final 's'. The coinage both parallels 'aesthetics' and correctly reflects the Greek middle voice for the sense 'to find out for oneself'. Riker mostly had in mind manipulation to increase or diminish the number of issue dimensions in politics. If the number of dimensions is two or more, the *median voter theorem does not apply, and *cycles in majority rule are possible. Therefore, politics may lead to surprising outcomes. Herestheticians are politicians who can glimpse such possibilities and perhaps achieve such an outcome. Riker and his followers have claimed the title for a number of politicians, including (in the USA) Gouverneur Morris and Abraham Lincoln; (in New Zealand) 'King Dick' Seddon; and (in the UK) Sir Robert Peel and David Lloyd George. Lloyd George had a motto over his bed from the Book of Job, 'There is a path which no fowl knoweth and which the eye of the vulture hath not seen'.

hermeneutics In Greek a *hermeneus* was an interpreter and the word probably originates from the name of Hermes, messenger of the gods and epitome of eloquence. In all its nineteenth-century uses and definitions hermeneutics was agreed to be the art and science of interpretation, primarily, though not exclusively, of religious texts. A more specific implication was that hermeneutics was concerned with real and hidden meanings, quite different from the elucidation and concern with practical application which was the concern of *exegesis*.

In the twentieth century, hermeneutics became one of many terms to shift from a primarily religious context into secular social theory. The principal individual responsible for this transition was probably *Heidegger. In the study of political theory, hermeneutics has become principally associated with the 'Cambridge School', which includes such writers as Quentin Skinner and John Dunn. For hermeneutical scholars the interesting questions about, say, John Locke would not be whether he offers us a coherent set of prescriptions for when we should obey government, but what meaning the text has when it is put in its social context and we fully understand what Locke understood (for example) by property and by 'servants'.

Up to a point hermeneutics can be treated simply as a different discipline, with different emphases from the kind of exegesis that looks at a text and asks, 'Irrespective of its context, what can this tell us now?' But certain practitioners of hermeneutics stand to be accused of abandoning any possibility of persistent or resoluble argument and treating the kind of meaning that comes from particular contexts and the interests within them as the only form of meaning.   LA

high and low politics Largely used in the study of *international relations, 'high politics' generally refers to issues of vital importance and survival of the state, such as national and international security. This is in opposition to 'low politics', which usually refers to secondary non-security issues such as economic policy and social policy.

Hindu nationalism Belief that politics should be organized in accordance with the precepts of the Hindu scriptures and way of life. In its more extreme form, this takes the form of the promotion of a Hindu *Rashtra* (nation) in the Indian subcontinent. Hindu nationalism emerged in the late nineteenth century, accompanied by the emergence of religious reform organizations such as the Arya Samaj, founded in 1875. The Arya Samaj sought to counter a perceived threat to Hinduism from conversion to Islam, Christianity, and Sikhism. Hinduism was seen as vulnerable because of its decentralized and non-hierarchical organization; its lack of a core of orthodox beliefs or practices; and because of the operation of the *caste system, which imposed social stigma and economic constraints on many Hindus. This was accompanied by a belief that Muslim and British rulers of India had sought to

undermine Hinduism, and promote conversion to Islam and Christianity. The Arya Samaj sought to combine the advocacy of a Hinduism based around ancient values alongside programmes of education, social reform, and the ritual of *shuddhi*, a purification ceremony which was used to reconvert people to Hinduism and to remove social stigma from the lower castes. At first Hindu nationalism ran alongside the Indian Nationalist movement, with leaders such as B. G. Tilak (1856–1920) who was both an organizer of Hindu revivalist festivals and leader of the *Congress. However, Congress's need to appeal to Indians of all religions led to tension with Hindu nationalists, particularly under the leadership of *Gandhi, who believed that all religions were equally valid. The Hindu Mahasabha, formed in 1915, articulated a much more strident pro-Hindu agenda, aimed at developing centralized organization which would promote a cohesive Hindu doctrine, and countering political concessions given by the British to Muslims. The Hindu Mahasabha could not match the mass appeal of the Congress, and played a peripheral political role in the run-up to Independence. Another Hindu nationalist organization, the Rashtriya Swayamsevak Sangh (RSS: National Volunteer Corps), founded in 1925, avoided direct involvement with politics, focusing on a programme of physical exercise, military drills, and Hindu teaching. The man who assassinated Gandhi was a member of both the RSS and Hindu Mahasabha, which tainted the reputation of both organizations.

After Independence the Hindu nationalist parties struggled to compete with Congress, which often absorbed Hindu nationalist issues—such as the promotion of the Hindi language in the northern States and the prohibition of cow slaughter—into its own programme. With the decline of Congress, however, opportunities arose to develop a mass appeal. The Bharatiya Janata Party (BJP: Indian People's Party: formed 1980) was able to exploit a vernacular religious enthusiasm, partly fostered by the broadcast of two Hindu epics (the Mahabharata and Ramayana) on national TV, with the strong organizational base provided by close links with the RSS, which had by then developed a large membership. This brought electoral success in 1989, and a pivotal position in government formation. The BJP became involved with two often violent agitations in the early 1990s; over the attempt to extend *reservations, and in the dispute over the destruction of a Muslim mosque (the Babri Masjid) in the town of Ayodhya. These events consolidated the BJP's support amongst the upper castes and devout Hindus, but alienated many others.

Electoral considerations have forced the BJP to temper its nationalist programme, and through successful coalition building the party's leader, A. B. Vajpayee, became Prime Minister in 1998. In power the party has been constrained in its ability to implement a Hindu nationalist agenda, although it carried out nuclear tests in 1998 in a bid to assert Indian power in the region, has pursued an aggressive policy in *Kashmir, and has attempted to influence the education system so as to promote the teaching of history in line with the Hindu nationalist agenda.

After further demonstrations in Ayodhya over the right of Hindus to build a temple on the site of the Babri Masjid in 2002, there were widespread riots in Gujarat targetting the Muslim population, which were seen by many to have been encouraged (or even orchestrated) by the incumbent BJP State government. Outrage following this violence, which some commentators likened to ethnic cleansing against the Muslim population, destabilized the national government. It has further exposed the tension between a populist nationalist programme and the upholding of acceptable limits of tolerance and democratic behaviour.

Hindutva Translated as Hinduness, it refers to the ideology of *Hindu nationalists, stressing the common culture of the inhabitants of the Indian subcontinent. The term originated in *Hindutva: Who is a Hindu?* (1923) by V. D. Savarkar (1883–1966), written whilst imprisoned by the British. Influenced by the Italian nationalist *Mazzini, Savarkar stresses the need to preserve the cultural purity of the Hindu nation, and resist the incursion of alien practices. Modern politicians have attempted to play down the racial and anti-Muslim aspects of Hindutva, stressing the inclusiveness of the Indian identity; but the term has *fascist undertones.

historical analysis A term referring to the methodological tools and general intellectual approach used to examine historical context, language, documentation, institutions, and processes so as better interpret and explain political events and outcomes. Often seen in opposition to *positivism and the analysis of history as a series of knowable 'facts', historical analysis employs methods of interpretation as well as the generation of historical narratives, since knowable historical 'facts' are often highly contested.

historical institutionalism A fashion (actually a number of convergent fashions) in political science for stressing that institutions matter because they shape behaviour, and that therefore it is important to study their history, both for its own sake and for the sake of understanding why political actors behave as they do within the framework they find themselves in. Leading figures of historical institutionalism include T. Skocpol, D. North, and W. H. *Riker. *See also* NEW INSTITUTIONALISM.

historical materialism The concept that social structures derive from economic structures, and these structures are changed through class struggles, each ruling class producing another class that will eventually supersede it. A *Marxist doctrine, which supposes that human history develops as the result of contradictions, mainly among social classes. The material element of the theory consists in the assertion, first, that human history is a form of more general natural development and, second, that the principal determinant of social organization is the manner in which people reproduce their lives. Thus, at the stage of 'primitive communism' humans found it necessary to work in common to survive, and class formation was absent. However, slave society emerged with the accumulation of surplus products and weaponry in the possession of a military caste. Feudal relations were characterized by the military protection of serfs in return for a proportion of their surplus agricultural product. Capitalism, in turn, was characterized by the emergence of a bourgeois class, using free labourers (proletarians) to operate machine technology to produce an even greater surplus product. Within each of these 'modes of production', at a certain point the existing class relations begin to act as a constraint on the further development of the material forces of production and revolutions occur. On this basis, socialism was expected to succeed capitalism under which private control of the material forces was increasingly at odds with their real potential. swh

historicism Doctrine that historical events are governed by natural laws, which in turn determine social and cultural developments, beliefs, and values specific to each period of history.

As a translation of the German *Historismus*, historicism in social philosophy originally meant an insistence on 'getting inside' a historical period in order to understand it, by learning the meaning of the language and concepts used in that period. However, since the publication of Karl *Popper's *The Poverty of Historicism* in 1957 the most generally recognized sense of the word has been entirely different: a belief in the unavoidable necessity of historical development following a certain path. Marx and *Marxism provide the most obvious examples of historicists, in this sense, but many others, including Oswald Spengler, *Hegel, and *Comte, qualify in different ways. Popper criticized historicism not merely as wrong, but as conducive to an ideological, potentially totalitarian outlook which encourages those who believe themselves to be 'on the side of history' to show contempt for alternative points of view and those who hold them. The range of historicist doctrine is, perhaps, wider than Popper suggests. The *Whig view of history, identified by Sir Herbert Butterfield as a belief in the necessity of the ultimate triumph of progress over reaction, is certainly historicist. So are many 'liberal' views, including Adam *Smith's account of historical development as culminating in the establishment of a commercial society. A more recent version of this thesis is Francis Fukuyama's *The End of History and the Last Man* (1992). All of these forms of historicism can be said to have been shown to be deficient in their understanding of history. LA

Hitler, Adolf (1889–1945) *See* NATIONAL SOCIALISM.

Hobbes, Thomas (1588–1679) One of the greatest of all political philosophers, the most brilliant and profound ever to have written in English. Hobbes was born in Malmesbury, Wiltshire (he joked that 'Fear and I were born twins' because his mother went into labour out of shock at the news of the Spanish Armada) and rescued from an unpromising background by a far-sighted schoolmaster. Hobbes studied at Oxford, where he learnt a contempt for the philosophy of *Plato and, especially, *Aristotle that stayed for life. He then joined the family of the Earls (later Dukes) of Devonshire as a tutor. He remained associated with the family until his death; he is buried at Ault Hucknall, in the parish of the Devonshire house at Hardwick. He had suggested that 'This is the true philosopher's stone' be inscribed on his tombstone, but settled for a more modest Latin inscription.

As a political theorist, Hobbes was a late starter. His first publication is a plain and muscular translation of *Thucydides' *History of the Peloponnesian War* (1628). Hobbes chose Thucydides because he was 'the most politick historiographer that ever writ'. Thucydides recounts the decline of *Athenian democracy from the high ideals of Pericles to incompetence and *realpolitik*. Hobbes saw Thucydides as a warning to the parliamentarians who in 1628 were mounting the challenge to royal authority that was to culminate in the English Civil War. Hobbes was then an anti-democrat first and an absolutist second. Soon after this, Hobbes had an encounter which changed his life. In the words of Hobbes's friend and biographer John Aubrey, 'Being in a gentleman's library ... Euclid's *Elements* lay open, and 'twas the 47 *El. libri I* [which is Pythagoras' Theorem on the relationship between the sides of a right-angled triangle]. "By G—", sayd he ... "this is impossible!" So he reads the demonstration of it, which referred him back to such a proposition; which proposition he read. That referred him back to another, which he also read. *Et sic deinceps* [and so on], that at last he was demonstratively convinced of that trueth. This made him in love with geometry', which Hobbes would later describe as 'the only science that it hath pleased God hitherto to bestow on mankind'.

Geometry seemed to him to give certainty in science. Hobbes was fascinated by scientific method, which he studied in the work of

Galileo (1564–1642), Sir Francis Bacon (1561–1626), René Descartes (1596–1650, of whom Hobbes said 'Had he kept himself to Geometry he had been the best Geometer in the world but ... his head did not lye for philosophy'), and Pierre Gassendi (1592–1655). Hobbes had briefly worked for Bacon as a young man, and visited Gassendi, Descartes, and Galileo when his patron toured Europe. Hobbes's resolutive-compositive method was influenced by Bacon and Descartes, but was closer to that of Galileo than either. It involved the following thought-experiment. Take something, such as civil society, apart. Examine its fundamental elements. Make a rational reconstruction of the necessary principles on which it works. Hobbes gave several expositions of his political theory, in *The Elements of Law* (written 1640, published 1650), in *De Cive* (*The Citizen*, 1642), and above all in *Leviathan* (1651). Here Hobbes sets out first what he takes to be axioms of human behaviour analogous to the geometrical axioms that underpin Euclid's system. Hobbes's axioms are that men are rational and desire above all their own preservation. Hence they are led by 'a perpetuall and restlesse desire of Power after power' to a condition of 'warre ... of every man, against every man' in the *state of nature. Realizing, however, that life in the state of nature would be 'solitary, poore, nasty, brutish, and short', rational men would agree to a social contract in which each conditionally hands over his arms to a third party if each other will do the same. The third party thus empowered is called the Sovereign, who has been authorized to do anything except order a subject to kill himself. Thus Hobbes derives absolutist conclusions from individualist premisses. Writing just after the English Civil War, Hobbes insists that one should not challenge authority, denouncing both the Puritan appeal to conscience against the State and the Catholic appeal to the Church against the State. But Hobbes's reasoning is ruthlessly unsentimental. Once Charles I has been overthrown by Oliver Cromwell, the argument for obedience to Charles immediately becomes an argument for obedience to Oliver. (Hobbes's philosophy does not tell the rational citizen when to make that leap.) It is absolutist first, and anti-democratic second. The Sovereign need not be one man. It may be an assembly,

so long as it is an assembly with an odd number of members to avoid becoming stalemated (a typically Hobbesian touch). Thus Hobbes's approach is entirely compatible with a doctrine of *parliamentary sovereignty. He repeats his arguments for undivided sovereignty in his later works *A Dialogue between a Philosopher and a Student of the Common Laws of England* (written 1666, published 1681) and *Behemoth* (a history of the English Civil War, written 1668, published 1679). With the restoration of the monarchy in 1660, Hobbes had once again become a monarchist (and indeed was protected by Charles II); however, this simply followed consistently from his views on sovereignty.

It is frequently objected that if people in the state of nature are as Hobbes says they are, they might sign the social contract but would immediately fail to carry out the promises they had made; whereas if people are not as he says they are, there is no need for the Sovereign to be given absolute power. It is still not clear whether Hobbes can be defended against this attack, but close reading of Hobbes's argument against the 'Foole' in chapter 15 of *Leviathan* suggests that he can.

Note that the state of nature in Hobbes is not, as it perhaps is in both *Locke and *Rousseau, an attempt to describe an actual state of affairs. It is a rational reconstruction of what would happen were people the sort of rational maximizers Hobbes has them axiomatically as being. Hobbes tries to construct both physical science and social science on these common deductive principles. On both fronts, his work is generally regarded as a magnificent failure. Hobbes is the main precursor of the modern *rational choice approach to politics, and many writers have tried to rework the central arguments of *Leviathan* in terms of *game theory.

Many of the arguments of *Leviathan* have set the terms of subsequent debate. For instance, Hobbes's discussion of sovereignty and authorization (*Leviathan*, chapter 16) insists that sovereignty cannot be divided—the opinion that it can leads to civil war, in his view—and that subjects are the authors of everything the sovereign does as their agent. The first of these claims is generally accepted, the second is not. But what has emerged in recent years as *principal–agent theory may be regarded as a long footnote to Hobbes. How can principals (citizens) control their agents (governments)? Hobbes sets the question but does not provide a satisfactory answer. As Locke sarcastically observed, the argument that people would hand over their right of self-preservation to one man 'is to think that Men are so foolish that they take care to avoid what Mischiefs may be done them by Pole-cats, or Foxes, but are content, nay think it Safety, to be devoured by Lions'.

Hobbes's religious position is much disputed. He was not a straightforward atheist or agnostic, although superstitious people blamed the Fire of London of 1666 on him. He was probably a deist, who believed that God was necessary, as a 'first cause', to explain how matter came into being. He was witheringly contemptuous of religion ('For it is with the mysteries of our Religion, as with wholsome pills for the sick, which swallowed whole, have the vertue to cure; but chewed, are for the most part cast up again without effect') but devotes half of *Leviathan* to theology, essentially in order to pre-empt all religious challenges to his doctrine of absolute sovereignty.

Hobbes is valuable not least because of the beautiful clarity and style of his language. He claimed that 'True and False are attributes of Speech, not of Things. And where Speech is not, there is neither Truth nor Falsehood'. In this he is one of the fathers of analytical philosophy.

Hobhouse, Leonard Trelawny (1864–1929) Political philosopher, journalist, sociologist, and political activist in the field of labour relations and social policy. Hobhouse was a crucial figure in the emergence of 'social liberalism', which justified increased state intervention as necessary for the achievement of both social and individual goods.

Hobhouse argued, and defended through a series of physiological, anthropological, and historical studies, that the human mind was the central force in human development. The culmination of this unfolding teleological process, he maintained, lay in the deliberate construction of certain social and political forms (such as common property) representing the ethical principles of cooperation and rational humanitarianism. The relationship between the individual and society was a symbiotic one, and their ends were harmonized by the regulative activity of the state.

Like nineteenth-century liberals, Hobhouse asserted the moral primacy of individual autonomy, but maintained that it was an impoverished liberalism that failed to appreciate the social bases of the formation and flourishing of human personality. Consequently, and contra Locke and other liberal predecessors, the individual and his claims to rights and property cannot be said to be prior to society and its claims on the individual in the name of its members. While arguing that, properly understood, individual liberty and the social good were complementary, Hobhouse suspected any group that defended sectional interests at the expense of other members of the social body. The state in Hobhouse's work is therefore conceived as an intelligent director of social interaction, sustaining the conditions for individual development while simultaneously preserving the priority of common over particularistic goods (and entitled to coerce individuals to this end). sw

Hobson, John (1858–1940) English economist, associated with radical liberalism before 1914 and later with the Labour Party. He is remembered for *Imperialism: A Study*, written in opposition to the Boer War and published in 1902. His explanation of imperialism depended on the idea of underconsumption in the imperial or metropole power. In the metropole the uneven distribution of wealth, and very low spending power of the working class, led to a fall in profits from manufacturing industry. Financiers thus tended increasingly to look abroad for markets for investment. Their interests dominated government, which was increasingly drawn in to protect these investments by force, involving the state in conflicts both with the regimes of the underdeveloped world and with other European governments intent on the same process. Hobson thought that radical economic and political reforms at home could channel energies into domestically based growth; he held utopian views on the international cooperation which could follow from radical reform at home. Underconsumption has been widely criticized as an explanation of imperialism, though Hobson's work was the basis of the

Leninist theory of *imperialism and continues to play a prominent role in the massive modern literature on the economic roots of imperialism. His work also anticipated in important respects Keynes's theories of underconsumption. PBY

Ho Chi Minh (1890–1969) Vietnamese revolutionary and politician. Leader of the Indo-Chinese Communist Party, and the League for the Independence of Vietnam. Gains a place in this dictionary more for the idealized vision of him held by many followers of the *New Left in the West in the 1960s than for his actual contribution to political institutions or theory. As his regime was successfully opposing the United States, and as the United States was the fount of all that was evil, Ho became the symbol of all that was good.

Holbach, Paul Henri Dietrich d' (1723–89) Writer of the French *Enlightenment, opposed to utilitarianism. Originally educated in the natural sciences, he wrote the articles on chemistry for the *Encyclopédie*. Holbach rejected Christianity, and was regularly condemned by the Church and the *Parlement de Paris*. He believed that the only way to long-term happiness was a severe morality. Despite these views, he was immensely rich, and was known particularly for the dinners he gave. He changed his opinion about the political system which might achieve his ideal. At first, he supported absolutism, in agreement with *Voltaire. Then he moved to support the legal aristocracy, in agreement with *Montesquieu. In terms of the ends to be achieved, he disagreed with both, and with the Enlightenment in general. CS

Homeland Security, Department of In the aftermath of the *September 11th 2001 attacks on the United States, President George W. Bush announced the establishment of a Department of Homeland Security. The aims of the department were to undertake counter-terrorism measures, and coordinate rescue and recovery missions in the event of any attack.

(⊕) SEE WEB LINKS

• US government Department of Homeland Security site.

Home Rule *See* DEVOLUTION.

homogenization A concept generally employed in debates about *globalization which suggest that diversity is being reduced culturally, politically, and economically by global processes. Used as a pejorative, homogenization is understood as an existential threat to valuable cultural and national identities and is therefore a form of *cultural imperialism and economic domination, predominately by the West.

Hondt, Victor d' *See* D'HONDT.

Hooker, Richard (*c.*1554–1600) English theologian and philosopher. Hooker grew up in a critical period for the Anglican Church, when the Calvinist wing was trying to gain the ascendancy. Though initially he was favourable to *Calvinism, he later moved away from it. His theory was published in eight volumes from 1592 entitled *Of the Laws of Ecclesiastical Polity*. Much of his theory reflects that of *Aquinas. He distinguished four types of law: (1) eternal—that by which God operates; (2) natural—a reflection of the eternal law, which natural agents observe and all human beings ought to observe; (3) positive divine—revealed by God; and (4) positive ecclesiastical and civil, which may vary from society to society and at different times.

Like Aquinas, he held that the state is founded on a natural inclination. But he introduced an element of contract: 'an order expressly or secretly agreed upon' governing the manner of living together (i. 10) (which had some influence on *Locke). Moreover, civil government depends on the consent of the governed: 'Laws they are not therefore which public approbation had not made so.' CB

House of Commons The elected house of the UK Parliament. It is composed of 650 Members of Parliament (MPs), representing single member constituencies (although the number fluctuates with each *Boundary Commission review). The constitutional authority of the House of Commons derives from features of historical evolution. Its political authority has, however, been undermined since the nineteenth century, and its effectiveness in particular roles has been brought into question. Debate upon the decline of the House of Commons and prescriptions for its reform have become commonplace.

The UK Parliament's composition was based initially upon the lords spiritual and temporal, but from 1295 Edward I formalized the extension of the political nation to be called to each parliament to include two knights to represent each of the shires, two citizens to represent each of the cities, and two burgesses to represent each of the boroughs. During the 1330s these came to be known as the Commons, and sat separately from the lords. The relationship between the Commons and the Crown was marked by incremental rather than revolutionary change between the fourteenth and seventeenth centuries. Nominally, the Crown dominated. The Commons sat only at the behest of the Crown and represented a narrowly defined political nation. Its composition was open to manipulation by the Crown, and, as a result, it was largely compliant to the wishes of the Crown when it did sit. At the same time, however, the Crown habitually sought the consent of the Commons in order to raise taxation and increasingly to lend political support to Crown policies, thereby establishing the basis for claims to greater power. Granting of taxation, for instance, was made dependent upon the Crown recognizing the Commons' right to redress of grievance. In this context the arbitrary rule of James I and Charles I aroused the bitter opposition of the Commons, and the English Civil War of 1642–6 represented a battle between Parliament, led by the Commons, and the Crown for supreme authority. Victory for Parliament, however, did not lead to lasting change. The Restoration of 1660 largely restored the pre-1642 relationship with superiority lying with the Crown.

More important was the Glorious Revolution of 1688 in which Parliament effectively rejected James II and invited William of Orange to take the throne. The Crown retained the right to appoint and dismiss governments, and draw the personnel of governments from any chosen source. However, the fact that William owed his position to Parliament established more firmly than ever before the central constitutional convention that the monarch must pursue government and the raising of taxation in consultation with Parliament, in particular the Commons. The 1689 Bill of Rights established for the Commons the sole right to authorize taxation and the level of financial supply to the Crown. The 1694 Triennial Act established the principle of the necessity of election within a given time period to continue service within the House of Commons, thus ending the Crown's ability to extend indefinitely parliaments which proved supportive, and ensuring parliamentary independence from the Crown. Crown/Commons relations were marked by consensus for much of the eighteenth century as their interests coincided over the need for political and social stability, the rule of law, and the preservation of property. A balanced constitutional monarchy emerged as the framework of British political life.

The constitutional adjustments of the seventeenth and eighteenth centuries were followed by similarly gradual but important changes in the role of the House of Commons during the nineteenth century. Parliamentary reform acts of 1832, 1867, and 1884 gradually extended the electorate, thus widening the political nation represented by the House of Commons to include members of the working classes. This had two main effects. First, MPs began to organize themselves much more rigorously on a party basis in order to capture the popular vote at election time, and subsequently to form party governments on the basis of electoral support. Secondly, the heightened democratic basis of the House of Commons secured its primacy over the House of Lords and the monarch within Parliament. 1834 was the last occasion on which a monarch changed a government to suit himself.

*Parliamentary sovereignty ensures that the House of Commons has considerable constitutional importance, retaining its centrality to the processes of granting taxation and making law. However, there is a widespread perception that its political authority to influence them has gone into decline. The party of government faces the official opposition and other opposition parties across the floor of the House of Commons, all indulging in debates which are often reduced to pure theatre by MPs generally voting on party lines. The party of government can usually dominate the Commons, making it the location of key decision-making but rarely its source.

The overwhelming workload for MPs consequent upon increases in the responsibilities and apparatus of government and an expansion of its fiscal and legislative business from the late nineteenth century has undermined the ability of the Commons to provide a good consultative forum. It is suggested that the adversarial party system militates against the exploration of new ideas and cooperative decision-making, and ensures that most decisions are taken outside the Commons within the party of government. At regular intervals since the 1920s there have been calls for special economic parliaments or councils of experts to provide alternative wider forums. Many have seen policy networks, encompassing interest groups, or corporatist arrangements involving the captains of industry and trade union leaders in the business of government as better forums for consultative decision-making.

In terms of its more modern role of holding the executive to account on behalf of the wider political nation, the House of Commons has again been found wanting. Facilities such as parliamentary questions, standing committees, and the parliamentary select committees created in 1979 provide routes to scrutiny and, of course, party government dominance over Parliament is contingent upon the size of governing party majorities. Nevertheless, it is widely perceived in the early twenty-first century that MPs are too obviously complicit in the operations and needs of the executive. They lack the facilities to provide for scrutiny of a kind to be seen in, for example, the US Congress.

The prescriptions for reform since the First World War have been many and varied: from symptomatic reforms of procedure and extension of committee powers to systemic reform involving a written constitution, electoral reform, and territorial decentralization of Commons powers. As yet, there has been no fundamental reform debate, but there have been changes. In 1997 a select committee on the modernization of the House was established to address procedural issues. This led to reforms which enhanced the ability of the Commons to hold the government to account: including a longer prime minister's question time session each Wednesday; requiring the prime minister to appear before a Commons liaison committee twice a year; increased resources for select committees; and the creation of Westminster Hall as a parallel debating chamber on issues for which the House of Commons cannot find sufficient time. There have also been efforts to remove the archaic practices of the Commons, for example ending the practice of wearing top hats to make a point of order during a division. Recent research has also highlighted the extent of parliamentary dissent shown by backbench members of the governing party since the 1970s. In a myriad of ways this has led to revisions to bills being taken through the Commons, and in certain celebrated cases has highlighted public opposition to government policy or indeed defeated it. The 2003 Commons debate on the decision to go to war in Iraq saw the biggest revolt in the governing party since the debate on the repeal of the Corn Laws. In 2005 a backbench revolt actually defeated the Government's proposals to detain terrorist suspects.

Nevertheless, the procedures and party dominance of the Commons remain generally deeply entrenched. The only systemic change followed devolution of some primary legislative powers to the Northern Ireland Assembly in 1998 and Scottish Parliament in 1999. Change was limited, however, to the territorial scope of legislation in the House of Commons despite the issues that *devolution raised, and did not lead to any fundamental reform of House of Commons procedures. Overall, it has remained in the interest of whichever party has been in power, in order to maximize its own autonomy, to foster the myth of the House of Commons as a cockpit of democracy whilst preserving its many real weaknesses. Equally, it has remained in the interest of British government to foster the myth of the House of Commons as an arena expressing the unity of British politics while allowing devolution to undermine its legislative and political power. It is apparent that the victory that was won by the Commons against domination by the unelected executive was replaced during the twentieth century by defeat at the hands of the elected executive. For the Commons to more systemically reassert itself against the executive in the twenty-first century would require more far-reaching changes in institutional arrangements and the party system. JBr

• House of Commons website.

House of Lords The upper house in the UK Parliament. It is composed of life peers, Church of England bishops and archbishops, law lords, and 92 hereditary peers. At the end of 2005 there were 721 peers on the roll, of whom 208 took the Conservative whip, 210 were Labour, 74 were Liberal Democrats, and 192 were not aligned with a party. Its composition was transformed by the 1999 House of Lords Act, which abolished the voting rights of many more hereditary peers and thus nearly halved the membership. Its composition, nevertheless, continues to be the subject of debate so long as it has Members of Parliament there by birth. The Wakeham Royal Commission, which reported in 2000, advocated the complete abolition of the hereditary peers. It recommended instead that the House of Lords should be made up of 550 members, of whom 12–35 per cent should be elected to represent the nations and regions of the UK, and the rest appointed by a statutory appointments commission. Critics argued strenuously for a fully elected House and in 2007 MPs voted either for a completely elected second chamber, or one that was 80 per cent elected and 20 per cent appointed. In 2008 the Government finally published a white paper which fleshed out these two options in a House of Lords with around 450 members, elected for terms of between 12 and 15 years.

The political authority of the House of Lords rests upon its historic role in the constitution. However, without a popular mandate, its legislative power has long been secondary to that of the House of Commons. Whilst it initiates some *private member's and *public bills, the bulk of government legislation, and all the most important, is initiated in the House of Commons. The Lords have little power to block a determined government. During the 1945–51 Labour Governments the 'doctrine of the mandate' principle was adopted by Conservative peers, by which they accepted the Labour programme which had received a clear electoral mandate. This doctrine has largely been followed ever since. The 1949 Parliament Act further stipulates that even if

minded to the Lords can only delay public bills for up to thirteen months (reduced from two years under the 1911 Parliament Act). Nevertheless, the House of Lords carved out a routine role of detailed scrutiny of legislation not possible in the House of Commons. This has led to many amendments without compromising the basic principles of bills, which governments have accepted. The work of the Lords select committees has also been influential on ministers and government departments. The Wakeham Commission recommended that the House of Lords should add to its existing roles an interest in the constitution through three new committees on the constitution, human rights, and devolution.

Despite the polite 'old world' atmosphere in which it implements its limited legislative and deliberative roles, the House of Lords has still been highly political in taking on government on specific issues. The Lords thwarted previous Labour Government attempts to reform the House of Lords in 1948–9 and 1968–9. Between 1979 and 1990 many saw the House of Lords as the only real parliamentary opposition to the Thatcher Governments. After 1997 the Lords also successfully thwarted attempts by the Blair Government to abolish section 28 of the Local Government Act, which allows positive material on homosexuality in schools. The creation of the largely appointed House of Lords in 1999 saw an increase in opposition to government bills, with the Government being defeated 245 times in the 2001–5 Parliament. There was particular opposition on Government proposals to combat terrorism. Many would suggest that an elected composition would enhance still further the legitimacy of the Lords' right to question legislation emanating from the House of Commons. Such a situation would create relations between the House of Commons and House of Lords that perhaps would be more typical of bicameral legislatures. JBr

• House of Lords website.

House of Representatives The lower house of the United States *Congress. It has 435 members elected from equal population districts, and a single elected non-voting delegate from each of the District of

Columbia, Puerto Rico, and Guam. It has an equal status with the *Senate on most matters, but a superior status in tax and spending.

• House of Representatives website.

housework Housework is seen by *feminists as 'work' within the domestic space. It involves labour and efficiency as any other job in the public sphere. Housework is often recognized as another dimension of 'natural' feminine attributes. Gender differences and job inequalities are sharpened due to the low status given to housework in hierarchical institutions.   STH

humanitarian intervention Entry into a country by the armed forces of another country or international organization with the aim of protecting citizens from persecution or the violation of their human rights. The creation of safe havens in north and south Iraq following the *Gulf War and intervention in Somalia, Haiti, Liberia, Rwanda, Bosnia, Kosovo, and Sierra Leone have seen (mostly American-led) military operations to protect certain groups in the population. The Russian government argued that its military intervention in Chechnya was necessary to protect the rights of the Russian minority (*see also* CRIMEA CRISIS). Whilst increasingly cited as a justification for armed incursions in crisis-ridden countries, the legal and political boundaries of humanitarian intervention are ambiguous. The United Nations Charter 2(4) states: 'All Members shall refrain in their international relations from the threat or use of force against the territorial integrity or political independence of any state', although the *United Nations Security Council has authorized specific interventions.

In 2005 the *United Nations General Assembly unanimously endorsed the *responsibility to protect (R2P) principle. The agreement is set out in paragraphs 138, 139, and 140 of the World Summit outcome document. These outline a threefold responsibility and 'triggering' for intervention. First, every state has a responsibility to protect their population (not just citizens) from *genocide, *war crimes, *crimes against humanity, and *ethnic cleansing. Second, the international community has a responsibility to encourage and assist states so that they can fulfil their primary responsibility to protect people from the four crimes. Third, if a state is 'manifestly failing' to protect their population from the four crimes then the international community has a responsibility to take timely and decisive action on a case-by-case basis. This includes a broad range of coercive and non-coercive measures under Chapters VI, VII, and VIII of the United Nations Charter. At the time of writing, R2P has been invoked in more than forty-five Security Council resolutions, such as Resolutions 1970 and 1973 regarding the *Libyan Civil War in 2011. That said, the justification of humanitarian intervention in order to protect the lives and rights of a minority still raises dilemmas over when it is right to intervene (or indeed when not to intervene) because what is meant as a 'manifest failure' remains unclear. Thus the balancing of minority and majority rights, the amount of death and damage that is acceptable in a humanitarian military operation, and how to reconstruct societies after intervention still remain the key questions.   AG

human rights Human rights are a special sort of inalienable moral entitlement. They attach to all persons equally, by virtue of their humanity, irrespective of race, nationality, or membership of any particular social group. They specify the minimum conditions for human dignity and a tolerable life.

The first generation of civil and political rights restricts what others (including the state) may do, for example, life, liberty, and freedom from torture. A second generation of social and economic rights requires active provision, such as by imposing an obligation on government. Some analysts call them ideals, often constrained in practice by inadequate resources. A third generation concerns such rights as peace, development, and humanitarian assistance. While many of the claims attach to individuals some belong to collectivities, such as the right to national self-determination.

Rights have been catalogued by the *United Nations in the Universal Declaration of Human Rights (1948)—a General Assembly resolution that is not legally binding—and elsewhere. Other accounts are present in many countries' constitutions and regional organizations of states including Europe.

Statements about human rights are normative and prescriptive. Critics reject the idea of universality, or allege particular accounts are ideological or culture-specific, as in the claim from Singapore's leadership that 'Asian values' offer a more appropriate account of rights to some East Asian societies. Some commentators argue that even human rights may be violated for reasons of state or public emergency. Human rights claims challenge state sovereignty and power. But increasingly respect for rights contributes to a state's international legitimacy and reputation, and increasingly the view is taken that external pressures should be brought to bear on governments that abuse basic human rights. A distinctive example is situations where there are accusations of genocide. PBl

Human Rights Act (1998) *See* EUROPEAN CONVENTION FOR THE PROTECTION OF HUMAN RIGHTS AND FUNDAMENTAL FREEDOMS.

human security The origins of the phrase 'human security' are often traced back to the 1994 United Nations Human Development report, which 'explores the new frontiers of human security in the daily lives of the people'. Set against the state-centric backdrop of *international relations, the value of the human-security approach lies in its innovative focus on the individual rather than the state. The report highlighted that whilst the vast majority of states had secured their right to freedom, individuals remained vulnerable to local, national, and global threats, such as disease, poverty, terrorism, and pollution. Although initially contextualized in relation to development, human security began to have broader resonance as scholars championed the idea that individuals, as opposed to states, should be the referent object of security in international relations/security studies. Both human security and *critical security studies challenged the state-centric orthodoxy of international relations and security studies. However, the emancipatory value of human security has come under scrutiny. This is captured in Edward Newman's 2010 call for scholars to develop critical human security studies (CHSS). The hope is that CHSS can

recapture the emancipatory foundation of human security by further challenging the conceptual underpinning of state-centric approaches. AG

human trafficking The illegal recruitment and transportation of human beings for the purpose of exploitation, often through the use of force and coercion, including fraud, deception, and abduction. The international legal definition was established in the Palermo Protocol and adopted by the *United Nations General Assembly in 2000. Exploitation can include forced labour, commercial sexual exploitation, or the removal and sale of organs. The form and degree of coercion required to qualify an incident as trafficking is controversial and frequently debated.

Vulnerability to trafficking is shaped by poverty, gender and racial inequality, and discrimination on the basis of ethnicity, caste, and other factors. Like other forms of illegal activity in the global economy, human trafficking is difficult to measure.

Politicians and advocacy groups often use the concept to describe a contemporary global trade in human beings which they argue is akin to the nineteenth-century slave trade. However, experts have argued that this characterization and analogy perpetuates common misconceptions about trafficking, including its scale, geography, and the agency of perpetrators and victims. Some critics claim that the discourse of trafficking has depoliticized debates about contemporary migration and is used as a discursive 'fig leaf' for restrictive migration policies by Western governments. GLB

Hume, David (1711–76) Scottish empiricist philosopher and historian, who, born in Edinburgh and remaining unmarried, held several posts in his life, but never achieved high office in the academic world or elsewhere. He did, though, achieve the 'literary fame' which was his sole expressed ambition: his work was widely admired and discussed in Scotland, France, England, and beyond, and his reputation, though viciously attacked by eminent Victorians such as Carlyle, has been maintained on a high level ever since.

This reputation is not primarily as a political theorist, but in the fields of epistemology and ethics, where his *Enquiry concerning Human Understanding* and *A Treatise of Human Nature* respectively have given him an undisputed eminent place in the history of philosophy. His position in the history of political thought is not generally considered to be so large. There is no work comparable to Hobbes's *Leviathan*, Rousseau's *Social Contract*, or even Locke's *Two Treatises on Civil Government*; it is a consequence of his approach to politics that there could not be. Hume's conventionally 'political' works consist of something between a dozen and two dozen essays, depending on what one means by politics. Yet Hume is, in many respects, a deeply political writer. His epistemology cannot be ignored by anyone seeking to explain politics, his consideration of the nature of morality, including convention, justice, and property, is an important political theory in all but conventional categorization and these are complemented by his overtly political essays and his *History of England* in six volumes.

Hume wrote forcefully, in elegant, common language: no British philosopher is further removed than Hume from the Germanic habit of inventing terms and creating concepts. Yet Hume's clarity is often said to be deceptively, even deceitfully, misleading: the contradictions and ambiguities of Hume's writings as a whole are legion and he can make an apparently simple concept, like 'the association of ideas', which he is often accused of overusing, into a puzzle as unclear as anything in Kant or Hegel. Take, for example, four famous Humean arguments:

1 '*Hume's fork*': the insistence, most clearly in the *Enquiry*, that true statements come in two forms, 'relations of ideas' (especially mathematics) and 'matters of fact'. Books full of claims which fall into neither category should be 'consigned to the flames'. This argument suggests Hume as an intellectual ancestor of the logical positivists.

2 *Atheism*: the *Dialogues concerning Natural Religion*, consistently with much of Hume's epistemological writings, appear to favour rejection of all the established arguments in favour of religion including the ontological argument, the necessity of a Creator, and so on.

3 *Causation*: Hume argued that causes did not have a separate existence, that the idea of causation must be reduced to the 'constant conjunction' of what we imagine to be causes and their effects.

4 *The gap between facts and values*: or, in Hume's terms, the impossibility of inferring an 'ought' from an 'is'.

Yet all of these arguments, put so forcefully by Hume in famous passages, are contradicted or mitigated elsewhere in his writings and have been interpreted in widely different ways. The 'relations of ideas' category is expanded far beyond the bounds allowed by the logical positivists and Hume insists on the untenability of complete scepticism. Not only is there private correspondence which seems to establish Hume as a religious believer, but the *Dialogues* contain convincing arguments in favour of an anthropomorphic analogy for any principle of order in the universe and for the necessity of religion reinforcing morality.

The argument from 'constant conjunction' can be cited as both a scepticism about science and as a redefining basic principle for Newtonian physics and thus modern science. Some critics have argued that Hume, far from instigating a rigid distinction between fact and value, collapsed such a distinction and convincingly portrayed certain kinds of morality as natural and compelling because of their naturalness.

Similar contradictions threaten the clarity of his political writings. In his essay, 'Of the Original Contract', he sustains, with great force and elegance, a contempt for the plausibility and usefulness of any idea of government being based on the kind of contract posited by Hobbes, Locke, or Rousseau. Government is founded on 'usurpation or conquest'; it must be supported because of its beneficial consequences and it would not last five minutes if subjected to the test of having to fulfil a valid contract. But in many other passages, including the essay *Of the Origin of Government*, he seems much more sympathetic to a contractual account. In *That Politics may be reduced to a Science* he argues against the possibility of general prescriptions of how government should be organized while in *Idea of a Perfect Commonwealth* he appears to offer us just such a general prescription, a devolved, elected, republic, based on a property franchise with a separation of powers.

The accusation must be considered that Hume was inconsistent and negative. Contesting such considerations must start with Hume's beliefs and prejudices about English history. His *History* ends with the 'Glorious Revolution' of 1689: 'we, in this island, have ever since enjoyed if not the best system of government, at least the most entire system of liberty, that ever was known among mankind.' Nothing could be stronger or more consistent in Hume's view of the world than the contrast between his abhorrence for the doctrinaire, vicious milieu of the seventeenth century, with its religious persecutions, civil wars, and political crises, and his gratitude for finding himself alive in the eighteenth century. His own age, as he portrayed it in his essays on economics and the arts, was an unprecedented period of peace, stability, prosperity, and freedom of expression. His disgust at the excesses of the seventeenth century is well shown in his version of the Popish Plot period of 1678-9 with its show trials (as we should now call them) and its hypocrisies, in which both sides, supporters of Parliament and monarch, were equally objectionable in his view.

How did the happy condition of the eighteenth century arise? On what principle was it based? How was it to be maintained? These were essential questions for Hume and he had subtle and important answers to them. The settlement of British political problems had not come about because the right side won, still less because the correct doctrine prevailed. Of William of Orange, the principal beneficiary of the Glorious Revolution, he says, 'though his virtue, it is confessed, be not the purest, which we meet with in history, it will be difficult to find any person, whose actions and conduct have contributed more eminently to the general interests of society and of mankind'. Thus he supports the same side as John Locke, but regards Locke as taking the right side, not just for the wrong reason, but for the wrong sort of reason. Acceptance of the Glorious Revolution and the subsequent Hanoverian Settlement starts with its good effects. One reason these effects are good is that they give a preponderant victory to the Whigs, but not a total victory: the monarchy remains, with

Hume's support, allowing a government which is 'mixed' in its principles and institutions and therefore moderate in its nature. Above all, political life is no longer a contest over abstract or religious truth; Hume had as much contempt for *divine right as for contract theory, and as much again for the popular political dogmas they generated: the Tory doctrine of passive obedience and Whig doctrine of the right of resistance. Whatever the subtleties of Hume's religious position, he was consistently opposed to religion in its seventeenth-century form, which claimed philosophical truth and moral substance. By contrast, he saw 'ancient religion' as a benign package of myths, morals, and allegiances which required no dogma.

Hume's philosophical arguments and historical judgements can be synthesized as follows: the purpose of government is the well-being of the people, but you cannot bring government into being or destroy governments in relation to that purpose, because to do so would not be beneficial. Governments arise by contingency; they are worthy of obedience not because of any rigorous principle, but because their maintenance allows the freedom and stability which is conducive to the general wellbeing. Human institutions are founded not on abstract principles, but on conventions; justice and property are necessary conventions in conditions of scarcity. Some conventions have a natural basis, not in that they can be derived naturally from reason, but in the sense that they flow from the sympathy which exists naturally in all of us and links us together. The question for political theorists is not, 'In what circumstances can we justify acceptance of and obedience to government?', but 'How can we understand the nature of the bonds which form a society and give us the habit of being governed without resorting to the kind of theological and moral dogmas which are intellectually unacceptable and practically dangerous?' Most elements of this body of theory are shared with Hume's contemporaries: the relativism and passion for moderate government is shared with Montesquieu; the ultimately sensual purpose is shared with the utilitarians, though without a linear concept of well-being or the apparent rigour of Bentham; the belief in a society based on convention, which grows in conditions of stability, is shared with Burke. Yet the whole constitutes one of the most subtle and important of modern political philosophies.   LA

hung parliament A term for the situation when after an election no political party has an overall majority in the UK House of Commons. Without a written constitution the response to such a circumstance is governed by statements by courtiers and senior civil servants as to what the constitution requires the monarch to do. The most famous of these statements were by Sir Alan Lascelles, private secretary to George VI, in a letter to *The Times* in 1950, and by Lord Armstrong, secretary to the cabinet between 1979 and 1987, in a radio interview in 1991. The incumbent prime minister may continue in office and offer a queen's/king's speech: that is, a speech delivered by the monarch but written by the government, outlining its programme. This is likely only if the prime minister's party still has the largest number of seats, or a pact with another party can be engineered to ensure an overall majority. If the prime minister cannot command the largest party in the Commons and has no pact then the prime minister may ask the monarch to dissolve Parliament and call a further election. In the absence of precedent it remains unclear whether the monarch would be obliged to accede to this request. More likely, the prime minister would resign and advise the monarch upon a successor. Usually the monarch would heed that advice, although in the last resort the monarch is not bound to do so. The new prime minister would then form a government, and if a working majority could again not be sustained, a dissolution of Parliament and calling of a second election would be sought and gained from the monarch.   JBr

Huntington, Samuel (1927–2008) American political scientist, best known for his 1993 theory and later 2006 book *The Clash of Civilizations*, in which he predicted that the post-*Cold War era would be characterized by conflicts between cultural identities and religious values instead of conflicts between states. Huntington argued that the biggest threat to Western-dominated world order would come from *Islamic fundamentalism and predicted that cultural wars would continue to increase as processes of *globalization brought civilizations into more immediate contact. Although often debunked as a form of *cultural imperialism and potential racism, his ideas continue to be debated, particularly after the *September 11th 2001 terrorist attacks and ensuing military operations in the *Afghanistan War in 2001 and the *Iraq War in 2003.

hyperglobalism A conceptual offshoot of *globalization theory arguing that globalization represents a historically unprecedented and potentially revolutionary form of cultural, social, political, economic, and technological advancement towards a more unified and borderless world. Hyperglobalism is underwritten by the notion that technologies such as the Internet, mobile phones, and computerized financial systems drive positive global interconnectedness and prosperous dynamism.

IAEA *See* INTERNATIONAL ATOMIC ENERGY AGENCY.

Ibn Khaldun (Abd al-Rahman Abu Zaid Wali al-Din ibn Khaldun) (1332–1406) Historian, sociologist, and philosopher, born in Tunis. His reputation rests on *The Book of Exemplaries and the Collection of Origins and Information respecting the History of the Arabs, Foreigners and Berbers and Others who possess Great Power* completed in 1377 and published in seven volumes in Cairo in 1384. His work, in a translation by Silvestre de Sacy, began to be noticed in Europe in 1806. Essentially a historical account of the peoples of North Africa, the introduction, the 'Muqaddima', attempted a systematic study of a methodology and an analysis of the development of Arab-Muslim history and society.

Ibn Khaldun was educated in the various branches of Arabic learning—Qur'an, grammar, language, law, logic, mathematics, philosophy, natural science, traditions, and poetry. His teacher was a student of Ibn Rushd (*Averroës). He held various positions in government in Spain. In Egypt in 1384 he began a new career in the judiciary, where on several occasions he served as the chief Qadi of the Maliki school of jurisprudence. Ibn Khaldun lived at a time of disruption and instability throughout the Islamic world. The lands of the Levant had been subject to the Crusades until the crusaders were swept away by the Ottoman Turks in the fourteenth century. In 1258 Genghis Khan and his Mongol forces swept through the Fertile Crescent, in the process destroying forever what was left of the Abbasid Caliphate, before being halted by the Mamluks in southern Syria (modern Palestine). However, within fifty years, the Mongols themselves became Islamized. In the early fourteenth century, Mongols from Central Asia under the leadership of Timurlane again invaded the northern Eurasian continent (today's Azerbaijan, North India, Afghanistan, Iran, Iraq) as far as Damascus before he turned north to defeat the Ottomans in Anatolia. In the west, the Spanish Reconquista was in the process of driving the Muslims from Spain.

Ibn Khaldun did not see this period as one of transition but of decline interrupted by vain attempts at renewal. He concentrated on the understanding and meaning of the history through which he had lived, focusing on the rise and fall of dynasties or states (*dawla*), examining the development of the internal structures of the society in which he lived. He concluded that the progress of history—the emergence of communities and the creation and decline of the dynastic state—hinged critically on group solidarity (*asabiyya*), culture (*umran*) and power. In his view, the social nature of man impelled him to form cooperative communities for survival. The form that the community took was conditioned by the specific circumstances of its material existence—the climate and material environment. Nomadic society based on kinship possessed the strongest characteristic of solidarity. By its nature, nomadic life was non-territorial, frequently marginal, distinctly egalitarian, and precarious. The coming together of tribal solidarity and vitality with the prophetic impulse of Islam transformed nomadic solidarity into an inspired historic movement. The expansion of Arab tribal power resulted in a dynastically ruled complex community pursuing both nomadic and sedentary lifestyles. A dynastically ruled state, however, contained within it the seeds of its decay and destruction. The security of existence in settled communities, the comparative luxury, the segmented character of labour, the conspicuous consumption of the elite eventually led to a decline in resolute boldness and integrity, and to rising corruption. Populations debilitated by desire and moral decline and most importantly by a loss of a sense of solidarity resulted in the fall of dynasties from internal decay or conquest.

Though not akin to Enlightenment thinking because of his combining both rationalism and religious assumptions, his approach to historical analysis has been thought modern because of rational characteristics, and social scientific quality with some similarities to historical materialism. BAR

Ibn Rushd *See* AVERROËS.

idealism 1. The doctrine that the external world must be understood through consciousness. *Plato, *Kant, and *Hegel all opposed the empiricist claim that knowledge of the world could only be gained by experience. On the contrary, claimed Kant, experience could only be made sense of by drawing on categories of thought and the concepts of space and time, and these were prior to experience. By extension, particular forms of experience could be ordered and judgements made about them only in relation to something beyond themselves: for instance, moral experience in relation to an ideal of the good, and religious experience in relation to God.

2. Loosely, any behaviour shaped by the pursuit of an unattainable objective such as equality or justice, or by a general principle such as public service.

3. Specifically, from sense 2, in a generally pejorative sense, to denote liberals who had sought to bring an end to war after 1918 through the *League of Nations and the principle of *collective security. They were charged with having advocated a system of international relations that set order above justice, so favouring the dominant powers of the day against revisionist states such as Germany, Japan, or the Soviet Union, and with supposing that desire alone could end war in spite of supposedly immutable realities such as human nature, national interest, the *security dilemma, or history.

Those *realists, such as E. H. *Carr, who argued for a foreign policy based on practical acquiescence in the tendency of history drew heavily on the German philosophical idealism of *Hegel and his successors in order to oppose the popular or common-sense idealism of their day, and this semantic shift has sometimes caused confusion. CJ

ideal-regarding principle A distinction was drawn by Brian *Barry between ideal-regarding and want-regarding principles employed in political argument. A want-regarding principle takes into account all the wants persons happen to have. An ideal-regarding principle is selective about those wants: for example, it might aim to exclude consideration of those wants which persons have, the fulfilment of which would be inimical to their welfare. There are, of course, many different 'ideals' which would license such selectivity. AR

ideology Any comprehensive and mutually consistent set of ideas by which a social group makes sense of the world may be referred to as an ideology. Catholicism, Islam, Liberalism, and Marxism are examples. An ideology needs to provide some explanation of how things have come to be as they are, some indication of where they are heading (to provide a guide to action), criteria for distinguishing truth from falsehood and valid arguments from invalid, and some overriding belief, whether in God, Providence, or History, to which adherents may make a final appeal when challenged.

The term has had very variable connotations, and at least in its dominant sense it has been necessarily pejorative, a term always to be used of the ideas of others, never of one's own. For some, notably Marxists, ideology has generally been used to describe the world-view of the dominant. Even for Karl *Mannheim, no Marxist, ideology sought to maintain the status quo and was to be distinguished from utopian thought, directed towards change. For others ideology might be applied to any set of ideas, such as the *Enlightenment, so abstract as to provide an impractical guide to policy-making and so ambitious as to advocate wholesale reform.

The Marxist account of ideology faces three hard questions. First, why should one class, the bourgeoisie, have an ideology consistent with its interests, while another, the proletariat, is afflicted with belief in the dominant ideology, resulting in action based on false consciousness and quite contrary to its true interests? Secondly, how is it that anyone brought up within society can attain a position of objectivity from which to describe and judge the ideologies which constrain others? Thirdly, what set of beliefs could such an independent judge possibly hold that were not themselves an ideology, subject to objective judgement in their turn or else as groundless as all others?

Materialist philosophies have claimed in the face of these objections that the intellectual, through consciousness of the relativity and historicity of ideas, is capable of liberation from the bonds of ideology. But once this is raised from the casual observation that intellectuals may be better able than most to see both sides of an argument, it is in immediate danger of collapsing into Hegelian idealism, an ideology if ever there was one, in which history takes the form of the progressive liberation of the human spirit from ideology, culminating in absolute freedom. CJ

images (three) of international relations

The three images of *international relations, also known as the 'three levels of analysis', were first introduced by Kenneth *Waltz in his 1959 book *Man, State and War*. According to Waltz there exist three levels of analysis that can help scholars better understand the causes of war: first image, second image, and third image. Under this framework of categorization, the first image seeks to examine the causes of war by studying the psychological and contextual dispositions of key individuals, statesmen, and politicians, such as Napoleon and *Hitler. Nevertheless, in *classical realism the examination of particular individuals is less important, preferring to examine elements of human nature more generally as the primary driver of conflict and war. Whereas the first image focuses on people, the second image examines the domestic make-up of states and its effect on how international actors are predisposed towards or away from conflict. For example, it is often argued that *authoritarian regimes are generally more prone to go to war due to a lack of checks and balances, while democratic states are often seen as *liberal promoters of *democratic peace. In the third image, the role of the *state system and its effects on state behaviour are the primary level of examination. This is also the preferred image of *neorealism, which focuses on the role of *anarchy within the *international system and how this structural

condition (or lack thereof) creates incentives for conflict and war. The key to this, argues neorealism, is that international anarchy (lack of world government) forces all states and peoples (regardless of internal make-up) to behave as independent rational actors in a *Hobbesian world of diffidence and self-reliance, which will incentivize *arms races, *alliances towards a *balance of power, and increased conditions for war. Although the three images have traditionally been associated with the study of war, they have also been adopted by international relations scholars who employ them for explanatory analysis in other areas within the discipline.

IMF (International Monetary Fund)

The International Monetary Fund was the centrepiece of the *Bretton Woods agreement of July 1944. It was agreed that primary responsibility for the regulation of monetary relationships among national economies, of private financial flows, and of balance of payments adjustment should rest in the hands of public *multilateral institutions and national governments with a view to underpinning a cooperative international economic order. The International Monetary Fund, alongside its sister institution the International Bank for Reconstruction and Development (IBRD or *World Bank), was to be the main vehicle for achieving these ends.

The IMF was to oversee the exchange rate mechanism and the international payments system, to act as the main source of liquidity to facilitate trade, and to monitor national economic policies with a view to avoiding policies in one country which would unduly prejudice the others. IMF member states provided the Fund with resources through a system of quotas more or less proportional to the size of respective national economies, and they received votes in the Fund relative to these quota contributions. In this way the power of the richest countries was entrenched, especially the United States, which still commands just under 17 per cent of the votes. As exchange rates were to be fixed (though adjustable if circumstances warranted), countries with balance of payments deficits might experience difficulties defending their par value and also shortages of foreign exchange. In this case, governments could avoid devaluation and shortages of foreign exchange, at least in the short term, by borrowing from the

Fund and thus finance the deficit without excessively disrupting the continuity of domestic macroeconomic policy or international monetary stability.

As the system evolved, a number of conventions were established (mostly under American pressure) concerning the working of the system. If borrowing began to exceed a country's original quota, increasingly onerous conditions (*conditionality) would be imposed on any further borrowing and would be enforced by Fund officials (backed by the richest members). These conditions concerned the domestic economic policies the debtor country was to follow, theoretically leading to a process of domestic *structural adjustment to overcome the underlying causes of the payments deficit and thereby maintaining the fixed exchange rate system, world payments equilibrium, and the cooperative nature of international economic relations on issues such as trade. Over time 'conditionality' has become more severely defined, especially as developed countries, as creditors, realized that they were unlikely ever to have to submit to it.

Initially, the Fund was severely underfinanced and could achieve little until most currencies could survive free convertibility with the US dollar. It never played the role foreseen at Bretton Woods, that of main provider of liquidity to the international monetary system. It did help with balance of payments lending, but often Fund resources were overwhelmed by the volume of short-term capital flows, and cooperation among central banks had to substitute in a crisis. In 1976 at its Jamaica conference the Articles of Agreement of the IMF were altered to usher in an era of floating exchange rates, in existence de facto since 1973. The IMF, however, became much more prominent in the 1980s when it emerged as the key institution in the management of the Less Developed Country (LDC) debt crisis. Here the development of conditionality came into its own, promoted by the small number of creditor countries holding the majority of IMF votes. The IMF became the designated coordinator of lending to facilitate continued debt repayment, often imposing painful restructuring programmes on indebted countries with a view to maintaining the stability of the international financial system and encouraging additional (if limited) lending from other

sources to troubled LDC economies. With the collapse of the Soviet bloc and the economically troubled transition of these countries to liberal market economic structures, the Fund has once again enhanced its role as a coordinator of international lending activity and associated liberal market reforms.

Despite the apparent failure of the IMF to fulfil its Bretton Woods promise, its officials have nonetheless functioned as a catalyst to international monetary and policy cooperation, and have helped galvanize cooperative management of monetary crises over the years. It remains an important symbol of international cooperation, albeit heavily weighted in favour of the interests of the developed market economies. As in the case of the *World Trade Organization and trade liberalization, IMF policy is shrouded in controversy. The tremendous growth of global capital flows, associated with the emergence of floating exchange rates and liberalization of financial markets and capital accounts, has been punctuated by frequent and severe financial crisis to which transition and developing economies have been particularly vulnerable. The success of structural adjustment policies in the weaker economies is seldom obvious in the longer run, though short-term stabilization measures have worked rather well if painfully. Countries taking the medicine of conditionality and liberal reform have frequently faced further rounds of crisis and adjustment. A range of scholars claim that global liberalization has been accompanied by growing inequality and that problems of poverty alleviation cannot be addressed in the current policy paradigm. IMF annual meetings have thus become magnets for protest against the policies the IMF and its most powerful government members promote. Recently, particularly since the Asian financial crisis (1997–8) and ongoing volatility, the IMF has begun to respond to criticism, taking up proposals for more orderly sovereign debt workouts with greater responsibilities for private investors and creditors. Another matter of controversy has been the shift of quotas and voting shares from member states with advanced economies to those with rapidly developing emerging economies, such as China and India. A member state cannot unilaterally increase its quota, and in 2001 China was prevented from doing so as much as it wanted. China and other countries were granted a further increase in 2005. In 2008, a major reform package was agreed to enable a more significant shift in quotas and voting rights. DH/GH

SEE WEB LINKS

• IMF website.

immigration When persons enter a destination country in order to settle, temporarily or permanently, sometimes with the intention of acquiring citizenship. Temporary immigration is distinct from tourism or business journeys, where there is no intention to settle. Immigration is an umbrella term and includes, *inter alia*, labour, asylum, student, and family immigration. Citizens of the destination country who are returning from having lived abroad may count as immigrants in official statistics.

Immigration policy is premised on the right of sovereign states to exclude foreign nationals at their discretion. Such a right to exclude is argued to be a cornerstone of national *self-determination and state *sovereignty. Those that dispute it argue that there is a *human right to freedom of movement and that immigration restrictions cement global inequalities by preventing the poor from immigrating to a developed state in order to improve their opportunities. The right of states to exclude is regulated and limited by international law relating to asylum seekers and *refugees, yet not all states have signed to or adhere to these Conventions.

Most states impose strong immigration restrictions, and policies often favour immigrants who are highly skilled or wealthy, or who have a family connection to the destination country. Immigration policy sometimes favours immigrants of a particular cultural or ethnic origin, such as the White Australia Policy of 1901–73. States control immigration at the territorial border as well as domestically. Examples of the latter include sanctions on employers and landlords if they hire or rent to illegal immigrants. States also control immigration by restricting the rights of immigrants and by limiting access to naturalization.

Since the end of the *Cold War, controlling immigration has become increasingly linked to states' security agendas, in particular since *September 11th 2001. Both the admission of immigrants and immigrant integration have witnessed *securitization in Western states as part of the War on Terror, amid fears of Islamist terrorism as well as increased prejudice against Muslims. The security dimension of immigration is also linked to perceived cultural, economic, and political threats. Native citizens may perceive of immigration as eroding their cultural way of life and national identity, as undermining their labour market and welfare state, and as politically disloyal or subversive. The extent to which such threats are perceived as strong by citizens is a good indicator of attitudes to immigration.

Voters in democratic states tend to express preferences for reducing the levels of immigration. Despite this, states cannot always control who enters their territories, as some enter without authorization ('irregularly'), some overstay their visas, and some are entitled to enter by international law, such as asylum seekers. Some states have been more relaxed about this kind of unauthorized immigration, as it becomes a desired supply of labour. Immigration is a policy area where most democratic states experience a gap between voters' preferences for closure and policy outcomes. At the same time, people tend to overestimate the share of immigrants in the population.

Depending on their status, immigrants often do not have access to the same rights as citizens. If they become permanent residents, they typically acquire social and some political rights. Complete political rights are acquired through naturalization. Temporary immigrants typically only have access to a narrow set of rights and may not have access to any routes for naturalization. This is often the case of so-called guest worker programmes, which were especially common in Europe during the 1960s and 1970s as a way of recruiting foreign workers. Germany's guest worker programme was one of the more extensive and granted few routes to citizenship even for the second and third generation of immigrants. CSA

immobilisme An expression associated with the French parliamentary regimes of the Third and *Fourth Republics, characterized by governmental instability and viewed as a serious obstacle to rapid socio-economic change and political adaptation. *Immobilisme* was the product of complex social cleavages which translated into weak, unstable coalition governments unable to agree on policy or programme. IC

impeachment A formal accusation of wrongdoing. To impeach a public official is to accuse him of crimes or misdemeanours in the execution of his duties. Impeachment proceedings normally occur in the lower house of a legislature, with any subsequent trial taking place in the upper house. In England, prior to the development of ministerial responsibility to Parliament, impeachment was used as a means whereby the legislature sought to call to account ministers who saw themselves as answerable primarily, if not exclusively, to the Crown. For example, in 1677 the House of Commons impeached the King's chief minister, the Earl of Danby, for negotiating a treaty with the King of France. The House of Lords declined to convict Danby although he was dismissed and committed to the Tower for five years. There have been only two cases of impeachment in Britain in the last two hundred years—Warren Hastings was impeached in 1786 arising from alleged misgovernment in India, and Lord Melville was impeached in 1806 for corruption in the use of public funds.

In the United States the Constitution provides for the impeachment of federal officials charged with 'Treason, Bribery, or other high Crimes and Misdemeanours'. The House of Representatives has 'the sole Power of Impeachment' and all impeachments are tried in the Senate with the Chief Justice of the US Supreme Court presiding. Conviction requires the agreement of two-thirds of the members present. Since 1787 seven federal judges have been removed following impeachment proceedings.

President Andrew Johnson was impeached in 1868, but survived in the Senate by one vote. In 1974 the House Judiciary Committee agreed three articles of impeachment against President Richard Nixon. Nixon was charged with the abuse of his power as President, obstruction of justice, and contempt of Congress. Before these articles could be voted on by the full House the President resigned, after being informed that his impeachment and conviction were otherwise inevitable. In 1998 the House agreed articles of impeachment against President Clinton on charges of lying about an extramarital relationship. The Senate failed to summon the necessary two-thirds to eject Clinton. The impeachment distracted all branches of the Federal government for more than a year. DM

imperialism Domination or control by one country or group of people over others. The precise nature and the causes of imperialism, the clearest examples, its consequences, and therefore the period which exemplifies it best, are all disputed.

The so-called new imperialism was the imposition of colonial rule by European countries, especially the 'scramble for Africa', during the late nineteenth century. Many writers construed imperialism in terms of their understanding of the motivating forces. Among these, *Hobson, *Luxemburg, *Bukharin, and especially *Lenin focused on economic factors, the rational pursuit of new markets and sources of raw materials. Lenin argued, in *Imperialism: The Highest Stage of Capitalism* (1917), that imperialism is an economic necessity of the industrialized capitalist economies, seeking to offset the declining tendency of the rate of profit, by exporting capital. It is the monopoly stage of capitalism.

*Schumpeter (1919) defined imperialism as the non-rational and objectless disposition on the part of a state to unlimited forcible expansion. Imperialism is rooted in the psychology of rulers and the effects of surviving pre-capitalist social structures, not the economic interests of nation or class. Alternative accounts view imperialism as: an outgrowth of popular nationalism; a device to underwrite the welfare state, which pacifies the working class (notably in Britain); personal adventurism; an application of *social Darwinism to struggles between races; a civilizing mission; and as simply one dimension of international rivalry for power and prestige. The latter implies that socialist states too were prone to be imperialistic.

All these 'push' versions share an endogenous or Eurocentric focus. Competing views emphasize pull factors: the contribution made at the periphery by local crises such as a power vacuum (perhaps induced by foreign intervention) and the collaboration of indigenous elites. Imperialism becomes a matter of accident as well as design.

'Informal imperialism' is said to render direct political control unnecessary, in the presence of other ways of exercising domination, for example through technological superiority or the free trade imperialism of a leading economic power, and cultural imperialism. Therefore, for modern neo-Marxists, capitalism in the West has been able to survive the process of decolonization; imperialism outlives the age of territorial annexation. Economic, financial, and social structures of *dependence remain, and are reproduced by *multinational corporations especially. The *developing countries are still *exploited and may even be subjected to indirect political control. Ghana's first President, Kwame *Nkrumah, depicted this imperialism without colonies in *Neo-Colonialism: The Last Stage of Imperialism* (1965).

Some analysts argue that the idea of imperialism loses its usefulness when equated with international capitalism, where asymmetries of economic power and integration are inevitable. They reject monocausal explanations, and stipulate that the political relationships must be specified closely before imperialism can be inferred from the existence of economic inequalities. Others argue that globalization, more specifically the global economic integration that applies the tenets of neo-liberal economics, makes forms of imperialism newly relevant in today's world. The same has been said of the drive by actors in the West and the United States in particular to disseminate their own political values and institutions more directly, through international democracy promotion. This too has been criticized as but another way of trying to maintain hegemony, through ideological and cultural means rather than by exerting physical or economic control. *See also* CULTURAL IMPERIALISM. PBl

imperial preference Rooted in a *geopolitical vision of enduring maritime Empire, the proposal that Britain and its dependencies should form a single *autarkic economy, raising tariffs against the rest of the world but extending preferential rates to one another, attracted considerable support once it was clear, by the 1890s, that the British economy was failing to keep pace with Germany and the USA. The persistent British attachment to *free trade survived the First World War but

was finally overcome in 1931 as the steeply declining relative competitiveness of the British manufacturing industry, coupled with more autarkic trade policies of the United States and elsewhere, coincided with an unprecedentedly sharp cyclical downturn in world demand and trade after 1929. The system of imperial preference was partially applied to the self-governing dominions following the Ottawa Conference of 1932 and was underpinned by formalization of a largely coextensive sterling area, especially after the imposition of exchange controls in 1939. The system gradually withered after 1945 as changing trade patterns reduced the importance of intra-Commonwealth commerce, while margins of preference were eroded by inflation and British membership of the European Free Trade Association (EFTA). The end, effectively, came with the twin blows of sterling devaluation in 1967 followed by British entry to the European Economic Community (now the *European Union) in 1973. CJ

imperial presidency *See* PRESIDENT.

impossibility theorem Proof that something cannot be done or cannot be had. The most famous such result in politics, due to K. J. Arrow, proves that if a choice or ordering system (such as an electoral procedure) produces results that are transitive and consistent (*see* ECONOMIC MAN), satisfies 'universal domain' (that is, works for all possible combinations of individual preference), satisfies the weak *Pareto condition, and is *independent of irrelevant alternatives, then it is dictatorial. 'Dictatorial' here has a technical meaning, namely, that the preferences of one individual may determine the social choice, irrespective of the preferences of any other individuals in the society. A non-technical interpretation of Arrow's theorem is as follows. In a society, group choices, or group rankings, often have to be made between courses of action or candidates for a post. We would like a good procedure to satisfy some criteria of fairness as well as of logicality. Arrow's startling proof shows that a set of extremely weak such criteria is inconsistent. We would like a good procedure to satisfy not only these but much more besides. But that is logically impossible.

Impossibility theorems save time. For instance, much work by electoral reformers amounts to trying to evade Arrow's theorem. As we know it cannot be done, this removes the need to scrutinize many such schemes in detail. This is not to say that all electoral systems are equally bad, however; there remains an important job for electoral reformers within the limit set by Arrow's and other impossibility theorems.

impoundment The refusal of the executive to spend funds which have been appropriated by the legislature. In the United States legislative control over the appropriations process allows members of Congress to play a substantial role in the shaping of public policy. Some occasional use of impoundment by the executive has traditionally been accepted as legitimate. Thus the Director of the Office of Management and Budget is authorized by law to make savings where changes in requirements allow. In addition, impoundments have on occasion been justified by reference to the chief executive's constitutional position as commander-in-chief. President Nixon, however, made much greater use of impoundment than before, appearing to use the device as a means of overturning policies that he found unacceptable. Members of Congress saw this as a serious assault on their constitutional prerogatives and responded by passing the 1974 Congressional Budget Reform and Impoundment Control Act. Under this legislation Presidents seeking to postpone or cancel the expenditure of appropriated funds must follow certain procedures. Postponement requires the chief executive to lay a specific deferral proposal before Congress which may be rejected by a resolution of either the House or the Senate. Cancellation of appropriations, on the other hand, requires the President to submit a 'rescission' proposal which is subject to approval by both houses. If Congress chooses not to act on such a proposal within forty-five days the executive is obliged to release the funds.   DM

incomes policy A government policy which seeks to regulate the rate of growth of wages and earnings through the use of such devices as norms, upper limits to the rate of increase expressed in cash or percentage terms, and review boards. Incomes policies became increasingly popular in advanced industrial countries as wage push inflation—that is, inflation (believed to be) caused by pressure from wage bargainers—under conditions of full employment became a central economic policy issue in the 1960s. Incomes policies were often linked with attempts at price restraint policies, and relied on either voluntary cooperation or statutory measures or some combination of both. They were associated with the development of a *corporatist pattern of politics. They fell out of favour with Western governments in the 1980s for a variety of reasons: reduced inflationary pressures in conditions of higher unemployment; the poor record of many of the policies implemented over the preceding twenty years; and the return of neo-liberal governments in the United States and Britain which believed that the task of governments was to exert monetary discipline so that workers would be dissuaded from seeking high pay rises, and employers would be better placed to resist them.   WG

incrementalism A model of the decision-making process in government which maintains that decisions are usually made on the basis of relatively small adjustments to the existing situation. As developed by Charles Lindblom, in an article on 'The Science of Muddling Through' published in 1959 and in subsequent books, the incrementalist model stated that policy-makers started the decision-making process not with some ideal goal in mind but from current policies. Only a limited number of policy options is reviewed, with changes being made at the margin. Yehezkel Dror criticized incrementalism on the grounds that it would apply only when: existing policy was broadly satisfactory; the nature of the problem did not change; and there was continuity of resources—conditions that would be met only under conditions of unusual social stability. Lindblom nevertheless maintained that in most stable political settings, the conditions for incrementalism were usually met. Incrementalism does seem to describe most budgetary decision-making in Western democracies. It is a less useful model when there is some considerable shock to the decision-making process such as that provided by a war or an economic crisis. WG

independence of irrelevant alternatives

The property that a group's choice between any *a* and *b* should be a function only of the choices of the individuals in the group between *a* and *b*. In particular, it should not change if some individuals in the group change their minds about the merits of *c* and/or *d*. To most, but not all, analysts of electoral systems, independence seems a highly desirable property, and the inconsistency of independence with other desirable properties which is proved by Arrow's *impossibility theorem therefore seems disturbing. Others, who disagree with the claim that independence is desirable, are less worried by Arrow's theorem and happier with voting systems, such as the *Borda count, which violate the independence of irrelevant alternatives.

To understand what is at stake, consider four skaters *A*, *B*, *C*, and *D*, and three judges *X*, *Y*, and *Z*. All four skaters are candidates for the open competition, and *A*, *B*, and *D* are also candidates for the under-25 competition. Both competitions are judged at the same time. The judges rank the candidates on their performance. Their rankings, in descending order, are:

Judge *X*: *ABCD*
Judge *Y*: *BCDA*
Judge *Z*: *CDAB*

By the Borda rule, *C* wins the open competition, and *B* wins the under-25 competition. Then an argument breaks out about the real quality of *C*'s performance. The judges look again at the video replay, and change their minds in various ways, now reporting the following rankings:

Judge *X*: *ACBD*
Judge *Y*: *BDAC*
Judge *Z*: *DACB*

No judge has changed her mind about the relative performance of the three under-25 contenders—their ranking remains unchanged. But the winner of the under-25 competition is now *A*, and *B* comes in only at third place. Thus the Borda rule violates the independence of irrelevant alternatives. *See also* PATH DEPENDENCE.

individualism Political individualism—in its most common, though not its only meaning—is a fundamental belief in the protection of the rights of the individual against the incursions of the state and of political power. However, there are many dimensions of individualism and it is possible to be an 'individualist' in several different fields. In general usage, an 'individualist' denotes a person with a distinctive or unusual personal style, who stands out from the mass. In metaphysics or ontology individualism is a belief that the universe consists fundamentally of individual particulars, separable entities. The opponents of individualism in this sense are holists or monists. The typical holist belief is that the relations (usually systematic relations in some sense) between entities have a more fundamental existence than the entities themselves.

Within the Christian religion individualism is closely associated with Protestantism and the belief in the human capacity for personal contact with God rather than the necessity of instruction through a hierarchy. 'Economic individualism' is usually taken to refer to a faith in the capacity of individual action and ambition, working through the market, to create wealth and to bring about progress. Political individualism, as defined above, is a more ambiguous idea.

The central question about individualism *per se* concerns the connections between these different dimensions. To what extent are they associated and what is the form of the association? Margaret Thatcher is often quoted as saying, 'There is no such thing as society, but only individuals', an overtly ontological statement which is ethically and politically suggestive. She actually added the words 'and families', which two words can be taken as the thin end of a more collectivist philosophical wedge. The connections between many of these dimensions is not logical entailment: there is no contradiction in being a philosophical monist, yet believing that individual initiative is the chief engine of economic progress or that persons possess rights which should be protected from the power of the state. But a desire for ideological consistency creates an association between the different dimensions of individualism.

There is also an important paradox at the heart of individualism. John Stuart *Mill offers one of the most morally appealing images of the individualist society, in which people are unconstrained by conformity and are able to advance civilization by the freest possible development of their own ideas and forms of expression. But how is this individualist society to be achieved? The society which most clearly embodies a belief in economic individualism in its norms and institutions, and the protection of individual rights in its constitution, is the United States. But the United States has often been criticized for its tendency to homogenize people, products, and places, and to require conformity from individuals. In the field of education, it has often been remarked that the withdrawal of authoritarian requirements for conformity in schools is often replaced by a more effective pressure for social conformity which arises from the pupils themselves. Many people believe that the 'totalitarian' Soviet Union produced greater individual artists and political thinkers than many more free societies. *In extremis*, the paradox implies that an element of despotism is required to produce the full flowering of the individual, that authoritarian political structures can serve to protect individuals from social and economic pressures to conform. *See* INTERESTS, INDIVIDUAL.   LA

individual ministerial responsibility
See MINISTERIAL RESPONSIBILITY.

industrial democracy (Participation in) government of a workplace by those who work there. Also known by its French name, *autogestion*, or more recently as cooperatively owned 'workplace democracy'. The idea of industrial democracy arose along with *socialism, but the two are not always intimate. A typical socialist commitment, from Clause IV of the constitution of the British Labour Party, as it was worded from 1918 until 1995, is to 'the common ownership of the means of production, distribution, and exchange, and the best obtainable system of popular administration and control of each industry or service'. But when, say, coal-mining is nationalized, do the mines then belong to the miners or to the people? The interests of the miners and the people as a whole are not identical: the former benefit from dear coal and the latter from cheap coal.

Socialist theorists have debated this many times: for instance in controversy between *Marx and *Bakunin in the 1870s, and especially between *c.*1900 and 1920, with the rise of revolutionary *syndicalism and of *guild socialism. Syndicalists believed that the workers in each industry should seize it, but had no theory of equitable or efficient distribution or exchange. Guild socialism supported non-revolutionary industrial democracy, but again without addressing issues of distribution or exchange. Therefore there was no sustained intellectual challenge to the standard pattern of nationalization, in which a railwayman might be appointed to the Coal Board and a miner to the Railways Board, but never a miner to the Coal Board.

The rise of *market socialism in the 1980s revived interest in industrial democracy, and concentrated attention on the relatively few successful experiments in it. The most notable of these is the network of producer cooperative enterprises at Mondragon, in the Spanish Basque country. Elsewhere, worker-controlled enterprises suffer chronically from shortages of capital and from conflict of interest between existing members and new entrants. These conflicts are least serious where a firm depends more on human capital (brain-power and skills) than on machinery, and so industrial democracy is commonest in service enterprises, notably in computing and information technology.

Not all advocates of industrial democracy are socialists: for instance Robert A. Dahl was a liberal who argued that people should have as much power to decide in the workplace as in the political marketplace.

industrial relations Interaction between employers, employees, and the government; and the institutions and associations through which such interactions are mediated. Government has a direct involvement in industrial relations, through its role as an employer; one that is particularly prominent in states where there are high levels of nationalization. Indirectly, government has a major role through the regulation of the economy and the relationship between employers and *trade unions. *See* CORPORATISM.

industrial society A society which exhibits an extended division of labour and a reliance on large-scale production using power-driven machinery. This characterization does not include any specification about markets, and thus industrial society has been seen as a common designation for recent capitalist and socialist formations. *Saint-Simon, who used the category of industrial society in historical contrast with military society, envisaged a technocratic future. Other writers who were conscious of the emergence of a new form of market society emphasized a further characteristic: widespread participation in the labour market, coupled with very limited participation of the direct producers in the product market. *Marx, for example, saw this as one characteristic of the capitalist form of industrial society. It has been suggested that post-industrial society has now emerged. In post-industrial society, division of labour may be looser than in industrial society because people have transferable skills; accordingly, the industrial discipline of *fordism is looser as well. Hence some Marxist scholars call modern post-industrial societies 'post-fordist'. AR

inflation A general and persistent increase in the price level. Inflation has been seen to lead to uncertainty, discouraging saving and investment, as well as affecting a country's international trade, via the exchange rate and balance of payments, and redistributing income, from those with savings to borrowers. With the increasing influence of *monetarist thinking during the 1970s, which itself was partly due to the jump in international inflation after the *OPEC crisis of 1973, the reduction of inflation became a key target of economic policy. Methods of controlling the price level centred first on *incomes policies, and when these failed, on *monetary policy. Since 1997, the standard method of inflation control has been an independent central bank.

INGO (international non-governmental organization) A not-for-profit organization, independent of governmental entities and not established by intergovernmental agreement, that is transboundary in its operations, collaborations, or resources. INGOs provide benefits to the public and may include, *inter alia*, *civil society and business organizations, trade unions, scientific organizations, religious organizations, and, under a broad but contested understanding, illicit organizations such as crime syndicates. *See also* NGO. FZ

initiative A particular form of the *referendum used especially in Switzerland and California. In the latter, to be placed on the ballot, an initiative needs signatures which equal 5 per cent of the vote for governor in the last election, or 8 per cent in the case of a proposal for a constitutional amendment. The initiative was used increasingly frequently in the 1970s and 1980s. Proposition 13 in 1978 severely restricted property taxes and was seen as the forerunner of taxpayers' revolts throughout the world. WG

institutional racism Phrase coined by the Macpherson Report (UK 1999; Cm 4262-I, paragraph 46:1) on Stephen Lawrence, a black teenager who was stabbed to death in London in 1993 by a gang of white youths. Nobody was ever convicted of his murder due to police blunders, which Sir William Macpherson's committee believed formed such a persistent pattern of prejudice (some of it unconscious) against black citizens that the Metropolitan Police was guilty of 'institutional racism'. The Metropolitan Police accepted the charge. So did the liberal heads of a number of other UK institutions, though not always those they led.

insurgency Armed uprising or rebellion against a government. The term has been used variously to describe revolutionary movements, civil wars, anti-colonial struggles, and terrorist agitation. The military campaign against the United States-led forces and government in Iraq after the 2003 war has been labelled an insurgency. *See also* ASYMMETRICAL WARFARE.

intelligence As *process* intelligence refers to the means by which information important to national security is requested, collected, analysed, and provided to policymakers. This generally contains an 'intelligence cycle' comprising five steps: planning and direction, collection, processing, analysis, and production and dissemination. The planning and direction process involves the management of the entire intelligence effort, from the clarification of the need for data to the final delivery of an intelligence product to a consumer. The collection phase involves the gathering, by various means, of raw data. This raw data is then interpreted or analysed in the next phase, giving the often fragmentary, contradictory, or seemingly valueless data meaning. The final step in the cycle, dissemination, involves the distribution of the finished intelligence to the correct consumer. Intelligence practice also includes counter-intelligence, safeguarding processes to protect one's own intelligence capability from the actions of other intelligence services, while undermining these 'foreign' efforts. Finally, intelligence practice covers covert action—operations designed to influence foreign governments, persons, or events in a particular direction, while keeping your own involvement secret. This can include propaganda and psychological warfare, whereby a state manipulates the news and media to influence the thinking of its people; political covert action, including providing physical and financial support to an enemy's enemy in order for them to gain strength; economic covert action to undermine or support the economic efforts of another to influence their stability; and paramilitary actions or support via arms supply, advice, and training. As *product* intelligence refers to the end result of the intelligence process; namely, that the information collected, analysed, and presented is important for making national-security decisions. For military intelligence this refers to the tactical and strategic information produced in order to inform military manoeuvres and decisions. RB

intelligence services All states gather intelligence about the 'enemies of the state' at home and abroad. The police and armed forces collect and act on intelligence, but the term intelligence services refers to services organized expressly for the collection of secret information. Such services also take covert (disavowable) activity on behalf of the state.

In Britain there are two such organizations, the Secret Intelligence Service (MI6), which is supposed only to operate abroad, and the Intelligence Service (MI5) which operates at home. They engage both in the collection of intelligence and in counter-intelligence—that is, in combating the activities of others, especially other intelligence services, working against British interests.

The evidence, much of it necessarily non-verifiable, is that the organizations devoted much energy into watching each other and that both were heavily penetrated by the very organization—namely, the Soviet intelligence service, the KGB—that they were supposed to be fighting. The existence and operations of both services raise problems of ministerial control and accountability to democratic or parliamentary procedures. Another general area of concern has been the extent of collaboration between intelligence services behind the backs of governments.

In the United States the Federal Bureau of Investigation (*FBI) (domestic) and the Central Intelligence Agency (*CIA) (overseas) play roles similar to the two British services, though they have always been much more open and, at least in theory, subject to democratic accountability. In the aftermath of the *September 11th 2001 attacks on the United States, a *Director of National Intelligence was given the role of coordinating the intelligence community. In the Soviet Union the KGB, the descendant of a series of intelligence organizations dating back to Tsarist times, was responsible for both domestic and external intelligence, and for a system of labour camps and prisons (the '*Gulag'). In Russia, the Federal Security Service (FSB) and the Foreign Intelligence Service (SVR) have taken over the domestic and external roles of the KGB. Other intelligence services which have attracted widespread interest include the French DGSE (Direction Générale de la Sécurité Extérieure) and the Israeli Mossad (external) and Shin Bet (internal). PBy

intelligentsia Russian word for intellectuals engaged in politics, as were most reformers in nineteenth-century Russia. After the *Russian Revolution, the word acquired a *Leninist tinge, being used both of and by intellectual supporters of Lenin(ism). Mostly now used sarcastically.

interdependence   Between   industrial democracies.

Influenced by the emergence of trade deficits after 1970, the rapid post-war spread of *multinational corporations, and the oil crisis of 1973–4, many political scientists in the United States reacted against the strong emphasis placed by the dominant *realist school of international relations upon the centrality of the state and the relative autonomy of its military and political power from social and economic pressures. R. O. Keohane and J. S. Nye coined the term 'complex interdependence' to describe the new pattern of relations between mature industrial democracies in which functionally defined international *regimes, comprising state agencies, specialized international organizations, and firms, managed matters as diverse as international trade, security, environmental issues, public health, and development assistance in ways which could no longer be relied upon to yield outcomes dictated by the United States as the conventionally pre-eminent power. Interdependence was also seen as an insurance against any collapse of Western security and the international economy that might follow a post-*Vietnam decline in United States hegemony, since it was argued that cooperative international regimes might outlast the *hegemon that had instigated them. Mere lexical coincidence has led to confusion between interdependence and neo-Marxist Latin American *dependency approaches to international relations, but the two are quite unrelated. CJ

interest groups Organizations seeking to advance a particular sectional interest or cause, while not seeking to form a government or part of a government. The term is often used interchangeably with *pressure group, and is being supplanted by *non-governmental organization. Interest groups may occasionally contest elections as a tactic to influence political parties, but they usually rely on a variety of campaigning and lobbying methods to influence government policy. Thus, *agrarian parties contest elections with the objective of forming a government or, more realistically, entering into a coalition with other governing parties, while farmers' organizations do not seek to enter government themselves. Yael Yishai has developed the term 'interest party' to refer to groups that straddle the fence between an interest group and a party such as the narrowly focused religious parties in Israel.

A considerable proportion of the literature on interest groups has focused on why individuals or institutions become members given that they can '*free ride' on the public policy objectives achieved by the group

without incurring the costs of membership. A variety of answers have been given to this problem, ranging from the selective incentives provided by the group in the form of services (M. *Olson, J. Q. Wilson), through the role of the entrepreneur–organizer in initiating the group (R. Salisbury), to the role of external patrons including government in assisting the group (J. Walker). In any event, the general tendency is for interest group memberships to increase while political party memberships decline.

Various attempts have been made to categorize interest groups to assist understanding of their methods of operation. The distinction between sectional groups and cause or promotional groups differentiates between those groups based on the representation of a particular defined interest (such as a trade union), and those which seek to advance a particular cause (such as animal welfare), and whose membership is open to all interested citizens. The distinction between insider groups and outsider groups draws a line between those groups that are regularly involved in the formulation of policy by ministers and civil servants, and those that have to rely on other methods of securing support such as letter-writing campaigns and demonstrations. The exact combination of methods used by interest groups to exert influence will vary from one political system to another. Indeed, the institutions on which interest groups focus their attention are one indicator of where power lies in a particular political system. Thus, in the United States, interest groups pay particular attention to influencing Congress, sometimes producing so-called iron triangles comprising interest groups, congressional subcommittees, and bureaucratic agencies. Interest groups are more likely to resort to the courts in the United States to secure their objectives than in many other political systems, reflecting the importance of the Supreme Court in the US political system. As the United States has a federal form of government, some attention has to be paid to developments at the state level. In Britain, where power is more concentrated in the executive branch, interest groups generally place a greater emphasis on influencing ministers and civil servants.

The influence of the media in Western societies, particularly in terms of political agenda-setting, has tended to increase, leading to a greater emphasis by pressure groups on securing media attention. This strategy has been particularly important for environmental groups as a means of placing their concerns on the political agenda. The development of political structures at the international level, notably the *European Union, has led to the development of increasingly effective international federations of national interest groups, and in some cases direct membership interest groups operating in Brussels. Concern is often expressed about the influence exerted by special or vested interests in democracies. This concern has particularly focused on the privileged status that appeared to be achieved by a limited range of economic interests in connection with the development of *corporatism, and the techniques used by some *lobbyists. *Freedom of association is, however, a basic principle of democratic societies, and interest groups provide a channel for special expertise to be made available to decision-makers, and for particular concerns to be brought to their attention. WG

interests, individual An individual's interests connect policies and actions adopted by him or her, or by other persons or governments, with want-satisfaction and possibly need-fulfilment. Interests express an instrumental relation between such policies and so forth, and an individual's preference-attainment. Hence if I claim that it is in my interests to receive a pay rise, I suggest that more pay will enable me to obtain more of what I want. Such judgements are often predictive, and may be wrong. Interests are important in political analysis because they are taken as guides to behaviour—if something is in my interests I may be expected to try to bring it about (*but see* COLLECTIVE ACTION PROBLEM). Again, in judging how others are likely to behave it may help to assess where their interests lie. When the relationship between a policy and its effects on a particular agent is a complex one, or where there is inequality in information, or when the agent is or has been subject to a power relation, the agent may not be the best judge of his or her own interests. In general, liberal political theory has given the agent a privileged position in the assessment of his

or her interests for two reasons: first, agents have knowledge of their own wants which may not be accessible to outsiders; and secondly, an external judgement may impose someone else's view of the good. Radical political theory has suggested that the real interests of agents are not those based on the whole set of their present wants, but those based upon the wants they would have if liberated in various ways from the heteronomy imposed by the society in which they live. Liberals recognize that agents can be mistaken about the impact of a policy or action on their want-satisfaction, and thus that they can be mistaken about their interests; radicals suggest that they may be systematically misled about their wants and needs, so that even if they correctly judge their interests on the basis of their perceived wants they will not pursue their real interests. *See also* PUBLIC INTEREST; INDIVIDUALISM. AR

intergovernmentalism Both a theory of integration and a method of decision-making in international organizations, that allows states to cooperate in specific fields while retaining their sovereignty. In contrast to supranational bodies in which authority is formally delegated, in intergovernmental organizations states do not share the power with other actors, and take decisions by unanimity. In the European Union, the Council of Ministers is an example of a purely intergovernmental body while the Commission, the European Parliament, and the European Court of Justice, represent the supranational mode of decision-making. Virtually all other integration initiatives, including those among developing countries, are almost fully intergovernmental.

As a theoretical approach to the study of European integration, intergovernmentalism was developed in the mid-1960s. Building on realist premisses, writers such as Stanley Hoffmann (1928–2015) highlighted the convergence of national interests and the will of states to cooperate as central to the analysis of regional integration. More recently Andrew Moravcsik's 'liberal intergovernmentalism' incorporates the role of domestic interests in helping define national state preferences, while still arguing that states have the ultimate control over the process and direction of integration. In studying

European integration, both the realist and the more liberal variants of intergovernmentalism have focused on major sets of inter-state bargains (especially intergovernmental conferences) and on the decision-making of the Council of Ministers, rather than on the role of the Commission, European Parliament, or societal actors.   AHu/LGm

intermestic A term used to denote the interconnectedness and relevance between domestic policy and international policy. Often used in relation to increasing processes of *globalization, intermestic is used both as an empirical signifier, such as 'globalization has blurred the lines between domestic and foreign policy issues' and/or as a normative claim, such as 'domestic policy should be reflected upon in light of its implications for foreign policy and its globalized results'. This is in contrast to mainstream views in *international relations, which often suggest that domestic policy and foreign policy are distinctively different and separate exercises.

internal colonialism Application of the theory of imperialism developed by *Lenin to *centre–periphery relationships within a country. The Leninist theory of imperialism argued that an imperialist country exported the exploitation of the proletariat to its colonies, or to other undeveloped countries whose terms of trade it could control; therefore the proletariat of the colonizing country were 'bought off' or subsidized by the proletariat of the exploited countries. Internal colonialism uses the same argument to account for the development of rich and poor regions within a country. Although the best-known such attempt—that by Michael Hechter (*Internal Colonialism*, 1975) to explain relationships between England, Scotland, Wales, and Ireland—is only patchily supported by the evidence (it fits Ireland well and Scotland badly), the idea of internal colonialism remains fruitful. Robert Blauner (*Racial Oppression in America*, 1972) used the concept to describe race relations in the United States and elsewhere.

internally displaced persons People who have been forced to leave their homes, often due to armed conflict, *human rights violations, *climate change, or natural or human-made disasters, but remain within the borders of their state. Distinct from refugees in international law, since *refugees have crossed a national border.   GLB

international aid *See* AID.

International Atomic Energy Agency (IAEA) Agency reporting to the United Nations, established in 1957 to promote the safe and peaceful use of nuclear technology. In the aftermath of the Chernobyl nuclear accident in 1986 it expanded its advisory role on the safety of nuclear power production, and it has played an important role in the *verification of nuclear weapons programmes and in gathering evidence relating to adherence to the *Nuclear Non-Proliferation Treaty.

(⊕) SEE WEB LINKS

• International Atomic Energy Agency site, including history of the organization.

International Court of Justice The judicial arm of the United Nations. Established in 1946 it is composed of fifteen judges appointed by the General Assembly and Security Council. It acts as a body of arbitration for consenting states in conflict over a particular issue, and makes its decisions according to international law. It also provides legal advice to other UN institutions.   JBr

(⊕) SEE WEB LINKS

• International Court of Justice site.

International Criminal Court Established in 2002, the International Criminal Court (ICC) is charged with jurisdiction over the crime of *genocide, crimes against humanity, and war crimes. As of November 2017, 123 states were signatories to the founding treaty and hence members of the ICC. China, India, and the United States were amongst states which did not support the establishment of the ICC. The ICC can investigate cases where citizens of member states are accused; incidents take place in member states; or where the United Nations Security Council refers a case. The ICC has opened investigations into crimes committed in the Central African Republic, the *Darfur region of Sudan, the Democratic Republic of the Congo, and Uganda. It has been criticized by African leaders as it has so far only considered cases in Africa. Concern was highlighted by the case against Uhuru Kenyatta, President of Kenya, which was dropped in 2015 because of lack of evidence. The jurisdiction of the court has also been questioned as a result of the ease with which Omar al-Bashir, the President of Sudan, has avoided warrants for his arrest. In 2016, South Africa, Burundi, and the Gambia withdrew from the ICC, and in 2017 the African Union advised that all its members should withdraw.

(⊕) SEE WEB LINKS

• International Criminal Court website.

internationalism A principle and ideology that promotes and defends greater political and economic cooperation and mutual benefit among states and people. An underwriting principle of internationalism is the idea that cooperation will better serve and secure the long-term interests of actors and people within the *international system. This view is often held in opposition to *classical realism and *nationalism, which argues that power and *sovereignty are the key motivating principles within the *state system, not cooperation. Historically, internationalists have been outspoken advocates for increasing the scope and strength of the *United Nations, and have often been associated with promoting the idea for a *world government and world federalism.

international law A set of rules generally recognized by civilized nations as governing their conduct towards each other and towards each other's citizens. How far international law may be thought to differ from municipal (national) law depends on whether one takes a positivist or a naturalist view. For positivists, law is the command of a sovereign backed by force. Since the international system is an *anarchy, with no supreme authority, international law is necessarily deficient. Naturalists take a different view, believing that positive law consists in the recognition and codification of other sources of law, such as custom, which do not rely upon a sovereign for their authority.

It is certainly true that custom and general principles as sources of international law have a strong flavour of the medieval natural law tradition about them, and the acceptance of the views of expert publicists only slightly less so. Thomas *Aquinas, summing up the European naturalist position in the thirteenth century, had argued that the world as created by God was orderly or law-governed. This made it possible for the physical world to be understood through mathematics and the strict deductive processes of theoretical reasoning. But because of the imperfection of man following the Fall, human affairs were afflicted with contingency or uncertainty. Practical reason, which concerned human conduct, was therefore a much less clear-cut business than theoretical reason. Yet the two were loosely analogous. Thus, law could be ascertained by a quasi-deductive process of reasoning from first principles such as 'Do unto others as you would be done by'; such practical reasoning called for skill and judgement in which expert jurists might have an advantage over sovereigns or statesmen; and similar laws and customs widely adopted by differing peoples (*jus gentium*) were good evidence of the success of human practical reason in discovering natural law.

By the early modern period, custom, general principle, and the views of expert publicists had yielded a body of international law on the use of force—to name only one area—in which states were generally content to acquiesce. There was general agreement within Christendom on the reasons for which a prince might go to war (*jus ad bellum*) and the right conduct of war once begun (*jus in bello*).

Subsequently, a general substitution of statute and other written forms of municipal law has led to a strong preference for convention as a source of international law. Treaties create international law, but commit only those states that are signatories to them. The term convention is more often applied to multilateral treaties with large numbers of signatories, and it is worth noting that even now, with an abundance of conventions, the source of law is often not what at first appears. Where non-signatories acquiesce in the provisions of a convention these may come to be regarded as customary international law, binding upon all states.

Such conventions now cover a wide range of subjects including territory, the sea, the responsibilities of states, human rights, treaties, dispute settlement, and the use of force. International law relating to territory covers not only the demarcation of frontiers, but airspace and outer space. The 1982 Convention on the Law of the Sea provides law relating to shipping, coastlines, territorial waters, exclusive economic zones, and rights to resources on and under the deep sea bed. Law relating to the responsibilities of states to each other's citizens covers both the care of refugees and asylum seekers and the expropriation and compensation of multinational corporations.

Until recently only states were subjects of international law, but individuals now have rights specifically recognized. Typical of the transition from customary to conventional international law is the fact that freedom from slavery, established as customary international law by 1815, has been secured under conventions only in the twentieth century. Again, since 1945 the *European Convention for the Protection of Human Rights and Fundamental Freedoms and the United Nations Universal Declaration on Human Rights (which is not a convention) have gone some way to committing states to provision of a broader range of human rights. The United Nations Charter, which does have the force of law, suggests suitable rights without conferring them on individuals; the final act of the Helsinki Conference on Security and Co-operation in Europe, which does not, is more specific.

The ways in which states may accede to, abrogate, and interpret treaties is covered by the 1969 Vienna Convention on the Law of Treaties, which came into force in 1980. Legal procedures for the settlement of disputes between states range from the exercise of good offices by a third party, through mediation and conciliation, to formal arbitration. Under the 1899 Convention on the Pacific Settlement of International Disputes and subsequent conventions states have been able to submit disputes for settlement, but the process depended on the consent of both parties. Only since the formation of the Permanent Court of International Justice in 1922 and its successor, the International Court of Justice, in 1946 has there been a court to which a state could unilaterally bring a complaint against another state.

The use of force is the area most often referred to by those who are sceptical about international law; they forget, perhaps, that municipal law does not prevent assault, but rather provides generally accepted ways of dealing with it. Under the United Nations Charter of 1945 the use of force by states against one another is illegal, except in self-defence. This has not prevented war, though it may have prevented some wars. Other conventions govern the kinds of weapons which states may use, the treatment of non-combatants and prisoners of war, and the conduct of UN peacekeeping forces.   CJ

International Monetary Fund *See* IMF.

international political economy International political economy (IPE) emerged as a heterodox approach to international studies during the 1970s as rising oil prices and the breakdown of the *Bretton Woods international monetary system alerted Anglo-Saxon academic opinion to the importance, contingency, and weakness of the economic foundations of world order. Traditional study of international relations was held to have placed excessive emphasis on law, politics, and diplomatic history. Conversely modern economics was accused of abstraction and inaccessibility. Drawing heavily on historical sociology, intellectual history, and economic history, IPE instead proposed a fusion of economic and political analysis. In addition, many adherents—both Marxist and liberal—protested against the reliance of Western social science on the territorial state as the unit of analysis, preferring a holistic approach to world politics. By the 1990s IPE had largely succeeded in transforming the old orthodoxy yet stood in some danger of succumbing to respectability as a tolerated subfield of *international relations. *See also* POLITICAL ECONOMY; POLITICS AND ECONOMICS.   CJ

international relations The discipline that studies interactions between and among states, and more broadly, the workings of the international system as a whole. It can be conceived of either as a multidisciplinary field, gathering together the international aspects of politics, economics, history, law, and sociology, or as a meta-discipline, focusing on the systemic structures and patterns of interaction of the human species taken as a whole. The discipline acquired its own identity after the First World War. Its principal branches additional to theory include international political economy, international organization, foreign policy-making, strategic (or security) studies, and, more arguably, peace research. If area studies is added to these, the label international studies becomes more appropriate. When spelled wholly in lower case, the term refers to the totality of interactions within the international system. The emphasis is often on relations between states, though other collective actors such as multinational corporations, transnational interest groups, and international organizations also play an important role.   BB

international socialism The doctrine that socialism ought to come by international revolution. *Marx and Engels called for 'Workers of all countries' to 'unite!' in 1848. The International Working Men's Association (First International) was founded by Marx in 1864 and dissolved in 1876 when he moved its headquarters to New York in order to prevent it falling into the hands of his opponents. The Second International was founded in 1889. It embraced both Marxists and non-Marxist socialists, but fell apart in 1914 when the majority of the socialists in all the combatant countries in the First World War embraced their country's war effort. The Third (communist) International was founded in 1919 and dissolved in 1943. Official doctrine in the Soviet Union promoted international socialism at some times, and *socialism in one country at others, according to the perceived needs of the USSR. *Trotskyists founded a rival 'Fourth International'. Groups calling themselves International Socialists in capitals are therefore Trotskyist.

international society The main concept of the so-called *English school of international relations, its central idea being that states can form a society by agreeing amongst themselves to establish common rules and institutions for the conduct of their relations and by recognizing their common interest in maintaining these arrangements. This idea goes back to *Grotius. It is related to the contemporary American concept of regimes which also stresses the development of common norms, rules, and institutions

among states as a way of regulating their relations. But whereas 'regimes' refers to specific instances of cooperation or coordination on particular issues, international society refers to what constitutes a system of states.

International society has states as its units, as opposed to world society, which is based on individuals and transnational actors. The exchange of sovereign recognitions establishes states as legal equals, and provides the basis for a shared identity as members of international society. It is sometimes argued that international society and world society are opposed ideas, with the state and national identity blocking the development of world society, and world society (especially *human rights) undermining the identity and purpose of the nation-state. But a case can be made that they are complements, with world society providing the political consensus to sustain the high levels of openness and interdependence of advanced international society, and international society providing the political framework for world society, so rescuing it from the fate of having either no political structure, or being dependent on an unattainable world government.

The most widely cited cases of international society are those of classical Greece and modern Europe. During their imperial heyday, the European powers imposed their own form of political order, the territorial state, onto the rest of the planet. This legacy provided the post-colonial foundations for a global international society by making almost universal the mutual recognition of claims to *sovereignty amongst all of the states in the system. It also raised the question of whether there can be a stable global international society in the absence of a global culture, and whether international society is necessarily global, or also operates at the regional level. The *European Union is a good example of a highly developed regional international society. The contemporary global international society is unevenly developed, with some states sharing many more norms, rules, and institutions than others. At its centre lies a Western core, surrounded by concentric circles of states in each of which states share fewer of the norms, rules, and institutions as one moves further outward. A few *rogue states are outside international society altogether.

By emphasizing the social bases for cooperation amongst states, and by seeing this as a natural outcome of relations in an anarchic international system, the idea of international society moderates the conflictual assumption about the nature of international relations associated with realism. It is a way of synthesizing many of the core elements of realist and liberal thinking, and it is vital to any understanding of rights and responsibilities concerning intervention by states into each other's affairs.   BB

international system A term used to describe the pattern of relationships between and amongst states as the key unit of study in *international relations. *See also* STATE SYSTEM; WESTPHALIAN STATE SYSTEM.

Internet and politics The Internet (World Wide Web) came into widespread use in the mid-1990s. Its main impact on politics is fourfold: (1) its ability to increase governmental transparency via allowing access to online content and governmental reports; (2) its ability to increase politically relevant information flows (both factual and spurious) between people; (3) its ability to facilitate the coordination of interest groups, extremist groups, and *civil society beyond traditional political spaces and borders; and (4) its creation of new forms of *cyber-crime, *cyber-terrorism, and *cyber-security issues.

In terms of increased transparency, governments, *non-governmental organizations, and institutions in *global governance have posted millions of Web pages of political information such as official reports, contact forums, and strategy rationalizations. Several governments, including that of the UK, have set increasing targets for the maximum proportion of citizens' business with government to be conducted via the Internet. In terms of information flows, the Internet provides a cheap and easy platform for *populist movements in the West, such as the *Tea Party, as well as to established political parties seeking to influence voters, such as those successfully used by the Democratic Party in the election of Barack Obama for US President in 2008. The Internet also allows for greater communication of identity politics, such as those witnessed during the UK's referendum to leave the *European Union (*Brexit), as well as the dissemination of extremist *propaganda, such as used in the recruitment strategies of *ISIS and other *Islamic fundamentalist groups. As part of this trend, the Internet and social media have also provided a vehicle for the greater dissemination of 'fake news', which is a form of uncorroborated media popularized by the number of online views generated, rather than from traditional forms of independent verification. In the case of the former, it is argued that both the promotion of 'fake news' as well as targeted viewer profiling on the Internet greatly aided in the election of Donald J. Trump for US President in 2016.

internment Internment without trial is a draconian device adopted by democracies during emergencies. Australia and the USA used it in war-time, as did Britain under the 1939 Emergency Powers (Defence) Act. More recently it has been used in the Middle East and in *Northern Ireland. Its introduction is an admission that normal democratic politics no longer prevail because it evokes the spectre of arbitrary government. Ireland serves as the ideal laboratory: during the nineteenth century 73 separate statutes of a coercive character were passed for Ireland and habeas corpus was suspended on four different occasions. Internment was a feature of security policy in Northern Ireland; it was used in 1920-4, 1931-4, 1938-45, and 1956-61. Its imposition aroused particular controversy when it was reintroduced on 9 August 1971. Of the initial 342 detained 116 were released within 48 hours. No loyalists were detained at first: only 109 suspected loyalists were interned in the period 1971-5—suspected republicans totalled 2,060. Interrogation techniques used in the beginning led to a *European Court of Human Rights judgment in January 1978 that found against Britain for degrading and inhuman treatment. Not surprisingly the exercise led to huge alienation in the Catholic community. Internment failed miserably to control the violence: of the 172 who died violently in 1971 only 28 were killed before 9 August. The RUC Chief Constable described it later as a 'disaster' and it acted as a tremendous boost for IRA recruitment. Conditions in the internment camps were to benefit the IRA where they operated under paramilitary structures. Once direct rule was imposed in

March 1972 the authorities introduced a 'quasi-judicial' element into the equation but when a committee chaired by Lord Gardiner reported in 1975 it said that the 'procedures are unsatisfactory, or even farcical'. In essence, Gardiner buried internment in 1975 by stating that it brought the law into contempt. PA

interval level variable *See* MEASUREMENT.

intifada *Intifada* is Arabic for 'a shaking off'. The term refers to the two Palestinian uprisings on the West Bank and Gaza (the territories occupied by Israel during the 1967 war). The first intifada arose spontaneously in 1987, lasting until 1993, and the second began in 2000. It has been suggested that the emergence of the first intifada was a response to the realization that the Palestinian issue and the Arab–Israeli conflict was slipping as a key concern of Arab governments, and that Palestinians in the Occupied Territories would have to take matters into their own hands. The second intifada, known as the Al-Aqsa Intifada, erupted when Ariel Sharon visited the Al-Aqsa Mosque, symbolizing a provocative violation of the holy site. Some Palestinian activists called for a third intifada during the summer of 2014, when Palestinian teenager Mohammed Abu Khdeir was burned alive by Israeli settlers. Khdeir was murdered in response to the kidnap and murder of three Israeli teenagers who lived in settlements in the West Bank. The subsequent period of increased violence, especially taking place in East Jerusalem, has been described as the 'silent intifada'.

Underlying these specific triggers is the question of whether the Palestinian people of the West Bank and Gaza will be allowed self-determination or autonomy or statehood, or whether these territories will ultimately be incorporated into the state of Israel. The background to this issue goes back to the end of the First World War and the establishment of the authority of Great Britain over the Palestine Mandate with its provision for a national home for the Jews, though not to be at the expense of the local population. The key difficulty was maintaining an appropriate balance between these stipulations that would be acceptable to the parties concerned.

The decades before 1948 saw an inflow of European Jews into the Mandate together with a land-purchasing policy of the Jewish Agency (allowed by Britain) designed to alienate land from the Arabs (i.e. stipulating that it could not be resold to Arabs). Unable to resolve the intensifying conflict between the demands of the Jewish and Arab communities, Great Britain passed responsibility for the Mandate over to the new *United Nations which in 1947 decided on the partition of Palestine into two states—one for the Jews and another for the Arabs. The stage was set for the settlement of the issue. Instead, in 1948, an Israeli state emerged from the Palestine Mandate at the expense of the founding of a Palestinian state in the process creating 700,000 Palestinian refugees who were either *ethnically cleansed or who had left temporarily in fear. Concurrently, the first Arab–Israeli war began ending in an armistice without a peace settlement. The state of Israel was seen, from the Arab point of view, as the last vestige of colonialism remaining in the Arab Middle East. From the Jewish point of view, carving out a state from the Mandate gave European Jews the opportunity to fulfil their nationalist aspirations to have a state of their own. From 1948 onward, Arab governments whether or not *Pan-Arab Nationalist in ideology had taken up the Palestinian cause that came to symbolize for the Arab nations of the Middle East the injustices and frustrations engendered by its involvement with the West in recent history.

For the Palestinian people, there was a further complication. Amir Abdullah, the Hashemite ruler of Transjordan, had argued that Palestine and Transjordan should be united under Hashemite rule. He was unable to convince the British government of the desirability of this plan. Unable to achieve this aim, in 1947–8, Abdullah struck a deal with the *Zionists that in the event of conflict his forces would occupy and annex the central area of Palestine, i.e., the West Bank, leaving the remainder of Palestine to the Zionists. As a result of this deal and annexation, Transjordan became the state of Jordan and the Amir a king. However, in 1948, no Arab government recognized Jordan's annexation of the West Bank. Nineteen years later, King Hussein of Jordan, the grandson of Abdullah, lost the West Bank to

Israeli forces in the June war of 1967. Twenty-one years later, after the Intifada was under way, he relinquished the claim which Jordan and his dynasty had to the territory, paving the way for the Palestine Liberation Organization's (*PLO) Proclamation of an independent Palestinian state in November 1988. The Gaza Strip results from the Egyptian military being able to hold it in 1948 when the armistice was signed. It was later occupied by Israel in the 1967 war.

The first intifada began as a revolt of the Palestinian youth throwing stones against the forces of the Israeli occupation, but became a widespread movement involving civil disobedience with periodic large-scale demonstrations supported by commercial strikes. The response of the Israeli government was brutal repression of the whole population of the Occupied Territories. The persistence of the intifada is believed to have played a part in contributing to the Israeli government's eventual acceptance of direct negotiation with the Palestinians in the Madrid Peace Process launched by Presidents Bush and Gorbachev in October 1991 and, subsequently, its eventual willingness to recognize the PLO in the Oslo Accord of 1993. The accord established the Palestinian National Authority (commonly shortened to Palestinian Authority) as an interim governmental body with a five-year lifespan, and tasked it with overseeing the transition between occupation and self-government. The PA is thus a product of the Oslo Accords while the PLO remains the Palestinian people's sole and legitimate representative to the United Nations.

The schedule for implementation of the Oslo Accord eventually broke down particularly after parties were elected in Israel which were hostile to the land for peace principle. The Oslo Accord called for a three-phased Israeli military withdrawal from the Occupied Territories after which there would be Final Status negotiations over the four most difficult items—right of return of refugees, Jerusalem, borders, and Jewish settlements. A series of Interim agreements (before the Final Status talks) then took place resulting in Palestinian authority being established in the main towns of the West Bank and Gaza, each of which were separated by a system of roads patrolled by Israeli forces. This provided Israeli settlements easy access to Israel proper at the same time isolating Palestinian communities from each other. In this way, Israeli settlements acquired a level of security while Palestinian unity was physically fragmented. As this arrangement began to take on an air of permanence and with continued settlement building, land confiscations, daily humiliations at frequent check points, sporadic Palestinian attacks were launched against Israeli settlements and occupying forces, and on occasion within Israel itself.

As a malaise set in resulting from a lack of progress in the Peace Process, the second intifada erupted. This intifada differs in many ways from the first intifada in that the economy of the West Bank and Gaza rapidly collapsed. The violence of the first intifada on the Palestinian side was mainly from stone throwing and only much later some use of small arms. This intifada encouraged the emergence of an Israeli government that was interested in a land for peace settlement of the issues between Israel and the Palestinians. The second intifada, on the other hand, has seen an escalation in the level of violence in which Israel has used its heavy military equipment, tanks, helicopters, missiles, and aircraft as well as snipers. It has targeted leaders of secular and religious groups and others that it has believed a threat, destroyed official buildings of the various security forces, and finally re-entered the towns with tanks to destroy family houses of those who had attacked it and any other buildings which it saw as part of the infrastructure of those attacking it. On the Palestinian side, once the intifada began, there was an escalation of attacks of settlements but more importantly, attacks inside Israel mainly by suicide bombers, not only by religious groups but by secular groups, which occurred in population centres throughout the country. It was believed by the Israeli government that these attacks were orchestrated by Yasir Arafat, the President of the Palestinian Authority. Eventually, in an escalating spiral of violence, the autonomous towns in the West Bank were reoccupied, Arafat was forceably restricted to a few rooms in his Ramallah headquarters until he would call off the Palestinian violence. Essentially, the gap between the two sides had become wider. The Israeli government wanted the violence to stop before negotiations could begin and was unwilling to consider the previous negotiations of Camp David II and the Clinton proposals as still on the table. Yasir Arafat, having lost the full support of the Palestinian population over the long years of what for them seemed fruitless negotiations, was unable to restrain the violence without having something positive to offer from the Israeli government which it was unwilling to give.

After the death of Arafat in November 2004, there was a weakening of Fatah control over the Palestinian Authority, with the radical Hamas faction gaining prominence and popularity. The Israeli construction of a separation barrier through much of the West Bank disrupted Palestinian communities, and disengagement from Gaza was challenged by rocket attacks on Israel. In 2006, after incursions into Israeli territory led to the killing and kidnapping of Israeli soldiers, Israel launched attacks on Lebanon and Gaza. The victory of Hamas in Palestinian Legislative Council (PLC) elections in 2006 led to the imposition of international economic and political sanctions, which undermined the viability of the government. Bitter fighting broke out between supporters of Fatah and Hamas, as the legitimacy and authority of the Palestinian Authority was challenged by Palestinians, Israelis, and the international community. *See also* PLO.   BAR/JHa

invisible hand Term introduced by Adam *Smith as a metaphor for the working of the uncoordinated market: 'every individual . . . intends only his own gain, and he is in this, as in many other cases, led by an invisible hand to promote an end which was no part of his intention' (*Wealth of Nations*, 1776). Smith, unlike some of his modern followers, did not believe that actual markets were necessarily coordinated only by the invisible hand of perfect competition.

Iraq War War launched on 20 March 2003 by coalition forces led by the United States against Iraq, to oust Saddam Hussein. The coalition referred to Iraq's failure to comply with the UN Resolution 1441's conditions for disarmament, and a perceived terrorist threat. Critics suggested the US were imposing military hegemony on the Middle East. UN diplomatic efforts floundered, and the war was supported by a narrow coalition.

The UK and Australia offered military support, and Turkey offered minimal cooperation. With massive air superiority and limited resistance from the Iraqi army, the US entered the capital, Baghdad, on 9 April 2003.

Expectations that a grateful Iraqi population would greet the invaders as liberators and that Iraq would become a model of a stable and democratic state in the Middle East were quickly confounded. Saddam Hussein was captured in December 2003 and, convicted of crimes against humanity by a military tribunal, hanged in 2006. The death of the Iraqi dictator did not legitimize the invasion, or make the task of reconstruction in Iraq easier. The failure to discover evidence of any weapons of mass destruction undermined much of the justification for the military action. The decision to dissolve the Iraqi army and ban prominent members of the Ba'ath Party from holding official positions led to instability and resentment, and was followed by an increased level of violent *insurgency. The economic reconstruction of Iraq was hindered by widespread corruption, violence, and instability. The award of contracts to US companies to rebuild infrastructure, operate as security forces, and exploit oil resources led to suspicion of US motives.

Although a limited transfer of power to an Iraqi civilian government occurred in 2004, and a provisional constitution was ratified in 2005, a stable and democratic Iraq did not emerge. Tensions between Sunni and Shi'ite groups, the uncertain federal relationship between regions, and the continued role and influence of the United States military weakened the authority and legitimacy of the government. According to Larry Diamond, an expert on democratization and adviser to the Coalition Provisional Authority in Baghdad, 'America's quest to stabilize and democratize Iraq seemed to be becoming one of the major overseas blunders in US history'.

The election of Barack Obama to the US Presidency in 2008 resulted in a drawdown of major combat forces in Iraq as well as accelerating the transfer of political and military authority to the largely dysfunctional Iraqi government. Given this new fragility of authority in Iraq, political infighting within the power-sharing government increased, creating disorder and power vacuums in large portions of the country. One consequence was the emergence and successful military campaign of the *Islamic fundamentalist group *ISIS, who took military control of large sections of northwest Iraq and eastern Syria, including Iraq's second-largest city, Mosul. Furthermore, the rise of ISIS and its call for an Islamic caliphate has destabilized the entire region, leading to both the *Syrian crisis and the *refugee crisis.

Irish Republican Army (IRA) *See* NORTHERN IRELAND.

iron curtain The boundary between Soviet-controlled eastern Europe and western Europe. The phrase was first used by Ethel Snowden, wife of a British Labour politician, in 1920, but was made famous by Winston Churchill, who said in Fulton, Missouri, in March 1946, 'An iron curtain has descended across the Continent'. Hence the countries of the Soviet bloc were called 'iron curtain countries', especially by right-wingers.

iron law of oligarchy Name given by Robert Michel (1875–1936) to his claim that even socialist parties which professed internal democracy would in practice be controlled by a small elite: 'who says organization, says oligarchy'. The aims of the organization would be undermined by the elite's self-interested pursuit of its own aims. In that no large organization is controlled from day to day by its membership at large, Michels' claim is true but trivial. But it remains painful for organizations which are formally committed to internal democracy.

iron law of wages A doctrine imputed by *Marx to the German socialist Ferdinand Lassalle (1825–64) and vituperatively denounced in Marx's *Critique of the Gotha Programme* (1875). It is the idea that under capitalism wages are necessarily held at the barest level of subsistence that allows the worker just to survive in order to work and reproduce the children who will be the next generation of the working class. Marx denounces this as no more than a reworking of *Malthus. Some of Marx's earlier work nevertheless gives the distinct impression that Marx also once believed in the iron law of wages.

iron triangles *See* INTEREST GROUPS.

irredentism The term 'irredentism' comes from the Italian, *irredenta*, meaning unredeemed. After the unification of Italy in 1870 with the annexation of the Papal States, there still remained certain pockets of ethnically Italian territory in Austrian hands, including Trieste (Austria's only port), Istria, Trentino, and South Tirol, which the irredentists claimed. The term has been extended to any movement or aspiration to recover territory claimed back for ethnic or linguistic reasons. CB

ISIS *See* ISLAMIC STATE OF IRAQ AND SYRIA.

Islamic fundamentalism (Islamism) A disputed term, widely used in the US and to a lesser extent in Britain to denote any movement to favour strict observance of the teachings of the Qur'an and the Shari'a (Islamic Law). On the continent, as well as in Britain and amongst many scholars of Islam and the Middle East, there is a preference for terms such as 'Islamism', 'Islamicism', 'Islamists', or 'Islamicists' in referring to the current activist political trend. Islamism emerges out of the reform (*islah*) project of the nineteenth and twentieth centuries that was launched by Jamal al Din al-Afghani (1837–97), Muhammad Abduh (1849–1905), and Rashid Rida (1865–1935). The reform envisaged was broadly defined to incorporate a revitalization of culture, society, and religion utilizing European science and techniques coupled with the requirement of drawing on the moral and cultural tradition of early Islam, of the pious forefathers (*al-salaf*, AD 610–855). Thereafter, the revitalization of Islam and Islamic society, and hence its defence, came to dominate this trend as the fate of the Islamic world was increasingly seen as being in the grip of European power to do with it as it would.

Reform (*islah*) was comprehensive in addressing the causes of backwardness. In their efforts against the conservative and traditionalist religious forces hostile to reform, Abduh and Rida focused on the *salaf* and condemned all innovations (*bida*) introduced into Islam after their time, including the law schools (*madhhabs*). They called for a return to the independent interpretation of the sacred sources (*ijtihad*), of the Qur'an and Sunna of the Prophet and consensus of his Companions which was said to have ended during the tenth to eleventh centuries. This would allow those in authority to pursue what was in the best interests of the Community in the secular sphere though it was never to be in conflict with the Qur'an and Sunna. This type of argument contributed to the emergence of a modern tendency to focus on the practices of the early years of Islam (*salafiyya*) which remains influential until the present time. All innovations in Islam that had occurred throughout its history after the *salaf* which were regarded as having caused schisms and accepted local customs which led Muslims away from the straight path were condemned. By returning to the pure practice of the Prophet and his Companions, the traditional structures of Muslim society including the secular domain could more easily be exposed to new cultural and social dynamisms leading to reform.

In 1928, the Muslim Brotherhood (Ikhwan al-Muslimun) was founded in opposition to these movements to renew the focus on the approach of the *salafiyya* (sometimes referred to as neo-*salafiyya* to distinguish it from the approach taken by Abduh and Rida), this time to bring its ideas to the 'man in the street' and to exclude the colonial society by recovering dominance of the public discourse, and to oppose Western imperialism and secularization. They would look deep into the roots of Islam in order to purify and renew it by focusing on the principles of the earliest generations of Islam, the *salaf*. In effect, they rejected the integrationist approach of the earlier reform movement as cooptation.

A further intensification of Islamic concern and activity can be discerned from the end of the 1967 Arab–Israeli war in which the Arab forces suffered a crushing and humiliating defeat. This sounded the death knell of Arab nationalism as a viable alternative strategy and ideology. Added to this was the successful Iranian revolution toward the end of the 1970s, the disorienting effects upon the region of the long-running Iraq–Iran War (1980–8), the *Gulf War (1990–1) which led to Western militaries being invited into Saudi Arabia, the proclaimed protector of the holy cities of Mecca and Medina, and the attacks in the US on 11 September 2001 which brought a return of Western militaries this time to Afghanistan. Events on both these last two occasions had transpired to bring almost all Arab governments to join in alliance with the West, some, in the first instance, sending forces to Saudi Arabia alongside those from the West to attack an Arab state. In the case of Afghanistan, no Arab military participated. The Iraq–Kuwait war is an indication of the degree of irrelevance to which Arab nationalism had fallen; Afghanistan indicated the degree of Arab governments' sensitivity to their populations' resistance to their governments' cooperation with US Middle East policy.

The Muslim Brothers themselves reinvigorated the position of moderate reform (though without abandoning the *salafiyya* approach) which at their founding had been condemned. Other groups, regarding this as cooptation, developed more militant and in some cases jihadist approaches, the most extreme example being *al-Qaeda and *ISIS.

Thus, Islamism expanded into the gaping vacuum of a dying nationalism and, by focusing on domestic issues, for a time, continued to particularize national identities, sometimes encouraged by governments. For example, President Anwar al Sadat of Egypt on attaining leadership in 1970 clothed his rhetoric in Islamic symbolism, invited Islamist activists in exile to return as a counterforce to an organized political left in Egypt, and reintroduced aspects of Shari'a Law into the legal system. This Islamist response with its neo-salafiyya tendency led to a proliferation of new-style voluntary benevolent associations (*jama'iyya*) whose registered numbers in Egypt alone in the early 1990s were over 12,800, all concerned with social services, together with an unknown number of unregistered associations. In this way, Islamist spokesmen emerged in many Arab and Muslim non-Arab countries with political agendas designed to relate Islam to state power, either openly, by stealth, or by violence. The most reinvigorated current form of Islamic fundamentalism is that posed by ISIS and its political and militaristic call for an Islamic caliphate. BAR

Islamic politics The mantra, there is no separation between religion and politics in

Islam: 'Islam din wa dawla' (Islam is religion and state) is of recent vintage in the Arab Middle East going back to the end of the nineteenth century. However, *secularization in the sense of the separation of state and religion has been a fact of social life in the Middle East for some considerable time. This is most evident in the generally accepted and widespread encroachment of the state on the jurisdiction of Islamic (Shari'a) law. During the time of the Ottoman Empire and the Qajar dynasty in Iran, imperial rule was most evidently secular. However, this occurred in a way that did not consciously secularize the population. As a consequence, while governments pursued policies reflecting 'reasons of state', Islam has remained an important part of the culture and identity of the masses in Middle Eastern societies. Western penetration of the Islamic world from the nineteenth century onward resulted in a conflict between secular and religious conceptions of politics because education and the legal system were being Westernized. Colonialism led to an emerging new public sphere. *Islamists set about to reconstruct the political discourse through utilizing the formula, 'Islam din wa dawla', to reconquer in the public arena, where *din* symbolizes people, and where the call for the implementation of the Shari'a critiques the lack of constitutional guarantees that would legitimize the political community.

With the Islamic Revolution in Iran in 1978–9, the profile of Islamism intensified and with it the question of whether secularism can be reconciled with Islam: Does Islam prescribe all matters including daily affairs? Should it be enforced? Are Muslims allowed any area which they can determine for themselves? On the other hand, among those who reject secularism, the debate among Islamists moved more sharply onto the terrain of pluralistic politics and human rights.

In this debate, distinctions are made between those matters that are absolute requirements of the Muslim for the maintenance of his or her relationship with God, for example, the five pillars of Islam (the Shahada—the profession of the faith, Salah—prayer, Ramadan—fasting, Zakat—almsgiving and the Haj—pilgrimage), and those matters about which adjustments are

allowed by the religion given the requirements and conditions of the time as long as these adjustments do not contradict the public good. These matters concern economic, political, and family affairs about which there is no explicit scriptural text in the sacred sources. Given these ambiguities, different positions are held among Islamists. There is general agreement that what is done must remain within the meaning of the Shari'a, and the role of the state is to maintain the conditions for the implementation of the Shari'a. This places the focus on two questions—what kind of state and what kind of Shari'a. What is clearer is that the state must be founded on certain principles based on the Qur'an and Sunna of the Prophet, in particular, the principles of justice, equality, and consultation (*shura*). What is important is that the principles are maintained, the type of government under which this is to occur is of less concern. As to the kind of Shari'a, there has been a debate between secularists and Islamists and amongst Islamists themselves as to what should constitute the Shari'a. The secularists have conceded that the Shari'a is based on God's Word in the Qur'an and also the Sunna. But they argue that its historical development and implementation has been the creation of men and, therefore, subject to question. There is a general consensus among Islamists that the Shari'a is both all-embracing and facilitating as long as any independent interpretation of the sacred sources (*ijtihad*) follows the established methodological rules in Islamic jurisprudence. The conceptualization of the Shari'a has come to encapsulate abstractly a social normative system expressing social justice. If the Shari'a is not implemented, there is not the possibility of social justice.

It is often observed in traditional literature that sovereignty belongs to God, and the ruler—even an unjust ruler—must be obeyed in order to maintain peace and stability. This led to arbitrary government. Modern Islamists are shifting away from a blanket acceptance of a ruler toward an emphasis on the authority of the community and the responsibility of each believer. With the emphasis upon the implementation of the Shari'a, as the ideal of social justice, Muslims' current concerns are to limit the arbitrariness of governments and to substitute instead the rule of law. The sort of system that is expected is no longer the Classical system in which the leader was chosen, ostensibly by the community via *shura*, but in reality by the ruling elite, then giving the leader the oath of allegiance leading to arbitrary rule. What is expected now is a constitutional system where there is continuous consultation in which the ruler and government could be constantly monitored and held responsible not only to God but to the electorate. For some, this is a system of a separation of powers between the ruler and the institution of *shura* with an independent judiciary, even a constitutional court. In effect, it is a system of checks and balances where governance is in accordance with the Shari'a.

There is still considerable debate about the actual relationship between the ruler and *shura*. Many see *shura* as a requirement binding on the ruler, that it consists of a formal process and an institution with elected members which would operate on the basis of the principle of majority decision. This may not necessarily be a parliament but more likely would be a council of experts giving Islamically correct advice based on the common good.

These ideas and debates are the results, after the First World War, of the further development and elaboration in the Sunni world of the Islamic reform movement (*see* ISLAMISM) challenging the basic character of the secularist, colonialist state. The key originators and contributors to the development of this perspective were Hassan al-Banna (1906–49, an Egyptian, founder of the Muslim Brotherhood in 1928), Abu al-A'la Mawdudi (1903–79, a British Indian Pakistani, founder of the Jamaat-e Islami in 1941), and Sayyid Qutb (1906–66, an Egyptian, Muslim Brother). This approach to Islamic reform which became ideologized spread widely in the Islamic world. It was an Islamic world that was still essentially traditional, with its orthodox and traditional establishment, its particular configuration of Sufi (mystical Sunni) orders, history, and conditions. In response to international and globalizing influences, Islamists have demonstrated a wide range of views from the moderate to the extreme or jihadist. Pakistan, on the other hand, has been under the influence of one of the most influential

Islamic movements of the subcontinent both before and after Partition. This is the Jamaat-e Islami, founded and led, from 1941, by Abu al-A'la Mawdudi, whose Islamic ideas were popularized for more general consumption and which have been a significant influence on the Muslim Brotherhood of the 1950s and 1960s. The Jamaat-e Islami have contributed to the long-running internal debate and struggle in Pakistan on whether or not it was to be an Islamic state or simply a state for Muslims. Since its founding, Pakistan governments have vacillated on defining the ultimate character of the state. Where attempts were made to give the laws an Islamic character, the measures that were proposed were seldom given institutional means of enforcement. Not only in Pakistan but elsewhere in the Middle East and South Asia, the intellectual heritage of Mawdudi has formed the ideological backdrop for the debates concerning the Islamization of the state.

Central Asia, where the new Muslim republics of Kazakhstan, Kirgizstan, Tajikistan, Turkmenistan, and Uzbekistan; and the Transcaucasian republic of Azerbaijan are to be found, has not had the same opportunity of association for the past 70 years with the mainstream of either the Sunni or Shi'i Islamist thought circulating in the Middle East. This region, having been dominated in the eighteenth and nineteenth centuries by Tsarist rule, was subjected to the restrictive policies of the Soviet government which promoted atheism and limited Muslim education and Qur'anic knowledge at the local level. The number of mosques was reduced and imams were officially appointed with the result that the development of traditional religious-philosophical thought was undermined and the modernist Islamic trends uprooted. On the other hand, what came to be called 'unofficial' Islam or popular Islam dramatically increased via the spread of Sufi orders and the lowest stratum of clergy. The result has been that, as far as Central Asia is concerned, there has been little influence of Sunni or Shi'i political theological arguments that are current in the Islamic world. The lowest stratum of clergy comprised the unofficial imams of the 'non-mosques' or underground mosques, teachers of secret schools and reciters of the Qur'an. It is from this stratum that an Islamic revival began.

This revival, in one sense, has been directed against the official imams and muftis. On the other hand, Central Asian Muslims comprise diverse linguistic, ethnic, and religious groups with differing historical experiences which made it difficult to cooperate in the past and unlikely to bring about cooperation in the future. In the post-Soviet transition to independent statehood, Islam has become an important symbol associated with national identity. It can be and has been utilized by all the forces unleashed by the new situation whether conservative, nationalist, democratic, or other. It is unclear whether any of these forces will combine politically.

Afghanistan, like other parts of the Islamic world, has had a rich and complex religious history with its traditional and orthodox establishments and Sufi orders. The population is largely Sunni with a Shi'i minority. Islamism is a fairly recent development in the religious life of Afghanistan emerging in the late 1950s as a challenge to the secular state. The inspiration for Islamist views came from those Afghans, some of whom later became leaders of the various Mujahedin groups, who had been educated at the al-Azhar University in Cairo and had absorbed the ideas of the Muslim Brotherhood. Islamists came to prominence after the Marxist coup of 1978 with the most effective Mujahedin groups opposing Soviet intervention and the Communist government. Though the struggle against the secular state and foreign involvement intensified, Islamists remained divided. After the fall of the Communist government, power coalesced around two main groups—Jamiat-i Islami (not to be confused with the similarly named group in Pakistan) led by Burhanuddin Rabbani and the other, Hezb-e Islami, led by Gulbuddin Hekmatyar. After the Soviet withdrawal from Afghanistan a transnational Islamist movement was given a boost, bolstered by the dispersal of the principally Arab Muslims who had answered the call of jihad. New networks created in Afghanistan followed those Arabs who returned to their countries of origin and those who turned their focus on other areas where Muslims were under attack, such as Bosnia, Chechnya, Philippines, and others. These latter have been described as a 'deterritorialized' movement of radicalized jihadis who move from one location to another unattached to any particular state. Success in defeating the Soviet Union in Afghanistan has led to their belief that other invaders of Muslim territory elsewhere should also be confronted and defeated. The United States, because of its suspect involvement in the Middle East and support of Israel and elsewhere, has itself became a target of the jihad. *See also* JIHAD.   BAR

Islamic State of Iraq and Syria (ISIS) A

transnational terrorist organization based in Iraq and Syria. Known also as the Islamic State of Iraq and the Levant (ISIL) and, derogatively, as Da'esh, its acronym in Arabic, ISIS renamed itself the Islamic State after the group captured the Iraqi city of Mosul and declared an Islamic Caliphate in June 2014. The origins of ISIS lie in a militant group, Jama'at al-Tawhid w'al Jihad (Organization of Monotheism and Jihad), founded by Jordanian jihadist Abu Musab Al Zarqawi in Jordan in 1999. Al Zarqawi operated militant training camps in Afghanistan and established loose links with *al-Qaeda and Osama bin Laden, but fled the country after the fall of the Taliban in November 2001 and resurfaced in Iraq in 2002.

Following the US-led invasion and occupation of Iraq in 2003, bin Laden named Al Zarqawi the Emir of al-Qaeda in Iraq, and Al Zarqawi played a prominent role in the Sunni insurgency that developed in Iraq from 2004. During this period, several fighters who later became prominent in ISIS, including its leader, Abu Bakr Al Baghdadi, fought against coalition troops and spent periods in US detention at Camp Bucca. In January 2006, al-Qaeda in Iraq merged with other Sunni militant groups to form the Mujahideen Shura Council and, after Al Zarqawi was killed by US forces in June 2006, relaunched as the Islamic State of Iraq. The Islamic State of Iraq was strongest in Anbar Province but lost territory to the US troop surge as well as hearts and minds among swathes of Iraq's Sunni communities of Iraq to the Awakening Councils after 2007.

Abu Bakr Al Baghdadi became leader of the Islamic State of Iraq in May 2010, one month after the death of his predecessor, Abu Omar Al Baghdadi, in a raid by Iraqi and US forces in Tikrit. Born Ibrahim al-Badri, Abu Bakr Al Baghdadi had close ties to former military and intelligence officers in the Ba'ath regime of Saddam Hussein that had been ousted in 2003, and used these networks to methodically overhaul the Islamic State of Iraq's management structure. A complex bureaucratic apparatus evolved after 2010 modelled on the intelligence agencies that had maintained the Ba'ath Party in power in Iraq for thirty-five years. A cleric himself, Al Baghdadi fused the religious elements of the Sunni insurgency with the remnants of Hussein's regime in the waning years of the eight-year US-led *Iraq War and occupation.

Regional developments after 2011 re-energized the Islamic State of Iraq and facilitated the expansion of operations into neighboring Syria in 2013. In Iraq, Prime Minister Nuri al-Maliki consolidated political and military power after the departure of US forces in December 2011, and ruled in an authoritarian manner that alienated many Sunni Iraqis. In Syria, the *Arab Spring uprisings that started in March 2011 with largely non-violent demonstrations against President Bashar al-Assad was violently suppressed by regime forces and by the middle of 2012 had morphed into a chaotic series of localized conflicts. Maliki's extension of power in Iraq and Syria's descent into civil war led to an escalation in communal tension that provided an enabling environment for the sectarian grievances that fed into groups such as the Islamic State of Iraq.

The Islamic State of Iraq expanded into northern Syria in early 2013 and found a vacuum of governing and security authority after two years of intense fighting between regime forces and an increasingly fractured opposition. The Islamic State of Iraq opened offices in Aleppo and Idlib Provinces in early 2013, as well as military camps for the significant flows of foreign fighters who began to arrive in Syria. Substantial numbers of fighters came from Tunisia, Saudi Arabia, Chechnya, Turkey, and Egypt, in addition to volunteer recruits from Europe. Their arrival strengthened the Islamic State of Iraq relative to other Sunni rebel groups in Syria and allowed the group to wrest control of the city of Raqqa during 2013. Simultaneously, the Islamic State of Iraq seized control of the Iraqi cities of Falluja and Hit and extended its control over western Iraq adjacent to the Syrian border. Fierce fighting for control of the border region and its checkpoints

erupted in April 2014 between the newly renamed Islamic State of Iraq and Syria and the al-Qaeda-linked Jabhat Al Nusra. ISIS prevailed, but at the cost of thousands of casualties on both sides and a formal split with al-Qaeda and its leader, Ayman Al Zawahiri.

ISIS came to global attention in June 2014 after it routed Iraqi military resistance and captured the country's second-largest city, Mosul. Later that month, Al Baghdadi announced the declaration of a Caliphate with himself as its Caliph, in a move rejected by most Arab and Islamic authorities, and ISIS shortened its name to the Islamic State. As the Islamic State consolidated territorial control over large parts of western Iraq and northern Syria it developed bureaucratic and financial mechanisms designed to govern the several million inhabitants under its control. In addition to raising funds from taxes, fees, and the sale of oil on the black market, funding streams came from the looting of antiquities and the seizure of bank assets, as well as private donations. The Islamic State additionally became a magnet for hundreds of would-be foreign jihadists attracted by the group's slick and technologically savvy online and broadcast media. The affiliation of previously unrelated militant organizations in West and North Africa, the Sinai and Arabian Peninsulas, and South East Asia added to a sense of momentum of the Islamic State in 2014 and 2015.

Reports of large-scale killings of civilians and international fears of a genocidal assault on Iraq's non-Arab communities prompted the international community to launch an anti-ISIS military coalition in August 2014. Led by the United States and including Arab states such as Jordan, Morocco, Saudi Arabia, and the United Arab Emirates, the Global Coalition to Counter the Islamic State commenced air strikes in Iraq in August 2014 and Syria in September 2014. The Global Coalition additionally sought to interdict financial and human flows to Islamic State territory in Iraq and Syria. In October 2016 the Iraqi armed forces launched the Battle of Mosul, a major offensive to recapture the city from Islamic State.

The rapid growth of ISIS has constituted the most fundamental challenge to the state system that emerged in the Middle East during the twentieth century. Although at root a violent non-state actor, ISIS has differed from other jihadist groups, such as al-Qaeda, through its control of territory and appropriation of the language of statehood. The violent ideology espoused by ISIS has attracted sympathizers worldwide and spawned acts of terrorism that have ranged from coordinated mass-casualty attacks in Paris and Brussels in 2015 and 2016 to 'lone wolf' and 'copycat' attacks. Moreover, the savagery of ISIS rule has intensified the displacement of millions of people in Iraq and Syria, accelerated the flows of refugees to *European Union (EU) states, and sparked a populist backlash against formative policies such as the Schengen Agreement that regulates the freedom of movement within many EU and European Economic Area states. *See also* SYRIAN CIVIL WAR/SYRIAN CRISIS; REFUGEE CRISIS.   KCU

isolationism Support for non-involvement in foreign affairs, especially by the United States. Applied particularly to American politicians who wished the United States not to be involved in the World Wars, or in postwar treaty-making.

issue voting The idea that voters' decisions are largely determined by the issues at stake in the election. Before *survey research, most writers assumed that issue voting was the norm in democratic elections (although there have always been sceptics, from *Condorcet to *Schumpeter, who denied this—Schumpeter even denying that it ought to be). The first surveys of the determinants of voting showed that habit and party identification played leading roles, and issue voting almost none, as most voters knew nothing at all about many of the issues discussed by politicians and journalists during elections. Since the late 1960s issue voting has enjoyed a modest revival. This is due partly to the influence of rational-choice theory on election studies, and partly to the recognition that the politics in the United States in the 1950s—when the most influential surveys of the party identification school were done—were unusually bland and consensual. When 'issues' are restricted to 'issues which are salient to the electorate', it can be shown that issue voting plays quite a prominent role in a typical election. The other main determinant is retrospective voting, or evaluation of the party (team) currently in office. Here voters must compare the performance of the government with the promises of the opposition, a comparison which most voters are well aware is lopsided.

item veto An item veto gives the governor in most US states the power to strike out specific sections of an *appropriations bill, while signing the remainder into law. Item vetoes allow the executive to keep a close control over financial legislation, cutting out *riders, and reducing *pork barrel legislation. The US President does not possess an item veto, although it has been frequently proposed.

Jacobinism Originally the name given to the ideas of members of the Jacobin Club, itself named after the religious order whose premises it had taken over during the *French Revolution. Founded in 1789, it became extremely revolutionary under the leadership of *Robespierre. Closed after his fall from power in 1794, it later reopened until its definitive closure in 1799. It favoured centralization of all power under whoever (in 1793 the Paris street demonstrators) controlled the one and indivisible Republic. The name Jacobin is still given to politicians and parties which adopt this centralist view in opposition to independent local government. Although Jacobinism was leftwing during the Revolution, it was later adopted by the right and (some of) the extremeright as well as by the French Communist Party. CS

Jacobitism Jacobites were the followers of James II (Latin: *Jacobus*), deposed in the 'Glorious Revolution' of 1688–9, and his heirs. There was some overlap between Jacobitism and the early Tories; Jacobites rejected the succession arrangements of 1689 and 1714, whereas Tories tended to be doubtful and troubled about them. During the Hanoverian period the main areas of support for the Stuart 'Pretenders' were outside England, principally in the Highlands of Scotland. The Jacobite cause was effectively dead after the last and greatest of rebellions, the '45', which was ended by the government victory at Culloden in April 1746. Since that time political theorists have continued to cite Jacobitism as an example of a body of belief which rejects the technical legitimacy of a particular system of government even if it is, in other respects, far from radical. LA

Jamaat-e Islami *See* ISLAMIC POLITICS.

janjaweed *See* DARFUR.

J-curve Illustration, developed by James C. Davis in a 1962 article, 'Toward a Theory of *Revolution', of the idea that 'revolutions are most likely to occur when a prolonged period of objective economic and social development is followed by a short period of sharp reversal'. A graph, mapping time (*x*-axis) and needs (*y*-axis) to represent rising expectations followed by their effective frustration, shows a letter J turned 135 degrees anticlockwise.

Jefferson, Thomas (1743–1826) American politician, scientist, educationalist, library cataloguer, architect, ambassador, winegrower, and writer. Born and brought up in Virginia, Jefferson was educated at the College of William and Mary in Williamsburg, then the state capital. Here he was introduced both to pre-Revolutionary politics and to the ideas of the Scottish *Enlightenment. He was elected as a delegate from Virginia to the Continental Congress of 1776. Jefferson drafted the Declaration of Independence, a statement of claims derived from *Locke of the equal right of all men to self-government. 'All men' did not include Indians or slaves, and Jefferson could never reconcile the universality of the Declaration with his practical views on slavery. (It would have been very difficult to run his marvellous and beautiful house at Monticello without slaves.)

Jefferson was disillusioned by the legislature of independent Virginia: 'All the powers of government . . . result to the legislative body. The concentrating these in the same hands is precisely the definition of despotic government . . . .173 despots would surely be as oppressive as one.' Some of his ideas on restraint of government, such as the Virginia Declaration of Religious Freedom, found their way into the First Amendment of the US Constitution. He was also much affected by the death of his wife in 1782. He therefore accepted with alacrity the offer of a post as American Minister in Paris (1784–9). Here he was a bridge between the American and French Revolutions. He coached the Marquis de Lafayette in writing the Declaration of the Rights of Man (1789), which Jefferson regarded as a somewhat inferior copy of the Declaration of 1776 necessitated by the survival of feudalism in Europe. He associated with *Condorcet, with whom he shared beliefs in the perfectibility of mankind and the applicability of scientific method to solving political problems. Jefferson succeeded in some of his Enlightenment-inspired plans for the United States (for instance, in the North-West Ordinance of 1787, which laid out the plans for future white settlement, reserving one block of land in each settlement for the support of education), but failed in others, including metrication.

Jefferson served in the administrations of George Washington from 1789 to 1793 and was President himself from 1801 to 1809. He was responsible for the system of *apportionment of House seats to states after each census which was used until the census of 1830, and is mathematically the same as the *d'Hondt system of proportional representation. In the first US party system, he was the leader of the Republican–Democratic party, which stood for rural self-sufficiency and (relative) trust in the ordinary voter as against the urban and pro-business policies of the Federalists (*see* ADAMS and HAMILTON). He is regarded as the co-founder (with Andrew Jackson, President 1829–37) of the *Democratic coalition—rural, populist, embracing North and South until 1860. After his retirement, Jefferson was intensely active, and left his mark on architecture, garden design, universities, and librarianship through his oversight of the building of the University of Virginia and his books and cataloguing system which formed the nucleus of the Library of Congress. His epitaph, chosen by himself, describes him as 'author of the Declaration of American Independence, of the statute of Virginia for religious freedom, and father of the University of Virginia'.

jerrymandering *See* GERRYMANDERING.

jihad Term to indicate struggle. Linguistically, in Arabic the root letters of the word 'jihad' (dʒ – h – d) mean 'to endeavour, to strive'. The derivative word 'jihad' (dʒ – h – a: – d) however, has different layers of meaning, including the term 'holy war'. The religious meaning of the word 'jihad' has been interpreted in different ways, and Islamic scholars have discussed ideas related to 'greater jihad' and 'lesser jihad'. Prophet Mohammed is said to have referred to a person's inner struggle—which could revolve around vices such as greed or jealousy, for example—as the 'greater jihad'. Those who follow this interpretation would thus argue that jihad primarily refers to an internal struggle. Others have argued that jihad primarily refers to the notion of a 'holy war' and an associated duty to establish an Islamic society. The ideas of Sayyid Qutb, for example, increasingly embraced a militant version of Islam in which the overthrow of existing order—rather than attempts to revise it or establish parallel societal alternatives—is the primary objective. Others have developed such ideas further, often relying on extremely selective interpretations of existing texts. It is through such connections that the link between Islam and violence has been elaborated in, for example, the ideology of militant Islamic groups and in areas of *Islamic fundamentalism.   JHa

Jim Crow laws Laws or practices designed to separate whites and blacks in public and private facilities. Used in Southern states of the United States to preserve segregated schools, transport facilities, and housing, until the doctrine of 'separate but equal' was declared unconstitutional in 1954.

jingoism From a British music-hall song of 1878: 'We don't want to fight, yet by jingo! if we do, | We've got the ships, we've got the men, and got the money too.' This was immediately taken up by those who wanted Britain to go to war with Russia, who were labelled 'jingoes' by the socialist G. J. Holyoake. Hence jingoism is aggressive militaristic patriotism.

Jinnah, M. A. (1876–1948) The first Governor-General of Pakistan, who led the struggle for the partition of India so that Muslims could form their own state. The call for the formation of Pakistan was made in 1940 by the Muslim League party led by Jinnah. The

League claimed that the results of the 1937 elections which were held under the Government of India Act of 1935, when the *Congress party failed to do well in the *separate electorates reserved for minorities, clearly showed that Muslims did not want to be ruled by a Hindu-dominated Congress. Between 1940 and 1945 the Muslim League led by Jinnah made concerted efforts to crystallize Muslim opinion behind the idea of an independent Pakistan. Its efforts bore fruit when Pakistan became an independent nation-state on 14 August 1947. Jinnah died soon after, in 1948. Himself a British-educated lawyer, the lasting legacy of Jinnah has been realizing the idea of a Muslim state in Pakistan rather than a wider vision of a post-colonial society. SR

joint committee In bicameral legislatures, joint committees, containing members of both houses, can be convened in order to coordinate activities, avoid duplicating work, or to discuss matters of common interest.

In the US Congress joint committees play an important legislative role. The two houses often pass substantially different versions of the same bill, in which case a joint committee, usually consisting of three members from each house, is convened. The joint committee seeks to find a compromise between the different versions of the bill, a procedure that often involves substantial redrafting. Joint committees are also convened to carry out congressional investigations, or to discuss business the two houses have in common, such as the running of common facilities, or arranging celebrations or memorials. There are also a number of permanent joint committees.

Jubilee 2000 Campaign which sought to remove the debt burden from a number of the poorest countries in the world through a unilateral gesture at the end of the twentieth century. It was supported by various religious groups, trade unions, and NGOs, and lobbied individual creditor nations and the *IMF and *World Bank. By unilaterally cancelling debt through a one-off gesture it was hoped that poverty could be alleviated, without what were seen as debilitating constraints of *conditionality and whilst avoiding undermining the international system of finance by encouraging debt default. The

campaign succeeded in putting public pressure on Western governments to address the problems of Third World debt, and the IMF and World Bank granted limited debt relief to 22 of the most debt-ridden countries.

(⊕) SEE WEB LINKS
• Jubilee 2000 website.

Judaism The religion of the Jews, characterized by: (1) its monotheism; (2) its belief in a special covenant with God making it his 'chosen people'; (3) ethnic and territorial identity (the 'promised land'); (4) specific laws and practices; and (5) Messianism.

Its origin dates either from Abraham's covenant with God or Moses' formulation of monotheism and of the laws attributed to him included in the Pentateuch. However, political Judaism is most closely associated with King David, who set up his capital in Judah and planned the temple of Jerusalem, built by his son Solomon. During the Babylonian captivity (586–538 BC) Judaism was consolidated and the Mosaic law was written down.

As befits a theocracy the distinction between divine and civil law is blurred. God is the supreme power and his command is law, be it religious or civil—a view shared by Islamic fundamentalists. Mosaic law (*torah*) was fixed by the fifth century BC. It was interpreted by the Talmud and the Midrash. The Talmud includes religious and civil laws not in the Torah proper, and gives explanations of them.

Unlike the Talmud, the Midrash keeps close to scripture and is exegetical. It covers a period from at least the second till the twelfth centuries AD. It consists of (*a*) the Halakah, a collection of traditional laws and minor precepts not in other written law, and (*b*) the Haggadah, free interpretation of scripture consisting of parable stories and other non-prescriptive material, used exclusively at Seder, the initial ritual of the Passover.

The high priest was usually the head of state and administered both religious and civil law, though, as in the Maccabean (Hasmonean) dynasty, there were kings. Rabbis were both interpreters of the law and civil judges. The scribes fixed the text of the law and recorded interpretations as they occurred through time. The Pharisees were a sect that devoted themselves to the exact observance of oral and written law. While the Babylonian captivity tended to unite the Jews, the Roman occupation of Palestine, the Herodian dynasty, and finally the destruction of the temple in AD 70 led to the dispersion of the Jews. Fragmentation accompanied dispersion, from the extremes of fundamentalism (Karaites who reject rabbinical tradition and rely on scripture alone) and orthodoxy, to rationalism, either purely philosophical or a mixture of philosophy and Talmudic and rabbinical tradition.

By the seventh century AD Palestine had been occupied by the Muslims. During the Middle Ages Jews spread throughout Europe, west, and east. For the most part they lived in enclaves (ghettos) and from time to time were persecuted, and at best tolerated and protected.

*Anti-Semitism became politically prominent in 1894 when Alfred Dreyfus, a French Jewish army officer, was wrongly convicted of spying for the Germans and deported to Devil's Island. In 1896 Theodor Herzl wrote a book, *Der Judenstaat*, advocating a Jewish homeland in Palestine. In 1897 he organized the first *Zionist Congress to further this aim. In 1917 the British minister Arthur Balfour promised the British Zionist Federation that when Palestine was liberated from the Turks limited quotas of Jews could settle there. From 1920 to 1948 Palestine was under British mandate. During this time increasing numbers of Jews availed themselves of the Balfour Declaration. This influx was accelerated during and after the Second World War as a result of the Nazi persecution of the Jews in occupied Europe. The state of Israel was established with the blessing of the UN in 1948. The Jews had returned to part of their homeland, but the state was secular, not a theocracy, and Jerusalem was divided.   CB

judicial activism/judicial restraint Alternative judicial philosophies in the United States. Those who subscribe to *judicial restraint* contend that the role of judges should be scrupulously limited; it is their job merely to say what the law is, leaving the business of law-making where it properly belongs, with legislators and executives. Under no circumstances, moreover, should judges allow their personal political values and policy agendas to colour their judicial

opinions. This view holds that the 'original intent' of the authors of the Constitution and its amendments is knowable, and must guide the courts.

For those who adhere to these views, typically in recent years conservative Republicans, the *judicial activism* of the United States Supreme Court led by Earl Warren between 1953 and 1969 was an outrage. By a series of intensely controversial decisions concerning matters such as segregation in education, legislative reapportionment, and the rights of those suspected of crimes, the Warren Court effectively made public policy in a number of sensitive areas. In so doing, it is charged, the Court violated both the separation of powers and federalism and wilfully inserted its political values into judicial decisions.

Presidents favouring judicial restraint such as Richard Nixon, Ronald Reagan, and George Bush Sr, have attempted to counter these developments by trying to appoint 'strict constructionists' to the federal bench, although they did not always distinguish sufficiently between judicial restraint and political conservatism. Strict constructionists believe that in interpreting the Constitution, judges should be bound by 'original intent'. Taken to extremes this position presents a number of difficulties. It is not at all easy to establish what the intentions of the drafters were and, in any case, the Constitution necessarily offers only an outline, designed more than two centuries ago, for a far smaller and profoundly different society. To cling to the intent of the framers of the Constitution is to deny the possibility of constitutional development; the essential updating that an antique instrument surely requires. And yet if judicial activism were to become rampant the Constitution would ultimately lose all meaning. Some strict constructionists can be surprisingly loose when they want to achieve a politically desired result. This is the serious charge against the Court majority that, by one vote in *Bush* v. *Gore* (2000), stopped the vote counts in Florida and thereby handed the presidency to George W. Bush.   DM

judicial restraint *See* JUDICIAL ACTIVISM.

judicial review The power to review legislative and executive acts and to nullify those that are believed to contravene a constitution. Used in a number of countries including Australia, Pakistan, Japan, India, Germany, Italy, and the United States.

Judicial review is not in fact mentioned in the US Constitution, nor was it discussed at the Constitutional Convention in 1787. It has, however, been suggested that the practice can be traced back to the colonial period when the Privy Council in London acted as a final court of appeal and assumed the right to strike down colonial legislation that did not conform to the English Constitution. The federal judiciary's right to exercise judicial review was boldly asserted by Alexander *Hamilton in *Federalist Paper* no. 78 when he said 'The interpretation of the laws is the proper and peculiar province of the courts. A constitution is, in fact, and must be regarded by the judges as, a fundamental law. It therefore belongs to them to ascertain its meaning as well as the meaning of any particular act proceeding from the legislative body.'

The principle of judicial review was further elaborated and justified in one of the most famous Supreme Court decisions, *Marbury* v. *Madison* (1803) when part of the Federal Judiciary Act of 1789 was declared unconstitutional. Chief Justice John Marshall, on behalf of the Court, noted that: 'the Constitution organizes the government, and assigns to different departments their respective powers...The powers of the legislature are defined and limited; and that those limits may not be mistaken, or forgotten the constitution is written. To what purpose are powers limited, and to what purpose is that limitation committed to writing, if these limits may, at any time, be passed by those intended to be restrained?...It is a proposition too plain to be contested, that the constitution controls any legislative act repugnant to it;...It is emphatically the province and duty of the judicial department to say what the law is.'

Theoretically, this makes a lot of sense. Those who set up the American political system were trying to construct a government of divided, limited powers and the whole purpose of having a written constitution was to ensure that those divisions and limitations were properly respected. The supremacy of the Constitution over legislative acts in such a system cannot be denied and there is plausibility to the argument that the federal courts must adjudicate when

disputes arise as to the constitutionality of legislation. In practice, however, such arrangements pose important problems. Those appointed to the courts are often selected for political reasons, and, many have not been slow to import their personal, political preferences into their judicial decision-making. This would matter less if the Constitution was not such a brief, ambiguous document subject to many interpretations and profound disagreement.

It is also a cause for concern among some observers that judicial review allows unelected judges, appointed for life, to become the ultimate arbiters of public policy-making, able to defy even the wishes of the majority, and thereby violating basic principles of liberal democracy. In response to such complaints it can be argued that the federal courts are not immune to the will of the people. The appointment process, for instance, allows elected officials to exercise influence on the judiciary—the President appoints federal judges subject to the advice and consent of the Senate.

Furthermore, as Hamilton observed in *Federalist Paper* no. 78, checks and balances incorporated in the Constitution ensure that the courts constitute the 'least dangerous' branch of the government. Thus the scope of the appellate jurisdiction of the Supreme Court is subject to the will of Congress and, while the latter possesses the power of the purse and the executive the power of the sword, the Court has no means of enforcing its decisions. It is also the case that the Supreme Court has shown itself capable of reversing earlier decisions that no longer meet with popular support. It is also possible to impeach judges, or to overturn their decisions by the process of constitutional amendment.   DM

judiciary The body of judges in a country. Four main issues concerning them commonly arise in political discussion.

1 *Judicial independence.* It is generally thought important for the rule of law that judges should not be easily dismissible. This is typically guaranteed in constitutions. For instance, the US Constitution, in Article III: 1, lays down that 'The Judges, both of the supreme and inferior courts, shall hold their offices during good Behaviour, and shall, at

stated Times, receive for their Services, a Compensation, which shall not be diminished during their Continuance in Office'. Similar arrangements are secured in Britain by charging judges' salaries to a fund which is not reviewable by Parliament. This leaves politicians with considerable control over the appointment of judges. Notoriously, American Presidents try to appoint Supreme Court justices who they think will support their politics; equally notoriously, they are often disappointed. President Eisenhower is said to have called his appointment of Chief Justice Earl Warren 'the biggest damfool mistake I ever made' (*see also* CIVIL RIGHTS; JUDICIAL ACTIVISM).

2 *Judicial review of legislation.* Written constitutions give the power to review the constitutionality of laws to the regular courts, to special constitutional courts, or in France, to the *Conseil Constitutionnel.* By contrast, the British doctrine of *parliamentary sovereignty gives judges no power to review the constitutionality of laws, only the power to declare what they really mean. In some cases, as in a Court of Appeal ruling on the powers and duties of the *Boundary Commission in 1983, this may turn out to be quite different from what Parliament intended them to mean. However, since 1990, British courts have been prepared to review legislation for consistency with European Union and (more recently) human rights law. This contradicts *parliamentary sovereignty.

3 *Judicial review of executive actions.* Because the US Constitution gives Congress the power 'to regulate Commerce with foreign Nations, and among the several States, and with the Indian Tribes', the courts were drawn early on into the regulation of executive acts and agencies dealing with interstate commerce. Most judicial systems, in this case including the British and French, have a similar power (*see also* ADMINISTRATIVE LAW). It is now common for aggrieved parties to ask for judicial review of executive actions in Britain.

4 *Their social origins.* Especially in Britain, the case against giving more independence to the judiciary is generally based on an argument that they are drawn from a narrow social stratum and cannot be expected to give a fair hearing to the poor or to ethnic minorities; and/or that they are biased in favour of individualism against collectivism.

That they are drawn from a narrow social stratum is undeniable, especially in Britain where most judges are recruited from the ranks of barristers (advocates) and where the recruitment of barristers is peculiar even by British standards. But it has never been satisfactorily shown that they are systematically biased in the ways suggested.

junta This Spanish word meaning 'council' referred in the sixteenth century to government consultative committees. In modern usage it refers to a military council that rules a country following a *coup d'état*, before constitutional rule is restored. In Latin America juntas are normally formed by the chiefs of the army, air force, and navy. RG

jurisprudence The science of law. More specifically, jurists are concerned to produce a systematic understanding of the nature of law, and its development, to expound the principles upon which it is, or should be, organized, including its relationship to other institutions and practices, like morality, and to elucidate its internal practices. 'Law' may be positive law, natural law (hence the important tradition of 'natural jurisprudence'), or even a regulatory code not part of a formal legal system. The abstract nature of these concerns might appear to distance jurisprudence from the content of law, but the principles it explores or adumbrates are those which do or could form part of the practice of lawyers or are those applied, or capable of being applied, within the legal system. Hence the relationship between law and jurisprudence is akin to that between *politics and *political theory. AR

jury (theorem) A body of people charged with deciding the truth of some claim. In democratic Athens, juries had 501, 1,001, or 1,501 members (an odd number to avoid tied votes). Then as now, jurors were selected randomly (at least in principle). The idea that it is fair that the guilt or innocence of the accused should be decided by a jury selected at random from his or her fellow-citizens was formalized by *Condorcet, whose jury theorem states that if each juror is on average more likely to judge correctly than wrongly whether the accused is guilty, then the verdict of the majority will be trustworthy. In particular, each juror need be only just more likely to be right than wrong for a majority of, say, 10 to 2 to be sufficient to conclude that the majority is correct. The jury theorem is again being studied and applied in politics and other social sciences.

justice The existence of a proper balance. Justice in law illustrates applications of the notion of a proper balance: a fair trial, which, among other things, achieves a proper balance between the ability of the defendant to establish innocence and the ability of the prosecution to establish guilt; a just sentence (*see* PUNISHMENT) which balances the precedent wrong with a present response. In political theory, justice has concerned both the terms of membership of a social group (*see* SOCIAL JUSTICE) and the distribution of burdens and benefits within that group (*see* DISTRIBUTIVE JUSTICE). In a legal context, distribution is sometimes contrasted with compensation, with restoring the proper balance which existed before a wrong, and this view informs some theories of punishment. *Plato's Republic* depicted a just society as one in which various social functions were properly fulfilled and balanced, thus tending to assimilate the virtue of justice with the pursuit of the common good. This assimilation makes justice the cardinal virtue of political order, but is resisted by those, for example, who might wish to consider how just a society is as only one of a number of guides to the desirability of a life within it. *See also* GLOBAL JUSTICE.   AR

just war A war held to be justly caused and humanely conducted.

Classical Greek thought, as represented most graphically in *Thucydides' History of the Peloponnesian War*, accepted war as an inherent aspect of politics. The early Christians were pacifist and practised abstention from politics. The Roman empire, once converted to Christianity, had to reconcile the pacifist teaching of Christ with the demands of politics, power, and war. *Augustine's City of God argued that day-to-day acceptance of political 'realities' was inevitable for Christians living in a fallen world. The theme was developed by *Aquinas, who distinguished between just and unjust war using two sets of criteria, the justice of the cause (*jus ad bellum*) and the justice of the conduct (*jus in bello*).

The two elements of just cause and just conduct have continued to dominate the debate. In the twentieth century, just cause has narrowed to self-defence against aggression and helping the victims of aggression. The doctrine of just cause has concentrated on discrimination between combatants and non-combatants and proportionality between the injustice suffered and the level of retaliation. The waging of 'total war' has strained practically to breaking point the doctrine of just war.

Nuclear deterrence has added an additional dimension to the debate because, while most theorists of just war have condemned nuclear war as unjust (on grounds of discrimination and proportionality, but also on grounds that there is no prospect of a successful outcome), some Christian thinkers have considered deterrence—the threat to use nuclear weapons—to be morally allowable. Some Catholics, for instance the American Bishops, have distinguished between the mere possession of nuclear weapons, constituting a so-called existential deterrent, and the intention to use those weapons, the former being allowable while the latter is disallowed. *See also* SUAREZ.   PBY

Kant, Immanuel (1724–1804) German philosopher of the idealist school. Kant lived a quiet academic life in the East Prussian city of Königsberg (now Kaliningrad). It has been a matter of much consolation to philosophers that Kant, renowned as one of the greatest of European thinkers, published all his most important works after the age of 57.

Kant is not normally thought of as a political theorist. But his philosophy of ethics and law makes such profound suggestions about the nature of duty, law, and freedom that it would trivialize political theory to exclude them from that subject. Kant is often claimed as an 'Enlightenment' theorist. In some respects, however, his project is the opposite of that of many of his contemporaries. *Holbach in France and *Bentham in England produced ethical theories which were hedonistic and *consequentialist, judging actions on their consequences for people's well-being rather than on their conformance to any natural or divine law. Kant, on the other hand, attempted the reconstruction of traditional doctrines on new, rational foundations.

The core argument of this enterprise is the derivation of a shape and a minimal content for our duties from the nature of our being as rational, autonomous agents. The nature of the argument is similar to that used by Kant to derive the universality of causation in his philosophy of science, the 'synthetic a priori'. It amounts to saying that there are propositions which we must accept not because they are logical necessities, nor because they are observably true in the world, but because they are presuppositions which must be made if we are to have a rational discourse of a certain sort. Thus we must assume that causation exists if we are to have a science and we must assume that universal rules exist if we, as rational beings, are to have moral arguments. This is the 'categorical imperative' which requires that we act only on precepts which we can will as

universal laws. The most general precept which follows from this is that we should treat other people as ends, not merely as means. Duty, derived from the categorical imperative, is a 'sublime and mighty name' for Kant and goodness is the performance of duty because it is duty. (This view was satirized by the poet Friedrich Schiller as a doctrine which made it impossible for a sympathetic person to be good since such a person derived pleasure from the well-being of his companions.) In *The Philosophy of Law* Kant took his view of duty to its ultimate conclusion by imagining a social contract in reverse, in which everybody decided to end society and to enter a state of nature. The dissolution must not be carried out, says Kant, until all existing criminals have completed their punishments. Such a view would, of course, make no sense within consequentialist assumptions because in their terms the purpose of law and punishment is to achieve order so as to maximize well-being in society. If society is to end, then punishment can serve no purpose.

Kant's most specifically political writings applied the universalism of his theories of ethics and law. In *Perpetual Peace*, published in 1795, he argued for a 'League of Nations' (called the Pacific Federation) to enforce the natural, rationally derivable and (therefore) international law, envisaging a decline in the power of individual states as that of the universal authority came to be established.

Many modern thinkers can be described as 'neo-Kantian' in so far as they attempt to derive the existence of universally valid moral precepts which should be obeyed regardless of the consequences from some essential feature of the human condition. *See* COSMOPOLITANISM. LA

Kashmir Disputed region, whose sovereignty is contested by India and Pakistan.

When the British announced their withdrawal from India and *partition in 1947, the ruler of the State of Jammu and Kashmir was reluctant to join with either India or Pakistan, but in the light of military incursions from Pakistan acceded to India. Continued fighting lasted until the United Nations negotiated a ceasefire, and the State was divided by a line of control. There was another war between India and Pakistan over Kashmir in 1965, and there have been periodic military flare-ups since the 1990s. The Indian State of Jammu and Kashmir is predominantly Muslim, but with significant areas populated by Hindus and Buddhists. In the face of hardening religious identities, set against a backdrop of a destabilizing and militarizing conflict in Afghanistan, and with value for both India and Pakistan as a key strategic location, the prospects for conflict resolution seem remote. Since both India and Pakistan now have nuclear weapons, such a source of tension is potentially disastrous.

Kautilya (*c.*300 BC) Kautilya (also known as Chanakya and Vishnugupta) is known as the author of the *Arthashastra* (which can be translated as *The Art of Well-being* or *The Science of Polity*), a book which is part political philosophy, part manual of statecraft. Although the *Arthashastra* had been referred to in other ancient books, a full text was only rediscovered in 1904, when an ancient copy, written on palm leaves, was handed over to an Indian librarian by an anonymous donor.

Kautilya was a political adviser in the service of Chandragupta, the founder of the Mauryan empire which stretched across the north of the Indian subcontinent. The *Arthashastra* describes the means by which a state should be established and maintained in the face of the threat of competing powers and an inherent danger of social instability. In the absence of the state, people are subject to the 'law of the fishes', whereby the stronger swallows the weak. The role of the king is to enhance the prosperity of his people, increasing the power of the state, and expanding the territory through conquest. The prosperity of the people is enhanced through the promotion of trade, the development of infrastructure (such as dams and communications), and the strict enforcement of a system of law and order.

A comprehensive list of crime and punishment is set down, ranging from being publicly smeared with dung for minor theft to being boiled alive for sleeping with a queen. The power of the state stems from a strong basis in trade which is harnessed through a taxation system run by a well-maintained civil service.

The issue of territorial protection and conquest is the basis of Kautilya's most incisive political thought, and can be taken to be an early guide to the field of *international relations. Here he deals with a wide variety of strategies, which can be used independently or in combination, to deal with different situations according to the relative strengths of the opposition. These strategies include conciliation (through flattery, bribery, or other inducements), sowing dissent amongst the opposition, forming coalitions with other rulers, consolidation, and the use of hostility and force. Different circumstances are described, along with the appropriate choice of strategy, the likely outcome, and the appropriate pay-offs for the actors involved. Kautilya has been compared to *Machiavelli in the breadth of his statecraft, and also for his willingness to use deceit and intrigue, not just against opponents but also to bolster the king's reputation with his people. However, the *Arthashastra* exhibits a repeated commitment to the welfare of the people and principles of order and justice. The duty of a conqueror, for instance, is to 'substitute his virtues for the defeated enemy's vices, and where the enemy was good he shall be twice as good'.

Kautsky, Karl (1854–1938) Chief theorist of the German Social Democratic Party before 1914. Co-author with *Bernstein of the Erfurt Programme (1891) which adopted *Marxism as the official party ideology. His most innovative work was on *imperialism. He argued that the contradiction between increased production and underconsumption led to colonial expansion, competition, and war between the industrialized powers (although he later conceived of an 'ultra-imperialism' which would divide the world into spheres of influence and so ensure peace). Kautsky rejected *revisionism, insisting upon the inevitability of class conflict. His view of Marxism as a predictive science led him to undervalue revolutionary strategy—what the Dutch Marxist Panne-koek called 'the theory of passive radicalism'. Thus in his debate with *Luxemburg over the mass strike, he viewed it as a defensive position rather than a means of seizing power.

In *The Road to Power* (1909) he stressed the democratic nature of the *dictatorship of the proletariat, interpreting it as meaning not class war but rather the majority rule of the *proletariat under democratic conditions. His criticism of the October Revolution (which provoked Lenin to write *The Renegade Kautsky and the Proletarian Revolution*) centred upon the impossibility of creating socialism in an underdeveloped society. The Bolsheviks had established a dictatorship over the proletariat resulting in a bureaucratization of the state and the rise of a new ruling class. GL

Kemalism The ideology promoted by Mustafa Kemal (Atatürk) and his associates after the creation of the Republic of Turkey. The basis for Kemalism is to be found in the Ottoman reforms which began in 1839. These reforms—known as the Tanzimat (reorganization) produced the Young Ottomans, followed by the Young Turks. They produced a class of civil servants, professional and military technocrats, imbued with knowledge, organizational skills, and technological adeptness of their counterparts in Europe together with aspirations and motivational drives engendered by modernizing influences and the adoption of secular legal codes. However, they also preserved the fundamental traditional institutions of the Shari'a (Islamic Law), together with its courts and the Islamic schools. Later reformers—Kemal included—regarded the maintenance of the latter as an important reason for the weakness of the Tanzimat reforms.

The Committee of Union and Progress—the political organ of the Young Turk movement—was formed in 1908 and produced the leadership of the Turkish Republic of 1923. The six principles of Kemalism were: (1) *Republicanism*; (2) *Secularism*, which meant that there would be no state religion and there would be secular control of law and education. In 1924, the Caliphate was abolished, followed by the abolition of the Shari'a courts (1925) together with the adoption of the Swiss civil and Italian penal codes

(1926). Included in this package was the suppression of convents, monasteries, and religious schools, the Latinizing of the alphabet, the enforced change to a Western style of dress, emancipation of women, and Turkification of the Qur'an. (3) *Nationalism* promoted the idea that the Turkish language identifies the nation, that it was devoid of racial, religious, or ethnic sense and encompasses all those found within the confines of Turkey. (4) *Populism* was a vague notion which stressed popular sovereignty, the mutual responsibility of state and individual and the absence of social class. (5) *Revolutionism* entailed the orderly transformation of society to bring it into the family of advanced nations. This meant transforming the outlook of people, the adoption of Western ways, confronting ignorance and superstition, and importing new techniques together with the promotion of economic development and science. (6) *Étatism* implied that the state should play an active role in economic development, social, cultural, and education activities when the general interests of the state are involved.

The modernization of Turkish society occurred after the First World War in a troubled international environment. Kemalists, disillusioned with the consequences of the war, opted for the establishment of a Turkish nation on a diminished territory of the Ottoman Empire inhabited largely by Turks. Lacking a credible power source other than its army, with an economy underdeveloped and in disarray, political discontent among minority groupings and the threat of the dismemberment of the territory that had been mapped out for the Turkish nation, Mustafa Kemal organized the administration of the new nation on authoritarian lines with the objective of modernizing its society on the model of a Western secular order to define itself as part of Western civilization. BAR

Keynes, John Maynard (1883–1946) British economist, who made a leading contribution to economic theory, particularly through *The General Theory of Employment, Interest, and Money* (1936), to economic policy, and to international economic negotiations. The use of the word 'Keynesian' to describe a particular mix of economic and social policy is a reflection of the success of his attempt to provide an intellectual justification for a form of government intervention that would save capitalism and liberal democracy, a task which appeared to be a compelling and urgent one in the 1930s. In a chapter entitled 'Concluding Notes on the Social Philosophy towards which the General Theory might Lead', Keynes admits that his theory is moderately conservative in its implications. The state would intervene in some areas, including the use of the tax system to influence the propensity to consume, but wide fields of activity would be unaffected. A comprehensive socialization of investment would be necessary to achieve full employment, but this could be achieved by what would later be called public–private partnerships. There was no obvious case for a comprehensive system of state socialism, and most of the necessary measures could be introduced gradually, and without a general break in the traditions of society.

Keynes was a product of an essentially Victorian milieu which had set aside religious belief, but maintained a strong interest in moral rules of conduct, underpinned by rational justification rather than faith in the existence of a deity. From Eton he went to King's College where he graduated in mathematics and then spent a fourth year reading economics, then dominated by Alfred Marshall and his *Principles of Economics*. While at Cambridge, Keynes wrote a long prize essay on *Burke which gives a good indication of Keynes's developing political beliefs. He emphasized Burke's advocacy of expediency against abstract rights, and, like Burke, he was uncertain about the value of basing action on absolute principles. Keynes supported Burke's view that war should be approached with prudence, and in the First World War he attempted to register as a conscientious objector, but was exempted because of his work at the Treasury. In 1919 he published a critique of the *Versailles settlement entitled *The Economic Consequences of the Peace*, which achieved substantial worldwide sales and had a considerable influence on political opinion. Keynes argued that the Versailles settlement would impoverish Europe.

In the early 1920s, Keynes became involved with the Liberal Party. In 1926 he became a member of a Liberal Industrial Inquiry, drafting substantial parts of the report *Britain's Industrial Future*, better known as the *Yellow Book*. One of the proposals was that the investment funds of all public concerns should be put into a separate capital budget under the direction of a national investment board. The disappointing performance of the Liberals in 1929, and their reactions to the depression, lessened his enthusiasm for the party. He gave some financial support to individual Labour candidates in the 1930s, and made some favourable comments about Labour policies. When he became a peer in 1942 he sat as an independent, although he continued to express some sympathy for the Liberals and gave them a small donation in 1945. As one of Keynes's biographers, Robert Skidelsky, has pointed out, Keynes was a political economist rather than a political animal, someone who was interested in influencing public policy, but who believed that the intellectual argument had to be won before the political argument. Although Keynes wrote extensively for the popular press in the middle period of his life, he was of a generation that believed that rational decision-making could be left to a well-informed elite based in London and the ancient universities. Keynes had the economist's habit of referring to political difficulties as second-order problems for which economists had no professional responsibility to provide solutions. He recognized that full employment could lead to upward pressures on wages, a problem which eventually led economists working in the Keynesian tradition to advocate *incomes policies. He argued that the task of keeping wages reasonably stable was a 'political rather than an economic problem', and that the combination of collective bargaining and full employment was an 'essentially political problem' where analytical methods were of little assistance. His involvement in important economic negotiations with the Americans during and immediately after the Second World War showed that he had good negotiating skills, and an awareness of political realities and the need for mutual accommodation. Keynes's advocacy of macroeconomic economic management did not provide an enduring solution to the problem of maintaining full employment, even less that of curbing inflation, but no discussion of the politics of economic management in the latter half of the twentieth century can proceed very far without reference to Keynes and his influential, if often ambiguous, ideas. WG

Key, V. O., Jr. (1908–63) US political scientist. Renowned first for *Southern Politics* (1949), the finest work in the electoral geographical tradition of André *Siegfried to appear in the United States, and subsequently for the first challenge to the *party identification perspective on the American voter in favour of *issue voting and retrospective voting. He was also noted for his writing on *interest groups.

Khaldun, Ibn *See* IBN KHALDUN.

Khmer Rouge A communist military faction in Cambodia (which they renamed Democratic Kampuchea) which took power under their leader Pol Pot in 1975. They were responsible for *genocidal massacres of people from many sectors of the population. Driven from power by the Vietnamese invasion in 1979, they lingered on as a guerrilla force.

Khrushchev, Nikita Sergeyevich (1894–1971) Soviet Communist Party Secretary from 1953 to 1964 (Premier from 1958). Khrushchev's denunciation of Stalin ('Secret Speech', 1956) marked a decisive break in post-war Soviet politics. In foreign policy, Khrushchev maintained the possibility of 'peaceful coexistence' with the West, despite stumbling into a superpower showdown over missile deployment in *Cuba in 1962. Domestically, the failures of his reorganization of the Party administrative apparatus and reform of agricultural policy contributed to his forced 'resignation' in 1964. swh

kibbutz Hebrew word meaning 'gathering'. A collective farm in Israel, whose members work cooperatively and do not hold private property. Kibbutzim were set up by Jewish settlers in Palestine before the establishment of the state of Israel. In the 1960s and 1970s they were popular among idealistic non-Jews in the West, but their popularity has faded.

King, Martin Luther, Jr. (1929–68) Baptist minister who rose to prominence in the 1950s and 1960s as the leader of the American Civil Rights Movement. Having studied theology at Crozier Seminary and Boston

University, King became a pastor in Montgomery, Alabama, in 1955, and was soon asked to head the 'Montgomery Improvement Association' in its campaign for desegregation of city buses. A year later, King founded and headed the Southern Christian Leadership Conference (SCLC), and travelled throughout the country to campaign for the emerging civil rights movement. King's prominence and oratory power served both to unite and to promote various local campaigns against practices of discrimination, some of which resulted in his arrest and imprisonment. On 28 August 1963, King led a 200,000 strong march on Washington, and delivered his famous 'I have a dream' speech from Capitol Hill. Support for the movement was a key factor in the passing of the 1964 Civil Rights and 1965 Voting Rights Acts. He was assassinated in Memphis on 4 April 1968.

King's contribution to the cause of civic activism lies in his justly celebrated doctrine of 'active non-violence' (inspired by the teachings and practice of *Gandhi). Undoubtedly the resolute pacifism of the movement served to promote its cause among white 'middle America', as did its concentration on those civil rights, such as the right to vote, which were difficult for most people to dispute. From 1963 onwards King was increasingly criticized by more radical black activist groups for his moderation (*see* BLACK POWER). In his last years, King turned towards more complex issues affecting black Americans (e.g. the Vietnam War), and attempted to launch a cross-racial coalition against poverty, but his contribution to the dismantling of segregation in the South remains his enduring achievement. sw

kinship Political institutions based on family relationships are the staple of *anthropology. Anthropologists have established that the structure of powers and rights may be patrilineal or matrilineal (in Western written codes it has been almost exclusively patrilineal—*see* FEMINISM). Some anthropologists have highlighted the importance of lineage (descent) in perpetuating political structures; others prefer to stress the role of marriage. There is a long ethical tradition of encouraging people to be as altruistic towards non-relations as they are (assumed to be) towards relations. This may be seen in writers as various as *Plato, the Christian Gospel writers, and *Rousseau. It has been boosted from an unexpected quarter by the recent emergence of kin selection as a central theme in evolutionary biology. The evolutionary advantage in being altruistic on behalf of one's relations lies in the transmission of one's own genetic pattern. Can this explain human impulses towards love of one's children?

kitchen cabinet Small group of close advisers to a prime minister or president, who informally gather to take decisions on government policy. The term was first used to describe the meetings in the White House kitchen between President Andrew Jackson and his friends to discuss government business. There is often tension between members of a kitchen cabinet, who are able to influence policy in an informal way, and those ministers who have direct and official responsibility for government departments but see themselves cut out of the decision-making process.

Korean War The Korean War began on 25 June 1950 when the forces of communist North Korea crossed the 38th Parallel of latitude to invade South Korea. At the time it was widely assumed in the West, and in the United States in particular, that this act of aggression had been planned and ordered by the Soviet Union as a test of Western resolve in the wider context of the Cold War. Nowadays, however, it is believed that the initiative came primarily from the North Korean regime which bitterly resented the artificial partition of the country that had followed the collapse of Japanese rule in 1945. So it may be that President Harry Truman's extremely robust response was based on a misapprehension of what was involved.

In any event, the upshot was that the United States persuaded the Security Council of the United Nations, which was being temporarily boycotted by the veto-wielding Soviet Union, to authorize the sending of military assistance to the victim. The United Nations forces, commanded by US General Douglas MacArthur, narrowly succeeded in preventing the total conquest of South Korea and then went on to drive the North Koreans back across the 38th Parallel. At this point Truman, perhaps unwisely, insisted on punishing the aggressor by taking the war into North Korea. This in turn provoked Chinese intervention in October 1950 which saved North Korea and eventually led to an armistice being agreed in 1953 on the basis of a virtual return to the *status quo ante*.

Late in 1950, however, Truman was urged by some Americans to go for all-out victory even if it meant bombing China, thereby risking a possible escalation to nuclear war if the Soviets then saw fit to intervene. But he resisted this advice and accordingly felt driven to dismiss MacArthur, who did not try to conceal his dissent. Thus the outcome of the Korean War was seen by some as the first war the Americans had failed to win and was held by others to be the first example of the UN-based collective security system actually succeeding in rescuing a victim of aggression. DC

Kropotkin, Peter (1842–1921) A Russian aristocrat by birth, Kropotkin renounced his title in 1872 and henceforth devoted himself to the cause of social revolution, spending most of his later life in Western Europe and Britain. He embraced principles of libertarian communist *anarchism, and expounded his ideas in a number of influential works, including *The Conquest of Bread* (1892), *Fields Factories and Workshops* (1899), and *Mutual Aid: A Factor of Evolution* (1902).

The expulsion of anarchists from the First International in 1872 opened up a wide split in the European revolutionary movement between anarchists and the followers of the 'scientific socialism' of *Marx and *Engels. Kropotkin continued to criticize what he considered to be the authoritarian and centralizing tendencies of Marxist theory, and offered an alternative vision of a new society based on principles of voluntarism, mutual aid, and federalist communitarianism. KT

kulak In official Soviet parlance, the kulak was a rich peasant who exploited private labour. He was designated for 'liquidation as a class' by Stalin during collectivization in the 1930s. In practice, however, the kulak was frequently the best farmer, whose destruction irrevocably harmed Soviet agriculture. swh

Kyoto Protocol (1997) *See* CLIMATE CHANGE.

labour movement Imprecise term referring to two ideas: first, that workers, especially blue-collar or manual workers, share common political and economic interests which may be advanced through organized trade union and political action; secondly, that trade unions can form an effective alliance with left of centre parties in Parliament with the objective of forming a government in which workers' interests would be of central importance.

Labour movements in Europe derive from the reaction of the newly urbanized workers to industrialization in the nineteenth century. *Marxism made a powerful impact on the emergence of labour movements in continental Europe and led to the formation of socialist political parties (Germany 1869); in Britain the labour movement was reformist rather than revolutionary and in the nineteenth century worked within the framework of the existing system of political parties (Labour Representation Committee formed 1900, Labour Party 1906).

The labour movement was strongly internationalist in character, emphasizing the shared interests between workers in different countries in opposing capitalist political regimes. However, in 1914 the socialist parties were swept up in a tide of nationalist fervour and, with the exception of a few individuals, supported the war efforts.

After 1917, labour movements were strongly influenced by the success of the Russian Bolsheviks. However, the established socialist and labour parties almost immediately turned their back on the 'Third International' organized from Moscow to coordinate revolutionary activity by the international communist movement, and separate communist parties were formed. Socialist and communist parties were locked in conflict during the inter-war period. In some countries such as Britain, Germany, and the United States communists played a role within a single trades union movement, while in countries such as France the communists controlled their own trade unions which competed with socialist and Christian trade unions.

After the Second World War, when antifascism provided an imperative for unity, the labour movements again divided and trade unions and socialist parties formed international organizations divided on Cold War lines into pro- and anti-Communist groupings. Further weakening of the significance of the labour movement has occurred with the decline of manual employment, and the declining influence of trade unionism on socialist parties, especially in government.

The idea of the labour movement was revived by the role played in the 1950s and 1960s in the Third World by trade unions in the movements for freedom from colonial rule. However, post-independence, the idea of independent trade unionism representing the rights of workers vis-à-vis governments, which often proclaimed themselves to be socialist, was often difficult to carry into effect. PBY

Labour Party The principal centre-left party in modern British politics. It was established as the Labour Representation Committee in 1900, becoming the Labour Party in 1906. Labour developed as a mass party, with its origins in late nineteenth-century working-class protest. Its strategy from its formation was electoral, eschewing direct action as a route to political power. Its structure formally placed a high premium on internal party democracy, putting responsibility for policy with the annual Party Conference. A key part of Labour's origins, however, lay in the desire of the trade union movement to seek political representation and throughout its history the trade unions have been the party's principal funder. Up to 1993, the Party constitution offered a unique role for the trade unions, who through the power of the block vote dominated decisions at Party Conference. They played a considerable role in the selection of parliamentary candidates, and had the largest share of the vote in the election of the Party's leader and deputy leader. In practice, though, the parliamentary leadership, especially when the Party is in government, has always enjoyed considerable autonomy on policy issues from both the party and trade unions.

Labour's electoral history makes tortuous reading. After allying with the Liberal Party in pre-1914 electoral pacts, it broke through as a party in its own right after the franchise was widened to the lower working class in 1918. Labour formed minority governments in 1924 and 1929–31. However, in 1931 Cabinet division over cuts in public spending led to Labour's leader, Ramsay MacDonald, deserting the party to lead a coalition of so-called 'national' Conservatives, Liberals, and Labour members. Labour later participated in Churchill's Second World War coalition government and after the Second World War Labour became one of the two parties which dominated government. However, Labour's electoral successes before 1997 were much more limited than the Conservatives', and the Party won a clear governing majority on only two occasions (1945 and 1966). In 1950 it won a small majority which it lost the following year. In 1964 it won a small majority which it consolidated in 1966, and in February 1974 it became the largest party but without an overall majority. In October 1974 it won a majority of three seats, though by April 1976 by-election defeats had removed the majority. For nine months in 1977 the Party governed on the basis of a parliamentary pact with the Liberal Party. Not once did Labour win a genuine two-term tenure on power at Westminster.

After 1918 the Party traditionally presented its policies as 'socialist', emphasizing the importance of a large state-controlled sector of the economy, relatively high levels of taxation, and comprehensive state-organized welfare provision. In office, the 1945–50 government of Clement Attlee is widely credited with successful radical reform which epitomized much of this progressive agenda.

The Attlee Government created a mixed economy through the nationalization of a number of strategic industries and public utilities, and promoted Keynesian ideas of economic management. A welfare state was established involving a commitment to full employment, universal social security, free universal state-funded healthcare and extensive state-funded social housing. Attlee also laid down a foreign and defence policy based on NATO, bilateral cooperation with the United States, and the development of nuclear weapons. Such approaches set the framework for government for the next twenty to thirty years.

The general picture, however, was that Labour governments were haunted by caution and failure. The inter-war minority governments lacked political power and were heavily influenced by the desire to show that they were fit to govern. Critics of the 1945 Attlee Government highlight that actually it should have gone a lot further in nationalization and in introducing greater industrial democracy. Post-war governments commonly were unable to develop state intervention as they were beset by economic crises. Both the 1945–50 and 1966–70 Labour governments were forced to devalue the pound. The Labour governments 1974–9 presided over the shock-waves from the oil crisis following the Arab–Israeli war and domestic industrial relations problems. Inflation rose to over 25 per cent and unemployment to over 1 million. Labour was forced to seek a loan from the *International Monetary Fund in 1976, and left government in 1979 tarnished by the image of the winter of discontent, 1978–9, when Britain was hit by a wave of strikes. Labour's common experience was to enter office with big plans and high expectations, only to retreat a few years later overwhelmed by events.

By the time Margaret Thatcher became Conservative Prime Minister in 1979 Labour had turned bitterly in upon itself. What emerged initially was a victory for the more radical left, leading to the departure of leading moderates, known as the 'gang of four', to establish the Social Democratic Party (SDP) in 1981. The Party entered the 1983 General Election committed to a fully planned socialist economy, defended by protectionism that made withdrawal from the European Community virtually certain, as well as withdrawal from NATO and the unilateral dismantling of nuclear weapons. Leadership and campaigning were shambolic and the policy programme was widely attacked. As Labour's vote plummeted to just above that of the Liberal–SDP alliance, one party figure described the 1983 manifesto as 'the longest suicide note in history'. The new leader, Neil Kinnock (1983–92), intent on making the party electable again, took on the left in 1985, denouncing the Militant Tendency as an *entryist organization that should be expelled. Kinnock's purging of the hard left by the early 1990s and the work of his successor, John Smith (1992–4), paved the way for effective party modernization. This included reform of party organization to reduce the power of the trade unions and to enhance the power of the central leadership to keep discipline in the Party. It also involved an embrace of social democratic policies that gave much more emphasis to market economics and defined a lesser role for the state, based on regulation rather than direct ownership or control of the economy.

The advent of Tony Blair as leader in 1994 hastened reform of party organization to move the party even more away from union control and the influence of the left. He also re-branded the Party as *New Labour to emphasize its abandonment of doctrinaire policies of state intervention. In a massive symbolic gesture Blair pushed through reform of Clause IV of the 1918 Party constitution, which had committed the Party to public ownership. It was replaced by a more general commitment to social justice, although cynics should note that the new Clause IV explicitly termed Labour a democratic socialist party where the original clause did not. From this basis Labour were able to offer themselves unambiguously as a modernized centre-left party, and develop policies that mixed state and market solutions to policy problems relatively free from ideological baggage. Blair talked instead of the politics of community, the third way, and of practical evidence-based approaches to managing the economy and the welfare state. Under Blair Labour became the most pro-business and pro-European Union the party has ever been.

Faced by a heavily factionalized Conservative Party, Labour won two landslide election victories in 1997 and 2001 to establish itself for the first time as a two-term party of government; in 2005 it won a third term with a reduced but substantial majority. Blair's New Labour established for itself a place in history comparable to the Attlee Government through its large-scale reforms of the constitution, including House of Lords reform and devolution. Blair's chancellor of the Exchequer, Gordon Brown, also won plaudits for establishing Labour's ability to manage the economy successfully, while gradually increasing investment in public services and directing resources to the poorest members of society. However, major divisions within the party were caused both by the drive to modernize public services after 2001 through a focus on diversification of service provider and a role for the private sector, and by the decision to go to war in Iraq in 2003. The subsequent problems of the Iraq war and controversies over the case for the war in the first place seriously weakened Blair and he eventually stood down in 2007, immediately leaving the Commons for a post as an international special envoy in the Middle East. He was succeeded by Brown who was faced with trying to secure the historic achievement of a fourth election victory in the context of international economic, security, and environmental problems, pressures from the centre-left of the party for a less Blairite approach to economic and social policy, and doubts about his leadership ability. In this he was unsuccessful, the party having one of its worse general elections, losing 91 seats, and being replaced by a Conservative and Liberal Democrat coalition. Gordon Brown resigned as leader and was replaced by Ed Miliband, who had union support and defeated his Blairite brother, David, in the leadership contest. Miliband lacked the charisma of a leader and failed to deliver a coherent policy alternative to the coalition. In Scotland the party was not seen as leading the campaign against independence in the 2014 referendum and the SNP gained significant influence in the traditional Labour heartlands in central Scotland. Labour lost 40 seats in Scotland in the 2015 general election, keeping just one MP north of the border. In the rest of the UK Labour made small gains but overall lost 26 seats. Early in the campaign Labour were expected to be the largest party in Parliament, but they ended with 99 seats fewer than the Conservatives, who gained an absolute majority. Miliband resigned as leader and the result reopened the debate over whether the party needed to move more to the left or more to the middle ground to establish its political future. While advocates suggest Blair, Brown, and other modernizers from Kinnock onwards have skilfully adapted democratic socialist principles for modern times, critics suggest that they more generally represent a betrayal within the party comparable to that of Ramsay MacDonald's in 1931 and the SDP's 'Gang of Four' in 1981. In September 2015, Jeremy Corbyn, a democratic socialist, was elected party leader, marking an official move towards the far left, yet also sparking a number of leadership challenges indicative of continued fractures within the party between old Blairites and left-leaning Corbynites. JBr

(∰) SEE WEB LINKS
• Labour Party website.

labour theory of value The proposition that goods have their value by virtue of the labour, or labour power, that has gone into producing them. The issue was raised by *Locke in chapter 5 of his *Second Treatise of Government* (c.1681). Here Locke argues that, although God left the earth for mankind to enjoy in common, yet individuals had a title, first, to their own bodies and persons, and in consequence, secondly, to whatever they removed from the common stock by their own labours: 'Whatsoever then he removes out of the State that Nature hath provided, and left it in, he hath mixed his Labour with, and joyned to it something that is his own, and thereby makes it his Property.' Locke's theory has been revived by Robert *Nozick in *Anarchy, State, and Utopia* (1974) as a theory of just *entitlement.

However, a labour theory of property rights is not in itself a labour theory of value, although it gives the Marxist version of the latter its ideological underpinnings. The labour theory of value was fully developed by *classical economists, especially David Ricardo and *Marx. Ricardo argued that the price (strictly, the exchange-value) of a good was in ideal conditions determined by the quantity of labour that had gone into producing it (including producing the capital

goods that helped to produce it). Marx argued that this was the price the worker deserved to get (thus making an unspoken connection with Locke before him and, paradoxically, with Nozick after him). However, the worker actually tended to get only enough wages to keep him at work and capable of producing children. The difference between the two was the worker's *surplus value. Under capitalism, surplus value was unjustly appropriated by capitalists; under socialism it would belong to the workers, as in the classically Marxist formula of Clause IV: 4 of the Labour Party constitution (1918–95), which defined its objective as being 'to secure for the workers...the full fruits of their industry'.

The labour theory of value takes no account of the role of demand in setting prices. Two labourers may burn up the identical number of calories in breaking up identical volumes of ore that they have mined on the common. But if one yields iron and the other silver, they will not fetch the same price.

laissez-faire 'Laissez-faire' means 'leave to do'; a more colloquial translation might be 'let them get on with it'. Since the late eighteenth century such phrases as 'a laissez-faire policy' and 'laissez-faire economics' have suggested a belief in the virtues of allowing individuals to pursue their interests through market transactions with minimal government interference.

However, laissez-faire in a broad sense, as opposed to the use of the phrase in particular contexts with respect to particular sections of production, is vague and its historical location elusive. Laissez-faire economics is not normally based on libertarian ethics but rather on the utilitarian calculation that absence of interference functions better than interference. But nearly all market theories are also theories of market failure and it is difficult to identify any leading economic thinker who thought that laissez-faire was the best solution to all problems. Adam *Smith, for example, did not believe that unregulated markets could provide the kind of educational system which a commercial society needed. LA

Lamarckism Term for all of those evolutionary theories which rest upon the inheritance of acquired characteristics, an evolutionary mechanism initially popularized and disseminated by the French thinker Jean Baptiste de Lamarck, notably in the *Philosophie Zoologique* of 1809. This belief is completely discredited. In fact, 'Lamarckism' is now generally held to be incompatible with the central doctrine of molecular biology which denies the transmission of information from soma—that is, the body considered generally and as a whole—to the chemical alphabet of DNA. No molecular mechanism exists that would make such transmission possible. JH

lame duck American term for a person, legislature, or administration that continues to hold office after losing an election.

The practice in the United States of holding presidential elections in November, with the winner taking office only in January (originally in March), means there are often lame duck presidents. Without a *mandate the power to make decisions is undermined, and it becomes easier for opponents of measures to utilize delaying tactics, knowing that the President will soon be out of office.

land reform State intervention to redistribute ownership of land. Often seen as a way of redressing entrenched socio-economic inequalities, attacking *feudalism, and challenging *colonial systems. Implementation of land reform schemes has been widespread, usually with the aim of giving agricultural workers and tenant farmers greater rights. Land reform is a highly politicized issue, challenging individual property rights in the interest of rural reform, and can have mixed consequences in terms of agricultural productivity and social development. It was brutally imposed in the USSR under the *collectivization programme.

language The essence of politics is argument between principles and theories of society. Thus language is to politics as oxygen is to air, its vital and distinct ingredient. Perception of the realities of politics is shaped by the structure and emotional power of language. Words do not merely describe politics, they are part of the politics they describe. It can be argued that almost every choice of word, in most of the discourse we engage in, is a political act. The

academic study of politics has almost entirely failed to develop the kind of agreed, 'neutral' vocabulary which exists in the physical sciences and, to a degree, in economics. The study of politics, like politics itself, is thus in large part a contest over words, a language game. Even *Mao Zedong, who said that 'Political power grows out of the barrel of a gun', saw the 'little red book' of his thoughts as more important than bullets in achieving his communist objective.

Much feminist theory claims that existing language embodies forms of patriarchy or male power: we talk of our species as mankind and refer to God as a male. These forms of language arguably inculcate or maintain the acceptance of a dominant role for the male in social institutions. It is extremely difficult, though, to demonstrate the effects of such usages or to refute the allegation that they are trivialities. It is even more difficult to show them to be forms or tools of 'power' in any workable sense that allows us to attribute control over society. *Orwell offers us, in *1984*, a vision of a society in which the state does control people through its deliberate manipulation of language, by introducing a turgidly jargonistic form of English, 'Newspeak', which blurs almost all significant moral and philosophical distinctions. This largely drew on Orwell's knowledge of totalitarian dictatorship, but it can also be taken as a satire on almost any political propaganda and speechifying, since politicians invariably try to manipulate people through their use of language and engage in 'doublespeak'. Since the late twentieth century the practice of presenting politicians' actions in favourable language in order to manipulate opinion has been known as 'spin' and the aides and press officers responsible for 'spinning' their masters' reputations are called 'spin doctors'.

Most states have more than one linguistic group within their borders. This situation persists because, although there is a tendency for 'big' languages (of which English is the biggest on a global scale) to eradicate smaller ones, this tendency is offset by both migration and deliberate policy. To some degree there is always a 'politics of language' in a multilingual society, because questions of educational resources, the language of bureaucratic and legal procedures, and the control of the mass media are bound to arise.

In Malta, a long struggle between English and Italian as potential 'official' languages ended with the elevation of the Maltese dialect into a full-blown language. In Israel, Hebrew has been successfully revived and is an important dimension of national unity. Black children in South Africa successfully revolted in the 1970s against education in Afrikaans, itself an African dialect of Dutch elevated into a written language as a 'Boer' nationalist project. The Canadian federal government has struggled to establish bilingualism (English and French) throughout Canada. In Belgium the struggles between French- and Flemish-speaking populations have led to an extreme form of federalism, and the establishment of strictly defined boundaries within one state, that determine the appropriate official language. A similar system has been operated in Switzerland, where a German-speaking majority coexists with French-, Italian-, and Romansch-speaking minorities, though the issue has never been so bitterly contested as in Belgium.

The political dimension of language raises complex and, ultimately, mysterious questions. Questions of culture, identity, and manipulative power are inseparable from linguistic structures. Language sometimes seems definitive of identity, at other times almost irrelevant. One must beware of simplification or generalization about language and politics, yet always remain aware that language is not separate from political reality, but part of that reality. LA

Laski, Harold (1893–1950) British political scientist. One of the most influential Marxist writers on British and American political institutions. In *A Grammar of Politics* (1925) Laski combined a radical critique of the economic structure of society with a pluralistic programme of political reform. He argued that inequalities of wealth and political access prevented the free development of the majority of society; and proposed a programme of state intervention in the economic sector combined with corporatist decentralization in order to widen access to political power. *Democracy in Crisis* (1933) responded to the economic depression by arguing that large-scale unemployment was an inherent feature of capitalism but incompatible with democracy; the solution was democratic socialism. Laski reacted positively to Roosevelt's *New Deal, but was also impressed by the economic reforms introduced in Soviet Russia under Stalin. His *Reflections on the Revolution of Our Time* (1943) sought to reconcile economic planning with personal self-expression, but Laski's work suffered from an imbalance between persuasive institutional analysis of political power and a rather idealistic approach to economic development and class relations. His advocacy of a pro-Soviet foreign policy saw him labelled as an extremist, particularly in the United States. However, his strident advocacy of socialism and opposition to imperialism gave him a following amongst the anti-colonial nationalist movements, particularly in India.

Laski was a prominent member of the *Fabian Society and the *Labour Party. When Laski pointed out in 1945 that the parliamentary Labour Party was, according to the Party constitution, subordinate to the extraparliamentary Party of which he was chairman, Winston Churchill claimed that to vote Labour was thus to hand over power to an unelected body. Clement Attlee, leader of the Labour Party, nevertheless won the 1945 General Election, having written to Laski, 'a period of silence from you would be welcome'.

Lassalle, Ferdinand (1825–64) Socialist thinker, democrat, and agitator. Born in Breslau, the son of a wealthy Jewish merchant, Lassalle was very idle as a schoolboy, constantly cheating and playing truant. Lassalle is remembered now for his endeavours to make socialism and private property compatible, and also for his attention to the *iron law of wages. He always believed that wages suffered from a downward pressure to mere subsistence. As he reached his maturity, his early hostility to Judaism broadened into anti-Semitism. JH

law Virtually all accounts of law acknowledge the existence of positive law, which can be loosely defined as the body of rules enforced by any sovereign state. Beyond that, theories of law diverge sharply in their answers to a range of questions about what the law is. For example: Do we have to accept that any rule enforced by any state is a law? Is positive law the only kind of law which exists? Must a rule, in order to be called a law, conform to certain universal principles or precepts? What is the relationship between laws in the legal sense and scientific laws? Answers divide generally into two camps, the *legal naturalists* and the *legal positivists*.

Legal positivism asserts that only positive laws exist. Laws are, therefore, made, or chosen by, legislators; they do not exist, awaiting discovery, before a law-making act occurs. The distinction between laws and non-laws is a question of judging whether the source of a rule is or is not a sovereign state. Moralizing about what the law ought to be is thus a logically separate activity from discovering or deciding what the law is. Legal laws bear only an etymological relationship to scientific laws: they are quite different kinds of statement.

Positivism can be traced back to Jeremy *Bentham's attending the lectures of William Blackstone (1723–80) in which the latter attempted to derive the content of English common law from the existence of a higher, natural law (*Commentaries on the Laws of England*). To Bentham it was clear that real laws were made by legislators, parliaments, and judges, and ought to be chosen because their consequences were better than those of alternatives and not because of their supposed conformance to some other body of law. He published his critique in the *Fragment on Government* in 1776.

John Austin (1790–1859), an associate of Bentham, developed a brutally clear form of positivism in *The Province of Jurisprudence Determined* (1832). In this version, laws are simply the commands of a sovereign, who is a person or institution whose general commands are habitually obeyed by the bulk of a reasonably numerous population. Austin has been criticized on the grounds that his theory is incapable of distinguishing between a legal system and the rule of a gangster, but an obvious Austinian response to this is to say that if the gangster has a capacity to enforce rules over an entire territory and to dominate or eradicate his rivals, then what he has is a state, and the rules that he enforces are laws.

Positivism has dominated twentieth-century thinking about law, at least in Western and Communist states. American legal positivists have argued that 'the law is what the judges say it is' and their account is strikingly concordant with that of Lenin in *State and Revolution* (1916). To Lenin, law is the expression of the will of the dominant class, whether the bourgeoisie before the revolution or the proletariat afterwards.

A more complex version of positivism is offered by H. L. A. Hart in *The Concept of Law* (1961). Hart characterizes law as 'a system of rules'. The most basic type of rules are primary rules which impose rights and obligations and which include the criminal law. Secondary rules stipulate how primary rules are 'formed, recognized, modified or extinguished'. A system is identified by its 'rule of recognition' that defines its legal status. A rule of recognition is, in effect, a definition of what Austin called a sovereign: in the United States it is the whole constitution, while in Britain it consisted traditionally of the single principle of *parliamentary sovereignty. This is now complicated by the existence of European law which has 'superiority' and 'direct effect' though it could still be argued that, should Parliament decide to assert its unequivocal sovereignty, there exists no mechanism to deny its claim.

Turning now to *legal naturalism*, if positivistic theories of law have been predominant in the 'developed' world in the twentieth century, naturalistic theories, defined as those which posit the existence of some kind of higher and permanent law not dependent on the actions of particular legislators, have dominated most other societies at most other times. Typically, such laws are derived from religious revelation or from the requirements of reason; in the synthesis of *Aquinas, our reason is the mechanism whereby religious truth is revealed. Reason may inform us, for instance, about the necessary structure of a legal system or about its core content. It may tell us that there must be laws against murder or that all laws, whatever their content, must treat equals equally. Thus, systems of laws are, in some respects, like scientific laws; both are necessary truths which our intellects can discover. In naturalistic theory some questions about the ethical quality of a 'law' are relevant to the question of whether or not it is a law at all. Of a racist law, say, which contradicts natural principles of law, the natural lawyer can say, 'It is a rule the current state attempts to enforce, but it is incompatible with natural law and, therefore, not properly a law at all'.

In the West, the theory of natural law has had a significant revival in the last decades of the twentieth century, led by such writers as Ronald Dworkin and John Finnis. In Islamic cultures, it has always remained dominant. There is room in an Islamic society for rules which are merely contingent to a particular society, covering such matters as driving on the left or the right. But positive law which contradicts holy law would not be law and there is no room, in principle, for divine rules which are not enforced as positive laws.

From a positivist point of view naturalism carries excessive philosophical baggage: it must be based on either revealed religion or a concept of reason which is dangerously wide-ranging and which objectifies ethical judgements. Thus, naturalism is potentially illiberal and must conflict with the canons of utility and democracy. On the other hand, positivists have only feeble answers to certain practical ethical problems. What do we do with people who did wicked things which were not illegal under a wicked regime? How do we distinguish between, say, burglars and political protestors who are imprisoned under a morally unacceptable government when both their activities were clearly illegal at the time they were committed? Positivists, rightly or wrongly, can have no answer to Heinrich Himmler's claim that he could not possibly be tried since he had committed no crime.

In some, more subtle, accounts, positivism and naturalism are not so far apart: legislators make law and judges interpret it, but they do so according to criteria which may be common to all legal systems and, in some sense, are deduced to be necessary preconditions of a legal system. *See also* JUDICIAL ACTIVISM; JURISPRUDENCE.   LA

leadership selection The process by which organizations produce a principal executive officer. In most countries political interest focuses on the means of selection adopted by parties for the identifiable party leader who is likely to become head of government either immediately or after an election.

Five common types of party leadership selection process may be discerned:

1 *By a single individual*. This occurs when individuals create parties as vehicles for their own political views, for example, the Reverend Ian Paisley and the Democratic Unionist Party in Northern Ireland, or when the outgoing leader may help to avoid a divisive succession battle by being allowed to name the successor, as has occurred in the Japanese Liberal Democrat Party.

2 *By a small elite party group, either by formal vote or apparent consensus*. This procedure is common in parties which originated prior to mass democratic politics, are located in relatively centralized political systems and espouse elitist values. It was practised by the British Conservative Party before 1965.

3 *By the party members of a legislature*. This method is common to many parties in parliamentary systems, the view being taken that as a leader is primarily a leader of a parliamentary party he or she needs to enjoy its support. In Britain this method was used by the Labour Party until 1981, the Liberal Party until 1976, and the Conservative Party between 1965 and 1997.

4 *By party conference/electoral college*. Party members of the legislature are joined by party members outside the legislature, either as representatives or delegates of specific parts of the wider party in an electoral college to vote for the leader. The selection process may occur as part of the regular party annual conference, as with the British Labour Party in the 1980s, or at a special conference, for example, the American party presidential nomination conventions. A variant, especially in the United States and for nominations to local offices in the Labour Party, is selection by a *caucus of party activists. Selection by party conference is appropriate for parties which are located in non-parliamentary systems, such as that in the United States, or where parties are composed of specific parts other than the parliamentary party that demand a role in the selection process: for example the trade unions and constituency parties in the British Labour Party.

5 *By ballot of the whole party membership*. This is considered to be appropriate where parties are based totally on individual membership, where the parliamentary party has become diminished in importance relative to the extra-parliamentary party and/or the party has been created since such direct methods of selection have gained credence.

In Britain, the Liberals after 1976, followed by the Social Democrats and the Liberal Democrats, have all favoured selection by a full member ballot. The 1994 leadership election of the Labour Party made some move to this method by providing for full member ballots in all three parts of the electoral college: elected members, trade union Labour Party members, and ordinary party members. After disquiet about William Hague being elected as Conservative leader solely by MPs in 1997, in 1998 the Conservative Party also adopted a full member vote to decide their leader. In each party, however, candidates have to meet prior requirements before going before the membership. In the Liberal Democrats candidates need the support of 10 per cent of party MPs and 200 party members from twenty different local parties. In the Labour Party, candidates need the support of 12.5 per cent of party MPs. In 2007 only one candidate, Gordon Brown, passed this threshold and he was therefore elected unopposed. In the Conservative Party, candidates only need the support of two party MPs but if more than two stand the Party uses an eliminatory ballot procedure among MPs to whittle the field down to two candidates before deciding the winner on a full member ballot.

Selection processes in the United States since the 1970s offer the best grounds for a possible sixth legitimate method of leadership selection. State primaries, the results of which may determine voting in presidential nomination conventions, are generally held on the basis of balloting only party members. In some cases, however, 'open' or 'wide open primaries' are held in which anyone, regardless of party affiliation, may vote. The principle of selection by popular vote is not followed systematically in any leadership selection process, but does offer the potential for further variation. JBR

League of Arab States *See* ARAB LEAGUE.

League of Nations The League of Nations was established at the end of the First World War by the victor powers meeting at the Paris Peace Conference. Its strongest advocate was US President Woodrow Wilson. But ironically his own country's Senate refused to ratify membership and hence the world's strongest state withdrew into a form of 'isolation'. Of the other great powers only Great Britain and France were to be members throughout the League's existence. Germany, the Soviet Union, Japan, and Italy joined late or resigned, or did both.

At Wilson's insistence the League was given the task of preventing international armed aggression through a system of so-called *collective security. False hopes were thus raised in many quarters that all aggressors henceforth would be deterred or effectively punished by the leading states in the League's establishment. During the 1930s this illusion was dramatically dispelled. Analysts have differed ever since as to whether such a system of collective security would in all circumstances have proved unworkable or whether the failure was due in the particular case to so few great powers being loyal members.

At all events, when in 1931 Japan invaded Manchuria, Great Britain and France, the only League members at the time with significant regional 'clout', proved unwilling and would perhaps in any case have been unable to impose effective sanctions on the aggressor. Next, in 1935, Italy invaded Abyssinia in whose fate no other great power had any direct interest. This, it was widely recognized, was the decisive test case for the League. For Great Britain and France clearly did on this occasion have the capacity to defeat Italy if matters came to an all-out war. But in neither London nor Paris was there sufficient support for the imposition of anything more vigorous than partial economic sanctions (which themselves were lifted in 1936). The British cabinet was satisfied that they could not risk the loss of even part of their fleet in a war with Italy at a time when their possessions in the Far East were thought to be menaced by Japan and when the US administration was seen to be hamstrung by congressional neutrality legislation. Similarly, the French held that war with Italy for the sake of Abyssinia would be quixotic at a time when all French forces were thought to be needed for a possible early showdown with Nazi Germany. Abyssinia was accordingly incorporated into the Italian empire in 1936. As a body for resisting international aggression the League had thus effectively perished. It continued to exist in a moribund condition until the end of the

Second World War when it was formally replaced by the *United Nations. DC

(⊕) SEE WEB LINKS

• The text of the Covenant of the League of Nations.

left In political terms, now indicative of the radical or progressive socialist spectrum, but originally literally a spatial term. In the French estates general of 1789, commoners sat on the left of the king, because the nobles were in the position of honour on his right. This is the connection with the root sense of 'left' as pertaining to 'the hand that is normally the weaker of the two', a pejorative association also found in French *gauche*, Latin *sinister*, and their derivatives. In the assemblies of the *French Revolution this evolved into a custom that the radical and egalitarian members sat towards the left-hand side of the assembly, viewed from the presiding officer's chair (and higher up, so that some of them were labelled the 'Mountain').

What it is to be 'left(-wing)' varies so much over space or time that a definition is very difficult, but the following issue orientations would normally be involved: egalitarianism, support for the (organized) working class, support for nationalization of industry, hostility to marks of hierarchy, opposition to nationalistic foreign or defence policy. 'Left' is used to distinguish positions within parties as well as among them. A left-wing socialist is one who takes extreme positions on (some of) the items on this list. Left-wing communism (described by *Lenin in a pamphlet of 1920 as 'an infantile disorder') may be cynically defined as all forms of communism not supported by the prevailing leadership of the Communist Party. However, in the 1920s and 1930s, left-wing deviation meant encouraging revolution among the people without caring sufficiently about the leading role of the Party; right-wing deviation meant too much support for *NEP and the market.

legislature A law-making assembly of elected members in a formally equal relationship to one another. Legislatures evolved from medieval bodies periodically assembled by kings in order to agree to levies of taxation to bodies which sat more or less continuously, or at least claimed the right

to do so as did seventeenth-century English parliaments. The legislature therefore took its modern form in the work of *Locke and the parliaments he had in mind. For specific legislatures *see* PARLIAMENT; CONGRESS (US). For division of powers by function *see* PARLIAMENTARY SOVEREIGNTY; SEPARATION OF POWERS. For division of powers by territory *see* CENTRAL–LOCAL RELATIONS; FEDERALISM. For the number of chambers, *see* BICAMERALISM; UNICAMERALISM.

legitimacy The property that a regime's procedures for making and enforcing laws are acceptable to its subjects. The term is derived from Weberian sociology. As *Weber emphasized, legitimacy constituted the basis of very real differences in the way in which power was exercised. There was a generally observable need for any power to justify itself. There were three broad grounds for exercising authority, based on: tradition; charisma; and rational legal authority, resting on a belief in the legality of enacted rules and the right of those in positions of authority to issue commands. Obedience is owed not to a traditionally sanctioned person or a charismatically qualified leader, but to the legally established impersonal order. It extends to the persons occupying a public office by virtue of the legality of their commands. Their authority is confined to the scope of the office and cannot be used in a capricious or self-interested way.

In his classic study, *Political Man*, S. M. Lipset argues that: 'Legitimacy involves the capacity of the [political] system to engender and maintain the belief that the existing political institutions are the most appropriate ones for the society.' Lipset contends that Western nations have had to face three difficult and potentially destabilizing issues: (1) the place of the church or of various religions within the nation; (2) the admission of the working class to full economic and political rights; and (3) the continuing struggle over the distribution of the national income. Some of the greatest challenges to the legitimacy of nation-states in the 1980s and 1990s have come from groups which do not accept the legitimacy of the territorial boundaries of the nation-state, for example many Québecois within Canada. In extreme cases, this has led to the dissolution of the former nation-state, for example in

Yugoslavia. The difficulty of maintaining government in the face of a challenge from a minority population which does not accept the legitimacy of existing territorial boundaries is shown by the case of Northern Ireland. As well as being a crucial problem in divided societies, the issue of legitimacy also arises in relation to new types of political formation such as the European Union. Because of the perceived problem of the *democratic deficit, the European Union is often regarded as lacking adequate means of legitimation from the citizens of the Union. The ability to issue commands which are seen as binding because they are legitimate is one of the central pillars of a stable political order. WG

legitimation crisis A theory developed in the mid-1970s by the German *Marxist turned *critical theorist Jürgen Habermas, a leading member of the *Frankfurt School. He suggests that people expect governments to intervene successfully in the economy to try and ensure economic prosperity. Failure to succeed can cause the validity of the capitalist system to be questioned, thus undermining its legitimacy. The term 'legitimacy crisis' has also been used in reference to the perceived *democratic deficit of the *European Union and has found more general expression making reference to the growth of voter apathy in Western liberal democracies, particularly in the United Kingdom. IF

Leibniz, Gottfried Wilhelm (1646–1716) German rationalist philosopher and mathematician. Born in Leipzig at the end of the Thirty Years War, Leibniz took a degree in law. He entered on a political and diplomatic career in 1666. This took him to the principal courts of Europe, from Paris to St Petersburg. There he met the learned men of the day. He was made a Fellow of the Royal Society. He and Newton arrived at the calculus independently. He held a debate by correspondence with Samuel Clarke on Newton's notion of space. His learned work was not isolated from his public; he wrote the *Theodicy* for the Queen of Prussia and the *Monodology* for Eugene of Savoy. He founded the Berlin Academy of Science. In Hanover he was in charge of the ducal library, from which his scientific and philosophical works have been abstracted with difficulty. (He turned down an offer to take charge of the Vatican Library.)

Leibniz was a practical rather than a theoretical political philosopher. Europe of his time was suffering the ravages of the Thirty Years War. The French had to be restrained in the interests of a united Europe if the Turks were to be constrained and ejected from their march westward. Standing in the way of unity were the religious divisions. Leibniz saw it as his task to bring about a reconciliation between the contending factions. To this end he wrote numerous treatises and letters on the subjects of contention—nature and grace, transubstantiation, and so forth. In these he tried to find a rational basis for discussion and, hopefully, for agreement. It can be argued that the whole of Leibniz's philosophy is designed to the same end, starting with the notion of the combinatory arts and proceeding to the notion of pre-established harmony, though the idea that these abstruse metaphysical notions would somehow mend the rift in Christendom is a testimony to Leibniz's optimism rather than a blueprint for religious and political harmony. CB

leisure class Consuming, parasitic class, represented by an idle elite engaged in continuous public demonstration of their status. The idea is particularly associated with the American sociological economist Thorstein Veblen, who published *The Theory of the Leisure Class* in 1899. Veblen saw the fundamental human motive as the maximization of status rather than orientation towards any monetary variable. In establishing status, expenditure was more important than income, enhanced status being often achieved by 'conspicuous consumption'. Thus a leisure class comes into being which dominates and trivializes leisure within a culture, though this pattern of consumption may be a necessary feature of the working of the economic system. Veblen's theories belong in the category of critical analysis of consumer society, a form of discourse embracing such writers as Lewis Mumford, J. K. Galbraith, and J. B. Priestley. The contemporary significance of Veblen's theories is that in an 'affluent society' large sections of the population may come to share the attitudes and behaviour of the 'leisure class'. LA

Leninism The doctrines of V. I. Lenin (1870–1924), especially his core contributions—on the *party, the *state, *imperialism, and *revolution—to Marxist theory.

In *What Is To Be Done?* (1902) Lenin addressed the question of party organization. The book's specific intention was to criticize the 'economists'' stress upon legal struggles, which Lenin argued lost sight of Social Democracy's maximum programme which was to challenge for state power. He later admitted that in denigrating minimum demands he had 'gone too far in the opposite direction' and *What Is To Be Done?* was not republished after 1917. Lenin distinguished between trade union and socialist consciousness. Those who promoted the idea of spontaneous revolutionary activity by the proletariat were really abdicating political leadership. Left to itself the working class would inevitably adopt bourgeois ideology (although Lenin wrote, in 1905, that 'the working class is instinctively, spontaneously social democratic' (*The Reorganization of the Party*). What was needed was a vanguard party of professional revolutionaries. Its strategy and tactics should be rooted in the working class and its task was to lead the latter to a socialist consciousness. Lenin argued for the creation of parallel secret and mass organizations.

The 1903 Bolshevik–Menshevik split revealed opposing views on the nature of revolution and how far Lenin was moving away from what was regarded as Marxist orthodoxy. In *The Development of Capitalism in Russia* (1899) Lenin had followed *Plekhanov in arguing that Russia was already capitalist but, because the bourgeoisie was weak, it was left to the proletariat to assume the tasks of the democratic revolution. Socialism was a distant prospect. However, the 1905 revolution caused a radical shift in Lenin's thinking. In *Two Tactics of Social Democracy in the Democratic Revolution*, he eschewed any alliance with the liberals who had sided with Tsarism against the revolutionary movement. The revolution would still have a bourgeois character but would be directed by 'a revolutionary democratic dictatorship of the proletariat and the peasants'. Traditionally Marxists had regarded the peasantry as a conservative even reactionary class. Lenin maintained an ambivalent attitude towards it throughout his life but he became convinced that the

social weight of the peasants would determine the immediate outcome of the revolution. When the Provisional Government refused to implement land reform after February 1917, Lenin placed the Bolsheviks firmly behind the peasants' demand for land.

His 1905 writings had indicated that there might be some 'growing over' between the democratic and socialist revolutions. *Imperialism, the Highest Stage of Capitalism* (1916) presented the possibility of an immediate socialist revolution based upon Lenin's analysis of a fundamental change in the nature of *capitalism—from competitive to monopoly. Banking cartels made enormous profits through exporting capital to backward countries; some of the repatriated profit was used to create a workers' aristocracy in Western Europe and so block the development of revolutionary consciousness. However, global capitalism and superexploitation provoked national self-determination movements and the contradictions of uneven development in peripheral countries (like Russia) which Lenin termed 'the weakest links'. Additionally, economic rivalry between the imperialist powers would result in war and international revolution.

By 1917 Lenin had reached the same conclusion as Trotsky—the idea of a continuous transition between the democratic and socialist revolutions. In the *April Theses* he rejected conditional support for the Provisional Government and demanded that the Bolsheviks agitate for 'All Power to the Soviets'. After government repression of the Bolsheviks in July, he realized that a peaceful development of the revolution was not possible and advised the party to plan for insurrection.

Whilst in hiding before October, Lenin wrote *State and Revolution*, which was a libertarian reappraisal of Marx and Engels' views on the *withering away of the state, stressing the commune rather than the *dictatorship of the proletariat as the organizational form for the transition to socialism and barely mentioning the role of the party. Lenin rejected both parliamentarism (anticipating the closure of the Constituent Assembly by the Soviet government in January 1918) and reformism, making a distinction between socialist and bourgeois democracy ('democracy for the people and not democracy for the money bags').

However, the revolutionary optimism of *State and Revolution* quickly evaporated in the post-1917 period. Amidst foreign intervention and civil war, the 'withering away' became increasingly problematic as a monolithic system emerged with centralized control by the party, the repression of opposition, and the decimation of independent working-class activity. Accused of state terrorism by socialist critics, Lenin responded with works such as *Left Wing Communism—An Infantile Disorder* and *The Proletarian Revolution and the Renegade Kautsky* (both 1919) which attempted to justify revolutionary violence. In his last years, however, and particularly after being incapacitated by a succession of strokes, he was preoccupied by the problems of cultural backwardness, the urban–rural dichotomy, and the bureaucratization of the state and party. His *Testament* of December 1922 called for greater political control over the *bureaucracy, and warned against Stalin, but was suppressed by him.

Possibly the most distinctive feature of 'Leninism' was what György Lukács (in *Lenin*, 1924) called its 'revolutionary realpolitik; a concrete, unschematic, unmechanistic, purely praxis-oriented thought'. Lenin's opposition to dogmatism in both theory and practice has been described as opportunism and as an imaginative adaptation of Marxist methodology to changing historical circumstances. GL

Levellers A group of radicals which emerged during the English Civil War. In the Putney Debates they argued for a more sweeping programme for the Parliamentary army than their generals, Cromwell and Ireton, were willing to adopt. They focused on a wide extension of the franchise and other 'democratic' reforms, but, unlike the Diggers (*see* WINSTANLEY), they accepted the principle of private property, if not its existing distribution. Indeed, they linked the claim that 'each had a property in his person' to the argument for a wider franchise, because they accepted that the franchise was based upon a property qualification. AR

Liberal Democratic Party (Japan) The product of the merger of the Liberal Party and the Democratic Party in 1954, the LDP is the hegemonic party in Japan. It is highly factionalized, although its factions have always been personal rather than ideological. The LDP is a right-wing party without a distinctive ideology.

(((()))) SEE WEB LINKS

• Liberal Democratic Party (Japan) site, with information on party organization and history.

Liberal Democrats (UK) *See* LIBERAL PARTY (UK).

liberal internationalism A broad theoretical approach to *international relations theory that includes many aspects of *liberalism, focusing specifically on the global behaviour of liberal states and their foreign-policy aim of reforming the *international system, both in terms of 'exporting' liberal principles to other states and creating organizations to facilitate cooperation on global issues. The foundation of liberal internationalism is often accredited to the writings of Immanuel *Kant, but its modern development is associated with the writings of Richard Cobden and Joseph *Schumpeter, among others, who made both empirical and normative claims relating to how domestic liberal principles produced international peace and cooperation. Cobden viewed elite interests as entrenching poverty domestically and encouraging violence globally. He argued that the key liberal principles of free trade and democracy would solve both domestic and global problems. Free trade would decrease the power of elites in favour of wealth generated from commercial trading, and democracy would empower wider sections of society, beyond male property-holders, who could then further support free trade. Schumpter expanded upon the ways in which the interaction between the liberal institutions of free trade (or, more generally, capitalism) and democracy would result in increasingly pacific foreign relations between states. *Capitalism would ensure that a population's focus was on production and trade rather than war, and people generally do not profit from war (save for particular sectors of industry) because it increases instability and decreases trade. Democracy would ensure that peaceful preferences were represented by their government in its international relations.

Early liberal internationalists differed in their views of how peaceful international relations would be established across the globe. One idea was that domestic reform towards capitalism and democracy was enough to bring about a gradual change in the global domain; others thought that domestic change alone was not enough to produce global reform, so that international organizations were needed as facilitators. The *League of Nations can be seen as emblematic of the liberal internationalist optimism popular at the time of its inception in 1920. It was a significant development in international cooperation through internationalization and sought to ensure that there were no further world wars. The League failed when Germany and other Axis powers withdrew and the Second World War started.

Modern liberal internationalists have advanced these theories to focus on empirically proving Kantian-inspired ideas of *democratic peace, which posits that democratic or republican states are more peaceful in their external relations and never (or almost never) fight each other. Many modern liberal internationalists also continue to argue for the promotion of greater economic and institutional *interdependence between states, claiming that greater global interdependence increases the cost of conflict and thus reduces incentives for war. Lastly, many contemporary liberal internationalists have adopted universal *human rights as part of their normative and legal lexicon, suggesting that they ground duties to promote, protect, and actively advance the needs of others beyond borders.

Despite many of its compelling arguments, liberal internationalist thought remains internally divided and open to external criticisms about *imperialism. For defenders, liberals have a duty to act on behalf of vulnerable people and to promote peaceful order by force if necessary. For critics, to engage in coercion or 'civilizing' acts is a paternalistic and often violent enterprise. As a result, whilst liberal internationalism remains a popular way of understanding world events, and making normative prescriptions about how things ought to be, there remain significant controversies in the study of international relations concerning both its explanatory and normative power.   AMB

liberalism In general, the belief that it is the aim of politics to preserve individual rights and to maximize freedom of choice. In common with *socialism and *conservatism, it emerged from the conjunction of the *Enlightenment, the Industrial Revolution, and the political revolutions of the seventeenth and eighteenth centuries. Liberalism retains a faith in the possibilities of improvement in present social conditions, which is related to the idea of *progress widely accepted in the late eighteenth and nineteenth centuries. That idea embraced the prospects for developments in knowledge, in welfare, and in morality. Although the confidence in the prospects for progress in some of these respects has now diminished (see POST-MODERNISM), liberalism retains an ameliorative ambition. The Enlightenment also shaped liberalism's perception of human agency, conceived as (at least potentially) rational and responsible. The political revolutions in France and America disclose an ambiguous heritage. The emphasis placed on equal rights remains, and this is the fundamental form of equality most liberals aim to achieve. On the other side, liberalism has been pictured by its critics as infected with *bourgeois values, those appropriate to the position of the emerging class of capitalists in present industrial society.

Apart from the concern with equality of rights and amelioration, liberalism has focused on the space available in which individuals may pursue their own lives, or their own conception of the good. The immediate threat to this 'space' was considered to be the arbitrary will of a monarch, leading liberals to consider the proper limits of political power. They explored the relationship between legitimate power and consent, and the characteristics of the rule of law. Other threats were seen in religious intolerance and the power of public opinion, or social intolerance. In a general way, liberalism has tried to define the line to be drawn between the public and the private, an approach which has several key components.

The first is the project of describing the peculiar features of political power, in contrast to the power which might be held or exercised in private domains. *Locke, for example, devoted considerable attention to the distinctions to be drawn between the power of a master over a servant, the power of a master over a slave, paternal power, and the power of a husband over a wife, on one side, and political power, on the other. None of those 'domestic' power relations illuminated the nature of political power, which was legitimate if, and only if, the governed consented to it. That power was to be directed at the public good, limited by its purposes and regulated by settled and known law. This notion of limited government has been in the centre of liberal concerns: the rule of *law, *separation of powers, constitutionalism, emphasis on civil liberties, for example, are consequences of a desire to restrict political power to what is conceived to be its proper domain.

A second aspect of the limitation of government has been an emphasis on the autonomy of the economic realm, and a defence of private property. This characterization, however, needs to be treated with caution. Liberals have not always been enthusiastic proponents of a laissez-faire policy, not least because they have recognized that a market system is not capable of guaranteeing the conditions of its own existence. Again, while private property has generally been supported as providing a bulwark against state power, allowing some prospect of independence, many liberals have been concerned about the effects of concentrations of private property. It has been a common, but not wholly justified, complaint against liberal thought that it takes insufficient notice of the effects of private power as a consequence of its concern to limit public power.

The advent of *democracy has posed particular problems for liberalism, which has given only a qualified endorsement to the idea of government by the people. Whilst democracy might be welcomed as a counter to the tendency of those who hold power to pursue their own interests, it may threaten individual liberty in new ways. *See* TYRANNY OF THE MAJORITY. More generally, liberals have been concerned lest the levelling tendencies of mass society suppress individual initiative and eliminate the space for experiments in ways of life. Just as liberalism has had an uncertain relationship with unrestrained democracy, so too it has had a

complex relationship with *utilitarianism. Some accounts of liberalism restrict their consideration to writers who have endorsed *natural rights, thus excluding all utilitarian contributions. Even if attachment to natural rights is not considered to be a qualification, some accounts regard utilitarianism as propounded by *Bentham and J. S. *Mill as a deviation from the main tradition of liberal thought: Benthamism seems to license greater state activity than is desired, while J. S. Mill was sympathetic to socialist experiment, and paid insufficient regard to the sanctity of private property. The controversy between rights theorists and utilitarians continues, but it is not clear that only the former have a claim to be regarded as liberals. At stake is the balance between the welfarist ambitions of utilitarianism, which are consonant with the liberal concern with amelioration, and the liberal emphasis on the protection of the individual from the effects of public power, which may be incompatible with unrestrained utilitarianism. All political ideologies can be seen as dynamic, in the sense that particular values to which they are attached have to be defended in the face of new threats, or reassessed in the light of changing conditions. For this reason, amongst others, there is no shared conception of *freedom within liberalism. The so-called new liberals, who were responding to conditions at the end of the nineteenth century, and the beginning of the twentieth century, adopted a more positive conception than many of their predecessors, a conception which re-emphasized the welfare concern of utilitarians with whom they otherwise had little in common. Contemporary liberalism has been much exercised by the notion of justice. Rawls (1921–2002), Dworkin, *Nozick, and Ackerman are perhaps the most highly regarded contributors to this discussion. This concern with justice has been linked to another characterization of contemporary liberalism, a concern with neutrality. The relevant neutrality may be variously conceived, but it certainly includes a neutrality with respect to citizens' conceptions of the good. *Communitarian critics have doubted whether the priority of the (justice-based notion of) right over the good can be sustained, but it is clear that in many spheres the liberal ambition is to produce neutral procedures which allow for, but do not discriminate between, the diverse conceptions of the good or ways of life adopted by citizens. Such neutrality suggests that the role of public power is merely instrumental, creating the necessary space for the exercise of individual freedom and providing for conflict-resolution; such an approach has been challenged not only by communitarianism but also by liberal *perfectionism.   AR

Liberal parties Liberal parties are as varied as the idea of liberalism is broad and vague. All liberals believe in the freedom of the individual, but that belief takes very different forms, varying from the 'classic' liberal belief in natural rights with which the state cannot interfere to the 'new' liberalism, which has dominated the English Liberal Party for over a century and which sees an important role for the state in liberating people from poverty, ignorance, and discrimination. There are liberal parties which some liberals would regard as not very liberal, and parties that do not contain a reference to liberalism in their name but which many liberals would recognize as essentially liberal in their aims. The nature of a liberal party in a particular state has very often been determined by the kind of main party to which it has been opposed: those parties which have seen a socialist party as their main rival tend to be more favourable to free markets than those which have opposed a conservative party.

Liberal parties tend to lack both the social base of socialist, communist, conservative, and agrarian parties and the territorial base of regionalist and nationalist parties. In most political circumstances in the twentieth century they have tended to find themselves in a moderate, centre position, typically between socialists and conservatives. For these reasons, their importance has generally declined. Most countries do not now have a recognizable liberal party and only in a tiny minority of states is the liberal party the government or principal opposition. Such countries are, however, an impressively wide variety. They include Australia, Canada, Colombia, Honduras, and Japan. In Australia and Japan the Liberal and Liberal Democratic Parties respectively are perceived as right of centre, in Honduras and Canada the Liberal Parties are left of centre, while the party in Colombia is perceived as holding the centre ground.   LA

Liberal Party (UK) A faction of the Whig Party whose members called themselves 'liberals' or 'radicals' emerged around the time of the Reform Act of 1832. Some of these MPs were influenced by the doctrines of classical economics and/or the utilitarians ('philosophical radicals') *Bentham and James *Mill. The proportion of Liberals to Whigs in the coalition gradually grew during a period of confusion in party labels from 1846 (when the Tory Party split over the repeal of the Corn Laws; many Tory supporters of repeal, including W. E. Gladstone, becoming Liberals) to 1868, when a majority Liberal government was formed. The Liberal Party split in 1886, when most of the remaining Whigs (who had been drifting towards the Tories) and some others refused to support Gladstone's proposal for Home Rule to Ireland. Nevertheless, alternation of Liberals and Conservatives in a two-party system continued until 1915. There is a lively debate as to whether the supplanting of the Liberals by Labour as the opposition to the Conservatives between 1918 and 1929 was an inevitable consequence of social change and of franchise extension, or whether, but for accident and personalities, it might have been the Liberals rather than Labour who emerged stronger from the First World War, in which case the plurality electoral system would have crushed Labour in the way in which it actually crushed the Liberals.

The Liberal Party survived at a low ebb until the early 1960s, always winning a handful of parliamentary seats in peripheral areas of the United Kingdom. Its slow and patchy revival since then can be variously attributed to the intensifying of centre-periphery conflict, to the growth of retrospective voting in which voters wished to punish the incumbent party without being willing to vote for its traditional rival, to some resurgence of nineteenth-century liberal ideology, and to the alliance with the Social Democratic Party (1981-7). However, the Liberals remained penalized by the electoral system. Though they supplanted Labour as the opposition to the Conservatives in parts of the periphery and in much of southern England, they were unlikely to achieve power without proportional representation, which it was not in the interests of the other parties to grant. Large elements of traditional liberalism are found in the other parties. For instance, Labour has inherited the mantle of the party of nonconformity, of idealistic foreign policy, and (for the most part) of peripheral resentment, while some Conservatives have appropriated the economic, although not the social, part of nineteenth-century liberalism.

In 1988 the Liberal Party merged with the Social Democratic Party to form the Social and Liberal Democrats, more usually referred to as the Liberal Democrats. Under the leadership of Paddy Ashdown it began to increase its influence and representation and by the 2005 election it had 62 MPs. Following the 2010 election, in which it lost five seats, the party held the balance of power and formed a coalition with the Conservatives, with Nick Clegg, then leader, becoming Deputy Prime Minister. It succeeded in tempering more radical Conservative polices, for example on immigration, human rights and on cuts to government expenditure. However, in the electorate's mind, the party had lost trust over some major policy reversals and in the 2015 general election, its support evaporated, losing 49 seats and leaving it with eight MPs. Nick Clegg, who managed to retain his seat, resigned as leader. He was replaced in July 2015 by Tim Farron.

((((SEE WEB LINKS))))
• Liberal Democrats website.

liberation theology Belief that the Christian Churches have a duty and a commitment to oppose social, economic, and political repression in societies where exploitation and oppression of humanity exist.

Liberation theology emerged in Latin America in the 1960s to challenge the Catholic Church's traditional role as defender of the status quo. Lay organizations and worker priests argued that the Church must identify itself with the interests of the poor. They became involved in grass-roots organization around development issues. A strong influence was the educationalist Paulo Freire (*The Pedagogy of the Oppressed*, 1972). Despite the misgivings of the Catholic hierarchy, in 1967 Pope Paul VI published his encyclical *Populorum Progressio* which condemned the differences between rich and poor nations. In 1968, the Latin American Episcopal Conference (CELAM) meeting in Medellín, Colombia, espoused liberation theology (the fullest expression of which is Gustavo Gutierrez's *Theology of Liberation*, 1971).

Since the 1970s, the Vatican has attempted to reassert its authority, attempting to neutralize the influence of the grass-roots organizations. National churches have experienced schisms. Nevertheless, liberation theology has had a profound impact, demonstrated, for example, by the Chilean Church's deep involvement in human rights activities during the Pinochet regime and the Nicaraguan Sandinistas' acknowledgement that it formed an integral part of their political heritage.   GL

libertarianism Refers primarily to a range of theories and attitudes whose common characteristic is that they seek to reverse the progress of collectivism and authoritarianism and to 'roll back the frontiers of the state'. Traditionally, 'libertarian' denoted a believer in free will, as opposed to determinism; the opposite was, therefore, a necessitarian. A further meaning referred to a kind of principled libertine, a person in favour of breaking down whatever inhibited and constrained natural or instinctive behaviour, whether it was religious belief, family ties, or the enforcement of laws by the state. But these meanings are now antiquated.

Libertarians as now defined can be divided into two main camps. The most precise form of libertarianism rests on a belief in the essential separateness of individual persons who possess, quite irrespective of whether or not they are part of a society or subject to the laws of a state, a set of inalienable rights, which necessarily include rights to acquire and retain property. The denial of these rights by states can never be defensible and people should only consider themselves subject to states in so far as those states enhance their rights or rest on voluntary procedures. The clearest modern statement of this doctrine is in Robert *Nozick's *Anarchy, State and Utopia* published in 1974. It has been described as a brilliant drawing of conclusions (such as that taxation is 'forced labour') from premises (the *a priori* existence of rights) which are merely asserted and which we have no good reason to accept.

Libertarianism in this sense is fundamentally opposed to utilitarianism: an individual's rights must never be abrogated in the general interest. Paradoxically, a variety of libertarians in the broader sense base their projects for the retreat of the state on arguments which are quite compatible with utilitarianism and even overtly utilitarian. The 'Austrian school' of economists, culminating in the influence of Ludwig von Mises and Friedrich von *Hayek, is more concerned with the ultimate aggregate benefits of free markets and with the need to counter the state's inherent tendencies to expansion and inefficiency. Some writers, like Samuel Brittan, have attempted to reconcile utilitarian and libertarian thought by stating that, although the aggregate benefit of the population is the only ultimate justification of policy, this is best interpreted as a maximization of individual autonomy and a minimization of dependence on the state.

Some libertarians call themselves 'minarchists', indicating a belief in the minimal or 'night-watchman' state which confines its activities to defence of its boundaries and the enforcement of contracts and a (minimal) body of criminal law. They are thus quite different from *anarchists, who wish to abolish the state in its entirety and the institution of property. Libertarians may be accused of taking the state too seriously and the idea of liberty not seriously enough. The dominant contemporary tradition of libertarianism sees only the state as constraining liberty whereas, considered more broadly, freedom is restricted by social norms, religious beliefs, family structures, and market forces. The most convincing libertarian reply to this criticism is that the determined individual can, ultimately, by strength of will, shrug off these constraints, but not the coercive power of the state. LA

liberty *See* FREEDOM.

Libyan Civil War(s) (2011 and 2014) The Libyan Civil War is often understood as involving two civil conflicts within the North African country. The first, often referred to as the 'First Libyan Civil War' or 'Libyan Revolution', erupted on the back of the *Arab Spring protests in 2011, in which forces loyal to Colonel Muammar Gaddafi were mobilized to crush uprisings and protests in several cities, principally the city of Benghazi in the east. These protests developed into rebellion against Gaddafi, with opposition forces organizing themselves into a loose alliance called the National Transition Council (NTC). On 26 February 2011, due to dramatic increases in violence by Gaddafi forces, the *United Nations Security Council passed a resolution to freeze Gaddafi's assets and passed a further resolution to enforce a 'no-fly zone' and protective area around Benghazi. These resolutions proved substantial, since they approved the use of 'all necessary measures' to counter advances by Gaddafi forces and to protect civilian populations. This protective area was effectively enforced (primarily led by the United Kingdom and France) through the use of aerial bombing and targeted aerial attacks on Gaddafi forces, which due to the open terrain of Libya, inflicted critical damage to Gaddafi's heavy weaponry, troop deployments, and general morale.

In August 2011, opposition forces staged a series of attacks on coastal cities leading toward the capital Tripoli, eventually taking Tripoli. Despite capturing the capital, Gaddafi remained at large. On 20 October 2011 Gaddafi was captured and immediately executed by opposition militia in the city of Sirte. On 23 October 2011, despite continued pockets of violence in Libya, the NTC declared Libya as 'liberated' and announced the end of the Libyan Revolution. However, the killing of Gaddafi did not end conflict in Libya, with militia groups and remaining loyalists continuing to fight for territory, resources, and control. This led to the country being carved up between different militia groups and political organizations that claimed authority.

Ongoing fighting between militias as well as the lack of authority and power by the NTC has led directly to what is often called the 'Second Libyan Civil War' and Libya's continued instability. Representing the period from 2014 to the present, the Second Civil War refers to continued conflicts between two main political factions: the 2014 nationally elected Council of Deputies (CoD) operating from Tobruk and the National Salvation Congress (NSC) which operates from Tripoli—granted authority by the General National Congress (which was established immediately after the Libyan Revolution by the NTC). The condition of instability is compounded by additional smaller militias seeking control of Libyan territory, such as the Shura Council in

Benghazi, the Tuareg in the south-west provinces, and with the emergence of *ISIS in Libya. Although the CoD and NSC signed a deal in 2015, creating a power-sharing agreement to form the 'Government of National Accord', peace in Libya remains elusive, with the Egyptian brokered peace talks in February 2017 failing to bring all the warring factions together.

lifeboat ethics A hypothetical thought experiment and metaphor used by ecologist Garrett Hardin in 1974 to describe the resource capacity of the earth and what considerations would be ethically required to 'keep the earth lifeboat afloat'. In the hypothetical, Hardin suggests that over-filling the lifeboat would jeopardize its overall worthiness, killing everyone. As a result, it is ethically and pragmatically justified to allow people to drown around the boat, even if there are places left on the lifeboat. The metaphor has often been used to describe the distributive resource capacity of the earth (as the lifeboat) and how it is justified for affluent cultures to allow weaker societies to die out via natural processes and without international aid. It is also often linked to the population theories of Thomas *Malthus. Although often debunked as oversimplified, lifeboat ethics has gained new followers as the world reaches 10 billion people and as environmental issues have become increasingly acute.

life peerage Under the Life Peerages Act of 1958, membership of the UK *House of Lords can be conferred on a man or woman for life. Life peers have exactly the same privileges and voting rights as hereditary peers, the only difference being that the peerage is not passed on to the peer's heir.

The House of Lords Act 1999 expelled all bar 92 of the hereditary peers, leaving a house dominated by life peers. Plans to replace these by elected or appointed peers had run into serious trouble by 2006, suggesting that life peers may remain as a long-term feature of the UK parliament.

(⊕) SEE WEB LINKS
• Parliament site, with details of types of peerage.

life-cycle effect *See* AGE.

limited vote An electoral procedure whereby each voter has fewer votes than there are seats to fill in a multimember district. The best-known examples are: (1) the division of a number of large cities in Britain between 1867 and 1885 into three-member seats, with each voter having two votes; and (2) the single non-transferable vote system in Japan, where each voter had one vote in a multimember seat.

The limited vote is one route to *proportional representation (although only C. L. *Dodgson understood its properties correctly), but it was abolished in the United Kingdom because the Birmingham Liberals found what contemporaries saw as a way to evade its intentions: by dividing the city into three zones and asking their supporters in each third to vote for a different pair of their candidates, they ensured that all three seats were won by Liberals.

Lincoln, Abraham (1809–65) US politician. He expressed his democratic ideals most famously at the dedication of a cemetery at Gettysburg, Pennsylvania, site of the battle of the Civil War where the Confederate armies had been turned back from their northernmost point. Lincoln stated that 'the world will little note, nor long remember, what we say here', but expressed the hope that 'government of the people, by the people, and for the people, shall not perish from the earth'. Lincoln's magnificent oratory may conceal more than it reveals. In particular he was not a principled opponent of slavery, but rather a principled defender of the Union. He was also a master of manipulation, being one of the most effective hammerers of the wedge between Northern and Southern Democrats, which led to the splintering of the Democrats in the 1860 presidential election and to Lincoln's election on under 40 per cent of the popular vote.

linkage 1. The interdependency of domestic and international politics. In studies of international relations, such as Robert D. Putnam's 1998 article 'Diplomacy and Domestic Politics: The Logic of Two-Level Games', an emphasis on linkage tends to highlight the constraints faced by actors in international negotiations due to domestic political factors. The determination of the national interest is seen to be less of a unitary process, rather a *pluralistic and contingent negotiation reflecting public opinion and partisan influences.

2. In diplomacy, the bringing together of ostensibly separate issues in negotiations (often carrots and sticks).

lobbyists The term 'lobbyist' derives from 'lobby', in the sense of areas adjacent to a legislative assembly where it is easy to meet members of the legislature. A lobbyist is one who is professionally employed to lobby on behalf of clients or who advises clients on how to lobby on their own behalf. Lobbying refers to attempts to exert influence on the formation or implementation of public policy. Lobbying as an activity is carried out by a variety of actors ranging from *interest groups through the government relations divisions of large firms to foreign embassies. Those lobbyists functioning as professional intermediaries, such as political consulting firms or lawyers specializing in offering political advice, are sometimes referred to as contract lobbyists as distinct from 'in house' lobbyists employed by firms or interest groups. Lobbyists are to be found in large numbers in the United States, particularly concentrating their activities on the Congress. This older type of lobbying which depends on mobilizing networks of influence with legislators has been supplanted by a newer form of lobbying in which political campaign firms package issues, mobilize voters, and raise campaign funds.

Political action committees (*PACs), set up by corporations, unions, and other organizations to act as conduits for funds to candidates who favour particular policy positions, have grown considerably in numbers and expenditure in the United States. Although it is on a much smaller scale than in the United States, professional lobbying has also expanded in Britain. This has led to concern about standards of lobbying, the possibility of the improper exercise of influence, and the question of some form of registration and code of practice for lobbyists. This concern has been reflected at the European Union level, where there has been a rapid expansion in professional lobbying activity, leading moves by the European Parliament to regulate lobbying activity. The 1946 Regulation of Lobbying Act in the United States requires lobbyists to file reports identifying themselves, their clients, and individuals lobbied, as well as detailing contributions received and expenditures made. The force of the Act was considerably narrowed by the 1954 Supreme Court decision in *United States* v. *Harris* which narrowed its reach to direct contacts with a member of Congress by individuals or organizations whose principal purpose is lobbying. The Act is seen as unenforceable and having little practical effect, although lobbyists have been successfully prosecuted for bribery and corruption. Registers of lobbyists can be used by lobbyists as a marketing device to emphasize that their activities are officially endorsed. Canada introduced a register in 1989 which is intended to identify each lobbying task. Lobbyists are divided into two groups, professional lobbyists and employees lobbying on behalf of an employer. Professional lobbyists in Canada consider that by making their activities more transparent, the register has reduced levels of suspicion about their activities. The development of professional lobbyists may be seen as part of a more general professionalization of politics in which, for example, being a politician is seen as a lifetime career, with perhaps a period in the legislature being followed by work as a professional lobbyist. WG

local government A governing institution which has authority over a subnational territorially defined area; in federal systems, a substate territorially defined area. Local government's authority springs from its elected basis, a factor which also facilitates considerable variation in its behaviour both between and within countries.

Structure in Europe is generally multi-tier. In Federal Germany below the state-level Länder are commonly found two tiers of local government: the upper-tier Kreise and the lower-tier municipalities. Regionalized states such as Italy, Spain, Portugal, Belgium, and France echo such arrangements by having three levels of local government: the region; provinces or counties; and communes as the lower-tier basic authority. By contrast, many Scandinavian countries, Britain, and many of its former colonies eschew three tiers of local government for two. In Britain the structure developed after 1888 was based upon lower-tier district authorities and upper-level county (in England and Wales) or regional (in Scotland after 1972) authorities. In the 1990s, debate in Britain reintroduced the idea of having only one tier of local government. In England some cities, and concise county areas with strong senses of community such as Rutland and the Isle of Wight, were given single-tier authorities, whilst other larger county areas retained two tiers. From 1996, the whole of Scotland and Wales was divided into single-tier authorities. Conversely, in 2000 two-tier local government for London was restored with the creation of the Greater London Authority to oversee strategic functions, above a lower tier of metropolitan boroughs. In the United States, beneath the state level there is one common tier of local government—the county—but the existence of a second tier of municipalities is piecemeal, entirely dependent upon petitioning by local residents. Often a state will have two-tier local government in some mainly urban areas but only one-tier local government in other mainly rural areas. Furthermore, specific functions such as education, responsibility for which has been concentrated in the tiered local government structure in Europe, have usually been placed under single-purpose elected local bodies in US states.

Organization of the elected executive in local government varies primarily between the mayoral system and the committee system. In the former, long found in France and the United States, a mayor is most frequently separately elected as the political leader of a council (in some smaller US cities, the mayor is a figurehead and the city is run by an unelected 'city manager'). In the latter, previously seen in the UK and Sweden, councillors are elected who then make decisions by committee. In 2000 the United Kingdom introduced arrangements by which most local authorities could be run either by directly elected mayors, by elected mayors with an unelected city manager, or by a party group nominated leader and appointed cabinet. Other non-executive councillors took on purely scrutiny and representative functions. Only in small authorities with a population of 85,000 or less could the committee system continue. Historically, development of council workforces was based upon the building up of large functionally defined departments of permanent staff. However,

since the 1980s, local bureaucracies have begun to be broken up in preference for the public contraction of work privately supplied.

Local government expenditure generally accounts for a significant proportion of GDP—between (in 2003/4) 10 per cent in Great Britain and over 30 per cent in Denmark (*see also* LOCAL GOVERNMENT FINANCE). Large-scale expenditure in Scandinavia reflects the fact that costly social services, including social security, secondary education, and healthcare, have been put in the charge of local government at the county/province level and public utilities such as water, gas, and electricity supply at the commune/municipalities level. In other countries this is not the case, but British local government, for example, retains significant responsibilities in education, planning and roads, environmental protection, and leisure service provision, and continues to expand its economic development role.

Local government's role in the political system has been considered primarily in terms of its relationship with central government. Observers from a liberal democratic standpoint have stressed two bases upon which such relationships have been formulated since the nineteenth century. First, local government has been considered important to the encouragement of political education and participation, and the basis upon which services could be provided according to local needs. Hence, relationships with the centre have been based on the partnership of free democratic institutions. Secondly, local government has been seen as rational from an administrative point of view as it allows for the efficient provision of public services at the point of service need under the direction of the centre. On this basis local government is seen as the agent of central government. France may be taken to typify the stress on both bases for the development of local government. Political participation has been maintained through the strong community identity underpinning commune local government, and a strong relationship between the operations of local government and the interests of the state has been maintained through the office of departmental prefect. Britain's leaning towards the utilitarian administrative efficiency purpose of local government is reflected in the fact that even its lowest-tier authorities may have bigger populations than some other countries' county/province level authorities.

Since the 1970s fiscal stress and changes in approaches to government have forced a reconsideration of relationships. Central governments have sought to control local government finance and expenditure, and where the community basis for local government has been weak, as in Great Britain, this has extended to the control of service policies. At the same time, in most countries the role of local government has been increasingly cast as that of the buyer of services on behalf of the public that can be provided best on a competitive basis by the private sector, and as a local governing institution which, having been overburdened, should have its responsibilities slimmed. Local government has also lost many responsibilities to non-elected local *quangos, created or encouraged by central government, so much so that the local political arena has increasingly been conceptualized as local governance, in which local government is reduced to the status of one player among many.

On the European mainland where local government is strongly territorially based, and in North America and Scandinavia where there is a greater concern to reinvent government than to privatize it, continued autonomy for local government will remain, perhaps not in the role of providing services directly, but in defining the local needs which other providers must meet. In contrast, British local government during the 1980s and 1990s followed a model in which it was expected to diminish into a contractor of services within a straitjacket of regulations imposed by central government. The Blair–Brown Governments after 1997 offered a continental-style community leadership role, symbolized in the granting of a general competence power for the first time 'to promote the economic, social and environmental wellbeing of their area'. It also changed the duty of councils to that of achieving best value in local services, in which private contraction was only one option and not imposed. The practical capability to assert local leadership and discretion nevertheless remained dependent upon improvements in local service delivery and a willingness to work with a range of local partners. Indeed the implications of failure became more serious as central inspection multiplied and a local council that did not meet centrally set standards could see the wholesale removal of such services as local schools to a private contractor.   JBr

local government finance The income raised by elected *local government. It includes local taxation, national grant subventions, local government service user charges, loan capital funding, and private financial partnerships. Variations are commonly rooted in the historical development of the role of local government in the political system, and agendas for reform are generally bound up with prescriptions for that role.

Historically, local taxation has been a principal source of finance where local independence against state formation is strongest, an appropriate local resource base exists, and services provided have been considered to be primarily of local interest. Both the United Kingdom and the United States reflect this pattern, with even the level of local taxation in the United Kingdom being left in local hands until rate-capping was introduced in 1984. Where the concept of the nation-state is stronger, as in France, national grants have been much more important than local taxation, and in the Third World the lack of local resource bases leaves localities highly dependent on central funding. The expansion of local government responsibilities across North America and Europe in the twentieth century as part of increased state intervention nevertheless necessitated increased central funding both to supplement local fiscal bases under severe pressure, and to reflect the national importance of the services that local government has undertaken. Even so, there remain huge variations between states, with local taxation as a proportion of total tax revenue among European states varying in 2005 from over 30 per cent in Sweden and Denmark to less than 5 per cent in the UK, Netherlands, Ireland, and Greece.

Equally, fiscal stress across many states has necessitated central government requiring local government to raise more of its income from user charges and through financial partnerships with private sector bodies. In the majority of Western states local government draws its local finance from a variety of sources and levies taxes on both taxpayers and service users. Only in some Scandinavian countries and the UK is there a continued reliance on one predominant form of local taxation. In Scandinavian countries this involves the usage of a local income tax; in the UK this has commonly involved the use of a property tax, formerly the local rates based on housing rateable value, and currently the council tax. Briefly, in the 1980s, the UK experimented with a flat rate personal tax, the community charge (or poll tax), but this received a hostile public reaction and was abandoned. In 2008 the Scottish Government proposed a local income tax just for Scotland.

On the assumption that he who pays the piper calls the tune, many analysts have concluded that regulation of capital funding and increased central revenue funding have inevitably meant increased central control since the 1970s. Some view this benignly as a necessary feature of public service improvement. Others criticize it for its erosion of local democracy and policy flexibility. Similarly, whilst advocates of marketization and private sector finance at the local level emphasize the stimulus this gives to long-term investment in services, critics complain that it essentially involves the public mortgaging its assets to the influence of corporate business and creates uncertainty over public service priorities. Such arguments reflect differing perspectives on the competing values of local government as rational–efficient bodies or arenas for political participation. JBr

local politics The politics of subnational units. Liberal theorists customarily assess the strength of local democracy, and thus focus on electoral politics, the politics of decision-making and governing accountability in elected local government. In comparative terms local politics appears to be heavily shaped by the degree of *federalism. Federal states have strong local politics although the autonomy of local politics in the United States from interest-group pressures has long been controversial (*see also* COMMUNITY POWER; PLURALISM; MACHINE). Unitary states such as France and Britain tend to have weak local politics (although in France this is tempered by the custom of national politicians doubling up as mayors of their local commune). In Britain the electoral politics of local government has been dominated by

political parties, whose fortunes in local elections have been determined by voters who turn out in relatively small numbers—rarely over 50 per cent—and who often vote in a second-order manner according to how they feel about national politics at the time. Debates about electoral reform have led to the adoption of the single transferable vote (STV) system in Scotland, but there remain underlying problems in the extent to which electors are knowledgeable about decision-making in local councils and relate to local representative democracy.

In recent decades innovation has focused on reconceiving the basis of local politics, decision-making, and accountability. Developments in local government from the 1980s increased the range and number of service-providing bodies at the local level, meaning that elected local authorities became one—although still the most important—amongst a number of institutions of local governance. Liberal optimists suggest that the required partnership working between local agencies has enhanced the accountability of elected local government in its community context. Pessimists suggest that the networks across local governance have exacerbated the closed, self-interested elite nature of the governing process.

More broadly, the *new right in the USA and Britain innovated by conceptualizing local politics as the local market-place for the provision of services. In the 1980s they advocated market solutions to service delivery problems and the contraction of local government in favour of a range of private, voluntary, and quasi-governmental agencies at a local level. They viewed this market-place of service providers which rose to replace the monopolistic control of elected local government as automatically a good thing. As a corollary to this the local citizen was conceived as a customer whose political participation was made through consumer actions in the local service market-place. In Britain the new public management revolution in the late 1980s and early 1990s focused on the development of market-based methods in the supply of services. The development of an active customer-orientated culture in demand was more problematic. The citizens' charters for local government launched in the early 1990s attempted to enhance local government accountability to service consumers and local tax-payers.

The Blair–Brown Governments after 1997 espoused a broader rhetoric of citizen participation, encouraging local government in the use of a wide range of consultation methods, forums, and approaches to deliberative democracy. At the same time, however, they did much to consolidate a customer-orientated culture through a stress on service league tables and service delivery satisfaction evaluation. The co-existence of consumerist and citizen-focused approaches to reactivating local politics has in itself been problematic, and both seem to have largely failed. Local councils widely report a halting take-up of opportunities to participate in local decision-making, and the new right model of local politics has failed to take root. One motivation for the *poll tax reform in the 1980s was to increase awareness of the true costs of local government, and hence make citizens behave as active consumers and vote for what they were prepared to pay for. In practice it had the opposite effect as central taxes were transferred to paying for local services in a vain attempt to relieve the tax's unpopularity. The episode ended with local participation weaker than when it began, and arguably little has really been achieved since.

Radical writers have seen local politics more in terms of a wider local system of power, conceptualized often as a local state. A major thesis for the UK advanced by Peter Saunders in *The Dual State* argued that the capitalist state had segregated itself according to social investment and social consumption functions. The latter were located in the local state, primarily provided by elected local government, but also by the National Health Service and other voluntary and quasi-governmental agencies, because they could be most efficiently tailored to ameliorating proletarian need by being located close to it. Later discussion has focused on how local politics has moved from being *fordist to post-fordist in fulfilling the needs of capitalism. However, as long as local politics moves its focus away from elected local government into unelected agencies where it is easier for business interests to predominate, the legitimacy of the local state may become increasingly hard to sustain. More recently interpretivist writers have reconceptualized local politics as a set of spaces for the promotion of varying discourses regarding what

local politics is and should be. What characterizes local politics is actually contestability rather than clarity, reflecting the fact that debate has moved a long way from a straightforward universal concern with the relative health of local representative democracy.   JBR

Locke, John (1632–1704) English philosopher widely regarded as one of the fathers of the Enlightenment and as a key figure in the development of *liberalism. Locke became a Student (i.e. Fellow) of Christ Church Oxford in 1658, but his tutorial activities came to an end in 1667, seven years after the Restoration, when Locke moved into the household of Lord Ashley (formerly Sir Anthony Ashley Cooper, and subsequently Lord Shaftesbury). His reputation as a political theorist rests upon *Two Treatises of Government* (1690); as a philosopher and founder of empiricism, on his *Essay Concerning Human Understanding* (1689). He also wrote the highly-regarded *Thoughts Concerning Education* (1693), the manuscript of which was based on letters written while he was staying in Holland (where Locke had travelled following the failure of Shaftesbury's political projects, and his death in 1683). His *Letter Concerning Toleration* (1693) deals with the proper extent of freedom of religious conscience. Its general claim was that rulers cannot have certain knowledge that the religion in which they believe is the true religion; but government is permitted to interfere if religion is a threat to order. Toleration could not be extended to atheists, who would not be bound by conventional oaths, nor to Roman Catholics whose allegiance lay elsewhere. *The Reasonableness of Christianity* (1695) stimulated considerable argument; Locke asserted that reason and revelation concurred in their specification of the law of nature (*see also* NATURAL LAW).

Two Treatises of Government is ostensibly written as a refutation of the ideas of *Filmer, who argued in his book *Patriarcha: or The natural power of kings* that the liberal jurisprudents *Grotius and *Pufendorf had set out from false premisses. Whereas they had claimed that the world was originally given to all, and that property and government had subsequently arisen from agreement, Filmer argued that the Creation conferred upon Adam private property and the right to rule. Political authority was thus God-given, not conferred by the individual choice of previously free persons. Locke wanted to explain the origins of property and political authority, maintaining an interpretation of the biblical story as the creation of natural equality, without falling foul of Filmer's criticisms of incoherence in earlier *natural rights theories. He conceived political authority to be the result of an agreement to introduce necessary protection for property, in which term he embraced 'life, liberty and estate'. The government was entrusted with authority for limited purposes, and was liable to removal if it exceeded or abused its powers. Private property was explained, not by agreement, but by the activity of labour. In his account of legitimate appropriation from the common gift, Locke referred both to the right of the labourer to that with which his labour was mixed, and to the capacity of labour to confer value on its object. Many writers subsequently deployed a labour theory of property entitlement, or a *labour theory of value, and the relationship between the two in the history of social thought is a complex matter. Locke's account of the origins of private property has led some commentators to see him as an apologist for a rising *bourgeoisie, while others emphasize what they see as his *Calvinism, and others an attachment to a landed interest. Locke aimed to depict political power as quite distinct from the power of a parent or from the power associated with property. He argued not only for limited government but for a *separation of powers, the rule of law, and the legitimacy of rebellion in some circumstances.

The possible connection between these arguments and Locke's role in Shaftesbury's household has led to close investigation of the circumstances in which the *Two Treatises* was written. Shaftesbury had wanted to exclude the Catholic Duke of York (later James II) from acceding to the throne, and supported the (failed) Exclusion Bill to that end. The Exclusion Crisis has been put forward as the proper *context for Locke's Second Treatise (which, some have argued, was written before the First, but placed after it when they were published in 1690). But Shaftesbury also thought of armed rebellion after that failure, and this has also been proposed as the context of the book's composition. This controversy about context has been invoked in assessments of the extent

of Locke's radical democratic commitments: was he arguing that it would be legitimate for the people to take up arms against James if he became king? Or that the political elite would be justified in negating his claim to the throne through law? While Locke's liberal credentials can scarcely be doubted, there is no agreement on just what sort of liberal he was. AR

logrolling Vote trading between legislators, in order to obtain legislation or appropriations favourable to the legislator's home district, with the understanding that 'you scratch my back, I'll scratch yours'.

Lomé Convention *See* EUROPEAN UNION.

longitudinal analysis The study of a population over time, as opposed to *cross-sectional analysis which is limited to a single point in time. *Time-series analysis and *panel studies are both examples. In general, panel surveys use individual-level data and time-series analysis uses aggregate-level data (*see* ECOLOGICAL ASSOCIATION). However, the chief difference is that panel studies have a relatively large number of units studied over a small number of time points (maybe just two), whilst time-series data have a small number of units (maybe just one) and a large number of time points. SF

Lord Chancellor Traditionally, an official with functions in the judiciary, the legislature, and the executive of Britain: thus held to prove that there was no separation of powers in the United Kingdom. As the head of the legal profession the Lord Chancellor presided over hearings of the Law Lords, and selected judges, QCs (Queen's Counsel—senior advocates), and the heads of tribunals. In the House of Lords, he (there was never a female Lord Chancellor) acted as the Speaker, presiding over debate. In government he was a member of cabinet and the chief legal officer.

In response to criticism that this fusion of powers was dangerous and possibly contrary to human rights law, the role was split up in 2005. The new post of Lord Speaker was created, to preside over the House of Lords. The judicial functions of the Lord Chancellor were transferred to the Lord Chief Justice, and the appointment of judges transferred to an independent commission. The government proposed to abolish the title of QC, but backed down in the face of lobbying; QCs are now appointed by an independent panel. It also attempted to abolish the title of Lord Chancellor, but failed to get the abolition approved by the House of Lords. The title remains, currently attached to the functional title of Secretary of State for Justice. The Lord Chancellor need no longer be a member of the House of Lords. Jack Straw MP (appointed Lord Chancellor and Secretary of State for Justice in 2007) is the first non-peer to hold the title.

Lord President of the Council UK political title without substantive duties. The post may be given by the Prime Minister to a member of the Cabinet in order to undertake *ad hoc* tasks.

loya jirga Pashto term for 'Grand Council'; a gathering of tribal leaders used in Afghanistan to select leaders and settle disputes. After the *Afghanistan War (2001) a *loya jirga* was convened, consisting of some 2,000 representatives chosen mainly by election, with the aim of finding a broadly acceptable consitutional settlement and choosing a head of state.

loyalty *See* EXIT; VOICE.

Lukács, György 1885–1971) Marxist philosopher, and communist, born in Budapest and educated at the University of Berlin. His early writings such as *The Theory of the Novel* (1916) were concerned with applying a form of neo-Kantianism to investigate problems within aesthetics. After reading Hegel and Marx, however, he began to concentrate on the problem of the relationship between theory and practice in terms of the dialectical method. *History and Class Consciousness* (1923) takes up these issues explicitly. Lukács emphasizes the importance of the proletariat as a class-conscious 'subject' within the 'object' of capitalist society. It is only the proletariat, from its privileged class position, that can grasp society as a totality, as a unity between theory and practice. It is in this sense that Lukács could see the proletariat as the bearer of historical development in a capitalist system which attempted to negate that very fact. To this end the fetishized appearances of capital had to be subjected to a thoroughgoing dialectical critique. Even the categories which orthodox theory used to explain social reality needed to be understood as specific to their historical context. They were therefore steeped in the very bourgeois ideology that the dialectical method had to penetrate in order to discover 'truth'. In *The Young Hegel* (1948), his emphasis on the direct influence of Hegel's thought on Marx was further established. Consequently Lukács has been seen as a founder of Hegelian Marxism. IF

Lull, Ramon (c.1235–1315) *See* SOCIAL CHOICE.

lumpenproletariat *See* BONAPARTISM; COMMUNISM.

Luther, Martin (1483–1546) German religious reformer. Luther's political thought was concerned with Church–State relationships, but he brought some new ideas to that protracted controversy. He was born at Eisleben in Saxony and studied classics and philosophy at Erfurt. In 1505 he entered the Augustinian Order, and, having studied theology, was ordained in 1507. He lectured at Wittenberg (1508–46) on philosophy and Scripture (mostly New Testament). Basing himself on Paul and *Augustine he evolved his doctrine of justification by faith alone. As was common at the time he became critical of Roman practices. In 1517, when the Dominican preacher, John Tetzel, was descending on Wittenberg selling indulgences (remission of punishment due to sin in return for a monetary consideration), Luther posted ninety-five theses against the practice and its implications on a church door.

This marked the beginning of Luther's break with Rome and led by a series of events to what came to be called Lutheranism, the Reformation, and Protestantism. These events of a purely theological and internally ecclesiastical nature do not concern us here, but they set northern Europe in turmoil. Luther had to revise the notions of Church–State relationship to accommodate his new theological ideas. This he attempted to do, but never did satisfactorily.

By 1523 he had clarified his ideas on the Church–State relationship along Augustinian lines in *On Secular Authority*. Like Augustine he distinguished between two kingdoms: the Kingdom of God; and the Kingdom of the World or Satan. First, Luther's Kingdom of God is free to follow its own conscience. It is a community bound together by love rather than coercion (unlike the Roman Church). The only authority is the word of God which is obeyed freely. There is no external form such as a church nor any distinction between clergy and laity; there is a 'priesthood of all believers'.

The other kingdom is secular and temporal. It is a divine institution but governed by its own will and reason, and designed to keep the peace by coercion. Christians can participate and hold office in it freely so long as its laws do not conflict with divine law set down in Scripture. Rulers could war with one another as equals and even against the emperor if he was acting tyrannically—this was a secular matter. But the secular kingdom could not interfere in spiritual matters. However, in practice Luther allowed secular authorities to appoint ecclesiastics, pay them, and even interfere in matters of doctrine and worship.   CB

Luxemburg, Rosa (1871–1919) Socialist writer and politician active in Polish, German, and Russian socialist movements. She led the Spartacus League out of the SPD (German socialist party) in 1917. She was murdered in January 1919 during the abortive Berlin insurrection.

Her *Social Reform or Revolution?* (1899) was an outstanding critique of *revisionism.

In *Mass Strike, Party and Trade Unions* (1906) she attacked Lenin's *democratic centralism, arguing that the party must provide political direction but must also be in touch with the spontaneous mobilizations of the masses. Influenced by the 1905 Russian Revolution, she focused upon the mass strike as the embodiment of spontaneity in that it represented a whole series of activities, combining economic and political demands, during a revolutionary situation. *The Accumulation of Capital* (1913)—her main work—described how the industrialized states solved the problem of surplus product by exporting it to non-capitalist states, involving them in a world system of exploitation. Once all had been absorbed, there would be no further destination for the surplus and capitalism would collapse. Although criticized for a misreading of Marx, Luxemburg's depiction of the relationship between centre and periphery influenced *dependency theory. Luxemburg's most trenchant criticism of the Bolsheviks in *The Russian Revolution* and *Leninism or Marxism?* was that they had established a party dictatorship which had resulted in 'the brutalization of public life'. She believed that there should be no distinction between revolutionary method and revolutionary aim, although she might be criticized for a refusal to confront the problems of power.   GL

Maastricht, Treaty of The Maastricht agreement (signed 7 February 1992) was an important amendment to the Treaty of *Rome and associated treaties of the European Communities. Building on the 1986 *Single European Act (SEA), the Maastricht agreement accelerated and enhanced the institutions and processes of European integration. Upon implementation (November 1993) the European Community was replaced by the European Union, the process leading to *economic and monetary union was outlined, and a *Common Foreign and Security Policy was developed. It became the focus of campaigns against further European integration, notably in Denmark and the United Kingdom.

( ) SEE WEB LINKS
• European Union treaties.

Machiavelli, Niccolò (1469–1527) Florentine political adviser and historian, often regarded as the first modern political theorist. After the fall of Savonarola's administration, Machiavelli became head of the Second Chancery of Florence at the age of 29. As a member of Florentine diplomatic delegations, Machiavelli became acquainted with the chief political actors of his region and time—notably, Cesare Borgia, Maximilian (the Holy Roman Emperor), and Pope Julius II. Following the invasion of Florence and restoration of the Medici family, Machiavelli was sacked and imprisoned for conspiracy. Upon his release in 1513 he sought employment as a political adviser to the new Medici Pope (Giovanni), to whom he dedicated *The Prince*. Political ambitions frustrated, Machiavelli turned to scholarship in the company of a group of 'literati' at the 'Orti Oricellari'. During this period he wrote (among other works) three *Discourses* on the first ten books of Livy's history of Rome (completed in 1519). From 1521 until his death, Machiavelli devoted his attention to writing a commissioned history of Florence.

Machiavelli's main contributions to political science are to be found in *The Prince* and the *Discourses*. Both works can be seen as expounding the requirements for the maintenance of political stability in two different regimes (principalities in *The Prince*, republics in the *Discourses*), addressing similar themes, and offering similar counsel to political leaders. The primary goals of political leaders must be to sustain government, and to acquire glory, honour, and riches for the rulers and their people. The bulk of the discussion in these works is concerned with what is required of those in power in order to secure these goods. Machiavelli's answer rests on the interplay of two key classical concepts—*fortune* and *virtú*.

Machiavelli's concept of *fortune* is very much a Roman rather than a Christian inheritance. Fortune is not a synonym for 'fate' or 'Providence' in Machiavelli's usage. Rather, it is a 'force' with which a state must 'ally' itself in order to reap greatness. Machiavelli argues that princes (and in republics the whole citizen body) must be prepared to do whatever is necessary to preserve liberty and earn glory on behalf of the state. This is the quality of *virtú*. Virtú uses luck and fortune when it can, but princes who possess it can achieve great things even without luck or fortune. In an evil world, Machiavelli warns, the wise prince must recognize that it is not always prudent to act according to conventional maxims of private morality. Nothing other than necessity should dictate a prince's actions. Much of *The Prince* is devoted to examples (drawn largely from Machiavelli's own diplomatic experience) of the art of political leadership—princes must imitate the cunning of the fox and the brawn of the lion; they must avoid the people's hatred but sustain their awe; they must consistently project an image of nobility and virtue irrespective of their deeds; they must be prepared to be cruel. His name has become associated with the exercise of cunning and expediency.

Whereas *The Prince* is concerned with the qualities of princes, the *Discourses* place a greater emphasis on the civic demands on citizens. Machiavelli's central claim in the *Discourses* is that liberty is a necessary precondition for the accumulation of power and riches. The protection of liberty is therefore the fundamental political task in a republic, and requires first and foremost a citizen body of the highest 'virtue'. What role should rulers play in a republic? Machiavelli's answer is that they should organize the polity in such a way as to promote the virtue of its citizens, and prevent its corruption (either by the substitution of private for general interests, or by creeping indifference). This requires men of great stature, exhibiting those qualities detailed in *The Prince*. In addition, a state can only secure its liberty through a perennial quest for dominion over other states (for which a large population, citizen militias, and strong allies are indispensable). Internally, a strong republic is characterized by a wisely designed constitution and basic institutions (*ordini*) whose chief function is to promote the civic patriotism required to secure liberty. Central to this project is state sponsorship of divine worship in order to inspire individuals to strive for excellence and glory. However, Machiavelli is at his most radical in urging that this utilitarian function is better fulfilled by Roman religion than by Christianity (with its enervating values of piety, humility, and general 'other-worldliness'). Machiavelli also rejects conventional Christian affirmation of social harmony by emphasizing the instrumental value of preserving the distinction between the 'orders' of rich and poor. Fearing the domination of one order by the other, Machiavelli embraced the notion of a 'mixed constitution', neither aristocracy nor democracy, but embracing elements of both forms. Similarly, laws should be designed not only to protect the rich (e.g. prohibition on slander) as well as the masses (e.g. limitation of emergency power provisions), but to keep people poor in order to avoid the dangers of factionalism.

Machiavelli remains an impenetrable figure—as Sabine observes: 'He has been represented as an utter cynic, an impassioned patriot, an ardent nationalist, a political Jesuit, a convinced democrat, and an unscrupulous seeker after the favor of despots.' His work excites similar controversy. Civic republican commentators (e.g. Skinner, Pocock) see Machiavelli as part of a broader contemporary renaissance of the virtues of classical humanism. Straussians (e.g. *Strauss, Mansfield), in contrast, view Machiavelli as a pivotal figure in the history of political philosophy in his elevation of 'liberty' above 'nature' as the defining object of political inquiry. To these interpreters, Machiavelli is the first modern political philosopher.   sw

machine Those who control the mass organization of a political party within a locality. The word was given its sinister connotations from its first use in the United States in the late nineteenth century. It was used to describe urban groups in which politicians solicited votes and delivered favours in return. The favours might be jobs, welfare, or (in the upper reaches) contracts. The machine is wittily described by one of its bosses in W. L. Riordon (ed.), *Plunkitt of Tammany Hall* (1905). The machine survived attacks on it by the Progressives but had died out even in Chicago by the 1970s.

The term was also applied to Joseph Chamberlain's machine in late nineteenth-century Birmingham, and entrenched Labour Party machines in some cities in the twentieth century. These, too, have disappeared.

Macpherson, Crawford Brough (1911–87) Political theorist and analyst of political thought, Professor of Political Science at the University of Toronto. Probably his most influential work is *The Political Theory of Possessive Individualism: Hobbes to Locke* (1962), an analysis of the ideas of seventeenth-century English political philosophy. Amongst thinkers as apparently diverse as Thomas *Hobbes, John *Locke, and the *Levellers, Macpherson claimed to discern a common philosophy of 'possessive individualism' according to which individuals are essentially owners of their persons, capacities, and fruits of their capacities, free insofar as they own themselves; society is a system of exchange between self-proprietors; and the state, merely an instrument for the protection of property and for securing orderly exchange. He claimed to show how tacit commitment to the assumptions of this philosophy undermined the democratic, egalitarian thrust of their work. According to Macpherson, the philosophy of possessive individualism reflected the circumstances of nascent market society, but came to look increasingly anachronistic as capitalist society developed. In later work, notably *The Life and Times of Liberal Democracy* (1977), Macpherson developed a contrast between a 'protective' model of liberal democracy, based on the philosophy of possessive individualism, and an alternative 'developmental' model of liberal democracy based on a different conception of the individual as a potential developer and exerter of valuable capacities. John Stuart *Mill is identified by Macpherson as the pioneer of this alternative developmental form of individualism and model of democracy. Macpherson argues that if the promise of the developmental model is to be realized, however, democrats will have at once to promote more participatory forms of democracy and entertain much more radical departures from capitalist economic organization than envisaged by Mill, or by developmental democrats of the early twentieth century (such as John Dewey, Ernest Barker, and L. T. *Hobhouse). His work represents a sustained argument to the effect that democracy must be detached from capitalism if it is to achieve its promise of equality of self-development. swe

macroeconomics The branch of economics which deals with aggregates such as capital and labour, and their interactions in an economy as a whole. Politics everywhere is deeply affected by changes in macroeconomic variables such as inflation, unemployment, and the exchange rate. Some writers have developed 'political business cycle' models which aim to predict the popularity of the government from the current or recent ('lagged') values of these variables.

Madison, James (1751–1836) US politician and political theorist. Madison entered Virginia politics in 1776 and national politics in 1780. He was instrumental in setting up the Constitutional Convention of 1787 and played a large role both in writing the Constitution and in its defence in *The Federalist Papers*, written jointly with Alexander *Hamilton and John Jay. In his successful campaign to persuade Virginia to ratify the Constitution, he promised to promote amendments to it protecting individual rights against the state: these became part of the Bill of Rights (the first ten amendments, ratified in 1791). As the first party system developed, Madison joined *Jefferson's agrarian and (relatively) democratic coalition; he was Jefferson's Secretary of State 1801–9, and succeeded him as President 1809–17. He was the shortest President of the United States to date (*Lincoln was the tallest).

Madison's numbers of the *Federalist Papers* raise issues of enduring importance in political theory. Most opponents of ratification believed that the federal government would have excessive powers. In papers nos. 10 and 45–51, Madison argues that the horizontal division between states and the federal government, and the vertical division among legislature, executive, and judiciary, are the checks and balances which are necessary (and sufficient) to balance democracy and liberty. Madison believed that unchecked majority rule (as he perceived it in several of the state legislatures of the time) could lead to expropriation of the rich by the poor, or of creditors by debtors, for instance through 'a rage for paper money, for an abolition of debts, for an equal division of property, or for any other improper or wicked project'. Madison's is one of the clearest statements of the '*tyranny of the majority'; but he was wrong to describe the US Constitution as either a necessary or a sufficient curb of it. In particular, it could do nothing for groups which were neither a local nor a national majority, such as black Americans.

Mafia An analytical concept that applies to criminal organizations that aspire to obtain a monopoly over the protection of illegal transactions, share a common ritual, rules of behaviour, and ways to coordinate activities, but ultimately retain a high degree of independence.

The Mafia is a males-only secret society that emerged in western Sicily at the beginning of the nineteenth century. The foremost scholar of the Sicilian Mafia, Diego Gambetta, has shown that the Sicilian Mafia is the product of a late and imperfect transition to the market economy. The end of feudalism in Sicily led to an increase in economic transactions and a demand for the protection of property. Because the Italian State could not meet that demand, property owners searched for alternative sources of protection. However, demand alone was not sufficient for the Mafia to emerge. Sicily, in the nineteenth century, possessed a ready supply of people trained in the use of violence, such as disbanded army soldiers and field guards. Demand met supply and the Sicilian Mafia thus emerged as an independent and rather stable supplier of private protection. Although at first the Mafia protected some Sicilians against theft and banditry, and regulated trade and markets in the agricultural sector, over time it specialized in protecting criminals dealing in illegal commodities or individuals dealing illegally in otherwise legal commodities. A specific role of the Mafia in the overworld is enforcing illegal cartel agreements. Although mostly genuine, Mafia protection is often imposed by force, is expensive, rough, and unjust.

Members join a given Mafia 'family' through a ritual, which has hardly changed since the nineteenth century and has significant religious overtones. At the ceremony the norms of the organization are presented to the novice. Contrary to widespread belief, the Sicilian Mafia is not a hierarchical organization with a 'Boss of the Bosses' at the top, but rather a confederation of independent 'families', who share the same ritual and rules of behaviour, each with its territorial bases. In the late 1950s, the 'families' created a forum to discuss inter-family matters (the *commissione*) but have always retained their independence. In fact, disputes among 'families' are not uncommon and can be bloody: two all-out Mafia wars have taken place since the Second World War (1961–3 and 1981–5) and claimed hundreds of lives. The *commissione* itself was dissolved between 1963 and 1973.

According to estimates, in 1987 the Mafia had 3,000 members distributed over some 100 'families' in Sicily (fifty-four of which were in Palermo alone). Membership ranges between two to 120 individuals per 'family'.

The Mafia's interactions with politics have been dictated mostly by expediency. Some evidence suggests that possibly two 'families'

supported an independent Sicily in the immediate post-Second World War period. The only two political parties the Mafia refused to deal with were the Italian Communist Party and the neo-fascist party (MSI). The most significant anti-Mafia trial took place in 1986–7. A team of Palermo prosecutors (including G. Falcone and P. Borsellino, both later murdered by the Mafia) charged some 500 people, nearly 400 of whom were found guilty.

Although the Mafia is a product of Sicily, are we justified in using 'Mafia' as an analytical concept that covers more than one case? Notwithstanding local variations, other criminal organizations (the Japanese Yakuza, the Hong Kong Triads, the American Cosa Nostra, and the Russian Mafia) emerged in similar ways, have a comparable structure, and perform a similar role in both the underworld and the overworld. The Mafias mentioned above all developed after major and rapid spread of property that was not matched by the establishment of adequate formal enforcement mechanisms by the State. This generated a demand for non-state sources of protection. Such a demand was matched by the presence of individuals who had acquired violent skills and found themselves unemployed. These people underwent a process of specialization and became *autonomous* suppliers of criminal protection. The Russian and the Japanese cases resemble the Sicilian one the most (disbanded Red Army soldiers, Afghan veterans, and unemployed sportsmen formed the supply in the post-Soviet period, while disenfranchised samurai, hoodlums, and poor peasants formed the supply of the early Yakuza when feudalism came to an end in Japan during the Meiji period, 1868–1911). The American Cosa Nostra emerged at the time of Prohibition, offering protection directly in the underworld to people illegally dealing in alcohol, its ranks formed by poor and unemployed Southern Italian immigrants.

By and large, each Mafia is a collection of independent groups that share the same ritual yet retain a high degree of independence and ability to mobilize violence. Within each group, specific roles (such as adviser, boss, deputy boss) exist as well as some possibility of advancement by either promotion or violent takeover. Although these arrangements may have a certain fluidity and instability,

Mafias are not loose networks of people who meet *ad hoc* to commit crimes. Also, by and large the Mafias' groups intersect but by no means coincide with blood families.

Differences among Mafias do exist as regards number of 'families', size of each 'family', relation to politics, intra-Mafia violence, and criteria to coordinate their activities. For instance, compared to its Sicilian counterpart, the American Mafia has proved to be less prone to internecine violence (with only one all-out war since the 1930s—the Castellamarese wars), has fewer and larger 'families' (only five in New York; estimates range from seventy-five to 400 members per 'family', for a total of 1,400 individuals in 1992). Also, the New York five 'families' divided their jurisdiction not according to territory but sectors of the economy.   FV

Maistre, Joseph de (1753–1821) Political philosopher, born in Savoy. Although a Catholic, he was for fifteen years a Freemason, and briefly supported the *French Revolution. But in 1793 the French invasion forced him into exile first in Switzerland, then in Russia as ambassador for the king of Savoy where he remained without his family until 1817. All Maistre's writings derived from his hatred of the Revolution, but instead of a critique of particular events, he started from the form of thought that for him explained them, summarized in the notion of pride. This was a denial of the knowledge of final causes that had existed before the Fall of Adam and Eve, and which was afterwards available only in an instinctive form in the traditions of different societies, or in an individual form, in the consciences of the virtuous. The thinkers who had inspired the revolutionaries believed that they could do better by applying abstract reason, something which the history of the Revolution showed to be ridiculous. After the defeat of Napoleon, Maistre returned to Turin, and established contact with pro-royalist circles in France. He rapidly became dissatisfied with the Restoration, and with the post-revolutionary settlement. In 1819, he published *Du pape* in which he proposed the Church as the only possible sovereign, but this seems to have been more a matter of disappointment with the situation in Europe than something derived from his social philosophy.   CS

majoritarianism The view that legitimate political authority expresses the will of the majority of those subject to this authority (also known as the majority principle). Some commentators regard the majority principle as self-evidently the appropriate way of determining law or policy where citizens disagree. According to John Locke: 'when any number of Men have, by the consent of every individual, made a *Community*, they have thereby made that *Community* one Body, with a Power to Act as one Body, which is only by the will and determination of the *majority*. For that which acts any Community, being only the consent of the individuals of it, and it being necessary to that which is one body to move one way; it is necessary the Body should move that way whither the greater force carries it, which is the *consent of the majority*; or else it is impossible it should act or continue one Body . . . '. Others, such as *Rousseau, claim that the majority will is more likely to be objectively correct in identifying what is in the common good than the minority's, a view that derives some support from *Condorcet's *jury theorem. This result depends, however, on whether the majority is indeed aiming at the common good, rather than its own sectional interests. Critics point out that since citizens need not aim for the common good, a simple majority will need not accord with what is objectively fair, leading to the view that there should be some constitutional limits on the majority's authority. The development of modern *social choice theory has also raised awkward questions about the very idea of a 'majority will'. Social choice theory suggests that where a group of people are choosing between more than two alternatives, the alternative that is selected as the winner can change depending on exactly which democratic institutions are used to aggregate individuals' preference orderings into a 'social choice'. The majority will is not something which exists prior to the process of aggregation, and which is reflected by it; rather, it is something which exists only following the process of aggregation, and different, apparently reasonable processes of aggregation may produce different majority wills (*see* CYCLE). If, however, there is a potential plurality of majority wills for any given set of individuals' underlying preference orderings, it is less clear why any specific majority will has the special legitimacy assumed by majoritarianism. swe

majority government Descriptively, majority government means a government formed by one party with a majority over all other parties in the legislature, a condition most likely to be fulfilled under *two-party systems. When used normatively, it refers to the belief that a government formed in this way offers the most effective and accountable form of government. Proponents of this view would argue that parties should have the maximum opportunity to implement their policies once they are in office, both because this makes the electoral choice made by electors meaningful, and because it leads to consistent and coherent policies. The merits of such a form of government are often emphasized by opponents of proportional representation who see electoral reform as reducing the chances of one party forming the government without engaging in bargaining with other parties. Such bargaining is seen as diluting the coherence of party policies, and diminishing the link between the elector and the government, while the poorer survival prospects of multi-party governments for a legislative term are seen as undermining political stability. So-called majority governments often, however, lack the support of a majority of an electorate, and may be less willing to take account of views of minority groups, or respond to evidence that their policies are not working. One-party majority government was once viewed as the desirable norm, but this is no longer the case. wg

majority-minority districting A rule by which the design of new electoral boundaries must where possible create electoral districts which have a majority population of some group which is a national minority (hence, majority-minority districts). In the US, such districts are required by the Voting Rights Act as amended in 1982. Section 2 of the Act includes language designed to prevent dilution of representation for minority groups, and to protect their ability to 'elect representatives of their choice', although not a right to proportional representation for protected classes. In *Thornburg* v. *Gingles* (1986) the US Supreme Court set out three

guidelines for 'dilution' which now broadly govern when majority-minority districts must be created: first, the minority group must be large enough and geographically situated such that a relatively compact district in which they are a majority can be drawn up; secondly, there must be a history of cohesive voting among the minority group; and thirdly, there must be a history of racially cohesive majority voting behaviour sufficient to prevent the election of most of the minority group's favoured candidates.

The creation of majority-minority districts has had a swift and substantial effect in increasing African-American representation in the House of Representatives and in state legislatures. It has also been used to create majority Hispanic and Native American districts, especially at the state level. The courts have continued to tinker with the system, concerned that overtly racial drawing of boundaries breaches the Fourteenth Amendment: in *Shaw* v. *Reno* (1993) the Supreme Court rejected a North Carolina plan which created an extra majority African-American district by stringing together a group of geographically dispersed communities along a freeway. Majority-minority districting in the era since has been controlled by the Court's concerns in that case: district boundaries cannot be drawn *solely* on the basis of race, as arguably they were in the North Carolina case, but majority-minority districting can permissibly be part of the entire redistricting scheme, albeit under close judicial supervision. Meanwhile, many supporters of the original scheme have begun to support a move to more proportional, multimember voting systems which may provide a more nuanced tool for increasing minority representation. pm

majority/minority leader In the US Congress the majority leader is the Representative or Senator selected by the majority party to organize the passage of legislation. The Senate majority leader controls the legislative schedule, sets party strategy, and is the party's chief spokesman. The House majority leader, although subordinate in rank to the *Speaker, has an important role in organizing the passage of legislation. Minority leaders organize the minority party's strategy, and are the party's main spokesmen in Congress.

majority rule Widely used as a synonym for 'universal franchise' (for instance in the slogan 'No independence before majority rule' or NIBMAR, which was the British Government's position on Rhodesia, now Zimbabwe, in the period leading up to the unilateral declaration of independence by the white minority regime there in 1965). As this instance shows, it is easy to recognize what is not majority rule, but harder to say what is. 'Majority' means 'more than half'; but most political choices involve more than two people or courses of action, and therefore no one may have the support of as many as half the electors. What then is majority rule? This is a deep and still unresolved question (*see also* BORDA; CONDORCET; DEMOCRACY; IMPOSSIBILITY THEOREMS).

maladministration Maladministration in UK public administration was defined by Richard Crossman, the minister responsible for legislating in 1967 for the UK parliamentary *ombudsman, as 'bias, neglect, inattention, delay, incompetence, ineptitude, perversity, turpitude, arbitrariness and so on' leading to perceived injustice. It refers to defective administration rather than defective policy. However, in practice, administration and politics are hard to distinguish and over time possible complaints of maladministration have been interpreted with increasing flexibility. Investigation is conducted by a range of ombudsmen including those established for Parliament, the National Health Service, local government, and the parliaments/assemblies created by *devolution. Evidence of the extent of complaints of maladministration provides a mixed picture. On the one hand, figures for 2003–4 indicate that the UK parliamentary ombudsman alone received 2,319 complaints. However, many were not taken forward, 919 were resolved by the organization which had been complained against taking appropriate action that satisfied the complainant, and only 148 were accepted for statutory investigation. The health service ombudsman generally investigates little more than a hundred complaints per year. The local commissioners for administration, nevertheless, receive rather more, the commissioner for England commonly receiving thousands rather than hundreds. The relative significance of these figures as a barometer of competence in public administration is impossible to state. However, the very investigation of maladministration has provided a legitimation for public provision made necessary by the shortcomings of other forms of accountability in central government, and by the need to reassure the public following state reform and territorial decentralization.   JBr

Malcolm X (1925–65) Black radical leader prominent in the United States in the late 1950s and early 1960s. Born Malcolm Little in Omaha, Nebraska, he became a Black Muslim (Nation of Islam) convert whilst in prison in the 1940s. Released in 1952, he subsequently became the principal lieutenant of Elijah Muhammad, the leader of the Muslims. Suspended from that movement in late 1963, he was assassinated in 1965. For most of his short political career, Malcolm X was a devout, totally loyal follower of Elijah Muhammad, espousing his leader's unorthodox version of the Muslim faith and the political doctrine that went with it. This included an emphasis on black pride and black culture; elaborate schemes to promote black rehabilitation and self-sufficiency; abstention from the political process; and a rigid commitment to separatism. As a strident and vivid spokesman for the Black Muslims, Malcolm X bitterly denounced the moderate, integrationist strategies of *civil rights leaders such as Martin Luther *King. The violence of his rhetoric alarmed many white Americans, but although he regularly used incendiary language as an attention-seeking device and as a means of awakening black consciousness, he was careful not to advocate violent methods by blacks, except in self-defence.

Towards the end of 1963 Malcolm X became increasingly frustrated by the fatalism and the narrow sectarianism of the Muslim faith. The break with Muhammad gave him the opportunity to set up new organizations of his own, the Muslim Mosque Incorporated and the Organization of Afro-American Unity. He now abandoned political abstentionism and urged upon blacks the need to organize voter registration drives and to develop political unity in order to exploit their pivotal position in elections. *See* BLACK POWER.   DM

Malthus, Revd Thomas Robert (1766–1834) Born in Surrey, his father was a country gentleman with broad-ranging intellectual interests, who was both a *Godwinian and a friend and executor of *Rousseau. Malthus himself was tutored privately for Cambridge. He obtained a fellowship at Jesus College. He took orders in 1788. His writings on population undoubtedly cast a long and deep shadow over Victorian optimism, and all editions of the *Essay on the Principle of Population*, 1798–1803, provoked virulent criticism. In brief, 'parson Malthus' argued that the natural rate of population increase was geometrical, while the increase in food production was arithmetical; population, then, would always tend to outstrip food supply. This observation, that scarcity, hunger, and poverty were natural and inevitable conditions, was flanked by a specific concern with the improvidence and imprudence of the poor, whose fertility was unchecked by contraception or moral restraint. Thus, in the popular mind at least, the Malthusian doctrine was that only continuing poverty would limit the numbers of poor. Malthus's doctrines played a crucial part in the formulation of the theory of natural selection, since the 'wedging' effect of population pressure results in a 'survival of the fittest'. JH

Manchester school Name given first by its opponents to the Manchester-based campaign to repeal the UK Corn Laws, 1838–46. The campaign mixed the self-interest of employers in export industries (for whom protectionist barriers to free trade in food added to their costs, as they increased the wages that must be paid to prevent working-class families from starving) with arguments of principle for free trade. The label is sometimes applied, less accurately, to any or all of the doctrines of *classical economics which were current at the time.

mandate An electoral victory is interpreted by the successful party or coalition as giving it a mandate from the people to govern in the best interests of the nation or a specific mandate to pursue particular policies. Given that in an election parties campaign on many issues, it is difficult to claim that the government has a specific mandate for every policy, though it can reasonably claim to have a general mandate to govern. If a particular issue dominates a party's successful election campaign, then it might reasonably claim to have a mandate to pursue that issue. In recent times, however, it is difficult to identify particular issues as dominating elections, because parties compete with each other in terms of very general competences to govern.

The doctrine of the mandate can be interpreted in a negative sense to mean that governments ought not to introduce policies for which they lack a specific mandate. This meaning is difficult to reconcile with the idea of a general mandate to govern, but *see* HOUSE OF LORDS. PBY

Mandeville, Bernard (1670–1733) Social theorist, who practised medicine in London, although born and educated abroad. He provided important analyses relating individual activity to social outcomes. For example, he drew attention to the advantages which accrued from division of labour. He was also interested in the advantages to society of the pursuit of self-interest and profit, and provided an account of the sort of unintended consequences of individual action within a social process that was later associated particularly with Adam *Smith's work. His notoriety amongst his contemporaries arose from his apparent denigration of dispositions or moral outlooks which encouraged the intentional promotion of that social benefit. He argued in *The Fable of the Bees: or Private Vices, Public Benefits* that the disappearance of what was conventionally regarded as vice would lead to impoverishment, because such 'vices', particularly those associated with acquisitiveness and jealous comparison with the lot of others, were engines of activity. The allegation that conventional virtues were destructive of the good at which they aimed was not well received. AR

manifesto A document in which a political party sets out the programme it proposes to follow if returned to office. The document may reflect compromises between different party groupings, rather than an agreed programme of action. The manifesto can be seen as establishing the *mandate for a governing party, although governments are often reluctant to be constrained by manifesto commitments. WG

manipulation The turning of a situation to advantage. Specifically, use of procedural devices such as changing the order of the agenda or the voting rules, or introducing new proposals not for their merits but to split an otherwise winning coalition.

Mannheim, Karl (1893–1947) Hungarian sociologist who made an important contribution to the sociology of knowledge, starting with *Ideology and Utopia* (1929). Like *Marx before him, Mannheim wanted to relate systems of belief and 'states of mind' which emerged in particular historical periods to the socio-economic and political conditions which seemed to stimulate and sustain them. But he differed from Marx in that he considered *utopianism to be a forward-looking, visionary tendency which was capable of breaking out of the constraints of the existing social order, and could thus point to the possibility of real change and transformation in the historical process. Thus Mannheim could identify a positive utopian element in *Marxism itself, whereas Marx considered 'utopian' to mean unscientific and incapable of producing real change in society. Similarly Mannheim rejected Marx's conclusion that proletarian consciousness is in some respects closer to the truth than is bourgeois consciousness: for Mannheim all social classes adhere to belief systems which are rooted in their own limited experience, and this must necessarily include working-class beliefs. Mannheim considered an *ideology to be any system of ideas firmly rooted within the confines of existing reality, and which basically expressed an acceptance of that which exists and a failure to see beyond that reality. Thus, for him the modern socialist tradition (including Marxism) must be considered highly utopian rather than narrowly ideological. Mannheim sought to develop an analysis of the link between systems of belief and the distinctive social groups which, at different times, embrace and promulgate those beliefs. He proceeded to argue that it was the task of social scientists to transcend the battleground of ideologies and utopias, and produce a more neutral and objective set of social principles which could help produce a free but also rationally planned society based on a true science of politics. This suggested a prominent role for intellectuals in society—a view which many critics of Mannheim have considered to be dangerously illiberal in its implications.   KT

Mao Zedong (1893–1976) Leader of the Communist Party of China from 1934 until his death in September 1976 and Marxist theorist. Mao is now remembered primarily for his two greatest campaigns, the Great Leap Forward of 1958, and the Great Proletarian *Cultural Revolution of 1965, both of which were disastrous failures. The first ended with one of the greatest famines in human history, the second deteriorated into bloody chaos. Yet it is not enough to write off 'the thought of Mao Zedong' as perverse or without substance. These two linked movements began from rational and intelligent attempts to create a humane and to some extent democratic alternative to Stalinism.

Mao was born in Hunan in 1893 into a family of prosperous farmers. By the time he reached his majority, China was plunged into the chaos which succeeded the fall of the imperial system in 1912, and at the same time plunged into a desperate revaluation of Chinese society and traditions. After some years of self-education he succeeded in entering one of China's new colleges as a mature student. There he came under the influence of the teacher Yang Changji (*see* CHINESE POLITICAL THOUGHT) who had been educated abroad in Germany and in Scotland and had created a philosophy combining elements of Western and Chinese thought. The main Western influences on Yang were *Kant, T. H. *Green, and the Scottish empiricists, and his philosophy stressed the importance for society of individual development in conditions of freedom. Through his teaching, Mao became passionately committed (like the young Marx) to this individualism, and to a belief in the power of consciousness in motivating action. At this time he had read little or no Marxism, but he had been introduced to socialist ideas through the translation of Thomas Kirkup's *History of Socialism*, which discusses the two alternative forms of socialism, the etatist and the communal. Mao read it 'with wild enthusiasm', and like most of his contemporaries agreed with Kirkup in approving the communal alternative; Mao was also profoundly impressed by the pragmatism of John Dewey, whose ideas were made popular in China via his student Hu Shi.

It was warlordism rather than capitalism which turned Mao into a Marxist; it was the possibility of uniting China through the mobilization of the masses by means of a Leninist cadre party which clearly attracted him. He worked briefly in the library of Beijing University, where the librarian Li Dazhao had just founded a Marxist group. From Li, Mao's ideas of the importance of consciousness were confirmed, and from then on his concept of leadership stressed the creation of consciousness rather than organization. This was at once the greatest strength and the greatest weakness of his thought.

In 1924 *Sun Yatsen invited China's new Communist Party to join a *United Front against the warlords, turning to the Soviet Union for the help which the West refused. Mao was more enthusiastic about this united front than many of his fellow Communists. With Soviet help Sun's successor Chiang Kaishek defeated the warlords, but he then repudiated his Communist allies in a bloody coup in 1927. Mao had already been arguing within the alliance for the importance of the peasants in the revolution (China's industrial proletariat was then minuscule). Chiang's coup, rather than Mao's eloquence, persuaded the Communist Party of China of this; driven into the hills, they had no option but to depend on the peasantry, and Mao set about creating the Jiangxi Soviet, a revolutionary rural state within the state. This was destroyed in 1934, but a new base was found in north-west China. Soon it was involved in guerrilla resistance to the Japanese. There, Mao's ideas were further developed in the course of attempting to develop the wartime economy of this poor region. He repudiated the forced cooperatives created by his fellow leaders and turned for help to the Chinese Industrial Cooperatives, a non-Communist movement which sought to bring appropriate technology to the villages. In these simple, democratic institutions Mao found the concrete form of his communal socialism.

Guerrilla warfare depended upon popular support. Mao opposed all attempts by his fellow leaders to force ideologically inspired policies upon the peasants, and in opposing them developed his mass-line theory of leadership, a process of mutual education between leaders and led. The close relation in Mao's mind between Marxist knowledge and mass-line action is shown in the last sentence of the key paragraph in his summary of the meaning of the mass line: 'In the practical work of our Party, all correct leadership is necessarily 'from the masses to the masses'. This means: 'Take the ideas of the masses (scattered and unsystematic ideas) and concentrate them (through study, turn them into concentrated and systematic ideas), then go to the masses and propagate and explain these ideas until the masses embrace them as their own, hold fast to them and translate them into action . . . . Such is the Marxist theory of knowledge' (*Selected Works*, iii. 119).

In power in 1949 Mao assumed that capitalism must be developed before socialism was attempted. However in 1953, under the threat from American hostility and the dependence on the Soviet Union thus made necessary, he accepted the Stalinist system in China's first five-year plan. Yet by 1959 in a series of speeches and documents he had condemned *Stalinism, on five grounds. (1) It was counter-productive to impoverish the peasants in order to build industry: 'this is draining the pond to catch the fish'. (2) The high priority given to the development of heavy industry was also counter-productive: 'if you are really serious about developing heavy industry, you will pay serious attention to agriculture and light industry'. (3) Stalin's command economy offered no place for popular participation and popular initiative: accumulation and investment spring not from the communities' consciousness of new possibilities but from state coercion, and accumulation was therefore severely limited. (4) Stalin argued that in socialist society there were no contradictions: Mao argued that contradictions continued, including contradictions between the people and the government, and he also argued that to deny and suppress such conflict was to 'abolish politics', and so to abolish progress, for contradiction is the motive force of progress. (5) A socialist society cannot stop merely at the nationalization of the means of production and treat the first institutions thus created as if they were permanent. These institutions are only the beginning, and they are not in themselves socialist: 'there is still a process to be gone through . . . there is work to do', in order to create new and truly socialist relations of production. The way to overcome all these faults is to decentralize decision-making as far as possible to the local communities; the job of socialist planners will then be to respond to community initiatives, not to dictate from above.

Thus Mao's mass line developed into a specific strategy of economic development, expressed in the *Great Leap and the Communes. The central part of his strategy was the creation of 'commune and brigade enterprises' using labour-intensive techniques. His new strategy, however, should not be seen as having been created by one man. The economic ideas involved—the use of surplus rural labour to create new infrastructure and to develop local industry, in a framework of 'integrated development'— were fashionable among Western development economists at that time. In a wider sense, Mao's ideas of the relations between centralized and local development and between agriculture and industry go back to *Bukharin. His resistance to the fossilization of Soviet institutions echoes *Kautsky, whom Mao read in his youth. And behind the whole complex of ideas there undoubtedly lies the affirmation of the seventeenth-century philosopher and patriot Gu Yanwu that 'China is at her weakest when the central government is strongest, and at her strongest when her local communities are strong'.

When in 1965 Mao launched his great campaign, the Great Proletarian Cultural Revolution, this time the enemy was not Stalin but his successors. Mao called them revisionists, but his hostility to them was not that they had repudiated Stalinism (he had done that himself), but that they merely confirmed the Stalinist managers in their power by adding profit to political authority. Mao said that 'the officials of China are a class, and one whose interests are antagonistic to those of the workers and peasants'. Privilege and the abuse of power were rampant, and the vested interests built up through the centralized command economy had created a massive obstacle to Mao's alternative strategy. In imitation of the 1919 May Fourth Movement, he called on China's students to criticize the Party establishment. The Cultural Revolution failed, as the Great Leap had failed. In the case of the Leap Mao tried to run a movement which could only have succeeded if carried through democratically; an authoritarian party could not succeed.

The Cultural Revolution failed because at the critical point Mao refused to dispense with the vanguard party, which he identified with Yang Changji's conscious elite which was to create consciousness among the masses. In spite of the failure of his two greatest campaigns, they left in some respects a positive legacy. First, his rural collective 'commune and brigade enterprises' were revived in the Cultural Revolution and by Mao's death in 1976 had grown so rapidly that they had become indispensable. Mao's successor Deng Xiaoping accepted and encouraged them, and they provided a buoyant new economy which allowed the reform of the inefficient state sector to be carried on gradually and experimentally. Second, Mao had told China's younger generation that 'to rebel is justified'. The Cultural Revolution rebellion ended in chaos and failure, and many Red Guards had learned that to be successful, rebellion would have to aim at the establishment of democratic institutions and procedures. From then until now, former Red Guards have led that section of China's democratic movement which repudiates as futile any attempt to seek democratization from the top, and have concentrated on mobilizing the people to secure democratization from below. The third part of Mao's positive legacy was the rapprochement which he reached with the USA. This gave China unprecedented security in which more relaxed policies became possible.   JG

Marcuse, Herbert (1898–1979) German philosopher. Member of the *Frankfurt School of *critical theory. Escaping Nazi persecution, he settled in the United States in 1934. As an enthusiastic supporter of the student and black movements of the 1960s, he became known as the 'father of the *New Left'. Arguing that 'the task of theory' was 'to liberate practice' (1928), he called for a reconstruction of Marxist social and historical theory. His work centred upon an attempted synthesis of *Hegel, Marx, and Freud (his most significant text on the latter being *Eros and Civilization* (1955).

Marcuse repudiated economic determinism in favour of an affirmation of human potential. Being and consciousness were dialectical partners with neither having priority over the other. In changing the world, humans re-create themselves (what his mentor *Heidegger termed 'authentic existence'). Here Marcuse was a precursor of phenomenological writers such as Sartre and Merleau-Ponty.

One Dimensional Man (1964) described how advanced technological society was able to contain the forces of revolution by co-opting the working class through consumerism, creating 'false needs', compounding alienation, and producing a system where people are enslaved but believe they have freedom ('unreal freedom'). In *Repressive Tolerance* (1965), he argued that liberal democracy defined the parameters of political debate and so blocked any real criticism (although this could be argued to be an un-*falsifiable statement).

Marcuse acclaimed the New Left for its confrontational politics and its creation of a new sensibility. It would act as a catalyst both for working-class and Third World revolutionary struggles. He saw the events of 1968 as an instinctual act of liberation.   GL

marginalism The technique of studying economic change by examining any small rate of change of any one variable (e.g. cost, revenue, consumer satisfaction) relative to another. Analytically powerful because it enables the rules of calculus to be directly applied to economic reasoning. Marginalism was imported into political thinking by economists who turned to politics. The benefit of marginalist thought is that it can dispel common fallacies, for instance 'We have spent £K (where K is a large number) on *Concorde so far and have got nothing to show for it; therefore we should spend the further £K? (where K? is a slightly smaller number) needed to complete the development, so as not to waste the money we have spent already'; or 'If everybody shirked, no cooperative benefit, such as reducing pollution, would ever occur; therefore I should do my bit'. In each case, only the marginal cost of contributing another pound or another hour is relevant to evaluating the costs and benefits of acting. Some critics have accused marginalism of introducing a selfish orientation to thinking about politics (*see* ECONOMIC MAN).

marginal seat A constituency in which the distribution of party support is relatively evenly balanced so that the incumbent party has a narrow majority and a small net movement of voters will lead to its changing hands. In many constituencies, the socioeconomic make-up of the electorate is such as to permanently skew support to one political party, and incumbents have substantial majorities which are normally unassailable by challengers. Such one-party 'safe' seats predominate in many political systems, in which case the outcomes of elections are decided in the 'marginals', the often small number of seats in which there are genuine prospects of change in the winning party. For this reason, the parties tend to concentrate their campaigning efforts on wooing voters in those marginal constituencies in which they are expected to come either first or second. It may be noted that seats can, of course, shift between the 'marginal' and 'safe' categories reflecting population movements, boundary changes, and political realignments.   ST

marginal utility *See* ECONOMIC MAN.

market The analogy between political exchange and market exchange has occurred to many thinkers over the centuries but has been formalized in the last 100 years (*see also* ECONOMIC MAN; EXCHANGE THEORY). Politics has been conducted in the market-places of cities at least since the ancient Greeks. In the market analogy, voters are compared with consumers, organized interests with producers of goods, and politicians with entrepreneurs and shopkeepers. Each political actor is regarded as maximizing utility, subject to a budget constraint (that is, with only a limited amount of money or number of votes to dispose of). Like any analogy, that from the market to politics can be dangerous if followed too slavishly.

market socialism The doctrine that socialism can and should be achieved without a massive state apparatus. Market socialists believe that while capital can and should be owned cooperatively, or in some cases by the state, decisions about production and exchange should be left to market forces and not planned centrally. Market socialism is intertwined with *industrial democracy because the most difficult practical questions often turn out to be: If capital is cooperatively owned, who decides how to dispose of it? And do cooperators get one vote each, or votes in proportion to the capital they have contributed? Robert *Nozick has argued (in *Anarchy, State and Utopia*) that the comparative scarcity of producer cooperatives shows that people have freely chosen to live under capitalism instead. Market socialists such as D. L. Miller have denied this, arguing that a capitalist economy is structurally biased against market socialist enterprises.

Marshall Aid The Marshall Plan—formally known as the European Recovery Programme—was announced by the US Secretary of State George C. Marshall on 5 June 1947. Sixteen European states—Austria, Belgium, Denmark, the Republic of Ireland, France, Greece, Iceland, Italy, Luxembourg, the Netherlands, Norway, Portugal, Switzerland, Sweden, Turkey, and the United Kingdom—became the beneficiaries of American grants. Although the sixteen nations (plus the German Federal Republic represented by the occupying powers) initially requested a total of $29 billion to cover each country's deficit over the period 1948-52, only $12.5 billion was actually delivered. Marshall Aid was phased out in mid-1951 and was replaced by Mutual Security Assistance which extended substantial military aid to Western Europe. Although the Marshall Plan has been dubbed the 'most selfless act in history', it was introduced not only to safeguard America's strategic political and military interests in Western Europe but also to take account of the need of the US to maintain its colossal export surplus in the face of a predicted domestic recession.   PBM

(⊕) SEE WEB LINKS
• Text of Marshall's speech initiating the Marshall Plan.

Marsiglio (Marsilius) of Padua (*c.*1275-*c.*1342) Philosopher involved in politics. He studied medicine and natural philosophy in Italy; and was rector of the university of Paris (1312-13). With the Aristotelian, John of Laudun, he wrote an antipapal treatise, *Defensor Pacis* (Defender of the Peace) (1324). It was condemned in 1327. Meanwhile he and John fled to the protection of the antipapalist, Ludwig of Bavaria. When, by popular acclaim, Ludwig was elected emperor

(and likewise Nicholas V), the pair were given bishoprics.

Marsiglio maintained that all civil strife is caused by religious conflict. This is caused by the Church claiming temporal power, which it does not and should not have, since its role is spiritual. The only power is coercive power, and only the State has that. The Church is not a perfect society (as *Aquinas held); the clergy are part of the State. Christ and the apostles submitted to the State. The papacy is not a divine institution and has no right to intervene in secular matters. The pope and the clergy must be elected. Evangelical law is prescriptive; canon and conciliar law have no force, since they have no coercive power in this life. Only law backed by power has the force of law.

Natural law is positive law agreed by all nations (*jus gentium*). The governing power (*legislator*) is either the whole people or their representative (*pars valentior*). The executive (*pars principans*) is appointed and removed by the *legislator*. An elected is better than an accepted government. The relationship between the executive and *legislator* is pragmatic, not contractual. The judiciary is part of the executive. This is not merely antipapal but a radical secular theory.   CB

martial law The resort to military force as a temporary expedient in exceptional circumstances to restore order and uphold civilian government. Troops may be deployed or the constitution suspended with the military assuming some or all of the functions of government.   IC

Marxism It was Karl *Marx and Friedrich *Engels who formulated the original ideas, concepts, and theories which became the foundations of a doctrine which has since come to be known as Marxism, but which they themselves designated as 'scientific socialism'. The relationship between Marxism and *socialism is a problematical one, but there can be no doubt that Marx and Engels saw many of their contemporary socialists as '*utopian' in the sense of being insufficiently objective in their understanding of how capitalist society was actually developing. Marx and Engels devoted their lives to the analysis of historical forces which they considered to be moving inexorably towards the eventual collapse of the capitalist system and a revolutionary crisis which would bring about a socialist transition and (eventually) full *communism. They gave particularly close attention to economic processes and structures, which they saw as the key 'material' factors in shaping social structure and class relations, and also the state and the distribution of political power.

Yet within the various schools of Marxist thought which have emerged in the last century or so there is no agreement as to how much weight should be attached to economic factors in explaining and predicting broader patterns of social and political change. Marx and Engels have been seen by some as economic determinists, but other interpretations have stressed the mutual interrelationships of economic and other socio-political factors. This dispute has become central to Marxism–*Leninism, which has inevitably sought to analyse and explain the actual processes of revolutions which have occurred throughout the world (starting with the 1917 *Russian Revolution) under the auspices of Marxist movements and political parties, and has become entangled in arguments over the importance of political leadership and the use of revolutionary state power in creating a socialist (and communist) society. Marx and Engels themselves did not produce any detailed analysis of such issues, and this is one of the reasons why twentieth-century Marxists such as *Lenin, *Stalin, *Mao, and *Castro added their own distinctive perspectives to the development of Marxist revolutionary strategy. The fact that many self-proclaimed Marxist revolutions have in fact led to the strengthening of state power and (frequently) the rule of one-party dictatorial regimes, rather than a society based on human freedom and the 'withering away' of the state, has also stimulated much disagreement over the relative merits of different Marxist strategies. Some Marxists deny the claims of such dictatorial regimes to be Marxist, and this has led to a persistent search for more democratic and pluralist strategies of change, for example in *Eurocommunism and also within some traditions of *social democracy.

Marxism may also be seen as a distinctive approach to the analysis of society, especially in terms of historical processes of change,

which has had a dramatic impact on numerous fields of study within the social sciences and the humanities. There is hardly any area of socio-economic, political, or cultural investigation which has not been scrutinized by the techniques of Marxist analysis. In particular this has involved *historical materialist methodology rooted in the belief that the structure of society and human relations in all their forms are the product of material conditions and circumstances rather than of ideas, thought, or consciousness. This raises the problem of 'determinism' in Marxism, since an emphasis on material forces of economic production and the social relations of production (i.e. class relations) inevitably suggests that these are the key factors which have shaped, and which continue to shape, the process of historical change. In particular these systems of thought, including political belief systems and cultural 'products' such as art and literature, are basically expressions of the class interests and socio-economic world-views of certain distinctive groups in society. Thus Marxism's analysis of capitalist societies focuses attention on issues of power and domination from the perspective not only of overt political supremacy but also through the supremacy gained from domination in the class structure (which is seen to be linked to political position) and domination in the realms of ideas, values, and cultural norms.

The Marxist analysis of capitalism and the conditions under which capitalism enters periods of economic crisis that eventually lead to social and political revolution is exceedingly complex and is essentially economic in its orientation. As capitalism has continued to develop and change its character since the death of Marx and Engels, numerous Marxist thinkers, from Lenin onwards, have added important theoretical dimensions, relating Marxism, for example, to new conditions of global economic production, *imperialism, and *colonialism, and the changing position of the *working class, or *proletariat, which has always been seen by Marxists as the most severely exploited class of capitalist society, and as the main agent of the eventual overthrow of capitalism. In the last century the working class of capitalist societies has undergone such a profound transformation that the 'classical Marxism' of Marx and Engels cannot be applied without sweeping changes of emphasis. Equally, Marxism has often been politically successful in peasant-based less developed societies rather than in the more developed industrial societies of the West. It may be, as some Marxists have suggested, that the focus of class exploitation has merely shifted to the *Third World, but if this is so, then critical shifts in emphasis in Marxist thought would seem to be necessary. Marxist thought in the Third World has focused on imperialism, colonialism, and post-colonialism.

The Marxist critique of capitalism places particular emphasis on the role of the institution of private property (of capital resources and land) as the basis of class exploitation and the dependency of employed workers on a privileged group of owners. And it follows that the vision of a future communist society embraces the idea of replacing private property by common ownership in the interests of all and exercised by some form of direct *workers' control. Marx and Engels did not produce any detailed blueprints for the precise mode of organization of a future post-revolutionary society, and did indeed criticize all such blueprints as 'utopian'. Marxist regimes have engaged in such a wide variety of practical experiments, and Marxist political parties have put forward so many different strategies, that it is impossible to identify one single agreed approach. In the end Marx and Engels believed that the tasks of socialist and communist construction must await the necessary conditions of historical change, and this raises the whole issue of how quickly or slowly capitalism would be transformed into socialism and communism, and also the question of whether such a transformation could be accomplished in individual countries or must become a genuinely worldwide movement. '*Socialism in one country' has become the actual strategy pursued by many Marxist regimes (including the Soviet Union under Stalin), but if capitalism has become a system of global economic power, it is perhaps questionable whether a single country can ever achieve the goals indicated by Marx, Engels, and Lenin. The collapse of many Marxist regimes in the late 1980s and early 1990s—including the disintegration of the Soviet Union—has cast further doubt on the

capability of such regimes to survive in an interdependent world dominated by capitalist countries. 'Marxism is dead' became a common slogan of political commentary during these years. But it seems almost certain, as capitalism continues to experience severe economic crises, and as environmental problems pose increasing threats for the very survival of the human race, that there will continue to be a significant measure of political space for Marxist ideas. KT

Marx, Karl (1818–83) German philosopher, sociologist, socialist, and economist. Marx was born in Trier in the Rhineland of Jewish parents who had converted to nominal Protestantism in order to escape legal restrictions. He was educated at the universities of Bonn and Berlin, and completed a doctorate on classical philosophy. He became an ardent *Young Hegelian, especially influenced by *Feuerbach's materialist analysis of Christianity, which saw religion as a form of *alienation. In 1842 Marx began his career as journalist and propagandist, moving around frequently as his newspapers were suppressed. In Paris in 1844 he met his lifelong collaborator *Engels. Intellectual landmarks from this period are the 'Paris Manuscripts' (usually known in English as *Economic-Philosophical MSS of 1844*), *Theses on Feuerbach* (1845), and *The German Ideology* (1846). These works are essentially about alienation, discussed in a materialist way but with little reference to the *proletariat and without Marx's later 'scientific' analysis of capitalism. Marx became more directly political with the *Communist Manifesto* (1848), with its peroration 'The proletarians have nothing to lose but their chains. They have a world to win. Working men of all countries, unite!' 1848 was the 'year of revolutions' in Europe, but Marx was unable to have any practical influence on them. In 1849 he was expelled from Prussia and settled for the rest of his life in London. Here he produced his main economic works: *Contribution to a Critique of Political Economy* (1859), and *Capital* (vol. i, 1867; vols. ii and iii published after Marx's death by Engels). He also wrote barbed and spiky comment on current affairs, especially in France, such as *The Eighteenth Brumaire of Louis *Bonaparte* (1852) and *The Civil War in France* (about the Paris *Commune of 1871). Marx and Engels helped to found the International Working Men's Association ('First International': *see* INTERNATIONAL SOCIALISM) in 1864, but it became divided between their followers and those of *Bakunin (expelled in 1872), and it was dissolved in 1876. However, socialist parties on Marxian lines emerged, especially in Germany, although in the *Critique of the Gotha Programme* (1875) Marx fiercely criticized the programme of the German socialist party for adopting slogans from *Lassalle that Marx regarded as simplistic.

Marx's health was poor, as was his family, especially in the early London years when he depended on Engels's generosity. Only three of his seven children survived to adulthood.

Marx's influence has been immense in all the social sciences, and concepts associated with him are scattered throughout this Dictionary. Discussion of these concepts is therefore not repeated here, but *see* especially ALIENATION; ASIATIC MODE OF PRODUCTION; BASE/SUPERSTRUCTURE; CAPITALISM; CLASS; CLASS CONSCIOUSNESS; COMMODITY-FETISHISM; COMMUNISM; CONTRADICTION; DIALECTICAL MATERIALISM; DICTATORSHIP OF THE PROLETARIAT; FACTORS OF PRODUCTION; FALSE CONSCIOUSNESS; FEUDALISM; FORCES OF PRODUCTION; HEGEMONY; HISTORICAL MATERIALISM; IDEOLOGY; IMPERIALISM; IRON LAW OF WAGES; PRIMITIVE ACCUMULATION; PRIMITIVE COMMUNISM; REIFICATION; RELATIONS OF PRODUCTION; RELATIVE AUTONOMY; REVISIONISM; SURPLUS VALUE; SYNDICALISM; WITHERING AWAY OF THE STATE. For Marxists and schools of Marxism, *see also* ALTHUSSER; BOLSHEVISM; BUKHARIN; FANON; FRANKFURT SCHOOL; GRAMSCI; GUEVARA; KAUTSKY; LENINISM; LUKÁCS; LUXEMBURG; MAO; MARCUSE; PLEKHANOV; POULANTZAS; SHINING PATH; SPARTACISTS; STALINISM; TROTSKYISM.

Marx's sociological insights (especially the importance of alienation in industrial society) are alive and central to political sociology. His economics, which he regarded as his most important work, is dead except to a few devotees. Most economic analysts agree that the Marxian *labour theory of value, including of surplus value, cannot be rescued from its internal contradictions. Marx's historical materialism remains an influential approach to both history and philosophy. His work on French politics combines insight with invective, and destruction of myths with their creation, in a way that will continue to fascinate readers for generations to come.

masses The body of common people in a society. Anxiety about 'the masses' is as old as anxiety about democracy (*see e.g.* PLATO; ARISTOTLE). It took clearer shape with eighteenth- and early nineteenth-century writing about the *tyranny of the majority (*see also* MADISON; TOCQUEVILLE). In his *Democracy in America* (1835–40), *Tocqueville expressed anxiety about the rootlessness and lack of social networks of Americans, who were, as they remain, much more mobile than Europeans: 'Each of them, living apart, is a stranger to the fate of all the rest.' However, this sits awkwardly with Tocqueville's admiration for American political activism and their enthusiasm for voluntary associations. Similar difficulties of definition have dogged all attempts to define the 'masses' and the nature of the threat they pose to elites or to democratic stability (*see also* MASS SOCIETY).

massive retaliation The *deterrence doctrine of the Eisenhower administration, that the United States would feel free to use nuclear weapons at the time and place of its choosing to prevent any further expansion of communist rule achieved by military aggression. BB

mass media The various agents of mass communication and entertainment: newspapers, magazines and other publications, *television, radio, the cinema, and the *Internet. They rely on widespread literacy, increased leisure, and ready access by the public to receiving equipment. Their entertainment function is usually predominant, attracting investment, providing revenue, and securing (and retaining) an audience. Other functions, however, have greater political relevance, including the collection, organization, and transmission of news and information, the formation of opinion, and, in more or less open societies, some contribution to public debate. Nowhere have the media escaped regulation, control, and some censorship. Regulation usually relates to ownership, funding, and licensing arrangements, as well as providing for supervision of the length, content, and balance of programmes. With the rapid advance of technology there has been a growing concentration of media ownership, particularly in sectors where the audience is extensive and production costs are high.

Governments are finding it increasingly difficult to maintain close control and supervision, especially with the spread of satellite, cable, and Internet, the advent of global media networks, and increased cross-media ownership. The emphasis has switched to deregulation, privatization, or a mix of public–private ownership. Meanwhile studies of media influence suggest that, outside elections and other big events, there is but a small audience for serious political debate and comment, and that even that restricted public is neither very receptive nor particularly retentive. Any effects are subtle and indirect. Nevertheless media access is indispensable to the main parties and groups and also allows minority candidates with unorthodox views to be heard.

Some have argued that the rapid advance of information technology has led to profound changes in political campaigning. Others retort that this is to confuse the medium with the message. IC

mass society The notion popularized by W. Kornhauser in *The Politics of Mass Society* (1959) that people have been vulnerable to the appeals of totalitarianism because of a lack of restraining social networks. Kornhauser found mass society in 'the sources of support for communism, fascism, and other popular movements that operate outside of and against the institutional order'. Like a number of his contemporaries, he wished to explain especially how Nazism in Germany and, to some degree, fascism in Italy, had erupted through the networks of the rule of law and of *civil society: the dictators had been able to appeal directly to the people and ignore all such constraints. Although Kornhauser is remarkably reluctant to define mass society, he seems to mean a society in which there is mass participation in politics but little *pluralism or variegated civil society. Thus the analysis of mass society looks back to the discussions of alienation and anomie in (especially) *Marx and *Durkheim. Other writers to use it include Erich Fromm (*The Fear of Freedom*, 1942) and David Riesman (*The Lonely Crowd*, 1950). The concept is so poorly defined that it is no longer used in political sociology, but Robert Putnam's recent discussions of the alleged decline of *social capital are reminiscent of Kornhauser.

master and slave A key section in *Hegel's *Phenomenology of Spirit* which illustrates the movement of the dialectic in terms of the search for a 'mutually recognizing' true self-consciousness. Although the master controls the slave the latter gains a degree of self-realization through his work. However, the fact that neither 'recognizes' the other as a free being means that true self-consciousness is not achieved. Hence, the division between them becomes concentrated in one individual, the 'Unhappy Consciousness'. IF

materialism Generally: belief that all that matters is material welfare, as opposed to spiritual or other ideals. Specifically: *Marx and *Engels developed what they called '*historical materialism' and '*dialectical materialism' in reaction to the idealism of earlier nineteenth-century thinkers, especially *Hegel. Since the seventeenth century, thinkers had been divided between those who insisted that, put crudely, physical matter is all there is, and those who gave an independent role to mind. A clear example of the first is *Hobbes, whose mechanical conception of nature (so labelled in an important study by F. Brandt, 1928) led him to claim, for instance, that our sensations of colour derived wholly from the coloured object we saw and not from anything in our minds. A clear example of the second was Bishop Berkeley (1685–1753), famous for his scepticism that we could prove that anything existed outside our mental images of it. Hegel sided with Berkeley, and Marx and Engels with Hobbes.

Marx wrote: 'My investigation led to the result that legal relations as well as forms of state are to be grasped neither from themselves nor from the so-called general development of the human mind, but rather have their roots in the material conditions of human life . . . . It is not the consciousness of men that determines their being, but, on the contrary, their social being that determines their consciousness' (Preface to *A Contribution to the Critique of Political*

Economy, 1859). This is Marx's historical materialism. It states that ideology, aesthetics, ideas about ethics and religion, and so on, are all parts of the superstructure, while economic relations are the base (*see also* BASE/SUPERSTRUCTURE). This idea has been widely criticized as self-refuting—if ideas are superstructural, how could the middle-class intellectual Marx and the capitalist Engels have developed Marxism—but has been ably defended in G. Cohen, *Karl Marx's Theory of History: A Defence* (1979).

Dialectical materialism is more associated with Engels. Briefly, this is historical materialism made dynamic. It includes the idea that each stage of society except the last contains the seeds of its own destruction, so that capitalism emerged out of feudalism and socialism will emerge out of capitalism.

matriarchy Generally, rule by women; more specifically, a society or kinship group in which authority descends down the female line. Matriarchy has been common in countries of Africa and Asia. The definition of matriarchy is as disputed as the definition of *patriarchy*. Matriarchy suggests some power negotiations between the sexes as opposed to the patriarchal tradition, where the male makes all the important decisions. Matriarchy takes cultural forms, especially in family and religious matters. A woman could often have the choice of a couple of husbands and the children from one particular union took the mother's name and the inheritance passed through her line. Children belonged to the mother's family and the mother could claim maintenance by the family. However, the eldest male of the family acted as the head of the house and this can be seen as an area of power negotiation. In certain parts of South India the heir to the throne was not the son of the king, but of his eldest sister, and the Marumakkathayam system prevailed, where there was common ownership of family property and it was indissoluble without the consent of all the members of the family.   STH

maximin In game theory, the strategy of maximizing one's own pay-off on the minimum (i.e. worst) assumption about the other player(s)' strategy. Thus for example in two-person *Chicken (see the pay-off matrix in that entry), my maximin strategy is 'Swerve'. If I 'Swerve' I cannot get less than c, whereas if I 'Keep going' I may get d.

The idea has also been used in political philosophy. John *Rawls (1921–2002), in *A Theory of Justice* (1971), argues that if people were placed behind a *veil of ignorance, so that they were asked to make rules of justice for a world in which they did not know what their views, wealth, or status would be, they would agree on a maximin conception of justice. The Rawlsian maximin is expressed in the first part of his *difference principle: 'Social and economic inequalities are to be arranged so that they are ... to the greatest benefit of the least advantaged.'

mayor Where separate direct election gives an electoral mandate, as commonly in the United States, the mayor is the political head of an urban local authority. In the United Kingdom a mayor was until 2000 simply the ceremonial head of a borough/district council, elected by councillors from among their own number. In that year, however, following the American model, the Greater London Authority was established under the executive leadership of a directly elected mayor. Since then some councils in England and Wales have also decided to organize executive leadership either through a directly elected mayor, or a directly elected mayor with the help of a city manager. Even so, the majority of councils continue to have a mayor as a ceremonial position and have adopted the executive model of a cabinet headed by a party group leader and appointed cabinet members.   JBr

May's law of curvilinear disparity A theory proposed by John D. May in his 1973 article *Opinion Structure of Political Parties*, which suggests that 'rank and file' members of a political party are more ideological than the party leadership as well as their constituents. Classifying parties into three levels—party elite, middle elite, and non-elite—May argued that each level will have competing political incentives to advance ideological positions, which result in greater ideological activity among the 'middle elite'. Although the theory remains controversial, it nevertheless has received considerable attention within *comparative politics and has delivered an overwhelming amount of conflicting research on the ideological activities of the United Kingdom's Labour Party.

Mazzini, Giuseppe (1805–72) Italian nationalist, born in Genoa, who spent most of his life in exile, campaigning for a united, republican, and democratic Italy. In 1831 Mazzini founded the Young Italy (*Giovine Italia*) movement—part political party and part subversive network. He was a tireless propagandist, with his ideas spread through a prolific correspondence and journalism. He established a number of periodicals, including *Giovine Italia* and *Pensiero ed Azione* (Thought and Action), and a selection of his articles were published as *The Duties of Man* (1860). In 1834, whilst in exile in London, he established a Young Europe movement, to foster nationalist movements throughout the continent, particularly in Italy, Germany, and Poland; and was described by John Stuart *Mill as 'the most eminent conspirator and revolutionist now in Europe'. Following the 1848 uprisings, Mazzini briefly headed a republican government in Rome, but was forced back into exile. He viewed the unification of Italy in 1861 with some disillusionment, as it failed to live up to his democratic or republican ideals.

Mazzini provided much of the political justification behind the *Risorgimento* (Rising Again), the period of cultural assertion and rebellion which led to the establishment of a unitary Italian state. He was influenced by *Condorcet, whose work he used to read at University during the celebration of mass. Mazzini hoped for a patriotic insurrection which would overcome regional divisions within Italy, and resist the influence of the imperial powers of Austria and France. His nationalism was moderate and somewhat romantic, based on the development of civic consciousness as a balance to individual liberty, rather than racial or historical determinism.

McCarthyism Generally, the use of unscrupulous methods of investigation against supposed security risks and the creation of an atmosphere of fear and suspicion. Specifically, Joseph McCarthy was a US senator for Wisconsin from 1946 until his death in 1957. He is remembered for his demagogic crusade between 1950 and 1954 to root out alleged communists and spies in American public life. As chairman of the Senate Government Operations Committee conducting investigations, he appalled observers by his coarse and brutal behaviour. Witnesses were remorselessly bullied, currency was given to wild and unsubstantiated charges, and evidence falsified. As a result an ugly mood of national hysteria was created, the careers of honourable men and women were damaged, and the reputation of the United States abroad suffered badly. McCarthy operated at the height of the *Cold War when international communism could be reasonably seen as a serious threat to the American way of life and many others shared McCarthy's fears. Eventually, however, the senator overreached himself in virulently attacking the Army on security grounds. He was subsequently censured by his colleagues in the Senate and ended his life as a broken and discredited figure.   DM

McDonaldization A term used by American sociologist George Ritzer in his 1993 book *The McDonaldization of Society* to denote the growth of new social paradigms based on rationalism and scientific management. The term is also often used to describe the *homogenization of cultures within processes of globalization as well as the more spurious suggestion that countries with a McDonald's restaurant do not go to war with each other. *See* DEMOCRATIC PEACE.

MDGs (Millennium Development Goals) Adopted in 2000 through the United Nations Development Declaration, the MDGs represented eight development goals aimed to end poverty and promote global development via eighteen time-bound targets with forty-eight indicators. Set against a deadline of 2015, the MDGs covered eight development goals ranging from ending the spread of HIV/AIDS to providing universal primary education. Although the MDGs had a number of individual target successes, the goals nevertheless went largely unmet, triggering the formulation and adoption of the *Sustainable Development Goals in 2015 to reunify a global partnership for development. Some critics of the MDGs suggest they represented a form of *cultural imperialism and *paternalism by the West. Yet, most critics of the MDGs prefer to highlight limitations in capacity, financing, and political will as the main reasons why the MDGs went largely unmet.

measurement (levels of) There is a hier-archy of four levels of measurement: nom-inal; ordinal; interval; and ratio. Nominal measurement is used for *discrete variables with unordered categories. Ordinal meas-ures are also discrete, but it is possible to order the categories. Interval level measure-ment involves the assignment of a number to each observation, so that the difference between the numbers is theoretically mean-ingful. For example, the difference between 10°C and 20°C is equivalent to that between 20°C and 30°C. However, with interval level measurement there is no true zero point, so it is not possible to say that 20°C is twice as hot as 10°C. Finally, the ratio level of meas-urement is the same as the interval level with the addition of a true zero point, so it becomes possible to make statements about the ratios of values. Whilst there is often a natural correspondence between the level of measurement and the nature of the variable, in practice some variables are measured or analysed in different ways. For instance, age is usually measured in years, which is a ratio scale; someone who is 40 is twice as old as someone who is 20. However, sometimes age categories are used so that measurement is at the interval or even ordinal level.   SF

median voter The voter (or pair of voters) in the exact middle of a ranking of voters along some issue dimension, e.g. from the most left-wing to the most right-wing. In the 1940s Duncan *Black proved the *median voter theorem*, which states that the median voter's preferred candidate (or policy) is bound to win against any one other, by any well-behaved voting system. This result was popularized in Anthony Downs's *An Eco-nomic Theory of Democracy* (1957). Downs further predicted that rational politicians would converge on the issue position of the median voter because, if they went anywhere else, the opposition could win by sidling up on the majority side of them. This centripetal force is often called Downsian competition. When there is more than one issue dimen-sion, the median voter theorem only applies in very unlikely conditions of balance. Instead, *cycles may exist, although they are often not revealed. *See* RIKER; HERESTHETIC(S).

medieval political theory Medieval pol-itical theory in Western Europe arose out of

the controversy between Church and State over the question of the investiture of bishops by the secular powers. Since the clergy were virtually the only people who were literate and numerate, emperors, kings, dukes, and other rulers relied on their help in the administration of their domains. It was, therefore, important that, at the highest level, clerics should be not only able administrators but also sympa-thetic to the sovereign. To ensure this rulers took to refusing to recognize an unfavour-able papal choice, and appointing a candi-date of their own choice whom they invested with both spiritual and temporal power.

The papacy resisted this from the advent of Gregory VII (1073–85). Before his time the papacy had a tenuous claim on ecclesiastical supremacy even in spiritual matters and was fortunate to control the appointment of arch-bishops. Gregory claimed the primacy of the Pope, even in temporal matters. These included the deposition of rulers and absolv-ing their subjects of allegiance. These claims were based on some texts of scripture (prin-cipally Matthew 16: 19, and Luke 22: 38), but above all on the eighth-century forged docu-ment, *The Donation of Constantine*, which states that, on his conversion, the emperor Constantine handed over to Pope Sylvester I the imperial power in the West. These papal claims were reiterated throughout the fol-lowing centuries and found their most extreme expression in the bull *Unam Sanc-tam* of Boniface VIII in 1302 which so pro-voked Philip IV of France that he had the Pope imprisoned.

Philosophers who supported the papal claims included Giles of Rome, John of Salis-bury, and *Aquinas. Those on the other side included *Dante and—most extremely—*Marsiglio of Padua. Giles of Rome (1247–1316) wrote two important political works while teaching theology in Paris between 1285 and 1292, *De regimine principum* and *De potestate ecclesiastica*. The first work was written for the future Philip IV. It was basic-ally *Aristotelian and Thomist. The second, which was papalist, was ironically the source on which Boniface VIII drew for the bull *Unam Sanctam*. The two can be reconciled only by saying that the first deals with the ruler merely in his temporal role whereas the second goes to the root of temporal and spiritual power. The first adds nothing to

Aquinas. The second states the extreme papalist position based on Augustinian arguments. Giles maintained that all power came from God through the Church and in particular the Vicar of Christ, the Pope. He conferred temporal power on secular rulers and could, if necessary, withdraw their power and absolve their subjects of allegiance. Temporal power involved the power over life and this only God had, so it could only be conferred by God's representative, the Church, and, in particular the Vicar of Christ. However, in Giles's phrase the temporal power belonged to the Church *non ad usum sed ad nusum*, that is, it had it but would/could not use it itself.

John of Salisbury (*c.*1115–80), an earlier papalist who had been secretary to Thomas à Becket, took a less extreme line. In his *Polycraticus* he maintained that temporal power came from the hand of the Church. But he did not give it the power to depose rulers. That he left to the subjects. Like many medieval theorists, he supported tyrannicide. In his view a ruler became a tyrant when he transgressed the laws of natural morality or of natural justice (*aequitas*). He interpreted the Roman lawyer Ulpian's dictum, *Quod principi placuit legis habet vigorem* (What the ruler decides has the force of law) not in an absolutist sense, as if the ruler can legally do what he likes, but in the juristic sense that the ruler's legitimate legislation has force in virtue of the powers invested in him by the people. Thus his object was to restrict the scope of the temporal power rather than to enhance the power of the papacy. However, he was not as thoroughgoing a political theorist as Aquinas.

Thus, out of this medieval controversy between *Church and State, emerged political theories that laid the foundations for political thought in more recent times. CB

Mensheviks The more moderate faction within the Russian Social Democratic Labour Party, which advocated gradual reform to achieve socialism. Representing 'the minority' (in fact a misnomer as it was the larger group in the party at the time), it emerged during the Second Congress in 1903 following a split with Lenin's more radical and revolutionary Bolsheviks (the final schism occurring in 1912).

The quarrel centred around the nature of party organization. Whilst Lenin argued for a professional revolutionary vanguard, Martov called for a mass party. Underpinning this debate were three important questions: Was capitalism the dominant mode of production in Russia? Should the RSDLP ally with bourgeois parties? What was the relationship between the party and the proletariat?

Following the February Revolution of 1917, the Mensheviks and Social Revolutionaries controlled the Petrograd Soviet and offered their conditional support to the Provisional Government. The period of 'dual power' developed with neither the Soviet nor the Government being willing to take control of the State. Although some Mensheviks joined the Kerensky coalition government in May, the party was divided and losing ground to the Bolsheviks. By September, the latter had majorities in both the Petrograd and Moscow Soviets. After the October Revolution, the Mensheviks were subjected to increasingly systematic repression and had ceased political activity by 1920. GL

mercantilism The system of relations between state and economy prevailing throughout Western Europe and its dependencies up to the nineteenth century under which those trades and industries were most encouraged that secured the accumulation of bullion, a national fleet and trained mariners, secure sources of strategic materials, and strong armaments production. Mercantilism was opposed by liberals like Adam *Smith from the eighteenth century onwards, because of its reliance on the granting of exclusive privileges to *corporations such as the British and Dutch East India Companies to the detriment of *free trade and a more rational division of labour at home. Subsequently acquiring an exclusively pejorative sense, *neo*mercantilism became in the 1930s and 1970s a convenient synonym for economic nationalism. CJ

MERCOSUR The Common Market of the Southern Cone, a product of a regional integration agreement signed between Argentina, Brazil, Uruguay, and Paraguay in March 1991. Encompassing a population of 200 million people, MERCOSUR is the fourth largest trade bloc in the world, and the second in the Americas, behind *NAFTA. MERCOSUR has a minimalist institutional structure characterized by six intergovernmental bodies, and a heavy reliance on presidential diplomacy. The origins of MERCOSUR can be located in the broader process of political rapprochement between Brazil and Argentina that developed in the 1980s. In that period the economic effects of the debt crisis, and the increasing trend towards the formation of economic blocs created incentives for the institutionalization of economic cooperation, beginning with the Integration and Cooperation Programme (PICAB) in July 1986. In March 1991, the Treaty of Asunción, gave formal birth to MERCOSUR and expanded the project to include Uruguay and Paraguay. A new strategy based on a programme of linear and automatic tariff liberalization was aimed at accelerating and deepening the process of economic integration. The Ouro Preto Protocol, signed in December 1994, brought integration a step forward with the establishment of a common external tariff, and the launch of the customs union. Regional trade and investment grew rapidly in the second half of the 1990s. However, increasing divergences in foreign and foreign economic policy goals (especially towards the negotiation of NAFTA) and the lack of macroeconomic coordination, especially following the Brazilian devaluation of January 1999 and the collapse of the Argentinian economy in 2001–2 have led to several episodes of tension and conflict between the two main partners. Venezuela, under President Hugo Chávez, applied for membership of MERCOSUR, but full entry was delayed by Brazil until 2012, and then its membership was suspended in 2016. Its associate countries are Chile, Bolivia, Colombia, Ecuador, Peru, Guyana and Suriname. Despite frequent pessimistic forecasts, ongoing political commitment has to date still compensated for its decreasing economic rationale.   AHU/LGM

(⊕) SEE WEB LINKS

• MERCOSUR site (Portuguese/Spanish), including information on history and organizational structure.

meritocracy An elite selected on the basis of ability rather than social background. In his 1958 fiction *The Rise of the Meritocracy*

1870–2033, Michael *Young emphasized the need to think of those who did not achieve elite membership even on a new basis of selection, presaging the contemporary debate on the 'under class'.   WG

meta-theory Reflecting on theories themselves or on their claims. Meta-theory might be considered in relation to the philosophy of (social) science, in particular, reflecting on the *ontological and *epistemological claims a theory makes or rendering explicit what might be implicit in the theoretical claims.   JJ

methodology The study of the methods to be used in any form of inquiry. The methods used in the study of politics include archival research; the study of previously printed materials; interview-based research; textual and *contextual analysis of the arguments of past political thinkers; *comparative government based on case studies, and quantitative research, often based on conducting one's own surveys or analysing other people's. All of these methods give rise to questions of methodology, although it is sometimes exclusively (but wrongly) associated with *quantitative analysis.

Mexican Revolution The first social revolution of the twentieth century (1910–20). It started as a political revolution against the more than thirty-year dictatorship of General Porfirio Díaz. This movement was led by Francisco I. Madero, whose motto 'Effective suffrage, no re-election' crystallized discontent around the country in 1910–11 against Díaz's permanence in power. Eventually Díaz went into exile in Paris, while Madero won democratic elections and became Mexico's president in 1911. However, the *ancien régime* forces, supported by United States ambassador Henry Lane Wilson, overthrew and assassinated Madero, and installed General Huerta in power in 1913. Under intense pressure from several revolutionary factions, Huerta fled to the United States in 1914.

After this the violent conflict became a social revolution. Leaders such as Emiliano Zapata in the south and Pancho Villa in the centre-north fought for land reform and social justice. Eventually these groups had to compromise with the more liberal-constitutional-oriented ones headed by Venustiano Carranza and Alvaro Obregón. The result was the drafting of the 1917 Constitution, a social liberal constitution, the first of its kind, which still rules Mexico today. The constitution granted liberal (civil and political) and social (land reform, progressive labour legislation) rights. The ideal was to create the conditions for the development of modern social citizenship. This new framework, probably the Mexican Revolution's greatest achievement, enabled Mexico's twentieth-century sociopolitical history to be more progressive than several other big Latin American countries such as Argentina, Brazil, Colombia, and Peru, where no social revolution took place.   FG

MFN *See* MOST FAVOURED NATION.

MI5 *See* INTELLIGENCE SERVICES.

MI6 *See* INTELLIGENCE SERVICES.

Michels, Robert *See* IRON LAW OF OLIGARCHY.

Michigan school The body of ideas and approaches associated with the Survey Research Center of the University of Michigan, which has been conducting national surveys of the US electorate since 1952. In their landmark study *The American Voter* (1960), they set out the evidence that voters' decisions on party support were determined much more by their long-term *political socialization, notably by tending to inherit their parents' orientations, than by ideology, issues, or evaluation of the competence of the candidates. The anchoring factor was thus a voter's *party identification, which was typically stable even if in a given election the voter might support another party for, say, the Presidency.

Michigan ideas were highly influential in election studies elsewhere, including the United Kingdom. They have been challenged by the rise of *rational choice approaches, and by new evidence showing the greater salience of *issue voting and retrospective evaluation of the incumbents' performance. Survey analysts, including those at Michigan, are more catholic in their approaches now than then.

microeconomics The branch of economics which deals with the choices of individual economic actors such as households and firms. Microeconomists are marginalists and use calculus extensively to build formal models of the interactions of numerous *market actors in (and out of) *equilibrium. Microeconomic models have been imported into politics by writers in the *rational choice tradition.

middle class The class or social stratum lying above the working class and below the upper class. It is a term that everybody uses every day, but hardly anybody ever defines. One of the earliest uses of it recorded in the *Oxford English Dictionary* was by Queen Caroline of Denmark in 1766; however, she denied its existence in Denmark. The term settles into something like its present meaning by 1843, when George Borrow talks about 'the middle class, shopkeepers and professional men'. The middle class are distinguished from the *working class by occupation and education. They are distinguished from the upper class, apparently, by seriousness, moral purpose, and earning a living. Nowadays, a large proportion of respondents class themselves as middle class—as many as 80 per cent in typical surveys in the United States.

The term clearly refers to status rather than to *class. People are judged to be middle class or otherwise more by their level of education, the physical conditions in which they work, and/or their consumption habits than by their relationship to the means of production. An example of each follows:

1 *Education.* In Victorian Britain, when the present system of school-leaving examinations supervised by the universities was introduced, they were sometimes called the 'middle class examinations'. For a century from the 1850s to the 1950s passing such examinations was regarded as a passport to the middle class.

2 *Physical conditions.* 'White collar' is a near-synonym for middle class, and 'blue collar' for working class. Thus a job is middle class if it is done in clean conditions and does not involve heavy manual work. A working-class job is perceived as one done in dirty conditions which require protective clothing. This distinction is also fading with the rapid change in the nature of work since the 1960s.

3 *Consumption habits.* The commonest measurements of class are those used by

the advertising industry to classify those who read or watch particular media. But advertisers are interested only in consumption habits, not in class properly defined.

The basis for the commonly expressed view that 'we are all middle class now' is therefore: (1) that many or most of us call ourselves middle class; and (2) that the old badges of status of the working class are no longer reliable.

migration The movement of individuals or groups from one place to another. Migration can be both domestic and international, and restrictions may apply at both levels, though it is more commonly restricted at the international level. About 3 per cent of the world's population are migrants; they live in a country other than their country of origin.

People migrate for a myriad of reasons, such as to work, to reunite with family members, to seek asylum, and to study. About one-third of all migrants move from a developing to a developed country, whereas most move either between developing or between developed countries. Transnationalism, the increased ability in a globalized world of migrants to stay in touch with their communities of origin, facilitates circular and temporary migration by making it easier for migrants to move between places several times. There are significant differences in the opportunities and barriers to migration depending on a person's nationality and resources. People from the poorest countries are the least mobile as often they lack the resources to move. People from poorer countries or countries struck by war and conflict also tend to be subject to the most limiting visa restrictions, as other states worry about the inflow of asylum seekers or low-skilled workers. Due to the restrictions on migration, many migrants undertake precarious and sometimes lethal journeys in order to seek asylum, improve their economic opportunities, a combination of both, or other reasons.

There is no coherent global governance of international migration, as states safeguard their ability to exert sovereign control over who enters their territories. Several international and intergovernmental bodies are tasked with certain aspects of international migration, such as the United Nations High Commissioner for Refugees and the International Organization of Migration. The European Union has, with some exceptions, no internal border controls, but instead cooperates to control the external border. Other states also have bilateral and multilateral agreements to control and manage migration.

Migration affects the migrant, the host country, and the sending country in different ways. Migrants benefit from enhanced opportunities in several areas and often gain access to better education and healthcare, though they may also be victims of exploitation and trafficking. The host country benefits, for example, economically and culturally. Even though the economic impacts tend to be positive overall, by increasing growth and innovation, some low-skilled domestic workers may suffer from the increased wage and job competition. The sending country benefits, for example, from the financial flow from remittances that creates jobs and increases consumption, from increased international links and the new skills, knowledge, and ideas that returning migrants bring. Migration from developing to developed countries has been identified as an effective way to improve development. Poorer sending countries may, however, be affected by 'brain drain', a shortage of highly skilled workers, as these seek better opportunities abroad. *See also* IRREDENTISM; POLITICAL ASYLUM REFUGEE. CSa

Militant Tendency Trotskyist political party that from the 1950s, when it was known as the Revolutionary Socialist League, pursued *entryism into the British Labour Party. By the 1970s it had succeeded in penetrating and controlling several local Labour parties, particularly on Merseyside, and the Labour Party's national youth organization. Militant denied that it constituted an organization, claiming to be merely an informal grouping of like-minded Marxists struggling for socialism within the Labour Party.

At its peak in the mid-1980s Militant probably numbered only about 5,000 members. It concentrated on a narrow range of economic and 'working class' issues (for instance, the nationalization of the 'largest 200 monopolies'); the essence of its tactics was to commit the party to direct action in support of a set of unattainable transitional demands, the inevitable failure to achieve which would lead to further overtly anti-democratic activity. For instance, its programme in Liverpool, where it controlled the city council, was based on a freeze on rents and rates, and no cuts in council services—inevitably leading the city into chaos and *de facto* bankruptcy.

The Labour Party took no action against the Militant Tendency until 1981. In 1983 the editorial board of Militant was expelled but Militant continued to dominate the party in Liverpool and to have three MPs. In 1986 expulsions on a larger scale were carried through and the party leader Neil Kinnock publicly denounced the Liverpool City Council at the Party Conference. By 1992 Militant Tendency had been removed from Parliament and its influence in the party extinguished. PBY

militarism A state of affairs where war, and the use or threat of military force, are accorded the highest priority by the state in the pursuit of its political ends. Alternatively, a situation where military values (patriotism, unity, hierarchy, discipline) come to permeate civil society. In practice the two usages overlap. The term had its origins in nineteenth-century concern about the threat the military posed to civilian supremacy and fears about the erosion of secular liberal values. The debate has continued, with divergent views about the best means of subordinating the military to civilian authority: whether consciously to promote a closer identity of views between civilian and military leaders, or rely instead on the latter's professional formation and career interests. Militarism in Third World countries appears to relate more to domestic than to external crisis: here political instability, social unrest, economic weakness, and, in some cases, the threat of revolution, have been the ostensible reasons for military intervention, not only to displace civilian governments but increasingly to impose their own authoritarian social order. IC

military–industrial complex Term coined by President Dwight D. Eisenhower to describe the powerful alliance of the military, government agencies, and corporations involved in the defence industry. Each sector has an interest, either financial or strategic, in expanding the government's arms budget.

millenarianism The belief that Christ's second coming would inaugurate a thousand-year period of divine rule on earth. Because Christ's second coming has been expected after the appearance of anti-Christ, and great misfortunes, this belief has been associated with political radicalism—especially hopes of overthrowing oppressive government—and some believers have seen revolution as the prelude to the millennium. AR

Millennium Development Goals *See* MDGs.

Mill, James (1773–1836) Born in the northeast of Scotland, the son of a mild-mannered shoemaker and smallholder, James Mill was subjected to a rigorous and detailed education at home, driven by the strong ambitions of his mother Isabel Milne. He showed considerable talent for composition, arithmetic, and Latin and Greek before the age of 7, and was given special treatment at the local parish school. His mother kept him away from other children as far as possible, and he was usually excused household chores. He was licensed to preach in 1798 and also became tutor to the family of Lady Jane Stuart of Fettercairn, the beginning, perhaps, of a lifelong dislike of hereditary aristocracy, but not preventing him from joining the Stuarts when they moved to Edinburgh. Here, Mill enrolled himself at the university. His courses at Edinburgh were rich and exciting and in Dugald Stewart he was instructed by one of the great bearers of the European and Scottish *Enlightenment. Mill's studies included history, political economy, and classics, especially Plato. In 1802 he went to London, ultimately establishing both his fame and his fortune with the publication of his *History of India* in 1817 and by gaining full-time employment in India House in 1819. Mill is now commonly remembered for two things: the education of his son John Stuart *Mill, and his long and fruitful association with Jeremy *Bentham. But other achievements need to be borne in mind. As an empiricist, James Mill extended and refined the classical view that the mind has no knowledge independent of experience. His *Analysis of the Phenomena of the Human Mind* stands as a monumental effort to reduce mental phenomena to banks of sensation associated by laws of resemblance and contiguity, a truly Newtonian exercise. His essay on *Government* (1820) established a sensible operational definition of human nature, from which any defensible science of man would have to proceed. The achievement of the philosophic radicals was to better inform the radical mind, to make it more methodical, and to infuse it with a dedicated enthusiasm. Without James Mill, this achievement would have been impossible.   JH

Mill, John Stuart (1806–73) Born in Pentonville, London, the first of six children by James *Mill and Harriet Burrows, educated at home by his father in a gloomy and humourless environment, with occasional extramural assistance from *Bentham and Francis Place, John Stuart began Greek at the age of 3, Latin at the age of 8—reading six of Plato's Dialogues before the age of 10—and chemistry and logic before the age of 12. He also acquired European languages, apparently quite easily, notably French and German. His domestic education was designed, above all else, to further the utilitarian creed and to make John Stuart the instrument of those reforms which Bentham and James Mill would not live to make themselves. The 'poor boy', as his dour father so patiently explained, was to be made 'a successor worthy of both of us'. In fact, although he studied Roman law with John Austin, an important and much neglected utilitarian thinker, John Stuart did not read Bentham systematically until he was 15. And he was not finally converted to Benthamism until he became familiar with Dumont's French edition of Bentham's writings in 1821–2. After this, apart from full-time employment at India House, there followed four years of confident political activism, including the advocacy of birth control, parliamentary reform, and universal male suffrage. In 1826–7, John Stuart suffered a severe and seemingly endless nervous breakdown. After this experience, nothing was ever quite the same again. And three important shifts away from his earlier philosophic radicalism can easily be identified. (1) The first of these led to a fervent belief in self-culture and self-improvement and a corresponding move away from the typical Benthamite indifference to personal character. John Stuart's new or revised utilitarianism was now squarely based on an ethic of self-culture

and not at all on hedonism, and it derived its inspiration, in part at least, from *Coleridge and the European romantics. The famous essay *On Liberty* of 1859 argues that a concern for personal character also meant the scrutiny of self-regarding conduct. The liberty principle itself required a disinterested concern to improve individual conduct and character. Like Wordsworth, Mill had come to the view that progress would only take place once the 'inward passions' and not merely 'outward arrangements' had been cultivated and developed. (2) The second shift is a little more elusive perhaps, but equally important. After the breakdown, John Stuart became increasingly concerned to promote agreement by avoiding an appeal to first or final principles. Now he preferred instead to recommend secondary or intermediate maxims capable of inspiring broad agreement. Even the *System of Logic* (1843) was conceived and written to avoid provoking philosophical controversy. And while the *Logic* could hardly be described as neutral, since it was an uncompromising defence of the inductive school in science, Mill thought that logic was an area upon which the most diverse of philosophic partisans could meet and join hands. In short, after the breakdown John Stuart counted very much on consensus, not just in philosophical discourse, but also in political practice. His view now was that the instructed or educated few had the crucial task of maintaining and developing a considered agreement amongst themselves. Without that agreement, political stability was less likely and clear, intellectual authority would either be diminished or lost entirely. (3) The third and final shift of ideas and belief was towards a quiet and contemplative 'toryism'. After the breakdown, John Stuart acquired an enduring concern for national character, as well as a strong distaste for those cultures, like the English and American, which were dominated by money-grubbing and by competition for material gain. What mattered more and more to him, was strong authority and noble ideals and this occasionally issued as an irritable and aristocratic disdain for the prosaic nature of the ordinary man. But no one ought to doubt his contempt for the usual English conservative. As a Liberal MP for the Westminster constituency, he was charged in the House of Commons with having said that all conservatives were stupid. He denied this, replying that what he had said was that all stupid people were conservative.

Mill was the leading liberal feminist of his day. He wrote *The Subjection of Women* (1869)—the only one of his books that was not a commercial success—and proposed an amendment to the Reform Bill of 1867 to substitute 'person' for 'man'. It failed, but got 73 votes. As with *On Liberty*, Mill stated that his views on the emancipation of women were deeply influenced by his wife, Harriet *Taylor. His intellectual relationship with his wife was very similar to *Condorcet's with Sophie de Grouchy. It enabled those who disagreed with the two books to put them down to his wife's meddling.   JH

Milton, John (1608–74) Poet and political pamphleteer. His pamphlets in support of divorce where the companionship of marriage had failed fell foul of parliamentary censorship in 1643, which led to one of the most powerful defences of freedom of the press, *Areopagitica*. His association with the Independents (Congregationalists) led him towards anti-monarchism. In *The Tenure of Kings and Monarchs* (1649) and in Latin pamphlets for foreign consumption, written as Latin Secretary to the Council of State, he defended the execution of Charles I on the grounds that kings were given power in trust for the good of the people and this power could be revoked if it was abused. With the Restoration he retired from politics to write his poetry.   CB

minimax In *game theory, sometimes used as a synonym for *maximin. Two more precise references are:

1 *The minimax theorem.* This is a fundamental result for zero-sum games. If such a game can be expressed in a matrix such as that given below (where, as the game is zero-sum, the pay-offs to You are simply the pay-offs to Me with the sign reversed), then it always has an equilibrium at its 'saddlepoint', for example the starred cell in the example below. A saddlepoint is simultaneously the lowest point in its row and the highest in its column. (Think of the shape of a horse's saddle and its position on the horse's back.) The reasoning is that I can guarantee myself at least 3 by choosing row I_2: I am *max*imizing my *min*imum pay-off

compared with row I_1, where I might get as little as –2. You can hold me to at most 3 (and therefore restrict your loss to –3) by choosing column Y_3, which *min*imizes your *max*imum loss. Therefore I will play my strategy 2; you will play your strategy 3. I will get 3; you will get –3. Not all games have such a saddlepoint; but there is a unique minimax point for every game, although it may involve a 'mixed strategy' of playing each of several different strategies with a certain probability.

Your strategy

		Y_1	Y_2	Y_3
My strategy	I_1	6	–2	2
	I_2	6	7	3*

2 *Minimax regret.* This is a decision principle proposed to explain why many people vote, even though they must know that it is highly unlikely that their individual vote will make any difference (*see* PARADOX OF VOTING (2)). If my side loses and I did not vote, I would regret my failure to vote much more than I would have resented the time it would have taken to vote. So I 'do my bit' in order to minimize the maximum regret I can feel after the event.

Minister Member of a national government, either in charge of a government department or available to work in a variety of policy areas at the behest of the head of government ('minister without portfolio').

In a Westminster system where members of the executive are drawn from the legislature, ministers are generally responsible for framing government policy and for steering government bills through Parliament. Ministers give political leadership to officials throughout the central machinery of government and in so doing may act in varying degrees as policy initiators, departmental managers, or policy publicists. They are criticized on several grounds. Ministers are rarely experts in the policy area to which they are appointed, and seldom have had experience of managing large organizations before entering government. Nor are they generally kept in the same position for more than two years. Confronted by a heavy workload and limited knowledge, ministers become heavily reliant on their civil servants, especially in relation to routine and reactive policy-making. JBr

ministerial responsibility The convention that a minister should be accountable to parliament for the conduct of their department, not just the decisions that the minister makes. There remains ambiguity about the operation of the convention: the interplay between responsibility and accountability, and the circumstances in which ministerial responsibility should lead to ministerial resignation. A classic case cited in discussions of ministerial responsibility in the UK is the resignation of Thomas Dugdale over the Crichel Down affair in 1954. The Ministry of Agriculture had been criticized over the handling of compensation claims after compulsory purchase of land, and Dugdale resigned on the basis that 'I, as Minister, must accept full responsibility to Parliament for any mistakes and inefficiency of officials in my Department'. Other examples of ministerial responsibility leading to resignation have included Peter Carrington's resignation as Foreign Secretary after the Argentine invasion of the *Falkland Islands in 1982, and Estelle Morris's resignation as Secretary of State for Education in 2002, over the failure to meet government targets on literacy and numeracy. However, there have been many more cases of ministers failing to resign or take responsibility for policy failures or mistakes made by their departments. Despite the legend of Crichel Down, resignation only occurs where personal involvement and parliamentary and political circumstances demand it.

minority government One which fails to command the guaranteed support of a majority of the members of a legislature. Minority governments have been judged to lead to political instability and ineffective government on the evidence of Germany during the Weimar Republic (1919–33), France during the *Fourth Republic (1946–58), and Italy between 1945 and the 1980s. In each case there was a rapid turnover of governments leading ultimately to a crisis of government legitimacy. The experience of minority governments in Scandinavia, notably in Denmark, presents alternative evidence of relative success, suggesting that the implications of minority government are dependent upon the underlying political culture. Since the First World War Britain has experienced minority government only in 1924, 1929–31, 1974, and 1976–9, in each case led by the Labour Party. However, the adoption of mixed member proportional electoral systems for the Scottish Parliament and National Assembly for Wales since 1999 has increased the likelihood not only of coalition governments but also of minority government where parties cannot agree majority coalitions. There have already been minority Labour administrations in Wales in 1999–2000 and 2005–7, and a minority Scottish National Party administration in Scotland in 2007–11. JBr

minority leader *See* MAJORITY LEADER.

minority politics Organized politics of groups that consider themselves under-represented in a political system. The minority characterization might be related to numbers or to influence in the public sphere, or both. Black, gay, and women's movements are examples. Minority politics tends to be both functional and normative, in that it generally has a 'consciousness raising' element to its politics; it is not simply organized around immediate or long-term issues of political representation. In the 1990s, liberal political theory revisited the issue of minority politics through the concept of group rights. It was argued that the historical focus on individual rights obscured the social inequalities which undermined the ability of marginalized groups to exercise their rights on an individual basis. Group-based rights, it was argued, would acknowledge the historical inequalities of marginalized groups and allow them more say in political rule-making. However, such a conceptualization has raised difficulties at both the practical and political level. Quotas based on group identities raise issues of merit and equal opportunities, and group-based politics raises the issue of representation of multiple identities in the fixing of group membership. SR

mobility *See* SOCIAL MOBILITY.

mobilization of bias *See* COMMUNITY POWER.

modernization View of historical progression as a series of stages, reflecting intellectual, technological, economic, and political development. The view is associated with the Marxist doctrine of *historical materialism, in its depiction of socio-economic synthesis, but also more broadly with approaches which view progress in terms of particular paths of transition. The association of modernization with a particularly Western model of development (and a *Whig interpretation of European history) has led to the charge of eurocentrism, and a denial of a neat dichotomy between the traditional and the modern in understanding political and socio-economic progress.

monadic Being, or related to, a single entity such as a regime or a state. In *democratic peace research, monadic peace is the proposition that democracies are inherently peaceful in their foreign relations with both democratic and autocratic regimes within the international system. *See also* SEPARATE PEACE. BBZ

monarchism Monarchy originally meant 'the rule of one', but the word has now come to be attached to the constitution of kingship (and queenship) that is usually conceived as hereditary, though many posts which we would consider as monarchs (Roman emperors, Holy Roman Emperors, and kings of Poland, for example) were, at least nominally, non-hereditary.

Monarchism is generally a belief in the necessity or desirability of monarchy. An extreme version of this would be to believe in a monarch who actually ruled and did not merely reign, who had an absolute, perhaps divinely ordained, right to do so, and who acquired this right by heredity. But all of these beliefs are very difficult to sustain in the early twenty-first century. Contemporary monarchists normally support a 'limited' monarchy, and ground their support in the general utility of the institution in a particular context. For example, they may believe it is best to have a head of state who is 'above' politics and does not have to compete for the role. Or they may believe in the ruling family as a symbolic embodiment of a country's history. Monarchy is often seen as a 'dignified element', in *Bagehot's phrase, which legitimizes the authority of the state without the need for precise constitutions and justifying principles which would prove divisive. It was largely on these negative grounds that the Australian electorate chose to retain the services of a monarch who lived more than ten thousand miles away in a referendum in 1999. LA

monetarism An economic doctrine which argues that changes in the supply of money in an economy cause changes in the general price level. Coupled with this is a stress on minimal economic intervention by government and an emphasis on the free play of market forces. The term was first coined by Karl Brunner in 1968 but its antecedents can be traced back to the quantity theory of money developed in the writings of classical theorists such as *Locke and *Hume. It was through the work of Milton Friedman, beginning in the 1950s, that the quantity theory was revived. Friedman and his associates, the so-called Chicago School of economists, argued that control of inflation could only be successful through restrictions in the growth of the money supply. By the 1970s these arguments found political succour due to the emergence of high levels of inflation and unemployment which suggested the breakdown of *Keynesian demand management policies. Hence, within Britain the Labour government adopted control of the money supply as an economic objective from 1976. The Conservative administration under Margaret Thatcher in 1979 continued this process although an emphasis on the free market was also fervently pursued. Strict control of the money supply had largely been abandoned by the mid-1980s. Despite this an emphasis on the free market and the importance of controlling inflation still pervades Conservative rhetoric. IF

monetary policy The control of the demand for, and supply of, money as a means of controlling the economy. The main tool of monetary policy is the level of interest, essentially the price of money, which a government can influence through its debt financing activities on the open market. During the 1980s, monetary policy became the central economic instrument used by the governments of the United States and Britain, in the belief that the control of inflation was the key to stable economic growth, and the level of inflation was determined by the growth in the money supply. However, the money supply proved very difficult to control (and even to measure), and interest rates a rather blunt economic tool, and a less dogmatically *monetarist stance was assumed. Hence by handing over control of the money supply to an independent *central bank, a policy pioneered in New Zealand and adopted in Britain in 1997, a government can escape blame when things go wrong and continue to praise itself when they go right.

Monnet, Jean (1888–1979) Jean Monnet is best known for developing French post-war indicative planning and the 'functionalist' Schuman Plan which led to the 1952 treaty establishing the European Coal and Steel Community (ECSC). Despite the 1954 failure of Monnet's other brainchild, the European Defence Community, the ECSC provided the impetus for the more thoroughgoing European integration of the Treaty of *Rome (1957), with Monnet once again playing an active part. As such, Monnet is regarded as the 'father of Europe', more correctly the *European Union. GU

monotonicity Of a line or function, the property that it either never decreases or never increases. Specifically, of an electoral or apportionment system, that a unit (e.g. a party or a state) never loses seats as it gains population or vote share. This property is violated by the greatest remainder rule (*see* HAMILTON), and by *single transferable vote.

Monroe Doctrine Originally promulgated by United States President James Monroe in 1823 as a warning to European powers that any expansionist activity by them anywhere in the Americas would be construed as a threat to the United States. Extended by Theodore Roosevelt and repeatedly used to justify US intervention in the affairs of Latin American countries. DM

(((•))) SEE WEB LINKS

• Text of Monroe's speech.

Montesquieu, Charles-Louis de Sécondat de (1689–1755) French political philosopher, historian, and novelist, often seen as one of the founders of sociology. As feudal landowner, magistrate, and president of the Parlement of Bordeaux, he was a complete member of the *ancien régime* establishment, but his extreme relativism cast doubt on all absolutes, not only the doctrines of the Church but even those of the French *Enlightenment to which he belonged.

Montesquieu saw human beings as fundamentally insecure. They have neither the certainty of instinct without any capacity for choice as have other animals, nor the certainty of perfect knowledge as has God. Individuals must accept the influence of their environment—perhaps Montesquieu's best known idea is the effect of climate—but as societies develop, more choices can be made although human beings must always use their limited reason with care.

In his best political work, *L'Esprit des lois* (usually translated as *The spirit of the laws*, 1748), Montesquieu divided political systems between despotism based on fear, republics based on virtue, and monarchies based on honour. Despotism is unnatural, whereas other political systems are natural. Which should be adopted depends upon particular circumstances.

In the modern world, Montesquieu preferred monarchy. One ideal form was the pre-modern French system, with the Church, the military aristocracy, and the legal aristocracy as three groups able to restrain the monarch and each other because of their independent moral or social positions. The other was the English system, which added the new commercial spirit to the monarchical principle of honour. This permitted the development of liberty in its modern form, as a sphere of life for each individual free from collective interference, as opposed to the ancient form, typical of the republic, which involved the direct exercise of power through participation by the citizen class, but excluded modern liberty.

Montesquieu argued that English government, unlike French, was characterized by a working separation of powers. Whether or not this was true, it deeply influenced the framers of the US Constitution. CS

Moral Majority Right-wing evangelical Christian group in the United States, founded by the Revd Jerry Falwell in 1979, partly supplanted by Falwell's Liberty Foundation from 1985, and formally dissolved 1989. The group connected directly evangelical concerns, such as school prayer and the teaching of creationism, with more political concerns such as opposition to abortion and gay rights. Since its demise, the term has become an umbrella one for groups within the US religious right. PM

Morgenthau, Hans (1904–1980) Hans J. Morgenthau was a German–Jewish émigré scholar of international relations who is most strongly associated with the school of *classical realism. Morgenthau was trained in Germany and Switzerland as a lawyer and international legal scholar. His early work in the 1930s argued that international law should be more responsive to social and political change. Throughout this period, Morgenthau's approach displayed two sets of commitments that would remain in tension throughout his later work. First, his arguments (like his politics) were broadly reformist. He defended sweeping changes to the international legal order and was critical of those who focused narrowly on questions of power politics. Second, like Carl Schmitt (with whom he had an uneasy intellectual relationship), Morgenthau conceived of conflict as constitutive of politics. Partly for this reason, Morgenthau was sceptical about ambitious projects of liberal international reform. He left Germany in 1932 and moved to the United States in 1937. Morgenthau spent most of his productive post-war academic career at the University of Chicago (1943–71), where he wrote his most influential works. *Scientific Man vs. Power Politics* (1946) offers a polemical critique of rationalism, 'scientism', and *liberalism. He argues that liberals like Woodrow *Wilson combine a faith in the power of human reason and science and technology to solve social and political problems. For Morgenthau, this reflects a dangerous hubris that is inattentive to human fallibility, the realities of power, and the complex and often tragic moral calculus of politics.

Morgenthau's most influential contribution to IR theory was his textbook, *Politics Among Nations*. First published in 1948, the book was the standard text for IR courses for several decades. Perhaps unfairly, *Politics Among Nations* is best remembered today for the 'Six Principles of Political Realism' that first appeared in its second edition (1954). These principles offer a picture of realism as an approach that seeks to identify unchanging and objective laws of politics that are grounded in human nature, relies on national interest 'defined in terms of power' to account for state behaviour on the international stage, and squarely faces the tension between the demands of morality and those of politics. The rest of the work is more nuanced than these principles suggest, examining the causes of international conflicts, the political mechanisms (e.g. the *balance of power) and the moral restraints that have successfully mitigated these conflicts in the past, and the likely efficacy of these mechanisms and restraints in a nuclear age. Arguing that a world state is the only stable bulwark against nuclear war (*see* NUCLEAR PROLIFERATION), Morgenthau concludes with a tragic observation: 'in no period of modern history was civilization in more need of permanent peace . . . [and] in no period of modern history were the moral, social, and political conditions . . . less favorable for the establishment of a world state.'

In his later writings, Morgenthau took an increasingly forceful stand on the dangers of nuclear war, arguing that deterrence was too fragile to be reliable and toying with various options for supranational nuclear oversight. While these writings began to put Morgenthau at odds with an American Cold War establishment that had previously welcomed him, his opposition to the *Vietnam War led to an enduring estrangement. Drawing on familiar realist arguments about the national interest (such as those offered in *In Defense of the National Interest*, 1951), he argued that Vietnam was a strategic and political disaster for the United States. It was also the result of a crisis in American liberal democracy. Morgenthau's later writings pushed in a more radical direction and were directed towards the prospects for both international and domestic political reform. AMQ

Mosca, Gaetano (1858–1941) Italian sociologist. His *The Ruling Class* (1896) was one of the first detailed statements of the claim that even in a representative democracy there was a small circulating elite which not only did rule but ought to. *See also* ELITISM.

Most Favoured Nation (MFN) The Most Favoured Nation principle is contained in

Article One of GATT and its successor, the *World Trade Organization (WTO). The name is confusing. It prohibits discriminatory treatment in international trade by providing that trade concessions or agreements with any one GATT partner must unconditionally be extended to all others. In this way any bilateral concession immediately becomes 'multilateralized'. Customs Unions are permitted as exceptions to Most Favoured Nation under certain conditions, and the principle may also be violated as part of 'anti-dumping' retaliation. In 1998, the US Congress renamed Most Favoured Nation 'Normal Trade Relations' because it was a misnomer (nearly all countries possessed this status), and because of opposition to applying the term Most Favoured Nation to authoritarian regimes. GU/DH

multiculturalism The term 'multiculturalism' emerged in the 1960s in Anglophone countries in relation to the cultural needs of non-European migrants. It now means the political accommodation by the state and/or a dominant group of all minority cultures defined first and foremost by reference to race or ethnicity; and also by reference to nationality, aboriginality, or religion. The latter groups tend to make larger claims; however, claims of national minorities now enjoy considerable legitimacy, whereas post-immigration claims have suffered a 'backlash' in the last decade.

Central to multiculturalism and the politics of difference is the rejection of the idea that political concepts such as equality and citizenship can be colour-blind and culture-neutral, and the argument that ethnicity and culture cannot be confined to some so-called private sphere but shape political and opportunity structures in all societies. It is the basis for the conclusion that allegedly 'neutral' liberal democracies are part of hegemonic cultures that systematically de-ethnicize or marginalize minorities—and thus for the claim that minority cultures, norms, and symbols have as much right as their hegemonic counterparts to state provision and to be in the public space, to be 'recognized' as groups and not just as culturally neutered individuals.

The African-American search for dignity has contributed much to this politics, yet, ironically, it has shifted attention from socio-economic disadvantage, arguably where African-Americans' need is greatest. For multiculturalism in the US seems to be confined to the field of education and, uniquely, to higher education, especially arguments about the curriculum in the humanities. Academic argument has, however, no less than popular feeling, been important in the formulation of multiculturalism, with the study of colonial societies and political theory being the disciplines that have most forged the terms of analysis. The ideas of cultural difference and cultural group have been central to anthropology and other related disciplines focused on 'primitive' and non-European societies. The arrival in the metropolitan centres of peoples studied by scholars from these disciplines has made the latter experts on migrants and their cultural needs. They also enabled critics from previously colonized societies, often themselves immigrants to the 'North', to challenge the expert and other representations of the culturally subordinated. These intellectual developments have been influenced by the failure of the economic 'material base' explanations of the cultural 'superstructure'.

The prominence of political theory too is due to a disciplinary dynamic. John *Rawls's focus on justice in a context of value pluralism has led the next generation of political theorists to define their questions more in terms of the nature of community and minority rights than in terms of distributive justice, no less than their social theory peers define it in terms of difference and identity rather than class conflict, and in each case the intellectual framework lends itself to multiculturalism, even when the term itself is not favoured. Multiculturalism has had a less popular reception in mainland Europe. Its prospect has sometimes led to the success of extreme nationalist parties in local and national polls. In France, where intellectual objections to multiculturalism have been most developed, multiculturalism is opposed across the political spectrum, for it is thought to be incompatible with a conception of a 'transcendent' or 'universal' citizenship which demands that all 'particular' identities, such as those of race, ethnicity, and gender, which promote part of the republic against the good of the whole, be confined to private life. The implosion of Yugoslavia, with its *ethnic cleansing, marks the most extreme reaction to multinational statehood and plural societies, and the political status of historic minorities, including the Roma (gypsies), is a conflictual issue throughout the territories of the former Austro-Hungarian, Ottoman, and Russian empires (*see* BALKAN POLITICS). Many post-colonized states in Asia and Africa are experiencing ethnonationalist and secessionist movements and some, such as India and Indonesia, are also struggling with non-territorial multiculturalism. Malaysia in particular seems to have managed ethnic conflict in a peaceful way.

The political accommodation of minorities, then, is a major contemporary demand across the world, filling some of the space that accommodation of the working classes occupied in most of the twentieth century, and constitutes powerful, if diverse, intellectual challenges in several parts of the humanities and social sciences. Since around the time of the *September 11th 2001 attacks on the US, however, there has been a strong reaction against multiculturalism, especially in Western Europe, such that it has become a 'dirty' word. With an almost exclusive focus on Muslims and their alleged failures of integration, it has come to be blamed for the rise of religious fundamentalism, cultural separatism, and even terrorism. The new watchwords are 'community cohesion', 'integration', and 'citizenship', but it is too early to tell whether this will lead to a modification or replacement of multiculturalism.   TM

multilateralism An approach to international trade, the monetary system, international disarmament and security, or the environment, based on the idea that if international cooperative regimes for the management of conflicts of interest are to be effective, they must represent a broad and sustainable consensus among the states of the international system. Multilateralism therefore lends itself to issues where clear common interests in the international community are identifiable. It should be thought of in contrast to strictly unilateral or bilateral initiatives.

Many recognized that during the inter-war years the exclusionary nature of bilateral bargains and the frequent resort to unilateral action had contributed to the breakdown of the international economy and the onset of war. Multilateralism therefore became the norm in such post-war agreements as *Bretton Woods, the *World Trade Organization/ GATT, the *United Nations, and, more recently, accords on the ozone layer or global warming. On questions of national security states have often proved reticent to accept the constraints of multilateral diplomacy, but there have been notable examples of multilateral action through the UN in the post-war period.

Global multilateralism has, however, been challenged, particularly with respect to trade, by emerging regional arrangements such as the *European Union or *NAFTA, not in themselves incompatible with larger multilateral accords. More seriously, the original sponsor of post-war multilateralism in economic regimes, the United States, has turned towards unilateral action and bilateral confrontation in trade and other negotiations as a result of frustration with the intricacies of consensus-building in a multilateral forum. As the most powerful member of the international community by far, the United States has the least to lose from a defection away from multilateralism, and the weakest nations the most, but the cost for all would be high.

In disarmament and arms control, important changes have also taken place in the post-war period. Initially it was felt that effective control of arms would require an ongoing multilateral forum in the context of the United Nations. As the nuclear arms race between the United States and the USSR emerged, however, it became clear that the two superpowers were unwilling to cede the issue of arms control policy to multilateral discussions. Despite consistent multilateral efforts, including the Partial Test Ban Treaty of 1963, the *Nuclear Non-Proliferation Treaty of 1970, and the Biological Weapons Convention of 1975, key arms control measures depended largely on bilateral superpower accords outside UN processes. Even the multilateral success stories rested on superpower cooperation.

The US–Soviet *SALT I agreement of 1972, coupled with the Anti-Ballistic Missile Treaty, was followed by SALT II in 1979. These opened the door to further multilateral agreements, especially with the changes in Soviet foreign policy under Mikhail Gorbachev that led to the end of the Cold War. This quickly resulted in the Conventional

Forces in Europe agreement of 1990 between NATO and Warsaw Pact members, as well as additional bilateral nuclear arms control agreements such as the Intermediate Nuclear Forces (INF) Treaty of 1987 and *START in July 1991. With the collapse of the Soviet Union, even nuclear arms control matters became multilateral because offshoots of the former USSR (e.g. Ukraine, Kazakhstan) possessed nuclear weapons that were once Soviet property. These smaller states subsequently agreed (Ukraine in 1994) to transfer their arms to the Russian Federation.

Multilateral agreements more often than not are underpinned by great-power understandings. The conclusion of the World Trade Organization Uruguay Round in December 1993 depended on prior EU–US agreements. But the powerful can wreck as well as underpin multilateral agreements. The arrival of the Bush administration in Washington in 2001 called many aspects of multilateral cooperation into serious doubt, including nuclear arms control treaties and environmental protocols to which the US was a signatory. Without US support the future of multilateral cooperation would become uncertain. GU

multi-level governance An influential theoretical perspective developed since the early 1990s in the context of studies of the European Union and especially its cohesion policies, with major contributions by Liesbet Hooghe and Gary Marks. Multi-level governance is contrasted to more traditional forms of state-centric governance and provides a framework for understanding the developing role of subnational governments in the emerging European polity. It is differentiated from theories of *federalism in terms of the dispersion of authority over a complex, flexible, and fluid patchwork of overlapping jurisdictions. This is sometimes summarized in terms of the acronym FOCJ (functional, overlapping, and competing jurisdictions). In contrast with more traditional forms of decentralization, the number of jurisdictions is not limited, the jurisdictions operate at diverse territorial scales rather than a few levels (even across national borders), and they are task-specific rather than multi-task. The networks of governance arrangements that emerge have been compared to a

'new medievalism' and have some similarities with polycentric forms of government developed at city level in the United States. Normative arguments in favour of such arrangements include the claim that they can better reflect the heterogeneous preferences of citizens and deal with the varying scale of externalities arising from public good provision. Critics have been concerned about transaction cost issues, what authority structures can resolve conflicts, issues of accountability, and whether there is an inbuilt bias towards effective problem-solving rather than issues of power. It has been questioned whether it is a coherent theory that can generate hypotheses or simply a useful account of how boundaries in government are becoming less clear. Provided that too much is not expected of the theory, it offers a useful lens on changing political opportunity structures in the European Union. WG

multinational corporation When clear managerial coordination and control together with some element of ownership link legally distinct businesses operating in several countries, the result is a multinational corporation (MNC). MNCs became common only from about 1890. Generally headquartered in developed industrial economies, they developed partly in response to market opportunity and partly in reaction to rising barriers to international trade and levels of state intervention. These forced firms, if they were to retain their share of a national market, to manufacture locally where they had formerly exported.

Multinationals have been held to be subversive of states, or even of the state system. This is partly because of a few infamous examples of corporate meddling in the politics of host states, but much more because of their ability to move capital across frontiers, and to manipulate the transfer prices at which their component firms exchange goods and services internationally in order to minimize tax liability. Multinationals have also been criticized for undermining national cultures through intensive use of advertising to achieve substitutions of synthetic and standardized goods for natural and distinctively local alternatives. Initially most prominent in extractive sectors, multinationals dominated the more capital-intensive forms of manufacturing in the later twentieth century before expanding into utilities and financial services in the wake of widespread neoliberal deregulation as the millennium drew to a close. The collapse of the ENRON corporation in 2001 provided a reminder of the mutual dependencies between multinational corporations and politicians (*see* GLOBALIZATION; ANTI-GLOBALIZATION).   CJ

multiparty system Regime where more than two political parties are in serious contention for power, alone or in coalition. Multiparty systems usually coexist with *proportional representation (PR) (*see* DUVERGER'S LAW), but the association is not unbreakable. For instance, Germany and Ireland have PR but relatively few parties; while Canada has had numerous parties contending for power, though usually only two or at most three in any one district, thanks to the effect of the electoral system. The pattern of political *cleavage is more fundamental than PR in determining the number of parties in a regime.

multipolarity An *international system characterized by four or more major centres of power and influence. This system is characteristically different from *unipolarity, *bipolarity, and tripolarity because power is distributed across a greater number of states, thus creating a unique system of constraints and incentives. For *classical realism, multipolarity creates constraints towards stability, incentivizing formal alliances and *balance of power. However, *neorealists suggest that multipolarity promotes insecurity and opportunities for military action, favouring *superpower bipolarity as a means to create system equilibrium. Examples of these systems are the *Cold War as bipolarity (USA and USSR) and the post-Cold War era as unipolarity (USA). More recent scholarship suggests that the current international system is transitioning towards a multipolar system due to the raise of the *BRICS and other emerging powers.

mutual assured destruction Usually rendered as 'MAD', the idea is that two nuclear rivals can make their relationship stable so long as each of them is capable of both destroying, and being destroyed by, the other. The logic is closely linked to possession of a secure *second-strike nuclear force, which guarantees the possibility of devastating retaliation, so deterring either from launching a first strike. MAD was an important element in the view that deterrence was easy, and that it could be made stable and effective with relatively small nuclear arsenals.   BB

NAFTA The North American Free Trade Agreement was negotiated between the United States, Mexico, and Canada between 1991 and 1993. It is the largest free trade area in the world, with a GNP of almost $5 trillion, and encompassing a population of over 360 million. Building on earlier US–Canada free trade accords, the final agreement establishes the progressive elimination of most tariff and non-tariff barriers to trade between these two countries and Mexico. The agreement also facilitates cross-border investment, and includes side-agreements addressing cooperation on labour and the environment.

NAFTA is best seen as the institutionalization of previously dense economic interdependence in the region. Incentives for the formalization, regulation, and deepening of this ongoing process came from changing global economic and strategic conditions. The instability introduced by the end of the Cold War and its related geopolitical developments made both a regional integration strategy, and good relations with Latin America, an attractive alternative for the US. NAFTA would, however, become a controversial domestic politics issue, being opposed mainly by unions and the environmental lobby, but eventually piloted through the US Congress by a bipartisan coalition. The Mexican government's decision to pursue a NAFTA had its origins in the desperate need for resources of capital and investment posed by the debt crisis and the exhaustion of the import substitution industrialization (ISI) strategy. Mexico saw in NAFTA an institutional structure that would bolster investor confidence by locking in the market-oriented reform package of which it was part. It was also seen as an effective response to the problems created by the growing interdependence between the two countries, given the profound asymmetry characterizing US–Mexican relations. Canada, which like Mexico is crucially dependent on the US market, decided to join the initially bilateral talks despite less apparent benefit from a free trade area with Mexico, due to lack of a more attractive alternative and fear of exclusion. The business community also pressed for a mechanism that would insulate Canada from protectionist pressures in America.

That said, the fate of NAFTA is uncertain with the *populist election of Donald J. Trump as US President in 2016. According to Trump, 'NAFTA is the worst deal ever negotiated—EVER!', yet he has said this about a number of treaties. Regardless, Trump has signalled an end to NAFTA and has additionally created political tensions with Mexico regarding immigration and trade, further threatening the free trade agreement. AHu/LGM

(((()))) SEE WEB LINKS
• NAFTA website.

Napoleonic Law As first consul of France in 1799, Napoleon Bonaparte (1769–1821) drew up a new constitution to provide a viable governmental machine, with an administration independent from the legislature and the judiciary. This resulted in the express exclusion of the civil courts from adjudicating administrative decisions of the administration, in favour of *Droit Administratif* (administrative law). French *Droit Administratif* became a model which was followed in other countries. *Droit Administratif* is regulated by the *Conseil d'État* which is also a product of Napoleon's influence. The *Conseil d'État* comprises the bulk of the elite of French administrators, organized into four administrative structures which comprise its administrative functions. The judicial function of the *Conseil d'État* is separate and known as the *Section du Contentieux*, which exercises the functions of *judicial review over administrative decisions.

Napoleonic Law remains the foundation stone of the French legal system. JM

Narodnik Literally, 'populist'. Supporter of the Russian revolutionary organization Narodnaya Volya (The People's Will) formed in 1879 to struggle for an alliance between peasants and intellectuals and espousing terrorism (notably the assassination of Alexander II in 1881). Transformed into the Social Revolutionary Party (in 1902), the Narodniks competed with the Marxist Social Democrats for popular support. GL

Nash equilibrium A concept invented in 1951 by John F. Nash Jr., Nobel laureate and hero of the 2001 film *A Beautiful Mind*. The strategies of the players in a game are in Nash equilibrium if no player would gain by a unilateral change of strategy. Unfortunately, some games, such as *Prisoners' Dilemma, have Nash equilibria with unsatisfactory properties. In Prisoners' Dilemma, it is a Nash equilibrium for both (all) players to defect even though it is common knowledge that it is better for one and all that each should cooperate.

National Front (France) Extreme rightwing movement, formed in 1972 by Jean-Marie Le Pen, ex-*Poujadist and militant supporter of a French Algeria. Its most successful period began in 1986, when the introduction of proportional representation and a vote of around 10 per cent ensured the return of a sizeable group of deputies. In the 1988 presidential contest Le Pen's support averaged over 14 per cent nationally, more in large industrial centres where unemployment was high, and in the Mediterranean departments with large concentrations of North African immigrants. In 1999 Bruno Mégret and more than half the party leadership left the FN to form the Mouvement National Républicain (MNR). This new party was sympathetic to coalition formation with the mainstream right, whilst Le Pen continued to pursue a 'neither left nor right' strategy. The extreme-right vote was split between the FN and the MNR, with the former marginally more popular, until the 2002 Presidential elections; in the first round Le Pen took second place with 16.9 per cent of the vote ahead of the socialist candidate Lionel Jospin. The shock result

led to major demonstrations against the extreme right, and Le Pen made little progress in the second round.

Since its loss in 2002 the National Front has undergone something of a public relations rebranding, which was led by Le Pen's daughter, Marine Le Pen. In efforts to garner more support, Marine Le Pen distanced the party from her father and moderated their message for a wider audience. Yet, the National Front continues its anti-European position and has gained increasing *populist support in response to perceived problems with Muslim immigrants as well as the *refugee crisis. In addition, the party received a considerable boost from the United Kingdom's June 2016 *Brexit referendum vote to leave the European Union. In similar fashion, the National Front has seen new gains in national polls due to their pledge to emulate the British referendum if they were to come to power. IC/SF

National Front (UK) A political party formed in 1967 by a merger between a number of fringe groups whose leaders hoped thereby to establish an extreme-right presence within the political system. The party's 'esoteric' or 'insider' ideology was neo-Nazi and centred upon nationalism, *anti-Semitism, and imperialism, but its 'exoteric' or mass appeal was based upon exploiting popular opposition to immigration from the New Commonwealth. As such, on occasions when the established parties were perceived to be flouting public opinion by allowing sudden influxes of immigrants, the National Front (NF) was able to benefit electorally, and the party gained dramatic increases in support in 1972–3 and again in 1976–7. On the last occasion, its success shocked both the left and the right, and the former responded by establishing organizations such as the Anti-Nazi League while the latter promised tougher immigration controls. These measures proved effective in countering the NF, which saw its vote collapse in the general election of 1979. In the wake of this, the party fragmented into a number of splinter groups. One of these, the British National Party, briefly won a local council seat in a traditional heartland of the far right, the East End of London, in 1993–4, and scored over 10 per cent of the vote in the 2001 General Election in two seats, both in the north-west of England, which had seen interracial violence. ST

national interest The interest of a state, usually as defined by its government. Two broad usages may be identified.

1 Use by politicians in seeking support for a particular course of action, especially in foreign policy. Given the widespread attachment to the nation as a social and political organization, national interest is a powerful device for invoking support. The term is used by politicians to seek support for domestic policy objectives, but here it is less persuasive given the normal extent of differences on domestic policy and hence employed less. In foreign policy in contrast, the term invokes an image of the nation, or the *nation-state, defending its interests within the anarchic international system where dangers abound and the interests of the nation are always at risk.

2 Use as a tool for analysing foreign policy, particularly by political *realists, such as Hans Morgenthau. Here national interest is used as a sort of foreign policy version of the term '*public interest'—indicating what is best for the nation in its relations with other states. This use of the term emphasizes not merely the threat to the nation from the international *anarchy, but also the external constraints on the freedom of manoeuvre of the state from treaties, the interests and power of other states, and other factors beyond the control of the nation such as geographical location and dependence on foreign trade. This analytical usage of the term places much emphasis on the role of the state as the embodiment of the nation's interest. The realists' use of the term national interest in evaluating foreign policy has focused on national security as the core of national interest. 'Interest of state' and 'national security interest' are closely allied terms.

The difficulty with the analytical usage of the term is the absence of any agreed methodology by which the best interests of the nation can be tested. Some writers have argued that the best interests are, nevertheless, objectively determined by the situation of the state within the international system and can be deduced from a study of history and the success/failure of policies. Other writers concede that national interest is subjectively interpreted by the government of the day. In this version, national interest is similar to the politician's rhetorical usage of the term—the national interest is merely what the politician says the national interest is. PBY

nationalism Nationalism, in the words of *Ernest Gellner, 'is primarily a political principle, which holds that the political and the national unit should be congruent'. However, this definition tells us little concerning different forms of nationalism or what motivates nationalist movements. Nationalism is a diverse and complex phenomenon. Part of this complexity derives from the difficulty in distinguishing nation from state, and from ethnic groups. A state is a political entity with (usually) clearly defined territorial borders. Nations are more fluid—defined at their most basic by a sense of belonging to a community, and possessing a sense of separatedness. This community can be defined according to many different criteria. Walker Connor has argued that a nation is a 'self-defined ethnic group', but what constitutes an ethnic group is contested. It is often defined as a community comprised of distinguishing elements which can include language, culture, religion, or race. Connor's definition of the nation also dismisses the possibility of civic nations created around an overarching political identity. India's first Prime Minister, Jawahar Lal *Nehru, sought to create such an identity, although this identity was contested by Hindu nationalists.

The rise of national and ethnic conflict after the end of the Cold War demonstrated how few of the states in the world were truly nation-states (in the early 1970s Walker Connor estimated that only 9 per cent of states could 'justifiably' be described as such). The break-up of Czechoslovakia, Yugoslavia, and the Soviet Union in the early 1990s testifies to this fact. Many other states have suffered from serious conflicts—notable among them the conflict between Hutus and Tutsis in *Rwanda in 1994—yet have maintained their territorial integrity. The latter example demonstrates that nationalist movements may not demand the creation of a separate state but may seek to control resources within a state (such as oil reserves), or to dominate an existing state (as in Afghanistan) or part of a state's territory (as do many movements in India). However, nationalist movements often do seek to acquire a state in order to make the political and the national borders congruent. They either seek to amalgamate territory over which they claim political sovereignty, as did the Italian and German nationalists of the nineteenth century, or seek to secede from an existing state, as did Croatian nationalists from Yugoslavia in the twentieth. Of course, the two can coincide: demands for a greater Kurdistan would require the secession, and amalgamation, of territory from several different states including Iraq, Turkey, and Iran.

Nationalism arose around the time of the *French Revolution, when the legitimacy of the concept of popular sovereignty, and the notion that the people should rule, was spreading. The concept of popular sovereignty became associated with the idea that 'my people' should rule, rather than other peoples, as Napoleon's conquering forces spread across Europe. But although this historical period is identified with the rise of nationalism, there are many different explanations for its emergence. One concerns the emotive pull of the ties that bind human communities together. Such opinions are especially associated with the work of Anthony D. Smith. Smith argues that nationalism and national communities have an *ethnie* at their core. Although this core may change over time, nations, for Smith, have historical depth. While nations may be modern, their constitutive parts are not.

Modernist explanations challenge these assumptions. Modernist theorists of nationalism include Ernest Gellner and Benedict Anderson. Gellner argued that the move from an agrarian to an industrial society necessitated the creation of a common culture and a standardized language. Anderson argued that the creation of printing presses led to the standardization of the written language around which a common culture could coalesce, leading to the creation of an 'imagined community'. Both believed that the processes of industrialization created the conditions for the rise of nationalism. This modernist perspective does not deny that individuals had identities before the processes of modernization, but argues that

they were localized, and that they are not *necessary* for the creation of nationalism. Theirs is a functionalist account: nationalism emerged as a necessary product of modernization. Therefore, in Gellner's words, '[n]ationalism is not the awakening of nations to self-consciousness: it invents nations where they do not exist'.

Many of the nationalist movements seen in the developing world at the time of decolonization were the product of different forces. The movements which emerged were generally not the product of processes of modernization, and involved multiple communities. Often, the colonized territories were ethnically heterogeneous and the bond unifying the nationalist movement was a shared sense of difference from the colonial power—'the other'. However, this bond against the colonial power did not always exist, as can be seen in the different approaches of the Indian National Congress (perceived to be a Hindu organization) and the Muslim League to Indian independence. And even when a shared interest in removing the colonial power existed, this often disappeared once the colonial power had departed.

What motivates nationalism and nationalist movements to emerge? The causes are multiple and differ between cases. Most explanations of nationalism and the creation of nationalist movements are united by their focus on the role of elites. Instrumentalist theorists of nationalism, notably Paul Brass, have argued that elites use certain elements within a community's tradition to mobilize that community, in the interests of maintaining or extending their power. Eric Hobsbawm, the Marxist historian, has argued that elites 'invent traditions' to maintain their power, or to perpetuate false consciousness. Even Anthony Smith accepts that elites play a role in nationalist movements. Others, such as Paul Collier, have argued that cost–benefit calculations explain the emergence of nationalist movements—and that greed is more powerful and pervasive a motive than a particular grievance. Most authors accept, however, that for elites to successfully mobilize a nationalist movement, real or perceived grievances have to exist.

The situation where a community is split between two or more states (e.g. Basques between France and Spain) can be the catalyst for the emergence of a movement, but this does not always lead to a nationalist movement. In addition, many within the divided community may not support the creation of a separate state, rather focusing on securing autonomy (as is the case for many within the Basque community). This is important to stress; nationalist movements may seek separate statehood, but many will settle for autonomy within existing borders (if they live concentrated in a specific territory) and/or a reconfiguration of power structures that gives them a greater say in the political process. The oppression of a community within a territory, or a regime's defection from an existing settlement (such as autonomy or power sharing), can also lead to a nationalist movement—as seen in Kosovo—as a means of seeking security. However, nationalism can also emerge when a community is not oppressed, but feels aggrieved, for example when a wealthy part of a country feels that it is subsidizing the rest, as was the case with Katanga in the Congo.

It is, however, important to emphasize that two or more nations can live peacefully within the same territorial borders, as the examples of Switzerland and India demonstrate. Nationalism can also emerge at a state-wide level, to be directed against other nations or states. A (usually) benign form of this type of nationalism can be seen in sporting fixtures, which unite the nation against others. But of course, this type of nationalism need not be benign—as the tensions between India and Pakistan demonstrate.

Nationalism remains an extremely powerful phenomenon. Despite predictions that national identities will be swept away by *globalization, the nation and movements associated with it show no signs of diminishing in importance. *See also* NEIGHBOURHOOD NATIONALISM. KA

nationalization The transfer of private assets into public ownership, in Britain usually in the form of a public corporation. The main wave of nationalization in Britain was under the Labour Government of 1945–51 when public utilities such as electricity, gas, and the railways, and basic industries such as coal, were brought into public ownership. The steel industry was nationalized, then partially denationalized by the succeeding

Conservative Government, only to be renationalized by the Labour Government of 1966–70. Aerospace and shipbuilding were nationalized by the Labour Government of 1974–9. By this time, failing companies such as British Leyland were also coming into public ownership, but with government shareholdings placed under the supervision of the National Enterprise Board rather than as public corporations. The political, constitutional, and administrative problems associated with nationalization created an active subfield of British political science which addressed such questions as what form the relationship between government and the public corporations should take and how Parliament could secure the accountability of the nationalized industries. WG

National Missile Defense (NMD) *See* STRATEGIC DEFENSE INITIATIVE (SDI).

National Security Council (NSC) American executive agency, part of the Executive Office of the President, that oversees issues concerning national security, both domestic and international. The agency was formed in 1947, and consists of the President, the Vice President, the Secretary of State, the Secretary of Defense, and other key advisers. The NSC is essentially a policy-recommending body, but because of its small size it can respond to crises quickly, and its powerful membership ensures that its decisions are influential. The NSC also has the function of overseeing the operations of the CIA. It is sometimes accused of operating as a rival State Department, often with better access to the President than the 'real' State Department.

⊕ SEE WEB LINKS
• National Security Council membership and functions.

National Socialism In Germany the National Socialist German Workers Party (NSDAP) rose to power under its leader Adolf Hitler (1889–1945) (who was appointed Chancellor in 1933) and sought to effect a complete transformation of state and society, creating in effect a ruthless dictatorship and single-party monopoly of power which has come to be seen as a form of *totalitarianism. Ideologically National Socialism combined an extreme form of *nationalism (including strongly racist and anti-Semitic beliefs in the superiority of the Germanic-Aryan community over all other peoples and cultures) and a distinctive concept of state-led *socialism which was far removed from both revolutionary *Marxism and *social democracy. The overriding aim was to inaugurate a new epoch of history embodied in a Third Reich or empire in which a territorially enlarged German nation would become the dominant force in world politics. A strongly militaristic focus drew National Socialist Germany into an acceptance of war as a necessary means of achieving national ambitions and in particular the goal of greater *Lebensraum* (or 'living-space' for the German *Volk*). Only with the military defeat of Germany in 1945 and the deliberate policies of de-Nazification which were subsequently implemented by the occupying powers was the National Socialist movement finally eradicated. *See also* FASCISM; NATIONALISM.   KT

national treatment Along with the *Most Favoured Nation clause, the principle of national treatment underpins the trade regime embodied in the *World Trade Organization. It means that a government must not apply regulations or restrictions to imported products any more strict than those applied to domestic producers.   GU

nation-state Literally, a sovereign entity dominated by a single nation. A mythical and intellectual construct with a highly persuasive and powerful political force. It is the primary unit in the study of international relations. Yet although it has a specific meaning it is also a highly abused political term, especially when too readily applied to the 'real' world. Its meaning is found in the coincidence of its two parent terms, 'state' and 'nation'. 'State' refers to the political organization that displays *sovereignty both within geographic borders and in relation to other sovereign entities. A world of nation-states implies an international system of pure sovereign entities, relating to each other legally as equals. 'Nation' refers rather to the population within, sharing a common culture, language, and ethnicity with a strong historical continuity. This manifests itself in most members in a sentiment of collective, communal identity. When the two concepts, 'nation' and 'state' are combined, this creates an enormously compelling mixture of legitimacy and efficiency for governing elites.

Unfortunately, there does not exist, has never existed, a nation-state in the perfect sense. Nevertheless, it has commanded a strong following, as governments have endeavoured to attain the legitimacy and political stability it brings. It was used most effectively in the nation-building of the nineteenth century, and has been the target more recently of many Third World governments hoping to build nations in support of their states as part of their socio-economic development. A common strategy of elites in building a sense of internal cohesiveness is in creating strong enemy images from outside or within the society. It is often this feature that causes dynamic instability for nation-states in the world system.

The later part of the twentieth century witnessed a decline in the power of the 'nation-states', as other bodies gained power in international relations, bodies such as large multinational corporations, international organizations, and other collectivities. The rise of supranationalism, most clearly in the *European Union, could well make the simple model of single-level sovereignty implied by the nation-state even more irrelevant. So could the problem of extranational minorities (such as Germans outside Germany, and Hungarians outside Hungary). For comparison, *see also* NATIONALISM.   PI

NATO The North Atlantic Treaty Organization (NATO), established in 1949, was the culmination of Western responses to a growing perception of threat from the Soviet Union in the years following the end of the Second World War. It followed on from the beginning of American re-engagement in Europe with Marshall Aid and the Truman Doctrine in 1947, from the formation of the Brussels treaty in 1948 among Britain, France, and Benelux, and from the joint allied response to the Berlin blockade in 1948–9. NATO originally had twelve members: the United States, Britain, France, Canada, Italy, the Netherlands, Belgium, Luxembourg, Denmark, Iceland, Norway, and Portugal. Greece and Turkey joined in 1952, the Federal Republic of Germany in 1955, and Spain in 1982. A post-Cold War round of enlargement began with the admission of Poland, the Czech Republic, and Hungary in 1999. They were joined by a further seven Eastern European states in 2004 (Bulgaria, Estonia, Latvia, Lithuania, Romania, Slovakia, and Slovenia), and by Albania and Croatia in 2009, meaning the original twelve states had increased to 28. The parties to NATO agree to treat an attack on any one of them as an attack against all, each member being obliged to assist those attacked by taking 'such action as it deems necessary, including the use of armed force, to restore and maintain the security of the North Atlantic area'. They agree to settle disputes among themselves by peaceful means, to avoid economic conflict, and to work towards economic collaboration with each other. The North Atlantic Council is the basic political directorate of the alliance, and its military command is centred on the Supreme Headquarters Allied Powers Europe (SHAPE).

NATO functioned successfully throughout the Cold War as the main bastion of Western defence (and of American containment policy and forward defence) against the Soviet Union. Despite nearly continuous internal wrangling over military policy and burden-sharing, the alliance sustained a solid front against Soviet political and military pressure. It survived the crisis of French military disengagement in 1966, and managed to contain, though not to solve, the antagonism of Greece and Turkey. NATO survived two serious crises over nuclear weapons. The first was in the early and mid-1960s, when the credibility of American military guarantees to Europe was weakened by the Soviet Union's development of the capability to mount nuclear strikes against the United States. The second was in the late 1970s and early 1980s, and concerned the controversial decision to deploy Cruise and Pershing II theatre nuclear weapons in Europe.

NATO's Cold War role can be summarized by the remark that its purpose was to keep the Americans in, the Germans down, and the Russians out. Between 1949 and 1989 it accomplished all three of these objectives successfully. The end of the Cold War and the dissolution of the Soviet Union created a crisis of function for NATO. The crises in the Balkans tested the alliance, and led to its first military engagement and then its first peacekeeping mission (both in Bosnia). The European Union's developments in the foreign and security policy areas pose awkward questions about the continued relevance of NATO and the division of labour between the two organizations. The expansion of NATO to Eastern European states poses questions about those states' and NATO's relationships with Russia. In light of this, NATO has worked to develop its relationship with Russia, one initiative being the establishment of the NATO-Russia Council (NRC) in 2002.

The role of NATO has again received much attention since the attacks on the US of *September 11th 2001. NATO invoked article 5 of the Washington Treaty for the first time in the organization's history, declaring the attacks on the US to be an attack on all NATO states. Despite this, the US went to war in Afghanistan without NATO. Disagreements about the 2003 *Iraq war prevented NATO engagement and caused much friction within the alliance. NATO's role has since increasingly expanded to 'out of area' and peacekeeping missions. This demonstrates a considerable shift in purpose for the alliance originally founded against the threat of the Soviet Union and limited to the North Atlantic area. Despite ongoing friction within NATO and questions about its future role, NATO members as a whole are reluctant to abandon the extensive network of military collaboration and integration that they have built up.   CT

⊕ SEE WEB LINKS
• NATO site, including list of members.

natural law Rules of conduct determined by reflection upon human nature, the natural conditions of human existence, or the requirements of human flourishing. 'Nature' has many meanings in the history of ideas, of which five (which overlap) are especially important in this context:

1 What is necessary for the development to occur or the aspiration to be realized.
2 What is common to all persons, or what is common to positive legal systems.
3 What the earliest conditions of human existence were.
4 What such an existence would be like in the absence of some event or institution, such as private property or government.
5 What God intended for man, and what is required of man.

The enforceability of natural law is problematic. In so far as it is associated with the will of God, its sanctions may be attributed to another world. In a secular version, in which natural law is depicted as rationally compelling, rights of enforcement may be attributed to all individuals, or the need for enforceability adduced as an explanation of the artifice of government. Natural law has therefore figured as an explanation of positive law and as a critical guide to its proper content. In so far as it specifies a universal standard, it provides a higher law than that of particular legal systems, and an external standard by which they may be judged. *Liberalism, in particular, has been shaped partly by a tradition of natural *jurisprudence, in which the writings of *Grotius, *Pufendorf, Barbeyrac, *Locke, and Adam *Smith are particularly important. Contemporary political philosophy, characterized as the exploration of the political consequences of the human condition, may reject many of these understandings of the 'natural', but can scarcely escape some depiction, however plastic, of the material of political life. *See also* PERFECTIONISM.   AR

natural rights *Rights which persons possess by nature: that is, without the intervention of agreement, or in the absence of political and legal institutions. Natural rights are therefore attributable to individuals without distinction of time or place. A contrast may be drawn with positive rights: that is, those rights conferred or guaranteed by a particular legal system. Natural rights have been derided as nonsensical (by *Bentham) on the ground that it is impossible to speak of rights without enforceable duties, and enforceability exists only when a potentially coercive legal system exists. Furthermore, there has been no unanimity even amongst those who recognize natural rights as to their content. Natural rights have been seen as gifts of God, as correlative to duties imposed on man by God, and as concomitants of human nature or reason. We might distinguish: (1) natural rights; (2) moral rights; and (3) legal rights. The third are those recognized by positive law. The first are those asserted to be universal and thus guides to the proper content of any legal system. The second are those which, it is claimed, should be recognized by particular legal systems or

which, while not universal, should be recognized under existing conditions. The classification of rights will depend in part on understandings of their purpose and of their consequences.   AR

nature, convention Generally, 'nature' connotes what comes as an inborn characteristic, while 'convention' connotes that which is suggested by custom and practice. The opposition between these two terms was an important feature of ancient Greek political thought. Until challenged by the *sophists, political thinkers seem to have thought of moral ideas as being natural in the sense that a morally mature person would come to acquire them. The sophist challenge lay in the idea that perhaps moral ideas were human inventions, which were proposed ultimately because they were convenient. A clear statement of this view is presented by Glaucon and Adeimantus in Book 2 of *Plato's *Republic*. People who have both meted out and received injustice 'began to set down their own laws and compacts and to name what the law commands lawful and just . . . . [J]ustice . . . is a mean between what is best—doing injustice without paying the penalty—and what is worst—suffering injustice without being able to avenge oneself'. Plato's Socrates devotes the rest of the *Republic* to arguments designed to rebut this and to show that ideas of justice are indeed natural.

The Greek word we translate as 'nature' is *physis*, from the verb *phyein*. This shows one of the classic perils of translation. English 'nature' is derived from Latin *natus*, 'born'. So if something comes naturally to us, the basic connotation is that it is inborn. But Greek *phyein* has the additional sense 'make to grow'. *Aristotle agreed with Plato that moral qualities were natural, not conventional. But he expresses himself in a biological rather than a metaphysical way when he states 'Man is by nature a political animal'. This carries the connotation that man grows to full moral maturity only by being the citizen of a Greek *polis* (city-state).

The Greek distinction between the natural and conventional has persisted. For instance, those writers who follow the *organic analogy are siding with Plato and Aristotle in thinking of the political institutions or ideas they praise as 'natural'. Those who deny the organic analogy and regard institutions and ideas as human artefacts side with the sophists.

Nazi *See* NATIONAL SOCIALISM.

needs A need refers to what is required in order to do something or achieve some state of being. 'Human needs', for example, have been taken to describe requirements which must be satisfied if harm to an agent is to be avoided. Thus theorists have spoken of needs for food, drink, shelter, and even love, on the grounds that deprivation of any of these 'goods' will constitute harm to an individual. A strong defence of the notion of needs contrasts it with the notion of *wants. Needs are universal, wants reflect the variety of circumstance and taste. Need-satisfaction is fundamental to welfare, want-satisfaction desirable but less urgent—and therefore needs have normative priority over wants. It is possible to be ignorant of one's needs, but not of one's wants.

There is, however, widespread scepticism about the distinction between needs and wants. Sceptics suggest that the notion of needs is socially relative and that of harm morality-dependent; that alleged needs may be met at so many different levels that they cannot define a baseline for considerations of welfare; that there is no less subjectivity in acknowledging needs than in asserting wants; and that purported needs merely represent someone's (contestable) view of the requirements of human flourishing. Although, in general, socialist political thought has been more sympathetic than other traditions to the notion of needs, and more willing to build theoretical prescriptions upon it, some contemporary radicals, particularly those concerned with societal shaping of our perceptions of 'need', are to be numbered amongst the sceptics. AR

negative rights Negative rights are often described as representative of 'rights from' or 'freedoms from' structures of authority and/or domination by others. A negative right denotes a key individual entitlement to inaction by others. In general, negative rights are often viewed as protecting key freedoms necessary for human *autonomy and freedom of action. This is said to be distinct from *positive rights, which often describe rights 'to something' and which

demand that others act to fulfil their duty to others or to fulfil an entitlement held by others. Despite their wide use there is considerable disagreement regarding how clearly distinctions can be drawn between negative rights and positive rights, since it is often the case that even inaction towards preventing harm will require positive acts.

Nehru, Jawahar Lal (1889–1964) Leader of the Indian National *Congress, and the first Prime Minister of independent India. He was the architect of India's developmental policy in the immediate post-independent era. Influenced by *Marxism, liberalism, and *Fabian socialism, Nehru was a modernizer who wanted India to become an industrialized and economically self-reliant nation. Impressed with the rates of economic growth in the Soviet Union, Nehru tried to combine markets and a planned economy in a model of mixed-economy for India, with a significant regulatory and productive role for the state. In foreign policy, Nehru was one of the initiators of the *non-aligned movement, and for India's friendly relations with the Soviet Union (*see also* PANSCHEEL). SR

neighbourhood nationalism Term used to refer to a form of identity politics that can embody both local and national discourses on race and nation. Common language and culture, and often a shared political cause (e.g. anti-colonialism, anti-racism, anti-establishment), can assist in generating a feeling of neighbourhood 'belonging'. The politics of neighbourhood nationalism can be inclusive but also can exclude those who are constructed as the 'others'. For example, the political goal of anti-colonial nationalism may influence mobilization for the 'nation' at the local level, which in specific contexts may override class, caste, and religious divisions in the neighbourhood. Similarly, national discourses (for example multiculturalism, or legislation on terror in the UK) can include or divide communities along ethnic and religious lines. What is unique about this form of nationalism is its ordinariness and embeddedness in everyday living patterns. In times of civil strife, simple acts such as communal cooking or eating, or looking after each other's homesteads, provide security and a sense of community identity. Neighbourhood nationalism also engenders many risks, so it is not uncommon to witness entire neighbourhoods and communities being implicated in certain traditional practices (such as female genital mutilation, honour killings, witchcraft, or political connivance) or subject to brutalities (as in *Rwanda) and becoming targets for a range of acts. STH

neoclassical economics The revival of classical economics which began when its statements were recast in a more mathematically exact form in the late nineteenth century. In political discussion, however, the term refers more particularly to the rejection of government intervention in markets. The fundamental neoclassical complaint against *Keynes is that he makes inconsistent assumptions about the rationality of economic actors. However, in the usual political use of the term it is merely a synonym for 'market economics'.

neo-colonialism The term 'neo-colonialism' was first coined by Kwame Nkrumah, who led Ghana to independence in 1957 and served as prime minister and president, and used it as the title of his 1965 book, *Neo-colonialism: The Last Stage of Imperialism.* Nkrumah used the term to describe what he saw as the continuing exploitative economic relations between developed and less developed countries even after the achievement of political independence. Though often used to critique relations between former colonial powers and their former colonies (of which France's relations with its former colonies in West Africa are a key example), it has also been used to describe relations between the *Global North and the *Global South more generally, and in particular relations between the USA and countries in Central and Latin America, the Middle East, and elsewhere in the developing world. As such, its meaning has extended beyond just referring to exploitative economic relations to political and cultural influence of developed countries (or simply foreign powers) more generally. Politically, the concept has been referenced by organizations such as the Organisation of African Unity, the Non-Aligned Movement, and various national liberation groups. Academically, a concern with neo-colonialism was a key influence in the development of *dependency

theory and in the field of *post-colonialism. *See* IMPERIALISM. WB

neoconservatism Heterogeneous intellectual tradition often portrayed as a unified ideology. In the early twenty-first century, neoconservatism became associated with the *Bush Doctrine and a group of political advisers perceived to ruthlessly pursue US interests and manipulate public opinion through a *politics of fear.

Neoconservatism began during the 1960s as an intellectual protest of disenchanted revolutionary-left liberals against a seeming social breakdown and liberal decadence. Neoconservative thought—often linked to the teachings of Leo *Strauss—was particularly critical of the *new left's radicalism, the societal permissiveness towards cultural taboos, and the non-discriminatory social policy of the federal government. Apart from a vigorous stance against Soviet communism, foreign policy considerations played only a minor role.

Contemporary neoconservatism lacks the defining characteristic that justified the prefix 'neo', as most advocates never undertook a political rightward journey. Neoconservatism today places its primary emphasis on foreign policy and has challenged isolationist tendencies in the *Republican Party. However, significant differences exist within neoconservative thought on the use of military force to advance American values and moral goals. Pragmatic neoconservatism promotes a realist-leaning foreign policy that restricts US intervention to cases where 'vital interests' are at stake. Radical neoconservatism favours a more 'hawkish' and unapologetically interventionist foreign policy. AHr

neocorporatism This prefix variant of *corporatism was frequently used by the new generation of corporatist theorists that emerged in the 1970s, largely as part of an effort to distinguish the corporatist model from earlier variants that had fascist or right-wing associations. WG

neo-fascism *See* FASCISM.

neofunctionalism Application of *functionalism to the study of European integration. The main impetus behind European integration during the 1940s was federalist and democratic. But the failure of France to accept the European Defence Community in 1954, and the apparent success of the less evidently political European Coal and Steel Community, led to a shift in emphasis towards the achievement of integration through the strengthening of economic and social ties. Some of the protagonists, and many political scientists observing the process, believed that this tactic would achieve a gradual withering of the power of nation-states, as functions of government directly pertinent to the welfare of Europeans came more and more to be performed by international agencies. European institutions would foster a governing elite free of national ties, and become the focus for interest groups and popular loyalties. This view was most clearly distinguished from earlier functionalist visions by its acceptance of a regional and centralized focus of power in place of the older ideal of global integration under dispersed functional agencies. In addition, its advocates placed less reliance than their predecessors on automatic progress toward integration, believing that tensions arising directly out of the process of integration would produce periodic crises, only to be resolved by the will of residual national governments, resulting each time in a broadening of the scope of integration.   CJ

neoliberalism There are two principal meanings of the term neoliberalism. The first refers to a set of market-liberal economic policies. In the developed world neoliberalism is often coupled with Thatcherism and grew up in opposition to Keynesianism. In the developing world it emerged in opposition to the development strategies based on import-substitution industrialization which had dominated the period 1945 to the early 1980s. Here it is often linked to the so-called 'Washington Consensus' (privatization and deregulation; trade and financial liberalization; shrinking the role of the state; encouraging foreign direct investment) and to the structural adjustment programmes promoted by the IMF and World Bank. More recently, it has been used (for example by the anti-globalization movement) to characterize the economic ideology behind capitalist globalization. Whilst all of these usages are related, the economic use of the term neoliberalism is somewhat general and imprecise.

The second use of the term is within academic International Relations. Here it describes a theoretical approach to the study of institutions (sometimes described as neoliberal institutionalism or regime theory). Developed in the mid-1980s as a reaction to the dominant neorealist paradigm, neoliberal institutionalism sought to demonstrate that international cooperation is possible, even on realist premises—namely that states are rational, unitary actors which seek to maximize their utility in an anarchic international system. Although recognizing that the absence of a sovereign authority at the international level creates opportunities for conflict, defection, and cheating, neoliberals argue that institutions and regimes help states cooperate by reducing uncertainty, linking issues, monitoring behaviour, and enhancing the importance of reputation. These arguments are countered by neorealist theorists who stress the importance of relative rather than absolute gains and the extent to which powerful states can shape institutions for their own purposes and avoid them when they are too constraining.   AHu/LGM

neo-Marxism A large corpus of work which identifies with *Marxism but seeks to build and improve upon the classical works of Karl *Marx and Joseph *Engels. While interstitial figures comprised Gyorgy *Lukács and Antonio *Gramsci in the inter-war period, neo-Marxism developed prolifically after 1945 and has entered all of the social sciences and humanities. An abiding driver of neo-Marxist thought is the desire to overcome economic determinism (as in *Stalinism) or class-reductionism—an initiative that began with the French structuralists Louis *Althusser and Nicos *Poulantzas and their notion of the 'relative autonomy' of the superstructure in general but the state in particular. This also has its political side, where evolutionary and democratic conceptions of revolution come to supersede the revolutionary politics of Marx, *Lenin, and *Trotsky (as in Gramsci's conception of 'counter-hegemony'). A further neo-Marxist initiative seeks to understand *globalization and development where, unlike Marx and Engels, who tended to believe in the European civilizing mission on political grounds, neo-Marxists have placed the critique of capitalist globalization as *imperialism front and centre. Despite various unifying themes, a striking aspect has been the proliferation of approaches which include Political Marxism, Gramscian Marxism, Open Marxism, World-systems theory, and those which revitalize Trotskyism and Leninism.   JMH

neorealism A theory in *international relations most closely associated with Kenneth *Waltz (1924–2013), neorealism, or structural realism, is a position within the *realist school that is critical of the classical realist focus on the self-interested motives of states and individuals, instead focusing on the structure of the *international system as the main explanation for state behaviour. It retains both the realist focus on the state as the main actor and on the self-interested motives for state behaviour, but insists that this self-interest—either to maximize power or security—derives from the anarchical nature of the international system and cannot be explained by either human nature or domestic politics.

Waltz argues that such attempts to apply individual- or domestic-level explanations to international relations are reductionist and should play no role in accounting for how the international system works. Seeking a more *positivist answer, he looks for repeatable patterns of behaviour at the international level, claiming that all states are functionally similar units operating under the same pressures generated by the international structure. Microeconomic theory is used to model how the system influences the behaviour of the units, imposing constraints and forcing states to adapt their behaviour in order to survive. *Balance of power now becomes a theory of equilibrium based on the number of *great powers. As well as the ordering principle—*anarchy—the international system is defined by the distribution of capabilities. If such a system produces two great powers, the system is more stable. This is described as bipolarity and is characteristic of the *Cold War period. By contrast, if the distribution of capabilities is more dispersed, or produces multipolarity, the system is less stable and less predictable. There is dispute as to whether the current system is unipolar or multipolar but agreement that it is less stable than Cold War bipolarity.

For Waltz there are only two kinds of structure: hierarchy and anarchy. Under anarchy there is no functional differentiation of units, so differences in the power of states is the result of states' position within the international system which in turn is the result of the distribution of material capabilities. Any changes in the system are the consequence of changes in this distribution. Internal events such as *regime change and *revolution are irrelevant. Regardless of internal politics or *ideology, the structure of the international system forces states to behave in a self-interested way.

The main dispute within neorealism is between *defensive and *offensive realists. Waltz believed that states were mainly concerned with their own survival and will normally be moderate in their behaviour. States are normally risk-adverse and will seek to balance rather than maximize their power. Offensive realists, notably John Mearsheimer, argue that the anarchic system produces more aggressive behaviour in states and that aspiring powers can be characterized as power-maximizing revisionists rather than balancers or supporters of the status quo. Rising powers will actively seek *hegemony as the best way of guaranteeing their own security. Mearsheimer is notable for his argument that the post-Cold War peace in Europe is temporary and a multipolar Europe is likely in the future. He also predicts that the rise of China is not likely to be a peaceful one.

A further theoretical development has been the emergence of neoclassical realism. Here scholars seek to combine the insights of neorealism about the determining influence of the international system with greater sensitivity towards domestic politics, the role of elites and societal actors, and cognitive factors such as perception and misperception of threats and opportunities.   JJ

NEP (New Economic Policy) Policy introduced in the Soviet Union in March 1921 in place of rigid central controls. It envisaged the end of grain requisitioning and the development of limited market relations in trade and industry. Originally a 'breathing space', it was then considered by many Bolsheviks, especially *Bukharin, as a long-term strategy for the transition to socialism.   SWH

networks See POLICY NETWORKS.

neutralism Neutralism describes the policy of non-alignment in the Cold War adopted by a large group of, for the most part, recently decolonized Afro-Asian states. It is not to be confused with neutrality. The principal forums for neutralism were the Non-Aligned Movement, the UN General Assembly, and the United Nations Conference on Trade and Development. Neutralist states rejected the Cold War as an organizing principle for international relations and tried to establish political space between the two superpowers. The ending of the Cold War has seriously undermined the relevance of neutralism. BB

neutrality Neutrality is a legal position by which a state either takes no part in a particular war, or adopts the policy that it will not take part in any war. Neutrals can claim rights of respect from belligerents in return for their strict impartiality. BB

New Deal In 1932 Franklin Roosevelt in accepting the Democratic nomination for the Presidency said, 'I pledge you, I pledge myself to a new deal for the American people'. At the time this was little more than campaign rhetoric, but the New Deal was subsequently widely used as an umbrella term to characterize the domestic reform programmes of the Roosevelt administration in the 1930s. These included banking and finance reform, various relief programmes for the unemployed, agriculture recovery legislation, the National Industrial Recovery Act, the act setting up the Tennessee Valley Authority, the National Labor Relations Act, the Social Security Act providing unemployment insurance and old age pensions, and much else besides. The phrase 'New Deal coalition' is often used to denote the coalition of blue-collar workers, blacks, 'ethnic' (non-Anglo-Saxon) white Americans, and Southerners which continued to support the Democrats until the 1960s. DM

New Economic Policy See NEP.

new institutionalism Phrase coined by J. G. March and J. P. Olsen (1984) to denote an approach to politics which holds that behaviour is fundamentally moulded by the institutions it is embedded in. This might seem a trivial truth, but during the long ascendancy of *behaviouralism in political science, it was often ignored.

New Labour Originally a label given to (but not by) supporters of Neil Kinnock's changes in the *Labour Party (UK) between 1985 and 1992. The label was then adopted as a brand by Tony Blair and his circle on Blair's accession to the party leadership in 1994 and to power in 1997, Blair then saying 'We were elected as New Labour, and will govern as New Labour'.

Kinnock first expelled the *Militant Tendency from the party, then set about changing party policies which he believed had caused voters to defect from Labour to the Liberal–Social Democrat Alliance. The party abandoned *unilateralism, distanced itself from the trade unions, and embraced the market. John Smith (Labour Party leader 1992–4) was more traditionalist, but Blair launched the theme 'New Labour, New Britain' at his first party conference in 1994. Blair barely concealed his admiration for Margaret Thatcher's programme of privatization, regulation of trade unions, and deregulation of utilities. In 1997 the Conservatives tried to turn the slogan back on its creators as 'New Labour, New Danger', and failed spectacularly. In social policy, New Labour has attempted to reduce *social exclusion by a mixture of targeted tax changes and moralizing. The moralizing blinded many to the fact that the targeting of the socially excluded helped to make the 1997 administration one of the most redistributive governments in British history.

new left Generic term encompassing diverse challenges to the doctrines, methods of organization, and styles of leadership of the 'old' *left.

The new left emerged from the disintegration of Soviet hegemony over the international communist movement after 1956; the East European revolts, Soviet response to them and the repercussions this had within individual communist parties, and the challenges made by Trotskyist and Maoist parties to Soviet ideological control. The Cuban Revolution of 1959, and anticolonial struggles in Africa and Asia suggested to some that there were different strategies of revolution and that other social groups, apart from the industrial proletariat, could be the agents of revolutionary change. Students, women, black power groups, and anti-Vietnam War activists in Europe and the United States mobilized, and claimed the support of peasants and 'lumpenproletariat' in the Third World. The apogee of the new left was witnessed in 1968 in the May 'events' in Paris, and its nadir in the Soviet invasion of Czechoslovakia and the end of 'socialism with a human face' there.

The new left's emphasis upon spontaneity left it vulnerable to fragmentation and an eclectic set of groups each with distinct agendas. However it left its mark on *feminism, *green parties, *Eurocommunism, and a renaissance in intellectual thought on the left (*see* GUEVARA, MARCUSE, and GRAMSCI) as well as renewed interest in Marx's views on *alienation and the *state.   GL

new right Theorists who stress the efficacy of the free market for economic and political freedom. The main principles of new-right philosophy can be found in the works of *Hayek and the American economist Milton Friedman. Some writers also consider J. M. Buchanan and the *public choice school to be part of the new right. Buchanan's school differs in important ways from those discussed here, but shares its eighteenth- and nineteenth-century liberal antecedents. The new right are 'new' not in the sense that their theories have no precedent. Indeed, they draw on Adam *Smith and closely reflect the preoccupations of nineteenth-century liberal thought. They can only be considered 'new' when contrasted with the 'old right' preoccupations with tradition, moderation, and support for the post-war political consensus.

These theories had a strong influence on the political process from 1979 to 1992 particularly in Britain and the United States. Within the British Conservative Party Margaret Thatcher and her mentor Sir Keith Joseph led a faction which adopted new right thinking while in opposition. The conflict between 'new' and 'old' right can be clearly encapsulated in her successful assault on the Tory leadership. Her predecessor Edward Heath and his colleagues were sidelined and depicted as being an accessory in Britain's economic and political decline. Their commitment to the corporate consensus of the post-war period was seen as the most damning evidence for Conservative failure to face up to harsh realities. For the new right this could only be done by an all-out attack on those institutions that were seen to interfere with free market clearing. These included trade unions, the government itself, in terms of interventionist economic policy, and excessive state expenditure, particularly in terms of welfare payments. *Monetarism, which emphasizes the need for strict control of the money supply to curb inflation, was also advanced as a main policy objective. A further, even more radical, aim was to eliminate socialism both as a philosophical doctrine and as a possible practical alternative to competitive capitalism.

Hayek's *The Road To Serfdom*, written in the early 1940s, and *The Constitution of Liberty* (1960) made a sustained attack on what he described as 'state socialism'. Hayek equated socialism with central economic planning. However, he indicates that market mechanisms can only work properly in the right social and moral context. To this end, and ironically reminiscent of 'old right' thinking, he stresses the importance of tradition in passing on the cumulative knowledge and experience of previous generations.

The attack on trade union power has its theoretical basis in Friedman's critique of the supposed trade-offs between lower unemployment and higher levels of inflation. Friedman argued that such trade-offs were possible only on a short-run basis. In the long run, the 'non-accelerating inflation rate of unemployment' (NAIRU), or natural rate of unemployment, indicates the equilibrium real wage at which the labour that is voluntarily supplied matches the amount of labour that firms voluntarily employ. Any unemployment at the natural rate is therefore frictional and structural. For Friedman the latter can only be dissipated by reducing the natural rate itself by attacking those institutions which interfere with the supply of labour. Hence, trade union power is particularly targeted because it restricts the unemployed from offering to work at a wage lower than the one determined at the natural rate. Only when this power is reduced will the labour market become more competitive and the natural rate of unemployment be reduced.

The *welfare state is another significant institution which has been a particular target for the new right. In particular the UK think-tank the Institute of Economic Affairs (IEA) propagated and expanded on Friedman's arguments in *Capitalism and Freedom* that government intervention distorted the labour market and created inefficient public monopolies for the provision of services. Although Friedman and the IEA suggest that a free market system would overcome such difficulties Hayek is more sceptical. He criticizes the reduction in freedom which taxation for the maintenance of the welfare state produces but suggests that some of its aims can be fulfilled without limiting personal liberty. Surprisingly, *Hayek suggests that government can fulfil this, and many other roles, as long as it does not operate through a centralized monopoly.

Aspects of new-right doctrines still find their way into the policies of many administrations throughout the world, including Labour governments in New Zealand (1984) and Britain (1997). IF

new social movements Term used to describe a diverse set of popular movements characterized by a departure from conventional methods of political organization and expression, and experimentation with new forms of social relations and cultural meanings and identities.

In advanced capitalist societies, the 'movements' have mobilized around *feminist, *ecological, peace, and anti-nuclear issues. In Africa, Asia, and Latin America their range has been wider, including Catholic base communities, neighbourhood and squatter associations, women's and human rights groups, peasant co-operatives, and environmental activists. New social movements aspire to a broadening of 'the political', popular empowerment, and the reappropriation of *civil society, away from the control of the *state.

However, their diversity creates both methodological and political problems. It is unclear whether there can be a universal definition of a 'new social movement'. Politically they encounter problems of sustainability and are vulnerable to co-optation by the state. Nevertheless their existence challenges the notion of the 'end of politics', representing as they do new types and levels of egalitarian struggle. GL

new wars The 'new wars' debate emerged in the 1990s as scholars debated how war had changed after the end of the *Cold War. The thesis is closely associated with Professor Mary Kaldor, whose book *New and Old Wars* was published in 1999. In this book, Kaldor argued that the conflicts seen in Africa and the Balkans in the 1990s marked a turning point in modern warfare, inasmuch as they were ethnically based, undertaken predominantly by non-state actors, *genocidal in nature, and rudimentary in their technology. A fight for natural resources may also be at the heart of such conflicts, in contrast to the fight for territory in 'old wars'. Kaldor urged that 'new wars' also needed to be placed within the context of the emerging process of *globalization and observed the increasingly blurred lines between war and criminality. Ostensibly taking a *cosmopolitan approach to understanding war, Kaldor advocates that the international response to 'new wars' needs to regenerate *civil society in the countries that such wars occur in given that the state has inevitably been eroded. Critics argue that the thesis was unnecessarily neologist, seeing something 'new' in a fundamentally age-old phenomenon. AM

New World Order Phrase used by President George Bush, in a speech made in September 1990, calling for a new era of international cooperation. It reflected optimism after the end of the the *Cold War, and his wish to avoid the need for a unilateral US response to the *Gulf War crisis. The mood of optimism soon dissipated, and the approach to international cooperation was not shared by Bush's son, President George W. Bush, when faced with his own crisis in *Iraq.

NGO *See* NON-GOVERNMENTAL ORGANIZATION; INGO.

Nice Treaty (2000) *See* EUROPEAN UNION.

Nietzsche, Friedrich Wilhelm (1844–1900) A nineteenth-century German philosopher and philologist, Friedrich Nietzsche was a radical critic of the Western moral and philosophical tradition and rejected both liberalism and socialism in favour of a radical elitism. His philosophical work is characterized by what he called a 'revaluation of values', a willingness to question and analyse the value of our most fundamental moral and philosophical beliefs, such as the existence of objective truth or the moral equality of all individuals. Indicative of his distinctive writing style and use of aphorisms, the often-cited passage in *The Gay Science* in which the madman declares that 'God is dead' conveys his rejection not only of the foundations of Christianity but of the metaphysical assumptions of the Western philosophical tradition more widely; in effect, we live in a disenchanted world in which we can no longer appeal to the conventional theological or philosophical presuppositions to justify many of our ethical and political beliefs.

In *On The Genealogy of Morality*, Nietzsche criticized Christianity as being a 'slave morality', a way for the weak, powerless, and oppressed (the slaves) to control the strong and the powerful (the masters) by positing that they will suffer revenge at the hands of God in the after-life for their supposed injustices in this world. Christianity is therefore based, Nietzsche believed, on the *ressentiment* (resentment) that the weak feel towards the powerful and the desire to control them by creating an imagined system of revenge. However, this slave morality is a disaster for humanity because it tames these masters, whom Nietzsche considered paragons of the life-affirming virtues of strength and self-assertion, and in doing so leads to the mediocrity of mankind.

Nietzsche's criticism of Christianity fed into his rejection of liberalism and socialism, the two dominant political ideologies of his time, on the basis that they both wrongly assumed that all individuals are morally equal and deserve to be treated as such. On the contrary, Nietzsche believed that there are some individuals of higher moral worth than all others; these are the *Übermensch* (higher men). The *Übermensch* are great individuals who are able to raise themselves above the constraints of the slave morality of Christianity and the prevailing moral norms intended to restrain them, and fashion both themselves and the world around them as acts of artistic creativity. The masses, Nietzsche thought, could legitimately be used by the *Übermensch* in order to further these creative projects, thus denying the Kantian categorical imperative that all individuals should be treated as ends in themselves rather as means to an end they do not

choose. Nietzsche therefore preferred an aristocratic social and political order in which the masses were ruled by the *Übermensch*.

Nietzsche's influence is considerable. Though his work made little impact during his own lifetime, his philosophy has been a major source of inspiration for existentialism and post-modernism, and continues to represent one of the most radical and compelling criticisms of both liberal and social theory. Infamously, his philosophy, and in particular the idea of 'will to power', were used by the Nazis as a justification for *National Socialism, though it is now commonly believed that this was based on a perversion of his thought.   MS

nimbyism NIMBY stands for 'Not in my back yard', referring to people who oppose projects for development because of the effects on their own quality of life and/or property values. The nimby motivation is therefore often in alliance with *environmentalism, but the two phenomena are quite different, as forms of nimbyism, by their nature, do not share consistent principles to justify their defence of interests.   LA

1922 Committee Committee of the back-bench members of the Conservative Party in the House of Commons, which acts as a link between the back-bench and the party leadership. So called because Conservative *back-benchers overthrew their leaders at a meeting in the Carlton Club, London, in October 1922.

Nkrumah, Kwame (1909–72) The first Prime Minister (1957–60) and subsequently the first President (1960–6) of the West African state of Ghana. Nkrumah gained worldwide prominence both as a proponent of African liberation and as one of the leading advocates of *Pan-Africanism. After studies in the United States and in Great Britain, Nkrumah returned to Ghana in 1947 and founded the Convention People's Party. During the 1950s this movement helped organize several major strikes which pressured the British colonial authorities to grant a greater degree of self-government in Ghana. After achieving independence in 1957, following a brief period of multi-party democracy, Nkrumah transformed Ghana into a one-party state, setting a pattern which would be followed in many other newly independent African states. He also imposed major restrictions on civil liberties at this time. Throughout his political career, Nkrumah was an ardent advocate of the ideology of Pan-Africanism, helping to found the Organization of African Unity in 1963. In the economic realm, Nkrumah promoted a strategy of rapid industrialization, and the keystone of this was the massive Volta Dam project which dramatically increased Ghana's electricity production. Ultimately, despite the completion of the Volta Dam, Nkrumah's attempt to move Ghana into producing heavy industrial goods proved a failure. The Ghanaian economy in these years also lapsed into a period of macroeconomic instability with very high rates of inflation. Due in large part to these economic failures, Nkrumah was overthrown by a military coup in 1966. DS

Nolan Committee *See* COMMITTEE ON STANDARDS IN PUBLIC LIFE.

nomenklatura Formally, the term refers to the fact that appointments to positions in the Soviet state apparatus, from factory manager to minister, were approved by party bodies from a list (nomenklatura) of suitable candidates. In general use, however, the nomenklatura consists of members of the party and state apparatus who were presumed to constitute the ruling elite. swh

nominal level variable *See* MEASUREMENT.

nominating convention *See* PARTY CONVENTION.

non-alignment The anti-colonial and anti-racist posture of mainly *Third World countries who have sought a collective identity separate from the capitalist and socialist blocs in the northern hemisphere. The Non-Aligned Movement originated in the Bandung meeting of leaders (1955) and first summit conference (1961), comprising mainly African and Asian states, but became a majority of *United Nations members. Triennial summits debated political and economic issues in South–South cooperation and North–South relations. The movement went into decline due to regional conflicts and differences over how to respond to the changes in the global distribution of power following the collapse of the Soviet Union. Efforts to revive the non-aligned movement in recent years have focused more on economic issues, with some of the more outspoken members like the leaders of Cuba, Venezuela, and Iran using it as a forum to castigate US imperialism. *See also* NEHRU. PBl

non-governmental organization (NGO) The term *pressure group has increasingly been displaced by non-governmental organization (NGO). This trend has been encouraged by the groups themselves who regard it as having more favourable connotations. The term originated with the *United Nations (UN), which made provision in its charter to give such organizations consultative status. As their numbers grew, the UN redefined and clarified the relationship in Regulation 1966/31 which defined NGOs 'as any international organization which is not established by a governmental entity or international agreement'. There are now about two thousand NGOs recognized by the UN including international, national, or subnational bodies. The UN definition covers sectional groups such as business organizations. The term has acquired a much wider application and is generally used to refer to various cause groups concerned with such issues as the environment, poverty, women's rights, racism, sexual minorities, and Third World debt. NGOs are prominent in the *anti-globalization movement. Levels of public trust in NGOs and their campaigning has been shown to be high in a number of surveys. Global governance agencies such as the *International Monetary Fund and the *World Trade Organization have sought to derive greater legitimacy by developing a relationship with them. However, questions have been increasingly raised about their lack of internal democracy, their governance arrangements, and the credibility and representativeness of some of their statements. This may lead to the introduction of codes of conduct and the replication of the 'insider–outsider' distinction found in relation to more traditional pressure groups. *See also* INGO. WG

non-refoulement The principle of not returning a *refugee or an asylum seeker to territories where his or her life or freedom may be threatened. Such territories may refer to the country of origin or to a third country. The principle is regulated in Article 33 of the 1951 Convention Relating to the Status of Refugees. *See also* POLITICAL ASYLUM. CSa

non-violence Non-violence seeks to oppose the use of state *violence by means such as peaceful demonstrations, sit-ins, civil disobedience, and so forth. It is a political strategy of opposition best known as adopted by *Gandhi in the Indian national movement. Gandhi insisted on the absolute nature of non-violence—there is no half-way house in a non-violent movement. This was because non-violence was regarded by Gandhi as a moral force, and hence could not be seen to be compromised in any way. His withdrawal from the first national non-cooperation movement in 1921 after the burning down of a police station at Chauri Chaura was on the grounds that there can be no exceptions to the rule of non-violence at any level. Many political leaders have been inspired by Gandhi in adopting non-violence as a form of political protest, the best known being the American *civil rights leader Martin Luther *King. *See also* QUAKERS; CIVIL DISOBEDIENCE. SR

non-zero-sum game *See* ZERO-SUM GAME.

norm 1. A standard which is statistically determined or is derived from a number of cases. The statistically normal means simply that which occurs most frequently. The confusing phrase *normal distribution relates to this sense, not to sense 2, nor to the everyday meaning of 'normal'.

2. A standard embodying a judgement about what should be the case. Hans Kelsen's theory of law portrayed it as a structure of such norms, containing statements about what ought to be done and what ought to be not done. Practical discourse about politics contains normative judgements which it is one of the purposes of political theory to examine. The two meanings may be confused with each other and with everyday usage, for example when normative weight is placed on behaving 'normally'. AR

normal distribution The normal distribution is a mathematical model of the distribution of a random variable which is *continuous, unimodal, and symmetrical, and in which frequencies fall away with increasing distance from the mean. The frequency curve is usually described as bell-shaped. The normal distribution is very useful in statistical analysis because with a reasonably large random sample, the sampling distributions of many statistics (including the sample mean) are approximately normally distributed regardless of the shape of the distribution of the population from which the sample was drawn. This allows the analyst to test hypotheses and estimate quantities of interest (and the uncertainty surrounding those estimates) about a population with just a small proportion drawn randomly from it. This sampling theory is the basis for most survey research, including opinion polls. The normal distribution is also referred to as the Gaussian distribution after its inventor Carl Friedrich Gauss. Although the distribution is commonly used it is not called 'normal' because things tend to be or should be distributed that way. SF

normal trade relations *See* MOST FAVOURED NATION (MFN).

normative analysis Approach which focuses on the moral and ethical context of political decisions, and examines the value judgements which underpin assumptions about the worth of different actions and outcomes. Often contrasted with *empirical analysis, normative studies address how people, politicians, and institutions ought to behave, not just how they do.

normative international relations theory A general term used in the study of *international relations to denote theoretical approaches aimed at delivering analysis and conclusions about what states and peoples normatively 'should' or 'ought' to do within global politics and the *international system. This is usually, although wrongly, held as contrasted with empirical or descriptive theories, which seek to explain empirical phenomena within the international system and which purport to offer more 'objective' insights and explanations. A more useful distinction would be to consider normative international relations theory as aimed at providing both empirical analysis as well as analytical normative response to human conditions, from which to reconceptualize, re-examine, and rethink new possibilities for global politics, progress, and global cohabitation.

normative power A term often used in the study of *international relations to denote the influence of ethical and 'best practice' behaviour within the *international system. This is often contrasted with *hard power and *soft power, since the emphasis is on the diffusion of norms and ideas (often by example) as a means of gaining influence and promoting socializing compliance by other states. It is often argued that the *European Union exerts a form of normative power, since it offers a real-world example of political cooperation and stability for others to emulate.

North See GLOBAL NORTH.

North American Free Trade Agreement See NAFTA.

North Atlantic Treaty Organization See NATO.

Northcote–Trevelyan Report See CIVIL SERVICE.

Northern Ireland Northern Ireland's position within the United Kingdom is easily misunderstood. It appears full of paradox: a successful implementation of the Westminster model that went horribly wrong; ultra-loyal territory prepared to demonstrate its loyalty through acts of disloyalty; and a deeply conservative polity which (since 1972) has become an adventure playground for constitutional tinkering. Insofar as we can speak of the 'settlement' of the historic British–Irish conflict (embodied in the Government of Ireland Act 1920 and the Anglo-Irish Treaty 1921), it was a British success. Lloyd George's genius had been to extricate Britain from the Irish imbroglio at minimum cost. By establishing two parliaments and governments in Ireland he had quarantined the issue from British politics; reduced Irish representation at Westminster to 13 Northern Ireland MPs; and security control was transferred to indigenous forces. But the settlement did not alter the fact that the same actors remained with their conceptual approaches fundamentally intact. Part of the ambiguity lay in the transitional status of Ireland. The 1920 Act was about political pacification and its designers settled for the fashionable post-war device of *partition. The first elections for the Northern Ireland Parliament, based at Stormont, established the dominance of the Ulster Unionist Party (UUP) winning almost 70 per cent of all seats between 1921 and 1969. They set about shaping it in their own image, a policy that met no resistance from Westminster where a philosophy of 'let sleeping dogs lie' was adopted.

Consequently it was fashionable to examine Northern Ireland as a peculiar form of devolution within the UK until the mid-1960s: indeed it was like an autonomous state with a federal relationship to the United Kingdom. It did not enjoy full legitimation and stability was ensured by a security policy in which citizens became accustomed to the belief that the rule of law could always be suspended. Westminster's limited control meant that it was a reasonably successful example of administrative devolution. The result was the absence of an informed Whitehall view of the more controversial aspects of Northern Ireland politics. This situation encouraged unionist illusions of self-sufficiency and it created unspoken separatist tendencies. These tendencies were put to the test after the campaign for full civil rights for Catholics erupted in 1968 and led to intercommunal violence. Both governments were caught unawares. There had been minimal contact between North and South since 1922. Dublin had claimed Northern Ireland's territory and wrote this irredentism into its 1937 Constitution. There was low-level functional cooperation on matters such as energy, fisheries, and railways. With scant knowledge of conditions on the ground Dublin was forced into acting as 'second guarantor' of a reform programme produced rapidly by the Wilson government (to respond to Catholic grievances). London reacted angrily by declaring that the Northern Ireland problem was purely an internal affair. Neither the reform programme nor a security response returned stability to the province and by March 1972 Stormont was prorogued and direct rule was imposed.

Increasingly London was reduced to using the instruments of war rather than those of civil administration. This set Northern Ireland apart from the rest of the UK. Violence was prevalent even before Northern Ireland had been established. Unionists had used it to resist the Home Rule threat in the period before the Great War. Nationalists retorted with the 1916 Rising. The Irish Republican Army (IRA) again mounted a violent campaign between 1956 and 1962 but it failed to win popular (Catholic) support. So when the 'Troubles' erupted both communities reverted to familiar tactics. It was the incident known as Bloody Sunday (30 January 1972) when the British Army killed thirteen unarmed Catholic protesters that meant that the decision was taken that London could not rule by proxy. Catholics had withdrawn compliance from the state and Westminster politicians in the person of the first Secretary of State for Northern Ireland, William Whitelaw, soon appreciated that Northern Ireland did not fit into the usual parameters of British political practice. Direct rule was meant to be temporary but it was impossible to find political leaders who had the authority to speak unequivocally for their respective communities. In an attempt to build a 'strong centre' and weaken the Unionist monolith the government reintroduced proportional representation for Stormont elections—the Unionist government had abolished it in 1929. They succeeded in that the UUP held only about 23 per cent of the popular vote by 1998. A March 1973 White Paper added to unionism's humiliation. The Stormont Parliament was to be an 'Assembly', the Cabinet an 'Executive', the office of Governor was to be discontinued and no more Privy Councillors were to be appointed. But the strong centre remained illusory and the 'politics of the last atrocity' endured. Whitehall veered between a security response and institutional tinkering. Between 1972 and 1984 there were six successive sets of institutions, all of them based on an internal settlement. Only the 1974 *power-sharing government that lasted five months, brought down by massive loyalist intimidation, began to address the fundamentals. The two communities were represented on it, it was answerable to London and it had an Irish dimension. So it encompassed the four contending parties and was a

cautious attempt to probe their conceptual approaches. But it was ahead of its time because there was not sufficient trust between the governments; factionalism was rife in each community; and loyalist and republican paramilitaries were rampant.

By 1980, and under some international pressure, the governments began a series of summits that culminated in the signing of the Anglo-Irish Agreement (AIA) in November 1985. Although deeply unpopular with unionists it had the merit of placing the conflict in its proper British–Irish context. The AIA had three features of note: it gave the Irish government a strong role (that fell short of joint authority) in the politics of Northern Ireland; it increased considerably British–Irish security cooperation; and its structures were flexible enough to withstand any sustained popular (Protestant) opposition. The IRA noted the significance of security cooperation—Sinn Fein had decided in 1986 to contest and take their seats in a Dublin parliament. This was hugely symbolic because, since partition, they had rejected Dublin rule as being illegitimate. Equally loyalist paramilitaries began to look for radical political alternatives to violence. The Agreement was a watershed. It received international endorsement particularly from the United States and it was registered at the UN under Article 102 of the Charter. The failure of the unionist community to bring down the Agreement represented a milestone in British–Unionist relations. It was the first occasion in the last century that London had withstood their pressure on a vital constitutional matter. The final realization that power resided in London (and Dublin) led to significant attitudinal change over time. It registered in two 1987 think-pieces, the Ulster Defence Association's *Common Sense* (1987) and a Democratic Unionist Party/Ulster Unionist Party joint report *The Way Forward*. Politics was moving from zero-sum to inclusion and process for the first time ever in Northern Ireland. Despite continuing violence historic talks occurred between Sinn Fein and the SDLP (Social Democratic and Labour Party) during 1988. They did not succeed but neither did they fail and they were to be resurrected in the 1990s in the Hume/Adams talks. Attempts to remove unionism from its internal exile (in protest against the AIA) began in 1989 through the Secretary of State Peter Brooke and his successor from 1992. In the meantime the IRA held secret talks with an emissary of the British government between 1990 and 1993. The outcome was the December 1993 Downing Street Joint Declaration signed by the British and Irish prime ministers. It was a deliberate piece of tortuous syntax with one aim in mind—to persuade the IRA to a ceasefire. That happened on 31 August 1994 followed by a loyalist ceasefire on 13 October. But it was to be a hiatus. One of the flaws of the Joint Declaration was its ambiguity on decommissioning. During 1995 the British government made decommissioning of paramilitary weapons a precondition for entering all-party talks. The IRA reacted by planting a bomb in Canary Wharf in February 1996 and the ceasfire was at an end. During 1995 both governments had published the 'Joint Framework Document' to establish accountable government in Northern Ireland and to 'assist discussion and negotiation involving the Northern Ireland parties'. In November they launched a 'twin track' process to make progress in parallel on decommissioning and all-party negotiations. An international decommissioning panel, chaired by former US Senator George Mitchell, was created. Despite the breakdown of the IRA ceasefire a constitutional architecture (for a new Northern Ireland and for relations within the archipelago) was in place with substantial international endorsement. The missing links for success were an IRA commitment to peace and the political will in Britain to push through an inclusive package. The latter became possible after Labour's overwhelming victory in the May 1997 general election: the former followed. Blair set the multi-party talks for one year later with George Mitchell chairing. The *Belfast Agreement was finally reached on 10 April (Good Friday) and was endorsed by 71.1 per cent of the North's electorate and 94.39 per cent of the Republic's voters on 22 May 1998.

The 1998 Agreement revisited the problems identified in 1920 with a stronger sense of realism. It was an acknowledgement that the problem was British–Irish and that the first version of Northern Ireland had not worked. It recognized the three strands to the solution: relations within Northern Ireland; those between North and South; and

relations between Britain and Ireland—all of these playing alongside developments in British devolution and in the EU. It gave the people of Northern Ireland the right to determine their constitutional future through a more inclusive range of political opinion. And it placed proper emphasis on equity, diversity, and human rights issues. By the turn of the century Northern Ireland might still be a place apart within the UK but the agreement was being heralded as a model for other societies coming out of conflict. PA

Nozick, Robert (1939–2002) Philosopher, educated at Princeton University, New Jersey, and for many years based at Harvard University, Cambridge, Massachusetts. His first book, *Anarchy, State, and Utopia* (1974), is a major contribution to contemporary political philosophy. The book develops a radical, rights-based philosophy which supports a minimal state, eschewing income redistribution, confined to the task of providing security of person and property. In defence of the minimal state, Nozick sets out a striking 'entitlement theory of justice'. Individuals are said to be inviolable and, therefore, to be self-owning: to have full private ownership of their bodies and abilities. The world's resources are assumed to be initially unowned, but Nozick argues that these resources may be appropriated as private property provided that the act of appropriation does not make others worse off than they would be in a world where appropriation has not taken place ('justice in acquisition'), a weak proviso which permits considerable inequality in the ownership of external resources. With these just original holdings of persons and external resources in place, exchange may take place, and any distribution of holdings which emerges on the basis of subsequent voluntary exchanges is itself just. Forcible redistribution of holdings to promote equality will violate rights, and redistributive taxation of labour incomes in particular is 'on a par with forced labor' since it involves giving the beneficiaries of redistribution a property right in the productive abilities of the taxpayers. A large critical literature has emerged in response to this theory, probing the adequacy of Nozick's theory of justice in acquisition and the relationship between self-ownership and individual dignity and freedom. Nozick, however, turned away from political philosophy following publication of his first book towards metaphysics, epistemology, and the theory of rationality (*Philosophical Explanations*, 1981; *The Nature of Rationality*, 1993). He did register a disagreement with the theory set out in his first book in later work (*The Examined Life*, 1989), specifically concerning the right to inherit wealth. He also sought in later work to develop further the philosophical foundations for his belief in individual rights, foundations which some critics argued were lacking in his original theory. swe

Nuclear Non-Proliferation Treaty (NPT)

Officially named the Treaty on the Non-Proliferation of Nuclear Weapons, the NPT came into force in 1970. It was extended indefinitely in 1995. The NPT has two types of signatories: those states that had tested nuclear weapons before 1967 (NWS), of which there are five, China, France, Russia (the Soviet Union in 1970), the United States, and the United Kingdom; and non-nuclear weapon states (NNWS). Under the treaty, NWS keep their nuclear weapons in the short term, but commit to disarmament. They may not assist another state to acquire nuclear weapons. NNWS commit never to receive or develop nuclear weapons, and to accept International Atomic Energy Agency (IAEA) inspections to verify this. This does not negate a state's right to pursue nuclear energy capabilities.

Many NNWS are dissatisfied with NWS for slow progress in disarmament. Although NWS made strong commitment to disarm in the 2000 review conference, little progress has been made since and the 2005 conference was widely seen to have failed to back this commitment up. Although the treaty has 187 signatories, four states continue not to sign: Cuba, Israel, India, and Pakistan. The Democratic People's Republic of Korea withdrew in 2003. In the light of India and Pakistan's nuclear weapon tests in 1998, and Israel's nuclear weapon capability, this continues to diminish the NPT's success and

causes security concerns for NNWS. The Democratic People's Republic of Korea's withdrawal and later nuclear weapon test also diminishes belief in the effectiveness of the treaty. CT

⊕ SEE WEB LINKS

• Information on NPT from the United Nations.

nuclear proliferation Specifically, the spread of nuclear weapons, and, more generally, the spread of nuclear technology and knowledge that might be put to military use. Most concern is given to horizontal proliferation: the spread of nuclear weapons to states not yet possessing them. Vertical proliferation—the increase in numbers or dispersion of nuclear weapons by nuclear weapons states—has become of less concern since the winding down of the superpower arms race, although slow disarmament is of concern to non-nuclear states. Nuclear proliferation is controlled by the Nuclear Non-proliferation Treaty (NPT), which recognizes five nuclear states. However, some states remain outside the treaty and have developed nuclear capabilities. Increasingly, the prospect of nuclear weapons in the hands of terrorist organizations, such as al-Qaeda, is creating concern. Nuclear proliferation is widely considered to be a problem because of the fear that it will increase the probability of nuclear weapons being used. Some argue that nuclear proliferation could enhance international security by spreading the paralysing effects of *deterrence in regions that otherwise have a high probability of recurrent conventional war. Because of the close links between civil and military nuclear technology, many states are able to reduce the time necessary to acquire a nuclear weapon by acquiring a range of nuclear technologies for civil purposes. Several states have already achieved threshold status, in which they either have unannounced nuclear weapon capabilities, or could develop them extremely quickly if necessary. CT

n

Oakeshott, Michael (1901–90) British conservative political philosopher. In his best-known work, *Rationalism in Politics* (1947), he denounces the 'sceptical and optimistic' rationalist: 'He has no sense of the cumulation of experience . . . the past is significant to him only as an encumbrance . . . . To the Rationalist, nothing is of value merely because it exists.' Oakeshott's list of rationalist policies included 'the *Beveridge Report . . . Votes for Women, the Catering Wages Act . . . and the revival of Gaelic as the official language of Eire'. For Oakeshott, rationalism ignored 'practical knowledge [which] exists only in use and . . . cannot be formulated in rules'.

Oakeshott's anti-rationalism sought to undermine proponents of idealistic political ideologies; his alternative being a limited government based on the preservation of traditional constitutionalism. His polemic was less strident than that of *Hayek, but they shared a belief that government intervention should be limited, and restricted to facilitating individual freedom. For Oakeshott this implies a distinction between high and low politics; the former concerned with foreign policy, macroeconomic policy, and the balancing of a pluralistic society, the latter with micro-management and redistributional issues. Government should, as far as possible, be restricted to high politics, in which it should use its power with restraint and in accordance with conventions and traditional practices.

Oakeshott vigorously reasserted *Burkean conservatism, but faces a contradiction in that his espousal of a conservative philosophy confounded his view that ideological abstraction was invalid. In *On Human Conduct* (1975), he sought to develop a mode of theorizing about politics which would reconcile (the right sort of) abstraction with prescription. He developed a distinction between practice-based and moral association, and between civil and enterprise areas of state intervention. Oakeshott espoused a civic authority which was organized to reflect the customs of the people, administered through the rule of law, and the development of a pluralistic institutional structure. However, the desire to theorize solely about political practice, denuded of moral considerations, left a rather sterile approach when considering justifications for political reform and solutions to real social conflict.

OAS (Organization of American States) A body established in 1948 to further peace, security, mutual understanding, and cooperation among the states of the Western hemisphere. In the early 1960s it imposed sanctions against Cuba. Deep internal divisions have prevented effective cooperation since then. Latin American members have frequently voiced opposition to US policy. RG

(((∯))) SEE WEB LINKS
• OAS site, including membership and an overview of functions and history.

OAU (Organization of African Unity) *See* AFRICAN UNION.

obedience The conformity of one person to the will of another by the implementation of that person's orders and instructions. Unquestioning obedience involves a willingness to implement instructions without exceptions. In despotisms and absolute governments, as well as in certain religious and military organizations, such obedience has been considered a virtue, but in liberal, individualist societies it is considered morally reprehensible and dangerous. In experiments published in *Obedience to Authority* in 1974, the psychologist Stanley Milgram claimed to show that people in modern Western societies (principally, the United

States, West Germany, and Australia) were far more obedient than they ought to be according to established ethical theories. In a variety of social situations people obeyed orders, involving the apparent infliction of harm on others, which they ought to have disobeyed according to doctrines of the limits of authority inherent in prevailing ideas about rights, law, and liberty. Milgram offered his experimental evidence as an insight on acquiescence to the Third Reich, *inter alia*. He diagnosed a 'fatal flaw' in mankind, an excessive propensity to obey others, probably developed during the hunter-gatherer stage of human society. Others have criticized his use of data as far-fetched and excessively generalized.   LA

obligation To become obliged to do something is to 'bind oneself' to do it; 'oblige' and 'bind' are Latin and Anglo-Saxon equivalents. Thus obligations must be incurred by a specific act; typically, this act will be a promise, but promises take many forms, including debts, contracts, partnerships, marriages, treaties, and conventions. Often, therefore, it is functionally necessary that the incurring of an obligation be accompanied by some solemn ceremonial, a symbolizing of the commitment, involving rings, seals, bibles, signatures, or other suitably symbolic actions and artefacts. It is also important for the meaning of the obligation that it be made, and be seen to be made, voluntarily and not under duress.

In this strict sense, political obligation is a rare and elusive thing. Naturalized citizens of a country and commissioned military officers may have political obligations of a conditional form, but the vast majority of us did not choose the state into which we were born, have no real option to leave it, and have made it no promises. To derive a general obligation in this sense, to accept the state and to obey the directives of its officials, is to attempt to square the circle. Some of the most determined attempts to achieve this end are to be found in *Locke's Two Treatises of Government*, published in 1690. Locke derives a 'tacit' consent to the laws of a state in the mere act of travelling through that state's territory and an act of choice from the failure to emigrate to the great unclaimed lands of America. The first argument stretches meaning to destruction and

the second is now outdated. More recent theorists, such as Robert *Nozick and John *Rawls, have posited a hypothetical contract between the individual and the state; this argument suggests that we should ask of a state whether it is the sort of state we would join if states were the sort of things that are joined. This form of argument posits an interesting standard for the appraisal of states, but generates only hypothetical obligations, not real ones.

The strict sense of obligation is not the only sense. People often refer to obligations as if the word meant the same as 'duties'; in this sense our obligations are what we ought to do according to a set of rules which are deemed to apply to us irrespective of any consent or contract we may have made. When A talks about P's duties, he may mean what the law prescribes that P should do, or what it is generally expected in society that he should do or what A thinks he ought to do. All of these senses suggest empty and tautologous ideas of political obligation: 'You ought to obey the state because the (state) law says so' would be a dangerous proposition if it were not so unconvincing. Strict senses of obligation may render the question of political obligation unanswerable, but looser senses leave it meaningless.

Perhaps the most profound question about political obligation concerns whether we need a theory of obligation at all. Locke was convinced that he did need such a theory, both to justify the Glorious Revolution and to prevent permanent revolution. *Hume and Adam *Smith, writing over half a century later, under a more stable regime, considered such a theory to be as unnecessary as it was impossible. Benevolence and sympathy lead us to cooperate with each other and the needs of the general wellbeing urge us to a tolerant cooperation with the state. These are the real foundations of the stable commercial society which both welcome, and Hume suggests that they are far more secure foundations than would be a precise doctrine of obligation, which would prescribe when we should and should not accept the order imposed by the state.   LA

Ockham, William of (*c.*1285–1349) Philosopher who developed ideas on sovereignty and discussed natural rights. On sovereignty, he was original in the emphasis he placed on the right and freedom of the people to choose their ruler and form of government. On rights, which were mainly rights to property, he distinguishes between natural and conventional right, and both from permission. A natural right is a legitimate power (in conformity with right reason) that is anterior to human convention. The Franciscans have the natural right to property, which they renounce, yet they have permission to use things that they do not own, which is revocable (*usus nudus* or *facti*), as distinct from permission, which gives a right, for example tenancy (*usus juris*).   CB

OECD (Organization for Economic Co-operation and Development) International organization of thirty-four members, mainly high-income Western states, which undertakes research on economic development. It was originally the Organisation for European Economic Co-operation, established in 1948 to administer the Marshall Plan (*see* MARSHALL AID), but renamed the Organisation for Economic Co-operation and Development in 1961. The data collected and published by the OECD has provided a rich resource for political scientists working on comparative politics and political economy.

(⊕) SEE WEB LINKS
• OECD site, including a history of the organization and its predecessor, the Organisation for European Economic Co-operation.

offensive realism A form of *realism suggesting that states act to maximize power and international influence so as to create a position of *hegemony and security. This is opposed to *neorealism and *defensive realism, which claim that states pursue moderate and defensive policies in order to assure state/international security.

Office of Management and Budget (OMB) US executive agency, created in its present form in 1970, with responsibility for the preparation and administration of the federal budget. The OMB was established to increase the President's control over the federal bureaucracy.

(⊕) SEE WEB LINKS
• Office of Management and Budget site.

Office of the Director of National Intelligence *See* DIRECTOR OF NATIONAL INTELLIGENCE.

Official Secrets Acts The UK Official Secrets Act 1989 declared it unlawful to disclose information relating to defence, security and intelligence, international relations, intelligence gained from other departments or international organizations, intelligence useful to criminals, or the interception of communications. The Act replaced the all-embracing 1911 Official Secrets Act. The origins of reform lay in the failure of governments to successfully prosecute under the 1911 Act. In 1985 Clive Ponting, a Ministry of Defence civil servant who had disclosed information on the Falklands War to an MP, was acquitted under section 2(1)(a) of the 1911 Act on the grounds that he had disclosed information which the jury decided was in the interests of the state. Further, in 1988 the Law Lords ruled that *Spycatcher*, a book written by a former security service employee, Peter Wright, and already published abroad, could not be suppressed by the government. Hence, the specification of categories in the 1989 Act was designed to render crucial the nature of information disclosed, leaving motives for disclosure irrelevant, and thus ensuring successful prosecution if such cases arose again. Claims that the Act can lead to more open government through freedom of information on matters not included in the categories for non-disclosure are generally dismissed on the grounds that the categories for non-disclosure themselves are very broad. Generally, the 1989 Act increased state secrecy. *See also* FREEDOM OF INFORMATION.   JBr

(⊕) SEE WEB LINKS
• Text of the UK 1989 Official Secrets Act.

oligarch Used to refer to Russian businessmen with strong (but often covert) political connections, who made huge fortunes out of market liberalization and *privatization programmes during the break-up of the USSR and the subsequent restructuring of the Russian economy.

oligarchy Government by the few. The logically exclusive categories of government by one, the few, or the many have been widely deployed, but the terminology has varied. For example, *aristocracy is a form of government by the few. *Aristotle distinguished between rulers who govern in the general interest (aristocracy) and rulers who govern in their own interest (oligarchy). Sociologists have made claims about a necessary connection between organization and oligarchy. *See also* ELITISM; IRON LAW OF OLIGARCHY. AR

oligopoly Market in which there are few sellers, so that they can control the price and/or quantity of goods supplied, by explicit collusion or game-theoretic strategy. Most political markets, such as the market in which political parties sell policies, are oligopolistic.

Olson, Mancur (1932–98) American economist with huge influence on political science. His first name was pronounced with a soft 'c'. He wrote three big books—big in ideas although not in bulk. The most influential was the first, *The Logic of Collective Action* (1965). Olson pointed out that all lobbies aim to change policy, and a policy is, in the technical sense, a *public good: it is jointly supplied (everybody gets it) and non-excludable. Some policies are, indeed, more public than others: environmental or income-tax policy affects everybody, whereas a tax break or protection for a particular industry benefits only those in that industry, although it is still a public good from the point of view of those in the industry. There is always a temptation to *free-ride on public goods. Almost always, the good will either be provided even if I do not contribute to the lobby for it, or will not be provided even if I do. Only in the case where the beneficiaries are few and the benefit per beneficiary large is it at all likely that my individual decision to contribute or not will make any difference to the chances of the lobby's success. Classical *pluralists had argued that there were as many, and as intense, interest groups as there were interests, and that the interplay of those groups was the essence of democracy. Those groups that succeeded represented the largest and/or most intense interests, and therefore all was as it should be. Olson showed that this could not be so. Each lobby must overcome its own free-rider problem. The fewer the potential members of the group, and/or the

greater benefit per member from the desired policy, the fewer will be the free-riders. Normally there are fewer producers than consumers in any industry, and among the producers, fewer capitalists than labourers. Therefore, expect trade associations to be the strongest lobbies; trade unions weaker; and consumers the weakest of all. In turn, therefore, expect policies to be biased in favour of producer interests such as industrial protection and against consumer interests such as free trade.

In *The Rise and Decline of Nations* (1982) Olson went on to argue that the older the traditions of free association in a polity were, the more 'sclerotic' would be its policies, because producer interests would have the strongest hold over policy. Therefore polities like Britain, the northern USA, Australia, and India were growing slowly, whereas those like Japan or Germany (whose special interests had been destroyed by war and conquest), the US south and west, or the newly industrializing countries of Asia were growing rapidly. When growth rates changed in the 1990s, with *Anglo-Saxon capitalism doing better than *Rheinish or Asian capitalism, some said that Olson had got it wrong; others that policy-makers had listened to Olson and broken up their producer-group lobbies. Certainly, the UK, Australia, and New Zealand did so. In *Power and Prosperity* (2000), Olson shifted ground. He first showed that it is better to be ruled by a stationary bandit than by a roving bandit. Even a Stalin or a Saddam Hussein has a rational interest in allowing his citizens to continue to lay enough golden eggs to be taken in future years, rather than in plundering and moving on. And the wider the suffrage, the more 'encompassing' becomes the interest of the rulers in the wealth and growth of the polity they rule. So the fast-growing countries are now those that have got good institutions, where investors have reasonable confidence that they will not lose their returns through default or expropriation. And the former Soviet empire was exposed as a place where, after Stalin's reign of terror ended, business could continue only by the cooperation of special interests, thus explaining its low or negative growth after the collapse of communism.

Olson died before the tensions between his second and third books could be resolved.

ombudsman Term of Scandinavian origin, the relevant meaning of which is grievance officer. Hence, throughout Europe an ombudsman is a public official who investigates citizens' complaints against maladministration in specified areas of public administration. The United Kingdom introduced three types in the 1960s and 1970s: the parliamentary commissioner for administration (PCA, created 1967); the health service commissioners (HSC, 1973); and the commissioners for local administration (CLA, 1976). This reflected concern to reform the *accountability of government on the basis of continental European models. Further types of ombudsman were established from the mid-1990s. This was due, first, to concern to ensure administrative redress following state privatization or deregulation. Hence, the independent (social) housing ombudsman was created in 1997, and ombudsman schemes for banking, insurance, building societies, and pensions were established under the Financial Services and Markets Act, 2000. Secondly, ombudsmen were established following devolution to ensure administrative redress accompanied the territorial decentralization of the state. The Scottish Parliament, Welsh Assembly, Northern Ireland Assembly, and Northern Ireland Police Service all appointed their own ombudsmen in 1998-9, and in 2002-3 in both Scotland and Wales integrated offices of public services ombudsmen were created. The application of the idea was also widened within British central government. In 1999 a further 158 public bodies were placed under the remit of the original PCA post. Parliament itself applied the idea in creating the parliamentary commissioner for standards in 1999, effectively an ombudsman for MPs. The Treaty of Amsterdam in 1997 further established a European ombudsman to investigate complaints of administrative error against EU institutions.

By international comparison the number of cases examined by British ombudsmen is low, a fact often taken as an indication of high standards in British public administration, but at least in part a function of public ignorance of the existence and role of ombudsmen. Elected representatives at all levels of government have been keen not to see alternative figures of public accountability arise at the expense of their perceived

competence, and have therefore under-resourced ombudsmen. The highly restrictive jurisdiction of ombudsmen also means that many complaints cannot be investigated. Reviews in the early 2000s of the proliferation of ombudsmen focused on the desirability of joint working and coordination to offer a clearer and more effective service. *See also* JUDICIAL REVIEW; MALADMINISTRATION. JBr

one member one vote (OMOV) *See* CANDIDATE SELECTION; LEADERSHIP SELECTION.

one-party states Those states where a single party is accorded a legal or *de facto* monopoly of formal political activity. This may be enforced under the constitution, or it may be a consequence of denying rival parties access to the electorate, or of a failure to consult the electorate at all. Alternatively, the electorate may be selectively defined, or consultation be otherwise manipulated, so as to ensure the return of the governing party. Until recently one-party states came under two main categories: so-called totalitarian states, mostly but not exclusively communist and East European; and numerous Third World states where authoritarian regimes have long had recourse to a single party to control administration, mobilize support, and supervise distribution of the available patronage. With the collapse of communism, the one-party state is now largely confined to areas of the Third World, including some former republics and autonomous territories of the Soviet Union. It is distinct from the dominant party system where, as in post-war Italy or post-independence India, a single party has predominated in central government, but sometimes sharing power and within an otherwise competitive party system with representative institutions. Military governments are also a distinct form of monist government; in the course of the 1990s some military regimes sought to gain a degree of legitimacy by converting themselves into party-based government.

The one-party state remains most entrenched in Africa, where it appeared shortly after independence and was able to draw on a legacy of autocratic colonial rule, with only a brief experience of contested elections at the very end of decolonization.

In a few cases, as in former Tanganyika, effective opposition to the ruling party had disappeared even before independence. Everywhere the ruling party had very considerable advantages denied its opponents. Starting as a successful nationalist movement or front, it was able soon after independence to profit from its control of the state and the expanded patronage now readily available. It sought to secure itself in office by suppressing its opponents. Usually, elections were restricted, or closely controlled, or replaced by the occasional plebiscite. Preventive Detention Acts, an unfortunate legacy of colonial rule, were revived and used extensively. The one-party state was presented as a means of achieving national unity, overcoming ethnic separatism, and hastening economic development and national independence. The stated justification was the need for nation-building above the sectional appeal of tribal loyalty which would, it was claimed, undermine imported 'Western' liberal democratic governmental institutions. Sometimes appeal was made to supposed pre-colonial government forms whose consultation process (analogous to the deliberations of tribal elders) was purportedly better suited to African circumstances. In most cases it was simply an adjunct of personal rule with the party confined in a strictly limited and essentially subordinate role: little more than an agency for recruitment to the government, a conduit for political patronage, and a check on the loyalty of the armed forces and the civil service.

Since 1989 the African one-party states have been under mounting domestic and international pressure to liberalize both politically and economically. Some African states, notably Botswana and the Gambia, have had a continuous history of contested elections, which, however, did not threaten the ruling party. Others, like Senegal since the 1970s, have experimented first with limited, and then with unrestricted, party competition, but without a change of government. With the 1990s, however, entrenched one-party regimes became vulnerable in the changing domestic and international environment. In the French-speaking states, representative national conferences were convened with the self-appointed task of drafting new constitutions and supervising free and open elections. By this means incumbent rulers were forced to quit in Benin, Congo, Niger, and eventually Madagascar. In Algeria the transition from a one-party state, under the Front de Libération Nationale (National Liberation Front), was already well advanced until the military intervened to reverse the process, fearing a landslide victory by the Islamic opposition party, Front Islamique du Salut (Islamic Salvation Front). In Zimbabwe, President Robert Mugabe's unwillingness to recognize the electoral success of the Movement for Democratic Change led to a political crisis in 2008.

In English-speaking Africa free elections were conceded in Zambia by President Kaunda, UNIP (United National Independence Party) leader, who was then himself defeated. President Arap Moi relaxed his opposition to multi-party elections in Kenya, previously a one-party state *de jure*, and won a plurality of votes mainly because of a split in the opposition ranks. Most important, the ruling National Party in South Africa, entrenched in government since 1948, surrendered power to the *ANC in the first democratic elections, in 1994. Since the first half of the 1990s, many of those one-party states whose ruling party lost power have reverted to the rule of a different single party. In others the entrenched position of the *de facto* single-party government has not been overcome in the absence of significant external pressure. IC/RTC

ontology The theory or philosophy of being. In contrast to *epistemology—or theory of knowledge—ontology is concerned with what exists and what should be considered real. Called 'first philosophy' by Aristotle, ontology is considered the basis of metaphysics or the real nature of things. Ontological questions include those that ask of the nature of these things. Are they independent of our knowledge? Are such things matter or forms? What are their main characteristics, features, or causes? One branch of philosophy which includes *hermeneutics, *phenomenology, and *constructivism would argue that such entities are inseparable from the knowledge we have of them. Realists would argue that they are mind-independent. This would be a view of the world as objective as opposed to the constructivist view of the world—or at least the social world—as intersubjectively constituted and the phenomenological view that objects are bound up with our mental activities. In politics, an ontological question might concern the main actors or the main causes of something. For example, are states real? Are nations the product of collective beliefs? Are nation states still the main actors in global politics? Rather than disputing our understanding of such things, an ontological approach would seek answers in an examination of the things themselves.   JJ

OPEC (Organization of the Petroleum Exporting Countries) OPEC, originally the inspiration of Venezuela and Iran, is an intergovernmental organization composed of thirteen oil-producing countries: Algeria, Angola, Ecuador, Gabon, Iran, Iraq, Kuwait, Libya, Nigeria, Qatar, Saudi Arabia, United Arab Emirates, and Venezuela (and formerly Indonesia). OPEC was founded in 1960 in reaction to the pricing and production policies of the major oil companies in 1959 and 1960. OPEC supplies approximately 40 per cent of world production and 60 per cent of oil exports.

Throughout most of the 1960s, the major Western oil producers in the Middle East and elsewhere pursued production strategies that led to a surplus of oil in the international markets, contributing to a downward push in real oil prices. By 1970, market conditions began an upward trend in oil prices. Demand rose dramatically and began to outpace the supply of oil. With the October War of 1973, a revolutionary change in the oil market occurred when Arab oil producers of OPEC—the Organization of Arab Petroleum Exporting Countries (OAPEC)—imposed an oil embargo upon the US and the Netherlands for their support of Israel. This was followed by the quadrupling of the price of oil by OPEC to $10.84 per barrel. These developments continued through to 1978 during which time many of the OPEC governments nationalized the oil companies operating on their territory. OPEC now had the ability to determine production and sales policies and to set oil policies.

This change in the structure of the oil market dramatically altered the balance of power in the energy markets and radically disrupted the financial flow of international reserves. Arab oil monarchies were in receipt of vast petro-dollar reserves which they invested mainly in Europe and the US. This dramatic increase in incomes financed the great economic boom of the 1970s and early 1980s in the Middle East while contributing to a slower more erratic economic growth in the industrialized world. A second oil price rise of 1979/80 to nearly $40 a barrel resulted in falling world prices, in particular in commodity prices. Oil prices, however, soon began to decline until the price collapse in 1986 to a low at one point of $8.

OPEC itself had and has no internal unity except on the matter of setting production limits on oil to their advantage—and even here unity is not always evident. Saudi Arabia is the only oil producer that can raise (as it did during the *Gulf War of 1991) or lower its oil production by millions of barrels per day without seriously affecting its own economy or polity. OPEC has come under increasing pressure resulting from its inability to devise production strategies that would appeal to the diverse interests of its members. Developments in extraction technology and pipeline transport have reduced costs significantly. In addition, substantial oil fields are continuing to be discovered in Central Asia, Russia, Latin America, and elsewhere. The dramatic rise in oil prices from 2001, exceeding $100 per barrel from January 2008, had little to do with OPEC production strategy and more to do with market speculation involved with the *Financial Crisis. In addition, with increased oil discoveries outside OPEC countries and new technologies such as 'fracking'—which allows for once economically unobtainable shale oil to be competitively welled—the strategic influence of OPEC continues to be questioned.   BAR

(⊕) SEE WEB LINKS
• OPEC site, including information on the history, structure, and functions of the organization.

open economy politics A research paradigm in the field of *international political economy. The paradigm is used to explain state behaviour in an open and globalized economy through rationalist theories and *quantitative methods. Open economy politics is closely associated with the so-called 'American School' of international political economy that itself is characterized by objective observation and systematic testing. LS

open primary Primary election at which voters are free to choose which party they wish to select the candidate for. Subject to manipulation, as supporters of one party can attempt to obtain the nomination of the weakest candidate of an opposing party by voting in their opponents' primary.

open rule See CLOSED RULE.

Operation Black Vote Campaign which seeks to improve the influence of members of African, Asian, and Caribbean communities in UK politics, aiming to broaden participation in electoral politics.

(⊕) SEE WEB LINKS

• Operation Black Vote website.

opinion polls Surveys designed to discover the attitudes and/or intended or recalled behaviours of political actors; these may be leaders, legislators, bureaucrats, or electors. Such polls may be conducted by a variety of means, including telephoning, face-to-face interviewing, and web questionnaires. Ideally samples should be random with each member of the target population having a known probability of selection, because with this method the range of error can be quantified. This is how telephone polls are conducted, although some have concerns as to the extent to which people are all equally available at the end of a landline. For face-to-face polls, random sampling is prohibitively expensive and too slow, and so the traditional method for such polls is quota sampling, whereby an attempt is made to replicate the social distribution of the population (according to factors such as age, gender, and social status) among the sample. The assumption is that if the sample is representative socially it will be similarly representative in its political views. This assumption led to poor forecasts at the 1992 general election in the UK. Quota polls are now rarely used, having been largely replaced by telephone and internet polls. Although the sampling is far from random and web users are a very unrepresentative subset of the electorate, internet polling companies can maintain large panels of respondents and produce predictions that adjust for selection bias and weight responses according to previous voting behaviour to ensure a more accurate result. See also SURVEY RESEARCH. SF

ordinal level variable See MEASUREMENT.

organic analogy Any form of explanation of politics by drawing an analogy to a human or animal body, or ecological system. For example, in Shakespeare's *Coriolanus*, the aristocrat Menenius Agrippa describes the plebeians' revolt by a parable beginning, 'There was a time when all the body's members | Rebelled against the belly.' In the philosophy of science, analogy has traditionally been regarded as a species of inductive reasoning. Consequently, the problem of the justification of analogical argument is usually understood in terms of the strength of inductive support. The new and unfamiliar is often explained analogically in terms of the familiar and intelligible. The notion that social entities are essentially like organic systems and capable of being explained by the laws of those systems is one of the commonest features of modern European thinking, a feature perhaps which reached its fullest development with Herbert *Spencer. What Spencer and many other Victorian organicists tended to ignore, however, was that individual organisms have a centre of consciousness, society does not. And while societies may well be more than the aggregate of their parts, in itself this does not constitute an argument that societies are organisms. JH

Organization for Economic Co-operation and Development See OECD.

Organization for Security and Co-operation in Europe (OSCE) The Organization for Security and Co-operation in Europe was originally the Conference on Security and Co-operation in Europe (CSCE) (renamed in 1994). Its origins lay in talks held in Helsinki in 1973, attended by the members of NATO, the Warsaw Pact, and the European neutral states. The Helsinki agreement (1975) was the outcome of several years of negotiation between the two Cold War alliances and represented one of the notable achievements of *détente, given that CSCE worked by consent and lacks any system of majority voting. The agreement covered a declaration of principles (including non-violability of boundaries, non-intervention, and territorial integrity of states), and three 'baskets' of areas of agreement including confidence-building measures such as advance notification of military manoeuvres (basket one), economic and other cooperation (basket two), and humanitarian and human rights cooperation (basket three). While the Soviets emphasized the declaration of principles and basket two, NATO gave greater emphasis to basket three.

The end of the Cold War transformed the situation, and the meeting in Paris in 1990 concluded the 'Charter of Paris for a new Europe', which normalized relations between the European states. Membership has expanded to over fifty, and includes the states of the former Soviet Union, including the new states of Central Asia. The OSCE played a part in the peacekeeping operation that followed the wars in Bosnia and Kosovo, and under the Charter on European Security (adopted in 1999) sought to consolidate this role. It is thus a part of the new architecture of European security but its consensual nature prevents it from playing a central role in the development of security arrangements for Eastern Europe. PBY

(⊕) SEE WEB LINKS

• Organization for Security and Co-operation in Europe site, including a history.

Organization of African Unity *See* AFRICAN UNION.

Organization of American States *See* OAS.

Organization of Petroleum Exporting Countries *See* OPEC.

oriental despotism Traditional concept used by *Montesquieu in his account of the influence of climate and physical geography on political structures ('power should always be despotic in Asia': *The Spirit of the Laws*). The idea was echoed in *Marx's account of the *Asiatic mode of production and revived by K. Wittfogel in his *Oriental Despotism* (1957). According to Wittfogel, oriental societies depended on massive irrigation which had to be centrally planned. He called the outcome 'hydraulic society'. Students of *comparative government now think that such generalizations are too broad to be useful.

orientalism From Orient and oriental as descriptions of the East, etymologically from '[the sun] rising'. Brought into recent political vocabulary through *Orientalism*, a study of historical literature and art in Europe by Edward Said (1978). Said argued that 'The Orient is not only adjacent to Europe; it is also the place of Europe's greatest and richest and oldest colonies, the source of its civilizations and languages, its cultural contestant, and one of its deepest and most recurring images of the Other. In addition, the Orient has helped to define Europe (or the West) as its contrasting image, idea, personality, experience. Yet none of this Orient is merely imaginative.' In other words, orientalism is underpinned by the material basis of imperialist exploitation and exercise of power. This is evident, according to Said, in the creating of a consensus about the 'other', the oriental nations, that encompassed not only the Western world but also the elites of those nations. Western education, literature, and art became dominant because of the economic and political dominance of the imperialist countries. Power, or the lack thereof, therefore, lies at the heart of the orientalist discourse and allows the stabilization of the consensus that is critical to the maintenance of dominance. Said emphasizes that orientalist discourses are not a thing of the past, and that they imbue the political vocabulary that we use today in our understandings of the nations of the developing world. SR

original intent *See* JUDICIAL ACTIVISM.

original jurisdiction The right of a court, usually a minor or trial court, to hear a case at its inception.

Orwell, George (1903–50) Pseudonym of the English novelist Eric Blair. Most of his novels, memoirs, and essays had a political content and contained sharply expressed prejudices against imperialism, capitalism, middle-class narrow-mindedness, and euphemistic and inelegant English. *Burmese Days* (1934) describes Orwell's experiences as an imperial policeman, *The Road to Wigan Pier* (1937) is an extended essay on socialism stimulated by a visit to Lancashire during the depression, and *Homage to Catalonia* (1938) is based on Orwell's experiences during the first year of the Spanish Civil War.

However, Orwell's writings would be of little interest to the scholar of politics *per se*, if it were not for the passionate antitotalitarian ideas which he began to develop in the late 1930s. Orwell put together his experience of the duplicity of orthodox communists (described in *Homage to Catalonia*) with the theory of power developed in Bertrand *Russell's Power: A New Social Analysis* (1938). A minor product of this combination was the satirical novel *Animal Farm* (1945) which portrays the communist revolution as a takeover of a farm by its animals. Its major product was *Nineteen Eighty-Four* (1949), which developed Russell's thesis of the limitless power of the modern state into a nightmare of the future. Orwell takes many of Russell's arguments almost verbatim and puts them into the mouth of O'Brien, a secret policeman. The state cannot be resisted; it can control thought. It can make its citizens believe that '2 + 2 = 5', that 'Freedom is Slavery' and that 'War is Peace'. Not only dissent and individual autonomy are eradicated, but also the capacity for clear thought in a Britain which has lost even its name.

Nineteen Eighty-Four was not an accurate prophecy. The vision, and the theory of power which inspired it, can be said to be dated, the product of a period which combined a vast, often newly urbanized, working class with the technological potential for a state monopoly of the means of communication. However, it remains one of the most powerful anti-utopian visions ever constructed and has functioned, to some degree, as a self-denying prophecy. LA

Oslo agreement *See* INTIFADA, PLO.

Osmotherly rules *See* SELECT COMMITTEE.

Ostpolitik 'Eastern policy': the Federal Republic of Germany's efforts to normalize relations with the Soviet Union, the German Democratic Republic, Poland, and other communist bloc countries from 1966 until German reunification in 1989. KT

Ostrogorski, Moisei (1854–1919) Russian political scientist, famous for *Democracy and the Organization of Political Parties*, published in 1902 in two volumes, one dealing with Britain and one with the United States. Ostrogorski dealt with masses of documentation that parties were under the control of unrepresentative enthusiasts—in this criticism of representative democracy he was a precursor of *Schumpeter.

Owen, Robert (1771–1858) Pioneer British communitarian socialist, advocating cooperative experiments on the scale of between 2,000 and 3,000 people. He put his ideas into practice at New Lanark in Scotland (founded in 1800) and at New Harmony, Indiana (from 1824 to 1829). The clearest exposition of the ideas which underpinned his approach to social reform is to be found in *A New View of Society* (1812–13), and in particular the theory is put forward that human character and behaviour are always shaped by the social environment. Accordingly, it was Owen's lifelong belief that the amelioration of social conditions and intelligent organization of the labour process were the necessary means for the creation of greater equality, justice, and human happiness. Like *Fourier and *Marx, Owen recognized the problem of the mechanization of the labour process under industrialism as a potentially enslaving force, and his own solution was to advocate the communal ownership and control of the means of production. This vision of small-scale *communism was also linked to pioneering ideas on the possibility of replacing money as a medium of exchange by the free distribution of essential goods and services according to need. Owen emphasized the process of gradual, peaceful reform as the only realistic way to improve society. In his later years he began to embrace religious fundamentalism as a source of inspiration for the creation of 'a new moral world', and he began to speak and write of the future socialist order as a new *millennium signalling the Second Coming of Christ. This inspirational gospel coloured Owenism as an influential social movement in Britain in the 1830s, and Owenite ideas also had an impact on the emergence and development of early trade unionism. KT

PAC (UK) *See* Public Accounts Committee.

PAC (USA) Political action committees, or PACs, are organizations in the United States that obtain contributions from individuals and distribute donations to candidates for political office. PACs may contribute no more than $5,000 per candidate per election, but may contribute larger sums for so-called party-building activities. The rapid growth in the number of PACs, the amounts of money involved, and the danger of their supplanting parties have been the subject of concern.

In 2010 a series of US court decisions (most notably *Citizens United* v. *Federal Election Commission*) allowed for the creation of what are known as 'Super PACs' or 'independent expenditure-only committees'. These Super PAC committees, unlike traditional PACs, cannot directly make contributions to candidates or to a party. However, also unlike traditional PACs, they are able to raise and spend unlimited donations on political activities and political campaigning as long as they operate independently of a candidate's official campaign and party. Although new donation disclosure rules and laws limiting aligned coordination strategies have been instituted, critics suggest that Super PACs have undermined both the primary process (the party leader election) as well as local and national elections. One particular side effect of Super PACs has been a sharp increase in political advertising for particular candidates and/or negative advertisement strategies against an opposition candidate or proposition. This has lead to hours of tedious and often spurious advertisements on television, particularly in 'swing states' where electoral races are close. Yet, the main argument against Super PACs is that they can raise tremendous amounts of money (in 2012 one Super PAC alone raised $40 million to support Mitt Romney for US President), thus having disproportionate influence on elections and their outcomes. DM

pacifism Rejection of war as a means of settling disputes. Associated with various schools of thought, for example *Gandhiism, *Quakerism. Some writers have reintroduced the word 'pacificism' (rejection of violent solutions to the particular question in dispute) to distinguish it from pacifism. Thus, most of those who opposed Britain's going to war with Hitler in the 1930s were pacificists; few were pacifists.

Paine, Thomas (1737–1809) Thomas (Tom) Paine, English deist and radical, born in Thetford, is best remembered in England for his outspoken republicanism, chiefly expressed in *Rights of Man* (1791–2), a vindication of the French Revolution written in reply to *Burke's *Reflections on the Revolution in France*. Paine had already achieved fame in the American colonies, where his anti-monarchical pamphlet *Common Sense* is credited with boosting the independence cause.

In England, Paine associated with reformers such as *Godwin. He fled to France in 1792, following a Royal Proclamation against seditious writings. He was subsequently outlawed *in absentia*. Initially honoured in France, where he mixed with *Condorcet and *Girondin moderates, he was imprisoned by the Jacobins.

Paine, a self-educated man, was more a propagandist than philosopher. He disseminated important ideas like natural rights, equality, majority rule, and a written constitution, in an easily accessible form. He said his country was the world and his religion was to do good. He died in relative obscurity in America in 1809. Thomas *Jefferson provided a fitting epitaph: 'it will be your glory to have steadily laboured, and with as much effect as any man living'. PBl

pairing Parliamentary practice where members voting opposite ways on legislation agree to be absent from the chamber when votes are taken, without affecting the outcome of the vote.

Palestine Liberation Organization *See* PLO; INTIFADA.

panachage In a list system of proportional representation, the procedure for allowing voters to select candidates from more than one party; the practice of such selection.

Pan-Africanism A movement, founded around 1900, to secure equal rights, self-government, independence, and unity for African peoples. Inspired by Marcus Garvey, it encouraged self-awareness on the part of Africans by encouraging the study of their history and culture. Leadership came from the Americas until the Sixth Pan-African Congress, in Manchester, UK, in 1945, which saw the emergence of African nationalist figures, notably Kwame *Nkrumah and Jomo Kenyatta, with a programme of African 'autonomy and independence'. With independence, however, the concept of a politically united Africa was soon replaced by the assertion—within colonial frontiers—of competing national interests. *See also* AFRICAN UNION. IC

Pan-Arabism The idea that the Arabs are a distinct people with a common language, history, and culture. Pan-Arabism emerged in the former Arab provinces of the Ottoman Empire. When the shock of the disappearance of the Ottoman Empire, followed by the imposition of the Mandates at the expense of the Arab Kingdom of the Amir Faisal in 1920, settled in upon the Arabs, some argued that Pan-Arabism had emerged as a substitution for Pan-Islamism with the more narrowed focus on the Arabs rather than on Muslims. For others, it was an expression of resistance to the colonialism of Britain and France which had imposed a territorial division upon the region. For yet others, Pan-Arabism was an expression of opposition to the effort of the newly formed states and governments of the mandates to encourage separate national identities.

Arab nationalism is generally referred to as a Pan-Arabist ideology incorporating the above ideas. This ideology was strongly influenced by the ideas of Sati' al-Husri (1879–1968), a Syrian who studied in France, Switzerland, and Belgium, who in turn had been influenced by German romantic nationalists and their ideas of the nation. Al-Husri saw the Arab nation, comprising the Arab east and North Africa, as a cultural community further united by a common language. It was a common language and a shared history that formed the basis for a national identity and a nation. It is only within the nation that a people could modernize and progress. His view of the Arab nation was inclusive of all groups and races speaking the Arabic language in the Middle East including North Africa. His was a secular concept of Arab nationalism with the added ultimate political objective of Arab unity. This latter was interpreted by the *Ba'athists as meaning the formation of a single independent Arab state incorporating the Arab nation. The other main view of Arab unity associated with Jamal Abd al-Nasir was that of solidarity among Arab governments, concerned less with the abstractions of nationalism than with the pragmatic economic and social concerns and the importance of unity of the Arab world in the face of predatory blocs.

While Arabism, the foundation of the *ethnos* in Arab nationalism, did not deny the Islamic element, the Pan-Arab nationalism that evolved was secular in character. Until the humiliating defeat by Israel in the June 1967 war, it attracted the hopes and support of the peoples of the Middle East and North Africa. This defeat had the corrosive effect of undermining faith in an already weakening ideology that had served as a guide, a strategy, and driving force in the region that competed with other developing local nationalisms. It was apparent that Arab governments were neither inclined to integrate, nor able to unite on the basis of solidarity, nor cooperate to defeat the Zionist state of Israel. From this point onward, Pan-Arab nationalism began to lose ground to political Islam. BAR

pancasila The official ideology of the Indonesian state. The word means 'five principles', which are democracy, humanitarianism, justice, monotheism, and unity.

panel study/survey A *longitudinal study in which variables are measured on the same units over time. For example, British Election Panel Studies have interviewed respondents after one election and again after the following election, and sometimes at various points in between. Panel surveys are particularly useful for understanding change at the individual level. Although *cross-sectional studies can be used to estimate change by asking questions about past behaviour, such as vote choice at the last election, the answers can be unreliable. Furthermore, panel studies help avoid relying on aggregate data across time (*see* ECOLOGICAL ASSOCIATION). However, they usually suffer from panel attrition—increasing levels of non-response with each successive 'wave' of the panel. Another potential problem is panel conditioning in which responses and/or behaviour are affected by membership of the panel.   SF

Pankhurst family Emmeline Pankhurst (1858-1928) and her daughters Christabel (1880-1958) and Sylvia (1882-1960). The mother and daughters were leaders of the English *suffragette movement. In 1903 they formed the Women's Social and Political Union (WSPU), and adopted the slogan 'Votes for Women'. They adopted tactics of disruption, arson, and window-breaking to argue for their rights.   STH

panscheel Five principles of *Nehru's foreign policy, arrived at in 1954 in negotiations with China. They were: mutual respect for each other's territorial integrity, mutual non-aggression, mutual non-interference, equality and mutual benefit, and peaceful coexistence.

pantouflage The practice of moving quickly on retirement from a public-sector position into a (usually lucrative) private-sector one, from the French *pantoufles*, slippers. The practice is common (and controversial) in Britain, the word less so.

paradox of voting 1. The majority-rule *cycle whereby, given at least three voters and at least three options, there may be a majority for x over y, for y over z, and for z over x simultaneousl y. In the minimal case where this may arise, one voter has $x>y>z$, a second has $y>z>x$, and a third has $z>x>y$, where > means 'I prefer the former to the latter'. This is not paradoxical, merely

surprising. The term cycle (sometimes *Condorcet cycle after its discoverer) is preferred.

2. In his highly influential *An Economic Theory of Democracy* (1957), Anthony Downs popularized the idea of treating political actors like economic ones, and analysing their actions with economists' tools. Thus the rational voter would vote for his or her favourite party if and only if the value to that voter of a government led by the party he or she favoured, multiplied by the probability that his or hers was the vote that brought this about, exceeded the cost of voting. However, the probability of being decisive in this sense is infinitesimally small in a normal election: so why does anybody vote? This has alternatively been labelled the 'paradox of rational abstention' on the argument that it seems to be rational to abstain but surprisingly few people do so.

pardon (Presidential) The US President may issue proclamations that have the force of law, freeing individuals from the legal consequences of any crime except impeachment. In 1974 President Gerald Ford pardoned Richard Nixon, preventing any prosecutions for crimes that may have been committed by Nixon during his Presidency.

Pareto, Vilfredo (1848-1923) Italian sociologist and economist. His sociology (*The Mind and Society*, 1935) was once highly influential, but now only his arguments about the inevitable domination of political structure by *elites survive. His work as an economist, by contrast, is much more influential than in his own day. He has given his name to a number of linked concepts which must be carefully distinguished:

1 *The Pareto condition*. If a move from state of affairs A to another (B) leaves nobody feeling worse off than before and at least one person feeling better off, the move satisfies the Pareto condition (or criterion or principle), and the move itself is called a Pareto improvement or just Paretian. B is then Pareto-superior to A, which is Pareto-inferior to B.

2 *Pareto-optimality*. If there is a state of affairs C such that no (further) Pareto improvements can be made, C is Pareto-optimal. That is, it is a situation in which nobody can be made to feel better off except

by making at least one person feel worse off. The set of all Pareto optima is called the Pareto frontier.

The various Paretian concepts are central to *welfare economics and *social choice, for both technical and ideological reasons. A choice procedure which ranked some A above some B, even though everybody prefers B to A, violates the Pareto principle even in its weakest possible formulation and therefore seems perverse; nevertheless, some apparently reasonable voting procedures do just that. This strange fact is used in the proof of Arrow's *impossibility theorem. Ideologically, welfare economists have seized on the Pareto principle because it has seemed value-free. Arguments about redistribution of income and wealth are necessarily value-laden, so it is regarded as uncontroversial to accept all and only Pareto improvements as improvements in welfare. This is linked to a defence of free trade, free markets, and libertarianism. A trade in which P offers money to Q in exchange for R is Paretian: P would rather have the goods than the money and Q would rather have the money than the goods. After the trade, they both feel better off, whether R happens to be an apple, a quantity of shares, or the rent of Q's property for a while.

Critics of the claim that the Pareto concepts are value-free argue variously:

1 that market transactions may impose external costs on others and/or corrupt the morality of the participants;
2 that Paretians slide too easily from saying 'at the Pareto frontier, only transactions which make at least one person feel worse off can be made' to saying 'at the Pareto frontier no further exchanges are admissible', which rules out any form of redistribution and regards all points on the Pareto frontier as equally justifiable; and
3 that Paretianism and liberalism are actually incompatible at the deepest level (A. Sen, 'The impossibility of a Paretian liberal', *Journal of Political Economy*, 1970).

parliament An elected assembly, responsible for passing legislation and granting government the right to levy taxation. Typically, it combines this role of a legislature with providing the personnel of government, thus fusing legislature and executive in a system of parliamentary government. The head of government and cabinet chosen from amongst the majority grouping in parliament are duly obliged to be accountable to parliament, accepting the principles of collective and individual responsibility which apply respectively to cabinet and ministers. If they can no longer command the support of a majority within parliament and receive a vote of no confidence, then they are obliged to resign to allow another government to be formed. Systems of parliamentary government are broadly distinguished from those based on the separation of powers principle, as in the United States. Here, the President and members of Congress are separately elected, and the executive is appointed by the President from among individuals outside Congress. Ministers are accountable only to the President who is directly accountable only to the electorate.

Systems of parliamentary government vary according to the constitutional role accorded to parliament and the electoral and party systems which determine their composition and political organization. Most parliaments face constitutional constraints. In Germany, for example, the national parliament's powers are limited by the federal constitution which ensures autonomous legislative power for individual *Länder* (provinces). A constitutional court exists to ensure that the parliament passes no law that is contrary to the written constitution. In contrast, the UK Parliament theoretically has unfettered authority to make, amend, or abolish any law, and no other body, including the courts, has a right to ignore its legislation. In practice, devolution of primary legislative powers to the Scottish Parliament in 1999 and Northern Ireland Assembly in 1998, although ultimately still subject to Parliamentary sovereignty, heavily amended this supremacy.

The distinctive qualities of parliaments may be explained by reference to the development of the UK Parliament and its international influences, and the varying historical contexts in which different countries have established parliaments. The UK Parliament is one of the oldest, its origins lying in the Witenagamot of the Anglo-Saxon period, the Norman great council, and the national council first called by Simon De Montfort in 1264. The parliamentary system of government that developed was seen in the nineteenth and early twentieth centuries to deliver political stability and efficient government at a time when other countries were experiencing political revolution and upheaval. Its historic role as the 'mother of parliaments' and its apparent virtues made it desirable to emulate in continental Europe and directly applicable in those countries subsumed in the British Empire. The *Commonwealth remains one of the most thriving homes of parliamentarianism. Yet the very historic nature of the development of parliament in Britain meant that its main features pre-dated the advent of electoral democracy. The doctrine of parliamentary sovereignty derived from a battle to overturn monarchical absolutism. Its electoral system was built upon the original calling of representatives of the shires, boroughs, and cities, thus antedating the later arguments for representation proportionally of party voters on a national basis. Its party system developed from within parliament rather than from among the people, and became adept at socializing latecomers such as the Labour Party to such shared assumptions as parliamentary sovereignty.

In the modern era it is frequently asked whether national parliaments still matter, given domestic tendencies towards executive domination, policy sectorization and the turn towards governance, and state decentralization. In post-parliamentary democracies it could be argued that parliaments are left primarily only with legitimizing and representative functions. Debates about the role and reform of the UK *House of Commons and *House of Lords are indicative of arguments both for and against the strength of these tendencies. Beyond this, however, the greatest challenge to national parliaments comes from the increasing international economic and political interdependence that orientates governing elites to more supranational processes of decision-making. This is starkly revealed in the case of the *European Union (EU), where collaborative decision-making between national leaders has been joined with an EU legislative process that assumes EU law to be superior to the law of each member state. Such a development challenges, for example, the doctrine of parliamentary sovereignty. At the same time, however, concerns over the lack of democratic accountability in the EU law-making

process may lead to continued expansion of the powers of the European Parliament, meaning that the focus of the study of parliaments may simply move from the national to the supranational context. This being the case, the historical context of the development of the European Parliament would suggest that its constitutional, electoral, and party basis would develop more on the lines of continental European parliamentary systems than that of Britain. It appears unlikely that a fully-fledged EU parliamentary system of government where legislature and executive are fused will develop.   JBr

SEE WEB LINKS
• UK Parliament website.

Parliamentary Boundary Commission *See* BOUNDARY COMMISSION.

parliamentary commissioner for standards *See* OMBUDSMAN.

parliamentary privilege Legal immunities conferred upon members of a legislature with regard to acts they may perform in the legislature or on its behalf. The principal parliamentary privilege in the UK Parliament is that of freedom of speech in its proceeding, given statutory expression in article nine of the 1689 Bill of Rights. This marked the parliamentary victory over the royal executive in the struggle that had lasted for most of the seventeenth century and ended with the flight of James II and Parliament's choice of William III to succeed him. No member may be held to account by an outside body or individual for words spoken within Parliament. Similar notions exist in most other democratic legislatures. Also surviving, but of diminished importance, are the privileges of freedom from arrest in civil process, freedom of access to the monarch, and rights of punishment against those abusing parliamentary privilege or those held to be in contempt of parliament.   JBr

parliamentary question Question addressed by members of a legislature to government ministers. In the UK Parliament oral questions, notice of which is given 48 hours in advance, are presented during question time; each MP called is also allowed to ask one unnotified supplementary question. At Prime Minister's question time special conventions apply, in particular allowing the Leader of the Opposition to ask up to three or four unnotified questions. Private Notice Questions, also delivered orally, are those which are allowed by the Speaker at short notice on the grounds of urgency. Written questions may be put to ministers at any time.

Formally, parliamentary questions offer one of the principal means by which members of a legislature may call ministers to account and scrutinize their operations. In practice, the regulation of questions by notification and limiting the number leads only to truncated debate and/or party political theatre. The long-term decline in the Prime Minister's availability for questions in the House of Commons reflects the extent to which the importance of parliamentary questions to good government has diminished and their potential for embarrassing ministers, particularly the Prime Minister, with party political rhetoric has increased. Parliamentary questions also came under scrutiny during the 1990s when it was alleged that in a number of cases MPs asked questions in return for money from outside interests. Following the work of the Nolan Committee on Standards in Public Life, Parliament imposed the requirement that all MPs make full disclosures of their financial dealings so as to revive faith in parliamentary questions.　JBR

parliamentary sovereignty The doctrine that 'Parliament can do anything except bind its successor', which is the official ideology of the British constitution. Acts are not subject to *judicial review, nor is constitutional or other legislation 'entrenched' (made more difficult to amend than ordinary legislation) because to do so would be to bind the sovereignty of future parliaments. One curious but logical consequence is that guarantees enshrined in Acts of Parliament are worthless. The Ireland Act 1949, s.1(2), states that 'It is hereby declared that Northern Ireland remains part of...the United Kingdom and...in no event will...any part thereof cease to be part of...the United Kingdom without the consent of the Parliament of Northern Ireland'. But as there is no entrenchment, this could simply be repealed should a future UK government wish to cede Northern Ireland to the Republic of Ireland.

Defenders of parliamentary sovereignty argue that it is essential to be clear where sovereignty lies, and that it should lie with elected politicians, not unelected judges or executive officers. Critics argue variously:

1 that parliamentary sovereignty has become a cover for executive despotism, because parliament neither can nor wishes to scrutinize executive actions purportedly done in its name;

2 that parliamentary sovereignty was ceded with the accession of the UK to the *European Union (*see also* STATUTE LAW); and

3 that rights ought to be entrenched, and/or that such constitutional matters as the maximum allowable length of a parliament should be kept out of the (allegedly sticky) hands of politicians.

Parliamentary sovereignty has been in rapid decline in the UK since 1990, when the courts first invalidated an act (the Merchant Shipping Act 1988) on the grounds of its incompatibility with an earlier statute, namely the European Communities Act 1972.

Parsons, Talcott (1902–79) *See* FUNCTIONALISM; STRUCTURAL FUNCTIONALISM.

participation, political Taking part in politics. The general level of participation in a society is the extent to which the people as a whole are active in politics: the number of active people multiplied by the amount of their action, to put it arithmetically. But the question of what it is to take part in politics is massively complex and ultimately ambiguous. It raises the question of what constitutes politics. We would, for example, assume that activity within a political party or an organization which regarded itself as a pressure group should count as political participation. But what about activity in other sorts of organization, such as sports associations and traditional women's organizations? Although not overtly political, these organizations set the context of politics, give their active members administrative experience and are capable of overt political action if their interests or principles are threatened. There is an opposite problem about political losers: if people act, but ineffectively, perhaps because they are part of a permanent minority in a political system, can we say they have participated in the making of decisions? One implication of this doubt is that possessing power is a necessary condition or logical equivalent of true political participation. If one is merely consulted by a powerful person who wants one's views for information, or if one is mobilized or re-educated within the control of another, one has not participated in politics in any significant sense. LA

partisan A term referring to a strong supporter or advocate of a particular party or movement as well as persons willing to take up armed and ideological resistance against a government in power or an occupying force. Partisans are the subject of a great Leonard Cohen song, and the term is used elsewhere alongside *guerrilla and *asymmetrical warfare. Resistance to *Franco during the Spanish Civil War and the French Resistance against *Hitler's occupation of France during World War II are often seen as exemplars of partisanship.

partition Attempt to resolve political disputes through the drawing of territorial boundaries. Ireland and India were both partitioned by the British rulers upon the granting of Independence, leading to the creation of *Northern Ireland and Pakistan. In both cases the drawing of the boundaries was contentious—since the religious groups that partition was meant to separate did not conform to compact geographical areas— and rather than resolving the underlying disputes can be seen to have exacerbated them. The island of Cyprus was partitioned after a conflict between Greece and Turkey in 1974.

party conference *See* PARTY CONVENTION.

party convention The periodic conference of a political party, used for deciding policy and/or for nominating candidates.

The policy-forming convention is characteristic especially of European socialist parties. Some, including the British *Labour Party, have had long arguments about whether the party convention, the parliamentary party, or the leader is finally responsible for deciding party policy. Whatever the formal position may be, no party leadership in practice allows the party convention to have the final say. In right-wing parties, the party convention is typically designed to be a rally of the faithful rather than a policy-forming body.

The nominating convention is a prominent feature of politics in the United States. The Democratic and Republican parties each hold a convention in the summer preceding each Presidential election (that is, in years divisible by four). The purpose is to nominate the party's candidate for President. States have votes roughly in proportion to the number of *Electoral College votes which they control. In recent years, nominating conventions have been foregone conclusions because one candidate has always amassed pledges from more than half of the delegates before the convention meets. However, that is a recent development. The 1880 Democratic convention went to thirty-six ballots before choosing James A. Garfield (who won the Presidency, and was assassinated shortly afterwards). State parties may give their pledges to *favorite sons, who are not expected to win, but who may be able to use their vote as a bargaining tool. Therefore, future conventions which do real work are not ruled out.

party identification The answer a respondent gives to a question of the form 'Generally, do you see yourself as a Republican, a Democrat, an Independent, or what?' and its equivalent in other countries. In the 1950s the *Michigan school of survey research argued that party identification questions tapped a stable underlying orientation which might be disturbed by current affairs without being permanently upset: thus Democrats who voted for the Republican President Eisenhower in 1952 were likely to return to Democratic voting in other times and other elections. Researchers in the UK have complained that the question is perceived as no different to the question 'If there were a General Election tomorrow, for whom would you vote?', and that the Michigan approach underrated the rationality of electors' choices. However, the two approaches are reconciled in current survey research, which accords a role both for party identification and for rational choice.

party list Any system of *proportional representation in which voters choose among parties, rather than among candidates, and seats are awarded to the parties in proportion to the votes they have received. Many party-list systems have supplementary provisions which enable voters to raise or lower particular candidates in their ranking (*see* PANACHAGE), but these schemes are generally little used. A party-list system was introduced for British elections to the European Parliament in 1999.

party organization The structures and procedures of political parties. Most interest has focused on party organization in competitive liberal democracies, which is initially focused on mobilizing electoral support.

Party organization in Western democracies was originally characterized by two principal types. Cadre parties developed as an expression of a small elite group. In the nineteenth century these were generally parties made up of social notables and their individual supporters. They were also commonly parliamentary in their origins. As social leaders who once assumed political power they simply now organized to garner the vote of expanding electorates. Such cadre parties were generally loosely organized, had low memberships, and were not ideologically programmatic. Most conservative and right of centre parties evolved in this manner. In contrast, mass parties grew out of the development of late nineteenth-century working-class protest and the political ambitions of trade unions, friendly societies, and cooperative movements. They were by definition extra-parliamentary parties, deriving from social groups and their quest for political power. They evolved more formal organization, full-time officials, a mass membership, and a systematic political programme that was accountable to the membership. Such parties tended to be social democratic or democratic socialist and were much more subject to internal party democracy.

The development of a broadened franchise, nevertheless, imposed similar pressures on cadre and mass parties to develop professional organization and a large membership whilst being pragmatic to the needs of winning elections. Otto Kirchheimer's catch-all model of party organization suggests that whilst historical origins have continued to give a distinctive flavour to parties, the logic of party competition has increasingly made them conform to common characteristics. Principally these have included: de-emphasizing the original social base so as to be able to appeal to a broader electorate; de-emphasizing a particular ideology so as to be able to respond to electoral views on short-term issues; strengthening central party leadership and hierarchic control to provide a clear electoral message; sacrificing internal party democracy so as to be able to present a favourable image of a united party; broadening social group links to enhance party funding opportunities; and a move from membership campaigning to leadership campaigning through the media.

Analysis by R. S. Katz and P. Mair identifies the further development of the cartel party as an ideal type towards which many established parties in Western democracies are moving. This confirms the common development of catch-all characteristics but adds that established parties take extra steps to preserve their position in volatile electoral market-places. This focuses on state funding of parties, a measure that enhances party autonomy from particular social group funding and the specific demands that might follow. Party leaderships thus become freer to tailor messages to the broader electoral middle ground. Equally, however, in that funding is provided in relation to existing representation it gives established parties a major resource advantage over newcomers.

In the modern era many parties in Western states are facing a range of fresh challenges to established patterns of party organization. Political parties face a crisis of both membership and activist decline, necessitating fresh approaches to local structures and member activities. They face severe pressures on party finance as whilst membership declines the costs of campaigning generally increase. It has become more commonplace for parties to look to the state for funding. State decentralization also demands that parties adapt their organizational structures and procedures to the demands of multi-level politics. Finally, social change demands that parties consider procedural changes, for example to provide for greater representation of women or black and minority ethnic communities. In these contexts political parties struggle to sustain their central roles in representative democracy.

In the United States, the Republican and Democrat parties are loosely organized, without the permanent structures normally found in European parties. In Eastern Europe differing organizational forms appear to result from the incidence of successor communist parties, the emergence of new state-organized parties, and a mass of tiny parties working in an electoral landscape where democracy is weakly rooted. In *one-party states or states dominated by one party, organization remains the most closely related to the assumed structure of state power. The failed communist parties of the Soviet Union and Eastern Europe were organized around the principle of *democratic centralism. PBY/JBr

party system Tautologically, the set of all the significant parties in a country, their interactions, and (sometimes) the electoral system and voter loyalties that produce it. Divided by some into '*one-party systems', 'two-party systems', and 'multi-party systems' (*see also* DUVERGER'S LAW); others doubt the analytical usefulness of the distinction. In the introduction to their influential *Party Systems and Voter Alignments* (1967), S. M. Lipset and S. Rokkan argue that party systems in Western democracies typically 'froze' the pattern of *cleavages that existed at the time of the enfranchisement of the working class, so that current party alignments reflected policy disputes and interest alignments of decades earlier. The study of parties in Europe is still heavily influenced by the Lipset/Rokkan typology, although their remarks about the effects of electoral systems on party systems have been superseded.

Pascal, Blaise (1623–62) French mathematician, scientist, and religious apologist. For Pascal, human misery is the result of the corruption of human nature at the Fall. Man without God is ruled by self-love which blinds him to true justice and is the origin of social and political disorders. Human greatness consists mainly in man's ability to realize his wretchedness. He may be a reed, but he is a 'thinking reed' (*Pensées*). But what can he do about it? Only an infinite being can save him from the social and political disorders that originate in his self-love, and help him to attain his aspirations. By implication Pascal is saying what *Augustine said before him: true justice on earth can only be attained through faith in God and God is found in Jesus Christ.

Pascal was also one of the founders of the theory of probability and statistics. This originated with problems in gambling, but soon spread to serious applications in all the social sciences including politics (for some modern ramifications *see also* COST-BENEFIT ANALYSIS; DECISION THEORY). His most famous argument in probability is 'Pascal's Wager' which has been described as a game-theoretic argument in favour of believing in God (or at least trying to believe, or going through the motions of believing). God either exists or He does not; if He exists He rewards believers with eternal life and punishes unbelievers with eternal punishment. Even if the probability of God's existence is very small, the penalty of eternal punishment is so devastating that the expected value of believing in God will always exceed that of not believing in Him. Given Pascal's premisses, the argument is valid; but all depends on God being the particular sort of God posited in the second premiss. However, the Wager is part of a broader argument that reasoning alone cannot lead to a knowledge of first principles. For Pascal, only religious belief can. CB

paternalism The exercise of power or authority over another person to prevent self-inflicted harm or to promote that person's welfare, usually usurping individual responsibility and freedom of choice. The paternalism of a parent (strictly, a father), even one who restricts the liberty of a child in the child's own interests, has not generally been thought to require extensive justification. It is alleged that children are incapable, through ignorance or inexperience, of sound judgement, and need protection from themselves as well as from other persons. Legal or state paternalism refers to the use of law or other state activity to prevent adult citizens, as well as children, from harming themselves, or to promote their welfare. A range of paternalistic interventions is available to the state, from the provision of advice and information, through taxation policies which make items expensive and less available, to the coercive prohibition of activities, or the prescriptive requirement of activities. Because some of the forms of intervention risk imposing the legislator's view of what is harmful or welfare-promoting, they have been seen as inimical to liberty. On the other side, citizens are certainly capable of bringing harm upon themselves (even on their own view of harm) through ignorance, short-sightedness, and so on. Treatments of the possible justifications for state paternalism consider whether a balance needs to be struck between liberty and welfare, the impact of different possible mechanisms of paternalist intervention, the relationship between 'preventing harm' and 'promoting well-being', the nature of *interests, and the legitimate purposes of the state.   AR

path dependence In *game theory and *social choice theory, the property that the same initial state may give rise to different outcomes by different routes. Any good choice procedure ought to be path-independent.

To understand what is at stake, consider four skaters A, B, C, and D, and seven judges. The judges rank the candidates on their performance. Their rankings, in descending order, are:

Three judges: ABCD
Two judges: BCDA
Two judges: CDAB

Note that every single judge considers that C is better than D. Now consider two variants of the *Borda count. Variant 1 says 'Rank every candidate'. Variant 2 says 'Eliminate any candidate who is unanimously beaten, then rank every remaining candidate'. By Variant 1, A gets 11 points, B gets 12 points, and C gets 13 points. So C wins, B comes second, and A third. By Variant 2, A gets 8 points, B 7 points, and C 6 points—the order of the candidates has been turned upside down! This shows that this version of the Borda count violates path-independence. Note the similarity (though not the identity) of *independence of irrelevant alternatives.

The term is also used loosely to signal that the options available now are constrained by previous choices. This usage is popular but empty as it is true of all choices.

patriarchy 'Rule by the father'. A doctrine especially associated with *Filmer: political authority was divine authority, descended from Adam through the kings of Israel to modern kings. Thus it justified the *divine right of kings. The word is also used by feminists to decry the practice, whether principled or unthinking, of giving primacy to fathers, sons, and/or men over mothers, daughters, and/or women. Patriarchal practices of all sorts are

widespread even in societies which claim to practise equal opportunities.

patriotism Patriotism has always been defined as love of one's country or zeal in the defence of the interests of one's country. Patriotism as such does not necessitate a programme of action; it stimulates and informs nationalism, but is not always nationalistic. In the eighteenth century reference to it was often ironic, as when Dr Johnson defined a patriot as 'a factious disturber of the government'. He also said that 'Patriotism is the last refuge of the scoundrel', referring particularly to the demagogue John Wilkes. Such ironic reservations about the virtue of patriotism are a frequent theme of much modern commentary, often prompting the bitter reflection by self-ascribed patriots that, 'Patriotism has become a dirty word'.   LA

patronage English 'patron' directly follows Latin *patronus* in the meaning 'protector, defender'. In the medieval church it also acquired the meaning of 'one who has the right to nominate a clergyman to occupy a parish'. These two senses are nicely blended in the concept of political patronage. In Victorian and Edwardian Britain, the civil service office of Patronage Secretary to the Treasury was charged with distributing favours to government supporters in return for votes. The patronage office existed until recently in the British Civil Service; its role is to check that political honours are not given to inappropriate people, as in the period from 1916 to 1922 when Lloyd George sold them.

In the United States, political patronage followed very similar lines, hence the *Progressive concern with civil service reform. However, some federal posts both high and low (ambassadorships, postmasterships) are still openly the subject of patronage. *See also* MACHINE.

peacebuilding A variety of measures aimed at solidifying peace and avoiding future conflict in a society, undertaken by actors such as government agencies and civil society organizations. Peacebuilding measures include overseeing the disarmament, demobilization, and reintegration into peaceful society of warring parties, electoral support, rebuilding political and economic institutions, and supporting local capacities to manage differences without turning to violence. The phrase has been in use since the 1970s to describe the promotion of sustainable peace, but has gained traction in the last thirty years within the *United Nations after the problems experienced by peacekeeping forces in the 1990s in places such as *Rwanda, Sierra Leone, and the Democratic Republic of the Congo. In 1992, then UN Secretary General Boutros Boutros-Ghali referred to peacebuilding in his 'Agenda for Peace' report, and in 2000 Lakdar Brahimi used the term 'peacebuilding' in his Report to the UN on the Panel of UN Peace Operations. These reports noted the importance to the UN of peacebuilding strategies, to ensure the continued success of the more traditional peacekeeping operations. The United Nations Peacebuilding Commission was set up in 2005 to encourage relevant actors to work together to improve the provision of peacebuilding measures. AMB

peace dividend A term referring to the money available for general domestic budgetary spending when less money is required for defence or war. Popularized by US President George H. Bush, the term was often used during the demilitarization of the post-*Cold War period and to justify cuts in military spending while highlighting its social benefit. This term was also used by Prime Minister Margaret Thatcher in the 1990s and more recently by US President Barack Obama at the end of the *Iraq War.

peacekeeping Intervention by a third party to separate and pacify participants in a conflict. The United Nations has performed peacekeeping operations since 1948, when it sent military observers to *Kashmir, to oversee the ceasefire between India and Pakistan, and the Middle East, in the aftermath of the Arab–Israeli conflict. Fifty years later the UN peacekeepers still had a presence in these regions. The number of UN peacekeeping operations has increased rapidly since the end of the *Cold War, with involvement in Somalia, *Rwanda, the *Balkans, and Kuwait, amongst others. Peacekeeping has tended to involve the introduction of military forces who have the job of observing the implementation of ceasefire agreements and providing a buffer between combatants.

There has been debate as to the extent to which peacekeeping forces could or should be involved in the active enforcement of ceasefires, the possibility and practicality of neutral intervention, and the balance between upholding the status quo and acting to change the strategic situation in order to enhance the prospects of conflict resolution.

peasantry Class of people, generally of low social status, who depend mainly on agricultural labour for subsistence.

Peasants work the land, and, even where they do not own the land that they work, they are distinguished from serfs by their freedom to move and to dispose of at least a part of any surplus output through the market. Still of great consequence in populous Asiatic societies such as India, they are a much diminished class in Europe. Their political role was problematic for the victorious *Bolsheviks in Russia after 1917 since *Marx had envisaged socialism growing out of the clash of bourgeoisie and proletariat in industrialized societies where the peasantry were no longer of much account. After an initial attempt to present their regime as one legitimated by an alliance of workers and peasants, the Bolsheviks effectively destroyed the Russian peasantry or *kulaks through collectivization of agriculture. For Chinese Communists, a generation later, the rural population was of such overwhelming importance that peasants had to be given greater ideological recognition in *Maoism, but they were once again deprived of effective access to markets by collectivization of agriculture until 1978. In both the Soviet Union and China the fall in agricultural output following collectivization provided a cogent empirical critique of practical socialism. In Western Europe and North America, by contrast, the productivity of peasant and family farming has been far outpaced by larger-scale corporate agriculture, although peasant politics have persisted (for instance, in the *Fourth Republic and the Common Agricultural Policy of the *European Union). CJ

Pedersen index *See* ELECTORAL VOLATILITY.

Pentagon So named because of its distinctive five-sided building (attacked by terrorists on *September 11th 2001), the Pentagon is the headquarters of the US Department of Defense. The department is responsible for the running of the armed forces and the formulation of military strategy.

SEE WEB LINKS

• Pentagon website.

people's democracy A phrase invented to describe countries of 'socialist orientation' which could not yet claim to have built socialism itself. It was used first in reference to the 'fraternal allies' of the Soviet Union in Eastern Europe after the Second World War and then those countries that adopted the Soviet model after decolonization.   swh

perestroika From a Russian word meaning 'restructuring', perestroika was adopted as the official policy of the Soviet Communist Party following the plenum of the Central Committee in April 1987. Although the term itself was not new in Soviet political parlance, the policy is inextricably linked in the popular mind with Mikhail Gorbachev. Its meaning, however, is still hotly debated. For many commentators, perestroika was another attempt to invigorate the Soviet system by fostering grass-roots initiative without allowing a challenge to the power of the Communist Party itself. For others, perestroika was an attempt by sections of the leadership to improve their position vis-à-vis rivals in the elite and sections of the recalcitrant bureaucracy by playing the democratic card. For others still, perestroika was an essentially democratic movement of those, including some in the leadership, who opposed the authoritarianism and inefficiency of the old system. Whatever the case, perestroika resulted in both democratization and the articulation of demands that went well beyond the capacity of the Communist Party to control. It allowed for the end to the *Cold War and of the division of Europe, and resulted in the demise of the Soviet Union itself.   swh

perfectionism The view that the role of the state is to promote morally acceptable conceptions of the good life, rather than simply to provide a neutral or impartial framework in which each person may pursue his or her own conception of the good

life. To the extent that liberalism has been identified with this second (instrumental) view, perfectionism has had an uncertain relationship with the liberal tradition, illustrated by J. S. *Mill's endorsement of the so-called higher pleasures within an apparently *utilitarian framework. Joseph Raz's defence of the promotion of *autonomy as a legitimate state activity provides a contemporary example of liberal perfectionism. Such liberal perfectionism may be usefully compared to accounts of the human good provided within the *natural law tradition (which need not issue in any liberal commitments). Perfectionism may be distinguished from eighteenth- and nineteenth-century ideas about human perfectibility. Liberal perfectionism requires moral discrimination by the state about valuable ways of life; the older doctrine referred to the capacity of persons to move towards perfection.   AR

Pericles *See* ATHENIAN DEMOCRACY.

permanent revolution The theory, due to *Trotsky, that a proletarian socialist revolution may develop continuously from a previous non-socialist revolution. The actual phrase is taken from Marx's *Address to the Central Committee of the Communist League* (1850).

Trotsky depicted Russia as an example of uneven development, combining the most modern and the most backward social and economic forces. Industrialization had been forced by an absolutist state and financed by foreign capital. As a result, the domestic *bourgeoisie would not establish *hegemony and thus could not lead a democratic revolution. In contrast, the *proletariat acquired a significance beyond its size because of the large scale and concentration of industry and its own levels of organization and consciousness.

Given the impotence of the bourgeoisie, it was left to the proletariat to accomplish the democratic revolution. However, a workers' government could not be restricted to those tasks because it would be influenced by the continuing class struggle. Once set in motion the revolution would become an uninterrupted process, the democratic stage merging into the socialist.

Trotsky acknowledged that the material base for socialism did not exist in Russia but he contended that this could be resolved by the second part of the theory—the international character of the revolution. Russia was just a link in the chain; it could not survive without the support of the European proletariat. GL

Perón(ism) The founder of one of Latin America's most durable political movements, Juan Domingo Perón (1895–1974) was twice President of Argentina (1946–55 and 1973–4).

Born the son of a Sardinian immigrant, Perón pursued a military career. An admirer of European fascism in the 1930s, he helped organize a military coup in 1943. In the ensuing regime Perón used the position of labour secretary to win favour among the unions—a tactic rewarded in 1945 when workers' protests secured his release following imprisonment by rivals.

Elected president in 1946, Perón legislated to improve the conditions of Argentine workers. Women were enfranchised thanks in part to his second wife, María Eva Duarte (Evita), who played a large role in Peronism. Perón used protectionist measures and state intervention in the economy to develop national industries. Re-elected in 1952, he was eventually deposed by the military in 1955. Perón then spent eighteen years in exile before returning to power in 1973.

Peronism was a populist movement whose social and political composition changed over the years, although generally it attracted strong labour support. Perón led the movement in an authoritarian manner, but believed in the value of mass mobilization and allowed local groups a degree of autonomy during his years in exile.

Justicialismo, the official doctrine of the movement, emphasized principles of social justice, international non-alignment, and economic nationalism. However, during the 1980s, leadership of the movement passed to Carlos Menem (President 1989–99), under whom labour influence declined and government policy was marked by economic liberalism and support for Washington. The Justicialist Party has again been in office since 2003, through the successive presidencies of Néstor Kirchner and his wife, Cristina Fernández. RG

personal as political The 'personal is political' is a frequently brandished slogan of women's liberation. It is held that a politics of analysing women's identities and personal experiences is liberatory for them. It is believed that there is not much difference between an individual's personal existence, belief, ideas, and the pursuit of politics, and that the more women transform their lives and consciousness, the more they realize the potential for change, they cannot be dependent on a revolution to liberate them. However, politics based on personal experiences and personal identity shares the danger of becoming too personalized. It also shares the danger of excluding issues affecting different women. STh

Petersberg Declaration/Tasks Signed on 19 June 1992, near Bonn in Germany, the Petersberg Declaration aimed to strengthen European defence capability; setting out a new role for the *Western European Union. This role was outlined in terms of a number of tasks: humanitarian and rescue missions, peacekeeping operations, and the deployment of combat forces in crisis management. The Treaty of Amsterdam (1997) incorporated the Petersberg Tasks as part of the *European Union Treaty. *See also* COMMON FOREIGN AND SECURITY POLICY; RAPID REACTION FORCE.

petite bourgeoisie Term used by Marx to describe a class intermediate between proletariat and bourgeoisie. Within this category he included artisans, shopkeepers, and peasants, those groups who depended upon self-employed labour and small productive property ownership (using their own tools and tilling their own plots). They were not capitalist because they were not involved in the exploitative extraction of surplus labour from wage-workers.

As a transitional class, the petite bourgeoisie were vulnerable to impoverishment and the risk of proletarianization and the anxiety this created, and yet also thought of themselves as 'bourgeois', aspiring to the lifestyle of the superior class. Marx argued that they joined in short-term alliances with the proletariat to agitate for democratic rights but would inevitably support the bourgeoisie in its suppression of revolutionary movements (the 1848 Revolution in France was a classic example of this). Petit bourgeois parties had played significant roles in social and political mobilization but were fundamentally reactionary. In *The Class Struggles in France* (1850), Marx warned against the danger of petit bourgeois socialism which had a radical facade, but was intrinsically reformist and whose aim was to maintain control over the proletariat.

Marx believed that the petite bourgeoisie would eventually disappear, caught up in the class polarization between bourgeoisie and proletariat and forced to choose between them politically. Here he anticipated some petit bourgeois intellectuals rejecting their class origins and adopting the cause of the proletariat.

The petite bourgeoisie has not disappeared, but it remains strongly right-wing. In some countries, including Britain, the petite bourgeoisie supports the right-wing party more strongly than do managerial and professional workers. GL

PFI *See* PRIVATE FINANCE INITIATIVE.

phenomenology A phenomenon is that which appears. In the political and philosophical senses of phenomenology, the basic concept therefore is 'the study of appearances (as unspokenly opposed to reality)'. The term was popularized by *Hegel's title *The Phenomenology of Spirit* and later, with a different meaning, by Edmund Husserl (1859–1938). For Husserl, phenomena can be studied only subjectively, not objectively—thus phenomenology is a close cousin of existentialism (*see* SARTRE). Some psychologists borrowed the term to mean 'as naive and full a description of direct experience as possible', and applied it to the perception of sensations of such things as colour and motion.

physiocrats Group of eighteenth-century French economists who believed that the land is the ultimate source of all wealth, and also in free trade in grain. The latter belief, but not the former, influenced Adam *Smith's development of classical economics. *See also* ENLIGHTENMENT, FRENCH; POLITICAL ECONOMY.

pillarization Deep social cleavages (e.g. between Catholics and Protestants) are recognized and legitimized by providing institutional autonomy to organized social groups in areas such as education and broadcasting. The Netherlands provides the most developed example of pillarization, the word being coined there, with official recognition provided to religious, secular, and territorial pillars (*Zuilen*). WG

pink tide Also referred to as 'left-of-centre', 'left-leaning', and 'radical social democratic' governments in Latin America. The term first came into public discourse following the victory of Hugo Chávez in the Venezuelan presidential elections of 1998. Subsequently, the election of governments in Chile, Brazil, Argentina, Uruguay, Bolivia, Nicaragua, Ecuador, and Guatemala consolidated the pink tide.

In terms of their regional and diplomatic policies, pink tide governments attempted to be more assertive in their response to US policy imperatives and that country's historical hegemony in the region. However, their ability to act together was hampered by the fact that other countries—such as Mexico, Colombia, and Peru—remained close to Washington and also by numerous rivalries and contentious issues. Thus, Brazil and Argentina have long vied with each other for regional leadership and Chile and Bolivia have been locked in a dispute over the latter's access to the sea since the former's victory in the War of the Pacific in 1881. While Venezuela, Bolivia, and Nicaragua have joined with Cuba to form the ALBA (the Bolivarian Alliance of the Peoples of Our America) with the aim of creating an alternative to Washington's proposed Free Trade Area of the Americas, Brazil, Chile, Argentina, and Uruguay have been more circumspect in their approach and distanced themselves from the radical rhetoric of Chávez's *Bolivarian revolution. GL

planning In its political usages, the term refers to any attempt to achieve a goal (such as economic well-being or a particular pattern of land use) by central direction. In the mid-twentieth century there was a widespread faith in forms of planning, including economic and urban planning. The success of the Soviet Union's 'five year plans' and the effectiveness in wartime Britain of comprehensive planning of production and the distribution of resources appeared to have given the future to the planners. A Conservative Prime Minister, Harold Macmillan, commented, 'Planning has become a rather emotive word; I myself have always rather liked it'.

Since the early 1970s, however, there has been a widespread perception that the best known forms of planning—economic and town planning—have failed in their objectives. The revival of arguments for *laissez-faire policies and the development of *public choice theories, which suggest that real planners cannot have the objectivity or length of vision which successful planning would require of them, have added theoretical justification to this perception.

The distinction between planning and other types of policy is a dubious one. Even those who believe in a clear distinction would have to confess that very little of what happens in the world is actually the consequence of planning. LA

Plato (*c.*427–347 BC) Greek philosopher. Born into an aristocratic Athenian family, he was expected to take up a political career, but circumstances and inclination persuaded him to turn to philosophy instead. The most significant factor in his disillusionment with contemporary politics was the execution in 399 of his close friend and teacher *Socrates at the hands of the Athenian democracy; he remained profoundly critical of democratic institutions and liberalism all his life. He did, however, make one foray into the world of *realpolitik*, when in middle age he attempted—entirely unsuccessfully—to put some of his political theories into practice in the Greek city-state of Syracuse.

He wrote a number of dialogues on a very wide range of issues; and the positions taken on various topics can vary considerably between works. The main character is almost always Socrates and it is often hard to know whether the views this 'Socrates' expresses are those of the historical Socrates or are original to Plato himself. It is generally agreed that the influence of the historical Socrates is particularly in evidence in the early dialogues, while the middle and late works articulate—constantly developing—positions original to Plato (though many of these still have clear Socratic roots).

Thus, while several early dialogues raise key political issues (cf. e.g. the *Apology*,

Crito, and particularly *Gorgias*, the last being a remarkable exploration of the nature of power and the philosophy of 'might is right' which influenced *Nietzsche considerably), it is the *Republic* that is usually considered to be Plato's first major contribution to political theory. In the first of its ten books, the sophist Thrasymachus issues a challenge to conventional views of justice. Justice, he claims, is simply the interest of whichever person or party is in power: all rulers make the laws to their own advantage and it is these laws that are called 'justice'. The shrewd and resourceful subject, therefore, will disobey the laws whenever he can escape detection and further his own interests instead. Being 'just' simply does not pay.

The rest of the *Republic* consists of an attempt by Plato to prove that, on the contrary, it does pay to be just. To show this, however, we first need to define justice. Given that justice is, Plato thinks, the same in both individual and state, it will be easier if we begin our search by examining the broader canvas of the just state and then see if our findings are applicable to the individual.

Plato locates the origin of all states, just or otherwise, in economic need. Such economic associations are best organized if each person performs the job for which they are naturally most suited: this will result in an efficient and harmonious state in which sufficient leisure is possible to allow for civilized life. Over time this minimal state will become more complex, until eventually it divides into three classes, corresponding to three natural types: the Producers, who supply all the economic needs of the state; the Auxiliaries, who act as a combined military, executive, and police force (the state is only ideally just, not just *simpliciter*, and the threat of war will still be a feature of life); and the Philosopher-Rulers, whose rule is sanctioned by the fact that only they have knowledge of an abstract and transcendent metaphysical entity called the Form of the Good, which alone enables one to act for the good of the whole. Most children will naturally be of the same type as their parents, and thus will form part of the same class; if they are of a different natural type, however, then the state must remove them to the appropriate class. Justice in the state consists in each member fulfilling the class function to which he or she is naturally fitted.

It is argued that these three classes correspond to three divisions within the psyche of the individual: the reasoning element, in virtue of which the individual is wise; the spirited element, in virtue of which he or she is courageous, and the appetitive element, the task of which is to obey. As in the state, justice in the individual consists in each part performing its own proper function. Furthermore it becomes clear that except in rare cases this internal harmony of the just individual can only fully develop in the harmony of the ideally just state. Plato claims that in the case of both individual and state this internal harmony will equal health and happiness; and—even more controversially—in being ruled by wisdom rather than by the tyrannical appetites, both just individual and just state will also be free. The interdependence in general of state and individual is illustrated by portraits of what Plato sees as the four degenerate types of individual and state: the timocratic, the oligarchic, the democratic, and the tyrannical, and their respective goals of glory, wealth, liberty (in the sense of acting without external interference), and an unspecified obsessive appetite.

The cornerstone of the just state is the government of the Philosopher-Rulers, supported by the Auxiliaries; the education of these two classes (collectively termed 'Guardians') is consequently of paramount importance, and its principal aim is to train the Auxiliaries to obey the Rulers and the Rulers to act for the good of the state as a whole. Plato describes the Guardians' training in great detail, and several times refers to it as the element which holds the entire state together. Until the age of 18 all future Guardians receive an identical education in literature, music, and athletics. There follow two years of military training, and then some are selected for further studies in mathematics and philosophy, followed by a period of study interspersed with practical administrative experience. Finally, when these select few are 50, they will be directed towards that knowledge of the Form of the Good which alone both legitimates and necessitates their becoming the Rulers of the state.

Plato also prescribes for the two Guardian classes an austere and communistic way of life, so that they may devote all their time and loyalties to the state. They are forbidden to possess private property or money, all their material needs being supplied by the Producers. The family unit is to be abolished, and both Rulers and Auxiliaries are to live together in common halls; children are to be conceived according to an organized breeding programme and brought up in state nurseries, having been removed from their natural mothers at birth. No one will know who their parents, siblings, or children are, and consequently everyone, Plato believes, will regard everyone else as a possible relative and be bonded accordingly. Amongst these two Guardian classes, too, women are to receive exactly the same education and perform exactly the same tasks as men, including ruling the state and going to war.

Plato's radical conceptions in the *Republic* of justice, social harmony, education, and freedom are enormously rich and have informed the thought of philosophers as diverse as *Rousseau, *Hegel, and J. S. *Mill; his attitudes to property, the family, and the position of women have also proved highly influential. His ideal, however, has also come in for some fierce criticism. The convenient match claimed between the division of natural talents and the class divisions required by the state has been regarded as entirely without foundation. In making the state more important than its parts, and allowing it to enter every sphere of the individual's life, Plato has been accused of totalitarianism, while charges of paternalism have been laid against the claim that the Philosopher-Rulers alone know what is best for the other classes. Nor are there any legal checks on the Rulers' behaviour. Their methods of rule are also problematic: the analogy drawn between the Producers and the unreasoning appetites raises questions about whether the Producers can really be willingly persuaded or whether they have to be forced, and Plato's language is ambivalent on this point. In any case, the means of persuasion are themselves disturbing, involving both propaganda and extreme censorship of the arts.

In the *Statesman* (*Politicus*), Plato takes a more pragmatic approach. While still maintaining that the best form of rule would be that of the true doctor-statesman, acting on the basis of trained judgement rather than formal law, he nevertheless allows that in the absence of such a statesman, a system of laws is a good second-best. Although too general and inflexible, laws at least have the merit of having been created by rational thought, and obedience to them makes for political stability. Another development is Plato's increased awareness of temporality and history and their relations to politics and political theory. The true art of statecraft weaves together opposing qualities in human nature and this can only happen over a period of time; it also requires an awareness of changing circumstances and an ability to select the fitting moment for action.

In Plato's last work, the *Laws*, laws are again promoted as a good second-best to the rule of the truly wise statesman, always providing that they are framed in the interests of the community as a whole; indeed, owing to the continuing failure of the ideal statesman to emerge, the rule of law is the only practicable system at all. Good (i.e. true) laws are perceived as the dispensation of divine reason, and their function is to establish and nurture the civic virtues; the most important of these virtues for the majority of citizens is the self-control that ensures obedience, and it is self-control that the basic education system is mainly designed to promote. In a sympathetic addition to conventional education, the self-control of the young is to be tested in state-organized drinking parties.

The state envisaged by the *Laws* remains authoritarian in the extreme, and is considerably influenced by the strict regimes of Sparta and Crete. There is legislation to cover the minutest details of both public and private life, and a large number of official bodies are established, headed by the Nocturnal Council, to ensure that the laws are maintained; the Nocturnal Council may also occasionally adjust the laws to suit changing circumstances. Religious belief, largely ignored by the *Republic*, is now viewed as a crucial factor in ensuring the cohesion and stability of the state, and recalcitrant atheists are to be put to death. In general, the individual continues to be perceived simply as part of an infinitely more important whole.

Nevertheless the imaginary state of the *Laws* is both more egalitarian and, except in religious aspects, more moderate than that of the *Republic*. Though the officials form a temporary ruling class, they are selected mainly by election, coupled with subsequent tests, and sometimes by lot from the main citizen body: there are no longer three castes purportedly in accordance with three natural kinds, though slavery is unequivocally condoned (the *Republic* is less explicit on this point, although 433d strongly implies that slaves are taken for granted in the ideally just state). All citizens are to receive the same basic education, including all females, and the restricted communism of the *Republic* is abandoned; everyone is to live within their family unit and possess a limited amount of private property.

It is important to emphasize, too, that for Plato the training in the civic virtues is not just social engineering for the sake of stability, but an attempt to educate the individual to love and wish to do what is true and fine. The good life is always objective for Plato and he always believes that it is the main task of the state to promote this good life for its citizens: he certainly desires stability, but only the stability of the good regime (this is admittedly made easier for him in that he believes all bad regimes to be inherently lacking in stability). Hence in the *Laws* the dispositional training of the child is not conceived as an attempt to stifle reason, but, as in the *Republic*, it is seen as the necessary introduction to it. This is shown by the novel and extremely important requirement that each law be preceded by a lengthy attempt rationally to persuade the citizens of its goodness. The laws must undoubtedly rule, but obedience to them should ideally be voluntary and intelligent. AH

plebiscite Latin for 'ordinance of the people', resurrected by *Voltaire to describe the *referendum in Switzerland. In the nineteenth century, 'plebiscite' was used in English as a derogatory term to describe the referendums called by Napoleon I and Napoleon III to boost their personal authority, but the term is no longer regarded as derogatory.

Plekhanov, Georgy (1856–1918) Intellectual leader of Russian *Marxism. Formed the Emancipation of Labour group in exile (1883), active in the Russian Social Democratic Party and an editor of *Iskra* (1900). Initially supported Lenin over the 1903 split but then went over to the *Mensheviks. Highly critical of the October 1917 Revolution (*see* BOLSHEVISM). GL

Plessy* v. *Ferguson *See* CIVIL RIGHTS.

PLO (Palestine Liberation Organization)
The PLO was created in May 1964 at the suggestion of President Jamal Abd al-Nasir of Egypt. The liberation of Palestine had increasingly become an issue in inter-Arab competition, with each government using or supporting different emerging guerrilla groups. While the PLO's creation indicated support for the Palestinian cause, it was also to the advantage of Arab governments to control and channel the energies and hopes of the Palestinians away from an independent use of violence. Attacks on the territory of Israel could lead to Israeli retaliation and expose the vulnerability of Arab governments. Initially supportive of the idea of the PLO, King Hussein of Jordan, in particular, was fearful that it could imply the formation of a 'Palestinian entity' which would include the West Bank: i.e. Palestinian land that had been annexed by his grandfather, the Amir Abdullah, in 1948 as a result of the first Arab–Israeli war. To avoid this implication, the objective of the PLO was defined in its constitution as 'the liberation of Palestine' rather than a formation of a 'Palestinian entity'.

The Palestinian National Covenant states that the Palestinian Arabs are 'part of the Arab nation' and have a 'legal right' to their 'homeland'; that Palestinians and their descendants, whether Muslims, Christians, or Jews, who were permanent residents in Palestine prior to 1947 would be citizens of Palestine. All the conditions and obligations imposed on the peoples of Palestine by the Balfour Declaration, the Mandate, the partition of Palestine and the establishment of the state of Israel that had abrogated the rights of Palestinian Arabs were declared 'null and void'. The Covenant declared that all Palestinians shall form a united front for the liberation of Palestine.

During its early years, the PLO set about establishing the organizational framework within which all Palestinian activities— social, economic, political, cultural, educational, and military—could be pursued. It built an army, parts of which were attached to the various Arab national armies. Despite a lack of sovereign territory, the PLO eventually was able to provide many of the complex needs of its dispersed population. Indeed, its aim was to prepare for, and achieve, statehood in Palestine.

However, in the aftermath of the humiliating Arab military defeat in the Six Day War in June 1967, many of the Palestinian guerrilla groups—fedayeen—which had emerged in the previous decade or more, coalesced into: the Popular Front for the Liberation of Palestine (PFLP) under the leadership of Dr George Habash, a marxist Christian Palestinian; the Democratic Front for the Liberation of Palestine (DFLP) led by Nayif Hawatmeh; the People's Party; and the most important guerrilla group, Fatah (the Palestinian National Liberation Movement) founded in 1957–8, led by Yasir Arafat. As the numbers attracted to the fedayeen grew, they came to dominate the PLO by 1968. At the next session of the Palestine National Council (PNC) in 1969, Yasir Arafat was elected Chairman of the Executive Committee. From this point on, the PLO drew under its umbrella many of the fedayeen organizations whose leaders were appointed to the Executive Committee and the strategy of PLO became that of 'armed struggle'.

This change of the PLO occurred in the aftermath of the Six Day War of June of 1967 which left an expanded Israel in control of the Golan Heights, the West Bank including all of Jerusalem, Gaza, the Sinai Peninsula. Israel and Egypt ended up facing each other across the Suez Canal in an uneasy ceasefire, rejecting negotiations. By 1970 the fedayeen in Jordan had created a state within a state, further weakening the position of King Hussein. After the PFLP hijacked three airliners, civil war soon broke out in Jordan (Black September) when King Hussein with a newly formed military government attacked the fedayeen. In the aftermath of the war, the fedayeen were expelled from Jordan. Throughout the civil war, the King's appeals to the US for military support were coordinated with Israeli preparation to come to his assistance if needed.

With the election of Yasir Arafat as chairman of the Executive Committee, the PLO became an independent actor, no longer under the control of any Arab government. The predominant view in the PLO was that of armed struggle but there was a lack of agreement among the fedayeen as to strategy and tactics. Though the PLO had gained an international profile, its ability to play a role in the solution to the Palestinian problem appeared as remote as ever. In the Jordanian crisis, Arab governments were not inclined to be drawn into confrontation with Israel unless of their own choosing. It also created the current strategic relationship between the US and Israel.

From this time until 1988, the role of the PLO was either peripheral or non-existent in the many wars as well as in the peace process. Each Arab government had a different strategy as regards Israel and expected the PLO policy and the activities of the Palestinians to be compatible with its strategy and whatever tactics it would be pursuing at the time. The PLO, having been declared a 'terrorist' organization by the Israeli government, was unable to become a negotiating partner on behalf of the Palestinians. The US government also came to accept this particular Israeli position as its official policy which meant that both the US and the PLO were reduced to quiet or secret intermittent back channels in their diplomatic contacts and negotiations.

This situation changed after King Hussein relinquished Jordan's legal and administrative ties to the West Bank in 1988 in favour of the PLO. Yasir Arafat then convened the PNC, where he declared the existence of a Palestinian state in the West Bank and Gaza (recognized by over 90 countries) with himself as president. Soon after, to the US government's satisfaction, Yasir Arafat confirmed the PLO's recognition of UN Resolution 181 of 1947 which partitioned Palestine into two states thereby recognizing *de facto* the right of the state of Israel to exist in the region, accepted UN Resolutions 242 and 338 and renounced all forms of terrorism, at which point the US lifted the ban on its dealings with the PLO.

However, in the ensuing Madrid Peace Process, the Israeli government of Yitzhak Shamir still would not negotiate with the PLO. In his view, to do so, would be to legitimize the PLO's position calling for a Palestinian state and the return of Palestinian refugees. Several 'covers' had to be constructed before the Israeli and Palestinian negotiators could sit together in the same room. These consisted of a Joint Jordanian–Palestinian delegation with all the Palestinians coming from the Occupied Territories (OT), all of whom were selected by the PLO. It appointed an advisory group to support the negotiating team which included those members which the Israeli government would not allow on the team: one from East Jerusalem, and one from the Palestinian Diaspora. In this way, the Palestinians, in effect, had a representative negotiating team and the Israelis could say that they were not dealing with the PLO nor had they recognized East Jerusalem as part of the Occupied Territories.

In 1991–3, conditions in the Occupied Territories deteriorated considerably and violence in the form of destruction, deaths, and arrests had escalated. The PLO had reportedly lost most of its financial support as a result of its pro-Iraqi stance in the *Gulf War. The Israeli economy was adversely affected by events in the Occupied Territories and the Israeli government was under pressure to renew the peace process. Secret negotiations between Israel and the PLO covering an eight-month period (January–September 1993) began in Oslo. The Israeli government of Yitzhak Rabin proposed to the PLO that initially Gaza (except for Jewish settlements) and the town of Jericho in the West Bank would be given self-governing status. Yasir Arafat and a majority of the PLO Executive Committee supported this proposal over the opposition of many Palestinians including members of the negotiating team. The resulting Oslo Declaration of Principles, based on UN Resolutions 242 and 338, provided for a phased Israeli military withdrawal over a five-year period, the establishment of the Palestinian Authority, and at the end of this period, Final Status negotiations regarding Jerusalem, the return of refugees, Jewish settlements, and borders. In September 1995 the Oslo 2 agreement was signed in Washington DC which provided for an extension of autonomy in the West Bank. About one month later, Rabin was assassinated by an Israeli right-wing extremist.

The launching of the Oslo era impacted negatively upon the PLO. When the PLO moved to the Occupied Territories, it left its Political Department in Tunis. There was dissension amongst the groups that made up the PLO over the wisdom of the concessions which Yasir Arafat had made to Israel in return for only a small presence in the West Bank and Gaza from which to secure the remainder of the Territories. However, to secure the remainder of the Territories depended upon continued Palestinian popular support, international donor support, and a Palestinian police force, the assumption being that this would strengthen Arafat's negotiating position in the Final Status talks. After the signing of Oslo, however, Israel continued to pursue 'terrorists', targeted assassinations and collective punishments in the Occupied Territories. The deepening dissension within the PLO exposed the lack of vision and strategy for developing a law-based democratic Palestinian state in the wake of the changed conditions after Oslo, again on the assumption that this might strengthen the Palestinians' position vis-à-vis Israel. Instead, the PLO found itself pushed increasingly into pursuing Israel's internal security requirements which did not satisfy Israel nor strengthen the PLO's position.

Once the Palestinian Authority was established in 1994, it and the PLO existed side by side. The Palestinians were at this stage formally organized and reasonably united. Initially, prospects for peace seemed promising. However, the negotiations soon stalled. Effective third-party involvement foundered on the inability of the US, for domestic and strategic reasons, to mediate impartially, the EU's inability to form a common policy on the issues and its reluctance to stand in opposition to the US. Conditions within the Occupied Territories deteriorated culminating in an escalating spiral of violence. The contending forces were unequal with the advantage lying disproportionately with Israel. In April 2002, Israel reinvaded the autonomous towns held by the Palestinian Authority in the West Bank and in the process destroyed the infrastructure for a future Palestinian state. Arafat was effectively confined in his Ramallah headquarters, until his final illness. Mahmoud Abbas (also known as Abu Mazen) became leader of the PLO in 2004, following Arafat's death. The Fatah political faction, associated with the PLO leadership, was heavily defeated in the 2006 legislative council elections for the Palestinian Authority, when the more radical Hamas took control. The increasing gap between the Palestinian Authority and its grassroots base

as well as widespread dissatisfaction over the failure of the peace process led to the election of Hamas. Conflict between Hamas and Fatah broke out, which has not been resolved despite efforts at mediation by Egypt, Qatar, and Switzerland. *See also* INTIFADA. BAR/JHa

pluralism Literally, a belief in more than one entity or a tendency to be, hold, or do more than one thing. This literal meaning is common to all the political and social applications of the word, but it has applied in contexts so varied that the uses seem like separate meanings. The most established of these is pluralism as the tendency of people to hold more than one job or benefice, most specifically in the context of the pre-Reformation Catholic Church. In the late nineteenth century, pluralism was applied to philosophical theories or systems of thought which recognized more than one ultimate principle, as opposed to those which were 'monist'. At the same time, the word came to be applied in the United States to the view that the country could legitimately continue to be formed of distinct ethnic groups, the Jewish-Americans, Irish-Americans, and so on, rather than that all differences should dissolve into a 'melting-pot' (*see also* MULTICULTURALISM).

All of these uses have had at least a slight influence on the primary contemporary meaning in which the pluralist model of society is one in which the existence of groups is the political essence of society. Pluralists in this sense contrast with *elitists because they see the membership of village and neighbourhood communities, trade unions, voluntary societies, churches, and similar organizations as being more important than distinctions between a ruling class and a class that is ruled: vertical distinctions in society are less important than horizontal.

The forerunner of this kind of pluralism was F. R. de Lammenais who edited the journal *L'Avenir* in France in the early nineteenth century. Lammenais attacked both the individualism and the universalism of the *Enlightenment and the Revolution. The individual, he said, was 'a mere shadow', who could not be said to exist at all socially except in so far as he was part of one or more groups. Both Lammenais and modern pluralists, including such notable

American writers as Robert Dahl and Nelson Polsby, tend to believe both that society consists essentially of groups, with its political life a competition for group influence, and that this state of affairs is a good thing. Thus pluralism is often a relatively conservative doctrine, at least in relation to Marxism or radical democratic theory, which both tend to portray society as a predominance of an elite over a non-elite rather than a competition between groups. LA

pluralist international society A disciplinary branch of the *English School that argues that human diversity and pluralist understandings of 'the good life' require a more limited conception of *international society: one which can best maximize independence, *self-determination, and difference, while also creating a minimal level of social norms and rules from which to maintain order and stability between plural entities. Unlike *solidarists, who promote universal principles, pluralists argue that state *sovereignty and the international commitment to non-intervention should be the paramount social norm.

pluralities of violence Refers to the myriad ways in which violence manifests itself: as structural, cultural, symbolic, and direct. Looking at the intersections between different forms of violence enables us to understand the intransigent and circular nature of violence. Structural violence shows up as unequal power and consequently as unequal life chances: for example, deprivation, poverty, colonialism, imperialism. Cultural violence is the way in which those who lack economic and political power have aspects of their 'culture' negated, denigrated, and delegitimized: for example, ethnic, religious, or caste discrimination. Symbolic violence involves relations and mechanisms of domination and power which do not arise from overt physical force or violence on the body. It clearly lacks the intentional and instrumental quality of brute violence, and works not directly on bodies but through them: through symbolic interactions, behaviour, language, and modes of conduct. Direct violence involves physical violence on the body. In specific contexts, plural forms of violence could nurture and support one another. Ethnic wars and the embedded impunity of dominant ethnic groups can be conceptualized as a form of structural violence which allows denigration and hatred for 'others' (cultural violence). This hatred can be reflected through language and symbols (symbolic violence) and provide legitimacy to all forms of direct violence (killings, wartime crimes). STH

plurality In a multi-candidate election in which no candidate has obtained as much as half of the vote, the largest single total of votes for any candidate. A plurality (or *first-past-the-post) electoral system is one which selects such a candidate as the winner.

pocket veto In the United States, before a bill that has passed the House and the Senate becomes a law the President must sign it. If he declines to sign a particular bill it automatically becomes law after ten congressional working days. However, if Congress adjourns before the required ten days have elapsed the bill is deemed not to have passed. The President has, in a sense, placed the bill in his pocket—thus a pocket veto. DM

Poisson distribution A probability distribution for the frequency of a particular event in a given period of time. It is named after Siméon-Denis Poisson (1781–1840) and famously describes the distributions of deaths due to horse kicks in the Prussian cavalry. In political science it is used for modelling variables such as the number of vetoes cast by a president in a year, or the number of strikes in a factory. SF

polarization Any general move of political actors from centrist to extreme political positions. Some factors that may lead to polarization include: ethnic or religious violence and counter-violence; political leaders taking up 'expressive' positions expressing ideology rather than 'instrumental' positions aiming to win the next election; and changes in the electoral system such that it becomes more profitable to woo one's core supporters than aim for the *median voter. Some writers argue that systems of *proportional representation have this last effect.

police Policing is the activity of enforcing the criminal law and it has taken place in any society which can be said to have such a law.

But in most societies the people doing the policing have also had other functions; typically they have been the military, church officials, citizens taking their turn, or persons hired by the magistrates. With the arguable exception of the Roman Empire, the existence of 'the police', a separate force designed entirely for enforcing the criminal law, is a product of modern urban society. The establishment of a metropolitan police force in London in 1829 is usually seen as the single most important event in this development. Police forces covered all of the United Kingdom by 1860 and many other states had imitated the development.

The existence of a police force, by its very nature, raises several related political issues. The oldest is summed up by the Latin question, *Quis custodiet ipsos custodes?* (Who guards the guardians?) That is, given the capacities and force of arms which the police must have to do their job, to whom are they accountable and how can they be prevented from abusing their position? Two related questions concern how the extent of police activity is to be defined and limited and the level of government at which responsibility for policing is treated. Subsidiary issues arise about how many police forces there should be and what should be the relations between them.

Accountability to local government suggests that the police will be responsive to local feelings and have good relations with the local community. But it might also imply that the police enforce local prejudices and are easily corrupted. The British solution is to have local police forces which are heavily regulated and partly funded by the central government. A more common solution is to have more than one police force with different crimes dealt with at different levels; typically, the more serious crime is the concern of the larger territorial unit. In an extreme case a crime in the United States might be contested by the jurisdiction of six different forces, including the sole police force for the US as a whole, the Federal Bureau of Investigation. The FBI deals with crimes of an interstate nature or those beyond the capacity of more local forces; necessarily, its job must be, to some extent, to police the police.

The largest single reason for the situation in the United States is the concept of 'police power', of a clearly defined limit on the sort of things that can be policed. Constitutionally, this is limited to the 'health, safety, morals, and general welfare' of the population. Although, in principle, these criteria might seem to suggest no real limit, the courts have actually used them to limit the criminal law. In other English-speaking countries the idea of the limits of police power is less well honed in the courts, but is informally applied.   LA

policy networks Policy network models were developed to explain differences in policy-making and power in different policy sectors. They suggest that informal pressure group activities are more important than constitutional or institutional approaches accept. Policy communities are networks with relatively few actors, close working relations and general agreements over the scope, aims, and general institutional processes leading to policy output. Issue networks are larger, with more internal conflict and less agreement over the aims of the policy network. Policy networks may also be involved in the delivery as well as the development of policy and some argue that government's failure to understand the nature of a policy network may lead to implementation failures. Formal network theory measures the number and type of interactions between actors within a network. By examining the nature of different institutional frameworks and differences between the actors within networks formal network models may elucidate the interaction between structural and individual factors in the generation of policy outputs. Policy network models tend to be better at explaining stability, demonstrating similarities across nations or sectors where different formal institutional processes exist but poor at explaining policy change or fundamental political processes.   KD

policy studies Analyses of the process of policy formation. It is, ultimately, difficult to distinguish the study of policy from that of politics, since there can be no politics without policy. Indeed, the French *politique* covers both, *la vie politique* meaning roughly what anglophones call politics, and *la politique publique* meaning policy. Only in the 1960s was any distinction made between the studies of politics and policy, in the belief that the understanding of policy outcomes required a more detailed analysis of the process of policy formation than was usually attempted by academic students of politics.

It is useful to distinguish two assumptions of policy studies, the normative and the analytical. Normative policy studies constitute a very broad church, stretching well beyond the confines of the study of politics: economists, operational researchers, organizational theorists, and public administrators are all involved in critical accounts of how policy is made and how the processes could be improved. The normative study of the making of policy overlaps into studies of policy evaluation and policy implementation which tend to be well funded by governments.

Analytic policy studies are largely confined to the discipline of politics *per se*. They seek to develop models and explanations of the policy process and the variety of methods employed can approach that of the study of politics as a whole. *Public choice theory and several kinds of comparative approach offer rival insights into policy-making, while some neo-*behavioural approaches which seek to explain policy outcomes in terms of general features of the political system, make policy studies difficult to distinguish from the study of political systems. LA

policy transfer The process whereby knowledge, policies, or administrative arrangements shift from one nation or policy domain to another. It is usually thought to be an intentional 'learning' process, rather than an unintentional 'evolutionary' one where governments facing the same problems discover the same trick. It is also thought to be voluntary though it can be coercive. National governments can compel different sectors or lower levels of government to follow others' practices. Policy transfer is thought to lead to policy convergence and to be part of globalization. Where governments buy services from the same multinational corporations, pressures from the corporations may also lead to convergence and policy transfer. Because policy transfer is largely about learning, modes of information acquisition is an important aspect of the idea and transfer is supposed to occur more now than in the past due to faster more efficient global communication. Largely descriptive and atheoretical, the policy transfer literature has not yet come to grips with the transfer of bad ideas or explained why transplanted ideas are often sub-optimally changed during the transfer process. KD

polis Transliteration of the Greek word for 'city-state'. In *Plato and especially *Aristotle, *polis* has the normative connotation of the best form of social organization. Aristotle's much quoted statement 'Man is by nature a political animal' would be more accurately rendered 'Mankind is an animal whose highest form of social organization is the city-state'.

Politburo The highest executive body of the Communist Party and the Soviet state, the Politburo was headed by the General Secretary and included powerful members of the party and the government. It did not function as an effective collective body under *Stalin, and while *Khrushchev was both head of the Council of Ministers and the Party, its position was uncertain. However, with the victory of Leonid Brezhnev, its pre-eminence was established. The Politburo remains the executive body of the Indian Communist Party (Marxist). swh

political action committee See PAC (USA).

political arithmetic Term coined by Sir William Petty (1623–87) to denote vital and economic statistics, of which he was the first systematic gatherer.

political asylum A place safe from persecution; usually a country which offers protection to a victim of torture or oppression. The Universal Declaration of Human Rights (1948), Article 14, states that 'Everyone has the right to seek and to enjoy in other countries asylum from persecution', and the United Nations Convention on the Status of Refugees (1951) reiterates the duties of states to uphold the rights and benefits of people displaced from their own country. However, enforcement of these commitments has been left to individual countries, and considerations of practical and political constraints have meant that the rights of those seeking political asylum have not always been upheld. It is often difficult for victims of persecution to prove the circumstances in which they suffered, and for officials to distinguish between those displaced for political reasons and those who wish to migrate for economic reasons. Hence the treatment of those seeking political asylum has become tied up with wider debates over immigration policy.

From the mid-1990s, the politics of asylum seekers moved sharply up the political agenda in Western Europe, because many more asylum seekers tried to enter, especially from the war-torn Balkans and Afghanistan. They presented an opportunity for politicians of the right, as witnessed by the success of the French *National Front leader Jean-Marie Le Pen, in reaching the run-off round of the 2002 presidential election. They presented a difficulty for politicians of the left, who had to sound 'tough' on asylum while actually having to deal with the intractable problem. Nevertheless, tensions involving issues of political asylum have become particularly salient due to the escalations of violence in Africa, Afghanistan, and the Middle East post-2008, particularly in regard to the *Syrian Civil War and its associated *refugee crisis. The influx of asylum seekers and refugees has also given rise to new anti-immigration movements in Australia, Europe, and the United States.

political behaviour The study of the behaviour of political actors such as voters, lobbyists, and politicians. It was a banner under which sociologists, survey researchers, and other empiricists gathered in the 1950s to distinguish themselves from those who studied constitutions, philosophy, or history. Much of the best work in politics studies behaviour as well as—not instead of—one or more of these other approaches.

political business cycle *See* POLITICAL ECONOMY.

political correctness Term, originally derisive, but accepted by some of its targets, for an influential movement on US campuses beginning in the late 1980s. Appealing to the principle of *affirmative action and to various understandings of '*multiculturalism', the movement for political correctness sought changes in undergraduate curricula to emphasize the roles of women, non-white people, and homosexuals in history and culture, and attacked the domination of 'Western' culture by dead white European males.

It promoted anti-sexist and anti-racist speech and behaviour codes, which opponents denounced as illiberal.

political culture The attitudes, beliefs, and values which underpin the operation of a particular political system. These were seen as including knowledge and skills about the operation of the political system, positive and negative emotional feelings towards it, and evaluative judgements about the system. Particular regional, ethnic, or other groups within a political system with their own distinctive sets of values, attitudes, and beliefs were referred to as subcultures. A greater awareness developed over time in the literature of the importance of studying elite political cultures, given that the influence of individuals in the political process varies significantly. One of the principal objections to political culture is that it can be used as a 'garbage can variable' to explain anything which cannot be accounted for in any other way. Hence, whilst appearing to explain everything, it actually explains very little. Cultural explanations can, nevertheless, assist the understanding of how reactions to political events and developments may vary in different societies, while the analysis of subcultures remains important in understanding tensions and cleavages within particular societies.   WG

political development Broadly, the development of the institutions, attitudes, and values that form the political power system of a society. Political development has been defined in many ways that reflect the passage of societies' and analysts' preoccupations.

One formulation dwells on the emergence of national sovereignty and the integrity of the state, demanding respect and upholding commitments in the international system. Others identify the domestic attributes of constitutional order and political stability, attained through the formation of a settled framework of government, reliable procedures for leadership succession, and a consolidation of the territorial administrative reach of government institutions. This conspectus owes to the fascination exerted by nation-building and state-building in new states of Africa and Asia. It also relates to earlier studies of legal-rational authority: an endowment of coercive powers and the ability to command obedience. The establishment of *bureaucracy, displaying characteristics like division of labour and functional specialization, hierarchy and chain of command, and merit-based recruitment, is connected.

Political development enhances the state's capacity to mobilize and allocate resources, to process policy inputs into implementable outputs. This assists with problem-solving and adaptation to environmental changes and goal realization. The contemporary notion of good governance also dwells on efficient, effective, and non-corrupt public administration.

Many *Marxists define political development in advanced industrial societies in terms of the growth of the class consciousness and political organization of the proletariat, leading, ultimately, to the overthrow of capitalism and the approach of communism. A more common (though *ethnocentric) and currently very fashionable view is progress towards liberal democracy, involving accountable government, and opportunities for participation (also seen by some as an aspect of modernization, rather than development), through the exercise of such freedoms as association and expression.

Linkages between economic progress and political development are much debated. The former has traditionally been seen as a begetter or facilitator of the latter, through the agency of intervening variables like the spread of literacy and rise of plural interest groups, the accumulation of independent financial power and economic strength in society. Cross-cutting *cleavages created by economic specialization and differentiation moderate social conflict.

More recently *democratization and good governance have been portrayed both as constitutive of political development and as conditions for sustained economic development in developing areas and post-communist societies. The rule of law (and thus respect for property rights) and the development of civil society are also included although the relationships with democratization are not well understood. For example, there is a debate over sequencing, that is to say over whether the rule of law and some amount of associational life must exist before movement towards liberal democracy becomes truly

possible. The embedding of *human rights is another central plank.

The enduring problem of political development for some divided societies, as in former Yugoslavia and especially in what the World Bank calls low income countries under stress, remains how to combine political stability with political liberalization and democratization. Another challenge is safeguarding democratic transition and consolidation in the midst of drastic economic restructuring (*see* STRUCTURAL ADJUSTMENT), where that engenders popular dissatisfaction and threatens a rise in political extremism. Political development touches not just on formal constitutional and organizational arrangements but also on such informal institutions as actual political relationships, for example patron clientelism. Thus changes in attitudes and the *political culture are relevant too. All this places limits on how far political development can be imported or imposed from without.

Political development is neither linear nor irreversible; not all countries are experiencing it, and some endure periods of political decline and decay, while a few suffer terminal political breakdown, like the former USSR. *See also* DEVELOPMENT. More specifically, the rising tide of democratization which was experienced around the world in the 1990s now seems to have come to a halt, and in some societies, Zimbabwe for instance, has been reversed.   PBl

political economy The traditional meaning of the term political economy is that branch of the art of government concerned with the systematic inquiry into the nature and causes of the wealth of nations, although it is now often used loosely to describe political aspects of economic policy-making. Since the seventeenth century the meaning of the term has fluctuated widely. It is possible nevertheless to identify three broad traditions of political economy which currently influence political science. These are, first, the tradition of classical political economy; secondly, the Marxian tradition; and finally, the tradition of political economics which uses statistical and modelling techniques to test hypotheses about the relationship between government and the economy.

The first recorded usage of the term political economy, is in the opening decades of the seventeenth century (generally attributed to Antoine de Montchretien in 1615). In the French courts of Henry IV the traditional meaning of economics as 'household management', when combined with *politique*, created the new science of the public management of the affairs of state. Under the influence of François Quesnay (1694-1774), physician to Louis XV, the study of political economy received its first systematic exposition in the work of the *physiocrats. Challenging the mercantilist view that value was synonymous with money and that trade itself was productive, the physiocrats defined value in terms of the production of physical goods with all prosperity dependent on a successful agricultural sector. This view overturned the mercantilist obsession with increasing the riches of the merchants, and by stressing the interdependence of individuals within society made political economy the doctrine of the whole nation. By the mid-eighteenth century in the hands of the Scottish *Enlightenment philosophers political economy was established as the forerunner of modern social science. Political economy was now seen as a study concerned with the chief domestic business of a statesman, which according to James Steuart (*Principles of Political Economy*, 1767) was to secure a certain fund of subsistence for all the inhabitants of a society.

Adam *Smith defined political economy as a 'branch of the science of a statesman or legislator' concerned with the twofold objective of 'providing a plentiful revenue or subsistence for the people ... and [supplying] the state or commonwealth with a revenue sufficient for the public service. It proposes to enrich both the people and the sovereign' (*The Wealth of Nations*, 1776). Smith built on the work of his Scottish colleagues Francis Hutcheson, Adam Ferguson, David *Hume, and John Millar to propose that the key to understanding the development of human society lay in identifying the mode of subsistence which was dominant at each stage. Although Smith worked with a crude four-stage model (hunting, pasturage, agriculture, commerce), his analysis of early industrial capitalism led him to conclude that commerce was the pinnacle of economic civilization and that liberty was fundamental to the growth of commerce. The human propensity to truck, barter, and exchange one thing for another had led, Smith argued, to the creation of that most perfect economic mechanism, the self-regulating market, which simultaneously satisfies self-interest and the needs of the community. The benefits of the division of labour, the true source of social progress and individual well-being, were limited simply by the extent or size of the market—hence Smith's preference for free trade and winding back the economic role of the state.

Unlike the later Marginalist approach to economics developed principally by Stanley Jevons (1835-82), Carl Menger (1840-1921), and Leon Walras (1834-1910), the economy is not seen by Smith as a self-propelling mechanism isolated from the wider society of which it is a part. From Sir William Petty to John Stuart *Mill the concern of the classical political economists was to identify the social classes which comprise society, define the economic relationships between these classes and discover the laws which regulate these relationships. The structure of society is thereby conceptualized on the basis of an understanding of its economic foundation. This view was well stated by William Robertson (1812) who argued that, 'in every inquiry concerning the operations of men when united together in society, the first object of attention should be their mode of subsistence. Accordingly as that varies, their laws and policy must be different.' In addition to an economic theory of historical progress, an understanding of wealth comprising commodities (not solely treasure), and a justification for free trade based on the principle of an unfettered global division of labour, the classical political economists developed the labour theory of value which saw labour as a measure, and occasionally as a source, of all value. This latter aspect of classical political economy was fully developed by David Ricardo (1772-1823) whose *Principles of Political Economy and Taxation* sought to determine the laws which regulate the distribution of rent, profit, and wages. A vociferous opponent of the Corn Laws and the Old Poor Law, both seen as fetters on production and distribution, Ricardo refined the 'embodied labour theory of value' and concluded that the national product available for distribution was determined principally by the productivity and availability of labour. Although Ricardo believed that competitive capitalism was the ideal form of society, his analysis of value enabled the so-called Ricardian Socialists to posit the existence of a conflict of interest between capital and labour, and his theory became a radical weapon in the unrest leading up to the 1832 Reform Bill.

The doctrines of classical political economy exert a significant though often unacknowledged influence on modern political science. The technical determination of social class (on the basis of the division of labour) and the harmony of interest which is said to obtain between the classes underpins many liberal and consensus theories of politics. Most liberal writers demonstrate the advantages of market economies in terms almost identical to those laid down by Adam Smith. Within *international political economy the liberal tradition draws heavily on Smith and Ricardo to justify arguments for the removal of all forms of protectionism in the world economy. In particular Ricardo's theory of 'comparative advantage' arguing that the distribution of industry among nations should not be regulated by absolute costs of production but by relative costs, occupies a central position in liberal views on *development and underdevelopment.

The latter half of the nineteenth century saw the rise of the marginal utility theories of Jevons and the Austrian school under Menger. The marginalists redefined economics as a branch of praxiology—the science of rational action. In an attempt to introduce a more scientific and mathematically precise discipline, political economy as an economic theory of society became 'positive economics', defined later by Lionel Robbins as 'the science which studies human behaviour as a relationship between ends and scarce means which have alternative uses'. Economics could now be narrowly interpreted as an isolated study of utility-maximizing individuals expressing their subjective preferences in a taken-for-granted market situation. This left space for the growth of complementary 'disciplines' studying social action (sociology) and political action (political science). The organic study of law, government, and society on the basis of the mode of subsistence as undertaken by the classical writers became a study of the determination of price

and resource allocation in accord with individual choice.

Karl *Marx, by contrast, developed his own organic conception of capitalist society through a thoroughgoing critique and reformulation of the theories of classical political economy. Marx's early economic and philosophical studies led him to question the naturalistic basis of classical political economy. The error of the classical writers was to naturalize (or present as universal) the historically specific social relations of capitalist society. Behind the formal abstractions of classical political economy (land, labour, and capital producing rent, wages, and profit) lay an unexamined historically specific postulate, private property. Only by taking for granted the existence of private property could the classical writers assume that classes were derived technically from the division of labour. The best exponents of classical political economy for Marx provided an analysis of value and its magnitude (however incomplete) but failed to ask the vital question, 'why this content has assumed that particular form' (*Capital*, vol. i). *Capital* begins therefore with an analysis of the commodity-form in order to emphasize, in contrast to the classical writers, that the products of labour only become commodities in historically specific and thereby transitory forms of society. On this historical and materialist basis Marx builds a theory of capitalist society rooted in the concepts of value, *surplus value, and *class. The isolated individual of liberalism is parodied since private interest is itself already a socially determined interest and the symmetrical exchange relation is shown to conceal exploitation thereby exploding Smith's theory of a harmony of interest existing between classes. Capitalist society is based on a particular social form of production within which the production of useful goods is subordinated to the expansion of surplus value. Although, therefore, Marx agrees with the classical writers that 'the anatomy of civil society is to be sought in political economy', his total reformulation of the classical concepts inaugurated a revolution in social and political theory the results of which have yet to be fully assimilated into mainstream political science.

Despite the dominance of marginalist definitions of economics in most orthodox academic circles, radical Marxian political economy continued to develop in the early part of the twentieth century and received a stimulus from the *Keynesian critique of neoclassical economics in the initial post-1945 period in Western Europe and the United States. In addition the new discipline of international political economy studies the reciprocal influence of politics upon economics in the global system, whilst radical *environmental politics is premissed on rejecting marginalist economics in favour of a more explicitly political conception of the world economy.

In an attempt to break free from the ideological connotations which surround the term political economy, a growing number of political scientists now work in the field of political economics. This principally studies the role of politicians in the making of economic policy and the effect of economic performance on the popularity/electability of governments. The methodology of modern political economics relies heavily on statistical and econometric modelling and emphasizes that hypotheses must be both logically formatted and capable of *falsifiability. The theory of the political business cycle, which claims that governments suspend their particular policy orientation in the run-up to an election in favour of policies which enhance popularity with voters, is a well-known hypothesis from the subdiscipline of political economics.

The traditions of classical and Marxian political economy have survived and are flourishing because the school of neoclassical economics is often reluctant to consider the political basis and the social implications of capitalist production and distribution. Political economy as a reflexive discipline analysing the fundamental political issues which arise from the accumulation and distribution of the surplus product in capitalism offers a vigorous challenge to the disciplinary boundaries which characterize modern social science.   PBM

political geography The geography of states, federations, and substate units. The term was first taken beyond the purely descriptive by *Montesquieu's suggestion that there was a link between types of climate and types of political regime. The father of modern political geography was

André *Siegfried, whose demonstrations of *ecological associations between soil types and voting behaviour in France have been more admired than copied (but *see* V. O. KEY). Ecological association fell under a cloud because of the risk of fallacious inference, but has recently revived.

political participation See PARTICIPATION, POLITICAL.

political philosophy The systematic elaboration of the consequences for politics of suggested resolutions of philosophical dilemmas (or of the intractability of those dilemmas). The greatest works of political philosophy try to present those consequences in relation to fundamental cosmological, ontological, and epistemological issues. They articulate a view of human nature which links the cosmological with the political. On a less grand scale, political philosophy explores the political implications of particular disputes, for example about the nature of the self (*see* COMMUNITARIANISM; FREEDOM; LIBERALISM; and AUTONOMY), or about the notion of moral responsibility (*see* PUNISHMENT). There is obviously a close connection between political philosophy and moral philosophy, because both involve exploring the nature of judgements we make about our values; consequently, when it was thought on epistemological grounds that it was not the place of philosophy to explore these normative matters, political philosophy was declared to be dead. Contemporary political philosophy flourishes because the epistemological argument once thought fatal to it has been rejected.

Political philosophy tries both to make sense of what we do, and to prescribe what we ought to do. Hence different conceptions of the nature of philosophy lead to different views of its status in relation to political activity. Many have contrasted the contemplative nature of philosophy with the active, practical character of politics, suggesting that the former provides a 'higher' form of activity which is in danger of corruption by the latter. Others have sought to ensure that their political practice is built upon a coherent philosophical foundation. When *Marx complained that philosophers had only interpreted the world, but that the point was to change it, he was proposing not the abandonment of philosophy, but a more adequate conception of it.

Both philosophy and political analysis raise issues which are timeless, but both have a history and both will, at a particular time, be engaged by contemporary circumstances or intellectual preoccupations. Perhaps the most abiding question in political philosophy is whether mankind has a nature, and, if so, what follows for political organization. Some answers to that question put human nature in a historical context. Perhaps the most abiding political issue is the legitimacy of government. But although these problems have constantly to be addressed, the situation and experience of those struggling to respond to them necessarily differ. For example, how is the experience of *totalitarianism to be described, understood, or explained? Political philosophy may thus be approached historically, and with an emphasis on the *context of an author's work, and analytically, with a critical approach to its internal coherence or inexplicit assumptions. Contemporary political philosophy also has its context, of course, while earlier writers struggled to find eternal truths, so these approaches are properly complementary in the exploration of the political consequences of the human condition.   AR

political science The study of the state, government, and politics. The idea that the study of politics should be 'scientific' has excited controversy for centuries. What is at stake is the nature of our political knowledge, but the content of the argument has varied enormously. For example, in 1741 when *Hume published his essay, 'That Politics May Be Reduced to a Science', his concerns were very different from those of people who have sought to reduce politics to a science in the twentieth century. Although concerned to some degree to imitate the paradigm of Newtonian physics, Hume's main objective was to show that some constitutions necessarily worked better than others and that politics was not just a question of personalities. Thus one of his main targets was the famous couplet in Alexander Pope's *Essay on Man*: 'For forms of government let fools contest, | Whate'er is best administer'd is best.'

The twentieth-century debate about political science has been part of a broad dispute about methodology in social studies. Those who have sought to make the study of politics scientific have been concerned to establish a discipline which can meet two conditions: it must be objective or value-free (*wertfrei*), and it must seek comprehensive and systematic explanations of events. The principal candidate for the role of core methodology of political science has been *behaviourism, drawing its stimulus-response model from behavioural psychology and thus being much concerned to establish 'correlations' between input phenomena, whether 'political' or not, and political outcomes. The chief rival, growing in stature as behaviourism waned after 1970, has been *rational choice theory, following economics in assuming as axioms universal human properties of rationality and self-interest.

Critics of the idea of political science have normally rested their case on the uniqueness of natural science. In the philosophical terminology of *Kant, real science is the product of the *synthetic a priori* proposition that 'every event has a cause'. The idea that the universe is regular, systematic, and law-governed follows from neither logic nor observation; it is what Sir Peter Strawson has called, more recently, a 'precondition of discourse'. In order for people to study physics rationally, they must assume that the universe is governed by laws.

It follows from this Kantian conception of the basis of science that there can only be one science, which is physics. This science applies just as much to people, who are physical beings, as it does to asteroids: like the theistic God, Kantian physics is unique or it is not itself. Biology, chemistry, engineering *et al.* are forms of physics, related and reducible to the fundamental constituents of the universe. The social studies are not, according to critics of political science, and become merely narrow and sterile if they attempt to ape the methods and assumptions of the natural sciences. The understanding we seek of human beings must appreciate their individual uniqueness and freedom of will; understanding people is based on our ability to see events from their point of view, the kind of insight that *Weber called *verstehen*. In short, the distinction between science and non-science, in its most significant sense, is a distinction between the natural sciences and the humanities; the two are fundamentally different and politics is a human discipline.

However, there are a number of objections to this harsh dichotomy between politics and science. Semantically, it might be said, this account reads too much into the concept of science which, etymologically, indicates only a concern with knowledge in virtually any sense. *Wissenschaft* in German, *scienza* in Italian, and *science* in French do not raise the profound philosophical questions which have been attached to the English word science. There are also many contemporary philosophers who seek to undermine the scientific nature of natural science. Inspired, particularly, by Thomas Kuhn's *The Structure of Scientific Revolutions* (1962) they argue that science itself is not determined by the absolute requirements of its discourse, but is structured by the societies in which it operates. Thus real physics is more like politics than it is like the Kantian ideal of physics, and it has no more claim to be a science than has politics.   LA

political socialization The process by which people come to acquire political attitudes and values. Socialization in childhood has been extensively studied. Children first acquire warm feelings towards authority figures who might appear in fairy stories (such as queens and princesses). Similarly warm feelings to elected officials (presidents, prime ministers) emerge later, *party identification later again, and something like a reasoned *ideology not until well into the teenage years. The earliest socialization is believed to be the deepest. Therefore one's awareness of one's sex and ethnicity precedes anything more directly political. Each layer of socialization colours those that come afterwards.

Critics of socialization research make a number of points:

1 There have been too few studies of children whose family position and early experiences might be expected to put them at odds with the values of most people in their society.

2 Socialization research cannot by its nature tap *false consciousness or any other way in which dominant values may be inculcated without the subjects of it being aware of it.

3 Party identification is not necessarily a reliable guide to voting, or political attitudes. Sex and ethnicity are genetically determined; political attitudes are not.

political sociology Political sociology broadly conceived is the study of power and domination in social relationships. It could thereby include analysis of the family, the mass media, universities, trade unions, and so on.

Political science and sociology began to develop as independent disciplines in the nineteenth century under the influence of marginalist economics which attempted to demarcate the study of the 'political' from that of the 'social' and the 'economic' (*see* POLITICAL ECONOMY). Political science became focused on the analysis of the machinery of government, the mechanisms of public administration and theories of governance. Sociology adopted a much broader definition of its subject matter. *Weber provided the theoretical underpinning for modern sociology defined as the interpretative understanding of social action linked to a causal explanation of its course and consequences. By concentrating on the reciprocal influence of social structure on social action, sociology is free to analyse all forms of social interaction (from language and sexuality to religion and industry).

Three main approaches to political sociology have considerably narrowed its subject area. The first builds directly on Max Weber's notion of 'politically oriented action'. Weber defined an organization as 'political' in so far as its existence and order is continuously safeguarded within a territorial area by the threat and application of physical force on the part of an administrative staff (*see* STATE). The study of the direct agents of the legitimate use of force could, Weber argued, be distinguished from the study of groups which attempt to influence the activities of the political organization. This latter study Weber designated as 'politically oriented' action. Weberian political sociologists have therefore traditionally focused attention on such issues as voting behaviour in communities, ideologies of political movements and interest groups, sociopsychological correlates of political behaviour and organization, and the relationship between economic power and political decision-making. In the late 1960s under the influence of Seymour Lipset and Stein Rokkan a second main approach to political sociology was developed. The subdiscipline now encompassed the comparative and historical study of political systems and nation-building. By analysing the role of political institutions in social development (and revolution) this branch of political sociology has contributed to the comparative analysis of welfare systems, to studies of the relationship between democracy and industrialization, and to charting the role of the state in the creation of national identity. The third focus of modern political sociology is on theories of the state, and here the subdiscipline draws particularly on currents in Western Marxism and contemporary political theory. Building on the Marxist critique of *pluralist approaches to the state, political sociologists have focused on the problem of state/society relations and developed detailed empirical studies of the exercise of power both within and between states. PBM

political theory Critical, systematic reflection about power in its public and private forms, particularly about the claims of government to possess legitimacy and authority; and, more generally, such reflection about the place of politics in social life. There is no generally accepted distinction between political theory and *political philosophy, but two differences of emphasis may be mentioned. First, political philosophers have developed and defended particular conceptions of human nature, before going on to explore the implications of their view for political life; but political theory may be less ambitious, exploring what follows if assumptions are made about that nature. Secondly, because political theory is eclectic, it draws upon the work not only of philosophers but also of lawyers and social scientists: particularly sociologists, economists, and psychologists—as well as, of course, political scientists. Its ambitions are to explain the political realm, to explore what is at stake in political practice, and to elucidate the values which motivate political action or which are affected by it.

One approach to the fulfilment of these ambitions is conceptual inquiry, aiming to elucidate the meaning and value-content of ideals by which political actors are guided,

like *liberty, *equality, and *fraternity, or terms of political debate and analysis like *power and *authority. A second approach has been the provision of models of behaviour generated by a restricted set of assumptions and compared to experience. In particular, there has been some emulation of the process of model-building in economics, and often the direct use of the assumption of self-interested behaviour associated with it. So, for example, *democracy has been modelled as a market in which parties (producers) meet voters (consumers). More generally, *game theory has been applied to explore what 'rational' actors would do in political contexts. Thirdly, reflecting its eclectic nature, political theory has aimed to synthesize the findings or insights of the many disciplines upon which it draws. For example, the political theory of *property has tried to embrace the philosophical, psychological, sociological, legal, and economic components of the social significance of property. Fourthly, there is the critical evaluation of the findings of political science, in particular a concern with the methodology of inquiry which is informed by the philosophy of the social sciences. Fifthly, prescription may result from analysis of contemporary conditions: for example, arguments in favour of greater participation are associated with a particular diagnosis of democratic malaise. Finally, there is a concern with the exploration of political *ideologies, particularly *socialism, *conservatism, and *liberalism. Because such exploration has a necessary historical component, political theory and political philosophy are brought together to the point where many practitioners would deny that a useful distinction may be made between them. AR

politics As a general concept, the practice of the art or science of directing and administrating states or other political units. However, the definition of politics is highly, perhaps *essentially, contested. There is considerable disagreement on which aspects of social life are to be considered 'political'. At one extreme, many (notably, but not only, feminists) assert that 'the *personal is political', meaning that the essential characteristics of political life can be found in any relationship, such as that between a man and a woman. Popular usage, however, suggests a much narrower domain for politics: it is often assumed that politics only occurs at the level of government and the state and must involve party competition. In the sense developed in Bernard Crick's *In Defence of Politics*, the phenomenon of politics is very limited in time and space to certain kinds of liberal, pluralistic societies which allow relatively open debate.

To say that an area of activity, like sport, the arts, or family life is not part of politics, or is 'nothing to do with politics', is to make a particular kind of political point about it, principally that it is not to be discussed on whatever is currently regarded as the political agenda. Keeping matters off the political agenda can, of course, be a very effective way of dealing with them in one's own interests.

The traditional definition of politics, 'the art and science of government', offers no constraint on its application since there has never been a consensus on which activities count as government. Is government confined to the state? Does it not also take place in church, guild, estate, and family?

There are two fundamental test questions we can apply to the concept of politics. First, do creatures other than human beings have politics? Second, can there be societies without politics? From classical times onward there have been some writers who thought that other creatures did have politics: in the mid-seventeenth century Purchas was referring to bees as the 'political flying-insects'. Equally there have been attempts—before and since More coined the term—to posit '*Utopian' societies with no politics. The implication is usually ('Utopia' means nowhere) that such a society is conceivable but not practically possible.

A modern mainstream view might be: politics applies only to human beings, or at least to those beings which can communicate symbolically and thus make statements, invoke principles, argue, and disagree. Politics occurs where people disagree about the distribution of goods, benefits, or statuses and have at least some procedures for the resolution of such disagreements. It is thus not present in the *state of nature where people make war on each other in their own interests, shouting, as it were, 'I will have that' rather than 'I have a right to that'. It is also absent in other cases, where there is a monolithic and complete

agreement on the rights and duties in a society. Of course, it can be objected that this definition makes the presence or absence of politics dependent on a contingent feature of consciousness, the question of whether people accept the existing rules. If one accepts notions of 'latent disagreement', there is, again, no limit to the political domain. LA

politics and economics Politics has been variously described as centrally concerned: (1) with civil government, the state, and public affairs; (2) with human conflict and its resolution; or (3) with the sources and exercise of power. Correspondingly, definitions of economics have generally focused upon: (1) systems of production and exchange; (2) rational behaviour directed towards the maximization of utility through optimal allocation of scarce resources; or (3) the accumulation and distribution of wealth.

However, agreed definitions in the social sciences are not to be held cheaply. Their ill-defined frontiers allow for periodic incursions and skirmishes. The border between politics and economics is peculiarly open, for the obvious reason that states dispose of substantial material resources while production and exchange can hardly take place without some framework of security. The main varieties of definition nonetheless deserve attention, since they help clarify the grounds on which challenges to the integrity of each discipline have generally been based.

Clearly the two sets of definitions are analogous. The first pair has to do with institutions; the second with means or processes; the third solely with ends. Taking them in turn, it is clear that few students of politics would readily abandon the study of warfare to economists simply because states are resorting to widespread use of mercenaries and contractors. They regard the production of at least this one essential service of the provision of defence as unequivocally public. Conversely, economists spend a great deal of their time studying the competitive behaviour of free rational actors in markets. But many concede that firms are hierarchical organizations within which authority substitutes for voluntary exchange, that contracts can hardly be relied upon without a framework of law backed up by the state, and that extensive command economies have from time to time existed in which the role of the free market was severely constrained. Large firms have been known to use a variety of means, including their influence over states, to compete by raising the costs of their competitors rather than cutting their own. Mercantilist states routinely do the same. But while many economists deplore such market imperfections, few would wish to concede the study of even the most grossly imperfect markets to political scientists. In short, the mixed character of even those institutions which seem archetypically political or economic often turns out on closer examination to call for forms of analysis more often associated with the rival discipline.

Notwithstanding the dominance of *rational choice approaches in many university departments of political science, especially in the USA, one of the more plausible lines of argument for those who wish to claim that politics is something more than the study of economics by the innumerate would seem to be to put their trust in irrationality as a defining feature of human social interaction, whether it be expressed in terms of the Thomistic concept of a sphere of practical reason shot through with contingency because of the Fall, the Hobbesian notion of mankind as the only species able to lie, or the Hegelian idea of absolute free will. Naturally, this poses methodological problems. How may the irrational investigate itself rationally, and why indeed might it really wish to? *See also* POLITICAL ECONOMY.   CJ

politics and psychology The methods and theories of psychology have been borrowed by politics on an increasing scale since the early twentieth century: in the academic interpretation of political behaviour; and in their utilization by practising politicians. The applicability of psychology in the interpretation and practice of politics nevertheless remains controversial.

In the early twentieth century human psychology was not widely seen as a key determinant of political development compared to structural or functional characteristics of the broader political system. In that it was, it was assumed that the self-perpetuating imprinting from one generation to another and the stabilizing aspects of the consequent wider culture determined basic personality structures consistent with the maintenance of political stability. The experience of fascist regimes, however, defied explanations within the conventional wisdom. The phenomenon of the *authoritarian personality was isolated, and political psychologists set about the explanation both of the phenomenon and the support that it attracted. They focused on the subject's family background, following the hypothesis that a perceived absence of parental love is the fountain of fantasized solutions to the problems of emotional deprivation which then become manifest in expansive desires for dominance. The conditions which created mass obedience to fascist regimes were analysed in terms of individuals: (1) giving up the private ego-ideal, embedded in the will of the leader; (2) regressing to infantile responses, thus allowing great scope for the group ideal; and (3) becoming easy prey to the imperatives of a collective paranoia against stated enemies.

Academic political psychology expanded to take in more mundane actions and events. Here the development of psychoanalysis has proved enriching, although inclined to foster a continuing obsession with the more rare authoritarian personality syndrome. Explanation of adaptation by political psychologists has also taken in the analysis of electoral behaviour, mass public opinion, and political activity, notably through political parties. Writers, such as Talcott Parsons and Gabriel Almond, propounded the thesis that participation in the democratic process was the principal determinant of adaptation. However, they differed over what determined participation, specifying causation variously to be the result of leadership styles or other elite political control processes or the first stage of *political socialization, in particular through school. Those who found no clear causes, however, were driven back to the normal assumptions of personality imprinting and political stability, looking for non-systematic causes of participation and adaptation as exceptional events in a similar manner to the analysts of the authoritarian personality.

Political psychology has also increasingly focused on group decision-making in executive elites or policy communities, as key areas of political activity. They have applied theories of bargaining and negotiation, culled from social psychology, to collective dilemmas of conflict resolution or policy coordination. However, this has been challenged by the economic approach to politics which stresses rational choice as the basis of political action, and hence asserted decision-making to be contingent upon the outcome of relations between rationally competing actors. Interestingly even some neo-Marxist writers have shown a tendency to embrace rational choice approaches to politics in the context of wider socio-economic pressures. In practice, it is likely that both rational and interrelational motives apply.

The development of approaches in academic political psychology was reflected in those applied by practising politicians. The mass propaganda strategies of Hitler's regime, notably through the work of Goebbels, gave way to more routine usage by political actors of the mass media, particularly from the 1960s in order to increase democratic participation and/or win election. During the 1980s political marketing was exported from the United States to a number of other countries, notably the United Kingdom. Party programmes are treated as products and the electorate as consumers, who are assumed to be individually rationally self-interested, and if not, are encouraged to be so. Parties both in government and opposition employ a large cadre of political advisers focused on the favourable presentation of policy. In that they are central to spinning stories in the media, and because the mass media has become such a key vehicle for political exchange, so-called '*spin doctors' have become major political figures in their own right. JBr

politics of fear Fear is an emotion and the processes of generation of fear, either 'imagined' or 'real' fear, are context and time contingent, often shaped by the specificity of places in which the events take place. Fear can be constructed and politicized in particular ways around certain groups, and widely used to serve certain political interests, for example in relation to ethnic, sectarian, or marginalized communities. Thus fear may come to control certain political discourses. Fear can be generated from terror and consent can be won through fear (through beatings, disappearances, forceful abductions). Consequently, people can come to live in a 'chronic' state of fear. There is a dialectical relationship between silence and fear. Fear engenders both silence and secrecy. Though silence can operate as a survival strategy, yet silencing is a powerful mechanism of control enforced through fear. Silence can also create more fear and uncertainty. People choose to remain silent because they are aware that talking could lead to repercussions and recriminations. Fear is not only a subjective experience but can be collectively experienced by communities. Geographical concentrations of fear can draw a wedge between communities as fear arises from distrust of strangers but also of each other. Fear feeds on the imagination and may be spread through rumour, myths, and stereotypes. STH

poll tax Two meanings, based on different meanings of 'poll', but with considerable convergence.

1 A tax levied at a flat rate per head on each inhabitant of a given district ('poll' meaning 'the human head', hence 'person on a list'). Two celebrated poll taxes have been levied in England: one in 1381 (actually the third of a series that started in 1377), and one in 1990. The tax of 1381 was described at the time as 'hitherto unheard-of'. It was difficult and intrusive to collect, and was widely evaded in places the collectors found difficult to reach, such as Cornwall. It led to serious rioting, and the Savoy Palace (near present-day Trafalgar Square) was burnt down. It was abandoned because of popular resistance. The tax of 1990 (1989 in Scotland) was difficult and intrusive to collect, and was widely evaded in places the collectors found difficult to reach, such as inner London. It led to serious rioting, and buildings at Trafalgar Square were set alight. It was abandoned because of popular resistance. Nevertheless, it may have had an unexpected benefit for the Conservatives who introduced it. By giving less affluent voters an incentive to disappear from the electoral register, it may have enabled the Conservatives to win more seats in the 1992 General Election, and therefore win that election by a wider margin, than they would otherwise have done.

2 A tax levied as a precondition of registering as an elector ('poll' meaning 'the counting of votes at an election'). They were used in Southern states of the United States as one of a number of ways of preventing black citizens from voting (*see* CIVIL RIGHTS) and were made unconstitutional in federal elections by the Twenty-Fourth Amendment to the Constitution (1964).

Because the electoral register was one of the sources that could be used for compiling the register for the British poll tax, it had an effect (no doubt unintentionally) similar to that of a poll tax in sense (2).

polyarchy Literally, 'rule by the many'. Term resurrected by R. A. Dahl (1971) to denote a representative democracy with substantial interest-group influence on government. Dahl defended the *pluralist institutions of a modern representative democracy both against those who claimed that countries were governed by narrow 'power elites' and against those who were fearful of the 'tyranny of the majority'; Dahl's case-studies showed that neither was true, at least in New Haven, Connecticut. In more recent work (notably *A Preface to Economic Democracy*, 1985), Dahl has been more critical of pluralist regimes for the lack of democracy inside institutions such as companies.

pooled sovereignty A term used to denote the sharing of decision-making powers between states in systems of international cooperation. Whereas unanimous decision-making between states leaves sovereignty unscathed, given the right of any state to unilaterally veto decisions, pooling of sovereignty implies a departure from unanimous decision-making. The most prominent system of international cooperation in which sovereignty is pooled is the European Union (EU). In a number of issue areas which have been defined in the treaty and subsequent treaty amendments, the member state delegates in the Council, one of the EU's legislative organs, decide by a qualified majority. Consequently, pooling creates the possibility that individual member states can be outvoted. The main reason why states choose to pool sovereignty is to reduce the likelihood of gridlock in policy areas where—on average—states expect to be better off by pooling sovereignty than by retaining the unanimity rule. This has been the case particularly in the context of creating a European single market for goods and services. The introduction of qualified majority voting in these issues demonstrated that EU member states valued the benefits of the abolition of trade barriers more than those that would have been associated with retaining the right to veto. However, in policy areas which governments consider particularly sensitive for domestic or ideological reasons or where the potential gains from pooling sovereignty are uncertain, governments are likely to retain the right to veto (for example, foreign and security policy, and redistributive policies). BR

Popper, Karl (1902–94) Philosopher of the social sciences. Born in Vienna, Popper was influenced by the intellectual debates around psychoanalysis, Marxism, and logical positivism; and inspired by a lecture given by Einstein on relativity theory. He sought to integrate scientific method with social inquiry by developing his criterion of *falsifiability; which distinguishes between testable hypotheses and other 'metaphysical' statements. In the *Open Society and its Enemies* (1945) Popper attacked philosophers, including Plato, Hegel, and Marx, who sought to constrain the development of social thought; be it through adherence to custom, religion, or moral absolutism. Both *utopianism and *historicism, Popper argues, are based on insubstantial assertions of abstract truths, which were not appropriate bases for political activity. Rather, he suggests, human development would thrive in societies which were open to self-criticism and which encouraged and sustained the free interaction of ideas. In the light of this, Popper presented a social theory which embraced limited government, the free market, and reform through gradual change. AM

popular front Broad collaboration between left-wing and bourgeois parties. Espoused, in a policy turnabout, at the Seventh Congress of Comintern in 1935 which focused upon the anti-fascist struggle. Other important examples were the Popular Front Governments in France and Spain 1936–8). GL

populism 1. A movement in the United States that gave expression to the grievances and disillusionment of (largely Western) farmers, who felt themselves oppressed by debt and let down by dishonoured promises of cheap land and cheap railroad rates. The movement began in the 1870s, peaked with the Populist Party's running of a candidate for President and electing four Senators in 1892, took a leading role in the *Democratic Party in 1896, and gradually merged into the more broadly based *Progressive movement.

2. A democratic and collectivist movement in late nineteenth-century Russia. 'Populist' is a direct translation of Russian *narodnik*, first recorded in the *Oxford English Dictionary* in an 1895 article by one of the leading populists, P. Milyoukov.

3. More generally, support for the preferences of ordinary people. The meaning has always been somewhat derogatory. In so far as a specific set of populist beliefs can be identified, they involve defence of the (supposed) traditions of the little man against change seen as imposed by powerful outsiders, which might variously be governments, businesses, or trade unions. These beliefs are disproportionately prevalent among the *petite bourgeoisie. Although the Russian populists were intellectuals going among the peasantry, most populism is anti-intellectual in tone. Movements which have been generally regarded as populist include *Peronism, *Poujadism, and the US Presidential campaigns of Ross Perot in 1992 and 1996. Politicians of any party may appeal to populist sentiment when it suits them, and denounce such appeals when that suits them.

pork barrel legislation Legislation that allocates government money to projects in a certain constituency. Particularly associated with US politics, where legislators seek to base military or transport facilities, and government agencies in their own constituency. Electoral prospects, especially for Congressmen, often depend on how much 'pork' they can divert to their home district, and members are reluctant to obstruct each other's pet projects in case their own are defeated. *See also* LOGROLLING.

pornography Literally, 'writing about prostitutes': obscene publications. Female pornography is seen by *feminists as a mode of oppression and exercise of power by the stronger sex. The woman's body is sexualized and various parts of her anatomy are used to provide pleasure to the male gaze. Pornography entails sexual exploitation and male violence. However, similar modes of exploitation can also be located in family life and certain state policies. Pornography is associated with the abusive and degrading portrayal of female sexuality through words and sexually explicit material. Another characteristic of pornography is the dehumanization and objectification of women's bodies.   STH

positional goods Term coined by F. Hirsch in *Social Limits to Growth* (1977) to denote goods which are valued for their scarcity alone: examples given include unspoilt countryside and high educational qualifications. Hirsch argued that competition for these goods was necessarily *zero-sum. Thus he distanced himself both from doomsters whose then-influential *The Limits to Growth* (ed. D. Meadows *et al.* for the Club of Rome, 1972) had argued that mankind was about to run out of natural resources and from conventional economists who saw no insuperable limits to growth through increasing material abundance. Critics of Hirsch have argued that the concept of positional goods disappears under close examination, but it has remained influential.

positive discrimination An institutionalized way of enabling those historically disadvantaged by a political system to participate in public life. Positive discrimination implies applying different criteria for selection to representatives of different groups as a way of addressing the existing social inequalities. It can be distinguished from positive or *affirmative action which implies taking proactive steps to encourage certain groups to participate in the social, economic, and political life of a country. So, for example, there might be a concerted effort made to spread information about job recruitment in particular geographical or social areas by advertising for jobs in local and/or targeted newspapers, magazines, and so on. At times positive discrimination is purely political in nature, as, for example, the quota system initiated by the Labour Party in Britain to increase women's representation within the party. In some cases it is seen more as a way of increasing opportunity, especially through better education. In the United States, for example, cases of positive discrimination in the 1970s focused on setting aside a fixed number of seats on courses in educational institutions. In India places are *reserved for those of the lowest castes under the Ninth Schedule of the Indian Constitution in state-supported employment, and in educational and political institutions at all levels. Supporters of the system see this as the dominant groups in society paying off a historical debt, and as an enabling process that will lead to more integrated societies. Critics point out that the system negates the principles of both equality and merit, and further, that it permits whole sections of society to avoid competition, which in turn reinforces prejudices. SR

positive rights Positive rights are often described as representative of a 'right to', 'entitlement to', or claim for action or mandatory obligation from others, including governmental authorities. In general, positive rights are often viewed as a set of social obligations required for individual well-being. This is distinct from *negative rights, which often describe negative rights as being left alone 'from something', or which command inaction from others. Despite their wide use there is considerable disagreement regarding how clearly distinctions can be made between negative rights and positive rights, since some combination of inaction and action will be required to fulfil either negative or positive duties, or entitlements, which are associated with the right.

positivism Term coined by *Comte to denote the rejection of value judgements in social science. Influenced by the French *Enlightenment even as he distanced himself from it, Comte believed in the development of science from its earlier theological and metaphysical stages to one which concerned itself only with observable facts and relationships. Though Comte himself later veered off into belief in a Religion of Humanity, these ideas have become unassailable in economics and strong (but not unassailable) in the other social sciences. In philosophy, they were restated as logical positivism in the 1930s. Supporters of positivism assert that science, including social science, is not the place for value judgements. Its critics assert that a 'fact' is not so simple a thing as Comte imagined, and that positivists' purported exclusion of value judgements is itself a value judgement (e.g. *see* PARETO).

In international relations, positivism denotes an epistemological position, which recognizes 'truth' as only that which can be naturally observed, scientifically measured, and/or mathematically proven. Advocates of positivism often contrast their position against metaphysical, theoretical, interpretivist, and *poststructural approaches, which they suggest lack empirical validity, scientific rigour, objectivity, and retestability.

post-colonialism Post-colonialism can be taken to refer to two distinct but related things. In general usage the hyphenated term 'post-colonialism' refers to the period since the end of colonialism and the conditions prevailing in societies and cultures that were previously colonized. As such it describes aspects of those societies and cultures that still bear the legacies of colonialism and the continuing presence of hierarchies of power, both within those societies and between the *Global North and the *Global South, whose roots lie in the era of colonialism. As such, the term has affinity with the concepts of *neo-colonialism and the *post-colonial state.

The non-hyphenated term 'postcolonialism' is generally taken to refer to the body of academic analysis and theory that seeks to understand, explain, and interrogate the continuing relevance of colonialism in today's world. Post-colonial theory includes work across the social sciences and humanities including cultural studies, history, anthropology, and literature, as well as politics and international relations. Key concerns of post-colonialism include analysing the perpetuation of colonial forms of power and knowledge; challenging historical and contemporary accounts which privilege western knowledge and interests; and promoting perspectives and views of 'subaltern' actors in the Global South. Research in post-colonialism often draws on sources from literature, culture, and personal testimonials to interrogate and critique western modes of thinking and governance WB

post-colonial state Term applied to the new nation-states that emerged out of the process of *decolonization in the post-World War II period. As with other uses of the term 'post-colonial', it refers both to this temporal characteristic—coming after colonialism—as well as to a number of other features related to the states' emergence from *colonialism. These other features include the ways in which post-colonial states exhibit aspects of statehood borrowed from the colonial power, such as the adoption of aspects of the British parliamentary system by ex-British colonies such as India. Attention has also been drawn to the ways in which the post-colonial states retained colonial-era boundaries, institutions, and political processes. Some scholars trace aspects of post-colonial politics, such as political *authoritarianism and highly ethnicized politics, to this history.

Post-colonial states have been characterized both in terms of their political and economic agenda and in terms of their 'infrastructural capacity'. Most post-colonial states embarked on interventionist programmes of development. However, their capacity to implement their programmes was affected crucially by their ability to implement political decisions and the strength of their political infrastructure. 'Strong' states are thus distinguished from merely 'despotic' ones and from 'weak' states where such infrastructure is lacking.

State capacity is, of course, linked to the economic resources available to the state but also to the evolving relations between the political executive and the bureaucracy on the one hand and state and civil society on the other. The 'embeddedness' of the state in society has been regarded by some as a feature of a 'strong' state, in the sense that it gains the cooperation of important state and societal interest groups, and by others as characterizing a 'weak' state, where the state is penetrated by *civil society and interest groups that are too strong for it to control. Weak capacity in post-colonial states is also linked to levels of political violence, in that the governability of a society is dependent upon the political infrastructure of the state, and where this is ineffective the state increasingly relies upon the use of violence. Governability is thus a continuing and growing concern for post-colonial states.

As a result of economic and political reform, processes of *globalization, and in some cases rapid economic growth, there is some debate as to whether the forms of statehood characteristic of the independence era are being transcended. While some point to the modernization of political systems and state institutions and the growth of civil society, others highlight the 'hollowing out' of the state and the prospect of further economic subordination to powerful external actors in a 'race to the bottom'. SR/WB

post-fordism *See* FORDISM; INDUSTRIAL SOCIETY.

post-industrialism *See* INDUSTRIAL SOCIETY.

post-materialism Concept due to the survey research of R. Inglehart in the 1970s, who argued that his results showed that younger and more affluent people in Western democracies were moving away from material concerns for income and security to post-material concerns such as a concern for civil liberties or for the environment. This has been weakly confirmed by subsequent research.

post-modernism A school of thought which rejects what is called modernism. Post-modernism is a broad term originating in literary studies, used by and of those thinkers who seek to respond in various ways to 'modernism'. For post-modernists, *modernity* begins sometime in the seventeenth century and ends sometime between 1945 and the present. It is characterized by the ascendancy of science and reason as means for both understanding and explaining the world. The success of the rational application of science to nature and the progress that ensued in this field, led to a belief that rational and scientific approaches to economics, politics, society, and morality would ensure progress in these fields too. Science and reason would be capable of providing firm, objective, and universal foundations with which to underpin social and moral reforms. It is in this sense that thinkers as diverse as *Hobbes, *Bentham, and *Marx may be described as 'modern'.

Writers who see themselves, or are seen by others, as post-modernist respond initially to what they perceive to be the twin failures of science and reason to deliver progress. (*Adorno, for example, remarked that no one can seriously believe in the idea of progress after the Holocaust.) The 'failure' of science and reason and the objective and universal claims made in their name undermines the possibility of ever producing 'totalizing' theories again—theories ('Grand Narratives') that seek to explain and predict individual behaviour and/or social formations on the basis of a set of incontrovertible, rationally derived propositions. Examples of such theories would be Marxism, *utilitarianism, and Freudianism.

On this basis, some post-modernists argue that knowledge claims can only ever be partial and local. *Foucault, for example, suggests that power is not a unified and uniform phenomenon centred on, say, the 'state' (as Marxists might take it to be). Resistance to power, therefore, must itself be 'decentred' or localized. Post-modernism in these terms is open to the charges both of relativism and conservatism. Relativism, because, if all that we have access to are local knowledges, practices, and so on, we can have no justifiable reason to judge other localities and their practices. Conservatism, because if we cannot judge even our own localities (institutions, practices, societies, etc.) in the light of standards or principles external to them, it is unclear what justification we could ever have for changing them. On the other hand, if one associates modernity with the rise and globalization of capitalism, and accepts that this phenomenon is itself a form of cultural and economic imperialism, then post-modernism can be represented as having radical potential in the attempt to formulate a defence of difference. AA

post-positivism An umbrella term for a range of IR approaches including *constructivism, *critical theory, *Marxism, *feminism, *post-structuralism, and *historical analysis. Post-positivists claim to challenge the dominance of *positivism through a critical or normative approach in contrast to what is seen as the rationalist or objectivist bias of the dominant theories. *See also* REFLECTIVISM. JJ

post-structuralism A loss of faith, most marked since 1968, in the entire family of social and political explanations, including

Saussurian linguistics, dialectical materialism, neoclassical economics, and neorealist international relations theory, held by post-structuralists to have obscured the world by privileging continuity over change, social structure over human agency, and generalization over detail. CJ

Poujadism A French movement (UDCA) created by Pierre Poujade after 1953, mobilizing the lower middle classes, shopkeepers and artisans, and the peasantry in the south, in opposition to big business and the unions, the state and the administration, but mainly to taxes. Right-wing and *populist, but also republican, the Poujadists exploited widespread discontent with the Fourth Republic, winning over two- and-a-half million votes in the 1956 election and returning fifty-three deputies. Within two years, lacking leadership and a programme, the movement collapsed. IC

Poulantzas, Nicos (1936–79) Greek neo-Marxist theorist whose primary contribution was the concept of the 'relative autonomy' of the capitalist state. Heavily influenced by *Gramsci and *Althusser, Poulantzas argued in his classic *Political Power and Social Classes* (1968) that despite its formal separation from the institutions of economic production, the state promotes accumulation by maintaining the cohesion of capitalist society and its characteristic class system. In the following year, Poulantzas and Miliband engaged in a celebrated debate in the pages of *New Left Review*. While Miliband envisaged a possibility for transformation through control of the state, Poulantzas maintained that the 'structural' position of the state ensured its status as a servant of capitalism. Poulantzas's work in the 1970s addressed a wide range of issues of strategic and theoretical importance for the contemporary European left—e.g. fascism and authoritarianism, the ending of military dictatorships in southern Europe, and the possibilities for democratic socialism. In 1979, Poulantzas committed suicide. Although considered highly influential in his country of residence, France, Poulantzas's work has suffered from relative neglect in Anglo-American Marxist-intellectual circles. SW

poverty Poverty is the state of being poor; that is, lacking the basic needs of life such as food, health, education, and shelter. Most frequently, poverty is discussed in relation to household income, though this is contested. In fact, a number of different approaches to defining and measuring poverty can be identified. One distinction is between 'absolute poverty' and 'relative poverty'. Absolute poverty is defined in terms of material deprivation defined in terms of income or other basic needs of life.

Absolute poverty is usually measured using a 'poverty line', of which there are national and international examples. The most frequently cited is the *World Bank's internationally agreed measure of 'extreme poverty'. The World Bank measure uses Purchasing Power Parity (PPP) US dollars to set the household income level below which people can be defined as living in extreme poverty. PPPs define the value of a dollar in relation to the cost of a set basket of goods and services and avoid problems of comparison between incomes in different currencies caused by exchange rate fluctuation and the differing costs of goods and services in different countries. Established in 1990 at an income of US$1 PPP per day, it has been revised on subsequent occasions to reflect changing prices and in 2015 was set at US$1.90 per day. The World Bank also uses a higher poverty line, sometimes referred to as 'moderate poverty', set in 2015 at US$3.10 PPP dollars per day. Many countries specify their own national poverty lines, with many developed countries setting their poverty line at a higher rate (to reflect their higher standards of living), and many developing countries defining poverty lines below the World Bank specified level.

Relative poverty defines poverty in relation to some average (such as mean or median income) of the society in question. Thus, relative poverty might be defined as those receiving less than a proportion (such as 50 per cent) of the mean average income. Whereas absolute poverty focuses on a material lack of income, health, or education, relative poverty focuses more on a person's capability to function within a given society and thus expands the idea of poverty to include aspects of social exclusion.

A multidimensional approach to poverty also seeks to move beyond a focus just on income to instead assess the multiple deprivations faced by the poor, including health

and education. Various indexes have been created to measure poverty in these terms, including the Human Development Index, the Gender Inequality Index, and the Multidimensional Poverty Index (MPI). The MPI was created by the Oxford Poverty and Human Development Initiative and the UN Development Program. It uses ten indicators across three dimensions of poverty—health, education, and standard of living—with a household defined as poor if it is deprived in up to six indicators.

A final distinction can be drawn between 'residual poverty' and 'relational poverty'. Those who conceptualize poverty as residual see it as affecting those who have not yet benefited from a general increase in standards of living. The task of policy in this view is to remove barriers (such as poor policy and governance, low economic growth, or the existence of conflict) so that all people can be lifted out of poverty. Those who conceptualize poverty as relational see it as a condition that is produced by wider structural conditions. In this view, economic growth itself is sometimes seen as producing poverty for some, while generating wealth for others.

Action to reduce poverty takes place at local, national, and international levels. Perhaps the most prominent example is the target of reducing the number of people living in extreme poverty between 1990 and 2015—a target that was adopted by the UN in 2000 as one of its eight *Millennium Development Goals (MDGs). The World Bank calculated that this target (defined in relation to its own measure of absolute poverty) was met by 2010. In 2015 the UN adopted a new set of *Sustainable Development Goals which aim to eradicate poverty 'in all its forms' by 2030.   WB

Powell, J. Enoch (1912–98) British Conservative politician. Powell's popular reputation will always rest on his 'rivers of blood' speech in 1968, when he prophesied that allowing unrestricted migration of non-white Commonwealth citizens to the UK would produce such rivers. But his political philosophy contained more than racialism. He was the first leading UK politician to embrace *neoclassical economics, and the last to make arguments of principle for *unionism. Fittingly, he ended his political career in Northern Ireland, the last redoubt of principled unionism in the UK. Powell's many enemies pointed out that neoclassical economics seemed to imply the free movement of goods, capital, *and labour*; Powell's ideology embraced the first two and abhorred the last.

power The ability to make people (or things) do what they would not otherwise have done. The purpose of the modern concept of power was recognized as early as 1748, with the publication of *Hume's essay 'Of the Original Contract', though, arguably, Niccolò Machiavelli in the late fifteenth century was the first person to write about politics as if it was essentially amoral, concerned with power rather than rights or legitimacy. 'Almost all of the governments, which exist at present', says Hume, '. . . have been founded originally, either on usurpation or conquest or both, without any pretence of a fair consent, or voluntary subjection of the people.' Describing the processes of political change—migration, colonization, and military victory—Hume demands, rhetorically, 'Is there anything discoverable in all these events, but force and violence?'

Hume's comments offer one of the first clear versions of the assumptions of a 'modern' age, which seeks to study politics positively, eschewing theological justifications and moral evaluations in favour of a causal assessment of how the political world works in reality. Politics is seen to be about might rather than right; indeed, in Hume, as in much social science, might is seen as creating right de facto because the seizure of power leads to the establishment of authority and the successful inculcation of belief. Power is the appropriate central concept for this world view because, in its modern form, it is concerned with which groups or persons dominate, get their own way, or are best able to pursue their own interests in societies. James March in his 1966 essay 'The Power of Power' stressed that the concept 'conveyed simultaneously overtones of the cynicism of *Realpolitik*, the glories of classical mechanics, the realism of elite sociology and the comforts of anthropocentric theology'. In other words the 'power' world view offers the would-be social scientist an immunity from moral evaluation and theoretical speculation, and the possibility of emulating the explanatory achievements of the physicist.

Bertrand *Russell defined power as 'the production of intended effects', but this serves better as an indication of what we want to mean when we talk about power than as a working definition. A large number of other writers have offered more complex definitions of power or paradigms of power relationships. The core of these, in respect of the expression 'A has power over B', are:

1 A has effects on B's choices and actions.
2 A has the capacity to move B's choices and actions in ways that A intends.
3 A has the capacity to override opposition from B.
4 The relationship between A and B described by propositions 1, 2, and 3 is part of a social structure (not necessarily *the* social structure) and has a tendency to persist.

Problems with any definition include:

1 *Intentionality.* If we do not include a condition of intentionality, then we are left with a paradoxical and useless concept of power. For example, the Victim has power over the Bully because his or her weakness and vulnerability are provocative to the Bully's action. On the other hand, there are intuitively satisfactory examples of power without intention: Subserviens may regard Superior as a powerful person and, therefore, try to please him, but he may respond in ways which are not according to Superior's intentions or even contrary to them. If Subserviens is so in awe of Superior that the only reaction of which he is capable is to throw his arms around Superior's ankles and kiss his feet, a practice which Superior detests, then Superior cannot be said to have power over Subserviens since he lacks the capacity to control him. We want the concept of power, ultimately, to tell us about who can get their own way, to distinguish between the Barrack Room Lawyer who appears to obey orders, but is generally capable of manipulating structures and relationships, and the Formal Authority who appears to be obeyed to the letter, but has no close control over his relationships. The solution to this paradox is to acknowledge that the possession of power can have unintended consequences, but that the test of whether a person has power or not must be conducted in terms of control, of the capacity to achieve intentions. If a person has power, the consequences of that power

must be attributable to that person, who is responsible for those consequences. Without intentionality and attributability the concept of power becomes vague to the point of meaninglessness, not like the concept of energy in physics (which Russell wanted it to be), but more like the concept of the ether, the presence of which could not be distinguished from its absence.

2 *Comparability and Quantifiability*. If the concept of power is to be the central concept for understanding certain kinds of politics, its use must go beyond isolated remarks of the form 'A has power over B' and at least extend to comparative analyses: 'A has more power than C in context x' and 'A has more power than anybody else in context x'. This raises issues of great complexity because the range of variables which might be used to compare the power of two people is considerable. Different writers have given different names to these variables, but an account of power must consider both the geographic and demographic range over which the power extends and the scope of issues affected. There is the question of the objective weighting of A's power in comparison to C's, that is, the extent to which the individuals affected care about the effects which A can control. There is also a question of subjective weighting, the extent to which A is able to control what he or she really cares about. This is complicated by the phenomenon of anticipated reactions: many shrewd political actors modify their aims to the political environment. For them, the possession of power may be an end in itself and the question of comparing the extent to which they can modify events according to their own will becomes obscure and irresoluble. Thus it is very difficult to compare the power of two individuals, groups, or institutions. Often the difficulty is as logically simple as comparing a person who has apples with a person who has oranges and coming to a conclusion about which possesses the more 'fruit'. It would be intuitively obvious that fifty apples was more fruit than five oranges, but a closer comparison might evoke alternative standards of market or subjective value, weight, volume, nutrient capacity, and so on. Thus ordinal comparisons of power are impossible in many circumstances, and dealing with the kind of cardinal

numbers we would need to make power 'like energy in physics' is usually out of the question.

3 *Time and Causation*. If A has the power to achieve x at time t and he or she wants x, does that mean x will necessarily occur? The answer must surely be no, because it must be possible for A to possess the power, but to fail to use it. This raises a profound doubt about the nature of power. How would we know at any one time what power a person had? Most exercises of power affect the possession of that power. The use of power may be self-diminishing, particularly where it 'spends' the resource (such as money or credibility) on which it is based. Equally it may be self-increasing, as when actors ranging from teachers to the leaders of military coups establish control over their domain. In many cases there are contingent increases and decreases in power: for instance, macro-economic conditions are bound to affect what can be achieved by entrepreneurs or trade union leaders. Thus the instances of A exercising power at t_1, t_2, etc., are of little value in estimating A's power at t. A series of exercises of power may be catastrophically self-diminishing: precisely because a person has succeeded n times, it may be that moves to thwart them are afoot on the $(n + 1)$th occasion. It is no help to say, as Dahl does, that power is best explained in terms of probability: statistical probability is no use, because it only works for a series of identical instances like the spins of a fair roulette wheel and inductive probability is merely an estimate of the odds which takes everything into account (including, presumably, the 'power' of the actors). The fundamental problem is that the concept of power seeks to make static statements about a dynamic reality and the consequent doubt must be as to whether the concept ever really helps us understand or predict real events such as the fall of a hitherto 'powerful' politician.

Power is often classified into five principal forms: force, persuasion, authority, coercion, and manipulation. However, only coercion and manipulation are uncontroversially forms of power.

1 *Force* in its narrow sense implies a control of the body rather than the person. We may kill, bind, or render comatose without being able to get a person's actions to

conform to our will. Only when they comply because of the threat of force can the relationship be called power and this becomes, strictly, coercion.

2 *Persuasion*, by which the slave may persuade the emperor or the professor the Prime Minister. In other words the powerless may persuade the powerful: the offering of ideas is not control until it creates a dependency and, therefore, the capacity to manipulate.

3 *Authority* is sometimes defined as 'legitimate power'. But it can also be understood as the existence (in various senses) of rights to command and corresponding duties to obey. Authority is therefore separate from power, though it constitutes a resource for power in the same way as does money and a capacity for rational persuasion. It can exist in a pure form, without power, as, for instance, the authority of a priest over his flock in a secular society.

4 *Coercion* is perhaps the paradigm form of power and is said to consist of controlling people through threats, whether overt or tacit. It is, though, extremely difficult to distinguish a threat from other forms of relationship. Is it a threat if we say we are going to make a person worse off than they expected to be? Or worse off than if we were not to act? Most modern relationships, whether the issue is children's pocket money or promotions at work, seem to exist in a middle territory between threats and offers for which we have no established word in English (though Hillel Steiner suggests 'throffers').

5 *Manipulation* involves control exercised without threats, typically using resources of information and ideas. Usually people do not realize they are being manipulated or the process would not work. Arguably, it is a more durable form of power: Subserviens' obedience to Superior is more securely founded on the belief that God wants him to obey than on the fear of being whipped. But arguments about manipulation can easily slide into unfalsifiable arguments about '*false consciousness*'. Increasingly, as power has failed as a concept for the positive investigation of political systems, it has been taken over by writers like *Foucault who see power as permeating all social relationships. This tradition of thought does not, generally, seek to measure or attribute power or to distinguish its forms, but is content to emphasize its transcendence and the effect of power in distorting social relations.

In summary, the concept of power has not filled the central role in the study of politics which many pioneers hoped it would. It has proved much easier to believe generally that 'Politics is about power', or, particularly, that individual P or group E possesses power, than it has been to clarify what such beliefs mean or what would constitute proof or disproof of them. Academic students of politics and journalists alike have continued to talk about power, but not with any pretensions to precision and often within the overtly evaluative, descriptively vague form suggested by such writers as Foucault and Lukes in which the discourse of power and powerlessness is within the genre of social criticism rather than that of empirical investigation.   LA

power elite Term used by C. Wright Mills in his 1956 study of the same name to refer to the 'overlapping cliques' at the helms of the chief political, economic, and military institutions in modern society. Mills argued that these elites share both membership and a set of common interests, and thus that the principal policy decisions for which they are responsible serve common goals.   SW

power index Any attempt to measure the power of a voting bloc in terms of the likelihood that it will be the swing voter, able to decide whether a proposition wins or loses. The first formal power index was proposed by Lionel Penrose in 1946 (although the idea was foreshadowed by the anti-*Federalist Luther Martin in 1787). The best-known index is the *Shapley–Shubik index. Unfortunately, different indices have different values in the same situation. Some critics deny that they have any meaning at all; supporters of the concept have been trying to produce a more general index, but none has caught on.

(⊕) SEE WEB LINKS

• Power index site, with index calculators.

power-sharing Within government, power-sharing refers to a coalition of two or more political parties which form the Executive. Such coalitions may be the outcome of either pre- or post-election bargaining between or among political parties. In deeply divided societies, such as Northern Ireland, power-sharing is associated with the model of *consociational democracy. Consociationalism is theoretically suited to deeply divided societies where majoritarianism, or single party government, is deemed—or has been demonstrated—to be unworkable. Such has been the case in Northern Ireland since the introduction of direct rule in 1972.

Power-sharing between or among rival ethnic blocs is an integral characteristic of consociational democracy. It refers to the inclusion in government of political leaders and parties that represent the divided communities—in the case of Northern Ireland, of nationalist and unionist parties. Since 1972, power-sharing has been a consistent feature of successive attempts by UK governments to restore devolved government to Northern Ireland. Following the 1998 *Belfast Agreement, it led to a four-party Executive Committee, comprising the Ulster Unionist Party, the Social Democratic and Labour Party, the Democratic Unionist Party, and Sinn Féin, allocated by means of the *d'Hondt rule. In 2010 the Alliance Party joined the power-sharing Executive.

Power-sharing is no guarantee of government stability, nor of wider social stability. Without the underpinning support of electors drawn from rival ethnic blocs, and a preparedness on the part of political leaders to practise the politics of accommodation, such a coalition may prove to be fragile. This was precisely the fate of the 1973–4 power-sharing administration in Northern Ireland. It was toppled by unionist and loyalist protestors, opposed to the inclusion in government of nationalist representatives.   RW

PPP *See* PUBLIC–PRIVATE PARTNERSHIP.

Prague Spring The period of Czechoslovakian politics following Alexander Dubcek's arrival as Party leader in January 1968, and ending with the Soviet invasion in August, during which reformist elements within the ruling Communist Party relaxed censorship restrictions, encouraged the formation of independent pressure groups, and attempted to gain some degree of national autonomy over foreign policy.   SW

Prebisch, Raúl (1901–86) Working as an economist for the Argentine government, Raúl Prebisch experienced directly the catastrophic impact of the Great Depression of the 1930s on what had long been a prosperous economy and a constitutional state. Generalizing from this, he reasoned that so long as industrialized states were able to react to adverse conditions with *mercantilist policies, as the United States and Europe had done in the 1930s, it was folly for less powerful states to settle for the gains from *free trade available to them as producers of primary commodities. Instead, he urged them to industrialize, however costly in the short run. Prebisch argued that the terms of trade were bound to move in the long run against producers of primary products because demand for their exports was bound to grow more slowly than for the manufactures they needed to import. Moreover any gains from improved productivity in agricultural production and extractive industry would be drained to the industrial economies by the superior bargaining power of their monopolistic labour unions and firms.

The political significance of Prebisch lies much less in the quality of his thought than in its reception. As he rose through the UN Commission for Latin America to become founding Secretary General of the United Nations Conference on Trade and Development (UNCTAD) in 1964, his proposed solutions to the dilemma of primary producers won widespread official acceptance, making him a much more powerful moulder of *Third World policies than the neo-Marxist *dependency school with whom he is often mistakenly associated. UNCTAD itself became, during the North–South dialogue of the 1970s, the vehicle for his programme, advocating the stabilization of international commodity markets, continued import-substituting industrialization and regional cooperation in the Third World, and the retraction of illiberal controls on market access for agricultural goods and textiles imposed by the advanced industrial economies.   CJ

(⊕) SEE WEB LINKS
• UNCTAD website.

prefect The principal local representative of the French state and member of an elite administrative corps (*see* GRANDES ÉCOLES).

Following the decentralization reforms implemented by the Socialists in March 1982, the prefect is no longer chief executive of the region or department, the administrative and financial powers having been transferred to local assemblies and their elected chairmen. Prefects are still responsible for coordination of regional planning and for supervision of the public services and any overall loss of power is probably more apparent than real. They were always constrained by local pressures, liable to frequent transfer, and subject to conflicting demands from centre and periphery. Their powers are now better defined and they enjoy more job security. IC

preference In the ordinary dictionary sense of 'liking or estimation of one thing before or above another', the concept of preference is important in *positivist social science. Economists regard behaviour as 'revealed preference' and usually regard a person's preferences as identical to her choices. Political scientists and sociologists are more cautious, especially when what people say differs from what they do.

preference ordering Simply, a (voter's or consumer's) order of preference among a number of candidates or options. Used to examine voting procedures: most procedures ask each voter only to reveal part of his or her preference ordering (his or her first preference in *first-past-the-post and in party-list systems of *proportional representation). Where full preference orderings are available or can be reconstructed, voting procedures can be evaluated by how faithfully they represent them.

prerogative Prerogative powers are those which are at the autonomous disposal of heads of state and which do not require sanction by a legislature. Their theoretical justification lies in *Locke's view of a need for a final arbiter to maintain order. In liberal democracies written constitutions vary in their definition of prerogative powers for heads of state. Constitutional monarchs and some presidents, for example in Germany, have almost entirely ceremonial powers, although in some cases, such as the Spanish monarchy under King Juan Carlos, important political roles can be played. More conventionally, presidents have reserve or emergency powers to be used in situations of political crisis, although by definition they are rarely invoked. In the United States, the President as head of state has considerable powers beyond those in an emergency which relate to the initiation of legislation, maintenance of internal order, diplomatic relations, and the command of the armed forces. In theory the Presidency is checked by Congress, federalism, and an independent judiciary, but in practice has asserted considerable autonomy in the use of such powers. The French Presidency in the *Fifth Republic has perhaps the most extensive constitutionally defined prerogative powers. In addition to unconstrained emergency powers the French President ordinarily has the right to chair the council of ministers, with the power to appoint, rather then merely nominate, and dismiss the prime minister, negotiate with foreign powers, and call referendums. This effectively makes the President the head of the government as well as head of state. In the United Kingdom in the absence of a written constitution prerogative powers have become discretionary powers of the political executive, carried out in the name of the monarch. These cover the making of foreign policy, the prosecution of war, and the making of appointments to the armed forces and the central machinery of government. In these policy areas, whilst still open to scrutiny, the UK executive is considerably more autonomous from parliamentary decision-making processes than executives in other Westminster-style systems, although the controversy over the decision to go to war in Iraq in 2003 led to proposals in 2008 for any such final decision in future to be made by Parliament. JBr

president Either the working chief executive or an honorific office with a working chief executive's post below it. In voluntary bodies, 'president' is more usually an honorific post. In political constitutions, 'president' is sometimes a working chief executive ('head of government'), sometimes an honorific post with occasional appointment or deadlock-breaking roles ('head of state'), sometimes both.

Presidents who are heads of government are common in non-democracies but less common in democracies. There are a number of examples in Latin America but the best-known examples are in the United States and France. The US Constitution, Article II, begins 'The executive power shall be vested in a President of the United States of America'. His specific powers, on the face of it, are limited to: acting as Commander-in-Chief of the US Army and Navy, and of state militias, 'when called into the actual Service of the United States'; 'requiring an Opinion, in writing' from the heads of executive departments; making senior appointments; and making treaties 'with the Advice and Consent of the Senate'. The actual power of the US President is much greater than this list would suggest. In a superpower and a world with nuclear weapons, the power of Commander-in-Chief is omnipresent. The restrictions on making treaties are evaded by calling them 'executive agreements'. Congress has tried to rein in the 'imperial presidency' but with no real success in foreign policy.

In domestic policy, the power of the President is much less. He may run executive departments however he pleases, but even this is subject to having their heads ratified by the Senate, which in recent years has been a substantial obstacle. Domestic policy-making is best regarded as a game in which the President, the two houses of Congress (separately), and the federal courts have a set of interlocking veto powers. For any policy to be implemented, a number of the players with vetoes must agree (the number varying with the policy area).

The Constitution of the French *Fifth Republic was written by Charles de *Gaulle and his allies in order to give far greater powers to de Gaulle than to the presidents of the *Fourth Republic which he overthrew. He strengthened his own powers in 1962 unconstitutionally but without penalty. The President of France has the power of arbitration (French *arbitrage*) to 'ensure the regular functioning of the public authorities, as well as the continuity of the state'. This power is extremely wide, and it is used extremely widely when the President and the government are from the same party, as they have been for most of the life of the Fifth Republic.

The duties of head of state entail dining, attending funerals, and presenting medals. The head of state may or may not be a unifying national symbol, as may be seen for instance in the contrasting examples of Mary Robinson (Ireland) and Kurt Waldheim (Austria). The constitutional roles of the post are similar, but the unifying Robinson could be a very effective head of state, while the divisive Waldheim could not. A head of state usually has back-up powers if the head of the government resigns or the government falls, and in national emergency. An unusual use of these was the dismissal of the government of Gough Whitlam in Australia, by the Governor-General in 1975. The Governor-General of Australia acts on behalf of the Queen as head of state. Although the powers of the Australian head of state escaped unscathed in 1975, the incident contributed to a long decline in support for the monarchy in Australia. This illustrates a constraint even on decorative heads of state.

Presidents may be directly elected, indirectly elected, or appointed. The more nearly they are to being directly elected, the more authority they have in their own right, as in the French and American cases.

president-elect Title given to victor of US presidential election during the transitional period between the election in November and taking office on 20 January.

pressure group An alternative term for *interest group, often used to indicate disapproval of the group concerned or its methods. Many analysts, however, use it interchangeably with interest group.   WG

Price, Richard (1723–91) Welsh dissenting clergyman, radical, and mathematician. A close follower of the French *Enlightenment and supporter of the *French Revolution, who prompted *Burke's attack on it, Price was perhaps the only person in England who understood the work on probability and its application to social science being done in France by Laplace and *Condorcet. Price was responsible for the posthumous publication, in 1761, of a paper by Thomas Bayes which is one of the foundations of probability as now understood.

primary election An intra-party election enabling voters to participate in the selection of candidates. In the United States there are two main forms of primary elections, presidential primaries and direct primaries. The former provide for the popular election of delegates to the national party conventions where presidential candidates are selected. Normally, where presidential primaries are used, the voters of a particular state identified with a given party choose between the various candidates seeking that party's nomination, with delegates then allocated either proportionally or on a winner-take-all basis. In a few cases voters directly elect delegates who will usually have declared a commitment to support a particular candidate at the convention. Where presidential primaries are not in use convention delegates are selected by arrangements that begin with local *caucus meetings. There are also non-binding 'beauty contest' primaries; some states hold these together with one of the other selection procedures.

The direct primary allows those who affiliate with a party to choose between candidates seeking that party's nomination to public office. Now used in some form in every state there are three types of direct primary—closed, open, and blanket. Most states have closed primaries. These require voters to indicate at some stage a party preference, which entitles them to participate in the primary of that party. In those states where primaries are open, voters may choose which primary to participate in. They have access to the ballots of each party and must select one. In three states, Alaska, Louisiana, and Washington, the blanket primary is in operation. This does not require any indication of party affiliation and voters are free to move back and forth across a blanket-sized ballot that includes all candidates of all parties. This makes it possible for voters to participate in, for example, the Republican primary contest for a seat in the US Senate and the Democratic primary to select a candidate for mayor.

Both the presidential primary and the direct primary came into widespread use in the early twentieth century. The *progressives who sponsored them wished to purify American politics, to destroy the power of party bosses and their machines, and restore the right of the people to govern themselves. Arguably these reformers have been altogether too successful in that primaries have savagely weakened American political parties, institutions which, despite their flaws, are indispensable in democratic political systems. DM

prime minister The head of the executive and, where it exists, the cabinet within a parliamentary system. The role of the post, however, varies depending on the institutional context, the nature of party government, and the political circumstances in which a prime minister governs. Constraints upon the power of a prime minister may be posed particularly by proportional electoral systems. Governments are commonly formed from a coalition of various parties, necessitating concessions to the differences in party interests in order to keep a government together. It has become common for prime ministers in some countries, notably the Netherlands, to act primarily not as leaders but as conciliators between opposing interests within a government. In some countries, such as Switzerland, political power is so fragmented that the role of the prime minister has been reduced to that of symbolic figurehead. Factionalized parties pose similar problems even in single-party government. Constraints are also posed by territorial devolution of power in federal systems, such as Canada, or regionalized systems, such as Spain and the UK; by a powerful second chamber such as the German Bundesrat; by constitutional courts; or by the political culture which gives power to extra-governing institutions such as business associations or trade unions. Consequently, a prime minister may need to govern in partnership with others for a variety of reasons.

In comparative terms, despite the recent development of devolution, the powers of the prime minister in the UK are among the largest. The electoral system generally produces one party government backed by a well-disciplined parliamentary party. This has facilitated the development of a range of powers for the Prime Minister not commonly applicable to those of other countries: the right to appoint and dismiss ministers; the right to establish policy guidelines for government; the right to arbitrate conclusively on differences between ministers in government; and the right to speak on behalf of the government in any area of policy. Since the 1960s concern has been expressed at the willingness of incumbents to exercise, enhance, and indeed abuse such powers. Analysis of the complex workings of the British cabinet and more broadly the political executive leads at best to an equivocal endorsement of this thesis. Experience of prime ministerial government is contingent upon the maintenance of solid parliamentary majorities, party cohesion, an electoral preference for strong leadership within the executive, and an activist style on the part of the incumbent. When such political circumstances do not occur then the Prime Minister may have or wish to play the role of bargainer or conciliator in a similar manner to counterparts in other systems. Margaret Thatcher and John Major are widely seen as the most clear-cut recent cases of strong prime ministerial government and prime ministerial conciliation respectively. JBr

primitive accumulation The process, described by *Marx, beginning with the gathering together of commodities, then gold and silver, and finally money by which nascent capitalism created the material base (through the systematic exploitation of labour, expropriation of resources, and colonial plundering) that facilitated its dominance in the economic and political spheres. GL

primitive communism A term reflecting *Marx and *Engels's interest in ethnology in general and in the research of Lewis H. Morgan (1818–81) in particular. There were societies, both ancient and modern, which existed without class and state and where the social and economic relationships themselves were broadly egalitarian. Such societies guaranteed a collective right to basic resources and allowed no space for authoritarian rule. Morgan gave detailed ethnographic support to this notion of primitive communism in *Ancient Society* (1877) and Engels, working with Marx's notes on Morgan, analysed the phenomenon and its relationship to historical materialism in *The Origin of Family, Private Property and the State* (1884). JH

principal–agent problem Whenever an individual (the principal) has another person (the agent) perform a service on her behalf and cannot fully observe the agent's actions, a 'principal–agent problem' arises. The underlying assumption is that the agent's interests may differ from those of the principal. In economics, the classical example is the potential conflict of interest between

ownership and management, but any delegation of authority gives rise to this quandary. A pre-eminent instance is the tendency of bureaucratic agencies to drift away from the goals of politicians and create official secrets. Indeed, an early subtle statement of the 'problem' is in Max *Weber's discussion of types of legitimate domination (*Economy and Society*, chapter III).

'Agency theory' (also known as 'principal-agent theory') focuses on mechanisms to reduce the 'problem', such as selecting certain types of agents, and instituting forms of monitoring and various amounts of positive and negative sanctions. As noted by Weber, such mechanisms include the practice among medieval and early modern rulers of rotating officials among different positions and creating collegiate monitoring institutions. He also submitted that an effective way to ensure the cooperation of officials is to foster a belief that the authority of the ruler is legitimate. In any case, strategies to mitigate the 'problem' produce 'Agency Costs', a type of transaction cost, reflecting the fact that without cost, it is impossible for principals to be sure that agents will act in the principals' interest. *See* DELEGATE; REPRESENTATION. FV

prior restraint The taking of legal action before an anticipated wrongdoing. Remedies to prevent a threatened illegality from taking place include the use of injunction or prohibition and declaration. In English law, an injunction may take the form of either a negative or positive requirement, depending on how best to deal with the illegality. In order to obtain an injunction, the plaintiff must show he has an arguable point of law and that on the balance of convenience an injunction ought to be given.

A prohibition will prevent any further action or wrongdoing, in effect telling the offending party to proceed no further. A declaration will issue to declare rights and clarify legal doubts over any potential dispute. Once awarded a prohibition, declaration, or injunction is effective against any potential wrongdoer, within the terms of the courts' decision. American law, especially the *First Amendment, outlaws many forms of prior restraint used in Britain, where reformers claim that it has protected rich bullies and fraudsters such as Robert Maxwell. JM

Prisoners' Dilemma The most famous of all non-*zero-sum games. Two prisoners are held in separate cells. The District Attorney knows that they jointly committed an armed robbery, but only if at least one of them confesses will he have the evidence to guarantee a conviction. If neither of them confesses, they will be sentenced to two years in prison for illegal possession of firearms. The sentence for armed robbery is twenty years. However, if they both plead guilty, it will be reduced to ten years. If one confesses and the other does not, the one who confesses will be set free altogether and the other sentenced to the full twenty years. The DA visits each prisoner, inviting him to confess. Should he?

The Prisoners' Dilemma may be expressed by the following matrix, where in each cell the number before the comma is the outcome for Row and the number after the comma is the outcome for Column. The numbers represent years in prison, and are preceded by minus signs because more years in prison are worse than fewer.

	Column:	
	Don't confess	Confess
Row: Don't confess	−2, −2	−20, 0
Confess	0, −20	−10, −10

Row does not know what Column will do. But he knows that if Column does not confess he will receive −2 if he does not confess and 0 if he confesses. If Column confesses he will receive −20 if he does not confess and −10 if he confesses. Irrespective of what Column does, it is therefore a 'sure thing' that Row is better off if he confesses. The reasoning is symmetrical for Column. Therefore, rational prisoners will confess, even though both of them knew all along that it would be better for each if neither confessed.

The Prisoners' Dilemma has been generalized for repeated interactions (*supergames) and for more than two players. With repeated interactions, it is no longer necessarily true that each player should always defect. For instance, players may agree on a tit-for-tat rule, or signal one to each other by their responses in repeated games. Tit-for-tat means 'I will cooperate in our first encounter; thereafter, whatever you do in each round, I shall do to you in the following round'. By this or another strategy of conditional cooperation, players may arrive at an 'evolutionarily stable' pattern of conditional cooperation.

Prisoners' Dilemma models have been applied to almost every form of human and animal interaction. Well-known examples from politics include *arms races, incomes policy, trade bargaining, and pollution reduction. There are dangers of overuse: the situation needs to be specified carefully, and what appears to be a prisoners' dilemma may not always be so.

There have also been extensive experimental tests of Prisoners' Dilemma in the laboratory. One of the best-established results is that economics students are consistently more prone to arrive at the selfish, rational, and suboptimal outcome than students of any other subject.

private bill *See* STATUTE LAW.

Private Finance Initiative British government initiative to involve the private sector in the provision of public services; part of the *public–private partnership programme. The system encourages public authorities to join with private companies in long-term contracts involving financing, building, and running infrastructure projects. Established under the Conservative government in 1992 to address problems of capital programme overruns and project mismanagement, it was enthusiastically taken on by the Labour government after 1997. Proponents of the system argue that the involvement of private sector brings in management expertise, new capital resources, and helps reduce public sector borrowing. However, critics argue that it has merely swapped government investment for a complex, unaccountable, and expensive form of service hire-purchase.

private member's bill Private members' bills, not to be confused with private bills, are public bills introduced to the UK Parliament by back-bench MPs or peers. They may be on any issue as long as the Crown's sole *prerogative to propose public expenditure is not breached. In the Commons they may be introduced by the first twenty MPs drawn in a ballot for each parliamentary session, for whom time is allocated on Fridays when they are given precedence over government bills.

They may also be introduced under the 'ten minute rule' at prescribed times during normal parliamentary business. Few of the latter achieve enactment, although success is more generally measured in the extent to which parliamentary and public attention has been drawn to the subject of the bill. Bills introduced by MPs successful in the ballot have a better chance of enactment, although many still fail for lack of parliamentary time. It is crucial that MPs presenting ballot bills do not excite the opposition of the government, so as to ensure assistance from government departments in preparing them, and to guard against fatal parliamentary opposition. They must also lobby support in both Houses.

Private members' bills have frequently aroused controversy, particularly in the 1960s when they resulted in legislation on contraception, homosexuality, abortion, and divorce. Opponents suggest that MPs do not have an electoral mandate to introduce bills and debates are far too rushed to deal with weighty moral issues. Advocates stress that it is in private members' bills that Parliament, sovereign and acting as a legislature independent of the executive, lives on. More pragmatically, private members' bills may be seen as vehicles to present legislation on matters for which the Government cannot find a place in its own parliamentary timetable, or upon which there is substantial social consensus outside Parliament but problematic dissenting voices in the governing party. Recent legislation resulting from private members' bills includes the Female Genital Mutilation Act, 2003, the Gangmasters Licensing Act, 2004, and the Sustainable Communities Act, 2006. JBr

(⊕) SEE WEB LINKS

• Parliament site for private members' bills.

privatization The transfer of public assets to the private sector, by sale, or contracting out. After some hesitant and small-scale experiments by the Heath Government of 1970–74, UK privatization on a large scale was undertaken by the Thatcher Government after 1979 with the electricity, gas, and telecommunications industries being sold. The advantages of privatization from the government's perspective included: raising large sums of money to offset public borrowing; weakening the power of public sector trade unions; widening share ownership; giving the management of former nationalized industries normal commercial autonomy; and reducing the burden of decision-making imposed on government by public ownership. Critics of the British privatizations argued that they were undertaken so that maximizing competition was sacrificed in the interest of ensuring the greatest possible revenue from the sales and protecting the monopolistic positions of the existing enterprises. The perceived policy success of privatization in Britain led to its imitation in many other countries. In particular, organizations such as the *World Bank encouraged developing countries to dispose of their loss-making state-owned industries. Privatization in the former Soviet Union has occurred more slowly than anticipated and has often involved acquisitions of enterprises by the management and *oligarchs on favourable terms. WG

Privy Council The British monarch's advisory group. Once a key part of executive power, it now exists as the formal machinery through which the monarch exercises *prerogative powers. Its role primarily is as a *dignified part of the constitution, although it retained an efficient role, for instance, in its facilitation of former polytechnics being granted university status in the early 1990s. The Privy Council is supervised by the Lord President of the Council, and, whilst its membership extends to all past and present cabinet ministers and other public figures, it is generally attended by a select few. The judicial committee of the Privy Council provides a constitutional basis for the Law Lords (from the House of Lords) to meet as a final court of appeal for certain commonwealth and colonial countries. As such it can act as a quasi-supreme court in interpreting state constitutions. It took on a heightened role with the advent of devolution in Scotland, Wales, and Northern Ireland in assuming the role of judging whether certain powers lay within the legislative competence of the devolved institutions.

In Canada, the Privy Council Office is the functional equivalent of a cabinet office. JBr

(⊕) SEE WEB LINKS

• Site of the UK Privy Council Office, which provides the Secretariat services for the Privy Council.

pro-choice An ideological position which defends a woman's right to have an abortion on the grounds of her inviolable autonomy over matters concerning her own body. In the United States, where the issue has become most politicized, the landmark *Roe* v. *Wade* decision of the Supreme Court in 1973 grounded a woman's right to have an abortion in an inferred constitutional 'right to privacy'. *See also* PRO-LIFE. SW

progressive movement An amorphous, cross-party tendency towards economic and political reform prevalent in the United States especially from 1896 to 1916.

In that era Democrats, Republicans, and non-partisans alike became alarmed by developments in American life that had been under way for some time. They viewed with concern the rise of trusts—monopolies in commerce and industry—and the parallel emergence of party bosses and political machines. Such concentrations of economic and political power, so it was argued, not only led to exploitation and corruption, but also ran counter to the values of equality, individualism, and democracy upon which the country had been founded. Progressivism and its forerunner *populism were responses to these concerns. Progressivism, while it drew strength from Populist agrarian protest, had its roots in the cities among the urban middle class, mainly of white Anglo-Saxon, Protestant origin.

All progressives were much exercised by the stranglehold on the American economy that the trusts were believed to have gained. However, they disagreed over solutions to the problem. Some such as Woodrow Wilson favoured restoring competition by enforcing and adding to legislation such as the Sherman Antitrust Act of 1890 which made structures 'in restraint of trade' illegal. Theodore Roosevelt, by contrast, saw trusts as inevitable, but wanted to bring them under the control of regulatory commissions.

There was greater agreement among progressives on political reform. They saw a need to purify politics by destroying the odious bosses and their *machines, and returning government to where it properly belonged, in the hands of the people. Progressives accordingly became enthusiasts for various devices of direct democracy such as the presidential *primary, the direct primary, the *initiative, and the *referendum, as well as the recall of public officials.

It is difficult to place progressives on a conventional left–right spectrum. Whilst they were committed to reform they were also, in a sense, deeply conservative. They harked back to an alleged golden age in American history—one of small farms, small towns, and small business where there was opportunity for all and where self-government was a reality. Although they sought to ameliorate some of the adverse consequences of capitalism, progressives were far from being anti-capitalist. They objected to trusts not out of any objection to capitalism itself, but because those organizations restricted or eliminated opportunities for small entrepreneurs and thereby curtailed equality of opportunity and individualism. Progressives also looked askance at organized labour and abhorred the collectivism associated with socialism even though the reform aspirations of trade unionists and socialists provided some common ground with progressives. DM

progressive taxation Income tax system which levies a proportionately higher tax rate on those with higher incomes.

proletariat A class of wage earner in a capitalist society whose only possession of significant material value is its labour power. Whatever its classical and medieval usages, where the term often applied to those required to give service, *Marx, *Engels, and the Marxists effectively captured the word. For them, the proletariat was that class which lived solely by its labour power, a class which could not live as the bourgeoisie could by profit from capital, or by ownership of the means of production, a class which had been totally dispossessed during the course of the industrial revolution. Engels in the *Principles of Communism* (1847) maintained that while there had always been a working class, just as there had always been poor people, there was a proletariat only in the nineteenth century. JH

pro-life An ideological position which opposes abortion on the grounds of the inviolable rights of the foetus as a moral subject. These rights are seen as 'trumping' all countervailing considerations claimed by *pro-choicers, though there are some differences of opinion on appropriate action in 'tough cases' (e.g. where the mother's life is threatened by continuation of the pregnancy). sw

propaganda Originating in an office of the Roman Catholic Church charged with propagation of the faith (*de propaganda fide*), the word entered common usage in the second quarter of the twentieth century to describe attempts by totalitarian regimes to achieve comprehensive subordination of knowledge to state policy. Based in the desire of fascists, Nazis, and Bolsheviks to develop legitimacy and social control by overcoming the broadly based cultural hegemony of antecedent regimes, propaganda soon came to be directed toward the populations of other states, provoking reactions from the industrialized democracies. Britain established its own Ministry, not of Propaganda but of Information, during the First World War (1917), its very title an exercise in rhetoric. In both world wars this ministry employed print, radio, film, graphic art, and the spoken word to put the best gloss on state policy and the fortunes of British arms (white propaganda) while also running down and misrepresenting Britain's enemies (black propaganda). Still important in international relations during the Cold War through radio stations such as Voice of America (US), propaganda both at home and abroad was frequently crude and ineffective, especially in communist states lacking the technical skills of advertising, marketing, and communications developed within the private sectors of a consumerist Western culture with largely unrestricted media. It has, however, been brought to a fine art in the advanced industrial economies in recent years, where the presentation of state policy and legislation in Britain, drawing heavily on the techniques of commercial advertising, sometimes seems to have received more attention than its content or drafting. cj

property (1) A legal relation between a person and a 'thing'; (2) the object of a legal relation with a person. The person may be a natural person or an artificial person. Property may be private, common, or public. The 'thing' may be quite concrete, for example, a computer, or abstract, for example the copyright in a computer's software. It may also be animate, when property in animals or in other persons is accepted. The legal relation of private property is often contrasted with that of contract, because the person who has private property usually has claims or *rights against all other persons, whereas a contractor acquires rights only against other contractors. For example, since the computer I am using is my own, I have the right to exclude all other persons from using it, but I have special rights against its supplier as a result of the contract of sale when I bought it.

An important element in the political theory of property is the justification of any favoured property system, be it private, common, or public. This requires examination of the sorts of titles to 'things' which are legitimate, an investigation of the ways in which titles may be acquired, transferred, and extinguished. In particular, the explanation of the legitimate transfer of private property (for example, through sale or gift) does nothing to explain how anyone became entitled to property in the first place. In some theories (like *Locke's and *Nozick's) this question is investigated by placing individuals in a *state of nature where property is absent, except the property persons are taken to have in themselves (*see* SELF-OWNERSHIP). In others it is explored by trying to see the consequences for property systems of promoting particular values, like *utility or *freedom.

Property is a centrally important institution because it is the consequence of, and has implications for, the economic, legal, and political systems of a society. This is true both of the sorts of property a society recognizes, and of the distribution of that property. Property is therefore at the heart of discussions about *power and *justice. In the first case, there are questions about the connection between power and resources. In the second, there are problems not only of intragenerational justice but also of intergenerational and international justice to be addressed. Once the question 'Why should anyone have any sort of property?' is asked, the particular location of individuals in time and within particular legal jurisdictions may look arbitrary. This is especially important for *natural rights theories, since the rights any individual can enjoy should, on that basis, be universal. Because of the dynamics of property systems, it has proved very difficult to design property institutions which genuinely embody natural rights. This is true of both individualistic private property theories and radical, communal property theories. Natural rights theories tend to see all rights as property rights, whereas alternative accounts try to specify the particular features of property. Many writers see property as the result of positive legal systems, arguing that in the absence of the law's coercion 'property' could not exist. Because positive law is a human artifice this approach recognizes that the institution is a consequence of decision which is in need of justification. AR

proportional representation Any scheme which seeks to ensure that each faction, group, or party in the electing population is represented in the elected assembly or committee in proportion to its size. For individual schemes of PR, *see* ADDITIONAL MEMBER SYSTEM; PARTY LIST; and SINGLE TRANSFERABLE VOTE. For a scheme which is often incorrectly described as PR, *see* ALTERNATIVE VOTE.

The concept of proportionality is surprisingly elusive (which is one reason for the proliferation of PR schemes); the consequences of PR are disputed; so therefore are arguments about its desirability. *Duverger's law posits an association between *first-past-the-post and two-party systems and one between PR and multi-party systems. The second association is weaker than the first. However, most argument on the merits of PR assumes that it is true. Opponents of PR then say that PR leads to instability and irresponsible government; its supporters argue that the alternatives are unfair. Thus there is usually no meeting of minds.

Constructive argument about the desirability of PR in any one case ought to concentrate on whether the second part of Duverger's law is (likely to be) true for the case in question, on whether any tendency to multi-partism would exist independently of PR, and on whether the electoral scheme is intended to elect a representative body or to take decisions. If the latter, those writing voting rules should seek a majoritarian rather than a proportional rule.

protection(ism) The doctrine or practice of restricting international trade to favour home producers, by tariffs, quotas, or (most frequently in modern times) by non-tariff barriers such as requiring all Japanese video-recorders imported to France to be cleared through a small customs shed in Poitiers.

Protectorate, protectorate 1. England between 1653 and 1659, when Oliver Cromwell appointed himself Lord Protector (1653–8), to be succeeded briefly by his son Richard.
2. A state under the protection of an imperialist power without being directly ruled as a colony. The distinction may have been nearly meaningless, as suggested by one of the defining quotations in the *Oxford English Dictionary* from 1889: 'H.M.S. *Egeria* has . . . just completed a remarkable cruise of annexation, formally declaring as protectorates of Great Britain no fewer than thirteen islands in the South Pacific.'

Protestant parties Protestant parties are political parties which seek to promote or defend the interests of Protestant religion against proponents of Catholicism, anticlericalism, or excessive liberalism in personal matters. The sectarian politics of Northern Ireland have led the Ulster Unionist and Democratic Unionist Parties to be clearly identified with the Protestant section of the population against the Catholic minority and the territorial claims of Eire, a Catholic state. Similarly, in Scandinavia Christian peoples' parties emerged during the 1960s on the back of Protestant revulsion at sexual permissiveness. Otherwise political promotion and defence of the Protestant religion is either one among other, non-religious, defining elements of a political party, as in the case of the British Conservative Party and its upholding of the established Church of England, or one among other religious causes promoted by a political party against secularism, as is the case with the Dutch Christian Democratic Appeal. Protestant beliefs have been promoted since the 1960s within more general religious backlashes against secularism in the context of populist 'moral majority' movements in established parties, such as the American Republican Party. The support of evangelical Christians has been assessed as critical to securing President George W. Bush a second term of office in 2004. Nowhere does an exclusively Protestant party form a government, a feature of political systems which is encouraged by an increasing stress on interdenominational toleration and general dominance of non-religious issues in defining party systems in the West. JBr

Proudhon, Pierre-Joseph (1809–65) French social theorist and the first thinker to make explicit use of the idea of *anarchism to denote an ideal community free from the constraints of law, government, and state power. In using this term he deliberately and provocatively challenged his opponents to distinguish between anarchism as a new, revolutionary way of life capable of securing order and justice, and anarchy as disorderly lawlessness.

Proudhon's influence spread rapidly after the publication of *What is Property?* in 1840. In this work traditional rights of property ownership were attacked, but at the same time *communism was rejected. For Proudhon the guiding economic principle of an anarchist community must be that of mutualism, which required a cooperative productive system geared towards genuine need rather than profit, and based on a moral respect for individuality within small-scale communities. KT

proxy war Proxy wars are conflicts in which a third party intervenes indirectly in a pre-existing war in order to influence the strategic outcome in favour of its preferred faction. Proxy wars are the product of a relationship between a benefactor who is a state or non-state actor external to the dynamic of the existing conflict (for example, a civil war) and the chosen proxies who are the conduit for the benefactor's weapons, training, and funding. In short, proxy wars are the replacement for states and non-state actors seeking to further their own strategic goals yet at the same time avoid engaging in direct, costly, and bloody warfare. Such responses are based on an intrinsic perception of risk, specifically that direct intervention in a conflict would be either unjustifiable, too costly (whether politically, financially, or materially), avoidable, illegitimate, or unfeasible. The recourse to proxy war was particularly prevalent during the *Cold War as the shadow of nuclear war ensured more acute selectivity in conflict engagement for the purposes of augmentation of national interests or ideological gains. Consider, for example, how the Carter and then Reagan administrations responded to the 1979 Soviet invasion of Afghanistan (*see* AFGHANISTAN WAR (1979–1989)) by arming, funding, and training the fledgling Afghan *mujahedeen*; or the Soviet use of Cuban proxies during the Angolan civil war, where conflict first broke out in 1974. More recent examples include Iranian sponsorship of Shia militias fighting the US Army during the occupation of Iraq (2003–2011) (*see* IRAQ WAR). AM

PSBR (Public Sector Borrowing Requirement) The quantity of money a government has to borrow in order to finance its annual expenditure. The PSBR covers the gap between the government's income and expenditure, and is usually financed by the sale of government securities. *Keynes argued that a high PSBR should be allowed when economic activity was depressed, enabling public spending when tax receipts are low, in order to encourage growth in the economy. Recent governments have reverted to the *neoclassical doctrine that government borrowing fuels inflation and crowds out private investment, and hence the PSBR should be tightly controlled at all stages of the economic cycle. Since 1997 the PSBR has been governed by two Treasury rules, the more important being the *golden rule.

psephology Term coined in 1952 by R. B. McCallum and popularized by D. E. Butler to denote the study of elections and voting behaviour. From Greek *psephos*, the pebble thrown into one or another urn to cast a vote in democratic Athens.

psychology *See* POLITICS AND PSYCHOLOGY.

Public Accounts Committee Established in 1861 to scrutinize the accounts of UK government departments and agencies, and ensure that money allocated to these bodies is spent as Parliament intended. The Public Accounts Committee is one of the most powerful, with backing from the independent National Audit Office.

- UK Parliament site for Public Accounts Committee, including history, functions, and list of members.

public administration Public administration (lower case) needs to be distinguished from Public Administration (upper case). Public administration denotes the institutions of public bureaucracy within a state: the organizational structures which form the basis of public decision-making and implementation; and the arrangements by which public services are delivered. At the heart of public administration in the UK is the *civil service, but it also includes all of the public bodies at regional and local levels. Definitional problems of 'public' have, however, been created by *quangos and *privatization or marketization of previously public bodies. Public Administration, as a subdiscipline of political science, is the study of public administration by means of institutional description, policy analysis and evaluation, and intergovernmental relations analysis. A shared project in Public Administration is that of developing a public sector organization theory which may topple the intellectual hegemony of private sector organization theory and market principles, although post-modernist, critical, and interpretivist approaches to Public Administration have all sought to reassert analytical concerns. JBr

public bill Any *bill concerned with public policy and affecting the rights and duties of the whole population or all of a certain specified class (e.g. all married women). In the United Kingdom they may be bills introduced by government ministers, or *private members' bills, introduced by back-bench MPs. Most public bills are presented first in the House of Commons, although a minority start in the House of Lords. Devolution to the Scottish Parliament (1999) and the Northern Ireland Assembly (1998) means that many public bills within their territorial remit are purely the preserve of these institutions. JBr

- UK Parliament site with list of public bills.

public bill committee Formerly known as standing committees, public bill committees in the UK House of Commons exist to examine *bills in detail after they have passed their second reading in the House so as to render them 'more generally acceptable' (*Erskine May) before they receive their third reading. All committees are composed in proportion to party strength in the House, although membership is reconstituted for each bill according to MPs' skills and interests. In some legislatures attempts have been made to create committees which combine public bill and select committee functions, notably the subject committees of the Scottish Parliament and National Assembly for Wales. JBr

- UK Parliament site with information about public bill committees.

public choice 1. Broadly, any study of politics using the methods and characteristic assumptions of economics. The methods are deductive and rely heavily on differential calculus because they depend on the marginal principle. The marginal principle stresses that changes in one quantity (say, propensity to vote for the incumbent party) depend on changes in another (say, the level of unemployment last month). A fully-fledged public choice application to politics would form a theoretical model, deduce its consequences, and then test them on observed behaviour. Most actual applications are less ambitious. The characteristic assumptions of economics are: that individuals, not groups or societies, are the appropriate unit of analysis; that tastes are taken as given; that people make choices under scarcity; that they would always rather have more than less, but that their preferences reflect diminishing marginal substitutability between any two goods. The last condition means that, faced with a fixed budget to split between goods A and B, the consumer will substitute more and more Bs in exchange for one A, the more As she already has.

Well-known work in this spirit includes:

a the *median voter theorem of Duncan *Black and its many derivatives;

b analysis of the logic of collective action (M. *Olson, 1965), which builds on the *prisoners' dilemma to explore why any interest groups exist (left to themselves, rational political actors would almost always leave the job of lobbying for somebody else to do), and which sort of interest groups are likely to be stronger than their relative weight in the population would warrant;

c the 'political business cycle' literature which tries to predict the popularity of parties from the state of the economy; and

d the properties of actual and potential voting systems, and the rational behaviour of political actors given that a particular voting system exists (this last shades off into *social choice).

2. More specifically, a school of writers founded in Virginia by J. M. Buchanan (Nobel laureate in economics, 1986) and Gordon Tullock in the 1960s. Their most important work is *The Calculus of Consent* (1962). In the *social contract tradition, this argues that only a constitution with unanimous support is legitimate: they regard such a constitution as embodying the *Pareto condition into politics because nobody would accept it unless he or she thought he or she would be at least as well off with it as without. The Virginia school are suspicious of governments, because they argue that political actors are no less likely to be driven by selfish motives than economic actors; therefore it is inconsistent to suppose simultaneously that the economy is driven by self-interested actions and the polity by altruistic ones. Recent Virginian research has concentrated on the alleged oversupply of *bureaucracy in modern democracies, and on *rent-seeking. Buchanan and Tullock are personally identified with the libertarian right, and many of their ideas have been adopted by right-wing politicians (*see* THATCHERISM), but nothing in the central ideas of public choice leads necessarily to right-wing conclusions.

public good Any good that, if supplied to anybody, is necessarily supplied to everybody, and from whose benefits it is impossible or impracticable to exclude anybody. A third requirement often added to the definition is that 'each individual's consumption leads to no subtraction from any other individual's consumption of that good' (Paul Samuelson, 1954). A public statue is a near-pure public good; other typical examples include national defence, national parks, and clean air. Many goods are partly public and partly private. Left

to itself, the market will not provide public goods because the rational egotistical citizen will free-ride. No national defence forces have ever been wholly provided from voluntary subscriptions (although some public statues have been).

Note that it is no part of the definition of a public good that it is, or ought to be, supplied by a public authority. Some public goods are privately provided; most public authorities supply private as well as public goods. *See also* COLLECTIVE GOODS.

public interest (1) The common interest of persons in their capacity as members of the public; (2) the aggregation of the individual interests of the persons affected by a policy or action under consideration. There is an obvious contrast between these two formulations because there is a distinction between a common interest and the aggregation of individual interests. A common interest is a shared interest, whereas an aggregation of individual interests depends upon an on-balance assessment of the position of individuals considered in isolation. The 'public interest' has been the subject of three different sorts of scepticism. First, it has been suggested that no coherent account can be given of the meaning of the term. Secondly, it has been suggested that even if such an account could be provided, it is impossible in practice to identify where the public interest lies, to know which policy fits the specification given. Thirdly, political scepticism has doubted whether the practices and institutions of modern politics are such that the public interest is pursued. A powerful contribution to political scepticism has been provided by *public choice theory. The first formulation of the public interest, above, refers to members of the public. The public is a group of non-specific persons: for example, a public house is licensed to sell alcohol to anyone (by contrast with a private club, which is licensed only to sell to members and guests). In this sense, the individuals constituting the public are inspecific—just anyone qualifies. But the membership of the relevant public when matters of public interest are raised is dependent on the context. For example, there is a public interest in security at airports, and a public interest in safety at sports stadia. While the group of persons using airports and the group of persons attending sports events may overlap, the two groups may be fairly distinct. The idea of the public nevertheless refers to an unknown group of individuals, in the sense that it is not known exactly who might be adversely affected by (for instance) an aircraft hijack or over-crowding in a stadium. The first formulation supposes that persons can share an interest when they consider themselves as potential members of a non-specified group, abstract-ing from their particular positions and pri-vate interests. For example, a person who never used airports might put that consider-ation aside and consider what arrangements for security he or she would favour suppos-ing he or she were a member of the relevant public. This way of looking at the public interest is closely related to *Rousseau's con-cept of the *general will.

The second formulation may be con-sidered as the '*cost-benefit' approach to the public interest. Adherents of this version deny the coherence or usefulness of the first formulation, and argue that the interest of the public can be no more than the sum of the interests of the relevant individuals, con-sidered in their concrete circumstances. The question of whether a policy is in the public interest is then settled by assessing the potential gains and losses which it is pre-dicted will follow from its adoption.   AR

public opinion The aggregation of the views of individuals in society. The idea of public opinion has roots in Western political thought that go back to the eighteenth cen-tury, although related ideas go back earlier and can even be found in the works of Plato and Aristotle. The term public opinion is derived from the concept of *l'opinion pub-lique* popularized by Rousseau.

Analysts continue to be divided on a pre-cise definition of the concept. Traditional definitions of public opinion had stressed the influence of elites and those best informed in society. The advent of scientific survey techniques in the early twentieth cen-tury led to a proliferation in the empirical analysis of public opinion. Based on the laws of probability sampling, opinion polls enabled a measurement of public opinion that represented the population. This view

of public opinion was espoused by George *Gallup who suggested that public opinion was the average opinion that could be meas-ured by summing up the opinions of every individual in society to form an aggregate opinion. Polling enabled public opinion to be measured relatively accurately and con-tinuously, but not without reservations. V. O. *Key summed up the difficulty in accur-ately measuring public opinion when remarking that 'to speak with precision of public opinion is a task not unlike coming to grips with the Holy Ghost' (1961). Public opinion is very closely tied to the democratic process since it forms a link between the mass of the people and their leaders. It is seen as a means of informing decision-makers of the will of the people, especially towards public policy.   SDC

public–private partnership (PPP) Agree-ment between government and the private sector regarding the provision of public ser-vices or infrastructure. Purportedly a means of bringing together social priorities with the managerial skills of the private sector, reliev-ing government of the burden of large capital expenditure, and transferring the risk of cost overruns to the private sector. Rather than completely transferring public assets to the private sector, as with *privatization, govern-ment and business work together to provide services. The British Government has used PPPs to finance the building of schools, hos-pitals, for defence contracts, and specific capital projects such as the Channel Tunnel Rail Link, the National Air Traffic Services, and improvements to the London Underground. In the latter case, the financial collapse of the Metronet consortium in 2007 meant that the provision reverted to public control. The system has been criticized for blurring the lines between public and private provi-sion, leading to a lack of accountability with regard to funding, risk exposure, and performance (*see also* PRIVATE FINANCE INITIATIVE).

public sector borrowing requirement *See* PSBR.

Publius Collective pseudonym adopted by James *Madison, Alexander *Hamilton, and John Jay as authors of *The Federalist Papers*

punishment

(1787–8). Publius Valerius, according to Plutarch's *Lives*, was a heroic figure responsible for establishing stable republican government in Rome after the fall of Tarquin. sw

• The Federalist Papers reproduced at the Library of Congress.

Pufendorf, Samuel (Puffendorf, Freiherr von) (1632–94) Jurist whose main contribution was to international law. Born near Chemniz, Saxony, he studied law at Leipzig and Jena, and taught at Heidelberg and Lund. He was imprisoned by the Danes because of his contact with the Swedish ambassador, whose sons he tutored in Copenhagen. While in prison he wrote *The Elements of Universal Jurisprudence* (1660). His main work, written at Lund, was *On Natural Law and the Law of Nations* (1670). He also wrote *On the Duty of Man and of the Citizen* (1671), and *On the Relation between Church and State* (1686).

Pufendorf followed *Grotius for the most part, but interpreted *jus gentium* more positivistically, thus breaking from the Aristotelian tradition. He introduced elements of *Hobbes's conventional, contractual idea, without carrying self-interest as far as Hobbes did. For him, as for Grotius, a firmer, more rational basis for a political society was necessary. In keeping with his positivistic approach, he came close to *Rousseau's notion of the *general will or the state as a moral individual whose will is the resultant when individual citizens' wills have cancelled each other out.

On Church–State relationships, while he conceded authority in religious matters to the State, he allowed authority in ecclesiastical matters (appointments, etc.) to the Church, with the proviso that the Church could make

over this power to the State. He did not favour a hierarchical Church. CB

punishment The deliberate infliction of harm, by authorized agents, on a person, in response to a breach of rules by which, it is claimed, the person is governed, and for which he or she is held responsible. Because of the concentrated coercive power at its disposal, state punishment has been a primary concern of political and legal theory. Here the rules are the laws of the state; the legitimacy of the legal system as a whole is contestable, as is the moral obligation to obey particular laws; and the purposes of the punishment may be variously understood. These purposes are usually identified as deterrence and retribution. Although denunciation, prevention, and reform are also mentioned, many theorists would reject these as objects of punishment (rather than possible side-effects or opportunities presented by it). Some accounts of state punishment define it as deliberate infliction of harm on a person who is guilty of breaking the law, in response to that breach, ruling out the possibility that an innocent person may be unjustly punished. Although this is unhelpful, justifiable punishment requires that there be compelling reasons to suppose the person to be punished is guilty; a realistic account of the practice must allow for the possibility of error, even if it hopes to minimize it. The connection between the breach of the rules and the person punished depends upon a conception of responsibility, which is again liable to be controversial, either because of different understandings of the 'causes' of a particular individual's behaviour or because of disagreement about the reasonableness of holding X (e.g. a parent, an army officer) responsible for what Y (e.g. a child, a soldier) did. AR

Quakers The Society of Friends was founded by George Fox in 1650 and nick-named Quakers because Fox told a judge to 'tremble in the name of the Lord' (in other accounts, because Quakers did so them-selves). Distinguished in religion for their silent meetings for worship and rejection of ministers and sacraments; and in politics chiefly for:

1 *Pacifism.* Fox rejected a request for army service because he 'lived in the virtue of that life and power that took away the occasion of all wars'. This and other founding statements form the basis of the Society's 'peace testimony'.

2 *Proceeding by consensus rather than by vote in business meetings.* This could be char-acterized as a unanimity rule.

Through their government of Pennsylva-nia prior to the 1750s, Quaker doctrines were influential out of proportion to the small size of the Society of Friends.

qualified majority rule Any decision rule that requires more than a simple majority (50 per cent + 1) of the votes to ratify a decision. Common examples are two-thirds or three-quarters majority rules (as required to ratify constitutional amendments in many countries) and unanimity rules (as required to return a Guilty verdict in many jury systems). Com-pared to simple majority rules, qualified major-ity rules make it harder to upset the status quo. Viewed positively, this property reduces instability and makes majority-rule *cycles less likely. Viewed negatively, it prevents some majorities from getting their way. There can be no absolute judgement as to whether quali-fied majority rules are better or worse than simple majority rules. Everything depends on the institution in which the rule is applied.

qualitative methods Methods of social research that do not depend on comparing quantities. The phrase is mostly used by people who wish to apply as many of the statistical techniques of *quantitative methods as they can, in order to ensure that the results of non-quantitative research are reli-able and valid. In survey research, a quan-titative approach uses a probability sample of the relevant population. This enables the researcher to establish how likely it is that the results obtained can be generalized to the population as a whole. But they do not permit detailed analysis of tastes and emotions. For that one needs qualitative research: for instance, to assemble a focus group and spend a morning talking to them. But one still needs to know as far as possible that the results from the group are repre-sentative of the population from which they are drawn. Similar issues arise with other research techniques, for instance elite inter-viewing; comparisons of small numbers of cases such as nations; and content analysis of written texts. In all of these cases, self-conscious qualitative researchers try to distinguish their efforts from what they regard as mere storytelling. Their bible has been *Designing Social Inquiry: scientific inference in qualitative research* by G. King, R. Keohane, and S. Verba (1994).

quango A quasi non-governmental organ-ization is one created and funded by govern-ment, and, therefore, held to account for its expenditure, but given operational inde-pendence. The term was invented by Alan Pifer, President of the Carnegie Corpor-ation, to describe such organizations which were appearing in the United States. Subse-quently, political scientists, observing the closeness to government of some quangos in their operations, have preferred the term to mean quasi-governmental rather than non-governmental. In the United Kingdom the term has been applied to many forms of arms-length public provision showing a great diversity of purpose, including the BBC, regional-development agencies, and the Commission for Racial Equality. During the 1980s and 1990s concerns were expressed at the tendency for power to flow from elected public bodies to unelected quangos, derisively dubbed 'quangocracy' by some. But subsequent efforts to cull quangos proved inconsistent, underlining their utility in modern governance to achieve specific objectives, free from political interference. JBr

quantitative methods The range of mathematical and statistical techniques used to analyse data. In order to test empirical theories and hypotheses, political scientists draw on a wide range of sources, including primarily qualitative data such as documents, unstructured interviews, and participant observation, and primarily quantitative data such as those derived from sample surveys or aggregate statistics such as election results, census materials, or cross-national statistical series.

In order to analyse quantitative data, it is first necessary to describe them, that is, to structure the information and to identify overall patterns. Once these patterns have been established then, secondly, it is important to examine the interrelationships between variables, to see whether they are associated or correlated and if so how strongly. Thirdly, assuming that the researcher has a priori reasons for asserting causal relations between variables, the question then arises of how far changes in the causal (predictor, independent) variables can explain changes in the caused (response, dependent) variables. Finally, if the data are from a sample, the issue arises of how far results can be inferred to be an accurate reflection of the population as a whole. To fulfil these four functions—description, association, explanation, and inference—political scientists use a range of techniques. The choice of such techniques varies according to a number of considerations, most notably the level of *measurement.

Quantitative methods have been widely used by political scientists in a range of contexts, including, for example, the study of arms races, of political stability, of political violence, and of the behaviour of legislators, but by far their most prominent application

has been in the area of electoral attitudes and behaviour, where data are easily quantified.

While such methods have enhanced the study of politics, there have been criticisms of quantifying for the sake of it, of equating results obtained with the results of scientific experiments (misapplying the methods of the natural sciences to social data), and over-emphasizing numbers at the expense of explanation (the establishment of the existence of a statistically significant correlation or regression coefficient may say little about its meaning). Such criticisms have led some to a more restrained and cautious use of quantitative methods. ST

Quartet on the Middle East Established in 2002 to represent the United Nations, Russia, the European Union, and the United States in mediation between Israel and the Palestinian Authority. The first international envoy representing the Quartet, James Wolfensohn, stepped down in May 2006, complaining that US and EU support for sanctions imposed on the Palestinian Authority after the election victory of Hamas threatened the peace process (*see* INTIFADA). Tony Blair took over the role of international envoy in June 2007, after stepping down as UK Prime Minister. He resigned in 2015, without being able to make any major progress in mediation. No direct replacement was made, with the head of mission of the Office of the Quartet, Kito de Boer, leading the its work in economic and institutional development in the Palestinian territories.

(⊕) SEE WEB LINKS
• Official website of the Office of the Quartet.

Queen's (or King's) Speech In the UK Parliament, a speech written by the government, read by the monarch to Parliament at the beginning of each session. It is followed by a debate ('Queen's Speech debate' or 'Debate on the Address'). Should the government not command a majority, it will be defeated at the end of this debate, and by convention must resign.

(⊕) SEE WEB LINKS
• State Opening of Parliament site, with recent Queen's Speeches.

queer theory Animated by a commitment to the radical contingency of the term 'queer' and thus subjectless critique, queer theory's scope and approach are notoriously difficult to define. At a minimum, queer inquiry challenges understandings of gender and sexuality as singular and stable. This critique extends also to the heterosexual/homosexual dichotomy underwriting traditional lesbian, gay, bisexual, and transgender (LGBT) studies. Conceptualizing sexuality and gender as part of wider relations of power and normalization, queer thought explores a wide range of pathologized sexual subjects and desires beyond the figure of the homosexual. This includes non-normative heterosexual subjects such as sex workers, single mothers, and a multiplicity of queered racial 'Others'. Queer theory's refusal of a clearly bound referent object has produced insight not only on the mutually constitutive relationship between 'normal' and 'perverse' sexual subjects and practices, and thus the contingent and *political* character of sexual norms and heteronormative logics, but has made possible an engagement with 'regimes of the normal' beyond the sexual, nationally and transnationally.

Queer theory has produced some of the most innovative scholarship on a range of core concerns in political science and international relations, including war, geopolitics, globalization, sovereignty, colonialism, nationalism, citizenship, norm diffusion, migration, austerity, and the welfare state. While the rise of queer theory is commonly associated with 'the poststructuralist turn' of the late 1980s/early 1990s, this concern with destabilizing—queering—fixed notions of sexuality and gender can be traced back to at least the 1970s and the scholarship of lesbian feminists, most of whom self-identified as black and women of colour theorists. In politics and international relations, scholars such as Spike Peterson and Cynthia Weber published explicitly queer work as early as the mid-1990s. Most recently, debates have focused on the increasing inclusion of LGBT subjects in liberal states and markets. Under rubrics such as 'homonormativity', 'homonationalism', and 'pinkwashing', queer theorists examine the ways in which these reconfigurations of sexual norms and normativities ('the respectable LGBT') shape national and transnational political and economic orders. MRM

Question Time *See* PARLIAMENTARY QUESTION.

quorum Minimum number of members that must be present to make proceedings of a political body, such as a legislature or committee, valid. In the British House of Commons the quorum is forty members, in the House of Lords three (although votes can only be taken if there are thirty members present). In the US Senate and House of Representatives the quorum is a simple majority of the membership.

race and politics The word 'race' is present in all languages of Latin origin; it is identical in English and French. In general, it merely refers to a group of common origin and is thus not clearly distinguishable from ethnicity or nationality. Eighteenth-century Englishmen would refer to 'the royal race' or 'the race of Smiths' or, as we still do, to 'the human race'.

Some eighteenth-century theory, such as Buffon's *Histoire naturelle de l'homme,* published in 1778, can be seen as moving towards a more precise and technical concept of race, but it was not until the 1850s that any such account of race became generally accepted. In large part this was because of the development of biological theories which culminated in the publication of *Darwin's *Origin of Species* in 1859. The Comte de Gobineau in France published his *Essai sur l'inegalité des races humaines* and Ronald Knox his *Races of Men* in England. Both argued that races of human beings were significantly different; such significance was scientific but of ethical importance in so far as the argument suggested that people of different races must be treated differently. Gobineau, for example, argued that 'Aryans' (roughly Europeans) were uniquely capable of spirituality and a love of freedom, while the 'black' races were unintelligent, and the 'yellow' races of Asia unimaginative and materialistic. Races, in this sense, occur in many species; they consist of any group with common genetic characteristics, members of which are capable of interbreeding with members of different races in the same species, but have generally not done so.

The concept of race, used in this way, creates the possibility of both racialism and racism, which can be precisely distinguished, even if the distinction is obscured in much argument and ordinary usage. Racialism in general is the doctrine that racial categories are important in determining human behaviour. Racism is the tendency to identify oneself racially and to show hostility or lack of moral respect for members of other races. It would be possible, therefore, to be a scientific racialist without drawing any ethically racial conclusions (Gobineau was an opponent of slavery and rejected anti-Semitism).

In considering the history of racialism and racism it is essential to keep in mind the core weakness of the concept of race. Increasingly, the natural history of man has posited a common origin for the species. In that light, it is hardly surprising that biology has not discovered any evidence for the kind of morally significant genetic differences between races which were posited by the early racialist theories. Such differences as exist are fairly superficial and could not reasonably be taken to justify the different moral treatment of people on racial grounds. Geneticists have shown that we are probably all descended from a 'mitochondrial Eve', who lived in Africa some 200,000 years ago. The different peoples of the earth have not lived and bred so separately as racialist theory assumes. The core weakness of the concept shows itself in the contradictory variety of categories created by racialist theory. Gobineau's category of Aryans, for example, later absorbed into the racial doctrine of Hitler's Third Reich, originally distinguished the relatively pale-skinned Persian and North Indian races from the dark-skinned Dravidians of South India, but came to mean a variety of things varying from 'Germanic' to 'white, non-Jewish' (the latter meaning is equivalent to the category of 'Caucasian' used in the United States in classifying racial origins for the purpose of maintaining policies of *positive discrimination). The use of this term is an extreme example of the mythology which often underlies racial terminology. 'Caucasians' are, strictly, inhabitants of the Caucasus, though often the term refers specifically to the Southern or 'trans' Caucasus which consists of Georgia, Azerbaijan, and Armenia. The term came to apply to 'white' people in the West because of a short-lived and entirely erroneous theory that white people evolved separately in that region. (Ironically, after the break-up of the Soviet Union, real Caucasians, who usually have darker skin and hair than Russians, were widely subject to ethnic prejudice within Russia.) Many textbooks divided Europeans into 'Alpine', 'Nordic', 'Slav', and 'Mediterranean' types. In the British Isles, the perceived racial difference was between 'Anglo-Saxon' and 'Celt'.

After the defeat of the Third Reich in 1945 racialism lost all semblance of scientific and moral respectability among international intellectual elites. We can, therefore, talk about 'the century of racialism' which lasted from the mid-nineteenth to the mid-twentieth century. Racism, though, remained very much alive, even if, given its lack of coherent theories or categories, it became indistinguishable from ethnic chauvinisms and nationalisms.

Much of the politics of race stems from the phenomenon, during that century, of racialism becoming an ideology justifying a range of political institutions. The situation in the 1850s was a paradoxical one: in Europe there were increasing demands for democratization and in America the movement to abolish slavery was reaching its climax. Yet Europeans were extending themselves into colonial empires and the United States was pursuing its 'manifest destiny' to dominate its continent. A justification was therefore required for practices which, increasingly, treated Europeans as equals, but non-Europeans as inferior to them. In British India, after the defeat of the mutiny of 1857, a formal Empire was declared and a much greater separation maintained between 'white men' and 'natives'. Segregation was also introduced in the 'reconstructed' South of the United States; racialist theory also served to justify the treatment of 'Red Indians' by white men, which amounted to genocide in extreme cases. In Africa, as it was colonized by Europeans, there was an even more widely shared assumption that the 'natives' were racially inferior. (It must

not be inferred, however, that imperialism was always justified racially; there were liberal imperialists who saw the differences between themselves and the indigenous population as developmental in nature.)

The kind of racialism which justified these practices did not, however, normally posit the existence of necessary hostility or a conflict of interests between races. Provided there was no interbreeding and the races stuck to their prescribed roles, race relations, it was assumed, could be harmonious and mutually beneficial. This was not true of the racial *anti-Semitism developed by such writers as Houston Stewart Chamberlain, which became the accepted policy of the German Third Reich. That saw the very existence of another race as a threat to German identity and culminated in the extermination camps as a 'final solution' to the 'Jewish question'.

The politics of race since 1945 can be described as the politics of post-racialist racist institutions. In its most important forms it has consisted of powerful interest groups maintaining the structures of power which had existed when racialism was predominant. Globally, the most notable example of this was in South Africa where the victory of the (Boer) Nationalist Party led by Dr Henrik Verwoerd in 1948 led to the institution of *apartheid, a policy of separate development for black, white, Asian, and 'coloured' (mixed race) peoples. Apartheid was often justified in purely cultural terms, but it operated on racial criteria and prohibited interracial marriage. It was a system maintained despite the opposition of a majority of the country and of the overwhelming majority of the world's states. South Africa became an international pariah until the 1990s.

In some respects, the position of the states of the 'Deep South' within the United States duplicated that of South Africa in the world as a whole (see CIVIL RIGHTS). In most respects, Southern segregation was dismantled by the 1970s, but it lingered on in obscure forms and places long after this. In the later period the politics of race in the United States focused on 'positive' moves to create social and economic equality for black people, such as the 'bussing' of children to mixed schools and the use of quota systems to ensure a proportion of good jobs for blacks. As a general rule, these policies were both less successful and less popular than the policies intended to secure equal political and legal rights.

Many European countries had a postimperial politics of race created by the immigration of large numbers of people from their former colonies: Indonesians and Surinamese in the Netherlands, North and West Africans in France, Asians and West Indians in Britain, Central Africans in Belgium. By the 1970s these minority groups averaged around 5 per cent of the population in those countries and was rising in all cases. To a varied extent, their existence aroused racist responses among some sections of the 'white' population and antiracist campaigns among the minorities themselves and liberal allies. Such anti-racist campaigns varied in their emphasis from street action to protect people from racists to intellectual efforts to expunge racism and the remnants of racialism from the culture of the white population. In general, racism has shown a capacity to survive long after the demise of racialism as a serious intellectual belief. LA

Radcliffe-Brown, A. R. (1881–1955) *See* FUNCTIONALISM; STRUCTURAL FUNCTIONALISM.

radical parties Radical parties were originally identified as those in the nineteenth century in favour of extending the franchise, popular participation in politics, civil liberties, and greater social welfare at a time when none of these were the established norm. As they became so in the twentieth century, radical parties were identified as those which sought further to widen established terms of political debate, for example European *green parties. In some countries where the Church-State relationship is strong and generally accepted, those parties representing anticlerical views may be termed radical. Some, but not all, analysts are prepared to admit a category of 'radical right' parties such as the *Poujadists, the French *National Front, and the British National Party. Confusingly, a number of parties across Europe retain the title 'Radical' from their time of formation when they perhaps deserved it, but have since become established parties advocating little systemic political change. 'Radical' means 'pertaining to a root', the metaphor being that radicalism is

root-and-branch reform. However, the etymology also leads to a famous satirical comparison between the French Radicals and radishes (*radis* in French)—red outside and white within. JBr

radical-right *See* EXTREME-RIGHT.

raison d'état Raison d'état (much less frequently in the English reason of state) dates from arguments in international law at the time of the formation of the modern statessystem in the seventeenth century. It means that there may be reasons for acting (normally in foreign policy, less usually in domestic policy) which simply override all other considerations of a legal or moral kind. *Raison d'état* is thus a term which fits easily into the language of political realism and *realpolitik. As those doctrines have declined in acceptability the term *raison d'état* declined with them. PBy

ranking member Member of legislative committee in the US Congress who has the longest continuous service on that committee for each party. Traditionally the ranking member of the majority party becomes the committee chairman. *See also* SENIORITY.

rapid reaction force (RRF) Term referring to specific formations of rapid deployment force, which can be defined as a 'shortnotice contingency force'. At the Helsinki summit of 1999, European Union leaders decided to give teeth to their *Common Foreign and Security Policy, by setting up a European Rapid Reaction Force (ERRF). Member states committed themselves to fielding a total of 60,000 group troops, deployable within 60 days, for periods of up to one year. The ERRF will provide the EU with its own military capability and allow it to undertake tasks from humanitarian and rescue missions to peacekeeping and actual combat; the so-called *Petersberg Tasks. The ERRF will come into action only 'where *NATO as a whole is not engaged'. YFK

ratio level variable *See* MEASUREMENT.

rational choice The division of, or approach to, the study of politics which treats the individual actor as the basic unit of analysis and models politics on the assumption that individuals behave rationally, or explores what would be the political outcome of rational behaviour. Rational choice writers usually define rationality narrowly in terms of transitivity and consistency of choice. An individual's choice is transitive if, given that he or she prefers A to B and B to C, he or she also prefers A to C. It is consistent if the individual always makes the same choice when presented with identical options in identical circumstances. The principal subdivisions of rational choice are *public choice and *social choice.

Rawls, John (1921–2002) Believed to have radically reinvigorated Anglo-American political philosophy, he is considered to be one of the most important political philosophers in the twentieth century. His most famous work, *A Theory of Justice* (1971), argues for a concept of 'justice as fairness': namely, that the demands of justice are satisfied when cooperators can equally accept reciprocal principles of justice and when their basic economic, political, and social institutions (the basic structure) are mutually understood as satisfying these principles. The foundations for justice as fairness stem from Rawls's rejection of *utilitarianism and his *Kantian belief that every individual has an interest in formulating a conception of the good, in being motivated by this conception, and in living cooperatively with others, under mutually consistent terms of respect and reciprocal benefit. In this regard, justice can be understood as fair when a cooperative scheme could be accepted and confirmed by every member involved.

However, unlike some traditional forms of contractarianism that treat political *contracts as possible historical events, Rawls's contract is purely hypothetical in formulation, suggesting that 'fairness' results from what could be reasonably considered as impartial procedures in an *original position* between deliberating cooperators. As Rawls states, 'the intuitive idea of justice as fairness is to think of the first principles of justice as themselves the object of an original agreement in a suitably defined initial situation . . . which rational persons concerned to advance their interests would accept in this [original] position of equality to settle the basic terms of their association.' In order to derive these fair procedures, Rawls places potential cooperators behind what he calls a *veil of

ignorance. The veil of ignorance is a thought experiment where we imagine that members are unable to consider all of their social standings, religious beliefs, cultural affiliations, and other individual interests that might bias the deliberative outcome. Participants do understand that they have a conception of the good and an interest in pursuing it, but are not aware of which conception of the good they hold while behind the veil of ignorance. In this regard, the veil forces individuals to create equal, impartial, and universal procedures of cooperation. If they do not, they might in fact be legislating against the possibility of being able to pursue their own conception of the good. For it is not until the veil is lifted that they know their true social position and particular self-interests.

From this original position, Rawls maintains that two principles of justice emerge as being mutually consistent and thus fundamentally just principles that should underwrite the political association. These principles emerge because '[individuals] do not know how the various alternatives will affect their own particular case and they are obliged to evaluate principles solely on the basis of general considerations'. According to Rawls, the two hierarchical principles of justice that emerge are:

1 A distribution of equal basic liberties. As Rawls maintains, 'each person has an equal claim to a fully adequate scheme of equal basic rights and liberties, which scheme is compatible with the same scheme for all.'

2 Social and economic distributive justice. (a) That social and economic procedures are to be arranged so that social opportunities remain equally open to all. (b) That economic procedures could be expected to be to everyone's advantage. In other words, social and economic structures should be organized so as to satisfy the standard of mutual benefit in that even the lowest member of the cooperative scheme improves (the difference principle).

The influence of Rawls's theory of justice on contemporary political philosophy has been enormous. Not only has his theory been seen as a viable alternative to utilitarianism, it has also proven to be heuristically valuable to liberal egalitarians who have applied Rawls's work to a broad range of interdisciplinary debates. However, his work has also influenced a large number of critical responses, especially from *communitarian and *libertarian theorists. For many communitarians, Rawls over-prioritizes individualism within the first principle of justice, thus undermining or ignoring the key role that societies play in human development and flourishing. Alternatively, many libertarians have argued that Rawls's egalitarianism, as argued under the difference principle, inappropriately limits the freedom of individuals to be rewarded for their natural ability to be competitive in an open and free society (market). Lastly, many *cosmopolitans have complained that there is no moral justification for limiting the original position to the state level as Rawls does and that the fundamental principles of Rawlsian justice should apply at the global level.

The most recent works by Rawls, *Political Liberalism* (1993) and *The Law of Peoples* (1999), offered reformulations and continued exploration of his principles of justice. In *Political Liberalism*, Rawls examines how we can have a stable and lasting agreement upon a conception of justice when we disagree fundamentally and seemingly intractably about 'the good' (reasonable pluralism). He argues that we must develop an 'overlapping consensus' through a form of 'public reason', where individuals construct and reaffirm principles of governance that all members can agree as not only just, but also as principles which maintain a sense of political stability (reflective equilibrium). In *The Law of Peoples*, Rawls responds to the cosmopolitan debate and to those who attempted to apply his work at the global level. In a rejection of cosmopolitan justice, Rawls focuses on a liberal notion of tolerance between all 'well-ordered' peoples, arguing that his principles of justice do not apply internationally and that 'liberal' and 'decent' (but non-liberal) people(s) can maintain different systems of social justice, while at the same time upholding a mutually consistent *law of peoples* that is based on human rights and a toleration of different ways of living.

reactionary A person or group of people who oppose progressive policies and political reform which deviates from the status quo. A reactionary tends to be conservative in nature and will oppose policies that do not re-establish a past condition or reaffirm existing policies that protect the status quo and what they see as their traditional cultural and national ideals. Examples of reactionary politics were involved in arguments advocating the continuance of *slavery in the 1800s, in opposition to women's *suffrage in the 1800s and 1900s (and still today in many countries), as well as against new *civil rights policies in the United States during the mid-1900s. In all of these cases, reactionaries viewed the policy changes as a direct attack on the fundamental foundations of societal norms and values.

realignment A change in underlying electoral forces due to changes in *party identification. It has been common to talk of 'realigning elections', or pairs of elections, in US political history. The generally accepted dates for such realignments are around 1828, 1860, 1896, and 1932. Because the concept is vaguely defined, there is no agreement on whether there has been a realignment since the *New Deal coalition was formed in 1932, although all writers agree that there has been a *dealignment since 1960.

realism Realism is the label given to the traditional orthodoxy in political approaches to understanding *international relations. It is conventional to counterpose realist thinking to *idealism. Realism dominated the discipline in the decades following the Second World War. It claims an intellectual heritage going back to *Thucydides, *Machiavelli, *Hobbes, and *Rousseau. Postwar realism was dominated by the writing of E. H. *Carr, Hans *Morgenthau, and John Herz. A revival under the label neorealism started in the late 1970s led by the work of Kenneth N. *Waltz. Realism in all of its forms emphasizes the continuities of the human condition, particularly at the international level. *Classical realists tended to find the source of these continuities in the permanence of human nature as reflected in the political construction of states. *Neorealists find them in the anarchic structure of the international system, which they see as a historically enduring force that shapes the behaviour and construction of states. On the basis of these continuities, realists see power as the driving force in all political life. Their analytical focus is on the group rather than on the individual, and because it commands power most effectively, the key human group is the state, whether understood as tribe, city-state, empire, or nation-state. Because relations between states are power-driven, and because the anarchic structure provides few constraints on the pursuit of power, realism emphasizes the competitive and conflictual side of international relations. The idea of the *balance of power is one of the most long-standing analytical tools of realism, and provides the link between the study of power politics generally, and the more specific analysis of military relations in strategic studies.

Realist analysis tends to model the state as a unitary rational actor operating under conditions of uncertainty and imperfect information. In this both realism and neorealism borrow consciously from microeconomic theory, seeing states as analogous to firms, anarchic structure as analogous to market structure, and power as analogous to utility.

From the late 1960s onwards it began to be argued and accepted that the methodology and theory associated with classical realism were anachronistic. Behaviouralists argued that the work of classical realists did not satisfy the canons of scientific investigation. There was a vigorous academic assault coming from those concerned with interdependence, political economy, and transnational relations. This included attacks on the centrality of the state and military power in realist thinking, an accusation that realism was unable to deal with either the issues or the character of international politics in an interdependent world, and a denunciation of the logic and the morality of realism's normative bias towards conflictual assumptions.

Neorealism reasserted the logic of power politics on firmer foundations, exposing the partiality of the interdependence view of international relations, and reaffirming the primacy of American power in the international system. It was much aided by the onset of the second Cold War in 1979, which caught off balance advocates of interdependence and transnationalism, who were still confidently generating explanations premised on the progressive redundancy of force in international relations and the fragmentation of state power. Increasingly,

neorealist and *neoliberal thinking merged in pursuit of *rational choice theory, sharing an opposition to the rising challenge from *constructivism. BB

realism (classical) Classical realism is a variant of *realism in *international relations theory and is most strongly associated with the work of twentieth-century thinkers such as E. H. *Carr, George Kennan, and Hans *Morgenthau, among others. Like all IR realists, classical realists take conflict to be an ineradicable feature of international politics and explain outcomes by appealing to the darker features of human nature (e.g. propensity to act on fear, the drive to dominate), the ordering principle of *anarchy, the distribution of power (e.g. *bipolarity, *multipolarity), or changes in the distribution of *power. However, three things distinguish classical realism from the dominant strand of IR realism called *neorealism. First, classical realists assign comparatively greater importance to explanations that appeal to human nature. Second, classical realists tend to be more attuned to the role of uncertainty and contingency in international politics. They are therefore comparatively less optimistic about our ability to reliably predict state behaviour. Third, classical realists rarely focus solely on *explaining* international political outcomes (i.e. what states do) and are comparatively more comfortable offering normative *prescriptions* (i.e. what states should do). AMQ

realpolitik A German term meaning the politics of the real, it refers to the *realist's determination to treat politics as they really are and not as the idealist would wish them to be. 'Machiavellianism' and *machtpolitik* or power politics are similar terms. *Realpolitik* is most commonly used in connection with foreign policy. PBY

recall Process whereby an elected official may be subject to an election which can lead to loss of office before his or her term of office has expired if a specified number or percentage of electors sign a petition calling for such an election. The recall device is widely available at state and local level in the United States and was used in California in 2003 to replace the Governor, Gray Davis, with Arnold Schwarzenegger. WG

redistricting *See* APPORTIONMENT.

referendum A mechanism which allows voters to make a choice between alternative courses of action on a particular issue. The result of the referendum may then be embodied in the particular state's constitution; it may be mandatory before an international treaty can be signed; it may serve as the equivalent of legislation; it may be necessary before public funds can be raised for a particular purpose; or it may simply be advisory. In some countries, such as Britain, the referendum has been effectively limited to big constitutional issues. In countries or states where there is more extensive use of the referendum, it is usual for a referendum question to be placed before the electorate if a given number or percentage of signatures can be obtained from electors in a specified time period, although there may also be provision for a referendum initiated by the head of government (as in France) or the legislature. Polities which make extensive use of the referendum, such as Switzerland or the state of California, encounter a number of difficulties. The ability of governments and legislatures to pursue coherent policies is weakened. Political parties become less important as mechanisms for developing policy options. Voters find it difficult to decide on complex issues, and may rely on politicians or the media to guide their choice, or use the referendum to make a general protest against current government policy. Too frequent use of the referendum may lead to 'voter fatigue' with declining turnout. Nevertheless, electors in those countries which use the referendum are generally reluctant to discard it. It can be defended as a means of ensuring that politicians do not lose touch with the preferences of the electorate. *See* BREXIT.   WG

reflective equilibrium A condition of balanced mutual rationalities and reasoning arrived at through reflective deliberation and intersubjectivity. In political theory, the idea of a reflective equilibrium is one where individuals deliberate, rationalize, and adjust their positions so as to come to a mutual agreement on a common set of principles that can reflect all positions to some degree. Famously used by John *Rawls in his book *A Theory of Justice*, reflective equilibrium was said to be generated through his hypothetical and deliberative *veil of ignorance. In this case, participants—who knew they had positions and interests, but not which ones—would rationally agree on a set of general principles that reflected the widest possible set of positions and interests, while also securing a level of mutual benefit for those who would be the worst off once the veil was lifted.

reflectivism Covers those approaches to *international relations that emphasize intersubjective meanings, historicity, values, norms, and social practices. The term derives from Robert Keohane's argument that IR can be divided into two approaches whereby reflectivism is contrasted with rationalism's reliance on formal models, transaction-cost analysis, and other arguments about rational, calculative behaviour. *See also* POST-POSITIVISM.   JJ

refugee The 1951 United Nations Convention relating to the Status of Refugees (as amended by a Protocol, 1967) defines a refugee as any person who, owing to a well-founded fear of being persecuted for reasons of race, religion, nationality, membership of a particular social group, or political opinion, is outside the country of his or her nationality and is unable or, owing to such fear, is unwilling to avail him-or herself of the protection of that country; or who, not having a nationality and being outside the country of former habitual residence as a result of such events, is unable or, owing to such fear, is unwilling to return to it.

The 1969 Convention Governing the Specific Aspects of Refugee Problems in Africa extends the definition to also include those who, owing to external aggression, occupation, foreign domination, or events seriously disturbing public order in either part or the whole of his or her country of origin or nationality, is compelled to leave their place of habitual residence in order to seek refuge in another place outside his or her country of origin or nationality. This reflects that the 1951 Convention was drafted in a European context of persecution following the Holocaust and during the *Cold War. In other regions, forced displacement tend to arise due to war, civil war, general disorder, or natural disasters. Definitions that focus more broadly on the deprivation of fundamental *human rights nonetheless distinguish between refugees, who have crossed an international border, and internally displaced persons, who remain in their country of residence. The latter constitute a majority of those forcibly displaced. A vast majority of refugees originate from, and are hosted in, developing regions. *See also* POLITICAL ASYLUM. CSa/PBl

⦿ SEE WEB LINKS

• Text of the Convention relating to the Status of Refugees.

refugee crisis A situation of acute humanitarian need, where conflict has created a large number of forcibly displaced persons within a short period of time. The crisis element may refer to the difficulties of neighbouring countries in hosting a large influx of *refugees, but it may also refer to exacerbated difficulties in providing protection due to reluctance by other states to host refugees or fund refugee camps.

'Refugee crisis' can refer to a situation where a large number of refugees enter a country or region irregularly, aided, for example, by smugglers. In Europe in 2015, though not a new phenomenon, this manifested itself in thousands of deaths as refugees attempted to cross the sea from Turkey to Greece, or from Libya to Italy. Due to so-called non-arrival policies, such as visa restrictions and carrier sanctions aimed at deterring asylum seekers, safer routes become closed off for refugees.

It is disputed whether the situation in Europe in 2015 should be called a 'crisis' at all, since European states host a comparatively low number of refugees. The main humanitarian crisis affected refugees themselves and developing countries in conflict regions (such as Lebanon or Turkey), not European states, even though some had to accommodate large numbers of refugees during a short space of time. CSa

regime A system of government or administration. The most common use of this promiscuous term in recent years has been in the phrase 'military regime'. So while any government may be termed a regime, be it monarchical, aristocratic, republican, or tyrannical, the term unavoidably conjures up memories of tanks in the streets in Latin American capitals. This is to be regretted, since it has two more technical senses in which it may not easily be replaced. First, when governments come and go with bewildering frequency, as in nineteenth-century Spain or post-1945 Italy, there may still be an absence of fundamental or revolutionary change. In these circumstances it is possible to speak of regime continuity. Alternatively, and more rarely, a change of regime (from constitutional monarchy to tyranny, or from dispersed to centralized government) may be achieved without a change in government, as in the move from parliamentary to personal rule by Charles I of England, or in Britain under Margaret Thatcher. Secondly, in international relations the difficulty of accommodating the rise of non-state actors and complex *interdependence within state-centric realist models of explanation has led to use of the term 'regime' to cover norm-bound interactions relating to issues such as the global environment or human rights, in which states, international organizations, transnational corporations, individuals, and worldwide pressure groups like *Greenpeace or *Amnesty International all take part. CJ

regime change Generally referring to the overthrow and replacement of a government by means of *hard power, military action, and/or support for a local militia who share the general aim to see a particular government toppled and replaced. In *international relations, 'regime change' often refers to a particular form of foreign policy activity, which mobilizes resources and *alliances so as to undermine and ultimately remove a particular governmental regime or administration in order to advance a favoured alternative regime. Regime change can also be furthered through non-military means via the weakening of a regime through economic sanctions and other means of *soft power. A recent example of regime change was promoted by US President George W. Bush and his instigation of the *Iraq War, which aimed to remove Saddam Hussein's *Ba'athist regime. *See also* PROXY WAR.

regionalization The theory and practice of economic, political, and social coordination and integration between states and peoples within a particular geographical region. Coordination can include the formation of supranational institutions, such as the *European Union, or more informal and policy-specific coordination mechanisms, such as the Association of Southeast Asian Nations (ASEAN). One argued feature of regionalization is its associated promotion of common norms, rules, regulations, and institutional structures. In addition, one often cited byproduct of regionalization is the formation of regional identities and realigned allegiances by citizens, which transfer from the state to the regional or supranational level.

regionalism The practice of or belief in regional government. Regionalism may be distinguished from *federalism, in which the lower tier of government has a protected sphere where the upper tier cannot intervene; and from *devolution, in which the upper tier devolves to the lower tier powers that are then difficult to take back (such as the power of internal self-government that the government of the United Kingdom gave to Northern Ireland between 1920 and 1972). The term regionalism is therefore better applied to regimes (such as France) in which there are, or might be, regions, but where regions are a creation of central government which may be as easily destroyed as created. England is divided into standard regions which are widely used for statistical and administrative purposes but have no political representation (unlike Scotland, Wales, and Northern Ireland). In 1993 the *European Union established a Committee on the Regions on which elected local officials serve. In the United Kingdom the process was introduced after a cross-party revolt against a government proposal to nominate its own appointees to the committee.

regressive taxation Taxation system which levies a proportionately higher rate on those with lower incomes. Taxes levied at a constant percentage on expenditure, such as VAT, and flat-rate taxes, such as the UK *poll tax or the TV licence fee, are regressive in effect. National lotteries, although not strictly taxes, are strongly regressive. The spending of the poor subsidizes the leisure of the rich.

regulation In its specialized political sense, the control of privately owned monopoly by government rules. It dawned in Britain with the Regulation of Railways Act 1844. Because railways were a natural monopoly—it is always cheaper for an established network to serve a new client than it would be for a rival network to start—Parliament tried (unsuccessfully) to regulate prices and (more successfully) to regulate safety. Regulation was exported to the United States during the *Progressive era from 1880 to 1920, and re-exported to the United Kingdom after *privatization of nationalized industries began in 1979. The theory of regulation has lagged behind the practice, so that the aim of regulation has sometimes been unclear. Some writers accuse industries of 'capturing' their regulators: that is, of bargaining with them for a pattern of regulation which the industry and the regulator can live with, but which fails to protect the public as the legislation intended.

'Regulation' is also used more broadly to cover any publicly imposed rules governing a firm or industry, especially safety and environmental rules.

reification The process of misunderstanding an abstraction as a concrete entity. *Lukács saw the origins of the concept in both Hegel and Marx, although the German word for 'reification', *verdinglichung*, cannot be found in any of their writings. Despite this Lukács relates the concept to *commodity-fetishism as explicated by Marx in the first chapter of *Capital*. For Marx, fetishism exists when social relations between men take the form of relations between things. Lukács discusses reification in this light by focusing on how men's productive activity takes an alien form in the capitalist mode of production. In contrast, *Adorno stressed the importance of understanding reification as a social category which indicates the way in which consciousness is determined. The emphasis on reification becomes not simply a relation between men that appears as a relation between things, but rather a relation between men that appears in the form of a property of a thing. Adorno relates this to Marx's distinction between use value and exchange value. Only exchange value is reified because it is the form in which the value of a commodity is expressed. IF

relations of production In general, this term—in German *Produktionverhältnisse*—

refers to those relationships which arise out of the actual production process and also, of course, to ownership relations of which the most important is property. Like *forces of production, it is a technical term from the theory of *historical materialism. According to *Marx, the most fundamental ownership relation, under capitalism at least, is bourgeois ownership of the means of production, an ownership which also manifests itself in a monopoly of political power. The precise relationship between forces and relations of production is ambiguous, and the sense or senses in which a contradiction between forces and relations constitutes the dynamic of history is obscure. JH

relative autonomy The theory that any social totality has four separate and distinct sets of practices—economic, political, ideological, and theoretical—which act in combination, but each of which has its own complete autonomy according to the limits set by its place in the totality. It is a term which has assumed particular significance in discussions of the *state. In Marxist theory the notion of relative autonomy was developed in response to the perceived bankruptcy of Soviet Marxism-Leninism which saw the state as an epiphenomenon whose actions could be reduced to the operation of an 'economic base' (see BASE/ SUPERSTRUCTURE). Whilst it could be argued that Marx and Engels first introduced the notion in discussing the *Bonapartist regime in France after Louis-Napoleon's *coup d'état* of 1852, the notion of relative autonomy was popularized by *Poulantzas in *Political Power and Social Classes* (1968). Poulantzas argued that the modern capitalist state best serves the interests of the capitalist class only when the members of this class do not participate directly in the state apparatus, that is, when the ruling class is not the politically governing class. This degree of relative autonomy from the capitalist class and from the interests of particular fractions of capital (finance, industrial sectors, etc.) enables the state to function as a 'collective capitalist' and maintain its legitimacy in the eyes of the electorate. The concept of relative autonomy has been heavily criticized for its *functionalist overtones and its tendency to tautology. Orthodox political theorists (in particular statists or state-centred analysts)

have also been preoccupied with the issue of state autonomy, usually defined as the ability of states to pursue goals in spite of the demands or interests of other social groups or classes. Rather than opt for notions of relative autonomy, statists have developed a continuum ranging from 'strong' to 'weak' states, which has been particularly influential in discussions of the developmental state. PBM

relative gains A term used in the study of politics and *international relations to measure differential gains in power and influence in comparison to other political actors or states. The term is widely used to depict the *international system as representative of a *zero-sum game, where states are concerned with relative *hard power gains versus 'absolute gains', which include economic gains and other gains in *soft power or *normative power.

relative power A term used in the study of *international relations to denote the measure of state power and influence as it relates to the power of other states. The term is often used to capture how states understand the distribution of power within the *international system and gauge where they stand hierarchically in relation to other states. It is said that relative power is useful in understanding insecurity within the international system and how states will behave differently based on their position and relative insecurities.

relativism See CULTURAL RELATIVISM.

religion and politics There can be no precise and agreed definition of religion. The origin of the word is of little help, for it descends from the Latin *religiare*, to bind, which suggests the broadest possible boundaries for the territory of religious belief and encourages the acceptance of the argument, frequently put in the twentieth century, that many kinds of belief which fall outside the bounds of the recognized religions, including forms of Marxism and nationalism, have the essential characteristics of religion. It is thus genuinely difficult to define religion for the purpose, say, of teaching children about comparative religion or of formulating laws against offending people's religious beliefs.

Are witchcraft and paganism a religion or set of religions? Is theosophy?

However, if the boundaries of religious belief are difficult to draw, the core territory is relatively easy to characterize. Religion is concerned with the worship of transcendent or supernatural beings whose existence is outside or above the realm of the normal, which is mortal and temporal. In its most historically important and ethically demanding form, monotheism, as exemplified in the Jewish, Christian, and Islamic religions, the religious concern is concentrated onto a single God who is omnipotent, omnipresent, and omniscient, the creator of the universe.

Religion is therefore normally of huge ethical significance. What people ought to do is derivable from the existence, nature, and will of God. It would be difficult to be seriously religious in any sense without that religion determining some of one's political beliefs. Indeed, the most natural relation between religion and politics is one in which the most important political questions have religious answers: the legitimacy or otherwise of regimes, the limits of a particular authority, and the rightness or wrongness of legislation can all be derived from religious revelation (*see e.g.* MEDIEVAL POLITICAL THEORY). The range of religiously justified regimes can be divided into theocracies, where divine revelation and the priests who interpret it rule directly, and those non-theocracies where the divine will has, nevertheless, sanctioned the particular form of secular rule (the doctrine of the *divine right of kings to rule being a typical form of religious, though non-theocratic, legitimation).

However, since the seventeenth century Western Europe and the Americas have been dominated by secular views which sought successfully to separate religion from politics, so that the state's existence is not justified by theology. Secularization arose out of the tension between science and religion and the schisms between forms of Christianity. It was essential to put religion beyond the sphere of truth and refutation and to justify the authority of the state without recourse to (disputed) theological premisses. Thus in 'Christendom', though not in the territory of Islam, there developed an acceptance that political disputes must be resolved on secular grounds. Paradoxically, this process evolved most rapidly in England,

which retained (and continues to retain) an established Church (*see* CHURCH AND STATE).

In a 'secular' society the principle that religion and politics are independent realms is accepted, but religion continues to influence politics in a number of ways. Although religious doctrines may be taken to be arbitrary or indeterminate on many political questions, there remain issues on which a Church must speak clearly and forcefully. Roman Catholic doctrine on abortion is one of the clearest cases. A particular form of religious belief can be strongly linked to national identity, as Catholicism has been for the Poles and the Irish, and Orthodox Christianity for the Armenians and Georgians. Where parties are freely formed, there are likely to be parties based generally on Christian social morality, like the many *Christian Democratic parties of contemporary Europe, or specifically on one Christian Church. For example, the Catholic People's Party in the Netherlands and the *Mouvement Républicain Populaire* in France have been specifically Roman Catholic parties, though both of these parties have now merged with others and there has been, since the late twentieth century, a tendency for parties based on one Christian Church to decline.   LA

rendition Legal term indicating transfer of a person or property from one jurisdiction to another. Used by the United States administration and the CIA to describe the movement of criminal or terrorist suspects from one country to another. *See also* EXTRADITION; EXTRAORDINARY RENDITION.

rent-seeking Seeking to capitalize on the scarcity value of a good or service. The term was coined by Anne Krueger, 1974, for an activity classically described by Gordon Tullock in 1967. Economic rent may be defined as the extra earnings a factor of production (land, labour, or capital) may secure from scarcity. Governments may artificially create this scarcity, for instance when they give a firm, a cartel, or a union the monopoly right to supply their factor of production. Tullock pointed out that it is worth while for those seeking such monopolies to bid anything up to the full scarcity value of the monopoly in an attempt to get it. Suppose, for instance, that a government will give just one airline the monopoly right to operate between two cities. Everyone knows that the winner of this licence will be able to charge a premium price for the whole duration of the licence. Each airline is therefore willing to spend anything up to the whole value of this premium in lobbying and bribing the government to try to get the licence. Thus the whole value of the monopoly would be dissipated in what Jagdish Bhagwati has labelled 'directly unproductive activities'.

reparations The act of providing restitution for a wrong or harm which has been committed. In the study of *international relations, reparations generally refer to compensation payments owed to countries or persons harmed or wronged by another state. The most famous form of reparations were those levied against Germany in 1919 by the *Treaty of Versailles, which demanded the transfer of money and land to the victors of the First World War.

report stage In Parliament, after a committee has examined legislation, it 'reports' the bill back to the house, when further amendments can be proposed. *See also* BILL.

representation One of the core concepts of politics, but elusive because it has incompatible meanings. The verb 'to represent' originally referred to the arts. To act a play was literally to 're-present' its characters through the actors. This usage survives in phrases like 'you represented to me that . . .'. Then from the sixteenth century it came also to mean 'to act for, by a deputed right'. Usually it implied one person acting for one other, as with a lawyer representing a client, or an ambassador representing a monarch. But it could also refer to one (legal) person acting on behalf of a group of people, as in the first and still the most influential discussion in political theory, chapter 16 of *Hobbes's *Leviathan*. Hobbes's Sovereign need not be literally one person—any assembly with an odd number of members may be the Sovereign. But he treats it throughout as a single legal person representing a group of clients, each pair of whom have made a pact to hand their rights of nature over to the Sovereign. From this it was an easy step, first taken during the English Civil War, to the third and now commonest usage: 'to be accredited deputy or substitute for . . . in a

legislative or deliberative assembly; to be a member of Parliament for' (*Oxford English Dictionary*, 'represent' senses 1 and 8; 'representation' senses 2, 7, and 8). Representation as picture leads to the 'microcosm' conception. During the American Revolution, John *Adams said that the legislature 'should be an exact portrait, in miniature, of the people at large, as it should think, feel, reason, and act like them'. This conception lies behind the phrase 'statistically representative'. Technically, a sample is representative of a population if each member of the population had an equal probability of being chosen for the sample. Informally, it is representative if the sample includes the same proportion of each relevant subgroup as the population from which it is drawn (*see* SURVEY RESEARCH). In political discussion, relevant subgroups are usually groups of a certain age, sex, class, and/or racial division (*see* GROUP REPRESENTATION).

The principal–agent conception ('acting on behalf of') has a clear meaning when one person acts on behalf of one other. The agent acts in the principal's interests, with a degree of leeway that varies from case to case. How much leeway political representatives ought to have is one of the hallowed debates of political theory (*see* BURKE; VIRTUAL REPRESENTATION). The interpretation of the principal–agent conception when one agent acts for many principals, as in the case of a legislator, is less clear. An electoral district may have interests, but only individuals can express interests. How is the legislator to decide whom to represent when his or her constituents disagree? One answer is that the legislator represents the majority of those who voted; but that is not necessarily true, unless a majoritarian electoral system such as *alternative vote was used. It is frequently untrue in *plurality electoral systems.

The microcosm and principal–agent conceptions may conflict. If MPs are a microcosm of the electorate in every relevant respect, but fail to do what the voters want, they are representative in the first sense but not the second; and conversely if they do what the voters want without being statistically representative of them. Microcosm conceptions of representation are associated with *proportional representation, and principal–agent conceptions with majoritarianism. The

PR school looks at the composition of a parliament; majoritarians look at its decisions.

Another dimension of fair representation concerns boundaries, districting, and the meaning of 'one vote, one value'. In the United States, since *Baker* v. *Carr* (1962), the courts have enforced exact mathematical equality of Congressional district populations, but have engaged in a futile struggle to obtain the proportionately correct number of *majority-minority districts—that is, districts where African-Americans or Hispanic Americans form the majority of the district population. By contrast, the United Kingdom tolerates, with almost no public discussion, fivefold variations in constituency electorates. Thus two regimes both regarded as representative democracies can rely on widely differing concepts of representation.

representative government Generally interpreted to refer to a form of government where a legislature with significant decision-making powers is freely elected. It is also sometimes argued that representatives should reflect the social and gender composition of the electorate. WG

republic Originally simply a synonym for 'state', as in the (Latin and) English title of *Plato's Republic*, from the seventeenth century the term came to mean a state without a king. Some definitions insist that only those states which have provisions for the (direct or indirect) election of the head of state may properly be called republics. *Madison distinguished between a republic ('a government in which the scheme of representation takes place') and a democracy ('a society consisting of a small number of citizens, who assemble and administer the government in person'). However, almost every state in the world without monarchy calls itself a republic, and this usage overwhelms nice distinctions.

republicanism 1. The belief that one's country ought to be a *republic rather than a monarchy.

2. Specifically, in Ireland, support for the militant (armed) branch of Irish nationalism.

Republican Party (USA) The term has had a very confusing history. Around 1800 the party system coalesced into Federalists and Democratic–Republicans. Broadly, the Federalists were urban and trade-orientated,

while the Democratic–Republicans were rural and orientated towards the interests of small farmers. The Democratic-Republicans became the *Democratic Party in 1828, Their opponents changed label from Federalist to Whig in the 1820s but this did not improve their fortunes. They coined the label Republican (probably because like Cortina or Escort it had vaguely good connotations without offending anybody) when the anti-Democrat forces coalesced on an anti-slavery campaign in 1854. The Republican victory in the presidential election of 1860 (*see* LINCOLN) and the ensuing Union victory in the Civil War led to Republican dominance until 1876. The pact of that year, in which the Republicans were allowed to win a disputed presidential election on condition that federal forces withdrew from the South (*see* CIVIL RIGHTS), reinstated the Democratic hegemony in the South. At federal level, the Republicans were again hegemonic from 1896 to 1932 because sectional interests captured the Democratic Party. This was overturned by the *New Deal coalition, which lasted until the 1960s. In the late 1960s some commentators predicted *The Emerging Republican Majority* (title of a book by K. Phillips, 1970), but no coherent majority has emerged.

Ideologically, the Republican Party favours business and opposes welfare. Because US parties are so weak and open, it is hard to pin any other ideological label on to it. A large but not dominant faction attempts to hitch the party to the values of *Christian fundamentalism, and under President George W. Bush there were charges that *neoconservatives wielded disproportionate influence. Yet, in 2016, influence from *reactionary grassroots movements such as the *Tea Party were able to influence the agenda, moving the Republican Party more towards conservatism and *populism, electing reality TV personality and real estate mogul Donald J. Trump to the US Presidency on a platform of anti-immigration, *hawkish foreign policy, reinvigorated *patriotism, and anti-globalization. The party is sometimes known by the acronym GOP (Grand Old Party). Its symbol is the elephant.

(⊕) SEE WEB LINKS

• The website of the Republican National Committee, including a history of the Party.

reselection The process by which organizations replace or endorse existing officers who have already successfully gone through previous candidate selection procedures. In political parties interest focuses on reselection for parliamentary candidates by parties prior to each general election. In Britain, where a first-past-the-post electoral system is used, reselection is the responsibility of local constituency parties. Three types of reselection have been used: first, reselection by a constituency party elected committee; secondly, reselection by an electoral college composed of delegates of affiliated groups within the constituency party; and thirdly, reselection by all local constituency party members on the basis of one member one vote. The second and third types of selection may be mandatory or discretionary, based on the will of a constituency party elected committee to trigger a full reselection procedure.

The first type is common in parties that are elitist in values, prefer to see their candidates as representatives rather than as delegates, and seek longevity in candidate service. The British Conservative Party takes this approach, meaning that candidates are generally very secure. The second type is common in parties that prefer to see their candidates more as delegates than as representatives. They wish to see different parts of a constituency party sit in judgement on their parliamentary performances and deselect them as candidates if they have failed to reflect local party interests. The British Labour Party took this approach between 1981 and 1990. However, the Labour Party switched to the third type at the 1993 party conference. This reflected desires to turn the party into a mass membership party, in which greater participatory democracy in reselection is achieved as an end in itself, without imposing constraints upon the autonomy of the nominated representative. During this period Labour also moved from mandatory full reselection procedures to discretionary trigger approaches. The Liberal Democrats have always followed the principle of one member one vote.

For the position in the United States, *see also* PRIMARY ELECTIONS. JBr

reservation Quota policy whereby a proportion of government jobs, educational places, and elected posts are set aside for members of particular groups. Extensively used in India, where the Constitution provides for reservation for the Scheduled Castes (Untouchables) and Scheduled Tribes (aboriginals). These two groups currently make up just under a quarter of the population, and should receive a proportionate share of reserved positions (although job and educational quotas often remain unfilled). Frequent attempts have been made to extend the scope of reservation, most notably in 1990 when the V. P. Singh government attempted to implement the recommendations of the Mandal Commission (1978) which would have extended reservation to 49.5 per cent of the population. The resultant political uproar brought down the government, and the clamour for special treatment amongst caste and religious groups has pervaded political debate. In the 1990s the reservation of seats in local government was extended to women, although caste-based interventions have undermined attempts to introduce legislation to secure a one-third quota for women in the Indian parliament. Reservation policy can be seen to have given opportunities to those who would otherwise have been excluded, but they have also perpetuated caste divisions, and their effectiveness in improving the social and economic position of the wider population, rather than just a 'creamy layer' of beneficiaries, is likely to be limited.

resilience Being able to withstand, recover from, or adapt in the face of shocks and stresses. Emerging from psychology and ecology debates, resilience looks at how individuals, communities, societies, and systems respond to crises and deal with risks. It can mean to restore previous functioning or to adapt and evolve. JJ

responsibility to protect (R2P) The *United Nations General Assembly unanimously endorsed the responsibility to protect (R2P) principle at the United Nations World Summit in 2005. The agreement is set out in paragraphs 138, 139, and 140 of the World Summit outcome document. These outline a threefold responsibility. First, every state has a responsibility to protect their population (not just citizens) from *genocide, *war crimes, *crimes against humanity, and *ethnic cleansing. Second, the international community has a responsibility to encourage and assist states so that they can fulfil their primary responsibility to protect people from the four crimes. Third, if a state is 'manifestly failing' to protect their population from the four crimes, then the international community has a responsibility to take timely and decisive action on a case-by-case basis. This includes a broad range of coercive and non-coercive measures under Chapters VI, VII, and VIII of the United Nations Charter. At the time of writing, the R2P has been invoked in more than forty-five United Nations Security Council Resolutions, such as Resolutions 1970 and 1973 on Libya in 2011 (*see* UNITED NATIONS).

The mainstream consensus is that the R2P is best understood as a multifaceted framework or a complex norm that embodies many different yet related components. Fleshing this out, in 2009 the UN Secretary-General divided the R2P into three pillars, which has had significant traction in the discourse to this day. Pillar I refers to the domestic responsibilities of states to protect people from the four crimes. Pillar II regards the international community's responsibility to provide international assistance with the consent of the target state. Pillar III focuses on 'timely and collective response' in that the international community takes collective action through the UN Security Council to protect the people from the four crimes, notably, without the consent of the target state. Although states have not formally 'signed up' to this three-pillar approach, they help distinguish between different forms of R2P action. For example, international assistance in Mali and South Sudan was provided with the consent of the Malian and South Sudanese government, yet the military intervention in Libya in 2011 was taken without the consent of the Libyan government. The former reflects pillar II action, whereas the latter is a pillar III operation.

Although the value of the R2P remains contested, advocates highlight seven key features. First, it reconceptualizes sovereignty, as it asks us to consider that state sovereignty is a responsibility rather than a right. Second, it focuses on the powerless rather than the powerful by addressing the rights of the victims to be protected rather than the rights of states to intervene. Third, it establishes a clear threshold, as it identifies four crimes as the benchmark for action. Fourth, the consensual support for R2P amongst states is important, as consensus helps shape international understandings of rightful conduct. Fifth, it is broader in operational scope than *humanitarian intervention, which posed a false choice between doing nothing and declaring war. The R2P overcomes this simplistic dichotomy by outlining the broad range of coercive and non-coercive measures that can be used to encourage, assist, and, if necessary, force states to fulfil their responsibility. Sixth, although it does not add anything new to international law, the R2P draws attention to a wide range of pre-existing legal responsibilities and therefore helps focus international response to a crisis. Seventh, in the aftermath of Iraq, the R2P was important in restating that the UN Security Council is the primary legal authorizer of any pillar III use of force. AG

responsible government Defined in A. H. Birch's *Representative and Responsible Government* in terms of a government that is responsive to public opinion, that pursues policies that are prudent and mutually consistent, and that is accountable to the representatives of the electors. WG

revenue sharing In general, any scheme for balancing taxing and spending between tiers of government, especially in federal systems. Without revenue sharing, rich regions of a country will be able to raise more than poor regions, but require to spend less. Therefore, any country in which there is pressure for redistributive politics will face pressure for revenue sharing, even if its constitution divides the power to tax among tiers of government. In particular, the term is used in the United States to denote arrangements whereby federal revenue is shared with state and local governments, with certain conditions attached.

revisionism Any critical departure from the original interpretation of (especially) Marxist theory. The term was originally associated with *Bernstein's critique of the theoretical premises and political strategies of *Marxism. He argued that the 'inevitable' crisis of capitalism was not in fact happening. Monopoly capital had proved resilient to crises of production and used imperialist expansion as a safety valve for surplus value. Social polarization was not occurring: the working class was not increasingly impoverished, a new middle class was emerging, and the peasants were not disappearing. Bernstein believed that it would be possible to move towards socialism with mass socialist parties seeking electoral collaboration with other progressive forces. He was influenced by *Fabian ideas concerning the permeation of the state. Bernstein contended that he was only giving a conceptual perspective to a situation that already existed in Germany and England. The label *revisionist* has been applied to other reinterpretations of socialism, *see* CROSLAND. GL

revolution The overthrow of an established order which will involve the transfer of state power from one leadership to another and may involve a radical restructuring of social and economic relations. Before 1789 the word often meant, truer to its literal meaning, a return to a previous state of affairs; since the *French Revolution, the modern meaning has expelled this one.

Revolutions are processes incorporating both elite competition and mass mobilization. Their causes are long in gestation—so that they may appear to occur spontaneously—and will have both domestic and international roots. Their outcomes differ from the original objectives of their participants. It is difficult to identify when revolutions begin and end. There have been many revolutionary situations which have not resulted in revolutionary outcomes. The small number of recognizably 'great' Revolutions creates methodological problems for comparative analysis.

One can differentiate between political and social revolutions. A political revolution produces changes in the character of both state power and personnel. It lasts until the monopoly of control and force of the old is broken and a new hegemonic group reconstitutes the sovereign power of the state. It may provoke a counter-revolution and sometimes a restoration. Social revolutions (which are far rarer) involve political and social transformations, class struggle, and pressure for radical change from below. This mobilization may be manipulated by other actors to achieve their own objectives,

which may be opposed to those of the popular classes. The depth of social transformation will depend upon the intensity of class struggle, the nature of class alignment, the strategy, organization, and leadership of the revolutionary forces, and the resilience of the incumbent authorities.

Karl Marx described revolutions as 'the locomotives of history'. According to his Preface to the *Contribution to the Critique of Political Economy* (1859), new modes of production (feudalism, capitalism, socialism) were generated within the confines of the existing one. Revolutions were caused by the development within a mode of production of a contradiction between the social forces and the social relations of production, with the latter acting as 'fetters' upon the former. This expressed itself in the intensification of class conflict, ushering in what Marx called 'the epoch of social revolution'. Each proto-revolutionary class developed consciousness of itself through economic and political struggles against the existing dominant class. The result would be the emergence of new relations of production and their accompanying ideological forms, and the eventual establishment of *hegemony by the triumphant revolutionary class.

Marx stressed that no social order ended until all scope for the development of its productive forces had been exhausted and the new relations of production had matured within its 'womb'. Although speculating on the possibility of peaceful transition in a few mature democratic states (Great Britain, United States), he argued that the bulk of socialist revolutions would be violent. His theory was based upon the premiss of revolutions occurring in highly industrialized states whereas experience has been of revolution in semi- and underdeveloped societies.

Rather than viewing them as progressive and inevitable, many writers have sought to understand the roots of social instability and political violence in order to pre-empt revolutions. Functionalism depicted society as being in a state of permanent, self-regulating equilibrium and viewed revolutions as profoundly antisocial—what Chalmers Johnson in *Revolutionary Change* (1966) termed 'dysfunctional'—events which must be avoided. Political authority was legitimized by social consensus concerning political

483

norms and roles. So long as this consensus persisted then governments could make necessary adjustments, even implementing quite radical reforms. A skilful government would be able to neutralize the impact of innovatory ideas, events, and processes (known as 'accelerators'), but a government which lost its political nerve would revert to coercion and might provoke revolution. Charles Tilly also stressed the importance of conflict management by elites (for example, in *From Mobilization to Revolution*, 1978).

Another approach has been to depict revolutions as socio-political crises produced by the dislocations of modernization. For *Tocqueville writing about the *French Revolution of 1789, revolutions occurred when previously encouraged expectations that things would continue to get better were dashed. Revolutions could be fed by both rising and deflated expectations in societies undergoing transition. A modern version of this argument is called the *J-curve hypothesis (imagine a letter J turned 135 degrees anticlockwise). For Samuel Huntington (*Political Order in Changing Societies*, 1968), revolution was caused by the mobilization of new groups into politics at a speed which made it impossible for existing institutions to assimilate them. Revolution did not happen in established democratic systems, because they had the capacity to broaden participation and incorporate counter-elites whilst maintaining political control. This model defined revolutions as characteristic of developing societies, with modernization emerging on an evolutionary sliding scale.

Theda Skocpol (*States and Social Revolutions*, 1979) criticized earlier models for reductionism (although she herself focused upon only two main causes of the French, Russian, and Chinese Revolutions: political crisis and peasant rebellion). Her structural analysis centred on the decisive and autonomous role the state could play in mediating between groups. Specific revolutions must be analysed in depth before causal patterns could be identified. Skocpol gave little weight to human agency or revolutionary organization. Her somewhat ahistorical model also had little sense of 'great' Revolutions influencing each other or other movements.   GL

Rhenish Capitalism A system of capitalism characterized by non-market patterns of coordination by economic actors and extensive state-regulation of market outcomes. The term Rhenish Capitalism was popularized by Michel Albert in his book *Capitalism vs. Capitalism* (1993) and is central to recent research on 'varieties of capitalism'. Rhenish capitalism is associated with Northern European economies—most centrally Germany but also the Netherlands, Denmark, and Sweden—and has also been used to characterize Japan. Non-market coordination refers to the engagement by firms, unions, and other social actors of a variety of associational bodies used to develop and renew economic institutions. Examples include collective wage bargaining, vocational training systems, technology transfer initiatives, and credit-based financial systems with 'stakeholder' patterns of corporate governance. State regulation supports non-market coordination through accepting many associational agreements as legally binding and through granting statutory bargaining rights to traditionally weak social actors, such as unions within collective bargaining law or employees within 'codetermination' or workplace representation law.

The varieties of capitalism literature has compared Rhenish and Anglo-Saxon economies to develop the idea of 'comparative institutional advantage'. According to this theory, differences in capitalism systems create different patterns of economic adjustment, particularly applied to patterns of commercial innovation. Deep patterns of non-market coordination associated with Rhenish capitalism create competitive advantages in industries associated with 'incremental' innovation or 'diversified quality production' such as the machine-tool or speciality chemical industries, but, through creating restraints on the short-term reallocation of resources, create comparative institutional disadvantages in newly developing or 'radically innovative' industries such as biotechnology or computer software.

Political research on Rhenish capitalism draws on the literature on democratic corporatism, suggesting that forms of social democracy characterizing the small European economies also exist at the level of the firm. Proponents of Rhenish capitalism argue that strong state regulation creates 'beneficial constraints' on employers such as limits on employee dismissals that encourage the development of substantial firm-specific training of employees and patterns of 'workplace democracy' that are lacking in Anglo-Saxon forms of capitalism. Critics of Rhenish capitalism argue that long-term employment norms limit the ability of firms to quickly adjust to technological and market changes and create labour market rigidities that contribute to higher unemployment than is typically found in Anglo-Saxon economies. Other critics note that Rhenish capitalism produces cross-class political coalitions between employers and skilled employees that exclude the unemployed and low-skilled (particularly immigrants and, until recent decades, women) from meaningful political representation.   SC

rhetoric Rhetoric is the persuasive use of language. Until the eighteenth century its study was one of the central disciplines in European universities alongside theology, natural and moral sciences, and law. Thereafter, empiricist and positivist methods of social inquiry led to its eclipse, on the ground that language, scientifically used, was no more than a transparent medium by which knowledge of the world gained by experience was mediated. Rhetoric, accordingly, came to denote the unnecessary or misleading embellishment and corruption of language—a view which *Plato had held of the *sophists. With the waning of faith in modernism, serious attention once again began to be devoted to language as a means to power. This was especially evident in the work of *Nietzsche, but was also strongly implied by the revival of *hermeneutics and Wittgenstein's attack on the correspondence theory of language.   CJ

Richardson, L. F. (1881–1953) English *Quaker scientist; pioneer of scientific meteorology and the study of *arms races. Studying the Anglo-German arms race in the years before the First World War, Richardson noticed that, as may happen with weather and other physical processes, English arms in one period may be a function of German arms in the last, and German arms in the next period may be a function of English arms in this period. This may lead either to catastrophe or to stable equilibrium. Richardson made numerous other contributions to the scientific study of politics, almost all unrecognized in his lifetime.

rider US term for a clause or provision added to an important bill, with no apparent link to the substance of the legislation. Although most riders would not pass into law if judged on their own merits, by attaching it to a bill that other members are reluctant to delay by tabling amendments to remove the riders, or the President to lose by invoking his veto, the measure may succeed. In many state legislatures the governor possesses a line-*item veto in order to prevent riders attached to a bill becoming law.

rights Legal or moral recognition of choices or interests to which particular weight is attached. Assertions that X has a legal right to Y are tested by whether the law does in fact recognize X's right to Y; assertions of a right in the absence of that legal recognition may be demands that the law be changed to accommodate the asserted right, or be a way of stating the perceived demands of morality. There are two principal theories seeking to explain what it is to have rights and the purpose of ascribing them to individuals. On the first view, a person who possesses a right has a privileged choice: it is recognized, if a legal right, because the law will ensure that it has effect, while if a moral right it identifies a person whose choice should have effect. To the extent that other persons have duties or liabilities as a consequence of the right, it is the right-holder who may choose to release them from those duties or choose not to trigger their liabilities. The point of rights, then, is to make available these sorts of choices, and a system of rights involves some sort of distribution of freedom. On the alternative view, rights give expression to important interests, and it is the purpose of rights to protect a person's significant interests by imposing duties on others. (Whether only persons are capable of having rights is a debated issue, but one affected by whether the capacity for choice or the possession of interests is thought fundamental.) Which choices or interests have the relevant importance or significance still needs to be specified, of course: for some writers the interests are those which would be threatened by *utilitarian calculations. One recurrent controversy about rights is just how weighty they should be. Are rights ways of establishing important claims, but claims which are defeasible or alienable? Or are rights vetoes ('trumps', according to Dworkin) which cannot be put into a balance? *See also* SIDE-CONSTRAINT. On the one hand, to respect a property right when the lives of thousands could be saved by overriding it looks fetishistic; on the other, to allow rights to be overruled by considerations of general utility is alleged to neglect the integrity and separateness of persons. In any case, if and when rights conflict we shall have to decide which to uphold, possibly on utilitarian grounds.

Two problems about freedom have parallels in the discussion of rights. The first concerns the distinction between a formal right to X and the substantive capacity to X. For example, A has a legal right to X, in a case where that means 'A is not to be forbidden to do X', does not guarantee that the action X is available to A, since its performance may require resources which A lacks. Similarly, with respect to *equality, *Marx criticized the rights held dear by the bourgeois revolutions of the eighteenth century: to guarantee to all a right of private property (for example) does not by itself give everyone equal amounts of property, or, indeed, any property at all. An equality of rights, in short, is compatible with great inequality in actual conditions. The second parallel with debates about freedom arises from the alleged differences between rights the primary purpose of which is to protect the individual from outside interference, and rights attributed to the individual which impose duties on others to provide the individual with resources. It is suggested that the latter (welfare rights) are unwarranted extensions of the former (claim rights) because of the different sort of duty they require. The alleged differences depend in part on whether we focus on choice/freedom or interests as explanations for the ascription of rights.

The relationships between rights and duties within systems of positive law cannot be assimilated to one model. Wesley Newcomb Hohfeld demonstrated over seventy years ago that 'rights' embrace four types of legal relation, and his analysis can also be applied to non-legal usage. Very often, statements about rights draw on more than one of the four relations identified:

1 A right is a liberty: a person has a liberty to X means that he has no obligation not to X.
2 A right is a right 'strictly speaking' or a claim right: a person has a right to X means others have a duty to him in respect of X.
3 A right is a power, that is, the capacity to change legal relations (and others are liable to have their position altered).
4 A right is an immunity, that is the absence of the liability to have the legal position altered.

The relation between the right-holder and other persons differs in the four cases. The importance of Hohfeld's analysis is not merely that it clarifies rights talk. Understanding how rights operate, characterizing them accurately, is a necessary precondition to decisions about their value. Sceptics have been critical of the importance rights seem to attach to the individual, particularly the acquisitive or egoistic individual: they see rights as the expression of the distance between a person and the community. Supporters have argued that rights are of crucial value in balancing the claims of persons, and that they have a potential to integrate society by providing a framework for action.   AR

right to life More a slogan than a precisely defined term. *Hobbes argued that each human being has a fundamental duty of self-preservation, and hence a natural right to do whatever conduces to it. In Hobbes's social contract, however, rational individuals hand over all their rights to the person or body they nominate as their sovereign, all of whose actions they are thereby deemed to authorize. Hobbes's absolutism has just one exception: that, as the purpose of signing the social contract was to preserve oneself, the Sovereign cannot order a subject to kill him- or herself. *Locke described civil society as an association for the 'mutual Preservation of their Lives, Liberties, and Properties', and this assertion is the ancestor of the claim in the American Declaration of Independence that: 'We hold these truths to be self-evident: that all men are created equal; that they are endowed by their creator with certain inalienable rights; that among these are life, liberty and the pursuit of happiness.'

Despite this high backing, the right to life is not an absolute right. Both Britain and

America have had provision for capital punishment: Britain until 1967, and many US states to the present day. Attempts to have capital punishment declared unconstitutional have failed. Both countries have had provision for military conscription. Hobbes recognized that his political theory did not grant a right to life guaranteed by discussing the biblical story of Uriah the Hittite, whom King David sent to the wars in the (correct) expectation that Uriah would be killed, as David was having an affair with Uriah's wife. Hobbes insisted that David had not violated Uriah's rights, which makes it hard to see what rights Uriah had.

The right to life is also used as a slogan in contemporary argument about abortion (*see also* PRO-LIFE) and euthanasia. 'Right to Life' is shorthand for the views of those militantly opposed to abortion, especially in the United States, because they argue that the foetus has an unconditional right to life. Those who favour euthanasia argue that if one has a right to one's life, one has a right to choose to end it. One might expect an association between opposing abortion and favouring euthanasia. However, the association tends the other way, partly because militant anti-abortionists are often *Christian fundamentalists, who are among those who think that the taking of the life of an unborn foetus and of someone who wishes to die are equally forbidden.

right(-wing) The opposite of *left. As with the term left-wing, the label right-wing has many connotations which vary over time and are often only understood within the particular political context. In advanced liberal democracies, perhaps more than anything else the right has been defined in opposition to *socialism or *social democracy. As a result, the ideologies and philosophies of right-wing political parties have included elements of *conservatism, *Christian democracy, *liberalism, *libertarianism, and *nationalism; and for *extreme-right parties racism and *fascism. As the policy platforms of parties have varied, so has the popular conception of the left-right dimension. In surveys, self-placement on a 'left-right' scale is associated with attitudes on economic policy, especially redistribution and *privatization/*nationalization, *post-materialism, and (particularly in Catholic countries) religiosity. SF

Riker, W. H. (1920–93) American political scientist, and pioneer of the *rational choice study of *Federalism, *coalition theory, and *structure-induced equilibrium. His most important work, *Liberalism against Populism* (1982), ranges widely through normative political theory and American political history. He argues that the probability of *cycling in a large society, which means that there will be no platform of policies that would not lose a majority vote to some other, renders the idea that the 'people should rule', associated with *Rousseau and his followers, vacuous. He attributes the stability of American political history since 1865 to the institutions which hide cycling from view, and interprets the Civil War, and the presidential election of 1860 which immediately preceded it, as a case of disequilibrium exploited by the previous losers, who formed the *Republican Party on the basis of a new coalition of forces to win in 1860.

risk Generally, the chance or hazard of some unpleasant outcome. To be carefully distinguished from uncertainty. The distinction usually made is that a risky event is one where the odds can (at least in principle) be calculated; an uncertain event is one where they cannot (e.g. in a game with no dominant strategy, such as the *Prisoners' Dilemma *supergame). Perceptions of risk are important in politics. There is massive evidence that people make systematic errors in their perceptions of risk: especially by believing that rare but newsworthy events are commoner than they are. As misleading perceptions of risk feed through to political attitudes and therefore to political decisions, politicians avoid some relatively safe actions, such as disposing of nuclear waste, and encourage some extremely risky ones, such as driving cars.

Risorgimento See MAZZINI, GIUSEPPE.

Robespierre, Maximilien (1758–94) French Revolutionary politician; one of the architects of the 'Reign of Terror' (1793–4) which claimed his own life. His deification of 'the people' using slogans loosely connected with *Rousseau has led writers of the left to hail him as a precursor of socialism, and communism, and writers (mostly but not entirely) of the right to hail him as a precursor of totalitarianism.

rogue state Label used by the Clinton administration (1993–2001) to characterize states 'beyond the international pale' who are hostile to the United States. Rogue states were portrayed as being contemptuous of international norms, bent on acquiring weapons of mass destruction, and being sponsors of terrorism. Rogue states were difficult if not impossible to deter, and their unpredictable behaviour was used as an argument by proponents of ballistic missile defence to argue in favour of installing such a system. The rogue state label was most consistently applied to Iraq, Iran, North Korea, Cuba, and Libya during the Clinton years. The policy implication was that such states ought to be isolated and contained, approaches that did not command universal agreement among America's allies. Toward the end of the Clinton administration, the term 'rogue state' was replaced by the more politically correct 'states of concern', an indication perhaps of the diplomatic disutility of the label. The label, however, has been resurrected by the George W. Bush administration, in part to justify its pursuit of National Missile Defense. YFK

Rokkan, Stein (1921–79) Norwegian political scientist with close American connections. Known for his work in such areas as state formation, nation building, *centre-periphery politics, *party systems, and historical political sociology. WG

roll-call Roll-call votes require a formal record of the presence and vote or abstention of each member of a legislature, traditionally by calling out each name, but increasingly through the use of electronic recording devices. Roll-call analysis seeks to identify voting blocs within legislatures where partisanship is a poor predictor of voting behaviour. WG

Roman law More commonly referred to, by lawyers, as civil law, meaning the collection of laws developed under codes promulgated by the Emperor Justinian in AD 528. Today, civil law systems are prevalent in all the member states of the European Union except Ireland and the United Kingdom. European Community law is itself influenced by the civil law tradition rather than the English common law. The characteristics of Roman law, most noticeable to English lawyers, are the use of codes, which are the written formulation of legal principles.

The four parts of Justinian's codification are as follows:

1 The *Institutes* setting out the basic elements of jurisprudence which appear in a didactic form.

2 The *Digest* or *Pandects* containing various rules which are derived from the *Institutes*. These rules are accompanied by opinions on the law and are organized on the basis of a compendium. The *Digest* is composed of fifty books divided into seven parts. The *Pandects* also contains fifty books; each book contains several titles. Taken together, the *Digest* and the *Pandects* are an important source of law and authority.

3 The *Codex Justinianis*, divided into twelve books; each book had several parts. The first nine books were called the *Codex*; the remaining three books contained the *Jus Publicum*.

4 The *Novels* (*Novellae Constitutiones*). About 168 books were placed into one volume which provided an explanation of Justinian's Codes. These were translated into various languages.

Roman law was influential in Britain for over three hundred years during the reigns of the Emperors Claudius to Honorius. However, it never took root and English law developed its own distinctiveness based on the common law rather than on the Justinian Codes. JM

Romanticism Associated with free and idealistic expression of and attitudes towards the passions and individuality, Romanticism is nevertheless an extremely vague term, more familiar in analysis of the arts than of politics. In literature, the adjective 'romantic' first appeared in French towards the end of the seventeenth century, and referred to a form of narrative fiction, involving passions rather than reason, which eventually became known in English as the novel. Romanticism as an explicit system of ideas appeared at the end of the eighteenth century, in Germany, as a critique of neoclassical aesthetics, an aspect of Enlightenment thought. It came to include history, philosophy, music, the plastic arts, and politics, as well as literature. The meaning in politics often seems to be a reflection of literary classifications, and

Romanticism cannot be associated with any specific political system or ideology. Some Romantics supported the *French Revolution, some opposed it, and some changed their minds about it.

Romanticism is often seen as an antithesis of the Enlightenment, but that is too simple. For the Enlightenment thinker, human nature is universal, or at least what is important about it is universal, and it can be analysed in terms of general laws on the model of physics. For the Romantic, this is impossible. What is important is the specificity and creativity of each individual, which cannot be reduced to any set of general laws. One aspect of this is the Romantic rejection of natural science, at least when applied to humanity but sometimes in any guise. Part of this denial of universalism involved the Romantic adoption of nationalism, but originally this was more cultural than political, and did not include the idea that one nation was 'better' than another.

Politically, Romanticism has been associated with every view from liberalism to extreme authoritarianism. One of its essential manifestations in the nineteenth century involved the rejection of individualism and industrial society in favour of sympathy for the factory worker, as in the case of *Coleridge.   cs

Rome, Treaty of Treaty signed in 1957 which inaugurated the European Economic Community (EEC, later the EC and EU: *see* European Union), establishing a common market in a variety of products between member states. The Community was seen by its signatories (the *Benelux countries, France, West Germany, and Italy) as complementing the success of the European Coal and Steel Community, created by the same countries in 1952.   sw

Rorty, Richard (1931–2007) A philosopher who straddled the pragmatist, analytical, and continental philosophical traditions, Rorty developed an anti-foundationalist approach to liberal political theory. Arguing that liberal democratic institutions would be better served by ignoring debates surrounding their philosophical foundations, or indeed lack thereof, Rorty believed that we should openly embrace their contingency. Liberals should not concern themselves with trying to ground liberal institutions in something

objective, be it human nature, metaphysics, or God, but instead get on with the practical task of reducing pain, cruelty, and humiliation. The ideal citizen of Rorty's liberal polity would be the 'liberal ironist', someone who committed themselves to liberal values in their public lives and engaged in innovative and novel acts of self-creation in their private lives.

Rorty's emphasis on the contingency of liberal values drew much criticism from the political right who often accused him of encouraging students towards a relativism which could provide no better reason to defend the ideals of liberal democracy than any other political creed. Though politically Rorty was of the left he received little support from that quarter either, for he was often accused by social democrats of offering nothing more than soft 'bourgeois liberalism'.   ms

rotten borough In the House of Commons before the nineteenth-century Reform Acts, a constituency that had very few electors and was in the pocket of a local landowner; indeed an alternative name is 'pocket borough'. Reformers highlighted the case of Old Sarum, which had no resident electors at all but returned two MPs up to 1832. But any borough with fewer than about 1,000 electors could be a rotten borough if the dominant local landowner was able to impose his candidate with no, or minimal, opposition. Not until after the 1867 Reform Acts were very small boroughs eliminated; not until after 1884 were district populations even roughly equal.

Rousseau, Jean-Jacques (1712–78) Moral, political and educational philosopher, novelist, composer, musicologist, and botanist. Not French, but born in Geneva, a French-speaking city-state of the Swiss confederation. Although his family was relatively poor, Rousseau was by birth a member of the citizen class, the highest in Geneva, and one of the only two classes out of five with political rights. They made up only a small percentage of the population. Rousseau left Geneva at 18 with nothing, to make his fortune. He rejected *Calvinism, especially the central place it gave to original sin, and became a Roman Catholic. Although readmitted to Protestantism in 1754, he increasingly rejected all formal religion. He educated himself, becoming familiar with, among others, the ideas of *Plato, the modern *natural law school, and the *Enlightenment. In 1749, inspired by the title set by the Academy of Dijon for an essay competition, Rousseau wrote his *Discourse on the Sciences and Arts*, and was awarded first prize. Published in 1750, this established his reputation as a writer. He wrote the *Discourse on Inequality* in 1755, again for the Academy of Dijon, but did not win. In both discourses, Rousseau contrasted the simplicity and innocence of solitary man in a *state of nature, living in terms of his own being, with the dishonesty of man in society who sees himself, and hence lives, only in terms of the opinions of others. Sciences and arts, on the one hand, and inequality on the other, are manifestations of this corruption. In between the state of nature and corrupt society, he puts (but only in one paragraph) the primitive family which is so small that no dishonesty can exist between its members, and which therefore provides a context for morality.

In 1762, he published both *Émile*, his tract on education, and *The Social Contract*, his most important work of political philosophy. Society is based upon a contract, but in contrast to other *social contract thinkers, Rousseau refuses to allow originally independent individuals to give to a government their capacity for will—it is inalienable. Rousseau therefore separates sovereignty—the legislative function—from government—the executive function—and makes the second the servant of the first.

The only legitimate form of sovereignty is a direct democracy in which all citizens have the right to participate in making the law. This solves to Rousseau's satisfaction the paradox of leaving each associate as free as before after joining a society. It depends upon his commitment to the ancient idea of liberty as participation instead of the modern one as a sphere of life free from social interference. The way to achieve ancient liberty is the *general will. This is the will of each individual in favour of the good of the whole community, and is superior to his own particular interest. This is based on the idea of a separation between real and apparent interests in which the realization of the latter would destroy the former, and the individual would lose the chance of achieving liberty in

the ancient sense. In this process, he may lose liberty in the modern sense, and this contrast lies behind Rousseau's paradoxical assertion that if anyone refuses to accept the general will, then he must be forced to be free. To ensure that the citizen body would come as close as possible to the ideal of voting laws unanimously, Rousseau relies upon the establishment of moral harmony between citizens. This must be a result of deliberate policy, but can only be achieved in a small and isolated society. There is some tension between Rousseau's view of the need for a tightly knit and artificial orthodoxy in society, and his view of education in *Émile* which relies largely on the effects of the individual pupil's natural contact with the world of things.

In practice, Rousseau recognizes that even the smallest possible society capable of independence could not give political rights to everyone. His models for legitimate society were some of the city-states of ancient Greece, republican Rome, and Geneva, which in different ways embodied the equality of citizens but inequality between them and the rest of the population. Rousseau rejected the possibility of applying his ideal to a large modern society, although in 1772 he wrote by invitation a constitution for Poland which was under threat of what became the First Partition by Prussia, Austria, and Russia. His plan involved taking account of Polish tradition, and attempting to turn it into a genuine national consciousness by educating the Polish equivalent of the citizen class in a city-state. At the same time, in order to approach as closely as possible the conditions for realizing the general will in a small state, Rousseau proposed to grant a large degree of self-government to each of thirty-three provinces which would be created, and connected by federal arrangements. Rousseau provided a *Romantic alternative to Enlightenment optimism, emphasizing the part played by feeling instead of reason in human motivation.   cs

royal commissions In the United Kingdom, royal commissions are committees of inquiry established by royal charter or warrant at the behest of the cabinet to look into issues of considerable public importance. Their membership and precise terms of interest will be set by a member of the cabinet, but it is then intended that their collection of evidence, deliberations, and submission of a report to the cabinet are carried out independently. Royal commissions have at least an educative impact, and may contribute policy proposals which are taken up by the cabinet. At worst they are used as vehicles for diffusing political problems, or are overtaken by the need to respond to events more rapidly. They fell out of favour after 1979 but are still occasionally used on major issues such as the future of the House of Lords (Wakeham Commission 1999–2000). The idea has been adopted by many Commonwealth countries. JBr

Royal Prerogative See PREROGATIVE.

Rules Committee An influential standing committee of the US House of Representatives which sets the timetable of the House, and the conditions under which debate takes place.

(⊕) SEE WEB LINKS

• Site for the US House of Representatives Committee on Rules.

rule utilitarianism See UTILITARIANISM.

Rushd, Ibn See AVERROËS.

Russell, Bertrand (1872–1970) English philosopher and political activist. Russell's main philosophical achievements are in the areas of logic and mathematics. Nevertheless, he became the best-known philosopher of his time because of the volume and clarity of his writing, and the vigour and prominence of his political activism.

If anybody could be said to be born to Liberalism, Russell could. His grandfather was Lord John Russell, a former Liberal Prime Minister; and his secular 'godfather' (a non-Christian appointed by Russell's non-Christian parents) was John Stuart *Mill. Many of Russell's political causes (such as support for female suffrage and opposition to the First World War) may be regarded as classically liberal; and so, in a sense, may his leading role in *CND in the early 1960s and even his fierce opposition to the American involvement in Vietnam in the late 1960s. Russell was not a lifelong *pacifist; for a short period after the Second World War he believed that, rather than allow the Soviet

Union to acquire nuclear weapons which could lead to a war in which human life was wiped out or almost so, the United States and its allies should be prepared to go to war, atomic war if need be, against the Soviet Union. As Alan Ryan put it in *Bertrand Russell: A Political Life* (1988), 'Russell was not a pacifist, because he was a *consequentialist'. This does not debar him from being viewed as the last Victorian Liberal.

Russian Congress of People's Deputies See CONGRESS OF PEOPLE'S DEPUTIES (RUSSIA).

Russian Federal Assembly See FEDERAL ASSEMBLY (RUSSIA).

Russian Revolution, 1917 There were two revolutions in 1917, the one in February which saw the collapse of Tsarism, and the Bolshevik insurrection of October.

With an economy crippled by Russian involvement in the First World War and the Tsar's political authority challenged by all social groups, the system imploded in a series of spontaneous demonstrations between 23 and 27 February (women against high prices, strikers in clashes with troops, desertions from garrison regiments) which culminated in Nicholas II's abdication on 3 March.

The Duma declared itself the Provisional Government which was dominated by the conservative Kadet Party. Simultaneously the Soviet of Workers' and Soldiers' Deputies emerged with a *Menshevik/Social Revolutionary majority and there began what came to be known as the period of dual power (although by June, Trotsky was calling it 'the dual powerlessness'). There was no state power—the Provisional Government exercising it theoretically, the Soviet potentially, but with the latter refusing to take it. The Soviet Order Number 1, for example, which established soldiers' soviets, began the dismantling of the hierarchical military structure. When Lenin returned to Russia in April he described the Soviet as having incipient state power but condemned the Mensheviks and Social Revolutionaries for compromising with the Provisional Government and being frightened of a real revolution. His *April Theses* demanded 'All Power to the Soviets' (under a Bolshevik majority) and highlighted peace, bread, and land as the central political issues.

On 18 April, the Kadets committed Russia to honouring its treaties with the Allies and to pursuing the war to a victorious conclusion. Anti-war demonstrations—the April Days—were the first signs of popular disaffection with the Provisional Government. On 1 May, a Coalition Government—including Kadets, Mensheviks, Social Revolutionaries, and led by Alexander Kerensky—emerged. It failed to address urgent economic and political problems (the breakdown of industry, land hunger, and the collapse of Russia's infrastructure) and instead launched the disastrous Galician military offensive in June.

On 10 June a mass demonstration in Petrograd called for the Soviet to confront the Provisional Government although Lenin argued that the workers were not ready for this. There was clear support for the Bolsheviks in Petrograd but they were gaining ground at a much slower pace in the provinces and at the front. And the Bolshevik party was itself divided over strategy.

Military defeat, accelerating inflation and scarcity, and the Provisional Government's desire to remove the Petrograd garrison to the front (away from agitators) provoked the mass mobilizations of the July Days. Again Lenin believed the time premature for a takeover (he described 'the Days' as 'far more than a demonstration and less than a revolution') but exhorted the Bolsheviks to support the masses because a revolutionary party could not abandon its constituency. In the ensuing repression (itself applauded by the Soviet leadership) the Bolsheviks were forced into hiding and the political climate swung to the right. Kerensky, urged on by the Allies, began discussions with the military High Command. The Social Revolutionaries now dominated the Coalition Government (Kadet ministers having left in July) and the Mensheviks, the Soviet. The latter were belatedly realizing that a counter-revolution would destroy them as well as the Bolsheviks but were not prepared to organize the workers against it. The country was polarized; lockouts and strikes, military plots, land invasions, the self-demobilization of soldiers, the creation of no-go areas by Red Guards. As the influence of the Bolsheviks grew, that of the Mensheviks and Social Revolutionaries declined (the latter party

now split with the Left Social Revolutionaries working with the Bolsheviks).

In September, the Cossack General Kornilov staged an abortive coup. By this time most soviets had a Bolshevik majority and Trotsky was elected President of the Petrograd Soviet. The Bolshevik Military Revolutionary Committee now began to prepare for the armed insurrection of 25 October. In Petrograd with the storming of the Winter Palace and the surrender of the Provisional Government it was practically bloodless, but there was protracted fighting in Moscow. On 26 October, Lenin announced the creation of the Soviet government and issued decrees on land and peace, proclaiming 'We will now proceed to construct the socialist order'.

The Bolsheviks were still a minority party in October (in the November Constituent Assembly elections they obtained 25 per cent as compared to 38 per cent for the Social Revolutionaries) but overwhelming public opinion supported them in the large industrial centres. Petrograd (St Petersburg, Leningrad) was the most significant political and industrial centre. This facilitated mobilization, organization, and a developing revolutionary consciousness, not found in other parts of Russia.

In a sense, the Bolsheviks were already 'in power' before 25 October—state power, which Lenin saw as the central question of every revolution, was there for the taking. GL

Russian Revolution, 1991 The so-called second Russian revolution occurred in August 1991 when the coup by hard-liners wishing to prevent the demise of communist power and the Soviet Union was defeated. The coup took place on the eve of the signing of a new union treaty that envisaged the transfer of power from the centre to the republics. Mikhail Gorbachev, the President of the USSR, was on holiday in the Crimea when the coup took place. On 19 August, a 'State Committee for the State of Emergency' appeared on television, headed by the Vice-President Gennady Yanaev and including the prime minister, and heads of the KGB and the Soviet Army, and declared itself in control. It was opposed by the Russian president Boris Yeltsin and the Russian parliament. World attention was focused on the parliament building itself, 'the White

House', where thousands of pro-democracy demonstrators congregated in defence of the Russian leadership inside. Despite repeated warnings of immanent military action, an attack never came and after three days the Committee surrendered and Mikhail Gorbachev returned to Moscow. The real victory, however, went to Boris Yeltsin. The failed coup exacerbated the centrifugal tendencies already evident and led to the collapse of the Soviet Union itself.   swh

Rwanda Rwanda was created out of the Great Lakes region by Germany during the age of European colonization of Africa (1885). After the First World War, Belgium gained possession of Rwanda-Urundi (Rwanda and Burundi) either as a colony or as a protectorate. Rwanda attained independence in 1962.

Rwanda has endured exceptional and consistent political turbulence. Colonial conquest—although very weak initially—imposed a form of political rule which generated tensions and conflicts. Although, broadly, the state of Rwanda follows the boundaries of a pre-existing socio-spatial structure based around a paramount and certain political relations of land ownership, colonization imposed a nation-state model which aimed to solidify the fluid social relations of the area and bend the peoples of the country to conform to colonial structures and more ambitiously to serve the needs of the colonizing state.

The most salient aspect of colonization was the formalized distinction between three aggregate social categories (called tribes by Europeans)—namely, Twa, Tutsi, and Hutu. Colonial state policy formulated these identities as irrevocable and politically charged so that the elites, parties, and ideologies prevalent during decolonization were substantially 'ethnicized'.

Rwanda's first president, Georges Kayibanda, was leader of the PARMEHUTU party, signifying an ethnic constituency and marginalizing others. In 1973, a military coup ushered Juvénal Habyarimana into power, also as a result of ethnic power politics. It was Habyarimana's assassination in 1994 that triggered the *genocide in which between 500,000 and a million people died.

The genocide was not the result of a single cause; nor was it the result of any innate or simple 'tribal' enmity. Rather, ethnic identities and their politicization provided the impetus for a state-led survival strategy. The insurgency by the Rwandan Patriotic Front (RPF) which commenced in 1990 created instability and a threat to the incumbent Habyarimana regime. Rwanda suffered a parallel economic crisis in the early 1990s, based around a debt crisis and a falling coffee export price. Other factors contributed to the genocide, but these points provide the main coordinates for the systemic killings that commenced in the capital, Kigali, and spread throughout the territory. Difficult questions remain concerning the weakness of the international community's response to the genocide.   GH

saddlepoint *See* MINIMAX.

Said, Edward (1935–2003) Palestinian-American scholar credited with founding the field of *post-colonialism. Most noted for his critique of Western *orientalism, Said was critical of how the Orient had been represented. Relying on tools borrowed from literary criticism, Said employed *discourse analysis and *poststructural methodologies to unpack and re-examine latent and dogmatic narratives used by the West to describe and malign the Orient. Said was also a noted activist against Israeli treatment of Palestinians, offering particular scorn for violations of Palestinian human rights.

Sainte-Lagüe, A. French mathematician who in 1910 proposed the fairest system of *apportionment of integer numbers of seats to each party in list systems of *proportional representation with multimember seats. The system had been independently proposed by Daniel *Webster in 1832 for the apportionment of seats in the US House of Representatives to states. The Sainte-Lagüe system of apportionment is apparently too fair to small parties to be used anywhere in Europe; the version in use in Scandinavia is deliberately biased in favour of large parties.

Saint-Simon, Claude-Henri de Rouvroy (1760–1825) A founding father of both modern social science and *socialism, and an important figure in nineteenth-century *utopianism. He was concerned mainly with the causes and consequences of social and political upheaval in the age of the *French Revolution, and sought to address the complex questions of the future direction of European society in the aftermath of the collapse of feudalism and the old monarchical, aristocratic, and Roman Catholic structures of the eighteenth century. His originality lay in his emphasis on the modernizing forces of science, industry, and technological innovation, and he spent the last twenty-five years of his life trying to convince his contemporaries of the need to adapt social and political systems to those new forces.

Saint-Simon's disciples, after his death, used the idea of 'socialism' to denote the collectivist orientation of his mature thought. Most nineteenth-century socialist thinkers—including *Marx—drew inspiration from his teachings.

Saint-Simon's attempts to found a scientific study of man and society were rooted in the rationalist philosophy of the *Enlightenment, and led towards *positivism through the link with Auguste *Comte, who worked as Saint-Simon's assistant in the early 1820s. Both Saint-Simon and Comte emphasized the importance of religion as a source of social integration, and tended—in the manner of many French social theorists of the nineteenth century—to work towards a reconciliation of modern scientific-rational thought and the religious order. Thus, in Saint-Simon's last and most influential work, *Nouveau Christianisme* (New Christianity, 1825), the emphasis was on the ethical and essentially Christian principles of social reform in the name of greater equality and social justice for the working classes. KT

salience The importance of a political issue, or issue dimension. The theory of *spatial competition allows for the possibility that there are several relevant dimensions. Since these dimensions may not be of equal importance, the concept of salience is used to reflect the relative weights voters place on each dimension. William *Riker noted that politicians can use rhetoric to manipulate the relative salience of different issues to achieve particular outcomes. For instance, he argued that Abraham *Lincoln won the 1860 election partly by emphasizing the slavery issue. SF

saliency theory The claim that when political parties compete through public statements they do so mainly by emphasizing particular policies or concerns. Since these can be linked to different sides of broader issue dimensions, such as economic left–right, issue emphasis is an indicator of party position. This theory has been applied through the content analysis of election manifestos, to compare the policy positions of parties in different countries, and across time. *See also* SALIENCE; SPATIAL COMPETITION, THEORY OF. SF

SALT (Strategic Arms Limitation Talks) Preliminary discussions to limit the long-range missiles and bombers of the two superpowers began in 1967. They were broken off by the Americans as a result of the Soviet occupation of Czechoslovakia in 1968, resumed in November 1969 under the name of Strategic Arms Limitation Talks (SALT) and concluded in May 1972. The treaty froze the numbers of strategic 'launchers' (missiles or bombers) for five years but permitted modernization and increases in the number of warheads which the launchers could carry. A second agreement, normally considered under the heading of SALT, prohibited permanent deployment of more than very limited defensive systems against offensive missiles. In 1979 a second SALT treaty was concluded which provided for very small reductions in the numbers of Soviet launchers and permitted considerable increases in the numbers of warheads deployed. Following the Soviet invasion of Afghanistan in December 1979 the Americans abandoned the ratification process and the treaty lapsed, though in practice both sides kept roughly within its very comfortable limits until the conclusion of the next round of strategic arms negotiations known as *START. PBY

sampling *See* SURVEY RESEARCH.

sanctions Punitive diplomatic, economic, and social actions taken by the international community against a state that has violated international law. Technically they may also refer to military actions with the same purpose. They range from suspension of diplomatic contact, and blockage of communication, through restriction or cessation of some or all trade, to military strikes. The United Nations Security Council has the legal right to instigate compulsory sanctions, but this was little exercised during the Cold War because of the paralysis of that body by the veto.

Sanctions were applied to Rhodesia in 1966, and more lightly to South Africa. Post-Cold War, they were applied to Iraq after its invasion of Kuwait, and to Serbia in the context of the messy war that followed the disintegration of Yugoslavia. Fierce arguments continue as to whether economic sanctions are an effective form of political pressure, or whether they merely inflict hardship on the population while strengthening the position of the offending government. There are also doubts about whether sanctions can be an alternative to war, or are merely a step in the build-up to war (as they were for example when Iraq invaded Kuwait in 1990). All sanctions against regimes attract profit-seeking smugglers, and the case of Iraq suggests that very harsh economic sanctions, even when accompanied by military action, do not guarantee either a change of policy or a change of government. Despite this, sanctions continue to be used, for example against Iran, the Democratic People's Republic of Korea, and Zimbabwe. CT

Sandinism The Sandinista National Liberation Front (FSLN) was created in 1961 by Nicaraguan admirers of the Cuban revolution of 1959. It took its name from the nationalist hero, General Augusto César Sandino, who fought a guerrilla war against US occupying forces in the late 1920s.

Early attempts to follow Cuban strategic advice led to guerrilla setbacks, but the FSLN gradually adapted its strategy and in the struggle against the dictatorship of Anastasio Somoza Debayle in the 1970s relied more on popular urban insurrection than rural guerrilla warfare.

Strategic and tactical internal differences did not prevent the Sandinistas from uniting to depose Somoza in 1979, but did leave the Front divided into three factions. The solution was a nine-member collective leadership, the National Directorate, which remained powerful even after Daniel Ortega's election to the Nicaraguan presidency in 1984.

Sandinism developed as an ideological hybrid, with influences from Marxism, nationalism, dependency theory, and Catholic Liberation Theology. In government between 1979 and 1990 Sandinista policies were based on political pluralism, a mixed economy, international non-alignment, and social reform.

In the early 1980s the Sandinista government enacted a land reform and achieved substantial improvements in healthcare, education, and social welfare programmes. Its radical policies antagonized the United States which sponsored attacks by 'contra' rebels and boycotted the Nicaraguan economy. Sandinista popularity declined due to compulsory military service, hyperinflation, and shortages.

The FSLN was defeated at the polls in 1990, having won elections in 1984. Subsequently it embraced social democracy and became the main opposition party.   RG

sans-culottes Literally, 'without breeches'. Urban supporters of extreme factions in the *French Revolution who wore trousers, rather than aristocratic breeches.

Sartre, Jean-Paul (1905–80) French political and literary writer and activist. Sartre was the best-known twentieth-century exponent of *existentialism, in *L'Être et le néant* (Being and Nothingness, 1943) and *Existentialism and Humanism* (English translation, 1980). Sartre's statements of the pain of existence ('Man is condemned to be free') are easier to understand in his philosophical and literary works (notably *Huis Clos* (In Camera, 1943) than in his political works. Sartre came to believe after 1945 that existentialism implied a particular sort of intellectual, activist, and (at least in principle) violent *Marxism by virtue of its assertion that there are no objective moral rules. Some have seen his later work (especially *Critique of Dialectical Reason*, 1978/1991) as a reconciliation of existentialism and Marxism; others as the rejection of the first for the second.

Saussure, Ferdinand de *See* STRUCTURALISM.

Schengen area (Schengenland) The zone of free movement of people consisting of (by 2017) twenty-three of the twenty-eight European Union (EU) member states, Norway, Iceland, Liechtenstein, and Switzerland. The area was constructed following a series of discussions and negotiations beginning at Schengen, Luxembourg, in 1985 by those European Community (EC) member states seeking the extension of the Single European Market to the free movement of people. Agreements were reached by the Schengen countries, outside the EC/EU framework, on the removal of all internal border controls, police and judicial cooperation, and common policies on external borders, visa arrangements for third-country nationals, asylum, and illegal immigration. After several delays, the area came into effect in 1994. The Schengen countries also agreed to the creation of a European Police Force (Europol), a European Drugs Unit (EDU), and common databanks for surveillance of criminal activity and asylum applicants in the area. The Amsterdam Treaty of 1997 incorporated the Schengen agreements into the Third Pillar of the European Union (Justice and Home Affairs), with many elements subsequently incorporated into the first (EC) pillar. Nonetheless, the term 'Schengen' continues to be widely used. Cooperation on Schengen matters has been considerably reinforced over the past decade through the adoption of numerous laws and other measures. The United Kingdom and Ireland continue to exercise their right to opt out established in the Maastricht Treaty, while Croatia, Cyprus, Romania, and Bulgaria have yet to participate in the free movement zone. Yet, the future of the Schengen has been questioned by the 2016 United Kingdom referendum to 'leave' the European Union (*Brexit), which was largely influenced by anti-immigration sentiment. This mirrors increasing free-movement hostility in other member states, particularly Denmark, France, and Holland. This has been compounded by the *refugee crisis and large numbers of *political asylum seekers entering Europe.   DH

Schmitt, Carl (1888–1985) One of Germany's leading political scientists and legal theorists during the inter-war years, and a fervent critic of the liberal democracy of the *Weimar Republic. In works such as *Political Romanticism* (1919) and *The Concept of the Political* (1932) Schmitt articulated a theory of political action based on practical necessity and the need for dynamic leadership and 'decisionism' rather than on any system of abstract philosophical argument. Such a view led to a defence of authoritarian dictatorship and, more specifically, to Schmitt's own personal support for the *National Socialism of Hitler and the Third Reich.   KT

Schumpeter, Joseph A. (1883–1950) Austrian economist, politician, banker, and horseman. Schumpeter is best known to political scientists for his *Capitalism, Socialism and Democracy* (1943; henceforth *CS&D*), the product both of his training as a theoretical economist and of his experiences of Marxist and fascist totalitarianism. Schumpeter was a respectful opponent of Marxism. He believed that most of Marxian economics was false, but that the Marxian prediction that capitalism would fall through its own contradictions might come true. In *CS&D* he illustrated this through the 'hog cycle', an example of individual farmers' rational behaviour leading to a foreseeable and undesirable outcome. However, it is the chapters of *CS&D* on democracy that have been most influential. Schumpeter forcefully argued that outcomes were not necessarily good just because they were reached democratically, giving examples of (near-)democracies which had persecuted Jews and burnt witches: democracy should therefore be evaluated only as a method whereby leaders acquire the power to give orders after a competitive struggle for votes. He contrasted this narrow basis for evaluation with what he misleadingly called 'the classical method', by which he really meant the approach of *Rousseau and his followers who call (appropriately reached) democratic outcomes 'the will of the people'.

Writing before *game theory had been developed, Schumpeter was unable to give his powerful insights a shape which would have defended them against the Rousseauvian attacks they encountered in the 1960s and 1970s. But he was an important precursor of the *rational-choice school of normative political theorists. *See also* RIKER.

Scottish Enlightenment *See* ENLIGHTENMENT, SCOTTISH.

SDGs (Sustainable Development Goals) Sustainable Development Goals were adopted by resolution within the *United Nations on 25 September 2015. SDGs act as the successor to the underperforming *Millennium Development Goals (MDGs) and were originally known as 'the 2030 Agenda for Sustainable Development'. The SDGs are made up of seventeen development goals with 169 associated targets. These goals are time-bound for delivery by 2030. The goals, like the MDGs, are meant to stimulate coordinated response to key development challenges, such as health and poverty. Unlike the MDGs, the formulation of the SDGs was done under extensive United Nations consultations and input from stakeholders. As a result, many advocates see the SDGs as representing a more legitimate and promising range of development interests. However, critics of the SDGs argue that many of the governance problems that plagued the MDGs remain unaddressed and that the addition of more goals and targets in the SGDs will equate to greater opportunities for underperformance.

SDI *See* STRATEGIC DEFENSE INITIATIVE.

SDP *See* SOCIAL DEMOCRACY.

SEA *See* SINGLE EUROPEAN ACT.

SEATO (Southeast Asia Treaty Organization) Outcome of treaty signed in 1954 by Australia, Britain, France, New Zealand, Pakistan, the Philippines, Thailand, and the United States, with the aim of discouraging communist expansion in South-East Asia.

Disagreement among members over the conduct of the Vietnam War meant a limited role for SEATO, which failed to contain communist insurgency in Vietnam or Cambodia. SEATO was formally disbanded in 1977.

secession The withdrawal of a group from the authority of a state. Disaffected members of a political community have a number of strategies available to them. They can seek amelioration of their grievances by working through the existing political system; they may strive to change the forms of the state, pressing for greater decentralization, arguing the case perhaps for a federal distribution of power. Seriously disaffected groups might despair of achieving their aims by such moderate means and feel obliged to resort to extremist strategies. They might counsel emigration, or work for a revolutionary overthrow of the state. Secession offers a further strategy for the profoundly disaffected. If successful, the group removes itself, and control of its territory and resources, from the authority of an existing state. This was the objective of the eleven states that sought to leave the United States and thereby precipitated the Civil War. In the past, Black Muslims in America included secessionist proposals in their programme. Currently numbers of Québecois are drawn to the idea of seceding from Canada, though 'sovereignty-association', as they call it, has just failed to carry twice in referendums.   DM

secondary legislation *See* STATUTE LAW; STATUTORY INSTRUMENTS.

second ballot Class of voting procedures in which candidates for a single-member seat first fight a *plurality election. Any candidate who wins more than half of the votes is elected. Otherwise, a second ballot is held, barred (by rule or convention) to all except those who came first and second in the first ballot. The winner of this round is elected. Second-ballot procedures have been the norm in France since 1789, although in that year they were first criticized by *Condorcet for their perverse properties. Their operation in France has supposedly illustrated the maxim 'Vote with your heart in the first ballot and with your head in the second'.

second chambers Legislatures have second chambers under *bicameral systems of government. The second chamber usually has a more limited role in the legislative process, but there are important exceptions such as the US *Senate.   WG

Second International *See* INTERNATIONAL SOCIALISM.

second reading Substantive stage of a bill's passage through Parliament, when the principles of the bill are discussed. *See also* BILL.

second-strike capacity The capability to retaliate after one's opponent has launched a first strike against one's own nuclear forces; essential to a policy of mutual assured destruction (*see* DETERRENCE).   BB

Secretary of State In Britain, the head of any of the more important government departments. In the United States, the head of the State Department, which deals with foreign policy.

Secret Service *See* INTELLIGENCE SERVICES.

secularization The detachment of a state or other body from religious foundations.

Among states where Christianity was the majority religion, the United States was unique in being secular from the start by virtue of the *First Amendment ('Congress shall make no law respecting an establishment of religion, or prohibiting the free exercise thereof . . . '). The secular institutions of the state coexist with higher churchgoing and religious belief than in any other Western democracy. Secularization has been a powerful movement in France since the French Revolution and the French state has been secular (and French state education militantly secular) for most of the time since 1789. Secularization is not complete in the United Kingdom. In England, the Church of England is established: some of its bishops sit in the House of Lords; its internal decisions are subject to review by Parliament; its finances are governed by the Church Commissioners (disastrously in the 1980s) of which the Prime Minister is a member. The Queen is the head of the Church of England, but in Scotland she is a member of the Church of Scotland, whose beliefs and organization are different. Some have questioned whether establishment is appropriate in a country in which Church of England (Anglican) churchgoers are equalled or outnumbered both by Roman Catholic churchgoers and by Muslim believers. Nevertheless, recent legislation confirms that state education must have a religious content which must be 'broadly Christian'.

The Indian Constitution (1949), written in the aftermath of the bloody partition which saw a predominantly Muslim Pakistan created, opens with a statement that India is a secular republic. Under *Nehru there was a clear commitment to a clear separation between the state and religion, and an avoidance of policies that discriminated on the grounds of religion. The *Hindu nationalist movement has challenged what has been labelled 'pseudo-secularism', claiming that religious neutrality was neither possible nor desirable, and sought to promote a political agenda which recognizes Hindu history and values. Such an agenda has been seen as threatening to religious minorities in the country, particularly Muslims and Christians, and associated with a heightening of communal tension.

The politics of secularization have been much more violent in some Islamic countries. The overthrow of the Shah of Iran in 1979, the collapse of government in Algeria in 1993–4, and the emergence of the al-Qaeda terrorist network are all examples of protest by *Islamic fundamentalists against secularizing regimes. *See also* RELIGION AND POLITICS; ISLAMIC POLITICS; CHURCH AND STATE.

securitization The process by which an issue becomes defined as a 'security issue', that is understood as an existential threat to a referent object (most commonly, but not necessarily, a state) requiring in response the adoption of exceptional emergency measures. Introduced into international relations through the work of scholars associated with the so-called *Copenhagen School, the study of securitization processes emerged in the context of debates occurring in the aftermath of the *Cold War. In this period it was recognized that 'new' forms of threat were appearing on the security agendas of Western nation states, including such issues as the environment, poverty, and migration. Thus, securitization theory proceeds from the idea that there is no fixed list of national security issues: defined through social processes that occur within particular institutional and political contexts.

Whilst the intricacies of securitization processes continue to be debated, there is general agreement over the core elements: that a 'securitizing actor' makes a 'securitizing move' (through a 'speech act' declaring x to be an existential threat to referent object y); that the securitizing actor's 'audience' accepts (or does not accept) this securitizing move; and that this acceptance allows for the enactment of 'exceptional measures', which would not be acceptable in response to 'normal' political (i.e. non-security) problems.

The application of this framework to a wide variety of empirical cases has led to scholarly disagreements over the specification of almost every one of these steps,

including which actors are likely to be in a position to make successful securitizing moves; the degree to which the likelihood of the purported existential threat occurring has to be supported by empirical evidence; the nature of the audience and the extent to which they have to be persuaded; the applicability of the theory outside the context of Western liberal democratic states; and whether securitization can only be said to have occurred once exceptional measures have actually been implemented, or whether agreement on the potential legitimacy of such measures is enough.

There have also been ongoing tensions between those who favour a more social constructivist-leaning form of securitization theory, which emphasizes the importance of audience acceptance in the social construction of security threats, and those who are closer to a post-structuralist account, which places a greater emphasis on the 'performative' effect of the speech act. A concurrent debate continues over whether the empirical focus should be on high-profile securitization processes that take place within institutions such as national parliaments or the *UN Security Council, or whether concentrating on such cases obscures the more mundane and everyday ways in which security is practised—a position often associated with scholars aligned with the so-called Paris School.

Whilst in general parlance 'security' might be thought of as something to be welcomed, the Copenhagen School express a clear preference for desecuritization, motivated by the idea that moving an issue out of the realm of 'normal' politics and into the realm of security can (and indeed has) led to the implementation of anti-democratic emergency measures that are injurious to human rights, civil liberties, and other social values. Thus the framework of securitization has perhaps most frequently been deployed as a way of critiquing securitization processes and highlighting the potential dangers of treating an issue as a security threat. To take one example, scholars engaged in health and international relations have critically examined the process through which HIV/AIDS came to be understood as an international security threat. Whilst some have argued that the successful securitization of AIDS brought positive effects in terms of high-level political attention and the deployment of resources, others have pointed to the downsides, which have included the imposition of restrictions on the freedoms of People Living with HIV and AIDS (PLWHA) and, arguably, the heightening of stigma and discrimination in respect of infected individuals who, by virtue of carrying the virus, could now be seen as posing a threat to national security. SRT

Security Council (UNSC) Cabinet of the *United Nations tasked with the maintenance of international peace and security. It originally consisted of eleven members, expanded in 1965 to fifteen, of whom five (Britain, China, France, Russia, United States) were permanent members, the rest being elected by the General Assembly for a two-year period. In 1991 Russia was awarded the Soviet seat. The Security Council exercises primary responsibility within the UN for the maintenance of international peace and security. The UNSC has the power to approve or decline all UN *peacekeeping missions, the official use of UN sanctions, as well as any UN decision for the use of military force. Beyond the remit of peace and security, the UNSC has the power to approve all changes to the UN Charter as well as the acceptance of new members. It can act only with the agreement of the five permanent members who exercise a veto; the lack of agreement on most issues throughout the Cold War severely restricted the role of the UNSC, although between the late 1980s and mid-2000s it enjoyed a much more active role. For example, the war to liberate Kuwait was organized by the United States in 1990-1 under a series of UNSC mandates and was considered an effective operation. Yet the UNSC has more recently been criticized for its lack of proportional balance, its often gridlocked decision-making process, the veto ability of the *great powers, and its frequent unwillingness to address key areas of conflict and instability when it is not directly in the interest of the permanent members (*see* RWANDA). In the study of *international relations, the UNSC is often seen as the UN body in most need of reform. PBy

(⊕) SEE WEB LINKS

• Security Council website.

security dilemma A state may arm itself with purely defensive intention yet, provided its forces are judged capable of attack, those states within range will feel unable to disregard this possibility and be obliged, perhaps reluctantly, to add to their own arsenals. So arises what John H. Herz (1950) identified as the security dilemma. Anticipated at least as early as the seventeenth century in Lord Rochester's 'Satyr against Mankind', this insight began to be modelled by game theorists as an instance of *Prisoners' Dilemma in the 1970s. A formal approach makes explicit the structure of the dilemma, which is that two independent states cannot attain the security both desire at least joint cost because each must guard against the heavy costs it will suffer should the other cheat.

Thus fear may prove a more pervasive and fundamental general cause of war than aggression. Many realists regard the dilemma as insurmountable. Optimists have argued that trust between states may be developed, and the dilemma surmounted, by means as varied as repeated interaction (Robert Axelrod) or efficacious grace (Herbert Butterfield). *See also* ARMS RACES. CJ

security studies Security studies is the examination, exploration, and analysis of what it means to be secure, and is a central part of the study of *international relations. At its core, security studies is simply how best to achieve the absence of threats. The field is therefore dominated by key questions on what it actually means to be secure, for whom, by what value system, from what threats, by what means, and at what costs. Its roots are often traced back to the First World War, when there was renewed interest in issues of war and peace. Before this, security studies was akin to strategic studies and was mostly studied by professionals in the military.

The history of security studies is linked to world events, with changes in perspective often coinciding with key events in world history. After the Second World War and throughout the *Cold War the field was focused on the study of war: how to fight better wars, policy-relevant military issues in the interests of national security, and nuclear strategy. This is often called the 'golden age' of security studies, and was dominated by *realist thought, where states

represented both the source and main referent object of security. States were seen as
unitary, self-interested, and rational actors
that were interested in increasing their *relative power. During this period there was a
strong imperative to look at ways that
nuclear weapons could and would be used,
which led to concepts such as *deterrence
and MAD (mutually assured destruction).
The *security dilemma was used to understand how states in search of security interact,
where military build-ups due to perceptions
of insecurity have knock-on effects to create
an arms race.

With the end of the Cold War, realist domination began to wane as the critical schools
of thought questioned realist assumptions.
This saw the decline in importance of military concerns as the main focus of security
studies, and was broadened to include military, economic, environmental, welfare, political, and social factors. There was also a
challenge to the importance of the state as
the only referent object and the inclusion of
the individual and society as key units.
Finally, there was an intellectual reposition-
ing that argued for seeing the world as being
constituted socially through intersubjective
interaction, where agents and structures are
mutually constituted, and that ideational factors shaped how security issues are formed
and viewed. For security studies this allowed
a refocus on the human as the referent object
and brought new forms of security concerns
to the fore (*see* HUMAN SECURITY). This
included economic security such as an
assured basic income; food security, including the need for physical and economic
access to basic food needs; health security;
environmental and resource security; personal security, including security from personal violence such as rape; community
security that highlighted the need for groups,
such as ethnic groups or family groups, to
have their identity secured; and political
security, including the role of human rights
and state repression as security issues. Other
post-Cold War challenges to the traditional
understanding of security studies includes
*feminist, *post-structuralist, and *post-colo-
nial approaches that seek to deconstruct
knowledge claims that underpin traditional
security thought and their distorting effects
on what counts as being an important security issue. RB

segregation *See* CIVIL RIGHTS.

select committee A legislative committee
which deliberates upon complex issues and/
or scrutinizes the executive on issues
broader than legislation. In the UK House
of Commons the *Public Accounts Committee, charged with examining accounts of
money appropriated by Parliament, dates
from 1861, and the system of departmental
select committees from 1979. In 2007 there
were 34 select committees, which also
included non-departmental scrutiny committees such as the Public Administration
Committee. The House of Lords has long
had select committees for procedural issues,
and subsequently introduced other committees, notably for the European communities
in 1974, science and technology in 1977, and
the constitution in 2001. House of Commons
departmental select committees are charged
'to examine the expenditure, administration
and policy of the principal government
departments . . . and associated public bodies'. They may invite written and oral evidence from witnesses, deliberate, and make
reports with recommendations to the House.
Their membership is determined in proportion to party strength in the House, and their
members normally serve for a full Parliament. Members attempt to work on a non-
partisan basis and it is normal for some
select committee chairs to go to members
of the opposition parties. Select committees,
nevertheless, are criticized for lacking information in undertaking inquiries. Only the
Public Accounts Committee in drawing
upon the work of the National Audit Office
has a substantial information base. The
Osmotherly rules (so named after the civil
servant who drafted them), governing what
civil servants can and cannot say before a
select committee, prevent revelations on
ministerial–bureaucratic relationships. Membership of select committees is also criticized
for being determined by party whips. Their
perceived undue influence led in 2001 to
the rejection by the House of Commons of
proposed new chairs for the Transport and
Foreign Affairs select committees. Nor do
committees' reports bind the executive, and
those which are heavily critical of government policy are often sidelined from further
parliamentary discussion by the government. Defenders of the status quo highlight

the policy-influencing and legitimizing functions of select committees. Critics seek greater powers reminiscent of the committee system in the US Congress.

In the United States a select committee is an ad hoc body. For instance, the official title of the Erwin Committee, which more than anything else toppled President Nixon over *Watergate, was the Senate Select Committee on Campaign Practices.   JBr

( ) SEE WEB LINKS
- Information on select committees from the UK Parliament site.

self-determination The philosophical idea of self-determination arose out of eighteenth-century concern for freedom and the primacy of the individual will. It has been applied to every kind of group which can be said to have a collective will, but in the twentieth century has come to apply primarily to nations. National self-determination was the principle applied to the break-up of the Austrian, German, and Ottoman Empires by President Woodrow Wilson's 'Fourteen Points' after the First World War. It is also embodied in the charter of the United Nations, in the 1960 Declaration on the Granting of Independence of Colonial Countries and Peoples, and in the 1970 Declaration of the Principles of International Law.

Unfortunately, for an idea so widely embraced, it can be argued that the principle of national self-determination is as vicious as it is vague. The justification of repressive national regimes as preferable to liberal empires is a travesty of the original idea of individual self-determination. What, in any case, is the 'self' of a nation and who can express its will? There would be reason to be suspicious of the application of this principle even if people were neatly divided into discrete nations on well-defined territories. They are not; and self-determination taken to its most vicious extremes leads to phenomena like the 'ethnic cleansing' practised by the Serbs in the 1990s.   LA

self-government The term may be applied both to the individual person and to a group or an institution. An autonomous person is, fundamentally, one able to act according to his or her own direction. An autonomous institution is one able to regulate its own affairs. The relation between the self-government of a group and individual autonomy is complicated by the need to distinguish between the collective self-government of a group and the self-direction of an individual member of that group. *Rousseau's writings illustrate the difficulties involved. Ideas about individual autonomy are closely linked to conceptions of *freedom. For example, to act according to my own direction may (on some views of freedom) require access to resources I presently lack, in which case to provide me with them would enhance both my liberty and my autonomy. This problem is, further, connected to notions of the constitution of the self. For example, it may be held that I am not truly 'self'-governing if my action is driven by powerful phobias 'I' cannot regulate, any more than if my actions are determined by external circumstances beyond my control.   AR

self-interest Regard exclusively to one's own advantage. The false belief that rationality and self-interest are the same thing has bedevilled *rational-choice approaches to politics. Because examples of altruism are all around us, many people have rejected rational choice out of hand. Some careless or provocative statements by leading rational-choice theorists such as Anthony Downs and Gordon Tullock have encouraged this misconception. A better approach is to say that, until evidence to the contrary is produced, it is best to assume that people are neither more nor less self-interested in politics than in the rest of social life.

self-ownership The claim of an individual to sovereignty over his or her person, typically taken to include not only his or her body (and possibly a foetus within it—*see* RIGHT TO LIFE), but also labour, talents, and 'moral space'. 'Ownership' confers a wide range of rights (and possibly duties) with respect to its object, so the claim to self-ownership is typically a claim to be allowed to dispose of or control one's person as one sees fit. Although the idea has plausibility when contrasted with slavery, an institution which allows one person to be owned by another, and although 'self-ownership' or 'self-propriety' have historically been used to assert freedoms, the identification of the subject and object of the ownership relation has led to the criticism that it is incoherent.   AR

self-regarding action An action that affects no one other than the agent. Some authorities locate this categorization of action in *Kant's treatment of the ordinary moral consciousness, others in Bentham's account of the relationship between pains, pleasures, and motives. But the most extended classical treatment is undoubtedly in J. S. *Mill's *On Liberty* (1859). Here Mill distinguishes a province of virtue from a province of duty. An action in the former province is self-regarding and subject only to personal persuasion and inducement. Such an action becomes other-regarding and open to public sanction if, and only if, it either harms an interest, violates a right, or neglects a duty owed to another person or persons. Hence a soldier or policeman merely drunk is self-regarding, a soldier or policeman drunk on duty is other-regarding. This kind of categorization is often regarded as one essential foundation of the liberty principle.   JH

senate Literally, 'council of old men'. The legislature in ancient Rome. Now, the upper house of the legislature in a number of countries, including the United States. The minimum age for a US Senator is 30 and for a member of the House of Representatives 25. The framers of the US Constitution intended the Senate to be a more conservative body than the House; not just because its members would be older on average, but because as originally arranged they were elected indirectly—by state legislatures, not by the people. Direct election of Senators was introduced by the Seventeenth Amendment (1913). *See also* CONGRESS (US).

seniority A convention, or unwritten rule, widely used in legislatures, especially in the United States, whereby status and other resources are allocated in proportion to length of service.

In the past seniority has been an organizing principle of great importance in both houses of the US *Congress. Seniority determined the size and situation of members' office space, the quality of their committee assignments, their speaking opportunities in those committees, and, above all, their chances of becoming a committee leader. In the early twentieth century, seniority was itself seen as a reform to modify the arbitrary power of the Speaker of the House. In the last two decades, the significance of seniority has diminished considerably but has by no means been eliminated.

It is in the House of Representatives where the changes in seniority have assumed greatest significance and as the Democrats controlled that chamber continuously from 1955 to 1994, it is the initiatives emanating from that party that are particularly worthy of attention. In the pre-reform Congress the chairmanship of standing committees went automatically to that member of the majority party with the longest continuous service on that committee. The rationale for such arrangements was twofold. First, it avoided the intrigue, the conflict, and the damage to personal relations that would otherwise result. Second, specialist committees are much dependent for their strength on expertise. In a seniority system the most senior members will normally have become experts and the career ambitions of others will encourage them to remain on committees where they will acquire the specialist knowledge and understanding needed for effective committee work.

Reformers, on the other hand, objected that seniority favoured members from one-party areas of the country, most notably the Democratic South, who were well placed to achieve the repeated re-election necessary to move up the seniority ladder. As a consequence, committee chairmanships in the House became the preserve of conservative Southern Democrats, unrepresentative of the nation as a whole. It was also argued that seniority allowed positions of great power to be bestowed on intellectually mediocre and sometimes tyrannically inclined legislators. Seniority, moreover, was destructive of party, allowing members hostile to the wishes of the majority of the congressional party to move into agenda control positions.

Early in the 1970s, the selection of committee chairmen was made subject to House Democratic *caucus approval and in 1975 three chairmen were actually removed. Ten years later the chairman of the House Armed Services Committee was deposed and replaced by a congressman who leapfrogged over several colleagues with greater seniority.

Seniority has been followed in the appointment of all other standing committee chairmen, but the fact that successful challenges have been made has profoundly altered the ethos. It has become particularly weak in the appointment of *sub*committee chairmen. DM

separate but equal See CIVIL RIGHTS.

separate electorates System of election to legislatures which divides voters along the lines of their religion or ethnicity; designed to ensure that each religious or ethnic group can elect their own representatives. Used in India, prior to Independence, to guarantee representation for religious minorities; and in New Zealand, for Maori representation. Separate electorates have been criticized as socially divisive, and for privileging one aspect of social identity above all others.

separate peace Variant of *democratic peace theory claiming that democracies do not go to war with one another. Unlike monadic peace, separate peace does not presuppose that democracies are inherently peaceful. Instead, democracies are thought to be amicable with one another due to shared values of mutual respect and accommodation. As a result, unlike democratic peace theory, they will often engage in warfare with non-democratic countries. BBZ

separation of powers The doctrine that political power should be divided among several bodies as a precaution against tyranny. Opposed to absolute sovereignty of the Crown, Parliament, or any other body.

Separation of powers was a leading idea in medieval Europe under the name of the 'two swords'. Most thinkers agreed that power should be shared between the State and the Church. But no convincing argument was produced for the supremacy of one over the other. Those who argued that the State was superior to the Church faced the fact that divine authority was supposed to be conferred on kings at their coronation, and that religious authorities claimed the power to excommunicate kings (as happened to King John of England). Those who argued that the Church was superior to the State had to explain away Jesus's command to 'Render therefore unto Caesar the things which are Caesar's; and unto God the things that are

God's'. Thus there was *de facto* separation of powers in medieval Europe.

The idea revived in the seventeenth century in response to renewed claims of divine right and absolute sovereignty (*see* FILMER; HOBBES). *Locke distinguished the executive, legislative, and federative (relating to foreign affairs) powers, although he did not intend them to be regarded as separate. He had in mind the British arrangement where the *executive was (at least partly) drawn from the *legislature and (at least in relation to finance) answerable to it. *Montesquieu developed this into a full-blown theory of the separation of the legislative, executive, and judicial powers (based, it is often said, on a misreading of contemporary British politics). From here it passed to the US Constitution and its justification in *The Federalist Papers*. The checks and balances of US government involve both the separation of powers among the executive (the Presidency), the legislature (the two houses of *Congress, themselves arranged to check and balance one another), and the judiciary (the federal courts), and separation between the federal government and the states.

Defenders of separation of powers insist that it is needed against tyranny, including the *tyranny of the majority. Its opponents argue that sovereignty must lie somewhere, and that it is better, and arguably more democratic, to ensure that it always lies with the same body (such as Parliament).

September 11th 2001 (9–11) Date of terrorist attacks launched by the *al-Qaeda network on targets in the United States, which caused thousands of deaths. Four passenger airliners were hijacked; two were flown into the twin towers of the World Trade Center in New York, and one into the Pentagon building near Washington. One plane crashed in Pennsylvania. The United States President, George W. Bush, described the attacks as an act of war, and responded by launching a military campaign in Afghanistan, where the Taliban government was seen to be harbouring terrorists and the leader of al-Qaeda, Osama bin Laden. *See also* AFGHANISTAN WAR (2001); TERRORISM.

In November 2002 President Bush established a National Commission on Terrorist Attacks Upon the United States (known as the 9-11 Commission) to investigate the 'facts and circumstances relating to the terrorist attacks of September 11, 2001'. The report, published in July 2004, presented a detailed account of the events leading up to the attacks, and addressed the US government's failures 'in imagination, policy, capabilities, and management' which allowed the attacks to take place. It was critical of the CIA and FBI, and argued that the administration failed to recognize the threat posed by al-Qaeda. Recommendations led to the establishment of the position of *Director of National Intelligence.

(⊕) SEE WEB LINKS

• Website of the National Commission on Terrorist Attacks Upon the United States (9–11 Commission) with report.

Seventeenth Amendment *See* SENATE.

sexism Sexism has been described as the practice of domination of women. It is a practice that is supported in many different ways that are critical to our socialization into our sex roles, and therefore make this domination acceptable in society—through language, visual association, media representation, and stereotyping, especially on the basis of the mothering/caring role of women. Sexism is important also because all women experience it in different ways, depending upon their social and economic situation—within the family and in jobs—and it limits the ways in which women seek to actualize their potential. SR

Shadow Cabinet The UK shadow cabinet is the front bench of the official parliamentary opposition party. It seeks to present itself as an alternative government for the next general election. It grew out of the practice that developed in the late nineteenth century of the ex-cabinet continuing to meet after election defeat in order to lead the opposition against the new cabinet. Since the 1950s it has become a key dimension of the formalized process of parliamentary adversarial politics. A Labour shadow cabinet would be based on members elected by the parliamentary Labour Party, whilst a Conservative shadow cabinet is appointed by the party leader. JBr

Shapley–Shubik index A measure of the power of a party in coalition bargaining,

based on the probability that the party can turn a winning coalition into a losing coalition. Formalizes the notion of 'balance of power' in coalition-building. *See also* POWER; POWER INDEX.

shari'a *See* FATWA; ISLAMIC POLITICS; SUNNI.

Shaw, George Bernard *See* FABIANISM.

Shi'i Shi'i or Shi'ite refers to those Muslims within the minority trend in Islam, who predominate in Iran, Tajikistan, Azerbaijan, northern Yemen, form the largest section of the population in Iraq and Bahrain, and are estimated to form the largest community in Lebanon. They are found in smaller numbers in many other Muslim countries—the Gulf countries, Afghanistan, Pakistan, and India, for instance.

The Shi'i trend in Islam developed as a result of the politics surrounding the rulership or governance of the early Islamic community, the Umma. The Shi'i believe in the significance of Ali, the fourth Caliph (successor) in 656-61, as the legitimate successor to the Prophet who had died in 632. Ali was cousin to the Prophet, married to Fatima, the Prophet's daughter, and produced the only grandsons of the Prophet. He was an early believer in the Prophet and those that supported him were referred to as the Shi'at Ali (Party of Ali). This later became elaborated into a religious doctrine complete with theology. At the time, though, the first civil war (fitna, 656-61) in the Islamic community occurred between Ali as Caliph and Mucawiyah, the leader of the Umayyads. The Umayyads won, establishing the Umayyad dynasty and caliphate (661-750). Hussein, Ali's second son and, in the Shi'i chronology, regarded as the third Caliph or Imam, was killed (680) at Kerbala (Iraq) by the forces of the Umayyad caliphate. This event gave rise to the annual Shi'i remembrance of the martyrdom of Hussein, and his place of death and tomb at Kerbala became a point of pilgrimage. These events form the political background to the later theological development of Shi'ism.

According to Shi'ism, the first Imam (divinely inspired leader) after Muhammad—as the Shi'i designate the legitimate leader of the Umma (Community of Believers)—was regarded to have been Ali, the fourth Caliph, and the proper succession should have been from Muhammad to Ali and then to his descendants according to the possession of those qualities of seniority and reputation such as charisma, experience, and others necessary to carry out the duties of the commander of the faithful (*Amir al-Mu'minin*) and head of state. In the view of the Imamis (beginning with Jafar al-Sadik, sixth Imam, 702–65, considered as founder of the Imamis, also known as *Ithna Ashari* or Twelvers), the largest subdivision in Shi'ism, there have been a succession of twelve recognized Imams descended from Ali. This succession became a matter of contention among the Shi'i leading to their fragmentation. The other two major subdivisions resulting from this contention are the Zaidis and Ismailis (both originating from the mid-700s). The Imami Shi'i believed that Muhammad had designated Ali as successor and, in this way, a special quality was, thus, transmitted through the succession. Only the Imam, in effect selected 'by divine right', could be the final interpreter of the law on earth. In the absence of the Imam (according to the doctrine of occultation, the twelfth or 'hidden' Imam disappeared in 260 H/878 AD, in effect, suspending the Imamate), the *mujtahid*—a scholar learned in Islamic Law—may interpret the Law.

The Shi'i have their own *sunna* (traditions) of the Prophet and their own *hadith* (sayings and doings of the Prophet). Each Shi'i subdivision developed separate schools of legal jurisprudence or interpretation. Within the Jafari law school of the Imamis two schools of thought emerged from the eighth century and crystallized during the seventeenth century: the Akhbari (traditions of the Imams as the source of religious knowledge) which took a restrictive approach to *ijtihad* (the application of reason to the solutions to legal matters), and the Usuli (roots) who utilized *ijtihad* by adopting reasoned argumentation in jurisprudence and theology. Usulis emphasized the role of the *mujtahid* who was capable of independently interpreting the sacred sources as an intermediary of the Hidden Imam and, thus, serve as a guide to the community. This meant that legal interpretations were kept flexible to take account of changing conditions and the dynamics of the times. The latter (Usuli) school became predominant in Iran in the eighteenth century and it is within this school that the Ayatollah Khomeini was located. The Akhbari are now located in Basra, its environs and Bahrain. *See also* SUNNI; ISLAMIC POLITICS; ISLAMIC FUNDAMENTALISM; FATWA.   BAR

Shining Path The Communist Party of Peru (*Sendero Luminoso*) launched a Maoist 'protracted people's war' in 1980, after years of careful preparation around Ayacucho. The name comes from an early pamphlet entitled *The Shining Path of José Carlos Mariátegui*, the founding father of Peruvian communism. By the late 1980s Sendero was Latin America's most successful guerrilla movement, distinguished by its frequent recourse to terrorism. Sendero leader Abimael Guzman Reynoso was captured in 1992 and the movement declined sharply thereafter.   RG

side-constraint Moral constraint on the pursuit of an individual's goals. In particular, Robert *Nozick, in *Anarchy, State and Utopia*, suggests looking at *rights as side-constraints. This perspective is presented as one model of the structure of our moral views. Another he mentions is that the violation of rights should be minimized. Since the latter view would allow someone's right(s) to be violated if such a violation prevented a greater violation of rights, the issues concern picturing how rights operate and determining what strength to attach to them.   AR

Sidgwick, Henry (1838–1900) Cambridge utilitarian philosopher best known for his *Methods of Ethics* (1874). Economists, political theorists, and philosophers have all regarded this as one of the most coherent and defensible statements of *utilitarianism.

Siegfried, André (1875–1959) French pioneer of electoral geography. Famed for his intensely detailed *ecological studies of the relationship between geographical and political variables, showing, for instance, how different types of soil conditions and farming patterns were associated with different patterns of voting. Because of both the volume of work involved and the difficulty of avoiding the 'ecological fallacy', he has had few English-speaking imitators except V. O. *Key and Henry Pelling. However, more sophisticated statistics and more powerful computers have revived an interest in electoral geography and in ecological association, which used with care can give valuable information about times and places where survey-based evidence is unavailable.

Simmel, Georg (1858–1918) An important figure in German social thought. Simmel was born, educated, and spent most of his career in Berlin. In 1885 he was appointed *Privatdozent* (unpaid lecturer), followed, fifteen years later, by an honorary professorship. He was repeatedly rejected for advancement despite support from *Weber and other academics. This rejection arose from reactions to his work and from anti-Semitic prejudice. Only in 1914 did he receive a full professorship at Strasbourg.

Simmel's work is diverse and difficult to categorize. His writings on groups, conflict, super- and subordination, all contribute to political theory. He wrote on *Kant, Goethe, Schopenhauer, and *Nietzsche; the philosophies of history, social science, and money; and the foundations of sociology. Like many German writers Simmel believed that the social sciences were distinct from the natural sciences. Interest in his work continues and is increasing among those who characterize modern culture as a fragmented and *alienating experience. IO

simple plurality electoral system *See* FIRST-PAST-THE-POST.

Single European Act The Act was signed in February 1986 by all member state governments of what was then the European Community (now the *European Union) and implemented in 1987. The Act amended the *Treaty of Rome and related treaties to give institutional expression to the Union's Single Market Programme and to reform decision-making processes.

While more ambitious integration proposals had previously met with objections from key member states, a consensus developed around the idea of returning to the original functionalist notion of step-by-step integration through the market and economic policy. As a result, the Act specifically recognized the Single Market Programme as a Community goal by 31 December 1992. The Single European Act streamlined *Council of Ministers legislative procedures:

qualified majority voting was introduced on all legislation related to the Single Market, the aim of which was to remove all barriers to the circulation of labour, capital, goods, and services within the European Community. The goal of *Economic and Monetary Union was given treaty basis. The role of the *European Parliament was strengthened through the 'cooperation' and 'assent' procedures, giving it amending power on Single Market legislation and the power to reject treaty reform and international agreements involving the European Union and third countries. Furthermore, there was a reorganization of the machinery for foreign policy cooperation among member governments in European Political Cooperation (although foreign policy nonetheless remained outside the legal framework of the Union until the Treaty of Maastricht was implemented in 1993). DH

(⊕) SEE WEB LINKS

• Information on the content and purpose of the Single European Act from the EU site.

single issue politics Broadly based political parties have declined in their ability to aggregate issues into coherent ideological packages linked to the aspirations of major social groupings. The vacuum created has been filled by fragmented forms of single issue politics. This is often characterized by a preoccupation with the particular issue to the exclusion of all others, an intensity of feeling about the issue, and a willingness to devote considerable resources of time and money to its pursuit. Because the attachment to the issue is often based on moral grounds, there is a reluctance to compromise. Typical examples of single issue politics are abortion, the debate about hunting with dogs and animal protection issues more generally, and the care of sufferers from specific diseases. Issues of this kind are often associated with single issue *pressure groups. The development of this type of politics poses problems for the polity as a whole. Advocates of single issues are often able to win media attention for an apparently well-argued case for more resources or new regulations. Decision-makers have to balance these demands against other equally well-founded ones within the constraints of limited budgets and legislative time. WG

single-peakedness The property that the available options can be ranked along a continuum in such a way that every voter's preferences can be represented in one of three ways:

1 she likes the 'left'most option best and each successively more 'right'ist option less the more 'right'-wing it is;

2 she likes the 'right'most option best and each successively more 'left'ist option less the more 'left'-wing it is;

3 she likes some intermediate option best and each other successively less as it becomes more 'left'- or 'right'-wing.

'Left' and 'right' are so printed because the continuum need not be literally from left to *right. If single-peakedness holds, the median voter's favourite option is the *Condorcet winner, and will win a simple majority vote against any other. If it does not hold (for instance, because some voters consider the 'centre' option the worst, however the options are arranged along the continuum), then there may be a *cycle in majority rule. *See also* CONDORCET; BLACK.

single transferable vote (STV) A system of *proportional representation in use in Ireland, Malta, for some elections in Australia, and since 2007 for local elections in Scotland; also popular among clubs and societies. A number (usually between three and seven) of seats are filled simultaneously. Each voter lists the candidates in order of preference. First preferences are counted. Those candidates who have achieved at least the *Droop quota ($v/(n + 1)$, rounded up to the next integer, for an n-member seat in which v valid votes have been cast) are elected, and their 'surplus' votes are transferred to the next candidate, if any, on those voters' lists. Surplus votes are weighted: thus, if the Droop quota was 1,200 and a candidate obtained 1,400 first preference ballots, each of those is assigned to the second preference named on it with a weight of 200/1,400. When no further candidates can be elected by this route, the candidate with the fewest first preferences is eliminated and his or her second preferences transferred with a weight of one. The process continues through redistribution of surpluses where possible and eliminations otherwise, until n candidates have been elected. (The process of vote transfers is similar to the *alternative vote system used in single-member constituencies.)

The main property of STV is that each faction or party is guaranteed as many seats as it has Droop quotas of first preference votes. A secondary property, in evidence in Ireland, is that it encourages candidates of the same party to compete against each other; as they cannot normally compete on ideology, they tend to compete on the conspicuous provision of local services. STV is more popular among electoral reformers than among *social choice theorists. The latter complain that the concept of 'wasted vote', on which the rationale of transfers depends, is ill-defined, and that the elimination process is arbitrary and non-*monotonic.

sittlichkeit Translated as 'ethical life' from the writings of *Hegel. It refers to the ethical norms which arise from the interaction of a person's own subjective values and those objective values present in the institutions of society. When these values coincide man, according to Hegel, is free.   IF

slavery The condition in which the life, liberty, and fortune of an individual is held within the absolute power of another. The English word derives from Slav, because Slavs were frequently slaves in the Dark Ages. The first challenges to slaveholding arose in ancient Greece, and *Aristotle produces a somewhat embarrassed justification of slavery, arguing that some people are slaves by nature. As has often been remarked, the movement for American independence produced the Declaration of Independence with its claim 'that all men are created equal; that they are endowed by their creator with inalienable rights; that among these are life, liberty and the pursuit of happiness'. But the Declaration was written by the Virginian slaveholder Thomas *Jefferson, who never freed his own slaves. First the slave trade and then slavery was abolished in the British Empire and in America during the nineteenth century through a combination of principled argument, political advantage, and the Union victory in the American Civil War (1861–5). Slavery is still found in a number of countries, notably Myanmar (Burma).

Smith, Adam (1723–90) Scottish philosopher and founder of classical economics.

Born in Kirkcaldy, Fife, Smith formed a bridge between the Scottish and French *Enlightenments. After his youthful studies at Glasgow, where he studied under Francis Hutcheson, one of the leading figures of the early Scottish Enlightenment, Smith went to Oxford, from which he concluded that 'In the University of Oxford the greater part of the professors have, for these many years, given up altogether even the pretence of teaching'. Thereafter, Smith had little intellectual or social contact with England. As a Scot with closer ties to France than to England, Smith much resembled his close friend David *Hume. From 1752 to 1764 Smith was Professor of Moral Philosophy at the University of Glasgow; *The Theory of Moral Sentiments* (1759: hereafter *TMS*) arose from his lecture course there. In 1764 the offer of a post as tutor to a young aristocrat enabled Smith to resign his chair in Glasgow and travel in France, where he met the *physiocrats, before returning to Scotland to work for ten years on *The Wealth of Nations* (1776: hereafter *WN*). His revelation of the dying Hume's stoical atheism in 1776 'brought upon me ten times more abuse than the very violent attack I had made upon the whole commercial system of Great Britain'. In 1778 he became Commissioner of Customs for Scotland. This curious choice enabled him to see at first hand the distortions of trade and (what would now be called) *rent-seeking that always surrounds the politics of tariffs. There are no signs that Smith felt unease at doing the sort of job—and doing it very conscientiously—which his economic and political theory castigated as useless. His last public role was as Rector of Glasgow University (1787).

The unity of Smith's thought is more clearly seen now than it once was. The moral sentiment on which he placed most trust in *TMS* was sympathy. Sympathy—the knowledge that one shares others' feelings—is presented as the basis for cooperation, both in fact and normatively: 'O wad some Pow'r the giftie gie us To see oursels as others see us!' (Robert Burns, *To a Louse*: Burns knew Smith's work, and the phrase 'if we saw ourselves as others see us' is Smith's). But *TMS* does not go so far as to say that there is enough benevolence to make the world go round unassisted; and it introduces the idea of the invisible hand in a passage describing how the investment of the surplus of the rich unintentionally benefits the poor. Smith's return to the invisible hand in *WN* moves the stress further from sympathy towards self-interest. Although 'it is not from the benevolence of the butcher, the brewer, or the baker, that we expect our dinner, but from their regard to their own interest', still each individual's pursuit of his own gain leads him 'by an invisible hand to promote an end which was no part of his intention'. 'Sympathy' for Smith has a wider meaning than in modern English, and in the wide meaning all these phenomena show sympathy at work.

Like *TMS*, *WN* is partly descriptive and partly normative. It opens with a description of the *division of labour, which Smith sees as the foundation of the wealth of nations. In his famous opening example, a workman in the 'trifling' manufacture of pins might at best make twenty pins a day if he had to do all the operations himself, whereas even an 'indifferent' factory where ten men worked, each on a different task, could produce 48,000 pins a day. Therefore the process in which labourers hire themselves to capitalists, who organize industry on the basis of the division of labour, makes everybody in a capitalist society richer than even the richest members of a non-capitalist traditional society. From this Smith argues towards his general prescription in favour of capitalism, laissez-faire, and *free trade.

Every school of political thought has found an Adam Smith to suit it. To *Marx, Smith advanced the *labour theory of value, making mistakes which it fell to Marx to correct. Marx also accepted that Smith was right descriptively about the division of labour, but failed to understand the *alienation to which it led. Defenders of laissez-faire have found a spiritual father in Smith, but their opponents have also found sustenance. Smith believed that defence, public works, and education ought not to be left to the market, and defenders of protectionism and of government intervention can quote Smith in their support.

Both of Smith's books are full of ironic asides ('*Place*, that great object which divides the wives of aldermen, is the end of half the labours of human life', *TMS*; 'the discipline of colleges and universities is in general contrived, not for the benefit of the students, but for the interest, or more properly speaking, for the ease of the masters', *WN*). The asides seem to make him a precursor more of *public choice than of any other school of political or economic theory.

social capital Social capital refers to the social networks, systems of reciprocal relations, sets of norms, or levels of trust that individuals or groups may have, or to the resources arising from them. Its recent popularity can be traced to three authors—Pierre Bourdieu (1930–2002), James Coleman, and Robert Putnam—each of whom has a distinctive conception of social capital.

Bourdieu discusses a range of different kinds of capital (economic, cultural, social) which interrelate and may substitute for one another. In his later work, social capital is identified as the actual or potential resources which arise from being part of a network of relationships of mutual acquaintance and recognition. Bourdieu was chiefly concerned with the way in which powerful elites retained their privilege.

Coleman's conception of social capital arose out of his empirical work in the 1980s examining the links between social disadvantage, community, and schooling. His claim is that children who are part of a group with high social capital (for example, a Catholic school) have better educational outcomes, even in the context of social disadvantage. More generally, he defined social capital as the set of resources which are inherent in a group (for example, a family or a community organization), and which facilitate certain actions of members of the group (for example, social and cognitive development of a child).

For Putnam, social capital refers to three features of social life—networks, norms, and trust—which enable participants to function more effectively in pursuing a common goal. In his much-quoted study *Bowling Alone* (2000), he documents the decline in civic engagement in the United States and points the finger of blame at the rise in television viewing. He also seeks to show that high levels of social capital are associated with a range of desirable societal outcomes, such as economic prosperity, improved health status, and low crime rates.

The literature distinguishes between structural and cognitive aspects of social capital. Structural social capital involves participation in groups and organizations, membership in networks that foster cooperation. Cognitive aspects of social capital revolve around norms, values, attitudes, and beliefs. Structural and cognitive aspects of social capital are complementary: participation in groups and associations fosters the adoption of social values and beliefs, and internalizing social norms reinforces the will to take part in associations.

Opinion is divided as to whether social capital is always positive. From the perspective of wider society, some forms of social capital are clearly damaging (for example, the *Mafia), while others are a barrier to equal opportunities (for example, old boys' networks). Even these forms of social capital may, however, be beneficial for those who possess them.

Putnam explicitly distinguishes between 'bridging social capital' in which bonds of connectedness are formed across diverse social groups—for example along ethnic/racial and socio-economic lines—and 'bonding social capital' which cements only homogenous groups. Bridging social capital is viewed as superior from society's perspective, even though more difficult to develop and sustain.

Social capital has also been conceptualized both as an individual property, indicating whether an individual participates in networks, trusts others, and shares social norms, and as a contextual feature, whereby the presence of strong networks affects everyone in a community, whether she participates or not and whether she trusts others or not.

The empirical evidence on the role of social capital in society is growing very rapidly. Attempts to operationalize the concept to capture different features—structural and cognitive, bridging and bonding, individual and contextual—are becoming more widespread. Studies examining the relationship between social capital and outcomes in domains as diverse as health, education, economic development, and the effectiveness of political institutions broadly support the notion that social capital is correlated with positive outcomes, although demonstrating causality remains a challenge.

However, the rich theoretical and empirical apparatus of writing on social capital seems to generate more controversies than it resolves. This may be because it is a 'broad church', able to accommodate diverse political perspectives. Neo-liberals in the World Bank can champion social capital as the missing link between free markets and economic growth, communitarians can point to the necessity of social capital for the maintenance of the social fabric, while radical egalitarians can argue that the destruction of social capital is yet another manifestation of the alienation inherent in capitalist society. TB/FB

Social Charter The Charter of the Fundamental Social Rights of Workers (Social Charter) was a declaration agreed to in December 1989 by all the *European Union (then European Community) member states, except Britain, on minimum standards of social security provision, health and safety at work, the labour market, equal opportunities, and vocational training. The Charter is a non-binding political instrument containing 'moral obligations'. Following the passage of the *Single European Act, which incorporated the Single Market Programme, there was concern amongst trade unionists and the Commission that the emphasis of the Single Market Programme on competition amongst enterprises might undermine social security provision and *corporatist labour market arrangements in the then European Community. Furthermore, some governments feared *social dumping by those member states with low wages and social security standards: these would attempt to attract investment away from states with comprehensive social security benefits. The Charter requests the Commission to make proposals for translating the content of the Charter into legislation. This non-binding request was further reinforced by the adoption of the Social Protocol of the *Maastricht Treaty. The Charter has also provided the basis for a range of European Union social action programmes and legislative proposals. Under the Labour Government, the United Kingdom signed up to the Social Charter in 1998. DH

(⊕) SEE WEB LINKS

• A discussion of the introduction and purposes of the Social Charter from the Council of Europe site.

social choice The study of the aggregation of individual preferences into a group choice, or group ordering. It had false dawns in medieval Europe, and again from 1785 to 1803, and from 1873 to 1876. In 1299 Ramon Lull proposed that the winner in a multicandidate election should be chosen by comparing the candidates with one another, two at a time. In 1435 Nicholas *Cusanus proposed what has come to be known as the *Borda or rank-order count for electing a Holy Roman Emperor. In 1785 *Condorcet first discovered that majority rule could '*cycle' so that there might be majorities for a over b, for b over c, and for c over a, all at the same time. When there is such a majority-rule cycle, the concept 'will of the people' is meaningless because every possibility loses by a popular majority to at least one other. Condorcet's ideas were extensively discussed in French academic circles until 1803, but then lost, to be independently rediscovered by C. L. *Dodgson (Lewis Carroll) in the 1870s and rediscovered by Duncan *Black in the 1950s. Social choice as now understood was founded jointly by Black and by Kenneth Arrow, whose general *impossibility theorem of 1951 uses majority-rule cycles on its way to the startling proof that any choice procedure which satisfies some apparently minimal conditions of fairness and rationality is potentially dictatorial.

Since 1951, social choice theory has grown explosively. Most work has been so mathematically uncompromising that neither politicians nor political scientists have understood it, nor have social choice theorists bothered to explain themselves. But its chief results matter for both political theory and political practice. They include: that the weak *Pareto rule ('if everybody prefers a to b, society should choose a') is inconsistent with libertarianism; that no fair and non-random voting procedure is proof against *manipulation; and that, when opinion is multidimensional, there is probably a global majority-rule cycle embracing all outcomes, even those which lose unanimously to some others. Social choice is starting to penetrate the practical discussion of *proportional representation.

social constructivism See CONSTRUCTIVISM.

social contract A contract between persons in a pre-political or pre-social condition specifying the terms upon which they are prepared to enter society or submit to political authority. For many authors, the social contract 'explained' or illuminated a transition from a *state of nature to a social and/or political existence. The 'terms' of such a contract depend for their plausibility upon the depiction of the gains and losses of such a transition, and thus upon the plausibility of the depiction of the state of nature. Adherents of social contract theory need not suppose the historical reality of the agreement, for they are often interested in exploring the limits of political obligation by reference to what a rational actor would be prepared to agree to, given such gains and losses. A great variety of social contract theories have been propounded, and despite the scepticism of authors like *Hume, the contract tradition is still important in political theory. AR

Social Credit A political movement which has enjoyed some success in various parts of the world, but has often been perceived as a populist fringe organization advancing unorthodox ideas. The ideas on which Social Credit were based were developed towards the end of the First World War by Major C. H. Douglas (1879–1952). Douglas was preoccupied by what he perceived to be the problem of underconsumption. He developed the $A + B$ theorem, a method of analysing costs which endeavoured to show that in peacetime there is a gap between the total buying power of individuals and the total prices of goods ready for sale. Additional purchasing power had to be created by manufacturers selling their goods below cost, the difference being made up by grants of credit through the issue of paper money. Every citizen was to be given a National Dividend as of right, although the inflationary implications of this injection of free money into the economy never seem to have been thought through. *Keynes, although critical of the 'mystifications' associated with Douglas's work, commented in the *General Theory* that 'Major Douglas is entitled to claim, as against some of his orthodox adversaries, that he at least has not been wholly oblivious of the outstanding problem of our economic system'. Social Credit as a political movement achieved its greatest electoral success in Canada. Under the leadership of the charismatic William ('Bible Bill') Abelhart it won

control of the Alberta provincial government in a landslide victory in 1935, providing the premier until 1970, and of the British Columbia provincial government in 1952, remaining the governing party for all but three years up to 1991. In New Zealand, Social Credit support peaked at 20.7 per cent in the 1981 general election. Small-scale business people and farmers have provided many of the party's activists in Canada and New Zealand. For such a movement, political education can be as important as electoral success, which Social Credit has never achieved at a national level. WG

social Darwinism A term not widely used in Europe and America until after 1880 and then almost invariably employed as a pejorative tag, to mean the belief, based on a (?mis-) reading of Darwin, that natural selection entails the elimination of weak societies, or people, by strong ones. Popular in the innocent 1890s, social Darwinism seemed wholly discredited after Nazism. Some have seen its recurrence in *sociobiology, which has therefore been controversial; but the 'new social Darwinism', if that is what it is, is based on the new genetics, which shows that Darwinism entails none of the *racist or eugenicist inferences that were widely made between the 1890s and the 1930s (that one part of the human race is genetically superior to another, or that it is feasible and desirable to breed exceptionally good offspring from exceptionally good parents).

Part of the difficulty in establishing sensible and consistent usage is that commitment to the biology of natural selection and to 'survival of the fittest' entailed nothing uniform either for sociological method or for political doctrine. A 'social Darwinist' could just as well be a defender of laissez-faire as a defender of state socialism, just as much an imperialist as a domestic eugenist. Many of the foremost thinkers conventionally labelled 'social Darwinist' established their arguments independently of the findings and methods of Darwinian biology. This is the case, for instance, with *Spencer and W. G. Sumner, the former being an unrepentant *Lamarckist and dedicated believer in the inheritance of acquired characteristics, the latter an enthusiastic disciple of *Malthus. With all of this in mind, it may very well be that the term 'social Darwinism' has merely a narrow rhetorical and ideological usage and consequently is of only passing historiographical interest.   JH

social democracy, social democrat

1. The title taken by most Marxist socialist parties between 1880 and 1914, especially the German and Russian Social Democratic Parties. In Britain, the Social Democratic Federation (SDF) was a late nineteenth-century Marxist group which was eventually absorbed into the Communist Party.

2. Beginning with the split of the Russian Social Democratic Party into *Bolsheviks and *Mensheviks, the more right-wing faction when socialist parties split. This has become the established usage.

By the 1960s there was a clear 'social democratic' faction in sense 2 within the British Labour Party. Its characteristic ideas were support for a mixed rather than a socialist economy, distrust of further nationalization, and to some extent liberal social policy. After many years of internecine tension some but not all of the social democrats in the Labour Party exited to form the Social Democratic Party (SDP) in 1981.

The SDP wished to 'break the mould of British politics'. It proposed a new—or at least rarely articulated—amalgam of strong social liberalism with fairly strong economic liberalism, under the slogan of 'the social market economy'. In conventional terms, therefore, it was *left-wing on social matters and *right-wing on economic matters. However, this strategy faced two problems:

a Although there was an increasing group of voters to whom this mixture appealed—typically well-educated people in professional rather than commercial occupations—they were not numerous enough to be electorally significant.

b Some members of the SDP preferred to present themselves as the continuing Labour Party when the real Labour Party was seen as having moved far to the left. This was the basis of an appeal to a quite different sector of the electorate; but it involved much stronger support for *corporatism and the traditional left in economic matters.

The narrow failure of the SDP/Liberal Alliance to push the Labour Party into third place in terms of votes in 1983 led to the crumbling of the vote under (*b*) except in places in the South of England where it was obvious to the rational voter that the SDP and its Liberal allies were the only force capable of beating the Conservatives. After acrimonious opposition from its leader, David Owen, most of the SDP voted to amalgamate with the Liberal Party in 1988 to form the Social and Liberal Democrats. Until 1992 Owen's supporters continued as a rival force to the detriment of both. The Liberal Democrats have dropped the word 'Social' from their title. All that is left of the SDP is a proportion of their membership and a constitution that is much more centralized than that of the former Liberal Party.

The German SPD (*Sozialdemocratisches Partei Deutschlands*) took its historic title from 'social democracy' in sense 1. However, at the party conference at Bad Godesberg in 1959, it voted to drop the Marxist programme which it had had since its foundation. It thus became, as it has remained, social democratic in sense 2.

Since 1932 the most consistently successful social democratic party in Europe has been the Swedish SAP. The Swedish model was a widely admired corporatist *welfare state which, however, ran into serious fiscal problems from the late 1980s onwards.

social dumping A careful definition of 'dumping' in the relevant sense is in the UK Customs Duties (Dumping and Subsidies) Act 1957: *For the purposes of this Act imported goods shall be regarded as having been dumped if the export price from the country in which the goods originated is less than the fair market price of the goods in that country.* By extension, social dumping would be the act of exporting goods from country A to B which were produced to worse social standards (such as restrictions on child labour or enforcement of environmental health) than those applied to domestic production in country *A*. On this definition, social dumping almost never occurs. But in popular discourse, goods are regarded as having been dumped if the export price from the country in which the goods originated is less than the price of producing the goods in the recipient country. Analogously, social dumping is the act of exporting goods from country A to B which were produced to worse social standards than those applied to domestic production in country *B*. To an economist, this is not dumping at all, but simply a normal feature of international trade. However, lobbies do not exclusively comprise economists.

social exclusion Social exclusion refers to lack of participation in society and emphasizes the multi-dimensional, multi-layered, and dynamic nature of the problem. Definitions of the concept emanate from diverse ideological perspectives, but most share the following features:

1 *Lack of participation.* Protagonists differ over which aspects of society are important and where responsibility for non-participation resides. Most agree that exclusion is a matter of degree, since individuals may be participating to a greater or lesser extent, and that it is relative to the society in question.

2 *Multi-dimensional.* Social exclusion embraces income-poverty but is broader: other kinds of disadvantage which may or may not be connected to low income, such as unemployment and poor self-esteem, fall within its compass.

3 *Dynamic.* The advent of dynamic analysis and a demand from policymakers to investigate cause as well as effect has generated an interest in the processes which lead to exclusion and routes back into mainstream society.

4 *Multi-layered.* Although it is individuals who suffer exclusion, the causes are recognized as operating at many levels: individual, household, community, and institutional.

The term 'social exclusion' probably originated in France, where it was used in the 1970s to refer to the plight of those who fell through the net of social protection—disabled people, lone parents, and the uninsured unemployed. The increasing intensity of social problems on peripheral estates in large cities led to a broadening of the definition to include disaffected youth and isolated individuals. The concept has particular resonance in countries which share with France a Republican tradition, in which social cohesion is held to be essential in maintaining the contract on which society is founded.

Social exclusion terminology was adopted at a European Union level in the late 1980s and early 1990s. Right-wing governments, including the Thatcher government in the

UK, did not recognize the existence of poverty in their own countries, while commentators on the left were becoming increasingly concerned about the social polarization associated with rapidly growing income inequality. 'Social exclusion' was sufficiently broad to accommodate both these perspectives, and allowed debates about social policy to continue at a European level.

By the mid-1990s, use of the term 'social exclusion' by Labour politicians in the UK was commonplace, and the Social Exclusion Unit (SEU) was set up shortly after the 1997 General Election. The SEU defined social exclusion as 'what can happen when individuals or areas suffer from a combination of linked problems such as unemployment, poor skills, low incomes, poor housing, high crime environments, bad health and family breakdown'. This conception fits into the tradition in British social science of investigating multiple deprivation.

Social scientists have increasingly placed emphasis on the duration and recurrence of spells in poverty. Just as the shift from income to multiple deprivation expanded the range of indicators of poverty, so the shift from static to dynamic analysis extended the range along the time dimension. Examining those in poverty at one particular time fails to differentiate between those who are in that state only transiently; those who are on the margins of benefit and work, with alternating periods of poverty and relative wealth; and the long-term poor, such as pensioners living below social assistance levels. A dynamic approach also facilitates an investigation of the processes which lead to poverty and, conversely, what helps people recover.

In the international arena, the United Nations Development Programme has been at the forefront of attempts to conceptualize social exclusion across the developed and developing world. A series of country studies led to the formulation of a rights-focused approach, which regards social exclusion as lack of access to the institutions of civil society (legal and political systems), and to the basic levels of education, health, and financial well-being necessary to make access to those institutions a reality. TB

socialism A political and economic theory or system of social organization based on collective or state ownership of the means of production, distribution, and exchange. Like capitalism, it takes many and diverse forms.

The word was first used in the early 1830s by the followers of *Owen in Britain and those of *Saint-Simon in France. By the mid-nineteenth century it denoted a vast range of reformist and revolutionary ideas in Britain, Europe, and the United States. All of them emphasized the need to transform capitalist industrial society into a much more egalitarian system in which collective well-being for all became a reality, and in which the pursuit of individual self-interest became subordinate to such values as association, community, and cooperation. There was thus an explicit emphasis on solidarity, mutual interdependence, and the possibility of achieving genuine harmony in society to replace conflict, instability, and upheaval. A critique of the social-class basis of capitalism was accompanied by the elevation of the interests of *working class or *proletariat to a position of supreme importance, and in some cases the principle of direct *workers' control under socialism was invoked as an alternative to the rule of existing dominant classes and elites. Images of a future 'classless' society were used to symbolize the need for the complete abolition of socio-economic distinctions in the future: an especially important idea in the Marxist tradition. However, socialists rarely agreed on a strategy for achieving these goals, and diversity and conflict between socialist thinkers, movements, and parties proliferated, especially in the context of the First and Second International Working Men's Associations (founded respectively in 1864 and 1889). Increasingly, as the nineteenth century developed, socialist aspirations focused on the politics of the nation-state (despite much rhetoric about socialism as an international and even global force) and the harnessing of modern science, technology, and industry. Yet other, alternative visions of a socialist future—emphasizing, for example, the potential of small-scale communities and agrarianism rather than full-scale industrialization—always coexisted with the mainstream tendency. In addition doctrines such as *anarchism, *communism, and *social democracy drew on the key values of socialism, and it was often difficult to separate the various schools and movements from each other. Thus *Marx and *Engels

regarded themselves as 'scientific socialists' (as opposed to earlier 'utopian socialists'), but saw socialism in the strict sense of the term to be a transitional phase between capitalism and full economic and social communism.

Once socialists moved into government, the focus of interest in socialism inevitably shifted from theory to practice. The most basic disputes amongst socialists have concerned the role of the state in the ownership, control, and organization of the economy (*see* STATE SOCIALISM), the relationship between socialism and democratic politics, and the tension between gradualist (e.g. parliamentary) and revolutionary strategies for change. By the 1930s two quite different systems of socialism could be seen to represent polar extremes of doctrinal interpretation: the socialism of the Soviet Union under *Stalin, and the *National Socialism of Hitler in Germany. Liberal, conservative, and even anarchist critics stressed the totalitarian tendency of all socialist thought. After the Second World War the division of Europe into a Western pluralist and liberal democratic bloc and an Eastern Marxist-dominated bloc further accentuated the distinction between alternative concepts of socialism. In Western Europe social democratic and Labour Parties used *Keynes to support a non-Marxist approach to the regulation and control of capitalism, stressing the need to achieve social justice and equality through effective management of the economy (and including some, but certainly not total, *nationalization of industry) and redistributive welfare policies (*see* WELFARE STATE). Social democrats accepted the reality of the 'mixed economy', and turned their back on the Marxist analysis of capitalism and the idea of socializing the main instruments of economic production, distribution, and exchange.

Socialism in the Western world entered a new phase of crisis and uncertainty in the 1980s and 1990s as the welfare state has found itself under increasing economic pressure, and as social democratic methods of Keynesian economic management fell victim to alternative neoliberal and *new right theories. The collapse of Marxist socialism in the Soviet empire in 1989, and the failures of many Third World socialist regimes, have added further uncertainty. Efforts to modernize, revise, and adapt socialism to new historical circumstances have led to a range of *New Left ideas and theories over the last twenty-five years, some of them contained within existing socialist movements and parties, others achieving mobilization and support in the arenas of 'new politics', *post-materialism, *feminism, and *environmentalism. There is also a conspicuous reawakening of interest amongst contemporary socialists in basic issues of radical democracy, including the changing relationship between state and *civil society, the new dimensions of social pluralism, the need for enhanced opportunities for *political participation, and the question of *citizenship rights. Some formerly socialist parties no longer support anything recognizable as socialism—*see* NEW LABOUR.   KT

socialism in one country Theory developed by *Bukharin and *Stalin and intended as a rebuttal of *Trotsky's model of *permanent revolution. Despite the failure of European revolutions, Russia could still build socialism through control over the commanding heights of the economy and under the political leadership of the Communist Party of the Soviet Union.   GL

socialist parties Socialist candidates and election programmes pre-dated socialist parties. The British *Labour Party was founded in 1900 as the Labour Representation Committee, one of its components being the Independent Labour Party, founded in 1893. The oldest socialist party in a leading country is the German Social Democratic Party, the SPD, which can trace its origins to the German Workers' Party, whose Gotha Programme of 1875 was fiercely criticized by *Marx. The first socialist candidate in a US presidential election ran in 1892 (and got 0.19 per cent of the vote); no socialist party has ever established itself there (*see* SOMBART). Although there were prominent socialists in France during the Revolution (*see* BABEUF) and during the uprising of 1848 (*see* BLANQUI), the continuous history of socialist parties in France dates back only to 1905. The reason for the late development of socialist parties was the late enfranchisement of the working class, where their mass support has always lain. Hardly had socialist parties started to benefit from the widening of the franchise when they were split

asunder by the First World War. Many of the leaders of the socialist movements in combatant countries continued to preach international socialism, but their followers deserted them. Only when the war was going very badly for all combatants did anti-war socialism revive, in 1916–18. But this merely deepened the splits in the socialist movement, as many socialist parties were now in governing coalitions, sometimes as in Britain for the first time. The most successful socialist parties at this time were therefore those in Australia and New Zealand, which were less affected by the war. Between the wars the most successful socialist parties were in countries which escaped extreme depression and fascism, particularly in Scandinavia (*see* SOCIAL DEMOCRACY).

After 1945, socialist parties spread worldwide, as many of the anti-colonial parties in the Third World were instinctively, or explicitly, socialist. Those where the socialist heritage ran deepest were perhaps *Congress in India and the *ANC in South Africa. In some other countries, 'socialism' was little more than a label for whatever the local anti-colonial elite happened to want.

Some argue that socialist parties are in permanent decline. Among the reasons for saying so are the decline in the *working class, however defined, as a proportion of the population, the increased difficulty of funding the *welfare state, and the (apparently) increasing unpopularity of socialist ideology among mass electorates. But parties and politicians have a vital interest in their own survival, and rational socialist politicians are no less clever than rational politicians of other persuasions, so that they may be expected to adapt their appeals to suit changed conditions.

social justice The requirements of *justice applied to the framework of social existence. The term has been attacked as involving redundancy, since justice is necessarily a social or interpersonal concern. Indeed, John *Rawls's magnum opus is entitled *A Theory of Justice*. What is usually intended by the term is a consideration of the requirements of justice applied to the benefits and burdens of a common existence, and in this sense social justice is necessarily a matter of distribution (*see* DISTRIBUTIVE JUSTICE). But the particular emphasis in 'social justice' is on the foundational character of justice in social life: we are invited to move from a conception of justice to the design of constitutions, to critical perspectives on economic organization, to theories of civil disobedience. In this way, social justice defines the framework within which particular applications of distributive justice arise. A concern with justification, with the appeal to just conditions of social cooperation, has been a marked feature of contemporary *liberalism. Furthermore, as *globalization has created greater interdependencies, arguments that social justice now applies to considerations at the global level have arisen. *See also* GLOBAL JUSTICE. AR

social market The phrase 'social market economy' gained currency at about the time of the foundation of the Social Democratic Party in the UK in 1981 (*see* SOCIAL DEMOCRACY). It was intended to denote an economy with capitalist modes of production but also a functioning welfare state. The trouble with the term is that, since the collapse of the Soviet empire in 1989, almost all politicians have believed in both capitalist modes of production and the welfare state. Therefore the term has no distinct meaning. It is used as a badge but is not a meaningful label.

social mobility Movement from one *class—or more usually status group—to another. There has been extensive and detailed study of social mobility both between generations and within individuals' careers. Those who study mobility from occupations of one status to those of another typically note that the proportion of occupations which require formal qualifications and where work is physically light and done in a relatively pleasant environment is increasing at the expense of their opposites. Thus there can be more 'upward' than 'downward' mobility despite the laws of arithmetic. Their opponents point out that a change of occupation is not necessarily a change of class: and that there is no long-term upward trend in the proportion of the population who are in higher-class jobs. Indeed, in so far as class is defined in terms of hierarchy at work, it could be argued that there never could be net upward mobility. The proportion of those who give orders to

those who take them is likely to be stable. Feminists point out that for decades social mobility and related subjects were studied by reference to the occupation of the head of the household, making women almost invisible to mobility researchers. *See also* SOCIAL STRATIFICATION.

social movements Social movements are change-orientated political formations, often using tactics such as direct action, with loose and informal organizational structures. They are organized around ideas which give the individuals who adhere to the movement new forms of social and political identity. The success of the feminist movement thus does not depend just on various forms of political action, but also on the way in which the ideas associated with the movement led women, and ultimately men, to rethink hitherto accepted and largely unchallenged notions about the roles of women in society. Social movements provide a means of introducing new ways of thinking to the political agenda. Their considerable potential for political displacement may, however, be offset by internal divisions over goals, strategies, and tactics, as in the case of the environmental movement. Partial achievement of the movement's goals may remove much of its dynamic energy, as in the case of the civil rights movement, or the movement may be overtaken by shifts in social and political attitudes, as in the case of the student movement of the late 1960s. Social movements may become institutionalized, as in the case of the British 'Labour movement', a term which remains a useful umbrella for the Labour Party, trade unions, cooperatives, and socialist organizations, but no longer conveys a sense of a dynamic force seeking radical change. WG

social security *See* WELFARE STATE.

social stratification The study of classes or strata in a society. This is usually centred on the social grading of occupations. Sometimes this is done by reference to power and control over the means of production (for which *see* CLASS). More usually, however, stratification is done by means of a mixture of class and status markers. For instance, the Registrar-General, responsible for the decennial census in the United Kindom, first produced a stratified table of occupations as long ago as 1911. Such a table must take note not only of a person's occupation ('farmer') but also his or her class or power position within that description ('farmer employing others', 'farmer employing nobody outside the family', and so on). Ultimately, the status of occupations means what most people think the status of occupations is.

social welfare function Taken over from other economists and adapted by K. J. Arrow, an 'Arrovian' social welfare function is any rule which derives a social ordering of available states of affairs from the set of individual orderings of them. It includes not only all voting procedures but also decision by dictators, oracles, and impersonal tradition. This is now the standard meaning.

society The English word 'society' can be stretched or narrowed to cover almost any form of association of persons possessing any degree of common interests, values, or goals. 'Society' in the nineteenth century meant the upper classes; one might now refer to 'international academic society' or 'European society', though these uses might be disputed. The primary and most normal sense refers to a society defined by the boundaries of the state, even though this usage is odd and potentially misleading in the many cases where there is more than one sizeable ethnic or cultural group in a society, like Canada and South Africa.

The influential German sociologists of the late nineteenth and early twentieth centuries, *Weber and Ferdinand Tönnies, suggested that societies take different forms in so far as the very nature of the association between people differs. Tönnies distinguished a *Gemeinschaft* form, where people are linked by assumption, tradition, and familiar ties, from *Gesellschaft*, where their association is agreed, self-conscious, and quasi-contractual. All societies contain elements of both.

A wide variety of contemporary writers choose to refer, in a Hegelian manner, to a '*civil society'. A civil society in this sense is not the population of a state as such and it is very far from being the mere amalgam of people on a particular territory. Civil society is a range of relationships and organizations which possess a tendency to form a political

system. The history of France from, say, 1780 exemplifies the distinction: the state has been re-formed and redefined many times but France has remained a distinct and continuous civil society throughout the period. Neither Europe nor Brittany or Provence separately, for all that they might have societies in some sense, have been a civil society in the way that France has.   LA

society of states *See* INTERNATIONAL SOCIETY.

sociobiology An attempt to explain social behaviour by reference to modern biological theories and by natural selection in particular. The 'new synthesis' of biology and the social sciences, promised by E. O. Wilson amongst others, rests squarely upon Darwinian population biology, comparative ethology, modern evolutionary theory—once that theory had been purged of *Lamarckism—and finally upon kin-selection. Consequently the sociobiologists' central belief is that, while not all biological phenomena are adaptive in each moment of time, nevertheless natural selection has a pervasive role in shaping all classes of traits in organisms. They have done best at explaining the natural selection of altruistic behaviour. In principle, then, all significant human social behaviour ought also to be explained by its biological basis. And, again in principle, it ought to be possible to establish the co-evolution of genes and culture. Whatever the truth of these claims, some practitioners of sociobiology have given the impression that they are genetic determinists. Debate about these issues has taken up a disproportionate amount of time and energy.   JH

sociology and politics *See* POLITICAL SOCIOLOGY.

Socrates (469–399 BC) Greek philosopher. In 399 BC he was put to death by the Athenian democracy on a charge of failing to worship the city's gods, introducing new deities, and corrupting the youth. It was commonly accepted that political motives lay behind the indictment (and religion in any case was a state concern). Socrates taught that politics is an art which requires for its basis knowledge of the good; most people, however, including most contemporary politicians, do not possess this knowledge and thus cannot acquire the political art. Such views ran counter to the Athenian democratic ideal, which required that in matters of general policy each male citizen's voice carry equal weight, and he was linked with the oligarchic faction which had briefly ruled Athens in 411 BC and 404–403 BC and which was still perceived as a danger. Its numbers also included several of his former associates. His death raises questions about the threat intellectuals may be thought to pose to the political order.

Socrates nevertheless believed that each citizen owed his state obedience in all matters which did not contradict his conscience. He consequently refused offers to help him escape from prison, giving three main reasons:

1 The relation between state and citizen is the unequal one of parent and child: the citizen owes the state gratitude for his upbringing.

2 By freely electing to remain in Athens and receive the benefits of her protection, he has made an implicit contract with her to abide by her laws (compare *Locke on *consent).

3 To break any of the state's laws, even if they are wrongly administered, would result in a dangerous undermining of the authority of law per se. One should never return wrong for wrong.

Socrates' influence on Greek political thought continued after his death through the seminal works of his younger associate *Plato. AH

soft power A term often used in the study of *international relations to denote the use of economic, cultural, and diplomatic incentives so as to shape the preferences of other actors in the *international system. This form of 'soft persuasion' is often contrasted with the notion of *hard power, which predominately focuses on the use of economic sanctions, military threats, and military deployment as a means to coerce compliance.

solidarist international society A branch of the *English School which argues that *human rights and notions of popular *sovereignty are the conceptual basis for the promotion of a robust *international society. Unlike *pluralists, who defend sovereign

*self-determination and a commitment to non-intervention, solidarists argue that a 'society of states' should do more to protect universal human rights and other normative principles that value human beings over state sovereignty, including military intervention if necessary.

Solidarity An independent union formed in Poland in 1980 under the leadership of Lech Walesa, Solidarity tapped into the public's disaffection with communist power. Following mass strikes, the communist regime was forced into unprecedented concessions to society. Although after martial law in 1981, the union was banned, its legacy devastated communism in Poland. It was allowed to reform in 1986, and was a partner in the Round Table talks which led to the orderly withdrawal of one-party rule beginning in 1988. Lech Walesa was elected president of Poland in 1990, and although party politics saw a fracturing of the Solidarity organization, the Solidarity Electoral Action coalition, formed in 1996, emerged as the largest party grouping in the 1997 election.   swh

Sombart, Werner (1863–1941) German social theorist. Opponent of *Marxism, because he denied the universal applicability of Marx's historical materialism. Well known for his book *Why Is There No Socialism in the United States?*: if (at least crude versions of) historical materialism were correct, the United States as the most advanced capitalist country ought to have the most advanced socialist movement.

sophisticated voting *See* TACTICAL VOTING.

sophists Professional itinerant teachers and philosophers, who flourished in Greece from *c.*450–400 BC. A fair appraisal of their work is difficult: our main source is *Plato, who is generally biased against them. They did not form a school, but differed widely in their interests and philosophical positions. Their main market, however, consisted of wealthy young men who desired political influence; consequently almost all sophists were concerned to teach the rhetorical skills politics required. Such skills were particularly in demand in democratic Athens, and this became their unofficial centre.

Their subject matter included metaphysics, epistemology, and linguistics, but their main focus was the relation between individual and society. Central to this relation was, they believed, the relation between '*nature' and 'convention'. Protagoras held that though the social virtues are not themselves innate, the capacity to acquire them is, and we all need to develop such virtues if we are to flourish both individually and as a species. In contrast, Antiphon argued that by nature we all pursue our own individual advantage, and that most man-made laws are inimical to this pursuit and should be evaded if we can escape detection. Some sophists took this view further and claimed that the dictates of nature represented a 'natural justice' which endorsed the supremacy of the strong over the weak; unsurprisingly, such radical claims aroused alarm and suspicion in some circles. Others opted for a *social contract theory by means of which individuals agree to forgo the ultimate 'good' of committing conventional injustice in order to avoid the ultimate evil of suffering it.   AH

Sorel, Georges (1847–1922) French philosopher and social theorist of *syndicalism whose *Reflections on Violence* (1906) put forward a highly original conception of the role of apocalyptic vision ('myth') in sustaining revolutionary struggle. He argued that the *general strike must be grasped as the great mobilizing myth capable of uniting the proletariat in its efforts to overthrow capitalism.   KT

sortition Selection by lot. *See also* DEMARCHY.

South *See* GLOBAL SOUTH.

sovereign debt crisis When a state is deemed to have (potential) problems repaying or refinancing its government debt (*see* DEBT CRISIS). The majority of states require some form of external funding for various reasons, which may include covering a shortfall in tax revenues or borrowing to accelerate the industrialization process. A crisis can occur when circumstances, such as the onset of recession or the loss of market confidence, change, which can directly or indirectly lead to difficulty in repaying debts.

The Latin American sovereign debt crisis of the 1980s is a prominent example. Due to a vast increase in oil prices and a recession in the Western world that affected imports, many Latin American countries faced domestic economic difficulties. In August 1982, Mexico announced that it could no longer pay its debts. Banks soon realized that they had similar exposure to other Latin American countries, such as Argentina and Brazil, and therefore enforced stricter conditions. In all, a further twenty developing countries rescheduled their external debt obligations in 1983. Many of these countries were forced to accept temporary assistance from the *IMF in return for enforced economic reforms that included, for instance, liberalizing trade and balancing national budgets. Following 2008, Greece became a modern example of sovereign debt crisis as part of the *Financial Crisis.   LS

sovereignty Sovereignty is the claim to be the ultimate political authority, subject to no higher power as regards the making and enforcing of political decisions. In the international system, sovereignty is the claim by the state to full self-government, and the mutual recognition of claims to sovereignty is the basis of international society. Sovereignty is the other side of the coin of international anarchy, for if states claim sovereignty, then the structure of the international system is by definition anarchic. Sovereignty should not be confused with freedom of action: sovereign actors may find themselves exercising freedom of decision within circumstances that are highly constrained by relations of unequal power.

The doctrine of sovereignty developed as part of the transformation of the medieval system in Europe into the modern state system, a process that culminated in the Treaty of Westphalia in 1648. In some ways the emergence of the concept of sovereignty ran parallel with the similar emergence of the idea of private property, both emphasizing exclusive rights concentrated in a single holder, in contrast to the medieval system of diffuse and many-layered political and economic rights. Within the state, sovereignty signified the rise of the monarch to absolute prominence over rival feudal claimants such as the aristocracy, the papacy, and the Holy Roman Empire. Internationally, sovereignty served as the basis for exchanges of recognition on the basis of legal equality, and therefore as the basis of diplomacy and international law. BB

soviet, Russian Elected council with legislative and/or executive functions.

Soviet Union (1924-91) The Union of Soviet Socialist Republics was formally formed on 30 December 1924 with the adoption of a federal treaty and constitution, and survived until 31 December 1991. Following the forcible incorporation of the Baltic states in 1940, it contained fifteen constituent republics: Armenia, Azerbaijan, Byelorussia, Estonia, Georgia, Kazakhstan, Kirgizia, Latvia, Lithuania, Moldavia, the Russian Socialist Federation, Tajikistan, Turkmenistan, Ukraine, and Uzbekistan. It was the largest country in the world in area, with a population of 293 million in 1991, composed of a multitude of ethnic groups, languages, and religions.

The Soviet period dates from the October 1917 *Russian Revolution. This triggered a break-up in the Russian Empire and independent states were formed in the Baltic, Ukraine, and Georgia; the latter two were reincorporated in 1921. *Soviets had been formed during the war among soldiers, workers, and peasants and had played a decisive role in mobilizing forces for the February 1917 revolution. Initially, they supported the *Mensheviks but, with the continuation of the war, gradually came under *Bolshevik influence. However, although the removal of the Provisional Government in October was approved *post hoc* by the soviets, it had in fact been the result of a Bolshevik coup.

The institutional structure of Soviet Russia took time to form, and there was considerable rivalry between the soviets, the Council of Peoples Commissars (Sovnarkom), the trade unions, the military, and the Communist Party. At the same time, even at this stage, the discrepancy between the legitimating claims of the regime and the real locus of decision-making can be discerned. Both the soviets and the trade unions were quickly sidelined as central sources of authority, though the former retained their status as the formal source of sovereignty. Trade unions were successfully attacked as too

sectional to run the economy, and there was even considerable debate about their continued existence in a socialist society where exploitation had been supposedly abolished. *Lenin defined them as 'conveyor belts of government and Party policy to the workers'; a subordinate position they retained until 1989. In conditions of civil war, which obtained from 1918 to 1920, the military played a significant role but *Trotsky's demand for greater power over industry via the 'militarization of labour' was also rebuffed. Gradually, the Party and Sovnarkom emerged as the main sources of executive power. Lenin's only official position was Sovnarkom chairman and from 1918 to his illness in 1922, the government was an effective body. However, even Lenin complained about the continuous drift of decision-making to the Party Central Committee; since all commissars were also on the Central Committee, this was not surprising. Despite this drift, the bicephalous executive was an ever-present feature of Soviet institutional life.

The Bolsheviks had come to power advocating the right of nations to self-determination, but for many of them nationalism was an inherently 'bourgeois' and parochial phenomenon; local interests, it was argued, were best served within the larger, more advanced Russian culture. Lenin again was instrumental in working out a fudge in which national boundaries would be retained and ethnic cultures strengthened provided they remained 'socialist in form'. At the same time, the general thrust of policy for many years was towards, first the 'drawing together' (*sblizhenie*) and then the 'merging' (*sliyanie*) of nations. Paradoxically, the national policy of the Soviet state, which entailed both the promotion of members of the titular majority in most of the non-Russian republics and the establishment, sometimes for the first time, of codified national languages backed up by the cultural apparatus of the state, in the end had profound consequences in terms of building the national separatist movements that arose in the late 1980s.

The period 1929-38 was decisive in creating the Soviet institutional system as it stood until 1989. At this time, under the leadership of *Stalin, who had been building a power base as General Secretary of the Party, the industrialization and collectivization drives were launched. Huge new industries were created and millions of people moved off the land into the towns. At the same time, the scale of repression was massively escalated. Estimates vary, but many millions of people died by execution, in the camps, or of starvation in the villages. Within the Communist Party itself, a series of purges took place that resulted in a massive change in leadership. In these ten years, the size of the state and its bureaucracy expanded enormously, with the biggest growth evident in the institutions responsible for administering the command economy.

The greatest threat to the Soviet Union's existence came with the German invasion of 1941. In 1940, the two countries had signed a non-aggression pact that contained a secret protocol allowing the Soviet Union to incorporate the Baltic states. Stalin was clearly unnerved by the loss of life and territory following the Germans' surprise attack. They advanced to within a few kilometres of Moscow before stalling in the winter. The Soviet Union eventually played the decisive role in defeating the German army, capturing Berlin and occupying most of Eastern Europe that then came under their domination. However, it did so at enormous cost to human life; at least 20 million Soviet citizens died in the effort.

In the aftermath of the war, the Soviet political system appeared vindicated: its institutions had managed the war effort and economic growth resumed at high levels by comparison with the capitalist West. Many Soviet people felt great optimism about the future prospects for their country, which were reflected in *Khrushchev's promise to build communism by the 1980s and stimulated by Soviet advances in space. However, a number of developments combined to shatter this confidence. First, Khrushchev himself revealed the connection between the system and repression. The revelations about Stalin fatally undermined the legitimacy of the regime. Second, there emerged a high degree of institutional conservatism, particularly among the bodies responsible for managing the economy. This resulted in declining growth and, alongside this, an increase in the amount of corruption. Beginning in the 1970s, the performance of the Western economies, knowledge of which became increasingly available, matched and then passed that of the Soviet Union. The claims to superiority of socialism evaporated in these conditions.

Growing awareness of the crisis in the country helped Mikhail Gorbachev to power in 1985 and led to his programme of *perestroika designed to reinvigorate the economy and society. However, the institutional framework proved unable to withstand the pent-up frustrations of various groups, particularly given the costs of reform itself. National unrest was especially virulent, and following two years of a 'war of laws' between the centre and governments of the republics, in late 1991 the Soviet Union was bypassed and then consigned to oblivion by an agreement among the republics to form the *Commonwealth of Independent States. swh

Sparta Ancient city-state in southern Greece. No state had a constitution quite like Sparta's. It has been said that it codified the customs of warrior tribes and its author is thought to have been one Lycurgus about whom little, if anything, is known for certain.

By the eighth century BC Lacedaemon, as it was then known, which had grown out of a collection of villages, had established itself as a strong state in the western Peloponnese. It was at the height of its power during the Persian War (500–449). It defeated Athens in the Peloponnesian War (431–404) (*see also* THUCYDIDES), and became the most powerful Greek state. However, it was defeated by Thebes at Leuctra (371), submitted to Philip II of Macedon, and went into decline in the third century.

The constitution of Sparta was sociomilitary. It was ruled by a dual hereditary monarchy, and an oligarchy consisting of magistrates (*ephors*), a council of twenty-eight elders (*gerousia*) (all over 60 and appointed for life), and a supreme consultative assembly of all those over 30, with power only to ratify war. The rest of the population were either *perioikoi* with some independence or *helots* (serfs).

Economically Sparta was remarkable for equality of possessions and the absence of moneyed wealth. These two principles were designed to achieve 'good order' (*eunomia*). All citizens were required to do military service, and children were trained (*agoge*) for war from the age of 7. In later times they were taught to be indifferent to pain and death. This (surreptitiously homoerotic) model influenced English public schools in the nineteenth century and was instrumental in the training of Empire builders. CB

Spartacists Internationalist, revolutionary group within the German SPD which adopted the name of the leader of a slave revolt in ancient Rome (and, later, Hollywood). Expelled from the SPD in 1917, it joined the Independent German Socialist Party (USPD), leaving in early 1919 to form the German Communist Party (KPD). Implicated in the January 1919 uprising against the SPD government during which its leaders, *Luxemburg and Karl Liebknecht, were assassinated. GL

spatial competition, theory of The division of *social choice theory which attempts to predict how politicians seeking to be elected will interact with voters attempting to vote for their favourite set of policies. The idea derives from the work of economists who tried to explain why shops are located together in the middle of town rather than being spaced equidistantly. By analogy, Anthony Downs argued (in *An Economic Theory of Democracy*, 1957) that politicians seeking (re-)election would position themselves on the set of policies favoured by the median voter (*see also* BLACK). Spatial theory assumes that voters can measure the distance between themselves and the candidates in multidimensional policy space, and vote either for the candidate nearest them or, tactically, for a more remote candidate with a higher chance of winning.

Like other subdivisions of social choice, spatial theory is usually set out in arcane mathematical language accessible only to other spatial theorists. Thus its strengths and weaknesses are opaque to everybody else. It is inappropriate for use either:

1 where voters do not regard issues as *salient, so have no real perception of issue space nor of their position in it; or
2 where issue space is so inherently multidimensional that majority rule is cyclical (*see* SOCIAL CHOICE) and there is no stable equilibrium point for politicians to seek.

But it can be a powerful tool for analysing the manoeuvres of sophisticated voters in one-dimensional arenas, such as Congressional committees. There, the basic insight that people who want to win elections will converge on the policy of the median voter remains robust. The sorry fate of those who conspicuously depart from the median (Barry Goldwater in 1964; George McGovern in 1972; Michael Foot in 1983; Margaret Thatcher in 1990) also suggests that the basic idea behind the theory of spatial competition is sound.

SPD (Germany) *See* SOCIAL DEMOCRACY.

Speaker The officer of the UK House of Commons, elected on a non-partisan basis by MPs from among their own number, responsible for the administration of the House, for presiding over its debates, and for its representation in relation to the monarch, official visitors, and other parliaments. The office of Speaker, or presiding officer, has been replicated in the devolved parliaments and assemblies in Scotland, Northern Ireland, and Wales, and by many other parliaments, particularly those in the Commonwealth. It is also to be seen in the US *House of Representatives, although there the Speaker's election and function are highly partisan. JBr

(⊕) SEE WEB LINKS

• Information on the office and role of the Speaker from the UK Parliament site.

special relationship Term used to describe post-Second World War Anglo-American relations, characterized by amiable diplomatic, military, economic, and cultural ties. The existence of shared history, language, cultural heritage, and close commercial relations in the pre-twentieth century significantly facilitated the formation of this relationship. The term, however, became popularized at the dawn of the Cold War, as the mutual security interests of the two powers became even more evident. Churchill's *Iron Curtain speech used the term to refer to the close Anglo-American relations that developed during the Second World War. For Britain, friendly relations with the United States were essential to counter aggressive Soviet policies in East Europe. For the United States, the relationship was important for the implementation of its policy of containment throughout the Cold War. In the post-Cold War world, this relationship is said to continue, as the two states continue as major trading partners and allies in the face of global terrorism.   YFK

species-being A concept (*Gattungswesen*) employed extensively by Hegelians in Germany in the 1830s and 1840s, used primarily to argue for the absolute uniqueness of man due to man's possession of consciousness: not just consciousness of self, which other social animals possessed, but rather consciousness of species or essential nature. Hence man was *sui generis* in his ability to reflect about his own species and also in the ability to make his own nature an object of thought. The contemplative life was distinctly and exclusively human. Indeed, man was taken to transcend a merely animal individuality in thought and for some, like *Feuerbach, this meant that human individuality was not *selbst-sein*, being oneself, but *mitsein*, being with another. *Marx extended the concept of species-being. While he accepted that man was unique, he also believed that the distinctively human attribute was not thought or consciousness *per se*, but rather free and conscious material production. It was, therefore, free labour which constituted man's active species life.   JH

Spencer, Herbert (1820–1903) English evolutionary philosopher. Born in Derby, the only survivor in a family of nine, Spencer was educated in austere Unitarian circumstances by his father and uncle. He worked first as a railway engineer and then, at the age of 28, he became sub-editor of *The Economist*, a London weekly committed to free trade and laissez-faire (*see* BAGEHOT). He is now amongst the most remote and forbidding of the eminent Victorians. The fourteen enormous volumes of *The Synthetic Philosophy*, which were painstakingly compiled over thirty-six years, are nowadays barely looked at, let alone read. And the *Autobiography* completed in 1889 spreads to over 400,000 words. In general, Spencer always endeavoured to subsume phenomena under his philosophy of evolution, a philosophy resting squarely on *Lamarckism. In the course of his life, he ranged under his definition of evolution not only the nebular hypothesis, the conservation of

energy, and the social organism, but also laissez-faire economics, political individualism, and a utilitarian ethic based on hedonism. However, Spencer stopped creative thinking around 1860, as he descended into despair and solitude, his own earlier and radical individualism increasingly giving way to a grumbling and pessimistic conservatism. Longevity was Spencer's worst enemy.

sphere of influence A determinate region within which a single external power exercises a predominant influence, limiting the political independence of weaker states or entities within it. The concept plays a central role in the analysis of imperialism and Great Power politics. Definitions and discussions of spheres of influence revolve around three dimensions. The first concerns the nature and scope of the imposed limits— whether the dominant power seeks to control only the foreign policies of weaker states or its domestic economic and political arrangements. Whilst different from formal empire which involves direct control and administration, the concept is often closely tied to notions of informal empire and to the concept of hegemony. The second dimension concerns the character of the power relationship, including the types of power involved (coercive, institutional, ideational) and the degree to which influence involves the active cooperation of elites or groups within the subordinate state (whether pro-US militaries in Latin America or local communist parties in Eastern Europe during the Cold War). The third dimension concerns the degree to which spheres of influence are recognized by other states or by international society more generally. This might involve formal agreement amongst particular states on the creation of spheres of influences—as in the practices of European imperialism in the period following the Conference of Berlin (1884–5), with the 1907 Anglo-Russian convention concerning Persia providing a very clear example. Or it might involve the attempt by a state to secure formal legal recognition of its sphere of influence, as in the failed attempt by the US to secure inclusion of the Monroe Doctrine in the Covenant of the League of Nations or Churchill's proposals for 'regional policemen'. Finally, and most importantly, spheres of influence may be embodied in the informal political norms that emerge as part of major power rivalry—as with the tacit understandings regarding the position of the US role in the western hemisphere or of the USSR in Eastern Europe and now Russia in its 'near abroad'. AHU

spin Putting a slant on the news that favours one's patron or employer; **spin doctor** one who does this. The words are new (the *Oxford English Dictionary* records 'spin' in this sense first in 1978, and 'spin doctor' in 1984); the activity is not. Lord Salisbury ended the political career of Lord Randolph Churchill in 1885 by leaking stories about him to the press and then denying that he had done so. Thomas Jefferson used James Callender as a spin doctor to besmirch members of the preceding Adams Administration in 1798–1800. Callender turned on his patron when he was not given a government job, and produced perhaps the most enduring spin of all time, namely the allegation that Jefferson had had children by his slave Sally Hemings. DNA analysis in 1998 showed that this could be (but may not be) true.

Spinoza, Baruch (Benedict) (1632–77) Dutch philosopher and theologian. Spinoza was born in Amsterdam, of Spanish-Portuguese-Jewish origin. His family had taken refuge there to escape persecution in Spain. His thirst for knowledge led him to study under Francis van den Enden, a freethinker. By 1656 his views were so unorthodox that he was accused of atheism and banned from the synagogue. He earned his living by grinding lenses, which put him in touch with developments in optics, and hence with the advances in mathematics of the time. Meanwhile he continued his reflections and wrote many philosophical works, especially on ethics.

In the *Tractatus Theologico-Philosophicus* of 1670, and the unfinished *Tractatus Politicus*, he advocated freedom of thought, religious thought in particular. Like *Hobbes, he believed that the state came into being to prevent anarchy. But unlike Hobbes he did not believe autocracy was the solution. He passionately believed in democracy, in the right to disagree and hold contrary opinions short of anarchy. The ultimate objective was wisdom, which, for Spinoza was reasoned judgement or rational behaviour. It was this that the state was established to promote. CB

spitzenkandidaten A German word that literally translates as 'top candidate', which refers to a general party leader or candidate to be presented for election to key leadership positions within the *European Union. The term first came to use in 2013, when the Party of European Socialists named a *spitzenkandidaten* for election to the *European Commission (EC). This was quickly followed by the European People's Party, who presented Jean-Claude Juncker as their *spitzenkandidaten* (who ultimately won the post). The main implication is that constituents are now able to vote in a candidate for a key leadership position within the EC, whereas their vote had traditionally been limited to electing members to the *European Parliament.

split-ticket voting *See* TICKET-SPLITTING.

spoils system The systematic sacking of one's opponent's appointees, and substitution by appointees of one's own, on winning an election. The spoils system was an accepted part of American federal government throughout the nineteenth century. It continues in a diluted form today with the presumption that the top appointed federal offices are vacated on a change of administration. The term is also applied to the systematic filling of low-level posts by one's own appointees as a reward for political loyalty such as helping in an election. Critics of *quangos and (since 1979) privatized agencies in British government argue that they give the incumbent party an opportunity to exercise a similar spoils system on behalf of their political supporters.

sponsored candidate In the British Labour Party, one sponsored by a trade union which meets a proportion of election and office expenses. In the past sponsorship was important in enabling working-class candidates to enter Parliament. Nowadays many sponsored candidates have no real connection with the sponsoring union, although they may undertake to liaise with the union. Sponsorship does not permit a union to dictate how a candidate or MP should behave.

Some trade unions and pressure groups such as the police, farmers', and teachers' unions sponsor MPs from all the main parties but do not contribute to campaigning activities. PBY

sport Sport is concerned with contests of skill and prowess, primarily, though not exclusively, athletic prowess. Until the last quarter of the nineteenth century 'sport' in the English language referred primarily to field sports; games were not included. However, many contemporary reference works on sport now exclude not only all of the field sports, but also many of the most popular games, including the cue games, card games, board games, and electronic games. Official definitions, such as those used by the Sports Council, are similarly exclusive. Thus, 'sport' can be said to have a shifting and contested meaning.

From its first conception modern sport had moral and political aims. It was conceived by such educators as Thomas Arnold of Rugby as a necessary means of training young men in loyalty, teamwork, and discipline while dissipating their excessive energy. These values were seen to be as relevant to an urban-industrial society as to a school and of particular value in the running of an empire. In the United States, English games like baseball and rugby developed separate American forms from the 1870s, highly trained and specialized, with an important role in both the educational system and the growing industrial conurbations.

The politics of sport has been subject to a mythical belief that sport had 'nothing to do with politics'. This myth was driven by the idealism, the purity of aspiration, which many people sought from sport and it functioned to help keep sport off the political agenda. But the reality was that modern sport was conceived, essentially, as a form of political socialization and the institution has contained political struggles at its core and lent itself to a number of political functions. The principal contest internal to sport has been between an amateur–elite ethos and a professional–commercial ethos. To the amateurs, sport was both recreation and moral training; these functions must necessarily be corrupted by the development of specialized professionalism. To the commercializers, sport offered a myriad of possibilities for making incomes and profits. The struggle between these ethoses was a long

one, with many battles and compromises on the way. Some sports, including rugby union and the Olympic Games, lasted much longer than most in resisting commercial professionalism, but, given the power of television, the defeat of amateurism was, by the late twentieth century, something of a rout.

It would be too simplistic to suggest that sport has functioned, or been successfully used, as an 'opiate of the people' as Leon Trotsky suggested it was (in *Where Is Britain Going*, 1926). Many politicians have tried to associate with sport and sporting success, though with mixed results. One consistent theme has been the development and preservation of national identities. Even in the early development of sport in the British Isles, the establishment of separate national competitions and teams in the most popular sports (and separate sports in Ireland) was important in redefining the relationship between the United Kingdom and its component nations. The Soviet Union after 1945 devoted enormous resources to success in Olympic sport in order to convince people of the virtues of its form of society. The fostering of and identification with sporting success have been an important element of attempts by post-colonial African states to meld multitribal societies into modern nations. The success of these enterprises was partial at best, but there can be no question that sport has had a distinctive part to play in modern politics. LA

Stable State Economics A movement within *ecological economics that suggests an economy with stable or mildly fluctuating levels of economic and population growth could be environmentally sustainable. Proponents of the approach often critique *capitalism for exceeding ecological limits. In addition to environmental concerns, notions of fair redistribution and *wellbeing are often central to the approach. *See also* DISTRIBUTIVE JUSTICE. LS

stakeholder Two main senses, one more collective, the other more individual.

1. One who has a stake in a business or a policy. In its modern usage, the word is deliberately contrasted with shareholder. A shareholder has a particular kind of stake, namely a share in capital. A stakeholder's stake may be labour, or land, or a consumer interest in the business or policy. Political writers who talk of a 'stakeholder society' therefore mean one in which interests over and above shareholders are effectively represented. The less well-defined the interest, the harder it is to see how the stake is to be claimed or protected. Workers' stake in a firm may be acknowledged in a supervisory board as in Germany and to a limited extent in the UK; but how are consumers' stakes to be claimed? Therefore, although in the early years of *New Labour, there was much talk of a stakeholder society, it is hard to point to institutions that have changed as a consequence of such rhetoric.

2. The term is increasingly used in connection with new forms of social policy based on individualized assets/accounts ('stakes'). In contemporary academic debate, this use of the term is exemplified by Bruce Ackerman and Anne Alstott's book, *The Stakeholder Society* (1999), which argues that each citizen (of the USA) should receive an $80,000 grant as of right on maturity. The UK's Child Trust Fund (inaugurated 2002), while much more modest than the policy Ackerman–Alstott propose, can be seen as a clear example of a stakeholding policy in this second sense. Another example was the invention of 'Stakeholder Pensions' under the first Blair government: these were designed to be personal pensions for middle income people not in an employer's pension scheme.

Stakhanovism Named after a prodigiously productive miner publicized by the Soviet authorities in the mid-1930s, Stakhanovism represented an attempt to maximize output by competitive record-breaking among politically motivated workers. It was despised by many employees who saw it as a management ploy to reduce piece-rates. Management itself was often opposed because of the disruptive effects record-breaking could have on overall performance.   swh

Stalinism Stalinism has come to stand for the whole of the repressive Soviet political system under Joseph Stalin (1879–1953) from at least 1928 until his death, although many commentators extend the term to include the period before *perestroika. He has been held personally responsible, as a total and arbitrary autocrat, for millions of

deaths and for the 'deviations of socialism' that went on under his rule. In recent years, however, a new historiography has appeared which seeks to distinguish Stalin and Stalinism from a range of competing ideological positions in Soviet politics. Many of the tenets of ideological Stalinism are considered by these historians to have lost ground in the 1930s, though adherents of this position continued to exercise influence and power throughout the Soviet period.

Josef Vissarionovich Dzhugashvili adopted the name Stalin (man of steel) as a pseudonym while in the Bolshevik underground before the revolution. He was a Georgian by birth and his education came first from an orthodox school and then a seminary where he learned Russian. He joined the Social Democratic Movement after his expulsion from the seminary in 1899. Stalin was not considered a significant theoretician among the intellectual Bolsheviks, though he had published works on the nationalities question among others, and *Trotsky in particular is famously said to have laughed at his writings. However, he possessed considerable organizational skills and acted as editor of *Pravda*.

He did not play a significant role in the October 1917 Revolution, despite latter-day efforts to paint him in at Lenin's right hand. However, until 1922 he occupied the positions of People's Commissar for Nationality Affairs and People's Commissar for State Control, and was a member of both the Communist Party's organizational bureau (*Orgburo*) and the Politburo. After his move from the government in 1922, he became General Secretary of the Communist Party. Though this position was regarded at the time as mainly administrative, Stalin was able to use the patronage available in the post and the network of connections he established to advance his power in the leadership struggles which followed Lenin's death.

Between 1924 and 1928, Stalin steered a middle course. He first opposed the Left Opposition to the line of the New Economic Policy (NEP), headed by Trotsky and later supported by Kamenev and Zinoviev. Following the defeat of these potential rivals, Stalin then adopted many of their positions in 1928 in his battle against *Bukharin. Many commentators have treated Stalin's shifting position in this period as a sign of his relentless and wholly personal drive for power. However, other scholars have seen a greater consistency in his position from 1929–38 when, though less extreme than some of his allies such as Zhdanov, he advocated strong central party control over both the regions and the various sectors of the growing economic bureaucracy.

The political difficulty for the Communist Party during NEP was that it had nothing significant to do: the regime depended on a deal with the peasantry, among whom the party had little support, and industry was run by (frequently bourgeois or Menshevik) experts in central bodies such as Gosplan and in the factories by the manager or technical director. Stalin was able to tap and mobilize growing disaffection with this position among party officials and cited dissatisfaction among workers with the pace of industrial development and supply of produce in support. The Stalinist revolution launched against NEP in 1929 was all encompassing: collectivization in agriculture, including the mobilization of 25,000 workers to the countryside; rapid industrialization with extraordinary targets set for output; and a cultural revolution, in which bourgeois experts would be quickly replaced by 'red directors'.

The slogans and motivations of this period were highly political—enthusiasm and creativity—as were the explanations for failure—wreckers and saboteurs. The central institutions of the period were the Communist Party, the party-dominated Workers' and Peasants' Inspectorate (Rabkrin) and the OGPU (Unified State Political Directorate). However, alongside these bodies, a new set of management institutions was being formed out of the old Supreme Council for the National Economy (VSNKh). Despite the claim that great success was achieved in the First Five Year Plan, fulfilled in four years between 1928 and 1932, there is considerable evidence of chaos and failure in the economy resulting from the highly politicized Stalinist programme. Gradually, ideological Stalinism of this sort was challenged by managerialism as the party itself underwent a degree of bureaucratization.

A considerable debate has taken place among scholars about the meaning, in this context, of the assassination of Kirov in 1935 and the fratricidal party infighting that followed. One school of thought blames Stalin for the death of Kirov, whom he had killed because of personal rivalry for the leadership. Stalin subsequently used Kirov's death as an excuse to launch purges against other opponents in the leadership, including Bukharin, Kamenev, and Zinoviev. The other school is neutral on who killed Kirov but maintains that the purges were politically motivated and connected to the battle between managerialists in the apparatus and their allies in the regions, and those advocating strong central party political control. On this account, ideological Stalinism was set back in 1938 by the establishment of a bureaucratic stranglehold over policy-making, though it remained a significant force in Soviet politics thereafter, as the anti-bureaucratic campaigns launched by Zhdanov in 1948, Khrushchev between 1957 and 1964, and Gorbachev after 1985 prove.

If this latter account is true, then it is ironic that Khrushchev in his secret speech to the twentieth party congress in 1956 and at the twenty-second congress in 1962, should have identified Stalin so completely with the Soviet system as it had evolved. Clearly, Khrushchev was taking a considerable political and personal risk in revealing the scale of repression that occurred under Stalin's rule. At the same time, by laying all of the blame for the 'deviations of socialism' at Stalin's feet Khrushchev was concealing the truth in order to limit the loss of legitimacy to the system itself. However, reforming the institutions that emerged in the Stalin period proved a far more difficult task, and Khrushchev's efforts to do so resulted in his ouster. Moreover the legacy of anger among all the repressed peoples and the loss of faith of the public in the 'friendliness' of socialism were never overcome. swh

standards in public life _See_ COMMITTEE ON STANDARDS IN PUBLIC LIFE.

standing committee _See_ PUBLIC BILL COMMITTEE.

stare decisis Latin phrase, meaning 'stand by past decisions'. Foundation of legal application of precedent, where a judicial decision on one case applies to all cases with similar principles.

START (Strategic Arms Reduction Talks)
Negotiations to succeed the *SALT process, initiated by President Reagan in 1981. The talks made no progress in the atmosphere of the New Cold War, were abandoned in 1983 and resumed in 1985 as President Reagan and General Secretary Mihkail Gorbachev re-established better relations.

The first START treaty concluded in July 1991, between Presidents Bush and Gorbachev, reducing each state's long-range launchers to 1,600 and warheads to 6,000, including further important limitations, especially on land-based missiles. In December 1992 Bush and President Yeltsin of Russia signed a second START treaty to reduce each side to about 3,500 warheads, including only 500 land-based missiles, each restricted to only one warhead.

START 2 marked the end of the nuclear arms race between the superpowers. Belarus and Kazakhstan had agreed by that time to hand over their former Soviet weapons to Russia, and by 1994 Ukraine had promised to trade its ex-Soviet weapons for Western assistance. The more ambitious New START, which was signed in 2010, set a target for a further 30 per cent reduction by 2018. However, the future of New START is now uncertain with the election of Donald J. Trump to the US Presidency in 2016. Within days of taking office, Trump informed the Russians that the treaty was disadvantageous to the US and indicated that it may not survive until its 2021 closure date.   PBY

state A distinct set of political institutions whose specific concern is with the organization of domination, in the name of the common interest, within a delimited territory. The state is arguably the most central concept in the study of politics and its definition is therefore the object of intense scholarly contestation. Marxists, political sociologists, and political anthropologists usually favour a broad definition which draws attention to the role of coercion-wielding organizations who exercise clear priority in decision-making and claim paramountcy in the application of naked force to social problems within territorial boundaries. By this standard, archaeological remains signal the existence of states from 6000 BC, with written or pictorial records testifying to their presence from 4000 BC.

Within Western Europe a number of state forms can be identified corresponding to historical epochs. In the slave-economies of antiquity, the state—in this context the instrument of the collective property-owners—existed either in the shape of a Hellenistic king and his henchmen or a Roman emperor and the imperial aristocracy. The high period of the Greek city-states can be dated from 800 to 320BC. Within these states, once the rule of the 'tyrants' had been overthrown, free members of society were granted citizenship rights. However, the democracy of the city-states was increasingly undermined by territorial colonization and conquest, leading to rule by royal succession by the time of Alexander the Great. In contrast, Rome did not introduce direct democracy but developed from a monarchy into a republic (Latin *res publica*, 'the things pertaining to the public realm'), governed by a senate dominated by the Roman aristocracy. The Greek city-states bequeathed direct democracy whilst Rome's contribution to the development of the modern state lies in *Roman law, and its clear distinction between the public and the private.

The dissolution of the Roman empire saw the fragmentation of the imperial state into the hands of private lords whose political, juridical, and military roles were at the same time the instruments of private appropriation and the organization of production. In early medieval Western Europe state power was not only divided up but also privatized, through local private proprietors whose property—gained from oaths of fealty, and which served as the basic economic unit of society—simultaneously endowed them with political authority. In these conditions, as Marx puts it tersely, their estate was their state. The feudal 'state-system' was an unstable amalgam of suzerains and anointed kings. A monarch, formally at the head of a hierarchy of sovereignties, could not impose decrees at will. Relations between lords and monarch are best seen in terms of mutual dependence, with the monarch an orchestrator rather than an absolute power. The lapse of universal taxation (central to the Roman empire) ensured that each ruler needed to obtain the 'consent' of each estate of the realm. The legal assumptions underpinning the feudal organization of society, and the Church's claim to act as a law-making power coeval with rather than subordinate to the secular authorities (*see* MEDIEVAL POLITICAL THEORY), show that a modern conception of the state is inappropriate as a basis for understanding politics in medieval feudalism.

The development of the modern form of the state, as a public power separate from the monarch and the ruled, and constituting the supreme political authority within a defined territory, is associated with the slow institutional differentiation of the 'political' and the 'economic' related to the growth of the centralized absolutist state and the spread of commodity production. Absolutist states arose in the sixteenth and seventeenth centuries in Western Europe under the Tudors in England, the Habsburgs in Spain, and the Bourbons in France. These European dynastic states exhibited many of the institutional features which characterize modern states. The introduction of a standing army, a centralized bureaucracy, a central taxation system, diplomatic relations with permanent embassies, and the development of the economic doctrine of mercantilism informing state trade policy, all date from this period. It is at this point that the term 'the state' is first introduced into political discourse. Although its derivation is disputed, *Machiavelli is often credited with first using the concept of state to refer to a territorial sovereign government in the widely circulated manuscript of the 'Prince' completed in 1513 and published in 1532. It is not, however, until the time of *Bodin and Sir Thomas Smith that a full account of the 'marks of sovereignty' is produced, and later modified by Sir Walter Raleigh, *Hobbes, and *Locke.

The most influential definition of the modern state is that provided by *Weber in *Politics as a Vocation*. Weber emphasizes three aspects of the modern state: its territoriality; its monopoly of the means of physical violence; and its legitimacy. Without social institutions claiming a monopoly of the legitimate use of force within a given territory, Weber argues, a condition of anarchy would quickly ensue. In raising the question of why the dominated obey, Weber draws our attention to a fundamental activity

of the state, the attempt to legitimate the structure of domination. Whilst he supplied the categories of 'traditional', 'charismatic', and 'legal' pure types of legitimation of obedience, historical sociologists have recently drawn on *Durkheim and *Foucault to extend our understanding of legitimacy as state power which 'works within us'. An emphasis is thus placed upon the violent establishment and continuous regulation of 'consent' orchestrated by that organization which has abrogated to itself the 'right' to use physical force (and to determine the conditions under which other institutions/individuals have that right) in society. Whilst, for Foucault, the state is the form in which the bourgeoisie organizes its social power, that power does not simply reside in the external repression meted out by 'special bodies of armed men having prisons, etc., at their command' (*Lenin, *State and Revolution*). Rather, state forms must also be understood as cultural forms, as cultural revolution and imagery continually and extensively state-regulated. Attention is thereby broadened beyond the usual focus on what the state does (defence of property rights, regulation of monopolies), to the equally important question of how the state acts, how it projects certain forms of organization on our daily activity. Studies of the administration of welfare emphasize this point showing how although claimants receive 'benefits' this is always bound up with submission to supervision and control.

There are three main traditions within political science which inform 'theories of the state': the pluralist, the Marxist, and the statist traditions. Robert Dahl and Nelson Polsby within the pluralist framework see the state as either a neutral arena for contending interests or its agencies as simply another set of interest groups. With power competitively arranged in society, state policy is the product of recurrent bargaining and although Dahl recognizes the existence of inequality, he maintains that in principle all groups have an opportunity to pressure the state. The pluralist approach to economic policy suggests that the state's actions are the result of pressures applied from both '*polyarchy' and organized interests. A series of pressure groups compete and state policy reflects the ascendancy of a particularly well-articulated interest. This approach is often criticized for its overt empiricism. It is argued that the attempt to explain state policy in terms of the ascendancy of pressure group interests introduces a pattern of circular reasoning.

Modern Marxist accounts begin with Miliband (*The State in Capitalist Society*), who offers an instrumentalist view of the state. Miliband attempts a literal interpretation of Marx's infamous statement that the executive of the modern state is but a committee for managing the common affairs of the whole bourgeoisie (*The Communist Manifesto*). Instrumentalists argue that the ruling class uses the state as its instrument to dominate society by virtue of the interpersonal ties between, and social composition of, state officials and economic elites. In an equally famous reply, Nicos *Poulantzas isolated the main defects of this approach, in particular its subjectivist view of the state and its unintended reliance on pluralist elite theory. The instrumentalist position has also been criticized empirically by case studies of the New Deal and industrial politics in the United States and by studies of nationalization and the labour process in Britain. For Poulantzas, the state is a regional sector of the capitalist structure, and is understood to have a *relative autonomy from capital: 'the capitalist state best serves the interests of the capitalist class only when the . . . ruling class is not the politically governing class' (*Political Power and Social Classes*). In addition to the problems of *structural functionalism introduced by Poulantzas, the concept of relative autonomy is often criticized as a hopeless catch-all which is used in a circular fashion to explain apparent dysfunctions in state activity after the event.

The realization that the internal structures of states differ has been the dynamic behind the development of post-Marxist approaches to state theory. Whereas there is no uniform agreement on what constitutes Marxian orthodoxy, post-Marxism argues against derivationism and essentialism (the state is not an instrument and does not 'function' unambiguously or relatively autonomously in the interests of a single class). This has led many *Gramscian approaches to stress the importance of interposing *civil society between the economy and the state to explain variation in state forms.

Empirical studies of the role of the state in foreign economic policy-making, and the theoretical critiques developed by post-Marxists, have led to the development of statist theories which conclude that states pursue goals which cannot be derived from interest group bargaining or from the class structure of capitalist societies. A focus has emerged on states as distinctive structures with their own specific histories, operating in a sphere of real autonomy. Writers influenced by this tradition (which claims allegiance to Weber and Otto Hintze) often utilize the distinction between 'strong states' and 'weak states', claiming that the degree of effective autonomy from societal demands determines the power of a state. This position has found favour in *international political economy. Recently, radical feminist writers, and those whose work is rooted in the analysis of racism, have questioned the assumptions of the pluralist, Marxist, and statist approaches arguing that the modern Western state has institutionalized and legitimized patriarchy and racism.

All states embedded in an international system face internal and external security and legitimation dilemmas. International relations theorists have traditionally posited the existence of an international system, where states take into account the behaviour of other 'like-units' when making their own calculations. Recently the notion of international society (a society of states) has been developed to refer to a group of states who by dialogue and common consent have established rules, procedures, and institutions for the conduct of their relations. In this way the foundation has been laid for international law, diplomacy, regimes, and organizations. Since the absolutist period, states have predominantly been organized on a national basis. The concept of national state is not, however, synonymous with nation-state. Even in the most ethnically 'homogeneous' societies there is necessarily a mismatch between the state and the nation—hence the active role undertaken by the state to create national identity (*nationalism) through an emphasis on shared symbols and representations of reality. PBM

state building An approach within the study and practice *international relations, which argues that *peacekeeping is best secured through promoting strong state-based political, economic, and social structures. State building is premised on the idea that order and stability are the foundation for peace and that an authoritative and effective state is required. The approach is often employed in relation to conflict and post-conflict strategies, and acts as a coordinating goal for intervening international actors. State building has underwritten post-conflict rebuilding within *Balkan politics and after the *Afghanistan War and the *Iraq War. Although state-building efforts in the Balkans arguably had some success in keeping peace, in Afghanistan and Iraq peace remains elusive.

state capture 'State capture' obtains when a small number of firms (or such entities as the military) is able to shape the rules of the game to its advantage through massive illicit, and non-transparent provision of private benefits to officials and politicians. Examples of such behaviour include the ability to control legislative votes, to obtain favourable executive decrees and court decisions. A relatively new concept, the main proponents being World Bank researchers, it echoes that of 'crony capitalism' and covers cases where high-level corruption is pervasive. (See MILITARY-INDUSTRIAL COMPLEX; CLIENTELISM.) FV

statecraft The practice of statecraft is the strategic utility of all components of national power to ensure peace and prosperity. The outcome of well-applied statecraft can be greater economic wealth or augmented international security. Practised poorly, the outcome can be conflict and poor governance. Good statecraft can be hindered by a weak civil society, corruption, and a dysfunctional civil service. Statecraft can require the use of traditional military means to coerce other states in the international system into doing something they otherwise would not have done (so-called '*hard power'); cultural or economic levers to persuade states to do something you want them to do (so-called '*soft power'); or a combination of these (which is often referred to as 'smart power'). Contemporary statecraft has become synonymous with 'public diplomacy', whereby states prioritize the communication of their goals using modern information channels such as the Internet to inform, engage, and influence people and governments beyond their borders. A close student of statecraft, Winston Churchill urged that we delve into the past in order to understand the applications of power and their consequences on international relations: 'Study history, study history! In history lies all the secrets of statecraft'. AM

State Department US government department responsible for foreign policy and the diplomatic service.

((⊕)) SEE WEB LINKS
• Site of the US Department of State.

state failure This concept achieved prominence in the 1990s, although states have failed throughout history. In fact, failure might be regarded as history's default setting for states and some of the most theoretically developed work is by archaeologists studying 'state collapse'. Failed states were understood as a by-product of the end of the *Cold War, characterized first by violence (often based on ethnicity), second by manifest failures of governance, and third by territorial fragmentation. These states were problematic because internal conditions made them attractive bases for terrorists or sources of other existential threats, such as pandemic diseases. The term enjoyed considerable popularity amongst academics and policy-makers and was an important part of justifying the limitation of state *sovereignty, *regime change, *humanitarian intervention, *state building, and even *empire. Definitional problems and difficulties in quantifying (let alone predicting) failure ensured that the term attracted heightened criticism in the 2000s. In contrast to the apocalyptic predictions of early analysts, much recent academic and policy work doubts state failure's utility as both an analytical concept and as a guide to policy. The Fund for Peace, for example, recently renamed its annual State *Failure* Index the Fragile States Index. AJT

((⊕)) SEE WEB LINKS
• Fragile States Index.

stateless society A term developed by political anthropologists which draws attention to the fact that 'the *state' has not always been present in human societies. Hunter-gatherer societies founded on the basis of kinship exhibited forms of political organization but they evolved no formal political division of labour or coercive institutions empowered to exercise force over (and rhetorically, on behalf of) the people. There is fierce debate over whether the impetus for the development of the 'pristine' states of the ancient Near East (from which our present-day 'secondary' states emerged) was endogenous, a consequence of the development of social stratification and class relations, or exogenous, resulting from military conquest.

The question posed by surviving stateless societies is: How and why do some non-literate societies manage to survive and cooperate without state coercion or authority? Various answers are given, some of them relying on the power of traditional authority and shared norms. An interesting answer of sorts is the evolutionary one: those stateless societies which have survived are the only ones available for the scholar to study; therefore the characteristics which cause a stateless society to collapse cannot generally be observed unless by chance an anthropologist comes on one in the process of extinction, as happened to Colin Turnbull (*The Mountain People*, 1972), who found the Ik of Uganda in a *Hobbesian state of war of all against all. PBm

state of emergency *See* EMERGENCY POWERS.

state of nature The condition of mankind before a (specified) event, intervention, or artifice. Whether treated as a historical reality or as the result of a mental experiment, the concept of a state of nature has been used to point up various contrasts important to particular writers. For *Hobbes, the state of nature depicted conditions in the absence of political power or authority—in the absence of the artifice of the state. For *Rousseau, the state of nature was associated with man in a pre-social, pre-linguistic world. In Christian thought, man's natural condition was likely to be assimilated to what was thought to be his biblical fate, and the story in Genesis contrasted natural innocence with sinfulness after the Fall. The many meanings of 'natural' in this context embrace a characterization of human nature: for example, the orthodox Christian account saw human

nature after the Fall as inevitably flawed. *See also* CONTRACT; SOCIAL CONTRACT. AR

State of the Union message The US President's annual message to Congress, setting out the administration's policies. The Constitution requires him to give the address, although it does not specify how often.

(●) SEE WEB LINKS

• White House site for the State of the Union message, with text and a webcast of the most recent speech.

States General *See* ESTATES GENERAL.

state socialism The form of socialist organization of production and distribution which is characterized by the control of resources by the organs of the state. In the nineteenth century, two distinct views of future socialist society were expressed. *Saint-Simon would have involved the mobilization of all major economic resources in the hands of a technocratic elite, to be rationally allocated. Robert *Owen contemplated the creation of small socialist communities united only in a fraternal relationship. In the writings of Marx and Engels, the conflict between these two contradictory views was not resolved. While Lenin professed to believe in the communalist form of socialism (his *State and Revolution* is an eloquent expression of this view), he contributed to creating an extreme form of state socialism. This was partly due to the need to defend the revolutionary state against internal resistance, independence movements within the Soviet Union, and external hostility. It was also partly due, however, to Lenin's economic naivety, which led him to a grossly exaggerated confidence in the economies of scale possible in both industry and agriculture, and to the belief that Western corporate management could provide the model for a centralized planned economy. The choice remained open, however, until Stalin disposed of *Bukharin. The issue was dramatically re-opened by Mao *Zedong in 1958, but by then in China as well as in Russia the strength of the state economic apparatus prevented effective change. However, as a result of Mao's influence subsequent economic reform in China under his successors has included a very large local, communal dimension of socialist development, and since 1971 local communal enterprises have been and continue to be the fastest growing sector of the Chinese economy, while creating at the same time the most likely basis for the renewal of a civil society.   JG

states' rights The Tenth Amendment to the US Constitution states: 'The powers not delegated to the United States by the Constitution, nor prohibited by it to the States, are reserved to the States respectively, or to the people.' This was a necessary part of the bargain which brought the United States into existence. The Constitution had to be ratified by at least nine of the then thirteen states. The nine had to include at least some Southern states, and therefore there could be no federal condemnation of slavery in the constitution. So on one interpretation, states' rights became, as it has always remained, an issue between the South and the rest of the country (*see* CALHOUN; LINCOLN). Since the end of the Civil War, the federal government has become more and more involved in states' spheres of influence. This arose in part from the attempt to enforce *civil rights in the Thirteenth to Fifteenth Amendments to the Constitution (ratified between 1865 and 1870). However, federal intervention in states' affairs did not increase significantly until the economic pressures of the *New Deal. The Thirteenth to Fifteenth Amendments were not enforced until the 1950s.

state system The state system (also often referred to as the *international system) refers to a relational formation or pattern of state-based relationships between and amongst states, which as a collective pattern of behaviour creates a measurable and stable condition of order as well as the allowance for mutual expectation and behavioural predictability. In the study of *international relations, the term 'state system' most commonly refers to the formation of mutually recognized state *sovereignty and *self-determination established in the Treaty of Westphalia and the *Westphalian state system.

statism In development studies, statism means the direction and control of economic and social affairs by the state. The practices included: investment in public enterprises; centralized economic planning; the regulation of employment; and other price-distorting interventions in the market. The economic aims are to promote industrialization and protection against foreign competition; politically, the state and the government might gain in domestic legitimacy. Inspired more by nationalism than by socialism, statism is compatible with state capitalism. Since 1980 statism has been challenged by economic liberalism and *structural adjustment reforms. Statism is also referred to as *dirigisme* and *étatisme*. France and Japan were classic statist examples.   PBl

statute law The body of laws passed by the legislature. Statutes may be broadly divided into two. First, Public General Acts—namely, Acts passed by the government of the day or prepared by *private members of Parliament winning a place in the ballot. Second, private Acts of Parliament prepared by private interests such as local authorities or companies. Relatively few private bills ever become law, as there are a number of procedural rules which make any objection to the content of the private bill amenable to rejection of the entire bill.

*Prerogative powers, the residual powers of the Crown, may be abolished by an express statement contained in an Act of Parliament. For example the Crown Proceedings Act 1947 abolished the immunity of the Crown from being sued in tort and contract.

Statutes may take different forms. Some consolidate previous law and provide a comprehensive code of up-to-date law. Others may simply amend or reform the law with technical changes which add to existing statutes and over a period of time build up to a comprehensive set of laws covering a particular subject.

A. V. Dicey's view was that Parliament could not bind itself and consequently Parliament may pass any kind of law whatsoever. The exact nature of Parliament's powers has since 1972 and the entry of the United Kingdom into the European Communities raised questions about the sovereignty of the United Kingdom's Acts of Parliament. In *Factortame* [1991] 3 All ER 769, the Law Lords were prepared to override an Act of the UK Parliament which the *European Court of Justice regarded as inconsistent with European Community (now European

Union) law. Dicey's orthodox view of British sovereignty is obsolete. UK Acts of Parliament are to be read as consistent with EU law. The extent to which there is inconsistency the UK Act may be held to be invalid or inoperative.

The complete collection of UK statutes are published as a whole in the *Statutes at large*. Modern Statute law is comprehensive, technical, and detailed. There is a heavy reliance on additional powers to make subordinate (secondary) legislation which grants further wide powers. This is in contrast to broadly drafted and general legislation favoured in the Victorian era. Statutes are of infinite variety and complexity. Since 1965 the Law Commissions have been charged by Parliament with the responsibility of codifying and simplifying the law. They also attempt to identify and keep under review any out-of-date statutes. A common criticism is that the drafting of statutes is over-elaborate with the result that the meaning is often obscure. JM

Statute of Westminster The Statute of Westminster was approved by the British Parliament in 1931. It gave legal form to a policy declaration made at the Imperial Conference of 1926. This had affirmed the equal status of the mother country and the other recognized Commonwealth nations (or Dominions), namely Australia, Canada, the Irish Free State, New Zealand, and South Africa. Thenceforth the Dominions were in the last resort to be masters of their own destiny in both domestic matters and international affairs. DC

(⊕) SEE WEB LINKS
• Text of the Statute of Westminster.

statutory instruments The principal basis of delegated (or secondary) legislation in the United Kingdom. Their scope and the nature of Parliamentary control (if any) of the legislation made under them is defined by their parent parliamentary Acts (primary legislation). The most significant statutory instruments are subject either to the negative procedure—they come into force unless either House passes a motion to annul—or the affirmative procedure—they do not come into force unless either House passes a motion to approve. A Scrutiny Committee

of both Houses decides upon those statutory instruments which simply may be accepted and not subjected to parliamentary debate. Procedures for the creation of statutory instruments vary for the Scottish parliament and Northern Ireland and Welsh assemblies. JBr

(⊕) SEE WEB LINKS
• The text of all UK statutory instruments from the Office of Public Sector Information.

Stirner, Max (1806–56) German philosopher (real name: Johann Kaspar Schmidt) whose best-known work *The Ego and His Own* (1845) had a lasting influence on nineteenth-century *anarchism, since it elevated the individual (or ego) and his will to a position of supreme importance, with the authority of all social and political institutions being rejected as obstacles to freedom. Stirner was much influenced by the Left or *Young Hegelians who sought to apply the philosophical principles of *Hegel in programmes of political radicalism. In *The German Ideology* (1846), *Marx and *Engels denounced Stirner's extreme *individualism as a contradiction of their own socialist and communist ideas. There was a revival of interest in Stirner's work in the European anarchist movement of the 1890s, and at the same time the nihilistic undertones of Stirner's egocentrism found further expression in the philosophy of *Nietzsche. KT

Stoicism With an initial capital, the word refers to the philosophy of Zeno (*c.*300 BC) and his followers. Stoics believed that the world was determined by necessity; that there is no point in humans' fighting necessity; and that humans should therefore confront it calmly. This last gives the link with the ordinary meaning of the word.

stop-go Characterization of macroeconomic policy, associated primarily with Keynesian methods of demand management during the post-war 'collectivist' period in Britain. Stop-go refers to a specific cycle of expansion and deflation. The stimulation of aggregate demand leads to increased volumes of imports, and a consequent balance of payments deficit. Governments usually responded by depressing demand (rather than devaluing the exchange rate). SW

straight ticket voting See TICKET-SPLITTING.

Strange, Susan (1923–98) British academic in the field of *political economy who is most noted for playing a pivotal role in developing the sub-discipline of international political economy. Her work focused primarily on what she described as the 'power–authority nexus' between political authority and international financial markets. In her work Strange highlights the role that international markets and *globalization play in challenging state authority as well as in incentivizing what she labelled as *casino capitalism.

Strategic Arms Limitation Talks See SALT.

Strategic Arms Reduction Talks See START.

Strategic Defense Initiative (SDI) Refers to United States President Ronald Reagan's programme for protecting the United States from incoming nuclear missiles. Announced during a televised address on defence policy on 23 March 1983, Reagan called for 'space-based defenses' against nuclear attacks on the United Sates. Assigned a special priority, the SDI resulted in the creation of the Strategic Defense Initiative Office (SDIO) in the Department of Defense and became the Pentagon's single most expensive research and development programme, costing some $30 billion. During Reagan's term, the Initiative was hotly debated: it was criticized for its high costs, dubious efficacy, and its potential for undermining the Anti-Ballistic Missile (ABM) Treaty. SDI did not progress very far in the latter part of the Reagan years partly because the initiative ran ahead of the technology; in the late 1990s, however, it resurfaced in the guise of National Missile Defense (NMD). Fear of small nuclear attacks from *rogue states and terrorists made NMD a priority for the George W. Bush administration; in December 2001 the administration gave notice of its intention to pull out of the ABM, thus paving the way for the development and testing of a comprehensive NMD system. YFK

strategic voting See TACTICAL VOTING.

strategy From the Greek, 'generalship'. In game theory, the sense of the distinction between 'strategic' and 'tactical' is retained. A strategy is a plan for dealing with every possible move by the other player(s) at every stage in the game. The number of strategies open to a player in a game of any complexity is astronomical. Even in a trivial game such as noughts-and-crosses (tic-tac-toe) the first player has nine legal opening moves. To each of the second player's eight legal responses the first player has seven legal replies, thus 504 strategies for the first two moves alone, and a total of 20,160 ($9 \times 8 \times 7 \times 6 \times 5 \times 4 \times 3$) strategies for the complete game. Most of these strategies would of course be extremely silly, and many of them are identical because of the rotational symmetry of the game. However, the example shows that analysis of strategies must depend on ruthlessly eliminating all but a tiny number of them. The usual way of doing this is to ask what is the best strategy against the best possible strategy by one's opponent(s). If everybody is playing a strategy such that nobody can better his or her chances by unilateral departure from his or her own strategy, the game is said to be in *equilibrium and the players' strategies are called equilibrium strategies.

strategy-proofness A voting procedure is said to be strategy-proof if it never rewards any voter for pretending that his or her preferences are other than his or her true ones. In the 1970s Allan Gibbard and Mark Satterthwaite independently proved that it was a corollary of Arrow's *impossibility theorem that no fair and non-random procedure was strategy-proof.

Strauss, Leo (1899–1973) Political philosopher, born in Germany. Strauss carried out research at the Academy of Jewish Research in Berlin from 1925, examining the relationship between religion and politics through the works of *Spinoza. Unable to remain in Germany under the Nazi regime, Strauss eventually settled at the University of Chicago. In *Natural Right and History* (1950), Strauss attacked the modernist development of politics, associated with writers such as *Machiavelli, *Rousseau, and *Heidegger. By suggesting that political systems could be constructed which would alter social structures, these authors moved away from a concept of natural right which sought government in accordance with underlying human characteristics. Strauss sought to reassert the virtues of *Greek philosophical thought which worked within the traditions and conventions of communities. Through his rejection of abstract political theorizing, the assertion of the importance of religion as a moral foundation, and his search for systems of natural justice underlying historical development, Strauss emerged as an influential conservative (and *neoconservative) theorist, his reputation bolstered by a generation of his students in the United States.

strict construction(ism) The belief that the interpretation of the US Constitution should be based only on adhering to the 'original intent' of those who drafted the Constitution or the amendment in question. It is not always easy to see how original intent can be found out. *See also* JUDICIAL ACTIVISM.

structural adjustment Industrial restructuring following economic liberalization. Structural and sectoral adjustment programmes initiated as part of *IMF and *World Bank conditional lending require governments to undertake policy reforms intended to stimulate the supply side and improve the public and national finances. Recent years have emphasized the desirability of giving structural adjustment a 'human face', that is mitigating the adverse effects on poverty. With an increase in pro-poor initiatives as part of international development cooperation, the idea of conditionality-based lending has been overtaken by more selective approaches to lending. These require countries to show a commitment to structural adjustment measures already, rather than seeing such lending to them as a way of obtaining promises to undertake this kind of change. PBl

structural functionalism A form of *functionalism—developed from the work of the social anthropologist A. R. Radcliffe-Brown (1881–1955) and systematically formulated by the American sociologist Talcott Parsons (1902–79) (*The Structure of Social Action*)—structural functionalism seeks out the 'structural' aspects of the social system

under consideration, and then studies the processes which function to maintain social structures. In this context, structure primarily refers to normative patterns of behaviour (regularized patterns of action in accordance with norms), whilst function explains how such patterns operate as systems. A recurrent criticism of the structural functionalist view is that functions seem to determine structures, with the consequence that it becomes impossible to derive structure from function in a coherent manner. This tendency of structural functionalist explanation has led to a resurgence of interest in the rival tradition of *structuralism. PBM

structuralism In general terms, the doctrine that the structure of a system or organization is more important than the individual behaviour of its members. Structural inquiry has deep roots in Western thought and can be traced back to the work of Plato and Aristotle. Modern structuralism as a diverse movement-cum-epistemology began with the Swiss linguist Ferdinand de Saussure (1857–1913). In social and political theory, structuralism refers to the attempt to apply methods influenced by structural linguistics to social and political phenomena. Its distinctive methodological claim is that the individual units of any system have meaning only in terms of their relations to each other. Saussure, who did not use the term 'structure', preferring 'system', saw language as a system of signs to be analysed synchronically, that is, studied as a self-sufficient system at one point in time (rather than in historical development). The French social anthropologist Claude Lévi-Strauss introduced Saussure's epistemology to social science, arguing that analysts should develop models to reveal the underlying structural mechanisms which order the surface phenomena of social life. Lévi-Strauss uncovered the 'unconscious psychical structures' which, he thought, underlay all human institutions. Within political science and international studies, structuralism has had an important influence. This is particularly evident in structuralist *Marxism and in critical realist philosophies of social science which often claim that Marx's theory of exploitation is an example of an underlying causal mechanism at work in society.

In international relations, structuralism has two distinct senses. Latin American structuralism refers to influential doctrines developed by *Prebisch and the UN Economic Commission for Latin America (ECLA). Prebisch argued not only for national strategies of import-substituting industrialization but also for regional integration and international cooperation between exporters of primary products. These policies, and the analysis underlying them, became the official doctrine of the Third World through the activities of the United Nations Conference on Trade and Development (UNCTAD), established in 1964 with Prebisch as founding chairman, and need to be carefully distinguished from the far less meliorative neo-Marxist ideas of the Latin American *dependency school.

Secondly, structuralism may refer to the twist given to realist international relations theory by Kenneth *Waltz and *neorealism. Instability and war were less the result of corrupt human nature or poorly constituted states than of changing distributions of power across states in an anarchical international system. Earlier realist explanations that had dwelt on the characteristics of individual states and their leaders were dismissed as reductionist. Debate between structuralists, often assisted by borrowings from microeconomic theories of imperfect competition, centred instead on which was likely to prove the more stable, a bipolar or a multipolar system.   PBM/CJ

structural violence Conceptualizing harm caused by embedded social structures rather than by violent physical acts. Socioeconomic and political factors that disadvantage certain individuals or groups are embedded into the structure of society, and cause harm to those individuals or groups by denying them the same privileges and life chances as the rest of society. It is difficult to pinpoint where the blame lies for this harm because the cause comes from social structures rather than any individual. In a domestic political system, structural violence is present when seemingly neutral decisions are taken (e.g. about healthcare funding) and these decisions have an unequal effect on different groups, with some groups experiencing long-term suffering or death from lack of access to basic medicines or sanitation.

In global politics, structural violence takes place where elites from states and international finance and development organizations implement projects that dispossess native populations of their land, without consultation, recompense, or any benefit from the project itself. Structural violence can lead to physical violence, particularly in fragile societies when other conflict triggers are present, as the oppressed groups try to gain control over the system and structures that cause them harm.   AMB

structuration A social theory which aims to grasp the importance of the concept of action in the social sciences without failing to highlight the structural components of social institutions. The approach was principally developed by the sociologist Anthony Giddens (*Central Problems in Social Theory*), and has become highly influential throughout the social sciences. Drawing upon (whilst attempting to transcend) the traditions of *hermeneutics, *functionalism, and *structuralism, the theory of structuration seeks to reinstate the importance of the concepts of time and space in social and political analysis. Central to structuration is the notion of the duality of structure. All social action consists of practices, located in time–space, which are the skilful, knowledgeable accomplishments of human agents. However, this 'knowledgeability' is always 'bounded' by unacknowledged conditions and unintended consequences of action. Duality of structure therefore attempts to convey the idea that structure is both the medium and outcome of the practices which constitute social systems. The theory of structuration is the latest in a long line of attempts to grapple with one of the central problems in social analysis, the agency–structure dilemma.   PBM

structure/agency Also referred to as the 'structure/agency debate'. In social science this debate revolves around what abilities agents have to make free choices against the structural opportunities or 'pathways' provided to them. For example, most people have a limited or fixed number of choices available, which are determined largely by social structures and the opportunities those structures afford. As a result, the structure/agency debate is about understanding how social structures determine social choice, how structures condition available choice, and what acts of agency are still permitted, even if those choices are conditioned in some way. In political theory, the debate is usually presented as a question between human *autonomy versus social determinism. In reality, the truth lies somewhere in the middle, since in most cases a significant level of free choice is available to people, despite the fact that social conditions limit the range and depth of those choices and that some options remain rationally suboptimal.

structure-induced equilibrium The notion that, as in a complex society majority rule is probably unstable (*see* CYCLE; SPATIAL COMPETITION), the observed stability of political control in many regimes results from institutions which suppress the underlying instability. Institutions which could have this effect include party discipline in the United Kingdom and the procedural rules of Congress in the United States.

Suarez, Francis (1548–1617) Jesuit theologian and philosopher of law, and in particular international law, called by some the last of the great scholastics. The notion of *jus gentium*, the law, recognized and agreed by all peoples, otherwise known as natural law, or, more simply, morality, had been in existence from ancient times. The notion of international law was new. It was generated by the expansion of the known Western world by the explorations of Columbus, Da Gama, and others. Suarez's theory of law is contained in *Tractatus de Legibus ac Deo Legislatore*. For the most part his theory of law is in the Thomist tradition, though he introduces refinements on law and right, natural law and *jus gentium* (which he regards as unwritten law or custom), the relationship between positive and natural law, penal law and conscience, and much else. On international law he drew up conditions for a just war that remain influential. CB

subsidiarity In broad terms, the investment of authority at the lowest possible level of an institutional hierarchy.

The origin of the principle of subsidiarity is in Catholic Social Theory (CST), although similar principles can be found in *Calvinist thought. The purpose of subsidiarity in CST

was, on the one hand, to limit the role of government as a whole in order to vindicate and protect the place of private institutions including the Church itself, while, on the other hand, justifying some role for government. This notion of subsidiarity was enmeshed in an understanding of society as an organism characterized by a hierarchy of organs. Subsequently subsidiarity has been used as a quasi-constitutional concept in some federal or federal-type political systems to provide a rationale for the allocation of powers between various levels of government. Wherever possible, powers are given to the least aggregated level of government; only when a particular task cannot be undertaken adequately by a 'low' level of government will it be handed 'up' to a higher level. It is this conception which is most useful in the analysis of German, Swiss, and *European Union politics, which provide the empirical context for most discussion of subsidiarity. Controversy over subsidiarity in the EU has shown it to be an *essentially contested concept. What to one person is of only local interest, to another is a matter of Union-wide concern. Transport of animals and working conditions are two examples. Although not inevitably incompatible with the CST definition, the use of the notion of subsidiarity in debates about federalism does not necessarily rest on an *organic conception of society, as it focuses exclusively on the institutions of government. DW

subversion A subversion is an overturning or uprooting. The word is present in all languages of Latin origin, originally applying to such diverse events as the military defeat of a city and a severe gastric disorder. But as early as the fourteenth century it was being used in the English language with reference to laws and in the fifteenth century came to be used with respect to the realm. This is the origin of its modern use, which refers to attempts to overthrow structures of authority, including the state. In this respect, it has taken over from 'sedition' as the name for illicit rebellion, though the connotations of the two words are rather different, sedition suggesting overt attacks on institutions, subversion something much more surreptitious, such as eroding the basis of belief in the status quo or setting people against each other.

Recent writers, in the post-modern and post-*structuralist traditions (including, particularly, feminist writers) have prescribed a very broad form of subversion. It is not, directly, the realm which should be subverted in their view, but the predominant cultural forces, such as *patriarchy, individualism, and scientific rationalism. This broadening of the target of subversion owes much to the ideas of *Gramsci, who stressed that communist revolution required the erosion of the particular form of 'cultural hegemony' in any society. LA

successive voting 1. A voting procedure (used, for instance, in the Norwegian parliament) in which the available proposals can be ranked in some natural order (for instance, by the amount which they propose to spend). Each is then compared with the status quo in succession starting with one of the extremes. Voting continues until an option wins a majority against the status quo.

2. The term is sometimes used to denote refinements of majoritarian or proportional voting procedures which elect candidates to some multimember body in a ranked order, so that the most popular qualifies for the best position, the second-most popular for the second-best position, and so on.

Suez crisis On 26 July 1956 the President of Egypt, Jamal Abd al-Nasir, announced that his government was nationalizing the Suez canal. The action was a response to the withdrawal of an offer by Britain and the United States to fund the building of the Aswan Dam, and led to a joint military attack on Egypt by Britain, France, and Israel.

Anthony Eden, the British Prime Minister, feared Nasir's brand of Arab nationalism, and harboured a deep personal dislike of Nasir, seeing him as a new Hitler. Eden wanted Nasir overthrown, and believed that a military operation to take control of the canal would enable this. However, the action of the Egyptian government was not against international law, and so the British and French had to find a *casus belli*. This led to the secret involvement with Israel, who offered to invade the Sinai Peninsula, and advance towards the Suez region, giving the British and French the excuse that shipping through the canal was at risk, and invasion necessary to protect it.

The Israelis attacked Egypt on 30 October, and British forces landed in Egypt on 4 November. Militarily the operation was successful, but politically it was a disaster. It was glaringly obvious that the grounds stated for the invasion were spurious, and merely an excuse for military action. This led to a schism between Britain and the United States, with President Eisenhower opposed to any military action. The United States invoked intense diplomatic pressure, and when Britain faced a run on the pound which threatened reserves, the United States withheld assistance until a military withdrawal was complete.

Faced with the humiliation caused by the failure of the Suez campaign Anthony Eden was forced to retire as Prime Minister. In France the failure was blamed on British and American duplicity, and was a factor in the collapse of the Fourth Republic in 1958. Israel was forced to withdraw from Sinai. Nasir became the hero of Arab opposition to the West. Although Eden's successor, Harold Macmillan, managed to restore Anglo-American relations, the Suez crisis symbolized Britain's reduced status in the post-war world, and the economic power of America.

suffrage Originally meaning prayers, especially for the souls of the departed, the senses relating to the right to vote emerged in the sixteenth century. In ancient Greek democracy, the qualifications to vote were not much discussed, as democracy depended more on the principle of random selection than on voting. From the emergence of modern democratic thought until the late nineteenth century, almost every commentator, radical as well as conservative, linked suffrage to property and accepted that only those who held some minimum amount of property should be allowed to vote. Universal suffrage had to await the supersession of that view. Universal male suffrage was introduced in the French constitution of 1793 and was in force in most countries which called themselves democracies by 1918 (the year in which it arrived in Britain). Enfranchisement of women was much slower. Universal adult suffrage arrived in Britain in 1928 and in Switzerland in 1971. In the United States it arrived in theory in 1920. However, the massive disenfranchisement of black citizens in the South, for federal as well as state and local elections, was not reversed until the court and legislative actions that culminated in the Voting Rights Act 1965.

suffragette Militant campaigner for the right of women to vote. After J. S. *Mill tried to introduce a motion for universal suffrage in the Second Reform Bill of 1867, societies agitating for extension of the franchise to women were formed, but the 'suffragists' had little success in persuading MPs to allow women to vote. In 1903 Emily *Pankhurst founded the Women's Social and Political Union, which instead of the peaceful means practised by the suffragists, advocated more violent methods, including demonstrations, disruption of House of Commons debates and public meetings, and the destruction of property. Pankhurst's 'suffragettes' stepped up agitation after the failure of legislation to enfranchise women in 1911, with increasingly violent measures, and, when imprisoned, resorted to hunger strike. In 1913 Emily Davison killed herself at the Derby by throwing herself under the King's horse.

Whether the suffragettes' campaign succeeded is debatable, and their violent methods alienated moderate supporters. Far more important in the move to female suffrage was the liberating effect of the First World War, which proved women were capable of the same work as men, and was quickly followed by the 1918 Representation of the People Act, giving the vote to women over the age of 30.

suffragist One who seeks extension of the franchise especially to women. In the UK between 1900 and 1918 the term was distinguished from *suffragette* on the basis that a suffragette was prepared to use direct action, whereas a suffragist was not.

Sunni Sunni, or Sunnite, refers to those Muslims in the majority trend in Islam. Sunnism and *Shi'ism split on the question of succession and the appropriate method of choosing a leader. The Sunni accepted the legitimacy of the first four Caliphs (successors to the Prophet). They would then accept as leader anyone from Muhammad's tribe, according to the consensus of the Umma or by the *ahl as-shura* as representatives of the Umma. Later, in effect, whoever became the leader by whatever route was acceptable to the Sunni. In the Shi'i tradition, Ali was seen as the successor to Muhammad.

The core beliefs of Muslims are based on the Qur'an and *sunna* of the Prophet Muhammad and centrally concern God, Muhammad, and the Umma. By the eleventh century, five hundred years after the Hijra (622, the flight of the Prophet and his followers from Mecca to Medina), a consensus on these beliefs emerged. Beyond these core beliefs, within Sunni Islam, is a diversity of interpretations and perspectives. While indicating what is meant by this diversity, it should be remembered that Islam is strictly monotheistic. The Qur'an is clear about God and his Oneness. As to the question about the relationship between God and man, the Qur'an is ambiguous. Exploring the oneness of God and His relationship with man, the Sunni focus on the 'immanence of God' or the 'transcendence of God'. One response to the ambiguity is the Sufi (mystic) tradition which expresses a yearning for personal communion with, and love for, God. In contrast, the answer to this and less crucial questions which the Qur'an did not answer was found in *hadith* which were used to elaborate the silent or ambiguous areas of the Qur'an. In this way, the *sunna* of the Prophet became a source of law. A legalistic response resulted from the search for answers or enlightenment from the sacred sources which produced a diversity of schools of law or more precisely, methods, doctrines, and schools of thought (*madhhab* (*madhahib*, pl.) *Madhahib* were networks of colleagues, masters, and disciples around the doctrines of a great Imam. These doctrines evolved through a constant interplay with politics. Eventually, these *madhahib* were reduced to the four that were equally accepted by all Sunnis. These *madhahib* elaborated and interpreted Islamic Law—the Shari'a.

The Hanafi *madhhab* uses reason and analogy based firmly on orthodoxy. It allows the use of subjective opinion and customary law, which made it more flexible and was also accommodating to secular needs (the Hanafi *madhhab* was officially recognized by Ottoman and Moghul Empires and other major states). The Maliki *madhhab*, which rejected rational interpretation of the

Qur'an though it allows reasoning by analogy as long as the public good is not injured, is dominant in much of Africa. The Shafi'i *madhhab* indicates a methodology (*usul al-fiqh* or roots of jurisprudence) whereby *ijtihad* (independent reasoning applied to legal interpretation of the sacred sources) can be safely utilized. It also recognized the validity of analogy via this methodology. This methodology influenced the other *madhahib* found in Africa, along the Arabian coastline, southern India, Indonesia. The Hanbali *madhhab* adheres to strict observance of the terms of the Qur'an and *sunna* with limited scope for *ijtihad* or analogy, and to this *madhhab* belong, Muhammad b. Abd al-Wahhab (1703–92), and through emphasis on the work of an earlier Hanbali, Ibn Taymiyya (1328d). Al-Wahhab focused on a recommitment to the Qur'an, Prophet and His Companions, and a strong commitment to anti-saint worship and anti-Sufism. Wahhabism became predominant in Saudi Arabia and Qatar. However, in Saudi Arabia, the other *madhahib* can be utilized where the Hanbali *madhhab* is silent.

Thus within Sunni Islam, there is a set of central core beliefs from which radiates a very diverse set of contrasting responses and institutions. *See also* SHI'I; ISLAMIC POLITICS; ISLAMIC FUNDAMENTALISM; ISIS; FATWA.   BAR

Sun Yatsen (1866–1925) The best-known early leader of the Chinese nationalist revolution, Sun was born into a poor peasant family in the southern province of Guangdong. At the age of 13 he joined an older brother in Hawaii, where he was educated in Western schools, from which he went to Hong Kong and took a medical degree. Concerned at the decay of China, he formed a small society, The Revive China Society (*Xing Zhong Hui*), which was reformist and moderate. However, the destruction of the 1898 Reform Movement and the execution of some of its leaders by the Manchu Empress Dowager, led Sun and many other Chinese to turn to revolution. He formed a new group, the Alliance Society (*Tongmeng Hui*). Support for this spread from the Chinese emigrant communities to the southern secret societies and then to young Chinese intellectuals, notably those studying in Japan. Meanwhile attempted reforms by the Manchus actually reduced Chinese as

opposed to Manchu power, so that disaffection spread to the Chinese gentry. In 1911, after ten failed risings organized by Sun and his followers, the eleventh succeeded. The Manchus abdicated and a Republic was proclaimed. Sun was elected provisional president, but was soon succeeded by Yuan Shikai, a much better known and acceptably conservative figure.

With the imperial focus of loyalty gone, China fell to pieces. Sun's task was to reunite the country, and to do so (as he perceived it) by the creation of a nationalist democracy. In 1923, in despair of assistance from the Western powers, he turned to the Soviet Union. He made an alliance with the new Communist Party of China (then minuscule, but backed by Russia), reconstituted his party on Leninist lines, and adopted a radical programme. He died in 1925 with China still fragmented among the warlords, but he had created a new climate of opinion and new political aims and expectations. Both Nationalists and Communists claim his inheritance.

His political ideas and programme were expressed in a series of published lectures called the *Three Principles of the People* (nationalism, democracy, and livelihood), and in his *Plan for National Reconstruction*. He was not a systematic philosopher. His ideas were often contradictory. He argued that the Western ideas of liberty and equality were not relevant to Chinese society in its existing state. As China (he believed) had not suffered from extremes of autocracy, liberty was not demanded. China's problem was too much liberty, by which he meant that the Chinese people were free to ignore appeals to national solidarity: 'on no account must we give more liberty to the individual; let us instead secure liberty for the nation'. He argued similarly that China did not demand equality; she had no aristocracy, few big landlords and few capitalists. In China, he said, there were no rich and poor, only poor and poorer. Yet he professed to be committed to democracy and even proposed the rights of recall, initiative, and referendum. He put forward a programme for the development of democracy, under tutelage, beginning with the village and culminating in the eventual creation of a national parliament.

He deplored Communism as expressing only 'the pathology of a particular society', but at the same time insisted that his Principle of Livelihood was 'practical Communism', and his plans for the economic reconstruction of China were fairly radical. The profits of expanding urban land values would be invested in state-sponsored industry, while lower rural rents and better security of tenure would prepare the way for the redistribution of land. On Chinese culture, he professed to believe that China's morality was on a higher level than that of the West, but admitted that the Chinese had been 'less active in matters of performance' than the foreigners.

Sun's successor Chiang Kai-shek, a traditionalist soldier who encouraged China's Blue Shirt fascists, made no serious attempt to apply Sun's ideology until he was chastened by defeat and confined to Taiwan. There land reform with compensation for the landlords, state control of upstream industry, and inducement planning of private enterprise, combined with a one-party system which while oppressive towards individuals was very responsive to peasant interests, produced an economic miracle—the more miraculous because rapid growth was most unusually accompanied by a rapid diminution of inequalities in income. Sun's ideas seemed vindicated, and this was not lost on the many Chinese of all communities who have always found Sun's modernization of tradition more comfortable than the repudiation of tradition in favour either of communism or Western democracy. Sun's Three Principles have life in them still. JG

supergame A series of repetitions of the same game between (among) the same players. Especially in *Prisoners' Dilemma and *chicken games, the supergame is important because it may (but need not) result in the cooperative equilibrium that rational players fail to reach in the single-shot (one-off) game. A well-known application of the prisoners' dilemma supergame is R. Axelrod, *The Evolution of Co-operation* (1984). Axelrod suggests that such phenomena as the live-and-let-live agreement between Allied and German troops on the Western Front in the First World War, and some forms of cooperation among animals, may be regarded as supergame equilibria.

Super PAC *See* PAC (USA).

superpower In its *generic* use, the term refers to those few states with power (defined by combining a series of variables together— e.g. economic wealth, population size, and above all, military strength, especially in the possession of sophisticated nuclear armaments) far transcending that of the rest of the states in the international arena. More specifically, the term refers to the two states, the United States and the Soviet Union, in the time of the *Cold War. After the Second World War, the United States and the Soviet Union emerged as the two leading powers, first in Europe, then, in the rest of the world, as the two powers competed against each other for influence in the global politics of the Cold War. It is widely conceded that in the aftermath of the Cold War there remains only one superpower, the United States; commentators have also coined the terms 'unipolar power' and 'hyper power' to describe the United States' post-Cold War power position. YFK

superstructure *See* BASE/SUPERSTRUCTURE.

supply side The side of an economy which determines how many goods are supplied at any given price. The supply side interacts with the demand side to produce an exact price and quantity at which the market exactly clears, with neither shortages of goods nor unplanned surpluses of them. (Neo)classical economists believe that most markets do clear in practice if the right political institutions exist; other schools including *Keynesians and *Marxists disagree. 'Supply-side policies' denote policies designed to make markets less sticky and more liable to clear. For instance, neoclassicists argue that the market for labour is often sticky because institutions such as national wage bargaining and statutory minimum wages prevent some bargains from being struck which, left to themselves, a worker with low earning potential and an employer seeking such a worker would strike. 'Loosening the supply side' means removing restrictions of this sort. Those who are opposed to it politically call it by less neutral names.

supranationalism Refers to the formal transfer of legal authority and decision-making power from member states to an institution or international body. In this context

Moravcsik distinguishes between 'pooled sovereignty' when governments agree to make future decisions by voting procedures other than unanimity; and 'delegated sovereignty' when supranational actors are given the authority to take certain sorts of decisions without either a vote amongst affected governments or the capacity of states to veto the decision. Although often used loosely to describe any set of institutions 'above the state', the term refers more properly to a particular characteristic of international institutions and international legal authority. The clearest examples of supranational institutions can be found in the European Union, where the Commission, the European Parliament, and the European Court of Justice, constitute common political structures with supranational authority—in contrast to the Council of Ministers, which is based on intergovernmental modes of decision-making.

Supranational institutions played a key role in neofunctionalist accounts of European integration. Neofunctionalists argued that high and rising levels of interdependence and cross-border exchange would generate increasing demands for the creation of supranational institutions to solve common problems. This, in turn, would catalyse a process of ever expanding collaboration between member states, leading eventually to political integration. More recently, theorists have challenged intergovernmental accounts of European integration both by highlighting the formally supranational components of the European Union but also by challenging the view that member-states have simply delegated certain powers for particular purposes and, as principals, remain in full control of an increasingly complex set of institutions and integration processes.   AHU

supraterritoriality A term largely associated with *globalization denoting the erosion of bounded state legal jurisdictions and/or the expansion of institutional legal authority across borders. As one example, a state is argued to have supraterritoriality when it can prosecute its own citizens or corporations even if they are no longer residing within the immediate territory of the state. In this example, various legal jurisdictions are blurred, since both the host state and the prosecuting state have transformed the

subjects and objects of claims to authority. The term is also often used to denote the ongoing erosion of trade and economic barriers between states as well as the abdication of state authority to *supranationalism and *transnational organizations, such as the *European Commission or *World Trade Organization.

supreme court A final court of appeal. The best-known example is the United States Supreme Court; there are also American state supreme courts, although in some cases they are named differently. Article III of the US Constitution provides for a supreme court at the apex of the federal judiciary while leaving to Congress the establishment of lower federal courts. The number of US Supreme Court justices has varied between five and ten, but has remained at nine since 1869. Justices are appointed by the President with the advice and consent of the Senate. These are lifetime appointments subject to good behaviour. Only one Supreme Court judge has ever been impeached, and he was acquitted, in 1805. The *original jurisdiction of the Court is very narrow in scope and it operates almost entirely as a court of appeal. Principally through its exercise of *judicial review the Supreme Court, from time to time, appears to assume great power and to become effectively a maker of public policy. However, the Court is also constrained by the checks and balances of the Constitution. Thus the appellate jurisdiction of the Supreme Court is determined by act of Congress, as is the structure of the federal judiciary and the number of federal judges. The Court has no means of enforcing its decisions. As *Alexander Hamilton observed in *The Federalist*, no. 78, the federal judiciary is the 'least dangerous' branch, possessing 'neither force nor will but merely judgment; and must ultimately depend upon the aid of the executive arm for the efficacy of its judgments'.

In the United Kingdom the court of final appeal (supreme court in the general sense) is the *House of Lords in its judicial capacity; but the Supreme Court as defined by the Judicature Act 1873 comprises the High Court and the Court of Appeal. In order to more clearly separate the role of the House of Lords as a legislative and judicial body, the

S

Constitutional Reform Act 2005 provided for the creation of a new UK Supreme Court, due to start work in October 2009. It will assume the jurisdiction of the current Appellate Committee of the House of Lords and the devolution jurisdiction of the Judicial Committee of the Privy Council.   DM

(((●))) SEE WEB LINKS

• United States Supreme Court site, including Constitutional background and information on rulings.

Supreme Soviet Until the creation of the *Congress of People's Deputies, the Supreme Soviet was formally the highest legislative body in the Soviet state. In practice, it was a merely symbolic institution until democratization in 1989, at which time it became a forum for serious debate and a check on government activity.   swh

surplus value A key concept within Marxist analysis that denotes the surplus labour (S) expended by a worker which is in excess of the necessary labour or variable capital (V) required to satisfy basic subsistence requirements. It is the ratio between necessary and surplus labour that Marx calls the rate of exploitation or rate of surplus value (S/V). The origin of surplus value is the labour power, the capacity to work, expended by the worker in the production process. The capitalist realizes this when the commodity is sold on the market and the surplus value takes the form of profit. Marx denoted two ways in which surplus value is extracted. Absolute surplus value refers to the way capitalists attempt to lengthen the working day and thereby increase surplus labour. Relative surplus value involves reducing necessary labour whilst still making the worker labour the full working day. This can be done through productivity increases by making people work harder or expelling labour and introducing machinery into the production process.   IF

survey research In 1936 the *Literary Digest* forecast that Franklin D. Roosevelt would lose that year's US presidential election. The forecast was based on some 2 million polls returned by telephone and car owners. Simultaneously some of the first *Gallup polls, having sampled only around

2,000 people, were correctly predicting that Roosevelt would win by a landslide. The *Literary Digest* poll failed because telephones and cars, in 1936, mostly belonged to the rich, who mostly opposed Roosevelt: thus it had an incorrect 'sampling frame'. In statistical theory a sample is *representative of a population if, and only if, each member of the population had an equal probability of being selected for the sample. The rigorous way to achieve a representative sample is to get a list of the eligible population (such as the electoral register, for voting samples), and select every (P/n)th member of the population, where P is the size of the population and n is the desired sample size. In practice most surveys use the rough-and-ready 'quota' method, in which the interviewer is instructed to interview the correct proportion of each principal social and demographic group in the population.

If a sample is correctly drawn, the laws of statistics enable us to predict how close its distribution of the trait being examined (such as voting intention) is to the unknown distribution of that trait in the population from which it is drawn. The form of this prediction is always that there is a high probability (usually 95 or 99 per cent) that the sample distribution varies by not more than a small proportion (typically 1 or 3 per cent) on either side of the true distribution. Headline writers, who typically overinterpret small shifts in voting intentions revealed by successive polls, insufficiently understand this form. One remedy is to take a 'poll of polls' including all the reputable polls taken at roughly the same time, and pool their results for the best available forecast of voting intentions.

The surveys of most interest to political science are not those of voting intention ('If there were a general election tomorrow, how would you vote?'; but every respondent knows there will not be), but rather those which tap attitudes and behaviour at deeper levels. Nationwide election surveys which have run continuously since 1952 in the United States and since 1963 in Britain have built up a full picture of why people vote in the ways that they do. The earlier surveys were held to justify the *Michigan school's picture of the electorate as ill-informed and responding more to their inherited 'party identification' than to the issues. More recent work suggests that voters are closer to the *rational choice school's image of people who choose the party which is closest to offering them what they want; current analysis accepts that both schools of thought have a valid contribution to make towards understanding what makes voters tick.

Survey research underpins almost all good empirical work on large populations in political science and sociology, as there is no other way of making reliable generalizations about them (which does not deter many self-confident people from making unreliable ones).

sustainable development Concept that stresses the balance between the interests of economic growth and environmental protection; emphasizing the importance of inter-generational transfers, the preservation of non-renewable resources, and a variety of loosely defined principles regarding the responsibilities and accountability of policy makers. Essentially a reiteration of the principles of *cost-benefit analysis with a full recognition of the *externalities involved in policy implementation, with an ecological veneer. *See also* SDGs (SUSTAINABLE DEVELOPMENT GOALS).

swing A measure of the change between one election result and the next. As originally defined and used by D. E. Butler, 'swing' was the average of the winning party's gain in share of the vote and the losing party's loss. This formula, while a valuable summary measure that is still in daily use, suffers from two problems:

1 It is hard to apply when more than two parties are in contention. Perhaps for this reason it has been little used for electoral analysis outside Britain, the United States, and Australasia.

2 It averages percentages of one thing (the vote shares at the first election) with percentages of another (the vote shares at the second). So what is the resulting percentage figure a percentage of?

Ingenious but cumbersome ideas of triangular swing have been put forward to deal with the first problem (but how do you summarize four-party movement, for instance in Scotland?) The second problem leads statisticians to eschew 'swing' altogether. Matrix measures of electoral change could be

substituted in the (rare) cases where details are available of every flow from one behaviour at the first election to another at the second. But no handy summary measure has been suggested.

syndicalism A doctrine of socialist transformation rooted in an emphasis on the role of the trade union (*syndicat* in French) as an agent of revolutionary class struggle. It spread rapidly in Europe, North and South America, and Australia between about 1895 and the mid-1920s. The general strike was considered to be the great weapon of syndicalist revolution, and was seen to be potentially more effective than the parliamentary route to socialism or the political overthrow of the state in establishing a new social order based on *workers' control. The anti-statist and anti-political tendency of syndicalism suggests strong similarities with *anarchism (hence the use of the term '*anarcho-syndicalism'). Amongst the many thinkers who contributed directly to the development of syndicalist theory, Georges *Sorel and Daniel de Leon (one of the founders of America's Industrial Workers of the World, 1905) were particularly important. KT

Syrian Civil War/Syrian Crisis The continued civil conflict in Syria between allies loyal to Syrian President Bashar al-Assad and numerous rebel groups seeking to either remove Assad's government by force and/or to gain separatist control of potions of Syria. The civil war was triggered by governmental responses to the *Arab Spring in 2011, in which protesters in various Syrian cities (primarily Aleppo, Damascus, Daraa, and Homs) demanded democratic reforms from Assad as well as the release of a number of political dissidents held in prison. In June 2011, as tensions increased, armed resistance and large-scale violence against Assad began in earnest with the burning of Assad's *Ba'ath Party headquarters and increased deadly clashes with police in several Syrian cities. Most significantly, as Assad's tactics increased in severity and Assad's authority waned, a group of seven military officers defected from Assad's regime, organizing themselves into the Free Syrian Army (FSA). In response to these events Assad launched a series of harsh police and military operations to regain control of key cities,

s

which quickly escalated on 31 July into the 'Ramadan Massacre', killing 142 people. Continued violence and diminished governmental authority led to the forming of a number of armed resistance and separatist groups. Each of these groups either formed loose *alliances with other anti-government militias against Assad or fought in opposition to any group unwilling to cede them control of specific territories or resources.

The main factions within the civil war include Assad's Syrian government and strategic allies (Russia, Hezbollah, Iran, and recently Iraq); the Free Syrian Army (FSA) and allied Sunni militia; the Kurdish Syrian Democratic Forces (SDF); the Salafi Jihadists (mainly the al-Nusra Front); and the Islamic State of Iraq and Syria (*ISIS—also known as Daesh, or the Islamic State of Iraq and the Levant: ISIL). These groups, and their foreign allies, have carved up Syria into militia-controlled zones. From March 2012, major insurgencies and military operations were underway in Homs, Damascus, Aleppo, and Eastern parts of Syria, as ISIS captured more territory and claimed its territory as a new Islamic Caliphate and Islamic state. Violence across Syria continues.

Despite a number of ceasefires brokered between Syria, Russia, the USA, Turkey, Iran, and the various rebel groups, peace remains elusive, with the civil war death toll estimated in 2016 to be approximately 400,000 people. Additionally, the continued war in Syria has caused a humanitarian crisis in key Syrian cities, where civilian populations live under heavy artillery fire (even chemical attack) and lack basic resources for subsistence. In addition to the rise in the death toll, the Syrian conflict triggered a *refugee crisis, with 4.8 million refugees leaving Syria for Lebanon, Turkey, Jordan, and Europe. According to the *United Nations, the ongoing crisis has also caused another 6.6 million internally displaced persons unable to return to their homes due to continued conflict.

At the time of writing, the Syrian Civil War remained a stalemate, with no one side powerful enough to regain control of the country and to exert political authority. In addition, the violence in Syria continues to destabilize the region and the *international system, with the crisis causing escalated political and military tensions between Turkey, Iraq, Iran, the SDF, the USA, and Russia. The civil strife and stalemate has been enhanced in Syria via US bombings of ISIS in the east, as well as Russian and Turkish aerial bombings in western and northern Syria. Lastly, there remains little agreement within the United Nations or its *Security Council on how to end the humanitarian and security crisis. This threatens to prolong the conflict as well as increase the humanitarian disaster in Syria into the foreseeable future. *See* RESPONSIBILITY TO PROTECT.

systems analysis Systems theory takes the political or social system as the proper unit of analysis. It was introduced to sociology and politics principally by Talcott Parsons (*The Structure of Social Action*, 1937; Parsons and Shils, *Toward a General Theory of Social Action*, 1951), and by David Easton (*The Political System*, 1953). Parsons, for instance, spoke of a social system as containing four subsystems, devoted to 'adaptivity', 'goal-seeking', 'integration', and 'latency', which relate respectively to the economy, politics, society, and the family. Both Parsons and Easton were influenced by biologists' models of ecological systems.

Except for its cousin *world systems analysis, systems analysis is no longer taken seriously. Its terms were too vaguely defined and its relationship with empirical evidence was too haphazard; it was never clear what would count as a test, still less a *falsification, of systems theory. However, systems theory did stress, however obscurely, some truths that have been periodically rediscovered since *Aristotle: especially that taking the individual as the unit of analysis misses interactions which can only be explained by reference to 'society'. Not many individualists are so extreme as to believe that 'there is no such thing as society' in the words of Margaret Thatcher.

tacit consent *See* CONSENT.

tactical voting In a *first-past-the-post electoral system a vote is tactical when it is cast for a candidate that the voter believes is more likely to win than their preferred candidate, to best influence who wins in the constituency. The classic example involves a supporter of a party placed third or lower in the constituency choosing to vote for one of the front-runners because they are wary of 'wasting' their vote. The wasted-vote logic is sometimes referred to as 'Duverger's psychological effect' and is one of the factors that is thought to drive *Duverger's law. Formal *rational choice theory shows us that it is not necessarily utility-maximizing to desert third or lower placed parties. Someone indifferent between the two front-runners will have little incentive to vote tactically for either of them. Also, tactical voting is not simply about voting against the incumbent, the most likely winner, or even the most disliked party. Although it often involves these things, people can vote tactically for the incumbent party even when the most disliked party is likely to come last. In recent general elections in Britain between 1987 and 2005, between 5 and 10 per cent of voters are estimated to have voted tactically. Perhaps as many as forty seats in 1997, 2001 and 2005 were lost by the Conservatives as a result, although not all tactical voting is anti-Conservative.

There are also strategic incentives to misrepresent one's preferences in other electoral systems (*see* GIBBARD–SATTERTHWAITE THEOREM). Typically they are much weaker and the frequency of strategic behaviour is correspondingly lower. Whilst the terms tactical voting and strategic voting are synonymous, sophisticated voting generally refers to behaviour in (particularly US Congressional) committees where there are defined agenda rules and legislators vote in a sequence of decisions. SF

Taliban *See* AFGHANISTAN WAR (2001).

Tamil Tigers Guerrilla and terrorist group in Sri Lanka fighting between 1983 and 2008 for a separate Tamil state against the majority Sinhalese community.

Tawney, R. H. (1880–1962) *Fabian socialist who achieved considerable reputation as both historian and social theorist. His *Religion and the Rise of Capitalism* (1926) examined the controversy between followers of *Marx and those of *Weber about whether capitalism explained Protestantism or vice versa. Tawney supported Weber, in so far as he argued that Protestant capitalism had a special character and was responsible for the development of modern Western society. His *Equality* (1931) was an influential book in developing the social objectives of the Labour Party. In that he believed that the 1944 Education Act and steeply progressive taxation would do much to enhance the 'life chances' of the least privileged in society, he can be said to represent a form of socialism which later became disreputable. But he also used to ask, 'Do the English still prefer to be governed by Old Etonians?', rhetorically suggesting the kind of opening of government to a wider social circle which has proved more persistent than socialism. LA

Taylor, Harriet (née Hardy) (1807–58) Feminist writer. Married in 1826 to a wholesale trader, John Taylor, through whom she soon met J. S. *Mill and became his companion. She married Mill in 1851 after her husband's death. They lived a lonely and ascetic life, having quarrelled with all their friends, but devoted themselves to providing 'mental pemmican' (preserved dried meat) for 'thinkers, when there are any after us'. This gloomy picture should be set against Mill's wholehearted praise for 'her who was the inspirer, and in part the author, of all that is best in my writings'. He stated that she was responsible for the chapter 'The Probable Future of the Labouring Class' in his *Principles of Political Economy* (1848). Her 'The Enfranchisement of Women' was published in 1851 under Mill's name. The intellectual partnership of the Mills is very like that of the *Condorcets, and has the common feature that contemporaries blamed the husband's commitment to feminism on the wife.

Taylorism *See* FORDISM.

Tea Party movement A political movement in the United States known for its conservative *reactionary views and 'alternative-right' (or 'alt-right') populist antagonisms within the *Republican Party and against the *Democratic Party. The main platforms of the Tea Party generally align with Christian values, lower taxes, smaller government, *hawkish foreign policy, *patriotism, anti-immigration, and anti-US President Barack Obama, as well as a dislike for the 'liberal media'. Although members of the Tea Party are more diverse than generally suggested, it is made up of largely white lower-middle-class Americans who claim to be frustrated with 'politics as usual'. The main political implication of the Tea Party has been its ability to alter the Republican political agenda as well as in mobilizing a *populist movement for the election of Donald J. Trump as US President in 2016.

television and politics The BBC opened a television service for the London area in 1936, first broadcasting from Alexandra Palace on 2 November. Widespread access to a medium which could accurately communicate both sounds and images must be assumed to have a considerable effect on political relations. For example, in democratic theory, at least some of the orthodox idea of a representative's role becomes irrelevant in circumstances in which national leaders can be seen or heard in nearly everybody's living room. The early period of mass television did produce observations of 'Caesarist' or 'Bonapartist' tendencies as politicians sought a direct relationship with the electorate. Harold Macmillan (British Prime Minister 1957–63), Charles de Gaulle (French President 1958–68), and John Kennedy (US President 1960–63) were all national leaders thought to have

succeeded by adapting to the 'television age'. Many people believed that Kennedy had won his narrow victory over Richard Nixon in 1960 because his 'clean-cut' image in television debate compared favourably with Nixon's 'five o'clock shadow'.

Early liberal fears of totalitarianism, such as those expressed by *Russell and *Orwell, tended to assume that television would prove a mighty mechanism for thought control by the established powers. But much research suggested that most people formed the core of their beliefs and values at an early stage of their lives through family influences and were capable of treating television very selectively, paying close attention only to ideas and evidence which confirmed their existing views. Counter-arguments have suggested that television is more important than this because it does tend to structure images, agendas, and beliefs in various ways, and that those ways function generally to support acceptance of the status quo.

From the 1980s onwards the political nature of television began to change rapidly. States increasingly abandoned their attempts to be monopoly providers of what was on the airwaves and to control what their populations were able to watch. This was partly because of political changes including the collapse of Communist regimes, but it was also the case that each technological change which occurred, including video and disc technology and the spread of the internet, made control more difficult. Global television companies such as CNN, the Murdoch empire, and Al-Jazeera were able to offer images across a variety of borders so that what people watched was increasingly determined by individual choice or community fashion rather than by the state whose boundaries they were within. By the twenty-first century the mid-twentieth-century liberal nightmare of a totalitarian state controlling the images and opinions its population could access was being replaced by fears of the power that new technologies were giving to private, 'extremist' organizations. LA

Tenth Amendment *See* CIVIL RIGHTS; STATES' RIGHTS.

terrorism Term with no agreed definition among governments or academic analysts, but almost invariably used in a pejorative sense, most frequently to describe life-threatening actions perpetrated by politically motivated self-appointed sub-state groups. But if such actions are carried out on behalf of a widely approved cause, say the Maquis seeking to destabilize the Government of Vichy France, then the term 'terrorism' is usually avoided and something more friendly is substituted. In short, one person's terrorist is another person's freedom fighter.

Terrorism as a pejorative term is sometimes applied, however, to the deeds of governments rather than to those of sub-state actors. The term 'state terror' is, for example, frequently applied to the actions of officially appointed groups such as the Gestapo, the KGB, the Stasi of East Germany, and the like, against dissidents or ethnic minorities among their own fellow citizens. And the term 'state-sponsored terrorism' is often used to describe the conduct of various governments in directly organizing or indirectly assisting perpetrators of violent acts in other states. But in practice this might be said to be simply a form of low-intensity undeclared warfare among sovereign states. In recent times many countries of divergent ideological persuasion have engaged in this kind of activity while in some cases strictly condemning others for the same practices. For example, the United States during the Presidency of Ronald Reagan denounced many regimes, most notably that of Libya, in this connection while simultaneously openly sponsoring sub-state violence against Nicaragua with whose government it had full diplomatic relations. Such apparent inconsistency should not perhaps surprise us when we recall that US dollar bills carry the portrait of a well-known perpetrator of politically motivated sub-state violence, or 'terrorist', or 'freedom fighter', namely, George Washington.

Public interest in these matters grew massively as a result of the assault by hijacked airliners on the World Trade Center in New York City and on the Pentagon in Washington DC on September 11th 2001. For it was now widely acknowledged that the world was facing a so-called 'new terrorism' whose first clear manifestations lay only in the early 1990s. By contrast, 'old terrorism' had had its heyday during the 1960s and 1970s. Then the emphasis had frequently been on territorial grievances involving demands for independence from imperialists

or for revision of allegedly unjust frontiers. Sometimes such terrorism was successful—for example when the French were driven from Algeria and the British from Cyprus. On other occasions terrorists obtained compromise concessions that usually failed to resolve the dispute but nevertheless kept the level of violence contained. The Provisional Irish Republican Army and the Basque terrorists Euzkadi ta Askatasuma (ETA) come into this category. But some terrorist groups, like Baader-Meinhof in West Germany and the Red Brigades in Italy, simply failed unambiguously and so faded away: typically these were motivated by ideology rather than by ethnic or cultural identity and had a tendency to misread the amount of popular support they commanded. What all these various 'old terrorists' had in common, however, was that their operations tended to focus on limited geographical areas and their methods, though certainly ruthless, were not intended to maximize bloodshed without any regard to the impression given to the constituencies they claimed to represent. In short, they wanted many people watching rather than many people dead; they usually had aims that were rationally defensible; and they pursued such aims with some sense of proportionality. So-called 'new terrorists', on the other hand, are nihilistic, are inspired by fanatical religious beliefs, and are willing to seek martyrdom through suicide. They rarely set out aims that appear remotely attainable; they give no warnings; they do not engage in bargaining; they find compromise solutions to problems unappealing; they are willing and even eager to carry out the mass slaughter of non-combatants; and they frequently do not even claim responsibility for their deeds—presumably because they feel ultimately accountable only to a deity.

The 'new terrorism' was maybe first seen in 1993 when an attempt was made to bring about the collapse of the World Trade Center in New York. The desire to kill thousands was clear even though in the event relatively few casualties resulted as the basement-based bombs proved insufficiently powerful to topple a tower. The US authorities blamed Islamic extremism and eventually a number of Muslims were brought to trial for the outrage. In the next major US manifestation of the 'new terrorism' it was Christian fundamentalism's turn to be involved: in 1995 168 people were killed when a US Government building in Oklahoma City was blown up—with an American White Supremacist, Timothy McVeigh, being found guilty of the attack. Even more alarming was the use of weapons of mass destruction, both biological and chemical, in Tokyo during the early and mid-1990s. Actual deaths amounted only to twelve as several attempts were made to spread botulism and anthrax in the streets and sarin in the subway. The desire to kill many thousands was undoubted but technological incompetence prevented a catastrophe. Those responsible were again motivated by religion—in this case that of the obscure Aum Shinriko sect.

The unambiguous emergence of a 'new terrorism' was finally put beyond question as a result of the attacks on the United States on *September 11th 2001. *Al-Qaeda, an Islamic fundamentalist network, was immediately blamed by the US Government. And, after much imprecise rhetoric about the intention to create a global coalition to wage 'War against Terrorism', US-led military action was taken against Afghanistan, whose Taliban-controlled regime was held to have harboured at least parts of the al-Qaeda network and, in particular, Osama bin Laden, who was eventually tracked down to the Pakistani town of Abbottabad, where he was killed by US troops in 2011.

Nevertheless, 'new terrorism' has not waned with the killing of Osama bin Laden. New forms of extremism have been witnessed by *ISIS and its military efforts for an Islamic caliphate. Although ISIS sponsors international terrorism, with 'pledged' followers conducting terror-suicide attacks in Florida, Paris, and Germany, the ISIS brand of terrorism has also moved beyond traditional tactics to include the use of more online beheadings, an increased use of rape and forced marriage as a means of terror, and the ability to conduct mass killings within occupied areas. DC

Thatcherism The economic and social policies pursued by Margaret Thatcher, British Prime Minister from 1979 to 1990. There are many different notions of what Thatcherism comprises, but core elements include deregulation and privatization, combined with authoritarian social policy.

The word was first coined in the late 1970s, when the Conservatives were still in opposition. After the Party's election victory in 1979 it became a regular item in the vocabulary of media comment on British politics. It also spawned a cottage industry of academic analyses. A minimalist definition of Thatcherism would push three themes: it is the most convenient shorthand description of what Conservative governments did between 1979 and 1990; it suggests that what they did had a heavy ideological or doctrinal base; and it implies that all the Conservative administrations in this period were dominated by their leader, Mrs Thatcher.

Much of the practice of Thatcherism is contested and debated. The classic interpretations of Thatcherism are rooted in the period of Mrs Thatcher's first two administrations, 1979 to 1987. Three emerged, all of which were associated with the predominant elite political cultures of the time, namely, the Thatcherite, 'middle opinion', and neo-Marxist.

For Thatcherites the origins were the Conservative Party's delayed realization that the post-war *consensus was responsible for Britain's decline in both economic and international status terms. Thatcherites argued that by the end of the 1970s Britain had reached the stage of 'last chance saloon': without the radical change of course instituted in 1979 Britain would have sunk to the status of an ungovernable 'banana republic'. The most important initial objective was to defeat inflation. After that the goals were the creation of a more competitive economy, raising Britain's status in the world, changing the 'hearts and minds' of the British people regarding the scope of government, and the defeat of British socialism (that is, the Labour Party). All this, the Thatcherite interpretation argued, had been achieved by 1987. In short, Thatcherism was a success. The principal cause of this success was Mrs Thatcher herself. It was her convictions, drive, and authority, which had ensured that Thatcherism had developed as a coherent doctrine, consistently and comprehensively applied, and one which suffered no serious 'U-turns'.

Middle opinion, which in Britain at the time ranged from the left wing of the Conservative Party (the so-called 'wets') through the Liberal/Social Democratic Alliance, to the right and centre of the Labour Party, rejected all this. It did not deny the short-term successes of the Thatcherite project, but it did emphasize the huge cost of those successes to the country and to particular groups in society. The moderate, and modern, social democratic consensus of the post-war period had been replaced by the politics of an ideology rooted in the harsh and outmoded principles of nineteenth-century *laissez-faire, the contemporary manifestation of which was the economic doctrine espoused by Thatcherism and labelled *monetarism. Inflation, so middle opinion argued, had been defeated, but only at the cost of mass unemployment and deindustrialization. Public expenditure and the size of the public sector had both been cut, but only at the cost of weakening the welfare state and creating vast profits for privatization speculators. Moreover the traditional and essential intermediate associations of British democracy, the trade unions, the professions, the civil service, and local government, had been fatally weakened. Finally, the foreign policy of Thatcherism was rejected both for its style, 'megaphonic diplomacy', and its substance, too close an attachment to Reagan's America and too hostile an approach to the European Community. For middle opinion the principal force behind this awful revolution, and hence its principal actor focus, was Mrs Thatcher, who had hijacked the Conservative Party, rejected its 'One Nation' doctrine, and who crudely and cruelly dominated her cabinet colleagues.

The neo-Marxist camp had been the first to spot this awful potential of Thatcherism. Hence in many ways their interpretations reflected the complaints of middle opinion. They, too, accepted that Thatcherism was an exceptional phenomenon in terms of post-war British political development. They, too, accepted the short-term successes of this revolution and its costs, especially to the working class. They, too, objected to the special relationship with the Reagan administration. But they went further than the simple negative hostility of middle opinion. Neo-Marxists were fascinated by, and envious of, the excesses of Thatcherism. Here was a party elite which actually pursued the interests of its class supporters. Here was a party elite which knew what had to be done to

bring about a revolution in post-*fordist Britain. Because of these concerns the neo-Marxist camp tried to analyse Thatcherism rather than simply praise or attack it. As a result it was far less interested in telling stories about Mrs Thatcher or providing dreary accounts of particular policies. It was far more interested in considering the global and domestic structural context in which Thatcherism operated and the governing techniques it employed to protect or promote its various projects.

After 1987 the provision of 'big-bang' interpretations of Thatcherism became a less popular exercise. First, there is general agreement that Mrs Thatcher's third administration made a number of serious mistakes, mistakes which eventually led to Mrs Thatcher's resignation. Examples commonly cited are the *poll tax, welfare state reforms, the return of inflation, and policies towards European Union. Secondly, even during the classic period of interpreting Thatcherism there were sceptics who denied its developmental exceptionalism, its ideological coherence, and its operational consistency. By the early 1990s this approach had assumed greater importance. In other words, commentators began to stress increasingly the implementation policy failures of the Thatcher-led governments. Finally, in the light of the problems encountered by John Major's governments, it could be argued that the wonder is that anything was done at all between 1979 and 1990. Privatization, industrial relations reforms, and the 1988 Education Act were successes achieved in a very difficult context. This highlights the fact that there are no agreed criteria for assessing the performance of British governments, apart from electoral victories. Until this is resolved Thatcherism will remain open to dispute and debate.   JBU

(⊕) SEE WEB LINKS

• Margaret Thatcher Foundation site including documents and speeches.

theocracy Theocracy means literally 'the rule of God' and the term was invented by Josephus (AD 38–c.100) to describe the ancient Hebrew constitution and the role of Mosaic law. However, if you do not literally believe that the law has been handed down by God on tablets of stone, it may be difficult to accept theocracies on their own terms.

A more secular version of the meaning of theocracy is that it is priestly rule. Arguably, however, the more important distinction is between regimes that have religiously revealed laws or policies unchallengeable even by a popular majority or by an inherited monarch, and regimes that do not. (It should be noted that even such regimes which claim that their laws are divinely ordained and thus immutable do not make this claim in respect of all laws. For example, the Islamic Shari'a recognizes a category of positive law, the *mubah*, covering such matters as driving on the right, which are religiously neutral. *See also* ISLAMIC FUNDAMENTALISM; SUNNI; SHI'I.) LA

think-tanks Policy research institutions of two kinds:

1. Organizations which seek to assist in the strategic coordination of government policies, establish relative priorities, offer new policy choices, and ensure that the implications of policy options are fully considered. They originated in America in the 1960s, and have been copied in the United Kingdom in such institutions as the Policy Studies Institute and the Central Policy Review Staff (CPRS), the government think-tank that existed between 1971 and 1983. The Constitution Unit, established in 1995, provided a major resource for considering the large programme of constitutional reform carried out by the Labour Government after 1997.

2. Organizations of an explicitly partisan interest that seek to offer policy advice to chosen recipients. These also originated in the United States, with, for example, the Urban Institute or the Brookings Institute for Democrats, and the Heritage Foundation and the American Enterprise Institute for Republicans. UK examples include the Centre for Policy Studies and Policy Exchange (Conservative-supporting) and the Institute of Public Policy Research and Demos (Labour-supporting). JBr

Third International *See* INTERNATIONAL SOCIALISM.

third reading Parliamentary debate on the final form of a piece of legislation. Usually the third reading is a formality, unless the measure is particularly controversial (*see also* BILL).

Third Republic, French The parliamentary regime that emerged almost by chance in 1871 after the defeat of France by the Prussians. Its chronic instability reflected the country's deep social and political divisions, its fragmented party system, and the parochialism of its politicians. Lacking legitimacy and unable to handle the domestic and external crises of the 1930s, it collapsed in 1940 under the impact of the German invasion. IC

third way Generally, any ideology that claims that it lies in between two traditional approaches that the writer believes are too limited. Specifically, the ideology claimed to underlie the actions of *New Labour in Britain after the succession of Tony Blair to the leadership of the Labour Party in 1994. In this case, the two old ways are often understood to be *socialism and capitalism. However, both its main ideologue in the UK (Anthony Giddens) and Prime Minister Blair emphasized that it was supposed to be a modernized form of *social democracy, rather than an alternative to it.

Although critics of the New Labour Third Way claimed that it had no empirical content, its defenders saw it as a route between what was seen as the excessive paternalism (and statism) of traditional left policies and the excessive individual personal responsibility of the right. The policy of welfare to work—dubbed 'tough love' by British thirdwayers—was an early example: a combination of a greater emphasis on personal responsibility to find work backed with the threat of withdrawal of benefits, but at the same time a reinforcing of a framework of public support. For a while in the late 1990s, the German Social Democratic Party imitated New Labour with a claim to pursue *die neue Mitte*, but that claim too disappeared in the 2000s. The concept has a modest salience in the USA where it became central to the philosophy of the Democratic Leadership Council, the centrist pressure group in the Democrats. *See also* SOCIAL EXCLUSION; SOCIAL MARKET.

Third World The precise historical origins of the term are disputed, but during the *Cold War it was applied to the less developed countries that belonged to neither the advanced industrial capitalist West (First

World) or the Soviet socialist bloc. The Third World, mostly former colonies, was politically non-aligned. It denoted the poor countries of Africa, Asia, and Latin America (also referred to as the South), distinguished from the North largely on economic, not ideological grounds.

Always liable to mislead, the term has outlived its usefulness. It suggests a uniformity among countries that are extremely varied economically as well as culturally, socially, and politically. They all share an objection to colonization, and to foreign domination generally (*see also* IMPERIALISM), but they hardly constitute a cohesive political force (*see also* NON-ALIGNMENT). The demise of the Second World following the end of communism there also renders the term anomalous. PBl

Thirteenth Amendment *See* CIVIL RIGHTS.

Thomism The philosophy of St Thomas *Aquinas.

Thoreau, Henry David (1817-62) American essayist. Born in Concord, Massachusetts, and educated at Harvard College. Thoreau is famous for having coined the term *civil disobedience. His most powerful and influential political essay, 'Civil Disobedience', originally published under the title 'Resistance to Civil Government' (1849), exalts the law of conscience over civil law. Incensed by the Mexican War (1846-8) and the Fugitive Slave Laws of 1793 and 1850, which ensured federal assistance to slave-catchers, Thoreau became concerned with widespread personal complicity in injustice. As a public act of protest against the Mexican War, Thoreau refused to pay his poll tax and was imprisoned overnight. In 1854 Thoreau published *Walden, or, Life in the Woods*, a plea for simplicity in everyday life. VB

three-line whip *See* WHIP.

Thucydides (460–*c.*404 BC) Thucydides' account of *The Peloponnesian War* between Athens and *Sparta is one of the classic pieces of writing on war. Thucydides, himself a failed Athenian admiral, wrote a detailed history of the war which, unlike the writings of his contemporaries, explained events by reference to the interplay of personalities

and power rather than by the divine intervention of the gods. Above all, his account is written from a *realist perspective which seeks to explain and understand rather than to moralize about war, although he does moralize implicitly and explicitly about the domestic pressures for war.

His analysis of the origins of the war is strictly realist: he refers to various complaints of Athens and Sparta against each other but notes that such complaints disguise the true cause, which was 'the growth of Athenian power and the fear which this caused in Sparta'. In the Mytilenian Debate and in the Melian Dialogue he represents the dilemmas which confront statesmen in war. In the Melian Dialogue the Athenians, who have occupied the small island of Melos, demand unconditional surrender from their opponents on the grounds of the superiority of their power which renders the Melians powerless to resist. The arguments used by the Athenians in persuading the Melians to surrender are immediately familiar to modern realists. The Melians are finally all killed or sold into slavery.

Thucydides explains the eventual Spartan defeat of Athens by the decline in the wisdom of Athenian statesmanship after the death of Pericles and a disastrous expedition to Sicily which caused, to use a modern term, an 'overextension' of Athenian power. PBy

Tiananmen Square Tiananmen, the Gate of Heaven's Peace, the main square of Beijing, where in the early hours of 4 June 1989 a huge pro-democracy demonstration was repressed by armed force.

The democracy movement began during the *Cultural Revolution when many Red Guards, while accepting *Mao's instructions to attack the Party establishment, realized that rebellion would be fruitful only if it aimed at the achievement of democracy. The first expression of this was the Li Yi Zhe Poster of 1974 which while supporting the aims of the Great Proletarian Cultural Revolution argued for democratic institutions. The second was Chen Erjin's book, *Crossroads Socialism*, written just before the death of Mao and published during the Democracy Wall demonstrations of late 1978. This sought to extend Marxism by arguing that violent socialist revolution inevitably produces yet another exploitative social formation, the rule of the authoritarian revolutionary elite. A second revolution is always necessary to put real power in the hands of the people, through the establishment of democracy.

Mao's successors, themselves victims of the Cultural Revolution, had an interest in strengthening the rule of law, and an interest in relaxing political control enough to prevent another outbreak. Deng Xiaoping had a personal interest in mobilizing democratic sentiment against the left. He supported the Democracy Wall protest of late 1978 until the young radical factory worker Wei Jingsheng demanded democracy 'as a right' and poured contempt on Deng's half-measures. Wei was sentenced to 15 years' imprisonment, fifty other participants were arrested, and the right to use 'big character' posters (which Mao had approved) was abolished. Thereafter, however, Deng sought to maintain a balance between the democratic elements within the Party and the conservative veterans. At the same time he supported his protégé Hu Yaobang (Secretary-General of the CCP from 1980), who had gone so far as to affirm (as Chen Erjin had done) that the forms of democracy have universal validity, whatever the content may be in terms of class.

However, when Hu refused to suppress the next great democratic demonstration in 1986 at Kei Da University where the radical democrat Fang Lizhi was Professor of Physics, Deng forced Hu's dismissal. In early 1989 Hu died. By this time he was the hero of the democratic movement. When the leadership arranged a demeaning low-key funeral, students marched to Tiananmen Square to protest. Thus the demonstration began.

There were at this point three groups involved in democratic dissent. The first was among intellectuals who hoped for democratization from the top. The second was led by former Red Guards who encouraged democratic revolution from below and were engaged in mobilizing workers and peasants. The third called themselves 'Neo-Authoritarians'; they argued that continued authoritarianism was required to carry through economic changes which would create a pluralist society capable of sustaining democracy. In spite of their views, they nevertheless supported the demonstrators.

In 2000, tapes and transcriptions of the debates within the Secretariat of the Politburo on how to handle the demonstration, drawn from materials to which only the five members of the Secretariat normally had access, were smuggled out to the USA (translated and published in A. J. Nathan and P. Link, *The Tiananmen Papers*, 2001).

It is obvious from the debate that most of the top leadership of the CCP had a good deal of sympathy with demands to abolish corruption, privilege, and the abuse of power, and some were also prepared to take further steps towards democracy to bring these evils under control. However, there was one step at which the majority baulked. Some of the demonstrators were demanding the right to form new political parties. Former Red Guard groups were encouraging the creation of autonomous groups of students, workers, intellectuals, and citizens; such associations could easily develop into political parties. The Politburo therefore refused to enter into dialogue with the newly formed nationwide Autonomous Federation of Students. Thus negotiation became impossible.

After an indecisive debate in the Secretariat, Deng Xiaoping demanded the publication of an editorial in the *People's Daily* to condemn the demonstration as 'turmoil', and asserted that it was controlled by a 'tiny handful' of people intent on destroying socialism and the CCP. Public support for the demonstrators soared. The students responded with a hunger strike, which further inflamed opinion throughout China until about four million people were involved in protest. The Secretariat met to consider the imposition of martial law. Two members voted in favour, two against. The fifth member abstained. Deng Xiaoping, the accepted arbitrator, used his casting vote for martial law. There was a national outcry, in which virtually every one of the Party's own institutions joined, and many army commanders showed great reluctance to become involved.

The Secretariat held firm, but insisted emphatically that there must be no bloodshed. This order was also repeatedly issued to the army. However, as the troops moved through the suburbs, a million or more Beijing citizens rose to beat them off. Harassed and humiliated and suffering casualties, by the time the army units reached the Square their mood was angry. They spared the students, who were allowed to evacuate the Square without molestation; but they took their revenge on the civilian crowds in the adjoining streets. The number of casualties is not known; it was probably in the hundreds.

The Secretary-General Zhao Ziyang, successor to Hu Yaobang, was dismissed for having opposed martial law. A new Secretariat was appointed. Surprisingly, it consisted mainly of moderates, led by Jiang Zemin; but these were for the moment powerless in the face of the enraged conservative veterans. Democratic leaders were rounded up and imprisoned, and the democratic debate suppressed. Attempts were also made to reverse economic reform. However, at the end of 1992 in a series of speeches Deng Xiaoping condemned this reaction. The precarious tolerance of debate was restored and economic reform speeded up. When Jiang Zemin, visiting the USA, was challenged to justify the Tiananmen suppression, he could only mumble that 'mistakes are sometimes made'. JG

ticket-splitting The propensity of voters in the United States to simultaneously cast votes for the candidates of different parties (where straight-ticket voting is the opposite). This widespread practice is a mark of the weakness of party, the importance of personal appeals in American electoral politics, and the effects of *federalism. It also helps to explain the prevalence of divided government, where one party controls the executive and another the legislature. DM

time-series analysis The statistical study of measurements (equally) spaced over time. There can be various aims which include understanding the phenomenon represented in a single series, forecasting the future, and explaining the relationships between variables that change over time. The major feature of time-series data is that observations are not independent of previous observations. The pattern of serial dependence, or autocorrelation, must be accounted for in statistical analysis for inferences regarding the relationships between variables to be valid. In British politics, time-series models have been used with opinion poll data to consider the effects of events, such as the Falklands war and departure from the *EMS (European

Monetary System), on government popularity. *See also* LONGITUDINAL ANALYSIS; PANEL STUDY. SF

Titmuss, Richard (1907–73) British sociologist who wrote extensively, both descriptively and normatively, on the *welfare state. His main works, written during and in the decade after the Second World War, argue that entitlement to benefits should be a mark of citizenship ('All collectively provided services are deliberately designed to meet certain socially recognized "needs"'). As needs do not rise in line with income, Titmuss argued fervently for universal non-means-tested benefits.

Titmuss's most enduring book has proved to be his last, The *Gift Relationship* (1970). This made a powerful case against the involvement of the market in the supply of human blood for medical procedures, and was influential in a shift of US policy (and the maintenance of UK policy) away from market provision and towards voluntary provision.

Titoism A variant of communism practised by Josip Broz Tito (1892–1980), who led an indigenous partisan army to military victory over the German occupiers in Yugoslavia. This victory gave his party, unlike other governing Communist Parties in Eastern Europe after 1945, a degree of independence that allowed it to introduce a distinctive brand of socialism—Titoism—after the break with Moscow in 1948–9. Titoist socialism abolished central planning and created a form of market economy based on workers' self-management in industry and private enterprise in agriculture; it transformed Yugoslavia into a genuine federal state; and it abandoned the 'leading role' of the Communist Party (renamed the League of Communists). Tito himself played a vital role in overcoming regional political and economic difficulties that his policy engendered, as well as historic communal antipathies particularly between Serbs and Croats. Nonetheless, Serbs continued to play the dominant role in the army and police force. After Tito's death, however, centrifugal tendencies grew and, with the crisis of communist rule across Eastern Europe, communists and anti-communists alike adopted extreme nationalist political strategies, leading to civil war in many parts of the country.   swh

Tocqueville, Alexis de (1805–59) French sociologist and political notable whose pioneering study of politics and society in the United States remains among the most empirically rich and theoretically innovative works in contemporary social science. After a spell as a junior magistrate Tocqueville travelled to America with his friend Beaumont, ostensibly to study the American penal system. Tocqueville spent most of the trip, however, gathering the impressions of American society that formed the basis of his classic *Democracy in America* (first part published in 1835, second part in 1840). Upon his return, Tocqueville entered the Chamber of Deputies, and served briefly as foreign minister under Louis Napoleon following the revolution of February 1848. After the dissolution of the Assembly in 1851, Tocqueville's efforts turned towards a planned multi-volumed study of French history (from the eighteenth century to the present). The first volume, a study of the pre-Revolutionary *ancien régime*, appeared in 1856. Plagued throughout his life with ill-health, Tocqueville died in 1859 of tuberculosis.

Tocqueville's study of America was premissed on the observation that the modern age had witnessed an 'egalitarian revolution'—the spread of the normative ideal of equality and of steadily equalizing social conditions had undermined the former aristocratic order throughout Europe. Tocqueville sensed (and through his study, confirmed) that the most viable political form for such a radically new sociological climate was democracy, whose 'image' he found in the American republic. Tocqueville's book should thus be read as an essay for a European audience uncertain of its own political future, and its tone is that of excitement at a genuine sociological discovery.

Tocqueville's concern in the book is with the civic dimensions of democracy. Using the (perhaps unrepresentative) model of the New England township, he details an elaborate institutional design that grounds the principle of 'popular sovereignty'. Power was decentralized to facilitate popular control, and participation promoted through institutions such as jury service and, most importantly, elections (which instil responsible citizenship and

'rational patriotism', and check the actions of public officials). Yet one of Tocqueville's most significant theoretical innovations was his observation of the democratic benefits of a rich associational life in sustaining the civic habits of self-government. More broadly, he understood that the vitality of democratic society rested on certain shared practices or republican 'mores'. Religion, for example, is important to the degree that it promotes civic values. For the sake of republican stability, religion should assure its followers of their future reward in heaven, and discourage any striving for transforming the earth.

Despite his obvious admiration for American republicanism, much of Tocqueville's analysis is devoted to the sociological problems engendered by democratic life. Democracy 'serves the well-being of the greatest number', yet it brings with it a tolerance for mediocrity that disturbed the aristocrat within Tocqueville. In politics, the electoral mechanism means that the most able do not necessarily govern, and that present goods are rarely sacrificed for future benefits. Of most concern is the possibility of the 'tyranny of the majority'. Tocqueville is worried not about majorities as persistent political factions in a Madisonian sense. Rather, he is referring to the oppressive effects of popular opinion, the contempt of the masses for the potentially enlightened minority. Tocqueville also laments the tendency to isolation (anomie) resulting from the destruction of the traditional institutions of the aristocratic order. The danger of 'individualism' is that citizens withdrawn from society are open to exploitation by potential despots. Participation in civic life should thus be understood as much more than altruistic activity—it is a necessary condition for sustaining individual liberty ('self interest rightly understood').

Tocqueville's second important work, *The Old Regime and the French Revolution* (1856), is as much profession of personal belief and a commentary on his own times as a historical account of eighteenth-century politics. Its themes are familiar—the intention is to show the way in which the Revolution displaced the aristocratic order and replaced it with a society of anomic individuals ripe for despotism in the form of Bonapartism. Yet Tocqueville finds the disjunctures between the 'old order' and the Revolution less striking than the continuities (bureaucratic paternalism, a large and independent peasantry, and, most importantly, excessive administrative centralization, a theme that had been anticipated in his reflections on the history of the Second Republic in the *Souvenirs*). Tocqueville's account of the collapse of the old order is liberal in its attribution of blame. His main targets are a persistently corrupt nobility, a monarchy embroiled in ill-judged legal and fiscal manoeuvres, and lastly a wild utopianism inspired by the spirit of equality but spearheaded by irresponsible rogue intellectuals. He argued that the Revolution occurred not at the depths of misery but when rising political expectations had been dashed.

Although often accused of inaccuracy in his empirical work and confusion in his use of theoretical terms (in particular, his interchangeable use of 'democracy' for 'equality', and of 'liberty' for 'self-government'), Tocqueville's conceptual and methodological innovations are undeniable. His insights on the relationship between the individual and society remain as brilliant and relevant today as they were 150 years ago. Put simply, Tocqueville studied politics by studying individuals and their associations, rather than constitutions. Tocqueville's work thus constitutes a vital landmark in the emergence of modern sociology and 'a new political science'. SW

toleration A willingness not to interfere with beliefs, attitudes, or actions despite a lack of sympathy for them or despite dislike of them. The value of toleration is said to lie in the absence of interference despite an initial reaction of dislike, even when the capacity (or power) so to interfere is available. Since 'interference' is a vague term, covering interventions ranging from the provision of persuasive arguments to legal coercion, the boundaries of toleration are inevitably unclear. For example, a person may claim to tolerate a practice of which he or she disapproves, on the ground that he or she does not support the legal prohibition (under penalty) of that practice. If, however, that 'legal toleration' is coupled to a willingness to make disapproval of the practice evident in social life, for example by ostracism or warning others against association with the person whose practices are disapproved, then the degree of toleration is disputable. In

political contexts, the toleration of religious diversity has, historically, been the most significant issue: To what extent is the state entitled to require particular religious observance? In a multicultural society, there is always the possibility that one group will think a particular practice incumbent upon it, while other groups will find that practice anathema. An especially troublesome issue about the limits of toleration may be posed thus: To what extent should toleration be extended to the intolerant? This question parallels a problem in democratic theory: To what extent should a democratic polity permit the activities of anti-democratic political organizations? AR

Tolstoy, Count Leo (1828–1910) Russian writer, ascetic, pacifist, and *anarchist. Moral critic of tsarism. Advocated the abolition of the state and property—the sources of exploitation—and the creation of a communal society based upon Christian principles. He stressed personal redemption rather than political resistance and was an important influence upon *Gandhi. GL

torture Most often understood as inflicting pain as a means of punishment, coercion, or especially interrogation, but often including sensory deprivation, pain produced through confinement or stress positions, and sometimes mental torture via solitary confinement. Defined in the UN Convention Against Torture (1984) as *'any act by which severe pain or suffering, whether physical or mental, is intentionally inflicted' for purposes of punishment, interrogation, or intimidation, by state / public officials*. The definition is a matter of contention, as the 'Bybee memo' narrowed torture to severe pain equivalent 'to the level of death, organ failure, or permanent impairment'. Both the permissibility and purpose of torture have evolved, from the medieval use of torture as the public expression of sovereign will on the condemned (as described by *Foucault) to the use of legal interrogatory torture in much of continental Europe, followed by large-scale legal prohibitions from the late eighteenth century onward, and a paradoxical reemergence in the twentieth century. Although an 'absolute' right from torture is now widely considered, it remains widely practised, and the right often ignored. For example, post-*September 11 2001 the US government engaged in, and attempted to legalize, torture. LSZ

Toryism More than just a colloquial synonym for *Conservatism, the word Tory is older. Derived from the Irish for 'pursuer', it was applied first to Catholic outlaws in mid-seventeenth-century Ireland, as in a proclamation of 1647 about 'roberies . . . committed by the Tories and Rebells upon the Protestants'. It was then applied by their enemies to those who opposed the exclusion of the Catholic James, later James II, from the throne ('the Word *Tory* was entertained, which signified the most despicable Savages among the Wild Irish'). From this it settled during the eighteenth century into meaning the party which was more pro-royalist, more in favour of the privileges of the established Church, and less in favour of parliamentary supremacy, than its *Whig rival. In the American Revolution, those who remained loyal to the king and the colonial administration (many of whom fled to Canada) were called 'Tories' because they often were.

'Conservative' superseded 'Tory' as the official title of the party in the mid-nineteenth century. Apart from its colloquial uses, however, Toryism survives as a useful label for a particular strand of Conservatism. It was classically characterized by Samuel Beer in *Modern British Politics* (1965), who opens by recording that Sir John Anderson warned his fellow-Conservatives in 1947, in the words of Shakespeare's Ulysses, 'Take but degree away, untune that string, | And hark, what discord follows' (*Troilus*, I. iii. 109).' (Michael Portillo, then one of the leaders of the intellectual right of the Conservative Party, quoted the same passage in early 1994.) In Beer's characterization, Tory thought is concerned with preserving existing hierarchies and traditions, because they are thought to protect social order. This may be reflected in such diverse policy areas as defending the establishment of the Church of England, promoting Shakespeare and/or Christianity in schools, and reinstating Rutland County Council.

totalitarianism A dictatorial form of centralized government that regulates every aspect of state and private behaviour. Although the term was originally intended to designate fascist and communist regimes, totalitarianism is mainly associated with characterizations of the *Soviet Union. Its proponents do not agree on when, if ever, the Soviet Union ceased to be totalitarian, but they tend to converge on the view that at some point the political leadership was both all powerful and totally illegitimate. For many commentators, the Soviet Union entered a new phase after the abandonment of mass terror on Stalin's death. However, others operating within the totalitarian paradigm point to institutional continuity, KGB harassment of dissidents, and the ever present possibilities of the reassertion of arbitrary state power until 1989. The total and sudden collapse of the Soviet Union since then casts doubt not only on this school, but perhaps on the whole concept of totalitarianism. In the 1970s, a new school of Sovietology emerged which pointed to evidence both for popular support for the regime and for widespread dispersion of power, at least in implementation of policy, among sectoral and regional authorities. For some of the 'pluralists', this was evidence of the ability of the regime to adapt to include new demands. However, totalitarian theorists claimed that the failure of the system to survive showed not only its inability to adapt but the formality of supposed popular participation. *See also* ARENDT.   swh

trade unions Collective organizations of workers whose purpose is to substitute a collective bargain for separate individual bargaining and thereby maintain and improve the standard of living of their members. They act as defensive organizations set up to counteract the economic weakness of propertyless wage-earners as unorganized individuals.

There is little evidence to support the view that trade unions emerged out of medieval craft guilds. Although the first forms of permanent organization among wage-earners were the combinations of handicraftsmen established in the eighteenth century, modern trade unionism began with the spread of factory industry in the early nineteenth century. The development of unions in Britain, as the first industrial nation, is particularly instructive when assessing their political role. The repeal of the UK Combination Acts in 1824 enabled the secret local associations of craftsmen to surface and become centralized in national amalgamated unions—the first of which was the Amalgamated Society of Engineers formed in 1850. These 'new model' unions, whilst national in scope, remained conservative in outlook and represented only skilled craftsmen eager to retain their privileged position in the labour market. The Trade Union Act of 1871 declared unions legal organizations, and further legislation in the nineteenth century established the legality of collective bargaining. The closing decades of the nineteenth century saw the growth of new 'general labour' unions (Seamen's, Dockers', General and Municipal Unions), who appealed to the mass of low-paid, unskilled workers previously excluded from the 'model' unions. This wave of 'New Unionism' sought to replace the methods of the skilled workers—control over apprenticeship and joint negotiating boards—with the strike weapon and all-embracing membership. Contemporary trade unionism in Britain is shaped by the often uneasy relationship which exists between the organizations of skilled and unskilled workers, a direct legacy of the nineteenth century.

The political role of trade unions can be analysed from three broad standpoints. Conservative pluralists (but also *Lenin) maintain that unions are 'economic' organizations whose role is to follow a narrow agenda concerned with terms and conditions of employment. In this view although their agenda may legitimately encompass welfare and training issues, trade unions are denied an immediate political role in society. Writers in the social democratic Weberian tradition insist that the purpose of trade unionism is democratic participation in job regulation. The primary focus of union activity remains the workplace but as democratic, representative organizations it is argued that they should play a more active broader role in social reconstruction. This tradition has been highly influential in Britain, where in exceptional circumstances, the *Labour Party developed out of the existing trade union movement. Marxist approaches to trade unionism are complex and centre on the extent to which unions both facilitate collective action and consciousness whilst simultaneously constraining and dividing the working class. Without unions, Marx

argued, workers would be degraded to one level mass of broken wretches past salvation; however, workers ought not to confine their efforts to 'a fair day's wage for a fair day's work', but inscribe on their banner the 'revolutionary watchword—abolition of the wages system' (*Wages, Price and Profit*).

European trade unionism has long been marked by national diversity in structure, ideology, and organizational form corresponding to differential historical development. Whilst in Germany industrial relations tends to be highly centralized, legalized, and cooperative, in Italy the impact of socialist and *syndicalist politics has fashioned an assertive local workplace form of trade unionism. From the American business unions of the 1930s to the Japanese company unions and single union deals of the post-war period, trade unions have been obliged to confront a plethora of management strategies aimed at restructuring labour/capital relations. Nevertheless European unionism looks set to enter a new vigorous phase with a series of large-scale mergers and opportunities for international organization in the light of moves to widen and deepen European integration. PBM

trade war A situation in which two or more nations restrict one another's exports. Trade wars are ancient and modern. Until Adam *Smith and the contemporary *physiocrats, no thinkers believed in free trade. All economists believed that the best policy was to maximize one's own exports; many added that it was good to restrict others' imports. If pursued worldwide, such policies were obviously self-defeating, but that does not lessen their attraction to individual national policy makers. The Napoleonic Wars were largely a trade war between France and her allies and the UK, which caused serious damage to third parties, such as the USA.

The nineteenth century saw the heyday of the bilateral trade treaty and the invention of the *most favoured nation clause. Between them, these devices restricted the scope for trade wars. However, the revival of *protection in the 1920s and 1930s revived trade wars. Since the 1960s, world trade politics has become multilateral rather than bilateral (GATT, *World Trade Organization). This has not eliminated trade wars, but has made them multilateral also. If the EU declares war on US hormone-fortified beef and export subsidies, then the USA may declare war on EU luxury goods and Caribbean bananas.

traditionalism Tradition originally referred to a handing over or handing down of anything, but the word came primarily to refer to the oral handing down of lore and legend. 'Oral tradition' is thus a tautology. In what are now called Western countries there was, therefore, for many years a distinction and potential conflict between traditional beliefs and the 'high', written culture of the classics and established religion. In contemporary non-Western countries there is a similar relation between local values and systems of thought and those which are imported from the West as more advanced or modern.

Traditionalists in religion (specifically in mid-nineteenth-century Roman Catholicism) held that religious truth consisted of a single revelation, the life of Christ, developed by tradition. Secular traditionalists, defined broadly, are people whose thought gives a high value to tradition. In its widest sense, tradition includes anything which is typical of the past, customary, or part of a cultural identity. It can thus include such diverse items as religious beliefs, sporting customs, linguistic practices, or dietary habits. There is, however, a distinction between two senses of traditionalism. We might say of a northern Englishman who keeps whippets and pigeons, speaks in dialect, and lives on a diet of black pudding, potato pie, and mushy peas that 'He's a great traditionalist'. But this kind of traditionalism might be entirely apolitical; the same man may have a liberal theory of taste and seek neither to promulgate nor protect his own traditional tastes for other people. In so far as he just happens to like these things and does not value them because they are traditional, then perhaps we should not call him a traditionalist at all. Traditionalism in a stronger sense therefore suggests a propensity to revive or defend traditions against non-traditional beliefs and values.

The power of political traditionalism is not to be underestimated, but usually has been. Both Marxist socialism and liberal capitalism are essentially progressive and rationalist doctrines with a limited capacity for tolerating traditional ways, but little capacity for valuing or defending them. The failures of both doctrines on the spiritual or cultural level of giving meaning to people's lives, of allowing them to experience a sense of belonging or permanent achievement, have enhanced the appeal of custom and tradition. Nationalism everywhere and religious revivalism in the developing countries are powerful expressions of traditionalism. They are paralleled in the West by weaker and less political forms, ranging from the defence of 'real' beer to the revival of folk music, dancing, and holiday customs.   LA

transitional justice Part of the process of post-conflict reconstruction of a society once major violence has come to an end. Transitional justice mechanisms aim to help a society 'come to terms' with the causes and effects of this violence. The field of transitional justice is largely concerned with matters of criminal justice and righting the wrongs associated with the conflict, rather than economic justice and the distribution of resources. Two main ways of implementing transitional justice are criminal trials or *truth and reconciliation commissions. Trials are often for international rather than domestic crimes, such as International Criminal Court prosecutions for *genocide, *war crimes, and *crimes against humanity. Trials are often associated with the aim of retribution, though judgements of these tribunals do refer to the aims of deterrence and rehabilitation on occasion. 'Truth and reconciliation' commissions do not involve punishment, but aim to establish an historical record of events and give victims a chance to tell their stories and have their experiences acknowledged. Critics suggest that neither trials nor truth commissions can really achieve justice, help people come to terms with past violence, nor help a society move towards peace.   AMB

transitivity *See* ECONOMIC MAN.

transnationalism A term often associated with *globalization, which denotes the social and global transformations of interconnectivity between peoples, states, economies, and cultures under the processes of globalization. The key to transnationalism is its focus on social transformations, which lie beyond the usual state borders associated within the *international system. In most cases, the term 'transnationalism' is used positively to suggest ongoing global integration, economic development, and political cooperation. However, critics of transnationalism associate these transformations with a form of *cultural imperialism and Western *hegemony.

Treaty of Rome *See* Rome, Treaty of.

Treaty of Versailles *See* Versailles, Treaty of.

Trotskyism Political movement originating with Leon Trotsky (1879-1940). Trotsky argued that the creation of a new International was necessary in order to compensate for the political bankruptcy of the Second and Third Internationals and to provide revolutionary leadership for the *working class during a period of growing capitalist crisis and fascist offensive.

Trotsky's critique of the Soviet Union as a 'degenerated workers' state' (in *The Revolution Betrayed*, 1936) was central to this strategy. Power had been transferred from the *proletariat to the *bureaucracy, which controlled state and party structures. The Soviet Union was a transitional society—it could either go forward to socialism or back to capitalism. The latter could only be prevented by a political revolution which could build upon the already socialized base.

The Fourth International would lead resistance to *Stalinist control, creating new working-class parties and unions and propagating world revolution. However, Trotskyism generally failed to establish a real base within the working class although it has exercised influence in certain countries (particularly in Latin America) and enjoyed bouts of notoriety (for example, *Militant). GL

Truman Doctrine The so-called Truman Doctrine was enunciated by President Harry S Truman in a speech to a joint session of the US Congress on 12 March 1947. In it he denounced the oppressive nature of the communist system of government and warned against the possibility that campaigns of subversion might bring even more countries under that system. He sought, and was given, Congressional authority to provide assistance to threatened regimes—

initially those in Greece and Turkey. The 'Doctrine' was thus the starting point for the strategy of containment of communism developed by successive US Presidents during the *Cold War. DC

((⊕)) SEE WEB LINKS
• Truman's speech of 12 March 1947.

trusteeship Now largely defunct, trusteeship was the system by which the United Nations, at its inception, appointed states to administer territories whose peoples, while regarded as units of self-determination, were deemed unfit to exercise immediate sovereignty. United Nations trusteeships replaced League of Nations mandates, providing a means by which administrative authority over the colonies of powers defeated in the two World Wars could be transferred to the victors without compromising their democratic and anti-imperialist aspirations. The UN Trusteeship Council, under the authority of the General Assembly, had the power to issue questionnaires and demand reports from states administering trust territories, to send missions to such territories, and to receive petitions from their inhabitants. Up to independence, all or part of the territory of Rwanda, Burundi, Tanzania, Togoland, the Cameroons, Nauru, and Somalia was ruled under trusteeship agreements by former colonial powers and the United States. CJ

truth and reconciliation In 1995, after the collapse of the *apartheid regime in South Africa, a Truth and Reconciliation Commission (TRC) was set up by the Government of National Unity in order to examine the human rights abuses that had been carried out between 1960 and 1994. The commission, chaired by Archbishop Desmond Tutu, concluded that 'The state, in the form of the South African government, the civil service and its security forces, was ...the primary perpetrator of gross violations of human rights in South Africa and, from 1974, in southern Africa', but also noted that in the course of its legitimate struggle against apartheid the *ANC and its armed wings committed gross violations of human rights. The aim of the commission was to uncover the real history of the apartheid period, through the examination of particular incidents and the testimony of those who took part in the political conflict in South Africa. Whilst the commission uncovered a huge amount of evidence about human rights abuses, and was generally seen to be a fair forum for discussion of the events which occurred during the apartheid era, there were questions about the objectivity and purpose of the TRC. The granting of amnesties to encourage witnesses to appear before the commission was seen as a distortion of the judicial process, and highlighted the conflict between the desire for reconciliation and the feeling that the perpetrators of human rights abuses should be punished. In Bolivia and Argentina national commissions were established (in 1982 and 1983, respectively) to investigate the disappearance of citizens during military rule. Other countries have used similar commissions to attempt to address the causes and consequences of state abuse of power and civil conflict; including Germany (to examine human rights abuses in East Germany between 1949 and 1989), East Timor (looking at the period between 1974 and 1999), and Yugoslavia (investigating war crimes carried out in the Balkans).

Tucker, Benjamin *See* ANARCHISM.

Ture, Kwame *See* CARMICHAEL, STOKELY.

Turgot, A. R. J. (1727–81) French politician and economist. A follower of the *physiocrats, Turgot tried to free the grain trade in France from internal tariffs during his brief career as Louis XVI's finance minister (1774–6). After protests from those whose *rent-seeking he had disrupted, he was dismissed. This episode drove Turgot's disciple *Condorcet away from the 'beautiful dream' that *Enlightened administrators could influence practical politics towards his highly theoretical study of voting and juries.

turnout The proportion of the registered electorate who vote in a given election. Turnout is both important and difficult to measure where registration is itself a costly process, especially in the United States. At the other extreme, regimes with compulsory voting (such as Australia), still have turnout well below 100 per cent, as the compulsory-voting laws are rarely enforced. There has been a general tendency in a number of countries including the United Kingdom for turnout to decline since a peak in the 1950s.

Some view this with alarm, others do not, either because too high a turnout has been argued to place too great a strain of conflicting demands on the political system, or because rational economic men and women who know that their own vote is highly unlikely to influence the election do not bother to vote. Some weak confirmation of the last view is provided by the association between turnout and the expected closeness of the election; but this explanation cannot explain turnouts of over 70 per cent in elections which nobody expected to be close, such as the British General Election of 1983. The collapse of turnout in that of 2001, when party policies were similar and everyone expected Labour to win, is, however, rationally explicable in this way.

two-party systems Political systems in which only two political parties effectively compete for government office. Minor parties may operate in such a system, although in some cases, as in the United States, they may have to surmount significant barriers to be placed on the ballot paper. Some theorists argue that two-party systems offer a superior form of electoral democracy because unless there are only two parties, there can be no guarantee that any party will have a legislative majority, without which government policy is formed on the basis of bargaining between political elites, which is seen as less accessible to popular control. However, in a two-party system much policy formation takes place within the political parties, also away from popular control. Two-party systems are most often found in association with *first-past-the-post electoral systems, as in the United States and Britain. WG

tyranny In classical thought, a corrupt form of monarchy in which a person ruled in his own interest. More generally, the abuse of the state's coercive force in the absence of the rule of law. This absence more particularly suggests government by the will of the tyrant (cf. *dictatorship) and the arbitrary treatment of citizens, if not the systematic use of terror. Democratic theorists like J. S. *Mill have been concerned to avoid the tyranny of the majority. They fear that the rights of minorities and the stability of expectations built on settled law could be neglected by the majority's abuse of its numerical superiority under a system apparently legitimating the carrying out of its will. AR

tyranny of the majority A fear expressed variously by *Plato, *Aristotle, *Madison, *Tocqueville, and J. S. *Mill. If the majority rules, what is to stop it from expropriating the minority, or from tyrannizing it in other ways by enforcing the majority's religion, language, or culture on the minority? Madison's answer in *The Federalist* is the best known. He argued that the United States must have a federal structure. Although one majority, left to itself, would try to tyrannize the local minority in one state or city and another majority, left to itself, would do the same in another, in a country as large and diverse as the United States there would not be one national majority which could tyrannize over a national minority. But if there was, the powers which the states retained would be a bulwark against it. The separation of powers among legislature, executive, and judiciary at federal level would be a further protection against majority tyranny.

Critics of Madison have pointed out that his formula gives no protection to minorities which do not form a local majority anywhere. In particular, the Madisonian constitution gave no effective protection to black

Americans until the 1960s, largely because the *states' rights which Madison thought it so important to protect were used by the white majorities in the Southern states to oppress the local black minorities.

J. S. Mill's solutions to majority tyranny were *proportional representation and extra votes for the rich and the well-educated. Neither solution bears close examination. Proportional representation is a solution to a different problem. If there is a majority, it is a majority, and proportional representation will not make it less so (although it may correct some overrepresentation of the majority). The majority of voters in Northern Ireland since 1921 has always been Protestant; the population votes almost entirely along religious lines; therefore any fairly elected Northern Ireland assembly must have a Protestant majority. Mill's solution of 'fancy franchises' is open to the same objection as Madison's.

The main danger that worried Aristotle, Madison, and Mill alike was that the majority poor citizenry would vote for confiscatory legislation at the expense of the rich minority. For whatever reason, this has never happened. At least we can be confident that the majority will not expropriate the *median voter.

UDI (Unilateral Declaration of Independence) Assertion by the white settler government of Rhodesia, made in 1965, in an attempt to resist the tide of decolonization and introduction of majority rule. Opposed by the British colonial power and the United Nations, the government, led by Ian Smith, resisted economic and political *sanctions until 1979. Rhodesia became Zimbabwe in 1980, after a prolonged civil war.

Ulster *See* NORTHERN IRELAND.

ultra vires Literally, 'beyond powers'. *Ultra vires* has two meanings: (1) substantive *ultra vires* where a decision has been reached outside the powers conferred on the decision taker; and (2) procedural *ultra vires* where the prescribed procedures have not been properly complied with. The doctrine of *ultra vires* gives courts considerable powers of oversight over decision-making. The range and variety of bodies amenable to the doctrine is large. Ministers, or any public body with statutory powers, may be included. The doctrine also applies to companies and corporations that are amenable to the remedies of declaration or injunction.

A local authority that enters an agreement or contract that is outside its statutory powers is said to be acting *ultra vires*. In *Hazel* v. *Hammersmith* [1991] 1 All ER 545, the House of Lords held that various speculative investments undertaken by local authorities lacked express statutory authorization and were void with severe consequences for those who had invested in local authority activities declared illegal by the courts.

The grounds for claiming *ultra vires* range from abuse of power, acting unreasonably (*Padfield* v. *Minister of Agriculture, Fisheries and Food* [1968] AC 997), or acting not in accordance with the rules of natural justice. *Ultra vires* is a formidable doctrine for the courts to intervene and challenge the legality

of decisions. *Ultra vires* may result in significant consequences for the body exercising legal powers. In many cases the decision that is *ultra vires* may be said, in law, never to have taken place, with often severe consequences from such a finding on the parties to any agreement.   JM

UN *See* UNITED NATIONS.

unanimity The rule that a decision is ratified only if every single voter supports it. The jury rule for conviction, in some legal systems, is a unanimity rule. Famous historical examples were the procedures to elect the king of Poland in the eighteenth century, and the Pope prior to the Third Lateran Council of 1179 which substituted a two-thirds majority rule (*see* QUALIFIED MAJORITY RULE). The unanimity rule gives each and every voter a veto over the outcome. Therefore, if any voter has corrupt or ulterior motives, they may have to be paid off. Contemporary observers thought that the Polish monarchy was weak for this reason; an outside power such as Russia or Austria need only bribe one Polish nobleman each to prevent any king from being chosen.

uncertainty *See* RISK.

UNCTAD (United Nations Conference on Trade and Development) *See* PREBISCH, RAÚL.

underclass A term used to signify members of a society who are at the very bottom of a hierarchical economic and social class structure. Members of the underclass tend to be poor, unemployed, or underemployed individuals with limited prospects for social mobility. A key element associated with the term 'underclass' is that it creates a 'poverty trap' or 'dependency cycle' in which members of the underclass become statically fixed within these social strata due to the lack of opportunity, education, and employment skills. The underclass is generally understood to be positioned under the *working class, with the term coming into predominant use in the 1960s as a means to respond to distributive inequalities and poverty in Western democracies.

UNGA (United Nations General Assembly) *See* GENERAL ASSEMBLY (UN).

ungovernability *See* GOVERNABILITY.

unicameralism Legislatures made up of one chamber are the exception rather than the rule, most national assemblies adopting a *bicameral form. The countries which have unicameral systems tend to be smaller countries (e.g. Finland, Greece, and Norway), or smaller states in federal systems: Nebraska has the only unicameral state legislature in the United States. There are cases of countries which have moved from a bicameral to a unicameral legislature (e.g. New Zealand, Sweden). These are both smaller unitary states, and it would be difficult to reconcile a federal system with unicameralism as a second chamber is generally seen as necessary to protect the position of the constituent units of the federation against the central government. *Second chambers are also seen as offering a protection against arbitrary decisions by a lower chamber dominated by one party. WG

unilateralism A term associated with foreign policy analysis and the study of *international relations to signify a state's foreign policy when it is pursued without consultation, alignment with, or reference to the foreign policies of other states and/or international norms. Basically, unilateralism is when a state decides to act alone and without the approval or affirmative recognition by other states.

unilateralism (UK) Literally 'one-sidedness', although unilateralists protested vigorously in the 1980s when opponents so translated it. A British movement against domestic involvement with nuclear weapons. All unilateralists have opposed British nuclear weapons, arguing *inter alia* that they are unnecessary for national security, positively destabilizing to international security, a bar on progress in disarmament, or immoral.

The most important unilateralist organization has been the Campaign for Nuclear Disarmament (*CND). PBy

unionism 1. Elliptical for trades unionism; therefore, support for the political aims of *trade unions.

2. Support for the Union (i.e. the North) before and during the American Civil War.

3. In the UK since 1886, support for the maintenance of the United Kingdom of Great Britain and Ireland (since 1921, Northern Ireland). Although the word in this sense is not attested before 1886, the concept goes back to the seventeenth century. The 1707 Union between England and Scotland was driven, on the English side, by the fear that the Scots might pass an act of succession that would give them a different (and possibly warring) king to the king of England. On the Scottish side, the unionists perceived that an independent Scotland was economically doomed to domination by the much larger English economy. The Irish Union of 1800–1 was likewise driven by strategic arguments on the British side. It was less stable than the Scottish Union, because the large majority of the Irish were Catholic, disenfranchised (a promise to enfranchise them after Union being broken), and not consulted.

Irish demands for Home Rule (what would now be called *devolution) led in 1886 to the regrouping of British politics into a unionist and an anti-unionist coalition. The centre of gravity of Unionism was always in the Conservative (for much of the time since 1886 it has been officially entitled the Conservative and Unionist) Party. But for most of the twentieth century the Labour Party was also unionist, for a principled and an unprincipled reason. The principled reason was that securing equal living standards throughout a nation implies unionism because it must entail redistribution from rich regions to poor ones, and therefore a central government strong enough to enforce that. The unprincipled reason was that Labour needed the parliamentary votes of its Scottish and Welsh MPs, where they were doubly overrepresented (Scotland and Wales had too many seats, and the *plurality electoral system gave them a majority of seats on a plurality of the vote).

u

Unionism has weakened substantially since 1997. Conservatives care less about the Union as such, now that they hold almost no seats outside England.

unipolarity An *international system characterized by one major centre of power and influence. This system is characteristically different from *bipolarity and *multipolarity because power is concentrated in one state or a collection of federated states. Although some theorists have argued that a *world government could be a positive form of unipolarity, most scholars of *international relations consider unipolar systems as prone to unchecked aggression and hegemonic exertions of power. For example, both *classical realists and *neorealists suggest that unipolarity can promote insecurity and opportunities for military action, since it allows for a sole *superpower to act largely at will without a *balance of power. The unilateral action in the *Iraq War by the United States in 2003 is often seen as a form of unchecked power associated with unipolarity.

United Front The Leninist strategy of alliance between Communists and other radical groups, particularly in the Third World but also for a time in Europe. It was based on two assumptions: that the new bourgeoisie in the colonial countries, especially in Asia, were sufficiently hostile to what Lenin described as economic imperialism to make common cause with the Communist Party, yet sufficiently weak to be unable to resist communist domination. M. N. Roy protested at these assumptions. Lenin won the debate but events proved Roy's case. In India the *Congress showed little sympathy with the Communist Party. In Indonesia the alliance ended in a massacre of the communists, and this was repeated on an even greater scale in China in 1927 when the Nationalist leader Chiang Kai-shek, having taken Shanghai and placated the capitalist powers, massacred his communist allies and drove the remnants into the mountains. In China, the Japanese threat eventually brought the two sides into a second United Front but it was scarcely a greater success than the first: cooperation, even military cooperation, against the invaders was negligible; considerable Nationalist and Communist forces were tied up in guarding their respective territories against their allies. After the Nationalists destroyed the Communist New Fourth Army in Central China in 1941, the United Front with the Nationalist Party virtually ended. Subsequently a new United Front was created to include the Communist Party of China and a number of third-force parties; this is still in existence, but the smaller parties have enjoyed little power or influence. JG

United Nations (UN) A voluntary association of over 190 member states signatory to the UN Charter (1945), whose primary aim is to maintain international peace and security, solve economic, social, and political problems through international cooperation, and promote respect for *human rights.

The UN, headquartered in New York, formally embodies the sovereign equality of states. The chief administrative officer is the Secretary-General. Primary responsibility for the maintenance of peace and security rests with the *Security Council. The *General Assembly is the main deliberative organ and plenary body. An Economic and Social Council coordinates the work of the many specialized intergovernmental agencies and bodies, and the *International Court of Justice. The Assembly delivers resolutions and not statutes; it can make external recommendations but not take binding decisions or enforcement action.

The hopes that the UN would play a larger role including in peacekeeping activities following the end of East-West hostilities have faced many challenges. The attitude of the US government is critical and has been a constraining factor. The 2003 invasion of Iraq sidelined the United Nations. In the 1990s the conventional understanding that the body has no right to intervene in matters essentially the domestic jurisdiction of any state (UN Charter Article 2:7) seemed to be weakening, especially regarding cases where governments abuse their own citizens' basic human rights. However, the attempts by US and allied governments to force regime change during the *Afghanistan War and *Iraq War have served to undermine this development, and states like Russia and China in particular remain firmly set against any erosion of sovereign rights. Funded by contributions from member states, the UN desperately needs larger and more secure funding. There are ongoing discussions about expanding the permanent membership of the Security Council to include such states as Japan, India, and Brazil, but securing universal agreement from the five existing members and other large states in developing world regions remains a major stumbling block. PBl

SEE WEB LINKS
• United Nations website.

universal domain In *social choice, the requirement that a procedure should be able to produce a definite outcome for every logically possible input of individual preference orderings. The rule 'Choose x over y if a majority of voters vote for x, and y if a majority of voters vote for y' fails to satisfy universal domain because it fails to cover the case where neither happens. The rule 'Choose x over y if a majority of voters vote for x, otherwise choose y' does satisfy universal domain, at the expense of giving y an edge over x.

UNMOVIC (United Nations Monitoring, Verification and Inspection Commission) *See* VERIFICATION.

UNSC (United Nations Security Council) *See* SECURITY COUNCIL (UNSC).

urbanism 'Urbanism' in English gains its contemporary meaning as a translation of the French expression *l'urbanisme*, which can be translated as 'town planning'. But it has implications which go beyond this translation. Urbanism suggests an approach which comprehends the city as a whole and contains a theory which seeks to explain urban relations. Perhaps the most influential such theory has been the neo-Marxist development, by such writers as Manuel Castells and Henri Lefebvre, of urbanism as a set of spatial relations which have distributive and class consequences independent of those generated by industrialism (the mode of production). LA

usual channels *See* WHIP.

utilitarianism The most famous definition of utilitarianism equates it with the belief that, 'That action is best which procures the greatest happiness of the greatest number'.

Although generally associated with *Bentham, who quoted it with approval, the statement was first made by Francis Hutcheson in his *Inquiry into the Original of our Ideas of Beauty and Virtue* (1725). The doctrine that actions should be judged on their capacity to produce happiness is an ancient one, recognizable as the classical Greek *eudaemonism*. However, it was only in the secular and commercial milieu of eighteenth-century Britain that it became an important and respectable philosophy, if not yet a dominant one. The works of Bentham, especially *An Introduction to the Principles of Morals and Legislation*, provide the most explicit statement of utilitarianism, but *Hume and *Burke were also utilitarians to some degree.

The 'greatest happiness of the greatest number' is an indication of the spirit and purpose of utilitarianism, but perhaps also a pointer to the intellectual problems which bedevil the philosophy. It seems to imply a prescription to maximize the population, since the maximization of xy is as well achieved by increases in y as in x. In so far as more people means less happiness per capita (as it means less space and fewer resources), then the definition sets up an indeterminate tension between numbers and individual happiness. It is clear that most utilitarians, including Bentham, intend the greatest happiness of a given number of people or of the whole existing population. 'Happiness' has not been successfully developed as a concept; nor have 'pain', 'pleasure', or '*utility'. Bentham offers a 'felicific calculus' to measure these concepts by considering their 'intensity', 'fecundity', 'duration', and so on, but even the most sympathetic contemporary utilitarian would not claim that the calculus actually offers us anything precise or capable of implementation. It is even crucially ambiguous as to whether 'pain' refers to states of very low pleasure, tending towards zero, or of negative pleasure, worse than death. Only biologists and *behaviourists, by concentrating on the physical concomitants of pain and pleasure rather than the sensations, have succeeded in making scientific concepts out of pain and pleasure. But these scientific meanings suggest that utilitarian policy-makers should look to pleasure machines or pleasure drugs as their principal instruments of policy, an implication which has been generally taken to be a *reductio ad absurdum* of the use of behavioural concepts of pleasure in utilitarian philosophy. The general aggregate which utilitarians would seek to maximize has been given several names including, recently, 'satisfaction' and 'human flourishing', but in the wake of the failure of the central concept, the philosophy has developed in two different directions, which can be called economic and broad utilitarianism. Economic utilitarianism replaces happiness as the central concept by the extent to which individuals get what they choose (or would choose, if they had a choice). It is thus able to develop a precise and sophisticated theory based on real and hypothetical choices and to allocate monetary values to outcomes; it generates such political and administrative applications as cost-benefit analysis.

Economic utilitarianism uses very different concepts from those used by Bentham, but it can be said to have developed in a Benthamite spirit. Broad utilitarianism, as it has been developed by moral philosophers, is more in the spirit of Hume and J. S. Mill in so far as it tends to eschew precise calculation in favour of more general utilitarian judgement and abandons the rigorous unidimensionality of the Benthamite concept of pleasure ('the quantity of pleasure being equal, pushpin is as good as poetry') to allow more qualitative judgements. The weakness of this approach is that it endangers the distinction between utilitarian moral and political philosophy and rival traditions. If we allow the possibility of qualitative judgement such as a presumption in favour of the profundity of the pleasure derived from poetry as against the triviality of that gained from pushpin, then have we not lost the rigorous insistence on the unbiased comparison of all goods which is typically utilitarian? Similarly, there is a problem about rules. Strictly, a utilitarian should acknowledge that 'rules are made to be broken' and calculate each individual act of obedience and disobedience on its consequences. But we are likely to be happier if at least some rules are obeyed habitually and generally. The doctrine of 'rule utilitarianism' suggests that we should always obey the rule which, if always obeyed, would have better consequences than any other

rule, always obeyed. Arguably, this cannot be called utilitarianism at all, its insistence on strict adherence to rules having crossed a philosophical boundary into neo-*Kantianism. Perhaps a more convincingly utilitarian solution to the problem of rules is John *Rawls's conception of 'summary rules', practices which we should generally, though not 'religiously', conform to in order to avoid the costs of endless calculations and to enjoy the benefits of social order.

A broad utilitarian outlook, by allowing a range of judgements about the quality of pleasure and the consequences of actions, is bound to allow utilitarian judgement to be informed by other philosophies to which the person making the judgement leans, whether traditionalist, libertarian, feminist, or whatever. However, even broad utilitarianism has its boundaries; the limits of what constitutes utilitarianism and what lies clearly in non-utilitarian territory can be delineated by three conditions, individually necessary and collectively sufficient to define it as a distinct form of political philosophy. Utilitarianism is necessarily:

1 *Consequentialist*. It judges, evaluates, and proposes actions according to their consequences and not, as deontological moralists do, according to conformance to a rule or rules, whether derived from reason, revealed religion, or the human condition.

2 *Aggregative*. It sums benefits for a population. This can be a state population (as a kind of summary rule about responsibility) or the global population. It may or may not take account of the interest of creatures other than *Homo sapiens*, but what it does not do is to allow any individual claims or rights to be wholly immune from inclusion in the aggregate sum.

3 *Sensualist*. What is aggregated must be reducible to the feelings of well- and ill-being of living entities. No virtue or advantage shall be counted which is not so reducible.

Utilitarianism entered politics as a radical philosophy, challenging orthodoxy, since its most famous development was stimulated by Bentham's hostility to Sir William Blackstone's lectures on law (published as *Commentaries on the Laws of England*). Blackstone attempted to derive English law from natural law, while Bentham was keen to establish that laws were made and not discovered by men and therefore could and should be chosen because of their consequences. Nor does utilitarianism necessarily support existing property rights, and early practical utilitarians such as Edwin Chadwick were instrumental in increasing the regulation of industry and the provision of public services. Utilitarianism does, after all, start from an egalitarian premiss: Bentham insisted that 'each is to count for one and no-one for more than one'.

But it is unlikely that a doctrine which seeks to maximize happiness over a foreseeable future could counsel revolution or even rapid social change. In *Anarchical Fallacies* Bentham rigorously opposed the natural rights doctrines of the French revolutionaries as 'nonsense on stilts', a new version of the old error of natural law. Utilitarianism has been, typically, the basis of liberal-conservative positions, realistic and reformist. With the demise of many of the traditional positions in political theory after 1945, utilitarianism came to hold a dominant position in non-Marxist thought. In 1979 Herbert Hart referred to this as 'the widely accepted old faith that some form of utilitarianism, if only we could discover the right form, *must* capture the essence of political morality'.

Economic utilitarianism is often attacked for the narrowness of its considerations and for its bogus precision. Broad utilitarianism meets two alternative criticisms: either it is treated as so broad and bland that it lacks proper boundaries as a philosophy or it is immoral in that the utilitarian approach to ethics profoundly contradicts our intuitive sense of right and wrong, most often our sense of justice or fairness.

The most important defence of utilitarianism is that there is no alternative to it as a public philosophy—in a secular and ethically pluralist age. Politicians cannot avoid causing the death of innocent people if they try to keep public expenditure in check or to help maintain a semblance of international order. Utilitarianism, uniquely, accepts this and yet makes an important moral demand of those who make policy: they must always consider the 'bottom line' of their decisions, who is gaining and who is losing and whether the net aggregate of well-being might not be better served by an alternative. Thus as a

'government house philosophy' (as Robert Goodin puts it) utilitarianism retains a leading, even unique, role. LA

utility The word has moved gradually from its general sense of 'usefulness' to its specific meanings in social science. The first philosopher to use it in the sense of the ability of something to satisfy wishes was *Hume, and this usage was systematized by the nineteenth-century *utilitarians. The cognate meaning in economics, that which leads someone to choose one thing over another, is traced by the *Oxford English Dictionary* to 1881, but the concept is far older. In particular, the idea that maximizing one's utility could not be the same thing as maximizing one's income was proved by Daniel Bernoulli in 1738. If they were the same, then anybody offered the opportunity to play the following game would rationally be prepared to pay all the money in the world to play it: A fair coin is tossed repeatedly until it lands for the first time on a head, when the game ends; your prize is two ducats if the coin comes down 'heads' on the first throw, four if the first head is on the second throw, eight if on the third throw, and so on. The expected value of this game is infinite, but as Bernoulli observed, nobody would be prepared to pay more than about twenty ducats to play it. This has become known as the 'St Petersburg paradox', which Bernoulli resolved by suggesting that the more money we already have, the less we want an extra ducat. This would now be labelled diminishing marginal utility for money.

Therefore when used as a technical term utility has no normative connotations. Utility furniture may be contrasted with beautiful furniture, but maximizing utility is the same as maximizing beauty if beauty is what the subject wants to maximize.

utopianism A disposition to embrace the vision of an alternative society from which present social evils have been eradicated and in which there is complete human fulfilment. Thomas More gave the name Utopia to the imaginary island in his book of the same name (1516): an island whose social, economic, and political arrangements were marked by a high degree of communism, undoubtedly inspired by More's own religious (Catholic) convictions and his monastic ideals. The imaginary society described by More was both a 'good place' (from the Greek *eutopia*) and a no-place (or *outopia*) in the sense that it did not actually exist.

Before More there had been a long tradition of speculation on the form and nature of an ideal human community: a tradition going back to *Greek political thought (especially in *Plato) and further developed in Christian doctrine (see, for example, Augustine's neo-Platonic *City of God*). From Plato to More the literary utopia served essentially as a way of articulating a moral sense of the ideal, and in this way the failings of real human societies and their political arrangements could be put into perspective. Often descriptions of utopia deliberately 'inverted' the real (e.g. private ownership of property) by putting forward an opposing principle (e.g. economic communism). In literary terms the effect of such contrasts was often highly satirical, as in More's celebrated description of gold and silver being used for the making of Utopian chamber pots.

The Renaissance gave renewed impetus to utopian thought, and authors such as Campanella (*The City of the Sun*, 1602) and Bacon (*New Atlantis*, 1627) began to inject a new spirit of modernity into political theory by describing societies transformed by the application of knowledge and economic-technological development. The utopian impulse found its way into movements of social protest, revolutionary sects and parties, and into the new all-embracing political ideologies of the age of the industrial and democratic revolutions. In particular, the new socialist doctrines of the early nineteenth century—articulated by *Saint-Simon, *Fourier, *Owen, Cabet, and others—were widely received as gospels of salvation by the industrial working classes in their struggle for liberation from the dehumanizing and exploitative effects of capitalist industrialism. The utopian socialists often described in considerable detail how such a society would be organized, whether on the level of a small-scale community (Fourier, Owen) or at a national and even international level (Saint-Simon and his disciples, and Cabet).

*Marx and *Engels sought to draw a strict distinction between utopian socialism and their own scientific socialism. They clearly believed that their utopian predecessors had put too much faith in reason and enlightenment as instruments of change in the direction of socialism, and stressed the importance of understanding the dynamics of class conflict in society and the need for revolutionary struggle as a means of overthrowing the existing social order. However, in terms of their own vision of a future socialist, and eventually communist, society, Marx and Engels, and indeed the whole tradition of modern *Marxism, can be seen to have embraced a strong (?utopian) conviction that the future would see the full realization of ideals of human liberation and equality.

Not only socialists and communists have produced utopias in modern times. Following Karl *Mannheim's analysis (in *Ideology and Utopia*) both liberal and conservative thought have found expression in utopian aspirations and (often) fully-fledged blueprints for the future. And today we must add the strongly utopian thrust of much contemporary environmentalist thought (Green utopianism), feminism (which has produced a rich literature of fictional utopias), and some social-scientific theories of post-industrial society. At the same time the strongly progressivist assumptions behind much utopian thinking in the nineteenth century have encountered widespread opposition in the twentieth century, and utopian blueprints and ideals have been widely rejected by their critics in a spirit of anti-utopian reaction. The literary dystopia—that is, a work deliberately seeking to reveal the awful consequences of trying to implement a rational blueprint for utopia—has exercised great persuasive power in the last half-century or so. Aldous Huxley's *Brave New World* (1932) and George *Orwell's *Nineteen Eighty-Four* (1949) are two of the most widely read accounts of possible 'nightmare'worlds of the future in which utopian ideas and principles have been put into effect through all-powerful dictatorial states.

However, utopianism does not necessarily lead to an advocacy of the all-powerful state and extreme forms of collectivism. As Robert *Nozick demonstrated in his *Anarchy, State and Utopia* (1974), it is possible to justify a minimalist state and extreme libertarian individualism on the basis of utopian arguments. KT

valence issue An issue that is uniformly liked or disliked among the electorate, as opposed to a position issue on which opinion is divided. *Corruption is a classic example of a valence issue; parties associated with corruption tend to be unpopular. Whilst all parties will claim to be virtuous and effective, parties do choose to emphasize particular issues over others (*see also* SALIENCY THEORY). Similarly, parties can develop reputations for (in)competence in particular areas. The idea that valence issues are important for understanding electoral success is a challenge to the theory of *spatial competition, which depends on the relevance of position issues. However, valence issues can become position issues once specific policies are proposed to deal with a commonly recognized problem. For example, unemployment is uniformly seen as bad, but there are important differences of opinion on how it should be tackled. SF

veil of ignorance Garment imagined by John *Rawls in his *Theory of Justice* (1971) as a mental device to enable individuals to formulate a standard of justice whilst remaining ignorant of their place in or value to their society. Rawls's social contract is that which he argues rational individuals would agree to if they were each placed behind a veil of ignorance. The veil permits them to know 'the general facts of human society' such as 'political affairs and the principles of economic theory . . . whatever general facts affect the choice of the principles of justice'. It prevents them from knowing any particular facts about themselves: 'no one knows his place in society, his class position or social status . . . his fortune in the distribution of natural assets and abilities, his intelligence and strength . . . his conception of the good . . . his aversion to risk or liability to optimism or pessimism.' Rawls argues that such people would agree on his principles of justice, including the controversial *difference principle. Critics of Rawls argue: (1) that people behind the veil of ignorance would not in fact choose the rules Rawls says they would as being just; and (2) that even if they did, that is no independent argument for the rightness of such rules. This latter point echoes a classic attack on social contract theory by *Hume.

Velvet Revolution The demonstrations and uprisings in Prague and other Czechoslovakian cities during 1989 which culminated in the ending of communist rule in November that year. SW

VER *See* VOLUNTARY EXPORT RESTRAINT.

verification The gathering of evidence as to compliance with agreements or undertakings. Issues of compliance and verification were prominent in the lead-up to the *Iraq war, when there was uncertainty about Saddam Hussein's compliance with UN resolutions demanding Iraq dispose of any *weapons of mass destruction (WMD) and accept a system of ongoing monitoring and verification. The United Nations Monitoring, Verification and Inspection Commission (UNMOVIC) was created in 1999, and its executive chairman, Hans Blix (previously head of the *International Atomic Energy Agency), led inspections of Iraqi facilities. The report that there was no evidence of an active WMD programme in Iraq was dismissed by President Bush of the US and Prime Minister Blair of the UK in the rush to war. In the aftermath of the war, the Iraq Survey Group conducted an exhaustive search, and found that Hans Blix had been right.

 SEE WEB LINKS
• UNMOVIC website.

Versailles, Treaty of Signed on 28 June 1919 at the Paris Peace Conference, seven months after the armistice ending the First World War, the treaty is seen as marking the end of the old order of Europe. It ascribed 'war guilt' to Germany, and imposed upon them huge reparations payments, territorial and colonial losses, and restrictions on military power. The treaty also comprised the Covenant of the League of Nations, an international organization established to promote collective security, and clauses ratifying the collapse of the Habsburg monarchy of the Austro-Hungarian Empire. SW

SEE WEB LINKS
• The text of the Treaty of Versailles.

veto Latin, I forbid. To prohibit, to block, to refuse consent to a legislative bill or policy proposal. Each permanent member of the United Nations *Security Council possesses a veto and during the Cold War this repeatedly prevented that organization from taking action. Presidents of the United States are endowed by the Constitution with a veto over congressional legislation. Bills that have passed the House and the Senate require the President's signature before they can become law. The President formally vetoes a bill by writing 'veto' across it and returning it to Congress with a statement outlining his objections. Members of Congress seeking to overturn such a veto can do so if they can muster two-thirds votes in support in both houses of the legislature. If the President declines to append his signature to a bill it automatically becomes a law after ten congressional working days. If the President fails to sign and Congress adjourns before the required ten days have elapsed that bill dies and the chief executive is said to have exercised a '*pocket veto'.

By preventing the passage of legislation that he deems unacceptable the President is able to play a prominent role in the making of public policy even when his party lacks majorities in Congress. Gaining one-third of the votes plus one in either house in order to sustain a veto is normally well within the reach of a determined chief executive and it is notable that presidents operating in conditions of divided government such as Eisenhower, Nixon, Ford, and Bush have made extensive and successful use of the veto.

The President of the United States can only veto bills in their entirety, whereas the governors of many states possess a line *item veto allowing them to veto specific parts of bills emanating from state legislatures. Proposals to give the President this weapon have been resisted on the grounds that this would shift the balance of power between the executive and the legislature to an undesirable degree. DM

Vice-President In the United States the Vice-President has few formal duties, and the importance of the position relies almost solely on the fact that the holder takes over the Presidency if the incumbent dies, retires, or is impeached; they are 'a heartbeat away from the presidency'. The Vice-President presides over the Senate, and votes in the case of ties. Presidents have tried to give the Vice-President roles in specific areas of policy, as roving ambassadors, or as heads of *ad hoc* agencies to deal with domestic issues.

Vice-Presidents are often chosen, not for the qualities they would bring to the administration, but in order to present a 'balanced ticket' at the election, broadening the appeal of the presidential campaign. The balance may be geographical—a Southern President choosing a Northern Vice-President—ideological—a conservative being paired with a liberal—or another consideration (e.g. religion, government experience, gender, ethnicity).

SEE WEB LINKS
• Site of the Vice-President of the USA.

Vichy The regime set up in unoccupied southern France after the French military collapse of 1940, named after the spa town which was its capital. Around the venerable figure of Marshal Pétain, there developed an authoritarian, collaborationist regime, organized on corporatist lines. The Third Republic was dissolved, strikes were banned, and 'Work, Family and Country' became the official motto. The regime undertook the reorganization of industry and agriculture, with an emphasis on central planning and coordination that would survive the war. Vichy attracted some early support, which, however, vanished as power gravitated into the hands of pro-Nazi, anti-Semitic elements, leaving Pétain isolated. Vichy was further undermined by the Resistance, the approaching Allied invasion and, finally, by the German occupation of the whole of France. At the liberation in 1944 the regime was completely discredited and its leaders later charged with treason.   IC

Vietnam War From the perspective of the present sovereign state of Vietnam, the Vietnam War began during the Second World War as a 'national liberation struggle' against Japanese occupation and only ended in 1975, after a series of victories over different adversaries, with the forcible incorporation of the state of South Vietnam into North Vietnam. The first victory came with the collapse of Japan in 1945. But a new enemy soon appeared in the form of France which sought to reimpose colonial rule on all of Indochina. By the early 1950s, however, the French were starting to wilt in the face of Vietnamese guerrilla resistance and were only with difficulty persuaded by the United States to stay in contention (even though in 1945 the Americans had urged the European colonialists to grant independence to Asian territories occupied by Japan). By the early 1950s, however, the Americans had been converted to the view that the anti-colonial forces in Indochina were communist-led and would, if successful, join the Soviet camp in the Cold War. Moreover the Americans came to fear that a *domino effect would ensue throughout South-East Asia with incalculable consequences for the Western policy of attempting to 'contain' communism.

In 1954 the French indicated their intention to withdraw from Indochina following the symbolic fall to Vietnamese guerrillas of the fortress of Dien Bien Phu. The Americans were fatally divided about their response. Secretary of State John Foster Dulles wished to intervene militarily to prevent any concession to communism, even if that meant that the United States had to act alone. President Eisenhower, on the other hand, insisted that such intervention must take a multilateral Western form. This left the British with the decisive voice, which Foreign Secretary Anthony Eden used, in association with the Soviet Union, to convene an international conference held in Geneva. Indochina was divided into four independent sovereign states: North and South Vietnam, Cambodia, and Laos. Of these, one, North Vietnam, was handed over to the communist-led insurgents

who had defeated the French. Eisenhower disapproved of this arrangement but lacked the resolution to use armed force to prevent it.

In the circumstances few believed that non-communist South Vietnam would survive for long. But its regime, encouraged by Washington, reneged on a promise given at Geneva for all-Vietnam so-called free elections to be held. And gradually successive US Presidents were drawn into taking South Vietnam under their wing as an insurgency, sponsored by North Vietnam, gathered momentum. Economic aid was presently supplemented with a degree of military support. In 1964 President Johnson, apparently reacting to a naval incident between US and North Vietnamese forces, obtained overwhelming support in Congress for the so-called Tonkin Gulf Resolution. This in effect authorized the US administration to render large-scale military assistance to South Vietnam and to wage an undeclared war against North Vietnam.

By 1968 it was apparent that the Americans had failed to defeat the insurgency in South Vietnam and that most other countries, even those belonging to NATO, had no enthusiasm for American policies. Facing much opposition at home and mounting evidence of low morale and indiscipline among US troops, Johnson decided not to seek re-election.

His successor, Richard Nixon, was elected in November 1968 on a platform of seeking to wind down the US presence in Vietnam but simultaneously to seek an honourable outcome in negotiations with North Vietnam. These aims proved to be incompatible but, as Nixon could not bring himself to admit this, the upshot was many more years of warfare. Only in 1973 did the North Vietnamese, under pressure from Moscow, consent to a negotiated settlement that enabled Nixon to order a withdrawal of all US forces and somewhat unconvincingly to claim that South Vietnam's independence had been saved. For the Americans, though not for the Vietnamese, the conflict was over.

Two years later South Vietnam's supposed independence disappeared as North Vietnamese forces marched into Saigon. The United States simply acquiesced in the takeover and hence in effect conceded that its longest war had ended in humiliation.   DC

violence Violence is endemic to political life. The pre-political *state of nature is often depicted as a place of indiscriminate violence, which we escape by forming a political society under the rule of a centralized authority (the State) that claims a monopoly on the legitimate use of violence. When the legitimacy of the State is challenged, and legal routes for voicing one's dissent are closed, citizens once again resort to violence. This can take different forms, from *civil disobedience, to *terrorism, to outright *revolutions.

The standard definition of violence refers to an act of force exerted to impart physical harm or injury on another person. This definition is inadequate on at least three accounts. It refers exclusively to physical harm or injury, neglecting psychological abuses or attacks. Only other persons are listed as the potential victims of violence, whereas animals or inanimate objects can also be the targets of violence. It assumes that there is a direct link joining the perpetrator and the victim of violence, overlooking the fact that violence often operates in indirect ways.

A more accurate but cumbersome definition of violence would be along the following lines: 'violence is the direct or indirect physical attack, injury, or psychological abuse of a person or animal, or the direct or indirect destruction or damage of property or potential property'. This richer definition of violence provides a more accurate standard for determining the conditions of non-violence. As Johan Galtung points out, apart from deliberately inflicting harm (direct violence), creating economic misery, repression and alienation should also count as types of violence (structural violence).

What distinguishes general 'violence' from 'political violence'? An act of violence is 'political' when it involves the actual or potential violation of someone's basic rights. Acts of political violence are illegitimate when the rights of the victim are unjustly violated. For example, sexual violence or domestic violence is the violation of a basic right to non-interference, or a right to self-ownership, which is why sexual or domestic violence are political issues. Under special circumstances, and as long as any divergence from the initial assumption of respecting the rights of others is justified, acts of political violence can be legitimate, even though the same act would normally

constitute a violation of rights. For example when the State punishes those who do not respect its laws, or when citizens rebel against the injustice of the State. *See also* PLURALITIES OF VIOLENCE. VB

virtual representation The essential idea of virtual representation is that one can be represented by a decision-making process without being able to vote for those who make the decisions. That the disenfranchised were virtually represented in Parliament was an argument often put by opponents of franchise reform in England in the nineteenth century. Twentieth-century social historians like E. P. Thompson have partly conceded this point by claiming that policy had to take some cognizance of the interests of the urban poor because of their capacity to riot, a form of anticipated reactions directly relevant to, for example, the Roman Empire, but also to the United States and United Kingdom in our own times in respect of people who do have the right to vote. Although the idea of virtual representation may seem paternalistic and undemocratic, it is perhaps the breadth of application rather than the concept itself which is offensive to modern susceptibilities: all modern societies accept it, in effect, in respect of children. LA

Voegelin, Eric (1901–85) Prolific and abstruse conservative political theorist; factors which have won him a committed following in the United States. He was born in Germany, and as a lecturer at the University of Vienna from 1929 attacked *National Socialism through books including *Race and State* (1933) and *Political Religion* (1938). The rise of Nazism forced Voegelin to emigrate to the United States, where he worked on *The New Science of Politics* (1952). This work attacked the *positivist approach to politics, arguing that it was methodologically flawed and based on a false belief in perfectibility. He developed a concept of 'gnosticism' (having, as with much of his terminology, a particular Voegelinian interpretation) which arose from a displacement from social reality and gave rise to a disruptive belief in the power of knowledge to transform reality. In five volumes of *Order and History* (published between 1958 and 1987) Voegelin sought to discover what lay beneath the gnostic turbulence, advocating a philosophy of human consciousness which would reveal the truth. The revulsion shown towards modernity and his theological style have seen him categorized as a conservative thinker, although he himself disputed this.

voice A. O. Hirschman's term to categorize the expression of grievances and demands on leaders by members of a political organization. Where the option of leaving the organization is reduced or eliminated, the threat of *exit becomes non-credible, and members will be forced to voice their discontent through internal pressure.   sw

Voltaire (François-Marie Arouet) (1694–1778) French political writer, journalist, and popularizer of every kind of knowledge. 'Voltaire' is an anagram of 'Arouet L I' (le jeune—the pairs I and J, and U and V, each being treated as the same letter). He was immensely successful in his own time, but is now little read apart from his satirical novel *Candide*. He rejected formal religion, which he saw as an insult to the supreme being in whom, as a deist, he believed. Voltaire was a relativist who believed that different political systems were appropriate to different societies. He praised the English system for its freedom, but saw a renewed and enlightened absolutism as the best form of rule for France. Unlike *Montesquieu, he supported the French monarchy against the Church and the aristocracy. For Geneva, however, he thought the existing system of *direct democracy was best, and tried to influence it in a more egalitarian direction. After failing to guide Frederick II of Prussia as a more enlightened despot, he concentrated on trying to achieve justice in particular cases, and produced his *Treatise on Toleration* in 1763.   cs

voluntary export restraint (VER) Agreement by an exporting country to limit exports to a specified importing country, for a price. The *World Trade Organization (WTO) prohibits discriminatory arrangements in international trade, and has led to a substantial reduction in tariff barriers. The resulting intensified competition among manufacturing producers often leads to painful industrial dislocation, generating a political dynamic which many governments

have difficulty resisting. One way around the problem is to negotiate voluntary export restraint agreements with those countries which are a source of rising import penetration. The successful exporter, such as Japan, 'voluntarily' agrees to restrict exports to the country whose products it is displacing. Japanese and other successful exporters tolerate VERs first because they risk facing the closure of the market in question, but also because despite making fewer sales than under free trade, they make more profit per sale. The resulting subsidy from the citizens of the protectionist country to Japan is unnoticed and therefore uncontroversial, although the flows can be enormous. It has been estimated that the VER between Japan and British car producers in the 1970s and 1980s involved a flow of some £50 per head per year from Britain to Japan.

As VERs do not involve any formal violation of WTO rules, they have provided an extra-legal channel for dealing with tensions in the international trade regime. However, their discriminatory character cannot be denied. In the context of the Uruguay Round (December 1993 agreement founding the WTO), member states agreed to eliminate most existing VERs over a four-year period and not to implement new VERs. Each member state could maintain a VER in one sector. This was partially successful. US and EU-imposed VERs against Japan were likewise to be removed. The most prominent VER arrangement, discriminating against textile and clothing exports from developing countries and known as the Multi-Fibre Arrangement, came to an end at the start of 2005.   GH/DH

vote bank Group of electors who vote *en masse* for a particular party or candidate. The term is often used in South Asian politics, where a feudal and caste-based social structure is seen to constrain individual choice when voting. Evidence suggests that vote banks are more a product of crude generalization amongst political commentators than an accurate description of voting behaviour.

voting There are three main subdivisions of the study of voting in political science: voting procedures, voting behaviour in mass electorates, and voting in smaller bodies such as legislatures.

In ancient Greece, voting was not much used for elections to offices, which were filled on the *jury principle of random selection. But it was used for decisions on propositions put before the democratic assembly, and on the fate of individuals. Periodically, assemblies voted on whether to 'ostracize'—that is, temporarily banish—somebody. The words *ostracize* and *ostracism* are derived from the Greek for 'tile' because bits of broken pottery were used as voting slips. Multiple voting slips with the same name in the same handwriting have been found, suggesting the earliest organized write-in (or rather write-out) vote.

There is a pioneering discussion of voting procedures in the Roman Senate in a letter of Pliny the Younger, AD 105, but the elaboration of voting procedures was next advanced in Europe by the medieval religious orders. As they had to choose their own officials independently of the papal authorities in Rome, they drew up elaborate procedures for doing so. At the same time, Italian city-states drew up elaborate voting procedures. The best-known of these were the rules for electing doges in Venice.

Voting re-emerged as a central theme in democratic theory in the eighteenth century with *Rousseau and *Condorcet. Democratic constitutions containing voting rules were written between 1787 and 1793 for the United States, France, and Poland. For the evolution of voting rules since then, *see also* SOCIAL CHOICE; PROPORTIONAL REPRESENTATION; PLURALITY.

The study of voting behaviour as opposed to voting procedures began in the twentieth century. The first studies were based on aggregate data such as election results. Electoral geographers in the *Siegfried tradition were able to establish the links between certain geographical features and patterns of voting behaviour. Herbert Tingsten in Sweden produced one of the first studies of the factors associated with *turnout, again based on aggregate data.

However, aggregate data must always be used cautiously (*see* ECOLOGICAL ASSOCIATION). Data about individuals required the development of the techniques of *survey research from the late 1930s onwards. Since then, vast quantities of evidence have accumulated on the relationships between such things as class, education, religion, and social attitudes ('independent' or 'predictor' variables), on the one hand, and voting behaviour (as 'dependent variable'), on the other. *See also* MICHIGAN SCHOOL; POST-MATERIALISM. Where, say, class and education both have an effect on voting, but are of course also related to each other because people in higher classes have or acquire more education, how do we disentangle the effects of each of the two on voting? Powerful computers enable more sophisticated statistical techniques based on multiple regression to attack these problems.

The study of voting in legislatures such as the House of Commons and the US Congress (often called '*roll-call voting') also dates back to early in the twentieth century. Initially, aggregate methods were used, notably by A. L. Lowell in his *The Government of England* (revised 1919). In the United States, where party discipline is weak, methods of analysing the divisions among Democrats or among Republicans by such predictors as their ideology, the length of time they had served in Congress, or the interests of their districts, are very well established. In the United Kingdom, the power of the party whips means that House of Commons division lists are usually quite uninformative. However, a few studies of roll-call voting have used more indirect measures such as floor revolts, membership of party factions, or *Early Day Motions.

v

Waltz, Kenneth (1924–2013) Waltz wrote his major work during the *Cold War period which had a profound impact on his arguments about the *international system. His earlier book *Man, the State, and War* (1959) is notable for introducing levels of analysis. The first 'image' relates to people, the second to the domestic situation, and the third to the anarchic structure of the international system, which is considered by far the most important. Anarchy here is not considered as chaos but the absence of hierarchical authority. This is developed in Waltz's main work *Theory of International Politics* (1979), which criticizes *classical realism for focusing on human behaviour instead of the structure of the international system and its ordering principles. Ultimately it is this structure—characterized by *anarchy—which forces states to behave in certain ways, rather than what goes on within or between states. The nature of the system is determined by the number of powers. For Waltz, the Cold War provided greater stability because the *balance of power was *bipolar rather than *multipolar. Waltz's theory became known as *neorealism or structural realism because of its focus at the level of the system rather than at the unit (state) level. JJ

want-regarding principles See IDEAL-REGARDING PRINCIPLE.

wants Unfulfilled desires for oneself or for others. Since individuals commonly aim to satisfy their wants, want-satisfaction may be a goal of public policy, either directly or through response to persons' *interests. For example, Benthamite *utilitarianism has been accused of seeing happiness as constituted by meeting desires. The 'efficient' satisfaction of wants is commonly taken to be a virtue of market allocation. The desire of individuals to satisfy their wants generates

only a weak normative weight, however, since such want-satisfaction may be inimical to the wellbeing of the agent, or of other people. Hence there may be a conflict between individual freedom and welfare considerations, prompting the distinction between want-regarding and *ideal-regarding principles. AR

war Armed conflict between two or more parties, usually fought for political ends. Its everyday meaning is clear, and the main focus of the idea is on the use of force between large-scale political units such as states or empires, usually over control of territory. The boundaries of the idea are, however, difficult to pin down. Some of this difficulty is suggested by the numerous adjectives that can be placed in front of it: *civil war, guerrilla war, limited war, total war, gang war, tribal war, *cold war, race war, *trade war, liberation war, propaganda war, class war, and so forth. Some of these are metaphors exploiting the image of ruthless and violent conflict over political ends taken from international relations, and transferred to actors other than states. In a legal sense, states can be at war without actually using force against each other, but merely by declaring themselves to be in a state of war (phoney war). Conversely, states can be using force against each other on quite a large scale without actually making formal declarations that they are in a state of war. The identification of war with a political motive means it can be applied to the international system and civil wars, preventing any clear location of the phenomenon at the interstate level. At both levels, wars are often about disputes over sovereignty and territory.

There are many theories about the causes of war, but no unified view. Some argue that war is simply a large-scale expression of the selfish, violent, and power-seeking elements in human nature. Others, notably neo-realists, argue that the regular recurrence of war throughout history is a consequence of the anarchic structure of the international system. Perhaps the most numerous source of theories is found amongst those who argue that war is caused by the political construction of states and the ideologies they express. During the nineteenth century, liberals argued that aristocratic states were aggressive because of the martial inclinations of their ruling class. Towards the middle of the twentieth century, almost everyone argued that fascist states were aggressive, including the fascists themselves. Marxists argue that capitalist states are driven to aggression by their ruthless competition for markets, while socialist states relate to each other peacefully. Liberals argue that communist states are inherently aggressive because of their totalitarian organization and their universalist ideology, while liberal democracies relate peacefully because of their economic interdependence with each other, and the constraints of democracy on the state's use of force. Empirically the liberals so far have the better of this argument. There are almost no cases of democracies going to war with each other.

Until quite recently, war was held to be a legitimate practice of states in pursuit of their national interest. European states fought regularly amongst themselves in pursuit of territory, dynastic claims, and colonies, and resort to war was an accepted mechanism for maintaining the balance of power. In the late nineteenth century laws of war began to develop to put some constraints on the use of some of the nastier technological possibilities for weapons. The shock of the unexpected cost and carnage of the First World War established war prevention firmly on the international agenda, but the collective security mechanism of the *League of Nations failed to expunge war from the practice of states. After the Second World War, a stronger legal regime against war was constructed, making war illegal for nearly all purposes except self-defence and collective security, and war was increasingly perceived as a morally dubious practice. However, the justification of wars in Afghanistan and Iraq following the *September 11th 2001 attacks has begun to move the criteria in the other direction, making pre-emptive and preventive attacks more acceptable in the eyes of many.

The lesson of the First, and even more so the Second, World War for the great powers was that their capacity to inflict destruction on each other had outrun the possible gains to be made from war amongst themselves except as a last resort of self-defence. This lesson was hugely reinforced by the arrival of nuclear weapons, whose obliterative powers were so great as to plausibly eliminate the distinction between total victory and total defeat. Despite great debate about whether war is becoming obsolete, these developments have not eliminated war amongst the lesser powers, or between great powers and lesser powers, although great powers often attempt to legitimize their role by claiming some humanitarian cause. Recent US-led wars against terrorism and wars on drugs reopen the prospect of non-state actors becoming principal players in the practice of war. *See also* RESPONSIBILITY TO PROTECT (R2P).   CT

war crimes Individual responsibility for violations of the laws or customs of war. Such responsibility covers both the commission of such crimes and the ordering or facilitating of them and the rule violated must belong either to the body of customary international law or be part of an applicable treaty. The first, although unsuccessful, attempts at the prosecution of war crimes took place after the First World War. The issue of individual responsibility re-emerged during the Second World War, with allied declarations in 1942 and 1943 expressing the determination to prosecute and punish major war criminals and to establish the tribunals that were to take place at Ñuremberg and Tokyo. Such crimes covered 'crimes against humanity', defined by the Charter of the International Military Tribunal established at Nuremberg as 'murder, extermination, enslavement, deportation, and other inhumane acts committed against a civilian population, before or during a war, or persecutions on political, racial, or religious grounds . . .'; and also the crime of aggression and crimes against peace, namely 'planning, preparation, initiation or waging of a war of aggression'. War crimes are also understood in terms of those acts that are defined as 'grave breaches' of the 1949 Geneva Conventions and Additional Protocol 1 of 1977. More recently they are defined in the 1993 Statute of the *International Criminal Tribunal for the former Yugoslavia, by the 1994 Statute of the International Criminal Tribunal for Rwanda, and in Article 8 of the 1998 Rome Statute of the International Criminal Court. The 1990s saw a greater willingness on the part of states to establish international courts to prosecute war crimes with the establishment of the tribunals dealing with the former Yugoslavia and Rwanda and the successful negotiation of the Rome Statute of the *International Criminal Court. *See also* RESPONSIBILITY TO PROTECT (R2P). AHu

ward The smallest unit of local administration or of vote counting; also known (especially in the USA) as a precinct.

warlordism A broad term used to denote a condition of weak central governmental authority within a state or region, in which a single warlord, or rival warlike militias, each headed by one dominant leader, control significant territory and exert power within that territory. In many cases warlordism is a result of a military coup within a country, which causes a division of that territory between warring parties. Warlordism can also occur when central authority fails (*state failure), where multiple warlords and their loyal militias fill vacuums of power through violence and fear. Although warlordism is a prominent feature in history (e.g. ancient China and feudal Europe), recent examples of warlordism exist in Afghanistan, Colombia, the Democratic Republic of Congo, Iraq, Libya, the Philippines, Somalia, and Sudan (to name just a few).

Warsaw Pact The Warsaw Pact, formally the 'Warsaw Treaty Of Friendship, Co-operation and Mutual Assistance' was formed in May 1955. The immediate reason given for its formation was the Paris Agreements amongst the Western powers that included West Germany in the North Atlantic Treaty Organization (NATO). To counterbalance this expansion of NATO, the Warsaw Pact set up a mutual defence organization, the Warsaw Treaty Organization (WTO), with a unified military command and headquarters in Moscow, which embraced the German Democratic Republic, as well as Albania, Bulgaria, Hungary, Poland, Romania, the Soviet Union, and the Czechoslovak Republic.

In practice the Warsaw Pact enabled the Soviet Union to station troops in these satellite states. In several satellites, these troops became a focus of protest during anti-Soviet uprisings, as in Poland and Hungary in 1956. Hungary sought to leave the organization at the time, but failed. Similarly, Czechoslovakia failed to leave the Warsaw Pact in 1968, when the Soviet Union invoked the treaty against it to crush the Prague spring. Only Albania successfully withdrew from the pact in 1968, having developed closer links with China. The Warsaw Treaty Organization became defunct with the East European Revolutions in 1989, and the German Democratic Republic's withdrawal from it in 1990 was a largely symbolic act, which foreshadowed the Warsaw Pact's final dissolution in July 1991. PS

Washington Consensus See NEOLIBERALISM.

Watergate Office block in Washington, DC, occupied in 1972 by the Democratic National Committee. A bungled burglary here, by agents of President Richard Nixon trying to disrupt the Democratic campaign, led eventually to the resignation of Nixon in August 1973. The suffix -gate is now widely applied to the name of people or places involved in alleged political scandal.

weapons of mass destruction (WMD) Collective term for chemical, biological, and nuclear weapons. The term, or its acronym, entered common usage after the *September 11th 2001 terrorist attacks on the United States, representing the dangers of proliferation and fears of similar outrages. The accusation that Saddam Hussein's Iraq regime possessed and was willing to use weapons of mass destruction was one of the main justifications for the US and UK decision to attack Iraq in 2003 (*see also* VERIFICATION).

Webb, Sidney James (1859–1947), **and Webb, Beatrice (neé Potter)** (1858–1943) *Fabian socialists, who married in 1892, and pursued a life of research and political activity together. Their published works included lengthy studies of the trade union movement and local government. Sidney Webb was active on the London County Council (LCC) from 1892 to 1910, and in the first two Labour Governments, ending his career as Lord Passfield.

For the Webbs, socialism was the most efficient possible social system rather than an end to be valued in itself. Sidney was a 'Progressive' (Liberal-Labour) on the LCC, and their first attempts at influence were on the Liberal Party. Their outlook combined a very British empiricism which insisted that ideas could only advance on a basis of massive detail with a stolid utilitarianism. The result was an outlook which perceived capitalism as wasteful and inefficient rather than as morally wrong or necessarily outdated. Disillusioned by the collapse of the Labour Government in 1931, they became interested in, and attracted by, the Soviet Union, publishing *Soviet Communism: A New Civilization?* in 1935. (The question mark was removed in the 1936 edition.) LA

Weber, Max (1864–1920) German sociologist; one of the most influential figures in the history of the discipline. Born in Erfurt, and moving to Berlin in 1869, Weber grew up in a prosperous household intimately connected with the academic and political life of Bismarckian Germany. His father, a worldly politician, became a member of the Reichstag whilst his mother was guided by a strong sense of religious duty. Weber read law, history, economics, and philosophy at the universities of Heidelberg, Göttingen, and Berlin, also attending seminars at Strasbourg during his military service. In 1886 he qualified as a junior barrister whilst working towards the first of his doctoral theses on the legal and economic history of medieval trading companies, awarded in 1889, and followed two years later by his 'habilitation' thesis on the agrarian history of Rome. Weber took up a professorship of economics at Freiburg after some teaching in Berlin. A chair in politics at Heidelberg (1896) marked a high point in his teaching career. The following year saw a quarrel with his father (mainly over the latter's treatment of Weber's mother) who died unreconciled to his son. This conflict seems to have precipitated the psychological and physical breakdown of Weber's health. He did not return to teaching until towards the end of his life

when he held professorships in Vienna and Munich.

Prior to his breakdown Weber had written on the stock exchange and 'traditionalism' amongst farm workers; topics which gave some impetus to later works. He became active in nationalist politics, joined the Pan-German League but withdrew on health grounds and because of disagreements over policy. After several years of illness a new phase of productivity began in the period 1902–4 when he took an honorary professorship at Heidelberg; worked on a series of methodological essays; and began his study of the formation of the modern world order, the first fruit of which was *The Protestant Ethic and the Spirit of Capitalism.* Thereafter Weber expanded his interests into a comparative study of the 'economic ethics of the world religions' which, when combined with the studies of Rome and the Middle Ages, provided an analysis of cultures on an unmatched scale. Even so he would be the first to admit that they were incomplete. Such incompleteness was both a practical matter and an issue of epistemological principle: all knowledge was necessarily partial. The last years of his life were mainly devoted to drawing together these strands in *Economy and Society: An Outline of Interpretative Sociology* (*see also General Economic History*). Like *Marx's Capital,* Weber's *Economy and Society* is a vast, complex, but ultimately incomplete text.

During the First World War Weber worked on the organization of military hospitals; he was a member of the German Delegation to the 1919 Versailles Conference; became a member of the executive of the German Democratic Party and, in that year, commenced his teaching at the University of Munich. After a short illness he died of pneumonia on 14 June 1920.

An outline of Weber's work can best set out from the philosophical, methodological, and ethical outlook which colours so much else. Epistemologically speaking, the essential antinomy is that between the infinite complexity of the potentially knowable and our finite capacity to know. For Weber, reality cannot be reduced to a set of brute facts; knowledge of that reality is formed by the interdependence of 'fact' and 'theory'. The central issue is the understanding and explanation of action. This focus is often misinterpreted as a will to believe in our psychological capacity to rethink or relive the actor's thoughts and to be incongruously matched to a model of explanation drawn from the natural sciences. Neither point does justice to Weber's methodology. The capacity to understand rests, not on psychological insights, but upon historical scholarship, empirical research, and ultimately upon the humanist assumption that the actor's intentions are in principle accessible, however difficult such access may, in practice, prove to be. Similarly the model of explanation is rooted, not in natural science, but in jurisprudence and legal theories of causality.

Weber's anti-empiricist stance rules out the possibility of direct observation of social life. His concepts or 'ideal types' are abstract exaggerations of phenomena which, in their pure form, cannot be found in reality. Idealizations of this kind (e.g. 'class', 'status', 'party', 'power', 'charisma', 'feudalism', 'sect', and so on) are, for Weber, not the main goal of sociological analysis but they do assist the understanding of the complexities of social phenomena. The very unreality of the ideal types highlights the empirical details, contradictions, and ambiguities of the subject-matter. Precisely because ideal types can be constructed from varying points of view, analysis knows no final resting point.

The analysis of power and domination illustrates something of Weber's approach. 'Power' is defined as any situation in which actors can realize their ends despite the resistance of others. 'Domination' is more specific, referring to the exercise of power through a command and the probability that such commands will be obeyed. Here the assumption is that power will normally be exercised through an administrative staff. The most enduring forms of domination are those to which, on whatever basis, 'legitimacy' is ascribed by the participants. Thus Weber seeks to develop a set of ideal types of legitimate domination through which the historical and contemporary variety of political arrangements might be analysed. These types are belief in legitimacy grounded in 'traditional' (an immemorial order), 'charismatic' (the special qualities—often divinely ordained—of the leader), or 'legal' (the due process of law) criteria.

The idea of legitimacy rests upon the actor's subjective belief (or lack of it) in the system—an orientation which blends with the focus on the 'meaningful'. Weber does not confuse these idealized forms with reality. A conceptual framework structured around an actor's subjective beliefs in legitimacy does not require acceptance of the claim that such legitimation actually exists. Nothing could be further from Weber's view of the political order as an arena of conflict—largely between classes, status groups, and parties, all of which are phenomena of the distribution of power. Finally, the typology of domination is not a portrayal of specific political structures but is, rather, a range of concepts through which a system can be analysed. The point being that the existence of all forms of domination is a contingent matter and this contingency rules out a deterministic progression from one form to another. Certainly legal and bureaucratic elements are very strongly present in Weber's view of the modern order but there is no neat development from, say, charisma to traditionalism to legality. Quite to the contrary, Weber saw, even in the modern world, the possibility of charismatic leadership as a source of revolutionary breakthroughs.

The analysis of domination forms a considerable part of Weber's sociology but it would be wrong to restrict the 'political' to this area. The social implications of religions are, for example, a theme to which he frequently returns. The concept of legitimacy resonates with theological issues—justification, salvation doctrines, and theodicies. Those having the good things in life wish to legitimate their holdings and one of the most powerful roots of such legitimation is a belief in divine approval of the existing arrangements. These observations raise the question of the relationship between morality, politics, and science. Weber's underlying premiss is that actors have a will to believe in the 'meaningful' nature of their endeavours and that social science must explore this. Such exploration confronts the world of values head on.

There are a number of strands to this confrontation. Weber had no intentions of rejecting the world of values in the search for scientific analysis. Often the aims of investigation included the desire to force both analyst and audience to face moral and political issues as well as the pursuit of knowledge. However, Weber found it both logically untenable and morally repugnant to claim that research could underpin questions of ultimate value. Science could not tell us how to live or what to do, but this prohibition did not prevent him from a vigorous advocacy of German national interests. Of course Weber never thought that these views could masquerade as science. The latter provided clarity, analysed means to ends, and indicated the possible consequences of action. None of these achievements replace the obligation to make political and moral choices. To live for science and for politics are, to Weber, matters of intense commitment (in contrast to the lack of passion in *Nietzsche's 'last men') the poignancy of which was heightened by the 'polar night of icy darkness and hardness' confronting post-1918 Germany. The politician confronts this darkness through the 'ethic of responsibility': that is, one in which responsibility for the consequences of action is ever at hand. Weber contrasts this with an 'ethic of conviction' rooted in absolute and ultimate ends which leave aside worldly consideration of the consequences of that action.

This concern with the demands of the day is rooted in Weber's analysis of the development of rationalization and of *capitalism in both its 'adventure' or 'booty' form and as the distinctive characteristic of the modern economic order. In this order, formally rational bourgeois capitalism and bureaucracy proceeded apace—although the growth of bureaucracy is, for Weber, by no means restricted to capitalism. He sees socialism as at least an equal contributor to this growth.

There are many views on the significance of Weber, and deep divisions remain as to the interpretation of his work. Criticisms include the 'unreality' of ideal types and, frequently, a rejection of his views on the separation of facts and values. Nevertheless, few would doubt his place as a thinker of the first rank. In methodology, comparative sociology, economic history, and the sociologies of law, religion, and politics, he left an enduring legacy in

1 A refusal to confuse scientific and moral propositions whilst maintaining an awareness of their complex relationships.

2 The production of a multilayered, multicausal, and self-consciously incomplete picture of the social world. Here explanation is frustratingly elusive and stands apart from closed meta-narratives based upon 'laws', 'structures', and the 'logic of history'.

3 An important perspective upon the great transformation to modernity. 10

Webster, Daniel (1782–1852) US Federalist (later Whig) politician notable for (1) his famous oratory, mostly in defence of retaining the Union of the United States in the years that led to the Civil War, a stance that alienated both Southern nullificationists (*see* CALHOUN) and Northern abolitionists; (2) his proposed solution to the problem of *apportionment. Webster's rule requires the scrutineers first to choose the size of the house to be apportioned. They must then find a divisor x such that, when x is divided into the qualifying number for each unit (population of each state, or votes cast for each party) and the quotients of all units are rounded off at ½, the entitlements of each unit (state or party) sum to the required number of seats. The Webster apportionment system is the fairest, and was used to apportion seats in the US House of Representatives to states between 1881 and 1931. It is exactly the same as the unmodified *Ste-Lagüe algorithm for allocation of seats to parties in list proportional representation, although the procedures for the two applications seem very different.

weighted vote *See* BLOCK VOTE.

Weimar Republic The federal republican system of government established in Germany in 1919, based on a new constitution drawn up at Weimar. From the start the Republic faced a range of political and socio-economic problems which made the achievement of order and stability extremely difficult. It has often been seen as a 'democracy without democrats' in the sense that it seemed to lack a solid basis of liberal support, and was also unable to secure the allegiance of key elites in German society. As world economic conditions worsened at the end of the 1920s, political disenchantment heightened and extremist movements and parties gained strength. From 1930 onwards the Republic was effectively transformed from a parliamentary to a presidential system, with President Hindenburg appointing cabinets which lacked a parliamentary majority and which made increasing use of powers of decree. Eventually this paved the way for the rise of *National Socialism, the appointment of the party leader, Adolf Hitler, as Chancellor in January 1933, and the ensuing suspension of the Weimar constitution. KT

welfare economics The branch of economics dealing with how well off people are, or feel themselves to be, under different states of affairs. Sometimes regarded as the normative branch of economics. Other branches ('positive economics') describe how economies work, and the consequences of any one person's actions or choices for everybody else. Mainstream welfare economics has nevertheless been fiercely attacked, from both inside and outside economics, for pretending to make fewer value-judgements than it actually does. One application of welfare economics is *cost-benefit analysis, which attempts to balance the gains and losses from some proposed policy, such as building an airport. Some critics say that the sort of technique involved, which must place a price on people's time at work and at leisure, and a price on any Norman churches that would be lost if the airport was built, must always be arbitrary and worthless. Defenders say it has to be done somehow.

welfare state A system in which the government undertakes the main responsibility for providing for the social and economic security of the state's population by means of pensions, social security benefits, free healthcare, and so forth. In 1942 the *Beveridge Report in the United Kingdom proposed a far-reaching 'settlement', as part of a wider social and economic reconstruction, once victory in the Second World War was secured, and became the blueprint for the British welfare state.

By 1944 a White Paper made full employment the first goal of government economic policy, and the Butler Act provided for universal secondary education. Labour, however, won the 1945 general election, to a considerable extent because they appeared more wholeheartedly in favour of the Beveridge plan. The key measures which followed, largely implementing the plan's essential features, were the National Insurance Act 1946, the National Health Service Act 1946, and the National Assistance Act 1948. An ambitious programme to build a million homes was also launched. By 1948 *The Times* newspaper proclaimed in an editorial that these measures had created 'security from the cradle to the grave' for every citizen.

These measures were the foundation of the 'welfare state', which was seen as synonymous with 'social security'. In a specific sense this meant entitlements to benefits under the newly established national insurance and assistance schemes. In a wider sense it referred to the other reforms implemented at the time, particularly the guarantees of full employment and access to a national health service free at the point of use. Underlying all this, however, was a new conception of the relationship between the state and the individual within a market-based society. This was based on an acceptance of the need for extensive intervention to ensure that its worst effects were mitigated, on the grounds that their causes were systemic rather than the fault or responsibility of individuals.

Nevertheless, behind the apparent consensus on the need for a welfare state, there was political conflict on its meaning between 'reluctant collectivists' in the liberal tradition (such as Beveridge himself) who saw the reforms of the 1940s as a high-water mark, and reformist socialists who saw it as a framework for developing a more concerted shift towards a planned and egalitarian society. A small minority of commentators, such as *Hayek, were never convinced of the need for the welfare state in the first place and remained resolutely 'anti-collectivist'.

The growing 'crisis' of the welfare state since the 1970s can be seen as due to changed economic and social circumstances, a disintegration of the post-war consensus, or both of these. Undoubtedly, growing economic pressures were making it harder to meet more insistent demands for improved services, and increased social needs due to changes in family patterns, more older people, and growing numbers of unemployed people. On the other hand, the 'welfare state' had been increasingly criticized within a more polarized political culture. Critics from the right argued that by removing responsibility from the individual, the welfare state stifled people's initiative to solve their own problems. Critics from the left agreed in part that the welfare state as it currently stood was often 'oppressive', but attributed this to a failure to attack the root causes of class, gender, and 'race' inequalities.

Even before 1979 there were discernible shifts by the 1974–9 Labour government after the expenditure crisis of 1976 towards retrenchment and 'restructuring' of welfare in ways that responded most to right-wing rather than left-wing critics. However, after the Conservative election victory of 1979, this shift occurred in a more concerted way and there have been substantial reforms in all of the services established as a result of the Beveridge Report, though only in one, housing, could there be said to have been significant retrenchment in provision. In other areas, there have been a tightening of eligibility rules and shifts to decentralization of managerial responsibility within tighter centralized control of finance. Perhaps most controversial of all has been the reform of the National Health Service in 1990, against widespread opposition, to create an 'internal' market within a socialized system.

In a wider sense, there has been a significant shift from Beveridge's assumptions. Most importantly, there was a shift in economic priorities from maintaining full employment to controlling inflation. The modest redistribution of income and wealth achieved up to the 1970s, was reversed by cuts in income tax and a shift to more regressive forms of indirect taxation like value added tax (VAT). Despite all this, by the end of the 1980s the welfare state had been 'restructured' rather than abolished. It was suggested that a new 'welfare pluralist' consensus had emerged in which it was accepted that private, state, and voluntary sectors could exist side by side. In the 1990s the growing internationalization of the global economy, which has undermined the autonomy of national governments, led to pressure to reduce wage and social security costs in order to attract highly mobile investment.

It is probably most helpful to situate the British variant analytically and comparatively as a 'welfare state regime'. These, G. Esping-Anderson argues in *The Three Worlds of Welfare Capitalism*, fall into three main types within market societies: 'conservative', 'social democratic', and 'liberal', depending on the extent to which they seek to work with, or to counter the effects of, the market on social inequalities. An example of a conservative regime is Germany, characterized by high welfare provision within a hierarchical and ordered society, while Sweden is closest to an egalitarian 'social democratic' regime. Though in 1948 the British welfare state was among the most developed, by the 1970s provision had become more extensive in conservative and social democratic regimes, and the British welfare state looked closest to the 'liberal' model, with only limited attempts to use welfare to mitigate social inequalities. Though all welfare state regimes have been under pressure, in Britain and the United States the shift towards liberalism has been particularly pronounced, nor was it reversed on Labour coming to power in 1997 or with the election of Democratic President Barack Obama in 2008. MC

wellbeing Wellbeing is understood in different ways in politics, but is a term often used synonymously with ideas about the 'good life' and the 'good society'. It has been an important theme in politics since the ancient Greeks. *Aristotle spoke of 'eudaimonia' or human flourishing as the highest purpose in life, while Epicurus provided a 'hedonic' account of wellbeing, emphasizing happiness—generally understood as the presence of pleasure (pleasant affect) and the absence of pain (unpleasant affect). Such distinctions remain present in contemporary debates on the role of wellbeing in politics.

Contemporary interest in wellbeing is the second of two waves of interest in the post-Second World War period. The first wave, which began in the 1960s, was driven by a combination of the desire to improve social conditions and an emerging post-materialism captured by US President Lyndon Johnson's (1964) description of the 'good society' as 'a place where men are more concerned with the quality of their goals than the quantity of their goods.' The political momentum behind the first wave fell away with economic recession in the 1970s and the election of right-wing governments in prominent states. The second wave emerged through awareness of growing environmental threats in the 1990s, but grew to incorporate a wider set of social concerns and—distinctive in public policy circles—an interest in promoting subjective wellbeing. Subjective wellbeing is closely associated with individual happiness, but is often seen by scholars as broader, combining pleasant affect, unpleasant affect, and life satisfaction. In both the first and second waves, concern with wellbeing has been closely related to challenging the status of GNP/GDP, which has been taken as a proxy of national progress. US Senator Robert F Kennedy (1968) famously argued that *GNP 'measures everything in short, except that which makes life worthwhile'.

A key feature of the second wave has been the emergence of a range of multi-indicator measurement frameworks both within and across states that seek to challenge the dominance of GDP. These frameworks typically include economic, environmental, and social indicators, often alongside indicators of subjective wellbeing. Examples within national contexts include the UK's Measuring National Well-being Programme, the Canadian Index of Well-being, and Measures of Australia's Progress. Examples at international level include the OECD Better Life Index and the EU's GDP and Beyond initiative. The UN's *Sustainable Development Goals (SDGs) agreed in 2015 can also be seen as part of these developments, providing a multidimensional framework against which all UN nations are now required to measure their progress.

These developments reveal significant political momentum behind new ways to capture the notion of progress and to reframe the goals of public policy. However, while measurement initiatives have proliferated and demonstrated an increasing convergence around 'what matters' for wellbeing, the policy response remains at an early stage. Thus far, GDP remains the dominant benchmark for national progress, and the dominance of economic indicators cascades down through different layers of policy-making. Yet for some, these developments have transformative potential in the longer term.

However, a number of controversies remain around wellbeing as a central goal

for public policy. For some, the 'science of wellbeing' is insufficiently advanced to provide a reliable and valid basis for reshaping overarching policy goals, while others argue that the pursuit of wellbeing should be left to individuals rather than be the focus of government activity. Others still are concerned that a greater focus on wellbeing may distract governments from other valued goals such as *freedom, *equality, and *justice.

Some debates stem from *meta-theory dispositions that cannot be reconciled empirically but underline the continuing relevance of the pursuit of wellbeing as a provocative but vital and enduring political issue. IB

West/Western As the neatest term available to refer to Western Europe, the United States, and other countries of European settlement in one breath, the word connotes an ideal of secular and democratic liberalism and economic growth which peoples in Russia, Turkey, China, and elsewhere have pursued and rejected by turns throughout the modern period. This was subsequently overlaid, from the later 1940s, by *Cold War ideological and military rivalry between an avowedly communist East under Soviet and Chinese leadership and a West, now clearly centred upon the United States and often taken to include Japan, in which the values of consumerism, economic growth, and personal liberty assumed heightened prominence. It is against this supposedly degenerate modern culture, in the aftermath of the Cold War, that Islamic states as different from one another as Iran and Saudi Arabia have continued to define themselves, though without abandoning the standards of technological and military sophistication and material well-being first achieved in the West. CJ

Western European Union (WEU) Established as the post-war repository of a specifically European conception of defence cooperation in 1954, the WEU was overshadowed by *NATO during the *Cold War. During the 1980s the WEU grew in importance as *European Union members sought to develop defence and foreign policy cooperation more systematically. France and Germany established a joint military brigade under WEU auspices, but since

2001 its part in European cooperation on defence matters has been subsumed by the *Common Foreign and Security Policy.

(⊕) SEE WEB LINKS
• Western European Union site, including historical information and documents.

West Lothian Question *See* DEVOLUTION.

Westminster Area of central London, including many of the institutions of the UK central government. The Palace of Westminster is the site of the Houses of Parliament, comprising the *House of Commons, and the *House of Lords. The oldest surviving building, dating from the eleventh century, is Westminster Hall, which hosts ceremonial occasions, and since 1999 has been used to hold debates on issues which cannot be fitted into the Commons' timetable.

Westphalian state system Term used in *international relations, supposedly arising from the Treaties of Westphalia in 1648 which ended the Thirty Years War. It is generally held to mean a system of states or *international society comprising sovereign state entities possessing the monopoly of force within their mutually recognized territories. Relations between states are conducted by means of formal diplomatic ties between heads of state and governments, and international law consists of treaties made (and broken) by those sovereign entities. The term implies a separation of the domestic and international spheres, such that states may not legitimately intervene in the domestic affairs of another, whether in the pursuit of self-interest or by appeal to a higher notion of sovereignty, be it religion, ideology, or other supranational ideal. In this sense the term differentiates the 'modern' state system from earlier models, such as the Holy Roman Empire or the Ottoman Empire (*see* SOVEREIGNTY). RTC

WEU *See* WESTERN EUROPEAN UNION.

Wheeler, Anna (1785–1848) Closely associated with Mary *Wollstonecraft, Anna Wheeler was a radical feminist and an Irish Protestant. A keen advocate of women's rights, she wrote that 'with the emancipation of women will come the emancipation of the useful class'. STH

Whig In British usage, originally a Scottish Presbyterian opponent of Anglican government; subsequently applied in 1679 to those who opposed the succession of the Catholic James II to the throne (*see* LOCKE) and thence to those who supported the 'Glorious Revolution' of 1689. They were in government for most of the eighteenth century, in opposition for most of the period following the French Revolution, and in government again after the 1832 Reform Act. In the nineteenth century the word was partly superseded by 'Liberal' but retained to denote the right-wing, aristocratic faction of liberalism. Most of its members joined the Tories in or after 1886.

In US usage, member of a party opposing the Democrats between 1834 and 1856; the name was chosen deliberately for its echoes of English resistance to the executive.

Whig interpretation Whig history, as it is usually called, was both a methodology and a series of messages about Britain's past. Its methodological assumptions were two: the study of British history should be rooted in political or constitutional developments; and the past could, indeed should, be assessed with the present, or present controversies, constantly in mind. Most professional historians now regard these assumptions with disdain. The general messages promoted by Whig history included the notions that Britain's past was the history of progress, that 'things' went well (certainly better than 'elsewhere'), that this progress was largely the work of accommodating elites and popular support for liberties, that its prime domestic product was the 'matchless' British constitution, and, finally, that the benefits obtained were graciously extended to other peoples scattered around the globe.

Whig history went through various phases. It started life in the seventeenth century as partisan history; English history as seen by those who opposed, in the name of the ancient constitution, the attempts by all Stuart monarchs between 1603 and 1688, to subvert that constitution and impose a foreign model of government: namely, absolutist monarchy. In the eighteenth century it became party history, that is to say, the Whig party's interpretation of the curious and embarrassing events of 1688 and 1714, when an essentially conservative national elite ditched kings they disliked for others (foreigners) they thought they would like. These episodes required an explanation and justification. Whig (party) history provided it. In the nineteenth century Whig history became the orthodox history of professional historians. Thomas Babington Macaulay's five-volume *History of England* published between 1848 and 1861 promotes with some style most of the general themes mentioned above.

Four criticisms are commonly levelled at Whig history. First, that the past should be studied for its own sake (and in manageable chunks), not as historical overviews designed to make a point about the present. Secondly, Whig history was winners' history, the history of the successful—wealthy conservative English Anglicans—and it has little to say about Ranters (or ravers), the lower orders, the 'crowd', Catholics, the Scots, and so on. Thirdly, it was altogether too contemptuous of foreign models of political development. Finally, it completely ignored, or was unable to digest, Britain's decline since the late nineteenth century. JBU

whip A member of a legislature appointed to facilitate party organization within the legislature. Generally, parties will each appoint a chief whip with a team of junior whips. The term is derived from the 'whipper in' of English hunting parlance, whose role it is to keep the pack together in chasing its quarry. In the UK House of Commons the whips' intentions are made clear by the weekly circulation of a document detailing important votes, three lines being scratched under an item indicating the whips' strongest call for support. In many legislatures the job of the whips has expanded to take some responsibility for the management of the legislative timetable itself, as well as facilitating the communication of views between party leaders and back-bench representatives. Whips also become the means through which opposing parties can communicate over the management of the work of the legislature. In the UK House of Commons this is known as the 'usual channels'.

The power of the whips is dependent upon the importance of consistent party loyalty to personal political advancement for members of a legislature. Where the latter is not critical, as in the US Congress, the power of the whips is weak. Where it is key, as in the UK House of Commons, the whips have much more power. The ultimate sanction against an MP who votes against the party line is the withdrawal of the party whip, which in the majority of cases effectively spells an end to parliamentary ambition. This said, Michael Foot and Harold Macmillan are both examples of MPs who had the party whip withdrawn early in their parliamentary careers only to go on to lead their parties, the Labour and Conservative parties respectively. For those who are appointed as whips and are seen to be successful, the position generally provides valuable experience in party management and a stepping-stone to ministerial appointment. JBr

(⊕) SEE WEB LINKS

- Information on the whip from the UK Parliament site.

white primary Primary election in which blacks are excluded. In the Southern states of the United States, where nomination in the Democratic primary was tantamount to election, 'white primaries' were used to exclude blacks from the electoral process. Declared unconstitutional in 1944.

Wilson, Woodrow (1856–1924) Began his career as a university politics teacher; President of Princeton University, 1902–10, Governor of New Jersey, 1910–12, and President of the United States, 1913–21. As President he first distinguished himself by presiding over an impressive programme of domestic reform legislation. After re-election in 1916 he led the United States into the First World War and was one of the main architects of the peace settlement negotiated in Paris. For Wilson the creation of machinery to preserve international peace was an essential part of that settlement, but he suffered a humiliating personal and political defeat when the Senate rejected the Treaty of *Versailles, thereby ensuring that the United States would not participate in the League of Nations.

Wilson was something of a rarity in that he began his career as an academic student of politics, attained considerable distinction in that field, and then had the opportunity to put into practice at the highest level some of his theoretical musings. In his early writings Wilson was severely critical of the US

Constitution and bemoaned the lack of opportunities for effective national leadership in the American political system. *Congressional Government*, first published in 1885, was trenchantly critical of Congress and bleakly pessimistic about the possibility of real leadership from the White House. This work remains to this day a constantly cited classic critique of Congress. *Constitutional Government in the United States*, published in 1908, had a distinctly more optimistic tone with Wilson now encouraged by the entrance of the United States on to the world stage and the example of Theodore Roosevelt's Presidency to believe that strong leadership by the chief executive was, after all, possible. Through his writings, his role as an opinion leader at the turn of the century, and his actions as President Wilson may be seen as one of the founders of the modern Presidency. DM

Winstanley, Gerrard (*c.*1609-60) The leader of the Diggers, a group who saw the earth as a 'common treasury' for all mankind. They consequently rejected the exclusion of anyone from the land. They believed this exclusion historically had been a consequence of illegitimate conquest, and incompatible with God's will. They advocated taking communal possession of existing commons and of land that was uncultivated, although Winstanley was pacific in argument and behaviour. They questioned the legitimacy of the authority that protected existing private property. Winstanley's ideas evolved, becoming rather more authoritarian at the end of his known writings. He has been claimed for both the *anarchist and the socialist traditions. The Diggers set up a short-lived community on St George's Hill in Surrey. AR

winter of discontent Name given to events in Britain during the winter of 1978/9, when as a result of industrial action taken by several public sector unions in protest at the centrally negotiated incomes policy, a number of key services were severely disrupted, many (e.g. hospitals, refuse collection) being brought to a virtual standstill. The term is a misquotation from Shakespeare's *Richard III*. SW

withering away of the state An argument of Engels and Marx that during the transition to communism, the state loses its bureaucratic and coercive functions and is replaced by collective and decentralized administration of society. GL

Wittfogel, Karl *See* ORIENTAL DESPOTISM.

WMD *See* WEAPONS OF MASS DESTRUCTION.

Wollstonecraft, Mary (1759-97) Mary Wollstonecraft is known as the first British feminist theorist. Her *A Vindication of the Rights of Woman* (1789) examines women's subordination in society in the light of the principles of rationality and equality that were so important to the Enlightenment. She argued that Reason—which she defined as the capacity of acquiring knowledge, making judgements, and forming moral frameworks of our own—is equal in both men and women. It is the denial of equal opportunities for education to women, on the one hand, and stereotyping women in their 'motherly' roles, on the other, that makes women behave differently from men. In her other influential book *Thoughts on the Education of Daughters*, Wollstonecraft argues for equal access to education for women. Her ideas about education and equality have been the inspiration for much equal opportunities legislation for women. SR

women's movement Or the Women's Liberation Movement (WLM), which has had multiple agendas for women, comprising: equal opportunities in education, employment, and pay, self-determination on issues such as contraception and abortion, improved public facilities for childcare, tightening of legal sanctions against violence against women whether in the public or the private sphere, and an end to discrimination on grounds of sexuality, race, religion, and ethnicity. The title of the movement was consciously adopted in the 1960s to move away from the objectification of women in political discourse as was represented by the construction of 'the woman question'. WLM drew its inspiration from the American New Left movement and represented a general shift in the radical political discourse of the time from a rights-based political language to one based on concepts of 'oppression' and 'liberation' and of activism. WLM depended on pooling women's lived experiences, and politicizing them through consciousness-raising programmes of meetings, demonstrations, exhibitions, and so forth. WLM, while challenging the frameworks of power within which women are oppressed in different contexts, also emphasized working within the system. This position led many radical feminists to dissociate themselves from WLM. SR

Woolsack A large square cushion, covered in red cloth; seat of the Lord Speaker (previously the Lord Chancellor) in the House of Lords, from where the Speaker, or his or her deputy, presides over debate.

workers' control This term covers a variety of schemes which have sought to give workers full democratic control over the organizations in which they are employed. It suggests something more than rights of consultation and participation, and points to a more fundamental achievement by workers (in their particular industry or occupational sphere) of the real power to take key decisions. It has permeated much of the socialist tradition of thought, including some strands of revolutionary *Marxism, and *syndicalism. Workers' control within a capitalist society—in the sense of significant measures of trade union and 'shop-floor' influence over managerial decision-making, known in German as *Mitbestimmung*—must be distinguished from complete self-management of industry by workers under conditions of socialized rather than private ownership of capital (as exemplified by the Yugoslav system of workers' councils in the 1950s and 1960s). KT

working class The class of people who are employed for wages, especially as manual workers. Narrower than Marx's *proletariat, comprising those who have nothing to sell except their labour power, because that describes almost everybody in a modern industrial society. In ordinary use the term denotes a *Weberian status-group rather than a Marxian class. To be working-class is to have some badge(s) of status such as wearing heavy protective clothes at work, being subject to tight discipline on attendance such as having to clock in and out of work at fixed times, and working in a heavily unionized occupation. The criteria are vague and it is not clear how they are to be fitted to

those not actually in work; nevertheless almost everybody uses and has subjective understanding of the term.

World Bank The Washington-based World Bank group of institutions comprises the International Bank for Reconstruction and Development (IBRD, established 1945) and its affiliates—the International Development Association (IDA, established 1960), the International Finance Corporation (1956), and the Multilateral Investment Guarantee Agency (1988). Their objective is to help raise living standards in developing countries by channelling financial resources from developed countries.

The IBRD is owned by the governments of 185 countries. It funds loans to governments or where there are government guarantees, chiefly from borrowings in world capital markets. The IDA depends heavily on subscriptions and replenishments by governments. The World Bank has evolved from financing mainly physical capital infrastructure, through addressing basic needs, to conditional lending in support of structural economic adjustment and, now, a stronger emphasis on poverty reduction. Governments are supposed to commit to a poverty reduction strategy process if they want to qualify for financial support, and this in turn is supposed to be done in consultation with civil society. In addition the World Bank has become more alert to environmental issues in development. However, it has been a favourite target of anti-globalization campaigners, who view the imposition of structural adjustment as an attempt to impose capitalism and consider the growing attention to poverty and the environment as inadequate. In reality the Bank's power has been under threat in recent years from the increasing ability of many developing countries to access other sources of international capital. The greater financial independence that commodity price increases have brought to some rentier states, oil exporters especially, has also made a difference. However, many of the poorest countries in Africa in particular still rely heavily on support from the IDA. PBl

⊕ **SEE WEB LINKS**

- World Bank site, including information on organization history, structure, and functions.

world government/world state World government is an ideal of political authority marked by full integration of all political units into a cohesive global institutional framework whose highest-level governing and legal bodies would exercise supremacy on a significant range of issue areas. A world state is a similarly integrated global political system, but one which also would control a legitimate global monopoly on the means of collective coercion, analogous to current states. A world government model could forego full monopoly control as a means of lessening potential threats from global institutions themselves.

In the 1940s' 'heyday' of world government, public and political calls were made in many countries for a global political authority capable of ensuring a global peace, especially after the 1945 nuclear destruction of the Japanese cities of Hiroshima and Nagasaki by the United States. During the *Cold War period, such advocacy was less popular, as it was typically equated with support for presumed Soviet designs on world domination. Since the break-up of the USSR, however, numerous prominent academics have renewed calls for full global political integration to promote security, democracy, or global justice. Others have predicted the emergence of a world government or world state, spurred by economic integration or continuing security vulnerabilities. LC

World Social Forum Network for *anti-globalization protest, describing itself as 'a plural, diversified, non-confessional, non-governmental and non-party context that, in a decentralized fashion, interrelates organizations and movements engaged in concrete action at levels from the local to the international to build another world'. Ambiguity about its role and purpose have led to criticism that it has been captured by *non-governmental organizations, and lacks any coherent ideology or programme.

(⊕) SEE WEB LINKS
• World Social Forum website, including Charter of Principles.

world system analysis A historical and sociological approach to political economy with a belief in the importance of interdependency and the global systemic structure

and connected processes. There are two strains to world system analysis. First, the strain that focuses on aspects of international capitalism and is associated most strongly with Immanuel Wallerstein (see his *Geopolitics and Geoculture: Essays on the Changing World System*, 1991). This uses a large-scale and long-term framework analysing structures, cycles, and trends. Three central processes are stressed: the rise and fall of hegemonic powers; the gradual expansion, with short-term shifts; and the core–periphery division of labour. The second strain emphasizes rather the global political system, and is associated most closely with George Modelski (see his *Long Cycles in World Politics*, 1987). Phases and cycles are identified in the hegemonic global structure, with processes associated with order, territorial rights, security, and trade stability. PI

World Trade Organization (WTO) The Uruguay Round of multilateral trade negotiations under the auspices of GATT (General Agreement on Tariffs and Trade, based on a 1947 agreement) established the World Trade Organization. Upon ratification of the Round's Final Act by members, the WTO replaced GATT as the global multilateral trade organization, and a series of agreements associated with but legally distinct from GATT were also placed under the WTO umbrella (such as the *GATS, the Agreement on Agriculture, on Textiles and Clothing, on Rules of Origin, etc.). In 2016 there were 164 members, including the 28 member states of the European Union which are also represented as the European Communities by the European Commission.

The 1947 General Agreement on Tariffs and Trade (GATT) emerged from wartime and post-war negotiations (*see* BRETTON WOODS) to establish a stable, multilateral economic order. The lengthy negotiating process (1944–7) reflected the controversial nature of the politics of international trade at domestic and international levels of bargaining: changing patterns of international trade could have dramatic and fairly immediate effects on domestic employment and income levels within and among national economies. While it has never proved possible to gain broad agreement on the extent of liberalization in most domains of international trade, it was accepted that the unilateralist and discriminatory practices of the inter-war period had had particularly negative consequences for all concerned.

GATT itself was an interim accord which sought to codify the rules of the emerging trade regime and to proceed with important reductions in national barriers to trade. The US delegation was determined to press other countries to reduce their discriminatory trade practices (particularly the British '*imperial preference') and in exchange the United States was willing to reduce its traditionally high tariffs. The USSR and its allies remained outside GATT, only considering membership at the end of the *Cold War in 1989. Following the signature of the Havana Charter in 1948, the GATT was supposed to form the 'rule book' of the newly established International Trade Organization (ITO). The ITO charter prescribed a far more ambitious multilateral institution than the eventual WTO, but this was in part its eventual downfall. When the US failed to ratify the ITO charter, the institution was dead and only the 'interim' GATT survived.

The GATT agreement enunciated the principles of reciprocity and non-discrimination, encapsulated in the *Most Favoured Nation (MFN) and National Treatment concepts. National Treatment implies that governments cannot treat foreign exporting firms any less favourably than domestic producers. Reciprocity meant that any negotiations among trading partners were to yield roughly reciprocal concessions and/or benefits in the eyes of the parties. Non-discrimination meant that any trade concession advanced by a country to one GATT trading partner had to be extended to all others simultaneously. In this way, bilateral negotiations among trading parties would be 'multilateralized', leading to the establishment of a liberal trading order.

GATT negotiating 'Rounds' were difficult due to the weak state of most post-war economies, and the extraordinary competitive edge of American industry at the time. Most economies would have experienced severe balance-of-payments difficulties had they removed barriers to imports, and domestic employment would have been adversely affected as well. As post-war recovery rendered more liberal trading policies acceptable, the American government sought to replace the piecemeal approach with reciprocal across-the-board tariff cuts by all participating parties on a wide range of traded products. This initiative developed into the 'Kennedy Round' agreements of June 1967 which stand as a watershed in post-war trade liberalization. Tariffs on manufactured goods were reduced by 36 per cent on average, and this progress was continued in the later Tokyo Round (1974-9).

The United States had originally taken unilateral measures to keep agricultural trade out of the GATT process in 1955, but had reversed this position in the Kennedy Round. This led to a long-running conflict with the *European Union (with its Common Agricultural Policy, which represented a delicate internal compromise difficult to disturb) and Japan, both with protected agricultural markets. Agriculture is still central to conflict over the trade regime, and held up the Uruguay Round of negotiations (completed in December 1993).

As tariffs were lowered, so-called non-tariff barriers (NTBs) became the remaining instruments of trade policy. Examples were *voluntary export restraint agreements and orderly marketing arrangements, running against the spirit of GATT non-discrimination. As these were 'voluntary', GATT rules theoretically did not apply. Furthermore, the principles of liberalization called into question many economic policy measures associated with successful national economic development strategies in the post-war period, particularly in Japan, Europe, and the developing world. Finally, the Less Developed Countries sought exemption from many of GATT's rules, pointing out that their weak economies benefited little from free trade arrangements. All governments abused the escape clauses in GATT (e.g. through anti-dumping measures) and attempts have been made to tighten up the rules over time. None of these disputes is likely to be resolved in any permanent fashion; it is the nature of the eventual compromise which will be crucial to the continued success of the WTO as GATT's successor. There nonetheless remains broad agreement on the need to continue the momentum of the liberalization process through further rounds of WTO negotiations.

The Uruguay Round negotiations successfully expanded the scope of GATT. It now includes multilateral rules applied to the services sector (*see* GATS), intellectual property, investment measures, and some aspects of agricultural trade. The Round also ended the provisional status of GATT by establishing the World Trade Organization with an enhanced institutional framework and dispute settlement procedure. The WTO's judgements on trade disputes now bind member countries to change their trade practices, though the US Congress formally refuses this implication and asserts the superiority of US laws.

The new WTO is not without tensions among its members and their societies, as its history would suggest is likely to be the case. Developing countries argue strongly that the WTO as constituted does not adequately take into account the difficulties and asymmetries of economic development under conditions of liberalization. Developed countries and the international organizations they control such as the *IMF have put strong pressure on developing countries to liberalize their trade laws despite uncertain consequences for long-run development prospects. Developed countries are often less than generous in opening their markets to developing country exports, especially in the domain of agriculture and garment production.

The present round of trade negotiations was launched in 2001 in a WTO meeting at Doha, Qatar. The Doha Development Round seeks to lower trade barriers further (in agriculture, industry, and services). A major split has developed between developed and many developing countries (led by China, India, Brazil, and South Africa) over the perceived fairness of existing trade rules for the latter. Because of ongoing disagreements between countries, the Round, which was initially intended to conclude by the end of 2006, was prolonged and, as of 2008, negotiations were stalled. The most prominent disagreement among countries concerns agriculture. Developing countries seek the elimination of price-distorting agricultural subsidies by the EU and the US. Negotiations in Geneva in July 2006 were suspended and negotiations in Potsdam in June 2007 broke down

because of differences over agricultural subsidies but also the opening of agricultural and industrial markets in various countries. In the end it was recognized that no agreement was going to be reached and the talks were abandoned at the start of 2016.

Perhaps the biggest challenge to the WTO comes not from member states but from civil society groups such as *non-governmental organizations. Many social activists in the *anti-globalization movement draw attention to the difficulties of liberalization in both developed and developing countries, especially for the weaker members of society and less market-competitive forms of economic organization which may nonetheless be crucial to local identities and cultures. Organized labour maintains an uneasy relationship with the liberalization process, for fear of job losses. Finally, the emergence of the European Union (EU), *NAFTA, and other nascent regional arrangements such as *MERCOSUR or the Asia Pacific Economic Co-operation Forum (APEC) are also potential challenges to the young WTO. So far these regional arrangements have not emerged as discriminatory trading blocs, and the WTO expressly permits regional economic integration if compatible with its rules. Despite the ultimate success of the long Uruguay Round, regional arrangements and indeed bilateral/unilateral solutions (especially on the part of the United States) may become the order of the day if ongoing agreement cannot be reached on outstanding issues in the Doha Round. However, global companies would be likely to put up stiff resistance to any attempt to substantially restrict the liberal or global nature of the trade regime. In short, conflict in the WTO continues to mirror socio-political tensions across its member economies and is intimately related to the tensions of global economic integration largely driven by liberalization policies. DH/GU

SEE WEB LINKS

- World Trade Organization site, including information on organization history, structure, and functions.

xenophobia Literally, fear of foreigners or strangers, though the term is often used to refer to attitudes of hatred or contempt rather than pure fear. Xenophobia is different from *chauvinisme* in French or *jingoism in English, which both suggest an excessive patriotism or national self-esteem, because it consists primarily of negative attitudes towards the outside group.

Xenophobic emotion has always played a part in the outlook of groups and communities. Its persistence defies the ideological universalism of most of the dominant movements of ideas, such as liberalism and socialism, in the past two centuries and drives the more doctrinaire political phenomena of racism and nationalism. Xenophobic tendencies seem most prominent where familiar structures and traditions have broken down, as in Germany after 1918 or Eastern Europe in the 1990s after the collapse of communism. They tend to manifest themselves in hostility towards immigrants and Jews. In the early twenty-first century migrants seeking *political asylum became the most frequent targets of xenophobia in many countries.   LA

Young Hegelians A label attached to those disciples of *Hegel in Germany who sought to develop and expand the dialectical spirit of Hegel's philosophy beyond the limitations of Hegel himself. 'Old' Hegelians, by contrast, saw the Hegelian system as the final and complete manifestation of that philosophic spirit. Nowadays, a list of the most famous of the Young Hegelians would certainly include, *inter alia*, Karl *Marx, David Strauss, Ludwig *Feuerbach, Bruno Bauer, Arnold Ruge, Max *Stirner, and Moses Hess. JH

Young, Iris Marion (1949–2006) American political philosopher. Young, who was Professor of Political Science at the University of Chicago, is best known for her works on justice, democratic theory (deliberative), democracy and difference, and feminist theory. Young's work can be seen as a fusion of her various interests into a coherent, and critical, re-examination of liberal conceptions of justice and democratic inclusion. She is most recognized for critically approaching these subjects from a feminist perspective, arguing that traditional and contemporary liberal arguments for inclusion, participation, and justice often under-represent, or fail to include, various members of a democratic society. In the case of *deliberative democracy,

Young was critical of 'rational procedures' that were meant to guide democratic discourse, where certain forms of meaningful communication might be excluded as being irrational. Although critical, the works of Young were not compelled by a wish to undermine these systems in their entirety, but to act as critical self-reflection, with the normative aim of furthering social justice and democratic inclusion.

Young, Michael (Lord Young of Dartington) (1915–2002) British sociologist and institutional designer. Author of the Labour Party's 1945 manifesto, he was not a conventional socialist. Most of his tireless innovation and institutional design focused on consumers and communities. Of the many institutions he created, the most enduring have been the Consumers' Association (1957); the Open University (endorsed by the incoming government in 1964); and the British arm of the University of the Third Age (created when Young and co-founder Peter Laslett were themselves at the statutory retirement age, in 1982). His satire *The Rise of the Meritocracy* (1958) warned in Orwellian fashion of the effect on the underclass of relentless sifting and screening by merit. It could be due for a revival.

zapatismo Derived from the Mexican revolutionary leader Emiliano Zapata (1879–1919), zapatismo has been an influential political tradition whose emphasis has been on the restoration of rights of the dispossessed and social justice. Zapata's basic ideas, spelt out in the *Plan de Ayala* (1911), were summed up in the mottoes 'Land and Freedom' and 'Land belongs to those who plough it'. The Mexican Constitution of 1917 incorporated the idea of land reform through the prohibition of large estates and the creation of the *ejido* system, or communal land-holding, which regulated land tenure in Mexico without substantial reforms between 1917 and 1992.

Hundreds of organizations which campaigned and fought for social justice and participatory democracy in Mexico throughout the twentieth century included the name Zapata in their names. The EZLN, or Zapatista army, became the best known after its dramatic public appearance in the state of Chiapas on 1 January 1994, the same day that NAFTA sealed the commercial integration of Mexico with the United States and Canada. Since then zapatismo has become an international social movement with strong support from progressive groups in the United States and in Europe. The new zapatismo has embraced indigenous' rights and cultural diversity as well as anti-globalization and anti-capitalist protests around the world. Rather than emphasizing class struggle they stress the need for broad coalitions and grassroots movements (globalization 'from below') to oppose the neoliberal world order. Likewise, rather than furthering their objectives through armed conflict they have concentrated their strategy and discourse on the international media (being dubbed the first 'virtual guerrilla' movement in the world). FG

zero-sum game A contest in which one player's loss is equal to the other player's gain.

Games may be divided into two classes, zero-sum and non-zero-sum. The class where the sum of the winnings of all the players is the same in all outcomes may be called 'constant-sum'. But as pay-offs can always be mathematically rescaled, it is convenient and normal to call them 'zero-sum'. In any change of outcome in a zero-sum game, the gain of the gainer(s) exactly equals the loss of the loser(s). Most games in the ordinary sense, without selective outside intervention, are zero-sum. Chess and football are zero-sum, and remain so even if an outside body awards a fixed prize for winning. But a football game where the participants are bribed to produce a score draw, or a Scrabble game where there is a prize for the highest aggregate score, would be examples of non-zero-sum games. 'Non-zero-sum' is preferable to 'positive-sum' and 'negative-sum'. Although these labels are commonly used, they are usually misleading and sometimes wrong, as they fail to specify what the positive sum is being compared with.

In 1944, J. von Neumann and O. Morgenstern proved that all two-person zero-sum games have a unique equilibrium in which each player plays that strategy which minimizes his or her losses for any possible strategy by the other player (*see also* MINIMAX; MAXIMIN). This is mathematically elegant but of limited practical use, although it shows that there exists a unique best strategy for chess. Luckily, that strategy has not yet been found.

The importance of zero-sum games in politics is more informal. In a zero-sum game there is no scope, in the long run, for cooperation among the players, although if there are more than two of them there is much, often infinite, scope for temporary coalitions of some players against the rest. Thus coalition games are zero-sum. Some writers view other political games as zero-sum, for example arms races or industrial conflict(s). This always leads to gloomy prognoses because there is no scope for long-run cooperation.

Non-zero-sum games offer scope for cooperation among the players to achieve one of the outcomes which is best in aggregate. This is true whether the game is regarded as cooperative or non-cooperative. Even in a non-cooperative game such as *Prisoners' Dilemma, players may reason about each other's reasoning. In repeated plays of non-cooperative games, they may send each other signals by their actions which enable the players to coordinate their actions on a cooperative (higher) equilibrium (*see* SUPERGAME). Most political games other than coalition games are probably best regarded as non-zero-sum.

Zionism *Zion* in Hebrew refers to the citadel of Jerusalem and also to the Kingdom of Heaven. Zionism refers to the movement among European Jews in the late nineteenth century to create a Jewish homeland. This movement was largely a consequence of the anti-Semitism which Jews were experiencing. In 1897 Theodore Herzl (1860–1904) formally initiated a Zionist movement at the World Zionist Conference in Basle. Since that time there have been organized attempts to persuade Jews to emigrate to the 'Land of Israel', otherwise known as Palestine. It was not at first unquestioned that the Jewish state must be in Palestine; Chaim Weizmann (1874–1952), later first President of Israel, was influential in establishing this objective and it was much encouraged by the declaration of the British Foreign Secretary, Arthur Balfour (the 'Balfour Declaration') in November 1917 that Britain favoured a homeland for the Jewish people in Palestine. Jews continued to emigrate to Palestine in relatively small numbers and a Jewish state might have been many decades or even centuries away had it not been for the persecution and extermination of the Jews by Hitler and his allies between 1933 and 1945, which legitimized the idea of a Jewish state to Jews and non-Jews alike as the only place where Jews might feel safe from persecution.

Zionism achieved its principal aim in 1948 with the establishment of a state of Israel which acknowledged, in its 'Law of Return',

the right of all Jews to live within its borders. Since that time 'Zionism' can be taken to refer to support for the continued existence of the state of Israel. Like many forms of nationalism, of which it is a special case, Zionism tolerates considerable ideological diversity: it is possible to be a religious or secular Zionist, and to believe in capitalism or socialism in the state of Israel.

Palestine was by no means unoccupied when Jewish settlement began, but populated by an Arab people, the Palestinians, who were, for the most part, forced into exile by a form of settlement which became, in effect, a military conquest (*see also* INTIFADA, PLO). Underlying this problem is the deeper question of the legitimacy of a national claim to territory which dates back to a dispersion of the Jews in AD 70 under the Roman Empire. Some historians have even claimed that European Jews are not, at least for the most part, descended from the original inhabitants of Palestine, but from Caucasian tribes who converted to Judaism under the later Roman Empire. LA

zipping The promotion and use of an all-women shortlist to increase female representation on electoral ballots and to increase the number of women holding parliamentary seats. Predominantly used in the United Kingdom by the *Labour Party. Zipping remains controversial, since critics argue that it limits the choice available to constituents as well as undermining *meritocracy. Advocates see the practice as a means to tackle structural and social inequalities and to provide more balanced representation within government.

zoning Zoning is the process whereby public authorities use whatever powers they have of controlling land-use in order to separate and concentrate different economic functions. Typically, they create residential, industrial, commercial, retail, and agricultural zones. Public authorities with powers over land-use almost invariably practise zoning in the belief that such policies produce better aggregate effects than an unzoned free market in land. For example, the belief that factories and dwellings should be kept apart is almost universal and has its roots in the traumas of early industrialization.

In many countries, such as Britain, zones are merely broad and flexible policies for land use. But in the United States, zoning has acquired a much more precise legal status. Arising, originally, out of the desire to keep Chinese laundries out of 'white' residential areas in San Francisco in the 1880s, the legal propriety of zoning was confirmed by the Supreme Court in the case of *City of Euclid* v. *Amber Realty Company* in 1926 and, with a few exceptions (of which Houston is the largest), most American cities have used zoning ordinances since. Zones usually distinguish densities of residence as well as uses. However, zoning goes to the limits of tolerance of the constitution, especially of the protection of property rights in the *Fifth and Fourteenth Amendments, and forms of zoning, including agricultural and undeveloped zones, have been declared to be 'confiscatory' and, therefore, unconstitutional. The history of American zoning has been a long conflict, largely taking place in the courts, between public authorities and environmentalists, who want to expand the powers of ordinances, and property owners and conservatives, who want to restrict them. LA

Timeline of Political Philosophers and Theorists

This timeline of political philosophers and theorists is designed to give a general chronological overview and show representatives of major traditions in the history of political philosophy. It is not designed to be comprehensive: not all the political philosophers and theorists included in this dictionary are shown, and (as with specific entries) we have not included people who are still alive.   MS

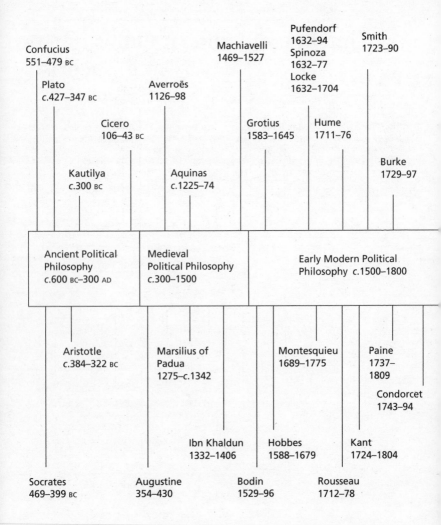

Confucius
551–479 BC

Plato
c.427–347 BC

Cicero
106–43 BC

Kautilya
c.300 BC

Averroës
1126–98

Aquinas
c.1225–74

Machiavelli
1469–1527

Grotius
1583–1645

Pufendorf
1632–94
Spinoza
1632–77
Locke
1632–1704

Hume
1711–76

Smith
1723–90

Burke
1729–97

Ancient Political
Philosophy
c.600 BC–300 AD

Medieval
Political Philosophy
c.300–1500

Early Modern Political
Philosophy c.1500–1800

Aristotle
c.384–322 BC

Marsilius of
Padua
1275–c.1342

Montesquieu
1689–1775

Paine
1737–
1809

Condorcet
1743–94

Ibn Khaldun
1332–1406

Hobbes
1588–1679

Kant
1724–1804

Socrates
469–399 BC

Augustine
354–430

Bodin
1529–96

Rousseau
1712–78

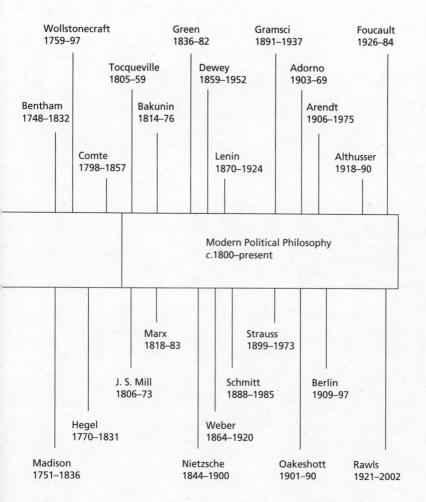

Wollstonecraft
1759–97

Green
1836–82

Gramsci
1891–1937

Foucault
1926–84

Tocqueville
1805–59

Dewey
1859–1952

Adorno
1903–69

Bentham
1748–1832

Bakunin
1814–76

Arendt
1906–1975

Comte
1798–1857

Lenin
1870–1924

Althusser
1918–90

Modern Political Philosophy
c.1800–present

Marx
1818–83

Strauss
1899–1973

J. S. Mill
1806–73

Schmitt
1888–1985

Berlin
1909–97

Hegel
1770–1831

Weber
1864–1920

Madison
1751–1836

Nietzsche
1844–1900

Oakeshott
1901–90

Rawls
1921–2002

Oxford Quick Reference

A Dictionary of Marketing
Charles Doyle

Covers traditional marketing techniques and theories alongside the latest concepts in over 2,000 clear and authoritative entries.

'Flick to any page [for] a lecture's worth of well thought through information'

Dan Germain, Head of Creative, innocent ltd

A Dictionary of Media and Communication
Daniel Chandler and Rod Munday

Provides over 2,200 authoritative entries on terms used in media and communication, from concepts and theories to technical terms, across subject areas that include advertising, digital culture, journalism, new media, radio studies, and telecommunications.

'a wonderful volume that is much more than a simple dictionary'
Professor Joshua Meyrowitz, University of New Hampshire

A Dictionary of Film Studies
Annette Kuhn and Guy Westwell

Features terms covering all aspects of film studies in 500 detailed entries, from theory and history to technical terms and practices.

A Dictionary of Journalism
Tony Harcup

Covers terminology relating to the practice, business, and technology of journalism, as well as its concepts and theories, organizations and institutions, publications, and key events.

Oxford Quick Reference

The Kings and Queens of Britain
John Cannon and Anne Hargreaves

A detailed, fully-illustrated history ranging from mythical and pre-conquest rulers to the present House of Windsor, featuring regional maps and genealogies.

A Dictionary of World History

Over 4,000 entries on everything from prehistory to recent changes in world affairs. An excellent overview of world history.

A Dictionary of British History
Edited by John Cannon

An invaluable source of information covering the history of Britain over the past two millennia. Over 3,000 entries written by more than 100 specialist contributors.

Review of the parent volume
'the range is impressive ... truly (almost) all of human life is here'
Kenneth Morgan, *Observer*

The Oxford Companion to Irish History
Edited by S. J. Connolly

A wide-ranging and authoritative guide to all aspects of Ireland's past from prehistoric times to the present day.

'packed with small nuggets of knowledge'   *Daily Telegraph*

The Oxford Companion to Scottish History
Edited by Michael Lynch

The definitive guide to twenty centuries of life in Scotland.
'exemplary and wonderfully readable'

Financial Times

Oxford Quick Reference

A Dictionary of the Bible
W. R. F. Browning

In over 2,000 entries, this authoritative dictionary provides clear and concise information about the important people, places, themes, and doctrines of the Bible.

The Oxford Dictionary of Saints
David Farmer

From the famous to the obscure, over 1,400 saints are covered in this acclaimed dictionary.

'an essential reference work' *Daily Telegraph*

The Concise Oxford Dictionary of the Christian Church
E. A. Livingstone

This indispensable guide contains over 5,000 entries and provides full coverage of theology, denominations, the church calendar, and the Bible.

'opens up the whole of Christian history, now with a wider vision than ever' Robert Runcie, former Archbishop of Canterbury

The Oxford Dictionary of Popes
J. N. D. Kelly and M. J. Walsh

Spans almost 2,000 years of papal history: from St Peter to Pope Benedict XVI.

'well-researched, extremely well written, and a delightful exercise in its own right' *Church Times*

Oxford Quick Reference

The Oxford Dictionary of Dance
Debra Craine and Judith Mackrell

Over 2,600 entries on everything from hip-hop to classical ballet,
covering dancers, dance styles, choreographers and composers,
techniques, companies, and productions.

'A must-have volume ... impressively thorough'

Margaret Reynolds, *The Times*

The Oxford Guide to Plays
Michael Patterson

Covers 1,000 of the most important, best-known, and most popular
plays of world theatre.

'Superb synopses ... Superbly formatted ... Fascinating and accessible
style'

THES

The Oxford Dictionary of Music
Michael & Joyce Kennedy & Tim Rutherford-Johnson

The most comprehensive, authoritative, and up-to-date dictionary of
music available in paperback.

'clearly the best around ... the dictionary that everyone should have'

Literary Review

Oxford Quick Reference

A Dictionary of Psychology
Andrew M. Colman

Over 9,000 authoritative entries make up the most wide-ranging dictionary of psychology available.

'impressive ... certainly to be recommended'
Times Higher Education Supplement

'probably the best single-volume dictionary of its kind.'
Library Journal

A Dictionary of Economics
John Black, Nigar Hashimzade, and Gareth Myles

Fully up-to-date and jargon-free coverage of economics. Over 3,400 terms on all aspects of economic theory and practice.

'strongly recommended as a handy work of reference.'
Times Higher Education Supplement

A Dictionary of Law

An ideal source of legal terminology for systems based on English law. Over 4,200 clear and concise entries.

'The entries are clearly drafted and succinctly written ... Precision for the professional is combined with a layman's enlightenment.'
Times Literary Supplement

A Dictionary of Education
Susan Wallace

In over 1,250 clear and concise entries, this authoritative dictionary covers all aspects of education, including organizations, qualifications, key figures, major legislation, theory, and curriculum and assessment terminology.

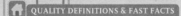